The Good Food Guide
2005

The Good Food Guide 2005

**Edited by
Andrew Turvil**

CONSUMERS' ASSOCIATION

Which? Books are commissioned and researched by
Consumers' Association and published by
Which? Ltd, 2 Marylebone Road,
London NW1 4DF

Distributed by The Penguin Group:
Penguin Books Ltd, 80 Strand,
London WC2R 0RL

Copyright © 2004 Which? Ltd

Base mapping © Map Marketing Ltd/
European Map Graphics 2004
Map information © Which? Ltd 2004

British Library Cataloguing in Publication Data
A catalogue record for this book is
available from the British Library

ISBN 0 85202 981 0

The Good Food Guide is a registered trade mark of
Which? Ltd.

Contributing writers: Elizabeth Carter, Bill Evans, Kieran Flatt, David Kenning, John Kenward,
Susan Low, David Mabey, Jane Middleton, Allen Stidwill and Stuart Walton

Sub-editors and proofreaders: Katharine Cowherd, Hugh Morgan, Katharine Servant, Richard John
Wheelwright and Alison Williams

Also warm thanks to Kevin Leamy and Jessica Turner for in-house research and administrative
support

For a full list of Which? books, please write to:
Which? Books, Castlemead, Gascoyne Way,
Hertford X, SG14 1LH
or access our web site at http://www.which.net

Photoset by Tradespools, Frome, Somerset
Printed in England by Clays Ltd, St Ives plc

Cover design: Price Watkins Design Limited
Cover photograph: ABPL/Ming Tang-Evans

Contents

COOKING MARKS

Marks are given out of 10, and are for cooking only, as perceived by the Guide and its readers.

1–2 COMPETENT COOKING Sound, capable cooking

3–4 COMPETENT TO GOOD COOKING Fine ingredients cooked appropriately, although there may be occasional inconsistencies

5–6 GOOD TO VERY GOOD COOKING High-quality ingredients, consistently good results

7–8 VERY GOOD TO EXCELLENT COOKING High level of ambition, finest ingredients consistently treated with skill and imagination

9–10 THE BEST The top restaurants in the country, highly individual and displaying impressive artistry

SYMBOLS

▲   accommodation is available

�   the wine list is well above average

♦   the restaurant has a truly outstanding wine cellar

NEW CHEF   is indicated instead of a cooking mark if there was a change of chef as we were going to press, too late for inspection

🍳   the chef has changed since last year's entry, and the Editor has judged that the change is of sufficient interest to merit the reader's attention

⊁   smoking is banned in all eating areas

⊁   there are some restrictions on smoking though it may be allowed in some eating areas or after a certain hour

£   it is possible to have a three-course meal, including coffee, half a bottle of house wine and service, at all sessions for £30 or less per person

NEW ENTRY   appears after the restaurant's name if the establishment was not a main entry in last year's Guide, although it may have been a Round-up or appeared in previous editions

(£5)   where this symbol appears, at the very end of an entry, the restaurant has elected to participate in *The Good Food Guide*'s £5 voucher scheme (see 'How to Use the Guide' for details)

How to use the Guide

FINDING A RESTAURANT

If you are seeking a restaurant in a particular area: *first go to the maps* at the centre of the book. Once you know the locality (or, for London, the restaurant name), go to the relevant section of the book to find the entry for the restaurant. The Guide's main entries are divided into seven sections: London, England, Scotland, Wales, Channel Islands, Northern Ireland, and Republic of Ireland. In the London section, restaurants are listed alphabetically by name; in all other sections, they are listed by locality (usually the name of the town or village).

In addition to the main entries are the Round-ups (a range of restaurants, cafés, bistros and pubs that are worth a visit but do not merit a full entry): those for London can be found just after the London main-entry section, and those for everywhere else are towards the back of the book just after the Republic of Ireland main-entry section.

If you know the name of the restaurant: *go to the index* at the back of the book, which lists both main and Round-up entries.

If you are seeking award-winning restaurants, those with outstanding wine cellars, etc.: *make use of the lists* starting on page 10. Additional helpful lists can be found at the back of the book.

HOW TO READ A GUIDE ENTRY

Please see page 6 for explanation of symbols and cooking marks. At the top of each main entry you will find the restaurant's name, map number, address, telephone and fax numbers, its email address or website, as well as any symbols that may apply to the establishment. The cuisine style is also given; this is not meant to be a comprehensive assessment of cooking style, but rather to act as a helpful pointer and in many cases has been suggested by the restaurant itself. At the top of entries you will also find the mark, from 1 to 10, awarded by the editor for cooking, and the cost range for one person having a three-course meal including wine. The middle part of the entry describes food, wines, atmosphere and so on, while the final section gives a wealth of additional information, explained below.

Cost

The price range given is based on the cost of a three-course meal (lunch and/or dinner) for one person, including coffee, house wine, service and cover charge where applicable, according to information supplied by the restaurant. The lower figure is the least you are likely to pay, from either á la carte or set-price menus, and may apply only to lunch. The higher figure indicates a probable maximum cost, sometimes based on a set-price meal of more than three courses, if that is what is offered. This figure is inflated by 20 per cent to reflect the fact that some people may order more expensive wine, extra drinks and some higher-priced 'special' dishes, and that price rises may come into effect during the life-time of this edition of the Guide.

Meals

At the bottom of entries information on the types of meals offered is given, with any variations for lunch (L) and dinner (D), and details of availability. An á la carte menu is signified by the letters *alc*. This is followed by a range of prices for main courses, rounded up to the nearest 50p. *Set L* denotes a set-price lunch; *Set D* means set-price dinner. Set meals usually consist of three courses, but can include many more. If a set meal has fewer than three courses, this is stated. If there is a cover charge, this is also indicated. Brief details of other menus, such as light lunch or bar snacks, are also given. If there is a cover charge, that is also mentioned here.

Service

Net prices means that prices of food and wine are inclusive of service charge, and this is indicated clearly on the menu and bill; *not inc*, that service is not included and is left to the discretion of the customer; *10%*, that a fixed service charge of 10 per cent is automatically added to the bill; *10% (optional)*, that 10 per cent is added to the bill along with the word 'optional' or similar qualifier; and *none*, that no service charge is made or expected and that any money offered is refused. *Card slips closed* indicates that the total on the slips of credit cards is closed when handed over for signature.

Other details

Information is also given on *seating, outside seating* and *private parties*. We say *car park* if the restaurant provides free parking facilities for patrons (*small car park* if it has only a few spaces), and say *vegetarian meals* only if menus list at least one vegetarian option as a starter and one as a main course (if this is not noted, a restaurant may still be able to offer vegetarian options with prior notice – it is worth phoning to check).

Any restrictions on children are given, such as *no children* or *no children under 6 after 8pm*; otherwise, it can be assumed that children are welcome. In addition, *children's helpings* are noted if smaller portions are available at a reduced price; *jacket and tie* if it is compulsory for men to wear a jacket and tie to the restaurant; *no smoking* if smoking is not permitted in all eating areas (or other restrictions on smoking are explained); *wheelchair access* if the proprietor has confirmed that the entrance is at least 80cm wide and passages at least 120cm wide in accordance with the Royal Association for Disability and Rehabilitation (RADAR) recommendations, and *also WC* if the proprietor has assured us that toilet facilities are suitable for disabled people (*not WC* means these are not available or the proprietor is not sure). *Music* indicates that live or recorded music is usually played in the dining-room; *occasional music* that it sometimes is; *no music* that it never is. *No mobile phones* means the restaurant requests these are switched off.

Accommodation

For establishments offering overnight accommodation, the number of rooms, along with facilities provided in the rooms (e.g. bath/shower, TV, phone), is set out. Prices are given usually for bed and breakfast (*B&B*). *D,B&B* indicates that the price also includes dinner. The first figure given is the lowest price for one person in a single room, or single occupancy of a double, the second is the most expensive price for two people in a double room or suite. *Rooms for disabled* means the establishment has stated that its accommodation is suitable for wheelchair-users. Restrictions on children, and facilities for guests with babies, are indicated.

Miscellaneous information

At the end of London entries, the nearest Underground station is given after the symbol ⊖. For restaurants that have elected to participate in the *Good Food Guide* £5 voucher scheme, a (£5) symbol appears at the very end of entries; see the reverse side of the vouchers themselves for a full explanation of how they work. *The Good Food Guide* is available on the Internet to Which? Online subscribers; details at www.which.co.uk.

The top-rated restaurants

(See page 6 for explanation of marking system)

Mark **10** for cooking

London
Gordon Ramsay, SW3

Mark **9** for cooking

England
Fat Duck, Bray
Le Manoir aux Quat' Saisons, Great Milton
Winteringham Fields, Winteringham

Mark **8** for cooking

London
The Capital, SW3
Pied-à-Terre, W1
Square, W1
Tom Aikens, SW3

England
Le Champignon Sauvage, Cheltenham
Gidleigh Park, Chagford
Hibiscus, Ludlow
Merchant House, Ludlow
Vineyard at Stockcross, Stockcross
Waterside Inn, Bray

Mark **7** for cooking

London
Le Gavroche, W1
Gordon Ramsay at Claridge's, W1
Lindsay House, W1
Pétrus, SW1

England
Anthony's, Leeds
Black Pig, Rock
Castle Hotel, Taunton
Castle House: La Rive, Hereford
Chester Grosvenor: Arkle, Chester
Cliveden: Waldo's, Taplow
Drake's Restaurant, Ripley
L'Enclume, Cartmel
Fischer's Baslow Hall, Baslow
Hambleton Hall, Upper Hambleton
Harry's Place, Great Gonerby

Holbeck Ghyll, Windermere
Hotel des Clos: Restaurant Sat Bains, Nottingham
Juniper, Altrincham
Mr Underhill's, Ludlow
Old Vicarage, Ridgeway
Pool Court at 42, Leeds
Whatley Manor, Easton Grey
Yorke Arms, Ramsgill

Scotland
Andrew Fairlie at Gleneagles, Auchterarder
The Creel, St Margaret's Hope
Restaurant Martin Wishart, Edinburgh

Wales
Tyddyn Llan, Llandrillo
Ynyshir Hall, Eglwysfach

Special awards 2005

These awards do not necessarily go to the restaurants with the highest mark for cooking, but rather to the ones which have shown particular merit or achievement during the year. It may go to an old favourite or to a new entry, but in either case the places listed below have been singled out because they have enhanced the eating-out experience in some special way.

UK Restaurant of the year: Gordon Ramsay, London, SW3

London

Anchor & Hope, SE1	*London newcomer of the year*
Chez Bruce, SW17	*London commended*
Cinnamon Club, SW1	*London commended*
Yauatcha, W1	*London commended*

England

Allium, Fairford	*Gloucestershire newcomer of the year*
Anthony's, Leeds	*West Yorkshire newcomer of the year*
Black Pig, Rock	*Cornwall restaurant of the year*
Le Champignon Sauvage, Cheltenham	*Gloucestershire restaurant of the year*
Dartmoor Inn, Lydford	*Devon commended*
Drake's Restaurant, Ripley	*Surrey newcomer of the year*
Fraiche, Oxton	*Merseyside restaurant of the year*
Glasshouse, Kew	*Greater London commended*
Little Barwick House, Barwick	*Somerset commended*
Hope Street Hotel: London Carriage Works, Liverpool	*Liverpool newcomer of the year*
Horse and Trumpet, Medbourne	*Leicestershire newcomer of the year*
Jessica's, Birmingham	*West Midlands newcomer of the year*
JSW, Petersfield	*Hampshire restaurant of the year*
Love's, Leamington Spa	*Warwickshire restaurant of the year*
Magpies, Horncastle	*Lincolnshire commended*
One Paston Place, Brighton	*Brighton & Hove commended*
Quartier Vert, Bristol	*Bristol commended*
Rish, York	*North Yorkshire commended*
Star Inn, Harome	*North Yorkshire restaurant of the year*
Talland Bay Hotel, Looe	*Cornwall newcomer of the year*
36 on the Quay, Emsworth	*Hampshire commended*
Yang Sing, Manchester	*Greater Manchester restaurant of the year*

Scotland

Andrew Fairlie at Gleneagles, Auchterarder	*Scotland restaurant of the year*
Kinnaird, Dunkeld	*Scotland commended*
Restaurant Martin Wishart, Edinburgh	*Scotland commended*
Seafood Restaurant, St Andrews	*Scotland newcomer of the year*

Wales

Bodysgallen Hall, Conwy	*Wales commended*
Chandlery, Newport	*Wales commended*
Le Gallois, Cardiff	*Wales commended*

The Guide's longest-serving restaurants

The Guide has seen many restaurants come and go. Some, however, have stayed the course with tenacity. (Qualification for this list is that the restaurant has been in each edition of the Guide subsequent to its first entry.)

Connaught, London W1	52 years
Gay Hussar, London W1	48 years
Gravetye Manor, East Grinstead	48 years
Porth Tocyn Hotel, Abersoch	48 years
Sharrow Bay, Ullswater	44 years
Walnut Tree Inn, Llandewi Skirrid	40 years
Black Bull Inn, Moulton	38 years
Rothay Manor, Ambleside	36 years
Le Gavroche, London W1	35 years
Summer Isles Hotel, Achiltibuie	35 years
The Capital, London SW3	34 years
Miller Howe, Windermere	34 years
Old Fire Engine House, Ely	33 years
Ubiquitous Chip, Glasgow	33 years
Druidstone, Broad Haven	32 years
Peat Inn, Peat Inn	32 years
Plumber Manor, Sturminster Newton	32 years
Waterside Inn, Bray	32 years
White Moss House, Grasmere	32 years
Isle of Eriska, Eriska	31 years
Airds, Port Appin	29 years
Farlam Hall, Brampton	28 years
Langan's Brasserie, London W1	28 years
Corse Lawn House, Corse Lawn	27 years
Gidleigh Park, Chagford	27 years
White House, Williton	27 years
Hambleton Hall, Upper Hambleton	26 years
The Pier Hotel: Harbourside Restaurant, Harwich	26 years
Sabras, London NW10	26 years
Grafton Manor, Bromsgrove	25 years
Magpie Café, Whitby	25 years
Champany Inn, Linlithgow	24 years
Drum and Monkey, Harrogate	24 years
Homewood Park, Hinton Charterhouse	24 years
Royal Crescent, Pimpernel's, Bath	24 years
RSJ, London SE1	24 years
Seafood Restaurant, Padstow	24 years
Sir Charles Napier, Chinnor	24 years
Y Bistro, Llanberis	24 years
Le Caprice, London SW3	23 years
Kalpna, Edinburgh	23 years
Little Barwick House, Barwick	23 years
Moss Nook, Manchester	23 years
Neal Street Restaurant, London WC2	23 years
Sportsman's Arms, Wath-in-Nidderdale	23 years

Restaurants with outstanding wine cellars
Marked in the text with a 🍾

London
Bibendum, SW3
Bleeding Heart, EC1
Chez Bruce, SW17
Le Coq d'Argent, EC2
The Don, EC4
Enoteca Turi, SW15
Fifth Floor, SW1
Le Gavroche, W1
Gordon Ramsay, SW3
Gordon Ramsay at Claridge's, W1
Great Eastern Hotel, Aurora, EC2
Greenhouse, W1
Mirabelle, W1
Orrery, W1
Oxo Tower, SE1
Pétrus, SW1
Pied-à-Terre, W1
Ransome's Dock, SW11
RSJ, SE1
Square, W1
Tate Britain Restaurant, SW1
La Trompette, W4
Zaika, W8

England
Birmingham, Hotel du Vin & Bistro
Bolton Abbey, Devonshire Arms: Burlington
    Restaurant
Bray, Fat Duck
Brighton & Hove, Hotel du Vin & Bistro
Bristol, Hotel du Vin & Bistro
Chagford , Gidleigh Park
Chester, Chester Grosvenor: Arkle
Chinnor, Sir Charles Napier
Corse Lawn, Corse Lawn House
East Grinstead, Gravetye Manor
Faversham, Read's
Grasmere, White Moss House

Harrogate, Hotel du Vin & Bistro
Huntingdon, Old Bridge Hotel
Kew, Glasshouse
Leeds, Fourth Floor Café and Bar
Leeds, Sous le Nez en Ville
Lewdown, Lewtrenchard Manor
Lyndhurst, Le Poussin at Parkhill
Manchester, Second Floor
Marten, Windmill
Masham, Swinton Park: Samuel's
Newton Longville, Crooked Billet
Oxford, Cherwell Boathouse
Padstow, Seafood Restaurant
Petersfield, JSW
Ross-on-Wye, Pheasant at Ross
Southwold, Crown Hotel
Stockcross, Vineyard at Stockcross
Tunbridge Wells, Hotel du Vin & Bistro
Ullswater, Sharrow Bay
Winchester, Hotel du Vin & Bistro

Scotland
Achiltibuie, Summer Isles Hotel
Anstruther, Cellar
Edinburgh, Forth Floor
Edinburgh, Valvona & Crolla Caffè Bar
Edinburgh, Witchery by the Castle
Glasgow, Ubiquitous Chip
Gullane, Greywalls Hotel
Champany Inn, Linlithgow
Peat Inn, Peat Inn

Wales
Aberdovey, Penhelig Arms Hotel
Llandrillo, Tyddyn Llan
Llandudno, St Tudno Hotel, Terrace
Pwllheli, Plas Bodegroes
Reynoldston, Fairyhill

Introduction

The main function of any guidebook is to inform. For fifty-three years the *Good Food Guide* team has been reporting on the UK restaurant scene and feeding the information back to our hungry readers. This book is based on the real experiences of people who choose to spend their money in restaurants. We try to convey a sense of what each restaurant is like, enabling you, our readers, to make choices about where you are going to eat, whether it is an anniversary dinner or a birthday, or simply because it's Wednesday night and you've nothing in the fridge. I am sure you all have your favourite restaurants and regular haunts, but with the help of the GFG, you can find out about other readers' favourite places, too. The rating out of ten that we give to each restaurant for its cooking is a further aid to decision-making. *Just* an aid, though: remember that every restaurant in this Guide is recommended and has impressed.

Places that do not receive support from our readers do not make the pages of this book. If you know of a restaurant that you think is deserving of inclusion, let us know, by letter or email (addresses are on the report form at the back of the book), as we want to hear from you. In fact, that is the whole point.

Up in the country

Let's start by *not* talking about London for a change. A glance at the list of Special Award winners for this edition (see page 11) shows a significant number of restaurants in villages and small towns among the recipients – places like Rock, Emsworth, Fairford, Dunkeld and Medbourne, for example. More and more over the last couple of years, some of the most interesting new restaurant openings have occurred in surprising places around the country. Most readers of the Guide will be familiar with Ludlow and its bewildering range of top-flight restaurants, but it remains unique among UK market towns. (I'm sorry to say that there is nowhere else quite like it, and we can only dream of a time when every small town is filled with such creative and exciting places.)

However, an increasing number of chefs do seem to be willing to eschew the bright lights in order to open in areas where they either have a past association, or simply want to move to for the lifestyle benefits. Or they might be drawn by the opportunity to head up their own team, perhaps in some refurbished trendy hotel, or to enter their first venture into ownership. It is always a pleasure to encounter talent in unexpected places. The maps in the centre of the book will reveal some real gems off the beaten track. The general rule has always been to head for a big city if you want great food in this country, but now it is fair to say you might be missing out if you don't spread your wings a little further.

In the past, too, the country restaurant has had a deserved reputation for being rather stuffy, a bit chintzy, perhaps, expensive and only worth a visit on high days and holidays. By contrast, many new openings apply a modern approach to the style of their dining rooms and menus, lightening the tone all round – and often take a more flexible approach to pricing. The gap between town and country is beginning to narrow. It is clear when talking to restaurateurs in rural locations that many still find customers hard to come by at midweek, and the relative sparseness of population is always going to restrict growth. Areas with high levels of tourism inevitably are more likely to be buoyant than those without seasonal influxes of hungry mouths to feed, and it is no surprise to note that Cornwall, for example, is one county with some especially promising openings over the past couple of years.

The pub is beginning to fulfil its promise as the natural home for a relaxed and casual kind of eating. The inn has long been a source of sustenance to weary travellers, though the poor quality of food served in so many of them has been a sticking point. There are more pubs listed in the Guide than ever before, and the standard of food they offer is often impressive. Let's hope that pubs continue to improve without losing their time-honoured virtues of informality.

Down in the city

Standards of restaurant food in many of the larger cities around the UK have been steadily improving over the past ten years or so as well. The revitalisation of many cities – Leeds, for example – has resulted in a thriving restaurant culture. Others have been slow to follow the lead, but still the signs are good. Taking a look at a copy of the GFG from ten years ago allows some interesting comparisons. In the main-entry section, Liverpool in 1995 had one entry, while the 2005 edition has six. Sheffield has increased its count from two to six, and Leeds from five to ten. Bristol has gone up just one – from nine to ten. Edinburgh is up from sixteen to twenty. These may not seem earth-shattering statistics, but they show a steady, positive trend. I dare say not every city has upped its number of entrants over those ten years, but the majority have. City restaurants reflect the diversity of our society, and it is here where the heartbeat of our restaurant culture can really be felt. This means choice, and a variety of cuisines such as Bangladeshi and Cantonese; it is impossible to imagine our present restaurant culture without this vibrant ethnic mix.

The London section in the Guide is big, very big, but then this is a fair reflection of the sheer number of good restaurants out there, and the vastness of the populace. London is in a super league along with a few other major cities around the world. The heavyweight, top-flight restaurants here are world beaters, and you can eat just about anything, from Brazilian street food to old-school haute cuisine.

Posh night out

There are two main elements to the fine dining experience: first, what it feels like (all that service, those hallowed rooms, the high cost) and second, what appears on the plate. The GFG office receives feedback on thousands of meals every year. Some are simply quick business lunches, others perhaps a routine dinner with a friend. Some are once-a-year (lifetime, even) trips to an expensive, grand restaurant, usually for a birthday or anniversary. The purpose of such a celebratory meal is to have a 'special' experience. So the fawning service, even the synchronised lifting of domes, can all be part of the appreciated theatre. These things make it special – for some people. For others the fine dining end of the spectrum is intimidating and tiresome. Is wearing a jacket and tie really the only way to be classified as presentable? Now, it doesn't do to turn up in a vest and combat trousers (unless you're a hot-news celebrity, in which case, 'your table is ready, sir'), but there is a considerable area of middle ground. Most restaurants nowadays have a much more relaxed attitude to dress, but if you look closely at the factual details at the foot of each entry in the Guide, you'll see a few that still stipulate what guests should wear.

By no means do all the top-rated restaurants in the Guide offer such formal service, or create a 'precious' ambience. The Fat Duck in Bray and the Merchant House in Ludlow are two examples of places where top-end food is delivered in a relaxed and relatively informal environment. Service can be well drilled and professional as well as friendly and approachable, and the most important thing is that staff are able to communicate effectively with both customers and the kitchen, that they understand the menu, and that they actually feel relaxed and comfortable themselves.

Nonetheless, the immaculately formal service found at, for example, the Waterside Inn in Bray, shows how that style of delivery can impress. Staff glide effortlessly around the room, wine glasses are filled a few moments before you think you might be running low – but never overfilled – and customers feel truly cosseted. If only everywhere offering this type of service were this good at it. There will always be a place for a bit of cosseting, and good service improves any dining experience considerably, but the twenty-first-century consumer is less likely to enjoy being treated like minor European aristocracy. It's all about the right kind of service for the right kind of place, and so many get it entirely wrong.

The fine dining experience is rightly going to be about the food above all else. If you're going to pay £150 to £200 for a meal for two, you expect to be eating something special, right? Well, that usually includes a succession of nibbles, 'courses between courses', and petits fours that are almost akin to another meal. The chef may spend a lot of energy planning your gustatory journey from start to finish, but by the time you've added bread and other extras to the equation, you might have to struggle to get out of your chair at the end of the evening. Sauces may have been getting lighter over the years, with cream used more sparingly, but just getting through the volume of food can be a struggle.

You might well say that, as you're paying mega-bucks, these freebies are all part of the experience, and chances are that you're dead keen to try as much of the kitchen's output as possible – maybe even eating off your dining companion's plate (that can't just be me, surely?). Although a few years ago a pre-starter or pre-dessert was a relatively unusual sight, saved for very special places, nowadays they are everywhere, and sometimes they are just not necessary – and many restaurateurs may find customers more appreciative of lower prices instead.

We are eating out in greater numbers than ever before in this country. Foods from Thailand, Sardinia, Algeria, France, and more – they are all out there, though, thankfully, not usually on the same plate at the same time! Diversity and choice are the strengths of the UK restaurant scene, and sometimes we want a posh night out, and sometimes we want no frills whatsoever; sometimes smart but never pretentious, sometimes casual but not slapdash.

You get what you pay for

Actually, you don't always. Sometimes an advertised scallop might be missing from the plate, and you swear you saw it listed among ten other things in the description of the dish, but that is another story. The point here is value for money. The cost of eating out continues to increase, with 12.5 per cent 'optional' seemingly the service charge of choice among restaurateurs these days. They would like us to eat our more frequently, and most of us would, if we could afford it.

It costs £35 for the set lunch (as we go to press) at Gordon Ramsay's flagship restaurant in Royal Hospital Road, and most reporters to the Guide consider that to be decent value for money. You get a similar experience at dinner – which is of course more expensive, but the food is of the highest order and so considered by most to be worth it. Eating out at lunch at the top-end restaurants can be a good way of getting to experience the thrill of a place, and some great food, at a less intimidating price.

The desire for cheap food could be said to be at the root of many problems seen today in the food and farming industries. The drive by supermarkets to bring down prices has had a negative impact on both farmers and consumers: the former in terms of falling profit margins, and the latter in terms of taste, choice, and even health. Food can be considered value for money only if it remains good (and safe) to eat and is full of flavour. A tasteless chicken pumped full of additives might catch the eye of a passing shopper for its low cost, but it cannot represent value for money (assuming your intention is to eat it). Cheapness is not a virtue by itself, and good food costs money. Former chef and restaurateur Carol Godsmark tells us about how restaurants source their ingredients (see her feature on page 20), and it should be clear to anyone reading the entries that follow that good produce is *the* main priority for any serious restaurant.

For a customer to leave a restaurant feeling truly satisfied he or she has to believe that the experience has been worth the money. When strolling out of the doors of Le Manoir aux quat' Saisons, for example, one is aware that a fair amount has been spent on goods and services, but most people who report back to us believe that it was well worth it. We all want a feeling of satisfaction when we leave any restaurant, not a sense of being stung.

Wine pricing is a constant source of frustration and confusion. This year we're hitting back in our own way by removing the 'bottle' and 'glass' symbols from lists that do not offer enough choice at the lower end of the cost spectrum. So the 'bottle' symbol goes to restaurants with outstanding cellars that offer a good selection for all pockets (a list of these places is on page 13). Each wine list has been looked at for its own merits, but if there is scant choice around the £20–£25 mark, and even a lack of interesting stuff up to £30, we have removed the award. Lists that qualify on quality but not on value will still get a 'bottle-length' write-up, but no award.

Quality from top to bottom?

The number of restaurants featured in the Guide has steadily increased over the years. Standards have undoubtedly improved, and though trends have come and gone, the trajectory – especially as regards innovation – is still very much upwards. The roll-call of chefs pushing out boundaries and exploring the nature of food and our appreciation of it is growing year on year. Many are challenging our perceptions, making us think about what we eat: for example Heston Blumenthal at the Fat Duck in Bray, Simon Rogan at L'Enclume in Cartmel, Paul Kitching at Juniper in Altrincham, and newcomer Anthony Flinn at Anthony's in Leeds. There are others, too, and their presence is putting the UK at the cutting edge of this new frontier. Exciting stuff. Not everybody is a fan of experimentalism, of course, but that comes with the territory.

Where the UK restaurant scene needs help, if not a life-saving operation, is at the other end of the spectrum. It's the simple things that are often done so badly. Picking a restaurant at random is likely to lead to disappointment. Poor ingredients, badly handled, and dependency on catering suppliers are still rife. We can scarcely afford to stop and celebrate the improvements that have been made when such rubbish is still being served up. The UK lacks a backbone of good, low-cost restaurants for everyday eating. There are plenty of chain restaurants, but – let me say it again – the UK lacks a backbone of good, low-cost restaurants for everyday eating. The pub is helping in this department somewhat; but we need more choice on the scene. There are restaurants in this country – and in the Guide – that make a virtue of simplicity, but they are the exceptions, not the rule.

The Guide lists a number of places that take a relaxed and multifarious approach to the restaurant business, often combining a delicatessen (or similar outlet) selling high-quality fresh produce, and serving it up to customers on site. Examples are Culinaria, Stephen and Judy Markwick's latest venture in Bristol; Chris Johnson's Ransoms in Ramsbottom, Greater Manchester; Flâneur in London's Farringdon Road; and Effings in Totnes. These places are little pieces of foodie heaven, and every town should have something along these lines.

Let's hope we see more of them in the Guide in the future.

Keep 'em coming

Thank you to anybody who sent in a report last year. And many, many, thanks to those who sent in large numbers. The book reflects all these experiences, endorsed by our team of volunteer inspectors. We are 53 years into a beautiful friendship, and long may it continue.

Good eating

Andrew Turvil
Editor

Real food sourced wisely

Carol Godsmark, food journalist, member of the Guild of Food Writers, and ex-chef/restaurateur looks at how the sourcing of food is no longer something that any of us can ignore

After decades of indifference to the question of where our food comes from, its sourcing is finally in the news and on people's minds. Modern production methods, labelling standards, and the nature of farming itself are being challenged, fuelling a debate on the food we eat at home and in restaurants. The adherence to 'pile it high and sell it cheap', and to the provision of year-round choice even if it means flying in produce from halfway across the world, is finally coming under scrutiny.

The increasing industrialisation of our food supply has led to a loss of flavour. Fruits and vegetables are grown for their shelf life and their uniform looks rather than for their taste; game is no longer necessarily wild and free-ranging; and much of the salmon we eat is farmed and flabby. Of all the hundreds of varieties of apples and potatoes, and the great regional breeds of cattle, poultry and pigs, only a handful are now regularly available to us.

But it's not just the dearth of flavour in intensively farmed food that gives cause for concern. The big wake-up call for many people has been the food scandals of the last 25 years: salmonella, BSE, E coli and GM foods – an ignominious roll-call that put our vast and anonymous supply system to shame.

Time to take control

If we are to gain a sense of control over the quality of the food we eat, then we have to know where it comes from. Good restaurateurs – the ones with a commitment to producing food with flavour and eschewing short cuts – are discovering that the best way of monitoring quality is to source at least a proportion of ingredients locally, and to buy direct. In this way they can see how the animals are reared, how the produce is grown, how the cheese is made. They can have a constant dialogue with suppliers, and perhaps ask them to hang their meat for longer, or grow crops they might not have considered before, specifically for the restaurant. They can be sure that everything they buy is fresh. And the real bonus is that good shopping is, as Jane Grigson pointed out, halfway to good cooking. Something that was picked yesterday needs much less doing to it to make it taste good than something that's been in cold storage for two weeks.

For customers, too, local ingredients provide a link to the community in which they were grown, and an escape from the dreary standardisation of our food supply – something they might not even have been aware of until they sampled the pleasures of locally caught fish with samphire gathered from the beach, or a dessert made with in-season rhubarb rather than air-freighted strawberries. There is a sense of rightness about local ingredients, a feeling that this food belongs to this place.

Although it would be pleasing to imagine that all restaurants are on a hunt for real food, grown by traditional methods on their doorstep, the reality is that too many of them (outside the realm of this Guide) still don't see the point of good sourcing. It's all too easy to rely on uninspiring wholesale outlets, supermarkets and, especially, the 'catering packs' supplied to the restaurant and pub trade. With catering packs, there is no need for chefs to do any cooking whatsoever – in fact, no need for 'chefs' at all. In many cases, all that's required is the ability to transfer food from freezer to microwave or deep-fat fryer. And as long as a largely indifferent public continues to eat in places such as these, there is no reason for them to change their ways.

Hard-working, responsible restaurants, cafés and pubs are fighting a difficult battle to increase awareness of good produce and skilful cooking. For chefs who care, 'local' and 'seasonal' have become the watchwords of good sourcing. But just how easy is it for them to find the kind of produce they want?

From Deben duck to Whitby crab

When I became chef/restaurateur of Soanes in Petworth, West Sussex, in the 1980s, sourcing local produce was very difficult. Quality fish, vegetables and cheeses were available, it seemed, only from Covent Garden or Rungis, the Paris market – though the local butcher and a mushroom forager were a help, and I grew herbs and some vegetables and salads myself. Local wholesale suppliers, by contrast, could only offer dull, tasteless vegetables and fruit, and I found their couldn't-care-less attitude deeply dispiriting. Writing for the Guide in 1985, Franco Taruschio, then proprietor of the Walnut Tree Inn at Llandewi Skirrid, bemoaned the loss of small stalls at the nearby market where he had once been able to obtain local butter, cheese, eggs, fruit, vegetables and game. He commented, 'It is easier to buy a mango from thousands of miles away than a precious offering [of strawberries] from our own soil.'

Even though, if anything, large wholesalers and the 'Big Four' supermarket chains have tightened their stranglehold on the nation's food supply since then, there has also been a renaissance of small, local suppliers. This has been boosted by the growth of the farmers' market movement, which has given suppliers a direct outlet for their produce and in turn made the public much more aware of alternatives to the supermarket, and more discriminating when they eat out.

If they choose to make use of the excellent supply network that is now available, today's restaurateurs have many more options than we did in the 1980s. It is getting much easier to acquire first-class ingredients according to the season without running up a huge tally of 'food miles', with their attendant pollution and excessive fuel consumption. There is also the satisfaction of knowing that you are supporting the local economy – which in turn can only be good news for your restaurant.

Those restaurants that do source locally are proud of the fact and usually advertise it on their menus. If you read the entries in this Guide you'll find plenty of mention of local (or regional) produce: Lincolnshire grey partridge; Goosenargh and Deben duck; Cromer crab and Skye scallops; Cumbrian fell-bred lamb; Dales-bred beef smoked and cured in Yorkshire ale; and Orkney potatoes, Lyth Valley damsons and Elmhurst strawberries. Well-hung, rare-breed beef such as Longhorn rump and Black Welsh fillet can be bought from butchers accredited by the Rare Breeds Survival Trust. Fish is not neglected: mindful restaurateurs are going after eco-friendly fish from Cornwall and Devon and elsewhere. Local and regional farmhouse cheeses made by traditional methods can be bought direct from the farm.

Weaver's Shed in Golcar, West Yorkshire goes one step further and produces its own chicken, duck, quails' eggs and vegetables. Co-chef/proprietor Stephen Jackson buys from his father, who grows cavolo nero, kohlrabi, leeks, salad vegetables, soft fruit and no fewer than 75 herbs and wild plants for the restaurant. This is, Stephen reckons, 'a sensible way of progressing and cooking within the seasons' – and the saving is £200 a week off the supplier bill.

Laurence Murphy, chef/proprietor of Fat Olives in Emsworth, Hampshire, says he 'gets local rabbit and game, and two guys fish for sea bass in the Solent for us'. The innovative menus reflect his enthusiasm, and he is a keen advocate of sourcing vegetables and fruit in season as well as game and fish.

The Star Inn at Harome, North Yorkshire, is a showcase of locally sourced food, with most dishes on the menu quoting their provenance. Yoadwath Mill salmon, Whitby crab, North Sea lobster, Pickering watercress, Sand Hutton asparagus, Ryedale lamb, local fallow deer, Yorkshire Blue cheese are just some of the goods sourced by chef Andrew Pern. For farming stock, Andrew looks to his own village to supply what he needs: Dexters bred for the table in view of the restaurant; Gloucester Old Spot pigs reared in a nearby orchard on apples; and honey and duck eggs also from Harome. 'We've set the benchmark in the area, with healthy competition from other pubs and restaurants upping the game,' Andrew says.

The global larder

Buying locally is becoming the Holy Grail for many restaurants, and rightly so, but this isn't always appropriate – not if we are to maintain the excitingly diverse restaurant culture on which we pride ourselves. For Peter Gordon, the New Zealand co-chef/co-owner of London's Providores, fusion is the name of game. Sourcing is equally important to him but for the kind of food he produces he must go beyond what's available locally: 'I treat the world's culinary resources as one huge and exciting larder.' His eclectic menus cover a lot of ground, from Exmoor-sourced duck, New Zealand venison and Suffolk Cross lamb to pomegranate molasses, plantains, tomatillos, jicama, yuzu, wasabi tobiko, and kirmizi biber – Turkish chilli flakes 'usually brought over from a friend in Turkey'. Cheeses are specifically British, with other ingredients sourced from specialist suppliers. Peter Gordon looks beyond national borders, but the important point is that he sources with attention to quality.

Obviously not all produce can come from this country, and the best foie gras, cured hams such as Parma and serrano, some cheeses, pistachios, limes, lentils and most wines are just a trickle of the global riches that have good reason to be brought to our shores.

Real food, real choices

Good-quality produce is available to chefs if they choose to seek it out, and thankfully, most of the restaurants listed in this Guide do exactly that. Others should follow their example. We – the public – need to make a point of asking about provenance when we eat out, encouraging restaurateurs to source responsibly. And in turn, we should be prepared to pay a little more for real food with real flavour. Our insistence on cheap food has already cost us dear – in terms of the pollution of our food supply, the destruction of our rural and culinary heritage, and the huge financial burden of dealing with crises such as BSE. Franco Taruschio commented when writing for the Guide, 'People are searching for real food again, and they are going to have to shout very loudly for it before we are lost in a sea of tasteless fruit, vegetables, meat and dairy products.' Let's vote with our feet and support those restaurants which have made it their mission to source real food and use it wisely.

Poetry and food: a celebration

Songs for the hunt, chants to make crops grow, incantations over the cook-pot, blessings spoken over food at the table: there is no doubting that food and poetry have had intimate interconnections since the beginnings of human history. And so when *The Good Food Guide* learned that this year's National Poetry Day, sponsored by the National Poetry Society, was to coincide with its own publication day, and that NPD's theme was 'food' – well. The Guide approached the Society to ask if it could recommend any top-quality poems about food by contemporary poets writing in the UK. We were delighted at the generous and very helpful response of the Society's Director, Jules Mann – a response quite possibly bolstered by her own experience of good food enjoyed with good wine in pleasant surroundings acquired during her years as a consultant to California wineries in the '80s and '90s – and we were amazed and pleased by the wonderful and varied poems she presented to us.

It took quite a bit of discipline to whittle the selection down to the four printed on the pages following. We based our choice on how the poems, though very diverse in subject, approach and technique, seem to complement each other; how they illustrate something special about the vibrant and compelling poetry scene in the UK today; and, of course, what they say, even if a little obliquely, about a subject we are rather impassioned about.

We wish to thank the Poetry Society for all its help, including providing the biographical notes supplied below, and organising permissions for printing the poems. More food poems can be found at www.poetrysociety.org.uk.

The poets:

Robert Crawford is Professor of Modern Scottish Literature and Head of the School of English at St Andrews (since 1989). He is author of several collections of poetry in English and Scots.

Katherine Gallagher is a widely published Australian poet resident in London; she is author of several collections of poetry, and works largely as a poetry tutor in schools and colleges.

Peter Finch is a poet, critic, author and literary entrepreneur living in Cardiff. He works in both traditional and experimental forms and is author of a number of works on poetry and book publishing.

Yuri Drobyshev has worked with Carol Rumens for many years in translating Russian Poetry; Rumens is a novelist, playwright, translator and editor as well as an award-winning poet. She currently teaches creative writing at the University of Wales, Bangor.

➤ For the poems, please turn the page.

Scotch Broth

A soup so thick you could shake its hand
And stroll with it before dinner.

The face rising to its surface,
A rayfish waiting to be stroked.

Is the pustular, eat-me face of a crofter,
Turnipocephalic, white-haired.

Accepting all comers, it's still our nation's
Flagsoup, sip-soup; sip, sip, sip

At this other scotch made with mutton
That intoxicates only

With peas and potatoes, chewy uists of meat.
All races breathe over our bowl,

Inhaling Inverness and Rutherglen,
Waiting for a big, teuchtery face

To compose itself from carrots and barley
Rising up towards the spoon.

– By Robert Crawford (from *Masculinity*, Jonathan Cape, 1996. Reprinted by permission of The Random House Group Ltd)

Poem for a Shallot

I am fooled.
You insist on the secret of skins –
how perfectly each wraps you.

You compartmentalize,
I don't know how.
I can peel you back to nothing.

I hunt for what isn't there –
layer upon layer –
down to your cagey heart.

When I try to get away
you've snuck into my breath, eyes,
making me cry

into my hands.

– By Katherine Gallagher (from *Tigers on the Silk Road*, Arc Publications, 2000)

The Tao of Dining

We go into the restaurant and the bill is thirty
before we sit. The waiter sells us five pound
Chardonnay for twenty. The menu reads like a
language test. Understanding creeps we go
limp and warm. I want a full plate three bread
rolls I get a biscuit and a pool of yellow in its centre a
centimetred fish. We are dining because this is
intimacy and the alcohol helps. I want life
it's here. Snazz blues in the backdrop the
waiter skips. "You enjoy, monsieur?" He's
Australian. The bill is already eighty I don't care.
The wine is a symphony I have no way of
judging. Crème Brulée makes our hair shine.
Our fellow diners glow like angels,
our souls are singing.
The bill is somewhere I have never been before,
read with joy, signed with ecstasy,
the whole restaurant is smiling.
Someone said dining is all experience.
Lao Tzu that only the one you are in right now
has any importance. Outside it's raining.

– By Peter Finch (from *Food*, Seren Press, 2004)

A Philosophical Gourmet

I eat good food, therefore I am:
Fresh spuds go down a treat with ham.
But you won't hear me say 'How nice!'
I always follow Mum's advice:
Full mouths don't mix with conversation.
Concentrate on mastication.

– By Yuri Drobyshev, translated from the Russian by the author and Carol Rumens

London

Adams Café £   map 12

77 Askew Road, W12 9AH	COOKING 3
TEL/FAX: (020) 8743 0572	NORTH AFRICAN
	£23–£31

Totally unpretentious and totally authentic, this is one of the best places in town for genuine North African food. Open your account with brik ('fans' of crisp filo with different fillings) or grilled sardines. The main event, however, is eight versions of couscous, closely challenged by a battery of Moroccan tagines: aromatic, sweet stews imbued with the flavours of pickled lemons, olives, prunes and apricots. Alternatively, you can take your pick from the list of assorted grills involving anything from merguez to marinated swordfish. Finish with crêpes berbères (Moroccan pancakes with honey sauce) or something like lemon and blackcurrant sorbet. The wine list is a modest collection of North African and French bins plus Ch. Musar. Prices start at £2.50 a glass, £9 a bottle.

CHEF: Sofiene Chahed   PROPRIETORS: Abdel and Frances Boukraa   OPEN: Mon to Sat D only 7 to 11   CLOSED: Christmas to New Year, bank hols   MEALS: Set D £10.50 (1 course) to £15.50   SERVICE: 10%, card slips closed   CARDS: Amex, Delta, MasterCard, Switch, Visa   DETAILS: 60 seats. Private parties: 24 private room. Vegetarian meals. Wheelchair access (not WC). Music   ⊖ Ravenscourt Park (£5)

Admiral Codrington 🍞   map 14

17 Mossop Street, SW3 2LY	COOKING 3
TEL: (020) 7581 0005 FAX: (020) 7589 2452	MODERN EUROPEAN
	£36–£58

At first glance, this looks like a 'workaday' watering hole (with an unapologetically Victorian-style bar) in SW3 Sloaneland. Wriggle through the crush, however, and at the back there's a light, banquette-lined conservatory-style dining room catering for gastro-pub appetites. John Rotherham delivers well-crafted dishes from a repertoire that plunders Europe and takes on a few Far Eastern flourishes. Ricotta and parsley ravioli has been notable for the quality of its pasta, and other openers might include crispy squid with sweet chilli dressing. 'The Admiral's Cod' (baked with tomato, mushrooms and a soft herb crust) is a favourite, or there's roast rack of veal with braised Belgian endive and truffle jus (vegetables extra). French cheeses are well kept, and the wine list is a fairly priced, globetrotting slate; Berry's house French is £12.

CHEF: John Rotherham   PROPRIETORS: Joel Cadbury, Ollie Vigors, Alex Langlands-Pearse and Eric Dunmore   OPEN: all week 12 to 2.30 (11 to 3.30 Sat, 12 to 4.30 Sun), 7 to 11 (10.30 Sun)   CLOSED: 25 and 26 Dec   MEALS: alc (main courses £10.50 to £16). Cover 80p. Bar and brunch menus available   SERVICE:

12.5% (optional), card slips closed   CARDS: Amex, Delta, MasterCard, Switch, Visa   DETAILS: 60 seats. 30 seats outside. Private parties: 20 main room, 1 to 50 private rooms. Vegetarian meals. Wheelchair access (not WC). Music. Air-conditioned   ⊖ South Kensington

Admiralty ☺ ⚹

map 13

Somerset House, Strand, WC2R 1LA
TEL: (020) 7845 4646   FAX: (020) 7845 4658
WEBSITE: www.somerset-house.org.uk

COOKING 5
FRENCH
£47–£74

There's no better way to impress foreign visitors than to book a table at this 'posh place' adjacent to the magnificent courtyard of Somerset House. Eat on the terrace to get views of the Thames, or inside in one of the two smartly set dining rooms, where large vases of flowers vie for attention against the bold colours on the walls.

There's a new order in the kitchen, and head chef Robert Spencer runs a tight ship. Raw materials are impeccable, and the kitchen's delivery is impressively consistent. A starter of confit duck leg on soft foie gras with champ showed excellent textural and flavour combinations, and red mullet with spring onions, bittersweet oranges and orange dressing was perfectly balanced, the fish with an impeccably crisp skin. Dishes are devoid of fussy presentation and over-elaboration, as in a main course of a perfectly formed, evenly golden rissole of summer truffle risotto, delivering pleasing contrasts of an oozing quail's egg, moist and creamy rice, crunchy wild asparagus and soft trompette mushrooms. Iced prune parfait with biscotti and dark chocolate mousse makes a restrained but 'magnificently executed' pudding. Admiralty's wine buyer sticks to what he knows best, with a well-researched, entirely French list offering a fair degree of interest and scope from beyond the classic regions. Two house bottles are £18; everything else is over £20, some in three figures.

CHEF: Robert Spencer   PROPRIETOR: Restaurant Associates   OPEN: all week L 12 to 2.15, Mon to Sat D 6 to 10.15   CLOSED: 25 to 28 Dec, D bank hols   MEALS: alc (main courses £15.50 to £21.50)   SERVICE: 12.5% (optional)   CARDS: Amex, Delta, Diners, MasterCard, Switch, Visa   DETAILS: 55 seats. Private parties: 60 main room, 15 to 30 private rooms. Vegetarian meals. No smoking in 1 dining room. Wheelchair access (also WC). Music   ⊖ Temple, Covent Garden

Alastair Little

map 15

49 Frith Street, W1D 4SG
TEL: (020) 7734 5183   FAX: (020) 7734 5206

COOKING 4
MODERN EUROPEAN
£42–£63

Mr Little is no longer associated with this Soho stalwart, but the cuisine he helped to pioneer – simple, Mediterranean-rooted, based on top-quality ingredients – remains the focus under Juliet Peston and Sue Lewis. The single, narrow room set a blueprint for cool and minimal dining rooms when it opened back in 1985, and it still looks remarkably contemporary nowadays. The menu changes daily, ensuring that seasonality is a priority, so an early June dinner might feature a starter of scallops with asparagus, broad beans, Jersey Royals and bacon, or grilled lamb served with farro and basil dressing. In winter, smoked eel might appear with potato cakes, rocket, beetroot and horseradish, and chicken breast with creamed spinach, ceps and mash. Desserts proclaim the kitchen's Italian leanings, with the likes of vin santo and cantuccini, or affogato al caffè. The wine list is adequate, covering most of the world's wine-growing territories, in a range of prices, with house wines starting at £17.

CHEFS: Juliet Peston and Sue Lewis   PROPRIETORS: Mercedes Andre-Vega and Kirsten Pedersen   OPEN: Mon to Fri L 12 to 3, Mon to Sat D 6 to 11.30   CLOSED: 24 to 26 Dec, bank hols   MEALS: Set L £29, Set D £38   SERVICE: not inc, 12.5% (optional) for parties of 8 or more   CARDS: Amex, Delta, Diners, MasterCard, Switch, Visa   DETAILS: 60 seats. Private parties: 25 private room. Vegetarian meals. Children's helpings. Wheelchair access (not WC). No music. Air-conditioned   ⊖ Tottenham Court Road

Al Duca ♥

map 15

4–5 Duke of York Street, SW1Y 6LA
TEL: (020) 7839 3090   FAX: (020) 7839 4050
WEBSITE: www.alduca-restaurant.co.uk

COOKING 4
ITALIAN
£35–£77

Any restaurant behind Fortnum and Mason must bring expectations of high prices, but – self-confident, upbeat and invariably crowded – Al Duca bucks the trend with good-value fixed-price menus (albeit with some supplements and extra charges for side dishes). Simple techniques are responsible for much of the output, including chargrilled squid with shaved fennel and blood orange salad, and salad of raw beef, celery, olives and mushrooms dressed with hazelnut oil. There's an inventive streak, too, seen in pasta dishes such as home-made cocoa tagliatelle with Savoy cabbage and duck ragoût; pan-fried halibut with potato fondant, Jerusalem artichoke purée and vermouth sauce; or pan-fried calf's liver served with sweet-and-sour onions and celeriac mash. Meals might end with orange jelly with Grand Marnier zabaglione and mint granita, or banana pannacotta with liquorice sauce. A modern textbook Italian wine list is extensive, if pricey – only the £16 house bottles are under £20 – but 15 are offered by the glass from £4.50 to £14.

CHEF: Antonio Cucchiara   PROPRIETOR: Cuisine Collection   OPEN: Mon to Sat 12 to 2.30 (12.30 to 3 Sat), 6 to 11   CLOSED: bank hols   MEALS: Set L £17.50 (2 courses) to £23.50, Set D Mon to Sat 6 to 7.30 and Mon to Wed 10.30 to 11 £13.50 (2 courses) to £16.50, Set D Mon to Sat £20 (2 courses) to £28   SERVICE: 12.5% (optional), card slips closed   CARDS: Amex, Delta, Diners, MasterCard, Switch, Visa   DETAILS: 65 seats. Private parties: 65 main room. Vegetarian meals. Children's helpings. No cigars/pipes. Wheelchair access (not WC). No music. No mobile phones at D. Air-conditioned   ⊖ Piccadilly Circus

Al Hamra

map 15

31–33 Shepherd Market, W1J 7PT
TEL: (020) 7493 1954   FAX: (020) 7493 1044
WEBSITE: www.alhamrarestaurant.com

COOKING 2
LEBANESE
£38–£72

The 'dated near-splendour' of Al Hamra is part of its enduring appeal but, two decades after it set out its stall as a serious Lebanese restaurant, some reporters think it's not quite the star it once was. Meals still begin with a harvest festival of vegetables plus huge rectangular pitta bread, and the long (and by no means cheap) menu opens with around 60 meze including good versions of hummus karwarmah topped with diced fried lamb, and foul moukala (cold broad beans with coriander and garlic). Main courses are mostly grills and roasts, and there's a display of everyday Lebanese puddings to finish. Old-school service is in tune with the plush formality of the place. French and Lebanese wines figure strongly on the list, which zooms skywards from £15.

CHEF: Mahir Abboud   PROPRIETOR: Alex Fansa   OPEN: all week 12 to 11.30   CLOSED: 24 Dec to 2 Jan   MEALS: alc (main courses £13 to £22.50). Cover £2.50   SERVICE: not inc   CARDS: Amex, Delta, Diners, MasterCard, Switch, Visa   DETAILS: 65 seats. 24 seats outside. Private parties: 70 main room. Vegetarian meals. Children's helpings. Wheelchair access (not WC). Music. Air-conditioned   ⊖ Green Park (£5)

Allium ♥

| | NEW ENTRY | map 13 |

Chichester Street, SW1V 3LX
TEL: (020) 7798 6888   FAX: (020) 7798 5685
WEBSITE: www.allium.co.uk

COOKING 5
MODERN EUROPEAN
£37–£83

Situated within the Dolphin Square hotel, Allium is a new venture under the aegis of Anton Edelmann, who was for 20 years maître chef at the Savoy. The design eschews the modern predilection for blond wood, instead going for a midnight-blue look, with soft leather armchair seating and chrome trimmings contributing to the feel of having boarded a luxurious ocean liner. The menus are firmly in the contemporary vein, featuring items such as pickled beetroot, butter-bean purée, caramelised artichoke and an almost casual use of foie gras. 'Allium' being the Latin genus for the onion family, we should not be surprised to come across a tartlet heaped with caramelised onion, itself topped with melting goats' cheese, surrounded by balsamic dressing. Frogs' legs are offered, pan-fried with a salad of endive, a garlic croûte and some spiced pepper cream. Dressings and sauces are top drawer, as is the case with a demi-glace accompanying a fillet of Buccleuch beef topped with roast foie gras. Good French cheeses might precede a showman's dessert such as apricot and chocolate soufflé with its own ice cream – a successful pairing of flavours – while a plate of variations on pineapple manages to include the diversions of chilli and clove seasonings among the more usual jelly and pastry. Smartly attired staff do everything well.

The wine list is less showy than you might expect – London prices, certainly, but nothing for the City bonus boys – sensibly mixing established producers, fashionable modernists and less familiar names. Prices start around the £15 mark, 11 come by the glass, and half-bottles and dessert wines round it all out well.

CHEFS: Anton Edelmann and Peter Wood   PROPRIETOR: Sodexho Restaurants   OPEN: Tue to Fri and Sun L 12 to 3 (2.30 Sun), Tue to Sat D 6 to 10.30   MEALS: alc exc Sun L (main courses £11.50 to £26). Set L £17.50 (2 courses) to £22.50, Set pre-theatre D £22.50 (2 courses) to £28.50, Set D £32.50   SERVICE: 12.5% (optional)   CARDS: Amex, Delta, Diners, MasterCard, Switch, Visa   DETAILS: 90 seats. Private parties: 90 main room, 5 to 70 private rooms. Vegetarian meals. Children's helpings. No-smoking area. No cigars/pipes. Music. No mobile phones. Air-conditioned   ⊖ Pimlico £5

Alloro

map 15

19–20 Dover Street, W1S 4LU
TEL: (020) 7495 4768   FAX: (020) 7629 5348

COOKING 4
ITALIAN
£41–£74

Alloro is in a quintessentially Mayfair neighbourhood. The frontage is quite discreet, opening into a dining room of earthy colours complemented by pistachio tones, with the laurel leaf theme ('alloro' means 'laurel') played out on some plaster casts hung on the walls. The emphasis is on high-quality raw materials treated with the utmost simplicity, delivering, for example, an unusual venison carpaccio that relies on exemplary ingredients to pull it off, 'and pull it off it did'. Sage gnocchi with sage and butter and black truffle liberally shaved over the top shows to good effect a deft hand and respect for simple flavours. The cooking is not shy of bold flavours when they are called for, as in chorizo and saffron sauce accompanying pan-fried monkfish with new potatoes. Light almond-flavoured biancomangiare ('like a stiff pannacotta') with rhubarb coulis gets the thumbs up for dessert, and bread is 'amazingly good'. Friendly, fuss-free service and a comfortable, relaxing atmosphere add to the appeal. As we went to press, a wine list had not been made available to us, though house wines begin at £16.50.

CHEF: Marzio Zacchi   PROPRIETOR: A To Z Restaurants Ltd   OPEN: Mon to Fri L 12 to 2.30, Mon to Sat D 7 to 10.30   MEALS: Set L £23 (2 courses) to £26, Set D £27.50 (2 courses) to £35   SERVICE: 12.5% (optional), card slips closed   CARDS: Amex, Delta, Diners, MasterCard, Switch, Visa   DETAILS: 65 seats. Vegetarian meals. No cigars/pipes. Occasional music. Air-conditioned   ⊖ Green Park

Almeida ▼

map 13

30 Almeida Street, N1 1AD
TEL: (020) 7354 4777   FAX: (020) 7354 2777
WEBSITE: www.almeida-restaurants.co.uk

COOKING **4**
FRENCH BISTRO
£31–£66

One for eternal Francophiles, Almeida is a smart, Conran-owned joint facing the Islington theatre of the same name and has been known to restore both cast and audience members after a show. Habitat-style furnishings meet 'pretty authentic high-end Parisian bistro' style cooking from a kitchen where fixed-price menus represent 'really good value', though carte prices seem to escalate a little. The menus are all-French and all in French: 'coquilles St Jacques, fondue de poireaux' delivers five medium-sized scallops on a bed of nicely made leek vinaigrette. Beautifully fresh halibut has been small, though a portion of braised calves' sweetbreads was huge; light main-course options may require side-order vegetables to quell a hearty appetite. Among the desserts, crème caramel has hit the spot, or there's a 'trolley of tarts' (they also have trolleys for charcuterie and for cheeses). Wine list mark-ups reflect the cost of living in this part of north London. There's plenty of choice by the glass, though, and bottles start a touch under £15; Roussette de Savoie is an unusual find, priced at £29.

CHEF: Ian Wood   PROPRIETOR: Conran Restaurants   OPEN: all week 12 to 2.30 (3 Sun), 5.30 to 11 (Sun 6 to 10)   CLOSED: 25 and 26 Dec, 1 Jan, Good Friday   MEALS: alc (main courses £12.50 to £19.50). Set L and D £14.50 (2 courses) to £17.50. Bar tapas menu available   SERVICE: 12.5% (optional), card slips closed   CARDS: Amex, Delta, Diners, MasterCard, Switch, Visa   DETAILS: 90 seats. Private parties: 90 main room, 8 to 20 private rooms. No pipes. Wheelchair access (also WC). No music. Air-conditioned   ⊖ Angel/Highbury & Islington

Al San Vincenzo

map 13

30 Connaught Street, W2 2AF
TEL: (020) 7262 9623

COOKING **2**
ITALIAN
£50–£60

This little shop-front restaurant, with its plain wooden tables and low-key air, has a proper Mom and Pop feel. The set-price, which has half a dozen choices per course and changes monthly, is handwritten and photocopied, service is personable, and chef/proprietor Vincenzo 'is always in the kitchen'. The cooking is home-style Italian, but with some rather bold flourishes: for example, a warm salad of organic breast of chicken cooked in organic orange juice with pickled quince. Black tonnarelle pasta could come with clams, and main dishes may include cotechino (a coarse, subtly spiced pork sausage from northern Italy) with zampone (pigs' trotters) served with lentils. Dessert lovers might yield to chocolate semifreddo, or pastiera, a Neapolitan-style ricotta cheesecake. House wine, from a short, all-Italian list, starts at £16 a bottle.

CHEF: Vincenzo Borgonzolo   PROPRIETORS: Elaine and Vincenzo Borgonzolo   OPEN: Mon to Fri L 12.30 to 1.45, Mon to Sat D 7 to 9.45   MEALS: Set L and D £28.50 (2 courses) to £34.50   SERVICE: not inc, 12.5% for groups of 5 or more   CARDS: Delta, MasterCard, Switch, Visa   DETAILS: 24 seats. Private parties: 20 main room. Vegetarian meals. No children under 12. No pipes/cigars. Music   ⊖ Marble Arch

Anchor & Hope £

NEW ENTRY   map 13

36 The Cut, SE1 8LP
TEL: (020) 7928 9898

COOKING 5
TRADITIONAL EUROPEAN
£28–£53

A gastronomic *quartier* has arisen in the area around the Young Vic theatre, Southwark Tube station and Waterloo. The Anchor & Hope fits snugly in with the prevailing air, its generously sized windows opening on to the street, and the chunky wooden furniture, ochre-coloured walls and bare-boarded floors proudly displaying its pub credentials. One half of the large open-plan space is most definitely for drinking, while in the other, close-together tables stand ready for eaters; a heavy curtain is sometimes drawn as a divide. The open kitchen delivers robust, unfussy, and 'downright appealing food'.

Outstanding sourdough bread presages the treats in store. The kitchen applies best culinary practice, arriving at its seasonal menus after dialogue with suppliers, and with an emphasis on shared dishes: for example, slow-cooked stuffed duck for three or four, suckling kid and fennel for two. The long cooking achieves majestic results, as with an 'unctuous, utterly captivating' oxtail stew with carrots, swede and buttery mash. Smoked herring comes with lentils, cuttlefish in a rich and inky risotto, skate with potato and aïoli, and rabbit cooked with wild garlic and sherry. Puddings will fill any corners with the likes of prune and almond tart, or a mountainous hunk of 'tall, dark and handsome' chocolate cake with a blob of crème fraîche. Friendly and knowledgeable service adds to the allure. A short, intelligently composed wine list stays mostly in Europe, encompasses a couple of Lebanese bottles, and opens at £10, or £1.80 a glass.

CHEFS: Harry Lester and Jonathon Jones   PROPRIETORS: Robert Shaw, Harry Lester, Jonathon Jones and Mike Belben   OPEN: Mon 6 to 10.30, Tue to Sat 12 to 2.30, 6 to 10.30   MEALS: alc (main courses £10 to £17). Bar menu available all day (from 5pm Mon)   SERVICE: not inc   CARDS: Delta, MasterCard, Switch, Visa   DETAILS: 80 seats. 9 seats outside. No cigars. Wheelchair access (not WC). No music   ⊖ Waterloo, Southwark

---

Anglesea Arms £

map 12

35 Wingate Road, W6 0UR
TEL: (020) 8749 1291   FAX: (020) 8749 1254

COOKING 2
MODERN EUROPEAN
£22–£51

It would be hard to think of a 'better neighbourhood restaurant', reckoned one reporter, extolling the virtues of this ground-breaking gastro-pub. Mingle with the young crowd in the bar if you want a pint of real ale or a plate of oysters; bag a table in the separate dining area (no bookings) if you fancy something more serious. The blackboard menu shows intriguing touches and a feel for rustic flavours: pigeon and duck foie gras terrine rubs shoulders with pork pie and piccalilli, while sea bass fillets with sautéed squid, pipérade and Swiss chard sit alongside slow-cooked pork belly with white beans, sage, apples and cider. A couple of cheeses and a few desserts like cheesecake with rhubarb and prunes close the show. The thoughtfully assembled, global wine list starts at £10.95.

CHEF: Jacky Lelièvre   PROPRIETOR: Fiona Evans   OPEN: Mon to Sat 12.30 to 2.45 (3 Sat), 7 to 10.30, Sun 12.30 to 3.30, 7 to 10   CLOSED: 23 to 31 Dec   MEALS: alc (main courses L £8.50 to £13.50, D £11 to £16.50). Set L £9.95 (2 courses) to £12.95. Bar menu available all day   SERVICE: not inc   CARDS: Delta, MasterCard, Switch, Visa   DETAILS: 80 seats. 18 seats outside. Vegetarian meals. Children's helpings. Wheelchair access (not WC). Occasional music   ⊖ Ravenscourt Park

Ark
map 13

122 Palace Gardens Terrace, W8 4RT
TEL: (020) 7229 4024   FAX: (020) 7792 8787
WEBSITE: www.thearkrestaurant.co.uk

COOKING 2
ITALIAN
£26–£57

Behind outside tables and the almost prefab-like exterior lies a relaxing flower-filled space – 'modern romantic' is the owner's categorisation. Seasonally changing robust combinations are typified by chickpea focaccia with marinated artichokes and prosciutto, or swordfish carpaccio as starters, and mains of roast monkfish with wild mushrooms and a basil and leek sauce, or pork with prune and balsamic jus and fennel gratin. In between lie 'primi piatti' that double as starter or main – asparagus ravioli in lemon sauce, say. Puds are the likes of pannacotta or pear tart. An all-Italian wine list starts at £12.50, has plenty around £20 and runs through to super-Tuscan Ornellaia and Gaja's Piedmontese reds at £150 plus. A generous number by the glass allows economical experiment.

CHEF: Simona Bonelli   PROPRIETOR: Louise Mayo   OPEN: Tue to Sun L 12 to 2.45, Mon to Sat D 6.30 to 11   CLOSED: bank hols   MEALS: alc (main courses £11 to £18.50). Set L £12.50 (2 courses) to £15   SERVICE: 12.5% (optional), card slips closed   CARDS: Amex, Delta, MasterCard, Switch, Visa   DETAILS: 55 seats. 16 seats outside. Private parties: 60 main room. Vegetarian meals. Children's helpings. Wheelchair access (not WC). Occasional music. Air-conditioned   ⊖ Notting Hill Gate £5

Armadillo
map 12

41 Broadway Market, E8 4PH
TEL: (020) 7249 3633
WEBSITE: www.armadillorestaurant.co.uk

COOKING 2
SOUTH AMERICAN
£28–£46

Contemporary South American restaurants are hardly thick on the ground in London, but this functionally decorated venue is intent on spreading the gospel. The menu has a few recognisable ideas – crispy duck and peppers in a roll with banana and tamarind chutney, grilled fillet steak with a mushroom-stuffed red onion – although the kitchen also throws down the gastronomic gauntlet by serving grilled 'smoky' salmon with jicama escabechada and chipotle mayonnaise and pairing braised pheasant with salsa negra, pancetta, sweet potatoes and chestnuts. Apple and cinnamon empanadas with orange sabayon figure among desserts, or you might go for chocolate and chilli truffles. Argentina, Chile and Mexico contribute to the wine list, along with some representatives from Iberia. Prices (from £10.50) are fair.

CHEF/PROPRIETOR: Rogerio David   OPEN: Tue to Sat D only 6.30 to 10.30   CLOSED: 1 week at Christmas, last week Aug   MEALS: alc (main courses £9.50 to £14.50). Cover £1   SERVICE: not inc, card slips closed, 12.5% for parties of 5 or more   CARDS: Amex, Delta, Diners, MasterCard, Switch, Visa   DETAILS: 50 seats. 8 seats outside. Private parties: 35 main room, 15 to 25 private rooms. Vegetarian meals. No cigars/pipes. Occasional music   ⊖ Bethnal Green

Assaggi
map 13

The Chepstow, 39 Chepstow Place, W2 4TS
TEL: (020) 7792 5501   FAX: (020) 7792 9033

COOKING 4
ITALIAN
£47–£69

Jet-black carpeted stairs lead to this popular Italian restaurant perched over a pub: a smallish room featuring lots of wood, with colour and texture lent by abstract canvases in soothing shades. There are only 11 tables, so dining here is an intimate affair (if not necessarily a quiet one). A genuine attempt is made at an Italian atmosphere and there is a disarming sincerity and unpretentiousness. Fine ingredients are treated with simplicity, and even the names of the dishes on the menu – in untranslated Italian – are also deceptively simple. There may be seppie con carciofi (squid with globe artichokes) to start, or a soup of farro (grain) and porcini. A main course listed as 'rombo all griglia' may see the turbot served on a bed of deep-fried strands of carrot and courgette, flecked with rocket and mint and interspersed with tiny cubes of steamed potato. Desserts, from a daily selection, continue the quality Italian route. Prices aren't cheap (not much change from £20 for most main courses), but ingredients are of the highest calibre, prepared with originality and served with care. Advance booking is essential, although a beguiled inspector felt it 'worth the wait'. The wine list is fairly brief and all-Italian; house wines from the proprietors' native Sardinia starting at £13.95 (£3.25 a glass), but not many bottles are under £25.

CHEF: Nino Sassu   PROPRIETORS: Nino Sassu and Pietro Fraccari   OPEN: Mon to Sat 12.30 (1 Sat) to 2.30, 7.30 to 11   CLOSED: 2 weeks Christmas, bank hols   MEALS: alc (main courses £16 to £20)   SERVICE: not inc, card slips closed   CARDS: Delta, Diners, MasterCard, Switch, Visa   DETAILS: 35 seats. Vegetarian meals. Children's helpings. No music. Air-conditioned   ⊖ Notting Hill Gate

Atlantic Bar and Grill ♥

map 15

20 Glasshouse Street, W1B 5DJ
TEL: (020) 7734 4888   FAX: (020) 7734 5400
WEBSITE: www.atlanticbarandgrill.com

COOKING 4
MODERN EUROPEAN
£37–£89

The Atlantic's glitz may have faded a little (the crowd somewhat older, perhaps), but meals are composed of fine ingredients and some good cooking goes on down in this subterranean restaurant. The vast room is split down the middle by a huge, imposing bar, featuring marble pillars and giant mirrors, and the dining area has well-spaced tables. There are long-established combinations on the menu, such as Caesar salad, or crispy duck with citrus and five-spice, and fish is given due attention in such dishes as roasted sea bass with poached asparagus and warm olive sauce. Delicately flavoured and textured octopus carpaccio might precede a main course of lamb of 'sterling-quality meat' accompanied by zingy aubergine caviar, cumin carrots and 'very good jus'. Buccleuch beef gets special mention on the menu, and vegetables are extra. Desserts extend to wild berry brûlée. Service is friendly but can be stretched, and the music gets louder as the night progresses. On the wine list, top-drawer names mingle with plenty that is more readily affordable, and all regions are approached with enthusiasm. Prices, starting with £14 house, are fair for the neighbourhood; options by the glass reflect the balance of the list with both a house range from £3.50 and some specials at up to £16.25 a shot.

CHEF: Ben O'Donoghue   PROPRIETORS: Oliver, Siobhan, Caitrina and Marie Peyton   OPEN: Mon to Sat D only 6 to 12   CLOSED: 24 to 26 Dec, bank hols   MEALS: alc (main courses £12 to £35). Set D £32. Bar menu available 12 to 2am   SERVICE: 12.5% (optional), card slips closed   CARDS: Amex, Delta, Diners, MasterCard, Switch, Visa   DETAILS: 180 seats. Private parties: 500 main room, 70 to 100 private rooms. Vegetarian meals. Music. Air-conditioned   ⊖ Piccadilly Circus

If customers are asked to switch off mobile phones while in a restaurant, this is noted in the details at the end of an entry.

Aubergine

map 14

11 Park Walk, SW10 0AJ

TEL: (020) 7352 3449   FAX: (020) 7351 1770

COOKING 6
MODERN FRENCH
£46–£115

The restaurant that put one Gordon Ramsay on the gastronomic map in the mid-1990s, Aubergine has forged its own singular identity since his departure. Its ambience is that of the upmarket restaurant du quartier, the quartier being well-heeled Chelsea, and the soft-focus décor, with maximal aubergine theming (you could see the beige-rolled walls as being the colour of aubergine flesh), helps to set a tone that is comfortingly a million miles away from domestic.

You'll know you're not at home when you peruse the menus, replete as they are with scallops, truffles, quail and foie gras. At the centre of the seven-course menu gourmand may be turbot with leeks and caviar in champagne sauce, preceding a breast of duck with prunes. Notwithstanding this high sheen, the approach is solicitous without over-familiarity, and the regular fixed-price menu reads quite straightforwardly. Marinated salmon with apple, mint and lime might encourage a moment of speculative tasting in the head, but braised oxtail with celeriac mash, best end of lamb with white onion purée and grain mustard sauce, and even sea bass with red wine and rosemary will orientate you in the familiar modern French idiom. Dishes are immaculately presented with a high degree of finish, and the quality of materials shines throughout. Desserts may be fashioned from a range of counterpointing flavours, as in lime chiboust with rhubarb compote and ginger sorbet, or may be as foursquare as banana parfait. Unsurprisingly, budget bottles are not the forte of the wine list. But if you are in a mood to feel the quality and hang the expense, then you won't be short of options, especially from classic French regions.

CHEF: William Drabble   PROPRIETOR: A To Z Restaurants   OPEN: Mon to Fri L 12 to 2.30, Mon to Sat D 7 to 11   CLOSED: last Sat before Christmas to first Mon Jan   MEALS: Set L £32 (inc wine), Set D £55 to £72   SERVICE: 12.5% (optional), card slips closed   CARDS: Amex, Delta, Diners, MasterCard, Switch, Visa   DETAILS: 52 seats. Private parties: 64 main room. No cigars/pipes. Wheelchair access (not WC). No music. No mobile phones. Air-conditioned   ⊖ South Kensington

Babur Brasserie ⅝ £

map 12

119 Brockley Rise, SE23 1JP

TEL: (020) 8291 2400   FAX: (020) 8291 4881

WEBSITE: www.babur-brasserie.com

COOKING 2
INDIAN
£28–£48

Brockley Rise makes a surprising location for this highly successful Indian restaurant, and there are more surprises on the menu. At a glance, it reads like the itinerary for a gastro-tour of the Subcontinent, with fish highlighting the regional scope of proceedings: Mangalore curry involves chunks of swordfish, potatoes and mango in a southern Indian sauce, sea bass is given a Keralan slant, and monkfish is used for a classic Madras curry. Elsewhere, the North contributes tandooris, while beef xacuti hails from Goa. Salmon samosas figure in the line-up of starters, vegetables are many and varied (miloni tarkari is a kebab of pumpkin and okra), and desserts include Raj throwbacks like booze-laden Byculla Club soufflé. House wine is £9.25.

CHEF: Enam Rahman   PROPRIETOR: Babur 1998 Ltd   OPEN: Sat to Thur L 12.15 to 2.15, all week D 6 to 11.15   CLOSED: 25 and 26 Dec   MEALS: alc exc Sun L (main courses £7.50 to £13). Sun buffet L £8.95   SERVICE: not inc, card slips closed   CARDS: Amex, Delta, Diners, MasterCard, Switch, Visa   DETAILS: 56

seats. Private parties: 35 main room. Vegetarian meals. No smoking in 1 dining room. Wheelchair access (not WC). Music. Air-conditioned £5

Back to Basics

map 15

21A Foley Street, W1W 6DS	COOKING 3
TEL: (020) 7436 2181 FAX: (020) 7436 2180	SEAFOOD
WEBSITE: www.backtobasics.uk.com	£35–£60

As the name suggests, this is a 'no-frills' restaurant: it can seem cramped, but the mood is entertaining and there are plenty of seats outside if the weather's kind. The kitchen relies on daily supplies of fish, which may be cooked simply or dressed up in modish style. A board listing 'Today's Catch' is the main attraction: wild sea bass, gilthead bream, and squid surface from time to time, along with dishes like mackerel fillet with spinach, grilled halloumi and spiced sweet red onion. Appetisers (from crab thermidor to a pint of prawns), salads and pastas are fixtures, and a few fish-free items broaden the choice: baby chicken with honey, cracked coriander and peppercorns is typical. Desserts are often spiked with alcohol, whether it's bread-and-butter pudding with whisky sauce or Baileys crème brûlée. The short wine list (from £13) is supplemented by an 'alternative cellar' of French gems.

CHEF: Andrew Dunbair   PROPRIETOR: Ursula Higgs   OPEN: Mon to Sat 12 to 3, 6 to 10.30   MEALS: alc (main courses £12.50 to £17)   SERVICE: 12.5% (optional)   CARDS: Amex, Delta, Diners, MasterCard, Switch, Visa   DETAILS: 35 seats. 50 seats outside. Private parties: 40 main room. Vegetarian meals. No-smoking area. Music   ⊖ Oxford Circus

Baltic

map 13

74 Blackfriars Road, SE1 8HA	COOKING 3
TEL: (020) 7928 1111 FAX: (020) 7928 8487	EAST/NORTH EUROPEAN
WEBSITE: www.balticrestaurant.co.uk	£24–£51

Behind the gunmetal grey frontage by Southwark Tube station, lie a long bar (where twenty-somethings photograph themselves on their mobiles to document the effects of the 25 vodka varieties available) and a cavernous, rackety rear space where food is served. Some more-Western dishes are now interspersed among the ethnic offerings, but the menu still impresses. Seared scallops on a pile of white cabbage with hotly peppered cherry jam offers great contrasts, while fried herrings on pickled vegetables is well flavoured and generous. Pot-roasted salt beef comes with an array of root veg and a little pot of horseradish, while a honey-roast pear makes an interesting garnish for venison. Pudding choices are less exuberant but vodka cherry ice cream with hot chocolate sauce has impressed. Wines are a reasonable but all-Western selection; prices open at £12.

CHEF: Nick Pound   PROPRIETOR: Jon Waroniecki   OPEN: Sun to Fri L 12 to 2.30, all week D 6 to 11.15   MEALS: alc (main courses £9 to £15). Set L £11.50 (2 courses) to £13.50, pre-theatre D 6 to 7 £11.50 (2 courses) to £13.50, Set D £22.50. Bar menu available   SERVICE: 12.5% (optional), card slips closed   CARDS: Amex, Delta, Diners, MasterCard, Switch, Visa   DETAILS: 220 seats. Private parties: 200 main room, 10 to 30 private rooms. Vegetarian meals. Children's helpings. Wheelchair access (also WC). Music   ⊖ Southwark, Waterloo

The Guide's top-rated restaurants are listed near the front of the book.

Bank Aldwych/Bank Westminster ♥

map 13

1 Kingsway, Aldwych, WC2B 6XF
45 Buckingham Gate, SW1E 6BS
TEL: (020) 7379 9797 (centralised number)
FAX: (020) 7240 7001 (centralised number)
WEBSITE: www.bankrestaurants.com

COOKING 3
MODERN EUROPEAN
£24–£82

Both Banks, the Aldwych original with its striking 'forest of glass' ceiling, and its Westminster sibling – a smart conservatory-like space with huge glass windows overlooking charming gardens – continue to draw the crowds. The food is every bit as stylish as the décor: witness sweet potato muffins and pickled fennel served with grilled cod and bouillabaisse sauce, or a starter of Thai red curry risotto served with chargrilled squid and ginger beurre blanc. For sheer indulgence there's well-timed roast veal cutlet topped by a gremolata walnut crust served with Roquefort polenta and cep confit, but what impressed one reporter most was a simple seminal sticky toffee pudding. Service from a trendily clad young team, though not always on the ball, is friendly and willing. Bank House Merlot (£14) gained the thumbs-up from an inspector, and in both Westminster and Aldwych branches this heads up an international list arranged by style. Prices are not too bad and a host of options come by the glass. As we went to press, we heard that a chef change was planned for Aldwych; reports please. There's a Bank in Birmingham, too (see entry).

CHEF: Matt Dawson (Westminster) PROPRIETOR: Bank Restaurant Group plc OPEN: Mon to Fri L 12 to 2.45, Mon to Sat D 5.30 to 11; Aldwych also open Sat and Sun brunch 11.30 to 3, and Sun D 5.30 to 9.30 MEALS: alc (main courses £9 to £28). Set L and D 5.30 to 7 and 10 to 11 £12.50 (2 courses) to £15. Bar and (Aldwych only) breakfast menus available SERVICE: 12.5% (optional) CARDS: Amex, Delta, Diners, MasterCard, Switch, Visa DETAILS: 220 seats. Private parties: 220 main room; 30 private room. Vegetarian meals. Children's helpings. Wheelchair access (also WC). Occasional music. Air-conditioned ⊖ Holborn, St James's Park

Belvedere Marco Pierre White

map 13

off Abbotsbury Road, W8 6LU
TEL: (020) 7602 1238   FAX: (020) 7610 4382
WEBSITE: www.whitestarling.org.uk

COOKING 4
MODERN BRITISH/MEDITERRANEAN
£32–£63

The luxurious green of Holland Park is the backdrop for this elegant restaurant, where the grand surroundings and eccentric interior call up images of Noël Coward. The table settings are sumptuously posh: lots of crisp linen and worn, polished silverware. Service is formal, in the silver-cloche-bearing French mode. A new chef is at the helm, with Billy Reid, latterly of L'Escargot and the Vineyard at Stockcross (see entries), having taken over in summer 2004.

Among starters a simple but perfectly turned out lobster linguine flavoured with a hint of vermouth and a few dill fronds showed accurate timings and seasonings, as did a crème Caroline, a soup containing 'fine, rich and sweet' salmon roe and sweetcorn, 'flawlessly silky' and splashed through with feather-light truffle and cream emulsion. For main courses, diners might find a neatly trimmed veal cutlet with morel jus, fondant potato and roast carrots revealed from beneath a silver dome. Desserts such as raspberry soufflé (pronounced 'unquestionably worth the 25-minute wait' by an inspector) and tarte Tatin replay the classic French theme. The wine list shows a keen eye for good producers from the New and Old Worlds, although France gets top billing. Bottle prices start at £15.

CHEF: Billy Reid PROPRIETORS: Jimmy Lahoud and Marco Pierre White OPEN: all week L 12 to 2.30 (3.15 Sun), Mon to Sat D 6 to 11 CLOSED: 25 Dec, 1 Jan MEALS: alc exc Sun L (main courses £12 to £18). Set L £14.95 (2 courses) to £17.95, Set L Sun £19.50 (3 courses) SERVICE: 12.5% (optional), card slips closed CARDS: Amex, Delta, Diners, MasterCard, Switch, Visa DETAILS: 144 seats. 20 seats outside. Private parties: 60 main room. No music. Air-conditioned ⊖ Holland Park (£5)

Benares map 15

12A Berkeley Square, W1J 6BS — COOKING **3**
TEL: (020) 7629 8886 FAX: (020) 7491 8883 — MODERN INDIAN
WEBSITE: www.benaresrestaurant.com — £51–£74

'Designed by a team of architects with a strong sense of symmetry, taste and style', according to one correspondent, Benares puts on a classy show with its sophisticated ambience, imperial staircase and 'two ponds with swimming blossoms'. Prices are steep and portions can seem small, but the kitchen finds favour with its original cooking. Set lunches are well reported, and the menu tries to move beyond the usual expectations: tandoori chicken is served as a salad with pickled tomatoes and star fruit, while tiger prawns appear with mango and coconut sauce. Side orders could include water chestnuts and haricot beans with onion seeds, or wadi aloo (crisp lentil dumplings), and desserts have featured grilled spiced pineapple with ginger ice cream. Service draws a mixed response, from 'cool and polite' to 'incompetent'. The global wine list has nothing below £18 a bottle, although ten are available by the glass.

CHEF/PROPRIETOR: Atul Kochhar OPEN: Mon to Fri L 12.30 to 2.30, all week D 5.30 to 10.30 (10 Sun) MEALS: alc (main courses £14 to £17.50). Set L £10 (2 courses), Set D £19.50 (2 courses) to £55 (inc wine) SERVICE: 12.5%, card slips closed CARDS: Amex, Delta, Diners, MasterCard, Switch, Visa DETAILS: 140 seats. Private parties: 140 main room, 10 to 22 private rooms. Vegetarian meals. No children under 10. No smoking. Music. Air-conditioned ⊖ Green Park

▲ Bentley, 1880 NEW ENTRY map 14

27–33 Harrington Gardens, SW7 4JX — COOKING **6**
TEL: (020) 7244 5555 FAX: (020) 7244 5566 — MODERN EUROPEAN
WEBSITE: www.thebentley-hotel.com — £58–£132

The recently opened Bentley Hotel is tucked away off Gloucester Road. Inside is a study in opulence, with silks, brocades and gilt everywhere you look. Enveloped in gilt, beneath twinkling chandeliers, you might well feel in the mood to play it cool and just nibble, which is where the indelicately named 'Grazing Menus' come into their own – five, six, seven or eight courses of miniaturised versions of the main menu dishes. There is skill at work in the cooking, as is indicated by the cavalcade of fabulous breads that arrives first. Not everything is as ornate as the interior design either. Tender lobster mounted on a cucumber and dill salad, honour-guarded by four spears of asparagus, made a convincing spring starter, while a pithiviers of confit pork, onion and tarragon was the centrepiece of a serving of fine, light rabbit velouté. Unusual combinations are skilfully achieved, with creamed cauliflower, capers and sultanas providing the partners for a main-course serving of plump, lightly seared scallops. Exemplary poulet de Bresse is more classically accompanied by artichokes, shallots, creamed cabbage and an intense red wine reduction. French cheeses look the part, but desserts at inspection suffered somewhat from the curate's egg syndrome, being good only in parts. Variations on pineapple run the gamut from an excellent caramelised ring of the fruit topped with high-intensity sorbet to a rather leaden jammy doughnut. Excellent petits fours come with premium coffee. The wine list majors on France and is reliably smart throughout. Prices are high by any standards, with very little under £25, but honour is salvaged by a breathtaking 200 options by the glass from £4.50 to £50.

CHEF: Andrew Turner   PROPRIETOR: International Luxury Hotels   OPEN: Mon to Sat D only 6 to 10 CLOSED: 26 Dec to 10 Jan   MEALS: Set D £40 to £70   SERVICE: not inc   CARDS: Amex, Delta, Diners, MasterCard, Switch, Visa   DETAILS: 50 seats. Private parties: 8 main room, 2 to 60 private rooms. Vegetarian meals. No smoking. Wheelchair access (also WC). Music. No mobile phones. Air-conditioned ACCOMMODATION: 64 rooms, all with bath/shower. TV. Phone. Room only £180 to £2,500. Rooms for disabled. Baby facilities

Berkeley Square Café   map 15

7 Davies Street, W1K 3DD   COOKING 6
TEL: (020) 7629 6993   FAX: (020) 7491 9719   MODERN FRENCH
WEBSITE: www.berkeleysquarecafe.com   £36–£80

The Berkeley Square Café – a café in name only – is as smart and stylish as you'd expect, given the location in one of London's most affluent neighbourhoods. Decking at the front allows for outdoor eating, and a blue awning adds to a general impression of Frenchness. Inside, walls in shades of purple and mauve and modern artworks principally in bright red create a warm feel, and well-spaced tables are laid with good-quality linen, small vases of flowers and candles. Service is 'correct' yet relaxed.

Steven Black's luxurious and classically orientated cooking demonstrates first-class workmanship without being showy, as in a starter of two fat, sticky, sweet, translucent scallops paired with foie gras and served on a bed of ceps, salsify and parsnip purée, and a main-course fillet of Aberdeen Angus, given added richness with a piece of seared foie gras and braised oxtail wrapped in caul, set off against bittersweet caramelised chicory and truffle fumet with good depth of flavour. Praise has also come in for poached turbot on an enticingly bright slick of bouillabaisse sauce, topped with three well-made Jerusalem artichoke tortellini. To finish, a 'variation on banana' has been a highlight, comprising five bite-sized portions of desserts, including a crème brûlée and a light, impressively flavoured parfait. Wines are expensive but well chosen, with ten house selections opening the list from £18.

CHEF: Steven Black   PROPRIETORS: Vince Power and Steven Black   OPEN: Mon to Fri L 12 to 2.30, Mon to Sat D 6 to 10   CLOSED: Christmas, bank hols   MEALS: Set L and D £15.95 (2 courses) to £47.50   SERVICE: 12.5% (optional), card slips closed   CARDS: Amex, Delta, Diners, MasterCard, Switch, Visa   DETAILS: 70 seats. 20 seats outside. Private parties: 60 main room, 8 to 16 private rooms. Vegetarian meals. Children's helpings. No-smoking area. No cigars. Wheelchair access (not WC). Occasional music. Air-conditioned

Bibendum ▮   map 14

Michelin House, 81 Fulham Road, SW3 6RD   COOKING 4
TEL: (020) 7581 5817   FAX: (020) 7823 7925   MODERN BRITISH
WEBSITE: www.bibendum.co.uk   £46–£100

The first-floor dining room feels luxurious and expansive, its stained-glass windows variously showing the Michelin Man on his bicycle and puffing on a fat cigar, while the curvaceous chairs at the larger tables are among the most comfortable around. A winning combination of France and Britain is the Conran culinary philosophy, bringing on starters of seasonal asparagus with sauce mousseline, or smoked eel with a poached egg and salt-beef hash. Choice is wide and alluring: pot-roast quails are done with chorizo and chickpeas as an unusual main-course option, sharing the billing with grilled rabbit with mustard sauce, deep-fried haddock with chips and tartare sauce, and fillet steak au poivre. Conclude with pear and almond tart with Jersey cream, or vanilla bavarois with passion-fruit sauce. The wine list appropriately centres on France, offering excellent bottles from all regions and laying on Bordeaux and Burgundy in magnificent style. Otherwise, Italy, Australia and California fare best. Some prices look high, but options under £20 are good, starting with £16.95 house white.

On the ground floor the Oyster Bar continues to offer 'an impeccable and lavish selection of simply handled shellfish' as well as mixed meze and crostini platters, tuna tataki with sweet pickled cucumber, and chicken Caesar salad.

CHEF: Matthew Harris   PROPRIETORS: Sir Terence Conran, Simon Hopkinson, Michael Hamlyn and Graham Williams   OPEN: all week 12 to 2.30 (12.30 to 3 Sat and Sun), 7 to 11.30 (10.30 Sun)   CLOSED: 24 to 27 Dec   MEALS: alc D (main courses £16.50 to £26.50). Set L £28.50   SERVICE: 12.5% (optional)   CARDS: Amex, Delta, Diners, MasterCard, Switch, Visa   DETAILS: 88 seats. Private parties: 90 main room. Children's helpings. No pipes. Wheelchair access (not WC). No music. No mobile phones. Air-conditioned

---

Bistro Aix   map 12

54 Topsfield Parade, Tottenham Lane, N8 8PT   COOKING 3
TEL: (020) 8340 6346   FRENCH
WEBSITE: www.bistroaix.co.uk   £28–£61

The fact that this bistro is personally run, intimate and decorated with an eye for quirky individuality may explain why it's a favourite destination for Crouch End locals. Black and white photographs, mirrors and oil paintings line the mustard-yellow and red walls, and there are chandeliers fashioned from wrought-iron hoops with little bulbs. The menu covers a lot of territory, from soups, salads and starters like foie gras terrine, and snails in hazelnut butter, to main courses of grilled prawn risotto, osso buco with horseradish potato purée, and a mighty provençale mixed grill (complete with boudin noir and onion relish). As a finale, order a cocktail or boozy digestif to go with, say, tarte au citron, or warm chocolate fondant with griottine cherries. France dominates the wine list, which leads off with vins de pays at £12.

CHEF: Lynne Sanders   PROPRIETORS: Lynne Sanders and Andrew Schutt   OPEN: Tue to Sun 12 to 2.30, 6.30 to 11   MEALS: alc (main courses L £8.50 to £15.50, D £11.50 to £15.50). Set L Tue to Sat £11.50 (2 courses), Set D Sun £13.50 (2 courses) to £16.50   SERVICE: 12.5% (optional), card slips closed   CARDS: Amex, Delta, Diners, MasterCard, Switch, Visa   DETAILS: 44 seats. Private parties: 50 main room, 25 private room. Vegetarian meals. Children's helpings. No-smoking area. No cigars/pipes. Wheelchair access (also WC). Music. Air-conditioned £5

Blandford Street   map 15

5–7 Blandford Street, W1U 3DB   COOKING 3
TEL: (020) 7486 9696   FAX: (020) 7486 5067   MODERN EUROPEAN
WEBSITE: www.blandford-street.co.uk   £35–£70

Blandford Street is a quiet side road off bustling Marylebone High Street, and the eponymous restaurant lies behind a glass frontage with a red awning. The white walls of the dining room are hung with big mirrors and abstract geometrical paintings in shades of red, and widely spaced tables are laid with crisp linen. The emphasis is on quality of ingredients, and while the cooking style seems old-fashioned it gives fine results. For starters, try tender, sweet seared cuttlefish with creamy brandade, crunchy poached leeks and a roast plum tomato, while to follow there might be a mixed grill of fish (swordfish, sea bass, mackerel and tuna) with 'proper' chips and tartare sauce, or succulent ribeye steak with fat, crisp rösti, French beans and a rich, creamy Diane sauce. For dessert, a traditional French-style apple tart with clotted cream has been well received. House vins de pays at £16 open a varied global wine list.

CHEF: Martin Moore PROPRIETORS: Nicholas and Emmaline Lambert OPEN: Mon to Fri L 12 to 2.30, Mon to Sat D 6.30 to 10.30 CLOSED: Christmas, Easter Sat, bank hols MEALS: alc (main courses £10.50 to £20) SERVICE: 12.5% (optional), card slips closed CARDS: Amex, Delta, Diners, MasterCard, Switch, Visa DETAILS: 50 seats. 8 seats outside. Private parties: 45 main room, 6 to 16 private rooms. Vegetarian meals. No-smoking area. Wheelchair access (not WC). Occasional music. Air-conditioned ⊖ Bond Street, Baker Street

Bleeding Heart map 13

The Cellars, Bleeding Heart Yard, Greville Street,
EC1N 8SJ
TEL: (020) 7242 8238 FAX: (020) 7831 1402
WEBSITE: www.bleedingheart.co.uk

COOKING 2
FRENCH
£36–£65

'Brilliantly designed', thought one reporter, commenting on Bleeding Heart's geranium-decked courtyard and beautifully illuminated cellar restaurant. It's 'wildly popular with suits at lunch', no doubt because it offers privacy, buzz and a feel of old-world refinement. A new chef is in residence, but the original style remains: menus are in English with French subtitles, flavours are robust, and ingredients come from all over. Scottish scallops are baked in their shells with caramelised shallots, while medallions of New Zealand venison could be paired with celeriac dauphinois; there's also Suffolk suckling pig and rack of Welsh lamb with sweet potato purée and rosemary jus. For dessert, try a dish of Agen prunes in little filo parcels. Legions of enthusiastic young staff are now 'armed with high-tech pocket computers'. Reporters are full of praise for the New Zealand section of the wine list, which looks well beyond the Wilsons' own Trinity Hill estate, but A-list France remains the focus. Magnums and larger bottles are on offer for big feasts. House white is £15.95, red £18.95, and 20 come by the glass.

CHEF: Pascal Even PROPRIETORS: Robert and Robyn Wilson OPEN: Mon to Fri 12 to 2.45, 6.30 to 10.30 CLOSED: 23 Dec to 4 Jan MEALS: alc (main courses £11 to £20) SERVICE: 12.5% (optional), card slips closed CARDS: Amex, Delta, Diners, MasterCard, Switch, Visa DETAILS: 120 seats. 30 seats outside. Private parties: 40 to 120 private rooms. Vegetarian meals. No music. Air-conditioned ⊖ Farringdon

Blue Elephant map 12

3–6 Fulham Broadway, SW6 1AA
TEL: (020) 7385 6595 FAX: (020) 7386 7665
WEBSITE: www.blueelephant.com

COOKING 1
THAI
£46–£85

'No other London restaurant is so capable of instantly transporting you to Thailand' as the glamorous and luxuriantly decorated Blue Elephant. Its gilt-edged bar resembles a dragon from a Royal barge, carp swim in little ponds, and the flowers would impress the RHS. The menu's extensive trawl though Thai staples has plenty for vegetarians, and dishes arrive on gold platters. Steamed dim sim and generously filled spring rolls are decent appetisers; other successes have included stir-fried prawns with oyster sauce and popular phad thai noodles. Curries, such as massaman lamb and roast duck with spiced coconut milk, are also up to scratch. Drink Thai beer, or there's a shortish wine list lifting off at £15.50.

CHEF: Sompong Sae-Jew   PROPRIETOR: Blue Elephant International plc   OPEN: Sun to Fri L 12 to 2.30, all week D 7 (6.30 Fri/Sat) to 12 (10.30 Sun)   CLOSED: 25 to 28 Dec   MEALS: alc (main courses £10 to £18). Set L £10 (2 courses) to £53, Set D £33 to £53   SERVICE: 12.5% (optional), card slips closed   CARDS: Amex, Delta, Diners, MasterCard, Switch, Visa   DETAILS: 350 seats. Private parties: 120 main room, 12 to 120 private rooms. Vegetarian meals. Children's helpings. Wheelchair access (also WC). Music. Air-conditioned   ⊖ Fulham Broadway

Blueprint Café   map 13

Design Museum, 28 Shad Thames, SE1 2YD   COOKING 3
TEL: (020) 7378 7031   FAX: (020) 7357 8810   MODERN EUROPEAN
WEBSITE: www.conran.com   £35–£82

Window seats are highly prized for their commanding views along the Thames to Tower Bridge and Canary Wharf. It's fitting that a tentacle of the Conran chain has intertwined with London's Design Museum – to pleasing effect, by all accounts. The plain-English menu reads enticingly and speaks of diverse European influences. Take your pick from the likes of jellied pork with pickles and toast, parsley-crusted razor clams, or lovage and celery soup before trying your luck with ox tongue and salsa rossa, onglet with watercress and mustard, or fresh-sounding cannelloni with asparagus, peas, sprouts and ricotta. There's plenty of fish too. Finish with a plate of British cheese, almond tart with quince jelly, or gâteau Ste-Victoire. There's some value to be had on the separate '20 under £20' wine list, while the main list is of a Francophile persuasion featuring some interesting bottles.

CHEF: Jeremy Lee   PROPRIETOR: Conran Restaurants   OPEN: all week L 12 to 2.45, Mon to Sat D 6 to 10.45 CLOSED: 24 to 26 Dec   MEALS: alc (main courses £12.50 to £21.50). Set L Sat and Sun £17 (2 courses) to £21, Set D Mon to Thur and Sat 6 to 7, Fri 6 to 11 £17 (2 courses) to £21   SERVICE: 12.5% (optional), card slips closed   CARDS: Amex, Diners, MasterCard, Switch, Visa   DETAILS: 120 seats. Private parties: 120 main room. Vegetarian meals. Children's helpings. Wheelchair access (not WC). No music   ⊖ Tower Hill, London Bridge

Boxwood Café   map 14

Berkeley Hotel, Wilton Place, SW1X 7RL   COOKING 3
TEL: (020) 7235 1010   FAX: (020) 7235 1011   MODERN BRITISH
WEBSITE: www.gordonramsay.com   £41–£83

The amply proportioned basement eatery at the 'seriously smart' Berkeley is intended as a homage to New York café society, replete with silver and gold wallpaper, huge monochrome photographs, and steel-stemmed lights adding a touch of Art Deco. Well-reported dishes have included crab minestrone with scallops and tomato, and pickled Arctic herrings with beetroot and crème fraîche to start, with main courses such as chargrilled sea trout with cherry tomatoes and lemon couscous, and grilled calf's liver with wilted cos, spring onion mash and black pepper sauce also getting the nod. The 'excellent' foie gras and veal burger manages to be light in texture and heavy in rich, livery flavour. Vegetable side orders can bump up the bill. Desserts try out some novel ideas, such as Scotch pancakes with poached rhubarb and cardamom ice cream alongside vanilla cheesecake or warm doughnuts. Polished service is efficient and well-drilled, and the wine list provides imaginative New World-led drinking, with wide and inspired choice by the glass from £4.75.

CHEF: Stuart Gillies   PROPRIETOR: Gordon Ramsay Holdings   OPEN: all week 12 to 3, 6 to 11   MEALS: alc (main courses £12.50 to £22.50)   SERVICE: not inc   CARDS: Amex, Delta, MasterCard, Switch, Visa   DETAILS: 140 seats. Private parties: 140 main room, 6 to 16 private rooms. Vegetarian meals. Children's helpings. Wheelchair access (not WC). No music. Air-conditioned   ⊖ Knightsbridge

Brackenbury ⚡ £

NEW ENTRY   map 12

129–131 Brackenbury Road, W6 0BQ
TEL: (020) 8748 0107   FAX: (020) 8748 6159

COOKING 4
MODERN EUROPEAN
£25–£49

An olive-green awning and outside seating on a quiet residential street in Hammersmith's Brackenbury 'village' announce this long-standing, relaxed and genial neighbourhood favourite. Under new ownership since July 2003, with a new head chef and redecorated, the restaurant has experienced an inspired revival. Large windows front its two rooms, which come decked out in a calm, subdued colour scheme, with unadorned walls and simple varnished wooden tables and black wooden chairs. The sensibly compact, regularly changing, Mediterranean-influenced menus hit just the right note and deserve 'praise for the reasonable prices'. The cooking is typically 'light and breezy', utilising sound ingredients, appealing presentation and little pretension. Expect the likes of roast hake accompanied by chorizo, potato and caper hash and saffron aïoli, or perhaps chargrilled calf's liver with fondant potato, baby gem lettuce and an 'accomplished' Marsala butter sauce. 'Rich' and 'sweet' lemon posset might head up the repertoire of puddings, while the wine list is a suitably modern global affair, with house vins de pays £12.

CHEF: Noel Capp   PROPRIETOR: Lisa Inglis   OPEN: Sun to Fri L 12.30 to 2.45 (3.30 Sun), Mon to Sat D 7 to 10.45   CLOSED: 25 to 28 Dec, 1 to 3 Jan, Easter bank hols, Aug bank hol   MEALS: alc (main courses £9 to £15). Set L Mon to Fri £12.50 (2 courses) to £14.50   SERVICE: 12.5% (optional), card slips closed   CARDS: Amex, Delta, MasterCard, Switch, Visa   DETAILS: 65 seats. 20 seats outside. Private parties: 60 main room, 20 to 40 private rooms. Vegetarian meals. Children's helpings. No smoking. Wheelchair access (not WC). No music   ⊖ Hammersmith, Goldhawk Road   £5

Bradleys ▼

map 13

25 Winchester Road, NW3 3NR
TEL: (020) 7722 3457   FAX: (020) 7435 1392

COOKING 3
MODERN EUROPEAN
£27–£64

Tucked behind Swiss Cottage Tube station, Bradleys is a good all-round neighbourhood restaurant often employing inventive techniques alongside simple grilling and frying to get the best from decent ingredients. Key skills in classic French cooking have delivered a top-notch sabayon and béarnaise, the latter served in a small copper pan to accompany accurately grilled ribeye steak. Starters may run from lemon and asparagus raviolo with burnt sage butter to tuna carpaccio with a quail's egg and pickled herring, with a main course of spinach crêpe, mushroom mousse and goats' cheese soufflé for vegetarians.

43

Presentation can be unorthodox, as with gnocchi and rosemary rolled up in calf's liver with slices of baked apple on the side, and quality is consistently good. Barbary duck breast might come with a cherry compote and cabbage and turnip dauphinois, and a theme on rhubarb – mille-feuille, brûlée, jelly and ice cream – has made an impressive dessert. The smart wine list presents a broad sweep of well-chosen wines arranged by weight, with reds pushing on into expensive and old bottles. Prices overall are good, starting from £12.50, and clued-up staff are a bonus.

CHEF: Simon Bradley   PROPRIETORS: Simon and Jolanta Bradley   OPEN: Tue to Fri and Sun L 12 to 3, Tue to Sat D 6 to 11   CLOSED: 1 week at Christmas   MEALS: alc exc Sun L (main courses £11 to £18.50). Set L Tue to Fri £12 (2 courses) to £16, Set L Sun £16 (2 courses) to £20, Set D £22   SERVICE: 12.5% (optional), card slips closed   CARDS: Amex, Delta, MasterCard, Switch, Visa   DETAILS: 60 seats. Private parties: 25 main room. Vegetarian meals. Children's helpings. No cigars/pipes. Wheelchair access (not WC). Music. No mobile phones. Air-conditioned   ⊖ Swiss Cottage £5

▲ Brasserie Roux
map 15

Sofitel St James Hotel, 8 Pall Mall, SW1Y 5NG   COOKING 3
TEL: (020) 7968 2900   FAX: (020) 7747 2242   FRENCH
WEBSITE: www.sofitelstjames.com   £25–£68

The solid, thick walls and high ceiling of the brasserie bear witness to its former life as a bank, and the space is now filled with huge lamp shades ('shades on steroids') and giant pictures on the walls. The brasserie has its own entrance, separate from the hotel. Polished wooden tables and brisk, professional service combine to create a proper Parisian feel, and Glen Watson cooks a textbook French menu under the aegis of presiding genius Albert Roux. A pair of pre-theatre diners enjoyed cheese and onion quiche with a wobbly filling and crisp short pastry, followed by 'excellent' roast breast of pheasant on 'sticky and satisfying' cep risotto, then pear crumble with a scoop of vanilla ice cream. These are simple dishes but brought off with convincing flair, ensuring bags of flavour in a starter such as marinated herrings with potato salad, and careful timing in the cooking of a main course of top-notch salmon with peppers. An extensive wine list finds room for plenty of non-French choice, with prices starting at £14.

CHEFS: Albert Roux and Glen Watson   PROPRIETOR: Accor Group   OPEN: Mon to Fri 12 to 3, 5.30 to 11.30, Sat 12.30 to 3.30, 5.30 to 11.30, Sun 12.30 to 3.30, 5.30 to 10.30   MEALS: alc (main courses £8 to £22.50). Set D 5.30 to 7 and 10.45 to 11.30 £15 to £20 (inc wine)   SERVICE: 12.5% (optional), card slips closed CARDS: Amex, Diners, MasterCard, Switch, Visa   DETAILS: 96 seats. Private parties: 3 to 12 private rooms. Vegetarian meals. Children's helpings. No-smoking area. Wheelchair access (also WC). Occasional music. Air-conditioned   ACCOMMODATION: 189 rooms, all with bath/shower. TV. Phone. Room only £220 to £280. Rooms for disabled. Baby facilities   ⊖ Piccadilly Circus

---

Brasserie St Quentin
map 14

243 Brompton Road, SW3 2EP   COOKING 2
TEL: (020) 7589 8005   FAX: (020) 7584 6064   MODERN FRENCH
WEBSITE: www.brasseriestquentin.co.uk   £29–£79

'Lively' and 'unpretentious' sum up the mood in this quintessential old stager opposite Brompton Oratory. Echoes of Paris still live on, and the menu proudly displays its Gallic brasserie lineage with feuilleté d'escargots, navarin of lamb, and seared scallops with pommes Parmentier and sauce Provence. England also makes a valuable contribution: seasonal game and meat from the Marquess of Salisbury's estate find their way into the larder, along with Morecambe Bay shrimps (dressed up with lobster oil, frisée and toasted Poilâne bread), smoked Irish eel, and Castle Brae fillet of beef (grilled and served with roast shallots and wild mushrooms). A 'temptation' of pineapple and basil, and the B.St.Q chocolate 'indulgence' are typically suggestive desserts. Three sherries and 11 wines come by the glass, and prices on the predominantly French list start at £14.50 a bottle.

CHEF: Nana Akuffo PROPRIETOR: Brasserie St Quentin Ltd OPEN: all week 12 to 1, 5.30 to 10.30 CLOSED: Christmas MEALS: alc (main courses £10 to £23.50). Set L and D 5.30 to 7.30 £14.50 (2 courses) to £16.50 SERVICE: 12.5% (optional) CARDS: Amex, Delta, Diners, MasterCard, Switch, Visa DETAILS: 55 seats. Private parties: 45 main room, 8 to 25 private rooms. Vegetarian meals. No cigars. Wheelchair access (not WC). Occasional music. Air-conditioned ⊖ Knightsbridge, South Kensington

▲ Brian Turner Mayfair 🍷 map 15

Millennium Hotel, 44 Grosvenor Square, W1K 2HP — COOKING **3**
TEL: (020) 7596 3444 FAX: (020) 7596 3443 — ENGLISH
WEBSITE: www.turnerrest@aol.com — £42–£93

In this ground-floor restaurant in a glitzy hotel in poshest Mayfair, with the adjacent bar a handy rendezvous, Brian Turner's name is much in evidence. Overlooking Grosvenor Square, the dining room has well-spaced tables, smartly set, and staff are 'particularly friendly'. Despite the 'traditional English' label, not all treatments and ingredients will be familiar: a starter of crispy fried cod's tongues with rocket and a tomato and caper dressing, for example, or flaked duckling with Cox's apples and celeriac with a chicken dumpling and walnut dressing. Moving on, some foreign influences creep in: slow-roast chump of pork on broad bean and tomato risotto, or a gratin of summer vegetables with red onion and cauliflower croquette and a herby shallot sabayon. For ardent traditionalists, there is bangers and mash with onion gravy (albeit with Stratford-upon-Avon best pork sausages) and, among starters, rare beef sirloin with English rocket and horseradish. Desserts may start from a traditional standpoint, but blueberry and fudge might go into bread-and-butter pudding, and rhubarb and champagne compote could come with nutmeg-flavoured custard, with Yorkshire Blue rarebit a savoury alternative. Wines start at £20 on a modern, manageable list arranged by grape variety and with a New World bias. Nine standard options by the glass are joined by some pricier specials.

CHEFS: Brian Turner and Paul Bates PROPRIETOR: Millennium Hotel OPEN: Mon to Fri L 12.30 to 2.30, Mon to Sat D 6 to 10.30 MEALS: alc (main courses £11.50 to £28). Set L £22.50 (2 courses) to £25.50 SERVICE: 12.5% (optional), card slips closed CARDS: Amex, Delta, Diners, MasterCard, Switch, Visa DETAILS: 80 seats. 20 seats outside. Private parties: 10 main room, 45 private room. Vegetarian meals. No-smoking area. Wheelchair access (also WC). Music. Air-conditioned ACCOMMODATION: 348 rooms, all with bath/shower. TV. Phone. Room only £190 to £335. Rooms for disabled ⊖ Bond Street, Green Park

Café du Jardin 🍷 map 15

28 Wellington Street, WC2E 7BD — COOKING **2**
TEL: (020) 7836 8769 and 8760 FAX: (020) 7836 4123 — MODERN BRITISH
WEBSITE: www.lecafedujardin.com — £23–£58

Try to get a ground-floor table to enjoy the bustle of the street through the wide windows of this 'café', which has stood firm while others have faded. First courses get things off to a promising start: a 'wonderful' dish of pasta with tomato, rocket, radicchio and a hint of chilli and pine nuts, or squid tempura offset by a colourful pile of pickled vegetables. Good-quality ingredients are in evidence at main-course stage, with perhaps tender, moist veal cutlet milanese with lemon butter alongside roast fillet of cod with butternut squash and smoked bacon risotto. Round things off in high style with pistachio and almond sponge served with frothy chocolate mascarpone. Staff are professional and accommodating. This being a pre-theatre kind of venue, it's good to see a large range of wines by the glass. The main list, bustling with goodies from France, Italy and Australia, is supplemented by a 'fine and rare' selection of considerable pedigree. House wines are £11 (in Covent Garden!), and prices are fair overall.

CHEF: Tony Howorth   PROPRIETORS: Robert Seigler and Tony Howorth   OPEN: Mon to Sat 12 to 3, 5.30 to 12, Sun 12 to 11   CLOSED: 24 and 25 Dec   MEALS: alc (main courses £9 to £16). Set L and D Mon to Sat 5.30 to 7.30 and 10 to 12, Sun 12 to 11 £10.95 (2 courses) to £14.50   SERVICE: 15% (optional), card slips closed   CARDS: Amex, Delta, MasterCard, Switch, Visa   DETAILS: 110 seats. 20 seats outside. Private parties: 65 main room. Vegetarian meals. Wheelchair access (not WC). Occasional music. Air-conditioned   ⊖ Covent Garden

Café Japan ✳ £   map 12

626 Finchley Road, NW11 7RR	COOKING 4
TEL: (020) 8455 6854	JAPANESE
	£20–£52

Simple charm is part of the appeal of Koichi Konnai's buzzy restaurant, with its rows of lacquered pine tables and a counter that seems more like a busy deli. Sushi and sashimi are the mainstays of the menu, and they come in all manner of permutations and styles. Hand rolls appear with an eclectic choice of fish, including turbot 'band', flying fish roe, and sea urchin, while vegetarian options bring on board pickled radish, fermented soy bean, and wild burdock. Added to these are 'inside-out' rolls (eel and cucumber, for example) and specials like salmon with avocado and mayonnaise. A few conventional appetisers are also listed, including hijiki (black seaweed) and boiled spinach marinated in sesame sauce, not to mention a smattering of cooked dishes, including salt-grilled yellowtail 'neck'. Desserts comprise flavoured ice creams and dorayaki (Japanese pancake with a sweet red-bean filling). Drink beer, saké or house wine (£2.50 a glass, £8.50 a bottle).

CHEF/PROPRIETOR: Koichi Konnai   OPEN: Sat and Sun L 12 to 2, Wed to Sun D 6 to 10 (9.30 Sun)   CLOSED: 3 weeks Aug   MEALS: alc (main courses £2.50 to £17). Set L £8.20 (2 courses) to £15, Set D £12 (2 courses) to £17   SERVICE: not inc   CARDS: MasterCard, Switch, Visa   DETAILS: 39 seats. Vegetarian meals. No smoking. Music. Air-conditioned   ⊖ Golders Green

Café Spice Namaste   map 13

16 Prescot Street, E1 8AZ	COOKING 2
TEL: (020) 7488 9242 FAX: (020) 7481 0508	INDIAN
WEBSITE: www.cafespice.co.uk	£35–£70

Cyrus Todiwala now divides his time between Prescot Street and Highgate (see entry, Parsee). Café Spice remains significant on London's progressive Indian scene. Huge banners flutter outside, and the Technicolor interior is still a talking point. The menu looks good, too: traditional regional styles are applied to sometimes non-Indian ingredients (as in kangaroo and venison sheek kavaab), and there are obvious influences from Goa (authentic pork vindaloo), Bombay street life (bhel puris), and Parsee cuisine (lamb dhansak). Dishes may not unfailingly meet expectations, but details like homemade pickles and chutneys, outstanding raita, unmatchable breads and rice highlight the kitchen's pedigree. The tandoor is deployed for everything from salmon to Suffolk wild boar chops, and there are also curiosities like smoked salmon, crab and tuna cake. Drink beer or dip into the food-friendly wine list (prices start at £13.50).

CHEFS: Cyrus Todiwala and Angelo Collaco   PROPRIETOR: Cyrus Todiwala   OPEN: Mon to Fri L 12 to 3, Mon to Sat D 6.15 to 10.30   CLOSED: 25 Dec to 1 Jan, bank hols   MEALS: alc (main courses £7 to £16). Set L and D £25 to £45   SERVICE: 12.5% (optional), card slips closed   CARDS: Amex, Delta, Diners, MasterCard, Switch, Visa   DETAILS: 110 seats. 40 seats outside. Private parties: 90 main room. Vegetarian meals. Children's helpings. Music. Air-conditioned   ⊖ Tower Hill £5

Calcutta Notebook ⚡✸ £

	NEW ENTRY map 12
201 Replingham Road, SW18 5LY	COOKING 3
TEL: (020) 8874 6603	BENGALI
WEBSITE: www.sarkhels.com	£28–£54

Udit Sarkhel has positioned his new venture right next to Sarkhel's itself (see entry), and all the food emanates from the same kitchen. Unlike its elder brother, this modest dining room is devoted to Bengali cooking, with many recipes reputedly from Udit's mother and grandmother. Snacks from the streets and Maidan of Calcutta include shingara (shortcrust samosas filled with potato, cauliflower and peanuts) and bhaja bagda chingri (a single, breathtakingly large marinated tiger prawn). Carnivorous curries involve goat, pot-roast lamb with liver and potatoes, and chicken with bamboo shoots. Vegetarians also fare well with baby aubergines in yoghurt and mustard sauce, and a superlative five-spice dhal. Rice and breads do their job, and you might finish with a glorious Alphonso mango 'as fresh as if it had been plucked that day'. The wine list globetrots for decent, affordable drinking. House South African is £10.90.

CHEF: Udit Sarkhel   PROPRIETORS: Udit and Veronica Sarkhel   OPEN: all week 12 to 2.30, 6 to 10.30 (11 Fri and Sat)   CLOSED: 25 and 26 Dec, 1 Jan   MEALS: alc (main courses £5.50 to £10). Set L £5 (2 courses), Set D £18   SERVICE: not inc   CARDS: Delta, MasterCard, Switch, Visa   DETAILS: 33 seats. Private parties: 33 main room. Vegetarian meals. Children's helpings. No smoking. Music. Air-conditioned   ⊖ Southfields £5

Cambio de Tercio 🍷

	map 14
163 Old Brompton Road, SW5 0LJ	COOKING 3
TEL: (020) 7244 8970 FAX: (020) 7373 8817	MODERN SPANISH
	£26–£67

'Sunset colours of yellow sand and the blush of the Mediterranean' give this Chelsea restaurant all the warmth of a true Spanish taverna, and the food has genuine ambition as well as authenticity. Sous-chef Alberto Criado has moved up the ranks, and his promotion is fully justified, judging by recent feedback. Starters are well above the London 'tapas-bar' norm, thanks to some unlikely twists, viz. a 'mosaic' of raw vegetables with razor clams, honey oil and squid ink, or grilled octopus on an 'ultra-fine' potato purée. Mains prove the attraction of rustic food – for example, acorn-fed Ibérico pork with Spanish black pudding, mange-tout and rice vermicelli, plus a side order of Padrón peppers, or maybe cod accompanied by quince paste and roast almonds in soft garlic juice. Desserts have included a 'harmonious' apple mille-feuille with lemon sorbet and chocolate-studded crème anglaise. A wine list was not made available to the Guide before we went to press, though an inspector noted an impressive range, from Martin Codax Albarino at £21 to 'Gran Reservas at considerable prices'. House wine is £17.

CHEF: Alberto Criado   PROPRIETOR: Abel Lusa   OPEN: all week 12.15 to 2.30, 7 to 9.30   CLOSED: 2 weeks at Christmas   MEALS: alc (main courses £14 to £17). Set L £11.95 (2 courses) to £14.95   SERVICE: not inc, 12.5% for groups of 6 or more   CARDS: Amex, Delta, MasterCard, Switch, Visa   DETAILS: 45 seats. 8 seats outside. Private parties: 45 main room, 15 to 20 private rooms. No-smoking area. Wheelchair access (not WC). Music. Air-conditioned   ⊖ Gloucester Road

Camerino

map 15

16 Percy Street, W1T 1TD
TEL: (020) 7637 9900   FAX: (020) 7637 9696
WEBSITE: www.camerinorestaurant.com

COOKING 3
ITALIAN
£34–£53

New name, new chef – but Camerino (né Paolo) still serves blisteringly authentic Italian food in stylish, relaxed surroundings. Expertly made pasta ranges from 'exceptional' tortellini with ricotta and spinach to organic chestnut tagliatelle with shrimps and wild mushrooms. Fish and meat succeed too: a large slice of scored, grilled squid had substance, flavour and added oomph from plenty of coarsely chopped garlic, while 'melt-in-the-mouth' calf's liver with spinach had a good dark sauce made with top-quality balsamic vinegar. Puddings may be simple (a perfectly ripe mango, fanned out, with a drizzle of passion-fruit seeds and a scoop of tangy sorbet) or complex (a tart containing an 'ambrosial mix of chocolate and almond' with strawberry ice cream). Service is enthusiastic and knowledgeable, and the all-Italian wine list starts in Sicily at £13.50, but prices rise quickly.

CHEF: Valerio Daros   PROPRIETOR: Paolo Boschi   OPEN: Mon to Sat 12 to 3, 6 to 11   CLOSED: 24 to 26 Dec, bank hols   MEALS: Set L £17.50 (2 courses) to £25.50, Set D £22.50 (2 courses) to £30.50   SERVICE: 12.5% (optional), card slips closed   CARDS: Amex, Delta, Diners, MasterCard, Switch, Visa   DETAILS: 65 seats. 6 seats outside. Private parties: 80 main room. Vegetarian meals. No pipes/cigars. Wheelchair access (not WC). Music. Air-conditioned   ⊖ Tottenham Court Road

Cantaloupe

map 13

35–42 Charlotte Road, EC2A 3PD
TEL: (020) 7613 4411   FAX: (020) 7613 4111
WEBSITE: www.cantaloupe.co.uk

COOKING 3
IBERIAN/SOUTH AMERICAN
£28–£48

When it opened in 1995, this was arguably the first new-wave bar/restaurant to take emerging Hoxton by storm. Nowadays its throbbingly noisy, pumped-up atmosphere is tailor-made for the throngs of young bloods who nightly invade the place. The open-to-view kitchen gets most of its inspiration from Iberia and Latin America, so expect dishes like fried chicken livers with chorizo, grapes, parsley and sherry vinaigrette followed by multi-ingredient main courses such as chargrilled chicken breast with spinach, jamón iberico, caper berries, pine nuts, olives, anchovies and saffron fondant potatoes. Alternatively, there are steaks from traditionally reared Charolais cattle, and you could finish with Spanish cheeses, or apple and vanilla crema catalana. A tapas bar menu is served all day (and from 4.30pm on Sundays). Cocktails and elite beers are challengers to the racy wine list, which opens with house French at £11.50.

CHEF: Henry Brereton   PROPRIETORS: Richard Bigg and Nigel Foster   OPEN: Mon to Fri L 12 to 3 (4 Sun), all week D 6 (7 Sat) to 11.30   CLOSED: 25 Dec, 1 Jan   MEALS: alc (main courses £9.50 to £16). Bar menu available Mon to Sat 12 to 12, Sun 4.30 to 11.30   SERVICE: 12.5% (optional), card slips closed   CARDS: Amex, Delta, Diners, MasterCard, Switch, Visa   DETAILS: 50 seats. Vegetarian meals. Wheelchair access (also WC). Music. Air-conditioned   ⊖ Old Street

---

▲ The Capital   map 14

22–26 Basil Street, SW3 1AT	COOKING 8
TEL: (020) 7591 1202 FAX: (020) 7225 0011	FRENCH
WEBSITE: www.capitalhotel.co.uk	£46–£155

By the time you read this, the dining room at the Capital will look quite different from how it looked at our last visit in spring 2004. A redesign during August was due to create a 1940s Parisian feel, with walls panelled in sycamore, chairs in cool cornflower blue, mirrored walls and flocked drapes. It should all provide a suitably chic backdrop for Eric Chavot's cooking. His style is to construct dishes in complex but logical layers from fine ingredients, with seasoning and spicing never less than spot-on, presentations a sight for sore eyes, and with dish after dish eating a lot more excitingly than the terse menu descriptions seem to suggest. With superb service and a wine list to travel for, there is no doubting that this is one of central London's premier addresses.

Rustic ingredients are a heartening forte: a knobbly piece of veal sweetbread sits on a base of gelatinous calf's foot, itself upholstered with a coating of crisp batter, alongside a quenelle of what appeared to be Jerusalem artichoke purée. Deceptively simpler in conception is a pile of crab ravioli over which a frothed bisque of langoustines is ladled at table, a dish nonetheless full of opulent concentration and flair.

A reporter who thinks nothing of making a 280-mile round trip to lunch here has enjoyed a briefly cooked pavé of salmon in red wine sauce, as well as a veal escalope with wild mushrooms. At inspection, the stirring main course was a pairing of roast venison and osso buco, balanced with creamed shredded cabbage and a tumulus of boulangère potatoes bound up in thin bacon. Fish can be just as good, as is the case with a brace of John Dory fillets, alongside a 'barigoule' fashioned from slivers of carrot and artichoke, with sauce diable adding depth.

Desserts maintain the pace. A plate of three mini brûlées is expertly conceived to allow gradations of texture and sweetness as you work your way down each one, the pink grapefruit sorbet on top giving way to crème brûlée seasoned with rosemary, with a compote of pink grapefruit at the base. Miniature rum babas with lime sauce, and pineapple tarte Tatin have been other impressive confections. Coffee and petits fours are in the highest class, and when you are offered the choice of salted or unsalted butter with the bread, and nobody blinks if you ask for tap water, it is clear that this is a place that treats its customers seriously.

Wine mark-ups have come in for a pasting from reporters, as provision for diners with less than £25 to spend is poor (house vin de pays is £25). Deep pockets give access to a fine cellar, where leading French bottles, the grandest of them offered in a huge range of vintages, rub shoulders with the global smart set, particularly from Italy and Australia. Interesting options come by the glass, including a sommelier's selection (at £47) to run alongside the tasting menu.

CHEF: Eric Chavot   PROPRIETORS: the Levin family   OPEN: all week 12 to 2.15, 7 to 11 (10.30 Sun)   MEALS: Set L £28.50, Set D £48 to £115 (inc wine)   SERVICE: 12.5% (optional), card slips closed   CARDS: Amex, Delta, Diners, MasterCard, Switch, Visa   DETAILS: 33 seats. Private parties: 33 main room, 24 private room. Vegetarian meals. Wheelchair access (also WC). Occasional music. Air-conditioned

ACCOMMODATION: 49 rooms, all with bath/shower. TV. Phone. Room only £195 to £250. Baby facilities
⊖ Knightsbridge

Le Caprice

map 15

Arlington House, Arlington Street, SW1A 1RT
TEL: (020) 7629 2239   FAX: (020) 7493 9040
WEBSITE: www.caprice-holdings.co.uk

COOKING 4
MODERN BRITISH
£35–£75

Hidden behind Venetian blinds, Le Caprice's discreet entrance gives way to a rather lively interior. Smoky mirrors, tiled floors and a black-and-white colour scheme leave a contemporary impression, while close-together tables and an 'animated pianist' add to the ambience. The menu leans toward comfort food, such as eggs Benedict, devilled lambs' kidneys on toast, or veal rump with Jerusalem artichokes, but there are lively ideas, too, like marinated octopus with enoki mushrooms, chilli and lime. Prawns piri-piri comprises five large prawns 'cooked to perfection' served with a hot, yet not overwhelming, sauce. A separate vegan/vegetarian menu might offer roast Italian onions with rocket and montassio cheese. Service is neither condescending nor reverential; despite the high celeb count, everyone gets the same care and respect. The wine list is well-considered and starts at £12.25 (£5.50 a glass); even if prices can be steepish, there is choice under £25.

CHEF: Kevin Gratton   PROPRIETOR: Caprice Holdings Ltd   OPEN: all week 12 to 3 (3.30 Sun), 5.30 (6 Sun) to 12   CLOSED: 25 and 26 Dec, 1 Jan, Aug bank hol   MEALS: alc (main courses £12 to £23.50). Cover £1.50. Sun brunch menu available   SERVICE: not inc   CARDS: Amex, Delta, Diners, MasterCard, Switch, Visa   DETAILS: 80 seats. Vegetarian meals. Wheelchair access (not WC). Music. No mobile phones. Air-conditioned   ⊖ Green Park

Cecconi's ▼ 🍽

map 15

5A Burlington Gardens, W1S 3EP
TEL: (020) 7434 1500   FAX: (020) 7494 2440
WEBSITE: www.cecconis.co.uk

COOKING 6
ITALIAN
£44–£80

For many, Cecconi's is a model of composed gentility. Seats are pulled back and napkins flurried out for you on arrival, while tables are sufficiently spaced to ensure nobody will overhear your indiscretions. Dark wood, cream walls and wooden floors aim for understatement, too, as does the lighting level, which some find on the gloomy side of dim. Excellent breads, including snappy grissini and the poppadom-like Sardinian carta da musica, are the prelude to some assured Italian cooking. The menus offer a nice balance of classic and bang-up-to-date restaurant food, whether you're in the market for a dish of penne with tomato and basil, or grilled squid with cannellini beans, roast peppers and pancetta. A salad of fine Italian artichokes is topped with a boiled duck egg, which on being tapped contributes to the dressing, while fresh egg ravioli are stuffed with mascarpone and garlic leaves to make an attractively pungent pasta dish. Veal milanese is two satisfying hunks of crumbed, succulent meat on the bone, rather than the usual escalope, or there may be roast black bream with crushed potatoes and a salsa of black olives and capers. Pineapple pannacotta is a 'magnificently creamy' dessert, or there might be chocolate tart with pistachio ice cream. The wine list naturally focuses on Italy, with a smattering of smart bottles from France and elsewhere. Top modern names such as Antinori, Gaja and La Spinetta are covered in depth but there's not much from south of Tuscany. Bottles start at £18, and ten options come by the glass.

CHEF: Nick Freeman   PROPRIETOR: Hani Farsi   OPEN: all week 12 to 3 (4 Sun), 6.30 to 11.30 (10.30 Sun)
CLOSED: 24 Dec to 5 Jan   MEALS: alc (main courses £11 to £24)   SERVICE: 12.5% (optional), card slips
closed   CARDS: Amex, Delta, Diners, MasterCard, Switch, Visa   DETAILS: 80 seats. Vegetarian meals.
Wheelchair access (also WC). Occasional music. Air-conditioned   ⊖ Green Park, Piccadilly Circus

---

▲ Le Cercle ♥ ⅍   NEW ENTRY   map 14

1 Wilbraham Place, SW1X 9AE   COOKING 5
TEL: (020) 7901 9999   FAX: (020) 7901 9111   FRENCH
EMAIL: info@lecercle.co.uk   £32–£64

This new Chelsea restaurant occupies a cool, neutral-toned basement with a double-height ceiling from which creamy voile curtains are suspended, acting as a room divider. For one evening visitor at least, the effect was romantic, with the 'lighting subdued' and spots picking out the centre of each (well-spaced) table. It's certainly a calmer, more relaxed space than its older sibling, Club Gascon (see entry). Thierry Beyris is clearly a gifted chef whose cooking seems very much at home in this chic, intimate setting.

Everything is served in small portions rather than following a standard three-course format, with the cooking a modern interpretation of classic regional French dishes; season, quality, flavour and technique all work hand in hand. Some are just first-rate assembly jobs (a delicate barigoule of baby artichokes, for example, lightly dressed with good olive oil and basil), while others show real skill and timing, as in 'intense, exquisite' asparagus emulsion with a black olive reduction and a vegetable cake. Praise, too, has been heaped on a light aniseed crab Parmentier, pot-au-feu de sot-l'y-laisse (chicken oysters in an 'intensely flavoured' chicken consommé), and a 'delicate, buttery' roast langoustine with warm foie gras flan and crispy bacon. If le Provençal – shot glasses filled with sweet green pepper purée, black olive purée, and tomato granita – sounds too avant-garde, go for the more mainstream dark chocolate fondant. All French regions are treated as equals on the wine list, so Languedoc-Roussillon, the south-west, Jura and Alsace fare better than usual. Much is good value and interesting, not least the regional tour of wines by the glass. Bottles start at £11.50.

CHEF: Thierry Beyris   PROPRIETOR: Phoenix House Restaurants   OPEN: Tue to Sat 12 to 3, 6 to 11   MEALS:
alc (main courses £5 to £15). Bar menu available all day   SERVICE: 12.5% (optional), card slips closed
CARDS: Amex, Delta, MasterCard, Switch, Visa   DETAILS: 80 seats. Private parties: 18 main room, 12
private room. Vegetarian meals. No smoking in 1 dining room. Wheelchair access (also WC). Music. Air-
conditioned   ACCOMMODATION: 33 rooms, all with bath/shower. TV. Phone. Room only £135 to £250.
Rooms for disabled. Baby facilities   ⊖ Sloane Square

Champor-Champor   NEW ENTRY   map 13

62–64 Weston Street, SE1 3QJ   COOKING 3
TEL: (020) 7403 4600   FAX: (07092) 812352   MALAYSIAN/ASIAN
WEBSITE: www.champor-champor.com   £38–£59

The name translates loosely as 'mix and match', which just about sums up this bewilderingly exotic, 'one-off' restaurant. The interior is ethnically 'funky', the music is Malaysian pop, and it can get 'as busy as Waterloo Station during the rush hour'. The food has its roots in Malayan village-style cooking, but it quickly takes flight with interesting breads (including a tofu version) and pre-starters like beetroot with Indian 'toddy' salsa. After that, expect convincing fusion ideas ranging from fried soft-shelled crab with slow-cooked garlic salad, chinchalok (fermented shrimp paste) and calamansi dressing to masala lamb fillet with aubergine mousse, and an onion and wasabi sauce. Wacky 'inter-course' granitas can let the side down, but desserts like tropical fruit in hibiscus and basil syrup with cracked peppercorns make a refreshing finish. There are fascinating 'Asia-Pacific' beers to drink, plus a well-considered wine list with prices from £12.50.

CHEF: Adu Amran Hassan   PROPRIETORS: Adu Amran Hassan and Charles Tyler   OPEN: Mon to Sat D only 6.15 to 10.15 (10.30 Fri and Sat). L by appointment   CLOSED: 2 weeks at Christmas, 5 days at Easter, bank hols   MEALS: Set D £19.90 (2 courses) to £35   SERVICE: 12.5% (optional), card slips closed   CARDS: Amex, Delta, MasterCard, Switch, Visa   DETAILS: 38 seats. Private parties: 18 main room, 6 to 8 private rooms. Vegetarian meals. Wheelchair access (also WC). Music   ⊖ London Bridge

Chapter Two 🍮 ✕

	map 12
43–45 Montpelier Vale, SE3 0TJ	COOKING 4
TEL: (020) 8333 2666 FAX: (020) 8355 8399	MODERN EUROPEAN
WEBSITE: www.chaptersrestaurants.co.uk	£32–£61

Blackheath's sister establishment to Chapter One (see entry, Farnborough) consists of a light, airy ground floor and basement which is less so. A new chef is at the helm, but the modern European cooking continues in the same vein. The menu revels in Mediterranean materials from brandade to tapenade. A 'heavy but satisfying' crab raviolo has come with a white onion purée and a puddle of 'excellent' red mullet bisque among starters, or there might be gnocchi with asparagus, Jerusalem artichokes and truffle dressing. Main courses tread a path between pot-roast Landes chicken breast with sweet potato fondant and red onion jam, and a 'robust and sophisticated' Barbary duck breast with candied beetroot and peach sauce. Details like side orders of vegetables can disappoint, but a dessert of honeycomb ice cream with chocolate feuillantine and caramelised baby banana was a fine finish at inspection. Six house wines at £15.50 to £17.50 head a respectable list.

CHEF: Trevor Tobin   PROPRIETOR: Selective Restaurants Group   OPEN: all week 12 to 2.30, 6.30 to 10.30 (11 Fri and Sat)   MEALS: Set L Mon to Sat £14.50 (2 courses) to £18.50, Set L Sun £14.50 to £16.50, Set D Sun to Thur £16.95 (2 courses) to £19.95, Set D Fri and Sat £23.50   SERVICE: 12.5% (optional), card slips closed   CARDS: Amex, Delta, Diners, MasterCard, Switch, Visa   DETAILS: 70 seats. Private parties: 50 main room. Vegetarian meals. Children's helpings. No smoking. Wheelchair access (also WC). Music. No mobile phones. Air-conditioned

Chez Bruce 🍷 ✕

	map 12
2 Bellevue Road, SW17 7EG	COOKING 6
TEL: (020) 8672 0114 FAX: (020) 8767 6648	MODERN BRITISH
WEBSITE: www.chezbruce.com	£40–£80

LONDON GFG 2005 COMMENDED

A two-storey building opposite one corner of Wandsworth Common, Bruce Poole's restaurant sits discreetly amid its leafy, affluent surroundings. Now entirely non-smoking, it is furnished in spare but elegant style, with crisp white linen and exposed floorboards, and with prints of modern art on the walls. The cooking is not restricted to physical borders, although a respect for classical and regional France is declared. A salad of baby squid with artichokes, Rosevale potatoes and rouille is 'a study in texture and flavour balance', garnished with paper-thin shavings of sourdough bread brushed with olive oil. There is no coyness about aiming for richness early on in a meal: a pithiviers of hare and foie gras with sauce soubise and balsamic has seen to that. Main courses can be large, as is the case with a rollicking interpretation of pot-au-feu, while even fish dishes aim for impact, as in well-timed sea bass with scallop and crab lasagne. Desserts rise to the occasion with rhubarb and champagne trifle, or meringue-topped passion-fruit tart scattered with toasted pistachios. Staff work hard to keep things flowing, and the young sommelier has been singled out for acclamation. Wine is generally viewed to be 'no bargain', but the focus is on quality and, as one reporter noted, 'there is a huge amount of scope'. Good, better and best bottles come from all over, including regions that are rarely taken seriously, such as Germany, Alsace and Austria, and the range of 30-odd by the glass would put many other lists to shame.

CHEFS: Bruce Poole and Matthew Christmas   PROPRIETORS: Bruce Poole and Nigel Platts-Martin   OPEN: Mon to Fri 12 to 2, 7 (6.30 Fri) to 10.30, Sat 12.30 to 2.30, 6.30 to 10.30, Sun 12.30 to 3, 7 to 10   CLOSED: 24 to 26 Dec, 1 Jan   MEALS: Set L £23.50, Set D £32.50 to £42.50   SERVICE: 12.5% (optional), card slips closed   CARDS: Amex, Delta, Diners, MasterCard, Switch, Visa   DETAILS: 75 seats. Private parties: 70 main room, 10 to 16 private rooms. Children's helpings at L. No children at D. No smoking. Wheelchair access (not WC). No music. No mobile phones. Air-conditioned   ⊖ Balham

---

Chez Moi
map 12

---

23 Richmond Way, Shepherds Bush, W14 0AS
TEL: (020) 7602 6004   FAX: (020) 7602 8147
WEBSITE: chezmoi-restaurant.co.uk

COOKING 2
FRENCH
£27–£56

Now settled into its new location after a generation in Holland Park, Chez Moi continues to defy fashion with classically rooted French haute cuisine that scores high in the comfort stakes. Bilingual menus deal in the likes of a pastry nest of soft-boiled quails' eggs with smoked salmon topped with sauce mousseline, or two terrines (foie gras and chicken liver) with toasted brioche and aspic. Main courses run the gamut from breaded cod goujons with tartare sauce to calf's liver with sage butter, via the odd daring turn such as fillet of hare seasoned with horseradish, nutmeg, cinnamon and port. Recline into an apple and Calvados pancake to finish, or the famous petit pot au chocolat slicked with Grand Marnier. The Francocentric wine list opens at £14.75.

CHEF: Mark Stapley   PROPRIETOR: Philippe Bruyer   OPEN: Mon to Fri L 12 to 2.30, Mon to Sat D 6.30 to 10.30   CLOSED: bank hols   MEALS: alc (main courses £15 to £17). Set L £12.50 (2 courses) to £14.50, Set D 6.30 to 7.45 £12.50 (2 courses) to £14.50   SERVICE: not inc   CARDS: Amex, Delta, Diners, MasterCard, Switch, Visa   DETAILS: 65 seats. 12 seats outside. Private parties: 12 main room, 10 to 30 private rooms. Children's helpings. No pipes or cigars. Wheelchair access (also WC). Occasional music. Air-conditioned ⊖ Shepherds Bush

---

Chisou £
NEW ENTRY   map 15

---

4 Princes Street, W1B 2LE
TEL: (020) 7629 3931

COOKING 3
JAPANESE
£22–£80

In the West End's 'Little Japan' between Hanover Square and Regent Street, Chisou looks 'like a Tokyo restaurant', with its clean lines, white walls and a plaster 'money-beckoning cat' by the entrance. The décor is uncluttered, the food creative, and the menu spans all the benchmark techniques and styles. Sushi is particularly praiseworthy: the mixed version arrives in a square lacquered box, while a visually stunning combination of eel sushi with spider crab maki rolls is presented on a wooden block. Elsewhere, reporters have praised seared scallop salad with lemony ponzu dressing, and grilled seasonal fish marinated in soy bean paste. The chef's recommendations (some written only in Japanese) provide a challenge (slivered burdock root and sliced fishcake with octopus and mayonnaise, for example), while pickles and rich home-made ice creams reinforce the restaurant's credentials. To drink, there are sakés, whiskies and a short list of wines from £13.

CHEF: Mr Funakoshi   PROPRIETORS: David Leroy and Mr Funakoshi   OPEN: Mon to Sat 12 to 2.30, 6 to 10.20   CLOSED: 24 Dec to 2 Jan, bank hols   MEALS: alc (main courses £6 to £22). Set L £9.90 to £12.80   SERVICE: not inc L, 12.5% D, card slips closed D   CARDS: Amex, Delta, Diners, MasterCard, Switch, Visa   DETAILS: 60 seats. Private parties: 14 main room, 3 to 14 private rooms. Vegetarian meals. No children after 7.30pm. No cigars/pipes. No music   ⊖ Oxford Circus

Chutney Mary

map 12

535 King's Road, SW10 0SZ
TEL: (020) 7351 3113   FAX: (020) 7351 7694
WEBSITE: www.realindianfood.com

COOKING 2
INDIAN
£30–£100

Opulent décor defines the mood in this seriously made-over Indian restaurant, and the kitchen's team of regional chefs takes customers on an intricate gastro-tour of the Subcontinent. Tokri chaat (a potato basket filled with vegetarian street food) is a popular starter, while tandooris include two kinds of chicken tikka (one with fenugreek and fig marinade, the other with plum chutney). Devon lamb finds its way into a korma with Himalayan screw-pine flower, French guinea fowl is stuffed and served with almond sauce, and vegetables look to the Punjab for much of their inspiration: baby aubergines, slow-cooked black Urad dhal, and okra with water chestnuts, for example. Desserts follow the new-wave path, as in banana fritters with chilli caramel and lime granita. The wine list is a seriously pitched, food-friendly slate, with prices starting at £15.

CHEF: Nagarajan Rubinath   PROPRIETORS: Ranjit Mathrani, and Nameeta and Camellia Panjabi   OPEN: Sat and Sun L 12.30 to 3, all week D 6.30 to 11 (10.30 Sun)   MEALS: alc exc Sat and Sun L (main courses £12 to £25.50). Set L £16.50   SERVICE: 12.5% (optional), card slips closed   CARDS: Amex, Delta, Diners, MasterCard, Switch, Visa   DETAILS: 110 seats. Private parties: 110 main room, 10 to 24 private rooms. Vegetarian meals. No-smoking area. Wheelchair access (also WC). Occasional music. Air-conditioned ⊖ Fulham Broadway

Cigala

map 13

54 Lamb's Conduit Street, WC1N 3LW
TEL: (020) 7405 1717   FAX: (020) 7242 9949
WEBSITE: www.cigala.co.uk

COOKING 2
SPANISH
£30–£58

Tables are closely packed at this strikingly light, simply decorated restaurant. A handsome wooden floor, plain white walls and a low ceiling tend to ratchet up the noise level – but shut your eyes and this could be Spain. Classics such as paella are given a modern workout when made with quail, chorizo and beetroot tops, but the kitchen knows when to leave well alone when it comes to the likes of sardines a la plancha. Good raw materials are apparent in straightforward dishes: say, marinated salmon with red onions, guindilla and caper berry dressing, or grilled chicken breast with new potatoes, spinach and artichoke salad and beetroot salsa. Patatas bravas wowed one visitor, while chickpea, garlic and parsley soup, and pan-fried scallops with deep-fried fennel, guindilla peppers and mint got the thumbs up from another. Service is friendly, and an interesting Spanish wine list (including a page of sherries) comes with helpful notes, fair prices and plenty by the glass. Prices start at £13.50.

CHEFS: Igor García and Ralf Wittig   PROPRIETOR: Jake Hodges   OPEN: Mon to Sat 12 (12.30 Sat) to 10.45, Sun 12.30 to 9.45   CLOSED: 24 to 26 Dec   MEALS: alc (main courses £10 to £18). Set L £15 (2 courses) to £18, Set D £18. Tapas menu available   SERVICE: 12.5% (optional), card slips closed   CARDS: Amex, Delta, Diners, MasterCard, Switch, Visa   DETAILS: 65 seats. 20 seats outside. Private parties: 70 main room, 10 to 40 private rooms. Vegetarian meals. Wheelchair access (not WC). No music. Air-conditioned   ⊖ Holborn (£5)

Cinnamon Club

map 13

Old Westminster Library, Great Smith Street, SW1P 3BU
TEL: (020) 7222 2555   FAX: (020) 7222 1333
WEBSITE: www.cinnamonclub.com

COOKING 4
MODERN INDIAN
£35–£128

In its present incarnation, the Old Westminster Library oozes slickness and confidence, with its luxuriously fashioned interior and glitzy clientele. But don't be seduced by the gloss, because seriously good Indian food is on offer here. Spices are flown in regularly, and the kitchen is fastidious about the provenance of its raw materials: beef is aged Charolais, and chicken is the French black-leg variety. Presentation is European, which means that dishes are ready plated rather than designed for sharing, and there's a fondness for exquisite 'tiny' starters: the visual impact of a stuffed zucchini flower with spring vegetables and tamarind dressing brought a 'beatific smile' to one vegetarian's face. By contrast, main courses aim for generosity, as in deeply spiced and 'disarmingly tender' Rajasthani goat curry, or king prawns simmered in creamy saffron and almond sauce with shrimp pickle. Accompanying rice comes in neat, 'separately grained' mounds. Desserts can be a letdown, but the overall impression is of fresh spicing, pure flavours and a kaleidoscope of 'clean and vibrant tastes'. The wine list is a good match for the food. Mark-ups are quite painful, but the quality is high. Prices start at £15.

CHEF: Vivek Singh   PROPRIETOR: Iqbal Wahhab   OPEN: Mon to Fri L 12 to 2.30, Mon to Sat D 6 to 11 CLOSED: 25 and 26 Dec, 1 Jan   MEALS: alc (main courses £11 to £31). Set L and D 6 to 7 £19 (2 courses) to £22, Set D £60 to £95 (inc wine). Bar D menu available   SERVICE: 12.5% (optional), card slips closed CARDS: Amex, Delta, Diners, MasterCard, Switch, Visa   DETAILS: 220 seats. Private parties: 40 main room, 40 to 80 private rooms. Vegetarian meals. No music. Air-conditioned   ⊖ Westminster

Cipriani

NEW ENTRY   map 15

25 Davies Street, W1R 3DE
TEL: (020) 7399 0500   FAX: (020) 7399 0501
WEBSITE: www.cipriani.com

COOKING 3
ITALIAN
£44–£111

The internationally expansionist group that owns Harry's Bar in Venice opened in London in 2004, aiming to bring a large dose of the cosmopolitan swish of the watery city to central London. Behind a double-fronted terracotta exterior lies a pulsating, multi-styled, tripartite dining room, where an Art Deco-style mural depicts modes of transport like hot-air balloons and ocean liners.

Giuseppe Marangi cooks in simple northern Italian style, and although prices may be West End at least they aren't Venetian. Smoked prosciutto with mozzarella looks generous and neat; there is asparagus risotto or gnocchi alla romana, and the pasta takes in excellent taglioni with veal ragù under a grilled cheesy top. Main courses are trim and well turned out: a succulent, glistening piece of monkfish is carefully timed and adorned with herby tomato sauce, while veal crops up plentifully again, perhaps as a tender chop with butter and sage. Cream-filled crêpes flamed with Drambuie should make a good winter warmer, and the signature selection of Cipriani cakes is vigorously pushed. Staff act as though trained to within an inch of their lives, which helps to make a memorable experience. A Bellini is the appropriate drink here. Wines are mostly Italian, mostly good, mostly expensive. Choices by the glass (£3.50 to £13) run to quality drinking. House bottles are £16.

CHEF: Giuseppe Marangi   PROPRIETOR: Arrigo Cipriani   OPEN: all week 12 to 3, 6 to 12   MEALS: alc (main courses £14 to £40). Set L £28 to £35, Set D £35 to £40   SERVICE: 12.5% (optional)   CARDS: Amex, Delta, MasterCard, Switch, Visa   DETAILS: 130 seats. Private parties: 130 main room, 8 to 30 private rooms. Vegetarian meals. Wheelchair access (also WC). No music. Air-conditioned   ⊖ Bond Street

Circus   map 15

1 Upper James Street, W1F 9DF   COOKING 3
TEL: (020) 7534 4000   FAX: (020) 7534 4010   MODERN EUROPEAN
WEBSITE: www.egami.co.uk   £27–£71

Large picture windows on two sides give directly on to the bustling streets of Soho, and the good-sized dining room is frequently buzzing, with well-spaced tables, white napery and tall candles. The up-to-date design pairs light and dark browns, suede textures, and lots of wood. Service is slick, smart and discreet. The set menu might offer a simple clam chowder or oak-aged feta with rocket, followed by shepherd's pie or roast cod with spinach and hollandaise. Asparagus with a poached egg and Parmesan from the carte was 'superbly fresh and expertly cooked' at inspection, its balsamic dressing powerful and sweet. Main-course honey-roast Gressingham duck breast with sweet potato and roast pumpkin comes on a robust dark jus, while chocolate truffle and honeycomb with chocolate and mint sorbet is a sensuous pudding with a complex mix of textures and flavours. Wine drinkers can choose from plenty by the glass. Few bottles come in under £20, although prices start at £14.50.

CHEF: Richard Lee   PROPRIETOR: Mirror Image Restaurants   OPEN: Mon to Fri L 12 to 3, Mon to Sat D 5.45 to 11.45   CLOSED: 25 and 26 Dec, 1 Jan, Easter Mon, summer bank hols   MEALS: alc D (main courses £11.50 to £18). Set L £12.50 (2 courses) to £19.50, Set D 5.45 to 7.15 and 10.30 to 11.45 £12.50 (2 courses) to £15   SERVICE: 12.5% (optional), card slips closed   CARDS: Amex, Delta, Diners, MasterCard, Switch, Visa   DETAILS: 130 seats. Private parties: 150 main room, 10 to 20 private rooms. Vegetarian meals. No-smoking area. No music. Air-conditioned   ⊖ Piccadilly Circus

Clarke's ▼ ⁵⁄✳   map 13

124 Kensington Church Street, W8 4BH   COOKING 4
TEL: (020) 7221 9225   FAX: (020) 7229 4564   MODERN BRITISH
WEBSITE: www.sallyclarke.com   £36–£68

Sally Clarke's restaurant was a beacon of innovation when it opened in the 1980s, and while the hustle of London food fashion might easily have swept a less confident operation aside since then, Clarke's sails on into its third decade. Set amid the antique shops of Church Street, the eating takes place on two levels, a small ground-floor area and the much more relaxing, low-lit basement room with its open-plan kitchen.

A set menu in the evenings consists of a possible four courses. An early-summer line-up produced a mousse of duck and chicken livers with San Daniele ham, followed by poached Alaskan halibut fillet with green mayonnaise, Jersey Royals and green vegetables, the standard brace of cheeses with oatmeal biscuits and quince, and a lemon-curd puff with strawberries and red fruit coulis. The care in cooking à la minute is firmly bolstered by formidable baking and buying skills, meaning that the incidentals are all good too. Lunch provides a choice, built around main-course options such as loin of Welsh lamb roasted with shallots, or chargrilled turbot sauced with Prosecco and chervil. Staff are friendly and knowledgeable. A café next door serves snacks and treats. France and California are the strongest suits on the wine list, but there's good quality elsewhere too. Prices are not excessive, opening with £14 house vins de pays, and seven by the glass look tempting.

CHEF: Elizabeth Payne   PROPRIETOR: Sally Clarke   OPEN: Mon to Sat L 12.30 (11 Sat) to 2, Tue to Sat D 7 to 10   CLOSED: 10 days at Christmas, bank hols   MEALS: alc L (main courses £14 to £16). Set D £49.50   SERVICE: net prices, card slips closed   CARDS: Amex, Delta, Diners, MasterCard, Switch, Visa   DETAILS: 80 seats. Private parties: 60 main room, 12 to 20 private rooms. Vegetarian meals. No smoking. Wheelchair access (not WC). No music. No mobile phones. Air-conditioned   ⊖ Notting Hill Gate

Clerkenwell Dining Room

map 13

69–73 St John Street, EC1M 4AN
TEL: (020) 7253 9000   FAX: (020) 7253 3322
WEBSITE: www.theclerkenwell.com

COOKING 3
MODERN EUROPEAN
£28–£64

Andrew Thompson and Zak Jones opened a second restaurant as we go to press (the Chancery, 9 Cursitor Street, EC4; tel: (020) 7831 4000), and installed Nelson Reposo as head chef here in St John Street. The dining room with parquet flooring and cream and blue colour scheme is an elegant and comfortable space, while the kitchen continues to aim for 'gutsy, bold dishes'. Expect starters in the modern vein, perhaps scallops with belly pork and cauliflower purée, or sushi-style tuna and scallops or artichoke and garlic soup. Main courses extend to fillets of sole with a potage of mussels, tomato and parsley with crisp aubergine, and saddle of lamb with chickpeas, macadamia nuts and apricot jus. Finish with chocolate fondant or tarte fine of plums and almonds. Service generally gets the thumbs up for friendliness, but can be elusive at busy periods. The straightforward wine list (organised by price) covers some interesting ground in New World and Old; bottle prices start at £13, and there's choice under £25.

CHEFS: Nelson Reposo and Andrew Thompson   PROPRIETORS: Zak Jones and Andrew Thompson   OPEN: Sun to Fri L 12.15 to 2.30 (Sun 12 to 3), Mon to Sat D 6 to 11 (Sat 7 to 11.30)   CLOSED: 24 Dec to 3 Jan   MEALS: alc (main courses £13.50 to £17). Set L and Set D 6 to 7 £13 (2 courses) to £16   SERVICE: 12.5% (optional), card slips closed   CARDS: Amex, Delta, Diners, MasterCard, Switch, Visa   DETAILS: 120 seats. Private parties: 70 main room, 16 to 40 private rooms. No-smoking area. Wheelchair access (also WC). Music. No mobile phones. Air-conditioned   ⊖ Farringdon

Club Gascon ▼

map 13

57 West Smithfield, EC1A 9DS
TEL: (020) 7796 0600   FAX: (020) 7796 0601

COOKING 5
FRENCH
£39–£97

In premises that were once a Lyon's Tea House, near Smithfield Market, Pascal Aussignac's restaurant draws plenty of support. The formula is experimental cooking, loosely based on the traditions of south-west France, presented in small portions from a multi-sectioned menu that offers generous choice. A 'variation' of duck with creamed caviar and sardine sorbet would indeed be most people's idea of a variation, as would roast John Dory with crunchy baby fern and an oxtail reduction. That said, there is method in the apparent madness, and no bashfulness about offering chips cooked in goose fat sprinkled with salt as one course, or an old-fashioned cassoulet toulousain. A pair of enthused reporters commended smoked salmon wrapped around pine needles with 'heavenly' basil sorbet, as well as a 'bar of chocolate' that turned out to be a long stick of chocolate parfait studded with violets, and what happens to foie gras is anybody's business: try it served sweet, with crystallised rose petals and champagne. Service is attentive and as helpful as it needs to be with explanations of the dishes. The wine list sticks to the brief with a tour around the intriguing corners of south-west France and the Languedoc, highlighting producers who are reinvigorating oft-forgotten regions like Gaillac and Irouléguy. Traditionalists can reorientate their senses with a strong list of classic Bordeaux. Prices start around £15. Le Cercle (see entry) has taken Pascal Aussignac's vision over to Chelsea.

CHEF: Pascal Aussignac   PROPRIETORS: Vincent Labeyrie, M. Mazouz and Pascal Aussignac   OPEN: Mon to Fri L 12 to 1.45, Mon to Sat D 7 to 9.45   CLOSED: 24 Dec to 4 Jan, bank hols   MEALS: alc (main courses £9 to £29). Set L £25 to £38, Set D £38   SERVICE: 12.5% (optional)   CARDS: Amex, Delta, MasterCard, Switch, Visa   DETAILS: 45 seats. Private parties: 45 main room. Vegetarian meals. No-smoking area. Music. Air-conditioned   ⊖ Barbican, Farringdon

Le Colombier 🍴   map 14

145 Dovehouse Street, SW3 6LB

TEL: (020) 7351 1155   FAX: (020) 7351 0077

COOKING 2
FRENCH
£36–£63

Right next to the Royal Marsden Hospital in a building that used to be a pub, Le Colombier is an authentic French restaurant in a traditional style. This goes as much for the extensive menu as anything else, with starters of soupe de poisson, goose rillettes, or oeufs en meurette, followed by sole meunière, or roast rack of lamb with flageolet beans. Pan-fried halibut with crab sauce has been favourably reported, featuring a generous piece of carefully cooked fish in a smooth, tasty sauce, and perfectly timed fillet steak in a well-flavoured peppercorn sauce has also been well received. Finish perhaps with classic tarte Tatin or crêpes suzette. Service from French waiters lacks the finesse suggested by their formal attire but is generally friendly and polite. The food represents good value for money – and so do the wines, which start at £13.50.

CHEF: Phil Coulter   PROPRIETOR: Didier Garnier   OPEN: all week 12 to 3 (3.30 Sun), 6.30 to 10.30 (10 Sun) MEALS: alc (main courses £12.50 to £20). Set L and D Mon to Sat 6.30 to 7.30 £14.50 (2 courses), Set L and D Sun 6.30 to 7.30 £16.50 (2 courses)   SERVICE: 12.5% (optional), card slips closed   CARDS: Amex, Delta, MasterCard, Switch, Visa   DETAILS: 50 seats. 30 seats outside. Private parties: 30 main room, 10 to 30 private rooms. Vegetarian meals. Wheelchair access (not WC). No music. Air-conditioned   ⊖ South Kensington

The Connaught, Angela Hartnett's Menu 🌿   map 15

16 Carlos Place, Mayfair, W1K 2AL

TEL: (020) 7592 1222   FAX: (020) 7592 1223

WEBSITE: www.angelahartnett.com

COOKING 5
MODERN EUROPEAN
£43–£98

Although much has changed at the Connaught in recent times, the dining room still 'evokes Edwardian Britain'. It is sumptuously panelled with mahogany of the kind that 'looks this way only after 50 years of polishing', set off against a checkerboard carpet in cream and brown and a stucco ceiling, with finishing touches provided by handsome floral displays. Bright modern paintings inject a dash of the contemporary.

Angela Hartnett's cooking is clearly influenced by her mentor Gordon Ramsay: highly refined, luxurious, with elaborate presentation and service stopping just short of silver domes. There is evident Italian influence in the menus, although it is more broadly European in real terms. There are flashes of brilliance: for example, a starter of caramelised foie gras with sweet and sour cherry tomatoes and vanilla; spaghetti with sweet, tender chunks of roast lobster and tomato fondue; 'melt-in-the-mouth' pan-fried wild salmon with a delicate stock sauce infused with garlic and chilli; and 'beautifully presented' roast quail with finely made ravioli, aged balsamic vinegar and Parmesan. A two-tier platter of ice creams and sorbets is presented before dessert of perhaps chocolate cake with cappuccino ice cream. There have been several reports this year, though, of meals falling short of expectation. The wine list concentrates on star names, starting with Italy, moving into France and on into smaller selections from elsewhere. Bottles under £25 are scarce, and, although the 14 options by the glass from £6 do offer some respite, these are heavily marked-up prices.

CHEF: Angela Hartnett   PROPRIETOR: Gordon Ramsay Holdings Ltd   OPEN: all week 12 to 3, 5.45 to 11   MEALS: Set L £25 to £50, Set D £30 to £60   SERVICE: not inc   CARDS: Amex, Delta, MasterCard, Switch, Visa   DETAILS: 120 seats. 30 seats outside. Private parties: 70 main room, 12 to 22 private rooms. Vegetarian meals. Children's helpings. No smoking in 1 dining room. Wheelchair access (also men's WC). No music. Air-conditioned   ⊖ Bond Street

Il Convivio   map 13

143 Ebury Street, SW1W 9QN   COOKING 2
TEL: (020) 7730 4099   FAX: (020) 7730 4103   ITALIAN
WEBSITE: www.etruscagroup.com   £32–£83

A slick, colourful décor, marble-effect floor tiles, and a glass roof bring a touch of the Mediterranean to this well-heeled Belgravia venue, where charming staff provide congenial, well-paced service. The menus follow the traditional Italian format, with pasta and starchy dishes placed second (crab and mustard leaf risotto has been highly commended). Fine ingredients are handled with dexterity, as in roast scallops with a warm salad of cucumber, watercress and preserved lemons, or thick veal fillet with glazed shallots, peas and mushrooms. To finish, 'utterly sinful' white espresso ice cream has proved more seductive than rhubarb tartlet with meringue and spiced strawberry sauce. The wine list offers a comprehensive tour of Italian regional grape varieties. Praiseworthy house selections start at £3.80 a glass, £12.50 a bottle.

CHEF: Lucas Pfaff   PROPRIETORS: the Quaradeghini brothers   OPEN: Mon to Sat 12 to 2.30, 7 to 10.45   CLOSED: bank hols   MEALS: alc L (main courses £10.50 to £17.50). Set D £26.50 (2 courses) to £38.50   SERVICE: 12.5% (optional), card slips closed   CARDS: Amex, Delta, Diners, MasterCard, Switch, Visa   DETAILS: 65 seats. Private parties: 70 main room, 6 to 14 private rooms. Vegetarian meals. No cigars/pipes. Music. Air-conditioned   ⊖ Victoria, Sloane Square

Le Coq d'Argent ▮   map 13

No 1 Poultry, EC2R 8EJ   COOKING 2
TEL: (020) 7395 5000   FAX: (020) 7395 5050   FRENCH
WEBSITE: www.conran.com   £43–£83

If Le Coq d'Argent is not the City's highest restaurant, splendid views from its roof-top garden still make it among the most dramatic. The dining room is plain but stylish, Conran fashion, and equally typical is the range of eating options, from breakfast, through simple tapas-style bar snacks and good-value fixed-price menus, to full à la carte. The kitchen offers classic French coq au vin, soupe de poisson, confit duck leg with pickled vegetable salad, and chateaubriand with béarnaise, but also more up-to-date options like ceviche of turbot with warm herb dressing, and scallops with chorizo, pepper confit and soft-boiled egg. Vegetables are extra. Oysters, caviar and lobster platters are menu fixtures. As for the wine list, never mind the prices, just thrill to the proximity of so many of the world's most sought-after and talked-about bottles. (If you're watching the pennies, look to southern France.) Prices start at £14.75, and 21 come by the glass.

CHEF: Mickael Weiss   PROPRIETOR: Conran Restaurants   OPEN: Sun to Fri L 11.45 to 2.45, Mon to Sat D 6 to 9.45   MEALS: alc (main courses £14 to £26). Set L Sun £23.50 (2 courses) to £25, Set L and D £24 (2 courses) to £28.50, Set L and D Anjou regional menu £36.50 (min 2)   SERVICE: 12.5% (optional), card slips closed   CARDS: Amex, Diners, MasterCard, Switch, Visa   DETAILS: 148 seats. 60 seats outside. Private parties: 148 main room. Vegetarian meals. Wheelchair access (also WC). Occasional music. Air-conditioned   ⊖ Bank

Cotto
map 12

44 Blythe Road, W14 0HA

COOKING 3

TEL: (020) 7602 9333   FAX: (020) 7602 5003

MODERN BRITISH

WEBSITE: cottorestaurant.co.uk

£28–£50

A minimally spare dining room behind the Olympia Exhibition Centre houses this popular neighbourhood restaurant that, despite its Italian name, serves comfortably 'modern British' food. Traditional ingredients are tweaked with ideas garnered from the Med (roast saddle of rabbit with Parma ham and cavolo nero purée), France (braised neck of lamb with pommes boulangère and onion sauce) and the Orient (steamed sea bass with pak choi and soy, ginger and garlic dressing), and the kitchen changes its fairly priced menu monthly to stay seasonal. Pleasing starters have included ham hock in a parsley jelly topped with a 'first-class piece of foie gras' surrounded by split peas and capers, while desserts could run to peanut butter parfait with chocolate sorbet. The contemporary wine list offers eight by the glass, choice under £25 and house French at £12.90.

CHEF: James Kirby   PROPRIETORS: James and Jane Kirby and Warren Barton   OPEN: Sun to Fri L 12 to 2.30, Mon to Sat D 7 to 10.30   CLOSED: 5 days at Christmas, bank hols   MEALS: Set L £13.50 (2 courses) to £16.50, Set D £17 (2 courses) to £19.50   SERVICE: 12.5% (optional), card slips closed   CARDS: Amex, Delta, MasterCard, Switch, Visa   DETAILS: 70 seats. 12 seats outside. Private parties: 50 main room, 10 to 35 private rooms. Children's helpings. No pipes. Wheelchair access (not WC). Music. Air-conditioned   ⊖ Kensington Olympia

Cow Dining Room
map 13

89 Westbourne Park Road, W2 5QH

NEW CHEF

TEL: (020) 7221 0021   FAX: (020) 7727 6771

MODERN EUROPEAN

EMAIL: thecow@thecow.freeserve.com

£37–£70

Climb a side staircase to find the small dining room, 'just like you'd imagine an upstairs room at a trendy West London pub'. It's slightly gloomy, and the background noise may be loud, but it's quieter than the bar downstairs. Service is calm, friendly and knowledgeable, and pre-booking is advisable. The former sous-chef was taking over as the top man as we went to press, but the inventive, fresh and seasonal food is set to continue. Start with oysters, penne alla genovese, or a tapas plate. Whole baked turbot might come with asparagus and hollandaise, and roast breast of guinea fowl with peas and morels. Desserts could include chocolate mousse cake with malted chocolate ice cream. Around a dozen wines on the short and varied list are served by the glass. Vins de Pays d'Oc kick things off at £12.50.

CHEF: Stefano Tancredi   PROPRIETOR: Tom Conran   OPEN: Sun L 12.30 to 3.30, all week D 7 to 11 (7.30 to 10.30 Sun)   CLOSED: 25 Dec, 1 Jan   MEALS: alc D (main courses £14 to £21). Set L Sun £21 (2 courses) to £26. Bar menu available all week   SERVICE: 12.5% (optional), card slips closed   CARDS: Delta, MasterCard, Switch, Visa   DETAILS: 38 seats. Private parties: 35 main room. Vegetarian meals. No music   ⊖ Westbourne Park

Crowthers   map 12

481 Upper Richmond Road West, SW14 7PU   COOKING 2
TEL/FAX: (020) 8876 6372   MODERN BRITISH/FRENCH
EMAIL: pacrowther@aol.com   £39–£47

Nothing much seems to change in this long-running neighbourhood restaurant. Philip Crowther continues to take on just about all the duties – greeting customers, waiting and washing up in addition to cooking. His set-price formula relies on well-tried fixtures, although the kitchen comes up with something new from time to time. A crab and tiger prawn raviolo with saffron, leek and Noilly Prat sauce made a fine opener for one correspondent, while main courses could range from noisettes of lamb baked with orange and ginger to fillets of sea bass delicately flavoured with mild Thai spices. To finish there might be praline and Marsala ice cream, or grilled fruit gratin with Calvados sabayon and mango sorbet. The short, well-chosen wine list has a useful showing of half-bottles, plus George Kinross house selections at £12.50.

CHEF: Philip Crowther   PROPRIETORS: Philip and Shirley Crowther   OPEN: Tue to Sat D only 7 to 10. L bookings only   MEALS: Set L £17.50 (2 courses) to £21.50, Set D £21.50 (2 courses) to £26.50   SERVICE: not inc   CARDS: MasterCard, Switch, Visa   DETAILS: 32 seats. Private parties: 32 main room. Vegetarian meals. Children's helpings. Wheelchair access (not WC). No music. Air-conditioned   ⊖ Richmond

Deca   map 15

23 Conduit Street, W1S 2XS   COOKING 4
TEL: (020) 7493 7070   FAX: (020) 7493 7090   MODERN EUROPEAN
WEBSITE: www.decarestaurant.com   £26–£90

Sharing a chef with its sister restaurant, Incognico (see entry), it is not surprising that much the same kind of food is offered in both, although the brasserie menu format is perhaps a little less overt here. Deca is set over two floors of a handsome four-storey building, and the main ground-floor dining room is a calm and discreetly smart space, with service that is correct and just-so. Roast red peppers with feta, and foie gras and green peppercorn terrine with a salad of French beans, have been among first-course options, and may be followed by Dover sole in one of four ways, tournedos Rossini, or the 'perfectly grilled' pigeon enjoyed by one reporter. Extra vegetables (usually necessary) include a salad of roasted beetroot with garlic mayonnaise, and you finish in classic style with lemon tart and raspberry coulis, or prune and Armagnac ice cream. There's also a good-value set lunch/ early evening dinner menu with two choices per course. The same wine list is offered here as at Incognico, starting with vins de pays at £15 for white, £16.50 for red.

CHEF: Jeremy Brown   PROPRIETOR: Chez Nico Restaurants Ltd   OPEN: Mon to Fri 12 to 3, 5.30 to 11   CLOSED: 10 days Christmas, 4 days Easter, bank hol Mons   MEALS: alc (main courses £14.50 to £25). Set L £12.50, Set D 5.30 to 7 £12.50   SERVICE: 12.5% (optional), card slips closed   CARDS: Amex, Diners, MasterCard, Switch, Visa   DETAILS: 80 seats. Private parties: 11 to 18 private rooms. Vegetarian meals. No pipes. Wheelchair access (also WC). No music. Air-conditioned   ⊖ Oxford Circus

Delfina Studio Café   map 13

50 Bermondsey Street, SE1 3UD   COOKING 4
TEL: (020) 7357 0244   FAX: (020) 7357 0250   GLOBAL
WEBSITE: www.delfina.org.uk   £33–£48

In the Delfina Studio Trust building Maria Elia offers her intriguing cooking in a painting-hung restaurant-cum-gallery that lunches artists from the upstairs studios as well as visitors, and contributes its profits to the Trust. A first course of oregano-baked feta with Turkish figs, crushed hazelnuts and Cabernet Sauvignon vinaigrette might precede main courses of confit pork belly, sage roasted spuds and confit fennel with tomato and cumin jam, or venison steak with spiced chocolate oil, mash, juniper-roasted apples and aubergines. Desserts may include coconut cream and rosewater bavarois with rose-petal banana fritters. Such adventurism is in safe hands here as it is supported by a culinary intelligence that yokes well-tried techniques and combinations to bold and novel approaches. With several by the glass and house bottles at £12.50, wines are mostly kindly priced and enhance the pleasure of food that already offers decent value for central London.

CHEF: Maria Elia   PROPRIETORS: Digby Squires and Bruce Watson   OPEN: Mon to Fri L 12 to 3, Fri D 7 to 10   CLOSED: 24 Dec to 3 Jan   MEALS: alc L only (main courses £10 to £13.50)   SERVICE: 12.5% (optional), card slips closed   CARDS: Amex, Delta, Diners, MasterCard, Switch, Visa   DETAILS: 100 seats. Private parties: 100 main room, 5 to 260 private rooms. Vegetarian meals. No cigars. Wheelchair access (also WC). Occasional music   ⊖ London Bridge (£5)

Le Deuxième ▼   map 15

65A Long Acre, WC2E 9JH   COOKING 3
TEL: (020) 7379 0033   FAX: (020) 7379 0066   MODERN EUROPEAN
WEBSITE: www.ledeuxieme.com   £24–£72

A sibling restaurant to Café du Jardin (see entry), in the heart of Covent Garden, Le Deuxième shares similar French-accented cooking with its elder relative. Escargots bourguignonne and crottin de Chavignol with toasted brioche, green bean and walnut salad might turn up among starters, while main courses reveal both Italian and Japanese influences, as in pan-fried veal fillet with mozzarella, or rare-grilled tuna in a sesame glaze with choi sum and water chestnuts. Classic French desserts such as lemon tart and crème brûlée have won diners' praise. This is a popular venue with the pre- and post-opera/theatre crowd, for which set menus represent good value and a strong line-up of wines by the glass and half-bottles comes into play. For those with time to linger, the full bottle list offers much to ponder and not just from France, and again prices look good given the high-rent location.

CHEF: Geoffrey Adams   PROPRIETORS: Robert Seigler and Tony Howorth   OPEN: Mon to Fri 12 to 3, 5 to 12, Sat 12 to 12, Sun 12 to 11   CLOSED: 24 and 25 Dec   MEALS: alc (main courses £9 to £16.50). Set L and D £10.95 (2 courses) to £14.50 (not available Mon to Sat 7.30 to 10.30)   SERVICE: 15% (optional), card slips closed   CARDS: Amex, Delta, MasterCard, Switch, Visa   DETAILS: 60 seats. Private parties: 60 main room. Vegetarian meals. Wheelchair access (not WC). No music. Air-conditioned   ⊖ Covent Garden

The Don 🍾

map 13

The Courtyard, 20 St Swithin's Lane, EC4N 8AD	COOKING 2
TEL: (020) 7626 2606 FAX: (020) 7626 2616	MODERN EUROPEAN
	£37–£68

The Don's bright modern interior, with paintings by John Hoyland, is housed in an eighteenth-century building tucked round the back of the Mansion House, amid the City's mingling of ancient and modern. In the ground-floor restaurant (there's a basement bistro, too), the carte deals in refreshingly robust and uncomplicated combinations, starting perhaps with seared tuna sashimi with crab and ginger mousse, or terrine of foie gras plus prune and cognac dressing, and finishing with polenta cake with a lime mousse, or chocolate tart and a mandarin sorbet. In between might be monkfish medallions wrapped in Serrano ham, Barbary duckling with sauce bordelaise, or rack of venison on pancetta. A fine range of ports and fortified wines reflects the site's earlier incarnation as Sandeman's bottling cellars, while a discerning collection of table wines runs from the proprietors' own Trinity Hill wines from Hawkes Bay (from £16) to expense-account trophy bottles. And you can drink by the glass throughout the meal, if you choose (particular treasures lurk amongst aperitifs and post-prandials). The owners also run the Bleeding Heart (see entry).

CHEF: Matt Burns   PROPRIETORS: Robert and Robyn Wilson   OPEN: Mon to Fri 12 to 2.30, 6.30 to 10 CLOSED: bank hols, 10 days at Christmas   MEALS: alc (main courses £12 to £22)   SERVICE: 12.5% (optional), card slips closed   CARDS: Amex, Delta, Diners, MasterCard, Switch, Visa   DETAILS: 50 seats. Private parties: 45 main room, 16 to 24 private rooms. Vegetarian meals. No children. No music. Air-conditioned   ⊖ Bank/Cannon Street

Drapers Arms

map 13

44 Barnsbury Street, N1 1ER	COOKING 3
TEL: (020) 7619 0348 FAX: (020) 7619 0413	MODERN BRITISH-PLUS
WEBSITE: www.thedrapersarms.co.uk	£34–£58

The first-floor dining room and a creative kitchen elevate this place from everyday Islington local to gastro-pub. While the homely, traditional downstairs bar offers the same menu (plus sandwiches) at lunchtime, the restaurant (dinner only, plus Sunday lunch) is more sophisticated and relaxed: high-ceilinged, large-windowed, with bare wooden tables and wooden floor. Expect the likes of linguini with mussels, peppers, garlic and flat-leaf parsley, or skewered monkfish and scallop with cardamom rice and muhummara purée. Among desserts are homely sticky toffee pudding and custard, or classic tarte Tatin with crème fraîche. The compact, modern wine list runs in price order, with a decent selection under £20, vin de pays from £12, and 18 by glass from £3.60.

CHEF: Mark Emberton   PROPRIETORS: Paul McElhinney and Mark Emberton   OPEN: all week L 12 to 3 (served in bar Mon to Sat), Mon to Sat D 7 to 10.30   CLOSED: 24 to 27 Dec, 1 and 2 Jan   MEALS: alc (main courses £9.50 to £15.50)   SERVICE: 12.5% (optional), card slips closed   CARDS: Amex, Delta, MasterCard, Switch, Visa   DETAILS: 40 seats. 50 seats outside. Private parties: 40 main room. Vegetarian meals. Children's helpings. No cigars/pipes. Music   ⊖ Highbury & Islington

---

The cuisine styles noted at the tops of entries are only an approximation, often suggested to us by the restaurants themselves. Please read the entry itself to find out more about the cooking style.

Drones

map 14

1 Pont Street, SW1X 9EJ

TEL: (020) 7235 9555   FAX: (020) 7235 9566

WEBSITE: www.whitestarline.org.uk

COOKING 4

ANGLO-FRENCH

£32–£80

Part of the Marco Pierre White stable, Drones is tucked away at the heart of fashionable Knightsbridge not far from Sloane Street. Large mirrors at the back make the sleek, confident dining room seem deceptively large, while black leather banquettes allow most a view of the action. Wooden flooring blends with light brown walls, offset by Cornel Lucas's alluring photographs of showbiz stars. Stiffly starched linen, table lamps, youthful Gallic service and a bar complete the stylish package.

The repertoire is trademark MPW, with reworkings of French classics alongside British favourites and presented on the menu as hors d'oeuvres, salads, pasta and risotto, fish and shellfish, entrées, roasts and grills, and desserts and cheese. Expect well-crafted dishes like eggs Benedict, potted shrimps with melba toast, Dover sole meunière, and ribeye steak with béarnaise, or step out from the more familiar with grilled sea bream accompanied by citrus fruits and coriander. Finish in classic mood with crème brûlée à vanille, egg custard, or sticky toffee pudding. The wine list is expensive but well put together, with a dozen interesting options by the glass. Prices start at £15.

CHEF: Joseph Croan   PROPRIETORS: Marco Pierre White and Jimmy Lahoud   OPEN: Sun to Fri L 12 to 2.30, Mon to Sat D 6 to 11   MEALS: alc (main courses £9 to £22). Set L £14.95 (2 courses) to £17.95   SERVICE: 12.5% (optional)   CARDS: Amex, Delta, Diners, MasterCard, Switch, Visa   DETAILS: 90 seats. Private parties: 90 main room, 12 to 40 private rooms. Vegetarian meals. Children's helpings. Wheelchair access (not WC). Music. Air-conditioned   ⊖ Sloane Square, Knightsbridge

Eagle £

map 13

159 Farringdon Road, EC1R 3AL

TEL: (020) 7837 1353

NEW CHEF

MEDITERRANEAN

£24–£43

'A place to relax, to get fed and watered,' noted a couple who relished the Eagle's laid-back vibes, music and full-blooded food. The chairs are hard, no bookings are taken, and there's always a crush, but this remains a lively venue 'for the young or young at heart'. There have been personnel changes in the kitchen since 2003, and the current incumbent arrived too late for feedback. It would be a brave soul who considered removing bife ana (marinated steak sandwich) or pasties de nata (Portuguese custard tarts) from the repertoire, and we expect the menu to continue in its own creatively Mediterranean way with the likes of courgette and saffron risotto, or cuttlefish stew with chilli and broad beans. Thirteen wines (from £2.50 a glass, £10.50 a bottle) are listed on a blackboard.

CHEF: Ed Mottershaw   PROPRIETOR: Michael Belben   OPEN: all week L 12.30 to 3 (3.30 Sat and Sun), Mon to Sat D 6.30 to 10.30   CLOSED: 1 week at Christmas, bank hols   MEALS: alc (main courses £8 to £14)   SERVICE: not inc, card slips closed   CARDS: Delta, MasterCard, Switch, Visa   DETAILS: 65 seats. 24 seats outside. Vegetarian meals. Music   ⊖ Farringdon

NEW CHEF *is shown instead of a cooking mark where a change of chef occurred too late for a new assessment of the cooking.*

Ealing Park Tavern £

map 12

222 South Ealing Road, W5 4RL
TEL: (020) 8758 1879

COOKING 2
MODERN BRITISH
£28–£44

On a busy suburban road not far from the M4, this corner pub houses an enormous bar area and a dining room with designer flourishes and lithographs on its walls. The menus change daily, and the geographical provenance of dishes is easy to spot: spiced parsnip soup, slow-roast Gloucester Old Spot belly pork with apple sauce, and rhubarb crumble fly the flag for England; while France has its say with ham hock and foie gras terrine, monkfish, and mussel and salmon bourride, and orange crème brûlée; and Italy chips in with spaghetti vongole, chicken cacciatora, and roast vegetable pancakes with red pesto. The wine list offers plenty of decent drinking for under £20, with 16 recommendations by the glass from £2.75.

CHEF: Vincent Morse   PROPRIETORS: Vincent Morse and Nic Sharpe   OPEN: Tue to Sun L 12 to 3 (4 Sun), all week D 6 to 10.30 (9 Sun)   MEALS: alc (main courses £9 to £14). Tapas menu available Tue to Sun 6 to 10   SERVICE: not inc, card slips closed   CARDS: MasterCard, Switch, Visa   DETAILS: 68 seats. 40 seats outside. Private parties: 24 main room. Vegetarian meals. Children's helpings. No-smoking area. Occasional music. No mobile phones (£5)

e&o

map 13

14 Blenheim Crescent, W11 1NN
TEL: (020) 7229 5454   FAX: (020) 7229 5522
WEBSITE: www.eando.nu

COOKING 4
ASIAN/FUSION
£34–£63

In trendy Notting Hill, this a honeypot for media celebs and star-watchers (there's a two-hour limit for tables before 7.30); the bar and sparsely decorated dining room throb, even on Sunday nights. 'Eastern and oriental' is the theme, and the kitchen pumps out classic and fusion ideas based on authentic ingredients (check the food glossary on the back of the menu). Dim sum and salads (duck with watermelon and cashews) share the stage with curries (green aubergine and pumpkin), BBQ/roasts and so on, and the roll-call of dishes reporters recommend includes prawn and chive dumplings, blackened cod with sweet miso, and fiery Korean bulgogi (barbecued beef). Fried rice 'cooked in stock' is an outright winner, while desserts are occidental (chocolate pudding) or crossovers (lychee granita). Cocktails feature, and the wine list is peppered with in-vogue New World numbers, plus some European challengers; house Pays d'Oc is £11, but there's little under £20. Eight Over Eight and Great Eastern Dining Room (see entries) are also owned by Will Ricker.

CHEF: Simon Treadway   PROPRIETOR: Will Ricker   OPEN: all week 12.15 to 2.45, 6.15 to 10.45   CLOSED: 25 and 26 Dec, 1 Jan, Aug bank hol Sun and Mon   MEALS: alc (main courses £9.50 to £21.50). Dim Sum bar menu available   SERVICE: 12.5% (optional), card slips closed   CARDS: Amex, Delta, Diners, MasterCard, Switch, Visa   DETAILS: 84 seats. 20 seats outside. Private parties: 6 main room, 12 to 18 private rooms. Vegetarian meals. No pipes/cigars. Wheelchair access (not WC). No music. Air-conditioned ⊖ Ladbroke Grove

---

'The puddings were no longer served from a trolley, but that may have had to do with the fact the main dining room was taken by an enormous party of Rotarians. They still weren't individually shaped or portioned. I mean the puddings, not the Rotarians.' (On eating in Dorset)

▲ East@West ▼

map 15

13–15 West Street, WC2H 9NE
COOKING **5**
TEL: (020) 7010 8600   FAX: (020) 7010 8601
MODERN EAST ASIAN
WEBSITE: www.egami.co.uk
£26–£82

The re-branding of this hotel and restaurant, formerly known as West Street, has been no mere cosmetic exercise. The change of name reflects a new oriental influence, illustrated by the stone Buddhas that now grace the windowsills of the spacious first-floor dining room, although the décor remains largely as before: predominantly black and white with minimal flourishes.

More significant has been the arrival of one of Australia's most renowned chefs, Christine Manfield, to take charge of the cooking. The menus have undergone a complete transformation, the cooking style switching from Italian with occasional oriental dishes to 'fusion food with attitude'. At dinner, there is a choice of menus, with titles such as Divine and Fabulous, although each in itself offers no choice (except for dessert), comprising five 'tastes' – similarly sized dishes presented 'in a suggested order', perhaps including grilled scallop with cape gooseberries, sweet tamarind, basil and salmon roe; a 'beautifully crafted' composition of lobster with caramelised coconut, bean sprouts, pomelo and mint; or hamachi and nori tempura with green tea noodles, ponzu cucumber, avocado, wasabi and flying fish roe. Although they may sound outlandish, the exotic flavour combinations have been created with great care and intelligent judgement to ensure that results are not merely successful but downright exciting to eat, eliciting rapturous praise from reporters. Each course is listed along with a recommended wine by the glass, but the full list (fairly short but bursting with quality flavours at manageable prices) offers plenty of tempting alternatives, with bottle prices from £14.50. The 'Shared Tastes' menu at lunch runs along more familiar lines, with bowls of high-quality Asian food: braised bean curd with hot bean sauce, for example, or tumeric chicken and rice noodle soup.

CHEF: Christine Manfield   PROPRIETOR: Image Restaurants   OPEN: Mon to Fri L 12 to 3, Mon to Sat D 5.30 to 12   CLOSED: bank hols   MEALS: alc (main courses L £4.50 to £6, D £9). Set D £40. Bar menu available   SERVICE: 12.5% (optional), card slips closed   CARDS: Amex, Delta, Diners, MasterCard, Switch, Visa   DETAILS: 85 seats. Private parties: 1 to 22 private rooms. Vegetarian meals. No cigars/pipes. Wheelchair access (also WC). Occasional music. Air-conditioned   ACCOMMODATION: 3 rooms, all with bath/shower. TV. Phone. B&B £250 to £450. Rooms for disabled   ⊖ Leicester Square

The Ebury, Dining Room

NEW ENTRY   map 14

11 Pimlico Road, SW1W 8NA
COOKING **2**
TEL: (020) 7730 6784   FAX: (020) 7730 6419
MODERN EUROPEAN
WEBSITE: www.theebury.co.uk
£33–£59

This former boozer in Pimlico looks inviting from the street, with huge and unusual arch-shaped windows allowing a view into the capacious ground-floor brasserie. The white walls of the upstairs Dining Room gain colour from flashes of red and rather kitsch chandeliers. The open-to-view kitchen is run by Michael Nadra, whose set menus include intriguing ideas like (as starters) smoked eel combined with chorizo and planchada beans, or duck hearts with Brillat-Savarin cheese and wild mushrooms. Grilled gilthead bream with pipérade and ruby chard gratin was less convincing at inspection than a platter of Majorcan black pig, the loin grilled and the cheeks braised, on sweet potato mash, or there might be stuffed leg of rabbit with black pudding and creamed Savoy cabbage, wholegrain mustard and glazed baby carrots. Praline mille-feuille with malt chocolate ice cream was a particularly successful dessert. A decent international wine list begins at £17, or £6 by the glass.

The downstairs Brasserie's à la carte menu runs from Toulouse sausage and mash with onion gravy to salmon ceviche with daikon and shiso cress; there's a seafood bar in there too.

CHEF: Michael Nadra   PROPRIETOR: Tom Etridge   OPEN: all week L 12 to 3, Mon to Sat D 6 to 10.30 CLOSED: 24 and 25 Dec, 1 Jan, L July and August exc Brasserie   MEALS: Set L £16.50 (2 courses) to £19.50, Sat and Sun L £21 (2 courses) to £25. Set D £24.50 (2 courses) to £29.50. Brasserie menu also available   SERVICE: 12.5% (optional), card slips closed   CARDS: Amex, Delta, MasterCard, Switch, Visa DETAILS: 50 seats. Private parties: 50 main room. Vegetarian meals. No children after 9pm. Music. Air-conditioned   ⊖ Sloane Square

Eddalino ♥

map 15

10 Wigmore Street, W1U 2RD
TEL: (020) 7637 0789   FAX: (020) 7637 2163
WEBSITE: www.eddalino.co.uk

COOKING 3
ITALIAN
£46–£73

Behind a stone-clad corner site on Wigmore Street, chef Francesco Pesce takes inspiration from his native Marches and other regions to produce authentic and interesting Italian dishes. An essential simplicity marked by dedication to well-defined flavours and properly sourced ingredients might bring on starters of chicory salad with wild mushrooms, vegetables, goats' ricotta and basil, and a 'very special' pigeon galantine. Main courses maintain interest in the form of perhaps chargrilled John Dory accompanied by a pastry case of tuna pâté, or pan-fried veal fillet with fried quail's eggs, sautéed lamb's lettuce and rösti, with a handful of daily specials extending the range of the carte. A star-studded Italian wine list also offers decent value at the bottom end (from £17.50), and ten wines by the glass (plus five options for fizz) are a step or two up from normal house Italian. Service of both food and wine has been described as 'professional'.

CHEF: Francesco Pesce   PROPRIETOR: Piero Zanelli   OPEN: Mon to Sat 12 to 3, 6.30 to 10.30   MEALS: Set L and D £25 (2 courses) to £36   SERVICE: 12.5% (optional), card slips closed   CARDS: Amex, Delta, MasterCard, Switch, Visa   DETAILS: 70 seats. Private parties: 70 main room. Vegetarian meals. No-smoking area. No cigars. No music. Air-conditioned   ⊖ Oxford Circus, Bond Street

Eight Over Eight

| NEW ENTRY | map 13

392 King's Road, SW3 5UZ
TEL: (020) 7349 9934   FAX: (020) 7351 5157
WEBSITE: www.eightovereight.nu

COOKING 2
ASIAN/FUSION
£37–£75

The latest addition to Will Ricker's mini empire (see e&o and Great Eastern Dining Room, both London) is a converted Chelsea theatre pub given a new persona and a new numerically charged name (it translates as 'lucky for ever' in Chinese). The elegant interior has been cleverly redesigned, with handsome furniture, silk ceiling lamps and vast sunflower-patterned dividers adding to the visual drama. Like Ricker's other restaurants, it attracts 'a great-looking crowd with many faces you see on magazines', and the food is an accessible fusion bonanza that plunders the Far East for dim sum (chilli salt-squid 'wrapped up in a Chinese newspaper'), sushi and tempura, salads (soft-shell crab with sweet tamarind), and meaty BBQ/roasts. 'Healthy drinks' are an alternative to the wine list, which is an eclectic choice that includes 12 by the glass from £3.30 (£14 a bottle).

CHEF: Neil Witney   PROPRIETOR: Will Ricker   OPEN: Mon to Sat 12 to 3 (4 Sat), 6 to 11, Sun 12.30 to 4, 6 to 10.30   MEALS: alc (main courses £8.50 to £26). Bar menu available   SERVICE: 12.5% (optional), card slips closed   CARDS: Amex, Delta, Diners, MasterCard, Switch, Visa   DETAILS: 95 seats. Private parties: 6 main room, 8 to 14 private rooms. Vegetarian meals. No cigars. Wheelchair access (not WC). No music. Air-conditioned   ⊖ Sloane Square

Embassy

map 15

29 Old Burlington Street, W1S 3AN   COOKING 4
TEL: (020) 7851 0956   FAX: (020) 7734 3224   MODERN BRITISH
WEBSITE: www.embassylondon.com   £34–£85

This popular, lively and, in the evening, noisy bar and restaurant is the creation of Garry Hollihead and Mark Fuller. The long, narrow dining room is decked out in brown, creams and golds, its awkward shape seemingly an afterthought to the much larger bar – a popular pre-club drinking spot for the downstairs nightclub. Wild mushrooms, truffles and foie gras might be expected in this sophisticated room, but they are balanced by humbler items like roast belly pork (with glacé carrots and parsley mash) and salmon and cod fishcakes (with baby spinach, a poached egg and tomato butter sauce). Lunch is a fairly sedate affair with expense accounts supplying much of the business, but an inspection lunch found a few dishes requiring more attention to detail, and 'doll-sized' portions didn't exactly win any friends. Hits, though, have included smoked duck salad with pickled cucumber and wild mushrooms, and exactly timed pan-fried salmon with champ and 'rich and deliciously flavoured' dill butter sauce. France dominates the wine list, but apart from French house wine at £16.50 (£4.50 a glass) only a few bottles are under £30.

CHEFS: Garry Hollihead and Mark Grogan   PROPRIETORS: Mark Fuller and Garry Hollihead   OPEN: Tue to Fri L 12 to 3, Tue to Sat D 6 to 11.30   MEALS: alc (main courses £13 to £27). Set L £16.95 (2 courses) to £25, Set D Tue to Fri £16.95 (2 courses) to £35, Set D Sat £35   SERVICE: 12.5% (optional), card slips closed, 15% for parties of 8 or more   CARDS: Amex, Delta, MasterCard, Switch, Visa   DETAILS: 120 seats. 20 seats outside. Private parties: 70 main room, 40 to 50 private rooms. Vegetarian meals. No children under 12. Music. Air-conditioned   ⊖ Green Park, Piccadilly Circus

Enoteca Turi ▮ ⅝✳

map 12

28 Putney High Street, SW15 1SQ   NEW CHEF
TEL: (020) 8785 4449   FAX: (020) 8780 5409   ITALIAN
                                                                 £32–£61

Giuseppe Turi's devotion to seasonal Italian ingredients and regional recipes defines proceedings in his smart but informal restaurant. Provisions are imported from artisan producers in his native land, and you can get a taste of things to come from the 'outstanding' olive oil and bread that kick things off. A new chef has been appointed, but the food is sure to remain distinguished by 'strong' authentic flavours. Puglia comes to Putney in the shape of antipasti; otherwise you might start with cured pork loin with broad beans, rocket and pecorino. Main courses could range from calf's liver with herb salad, crisp potatoes and a balsamic reduction to wild sea bass alla acqua pazza (a Neapolitan speciality involving cherry tomatoes, herby fish stock and toasted bread). The traditional option of a risotto or pasta is offered as a second course (perhaps ravioli with Sicilian aubergine, scamorza and basil), while desserts have included Vin Santo with cantuccini.

The wine list gives an outstanding account of the Italian wine scene at all price levels (starting with house at £12) as well as rounding up top bottles from elsewhere. For those who lack the tenacity to plough through its many pages, every dish on the menu is marked with a recommended bottle (available by the glass). However, wine service has not lived up to the fine standard of the list for some reporters.

CHEF: Kodajo Ginevry   PROPRIETOR: Giuseppe Turi   OPEN: Mon to Sat 12 to 2.30, 7 to 11   CLOSED: 25 and 26 Dec, 1 Jan, L bank hols   MEALS: alc (main courses L £8.50 to £12, D £10.50 to £16.50). Set L £12.50 (2 courses)   SERVICE: 12.5% (optional), card slips closed   CARDS: Amex, Delta, Diners, MasterCard, Switch, Visa   DETAILS: 90 seats. Private parties: 10 to 30 private rooms. Vegetarian meals. No smoking in 1 dining room. Wheelchair access (also WC). Music. Air-conditioned   ⊖ Putney Bridge

L'Escargot, Ground Floor   map 15

48 Greek Street, W1D 4EF	COOKING 4
TEL: (020) 7439 7474 FAX: (020) 7437 0790	MODERN FRENCH
WEBSITE: www.whitestarline.org.uk	£28–£57

Plumb in the heart of Soho, this old institution, which has gone through many guises in the last few years, can be spotted by its sign depicting a jolly Frenchman riding a snail. The eponymous lower room is a wooden-floored space adorned with a collection of original twentieth-century paintings, as well as the setting for some resonantly French cooking which would be at home in a Parisian brasserie. Simple lunch dishes please: Bayonne ham with rémoulade, and good pannacotta with summer berries and raspberry coulis. Dishes from the main menu take in sea bass croustillant with mussels provençale and shellfish vinaigrette, roast poulet des Landes with roast salsify, and a straightforward tranche of calf's liver with mash and sauce diable. None of it will frighten the horses, but nor is it supposed to, and the level of finish is mostly impressive, even if one reporter remarked that it all looked a little too 'nouvelle' for the twenty-first century. Finish with strawberry soufflé, apple tarte fine, or hot chocolate fondant. Service copes well with the crowds. Wine prices are high, and for those with money to burn the furnaces are well primed with venerable bottles from Bordeaux and Burgundy – California is another speciality. The rest of France is interesting, especially Alsace, and the south has some more affordable options, including the £14 house bottles.

CHEFS: Jeff Galvin and Dominic Teague   PROPRIETORS: Jimmy Lahoud and Marco Pierre White   OPEN: Mon to Fri L 12 to 2.15, Mon to Sat D 6 to 11.15   CLOSED: 25 and 26 Dec, 1 Jan   MEALS: alc (main courses £13). Set L and D 6 to 7 £14.95 (2 courses) to £17.95   SERVICE: 12.5% (optional)   CARDS: Amex, Delta, Diners, MasterCard, Switch, Visa   DETAILS: 80 seats. Private parties: 80 main room, 10 to 60 private rooms. Vegetarian meals. Wheelchair access (also men's WC). Music. Air-conditioned   ⊖ Tottenham Court Road, Leicester Square

L'Escargot, Picasso Room   map 15

48 Greek Street, W1D 4EF	COOKING 5
TEL: (020) 7439 7474 FAX: (020) 7437 0790	MODERN FRENCH
WEBSITE: www.whitestarline.org.uk	£42–£87

Progress from the relative hurly-burly of the Ground Floor (see entry above) to the Picasso Room upstairs for L'Escargot's take on fine dining. With its calm atmosphere and punctilious, unintrusive service, it feels like a private dining room, the more so when you take in the prints and ceramics and the row of mask-like heads along the picture rail that are all by Picasso.

Jeff Galvin's food is as French as it gets, with snails, frogs' legs and the likes of poulet en cocotte much in evidence. A single lobster raviolo comes in a chicken stock reduction boldly flavoured with fennel, while smoked salmon arrives en paupiette, daubed with oscietra caviar, with a petite salade of herbs. Main courses impressed at inspection, both for fish and meat: a piece of 'excitingly fresh' turbot accompanied by wild mushroom mousseline and a 'courageously sweet' Sauternes sauce, offset by roast salsify, garlic and truffle; while rabbit gained in depth and savour from a cheesy, herbed risotto, asparagus, baby leeks, and a powerful rosemary cream sauce. Fingers of poached quince, instead of the usual sponge, make an inventive surround for blackberry and quince charlotte; trois desserts au chocolat use fine chocolate for the various elements; or there is iced banana parfait with butterscotch sauce. The wine list is the same as for Ground Floor.

CHEF: Jeff Galvin   PROPRIETORS: Jimmy Lahoud and Marco Pierre White   OPEN: Tue to Fri L 12 to 2, Tue to Sat D 6 to 11.15   CLOSED: 25 and 26 Dec, 1 Jan, 2 weeks Aug   MEALS: Set L £19.50 (2 courses) to £42, Set D £42   SERVICE: 15% (optional)   CARDS: Amex, Delta, Diners, MasterCard, Switch, Visa   DETAILS: 80 seats. Private parties: 45 main room. Vegetarian meals. No cigars/pipes. Music. Air-conditioned   ⊖ Tottenham Court Road, Leicester Square

L'Estaminet   map 15

14 Garrick Street, WC2E 9BJ   COOKING 2
TEL: (020) 7379 1432   FAX: (020) 7379 1530   FRENCH
                                                           £24–£70

Affordable pre-theatre deals are just one of the options at this long-running, 'comfortable and couth' brick-walled restaurant between Leicester Square and Covent Garden. The full menu – written in French with English translations – offers a posh version of bourgeois bistro food in the shape of warm Lyons sausage on potato salad, marmite de la mer (an abundant fish stew, served in a soup plate rather than its traditional 'marmite'), roast breast of guinea fowl in red wine sauce, and 'les grillades'. One correspondent thought the impressively varied cheeseboard 'outstanding for London', and a 'chariot' of desserts comes laden with ever-so-traditional creations such as tarte aux pommes and crème brûlée. The concise, all-French wine list opens with house offerings at £11.50.

CHEF: Philippe Thamet   PROPRIETOR: Cassis Restaurant Ltd   OPEN: Mon to Fri L 12 to 2.30, Mon to Sat D 5.45 to 11   CLOSED: 24 Dec to 3 Jan, last 2 weeks Aug, bank hols   MEALS: alc (main courses £13 to £25). Set D 5.45 to 7.15 £13.99   SERVICE: 12.5%, card slips closed   CARDS: Amex, Delta, MasterCard, Switch, Visa   DETAILS: 80 seats. Private parties: 12 to 16 private rooms. No cigars/pipes. Music. No mobile phones. Air-conditioned   ⊖ Leicester Square, Covent Garden

L'Etranger ▼   NEW ENTRY   map 14

36 Gloucester Road, SW7 4QT   COOKING 2
TEL: (020) 7584 1118   FAX: (020) 7584 8886   MODERN FRENCH-PLUS
WEBSITE: www.etranger.co.uk   £26–£83

The plain aubergine colour scheme of this corner site in smartest Kensington makes a suitably muted backdrop for Jérôme Tauvron's speculative cooking, which is categorised (if that is the word) as French with splashes of Indochinese. Some long-staying dishes – confit lamb shoulder with grilled aubergine – are just French, but others more in fusion vein make seasonal appearances. Brilliantly timed Chilean sea bass is lathered with a grill-singed honey glaze, while pieces of lacquered duck are spiked with tamarind and accompanied by a marmalade of rhubarb and ginger. A starter of five fish tartares (sea bass, tuna, salmon, sea bream and trout), presented on black spoons, are both generous and convincingly seasoned. Black sesame ice cream looked like 'freshly mixed cement' to our inspector; a better way to finish could well be an unabashedly French passion-fruit soufflé. Service takes it all very seriously. Wines by the glass are a speciality – choose your grape then choose again for your favourite style – but beware the mark-ups on the bottle rates. The main list is a roll call of droppable names from both classic and upstart regions, strong in Australia and California as well as Europe. Prices are inevitably high, but £20 won't leave you out in the cold.

CHEF: Jérôme Tauvron   PROPRIETOR: Ibi Issolah   OPEN: Sun to Fri L 12 to 2.30 (11.45 to 3 Sun), all week D 6 to 10.45   MEALS: alc (main courses £15.50 to £22). Set L Mon to Fri £14.50 (2 courses) to £16.50, Set L Sun £16.50 (2 courses) to £18.50   SERVICE: 12.5% (optional)   CARDS: Amex, Delta, Diners, MasterCard, Switch, Visa   DETAILS: 70 seats. Private parties: 50 main room, 8 to 18 private rooms. Vegetarian meals. No-smoking area. Music. Air-conditioned   ⊖ Gloucester Road (£5)

Eyre Brothers ▼   map 13

70 Leonard Street, EC2A 4QX   COOKING 2
TEL: (020) 7613 5346   FAX: (020) 7739 8199   MEDITERRANEAN
WEBSITE: www.eyrebrothers.co.uk   £37–£69

Mahogany floor and ceiling, room-height windows and black walnut and leather (for chairs, banquettes, sideboards and bar) create a trendy, contemporary, upmarket metropolitan space with 'in-built quality and comfort'. And, though the food and service hasn't always matched the dizzy heights of the décor, customers revel in its rustic, robust, busy Mediterranean style, and, in particular, the Spanish and Portuguese dishes that inspire much of the menu. Expect top-quality ingredients in dishes like baked salt cod with garlic, onions, black olives, mashed potato and accompanying fried bread and aïoli, or fillet of Iberico pork, marinated with thyme and garlic, and served with patatas panaderas. You could precede these with starters like fried cuttlefish with aïoli, or escabèche of quail, and finish with a rich chocolate and prune terrine served up with raspberry ripple ice cream. The wine list is suitably stylish, with a welcome Iberian bias. Prices start at £13.50, and a dozen or so come by the glass.

CHEFS: David Eyre and João Cleto   PROPRIETORS: David and Robert Eyre   OPEN: Sun to Fri L 12 to 2.45, Mon to Sat D 6.30 to 10.45. Tapas menu also available   CLOSED: 25 Dec, bank hol weekends   MEALS: alc (main courses £14 to £21)   SERVICE: 12.5% (optional), card slips closed   CARDS: Amex, Delta, Diners, MasterCard, Switch, Visa   DETAILS: 87 seats. Private parties: 60 main room. Vegetarian meals. No-smoking area. Wheelchair access (also WC). Music. Air-conditioned   ⊖ Old Street

Fifteen ✗   map 13

15 Westland Place, N1 7LP   COOKING 3
TEL: (0871) 330 1515   FAX: (020) 7251 2749   MODERN EUROPEAN
WEBSITE: www.fifteenrestaurant.com   £39–£142

What started as an experiment to get underprivileged kids into gainful employment and enthused about food is now a well-established and thriving business. This year has seen the conversion of the ground-floor bar into a traditional trattoria, with a snazzy retro décor to match the basement restaurant, featuring black and white designer chairs, bright pink banquettes, bare wooden floorboards and lively, colourful murals. The emphasis in both dining rooms is on quality seasonal produce prepared simply in a style that blends British and Mediterranean themes. In the trattoria this translates into a 'superb' salad of intensely flavoured smoked duck with watercress, pickled shallots and shaved horseradish ('the price alone was sufficient to say that it ought bloody well to be good'), and tender monkfish with robust accompaniments of chicory, caper berries, lemon and parsley. Dishes in the restaurant are only slightly more elaborate, although descriptions are more enthusiastic, as in 'melt-in-the-mouth organic veal cheek with oozy wet polenta', or roast tranche of line-caught turbot with potatoes, fennel and 'the best black olive sauce in the world!' Some respondents herald skilful execution, accurate timing, and well-balanced flavours, but disappointments are reported, and prices are high for one and all. The restaurant's extensive wine list is arranged by style and grape variety, with prices starting at £18. The list in the trattoria is shorter and almost exclusively Italian, prices opening at £15.

CHEF: Jamie Oliver   PROPRIETOR: Cheeky Chops Charity   OPEN: all week L 12 to 2.15, Mon to Sat D 6.30 to 9.30   CLOSED: 25 Dec, 1 Jan   MEALS: trattoria: alc (main courses £12 to £15); restaurant: alc L (main courses £20 to £32). Set D £65 to £105 (inc wine)   SERVICE: 12.5% (optional), card slips closed   CARDS: Amex, Delta, Diners, MasterCard, Switch, Visa   DETAILS: trattoria: 40 seats. Vegetarian meals. No-smoking area. Wheelchair access (also WC). Music. Air-conditioned; restaurant: 70 seats. Vegetarian meals. No smoking. Music. Air-conditioned   ⊖ Old Street

Fifth Floor ▮   map 14

Harvey Nichols, 109–125 Knightsbridge, SW1X 7RJ   COOKING 4
TEL: (020) 7235 5250   FAX: (020) 7823 2207   MODERN BRITISH
WEBSITE: www.harveynichols.com   £31–£90

The ultramodern décor in Harvey Nicks' vibrant and bustling fifth-floor food court may not be to everyone's taste, but it is undoubtedly impressive. There's a sushi bar, wine boutique and one of Britain's most upscale groceries in this temple to fine comestibles. The centrepiece is the impeccably furnished Fifth Floor restaurant, which oozes glitz and glamour. One diner, surrounded by 'serial telephone users and chain smokers', commended the efficiency of the air-conditioning.

Here is a kitchen that seems quite at home with a range of modern European ideas but is unafraid to lob a bit of fusion into the mix. You might find a tempura of Whitby cod with pea purée alongside roast quail breast with veal sweetbreads, celeriac and apple purée and crispy Savoy cabbage – and they are just starters. Classic main courses such as grilled Dover sole meunière and tournedos Rossini jostle for place beside more modern renditions of, say, roast fillet of monkfish polonaise with cauliflower purée, salsify and chorizo oil and the like. Desserts are simpler constructions on the whole, with an emphasis on traditional British favourites such as rhubarb crumble with vanilla ice cream, or sticky toffee pudding. If indulging in small treats rather than going the whole hog on a designer frock is one of the joys of shopping here, then the wine list offers similar pleasures with its outstanding range by the glass. But if a splurge is on the cards, this definitive collection of good and great wines from around the world is reason enough to come. Prices, starting at £13.50, aren't at all bad, and on Monday nights an exciting selection is offered at shop prices.

CHEF: Simon Shaw   PROPRIETOR: Harvey Nichols   OPEN: all week L 12 to 3 (4.30 Fri and Sat, 3.30 Sun), Mon to Sat D 6 to 11   MEALS: alc (main courses L £15.50, D £16.50 to £24.50). Set L £22 (2 courses) to £25, Set D Mon to Wed, Thur to Sat 6 to 7.30 £18.50   SERVICE: 12.5% (optional)   CARDS: Amex, Delta, Diners, MasterCard, Switch, Visa   DETAILS: 114 seats. Private parties: 12 main room. Vegetarian meals. Children's helpings. Wheelchair access (also WC). Occasional music. No mobile phones. Air-conditioned   ⊖ Knightsbridge

Fina Estampa ✲

150–152 Tooley Street, SE1 2TU
TEL/FAX: (020) 7403 1342

COOKING 2
PERUVIAN
£27–£52

map 13

Tooley Street still has a vaguely Dickensian air about it, so a Peruvian restaurant may seem at odds with the setting. It is restrained enough not to overplay the South American card, being simply and tastefully, if inexpensively, done out. Ceviche of white fish topped with sliced red onion, coriander, a few tiny shrimp and sweet potato, and chupe de camarones – seafood bisque with a spicy kick from aji (Peruvian chillies) – are typical starters. Dried potato (a staple in Peru) is the mainstay of a well-made carapulcra, which comes with chicken, pork, cumin, aji, onions and garlic, and aji de gallina is a generous portion of poached and shredded chicken in a piquant sauce of chillies, walnuts and spices. All 11 bottles on the wine list are from either Chile or Argentina. Prices open at £13.50 and are reasonable throughout.

CHEF: Bianca Jones   PROPRIETORS: Bianca and Richard Jones   OPEN: Mon to Fri 12 to 10.30, Sat 6.30 to 10.30   CLOSED: 24, 25 and 31 Dec, 1 Jan, bank hols   MEALS: alc (main courses £7.50 to £16). Tapas bar menu available   SERVICE: 10% (optional)   CARDS: Amex, Delta, Diners, MasterCard, Switch, Visa   DETAILS: 70 seats. Private parties: 70 main room. Vegetarian meals. Children's helpings. No smoking in 1 dining room. Music   ⊖ London Bridge

Fino

33 Charlotte Street (entrance on Rathbone Street),
W1T 1RR
TEL: (020) 7813 8010   FAX: (020) 7813 8011
WEBSITE: www.finorestaurant.com

COOKING 2
SPANISH
£26–£74

map 15

A discreet entrance off Charlotte Street, with heavy oak doors, creates a rather grand first impression, which continues as you descend the oak staircase past bright floral displays and contemporary art to the large, open-plan and airy basement dining room, where pale wood dominates. The food is strictly traditional Spanish, with a long menu of small, tapas-style dishes featuring plenty of grilled and fried seafood, cold cured meats and classics such as patatas bravas, tortilla, and escalivada. Golden, crisp, soft-centred fried veal sweetbreads have been a highlight, as have soft, tender chunks of octopus lusciously covered in olive oil and sprinkled with paprika. The wine list opens with a good choice of sherry by the bottle or glass, and the rest of the list concentrates on Spain with a few bottles from elsewhere. Prices start at £14.

CHEF: Jean-Philippe Patruno   PROPRIETORS: Sam and Eddie Hart   OPEN: Mon to Fri L 12 to 2.30, Mon to Sat D 6 to 10.15   CLOSED: bank hols   MEALS: alc (main courses £8 to £15.50). Set L £14.95 to £28, Set D £17.95 to £28 (min 2). Bar menu available   SERVICE: 12.5% (optional), card slips closed   CARDS: Amex, Delta, MasterCard, Switch, Visa   DETAILS: 99 seats. Private parties: 12 main room. Vegetarian meals. Wheelchair access (also WC). No music. Air-conditioned   ⊖ Goodge Street, Tottenham Court Road

'The maitre d' expressed frustration that the chef did not even know what kind of mushrooms he put in his own soup. I asked if he found it worrying that he seemed to know more about the food than the chef. He admitted as much.' (On eating in the Home Counties)

Fish Hoek

map 12

8 Elliot Road, W4 1PE
TEL: (020) 8742 0766   FAX: (020) 8742 3374
EMAIL: info@fishhoek.co.uk

COOKING 3
SEAFOOD/SOUTH AFRICAN
£29–£89

Between a frosted window with the name etched in the glass, and walls lined with black-and-white photos of great catches, one chooses from a list of fish, mainly South African (stumpnose, snoek, emperor, kabeljou, etc.), all available in half or full portions. Treatments are straightforward, very much 'braai'-style (roasting, grilling, or frying), and accompaniments like Santa Rosa tomatoes, shallots, baby marrow, and spiced vanilla oil partner pan-fried gilthead bream, or pickled mushroom, pak choi and danhia dressing go with seared yellowfin tuna, and lime-infused turmeric rice with Cape seafood curry. Desserts are light fruits and sorbets, infused fruits and fuller puddings, like chocolate mielie meal pudding (a kind of chocolate fondant 'supremely cooked and presented'). Young South Africans serve good humouredly, and white wines dominate an all–South–African list, with most under £25. Owner Pete Gottgens also owns and runs the Ardeonaig Hotel, Ardeonaig, in Scotland (see entry).

CHEFS: Pete Gottgens, Joe Alexander and Mark Lythgoe   PROPRIETOR: Pete Gottgens   OPEN: Tue to Sun L 12 to 2.30 (3 Sun), all week D 6 to 10.30 (11 Fri and Sat)   CLOSED: 22 Dec to 7 Jan   MEALS: alc (main courses £11.50 to £32). Set L £11.50 (2 courses) to £16.50, Set D 6 to 8 £11.50 (2 courses) to £16.50   SERVICE: not inc, 12.5% (optional) for parties of 6 or more   CARDS: Delta, MasterCard, Switch, Visa   DETAILS: 54 seats. Private parties: 54 main room. Wheelchair access (not WC). Music. Air-conditioned   ⊖ Turnham Green

---

Fish Shop 🍴 ✂

map 13

360–362 St John Street, EC1V 4NR
TEL: (020) 7837 1199   FAX: (020) 7837 3399
WEBSITE: www.thefishshop.net

COOKING 2
SEAFOOD
£28–£71

Handy for Sadlers Wells, this neo-Georgian building has well-spaced tables in ground-floor and (non-smoking) basement eating areas. The menu offers predominantly simple, but skilful and often inventive, modern European treatments of good-quality seafood. Savour creamy smoked haddock soup, or maybe grilled squid and chorizo with rocket and balsamic dressing, then gilthead bream dressed with Pernod and olive oil, or perhaps smoked haddock brandade and poached egg. And there's fish 'n' chips: haddock in egg-and-matzo batter with chips that were 'special' for one reporter. Desserts include sticky toffee pudding or pink grapefruit sorbet with Plymouth gin. International wines start with a £12.75 Pays d'Oc and bottles from Luxembourg and Canada alongside Cheverny and Albariño.

CHEF: Didier Liberre   PROPRIETOR: John Moyle   OPEN: Tue to Sat 12 to 2.30, 5.30 to 10.30   MEALS: alc (main courses £11 to £30). Set L £13.50 (2 courses) to £17, Set D 5.30 to 7 £13.50 (2 courses) to £17   SERVICE: 12.5% (optional), card slips closed   CARDS: Amex, Delta, Diners, MasterCard, Switch, Visa   DETAILS: 80 seats. Private parties: 40 main room, 8 to 40 private rooms. Vegetarian meals. Children's helpings. No smoking in 1 dining room. Wheelchair access (also WC). No music   ⊖ Angel

---

'[The restaurant is in] a beautiful sixteenth-century building with a courtyard for al fresco eating, and the food tastes of nothing. They will probably make a million.' (On eating in the Home Counties)

FishWorks ✵

6 Turnham Green Terrace, W4 1QP	**map 12**
TEL: (020) 8994 0086 FAX: (020) 8994 0778	COOKING **2**
WEBSITE: www.fishworks.co.uk	SEAFOOD
	£36–£86

The formula of combining a fishmonger's and fish restaurant has been successful enough to turn FishWorks into a mini chain, with branches in Bath, Bristol and Christchurch (see entries). The focus is purely on fish and seafood, sourced from the South Coast and major European ports and markets. Native lobsters come from Cornwall, Devon or Scotland, and crab from Dartmouth. From the 'classic dishes' section of the menu, choose starter- or main-course-sized portions of Spanish prawns cooked with olive oil and sea salt, or River Fowey mussels steamed with wine and parsley. Cooking tends towards the unadorned (or 'plain', if you will), so among main courses might be roast hake with black butter and capers, or whole sea bream baked in sea salt. Side dishes of vegetables (charged extra) such as braised fennel with parsley, olive oil and chilli add pizzazz. Lemon tart has been a successful dessert. The wine list intelligently focuses on European fish-friendly whites, although three reds make an appearance. Bottle prices start at £15.25. A second London branch is due to open in Marylebone High Street after we've gone to press.

CHEF: Jack Scarterfield PROPRIETOR: FishWorks plc OPEN: Tue to Sat 12 to 2.30, 6 to 10.30, Sun 11 to 5 CLOSED: Christmas, bank hols MEALS: alc (main courses £11 to £35) SERVICE: not inc CARDS: Amex, Delta, MasterCard, Switch, Visa DETAILS: 48 seats. 22 seats outside. Vegetarian meals. Children's helpings. No smoking. Wheelchair access (not WC). Music. Air-conditioned ⊖ Turnham Green

Flâneur ✵

41 Farringdon Road, EC1M 3JB	**map 13**
TEL: (020) 7404 4422 FAX: (020) 7831 4532	NEW CHEF
EMAIL: mail@flaneur.com	MODERN EUROPEAN-PLUS
	£32–£65

Flâneur is an upmarket delicatessen with dining tables placed among the merchandise, and would certainly feel at home in Paris – 'pure heaven for foodies'. A new chef took over as the Guide went to press, but if the style of the new regime continues as before you can expect to find a mixture of classic and modern ideas. Start with a plate of charcuterie, or pork rillettes with sourdough bread, and proceed to pan-fried halibut with parsley sauce, roast rump of lamb with rosemary jus, or vitello tonnato. 'Puds are the thing here,' noted a reporter, impressed by lemon and ricotta cheesecake. Two bottles from Spain are the only interlopers on the otherwise entirely French wine list. Nothing is less than £15, but around ten, in a variety of styles, come by the glass from £4.50.

CHEF: Simon Phelan PROPRIETOR: Gavin Monk OPEN: Mon to Fri 12 to 3, 6 to 10, Sat 9 to 4, 6 to 10, Sun and bank hols 9 to 4 CLOSED: 25 and 26 Dec, 1 Jan MEALS: alc (main courses £9 to £16) SERVICE: 12.5% (optional), card slips closed CARDS: Amex, Delta, Diners, MasterCard, Switch, Visa DETAILS: 55 seats. Private parties: 55 main room. Vegetarian meals. No smoking. Wheelchair access (not WC). No music ⊖ Farringdon

---

If customers are asked to switch off mobile phones while in a restaurant, this is noted in the details at the end of an entry.

Four Seasons £

map 13

84 Queensway, W2 3RL
TEL: (020) 7229 4320

COOKING 3
CANTONESE
£20–£59

'Captures the hustle and bustle of Hong Kong,' observed one well-travelled reporter, who also noticed that the interior of this high-turnover Cantonese restaurant has been spruced up with new blue furnishings and a lick of magnolia paint. Inside, it can still seem 'cramped and humble', but the kitchen serves some of the most forthright Cantonese food in town. Whole ducks, slabs of barbecued pork, and other roast meats hanging in the window make an impact, and they are great for a quick lunch with a plate of rice. In addition to diehard dishes like steamed sea bass with ginger and spring onions, or beef with oyster sauce, the menu features around 50 specials, including a hotpot of braised chicken with yam and coconut sauce, clams with jellyfish, and stewed brisket of lamb with black pepper. Service has been noticeably friendly of late. House wines are £9.

CHEF: Mr Tong PROPRIETOR: Paul Chung OPEN: all week 12 to 11.15 MEALS: alc (main courses £5.50 to £20). Set D £12.50 to £17 (all min 2 or more) SERVICE: 12.5% CARDS: Amex, MasterCard, Switch, Visa DETAILS: 80 seats. Private parties: 30 main room. Vegetarian meals. Music. Air-conditioned ⊖ Bayswater, Queensway

Fox Dining Room £

map 13

28 Paul Street, EC2A 4LB
TEL: (020) 7729 5708
EMAIL: fox.ph@virgin.net

COOKING 3
MODERN EUROPEAN
£30–£38

'Rustic European' is one description of the food at this dining room over a pub, which could equally be applied to the dark interior with its added spicy dash of Dickensian Gothic. One reporter admired the 'confidence and maturity' of the kitchen that allows ingredients to speak for themselves. The menu description of asparagus and feta brings precisely that – crumbly cheese with six perfectly cooked spears – while a main course of gamey, moist, slow-cooked saddle of rabbit comes on top of full-flavoured caponata. Puddings might include lemon tart or satsuma and cranberry jelly with custard. Service bounds with enthusiasm, and the moderately priced, succinct list of predominantly French wines starts at £10.50; nearly all are available by the glass, from £2.50.

CHEF: Trish Hilferty PROPRIETOR: Michael Belben OPEN: Mon to Fri 12.30 to 3, 6.30 to 10 CLOSED: 24 Dec to 4 Jan, bank hols MEALS: Set L and D £15 (2 courses) to £19.75. Bar menu available SERVICE: not inc CARDS: Delta, MasterCard, Switch, Visa DETAILS: 34 seats. 20 seats outside. Private parties: 40 main room. Vegetarian meals. Children's helpings. No music ⊖ Old Street, Liverpool Street

Franklins

NEW ENTRY map 12

157 Lordship Lane, SE22 8HX
TEL: (020) 8299 9598
EMAIL: franklins@madasafish.com

COOKING 2
BRITISH
£21–£50

With the blue-tiled frontage standing out on this busy South-east London thoroughfare, this buzzy, basic, brasserie-cum-pub with paper cloths and plain wooden chairs makes a thing of a certain sort of Britishness. Service is briskly efficient, portions are large, and subtlety is not a strong point, but carefully sourced, interesting ingredients treated with the minimum of culinary faff add up to a good experience. Chunky dishes like deep, dark mutton and Guinness stew, or monkfish with lentils and bacon (although here the salty bacon gave the fish rather a run for its money) exemplify an admirably robust simplicity that doesn't lapse into coarseness of touch unless attention wavers. The shortish wine list, compiled with enthusiasm and knowledge, spotlights France; a good range by the glass, house bottles from £11, and fair mark-ups throughout encourage exploration.

CHEFS: Tim Sheehan and Phil Greene PROPRIETORS: Rodney Franklin and Tim Sheehan OPEN: Mon to Fri 12 to 4, 6 to 10.30; Sun 1 to 10 CLOSED: 24 to 26 Dec, 31 Dec, 1 Jan MEALS: alc (main courses £11 to £16.50). Set L Mon to Fri (exc bank hols) £9 (2 courses) to £12. Bar menu available SERVICE: not inc CARDS: Amex, Delta, MasterCard, Switch, Visa DETAILS: 60 seats. 12 seats outside. Private parties: 60 main room, 4 to 24 private rooms. Vegetarian meals. Children's helpings. Wheelchair access (also WC). No music (£5)

Fung Shing

map 15

15 Lisle Street, WC2H 7BE
TEL: (020) 7437 1539   FAX: (020) 7734 0284
WEBSITE: www.fungshing.co.uk

COOKING 3
CHINESE
£32–£69

A long-standing Chinatown fixture, Fung Shing continues to be popular with everyone who appreciates authentic traditional Chinese cooking, attracting a broad mix of Westerners and Chinese. Behind the blue frontage, the dining room is a calm, restful environment (a stark contrast to the bustling Chinese supermarket next door). Seafood and exotic dishes are the specialities, although the vast menu keeps most bases covered. Traditional favourites are done well: 'delicate' battered soft-shell crab with diced garlic and red chillies, for example, and 'tender and moist' spicy aromatic duck with the usual accompaniments. A hotpot of pork belly and yams has been a particular hit, featuring 'meltingly tender' meat and vegetables deeply infused with flavour during long, slow cooking. The above-average wine list includes a handful of house selections at £14.50 and £16 and a short choice of pricier fine wines.

CHEF: Chun Fat Cheung PROPRIETOR: Fung Shing Partnership OPEN: all week 12 to 11 CLOSED: 24 to 26 Dec MEALS: alc (main courses £8 to £26). Set L £17 (2 courses), Set D £17 to £30 (all min 2 or more) SERVICE: 10%, card slips closed CARDS: Amex, Delta, Diners, MasterCard, Switch, Visa DETAILS: 115 seats. Private parties: 50 main room, 20 to 40 private rooms. Vegetarian meals. Music. Air-conditioned ⊖ Leicester Square

Gate ⚘ £

map 12

51 Queen Caroline Street, W6 9QL
TEL: (020) 8748 6932   FAX: (020) 8563 1719
WEBSITE: www.gateveg.co.uk

COOKING 2
VEGETARIAN
£24–£45

They pack 'em in tight at this inventive and popular vegetarian venue, all the more so, perhaps, since its north London sister establishment closed. The curious setting is that of a former church hall (later an artists' studio), where natural light pours through large glass panels in the sloping ceiling into the yellow-painted dining room. Dishes take in European, North African, South-east Asian and Indian influences, a myriad ingredients in each of the kitchen's complex creations. To start, savour the aromatic kick of a pan-fried mustard seed potato cake stuffed with Indian-spiced vegetables with a sweet-and-sour tamarind sauce, or try beer-battered baby artichoke stuffed with duxelles with a Puy lentil salsa and aïoli. To follow might be fragrantly curried Caribbean vegetables, or pied bleu mushrooms, butternut squash and goats' cheese wrapped in thyme-infused potato on French beans with cep cream sauce and deep-fried leeks. Calvados ice cream, accompanying an apple frangipane tart, was the 'wow moment' of one meal. Service is informal and 'highly efficient', and the short wine list, priced from £11 to £27, contains a number of organic wines.

CHEF: Adrian Daniel   PROPRIETORS: Michael and Adrian Daniel   OPEN: Mon to Fri L 12 to 2.45, Mon to Sat D 6 to 10.45   CLOSED: Christmas, New Year, Easter, bank hols   MEALS: alc (main courses £8 to £11.50). Set L £12.50 (2 courses) to £15.50, Set D £17 (2 courses) to £20   SERVICE: not inc, 12.5% for parties of 6 or more   CARDS: Amex, Delta, MasterCard, Switch, Visa   DETAILS: 50 seats. 20 seats outside. Private parties: 50 main room. Vegetarian meals. No smoking. No music   ⊖ Hammersmith

Le Gavroche 🍴

map 15

43 Upper Brook Street, W1K 7QR
TEL: (020) 7499 1826   FAX: (020) 7491 4387
WEBSITE: www.le-gavroche.co.uk

COOKING 7
FRENCH
£47–£158

Few dining venues can claim the level of prestige that has been associated with this Mayfair address for what seems like for ever. A discreet entrance leads to a small reception area where pre-meal drinks can be taken while you browse the menu before being led downstairs to the dining room. Dark green walls hung with a few abstract paintings, a dark blue and pink patterned carpet, and widely spaced tables laid with crisp linen, silver cruet sets and candles in brass holders give an exclusive, luxurious feel. There is no music, emphasising the air of hushed reverence in this temple of gastronomy.

When it is firing on all cylinders, the kitchen can turn out cooking to match the best you will find anywhere. A recent inspection found it at the peak of its powers. A succession of finely crafted appetisers gets proceedings off to a fine start, with smoked eel and cabbage in a delicate pastry case particularly impressive. These set the tone for a meal in which finely honed classic techniques and abundant luxury ingredients are to the fore. For starters, seared tuna is served prettily in squares on a black plate with matching slices of chorizo, the richness of the combination balanced with lightly steamed asparagus of the highest quality. The traditional nature of the cooking is no more evident than in main courses such as wild salmon fillet with fennel, a velvety purée of Jerusalem artichokes and a decadent lobster sauce, or a substantial beef fillet topped with caramelised shallots, set next to a heap of gratinated macaroni and a couple of large ceps, and finished with a highly reduced and intensely flavoured red wine sauce. The cheese course involves choosing from no fewer than 36 fine French examples, and, to finish, passion-fruit soufflé has 'the lightest, fluffiest consistency that could be hoped for'.

The wine list is a hymn to the finest that France has to offer but is not restricted to the classic regions and also shows a healthy interest in non-stellar options. Short selections from elsewhere, mostly Italy, are choice but stick exclusively to top names. It starts with red or white Bergerac at £16.50.

CHEF: Michel Roux   PROPRIETOR: Le Gavroche Ltd   OPEN: Mon to Fri L 12 to 2, Mon to Sat D 7 to 11 CLOSED: Christmas, New Year, bank hols   MEALS: alc (main courses £27 to £39). Set L £42 (inc wine), Set D £82   SERVICE: 12.5% (optional), card slips closed   CARDS: Amex, Delta, Diners, MasterCard, Switch, Visa   DETAILS: 60 seats. Vegetarian meals. Jacket. No cigars/pipes. No music. Air-conditioned ⊖ Marble Arch

Gay Hussar
map 15

2 Greek Street, W1D 4NB
TEL: (020) 7437 0973   FAX: (020) 7437 4631
WEBSITE: www.simplyrestaurants.com

COOKING 1
HUNGARIAN
£29–£51

'Nothing changes ... it's always great' – thus writes one devotee of an institution that has graced Soho since 1953. No music now competes with the buzz of conversation from old-stagers, tourists and political types dining on beef goulash soup, or fried mushrooms with tartare sauce, before moving on to fish dumplings, smoked goose breast, crispy roast duck, or stuffed cabbage with sauerkraut, smoked bacon and sausage. Fruit pudding, or túrós palacsinta (cottage cheese pancakes) are favourite ways to finish, and portions are not for the fainthearted. Hungarian house wine (from £12.50), along with Bull's Blood and Tokaji (dry and sweet), heads the wine list, and Hungarian liqueurs include Slivovitz and Unicum.

CHEF: Carlos Mendonca   PROPRIETOR: Restaurant Partnership plc   OPEN: Mon to Sat 12.15 to 2.30, 5.30 to 10.45   CLOSED: public and bank hols   MEALS: alc (main courses £9.50 to £17). Set L £17.50 (2 courses) to £19.50   SERVICE: 12.5% (optional), card slips closed   CARDS: Amex, Delta, Diners, MasterCard, Switch, Visa   DETAILS: 75 seats. Private parties: 38 main room, 12 to 26 private rooms. Vegetarian meals. Children's helpings. No pipes/cigars. Wheelchair access (not WC). No music. Air-conditioned
⊖ Tottenham Court Road (£5)

Giardinetto ⁂
NEW ENTRY   map 15

69 Charlotte Street, W1T 4PJ
TEL: (020) 7637 4907   FAX: (020) 8993 2665

COOKING 3
ITALIAN
£46–£64

Large mosaic tiles on the floor, young customers, and shiny dark wooden tables keep the decibels up and the atmosphere animated, which is just as well as this basement restaurant gets the thumbs down for décor. Yet there's no doubting that the money has been spent on the right priorities – food and wine – and there is a palpable sense of honesty and passion about the cooking. Classic Genovese and Ligurian cuisine is the preoccupation, 'as true to its roots as it can be', producing starters of swordfish carpaccio with cinnamon and orange julienne, exemplary mussel casserole with white wine, garlic and parsley, and 'perfect' ciapazoi (pasta made from chestnut flour topped with pesto and a sprinkling of potatoes). Accurate timing makes the most of materials, as do the generally simple treatments: Scottish prime beef fillet wrapped in lard, rosemary and garlic, steamed monkfish topped with pesto and cherry tomato concasse with fennel salad, or 'wonderfully light and wobbly' pannacotta for dessert. An interesting list of predominantly regional wines from Italy, with some 20 from France, is not for the budget conscious, with seven by the glass and only a couple under £20.

CHEF: Maurizio Vilona   PROPRIETOR: Giardinetto Ltd   OPEN: all week 12.30 to 3, 6.30 to 11   CLOSED: 24 to 26 Dec   MEALS: Set L and D £24.50 (2 courses) to £33   SERVICE: 12.5% (optional)   CARDS: Amex, Delta, Diners, MasterCard, Switch, Visa   DETAILS: 36 seats. Private parties: 36 main room, 4 to 10 private rooms. Vegetarian meals. Children's helpings. No smoking in 1 dining room. Occasional music. Air-conditioned   ⊖ Goodge Street (£5)

Ginger

map 13

115 Westbourne Grove, W2 4UP
TEL: (020) 7908 1990   FAX: (020) 7908 1991
WEBSITE: www.gingerrestaurant.co.uk

COOKING 2
BANGLADESHI
£18–£57

'Proud to be Bangladeshi' might be the slogan and 'old Barclays Bank turquoise' is the predominant colour in this eye-catching restaurant. The wide-ranging menu gives seafood prominence, as in king prawns roasted in the tandoor with ginger, salmon kodi (a yoghurt-based curry), and specials like battered soft-shell crab 'embedded on aloo burjee' (Indian mashed potato). Meat and poultry also receive distinctive treatment: kashi bhuna is a classic Bengali goat curry, and other regions contribute barbecued lamb chops served on upma (South Indian-style semolina), and chicken cafereal (a Goan speciality involving roast potatoes). Vegetables and rice are capably handled, while desserts like warm halva and home-made honey and ginger ice cream uphold the Bengali sweet-making tradition. Plenty of New World bottles appear on the 'simple and sensible' wine list. House selections are £11.95.

CHEF: Cruz Gomes   PROPRIETOR: Ollie Rahman   OPEN: Mon to Thur 5 to 11, Fri 5 to 12, Sat 12 to 12, Sun 12 to 11   CLOSED: 25 Dec   MEALS: alc (main courses £7.50 to £13). Set L £9.95   SERVICE: 12.5%   CARDS: Amex, Delta, MasterCard, Switch, Visa   DETAILS: 60 seats. Private parties: 100 main room, 25 to 30 private rooms. Vegetarian meals. Children's helpings. Music. Air-conditioned   ⊖ Notting Hill Gate

Golden Dragon £

map 15

28–29 Gerrard Street, W1V 7LP
TEL: (020) 7734 2763   FAX: (020) 7734 1073

COOKING 2
CHINESE
£27–£58

A big and colourful player in Gerrard Street's Chinese razzmatazz, the Golden Dragon is a magnet for the crowds: dim sum draw plenty of custom at lunchtime, and the array of one-plate rice, noodle and ho-fun dishes suits those wanting an express meal. The cooking is predominantly Cantonese with a few nods to Peking and Szechuan along the way. A sizeable contingent of appetisers and soups starts the ball rolling, and seafood gets a good airing (from deep-fried crispy oysters and 'clear' steamed lobster to baked sliced eel with garlic and chilli). Elsewhere, the kitchen does a good line in barbecued meats (most of which are served authentically 'warm'): expect anything from roast duck and belly pork to salt-baked chicken and grilled pigeon. House wine is £9.

CHEF: Mr Wong   PROPRIETOR: Grandpord Ltd   OPEN: Mon to Sat 12 to 11.15 (11.45 Fri and Sat), Sun 11 to 10.45   CLOSED: 25 Dec   MEALS: alc (main courses £6.50 to £18). Set L and D £12.50 (2 courses) to £22.80 (all min 2 or more)   SERVICE: 10%   CARDS: Amex, Delta, Diners, MasterCard, Switch, Visa   DETAILS: 200 seats. Private parties: 200 main room, 10 to 40 private rooms. Vegetarian meals. Music. Air-conditioned ⊖ Leicester Square, Piccadilly Circus

Gordon Ramsay 🍶

map 14

68–69 Royal Hospital Road, SW3 4HP
TEL: (020) 7352 4441   FAX: (020) 7352 3334
WEBSITE: www.gordonramsay.com

COOKING 10
FRENCH
£51–£131

It may have come to readers' attention that Gordon Ramsay has spent a fair bit of time on the telly over the past year or so. In some cases a preoccupation with the glamorous world of celebrity can have a detrimental effect on the bread-and-butter business of running a restaurant. Not here. In fact, this is a restaurant that is cruising in high gear, with a chef at the top of his game, his cooking displaying superlative confidence and flair, buoyed by consistently faultless technical precision.

The venue is surprisingly modest but plays on the high expectations of diners with a translucent glass wall creating a passageway from the entrance to the dining room, as if to heighten the sense of anticipation. Flamboyantly colourful Venetian glassware in mini shrines on the walls adds a touch of opulence, while tables are laid with immaculate linen, Riedel glasses and pretty flower arrangements. The air of hushed reverence is punctuated by the singsong voice of maître d' Jean-Claude Breton, who greets even first-time guests with warm bonhomie – he runs a tight ship, with fast, controlled and perfectly orchestrated service that combines formality with an easy, friendly manner.

The quality of service ensures that there are no distractions from the serious business of enjoying the food. And serious business it is, too, as haute as cuisine comes, very French and very refined. Luxury ingredients are a given, as in the ever-popular foie gras starter, which features three globes of seared liver set on braised endive with a sweet Sauternes sauce and caramelised shallots. And yet there is no sense of a kitchen retreating to the safety of tried and tested ideas. Menus and dishes constantly evolve in exciting new ways. Among recent innovations is a dish of roast sea bass fillet with crackling-like crisp skin and glistening white and moist yet resolutely firm flesh, partnered to great effect by a mini lasagne constructed of super-fine pasta layered with richly flavoured, unctuous slow-cooked meat giving an extra textural dimension to the dish, its reduced red wine sauce combining pungency with lightness. Indeed, combinations of meat and seafood are a forte, another highlight including braised pork belly with langoustines, the 'wonderfully aromatic' pork braised to a delicately soft fusion of meat and fat and served on a bed of sweet, crunchy, tiny broad beans and spinach with a pair of 'huge, voluptuous and amazingly sweet' shelled langoustines. The dish is finished with a rich, meaty sauce, poured at table, that 'marries shellfish and meat together in a most elegant way'.

When judged by the high standards of everything else, desserts may impress less, but they still impress: a delicate, crisp tarte Tatin has been praised, as has a light, foamy pistachio soufflé served with chocolate sorbet. The cheeseboard, however, is legendary, featuring 30 fine examples, all in a state of perfect ripeness.

If trawling the excellent wine list seems an unnecessary chore, the 'helpful, friendly and wise' wine waiter will take care of everything without leaving an unexpected bomb on the bill. Those who take matters in their own hands will find monumental collections of fine Bordeaux and Burgundy plus interesting round-ups from other French regions. Germany (where dry wines are helpfully indicated), Italy, Australia and the US provide the bulk of the alternatives. The list is not exactly brimming with options under £25, but prices begin at just £12.

CHEF/PROPRIETOR: Gordon Ramsay   OPEN: Mon to Fri 12 to 2.30, 6.45 to 11   CLOSED: 2 weeks at Christmas, bank hols   MEALS: Set L £35, Set D £65 to £80   SERVICE: not inc   CARDS: Amex, Delta, Diners, MasterCard, Switch, Visa   DETAILS: 45 seats. Private parties: 45 main room. Vegetarian meals. Children's helpings. Jacket and tie. No pipes/cigars. No music. No mobile phones. Air-conditioned   ⊖ Sloane Square

---

denotes an outstanding wine cellar; ♥ *denotes a good wine list, worth travelling for.*

Gordon Ramsay at Claridge's ▮

map 15

Brook Street, W1A 2JQ
TEL: (020) 7499 0099   FAX: (020) 7499 3099
WEBSITE: www.gordonramsay.com

COOKING **7**
FRENCH
£48–£104

Stepping through the small revolving door into the interior of Claridge's is truly a step back in time, the foyer's Art Deco style lovingly restored, with stunning chandeliers. Turn right for the restaurant, its centrepiece the light fittings, which hover in orangey-pink with purple fur trims. Despite the classy setting, there is a sense of relaxed enjoyment in the air, reinforced by the classical polish of Mark Sergeant's cooking.

Excellent bread comes with a choice of salted or unsalted butters accompanied by nibbles – perhaps a blob of 'extraordinary' taramasalata and a spoonful of foie gras mousse with black truffle. Menu dishes deliver powerfully on the palate, even though the touch may seem to be quite light. A translucently cooked fillet of brill is served on cep risotto, garnished with white asparagus and a five-spice sauce, the last enhancing the overall flavour without dominating, while boiled beef cheeks also come delicately spiced, in a world-class consommé with achingly tender spring vegetables, a flash of Périgord truffle and smooth pomme purée spiked with horseradish. These may have been preceded by first courses equally adept at marrying lightness of impact with earthiness of flavour: perhaps a soup of smoked eel and celeriac built up with crushed ratte potatoes, crisp ventrêche bacon and poached quail's eggs, or – lighter still – a tian of Cornish crab with a salad of fennel, rocket and herbs. The dessert menu may not be a hotbed of inventiveness, but an assiette of passion fruit (tart, parfait and ice cream) manages to include a scoop of bitter chocolate sorbet too. A soup of Williams pear and champagne with caramelised star fruit made a 'stunning' pre-dessert. One diner was particularly impressed by the 'completely unstuffy and helpful' approach of the sommeliers – good news, as the wine list is an imposing tome and there's no such thing as a bottle of house wine to fall back on. Mark-ups are high, but quality across the board is stronger than ever.

CHEF: Mark Sargeant   PROPRIETOR: Gordon Ramsay Holdings Ltd   OPEN: all week 12 to 3, 5.45 to 11   MEALS: Set L £30 to £65, Set D 5.45 to 6.45 £30 to £65, Set D £55 to £65   SERVICE: not inc   CARDS: Amex, Delta, MasterCard, Switch, Visa   DETAILS: 115 seats. Private parties: 100 main room, 8 to 60 private rooms. Vegetarian meals. Children's helpings. No cigars/pipes. Wheelchair access (also WC). No music. Air-conditioned   ⊖ Bond Street

Great Eastern Dining Room

map 13

54–56 Great Eastern Street, EC2A 3QR
TEL: (020) 7613 4545   FAX: (020) 7613 4137
WEBSITE: www.greateasterndining.co.uk

| NEW CHEF |

PAN-ASIAN
£32–£53

Atmosphere, location and mind-blowing cocktails make the bar here a high-decibel playground for young, affluent City types, while the minimalist dining room in this converted fabric warehouse sets off a menu that plunders China, Thailand, Malaysia and Japan, dividing neatly into dim sum (chilli salt squid, maybe), maki rolls and sashimi, tempura (say, avocado and sweet potato with orange ponzu dip), salads and 'house dishes' (perhaps roast duck with plum and cinnamon caramel). Desserts are mostly orientalised versions of western ideas, like warm chocolate pudding with coconut pandan ice cream. Mercifully, there's a food glossary on the back of the menu. Teas or saké are alternatives to a lively wine list with plenty of southern-hemisphere bottles; ten come by the glass, and vin de pays is £11 a bottle.

CHEF: Mark Adler   PROPRIETOR: Will Ricker   OPEN: Mon to Fri L 12.15 to 3, Mon to Sat D 6.30 to 11   MEALS: alc (main courses £8 to £16)   SERVICE: 12.5% (optional), card slips closed   CARDS: Amex, Delta, Diners, MasterCard, Switch, Visa   DETAILS: 65 seats. Vegetarian meals. No music. Air-conditioned   ⊖ Old Street

▲ Great Eastern Hotel, Aurora ▮ map 13

Liverpool Street, EC2M 7QN
TEL: (020) 7618 7000   FAX: (020) 7618 5035
WEBSITE: www.aurora-restaurant.co.uk

COOKING 4
MODERN EUROPEAN
£42–£81

Five restaurants cluster under the Great Eastern's dome. Aurora is particularly notable for handsome décor, spacious urban ambience – and wine. Evenings get a noisy start as the adjoining bar is packed with jolly City types shouting to compete with the pianist, but the hubbub fades after 8.30, as trains soak up the celebrants. New head chef Allan Pickett retains the lunchtime carving trolley and embraces the Aurora's modern European slant. Starters take in Dorset crab ravioli with warm asparagus and vine tomatoes, as well as pastilla of five-spiced duck confit with beetroot carpaccio and hot foie gras. An inspector enjoyed a generous portion of fresh sea bass with truffled celeriac purée and Burgundy jus, and a sound rendition of chocolate fondant to finish. Alternatives might be calves' sweetbreads with romaine lettuce and morels, or poached and roasted lamb rump with braised onion and red pesto mash, plus tiramisù, or strawberry soup with crème Chantilly. Wine service is knowledgeable and unstuffy – a big bonus with a 45-page list to navigate. Famous bottles from all over will suit big spenders, but there's also much that is non-mainstream. Cheaper bottles, well-chosen and fair value, start with the £15 house wines from Spanish prodigy Telmo Rodríguez.

CHEF: Allan Pickett   PROPRIETOR: Conran Holdings   OPEN: Mon to Fri 12 to 2.30, 6.45 to 10   CLOSED: 2 weeks at Christmas, bank hols   MEALS: alc (main courses £16 to £25). Set L £28, Set D £50. Bar menu available   SERVICE: 12.5% (optional)   CARDS: Amex, Delta, Diners, MasterCard, Switch, Visa   DETAILS: 90 seats. Private parties: 90 main room. Vegetarian meals. Wheelchair access (also WC). Music. Air-conditioned   ACCOMMODATION: 267 rooms, all with bath/shower. TV. Phone. Room only £225 to £495. Rooms for disabled. Baby facilities   ⊖ Liverpool Street

The Green ⁵⁄₄ £ map 12

58–60 East Dulwich Road, SE22 9AX
TEL: (020) 7732 7575
WEBSITE: www.greenbar.co.uk

COOKING 2
MODERN EUROPEAN
£19–£54

The younger, trendier sibling of nearby Le Chardon (see entry, Round-ups) combines a lively bar with a fashionably styled dining area: sage-green walls decked with bright abstract paintings, halogen spotlights, bare wooden floors and simply adorned dark wood tables. There are various eating options, including breakfast seven days a week, all-day bar snacks and a full à la carte menu with a global outlook. Starters take in old-fashioned deep-fried breadcrumbed Brie with plum compote as well as more up-to-date ideas such as coriander salmon fishcakes with Thai chilli jam, while main courses range from pan-fried red mullet with basil and spinach sauce to confit pork shank with Calvados and caramelised apples, with vegetables as extras. Tuesday and Thursday dinners are served to the accompaniment of live jazz. Most of the wines on the short, global list are under £20, including two house French at £9.95.

CHEF: Damien Gillespie   PROPRIETOR: Robert Benyayer   OPEN: all week 12 to 4 (5 Sun), 6 to 11   MEALS: alc (main courses £9 to £12). Set L £7.95 (2 courses) to £10.95, Set L Sun £13.95 (3 courses). Breakfast and bar menus available   SERVICE: 10% (optional), card slips closed   CARDS: Amex, Delta, MasterCard, Switch, Visa   DETAILS: 120 seats. Private parties: 100 main room. Vegetarian meals. Children's helpings. No smoking in 1 dining room. Wheelchair access (also WC). Music. Air-conditioned (£5)

Greenhouse 🍾   map 15

27A Hays Mews, W1J 5NY   COOKING 6
TEL: (020) 7499 3331   FAX: (020) 7499 5368   MODERN EUROPEAN
WEBSITE: www.greenhouserestaurant.co.uk   £54–£112

The Greenhouse reopened in April 2004, having undergone another design makeover. Last season's pale green has been replaced by sober taupe, offset by laminate display cabinets stocked with ornamental glassware, and the verdict thus far is that it is an improvement. Bjorn van der Horst took over in the kitchens from Paul Merrett, and while there is a line of continuity in the menus, with the refined eclecticism of recent years maintained, there is also evidence of a new ingenuity. Baklava of quail consists of two hunks of tender meat encased with spinach in filo, accompanied by mousserons, a little warm foie gras, and rhubarb marmalade. A Chinese mood brings on steamed scallops with a green tea broth, with Westernised dim sum of pork and leek, and a tri-coloured tangle of Chinese black fungus, Japanese enokitake and samphire. Main courses aim for the skies, and sometimes get there – roast Périgord duck breast is served on a 'dhal' of cumin-spiced lentils dotted with foie gras – but sometimes fall a little short, as with roast fillet of Limousin veal garnished sparingly with asparagus and tomato, a dish lifted by a separate serving of pasta rings in blue cheese sauce. Pre-desserts and – yes – post-desserts might well be better than the dessert itself, where complexity can undermine, as in passion-fruit and chocolate ravioli with lime-leaf mousse and lemongrass consommé. Combinations can excite and, with comments like 'the food sparkles on the plate', it is clear that Mr Van de Horst has won over a lot of people in his first few months in London. The vast wine list has evoked gasps from a number of reporters – but of dismay at the prices rather than delight at the exceptional range, especially when a glass of house champagne proffered on arrival turned out to cost £12, yet decent options under £25 do exist. Lovers of top-class Bordeaux and Burgundy will be in heaven. Some smart options by the glass are £6 to £18.

CHEF: Bjorn van der Horst   PROPRIETOR: Marlon Abela   OPEN: Mon to Fri L 12 to 2.45, Mon to Sat D 6.45 to 11   MEALS: Set L £28 (2 courses) to £32, Set D £55   SERVICE: 12.5% (optional), card slips closed   CARDS: Amex, Delta, Diners, MasterCard, Switch, Visa   DETAILS: 62 seats. Private parties: 10 private room. No cigars/pipes. No music. Air-conditioned ⊖ Green Park

Green Olive   map 13

5 Warwick Place, W9 2PX   [NEW CHEF]
TEL: (020) 7289 2469   FAX: (020) 7289 2463   ITALIAN
                                                               £35–£63

A vibrant neighbourhood place just a few steps from Warwick Avenue Tube station in Maida Vale, the Green Olive is next to a busy pub. Traditional and often authentic Italian dishes grace the menu, which lists four courses from antipasti through primi and secondi piatti to dolci. The new chef (who joined as we went to press) is turning out tiger prawns with rocket and spicy tomato, and San Daniele ham with figs among antipasti, and main courses such as fillet of beef with aubergine compote. Finish on a high note with raspberry pannacotta. Mark-ups on the all-Italian wine list (apart from champagne) are on the high side, but prices start at £14.50, glasses from £4.

CHEF: Luca Isiola   PROPRIETOR: Red Pepper Group   OPEN: all week 12 to 3, 6.30 to 10.30   CLOSED: bank hols   MEALS: Set L £18 (2 courses) to £23, Set D £21.50 (2 courses) to £30   SERVICE: 12.5% (optional) CARDS: Amex, Delta, MasterCard, Switch, Visa   DETAILS: 60 seats. Private parties: 35 main room, 10 to 20 private rooms. Vegetarian meals. Children's helpings. Wheelchair access (not WC). Music. Air-conditioned   ⊖ Warwick Avenue

Haandi
map 14

136 Brompton Road, SW3 1HY   COOKING 4
TEL: (020) 7823 7373   FAX: (020) 7823 9696   INDIAN
WEBSITE: www.haandi-restaurants.com   £35–£67

'The kitchen just keeps rolling on here,' noted a frequent visitor to this rather swish but unpretentious restaurant and bar opposite Harrods. An encouraging number of Indians regularly use the place, which is perhaps testament to the food's authenticity. Tandooris and other specialities from the North-west Frontier dominate the extensive menu: sublimely tender chicken burra tikka is a 'marvellous example', while vibrantly spiced 'chilli garlic fish Amritsari' fully lives up to its name. There are also representatives from further afield, including Goan lamb vindaloo and jeera chicken spiked with cumin. Vegetables are cooked with panache and a feel for texture as well as flavour: witness adraki aloo gobi (potatoes with cauliflower and ginger), bhindi masala, and Punjabi-style chickpeas. Paratha is the pick of the breads, and rice impresses with its 'well-defined grains'. The wide-ranging wine list has a helpful chart listing recommended bottles with particular dishes. House Italian is £10.95. A second branch has opened at 301–303 Hale Lane, Edgware, tel: (020) 8905 4433.

CHEF: Ratan Singh   PROPRIETOR: Haandi Restaurants Ltd   OPEN: all week 12 to 3, 6 to 11 (11.30 Fri and Sat)   MEALS: alc (main courses £8 to £13). Set L £7.95 to £13.95 (inc wine)   SERVICE: 12.5% (optional) CARDS: Amex, Delta, Diners, MasterCard, Switch, Visa   DETAILS: 80 seats. 8 seats outside. Private parties: 15 main room. Vegetarian meals. No-smoking area. Music. Air-conditioned   ⊖ Knightsbridge £5

Hakkasan
map 15

8 Hanway Place, W1T 1DH   COOKING 5
TEL: (020) 7927 7000   FAX: (020) 7907 1889   CHINESE
EMAIL: reservation@hakkasan.com   £46–£159

'Do not be put off by the approach down narrow alleys,' writes one reporter reassuringly, because all is cool, calm, spare and inviting once you pass through the huge blue-glass door to the dimly lit basement. Lunchtime dim sum continue to generate excited reports from regulars and new converts alike: all manner of refined and exquisite morsels have been applauded, including steamed scallop siu mai dumplings with tobiko caviar, baked venison puffs, 'wonderfully delicate' har-kow, and char siu buns 'fluffy as a cloud'. The choice extends to roasts (from sesame chicken in spicy Malay sauce to jasmine tea-smoked organic ribs), vegetables (incomparable steamed gai lan), and tofu in various guises, not forgetting spot-on Singapore noodles.

A few minor lapses have been noted in the evening, when the menu is fleshed out with dishes like stir-fried spicy prawns with bell peppers, lily bulb and almonds, gloriously tender sweet-and-sour organic pork with pomegranate, and roast silver cod with champagne and Chinese honey. Desserts take a European view of things, with both ginger pudding and cherry croquettes receiving plaudits. Seven kinds of tea are a connoisseur's treat, and 'fascinating' cocktails add a trendy kick to proceedings. The wine list makes impressive reading, although prices are emphatically in the expense-account bracket (the cheapest bottles are £22). Afternoon tea with pastries in the lounge is a forthcoming attraction.

CHEF: Chee Hwee Tong   PROPRIETOR: Alan Yau   OPEN: all week 12 to 2.45 (4.30 Sat and Sun), 6 to 11.30 (12.30 Wed to Sat)   CLOSED: 25 Dec, 1 Jan   MEALS: alc (main courses L £8 to £18, D £9.50 to £48). Bar menu available   SERVICE: 13%   CARDS: Amex, MasterCard, Switch, Visa   DETAILS: 160 seats. Private parties: 160 main room, 65 to 150 private rooms. Vegetarian meals. No children after 7pm. Wheelchair access (also WC). Music. Air-conditioned   ⊖ Tottenham Court Road

Highgate   map 13

79 Highgate Road, NW5 1TL	COOKING 2
TEL: (020) 7485 8442 FAX: (020) 7482 0357	MODERN EUROPEAN
EMAIL: thehighgatebar@aol.com	£29–£52

This roomy bar/restaurant is in confident mood, sporting a look that 'is very brown' – leather sofas, walls, floorboards – with chandeliers, potted palms and draped curtains creating a luxury feel. The atmosphere is informal, staff are charming, and the food is generally straightforward. Casual eating appears to be one of the operation's main targets, given hummus with flat bread, and sausage sandwich in the bar for lunch, and a short dinner menu that deals in sirloin steak with Roquefort butter, mixed-leaf and herb salad and chips, and grilled lamb with a salad of new potatoes, green beans, red onions, olives and pesto. For those wishing to go the full hog, starters include 'buttery, delicate' raviolo of asparagus and spinach, and there could be raspberry and lemon tart for dessert. The short wine list focuses on Europe and the southern hemisphere. Prices start at £10.95, and 12 are served by the glass.

CHEF: Jamie Polito   PROPRIETORS: James McDowell, Mark Slade, Jamie Polito and Nick Rouse   OPEN: Mon to Sat D only 6.30 to 10.30   CLOSED: 25 and 26 Dec, 1 Jan   MEALS: alc (main courses £9.50 to £15.50). Bar L menu available all week   SERVICE: 12.5% (optional), card slips closed   CARDS: Amex, Delta, MasterCard, Switch, Visa   DETAILS: 100 seats. 20 seats outside. Private parties: 150 main room, 30 to 100 private rooms. Vegetarian meals. Children's helpings. No children after 8pm. No pipes. Wheelchair access (also WC). Music. Air-conditioned   ⊖ Kentish Town   £5

The House   map 12

63–69 Canonbury Road, N1 2DG	COOKING 2
TEL: (020) 7704 7410 FAX: (020) 7704 9388	MODERN EUROPEAN
WEBSITE: www.inthehouse.biz	£26–£69

Drinkers congregate in the bar and spill out on to the courtyard in fine weather at this red-brick street-corner pub in a rather verdant quarter of Canonbury. Those looking for solid sustenance head for the simply decorated cream-painted dining room. The menu aims to please with modern French/Italian-inclined assemblages such as Tatin of red onions and grilled goats' cheese, and roast sea bass with pipérade, tapenade and langoustine oil alongside shepherd's pie made from chunks of lamb shank. Tarts, parfaits and warm gingerbread with clotted cream find their way on to the desserts list. Brunch is served at weekends, and the wine list is a whimsically arranged collection of good-value bottles, with prices starting at £12.50.

CHEFS: Jeremy Hollingsworth and Robert Arnott   PROPRIETOR: Barnaby Meredith   OPEN: Tue to Fri 12 to 2.30, Mon to Fri 5.30 to 10.30, Sat 12 to 3.30, 6.30 to 10.30, Sun 12 to 3.30, 6.30 to 9.30   CLOSED: 24 to 27 Dec   MEALS: alc (main courses £9.50 to £22.50). Set L Tue to Fri £12.95 (2 courses) to £14.95, Set D Mon to Fri 5.30 to 6.30 £12.95 (2 courses) to £14.95   SERVICE: 12.5% (optional), card slips closed   CARDS: Delta, MasterCard, Switch, Visa   DETAILS: 90 seats. 80 seats outside. Private parties: 120 main room. Vegetarian meals. Children's helpings. No-smoking area. Wheelchair access (also WC). No music ⊖ Highbury & Islington

---

Huong-Viet 🍳 £   map 13

An-Viet House, 12–14 Englefield Road, N1 4LS   COOKING 1
TEL: (020) 7249 0877   VIETNAMESE
         £23–£39

The word 'canteen' is writ large above the front door of this bustling neighbourhood venue housed in a Vietnamese community centre. You can 'easily feel at home here,' noted a visitor: the atmosphere is comfortably soothing and prices won't break the bank. The kitchen delivers authentic dishes with delicate flavours: witness steamed pork roll wrapped in a soft rice-flour casing served with a crunchy salad and a fish sauce/rice vinegar dip on the side. 'BBQ' specialities include spicy chargrilled lamb with galangal, and clay-pot chicken is 'simplicity done well'. Vegetarian options like stir-fried tofu with chilli and black-bean sauce are deftly handled, and the kitchen conjures up a novel 'toffee-ball' take on banana fritters. Service has been good-natured but can be rather disorganised. Drink tea, Vietnamese beer or house wine at £7.45.

CHEF: Truong Lieu   PROPRIETOR: Huong-Viet Ltd   OPEN: Mon to Sat 12 to 3.30, 5.30 to 11   MEALS: alc (main courses £5 to £7). Set L Mon to Fri £6 (2 courses), Set D £13 (min 4)   SERVICE: 10%, card slips closed, 12.5% for parties of 5 or more   CARDS: MasterCard, Switch, Visa   DETAILS: 70 seats. 8 seats outside. Private parties: 25 private room. Vegetarian meals. Wheelchair access (also WC). Occasional music   ⊖ Angel, Liverpool Street

---

Incognico   map 15

117 Shaftesbury Avenue, WC2H 8AD   COOKING 4
TEL: (020) 7836 8866   FAX: (020) 7240 9525   FRENCH
WEBSITE: www.incognico.com   £26–£90

The buzz and bright lights around this part of town, just a few paces from Cambridge Circus and handy for theatreland, rather belies the calm atmosphere and brown-toned setting of the dining room. Incognico shares a chef with its sister restaurant, Deca (see entry), and the bright, modern brasserie menu doesn't stand on ceremony. They batter the salt cod and serve it with aïoli, dress the smoked salmon in dill-infused oil, and drape the stuffed artichoke (and much else) with hollandaise, and it all works to satisfy an informal West End clientele. Main courses (with vegetables extra) run the gamut from veal kidneys in Madeira, through skate with capers, to herb-crusted best end of lamb with roast garlic, and you can finish with pear tart, chocolate mousse, or pineapple anointed with kirsch. The pre-theatre set menu is still much appreciated. A decent spread of international wines includes Corsica and Uruguay and opens with vins de pays at £15 (white) and £16.50 (red).

CHEF: Jeremy Brown   PROPRIETOR: Chez Nico Restaurants Ltd   OPEN: Mon to Sat 12 to 3, 5.30 to 12
CLOSED: 10 days Christmas, 4 days Easter, bank hol Mons   MEALS: alc (main courses £14.50 to £25). Set L
£12.50, Set D 5.30 to 7 £12.50   SERVICE: 12.5% (optional), card slips closed   CARDS: Amex, Diners,
MasterCard, Switch, Visa   DETAILS: 80 seats. Vegetarian meals. No pipes. Wheelchair access (also WC).
Music. Air-conditioned   ⊖ Leicester Square

Inn the Park ⅝✳

NEW ENTRY   map 15

St James's Park, SW1A 2BJ
TEL: (020) 7451 9999   FAX: (020) 7451 9998
WEBSITE: www.innthepark.co.uk

COOKING 2
MODERN BRITISH
£28–£68

Getting something to eat in a public park in London has traditionally been a matter of hot dogs and ice lollies until now. A collaboration between the Royal Parks and Oliver Peyton's restaurant group has brought this punningly named dining experience to St James's Park. 'Grab & Go' items such as sandwiches, salads, cakes, biscuits and ice creams are sold, but there are also menus for sit-down eating from breakfast to dinner. Its light wooden structure is something like a giant sauna, with chrome chairs and UFO lights adding a fun retro touch to the design, while the covered terrace with handsome decking has overhead heaters. Cornish crab mayonnaise is boldly flavoured, generous and fresh, served with toast, and prawn cocktail with marie-rose dressing will satisfy too. Main courses run from roast suckling pig with fine crackling, rib-sticking champ and apple sauce, through seared salmon fillet with minted peas, to grilled Buccleuch ribeye with green beans and horseradish cream, the sizeable portions stilling any flinching at the prices. 'Chips are fabulous', and desserts take in chocolate and hazelnut tart with impressive pastry, as well as vibrantly flavoured sorbets and English cheeses. Early reports suggest that unfocused service needs a bit more drilling. A single-page wine selection comes mostly under £20, with glass prices from £3.20.

CHEF: Mark Bradbury   PROPRIETOR: Gruppo Ltd   OPEN: all week 12 to 2.45 (3.45 Sat and Sun), 6 to 10.45
(9.45 Sun)   MEALS: alc (main courses £8.50 to £17.50). Terrace bar D menu available   SERVICE: not inc
CARDS: Amex, MasterCard, Switch, Visa   DETAILS: 87 seats. 56 seats outside. Vegetarian meals. No
smoking. Wheelchair access (also WC). Music. Air-conditioned   ⊖ St James's Park

Inside

NEW ENTRY   map 12

19 Greenwich South Street, SE10 8NW
TEL: (020) 8265 5060
WEBSITE: www.insiderestaurant.co.uk

COOKING 1
MODERN BRITISH
£27–£51

'Small, noisy, fun' sums up this sparsely decorated, popular neighbourhood venue just outside the centre of Greenwich. The open-plan kitchen delivers lots of 'quick assembly food' based on smart ingredients – as in grilled king prawns with red lentil dhal, yoghurt, and baby spinach topped with home-made flat bread – and also turns its hand to sautéed scallops on a 'properly cooked' saffron risotto, and seared beef fillet served the old way with rösti, green beans, broccoli and cauliflower cheese. Desserts like dark chocolate tart with home-made white chocolate ice cream close the show. The set-price deals attract theatre-goers, and on Saturday there's a 'very attractive' brunch menu. House wines start at £10.95.

CHEFS: Guy Awford and Brian Sargeant   PROPRIETORS: Guy Awford, Pavlin Petrov and Brian Sargeant
OPEN: Wed to Sun L 12 (11 Sat) to 2.30 (3 Sun), Tue to Sat D 6.30 to 11   CLOSED: 24 Dec to 6 Jan   MEALS:
alc (main courses £11 to £16.50). Set L Wed to Fri £14.95 (2 courses) to £17.95, Set D Tue to Thur 6.30 to 8
£14.95 (2 courses) to £17.95   SERVICE: not inc, 10% for parties of 8 or more   CARDS: Delta, MasterCard,
Switch, Visa   DETAILS: 38 seats. Private parties: 40 main room. Vegetarian meals. Children's helpings.
No-smoking area. Wheelchair access (also WC). Music   ⊖ Greenwich DLR (£5)

Isola ▼

map 14

145 Knightsbridge, SW1X 7PA
TEL: (020) 7838 1044   FAX: (020) 7838 1099
EMAIL: reception@isola-restaurant.co.uk

COOKING **4**
ITALIAN
£30–£77

Although the indebtedness to Italy remains, contemporary pan-European cooking is more
the modus operandi at this striking, spacious basement restaurant (with a ground-floor bar
area) that's all shiny chrome, black marble and polished wood. The scope of Mark
Broadbent's repertoire is demonstrated by starters such as straightforward carpaccio of
Buccleuch beef with wild rocket and Parmesan, linguine with Cornish crab and chilli, and
more complex cannelloni of English asparagus with prosciutto and Parmesan. Main
courses, meanwhile, might take in a rustic-sounding roast rump of South Downs lamb
with baked aubergine and ricotta and spiced tomato fonduta alongside roast wild sea bass
with a simple accompaniment of cherry vine tomatoes, spiny artichokes and basil. For
dessert, there might be pine-nut praline semi-freddo with chocolate fonduta, or Sicilian
lemon cake with lemon curd and blueberries. The wine list is a directory of top Italian
names grouped into broad regions. Prices soon zoom skywards from £13.50, but the huge
selection by the glass, along with 'taster trays' of five different whites or reds priced at £17
and £20, put a brush with la dolce vita within reach.

CHEF: Mark Broadbent   PROPRIETOR: Oliver Peyton   OPEN: Mon to Sat 12 to 2.45 (3.30 Sat), 6 to 11
MEALS: alc (main courses £12.50 to £24). Set L £16 (2 courses) to £18.50   SERVICE: 12.5%, card slips
closed   CARDS: Amex, Delta, Diners, MasterCard, Switch, Visa   DETAILS: 153 seats. Private parties: 350
main room. Vegetarian meals. Wheelchair access (not WC). Music. Air-conditioned   ⊖ Knightsbridge

Itsu ⁙✳

maps 14 and 15

118 Draycott Avenue, Chelsea, SW3 3AE
TEL: (020) 7590 2400   FAX: (020) 7590 2403
103 Wardour Street, Soho, W1V 3TD
TEL: (020) 7479 4790   FAX: (020) 7479 4795
WEBSITE: www.itsu.co.uk

COOKING **2**
JAPANESE
£31–£45

The idea of watching your food pass by on a conveyor belt (kaiten) and grabbing what
catches the eye is now familiar across the capital, but here it is done with undoubted style.
The design of both venues (there's a third at Canary Wharf, too) is cool and functional,
using flashes of bold colours (on lampshades, for example) to add vibrancy, and leaving
centre stage to the kaiten, which snakes tantalisingly around the room. Classic sushi and
sashimi dishes will pass before your eyes (tuna and salmon, all fresh and feisty), but there is
more adventurous, Californian-inspired stuff, too. Chilli crab crystal roll, Thai chicken
salad, or duck crystal roll with hoisin dip are well considered, and flavours are bold. Press a
buzzer to gain the attention of the 'friendly, cheerful and frightfully trendy' staff to order
drinks or from the grill – 'excellent' eel sushi, for example, or chicken teriyaki. The music

can be loud. Drink Asahi beer, cocktails, or wine from the short list kicking off at £13.80. The third branch is at Cabot Place East, Canary Wharf; tel: (020) 7512 9911.

CHEFS: Roberto Campana (Chelsea) and Angela Baird (Soho)   PROPRIETORS: Julian Metcalfe and Clive Schlee   OPEN: all week 12 to 11/11.15 (10 Sun; 12 Sat and Sun Soho)   CLOSED: D 24 Dec, 25 and 26 Dec, D 31 Dec, 1 Jan   SERVICE: not inc, card slips closed   CARDS: Amex, Delta, MasterCard, Switch, Visa DETAILS: 67/70 seats. Private parties: 40/100 main room; 20 to 40 private rooms (Chelsea only). No smoking in 1 dining room (Chelsea), no smoking throughout (Soho). Music. Air-conditioned   ⊖ South Kensington (Chelsea), Piccadilly Circus (Soho)

Ivy
map 15

1–5 West Street, WC2H 9NQ
TEL: (020) 7836 4751   FAX: (020) 7240 9333

COOKING **4**
MODERN BRITISH
£32–£91

In the heart of theatreland, the Ivy plays its role as a West End institution well. That is to say, it serves an up-to-the-minute brasserie menu with confident flair and minimal standing on ceremony, in a starry atmosphere of hustle and haste, so that ticket holders won't miss their performances. Whether you're in the mood for sashimi in hot soy and ginger; dressed crab with rémoulade; ink spaghetti with baby squid; sausages and mash; or corned-beef hash with fried eggs – they're all here, and much more besides. Fishy things are good, as was confirmed by reporters who got through kedgeree, salmon fishcake, and fish 'n' chips. Finish with a savoury of Yorkshire Blue cheese with blackcurrant jelly, perhaps, if the puddings (sherry trifle, baked Alaska, vanilla cheesecake with roast apricots) don't tempt. Service may be tested to the uttermost in the huggermugger of it all, meaning that wine isn't topped up as promptly as might be. At the mark-ups, you may not mind that. French Merlot is £12.25, but most bottles are comfortably north of £20.

CHEFS: Alan Bird and Tim Hughes   PROPRIETOR: Signature Restaurants plc   OPEN: all week 12 to 3 (3.30 Sun), 5.30 to 12   MEALS: alc (main courses £9.50 to £30). Set L Sat and Sun £19.50. Cover £1.50 SERVICE: not inc   CARDS: Amex, Delta, Diners, MasterCard, Switch, Visa   DETAILS: 100 seats. Private parties: 25 to 60 private rooms. Vegetarian meals. No cigars/pipes. Wheelchair access (not WC). No music. No mobile phones. Air-conditioned   ⊖ Leicester Square

Iznik £
map 13

19 Highbury Park, N5 1QJ
TEL: (020) 7704 8099   FAX: (020) 7354 5697

COOKING **2**
TURKISH
£19–£32

'Zillions' of hanging lamps flicker in this delightfully decked-out and well-tended restaurant, which is crammed with antiquities, carved wooden screens and decorative tiles. It makes an atmospheric setting in which to enjoy genuine Turkish food. The menu holds no great surprises, and you can easily make a meal from the list of meze: mücver (courgette and feta fritters) and ispanak tarator (hot spinach purée with yoghurt, garlic and butter) have been applauded. Main courses centre on rather plainly presented kebabs and grills, including beykoz kebabi (lamb cubes stacked with sliced aubergine and green pepper), while desserts such as armut tatlisi (poached pears with pistachios and chocolate sauce) are reckoned to be a notch above the Turkish norm. Drink organic mint tea, Efes beer or Turkish house wine at £9.95.

CHEF: Adem Oner   PROPRIETORS: Adem and Pirlanta Oner   OPEN: all week 11 to 4, 6 to 11   CLOSED: 25 and 26 Dec   MEALS: alc (main courses £6.50 to £9.50)   SERVICE: 10%   CARDS: Delta, MasterCard, Switch, Visa   DETAILS: 76 seats. Wheelchair access (not WC). No music   ⊖ Highbury & Islington

J. Sheekey

map 15

28 St Martin's Court, WC2N 4AL   COOKING 4
TEL: (020) 7240 2565   FAX: (020) 7497 0891   BRITISH/SEAFOOD
EMAIL: reservations@j-sheekey.co.uk   £31–£107

'Inhale the ozoney, sea-fresh vapours of fish on the stove as you go through the door,' observed one visitor to this venerable – but reborn – West End institution. Customers are ushered into a warren of dark-panelled rooms with old photographs and contemporary artwork on the walls and a menu that offers ancient and modern dishes in equal measure. The old guard is cajoled by eggs Benedict royale and fish pie, but the kitchen also has plenty of contemporary aces up its sleeve. A special starter of razor clams with baby broad beans and chorizo comprises 'all things bright and colourful', while main courses are notable for their 'big, pugnacious flavours', as in braised monkfish with sweetbreads and summer vegetables, or Cornish fish stew with braised celery hearts. There's a separate vegetarian/vegan menu and, according to the menu, 'meat dishes also available'. Finish with something like rice pudding with raspberry jam, or cappuccino ice cream. A big contingent of French names shows up on the mainly European wine list, where prices zoom skywards from £12.75.

CHEFS: Martin Dickenson and Tim Hughes   PROPRIETOR: Signature Restaurants plc   OPEN: all week 12 to 3 (3.30 Sun), 5.30 to 12   CLOSED: 25 and 26 Dec, 1 Jan, Aug bank hol   MEALS: alc (main courses £10 to £30). Set L Sat and Sun £14.25 (2 courses) to £18.50. Cover £1.50   SERVICE: not inc   CARDS: Amex, Delta, Diners, MasterCard, Switch, Visa   DETAILS: 106 seats. Vegetarian meals. Children's helpings. No cigars/pipes. Wheelchair access (not WC). No music. No mobile phones. Air-conditioned   ⊖ Leicester Square

Kastoori £

map 12

188 Upper Tooting Road, SW17 7EJ   COOKING 3
TEL: (020) 8767 7027   GUJARATI VEGETARIAN
                                                            £18–£36

Reflecting the Thanki family's roots, this friendly, low-ceilinged restaurant mingles Gujarati dishes from their native Katia Wahd and ideas gleaned from time spent in Uganda. Starters might include samosas, mogo (cassava) bhajias and crisp pani puris; distinctive, freshly spiced curries on the 60-dish menu could take in panir pasanda (pockets of stuffed panir cheese in a cashew-nut and melon-seed sauce), special koftas (fried mixed vegetable balls) and cauliflower in a mild creamy sauce. African influence also shows in specials like kasodi (sweetcorn in coconut milk), chilli-stuffed bananas and green pepper curry in sesame and peanut sauce. Incidentals are up to the mark, and it's worth leaving room for the home-made shrikand topped with pistachio nuts. A decent, informative list of 20 wines begins with house French at £7.95.

CHEF: Manoj Thanki   PROPRIETOR: Dinesh Thanki   OPEN: Wed to Sun L 12.30 to 2.30, all week D 6 to 10.30   CLOSED: 25 and 26 Dec   MEALS: alc (main courses £5 to £6.50), thalis £8.25 to £16.25   SERVICE: not inc, card slips closed   CARDS: MasterCard, Visa   DETAILS: 82 seats. Private parties: 20 main room. Vegetarian meals. Children's helpings. Wheelchair access (not WC). Music. Air-conditioned   ⊖ Tooting Broadway

Kensington Place ▼

map 13

201–209 Kensington Church Street, W8 7LX
TEL: (020) 7727 3184   FAX: (020) 7229 2025
WEBSITE: www.egami.co.uk

COOKING 5
MODERN BRITISH
£29–£78

Eighteen years on, Kensington Place has lost none of its contemporary feel and continues to set the standard for simple, modern cooking. The décor still delights and dismays in equal measure: a striking glass façade overlooking the street on one side, brash colours and an incongruous mural on the other. With 'not a soft furnishing in sight' and tables packed close, noise levels can be high and cigarette smoke intrusive. Enthusiastic staff provide warmth, combining efficiency with informality and seeming genuinely pleased to see their customers.

The cooking displays an enviable grasp of technique and a sensitive approach to flavours. Seasonality dictates what's on offer, and the kitchen is not afraid to let good ingredients shine: hence the unexpected simplicity of morels on toast, or langoustines with mayonnaise. This respect for raw materials extends to more complex dishes, such as well-cooked organic chicken served with an intensely flavoured chicken liver sauce, or grilled sea trout with samphire and peppered hollandaise. Rowley Leigh's signature dish of scallops with pea purée is 'as good as ever', as is lemon tart, with its 'great pastry and perfectly balanced filling'. The wine list still looks ground-breaking, from the opening page of six sherries and 25 table wines by the glass. The main range is grouped by style, with good bottles from both classic and modern regions. Prices, starting at £14, are not outlandish.

CHEF: Rowley Leigh   PROPRIETOR: Image Restaurants   OPEN: all week 12 to 3.15, 6.30 to 11.45 (10.15 Sun)   CLOSED: 24 to 26 Dec, L 31 Dec, 1 Jan   MEALS: alc (main courses £15 to £22.50). Set L Mon to Sat £16.50, Set L Sun £21.50, Set D Mon to Fri £24.50 to £39.50 (inc wine)   SERVICE: 12.5% (optional), card slips closed   CARDS: Amex, Delta, Diners, MasterCard, Switch, Visa   DETAILS: 140 seats. Private parties: 45 private room. Vegetarian meals. Children's helpings. Wheelchair access (also WC). No music. Air-conditioned   ⊖ Notting Hill Gate

Kiku

map 15

17 Half Moon Street, W1J 7BE
TEL: (020) 7499 4208   FAX: (020) 7409 3259
WEBSITE: www.kikurestaurant.co.uk

COOKING 3
JAPANESE
£23–£89

Occupying a prime slice of Mayfair real estate, Kiku is a smart, modern venue with a bold, simple décor that aims to make a statement. Plain black tables and black and chrome wicker-backed chairs are set against lots of blond wood and blinds made from natural materials, while pleasant service combines the virtues of friendliness and discretion. The menu is divided into various sections dealing with the different areas of Japanese cuisine, although a good way to sample the cooking is one of the kaiseki set dinners, which comprise a selection of items from each section. Should you choose to eat à la carte, there is a vast range of sushi and sashimi, traditional appetisers, such as shredded squid with fermented soy or grated yam with a quail's egg yolk, and an extensive list of casseroles and grilled and fried dishes ranging from chicken teriyaki to mackerel casseroled with grated white radish. Drink green tea, saké or something from the rather pricey wine list, where house red and white are £12.50.

CHEFS: H. Hattori and P. Nishimura   PROPRIETORS: Hisashi and Mariko Taoka   OPEN: Mon to Sat L 12 to 2.30, all week D 6 to 10.15 (5.30 to 9.45 Sun and bank hols)   CLOSED: 25 and 26 Dec, 1 Jan   MEALS: alc (main courses £7 to £30). Set L £12 to £23, Set D £42 to £60   SERVICE: 12.5% (optional), card slips closed   CARDS: Amex, Delta, Diners, MasterCard, Switch, Visa   DETAILS: 96 seats. Private parties: 30 main room, 6 to 8 private rooms. Vegetarian meals. Wheelchair access (also WC). Music. Air-conditioned   ⊖ Green Park

K10 ⁵⁄₊ £

map 13

20 Copthall Avenue, EC2R 7DN
TEL: (020) 7562 8510   FAX: (020) 7562 8515
WEBSITE: www.k10.net

| NEW CHEF |
JAPANESE
£23–£41

Punningly named after the 'kaiten' (conveyor belt) that circulates around the pristine white dining room, this is an energetic, sociable and cheery pit-stop for decent sushi and more besides. A new chef arrived too late for inspection, but the menu remains as much as before. Colour-coded plates deliver a range of nigiri, maki and sashimi ('gourmet' versions might include seared peppered beef in tataki dressing); added to this are inventive salads ranging from classic sunomono to green-tea soba noodles, mushrooms and asparagus, plus teriyaki and curry for those in need of hot sustenance. Tea, saké and beer are the drinks of choice; alternatively opt for wine (from £12.95 a bottle). There's an unlicensed, scaled-down outlet at the Moorgate Northern Line tube station.

CHEF: J.T. Mohamed   PROPRIETOR: K10 Ltd   OPEN: Mon to Sat L only 11.30 to 3.30   CLOSED: 1 week over Christmas   MEALS: plate prices £1.25 to £5.50   SERVICE: not inc   CARDS: Amex, Delta, Diners, MasterCard, Switch, Visa   DETAILS: 68 seats. Private parties: 71 main room. Vegetarian meals. No smoking. Music. Air-conditioned   ⊖ Moorgate/Liverpool Street

Kulu Kulu Sushi ⁵⁄₊ £

map 15

76 Brewer Street, W1F 9TX
TEL: (020) 7734 7316   FAX: (020) 7734 6507

COOKING 3
JAPANESE
£21–£36

The conveyor belt in this Soho sushi joint started rolling in 1995, making it one of London's earliest examples of the genre. Expect queues and a cosmopolitan scrum (and a 45-minute limit on tables) in the tiny, utilitarian dining room, where the 'kaiten' carries a big selection of consistently good traditional sushi and sashimi at knockdown prices. Nigiri run from salmon roe to whelk and sweet shrimp, handrolls include eel, tuna and cucumber, and mixed plates are handy for the uninitiated. For something hot, try a bowl of udon noodles with prawn tempura or chicken teriyaki. Help yourself to complimentary green tea; alternatively go for soft drinks, beers, saké or house wines (£3.60 a glass, £12 a bottle). There are branches at 39 Thurloe Place, SW7, tel. (020) 7589 2225 and 51–53 Shelton Street, WC2, tel. (020) 7240 5687.

CHEF/PROPRIETOR: Mr K. Toyama   OPEN: Mon to Sat 12 to 2.30 (3.30 Sat), 5 to 10   CLOSED: bank hols   MEALS: àlc (main courses £8.50 to £12)   SERVICE: not inc, card slips closed   CARDS: Delta, MasterCard, Switch, Visa   DETAILS: 30 seats. No smoking in 1 dining room. Music. No mobile phones. Air-conditioned   ⊖ Piccadilly Circus

⁵⁄₊ *indicates there are some restrictions on smoking, though it is not banned altogether.*

Lahore Kebab House £

NEW ENTRY map 13

2 Umberston Street, E1 1PY
TEL: (020) 7488 2551

COOKING 1
PUNJABI
£20–£29

The 'Original' Lahore Kebab House off Commercial Road has been a jolly, Technicolor landmark since 1972, and it's still a crowd puller. The surroundings may be well worn and functional (no knives, no tablecloths), but it's the cracking Punjabi food that matters. Prices are remarkable: 'for 75p, I consumed the best samosa I have ever eaten,' raved one convert. The kitchen is famed for its kebabs and 'darkly seductive' grilled lamb chops, but the no-nonsense menu also promises elemental curries like karahi chicken, sag gosht, and vegetable biryani. Sweets are limited to home-made kheer, which has the true taste of 'Asian milky rice puddings'. Drink foamy lassi or BYO wine. There are branches at King's Cross Holiday Inn, 56 Calthorpe Street, WC1, tel: (020) 7833 9787, and 148–150 Brent Street, NW4, tel: (020) 8203 6904.

CHEF: Mohammed Shafique PROPRIETOR: Mohammed Siddique OPEN: all week 12 to 11.30 MEALS: alc (main courses £5 to £6.50) SERVICE: not inc CARDS: Delta, MasterCard, Switch, Visa DETAILS: 100 seats. Private parties: 50 main room. Vegetarian meals. Wheelchair access (not WC). No music. Air-conditioned ⊖ Whitechapel (£5)

Langan's Brasserie

map 15

Stratton Street, W1J 8LB
TEL: (020) 7491 8822 FAX: (020) 7493 8309
WEBSITE: www.langansrestaurants.co.uk

COOKING 1
ANGLO-FRENCH
£39–£67

Langan's has weathered the storm of passing fashion well, maintaining its popularity among a certain clientele, remaining a beacon of shimmering glitz beside Green Park Tube station. Eat on the ground floor if possible – the Venetian room upstairs can feel a little isolated – and allow for extra vegetables. The simple British food still appeals: perfectly cooked sea bass with light parsley sauce, and richer options like poached chicken in a creamy Stilton sauce, are highly spoken of. The extensive menu caters for all appetites. Try hot potted shrimps or Caesar salad to start and blackcurranty summer pudding in season to finish, or perhaps apple and ginger crumble. Three dozen wines start at £14.

CHEF: Ken Whitehead PROPRIETOR: Richard Shepherd OPEN: Mon to Fri L and D 12.15 to 11.45, Sat D only 7 to 12 CLOSED: bank hols MEALS: alc (main courses £12.50 to £19.50). Cover £1.50 SERVICE: 12.5% (optional) CARDS: Amex, Delta, Diners, MasterCard, Switch, Visa DETAILS: 240 seats. Vegetarian meals. Wheelchair access (not WC). Music. Air-conditioned ⊖ Green Park

Lansdowne £

map 13

90 Gloucester Avenue, NW1 8HX
TEL: (020) 7483 0409 FAX: (020) 7586 1723

COOKING 2
MODERN BRITISH
£27–£53

Good real ales, a laid-back atmosphere and food with plenty of gusto are the reasons why the Lansdowne is a prime example of a neighbourhood gastro-pub. You can choose to eat among the drinkers in the well-used ground-floor bar, or book a table and receive full table service in the upstairs dining room. The kitchen has a modern European outlook, with dishes like squid stew with Manzanilla sherry and parsley, or pork chop with glazed

Jerusalem artichokes, braised fennel and celery leaf showing up on the daily menu. Generous old acquaintances such as roast sirloin of beef with Bull's Blood chard and horseradish dauphinois also put in an appearance, and you could finish off with apricot tart, or polenta saffron cake. The concise, unaffected wine list keeps its prices in check, with house white £11.90, red £12.90.

CHEF: James Knight   PROPRIETOR: Amanda Pritchett   OPEN: Sun L 1 to 3.30, Tue to Sat D 7 to 10.30   MEALS: alc (main courses £8.50 to £16.50). Bar menu available Mon D, Tue to Sun L and D   SERVICE: 12.5%, card slips closed   CARDS: Delta, MasterCard, Switch, Visa   DETAILS: 55 seats. Private parties: 55 main room. Vegetarian meals. Music. No mobile phones   ⊖ Chalk Farm

Launceston Place ▼

map 14

1A Launceston Place, W8 5PU	COOKING 2
TEL: (020) 7937 6912 FAX: (020) 7938 2412	MODERN BRITISH
WEBSITE: www.egami.co.uk	£32–£62

Standing firm against trendy open spaces and minimalist décor, this quietly elegant, intimate venue in a decidedly posh part of town has luxurious table settings, plush banquettes and carpets throughout its several nook-like dining rooms. And solicitous service enhances the aura of exclusivity. Menus show the confidence not to over-describe dishes, and the cooking stays just as simple, with the focus on careful preparation. Fashionable flavours abound in starters ranging from roast pumpkin and sage risotto to grilled king prawns with crab wontons, cucumber salad and chilli sauce. Main courses tend to the traditional – roast skate with lemon, capers and parsley butter, crispy confit duck with spiced plums, or pan-fried calf's liver with Stroganoff sauce – while desserts range from sticky toffee pudding to pannacotta with roast figs. The wine list is appropriately understated and focused on quality. Classic France is its natural territory but favoured names like Plantagenet, Mulderbosch and Seresin represent the New World. Prices start at £15, and six (plus seven post-prandials) come by the glass.

CHEF: Philip Reid   PROPRIETOR: Moving Image Ltd   OPEN: Sun to Fri L 12.30 to 2.30 (3 Sun), all week D 7 to 11.30 (10 Sun)   CLOSED: 24 to 26 Dec, Easter   MEALS: alc (main courses £11 to £18.50). Set L £15.50 (2 courses) to £18.50   SERVICE: 12.5% (optional), card slips closed   CARDS: Amex, Delta, Diners, MasterCard, Switch, Visa   DETAILS: 90 seats. Private parties: 70 main room, 8 to 30 private rooms. Vegetarian meals. Children's helpings. No children under 6. No pipes. Wheelchair access (not WC). No music. Air-conditioned   ⊖ Gloucester Road

Light House

map 12

75–77 Ridgway, SW19 4ST	COOKING 3
TEL: (020) 8944 6338 FAX: (020) 8946 4440	MODERN EUROPEAN
EMAIL: lightrest@aol.com	£28–£57

This bright and breezy contemporary restaurant remains ever popular with the residents of Wimbledon. One reporter thought it struck exactly the right note for a neighbourhood restaurant, with service in particular 'pleasingly informal and helpful'. The menu may follow a traditional Italian four-course structure, but the kitchen tends to look further afield than any standard Italian dining room – dishes run the gamut of current fashion with influences from all over the Mediterranean and Asia, ensuring that there's something to please all tastes. Flourishes like sashimi-seared springbok on soba noodles with hijiki and pickled ginger salad are bolstered by braised squid with Kalamata olives and rocket, and tagliatelle with morels, oyster mushrooms and spinach. Puddings extend to Tunisian orange cake with Greek yoghurt, and rich, dark chocolate mousse cake with crème fraîche. The wine list has an equally global outlook but with little of interest below £25. House Italian is £13.50.

CHEF: David Winton   PROPRIETORS: Bob Finch and Ian Taylor   OPEN: all week 12 to 2.30 (12.30 to 3.30 Sun), 6.30 to 10.30   CLOSED: 25 and 26 Dec, 1 Jan, Easter Sun and Mon   MEALS: alc (main courses £11 to £15). Set L Mon to Sat £14 (2 courses) to £16.50, Set L Sun £17.50 (2 courses) to £22   SERVICE: 12.5%, card slips closed   CARDS: Amex, Delta, MasterCard, Switch, Visa   DETAILS: 80 seats. Private parties: 30 main room. Vegetarian meals. Children's helpings. No-smoking area. Wheelchair access (also WC). Occasional music   ⊖ Wimbledon

Lightship Ten

map 13

5A St Katharine's Way, E1W 1LP
TEL: (020) 7481 3123   FAX: (020) 7702 0338
WEBSITE: www.lightshipx.com

COOKING 2
MODERN EUROPEAN
£23–£61

The oldest lightship in the world (built in Copenhagen in 1877) now serves as a smart restaurant. Once occupied by German forces and assaulted by British machine-gun fire, today it is boarded only by diners keen to experience sound modern cooking with a Scandinavian twist. There's a bar on the top deck and two dining rooms below, with soft leather banquettes, crisp white tablecloths and subdued lighting. Straightforward European-style dishes (tomato gazpacho with basil croûtons, honey-roast pork belly with apples and smoked black pudding) share the menu with some interesting Scandinavian ideas: Danish blue-lip mussels with fennel and aquavit, meatballs with crushed potatoes, or perhaps a 'Swedish fusion' starter of subtly flavoured herring timbale with wasabi potatoes, cucumber linguine and dill pesto. For pudding, tarte fine aux pommes comes with an outstanding rich, buttery toffee sauce. The brief wine list starts with French house wines at £12.50 a bottle.

CHEF: Laurent Pruvost   PROPRIETOR: David Joul Hansen   OPEN: Mon to Fri L 12 to 3, Mon to Sat D 6 to 10   MEALS: alc (main courses £12.50 to £18). Set L £9.99 (2 courses) to £12.50   SERVICE: 12.5% (optional)   CARDS: Amex, Delta, Diners, MasterCard, Switch, Visa   DETAILS: 70 seats. 50 seats outside. Private parties: 70 main room, 30 to 100 private rooms. Vegetarian meals. No children under 10. Music. Air-conditioned   ⊖ Tower Hill

Lindsay House

map 15

21 Romilly Street, W1D 5AF
TEL: (020) 7439 0450   FAX: (020) 7437 7349
WEBSITE: www.lindsayhouse.co.uk

COOKING 7
MODERN BRITISH
£51–£95

The two small dining rooms in this 150-year-old Soho townhouse are imbued with a mix of elegance and rusticity, with rough wooden floorboards, well-spaced white-clothed tables and plain cream walls hung with large paintings. Richard Corrigan has a fondness for robust, hearty dishes and a strict regard for seasonality and for top-quality produce sourced from specialist regional suppliers. His dishes, simply described on the menu, make their impact in the mouth. Meals get off to a good start with interesting appetisers, such as smoked salmon with potato and soda bread, which reveals the influence of Corrigan's native Ireland, while a starter of cured foie gras rolled in spiced ginger bread and apple shows off the full extent of his creative approach. Main courses typically take in scallops with pork belly and spiced carrot, saddle of rabbit with black pudding, polenta and confit garlic, or pan-roasted red mullet with bone marrow and braised baby gem lettuce. Rhubarb and blood orange with ewes' milk yoghurt sorbet ended one reporter's meal on a high note. The wine list is a well-balanced and varied selection, albeit with a heavy leaning towards expensive French wines and few concessions to bargain-hunters (only two or three bottles under £25).

CHEF/PROPRIETOR: Richard Corrigan   OPEN: Mon to Fri L 12 to 2.30, Mon to Sat D 6 to 11   CLOSED: 1 week Christmas, 2 weeks summer   MEALS: alc (main courses £26). Set L £25 and Set D 6 to 7 £25, Set D £48 to (whole table only) £59   SERVICE: 12.5% (optional), card slips closed   CARDS: Amex, Delta, Diners, MasterCard, Switch, Visa   DETAILS: 60 seats. Private parties: 38 main room, 4 to 38 private rooms. Vegetarian meals. Children's helpings. No-smoking area. No music. No mobile phones. Air-conditioned
⊖ Leicester Square

Locanda Locatelli ▼

map 15

8 Seymour Street, W1H 7JZ

COOKING 6

TEL: (020) 7935 9088   FAX: (020) 7935 1149

ITALIAN

WEBSITE: www.locandalocatelli.com

£41–£93

Giorgio Locatelli's elegant, stylishly designed restaurant inhabits the Churchill Inter-Continental Hotel, yet benefits from the press of custom that an elevated reputation and some TV performances can provide. The stated business is seasonally changing menus of new-wave Italian cooking presented in the old-school format, with antipasti and pasta preceding the principal dishes. Chargrilled calamari with chilli and garlic administers a kick-start to the palate, perhaps as a prelude to lobster linguine, or pheasant ravioli in rosemary sauce. Presentations are kept simple, as is only fitting, with sea bass baked under a herb and salt crust, or veal kidneys fried with red onions, served with mash and sauced with Marsala. Goose is a rarely seen meat, its breast here roasted and partnered by Savoy cabbage and its own fegato grasso (foie gras), while leg of rabbit is swaddled in Parma ham and served with polenta. Enlivening dessert ideas include chocolate and blood orange tart with lemon and thyme ice cream, and ricotta cannoli with Amaretto ice cream, while for many the satisfaction is completed by service from handsome young Italian men. The Italian wine list has something from all regions, plus a majestic collection of top reds from Piedmont and Tuscany in a range of vintages. House wines are a mere £12, but most bottles are considerably smarter, leaving few options under £25.

CHEF: Giorgio Locatelli   PROPRIETORS: Giorgio and Plaxy Locatelli   OPEN: Mon to Sat 12 to 3, 7 to 11 (11.30 Fri and Sat)   MEALS: alc (main courses £16 to £28)   SERVICE: not inc   CARDS: Amex, Delta, MasterCard, Switch, Visa   DETAILS: 85 seats. Vegetarian meals. Children's helpings. No cigars/pipes. Wheelchair access (also WC). Music. No mobile phones. Air-conditioned   ⊖ Marble Arch

Lola's ▼

map 13

The Mall, 359 Upper Street, N1 0PD

NEW CHEF

TEL: (020) 7359 1932   FAX: (020) 7359 2209

MODERN EUROPEAN

WEBSITE: www.lolas.co.uk

£31–£67

Lola's occupies a prime site in the heart of happening Islington at the top of a handsome building that once was a tram shed. The girdered roof speaks of its former calling, but the singular décor of pink walls under a glass roof, enhanced by a hexagonal Moorish mosaic, unequivocally shouts 'now!' Much changing of the kitchen guard has been the norm here in recent years, and Brian Sparks is the latest incumbent, moving up from sous-chef to ensure continuity in the style. Bold combinations are the kitchen's forte, offering smoked eel with potato tuiles, asparagus vinaigrette and saffron, or Challans chicken accompanied by harissa-spiced couscous. Visual impact is high, with violet potatoes, baby fennel and a Pernod-laced beurre blanc accompanying a piece of halibut, but fillet of beef is accorded more classic treatment, with onion confit, chips and Madeira jus. Savoury seasonings are virtually expected with desserts today, and so there is a risotto of strawberries and basil as well as lemongrass sorbet to go with a poached peach, fennel mousse with coffee génoise. Lola's has an individual and exciting approach to wine, including not just a good range by the glass but also the option to try 'flights' of several small glasses on a particular theme. Bottle prices start at £11.75 on the quality-focused main list.

CHEF: Brian Sparks   PROPRIETOR: Morfudd Richards   OPEN: Mon to Sat 12 to 2.30 (3 Sat), 6 to 11, Sun 12 to 4, 7 to 10   CLOSED: 25 and 26 Dec, 1 Jan, Easter Mon, Aug bank hol   MEALS: alc (main courses £12.50 to £19.50). Set L Mon to Sat £15.50 (2 courses) to £33.25 (inc wine), Set L Sun £18.75, Set D Mon to Sat 6 to 7 and 9.45 to 11 £15.50 (2 courses) to £33.25 (inc wine). Cover £1   SERVICE: not inc   CARDS: Amex, Delta, Diners, MasterCard, Switch, Visa   DETAILS: 85 seats. Private parties: 85 main room, 6 to 14 private rooms. Vegetarian meals. Children's helpings. No music. Air-conditioned   ⊖ Angel

Lou Pescadou ⅜✻ £

241 Old Brompton Road, SW5 9HP
TEL: (020) 7370 1057   FAX: (020) 7244 7545

map 13

COOKING 3
SEAFOOD
£21–£66

Rugby and seafood come together here; the former figures in the basement bar, hung with pictures and jerseys documenting the French team's glory days, while the ichthyophagy goes on upstairs. Fish (as much as possible wild) is delivered daily and transformed into the textbook French dishes one might eat over the Channel. Queen scallops with leeks, or smoked herrings, or maybe squid cooked in tomatoes, garlic and olives, lead on to main courses like monkfish with mustard sauce, poached halibut in beurre blanc, or roast bream with garlic. There are steaks or corn-fed chicken in lemon sauce for those who must, and meals end with an assiette de fromages or crème brûlée. Service is brisk and friendly; note it is added to the bill at 15%. Wines (from £11.80) are mostly French: fish-friendly whites, plus some smart mature reds to partner those steaks.

CHEF: Laurent David   PROPRIETORS: Daniel Chobert and Laurent David   OPEN: all week 12 to 3, 7 to 12   CLOSED: Christmas   MEALS: alc (main courses £7 to £20). Set L £10.90, Set D Sat/Sun £14.50. Cover £1.50   SERVICE: 15% (optional), card slips closed   CARDS: Amex, Delta, Diners, MasterCard, Switch, Visa   DETAILS: 60 seats. 24 seats outside. Private parties: 45 main room, 14 to 45 private rooms. Vegetarian meals. Children's helpings. No smoking in 1 dining room. Wheelchair access (not WC). No music. Air-conditioned   ⊖ Earls Court (£5)

Lundum's

117–119 Old Brompton Road, SW7 3RN
TEL: (020) 7373 7774   FAX: (020) 7373 4472
WEBSITE: www.lundums.com

map 14

COOKING 3
DANISH
£27–£73

With staff 'among the nicest in the city', according to one reporter, this popular Danish eatery has had a face lift and expanded into neighbouring office space. The slightly baroque brick exterior remains, but inside, London chic yields to Danish design and tradition. A 'simply stunning' main dining room has colour and vitality, while the cooking makes best use of well-sourced seasonal ingredients. Lunch and dinner show the two sides of Danish cuisine. Lunchtime dishes are based on traditional Danish recipes and aim for clear flavours: herring, unsurprisingly, figures prominently, paired with onions and capers, spiced with cloves and wine, or sauced with mustard. Main-course platters offer tastes of plaice, gravad lax, prawns, meatballs, beetroot, soft cheese, dill and parsley. Finally, there are several Danish cheese options, plus traditional Æblekage apple cake, and spiced soup of wild berries. Dinner delivers a more contemporary take, with seared scallops on apple and tomato compote, or roast lamb with cherry tomato confit, but there are still dishes like Skagen ham with feta mousse, olive tapenade and sun-dried tomatoes, or Danish meat balls. The extensive wine list is organised by region, kicks off at £13.25 and rises into three figures for some quality bottles; nine come by the glass from £3.35. The optional service charge is 13.5%.

CHEF: Kay Lundum   PROPRIETORS: the Lundum family   OPEN: all week L 12 to 3, Mon to Sat D 6 to 11   CLOSED: 22 Dec to 4 Jan   MEALS: alc (main courses L £8.50 to £17.50, D £14 to £23). Set L £12.50 (2 courses) to £15.50, Set D £17.25 (2 courses) to £21.50. Sun brunch and Mon to Sat snack menus available   SERVICE: 13.5% (optional)   CARDS: Amex, Delta, Diners, MasterCard, Switch, Visa   DETAILS: 86 seats. 20 seats outside. Private parties: 12 main room, 18 private room. Vegetarian meals. No pipes/cigars. Wheelchair access (also WC). Music. Air-conditioned   ⊖ Gloucester Road

Mandarin Kitchen £   map 13

14–16 Queensway, W2 3RX   COOKING 1
TEL: (020) 7727 9012   FAX: (020) 7727 9468   CHINESE
     £27–£79

Seafood gets top billing at this long-running and bustling eating house in Queensway's mini-Chinatown. Lobsters and crab are the main contenders, but the kitchen rings the changes with sea bass, Dover sole and monkfish, as well as eel in various guises (braised with pork and mushrooms, for example). The mainly Cantonese menu also lists appetisers like steamed razor clams (in season), and other maritime delicacies including braised sea cucumber with sliced abalone. Away from the sea, expect stir-fried chicken with cashew nuts, veal chop in black pepper sauce, and crispy minced bean curd with oyster sauce. House wine is around the £11 mark. Details below may not be accurate, because the restaurant has not returned our questionnaire.

CHEF: Paul Ngo   PROPRIETOR: Steven Cheung   OPEN: all week 12 to 11.30   MEALS: alc (main courses £6 to £28). Set L and D £10.90 (2 courses) to £20   SERVICE: not inc, card slips closed   CARDS: Amex, Delta, Diners, MasterCard, Switch, Visa   DETAILS: 100 seats. Private parties: 100 main room. Vegetarian meals. Wheelchair access (not WC). No music. Air-conditioned   ⊖ Queensway

▲ Mandarin Oriental Hyde Park, Foliage   map 14

66 Knightsbridge, SW1X 7LA   COOKING 6
TEL: (020) 7235 2000   FAX: (020) 7235 2001   MODERN EUROPEAN
WEBSITE: www.mandarinoriental.com   £42–£111

In the middle of Knightsbridge and backing onto Hyde Park, the Mandarin Oriental is an 1880s fantasy in stone and brick, ornately turreted and balconied in wrought iron. The Foliage restaurant, though, could be in twenty-first-century New York or Tokyo: a glass-walled haven of studied opulence with a central raised section expressly designed to exploit the view of Hyde Park.

Much of the kitchen's output befits the glamorous setting. Appetisers are varied and extraordinary, from deep-fried frog's leg spiked with curry to sweet melon soup in a glass. Inspection highlights included a stunning first-course 'mille-feuille' – crisp slices of garlic caramel sandwiching plump roast sweetbreads, pointed up with a discreet sweet onion compote – and the show-stopping whole leg of Pauillac lamb, presented at the table then carved into superb, tender slices, their full flavour gently enhanced with herbs. Less convincing was a clumsy onion tart, and carefully cooked fillets of sole were let down by a crude bed of spiced shredded lettuce. More encouraging reports come in for the raviolo of scallops with langoustines, asparagus, truffles and an artichoke velouté, and for impressive desserts, among them classic tarte Tatin with a sharply refreshing green apple sorbet, and assertively flavoured Earl Grey soufflé with milk chocolate sorbet. Coffee has been 'very weak'. Reporters have enjoyed the policy of offering smart wines by the glass, such as super-Tuscan Tassinaia (£12.50). The main list drips class and is particularly strong in France, but mark-ups are high and options severely restricted below £25. House is £19.50.

CHEF: Chris Staines PROPRIETOR: Mandarin Oriental Group OPEN: all week 12 to 2.15, 7 to 9.30 MEALS: Set L £25, Set D £47.50 to £70 SERVICE: 12.5% (optional), card slips closed CARDS: Amex, Delta, Diners, MasterCard, Switch, Visa DETAILS: 42 seats. Private parties: 150 to 250 private rooms. Vegetarian meals. No pipes/cigars. Wheelchair access (also WC). No music. Air-conditioned ACCOMMODATION: 200 rooms, all with bath/shower. TV. Phone. Room only £375 to £4,500. Rooms for disabled. Baby facilities ⊖ Knightsbridge

Mash   map 15

19–21 Great Portland Street, W1W 8QB	COOKING 2
TEL: (020) 7637 5555 FAX: (020) 7637 7333	MODERN EUROPEAN
EMAIL: reception@mash-restaurant.co.uk	£34–£57

Behind the two-storey plate-glass exterior, a bold, modern design and bright colours set the scene at this microbrewery-cum-restaurant, known for its lively (and noisy at peak times) atmosphere. The ground floor is mainly for drinkers, while, upstairs, the eating area is bordered by an open kitchen and a glazed partition giving views of the brewery. The menu lists pizzas from the wood-fired ovens, salads, pasta and bistro classics, emphasising British ingredients. Start with Falmouth Bay crab on toast, moving on to steamed sea bass with tomato and watercress salad, or chicken breast with spring vegetables and saffron consommé, and finish with banana split or apple pie. Wash it all down with Mash's own beer, or choose a bottle or glass from the short list of wines, from £14.50 and £4.50 respectively.

CHEF: Simon Wadham PROPRIETOR: Gruppo Ltd OPEN: Mon to Fri L 12 to 3, Mon to Sat D 6 to 11 CLOSED: 25 Dec, some bank hols MEALS: alc (main courses £9.50 to £16.50). Bar L menu available SERVICE: 12.5% (optional) CARDS: Amex, Delta, MasterCard, Switch, Visa DETAILS: 150 seats. Private parties: 150 main room, 25 private room. Vegetarian meals. Wheelchair access (also WC). No music. Air-conditioned ⊖ Oxford Circus

The Guide is totally independent, accepts no free hospitality, and survives on the number of copies sold each year.

Matsuri High Holborn

map 13

Mid City Place, 71 High Holborn, WC1V 6EA
TEL: (020) 7430 1970   FAX: (020) 7430 1971
WEBSITE: www.matsuri-restaurant.com

COOKING **4**
JAPANESE
£31–£121

A Zen-like mood is set by the sophisticated minimalist style of this ultra-smart Japanese restaurant. High ceilings and plain white walls are enhanced by an open-plan kitchen and staff in 'ethnic but cool' costume. The menus aim to appeal to a non-Japanese clientele who might not be familiar with the finer workings of the cuisine, and there are some unusual Westernised ideas such as 'Japanese fish and chips', although dining options include authentically traditional omakase set menus, where the choice of dishes is left entirely to the whim of the chef. The food generally makes a positive impact, although it doesn't always match the wow factor of the setting. Nonetheless, this remains among the foremost venues in London for authentic Japanese cooking, and everything is done properly, from the sushi rice to the ritualised serving of tokkuri pot dishes in elaborate tripartite containers. Drinks include hot or cold saké by the flask and a wine list priced from £13.50.

CHEF: Hiroshi Sudo   PROPRIETOR: Mr Yamaguchi   OPEN: Mon to Sat 12 to 3, 6 to 10 (9 Sat)   MEALS: alc (main courses £8 to £25). Set L £15 to £22 (both 2 courses), Set D £25 to £80   SERVICE: 12.5%   CARDS: Amex, Delta, Diners, MasterCard, Switch, Visa   DETAILS: 135 seats. Private parties: 60 main room, 2 to 10 private rooms. Vegetarian meals. No cigars/pipes in sushi bar. Wheelchair access (also WC). Music. Air-conditioned   ⊖ Holborn, Chancery Lane

Metrogusto Islington ♟ ⅙✳

map 13

13 Theberton Street, N1 0QY
TEL/FAX: (020) 7226 9400
WEBSITE: www.metrogusto.co.uk

COOKING **3**
MODERN ITALIAN
£33–£57

In simple, bright surroundings with tiled floors and *naif*-style paintings on the walls, one writer enjoyed excellent alla siciliana salad, a clean-tasting authentic minestrone, superb bass with a balanced barbecue taste and 'gorgeous tiramisù'. The menu, written largely in English or accessible restaurant Italian, and with Sicily a particular focus, deals in simple subtleties from stuffed baby squid with piquant sauce to cantuccini with a glass of vin santo, via gnocchi, ravioli of fresh ginger and tuna, or veal escalope with fennel sauce. The all-Italian wine list opens with a fistful of rugged southern charmers (available by the glass from £4.50) and meanders its way gradually northwards in terms of both region and price.

CHEF: Antonio Di Salvo   PROPRIETORS: Ambro and Susi Ianeselli   OPEN: Fri to Sun L 12 to 2.30 (3 Sat and Sun), Mon to Sat D 6.30 to 10.30 (11 Sat), Sun D 7 to 10   CLOSED: 25 Dec, 1 Jan, Easter Sun and Mon, bank hols   MEALS: alc D (main courses £11.50 to £16.50). Set L £14.50 (2 courses) to £18.50, Set D 6.30 to 7.30 £14.50 (2 courses) to £18.50   SERVICE: 12.5% (optional), card slips closed   CARDS: Amex, Delta, MasterCard, Switch, Visa   DETAILS: 60 seats. 10 seats outside. Private parties: 30 private room. Vegetarian meals. Children's helpings. No babies after 10pm. No smoking in 1 dining room. Music. Air-conditioned   ⊖ Angel, Highbury & Islington   (£5)

'It was entertaining to see (through one of the dining room windows) how regularly kitchen staff would be running to and from the herb garden: there was that much attention to freshness!'
(On eating in Lancashire)

Mims

map 12

541A King's Road, SW6 2EB
TEL/FAX: (020) 7751 0010
EMAIL: al-sersy@mimsrestaurant.co.uk

COOKING 3
MODERN EUROPEAN
£27–£37

Short on comfort, frills, and coordinated décor, this relative newcomer to the Chelsea scene does offer quite a bargain for the area with its short choice, set menu that changes daily. Ali Al-Sersy is an accomplished exponent of the modern European style. The day's menu could typically take in lamb's tongue, penne and mushrooms with a curry broth, followed by poached rabbit with Jerusalem artichoke purée, lemon and mustard, or roast monkfish with spinach, chilli, garlic and coriander. Finish with white chocolate and vanilla mousse, or the enigmatic 'bread-and-butter'. Extras such as bread are good. Service can be slow at times, but at its best is considered 'friendly and helpful'. Most wines on the short, all-French list are under £20. Seven by the glass start at £3.40.

CHEF/PROPRIETOR: Ali Al-Sersy   OPEN: Tue to Sun 12.30 to 5, 6.30 to 11   MEALS: Set L £10.50 (2 courses) to £15, Set D £14 (2 courses) to £18.50   SERVICE: 10%, card slips closed   CARDS: MasterCard, Switch, Visa   DETAILS: 45 seats. Private parties: 60 main room. No children under 7. No-smoking area. Wheelchair access (not WC). Music   ⊖ Fulham Broadway £5

Mirabelle ▮

map 15

56 Curzon Street, W1J 8PA
TEL: (020) 7499 4636   FAX: (020) 7499 5449
WEBSITE: www.whitestarline.org.uk

COOKING 5
FRENCH
£36–£85

'My, what a civilised place!' commented one reporter on this chic Mayfair stronghold of Marco Pierre White's culinary empire. The bar is reminiscent of a 1920s ocean liner, while the sub-basement dining room impresses with its spacious feel and strong yet subtle features: dark parquet flooring, brown leather banquettes, and smartly set, well-spaced tables that are big enough for four even when laid for two. Service from well-drilled staff can be lacking in warmth, but everything proceeds smoothly at a comfortable pace.

French classics in the grand style dominate the lengthy menu, which rattles along in a confusingly franglais fashion (grilled sea bass au fenouil, ribeye of Aberdeen Angus aux escargots). There's no confusion on the plate, however. This is skilfully rendered, well-presented cooking displaying some unmistakable Marco Pierre White hallmarks. These have included a light, wobbly foie gras mousse, enriching a starter of pigeon that was 'moist and full of gamey flavour', and a large, plump, well-flavoured oxtail raviolo, served in a pool of oxtail consommé with pearl barley and garnished with deep-fried beetroot, providing excellent texture contrasts. A 'perfect' crème brûlée or pear tarte Tatin make an impressive end to proceedings. You may need a magnifying glass to read the wine list, but such close scrutiny will reveal no flaws in this dream of a line-up, mainly from France but with other countries equally on song. House white at £18.50 is tiptop Sauvignon de Touraine. Further treats are promised on the fine wine list, of which 50 different vintages of Yquem on the dessert menu give a taster.

CHEF: Philip Cooper   PROPRIETORS: Marco Pierre White and Jimmy Lahoud   OPEN: all week 12 to 2.30, 6 to 11.30   MEALS: alc (main courses £14.50 to £25). Set L £16.50 (2 courses) to £19.50   SERVICE: 12.5% (optional)   CARDS: Amex, Delta, Diners, MasterCard, Switch, Visa   DETAILS: 120 seats. 40 seats outside. Private parties: 120 main room, 12 to 48 private rooms. Children's helpings. Music. Air-conditioned ⊖ Green Park

Mr Kong £

map 15

21 Lisle Street, WC2H 7BA
TEL: (020) 7437 7341   FAX: (020) 7437 7923

COOKING 2
CHINESE
£24–£53

Since opening in 1984, the Kong family's restaurant has earned a reputation as one of the more reliable Cantonese venues in Soho Chinatown, although fluctuating standards have been reported of late. When it's on target, the kitchen delivers high-class renditions of stir-fried prawns with cashew nuts, lightly steamed gai lan (Chinese broccoli), and stupendously good Singapore noodles. The menu also boasts a challenging selection of 'manager's recommendations': steamed prawn dumplings have been capably handled; otherwise the choice extends to roasted pork with garlic sprouts and vegetarian specials like sautéed bean curd and asparagus with fresh mango. The mood in the ground-floor dining room is casual, and service is – for the most part – efficient; the basement is not such a good bet. House vin de pays is £7.80.

CHEFS: K. Kong and Y.W. Lo   PROPRIETORS: K. Kong, Y.W. Lo, M.T. Lee and C.Y. Chau   OPEN: all week noon to 2.45am (1.45am Sun)   MEALS: alc (main courses £6 to £12). Set meals available from £9.30 (min 2)   SERVICE: 10%   CARDS: Amex, Delta, Diners, MasterCard, Switch, Visa   DETAILS: 110 seats. Private parties: 40 main room, 30 to 40 private rooms. Vegetarian meals. No pipes/cigars. Music. Air-conditioned
⊖ Leicester Square

▲ Mju ▼

map 14

Millennium Knightsbridge Hotel, 17 Sloane Street,
SW1 9NU
TEL: (020) 7201 6330   FAX: (020) 7201 6302
EMAIL: mju@mill-cop.com

NEW CHEF
GLOBAL
£32–£95

Mju is essentially the hotel dining room of the swish, modern Millennium hotel, and occupies a capacious first-floor atrium. Décor combines modern touches, including abstract metallic paintings, with a hint of the orient in features such as floating candles on tables. A new chef arrived shortly before the Guide went to press. Menus have been revised, now leaning towards a fusion of Pacific Rim and European ideas, taking in starters of seared scallops with miso, grilled watermelon and bonito, or pan-fried foie gras with caramelised banana and coconut sorbet. Main courses might include a modernised duck à l'orange, comprising duck confit with a sesame orange mousseline and shiitakes, or lobster linguini with aromatic oil, garlic, konbu and laksa leaves, and for dessert, floating island is another updated version with lemongrass crème anglaise, mocha sorbet and coriander. An eclectic line-up of wines is particularly strong on smart Australian reds but has much of interest from all points of the compass. The best value is, unusually, in France. Bottles start at £17, or pick from the attention-grabbing range by the glass.

CHEF: Tom Thomsen   PROPRIETOR: Millennium Copthorne Hotels   OPEN: Mon to Fri L 12 to 2.30, Mon to Sat D 6 to 10.30   CLOSED: bank hols   MEALS: alc (mezze menu L £3.50 to £12.50, main courses D £14 to £22). Set L £19.95 (2 courses) to £24.95, Set D £40 to £60. Bar menu available   SERVICE: 12.5% (optional)   CARDS: Amex, Delta, Diners, MasterCard, Switch, Visa   DETAILS: 110 seats. Private parties: 152 main room, 10 to 100 private rooms. Vegetarian meals. Children's helpings. No-smoking area. Wheelchair access (not WC). Occasional music. Air-conditioned   ACCOMMODATION: 222 rooms, all with bath/shower. TV. Phone. Room only £270 to £552. Baby facilities   ⊖ Knightsbridge   £5

▲ Montcalm Hotel, Crescent Restaurant   map 15

34–40, Great Cumberland Place, W1H 7TW   COOKING 3
TEL: (020) 7402 4288   FAX: (020) 7789 9180   MODERN BRITISH
WEBSITE: www.montcalm.co.uk   £31–£63

The gentle colour scheme and chic table decorations of this hotel overlooking a quiet crescent, just near one end of Oxford Street, form a soothing backdrop for Ian Medas's inspired pan-European cooking. Menus are fixed-price and good value (they include a half-bottle of house wine per person), and mobilise some striking flavours – such as lightly grilled tuna with pear and the Japanese herb shiso – against a background of solid classical technique. A meal might proceed from crab and haddock fishcake with caviar beurre blanc, or Caesar salad, via noisette of lamb with aubergine purée, pommes dauphinoise and rosemary jus, before coming in to land with crème brûlée spiked with passion fruit. Service is commended as impeccable, and the wines are a French-centred collection starting at £17.

CHEF: Ian Medas   PROPRIETOR: Nikko Hotels (UK) Ltd   OPEN: Mon to Fri L 12.30 to 2.30, all week D 6.30 to 10.30   MEALS: Set L and D £20 (2 courses) to £25. Bar menu available   SERVICE: not inc, card slips closed   CARDS: Amex, Diners, MasterCard, Switch, Visa   DETAILS: 50 seats. Private parties: 60 main room, 2 to 20 private rooms. Vegetarian meals. Children's helpings. Wheelchair access (not WC). Occasional music. Air-conditioned   ACCOMMODATION: 120 rooms, all with bath/shower. TV. Phone. Room only £120 to £250. Rooms for disabled. Baby facilities   ⊖ Marble Arch £5

Morgan M ⚞✳   NEW ENTRY   map 13

489 Liverpool Road, N7 8NS   COOKING 6
TEL: (020) 7609 3560   FAX: (020) 8292 5699   MODERN FRENCH
    £38–£76

Morgan Meunier – formerly at Admiralty, Somerset House (see entry) – now runs his own restaurant, where a bare wooden floor and plain white walls are enlivened by the chef's own artworks (one of which adorns the menu cover). Attentive and agreeably professional service complements a menu with much to surprise and delight at prices that seem like kindness itself. Grilled langoustines gain earthy contrast from a caviar of aubergine and red pepper, and are further enhanced by a frothed shellfish sauce, while a main-course Anjou squab profits by its fine underlay of Puy lentils and a capably rendered sauce soubise. The 'Garden' menu gives vegetarians a studied six courses with suggested accompanying wines by the glass, and the £39 set menu does the same for omnivores. Cheeses from La Fromagerie are a pedigree French selection, while intricate desserts are cumulatively quite rich, pairing a creamy orange tart with chocolate ice cream, and adorning expert raspberry soufflé with strawberry coulis and an ice cream of rhubarb and sweet Jurançon. Decent coffee comes with an array of petits fours.

An entirely French wine list works methodically through the main regions, and includes some attractive-looking mature vintages; house wines at £15 are a south-western white and a Loire Cabernet Franc. Wines by the small glass are £4.50 to £6.50.

CHEFS: Morgan Meunier and Sylvain Soulard   PROPRIETOR: Morgan Meunier   OPEN: Wed to Fri and Sun L 12.15 to 2.30, Tue to Sat D 7 to 10   CLOSED: 24 to 30 Dec   MEALS: Set L £19.50 (2 courses) to £23.50, Set D £30 to £39   SERVICE: 12.5% (optional), card slips closed   CARDS: Delta, Diners, MasterCard, Switch, Visa   DETAILS: 48 seats. Private parties: 12 main room, 12 private room. Vegetarian meals. Wheelchair access (not WC). No music. No mobile phones. Air-conditioned   ⊖ Holloway Road

Moro

map 13

34–36 Exmouth Market, EC1R 4QE
TEL: (020) 7833 8336   FAX: (020) 7833 9338
WEBSITE: www.moro.co.uk

COOKING 5
SPANISH/NORTH AFRICAN
£33–£51

'It's probably the restaurant I go back to more than any other,' says one visitor. Much of the food is cooked in wood-fired ovens in the open-plan kitchen – 'addictive viewing' – and the hustle and bustle and general informality of the place are all part of the appeal. If you can't get a table, turn up for tapas at the long zinc bar. Perhaps the most enduring legacy of Spain's Moorish culture is its culinary tradition, evoked with passion and style as the central attraction here – although the restaurant draws inspiration from further afield, putting the length and breadth of the Muslim Mediterranean to good use. Get going with 'beautifully fresh' white and green asparagus with grainy almond sauce, or perhaps deeply rich and intensely flavoured fish soup, served with distinctive home-made sourdough bread and lashings of aïoli. Main courses might include seafood bisteeya – a light, flaky Moroccan-style pie accompanied by chard – or chargrilled turbot with a 'wonderfully earthy' stew of artichokes, green beans and peas. Finish with the simple pleasure of yoghurt and pistachio cake, or nectarine sorbet. The imaginative wine list focuses on Spain and kicks off with nine sherries by the glass. House Italian white and Spanish red are £12.50.

CHEFS: Samuel and Samantha Clark   PROPRIETORS: Mark Sainsbury, and Samuel and Samantha Clark
OPEN: Mon to Fri L 12.30 to 2.30, Mon to Sat D 7 to 10.30   CLOSED: Christmas to New Year, bank hols
MEALS: alc (main courses £13 to £17.50). Tapas menu available Mon to Fri 12.30 to 10.30, Sat 7 to 10.30
SERVICE: not inc, 12.5% for parties of 6 or more   CARDS: Amex, Delta, Diners, MasterCard, Switch, Visa
DETAILS: 85 seats. 12 seats outside. Private parties: 85 main room. Vegetarian meals. Wheelchair access
(also WC). Occasional music. Air-conditioned   ⊖ Farringdon

Mosaica @ the factory

map 12

Chocolate Factory, Clarendon Road, N22 6XJ
TEL: (020) 8889 2400   FAX: (020) 8889 1226
WEBSITE: www.mosaicarestaurants.com

COOKING 3
MODERN EUROPEAN
£24–£50

The unlikely incarnation of factory unit as eating establishment has put Wood Green on the map (well, the GFG map at least). No clever, post-industrial chic here, just a commitment to reducing the overheads of a good restaurant by placing it in a part-metal-clad building on an industrial estate shared with various warehouses and workshops in what might be regarded as a culinary desert. Success has assured the recent launch of a sister restaurant in Tottenham Hale (see entry below).

Start with asparagus with a fried duck egg and Parmesan, or foie gras with toast and pickles, and follow up with fillet of sea bass with baby vegetables and garlic potatoes, or belly pork with red cabbage and mash. Finish simply with tiramisù or chocolate mousse. The downside of popularity and acclaim, coupled with the venue's huge capacity, is that kitchen and service may be overstretched during peak periods. A child-friendly policy means it's often packed at Sunday lunch. Wine begins at £11.95 a bottle, and the brief list is bolstered by a few good bottles at the high end.

CHEFS: David Orlowski and Keith Kelly   PROPRIETORS: David Orlowski and John Mountain   OPEN: Tue to
Fri and Sun L 12 to 2, Tue to Sat D 7 to 10   MEALS: alc (main courses L £6 to £12.50, D £12 to £15.50)
SERVICE: not inc, 10% for parties of 8 or more   CARDS: Amex, Delta, MasterCard, Switch, Visa   DETAILS:
90 seats. Private parties: 120 main room. Car park. Vegetarian meals. Children's helpings. No-smoking
area. Wheelchair access (also WC). Music. Air-conditioned   ⊖ Wood Green

Mosaica @ the lock

NEW ENTRY   map 12

Heron House, Hale Wharf, Ferry Lane, N17 9NF
TEL: (020) 8801 4433   FAX: (020) 8801 1661
WEBSITE: www.mosaicarestaurants.com

COOKING 3
MODERN EUROPEAN
£27–£57

Word has spread, and Mosaica, which shares a building with the College of North-East London (the restaurant occupies the ground floor), appears to be going great guns: the success of its older sister in Wood Green (see entry above) seems to be rubbing off.

To begin with, there might be seared scallops with black pudding, or a simple and effective dish of marinated artichokes with tomatoes, pesto and Parmesan. Among successful main courses have been roast John Dory perched on Mediterranean vegetables and Jersey Royals, and grilled swordfish steak on Caesar salad. Finish with brazil nut parfait, or a refreshing pannacotta topped with espresso. House French at £13.90 opens the short wine list. Prices are generally below £20, although those celebrating could opt for a bottle from the fine wine selection.

CHEFS: John Mountain and Joshua Gale   PROPRIETORS: John Mountain and David Orlowski   OPEN: Tue to Fri and Sun L 12 to 2.30, Tue to Sat D 7 to 10   CLOSED: 20 Dec, 25 to 30 Dec, 1 to 4 Jan, Tue after bank hols   MEALS: alc (main courses L £6.50 to £13, D £12.50 to £16)   SERVICE: not inc, 10% for parties of 6 or more   CARDS: Amex, Delta, MasterCard, Switch, Visa   DETAILS: 80 seats. 40 seats outside. Private parties: 150 main room. Car park. Vegetarian meals. Children's helpings. No-smoking area. Wheelchair access (also WC). Occasional music   ⊖ Tottenham Hale

---

MVH

map 12

5 White Hart Lane, SW13 0PX
TEL: (020) 8392 1111   FAX: (020) 8878 1919

COOKING 4
ECLECTIC
£38–£58

This theatrical and quirky Barnes restaurant and bar is named after its chef/proprietor, Michael Von Hruschka. Prepare yourself for a dining experience with a difference. The ground floor, called 'Heaven', comes decked out in angelic white, with Italian-style glass chandeliers, tablecloths and high-backed chairs all following the ethereal theme. Upstairs is a blood-red 'Hell'-themed bar with décor just as wacky. The innovative set-price menus, backed by a veritable myriad of intermediary courses, travel the globe for inspiration. So expect the unexpected: perhaps red mullet tempura with wasabi and yuzu dip to start, and a kalamansi crème brûlée to finish, with, in between, maybe roast rump of lamb with spiced lentils and peperonata, or blackened cod with herb tagliolini and beetroot purée. The compact, globetrotting wine list kicks off with house vins de pays at £18 and offers seven wines by the glass from £3.50.

CHEF/PROPRIETOR: Michael Von Hruschka   OPEN: Thur to Sun L 12 to 2.30, Tue to Sun D 6 to 10.30   MEALS: Set L £19 (2 courses) to £22, Set D £26 (2 courses) to £29   SERVICE: 12.5% (optional), card slips closed   CARDS: Amex, Delta, MasterCard, Switch, Visa   DETAILS: 30 seats. Private parties: 30 main room, 18 to 30 private rooms. Vegetarian meals. Music. Air-conditioned

---

'Whilst I like harp music and whilst she was good, I would have preferred to have had her more than three feet from my right elbow all night. Preferably in another room or another city.'
(On eating in the West Country)

Nahm

map 14

Halkin Hotel, 5 Halkin Street, SW1X 7DJ
TEL: (020) 7333 1234   FAX: (020) 7333 1000

COOKING 4
THAI
£45–£102

'You wouldn't guess that this was Thai until the heady aromas of lemongrass, kaffir lime leaves and chillies seduce your olfactory sense-buds,' observed a visitor to this sophisticated venue in the auspicious Halkin Hotel. Nahm is a cool, discreet place decorated in plain earthy colours and staffed by a knowledgeable team who seem very 'un-Thai' with their European accents and crisp black suits.

David Thompson's version of the cuisine encompasses highly individual interpretations of the classics and occasionally wayward crossover ideas. At its best, the food is a true amalgam of delicacy, pungency, fire and sweetness, with mysterious ingredients and flavours to the fore (including, of course, intense nam prik relishes). Go for the eight-dish, four-course Nahm Arharn menu or plunge into the carte, which is divided into salads (grilled pork and squid with young ginger), rice, soups, curries (braised longhorn beef with steamed eggs and betel leaves), stir-fries, and so on. Prices reflect the Belgravia postcode, although the substantial wine list has been assembled with care. House selections start at £23.

CHEF: David Thompson   PROPRIETOR: Christina Ong   OPEN: Mon to Fri L 12 to 2.30, all week D 7 to 10.45 (10 Sun)   CLOSED: Christmas, bank hols   MEALS: alc (main courses £16.50 to £20.50). Set L £18 (2 courses) to £26, Set D £47   SERVICE: 12.5% (optional), card slips closed   CARDS: Amex, Delta, Diners, MasterCard, Switch, Visa   DETAILS: 76 seats. Private parties: 80 main room. Vegetarian meals. No cigars/pipes. Wheelchair access (also WC). Music. Air-conditioned   ⊖ Hyde Park Corner

Neal Street Restaurant

map 15

26 Neal Street, WC2H 9QW
TEL: (020) 7836 8368   FAX: (020) 7240 3964
WEBSITE: www.carluccios.com

COOKING 2
ITALIAN
£39–£79

Antonio Carluccio's restaurant still proves a place of pilgrimage for lovers of Italian food after 24 years in business and the roll-out of the Carluccio Caffè concept (see London round-ups). It's smart but informal, with plain white walls and table linen, and cuts a friendly, relaxed atmosphere away from the Covent Garden bustle. Carluccio is famous for his passion for funghi, and the menu always includes mushrooms and truffles: perhaps hand-cut tagliolini with a black winter truffle sauce and black truffle shavings, for instance, or 'truly first-rate' mixed sautéed mushrooms. Seasonality, freshness and carefully sourced ingredients are the keys to light, modern dishes, as in a main course of rolled saddle of rabbit with San Daniele ham, Savoy cabbage and a potato cake, while desserts run to classics of tiramisù, or hazelnut semi-freddo with pistachio and chocolate sauce. Not surprisingly, the wine list is almost exclusively Italian, starting at £14.50 (although prices quickly escalate).

CHEF: Andrea Cavaliere   PROPRIETORS: Antonio and Priscilla Carluccio   OPEN: Mon to Sat 12 to 2.30, 6 to 11   CLOSED: 24 Dec to 1 Jan   MEALS: alc (main courses £15 to £21.50). Set L £21 (2 courses) to £25   SERVICE: 12.5%, card slips closed   CARDS: Amex, Delta, Diners, MasterCard, Switch, Visa   DETAILS: 80 seats. Private parties: 10 main room, 10 to 24 private rooms. Vegetarian meals. No music. Air-conditioned   ⊖ Covent Garden

New Diamond £

map 15

23 Lisle Street, WC2H 7BA
TEL: (020) 7437 2517   FAX: (020) 7437 7221

COOKING **2**
CANTONESE
£24–£61

'Algae with salted eggs and pork soup' is just one of the unexpected treasures to be unearthed in this neat, white, narrow dining room, sparsely decorated but with a cheerful feel. Cantonese dishes dominate the menu, which takes in promising-sounding ideas like baked turbot in spicy salt, and scrambled eggs with oysters and chives, as well as sizzling frogs' legs, veal cutlet with honey sauce and even sweet-and-sour spring pigeon; there are also popular specials including razor clams with asparagus in XO sauce. Traditionalists can take their pick from staples such as crispy prawn balls, sliced beef with ginger and spring onions, and duck with ginger and pineapple. House French at £7.80 tops the predominantly Gallic wine list.

CHEF: Phat Van Ly   PROPRIETORS: Wai Cheung Lam and Kwai Li Ku   OPEN: all week noon to 2.45am   CLOSED: 25 Dec   MEALS: alc (main courses £5 to £20). Set D £9.50 to £25 (all min 2 or more)   SERVICE: 10%   CARDS: Amex, Delta, Diners, MasterCard, Switch, Visa   DETAILS: 80 seats. Vegetarian meals. No children under 5. Music. Air-conditioned   ⊖ Leicester Square

New Mayflower £

NEW ENTRY   map 15

68–70 Shaftesbury Avenue, W1D 6LY
TEL: (020) 7734 9207

COOKING **3**
CHINESE
£28–£99

You will be rewarded once you get beyond the crush of the queue waiting for a table in the tiny front dining room: the small spaces and alcoves further in and in the basement below, all done out in deep reds and white, are comfortable, and the place positively bustles. The draw is classy Chinese food, and though the menu may seem fairly standard – sizzling dishes, duck with pancakes, and a long list of seafood, chicken, pork, beef, noodle and Chinese porridge dishes – what you get on the plate is leagues ahead of the norm. Soups like crab and sweetcorn, and mixed meat (pork, squid, fish ball) with vegetables have good stock and the freshest of ingredients; 'pe pa' bean curd (stuffed with minced prawns and pork) is beautifully textured and sauced; and the simple-sounding 'stewed duck with yam in pot' yields unctuous textures and wonderful flavours. Wines are basic, though Chinese tea is good and refillable. Service can become a little disjointed when pressed but is friendly. Night owls note: last orders are at 3.45am.

CHEF: Raymond Mann   PROPRIETOR: To Yeung Tang   OPEN: all week D only 5pm to 3.45am   MEALS: alc (main courses £6.50 to £45). Set D £12 (min 2) to £22 (min 4)   SERVICE: 10%   CARDS: Amex, Delta, MasterCard, Switch, Visa   DETAILS: 120 seats. Vegetarian meals. Music. Air-conditioned   ⊖ Piccadilly Circus

Nicole's

map 15

158 New Bond Street, W1S 2UB
TEL: (020) 7499 8408   FAX: (020) 7409 0381
EMAIL: nicoles@nicolefarhi.com

COOKING **3**
MODERN EUROPEAN
£53–£75

This restaurant within the Nicole Farhi store is cream-painted with wood floor, chairs and picture frames, and has a classy '30s Art Deco feel. It heaves at lunchtime, but few realise it does dinner too – a shame, since it provides not just welcome banquettes for bag-burdened shoppers but decent food as well. Good breads with pungent olive oil exemplify the pervading simplicity and sound execution. Caesar salad with a proper oeuf mollet and a hint of anchovy in the dressing, subtly spiced duck breast with light, fragrant couscous, and unsweetened fresh fruits smothered in zabaglione and lightly grilled, all develop the theme with flair. A £1 cover charge, 15% service and pricey extras can be set against carefully chosen wines from £15.25 (18 available by the glass).

CHEF: Annie Wayte   PROPRIETOR: Stephen Marks   OPEN: Mon to Sat L 11.30 to 3.30, Mon to Fri D 6.30 to 10   CLOSED: bank hols   MEALS: alc (main courses £18 to £22). Cover £1. Bar L menu available   SERVICE: 15% (optional), card slips closed   CARDS: Amex, Delta, Diners, MasterCard, Switch, Visa   DETAILS: 100 seats. Private parties: 100 main room. Vegetarian meals. Wheelchair access (also WC). Music. Air-conditioned   ⊖ Green Park

Noble Rot

map 15

3–5 Mill Street, W1S 2AU
TEL: (020) 7629 8877   FAX: (020) 7629 8878
WEBSITE: www.noblerot.com

COOKING 5
MODERN EUROPEAN
£35–£126

Behind the privacy of wooden Venetian blinds this celebrity-haunted restaurant has chocolate-brown walls, cream and green upholstered chairs, and a stone floor scattered with antique rugs. The smartly dressed staff are 'approachable and efficient', and caviar and other luxuries are skilfully deployed by Julian Owen-Mold: 'a dab hand with foie gras'. Lobster might surface as a main course, with 'laitue de mer', asparagus and Tahitian vanilla butter sauce, while its essence enriches a starter of spiced crab and 'strikingly delicate' white tomato sorbet. Foie gras comes fried with a cassonade of cherries, or in a delicate mousse with beef carpaccio enhanced by a Sauternes reduction, mâche salad and truffled pecorino. Unusual meat and fish alliances have included 'mer et montagne' (rabbit with smoked bacon, mussels and sole) and roast turbot with confit of ceps, salsify and braised oxtail. Vegetables are charged extra. The highlight of the night for an inspector was a trio of chocolate: a beautifully textured tart, a chocolate pot, and a mousse incorporating foie gras and pistachio. Ten percent of the wine list is dessert wines (not all botrytised), many at A-list prices, though several come by the glass; the rest of the list starts at £16 but rises steeply.

CHEF: Julian Owen-Mold   PROPRIETOR: Soren Jessen   OPEN: Mon to Sat 11.30 to 2, 6 to 11   CLOSED: Christmas, Easter, bank hols   MEALS: alc (main courses £16.50 to £32). Set L £15.95 (2 courses) to £19.50, Set D £40 to (whole table only) £60   SERVICE: 12.5% (optional), card slips closed   CARDS: Amex, MasterCard, Switch, Visa   DETAILS: 70 seats. 20 seats outside. Private parties: 150 main room, 6 to 150 private rooms. Vegetarian meals. Wheelchair access (also WC). Music. Air-conditioned   ⊖ Oxford Circus

Nobu

map 15

19 Old Park Lane, W1Y 4LB
TEL: (020) 7447 4747   FAX: (020) 7447 4749
WEBSITE: www.noburestaurants.com

COOKING 5
MODERN JAPANESE
£45–£119

The long dining room on the first floor of the Metropolitan Hotel remains a hugely popular spot with the 'youngish', well-heeled Mayfair set. The attraction is not the view over the traffic towards Hyde Park, nor yet the minimal décor and bare wooden tables, simply set with chopsticks and glassware. The star here is first-rate modern Japanese cooking (with some South American influences), characterised by top-quality ingredients and clear, fresh flavours. The extensive menu never changes, except for daily specials, which is partly due to popular demand. Shockwaves would spread far and wide should the signature black cod ever be dropped from the repertoire; the combination of its moist, flaky flesh and the sweet, fruity flavour of the accompanying miso is as much of a hit as ever, judging from the latest round of reports. Other palate-pampering dishes have included yellowtail sashimi with garlicky marinade and slivers of jalapeño peppers, and tempura of pumpkin and courgette with a fermented bean curd dipping sauce; among non-Japanese offerings, there is Peruvian-style skewered chicken. Pleasant and efficient service puts diners at their ease, which is just as well because wine prices (starting at £23) are liable to cause anxiety to some. Time limits are applied to tables: an hour and a half at lunchtime and two hours at dinner.

CHEF: Mark Edwards   PROPRIETOR: Nobuyuki Matsuhisa   OPEN: Mon to Fri L 12 to 2.15, Sat and Sun 12.30 to 2.30; all week D 6 to 10.15 (11 Fri/Sat, Sun 9.30)   CLOSED: 25 Dec   MEALS: alc (main courses £13.50 to £23.50). Set L £50, Set D £70   SERVICE: 15% (optional), card slips closed   CARDS: Amex, Delta, MasterCard, Switch, Visa   DETAILS: 150 seats. Private parties: 12 main room, 14 to 40 private rooms. Vegetarian meals. No smoking area. Wheelchair access (also WC). No music. Air-conditioned   ⊖ Hyde Park Corner

Notting Hill Brasserie

NEW ENTRY   map 13

92 Kensington Park Road, W11 2PN
TEL: (020) 7229 4481   FAX: (020) 7221 1246
EMAIL: enquiries@nottinghillbrasserie.com

COOKING 3
MODERN EUROPEAN
£32–£64

Live jazz in the piano bar adds a touch of 'cool' to this 'really stunning' restaurant converted from three period town houses. 'Brasserie' underplays the 'very swish, dramatically lit' interior: three serene rooms with intricately corniced ceilings, floral displays and huge African artefacts. Decorative flourishes also find their way onto the plate. 'Buttery' butternut squash soup and a 'fine concoction' of scallops with herb gnocchi have opened proceedings impressively, while main courses have included wild sea bass atop tomato couscous with shellfish dressing, and roast loin of lamb with spring vegetables and globe artichoke purée. To finish, poached fig with a bay-leaf brûlée has been perfectly executed. Well-informed staff earn 'full marks', and the wine list divides equally between France and the rest of the world; vin de pays is £14.

CHEF: Mark Jankel   PROPRIETOR: Restaurant Associates Ltd   OPEN: Mon to Sat 12 to 3.30, 7 to 11 CLOSED: 25 and 26 Dec   MEALS: alc D (main courses £16 to £19.50). Set L £14.50 (2 courses) to £18.50 SERVICE: 12.5% (optional), card slips closed   CARDS: Amex, Delta, MasterCard, Switch, Visa   DETAILS: 110 seats. Private parties: 12 main room, 4 to 44 private rooms. Vegetarian meals. Wheelchair access (not WC). Music. Air-conditioned   ⊖ Notting Hill Gate

Noura Brasserie

map 13

16 Hobart Place, SW1W 0HH
TEL: (020) 7235 9444   FAX: (020) 7235 9244
WEBSITE: www.noura-brasseries.co.uk

COOKING 4
LEBANESE
£30–£66

Within walking distance of Victoria Station and Buckingham Palace, this is a suitably elegant, marble-floored restaurant with high levels of atmosphere and smartly groomed staff. New chef Badih Asmar cooks to a well-tried Lebanese menu. To start, pick your favourites from the long list of attractively presented meze, ranging from rustic foul medames and 'racy' sawdat djaj (flambé chicken livers) to kibbey nayeh (lamb tartare with cracked wheat) and batrakh (grey mullet roe). Main courses revolve around hefty doses of grilled animal protein, from lamb cutlets and quail to good-looking red mullet, while desserts rely heavily on exotic ice creams and sweet pastries. The wine list has some interesting offerings, although the cheapest bottle is house Saumur Blanc at £18.

CHEF: Badih Asmar   PROPRIETOR: Bou-Antoun Nader   OPEN: all week 11.30 to 11.45   MEALS: alc (main courses £9 to £18). Set L £14 (2 courses), Set D £23 to £31 (all min 2). Bar menu available   SERVICE: not inc   CARDS: Amex, Delta, Diners, MasterCard, Switch, Visa   DETAILS: 125 seats. Private parties: 125 main room. Vegetarian meals. Wheelchair access (also WC). Music. Air-conditioned   ⊖ Victoria £5

Novelli in the City   NEW ENTRY   map 13

London Capital Club, 15 Abchurch Lane, EC4N 7BW   COOKING 2
TEL: (020) 7717 0088   FAX: (020) 7717 0099   MODERN EUROPEAN
WEBSITE: www.londoncapitalclub.com   £32–£76

A restaurant in a private members' club, a few steps down a narrow alleyway near Bank tube station, is the setting for the latest venture from Jean-Christophe Novelli (see also Auberge du Lac, Welwyn Garden City). The London Capital Club (established 1915) is convenient for City slickers, but note lunchtime is for members only. The basement dining room has dark wooden panelling, a bare wooden floor, and caricatures of famous faces providing light relief.

An inspector's meal did not encourage an early return, although highlights were a pleasantly textured flan of steamed spinach, sliced tomatoes and vanilla-flavoured cream sauce, and another starter of roast scallops and black pudding, served on herb mash with smears of horseradish and balsamic sauces. Chorizo has made an appearance with fillet of sea bass (much to the surprise of the non-meat eating recipient), and to finish, expect a competent rendition of tarte Tatin, and sticky toffee pudding that lives up to its name. The main wine list is what you'd expect at a City club: it's geared up to serve Burgundy and claret, although a short, separate list takes a more global approach. Prices start at £16.50.

CHEF: Jean-Christophe Novelli   PROPRIETOR: Dieter Klosterman   OPEN: Mon to Fri 12 to 2.30 (members only), 5.30 to 9   CLOSED: 24 Dec to 2 Jan, bank hols   MEALS: alc (main courses £14.50 to £25). Set L and D £16.25 (2 courses) to £18.50   SERVICE: not inc, card slips closed   CARDS: Amex, Delta, Diners, MasterCard, Switch, Visa   DETAILS: 50 seats. Private parties: 50 main room, 10 to 150 private rooms. Vegetarian meals. No-smoking area. Music. Air-conditioned   ⊖ Bank £5

No. 6 George Street ✸✗ £   map 15

6 George Street, W1U 3QX   COOKING 2
TEL: (020) 7935 1910   FAX: (020) 7935 6036   MODERN BRITISH
                                                                £31–£53

Just off Marylebone High Street, No. 6 is a quality food store, shelves lined with loaves, hams, salamis, cheeses and preserves, arranged with appealing rustic simplicity. It doubles as a breakfast-to-teatime eatery, with a few simple, dark wooden tables and chairs crammed in to the compact space. Old-fashioned simplicity prevails in the kitchen, with lunch dishes ranging from straightforward assemblies, such as Serrano ham with balsamic figs and buffalo mozzarella, to classic home cooking like grilled lamb cutlets with roast new potatoes and an aubergine and mint salad, or an 'excellent' fish pie – 'big on fish and light on spuds'. To finish, there might be chocolate brownies with vanilla ice cream, and there's a modest wine selection from £12.50, plus a few beers and juices.

CHEF: Emma Miller   PROPRIETORS: the Miller family   OPEN: Mon to Fri L 12 to 3   CLOSED: bank hols, 2 weeks Aug   MEALS: alc L (main courses £10.50 to £16.50)   SERVICE: not inc   CARDS: MasterCard, Switch, Visa   DETAILS: 32 seats. Private parties: 32 main room. Vegetarian meals. Children's helpings. No smoking. No music. Air-conditioned   ⊖ Bond Street

Numidie £   `NEW ENTRY`   map 12

48 Westow Hill, SE19 1RX
TEL: (020) 8766 6166
WEBSITE: www.numidie.co.uk

COOKING 2
NORTH AFRICAN
£23–£44

'Walking right past would be a big mistake'. The looks and setting – opposite Woolworths in an 'unprepossessing' suburb near Crystal Palace Park – may not catch the eye, but this restaurant is worth a detour. Numidie has its own clear identity, avoids clichés, and has a relatively simple, if static, menu, supplemented by a few daily specials. Expect confident, enjoyable cooking. Although the theme is North African, there are some odd posh choices reflecting French North Africa: say, duck breast with quince purée, chicory and asparagus, or veal rib in truffle jus. The rest is a more traditional slate of couscous, tagines, merquez, and brochettes, with some good vegetarian choices like assiette mediterranéenne that takes in things like stuffed aubergine, falafel, steamed couscous, hummus and harissa sauce. House wine is £9.50.

CHEF: Serge Ismail   PROPRIETORS: Serge Ismail and Ashleigh Hope   OPEN: Sun L 12 to 4, Tue to Sun D 6 to 10.30   MEALS: alc (main courses £7.50 to £14). Set D Tue to Thurs and Sun £9.50 (2 courses)   SERVICE: not inc, card slips closed, 10% for parties of 6 or more   CARDS: Delta, MasterCard, Switch, Visa   DETAILS: 35 seats. Private parties: 10 to 30 private rooms. Vegetarian meals. Children's helpings. No-smoking area. Wheelchair access (not WC). Music. Air-conditioned   (£5)

Nyonya ⚡✳ £   `NEW ENTRY`   map 13

2A Kensington Park Road, W11 3BU
TEL: (020) 7243 1800   FAX: (020) 7243 2006
WEBSITE: www.nyonya.co.uk

COOKING 2
MALAY/CHINESE
£18–£50

Considered by some to be the mother of all fusion food ('but not as we know it today'), Nyonya cuisine is the culinary offspring of Singapore's Malay/Chinese community. This humble little restaurant is the setting for some of the 'most authentic and lively' food of its kind in town, and everything on the short menu is the result of painstaking effort. 'Hawker favourites' (street-stall food like Penang char kway teow noodles with prawns) share the billing with curries (classic beef rendang) and a few other specialities such as cashew nut prawns in a broth spiked with lemongrass. Side dishes range from chicken satay to otak-otak (an exotic fish sliced and steamed in a banana leaf), and you could finish with colourful 'kuih' pancakes. Asian beers are bolstered by a handful of wines from £13.50.

CHEFS: Mary Chong and Yeoh Teng Chye   PROPRIETOR: Nyonya Ltd   OPEN: Mon to Fri 11.30 to 2.45, 6 to 10.30, Sat and Sun 11.30 to 10.30   MEALS: alc (main courses £6.50 to £8.50). Set L £8   SERVICE: not inc   CARDS: Amex, Delta, Diners, MasterCard, Switch, Visa   DETAILS: 60 seats. Private parties: 30 main room. Vegetarian meals. No smoking. Wheelchair access (not WC). Music. Air-conditioned   ⊖ Notting Hill Gate

Odette's

map 13

130 Regents Park Road, NW1 8XL
TEL: (020) 7586 5486   FAX: (020) 7722 5388
EMAIL: rboulert@aol.com

COOKING 3
MODERN BRITISH
£32–£74

A fixture in Primrose Hill, this old favourite still draws crowds. The nooks and crannies of its Tardis-like interior are packed closely with linen-draped tables bathed in candlelight. Dishes tend to be fairly complex creations with busy flavour interactions, as in a first-course tartlet of morels and Gruyère accompanied by a pea shoot and broad bean salad. Sound-quality spit-roast milk-fed lamb has come with vine tomatoes, feta and courgettes, or there might be a casserole of sea bass, red mullet and mussels with garlic mayonnaise, croûtons and a spicy fish broth. Round things off with bitter chocolate torte and blood orange salad, or cheeses from La Fromagerie. Service has received the thumbs-down of late. France dominates a wine list that matches an affluent clientele; just three bottles come in under £20.

CHEF: Simon Bradley   PROPRIETORS: Simon Bradley and Richard Boulert   OPEN: Tue to Sun L 12 to 2.30, all week D 7 to 11   CLOSED: bank hols, exc Christmas/New Year   MEALS: alc (main courses £14 to £25). Set L Mon to Fri £12.50 (2 courses) to £17   SERVICE: 12.5% (optional), card slips closed   CARDS: Amex, Delta, Diners, MasterCard, Switch, Visa   DETAILS: 70 seats. 12 seats outside. Private parties: 30 main room, 10 to 30 private rooms. Vegetarian meals. Children's helpings. No music   ⊖ Chalk Farm

Olivo

map 13

21 Eccleston Street, SW1W 9LX
TEL: (020) 7730 2505   FAX: (020) 7730 7906

COOKING 2
ITALIAN/SARDINIAN
£32–£59

Friendly, bustling Olivo has plenty going for it, including the Sardinian-accented Italian cooking. As well as island-influenced dishes such as carta di musica bread and cassola di pesce (Sardinian seafood stew), there are mainland flavours such as carpaccio, risotto with artichokes, plus plenty in the way of fish and seafood. Start with chargrilled stuffed baby squid with plum tomatoes and basil, then try chargrilled (yes, there's a lot of that here) marinated lamb with rosemary. Desserts include standbys such as pannacotta and tiramisù, plus sebada (deep-fried pastry shells filled with ricotta and drizzled with honey), or Sardinian cheeses. Flavours are true, but prices tend to reflect the poshness of the postcode, particularly at dinner. Wines – all Italian – include interesting bottles from Alto Adige in the north to Sicily in the south, and the Sardinian selection is well worth a look. House wines are £14.

CHEF: Marco Melis   PROPRIETOR: Mauro Sanna   OPEN: Mon to Fri 12 to 2.30, all week D 7 to 11 (10 Sun)   CLOSED: bank hols   MEALS: alc (main courses £10.50 to £15). Set L £16.50 (2 courses) to £18.50. Cover £1.50   SERVICE: not inc   CARDS: Amex, Delta, Diners, MasterCard, Switch, Visa   DETAILS: 40 seats. Vegetarian meals. Wheelchair access (not WC). No music. Air-conditioned   ⊖ Victoria

▲ One Aldwych, Axis

map 15

Aldwych, WC2B 4RH
TEL: (020) 7300 0400   FAX: (020) 7300 0401
WEBSITE: www.onealdwych.com

COOKING 4
MODERN EUROPEAN
£35–£72

The One Aldwych hotel enjoys a commanding position, looking southwards over

Waterloo Bridge and the Thames. Axis restaurant, however, is in the basement. It's a striking venue nonetheless, 'a dramatic use of subterranean space' with a large cityscape mural that puts you back on the pavement, so to speak. An appealing, ambitious and eclectic repertoire of modern European dishes, light and well executed, sits well in the smart, cosmopolitan surroundings. Start with crispy duck noodle salad or sweetcorn vichyssoise with poached lobster, and move on to hay-baked leg of lamb, seared lemongrass tuna with artichokes and broccoli, or rump of venison with fondant potato, butternut chicken and red wine and pear chutney. Simpler options from the grill include snapper, steak and corn-fed chicken with various permutations of sauces and vegetables. Puddings are no less accomplished and range from banana profiteroles with chocolate and caramel sauce to hot apple and almond cake with vanilla ice cream and apricot sauce. An international wine list starts at £16.50 and is grouped into 'France' and the 'New World'; eight bottles come in under £20.

Indigo, the hotel's other restaurant, offers breakfast, brunch options from pumpkin and Brie tart to burgers and eggs Benedict, plus a full bistro-style lunch and dinner menu.

CHEF: Mark Gregory   PROPRIETOR: Gordon Campbell Gray   OPEN: Mon to Fri L 12 to 2.45, Mon to Sat D 5.45 to 10.30 (11.30 Sat)   CLOSED: 23 Dec to 6 Jan, bank hols   MEALS: alc (main courses £13 to £22). Set L £16.75 (2 courses) to £19.75, Set D 5.45 to 7.15 and 10 to 10.30/11.30 £16.75 to £19.75   SERVICE: 12.5% (optional), card slips closed   CARDS: Amex, Delta, Diners, MasterCard, Switch, Visa   DETAILS: 120 seats. Private parties: 120 main room. Vegetarian meals. Children's helpings. Wheelchair access (also WC). Music. Air-conditioned   ACCOMMODATION: 105 rooms, all with bath/shower. TV. Phone. Room only £179 to £965. Rooms for disabled. Baby facilities. Swimming pool   ⊖ Covent Garden

1 Lombard Street ▼   map 13

1 Lombard Street, EC3V 9AA   COOKING 6
TEL: (020) 7929 6611   FAX: (020) 7929 6622   MODERN EUROPEAN
WEBSITE: www.1lombardstreet.com   £63–£94

There was once a bank at this prestigious address deep in the financial heart of the City. In keeping with tradition, numerous deals are forged in the dining room to this day by a clientele of brokers and bankers. Walk past the informal bar and brasserie to reach the more serious restaurant – a spacious, high-ceilinged room in sober shades of coffee and chocolate, with a replica of Titian's *Rape of Europa* hung on one wall. Service from formally attired young men is discreet and professional, and while the brasserie offers an easy-going, well-priced menu encompassing salmon fishcakes and bangers and mash, the restaurant, under Herbert Berger's accomplished command, is a culinary big hitter.

Berger's classical pedigree ensures that technique and timing are absolutely precise, yet he is not above giving well-known dishes an unexpected twist. Carpaccio of tuna, for example, comes with black radish and a ginger and lime vinaigrette, while roast lamb is assigned parsnip purée and black truffles, plus a crispy potato and quince galette and caramelised foie gras. An inspector was struck by the careful balance of luxury and restraint, first in a superbly made timbale of crab with langoustines, tempered by avocado sorbet, then in mignon of veal with a paprika and crème fraîche sauce – 'a clever take on beef goulash' – given a seductive undertone by the paprika and served with 'faultless companions' of braised baby onions and girolles. A first-rate feuillantine of caramelised Granny Smiths was characterised by deft pastrywork and layered with a 'ravishing' Guinness ice cream that added an extra dimension of flavour and texture. The wine list covers the globe with assurance and includes plenty of blue-chip bottles, especially the older vintages from the 'Lombard vault'. Yet there is fair choice under £20 for non-power diners, and prices are not remarkable for London.

CHEF: Herbert Berger   PROPRIETOR: Jessen & Co   OPEN: Mon to Fri restaurant 12 to 3, 6 to 10, brasserie 12 to 10   CLOSED: bank hols   MEALS: alc (main courses £28.50 to £29.50). Set L £34 (2 courses) to £39   SERVICE: 12.5% (optional)   CARDS: Amex, Delta, Diners, MasterCard, Switch, Visa   DETAILS: 150 seats. Private parties: 150 main room, 5 to 40 private rooms. Wheelchair access (also WC). Music. Air-conditioned   ⊖ Bank

▲ One-O-One
map 14

Sheraton Park Tower Hotel, 101 Knightsbridge,
SW1X 7RN
TEL: (020) 7290 7101
EMAIL: oneoone@luxurycollection.com

COOKING 4
SEAFOOD
£45–£98

This ambitious seafood restaurant, which occupies prime pavement space on the famous shopping street, is part of the 1960s honeycomb-effect Sheraton Park Tower, where cavernous windows flood the ground floor dining room with natural light. The place makes its intentions clear with turquoise furnishings and conspicuous fish motifs, and excellent and attentive service helps to carry them out. Fine smoked salmon is sliced table-side from a handsome slab, while the chef's signature sea bass is presented theatrically and broken free of its heavy salt cocoon. The assembled luxuries are generally well sourced. Turbot and scallops have impressed with their freshness, the latter paired with wild mushroom fricassée, truffle and foie gras, the former beautifully timed and served with a creamy sauce. That skills extend beyond fish was apparent from a perfect chocolate fondant and passion-fruit sorbet that was the real star of a recent inspection meal – or try roast mango with creamy cardamom rice pudding. The wine list, mainly French with some nods abroad, is substantial and pricey in equal measure; the cheapest bottle listed is £24.

CHEF: Pascal Proyart   PROPRIETOR: Starwood Hotels and Resorts   OPEN: all week 12 to 3, 7 to 10.30   MEALS: alc (main courses £22 to £28). Set L £21 (2 courses) to £25, Set D 7 to 9.30 £50 (whole table only)   SERVICE: not inc   CARDS: Amex, Delta, Diners, MasterCard, Switch, Visa   DETAILS: 60 seats. 100 seats outside. Private parties: 100 main room. Children's helpings. No-smoking area. Wheelchair access (also WC). Music. Air-conditioned   ACCOMMODATION: 280 rooms, all with bath/shower. TV. Phone. Room only £255 to £3,000. Rooms for disabled. Baby facilities   ⊖ Knightsbridge

Original Tagines 🍲
map 15

7A Dorset Street, W1U 6QN
TEL/FAX: (020) 7935 1545
WEBSITE: www.originaltagines.com

COOKING 2
MOROCCAN
£16–£35

In sunshine, the open double-doors, tiled floor, mosaic tables and wrought-iron chairs make the Moroccan feel especially strong, but year-round the food here fragrantly recalls North Africa. Start with a crisp chicken b'stilla, kidneys with a mustard sauce, or something as light as broad bean salad. Then grills and couscous should not be ignored. Nor should the eponymous tagines. Remove the conical lid: instant aroma impact – lamb, perhaps, flavoured by its black pepper sauce, with sweet prunes and toasted almonds. Cracked wheat flavoured with tomato and a simple undressed salad (just chopped tomatoes, cucumber and red pepper) are uncomplicated partners. Finish with pastries and Moroccan coffee. Service is relaxed and efficient. House French is £10.50 (£2.85 a glass), and the multinational list includes a dozen Moroccan wines.

CHEF: Getin Orgun   PROPRIETOR: Kenan Duran   OPEN: Mon to Fri L 12 to 3, Mon to Sat D 6 to 11   MEALS: alc (main courses £9 to £12). Set L £7.50 (2 courses) to £9.50   SERVICE: not inc   CARDS: Amex, Delta, Diners, MasterCard, Switch, Visa   DETAILS: 36 seats. 30 seats outside. Private parties: 40 main room. Music   ⊖ Baker Street

Orrery 🍷

map 15

55–57 Marylebone High Street, W1M 3AE
TEL: (020) 7616 8000   FAX: (020) 7616 8080
WEBSITE: www.orrery.co.uk

COOKING 6
FRENCH
£38–£119

The Marylebone restaurant of the Conran galaxy is a long, narrow first-floor room full of clean lines, fronted by an orrery – a mechanical model of the solar system. Banquette seating runs down one side, divided into sections by wooden baffles, with angled mirrors giving diners facing the wall a view of the goings-on. The France-orientated carte opens with interesting combinations, such as crab ravioli with étuvée leek and grapefruit; partridge mousseline with toasted pearl barley, turnip velouté and consommé; frogs' legs with langoustine; and foie gras with marinated beetroot. Move on to roast sea bass en marmite with fennel, crayfish and crushed potatoes, or perhaps an assiette of Pyrenean suckling lamb with baby artichoke and onion soubise. Beef fillet may be presented with old-school creamed spinach and a bone-marrow beignet. A crisp-topped raspberry soufflé 'packed with fruit flavour' might come topped with a dollop of vanilla ice cream, and cheese is taken seriously, with guidance offered by formal but friendly staff. A breathtaking collection of wines digs deep in all French regions and includes rarely seen producers such as F Cotat in Sancerre and Peyre Rose in the Languedoc. Italy, Australia and California are strongest of the other countries. Barring the £14 house, very little is available under £25, although 16 classy options come by the glass.

CHEF: André Garrett   PROPRIETOR: Conran Restaurants   OPEN: all week 12 to 3 (2.30 Sun), 7 to 11 (10.30 Sun)   CLOSED: 25 and 25 Dec, 1 Jan, Good Fri   MEALS: alc (main courses £16.50 to £30). Set L £23.50 to £85 (inc wine), Set D Mon to Sat £55 to £85 (inc wine), Set D Sun £30 to £85 (inc wine). Bar menu available   SERVICE: 12.5% (optional), card slips closed   CARDS: Amex, Delta, Diners, MasterCard, Switch, Visa   DETAILS: 80 seats. Private parties: 80 main room. Vegetarian meals. No pipes. Wheelchair access (also WC). No music   ⊖ Baker Street, Regent's Park

Osia

map 15

11 Haymarket, SW1Y 4BP
TEL: (020) 7976 1313   FAX: (020) 7976 1919
WEBSITE: www.osiarestaurant.com

COOKING 2
CONTEMPORARY AUSTRALIAN
£30–£72

Osia's ground-floor dining room, 'swish, spacious and quite chic' with linen-covered chairs, olive banquettes and cosy alcoves, feels rather crepuscular at night, though cheery staff liven the atmosphere. But there is excitement in a high-octane fusion menu involving exotic ingredients drawn from antipodean flora. Sea bass ceviche with pineapple vinaigrette is straightforward, and king prawns with wasabi mayonnaise a take on prawn cocktail, but a big, tender beef fillet is partnered by Moreton Bay bugs (squat lobsters from Queensland), and dorrigo-herbed rack of lamb with wilted pea shoots comes with mashed kumara (a New Zealand sweet potato). One reporter finished with a 'divine' chocolate soup, but found the accompanying black pepper ice cream unconvincing. The short, rather modest wine list is quite highly priced, though it starts at £18.

CHEF: Koenrad Inghelram   PROPRIETORS: Raymond De Fazio and Scott Webster   OPEN: Mon to Fri L 12 to 3, Mon to Sat D 5.30 to 11   CLOSED: 25 and 26 Dec, 1 Jan, bank hols   MEALS: alc (main courses £15 to £19). Set L £15 to £23, Set D 5.30 to 7 £19 (2 courses) to £23. Bar menu available   SERVICE: 12.5% (optional), card slips closed   CARDS: Amex, MasterCard, Visa   DETAILS: 72 seats. Private parties: 80 main room. Vegetarian meals. Children's helpings. Wheelchair access (also WC). Music. No mobile phones. Air-conditioned   ⊖ Piccadilly

Oxo Tower ▮

map 13

Oxo Tower Wharf, Barge House Street, SE1 9PH
TEL: (020) 7803 3888   FAX: (020) 7803 3838
WEBSITE: www.harveynichols.co.uk

NEW CHEF
MODERN BRITISH
£42–£96

The Oxo Tower (incorporating brasserie as well as restaurant) rises amid the South Bank's concrete wasteland. Once lifted to the eighth floor and seated (by a window if you're lucky), the vista is as good as you'll find in London. The restaurant's undressed tables, armless chairs, hardwood floors and blue neon backlighting recall a nightclub chill-out room. A new chef arrived in the summer of 2004. His menus might start with sea trout, fromage blanc, apple and yuzu jelly, or chicken terrine with cos lettuce and anchovy cream, and move on to main courses like roast loin of rabbit, chorizo and summer cassoulet. Finish with coconut rice pudding with a mango sorbet, or there's a wide selection of Anglo-Irish cheeses. As for wines, the 40-strong house selection interleaves names like Pieropan (Italy) and Torbreck (Australia) with £13.50 house wine and top white burgundy, so what could the main list add? Plenty – right up to four Pétrus vintages at thousands apiece (though the New World looks thinnish outside Australia). A dozen table wines come by the glass, plus loads of sherries, ports, Madeira and other sweeties.

CHEF: Jeremy Bloor   PROPRIETOR: Harvey Nichols   OPEN: all week 12 to 3, 6 to 11.30   CLOSED: 25 and 26 Dec, Easter   MEALS: alc D (main courses £16 to £31). Set L £28.50   SERVICE: 12.5%, card slips closed   CARDS: Amex, Delta, Diners, MasterCard, Switch, Visa   DETAILS: 120 seats. 80 seats outside. Private parties: 120 main room. Vegetarian meals. Wheelchair access (also WC). No music. Air-conditioned   ⊖ Blackfriars/Waterloo

Painted Heron

NEW ENTRY   map 13

112 Cheyne Walk, SW10 0DJ
TEL: (020) 7351 5232   FAX: (020) 7351 5313
WEBSITE: www.thepaintedheron.com

COOKING 3
MODERN INDIAN
£39–£61

This is 'a curry house for the twenty-first century' opposite the houseboats near Battersea Bridge, eschewing traditional design features in favour of blond wood floors and modern artwork. And the daily menu abandons 'authentic' dish names for plain English (rock oyster with mini lamb kebabs; tandoori veal rack with masala mash and curry sauce). Stylish starters include a cake of spiced yoghurt, red onions and aubergines concealing a whole cherry tomato. Mains enjoy judicious spicing and fresh sauces: star turns have included cod in Bengal mustard and coconut curry, and roast duck breast in coriander and mint chutney with coconut, a sauce of 'some complexity'. Westernised desserts aren't in the same league. The short wine list's prices are 'not ruinous'; house French is £13.50. A second branch is at 205–209 Kennington Lane, SE11, tel: (020) 7793 8313.

CHEF: Yogesh Datta   PROPRIETOR: Charles Hill   OPEN: Sun to Fri L 12.30 to 2.45, all week D 7 to 10.45
CLOSED: 25 Dec   MEALS: alc (main courses £11.50 to £18). Set L (1-plate meals) £9 to £12   SERVICE:
12.5% (optional), card slips closed   CARDS: Amex, Delta, MasterCard, Switch, Visa   DETAILS: 70 seats.
25 seats outside. Private parties: 30 main room. Vegetarian meals. Children's helpings. No-smoking area.
Wheelchair access (not WC). No music. Air-conditioned   ⊖ Gloucester Road

Parsee ⅄*

map 12

34 Highgate Hill, N19 5NL	COOKING 1
TEL: (020) 7272 9091 FAX: (020) 7687 1139	PARSEE
WEBSITE: www.theparsee.com	£18–£57

This informal relative of Café Spice Namaste (see entry) is devoted to the cooking of
India's Zoroastrian Parsees. Eggs and potatoes are prominent, and much is made of classic
'dhaansaak' – served in all its glory with lamb meatballs and a star-anise-flavoured pilau.
The kitchen also produces specialities like chargrilled kingfish marinated in a 'green
chutney', and papeta nu saak (potatoes tossed with mustard seeds and other spices). Service
has been 'lacklustre' of late. Rice is well handled, and stuffed coconut pancakes are a
creditable dessert. Around 20 decent wines are tailored to the food; house South African is
£12.90.

CHEF: Cyrus Todiwala   PROPRIETOR: The Parsee Ltd   OPEN: Mon to Fri L 12 to 3, Mon to Sat D 6 to 10.45
CLOSED: Christmas and New Year, bank hols   MEALS: alc (main courses L £4.99, D £9 to £13.50). Set L (2
courses) £5.50 to £6.99, Set D £20 (2 courses) to £30   SERVICE: 10% (optional), card slips closed   CARDS:
Amex, Delta, Diners, MasterCard, Switch, Visa   DETAILS: 50 seats. Private parties: 35 main room, 18 to 20
private rooms. Vegetarian meals. Children's helpings. No smoking in 1 dining room. Wheelchair access
(not WC). Music. Air-conditioned   ⊖ Archway   (£5)

Passione

map 15

10 Charlotte Street, W1T 2LT	COOKING 4
TEL: (020) 7636 2833 FAX: (020) 7636 2889	MODERN ITALIAN
WEBSITE: www.passione.co.uk	£42–£73

In a street of wall-to-wall restaurants, one can easily walk right past Passione, despite the
'orange paint-job'. It has carved out a well-defined niche in the 'peasant cuisine bracket'
with food that is simple, rustic even, its focus somewhere in southern Italy, Geraldo
Contaldo's native region. Pasta and risotto dishes – all of which can be sized as starters or
mains – are a strong suit: agnolini of mixed game with a truffle sauce, for example, which
was the pick of an inspection meal. King prawns are cooked with garlic, olive oil, white
wine and chilli and served with deep-fried courgettes, and there are some interesting
combinations, such as a carpaccio of wild sea bass partnered with Sicilian blood oranges.
Gelato passione (limoncello and wild strawberry ice cream) and pears cooked in red wine
with vanilla ice cream are highly commendable, as is the espresso: 'it gets my vote for best
coffee outside Naples'. The all-Italian list opens with house wine at £13.50 and covers
most regions.

CHEFS: Gennaro Contaldo and Margherita Capuozzo   PROPRIETORS: Gennaro Contaldo, Gennaro d'Urso
and Liz Przybylski   OPEN: Mon to Fri L 12.30 to 2.15, Mon to Sat D 7 to 10.15   MEALS: alc (main courses
£13.50 to £22.50)   SERVICE: 12.5% (optional), card slips closed   CARDS: Amex, Delta, Diners,
MasterCard, Switch, Visa   DETAILS: 40 seats. 6 seats outside. Private parties: 12 main room, 10 to 16
private rooms. Vegetarian meals. No music   ⊖ Goodge Street

Patterson's

| NEW ENTRY | map 15 |

4 Mill Street, W1S 2AX

TEL: (020) 7499 1308   FAX: (020) 7491 2122

WEBSITE: www.pattersonsrestaurant.com

COOKING 4

MODERN FRENCH

£33–£63

The glass-fronted restaurant is an impressive newcomer to the Mayfair scene; family-run restaurants are unusual in this part of town, but Raymond Patterson, a former head chef at the Garrick Club works with his wife, son and daughters in this venture. The décor is minimalist 'in the safest possible way', with comfort provided by soft, high-backed leather chairs, and 'sumptuously thick' linen cloths on the tables. The food is contemporary without being overly fashionable, not only mixing the tried and true but also willing to give unusual combinations a whirl: a starter of ravioli of ham hock and a duck egg in a ham consommé, for example, or a main-course monkfish tail stuffed with braised oxtail and served with black and white cannelloni. Roast sea bass might be served with salsa verde and baby artichokes, and saddle of rabbit has come with the leg meat coated in a 'sticky, sweet, almost candied' reduction from the accompanying civet. Presentation of dishes is universally impressive. Finish with a straight-up apple Tatin, or cheeses from La Fromagerie. A short, France-dominated wine list offers little under £20. Six house wines are £13.50 to £23.

CHEF: Raymond Patterson   PROPRIETORS: Raymond and Thomas Patterson   OPEN: Mon to Fri L 12 to 2.30, Mon to Sat D 6 to 10.30   CLOSED: bank hols   MEALS: alc (main courses £14 to £17). Set L £15 (2 courses) to £20   SERVICE: 12.5% (optional)   CARDS: Amex, Delta, MasterCard, Switch, Visa   DETAILS: 100 seats. Private parties: 70 main room, 30 private room. Vegetarian meals. Children's helpings. No-smoking area. Music. Air-conditioned   ⊖ Oxford Circus £5

▲ Pearl £✳

map 13

252 High Holborn, WC1V 7EN

TEL: (020) 7829 7000   FAX: (020) 7829 9889

WEBSITE: www.pearl-restaurant.com

COOKING 3

MODERN FRENCH

£44–£78

The old Pearl Assurance building is now the Chancery Court Hotel, and 'whatever you do, don't forget to walk around the courtyard and the inside of this national treasure'. Its enormous, handsome main dining room has had a makeover by the team that designed Nobu – 'if this room were a man, it would be Brad Pitt in *Troy*' – and has been relaunched as Pearl under Jun Tanaka, head chef in its preceding incarnation as QC.

The menu starts strongly with a pairing of foie gras and beetroot Tatin achieving 'lovely balance', or feuilleté of Anjou quail, another success. Main-course veal loin with candied lemon and osso bucco jus exemplifies the aesthetic presentation here. Puddings could include banana Tatin with balsamic vinegar and peanut caramel ice cream. It was early days when we inspected, which might explain some of the inconsistencies experienced – a poor piece of sea bass, for example – so more reports, please. An extensive wine list with mark-ups to frighten the horses starts from £18, with some 50 by the glass.

CHEF: Jun Tanaka   PROPRIETOR: Hotel Property Investors   OPEN: Mon to Fri L 12 to 2.30, Mon to Sat D 6 to 10   CLOSED: bank hols   MEALS: Set L and D 6 to 7 £21.50 (2 courses) to £24.50, Set D £42.50   SERVICE: 12.5% (optional), card slips closed   CARDS: Amex, Delta, Diners, MasterCard, Switch, Visa   DETAILS: 70 seats. Private parties: 10 main room, 10 private room. Vegetarian meals. No smoking. Wheelchair access (also WC). Occasional music. No mobile phones. Air-conditioned   ACCOMMODATION: 356 rooms, all with bath/shower. TV. Phone. Room only £195 to £645. Rooms for disabled. Baby facilities   ⊖ Holborn

Le Petit Max

NEW ENTRY   map 12

Riverside Plaza, Chatfield Road, SW11 3SE
TEL: (020) 7223 0999   FAX: (020) 7223 2558

COOKING **2**
FRENCH
£30–£62

Max Renzland remains vigorously Francophile. His latest location, in a riverside development on the Thames Path, has dark polished oak floors, undressed tables and an old map of Paris etched on the windows. It's a 'jolly good little neighbourhood restaurant', serving mostly 'unfussed' bistro food of yore. Ingredients are impeccably sourced, timing is spot-on, and flavours are upfront: the speciality shoulder of Pyrenean milk-fed lamb navarin with Norfolk asparagus and Charlotte potatoes (for two) typifies the style. Elsewhere, there might be ballottine of foie gras, and tronçon of 'snow-white' Cornish turbot, girolles and beurre blanc, then oozingly rich pot au chocolate. Max is in evidence as 'patron', and staff are attentive. Respected French names dominate the wine list; vin de pays is £12.50.

CHEF/PROPRIETOR: Max Renzland   OPEN: all week L 12.15 to 2.30, Mon to Sat D 7 to 10.30   MEALS: alc (main courses £8.50 to £22). Set L Mon to Fri £14.50 (2 courses) to £18.50, Set D £18.50   SERVICE: 12.5% (optional)   CARDS: Delta, MasterCard, Switch, Visa   DETAILS: 120 seats. 40 seats outside. Private parties: 50 main room. Wheelchair access (also WC). Occasional music. Air-conditioned

Pétrus ▮

NEW ENTRY   map 14

The Berkeley, Wilton Place, Knightsbridge, SW1X 7RL
TEL: 020 7235 1200   FAX: 020 7235 1266
WEBSITE: www.marcuswareing.com

COOKING **7**
MODERN FRENCH
£47–£133

In 2003 Pétrus drew stumps in St James's Street and moved into the Berkeley Hotel, just off Knightsbridge. Off the hotel's marble foyer is a low-lit, spacious dining room in deepest claret (bien sûr!), with white metal window shutters like giant interlinked chains. Sink into ample, claret-coloured, leather-upholstered chairs with 'expensively clad people from all over the world'.

Executive chef Marcus Wareing, via head chef Darren Velvick, brings dazzling polish to some of the richest – and most richly detailed – cooking in the capital, and the menu proudly proclaims the provenance of fine ingredients. Ravioli of Ardennes frogs' legs offers first-rate pasta with a pleasingly chewy, tasty filling, its flavours deepened with garlic, lemon, foie gras and a sauce of port and cream. Lobster 'Arnold Bennett' is a smoked haddock omelette supplemented with tender Scottish lobster, plus intense lobster bisque added at the table. Main courses up the ante again. Anjou pigeon is poached and then sautéed, set on a croûton of truffled liver, the leg served confit with garlic, accompanied by red wine shallots and a magnificent sauce of the cooking juices. Meanwhile red mullet is sautéed and served on beetroot carpaccio with cauliflower beignets, plus scallop and anchovy vinaigrette. Fine French cheeses from a trolley are a prelude to desserts like gâteau opéra (layers of coffee and dark chocolate, served with 'wicked' espresso ice cream and caramelised hazelnuts). Appetisers, pre-desserts and petits fours to beat the band (don't miss the salted caramel or the honeycomb laced with chocolate), not to mention 'friendly and civil' service – it all adds up to a formidable addition to London's fine dining.

In a restaurant named after the world's most expensive wine (the 1994 is available at £89 a 125ml glass), a list of dazzling, irreproachable quality is not surprising, even if most bottles are beyond the wallets of ordinary mortals. Indeed, there is a sense of charge-what-you-dare pricing of the finest bottles from all over France and from Italy, Australia and California. So the surprise is a 'sommelier's selection' of 24 extremely drinkable bottles under £20 that will muzzle party-poopers, plus some distinctly affordable options by the glass.

CHEF: Darren Velvick   PROPRIETOR: Marcus Wareing   OPEN: Mon to Fri L 12 to 2.30, Mon to Sat D 6 to 11   CLOSED: 2 weeks at Christmas   MEALS: Set L £30, Set D £60 to £70   SERVICE: not inc   CARDS: Amex, Delta, Diners, MasterCard, Switch, Visa   DETAILS: 68 seats. Private parties: 70 main room, 8 to 12 private rooms. Vegetarian meals. Children's helpings. No pipes/cigars. No music. Air-conditioned

Philpott's Mezzaluna

map 13

424 Finchley Road, NW2 2HY
TEL: (020) 7794 0455   FAX: (020) 7794 0452
WEBSITE: www.philpotts-mezzaluna.com

COOKING 3
ITALIAN
£28–£50

This shop-front restaurant, with its floor-to-ceiling windows offering views of the 'bonhomie' within, has been in the capable hands of Messrs Philpott and Ross since the turn of the millennium, and continues to shows its mettle on the plate, with robust, classic bourgeois Italian food. Seasonal ideas get a look-in; on a hot summer evening a bowl of buttered samphire was much enjoyed by one reporter. The menu is prix-fixe for two, three or four courses, which might take in the likes of smoked aubergine and truffled Pecorino bruschetta, a simple spaghetti with tomato and basil, and stinco (shank) of lamb with crushed artichokes, rosemary and Frascati. Desserts, say some, are the best part of the meal and might include berry brûlée or panettone bread and butter budino. It's all very good value for money. A mostly Italian wine list features some good producers at benevolent prices.

CHEF: David Philpott   PROPRIETORS: David Philpott and Alex Ross   OPEN: Tue to Fri and Sun L 12 to 2.30 (3 Sun), Tue to Sun D 7 to 11   CLOSED: 25 and 26 Dec, 1 Jan, bank hols   MEALS: Set L £15 (2 courses) to £19, Set D £10 (1 course) to £23 (4 courses)   SERVICE: not inc, 12.5% for parties of 6 or more, card slips closed   CARDS: Amex, MasterCard, Switch, Visa   DETAILS: 60 seats. 9 seats outside. Private parties: 60 main room. Vegetarian meals. Children's helpings. Wheelchair access (not WC). No music. Air-conditioned (£5)

Phoenix

map 12

162–164 Lower Richmond Road, SW15 1LY
TEL: (020) 8780 3131   FAX: (020) 8780 1114
EMAIL: phoenix@sonnys.co.uk

COOKING 3
ITALIAN/MODERN EUROPEAN
£27–£52

Well back from the main road, this place hides its light behind some bushes and its entrance in a side road. Once found, it proves to be a smart, relaxed and friendly neighbourhood restaurant with strong Italian influences in both menu and wine list. Starters like scallops and endive salad with a beetroot dressing, and mains of perfectly cooked monkfish rolled in prosciutto with a daube of aubergine, or taleggio-stuffed chicken breast on truffled linguini, exemplify the robust approach, as does an intense almond ice with warm chocolate cake. Details like fine Italian breads and top-class coffee reinforce the favourable impression. Wines are not exclusively Italian; a wide range by the glass, house bottles at £10.95 and fair pricing at all levels allow for experiment.

CHEF: Heikki Purhonen   PROPRIETORS: Rebecca Mascarenhas and James Harris   OPEN: all week 12.30 to 2.30 (3 Sun), 7 to 11 (11.30 Fri and Sat, 10 Sun)   CLOSED: bank hols   MEALS: alc (main courses £11.50 to

£15). Set L £13.50 (2 courses) to £15.50, Set L Sun £19.50, Set D Sun to Thur £15.50 (2 courses) to £17.50
SERVICE: 12.5% (optional), card slips closed   CARDS: Amex, Delta, Diners, MasterCard, Switch, Visa
DETAILS: 100 seats. 50 seats outside. Private parties: 100 main room, 24 to 40 private rooms. Vegetarian
meals. Children's helpings. No smoking in 1 dining room. Wheelchair access (also WC). Music. Air-
conditioned   ⊖ Putney Bridge £5

Phoenix Palace £ map 13

3–5 Glentworth Street, NW1 5PG
TEL: (020) 7486 3515   FAX: (020) 7486 3401

COOKING 2
CHINESE
£25–£83

The location – underneath a block of flats not far from Baker Street tube station – may
seem unlikely, but this spacious Chinese restaurant, with silk flower displays and a mini-
waterfall has a hefty 200-dish menu that boasts a strong showing of seafood, hotpots and
one-plate rice and noodle specialities. Reporters have been impressed by the kitchen's
light touch and its use of decent ingredients, witness pork dumplings enlivened with chilli
sauce, prawns with cashew nuts and vegetables in a fried potato basket, and ultra-fresh gai
lan (Chinese broccoli), as well as Singapore noodles. Chef's specials like sea bass roll with
ham and shiitake mushrooms broaden the repertoire, and the restaurant also puts on
seasonal feasts (look for game dishes like venison with yellow chives). House French is
£9.80.

CHEF: S.C. Lee   PROPRIETOR: Topmart Catering Ltd   OPEN: all week 12 to 11.30 (11 to 10.30 Sun)   MEALS:
alc (main courses £5.50 to £22). Set L £10 (2 courses) to £19.80, Set D £13.80 (2 courses) to £23.80
SERVICE: 12.5%   CARDS: Delta, MasterCard, Switch, Visa   DETAILS: 230 seats. 30 seats outside. Private
parties: 200 main room, 2 to 30 private rooms. Vegetarian meals. Occasional music. Air-conditioned
⊖ Baker Street

Pied-à-Terre ▌ ❧ map 15

34 Charlotte Street, W1T 2NH
TEL: (020) 7636 1178   FAX: (020) 7916 1171
WEBSITE: www.pied.a.terre.co.uk

COOKING 8
FRENCH
£44–£153

Reporters who have been to Pied-à-Terre tend to speak of the civilised, haven-like
atmosphere that has been created with the design. It is effectively a darkened, windowless
back room (although smokers are separately provided for at the front), with a muted
aubergine colour scheme, low lighting, and the odd abstract print to divert the eye.
Regulars have noted that Shane Osborn's cooking has travelled an almost imperceptible
distance back along the spectrum towards the classical end of things but without any loss of
confidence. Dishes still please mightily, look great and deliver the kind of flavour that's all
quiet power rather than upfront brashness.

Four appetisers arrive on an oblong plate, each exquisitely constructed and highly
original, and may well include the famous foie gras filo crisp. A first course of fat scallops
topped with crisscrossed asparagus gains depth from the addition of a cumin-seasoned
purée of parsnip, the sweetness of the root complementing the delicate sweetness of the
shellfish. Oysters poached in lightly Indian-spiced broth, each balanced on a soft, warm
blini, make for a starter of high comfort value, or there may be quail accompanied by
Parmesan gnocchi and red onion crisps. Main courses raise the game still further,
producing 'perfectly cooked' pigeon, with its own 'wonderful, meltingly soft and tasty'
sausage. The palm at inspection went to a main course of Gressingham duck breast of

astonishingly rounded flavour, alongside a boudin of confit and gizzards, the whole scattered with deep-fried salsify, in a gently sticky, weighty port reduction. Fish could well be pan-fried John Dory, decked out with a leek terrine, ginger cream and crab bisque.

Memorable desserts have included a parfait of lemon curd in blood orange coulis, adorned with cylinders of soft meringue and mandarin sorbet, presenting a cleansing succession of flavours; and honey-poached apricot partnered by a pistachio beignet and honey ice cream. An unusual ice cream of stout ale is the accompaniment for bittersweet chocolate tart. Sad to say, service can be a little patchy, even abrupt, considering the prices. The densely packed wine list sets out a huge range of French wines, especially Burgundy, followed by serious global coverage. Offbeat bottles such as a very good Limoux (£25) or some German reds add interest. There are bottles to please most pockets (house is £18), although prices are not cheap. A good range by the glass is complemented by a line-up (at £45) to accompany the tasting menu.

CHEF: Shane Osborn   PROPRIETORS: David Moore and Shane Osborn   OPEN: Tue to Fri L 12.15 to 2.30, Mon to Sat D 6.15 to 11   CLOSED: last week Dec, first week Jan   MEALS: Set L £21.50 (2 courses) to £110 (inc wine), Set D £45 (2 courses) to £110 (inc wine)   SERVICE: 12.5% (optional), card slips closed   CARDS: Amex, Delta, MasterCard, Switch, Visa   DETAILS: 49 seats. Private parties: 7 main room, 4 to 14 private rooms. No smoking in 1 dining room. Wheelchair access (not WC). Occasional music. Air-conditioned
⊖ Goodge Street

Plateau
NEW ENTRY   map 12

Canada Place, Canary Wharf, E14 5ER   COOKING **3**
TEL: (020) 7715 7100   FAX: (020) 7715 7110   MODERN FRENCH
WEBSITE: www.conran.com/eat   £37–£93

'A welcome addition to Canary Wharf', this latest Conran restaurant is stylish, informal, and, as one reporter put it, 'makes power-dining user-friendly and accessible'. Floor-to-ceiling windows provide a fantastic view of towering corporate monoliths. Food treatments are straightforward, typically focusing on a single main component: a 'beautifully medium-rare' breast of Barbary duck accompanied by a roll of confit with a 'lovely earthy flavour' and celeriac, or wild sea bass given an interesting twist with pistachios served with crushed potatoes. Starters have included a combination of seared scallops (not sufficiently so at inspection) with celery and cranberry sauce, or butternut squash and mascarpone ravioli. Puddings have been on form, with successes taking in rhubarb parfait with toffee, and mandarin charlotte. The extensive and well-constructed wine list offers plenty of choice, with around a dozen by the glass and a reasonable selection under £30, starting at £15.50.

CHEF: Tim Tolley   PROPRIETOR: Conran Restaurants   OPEN: all week L 12 to 3, Mon to Sat D 6 to 11 CLOSED: 25 and 26 Dec, 1 Jan   MEALS: alc (main courses £14.50 to £27). Set D £16.50 (2 courses) to £47. Bar and Grill menus available   SERVICE: 12.5% (optional), card slips closed   CARDS: Amex, Delta, Diners, MasterCard, Switch, Visa   DETAILS: 210 seats. 60 seats outside. Private parties: 24 main room, 24 to 40 private rooms. Vegetarian meals. Wheelchair access (also WC). Music. Air-conditioned   ⊖ Canary Wharf

---

The text of entries is based on unsolicited reports sent in by readers, backed up by inspections conducted anonymously. The factual details under the text are from questionnaires the Guide sends to all restaurants that feature in the book.

Le Pont de la Tour

map 13

36D Shad Thames, SE1 2YE

TEL: (020) 7403 8403   FAX: (020) 7403 0267

WEBSITE: www.conran.com

NEW CHEF

MODERN EUROPEAN

£47–£99

A restaurant making the most of its location, the Pont de la Tour is pre-eminent on the Butler's Wharf strip, with a terrace for the pleasurable experience of eating outdoors in the shadow of Tower Bridge and watching the tourist boats go by. Smartly turned-out staff extend a warm welcome. A new chef took over in 2004, but the French-inspired evening carte continues, with the trademark Conran emphasis on fresh, well-presented seafood, together with brasserie-style dishes. Expect tuna carpaccio with baby beetroot and Sevruga; sea bass with brandade, carrots and ceps; and roast veal sweetbreads with pea purée and fondant celeriac. Further vegetables and salads are extra, though possibly not needed, and desserts range from poached pear with a granita of St Emilion to caramel soufflé with matching ice cream. The lunchtime set menu offers dishes like sautéed frogs' legs, salmon with peas and broad beans, or corn-fed chicken with polenta and asparagus, followed perhaps by orange tart or cheese. Wine lists don't come much better than this one, with France, Italy and Australia standing out. But prices – always an issue – seem to have ballooned in the last year, leaving very slim pickings below £25 (house red is £26). Wines offered by the 175ml glass (from £6) are serious propositions.

CHEF: James Walker   PROPRIETOR: Conran Restaurants   OPEN: Sun to Fri L 12 to 2.45, Mon to Sat D 6 to 10.45   MEALS: alc D (main courses £18 to £26). Set L £29.50. Bar/grill menu available   SERVICE: 12.5% (optional), card slips closed   CARDS: Amex, Diners, MasterCard, Switch, Visa   DETAILS: 120 seats. 65 seats outside. Private parties: 10 to 20 private rooms. Vegetarian meals. Children's helpings. Wheelchair access (not WC). No music   ⊖ London Bridge

---

Popeseye

map 12

108 Blythe Road, W14 0HD

TEL: (020) 7610 4578

COOKING 1

STEAKS

£24–£83

'The steaks are excellent, the chips crunchy and there's a good selection of red wine to suit the food', and you can't ask much more of a neighbourhood steak house. There are no starters. In a square room with a grill in one corner, well-hung Aberdeen Angus rump steak (popeseye), sirloin and fillet are priced by weight (from 6oz to 30oz) and cooked 'absolutely as requested'. Chips arrive automatically, but you pay extra for a mixed salad. Finally – if you still have room – order cheese rather than dessert. Staff wear T-shirts, and the 'jolly decent' wine list roams from vins de pays (£11.50) to pedigree clarets. There's a second branch at 277 Upper Richmond Road, SW15, tel: (020) 8788 7733.

CHEF/PROPRIETOR: Ian Hutchison   OPEN: Mon to Sat D only 6.45 to 10.30   MEALS: alc (main courses £10 to £45.50)   SERVICE: 12.5% (optional)   CARDS: none   DETAILS: 34 seats. No pipes/cigars. Wheelchair access (not WC)   ⊖ Olympia   £5

Net prices *in the details at the end of an entry indicates that the prices given on a menu and on a bill are inclusive of VAT and service charge, and that this practice is clearly stated on menu and bill.*

Portrait Restaurant ✠✗

map 15

National Portrait Gallery, Orange Street, St Martin's
Place, WC2H 0HE
TEL: (020) 7312 2490   FAX: (020) 7925 0244
WEBSITE: www.searcys.co.uk

COOKING **3**
MODERN BRITISH
£30–£61

This stylish rooftop restaurant, 92 feet up on the Gallery's new Ondaatje Wing, is long and sleek, light and airy, with a wall of glass revealing superb views of Whitehall, Big Ben and the London Eye. Decked in dark grey with chrome and black seating and blond-wood floors, it's a buzzy, minimalist space, though its hard surfaces and bar don't diminish noise. This is primarily a lunchtime joint, so deals in light, modern, bistro-style dishes, well-presented and based around quality ingredients. Expect the likes of roast fillet of salmon with a broth of chorizo, white beans and tomato, or Goosnargh duck breast, creamed cabbage and bacon with Madeira sauce, and finish maybe with spiced chocolate fondant and hazelnut ice cream. The compact wine list offers six by glass and bottles from £14.75.

CHEF: Brendan Fyldes   PROPRIETOR: Searcy Tansley & Co. Ltd   OPEN: all week L 11.45 to 2.45 (11.30 to 3 Sat and Sun), Thur to Fri D 5.30 to 8.30   MEALS: alc (main courses £11 to £19). Set L Sat and Sun £19.50 (2 courses) to £24.50, Set D 5.30 to 6.30 £13.95 (2 courses) to £16.95   SERVICE: 12.5% (optional), card slips closed   CARDS: Amex, Delta, MasterCard, Switch, Visa   DETAILS: 120 seats. Private parties: 200 main room. Vegetarian meals. No smoking. Wheelchair access (also WC). No music. Air-conditioned ⊖ Leicester Square

Potemkin £

map 13

144 Clerkenwell Road, EC1R 5DP
TEL: (020) 7278 6661   FAX: (020) 7278 5551
WEBSITE: www.potemkin.co.uk

COOKING **4**
RUSSIAN
£24–£56

The downstairs dining room at this vodka bar-cum-restaurant is done out in shades of red and maroon. Russian restaurants aren't ten a penny in London, despite the ever-increasing profile of certain expats from the motherland. There's the practically inevitable caviar, of course, plus plates of pickles specifically to accompany vodka: gribochki (wild mushrooms pickled with herbs) and raznosoly (pickled vegetables). Many zakuski – starters for sharing – are fish-based, such as pod shuboy (herring cake) and assorted cold smoked fish, but there's spiced roast pork as well. Alternatively, go for borscht, or try sturgeon soup. Main courses such as pelmeni (Siberian pork dumplings) and Cossack lamb casserole (a southern Russian dish served in a clay pot) are attractively presented and tasty variations on sweet/sour or mildly spicy themes. The four desserts are pleasantly unexceptional, and there are a (potentially) staggering 100-plus vodkas – clear, or supplemented with herbs, spices, fruits and flavourings from butterscotch to bison grass. The short Franco–New World wine list is tame in comparison, though enlivened by four Georgian wines from £16 to £35; house wines are £12.

CHEF: Elena Fisher   PROPRIETOR: Southside Limited   OPEN: Mon to Fri L 12 to 2.30, Mon to Sat D 6 to 10.30   CLOSED: bank hols   MEALS: alc (main courses £9.50 to £18). Set L £5.99 (1 course) to £10 (2 courses), Set D Jan to Aug £12.50 (2 courses) to £15.50   SERVICE: 12.5% (optional), card slips closed CARDS: Amex, Delta, Diners, MasterCard, Switch, Visa   DETAILS: 38 seats. Private parties: 38 main room. Vegetarian meals. Music. Air-conditioned   ⊖ Farringdon, Chancery Lane

La Poule au Pot

map 14

231 Ebury Street, SW1 8UT
TEL: (020) 7730 7763   FAX: (020) 7259 9651

COOKING 4
FRENCH
£26–£66

This is one of the most self-consciously Gallic places in the capital. Tables are packed closely together, perhaps in the interests of authenticity, and you'll find scarce a word of English on the menu. The place's popularity makes booking essential. Rustic *cuisine grandmère* disdains the presentational fripperies of the modern French fashion and, at its best, emulates the peasant cooking that inspired the doyenne of British cookery writing, Elizabeth David. From the lunchtime two-course table d'hôte, starters of moules or ratatouille, followed by skate in black butter, cassoulet, or boeuf bourguignon, along with coffee and a reasonable tip, should work out just under £20 a head. The evening carte, equally traditional, includes such fancier fare as pan-fried foie gras with a glass of Monbazillac, and the classic sole meunière. And then there may be veal escalope with mushrooms, or stews – of rabbit and veal, perhaps, alongside the signature poule au pot – served in copper or earthenware pots. Expect crème brûlée, mousse au chocolat and tarte Tatin among the desserts. The all-French wine list is divided into the classic regions (less Alsace) and 'regionals'; house wines are £25 a magnum (£3.30 a glass).

CHEF: Andrew Cafferkey   PROPRIETOR: Peter Frankel   OPEN: all week 12.30 to 2.30 (3.30 Sun), 7 to 11 (10 Sun)   CLOSED: 25 and 26 Dec   MEALS: alc (main courses £14 to £20). Set L £15.50 (2 courses) to £17.50   SERVICE: 12.5% (optional), card slips closed   CARDS: Amex, Delta, Diners, MasterCard, Switch, Visa   DETAILS: 70 seats. 40 seats outside. Private parties: 20 main room, 16 to 20 private rooms. Wheelchair access (not WC). No music. Air-conditioned   ⊖ Sloane Square

---

Providores ▼ ⁵⁄✳

map 15

109 Marylebone High Street, W1U 4RX
TEL: (020) 7935 6175   FAX: (020) 7935 6877
WEBSITE: www.theprovidores.co.uk

COOKING 5
FUSION
£40–£69

Peter Gordon's cooking may be thought of as the very paradigm of that overused term 'fusion food'. Presented here on two floors – a lively ground-floor Tapa Room, and the main, minimally decorated, low-lit upstairs Providores restaurant – it aims to create culinary magic by finding novel and illuminating ways to bring different idioms together. Even experts will find themselves asking for enlightenment as to the menu terminology, as when a lobe of foie gras is marinated in lychee juice and shichimi togarashi (a Japanese spice mix) before being fried. Its accompanying lychee and rhubarb salad is a sweet-and-sour inspiration. Complexity is at a premium, meaning you will have got through quite a few ingredients with the starters alone: caramelised ham hock with green chilli, jicama and mango salad comes with spiced nuts, coriander, and a hazelnut and plum wine dressing. This is the kind of cooking that gives vegetarian dishes full rein, as evidenced by pickled butternut squash and pine nuts with pomegranate molasses, plenty of prunes and horseradish tofu cream. Suffolk Cross, a lamb that feeds on windfall cherries, giving particularly tender meat, is served here with cumin-roast parsnips and plantain mash, or there may be roast sea bass on akadjura lentils and buttered Savoy cabbage with anchovy aïoli and salmon roe. If you're looking to relax into something familiar at dessert stage, don't. Expect instead something like tamarind caramel and coconut sorbet on shortbread with a saffron-poached quince. Service is as sharp and lively as the food. Cocktails in the bar get the thumbs up, then it's on to a New Zealand-dominated wine list that offers great quality at fair prices – and well matched to the food. Prices start at £12.50, and lots come by the glass.

CHEFS: Peter Gordon and Anna Hansen   PROPRIETORS: Peter Gordon, Anna Hansen, Michael McGrath and Jeremy Leeming   OPEN: all week 12 to 2.45, 6 to 10.30 (10 Sun)   CLOSED: 25 and 26 Dec, 1 and 2 Jan, Easter   MEALS: alc (main courses £15.50 to £20.50). Tapas bar menu available   SERVICE: 12.5% (optional), card slips closed   CARDS: Amex, Delta, MasterCard, Switch, Visa   DETAILS: 40 seats. 6 seats outside. Private parties: 40 main room. Vegetarian meals. Children's helpings. No smoking. Music. Air-conditioned   ⊖ Baker Street, Bond Street

Putney Bridge Restaurant ▼

map 12

Embankment, Putney, SW15 1LB
TEL: (020) 8780 1811   FAX: (020) 8780 1211
WEBSITE: www.putneybridgerestaurant.com

COOKING 6
MODERN FRENCH
£38–£84

A modern architectural masterpiece, the restaurant has floor-to-ceiling windows giving sweeping views of the Thames, and lighting pitched at a discreet level in the evening so as not to detract from them. Tables are smartly dressed, and brisk, attentive staff manage not to intrude unnecessarily.

Cutting-edge cooking intermingles East and West, the luxurious and the quotidian. Roast Scottish scallops come with a coral-based sauce spiked with chorizo, plus a bowl of carrot and ginger milk, while Aylesbury duck comes via Peking, lacquered with Szechuan pepper and blossom honey and served with purple sprouting broccoli. Fish figures in a resonant smoked haddock velouté topped with fried quails' eggs, or in a harmonious main course of sea bass with potato and hazelnut gnocchi, smooth pumpkin purée and a trickle of meat stock. Slow braises are a feature, enjoying their own subsection of the menu: perhaps belly pork with smoky barbecue sauce. A pre-dessert (rhubarb with mascarpone cream one night) foreshadows treats like well-textured arabica manicotti, with two warm 'cigarettes' of Valrhona cooked in a pancake, counterpointed by cardamom and orange ice cream; however, cheeses have disappointed. There is a nagging lack of consistency among reports, but when on song, the kitchen can show undoubted talent. The substantial wine list covers the world with discernment, not overlooking less mainstream wines like Germans, Alsatians and Loire reds. A couple of pages of Bordeaux add gravitas, and diners on a budget are not completely ignored, with house wines at £15 and 11 good options by the glass.

CHEF: Anthony Demetre   PROPRIETOR: Gerald Davidson   OPEN: all week L 12 to 2 (2.15 Sun), Mon to Sat D 7 to 10 (6.30 to 10.30 Sat)   MEALS: alc (not Sun L; main courses £17.50 to £23). Set L £22.50, Set L Sun £25. Set D £55 (whole table only)   SERVICE: 12.5% (optional), card slips closed   CARDS: Amex, Delta, Diners, MasterCard, Switch, Visa   DETAILS: 90 seats. Vegetarian meals. No children under 5 at D. Wheelchair access (also WC). No music. Air-conditioned   ⊖ Putney Bridge   £5

Quo Vadis

map 15

26–29 Dean Street, W1D 3LL
TEL: (020) 7437 9585   FAX: (020) 7734 7593
WEBSITE: www.whitestarline.org.uk

COOKING 3
ITALIAN/MEDITERRANEAN
£32–£63

The 'idiosyncratic' interior combines parquet flooring, stained-glass windows and such artworks as a pyramid of sheep's skulls and framed flatfish skeletons. Notwithstanding, the dining room has a comfortable, clubby feel, enhanced by leather banquettes, roomy tables and verdigris-toned walls. The menu interleaves classic Italian (bollito misto, linguine alle vongole) and modern (pan-fried John Dory, sautéed asparagus and open clams with almond sauce). Ideas are generally well conceived, with proper attention to flavour. Successes included pearl barley soup with cured speck and pecorino cheese, and loin of tuna wrapped in aubergine with orange and grapefruit segments and lavender. Finish with something like confit rhubarb with white chocolate and lavender jelly. Service is polite and willing, and the heftily priced wines are rescued for ordinary mortals by ten that come by the glass from £4.

CHEF: Richard McLellan   PROPRIETORS: Marco Pierre White and Jimmy Lahoud   OPEN: Mon to Fri L 12 to 3, Mon to Sat D 5.30 to 11.30   CLOSED: 25 and 26 Dec, 1 Jan   MEALS: alc (main courses £9.50 to £18.50). Set L and D 5.30 to 6.45 £14.95 (2 courses) to £19.95   SERVICE: 12.5% (optional), card slips closed   CARDS: Amex, Delta, Diners, MasterCard, Switch, Visa   DETAILS: 90 seats. Private parties: 90 main room, 8 to 90 private rooms. No cigars. Wheelchair access (not WC). No music. Air-conditioned   ⊖ Tottenham Court Road

---

Racine

map 14

239 Brompton Road, SW3 2EP
TEL: (020) 7584 4477   FAX: (020) 7584 4900

COOKING 4
RUSTIC FRENCH
£30–£65

Racine is 'French to its fingertips', mused one reporter. Another found it 'surprisingly formal' for somewhere delivering 'cuisine bourgeoise that follows the seasons', the stated aim. This results in an appetising menu of the kinds of dishes that introduced many people to French food in bygone days. Simple things like an assiette de charcuterie are composed of quality ingredients packed with earthy flavour, while the melted raclette comes with shallots and cornichons. Not all is straight from the post-war repertoire – Scottish scallops are served as a main course with a purée of Jerusalem artichokes and saffron – but the sight of skate with black butter and capers, or rabbit with mustard sauce, will arouse sighs of nostalgia in some. It is all presented with a distinctly modern eye for detail, though, whether it be the cranberry and orange relish with pheasant pâté, or the cross-hatching of powerful chocolate sauce on poire belle-Hélène. Top-notch coffee and humdrum baguette bread are both, in their different ways, in keeping. The classical French wine list offers a fair spread of prices, opening with house wines at £13.50.

CHEFS: Henry Harris and Chris Handley   PROPRIETORS: Eric Garnier and Henry Harris   OPEN: all week 12 to 3 (3.30 Sat and Sun), 6 to 10.30 (10 Sun)   CLOSED: 25 Dec   MEALS: alc (main courses £10 to £20). Set L £15.50 (2 courses) to £17.50, Set D 6 to 7.30 £15.50 (2 courses) to £17.50   SERVICE: 12.5% (optional), card slips closed   CARDS: Amex, Delta, Diners, MasterCard, Switch, Visa   DETAILS: 65 seats. Private parties: 8 to 20 private rooms. Vegetarian meals. No pipes or cigars. No music. Air-conditioned

---

Radha Krishna Bhavan £

map 12

86 Tooting High Street, SW17 0RN
TEL: (020) 8682 0969
WEBSITE: www.mcdosa.com

COOKING 1
SOUTH INDIAN
£14–£35

The décor here, with its huge tropical murals and life-size statue, evokes the Indian region of Kerala, as does the food. High points are starters, including utthappam (a light-textured 'pizza' topped with onions, green chillies and tomatoes) and Mysore bonda (spiced lentil balls). There are also 'tiffin' and Cochin specialities ranging from iddly vadai sambar to a fish fry masala (a whole fried pomfret), and the kitchen produces distinctive versions of curry-house favourites like methi chicken and lamb dhansak. Vegetables can be variable, though breads and rice generally pass muster. Thalis are the mainstay at Sunday lunchtime. Drink juice, lassi or beer; basic wines start at £8.

CHEFS: Mr Salam and Mr Madhu   PROPRIETORS: T. Haridas and family   OPEN: all week 12 to 3, 6 to 11 (12 Fri and Sat)   CLOSED: 25 and 26 Dec   MEALS: alc (main courses £2.50 to £7)   SERVICE: 10%, card slips closed   CARDS: Amex, Delta, Diners, MasterCard, Switch, Visa   DETAILS: 50 seats. Private parties: 60 main room. Vegetarian meals. Children's helpings. Wheelchair access (also WC). Occasional music. Air-conditioned   ⊖ Tooting Broadway

Ransome's Dock ▮ ⁵⁄× map 12

35–37 Parkgate Road, SW11 4NP   COOKING **4**
TEL: (020) 7223 1611   FAX: (020) 7924 2614   MODERN EUROPEAN
WEBSITE: www.ransomesdock.co.uk   £34–£73

Sitting by the side of the canal, where you might see the odd barge glide by, Martin and Vanessa Lam's well-established restaurant is a calming, relaxed place. Vibrant blue walls enhance the bright atmosphere, particularly enjoyed on summer evenings, and the cooking maintains a steady pace. Organic meats such as Devon lamb, perhaps served with shallot sauce, roasted root vegetables and broccoli, exercise strong appeal, as do starters such as Norfolk smoked eel with a buckwheat pancake and crème fraîche, or chargrilled quail with grapes and grappa-soaked raisins. Continuing its tour of the English counties, the main-course menu might offer Yorkshire pheasant breast with smoked pancetta and gratin savoyard as an alternative to a warming winter dish of beef, Guinness and mushroom pie. Simple desserts have included mango with strained yoghurt, pistachios and orange blossom syrup, as well as gingerbread pudding sauced with ginger wine. 'Relaxed, friendly and knowledgeable' service augments the sense of enjoyment, and the wine list sets out to surpass expectations whatever the style, high price or low. The house selection, all under or around £20, knocks the socks off the competition, while smart bottles from California, Italy and France head the big league.

CHEFS/PROPRIETORS: Martin and Vanessa Lam   OPEN: all week L 12 to 5 (3.30 Sun), Mon to Sat D 6 to 11 CLOSED: Christmas, Aug bank hol   MEALS: alc exc Sat and Sun L (main courses £10.50 to £20). Set L Mon to Fri £14.75 (2 courses). Brunch menu available Sat and Sun L   SERVICE: 12.5% (optional), card slips closed   CARDS: Amex, Delta, Diners, MasterCard, Switch, Visa   DETAILS: 56 seats. 20 seats outside. Private parties: 14 main room. Car park (evenings and weekends only). Vegetarian meals. Children's helpings. No smoking in 1 dining room. Wheelchair access (also WC). Music (£5)

Rasa ⁵⁄× £ map 12

55 Stoke Newington Church Street, N16 0AR   COOKING **2**
TEL: (020) 7249 0344   INDIAN VEGETARIAN
WEBSITE: www.rasarestaurants.com   £22–£33

Since opening in 1994, Rasa has spawned three siblings (plus a couple of 'express' takeaways), each providing a different view of Keralan cuisine (see Rasa Samudra, below; Rasa W1 and Rasa Travancore are listed in the London Round-ups). This one is resolutely vegetarian. The 'somewhat cramped' dining room has been given a lick of paint. Meals still begin with a 'trademark' snack tray of crisp nibbles plus an array of distinctive home-made pickles and chutneys. Beyond that are impressive appetisers like Mysore bonda (deep-fried potato balls) and masala vadai (crunchy mixed-lentil patties). Dosas come with a top-drawer sambhar, and curries make use of sweet mangoes, green bananas and even beetroot. Stir-fried blackeye beans with 'a well-balanced set of spices' is a fitting side order, alongside impressively wrought uzhunappam (rice-flour bread). The modest wine list has house selections at £8.95.

CHEF: Rajan Karattial   PROPRIETOR: Das Sreedharan   OPEN: Sat and Sun L 12 to 2.45, all week D 6 to 10.45 (11.45 Fri and Sat)   CLOSED: 3 days at Christmas   MEALS: alc (main courses £4 to £6). Set L and D £15.50   SERVICE: 12.5% (optional), card slips closed   CARDS: Amex, Diners, MasterCard, Switch, Visa DETAILS: 64 seats. Private parties: 25 main room, 6 to 11 private rooms. Vegetarian meals. No smoking. Wheelchair access (not WC). Music. No mobile phones. Air-conditioned

Rasa Samudra ✳

map 15

5 Charlotte Street, W1T 1RE
TEL: (020) 7637 0222   FAX: (020) 7637 0224
WEBSITE: www.rasarestaurants.com

COOKING 4
INDIAN SEAFOOD/VEGETARIAN
£33–£56

The Charlotte Street branch of the Rasa group (see entry above and in the London Round-ups) is reckoned by some to be the best of the bunch. An instantly recognisable pink frontage and exotic native décor define the place, and the kitchen has made its mark by spotlighting Kerala's seafood cookery as well as its vegetarian traditions. There's prowess in every department, from the crunchy nibbles and pungent home-made pickles that crank up the palate to 'flawless' home-made kulfi (a recommended finale). In between, varutharacha meen curry is a notable fish speciality comprising whole tilapia with a complex sauce of roast coconut, chillies, tomatoes and tamarind. Vegetarian options include multi-flavoured Mysore bonda (potato balls fried in chickpea flour batter) and crisp fried vendakka thoran ('the best okra dish I have ever eaten'). Rice has plenty of texture, and breads are fashioned with deftness and safe hands. Staff in flowing robes provide friendly, helpful service, and the 'surprisingly good' wine list leans towards the New World, with prices starting at £11.50.

CHEF: Prasad Mahadevan   PROPRIETOR: Das Sreedharan   OPEN: Mon to Sat L 12 to 2.30, all week D 6 to 10.30   CLOSED: 24 to 30 Dec, 1 Jan   MEALS: alc (main courses £10 to £13). Set L and D £22.50 to £30 SERVICE: 12.5% (optional), card slips closed   CARDS: Amex, Delta, MasterCard, Switch, Visa   DETAILS: 99 seats. Private parties: 40 main room. Vegetarian meals. No smoking in 1 dining room. Wheelchair access (not WC). Music. Air-conditioned   ⊖ Tottenham Court Road, Goodge Street

Rasoi Vineet Bhatia ♥ ✳

NEW ENTRY   map 14

10 Lincoln Street, SW3 2TS
TEL: (020) 7225 1881   FAX: (020) 7581 0220
WEBSITE: www.vineetbhatia.com

COOKING 5
MODERN INDIAN
£64–£117

The Victorian residence that once housed the English Garden has been claimed by Vineet Bhatia of Zaika fame (see entry) and transmuted into his very own contemporary Indian restaurant with black-stained wood floors, walls of many colours and 'weirdly-shaped' crockery arranged on cloth-free tables.

Creatively contrived trios and platters constitute the lion's share of the starters: the scallop version comprises three perfectly seared specimens sitting on, respectively, a tiny bed of date chutney, chilli oil and finely diced potato. Vineet Bhatia's feel for the core

Indian repertoire shows in poached prawns with coconut and chilli masala and in 'pickle-flavoured' chicken biryani correctly cooked in a pot sealed with pastry, but his eagerness to fuse influences is never far away: marinated duck escalopes come with hot tamarind chutney, sauté shiitake mushrooms and crispy onion fritters, while a whole tandoori pineapple set on a pineapple 'carpaccio' with a tuile of coconut ice cream is typical of his desserts. Amuse-bouche and espresso in tiny French cups reinforce the impression that this is restaurant without frontiers. This all comes at a price, with the nine-course 'Rasoi Gourmand' menu weighing in at a hefty £65. The wine list is earnest but kept to a manageable length. Germany and Alsace are unusually good and Bordeaux mines some important older vintages. Only one bottle is under £20. but there's acceptable value in the mid-£20s and quality options come by the glass.

CHEF: Vineet Bhatia PROPRIETORS: Vineet and Rashima Bhatia OPEN: Mon to Sat D only 6.30 to 10.30 CLOSED: bank hols MEALS: alc D (main courses £14 to £34). Set D £65 SERVICE: 12.5% (optional), card slips closed CARDS: Amex, Delta, MasterCard, Switch, Visa DETAILS: 36 seats. Private parties: 16 main room, 8 to 16 private rooms. Vegetarian meals. No smoking. No music. Air-conditioned ⊖ Sloane Square

Real Greek £

map 13

15 Hoxton Market, N1 6HG	COOKING 4
TEL: (020) 7739 8212 FAX: (020) 7739 4910	GREEK
WEBSITE: www.therealgreek.co.uk	£29–£58

The primary standard bearer of Hellenic cuisine in the UK, slap in the centre of Hoxton, the Real Greek spurns most culinary stereotypes. It presents, instead, the sort of food that Greeks cook for themselves at home. Forget souvlaki (for those, try the adjacent Mezedopolio, or the sister establishment in St John Street, see entry below); here you'll find Thracian-style yellow pumpkin cutlet and spicy soutzouki sausages among the meze selections, plus nettle pie with sheep's milk yoghurt, and venison with artichokes and peas to follow. There's plenty of scope among desserts, too, with Kymian fig and chocolate pot, for example. An all-Greek list of table wines makes instructive reading for wine buffs; from Crete to Thrace there are plenty of different styles and grape varieties to try out (even the retsina is reliably reported as 'delicate and crisp'). Mezedopolio is an open-plan annexe to the main restaurant – it's less formal, noisier, opens all day and focuses purely on mezedes.

CHEFS: Theodore Kyriakou and George Logothetis PROPRIETORS: Paloma Campbell, Mark Yates and Theodore Kyriakou OPEN: Mon to Sat 12 to 2.30, 5.30 to 10.30 MEALS: alc (main courses £8.50 to £16.50) SERVICE: 12.5%, card slips closed CARDS: Delta, MasterCard, Switch, Visa DETAILS: 65 seats. 30 seats outside. Vegetarian meals. No pipes/cigars. Wheelchair access (also WC). Music ⊖ Old Street £5

Real Greek Souvlaki and Bar £

map 13

140–142 St John Street, EC1V 4UA	COOKING 2
TEL: 020 7253 7234 FAX: 020 7253 7235	GREEK
WEBSITE: www.therealgreek.co.uk	£19–£39

Greek street food washed down with wines, beers, ouzo and cocktails is offered at this industrial-looking venue on fashionable St John Street. Deep-sea-blue awnings and full-height windows create a welcoming first impression. Just inside, contented locals eat, drink and chat, perched on stools at high bar counters; if you want a more leisurely, relaxed experience, head for the more conventional dining area at the rear. The eponymous souvlaki – skewered-and-grilled dishes – are the highlight of the menu, made with pork in winter and lamb in summer (plus fish and chicken versions), served in flat bread. Otherwise there's a choice of around a dozen meat and vegetarian mezedes, plus grills: liver and lentils, pork cutlets, or crevettes with salad. Half a dozen sweets include yoghurt with honey and walnuts. Greek wines come by the bottle from £11.50 or in 250/500ml carafes. A second branch has opened at Riverside House, 2A Southwark Bridge Road, SE1; Tel: (020) 7620 0162.

CHEFS: Theodore Kyriakou and George Logothetis   PROPRIETOR: Clapham House Group   OPEN: Mon to Sat 12 to 11   CLOSED: Bank hols   MEALS: alc (main courses £3.75 to £8)   SERVICE: 10% (optional), card slips closed   CARDS: Delta, MasterCard, Switch, Visa   DETAILS: 130 seats. 12 seats outside. Private parties: 150 main room, 4 to 60 private rooms. Vegetarian meals. Wheelchair access (not WC). Music. Air-conditioned   ⊖ Farringdon

---

Red Fort 🍴

77 Dean Street, W1D 3SH
TEL: (020) 7437 2525   FAX: (020) 7434 0781
WEBSITE: www.redfort.co.uk

map 15

COOKING 2
MODERN INDIAN
£33–£87

'Pristine visions of the East in the best possible taste of the West' is one snapshot of the décor here. The walls comprise Mughal sculpted faux-archways, a soothing waterfall cascades at one end and 'arresting' artefacts loom from alcoves. An 'incredibly delicate' selection of breads proves the kitchen can deliver, but elsewhere results have been erratic. The menu takes a broad sweep, from tandooris (seared salmon tikka has been praised) and French corn-fed chicken with coriander and yoghurt sauce to such as Scottish lamb chops in star anise and pomegranate juice, or goose 'ke parchey' (in a cinnamon, poppy-seed and blueberry sauce). Service, too, has been noticeably inconsistent. The ambitious wine list suits the food but is not cheap: house white is £18, red £25.

CHEF: Sayeed Naseer   PROPRIETOR: Amin Ali   OPEN: Mon to Fri L 12 to 2.15, Mon to Sat D 5.45 to 11   MEALS: alc (main courses £12 to £19.50). Set L £12 (2 courses), Set D 5.45 to 7 £16 (2 courses)   SERVICE: 12.5% (optional), card slips closed   CARDS: Amex, Delta, MasterCard, Switch, Visa   DETAILS: 77 seats. Private parties: 100 main room. Vegetarian meals. No-smoking area. Wheelchair access (1 step; also WC). Music. Air-conditioned   ⊖ Tottenham Court Road

---

Redmond's 🍷

170 Upper Richmond Rd. West, East Sheen, SW14 8AW
TEL: (020) 8878 1922   FAX: (020) 8878 1133
WEBSITE: www.redmonds.org.uk

map 12

COOKING 5
MODERN BRITISH
£27–£53

Redmond and Pippa Hayward's place is 'everything a neighbourhood restaurant should be', with relaxed atmosphere, creativity and care in the kitchen, an engaging and reasonably priced wine list, and cheerful, welcoming staff (not to mention a display of works for sale by a local artist). Large windows show off the simple, bright décor, which is further enhanced by a huge floral centrepiece.

The modern cooking style shows the eternal triangle of France, Italy and Britain as the main influences. A mixed hors d'oeuvres based on duck brought forth feather-light parfait, tangy rillettes, slices of smoked breast, and warm foie gras with pear. Peppered medallions of raw tuna came with lemon mayonnaise, balsamic and slightly assertive tapenade. Main courses show care and balance: thick fillets of cod, partnered with ceps, courgettes and mustard mash, perhaps, or a 'properly rare' sirloin, which came with a pile of assorted wild mushrooms and boldly flavoured truffled mash. The present vogue for savoury flavours in desserts surfaces here too, with a tower of red pepper ice cream accompanying a tarte Tatin of pears and basil, while rosemary-scented caramel might be the garnish for a Calvados and sultana parfait with 'sharp, cleansing' green apple sorbet. Wines are an evolving line-up from passionate winemakers around the world, presented with great enthusiasm; house white is £14.50. The Haywards have opened a new sister restaurant, The Burlington, by Chiswick station (see Round-up entry).

CHEFS: Redmond Hayward and Alberto Landgraf PROPRIETORS: Redmond and Pippa Hayward OPEN: Sun L 12 to 2.30, Mon to Sat D 6.30 (7 Fri/Sat) to 10 CLOSED: 3 days at Christmas, bank hol Mons MEALS: Set L Sun £19 (2 courses) to £23, Set D Mon to Fri 6.30 to 7.45 £12.50 (2 courses) to £15, Set D £27 (2 courses) to £31 SERVICE: not inc, 10% for groups of 6 or more CARDS: Delta, MasterCard, Switch, Visa DETAILS: 48 seats. Private parties: 48 main room. Vegetarian meals. Children's helpings. No cigars/pipes. No-smoking area. Wheelchair access (not WC). Occasional music. Air-conditioned

▲ Refettorio

NEW ENTRY map 13

Crowne Plaza – the City, 19 New Bridge Street,
EC4V 6DB
TEL: (020) 7438 8052 FAX: (020) 7438 8004
WEBSITE: www.london-city.crowneplaza.com

COOKING 2
ITALIAN
£36–£84

Refettorio is on the ground floor of the recently opened Crowne Plaza, a short walk from Blackfriars Bridge, reached either via its own entrance on New Bridge Street or through the hotel lobby. A large display of Italian goodies, as in an upmarket deli, confronts you on entering, and you can either sit at the bar, join fellow diners at a long, central refectory table, or slide into the booth-type seating. Star consultant Giorgio Locatelli (see Locanda Locatelli, London) has put Pasquale Amico in charge of proceedings here. One way to start is to order a plate of regional cured meats or cheeses. Fritto di verdure are crisp-fried vegetables, offering an array of 'keen, lively flavours', with an agrodolce dipping sauce. Taglioni with ham and mushrooms is a well-timed pasta course, while a main course of chargrilled calf's liver with roast red onions comes tenderly pink and flavourful. Simply presented fish include sea bass in white wine, garlic and tomato, and chargrilled tuna with black olives and oregano. Desserts are worth leaving room for, whether a fine ice cream and sorbet selection, or well-made and not-too-sweet mille-foglie with Marsala cream. A compact selection of modern Italian wines (plus champagnes) offers better value in whites than reds, with glass prices from £3.75.

CHEFS: Giorgio Locatelli and Pasquale Amico PROPRIETOR: Crowne Plaza Hotels OPEN: Mon to Fri L 12 to 2.30, Mon to Sat D 6 to 10 CLOSED: bank hols MEALS: alc (main courses £9.50 to £21.50). Set D £35 to £55 SERVICE: 12.5% (optional) CARDS: Delta, Diners, MasterCard, Switch, Visa DETAILS: 110 seats. Private parties: 50 main room, 10 to 20 private rooms. Vegetarian meals. Children's helpings. No-smoking area. Wheelchair access (also WC). Music. Air-conditioned ACCOMMODATION: 203 rooms, all with bath/shower. TV. Phone. Room only £179 to £220. Rooms for disabled ⊖ Blackfriars

---

Prices quoted in the Guide are based on information supplied by restaurateurs. The prices quoted at the top of each entry represent a range, from the lowest price of a three-course meal with service and wine to the highest; the latter is inflated by 20 per cent to take account of likely price rises during the year of the Guide.

Rhodes Twenty Four

NEW ENTRY map 13

Tower 42, 25 Old Broad Street, EC2N 1HQ
TEL: (020) 7877 7703   FAX: (020) 7877 7788
WEBSITE: www.rhodes24.co.uk

COOKING **5**
BRITISH
£42–£80

Reaching Gary Rhodes's newest venture, on the twenty-fourth floor of the former NatWest Tower, is like pre-flight check-in. You negotiate the desk, a walk-through security scanner and an X-ray belt for your baggage before boarding Lift B for takeoff. But the view up there is staggering (a head for heights helps): a panorama of London rolling away to distant hills, with the Swiss Re 'gherkin' for company. Tables not beside the window are on a dais to help you drink it all in.

Once again Rhodes applies haute cuisine technique to English vernacular dishes – cottage pie, piccalilli, fried bread, rhubarb and custard. They look simple (even spare) but pack punch, whether hot-smoked eel with that lurid yellow piccalilli, a smooth sausage of veal kidney in Turbigo sauce, or a main-course steamed suet pudding of mutton and onion, served with buttered carrots. Occasional lack of focus has caused wobbles: sea trout with cabbage and smoked salmon, lacking its advertised gravad lax sauce. A spring riff on a favourite pud produces an amply proportioned yellowy cheesecake singing with rhubarb, cream cheese and vanilla, plus a sour compote of rhubarb and a sorbet with equal bite. Otherwise, it's nostalgia in spades: jam roly-poly, Jaffa cake, rice pudding. Service is impeccable. Wines are almost depressing in their three-figure opulence, but there are ten reds and whites by the glass, and the base price for bottles is £17.

CHEF: Gary Rhodes   PROPRIETOR: Restaurant Associates   OPEN: Mon to Fri 12 to 2.30, 6 to 9   CLOSED: 25 Dec, bank hols   MEALS: alc (main courses £12 to £23)   SERVICE: 12.5%, card slips closed   CARDS: Amex, Delta, Diners, MasterCard, Switch, Visa   DETAILS: 75 seats. Private parties: 75 main room. Vegetarian meals. No pipes/cigars. Wheelchair access (also WC). Music. Air-conditioned

▲ Ritz Hotel

map 15

150 Piccadilly, W1J 9BR
TEL: 020 7493 8181   FAX: 020 7493 2687
WEBSITE: www.theritzlondon.com

NEW CHEF
FRENCH/ENGLISH
£56–£113

The Ritz's dining room is a chunk of living history – surely the best place (just so long as you're wearing a jacket and tie) to soak up a little nineteenth-century ambience, or is that eighteenth-century? It is certainly rich and luxurious. The splendidly high-ceilinged room is the setting for the cooking of new chef John Williams, who allows old favourites to sit comfortably with newer ideas. Start with a ballottine of wild rabbit with quince chutney, or Caesar salad with bacon lardons, prepared at table. Soups can be as luxurious as lobster bisque with Armagnac, and the grill offers up fillet of sole Normande and steak Diane (another one prepared at table). Meat main courses include noisettes of lamb Edward VII. Rosemary-infused fruit crumble with a chestnut ice cream is a contemporary-sounding finish. The menu is not much smaller than a gatefold LP and contains plenty of background reading material, should you tire of staring agog at the surroundings. Prices quoted on the gilt-edged pages may not aid the digestion – but this is the Ritz, for heaven's sake. Wine mark-ups are what one might expect, but the list opens at about £20 and provides plenty of interest – although most of the action tends to be centred in France.

CHEF: John Williams   PROPRIETOR: The Ritz Hotel (London) Ltd   OPEN: all week 12.30 to 2.30, 6 to 11 (6.30 to 10.30 Sun)   MEALS: alc (main courses £26 to £62). Set L £39, Set D £60. Palm Court and Rivoli Bar menus available   SERVICE: net prices, card slips closed   CARDS: Amex, Delta, Diners, MasterCard, Switch, Visa   DETAILS: 140 seats. 20 seats outside. Private parties: 14 main room, 2 to 50 private rooms. Vegetarian meals. Children's helpings. Jacket and tie. Wheelchair access (also WC). Music. Air-conditioned   ACCOMMODATION: 133 rooms, all with bath/shower. TV. Phone. Room only £300 to £430. Rooms for disabled. Baby facilities   ⊖ Green Park

River Café ♥ map 12

Thames Wharf Studios, Rainville Road, W6 9HA
TEL: (020) 7386 4200   FAX: (020) 7386 4201
WEBSITE: www.rivercafe.co.uk

COOKING 6
ITALIAN
£48–£83

Not surprisingly, given the architectural associations, the most is made of the space, and light floods in through floor-to-ceiling windows that open up to the terrace in fine weather; you can't quite see the Thames when you're sitting down, but it's nice to know it's there. Note that two-hour dining slots are often enforced, such is the popularity of the place.

Seasonal ingredients are an integral part of the plan, so a June menu may feature pea and vongole risotto with fish stock and parsley, and among main courses chargrilled tuna is marinated with chilli and summer savory, and comes with fine green beans and fresh plum tomato. The simplicity of many of the ideas is easily supported by the exceptional quality of the produce. The wood-fired oven comes into play for wood-roasted langoustines with wild oregano and chilli, or an impressively flavourful wood-roasted pigeon. Chocolate nemesis is a stalwart of the dessert menu, but there may also be Seville orange marmalade ice cream – and cheese-lovers may want time to peruse the list of Italian cheeses. A map of Italy announces the focus of the wine list, and every region has its representatives, led by reds from Tuscany and Piedmont. While there are plenty of smart bottles, this is a commendably balanced cellar, offering good drinking at all price levels from £10.50, including over a dozen by the glass.

CHEFS: Rose Gray, Ruth Rogers and Theo Randall   PROPRIETORS: Rose Gray and Ruth Rogers   OPEN: all week L 12.30 to 3 (12 to 3.30 Sun), Mon to Sat D 7 to 9.30   CLOSED: 10 days at Christmas, bank hol Mons   MEALS: alc (main courses £20 to £30)   SERVICE: 12.5% (optional), card slips closed   CARDS: Amex, Delta, Diners, MasterCard, Switch, Visa   DETAILS: 106 seats. 50 seats outside. Car park (eves and Sat and Sun only). Children's helpings. No cigars/pipes. Wheelchair access (also WC). No music   ⊖ Hammersmith

Roussillon ♥ map 14

16 St Barnabas Street, SW1W 8PE
TEL: (020) 7730 5550   FAX: (020) 7824 8617
WEBSITE: www.roussillon.co.uk

COOKING 5
MODERN FRENCH
£44–£105

Consistency is a watchword at this restaurant just off Pimlico Road. Alexis Gauthier continues to treat first-class ingredients skilfully and brings a light touch to imaginative and ingenious dishes that have a classic base. A British slant to raw materials complements a fairly discreet French flavour, the long, enterprising seasonal menus giving top billing to English meat and game, Welsh duck eggs, Aberdeen Angus beef, and Scottish lobster, as well as to Anjou pigeon, Pyrenean milk-fed lamb and a slate of French cheeses.

Start with Jersey Royal potato gratin with wild rocket, crispy bacon and truffle, or lobster velouté and morels, and move on to grilled halibut with sautéed squid, lemon and parsley cream, or calves' sweetbreads with wild asparagus and summer truffles. Desserts might feature steamed English rhubarb tartlet with pomegranate jus and sorbet, or spicy duck egg soufflé, maple syrup and gingerbread. Vegetarians fare well with a Garden Menu, and there is a seasonal seven-course tasting menu of dishes from the carte for £65. Tables are well spaced, and the service professional and informed. Appropriately, the sommelier is an avid fan of the Roussillon region, although the mighty wine list does reach out to all corners of France; other countries make minor contributions. Prices start at £18 and aim high, but a cracking range by the glass widens the possibilities.

CHEFS: Alexis Gauthier and Gérard Virolle   PROPRIETORS: James and Andrew Palmer   OPEN: Wed to Fri D 12 to 2.30, Mon to Sat D 6.30 to 11   MEALS: Set L £30, Set D £45 to £65   SERVICE: 12.5% (optional), card slips closed   CARDS: Amex, Delta, MasterCard, Switch, Visa   DETAILS: 46 seats. Private parties: 26 main room. Vegetarian meals. No children under 10. No pipes/cigars. No music. Air-conditioned   ⊖ Sloane Square ⑤

Royal China   maps 12/13/15

24–26 Baker Street, W1V 7AJ
TEL: (020) 7487 4688   FAX: (020) 7935 7893
68 Queen's Grove, NW8 6ER
TEL: (020) 7586 4280   FAX: (020) 7722 4750
13 Queensway, W2 4QJ
TEL: (020) 7221 2535   FAX: (020) 7792 5752
30 West Ferry Circus, E14 8RR   COOKING 3
TEL: (020) 7719 0888   FAX: (020) 7719 0889   CHINESE
WEBSITE: www.royalchinagroup.co.uk   £34–£95

Trademark black-and-gold lacquered walls with bird motifs set the tone for this gang of four high-ranking Chinese restaurants. The Queensway branch is considered 'the most reliable Chinese restaurant in London', according to one who knows his way around the scene; Baker Street is also favourably endorsed but there are a few doubters in the ranks who believe that the Royal China group is not as reliable as previously. All branches offer an extensive selection of 'reasonably consistent' daytime dim sum, and their menus move quickly beyond the familiar world of beef with chilli and black bean sauce. Rainbow soup is an outstanding broth with seven well-balanced ingredients in a 'great stock', while steamed whole sea bass (filleted at the table) has few rivals in the capital. Other highly commended dishes have included pork and chilli dumplings, deep-fried soft-shelled crab in spicy salt, juicy jumbo prawns in batter with spring onions, and 'stunningly delicate' Chinese broccoli with garlic. Service is on the ball but a shade 'impersonal'. House wine is £14. Note that the Baker Street branch has moved a few doors south from its address last year.

CHEF: Man Yuk Leung (executive chef)   PROPRIETOR: Royal China Restaurant Group   OPEN: all week 12 (11 Sun) to 11 (later Fri and Sat, 10 Sun)   MEALS: alc (main courses £7 to £50), Set L and D from £28 per person (min 2); dim sum menu available to 5pm   SERVICE: 12.5% (optional)   CARDS: Amex, Delta, Diners, MasterCard, Switch, Visa   DETAILS: (for Baker Street branch; may vary across other branches) 190 seats. Private parties: 190 main room, 12 to 36 private rooms. Vegetarian meals. Wheelchair access (also WC). Music. Air-conditioned   ⊖ Baker Street/Bond Street, Bayswater/Queensway, St John's Wood, Westferry DLR

Occasional music *in the details at the end of an entry means live or recorded music is played in the dining room only rarely or for special events.* No music *means it is never played.*

RSJ 🍾

map 13

33 Coin Street, SE1 9NR
TEL: (020) 7928 4554   FAX: (020) 7928 9768

COOKING 3
MODERN FRENCH
£31–£51

After 25 years, this 'relaxed, quiet and civilised' establishment has built up a loyal following, not least because its early kick-off makes it convenient for a meal before a visit to the National Theatre and other South Bank attractions. If the décor is getting a little tired, then RSJ is still 'a big hit' when it comes to food and service. Waiters don't intrude but are there when needed, and the well-sourced menu provides plenty of sustenance for comfort-food lovers: satisfyingly spicy sweet potato soup with crisp aubergine croûtons for a textural contrast, 'super-tender' roast Gressingham duck breast with a confit of the leg and creamed cabbage cooked with smoked bacon, or baked ham with buttered swede and quince jelly. Vegetarian dishes are treated thoughtfully, as in an impressive roast Mediterranean vegetable tart with goats' cheese, basil and pine nuts, all melding into a perfectly seasoned whole. Desserts lean towards the English, with treacle tart and Kent Lent pie. RSJ has long been *the* place at which to drink Loire wines, and it continues to scour the region for exciting finds to add to the list. There's plenty to be had for under £20, but a stretch to £30 will put stunning wines within your grasp.

CHEF: Ian Stabler   PROPRIETOR: Nigel Wilkinson   OPEN: Mon to Fri L 12 to 2, Mon to Sat D 5.30 to 11   MEALS: alc (main courses £13 to £16). Set L and D £15.95 (2 courses) to £17.95   SERVICE: 12.5% (optional), card slips closed   CARDS: Amex, Delta, Diners, MasterCard, Switch, Visa   DETAILS: 90 seats. 10 seats outside. Private parties: 50 main room, 10 to 30 private rooms. Vegetarian meals. No cigars/pipes. No music. No mobile phones. Air-conditioned   ⊖ Waterloo £5

Sabras ⚡✕ £

map 12

263 High Road, Willesden Green, NW10 2RX
TEL: (020) 8459 0340   FAX: (020) 8459 0541

COOKING 4
INDIAN VEGETARIAN
£19–£43

Hemant and Nalinee Desai's pioneering restaurant has showcased Indian vegetarian food since it opened in 1973 in the suburban backwaters of Willesden. Gujarati cooking is the bedrock of the menu, although the kitchen dips into other culinary traditions. 'Dazzling' deluxe sev puris make an outstanding appetiser or you might go for farshaan snacks like samosas and ghughara-kachori (half-moon pastries filled with peas, seeds and spices). Crisp, regionally diverse dosas are some of the finest in town, with freshly spiced fillings, sambal and coconut chutney (made to a 'brand new recipe'). Vegetables might involve sakkariya (sliced sweet potato) and ravaiya (based on baby aubergines, potatoes and banana), while four kinds of dhal are enlivened with tamarind, lemon and jaggery (unrefined cane or palm sugar). To finish, there are desserts ranging from chilled Alphonso mango pulp to basudi (thickened milk enriched with sugar, ground almonds, pistachios and cardamoms). Thirst-quenchers include five versions of lassi, tropical fruit juices, Indian beers and a minimal wine list with prices from £9.50

CHEF: Nalinee Desai   PROPRIETOR: Hemant Desai   OPEN: Tue to Sun D only 6.45 to 10.30   CLOSED: Dec 15 to Jan 15   MEALS: alc (main courses £6.50 to £7.50). Set D 6.45 to 8.30 £6.50 to £8.50.   SERVICE: 12.5%, card slips closed   CARDS: MasterCard, Switch, Visa   DETAILS: 32 seats. Private parties: 20 main room. Vegetarian meals. No smoking. Wheelchair access (not WC). Music. No mobile phones   ⊖ Dollis Hill £5

St John

map 13

26 St John Street, EC1M 4AY

TEL: (020) 7251 0848   FAX: (020) 7251 4090

WEBSITE: www.stjohnrestaurant.com

COOKING 5

BRITISH

£40–£70

Upstairs, beyond its bustling bar, the celebrated dining room at this former smokehouse close to Smithfield Market is a pared-down affair of plain cream walls, wooden floors, tables in serried ranks and an open-to-view kitchen. Hospitality is 'friendly and welcoming', service knowledgeable and enthusiastic. And then there is the food. Fergus Henderson's gutsy take on real British cooking is distinguished by honesty, simplicity and full-on flavours. Humble ingredients seem consistent with the minimalist approach to décor, and the twice-daily changing menus, bolstered by specials, are notable for their succinct descriptions (roast bone marrow and parsley salad, or tripe and chips). Start with smoked cod's roe on toast, or 'simple, tasty' dandelion and shallots, then share a (twosome) circular beef and pig's trotter pie with 'crisp pastry', or braised hare and swede, and finish with buttermilk pudding and prunes, or rhubarb cobbler and custard. Altogether, a 'truly distinctive' restaurant experience. The well-chosen, all-French wine list is ordered by price and kicks off at £13.50 a bottle; there are ten by the glass. There are no restrictions on smoking, and the atmosphere has been reported as 'rather fuggy'.

CHEF: Fergus Henderson   PROPRIETORS: Trevor Gulliver and Fergus Henderson   OPEN: Mon to Fri L 12 to 3, Mon to Sat D 6 to 11   CLOSED: Christmas and New Year, Easter bank hol   MEALS: alc (main courses £14 to £19.50)   SERVICE: not inc   CARDS: Amex, Delta, Diners, MasterCard, Switch, Visa   DETAILS: 100 seats. Private parties: 150 main room, 1 to 20 private rooms. Vegetarian meals. No music. No mobile phones. Air-conditioned   ⊖ Farringdon

St John Bread & Wine

NEW ENTRY   map 13

94–96 Commercial Street, E1 6LZ

TEL: (020) 7247 8724   FAX: (020) 7247 8924

WEBSITE: www.stjohnbreadandwine.com

COOKING 3

BRITISH

£26–£58

At this all-white, schoolroom-plain St John offshoot the pared-down simplicity of printed and blackboard menus are entirely in keeping, and one has to warm to somewhere offering 'peas in the pod', 'brace of slip soles' or 'bowl of Kent cherries'. Some feel this 'more a place for a nibble than a three-course meal' (they do breakfast and elevenses too), although you can stretch your lunch hour till dinner takes over at six if you want. Meat is carefully sourced, but it's not always the usual bits you meet (chitterlings, chicory and mustard, or ox heart with beetroot and watercress). And there could be deliciously tender grilled razor clams; lobster and samphire; or tomatoes, goats' curd and mint with 'terrific dressing, lovely cheese and fresh-tasting, sweet tomatoes'. Chocolate terrine with black pepper ice cream is richly indulgent; alternatively the Eccles cake is 'the real McCoy'. Wine, from £14 in the restaurant (like the outstanding breads, it's available retail too), is entirely French, with a good choice by the glass.

CHEFS: Karl Goward and Justin Gellatly   PROPRIETORS: Fergus Henderson and Trevor Gulliver   OPEN: all week noon to 10.30 (10 Sun)   CLOSED: 25 Dec, bank hols   MEALS: alc (main courses £8 to £16)   SERVICE: not inc, 12.5% for groups of 6 or more   CARDS: Amex, Delta, MasterCard, Switch, Visa   DETAILS: 60 seats. Private parties: 70 main room. Vegetarian meals. Wheelchair access (not WC). No music. Air-conditioned   ⊖ Liverpool Street

Salisbury Tavern

map 12

21 Sherbrooke Road, SW6 7HX
TEL: (020) 7381 4005   FAX: (020) 7381 1002
EMAIL: the salisburytavern@longshotplc.com

COOKING 3
MODERN EUROPEAN
£30–£53

A few photos of the glory days of Fulham FC are the only signs of nostalgia in either area of this sister to the Admiral Codrington (see entry), set among residential Fulham streets. The pub part does have TV screens showing sport from time to time and gets lively with drinkers, but this is an upmarket pub-cum-restaurant. The separate dining room gets added luminosity from skylights, while the kitchen goes about the business of producing well-conceived and carefully executed dishes. High spots at inspection were a well-balanced, meaty crayfish risotto with creamy but slightly crunchy rice; succulent belly of pork with sweet cabbage and crispy bacon; and an oozy chocolate fondant that avoided over-sweetening. Friendly and knowledgeable staff show healthy teamwork between kitchen and front-of-house. It can get smoky, and you can expect taped music, too. Decent wines, some from Berry Brothers, are all available by the glass; prices range from £12 (£3.30 a 125ml glass) to £40 (£11.20).

CHEF: Micky O'Connor   PROPRIETOR: Longshot plc   OPEN: all week 12 to 2.30 (3.30 Sat, 4.30 Sun), 7 to 10.45 (10.15 Sun)   CLOSED: 25, 26 and 31 Dec   MEALS: alc (main courses £8.50 to £15). Set L £15.75 (2 courses) to £18.50. Cover 50p at D   SERVICE: 12.5% (optional), card slips closed   CARDS: Amex, Delta, MasterCard, Switch, Visa   DETAILS: 75 seats. Vegetarian meals. Wheelchair access (also WC). Music. No mobile phones. Air-conditioned   ⊖ Fulham Broadway

Salloos

map 14

62–64 Kinnerton Street, SW1X 8ER
TEL: (020) 7235 4444

COOKING 3
PAKISTANI
£30–£60

Muhammad Salahuddin ('Salloo' to his friends) opened this restaurant in a Knightsbridge mews house nearly thirty years ago. It remains a family affair, with his daughters out front and many recipes handed down through the generations. Chef Abdul Aziz, trained by Salloo's mother, has been at the stoves since the start, purveying a genuine version of affluent Pakistani home cooking based on top-notch ingredients and forthright spicing. A genuine charcoal-fired tandoor cooks the 'colour-free' shish kebabs, quails, king prawns, lamb chops and more. Many dishes should be familiar to curry-house devotees (chicken jalfrezi, bhuna gosht, etc.), but look also for less familiar specialities like chicken taimuri (marinated thighs deep-fried in seasoned batter). Desserts include home-made kulfi, and hot carrot halwa gajar. The wine list, from Corney & Barrow, starts with house selections at £12.50.

CHEF: Abdul Aziz   PROPRIETOR: Muhammad Salahuddin   OPEN: Mon to Sat 12 to 2.30, 7 to 11.15   CLOSED: bank hols   MEALS: alc (main courses £10 to £17). Set L £12.50 (2 courses) to £16.50. Cover £1.50   SERVICE: 12.5% (optional), card slips closed   CARDS: Amex, Delta, Diners, MasterCard, Switch, Visa   DETAILS: 65 seats. Vegetarian meals. No children under 8. No pipes/cigars. No music. Air-conditioned   ⊖ Knightsbridge

---

All entries in the Guide are re-researched and rewritten every year, not least because restaurant standards fluctuate. Don't rely on an out-of-date Guide.

Salusbury £

map 13

50–52 Salusbury Road, Queens Park, NW6 6NN
TEL: (020) 7328 3286   FAX: (020) 7604 3300

COOKING 3
ITALIAN
£27–£47

This Kilburn gastro-pub takes care over everything, from the décor, via the cooking – mostly hearty and Italianate – to a wine list compiled with flair. It is a casual place, with an appealing bar area and separate restaurant, each bedecked with mirrors and nothing as fussy as soft furnishings. It can generate quite a hum of happy contentment when busy. Start with red onion soup with ewes' milk cheese - a large and comforting bowlful - or a winter salad of anchovies and a walnut dip. Pasta might appear in the form of pappardelle with duck ragù, or tagliolini with smoked haddock, leeks and cream. Main courses can be as straightforward as 'well-flavoured' ribeye steak with roast parsnips, or as 'fancy' as king scallop lasagnette with broccoli and chestnuts. Puddings include vin santo with cantuccini biscuits, and pannacotta with oranges, and wines (mainly from Romance Europe, with odd Antipodeans added) begin at £10.50, with a dozen by the glass.

CHEF: Enrico Sartor   PROPRIETORS: Robert Claassen and Nicholas Mash   OPEN: Tue to Sun L 12.30 to 3.30, all week D 7 to 10.15 (10 Sun)   MEALS: alc (main courses £9.50 to £16)   SERVICE: 12.5% (optional) CARDS: Delta, MasterCard, Switch, Visa   DETAILS: 80 seats. Vegetarian meals. No children under 7. No cigars. Music   ⊖ Queens Park

Sardo £✳

map 15

45 Grafton Way, W1T 5DQ
TEL: (020) 7387 2521   FAX: (020) 7387 2559
WEBSITE: www.sardo-restaurant.com

COOKING 4
SARDINIAN
£29–£59

A minute from Warren Street Underground is this stylish reference point for Sardinian cooking. The décor is a clever mix of the 'cool and classic' (literally classic in the case of the small Corinthian columns attached to cream-painted walls), and tables are immaculately set. Right from the chewy breads or the crispy *fogli di musica* dripping in fine olive oil, the kitchen shows its commitment. An 'utterly simple' salad of fleshy lettuce interspersed with light but potently flavoured pecorino cream shows real confidence. Superb cured tuna, with the quality of the finest prosciutto, is supported by diced French beans and thin slices of sun-dried tomato, and there are pasta dishes, such as linguine with a crabmeat sauce and chillies. Main courses include generous slices of rare venison with an intense honey-and-red-wine reduction, or there might be grilled swordfish with rocket and tomatoes. You can finish with an 'excellent' pannacotta with raspberries, a selection of Sardinian pecorino cheeses, or sweet polenta with stewed pears and sour cream. Modern Sardinian wines (four of which can be enjoyed by the glass) are the focus of the list, with Italian bottles in support and a few French also-rans; house bottles are £14.

CHEF: Roberto Sardu   PROPRIETOR: Romolo Mudu   OPEN: Mon to Fri L 12 to 3, Mon to Sat D 6 to 11 CLOSED: Christmas, bank hols   MEALS: alc (main courses £9 to £18). Cover £1.50   SERVICE: 12.5% (optional), card slips closed   CARDS: Amex, Delta, Diners, MasterCard, Switch, Visa   DETAILS: 55 seats. 10 seats outside. Private parties: 30 main room. Vegetarian meals. No smoking. Wheelchair access (not WC). Music. Air-conditioned   ⊖ Warren Street

---

All entries, including Round-ups, are fully indexed at the back of the Guide.

Sarkhel's £

map 12

199 Replingham Road, Southfields, SW18 5LY	COOKING 3
TEL: (020) 8870 1483	INDIAN
WEBSITE: www.sarkhels.com	£19–£49

Diners at this dependable south London restaurant regularly take a cook's tour of the Subcontinent, via Udit Sarkhel's special regional menus. But his regular repertoire also covers a lot of territory, looking north for chicken tikka with fenugreek and Kashmiri gade pakore (fennel-flavoured freshwater fish in batter dusted with powdered pomegranate seeds), then south to seek out spicy kozhi vartha kozhambu (a chicken curry with tomatoes, ginger and black pepper) and Karnakata lamb and coconut fry. Rice includes a lemon version with cashew nuts, while breads run to onion kulcha and laccha paratha. Thalis are fair value, and Sunday lunch is a buffet. The well-annotated, 50-strong wine list includes 11 by the glass and house selections at £10.90. Sarkhel's kitchen also supplies the Calcutta Notebook restaurant next door (see entry).

CHEF: Udit Sarkhel   PROPRIETORS: Udit and Veronica Sarkhel   OPEN: all week 12 to 2.30, 6 to 10.30 (11 Fri and Sat)   CLOSED: 25 and 26 Dec   MEALS: alc (main courses £7.50 to £10.50). Set L Tue to Sat £5 (2 courses) to £10, Set Sun L £10, Set D 6 to 8 £10   SERVICE: not inc   CARDS: MasterCard, Switch, Visa DETAILS: 98 seats. Private parties: 108 main room, 28 private room. Vegetarian meals. Children's helpings. No smoking area. Wheelchair access (also women's WC). Music. Air-conditioned   ⊖ Southfields £5

Savoy Grill

map 13

The Strand, WC2R 0EU	COOKING 4
TEL: 020 7592 1600 FAX: 020 7592 1601	MODERN FRENCH-PLUS
WEBSITE: www.marcuswareing.com	£48–£98

Despite its much-publicised makeover, the Savoy Grill remains quite sober; flashes of modern art notwithstanding, the colour scheme is still largely muted, beneath the shimmering elegance of a silver-leaf ceiling. Marcus Wareing has coaxed the menus into the present, though without entirely abandoning traditional elements the Grill has always been famous for. One pair explored both routes: one lunching on smoked salmon and gravad lax sliced from a trolley, followed by steak and kidney pudding; the other choosing scallops on a bed of minted pea purée, and then squab pigeon garnished with a tranche of foie gras. There may be basil in the crème brûlée these days, but another reporter was delighted with a simple serving of fine vanilla ice cream, albeit sprinkled with crystallised pineapple. Service is old-school in its blend of formality and charm, while the wine list is just old-school – a magnificent tour d'horizon at imperious prices. You can have a simple dry white Bordeaux, but after that the only way is up.

On the first floor, overlooking the grand entrance, is Banquette, where the food is reconstructed vernacular: duck spring rolls with sweet chilli sauce, fishcakes or battered goujons of sole with tartare sauce, grilled ribeye with garlic butter, and sandwiches and soups for the snackers. Food is served all day, and there is a truncated version of the Savoy wine list, with wines by the glass from £5.

CHEF: Joshua Emmett   PROPRIETORS: Marcus Wareing and Gordon Ramsay Group   OPEN: all week 12 to 3, 5.45 to 11   MEALS: Set L £30 to £50, Set D £50 to £60   SERVICE: not inc   CARDS: Amex, Delta, MasterCard, Switch, Visa   DETAILS: 110 seats. Private parties: 100 main room. Vegetarian meals. Children's helpings. Wheelchair access (not WC). No music. Air-conditioned   ⊖ Charing Cross

Searcy's

map 13

Level 2, Barbican Centre, Silk Street, EC2Y 8DS
TEL: (020) 7588 3008   FAX: (020) 7382 7247
WEBSITE: www.barbican.org.uk

COOKING 3
MODERN BRITISH
£39–£68

'I reckon Searcy's is a bit of a gem,' says a reporter, somewhat surprised to find the dining room so quiet at a Thursday lunch. Find it on the second floor of the main concrete mothership. It overlooks the lake, but lacks a terrace to make the best of it, although there are huge south-facing windows. Dishes can be complex, and ingredients include plenty from the more expensive end of the spectrum: a deceptively simple-sounding starter of langoustine boudin, for example, is presented in its own jus with some buttery clams and mussels, and pea and prawn raviolo. Main courses might include a heartily satisfying, earthy (and enormous) rendition of lamb shank, the tender meat sitting on a dollop of parsnip mash, with a frothy root vegetable cappuccino. For dessert, a 'tasting of lychee' has impressed, comprising of the fruit served in a variety of 'delicious' guises, including a soufflé. The wine list, divided by style, has a good selection of half-bottles and is well judged if not great value. Prices start at £17.50.

CHEF: Fergal O'Neill   PROPRIETOR: Searcy's   OPEN: Mon to Fri L 12 to 2.30, Mon to Sat D 5 to 10.30
CLOSED: 24 to 26 Dec   MEALS: Set L and D £21 (2 courses) to £25, Set D £18 (Performance menu 2 courses). Bar menu available   SERVICE: 12.5% (optional), card slips closed   CARDS: Amex, Delta, Diners, MasterCard, Switch, Visa   DETAILS: 90 seats. Vegetarian meals. No-smoking area. Wheelchair access (also WC). Music   ⊖ Barbican, Moorgate

Singapore Garden

map 13

83–83A Fairfax Road, NW6 4DY
TEL: (020) 7328 5314   FAX: (020) 7624 0656

COOKING 2
SINGAPOREAN
£19–£86

'The personification of a good family and neighbourhood restaurant' says one fan of this enduring venue; mother is head chef, while relatives often help out in the two spacious dining rooms. Authentic flavours and good value make it one of the top Singaporean/ Malaysian restaurants around. Singaporean chilli crab is a must, but also impressive are Malaysian satays, hoi jien (a 'decadent' omelette with oysters and chives) and benchmark versions of fried kway teow, and of chicken rice. The kitchen also has 'the rare ability' to produce commendable Chinese dishes: witness a fine example of crispy duck with pancakes. Loyal, batik-attired waitresses provide 'engaging' service, and the wine list combines unfussy quaffing (from £13.50) with some gems for deep-pocketed claret lovers.

CHEF: Mrs S.K. Lim   PROPRIETORS: the Lim family   OPEN: all week 12 to 2.45, 6 to 10.45 (11.15 Fri and Sat)
CLOSED: 4 days Christmas   MEALS: alc (main courses £6 to £32). Set L Mon to Fri (not bank hols) £7.50 (2 courses) to £9, Set D £20 to £32.50   SERVICE: 12.5% (optional), card slips closed   CARDS: Amex, Delta, Diners, MasterCard, Switch, Visa   DETAILS: 100 seats. 12 seats outside. Private parties: 60 main room, 6 private room. Vegetarian meals. No cigars. Music. Air-conditioned   ⊖ Swiss Cottage

The Guide is totally independent, accepts no free hospitality, and survives on the number of copies sold each year.

Sketch ✳

map 15

9 Conduit Street, W1S 2XG
TEL: (0870) 777 4488   FAX: (0870) 777 4400
WEBSITE: www.sketch.uk.com

COOKING **6**
MODERN FRENCH
£58–£218

It all looks quite unassuming from the outside. The presence of doormen might give an indication that it isn't for everybody, and many readers will flinch when they see the prices: a starter called 'Essence of Spring' is £42, a price at which you might reasonably expect the whole of that season, swallows and all. The results of the £10 million refurbishment of this former RIBA building in 2002 remain eye-catching, and the photographs of famous faces on the walls of the marble-floored lobby show where its heart lies: 'it's like an exclusive club for the phenomenally rich – young, flashy celebrities in particular.' The ground-floor Gallery restaurant is the best option for those wanting to get a taste of the high life without breaking the bank: from traditional soups (warm split pea, for example) to lamb in a spicy crust, served in a futuristic, starkly white and minimalist room. There's also the Parlour, which is open for breakfast, lunch and snacks, and offers everything from cakes to a hamburger with grapefruit, lime, mango and spring onion salad (£12). And a bar.

Upstairs in the Lecture Room and Library dining room (adjoining rooms, equally plush) is where super-chef Pierre Gagnaire's ideas are given free reign under the charge of head chef Pascal Sanchez. Prices are high, but this is an experience from start to finish, and an opportunity to try some of the ideas emerging from the creative mind of one of France's most lauded chefs. The tasting menu at £65 for three courses, or £80 for five, is, believe it or not, relatively cost-effective compared with the carte. Soft and delicate pieces of gingerbread, and a dish of powdered chestnut ('looking like a sandpit') stuck with wafers of crispbread are among the intriguing amuse-bouches. Starters of langoustines 'addressed in four ways', or the French Garden (pearl onion gratin and Sicilian cherry tomato crumble, and cider-braised chicory and cauliflower cream with a pea and sorrel velouté) show top-notch ingredients in complex constructions. A piece of veal fillet has seemed a little lost on the plate with a slick of heavily reduced sauce, or there might be turbot, roasted in spices accompanied with a Mac wine sabayon, grilled leeks, braised turnips and potatoes Heidi. Desserts are a strong point, with some strong flavours and clear contrasts. An 'uplifting rather than rich' chocolate ganache has come on a disc of chocolate with a 'strongly alcoholic foam' and a base of fruit compote with a 'vicious kick' of sharp berry flavour, and, as part of a 'lemon medley', an intense lemon and lime sorbet lived long in the memory for one recipient. Service is formal but genuinely passionate about the product. You can count the number of bottles under £30 on the fingers of one hand on a wine list that kicks off at £25.

CHEFS: Pierre Gagnaire and Pascal Sanchez   PROPRIETORS: Mourad Mazouz and Pierre Gagnaire   OPEN: Tue to Fri L 12 to 2, Tue to Sat D 7 to 10.30   CLOSED: Christmas, bank hols   MEALS: alc (main courses £40 to £65). Set L £22 (1 course, inc wine) to £80, Set D £65 to £80   SERVICE: 12.5% (optional), card slips closed   CARDS: Amex, Delta, Diners, MasterCard, Switch, Visa   DETAILS: 40 seats. Private parties: 150 main room. Vegetarian meals. No smoking in 1 dining room. Wheelchair access (also WC). Music. Air-conditioned   ⊖ Oxford Circus

---

All details are as accurate as possible at the time of going to press, but chefs and owners often change, and it is wise to check by telephone before making a special journey. Many readers have been disappointed when set-price bargain meals are no longer available. Ask when booking.

Smiths of Smithfield, Top Floor ▼   map 13

67–77 Charterhouse Street, EC1M 6HS   COOKING **4**
TEL: (020) 7251 7950   FAX: (020) 7236 5666   MODERN BRITISH
WEBSITE: www.smithsofsmithfield.co.uk   £33–£45

This four-floor gastrodome is a cornerstone of Smithfield's nightlife. With bouncers on the door and a heaving throng of young bodies in the ground floor bar at 8pm, one could be forgiven for confusing Smiths with its next-door neighbour, Fabric, London's über-club. Accessed by lift from the bar (or by a lot of stairs), the Top Floor restaurant is peaceful and refined, with good views of St Paul's and the City, plus plenty of business suits among the clientele.

Proximity to London's premier meat market means meat is the main event here. The house speciality is well-hung steaks, ordered from a separate 'rare meats' menu. Fish, including a beautiful Dover sole served with brown shrimp butter, also appears well-sourced. Prices are on the high side, but all the food seems to be of excellent quality, competently cooked and presented. To finish, there might be chocolate fondant with orange ice cream, topped with hot, just-candied, strips of orange peel. The wine list is international, well-chosen and pricey. Nevertheless, you can get by with £25 (the baseline is £15), and there is an inspiring range by the glass.

CHEF: Tony Moyce   PROPRIETOR: John Torode   OPEN: Sun to Fri L 12 to 2.45, all week D 6 to 10.30 CLOSED: 25 and 26 Dec, 1 Jan   MEALS: alc (main courses £10.50 to £11.50)   SERVICE: 12.5% (optional), card slips closed   CARDS: Amex, Delta, Diners, MasterCard, Switch, Visa   DETAILS: 180 seats. 32 seats outside. Private parties: 26 main room. Vegetarian meals. Wheelchair access (also WC). Music. Air-conditioned   ⊖ Farringdon

---

Snows on the Green ⅚✳   map 12

166 Shepherd's Bush Road, W6 7PB   COOKING **4**
TEL: (020) 7603 2142   FAX: (020) 7602 7553   MODERN BRITISH/MEDITERRANEAN
WEBSITE: www.snowsonthegreen.co.uk   £28–£53

Coffee, chocolate and golden beige colours mingle with gentle yellow gold and sage, giving a 'very in vogue' look to Sebastian Snow's restaurant. His menu, European with Italian leanings, involves a wide range of ingredients and cooking techniques (the tone is firmly set by a plate of bruschetta that comes with a whole head of roast garlic, tomatoes and basil and olive oil and balsamic). It is also market-orientated; a spring inspection meal opened with linguine topped with plump, freshly shelled mussels, some asparagus spears, young broad beans and wilted wild garlic. That same meal produced a large crisp-skinned red mullet fillet of 'ultra-fresh' flavour, complemented by rosemary and crisp pancetta, smooth mash, and flageolet beans slightly squashed into a creamy sauce, and also a finely balanced duck 'à la ficelle' (cooked in a sausage skin) offset by gutsy cotechino sausage and baby fennel, asparagus, French beans and marrow crostini. Desserts maintain the balance with a sophisticated coffee crème caramel with Armagnac prunes, or a trio of unpasteurised cheeses in perfect condition. There are 40-plus wines on a largely Franco–Australian list that includes 14 or so by the glass (£3.65–£8.25) and house Italian from £11.95.

CHEF/PROPRIETOR: Sebastian Snow   OPEN: Sun to Fri L 12 to 3, Mon to Sat D 6 to 11   CLOSED: 4 days at Christmas, bank hol Mons   MEALS: alc (main courses £12.50 to £16). Set L and D £12.50 (2 courses) to £16.50. Cover 95p   SERVICE: not inc, 12.5% for parties of 6 or more   CARDS: Amex, Delta, Diners, MasterCard, Switch, Visa   DETAILS: 80 seats. 10 seats outside. Private parties: 80 main room, 2 to 26

map 15

J 6PU

COOKING **8**

AX: (020) 7495 7150

MODERN FRENCH

staurant.com

£47–£124

e-wide glass frontage, the Square's interior feels discreet: restful to
oured walls punctuated with sizeable abstracts, smartly set tables all
whites.

his second decade here, still inspires comments like 'breads are
don', or 'how they produce wild duck with such tenderness and
Fish dishes are nervelessly executed; delicate crab tortellini, then
um asparagus, constituted a memorable lunch for one, while a trio
gently cooked as not to show any browning, their three teardrops
olstered by a mirepoix of meaty ceps in reduced red wine. The
e the intrinsic flavour of fine materials, so herb-crusted saddle of
s wrapped in a further, more astringent coat of spinach. Calves'
ated up with jamón Ibérico and roasting juices, while a tarte fine of
ompanied saddle of hare. For some, treatments can be slightly too
cod coming with 'almost liquid' mashed potato, buttered leeks and
esserts tend to richness. Bitter chocolate fondant comes in a casket
ate filigree handle) that exudes molten dark chocolate when
n cheesecake is served with wild strawberries, and the rhubarb
s.

e combines formality and efficiency with charm and humour, and
hailed, not for the first time, as a paragon. Wine guidance is
a list of such awesome size and quality, especially if you choose to
white Burgundy, red Bordeaux, the Rhône and Italy. But a huge
tempting options under £25 and good choices by the glass put
ce within reach of diners on a budget. House Chablis is £16.95.

ETORS: Nigel Platts-Martin and Philip Howard OPEN: Mon to Fri L 12 to 2.45,
OSED: 24 to 26 Dec, 1 Jan, L bank hols MEALS: Set L £25 (2 courses) to £55,
le table only) £75 SERVICE: 12.5% (optional), card slips closed CARDS:
Card, Switch, Visa DETAILS: 90 seats. Private parties: 90 main room, 8 to 18
eals. Wheelchair access (also WC). No music. No mobile phones. Air-

map 13

Soho, W1B 5NE

COOKING **4**

K: (020) 7437 7778

FUSION

ub.co.uk

£41–£88

ooking Soho back street parallel to Regent Street, Sugar Club
ays the effort. Large windows, dark wood and pale walls create a
l excitement is in the strikingly imaginative and exotic menu –
by some of the ingredients listed. The more conservative tastes
agus accompanied by goats' cheese crostini and rocket pesto, or
arrocina beans and rosemary, but a sense of adventure reaps
h plantain, Chinese black beans and a lime and spicy red pepper
lend of complementary flavours, while a main course of fried

The Good Food Guide 2005 voucher scheme

£5

Valid at participating restaurants, as listed in The Good Food Guide 2005, until 30 September 2005

See terms and conditions ov

Terms and Conditions

- The vouchers in *The Good Food Guide 2005* are valid from 1 October 2004 until 30 September 2005. Only one £5 voucher can be used per table booked (for a minimum of two people). No photocopies or any other kind of reproduction of vouchers will be accepted. The vouchers may not be used in conjunction with any other promotion scheme.

- The vouchers are redeemable against a pre-booked meal for a minimum of two people. For a voucher to be redeemable, the customer must mention at the time of booking his or her intent to use a voucher. The £5 is to be deducted from the final bill inclusive of VAT (and, if applicable, service), with the participating restaurant bearing the cost of the £5 discount.

- Participating establishments, which are highlighted in the pages of *The Good Food Guide 2005* by a symbol (£5) at the end of entries, may exclude certain times of day, certain days of the week, or specific menus from the scheme, as long as they (a) advise customers of the restrictions at the time of booking, and (b) accept the vouchers at a minimum of 70% of sessions when the restaurant is open.

Terms and Conditions

- The vouchers in *The Good Food Guide 2005* are valid from 1 October 2004 until 30 September 2005. Only one £5 voucher can be used per table booked (for a minimum of two people). No photocopies or any other kind of reproduction of vouchers will be accepted. The vouchers may not be used in conjunction with any other promotion scheme.

- The vouchers are redeemable against a pre-booked meal for a minimum of two people. For a voucher to be redeemable, the customer must mention at the time of booking his or her intent to use a voucher. The £5 is to be deducted from the final bill inclusive of VAT (and, if applicable, service), with the participating restaurant bearing the cost of the £5 discount.

- Participating establishments, which are highlighted in the pages of *The Good Food Guide 2005* by a symbol (£5) at the end of entries, may exclude certain times of day, certain days of the week, or specific menus from the scheme, as long as they (a) advise customers of the restrictions at the time of booking, and (b) accept the vouchers at a minimum of 70% of sessions when the restaurant is open.

Terms and Conditions

- The vouchers in *The Good Food Guide 2005* are valid from 1 October 2004 until 30 September 2005. Only one £5 voucher can be used per table booked (for a minimum of two people). No photocopies or any other kind of reproduction of vouchers will be accepted. The vouchers may not be used in conjunction with any other promotion scheme.

- The vouchers are redeemable against a pre-booked meal for a minimum of two people. For a voucher to be redeemable, the customer must mention at the time of booking his or her intent to use a voucher. The £5 is to be deducted from the final bill inclusive of VAT (and, if applicable, service), with the participating restaurant bearing the cost of the £5 discount.

- Participating establishments, which are highlighted in the pages of *The Good Food Guide 2005* by a symbol (£5) at the end of entries, may exclude certain times of day, certain days of the week, or specific menus from the scheme, as long as they (a) advise customers of the restrictions at the time of booking, and (b) accept the vouchers at a minimum of 70% of sessions when the restaurant is open.

private rooms. Vegetarian meals. Childre (not WC). Music. Air-conditioned ⊖ Ha

Sonny's ▼

94 Church Road, SW13 0DQ
TEL: (020) 8748 0393   FAX: (020) 87

This 'bright, airy and spacious' neigh when operating at full speed, and tha room by modern art on the walls. T who arrived here via the famous continues to impress. A moist and s palate in need of titillation', and a 'su foie gras coaxed delicate flavours from cinnamon-glazed turnips, while scallo with herring tuile. Main-course Mid and French beans, and grilled sea brea well kept, and desserts run from ba carpaccio, chilli syrup and coconut international mix at good prices (from on. A separate café does lunches and li

CHEF: Helena Puolaaka   PROPRIETOR: Rebe
Mon to Sat D 7.30 to 11   CLOSED: 25 Dec, b
courses) to £16.50, Set D £16 (2 courses
CARDS: Amex, Delta, MasterCard, Switch, Vi
20 private rooms. Vegetarian meals. Childre
access (not WC). No music. Air-conditioned

South

128 Curtain Road, EC2A 3AQ
TEL: (020) 7729 4452
EMAIL: southrestaurant@aol.com

South brings a touch of southern F unpretentious as the food. Decent ra combinations delivered in simple, str here and there. Menus (in French, w pears and walnuts, or crab and avoca chicken with tomato, basil and chick there's pear tart or chocolate mousse make this the kind of place to drop in wine is £12.50 on the short, all-Fren

CHEFS: Cathy Bolton and Barry Atkins   PRO
to Sat 12 to 3, 6 to 10.30   CLOSED: 10 days
£18). Set L and D 6 to 7.30 £12.95   SERVIC
MasterCard, Switch, Visa   DETAILS: 45 sea
meals. Children's helpings. No-smoking ar

Square ▼

6-10 Bruton Street,
TEL: (020) 7495 7100
WEBSITE: www.squa

Behind a seemingly the eye, with sandy turned out in their

Philip Howard, perhaps the best in juiciness is beyond wild salmon with p of scallops have be of white onion pu cooking seeks to e lamb, fringed wit sweetbreads may b celeriac and pear h soft and luxurious a truffled cream sa (sponge lid and opened. A Brilla soufflé is as good

Largely French the sommelier h virtually obligato explore the wone splurge is not ob some sips of self-i

CHEF: Philip Howard
all week D 6.30 to 10
Set D £55, Set L ar
Amex, Delta, Diners
private rooms. Veg
conditioned ⊖ G

Sugar Clu

21 Warwick Stree
TEL: (020) 7437 7
WEBSITE: www.the

Hidden down a takes some findin smart interior, b many reporters a may choose stear roast saddle of la rewards. Grilled s sauce proves an wild sea bass with Japanese aubergine, hijiki and enoki mushrooms and truffle miso dressing 'looked marvellous and was an adventure to eat – fascinating flavours and texture, all going well together'. A relatively simple sweet of oven-cooked young, tender rhubarb with raspberries and vanilla ice cream has been enjoyed. Service isn't always friendly and on the ball, and beware asking the sommelier's advice unless you have a generous wine budget – not that there are many bargains anyway, with house selections starting at £24. The Sugar Club was closed for refurbishment as we went to press.

CHEF: David Selex   PROPRIETORS: Ashley Sumner and Vivienne Hayman   OPEN: Mon to Fri L 12 to 3, all week D 5.30 to 11 (6 to 10.30 Sun)   CLOSED: 24 to 26 Dec, bank hol Mon L   MEALS: alc (main courses £15 to £23.50). Set L and 5.30 to 6.30 D £16.50 (2 courses)   SERVICE: 12.5% (optional), card slips closed   CARDS: Amex, Delta, Diners, MasterCard, Switch, Visa   DETAILS: 120 seats. Private parties: 95 main room, 15 to 55 private rooms. Vegetarian meals. No smoking. Wheelchair access (not WC). No music. Air-conditioned   ⊖ Piccadilly Circus

Sumosan
map 15

26 Albemarle Street, W1S 4HY
TEL: (020) 7495 5999   FAX: (020) 7355 1247
WEBSITE: www.sumosan.com

COOKING 4
MODERN JAPANESE
£33–£150

'A great place to go and see the beautiful people at play in a beautiful environment,' reckoned a correspondent. The blue-tinted glass step over a mock-Japanese garden makes an impressively spectacular entrance, and the dining room is awash with modish gestures. 'Japanese fusion' is the style, and dishes look oh-so dramatic on the plate – no wonder it's the 'fashionistas' grazing food of choice'. Sushi and sashimi cast their net wide for everything from hokki clams and flying fish roe to goose liver and Peking duck, and *de rigueur* freshness also shows in a stunning plate of three tartares: salmon, toro (tuna belly) and yellowtail. The kitchen copes impressively with classic specialities like nasu miso (deep-fried aubergine on a bamboo leaf topped with mirin-sweetened yellow miso) and jumps several borders for roast leg of wild rabbit with girolle sauce. As a pyrotechnic finale, order wild berry doriyaki with almond and plum wine sauce, which arrives at the table in flames. Service is 'young and groovy'. Equally groovy cocktails are alternatives to the wide-ranging wine list, where prices start at £15.

CHEF: Bubker Belkhit   PROPRIETOR: Janina Wolkow   OPEN: Mon to Fri L 12 to 2.45, all week D 6 to 11.30 (10.30 Sun)   CLOSED: bank hols   MEALS: alc (main courses £11.50 to £55). Set L £19.50 to £45, Set D 6 to 7 £27.50, Set D £65   SERVICE: 12.5% (optional)   CARDS: Amex, Delta, Diners, MasterCard, Switch, Visa   DETAILS: 140 seats. Private parties: 160 main room, 30 private room. Vegetarian meals. No-smoking area. Wheelchair access (also WC). Music. Air-conditioned   ⊖ Green Park

Sushi-Hiro £
NEW ENTRY   map 12

1 Station Parade, Uxbridge Road, W5 3LD
TEL: 020 8896 3175   FAX: 020 8896 3209

COOKING 3
JAPANESE
£21–£31

'Well worth the drive to Ealing' is one reporter's considered view of this scrupulously clean little sushi joint opposite Ealing Common station (and no, he doesn't live in Acton).' Ever so friendly, smiling chefs' produce a wide variety of nigiri: the seven-piece deluxe set comprises tuna, organic salmon, surf clam, turbot and more besides. Pickled plums, gourds, radishes and fermented beans add diversity to the choice of maki rolls, and there are chirashi sets comprising bowls of sushi rice topped with seaweed, egg and fresh seafood. Assorted sashimi and bowls of miso soup complete the repertoire. Ingredients are 'sparklingly fresh' and rice is 'a cut above most other competitors in London', according to one with well-travelled taste buds. Prices across the board are remarkably low, but note that payment is by cash only. Drink beer, sake or something soft.

CHEF/PROPRIETOR: H Shimakage   OPEN: Tue to Sun 11 to 1.30, 4.30 to 9   MEALS: alc (main courses £5 to £14)   SERVICE: not inc   CARDS: none   DETAILS: 21 seats. Music. Air-conditioned   ⊖ Ealing Common

Sushi-Say ⅍ £

map 12

33B Walm Lane, NW2 5SH
TEL: (020) 8459 2971 and 7512   FAX: (020) 8907 3229

COOKING 3
JAPANESE
£27–£76

The location may be downtown Willesden Green, but this spruce family-run restaurant succeeds in delivering Japanese food without compromise. The place hums every evening, and there's something very personal about its mood: chef Katsuharu Shimizu looks the part, while his wife presides over events in a kimono. Lunch plates and user-friendly set dinners are good value, while the regular menu encompasses sushi, sashimi, a host of appetisers and other staples from the traditional repertoire. Also check out the daily specials, which could include rarely encountered items such as deep-fried hairtail fish and hijiki seaweed with chopped vegetables. Wasabi ice cream sounds like an adventurous dessert, and you could cleanse your palate with the house digestif (vodka and pressed apple juice). Prices on the promising little wine list start at £9.95.

CHEF: Katsuharu Shimizu   PROPRIETORS: Katsuharu and Yuko Shimizu   OPEN: Sat and Sun L 1 to 3.15, Tue to Fri D 6.30 to 10.30, Sat and Sun D 6 to 11   MEALS: alc (main courses £6.50 to £19). Set L £8.20 to £12.80 (all 1 or 2 courses), Set D £18.30 to £28.80   SERVICE: not inc   CARDS: Amex, Delta, MasterCard, Switch, Visa   DETAILS: 36 seats. Private parties: 20 main room. Vegetarian meals. No smoking. Wheelchair access (also WC). No music. Air-conditioned   ⊖ Willesden Green

▲ Swissôtel The Howard, Jaan

map 13

Temple Place, WC2R 2PR
TEL: (020) 7836 3555   FAX: (020) 7240 7186

NEW CHEF
FRENCH/SOUTH-EAST ASIAN
£49–£108

The Howard's exterior belies a foyer that seems to have 'overdosed on opulent marble' and a light and spacious rectangular-shaped dining room with polished oak flooring, silk-upholstered chairs and floor-to-ceiling windows overlooking a central garden. Australian-born Paul Peters took over the kitchen as the Guide went to press, and he seems set to maintain the style of modern French dishes strongly influenced by South-east Asia. This translates into such starters as oriental mushroom consommé with Chinese chives, truffle and shiitake ravioli, and lobster salad with pickled daikon, cucumber, mango, paw-paw and yuzu dressing. Rack of lamb makes a reassuring main course, here served with aubergine caviar, pak choi, water chestnuts, miso and a natural jus, while puddings such as chocolate crème brûlée with raspberry sorbet steer a more European route. With only one bottle below £20 on the wine list – the bulk are well above £30 – older clarets and Super-Tuscans jostle with top New World wines.

CHEF: Paul Peters   PROPRIETOR: Swissôtel   OPEN: Mon to Fri L 12 to 2.30, all week D 5.45 to 10.30   MEALS: Set L £28 to £31, Set D £39 to £45   SERVICE: 12.5%   CARDS: Amex, Diners, MasterCard, Switch,

Visa   DETAILS: 56 seats. 24 seats outside. Private parties: 90 main room, 10 to 130 private rooms. Car park. Children's helpings. No children under 4. Wheelchair access (also WC). Music. Air-conditioned ACCOMMODATION: 189 rooms, all with bath/shower. TV. Phone. Room only £295 to £650. Rooms for disabled. Baby facilities   ⊖ Temple

Tamarind ✻

map 15

20 Queen Street, W1J 5PR	COOKING 3
TEL: (020) 7629 3561 FAX: (020) 7499 5034	MODERN INDIAN
WEBSITE: www.tamarindrestaurant.com	£31–£99

On a quiet Mayfair side street, this swish and opulently decorated Indian restaurant in a low-ceilinged basement is comfortably in tune with its upper-crust W1 postcode. The kitchen scours the Subcontinent for inspiration, and the tandoor gets plenty of use – handling everything from king prawns and lamb cutlets to broccoli with paneer cheese. Seafood receives contemporary treatment: spicy herb-crusted John Dory was the dazzling high point of one thoroughly enjoyable meal. Elsewhere, innovation shows in appetisers like chicken breast in a crisp batter of lentils and rice-flour flavoured with ginger and curry leaves and accompanied by an avocado dip, while interesting vegetable dishes take in paneer with cherries in creamed tomatoes and fenugreek leaves. Rice and breads are 'well above normal standard', and desserts are the real thing. Prices are 'not cheap', and the wine list zooms skywards from house selections at £16.50.

CHEF: Alfred Prasad   PROPRIETOR: Indian Cuisine Ltd   OPEN: Sun to Fri L 12 to 2.45, all week D 6 to 11 MEALS: alc (main courses £13 to £26). Set L £14.95 (2 courses) to £16.95, Set D £48 to £65 (some min 6) SERVICE: 12.5% (optional), card slips closed   CARDS: Amex, Delta, Diners, MasterCard, Switch, Visa DETAILS: 100 seats. Private parties: 100 main room. Vegetarian meals. No children under 6. No smoking in 1 dining room. Music. Air-conditioned   ⊖ Green Park £5

Tandoor

NEW ENTRY   map 12

232–234 Kingsbury Road, NW9 0BH	COOKING 2
TEL: (020) 8205 1450 FAX: (020) 8205 6613	INDIAN
EMAIL: tandoorlondon@aol.com	£31–£56

A 'barely converted' pub is the unexpected setting for this recently opened venue, which serves authentic Mughlai and North Indian food. Influences are drawn from the Awadhi, Rajasthani, Punjabi and Kashmiri traditions, say the owners, and the menu shows a neat balance of meat, fish, and vegetarian dishes. Chicken biryani is the real thing (sealed in a pot with pastry), and successful vegetables have included aloo jeera (potatoes and spinach laced with cumin), and khumb kaju mattar (mushrooms and peas in a cashew-based gravy). Breads – such as ultra-thin, folded romali roti – are not to be missed, and excellent kulfi is made on the premises. Drink beer or something from the minimal wine list. House wine is £10.95.

CHEF: Raman Sharda   PROPRIETOR: Nitu Khurana   OPEN: all week 12 to 3, 6 to 11   CLOSED: 25 Dec, 1 Jan MEALS: alc (main courses £6 to £13). Set L Mon to Fri £6.99 (1 course)   SERVICE: not inc   CARDS: MasterCard, Switch, Visa   DETAILS: 72 seats. 24 seats outside. Private parties: 50 main room, 30 to 50 private rooms. Car park. Vegetarian meals. No-smoking area. Wheelchair access (also WC). Music ⊖ Kingsbury £5

Tas ✷ £

map 13

33 The Cut, SE1 8LF
TEL: (020) 7928 1444   FAX: (020) 7633 9686
WEBSITE: www.tasrestaurant.com

COOKING 2
TURKISH
£21–£44

The Old Vic and the Festival Hall are within easy reach of this buzzily atmospheric Turkish brasserie, which scores with its bubbly service, music and keen prices. 'Tas' means a traditional Anatolian casserole pot: hence the presence of these comforting stomach-fillers on the menu. Recommended starters have included triangular borek pastries and patlican-biber kizartma (fried aubergines with peppers), and the kitchen also provides a healthy balance of salads, pilaffs, high-protein grills and fish specials like fried squid with walnut sauce. Desserts are traditional recipes, including kayisi tatlisi (home-made cream with sun-dried apricots, almonds and pistachios). A few gluggable Turkish wines pop up on the list. Villa Doluca is £10.95. There's a branch at 72 Borough High Street, SE1, tel: (020) 7403 7200, with a café close by.

The group's latest venture, Tas Pide, gives pride of place to 'pides' (boat-shaped Turkish versions of pizza): outlets are at 37 Farringdon Road, EC1, tel: (020) 7430 9721, and 20–22 New Globe Walk, SE1, tel: (020) 7928 3300. Another restaurant complex, Tas Gurme, is due to open in September 2004 at The Arches, 97–99 Isabella Street, SE1.

CHEF: Onder Sahan   PROPRIETORS: Onder Sahan, Ali Selim, Ismail Duman and Dervis Aslan   OPEN: all week 12 to 11.30 (10.30 Sun)   MEALS: alc (main courses £5.50 to £14.50). Set L and D £7.95 (2 courses) to £18.50   SERVICE: 10%   CARDS: Amex, Delta, MasterCard, Switch, Visa   DETAILS: 140 seats. 8 seats outside. Private parties: 55 main room. Vegetarian meals. No smoking in 1 dining room. Wheelchair access (also WC). Music. Air-conditioned   ⊖ Southwark

---

Tate Britain Restaurant 🍾

map 13

Millbank, SW1P 4RG
TEL: (020) 7887 8825   FAX: (020) 7887 8902
WEBSITE: www.tate.org.uk

COOKING 3
MODERN BRITISH
£34–£63

If the murals are your cup of tea, this must be one of London's prettiest dining rooms: 'ravishing rural murals bathe in a romantic golden glow', as one reader put it. Perhaps they inspire cooking based on seasonal and carefully sourced British produce. A new chef arrived in May 2004, and inspection showed the kitchen delivering food worthy of the setting, although the 'pleasant' service needed better coordination. Silky potato and watercress soup came with fresh pea shoots and perfectly coddled egg, but marinated herrings succumbed to a crudely seasoned curried dressing. Chargrilled spring vegetables and goats' cheese curd have been nicely assembled on sourdough toast, or else there might be herbed calf's liver with Swiss chard, runner beans and buttered carrots. Finish with simple but toothsome rhubarb and custard. One of the joys of dining here is dipping into one of the best wine lists in London. Since this is a lunchtime-only venue, options by the glass and half-bottle are important, and they are good and plentiful. The Francocentric list makes successful forays into other countries, and is always good value. Well-chosen house is £15.

CHEF: Andy Barber   PROPRIETOR: Tate Catering   OPEN: all week L only 12 to 3 (4 Sun)   CLOSED: 24 to 26 Dec   MEALS: alc L (main courses £11 to £18.50). Set L £17.50 (2 courses) to £20.50   SERVICE: not inc, card slips closed   CARDS: Amex, Delta, Diners, MasterCard, Switch, Visa   DETAILS: 90 seats. 20 seats

Square 🍾

map 15

6-10 Bruton Street, W1J 6PU
TEL: (020) 7495 7100 FAX: (020) 7495 7150
WEBSITE: www.squarerestaurant.com

COOKING **8**
MODERN FRENCH
£47–£124

Behind a seemingly mile-wide glass frontage, the Square's interior feels discreet: restful to the eye, with sandy-coloured walls punctuated with sizeable abstracts, smartly set tables all turned out in their best whites.

Philip Howard, into his second decade here, still inspires comments like 'breads are perhaps the best in London', or 'how they produce wild duck with such tenderness and juiciness is beyond me'. Fish dishes are nervelessly executed; delicate crab tortellini, then wild salmon with premium asparagus, constituted a memorable lunch for one, while a trio of scallops have been so gently cooked as not to show any browning, their three teardrops of white onion purée bolstered by a mirepoix of meaty ceps in reduced red wine. The cooking seeks to enhance the intrinsic flavour of fine materials, so herb-crusted saddle of lamb, fringed with fat, is wrapped in a further, more astringent coat of spinach. Calves' sweetbreads may be pointed up with jamón Ibérico and roasting juices, while a tarte fine of celeriac and pear has accompanied saddle of hare. For some, treatments can be slightly too soft and luxurious: roast cod coming with 'almost liquid' mashed potato, buttered leeks and a truffled cream sauce. Desserts tend to richness. Bitter chocolate fondant comes in a casket (sponge lid and chocolate filigree handle) that exudes molten dark chocolate when opened. A Brillat-Savarin cheesecake is served with wild strawberries, and the rhubarb soufflé is as good as it gets.

Largely French service combines formality and efficiency with charm and humour, and the sommelier has been hailed, not for the first time, as a paragon. Wine guidance is virtually obligatory with a list of such awesome size and quality, especially if you choose to explore the wonders of white Burgundy, red Bordeaux, the Rhône and Italy. But a huge splurge is not obligatory: tempting options under £25 and good choices by the glass put some sips of self-indulgence within reach of diners on a budget. House Chablis is £16.95.

CHEF: Philip Howard PROPRIETORS: Nigel Platts-Martin and Philip Howard OPEN: Mon to Fri L 12 to 2.45, all week D 6.30 to 10.45 CLOSED: 24 to 26 Dec, 1 Jan, L bank hols MEALS: Set L £25 (2 courses) to £55, Set D £55, Set L and D (whole table only) £75 SERVICE: 12.5% (optional), card slips closed CARDS: Amex, Delta, Diners, MasterCard, Switch, Visa DETAILS: 90 seats. Private parties: 90 main room, 8 to 18 private rooms. Vegetarian meals. Wheelchair access (also WC). No music. No mobile phones. Air-conditioned ⊖ Green Park

Sugar Club ⅝✳

map 13

21 Warwick Street, West Soho, W1B 5NE
TEL: (020) 7437 7776 FAX: (020) 7437 7778
WEBSITE: www.thesugarclub.co.uk

COOKING **4**
FUSION
£41–£88

Hidden down a murky-looking Soho back street parallel to Regent Street, Sugar Club takes some finding but repays the effort. Large windows, dark wood and pale walls create a smart interior, but the real excitement is in the strikingly imaginative and exotic menu – many reporters are baffled by some of the ingredients listed. The more conservative tastes may choose steamed asparagus accompanied by goats' cheese crostini and rocket pesto, or roast saddle of lamb with arrocina beans and rosemary, but a sense of adventure reaps rewards. Grilled squid with plantain, Chinese black beans and a lime and spicy red pepper sauce proves an exciting blend of complementary flavours, while a main course of fried private rooms. Vegetarian meals. Children's helpings. No smoking in 1 dining room. Wheelchair access (not WC). Music. Air-conditioned ⊖ Hammersmith Broadway

---

Sonny's ♟

map 12

94 Church Road, SW13 0DQ
TEL: (020) 8748 0393   FAX: (020) 8748 2698

COOKING 5
MODERN EUROPEAN
£27–£56

This 'bright, airy and spacious' neighbourhood restaurant can generate a considerable buzz when operating at full speed, and that seems to be much of the time. Colour is added to the room by modern art on the walls. The highly professional cooking of the Finnish chef, who arrived here via the famous French kitchens of Messrs Gagnaire and Koffman, continues to impress. A moist and succulent quail has been deemed 'ideal for the jaded palate in need of titillation', and a 'superbly crafted' pressée of smoked eel, pork belly and foie gras coaxed delicate flavours from robust ingredients. Foie gras may be fricasséed with cinnamon-glazed turnips, while scallops with pea and mint sauce and spinach come topped with herring tuile. Main-course Middle White pork loin has come with truffled gnocchi and French beans, and grilled sea bream with langoustine sauce on pappardelle. Cheeses are well kept, and desserts run from banana Tatin with butterscotch ice cream to mango carpaccio, chilli syrup and coconut sorbet. Two pages of wines pack in an inspired international mix at good prices (from £12). Fourteen of them also come by the glass. Spot on. A separate café does lunches and light bites.

CHEF: Helena Puolakka   PROPRIETOR: Rebecca Mascarenhas   OPEN: all week L 12.30 to 2.30 (3 Sun), Mon to Sat D 7.30 to 11   CLOSED: 25 Dec, bank hols   MEALS: alc (main courses £11 to £16). Set L £13 (2 courses) to £16.50, Set D £16 (2 courses) to £19.50   SERVICE: 12.5% (optional), card slips closed   CARDS: Amex, Delta, MasterCard, Switch, Visa   DETAILS: 100 seats. Private parties: 80 main room, 12 to 20 private rooms. Vegetarian meals. Children's helpings. No pipes/cigars. No-smoking area. Wheelchair access (not WC). No music. Air-conditioned ⊖ Hammersmith £5

South

map 13

128 Curtain Road, EC2A 3AQ
TEL: (020) 7729 4452
EMAIL: southrestaurant@aol.com

COOKING 2
FRENCH
£24–£54

South brings a touch of southern France to Hoxton, its modern interior as light and unpretentious as the food. Decent raw materials underlie generally colourful, balanced combinations delivered in simple, straightforward style with 'shades of Elizabeth David' here and there. Menus (in French, with translation) offer things like salad of Roquefort, pears and walnuts, or crab and avocado salad with dill and flatbread, followed by braised chicken with tomato, basil and chickpeas, or duck breast with red chicory and fig sauce; there's pear tart or chocolate mousse to finish. Neighbourhood feel and reasonable prices make this the kind of place to drop into regularly, rather than on special occasions. House wine is £12.50 on the short, all-French list.

CHEFS: Cathy Bolton and Barry Atkins   PROPRIETORS: Cathy Bolton and Jonathan Mortimer   OPEN: Mon to Sat 12 to 3, 6 to 10.30   CLOSED: 10 days at Christmas, bank hols   MEALS: alc (main courses £9.50 to £18). Set L and D 6 to 7.30 £12.95   SERVICE: 12.5% (optional), card slips closed   CARDS: Amex, Delta, MasterCard, Switch, Visa   DETAILS: 45 seats. 6 seats outside. Private parties: 45 main room. Vegetarian meals. Children's helpings. No-smoking area. Wheelchair access (also WC). Music £5

Terms and Conditions

- The vouchers in *The Good Food Guide 2005* are valid from 1 October 2004 until 30 September 2005. Only one £5 voucher can be used per table booked (for a minimum of two people). No photocopies or any other kind of reproduction of vouchers will be accepted. The vouchers may not be used in conjunction with any other promotion scheme.

- The vouchers are redeemable against a pre-booked meal for a minimum of two people. For a voucher to be redeemable, the customer must mention at the time of booking his or her intent to use a voucher. The £5 is to be deducted from the final bill inclusive of VAT (and, if applicable, service), with the participating restaurant bearing the cost of the £5 discount.

- Participating establishments, which are highlighted in the pages of *The Good Food Guide 2005* by a symbol **(£5)** at the end of entries, may exclude certain times of day, certain days of the week, or specific menus from the scheme, as long as they (a) advise customers of the restrictions at the time of booking, and (b) accept the vouchers at a minimum of 70% of sessions when the restaurant is open.

Terms and Conditions

- The vouchers in *The Good Food Guide 2005* are valid from 1 October 2004 until 30 September 2005. Only one £5 voucher can be used per table booked (for a minimum of two people). No photocopies or any other kind of reproduction of vouchers will be accepted. The vouchers may not be used in conjunction with any other promotion scheme.

- The vouchers are redeemable against a pre-booked meal for a minimum of two people. For a voucher to be redeemable, the customer must mention at the time of booking his or her intent to use a voucher. The £5 is to be deducted from the final bill inclusive of VAT (and, if applicable, service), with the participating restaurant bearing the cost of the £5 discount.

- Participating establishments, which are highlighted in the pages of *The Good Food Guide 2005* by a symbol **(£5)** at the end of entries, may exclude certain times of day, certain days of the week, or specific menus from the scheme, as long as they (a) advise customers of the restrictions at the time of booking, and (b) accept the vouchers at a minimum of 70% of sessions when the restaurant is open.

Terms and Conditions

- The vouchers in *The Good Food Guide 2005* are valid from 1 October 2004 until 30 September 2005. Only one £5 voucher can be used per table booked (for a minimum of two people). No photocopies or any other kind of reproduction of vouchers will be accepted. The vouchers may not be used in conjunction with any other promotion scheme.

- The vouchers are redeemable against a pre-booked meal for a minimum of two people. For a voucher to be redeemable, the customer must mention at the time of booking his or her intent to use a voucher. The £5 is to be deducted from the final bill inclusive of VAT (and, if applicable, service), with the participating restaurant bearing the cost of the £5 discount.

- Participating establishments, which are highlighted in the pages of *The Good Food Guide 2005* by a symbol **(£5)** at the end of entries, may exclude certain times of day, certain days of the week, or specific menus from the scheme, as long as they (a) advise customers of the restrictions at the time of booking, and (b) accept the vouchers at a minimum of 70% of sessions when the restaurant is open.

Terms and Conditions

- The vouchers in *The Good Food Guide 2005* are valid from 1 October 2004 until 30 September 2005. Only one £5 voucher can be used per table booked (for a minimum of two people). No photocopies or any other kind of reproduction of vouchers will be accepted. The vouchers may not be used in conjunction with any other promotion scheme.

- The vouchers are redeemable against a pre-booked meal for a minimum of two people. For a voucher to be redeemable, the customer must mention at the time of booking his or her intent to use a voucher. The £5 is to be deducted from the final bill inclusive of VAT (and, if applicable, service), with the participating restaurant bearing the cost of the £5 discount.

- Participating establishments, which are highlighted in the pages of *The Good Food Guide 2005* by a symbol **(£5)** at the end of entries, may exclude certain times of day, certain days of the week, or specific menus from the scheme, as long as they (a) advise customers of the restrictions at the time of booking, and (b) accept the vouchers at a minimum of 70% of sessions when the restaurant is open.

The Good Food
Guide 2005
voucher scheme

£5

*Valid at participating
restaurants, as listed in*
The Good Food Guide 2005,
until 30 September 2005

See terms and conditions over

The Good Food
Guide 2005
voucher scheme

£5

*Valid at participating
restaurants, as listed in*
The Good Food Guide 2005,
until 30 September 2005

See terms and conditions over

The Good Food
Guide 2005
voucher scheme

£5

*Valid at participating
restaurants, as listed in*
The Good Food Guide 2005,
until 30 September 2005

See terms and conditions over

The Good Food
Guide 2005
voucher scheme

£5

*Valid at participating
restaurants, as listed in*
The Good Food Guide 2005,
until 30 September 2005

See terms and conditions over

wild sea bass with Japanese aubergine, hijiki and enoki mushrooms and truffle miso dressing 'looked marvellous and was an adventure to eat – fascinating flavours and texture, all going well together'. A relatively simple sweet of oven-cooked young, tender rhubarb with raspberries and vanilla ice cream has been enjoyed. Service isn't always friendly and on the ball, and beware asking the sommelier's advice unless you have a generous wine budget – not that there are many bargains anyway, with house selections starting at £24. The Sugar Club was closed for refurbishment as we went to press.

CHEF: David Selex   PROPRIETORS: Ashley Sumner and Vivienne Hayman   OPEN: Mon to Fri L 12 to 3, all week D 5.30 to 11 (6 to 10.30 Sun)   CLOSED: 24 to 26 Dec, bank hol Mon L   MEALS: alc (main courses £15 to £23.50). Set L and 5.30 to 6.30 D £16.50 (2 courses)   SERVICE: 12.5% (optional), card slips closed CARDS: Amex, Delta, Diners, MasterCard, Switch, Visa   DETAILS: 120 seats. Private parties: 95 main room, 15 to 55 private rooms. Vegetarian meals. No smoking. Wheelchair access (not WC). No music. Air-conditioned   ⊖ Piccadilly Circus

Sumosan
map 15

26 Albemarle Street, W1S 4HY
TEL: (020) 7495 5999   FAX: (020) 7355 1247
WEBSITE: www.sumosan.com

COOKING 4
MODERN JAPANESE
£33–£150

'A great place to go and see the beautiful people at play in a beautiful environment,' reckoned a correspondent. The blue-tinted glass step over a mock-Japanese garden makes an impressively spectacular entrance, and the dining room is awash with modish gestures. 'Japanese fusion' is the style, and dishes look oh-so dramatic on the plate – no wonder it's the 'fashionistas' grazing food of choice'. Sushi and sashimi cast their net wide for everything from hokki clams and flying fish roe to goose liver and Peking duck, and *de rigueur* freshness also shows in a stunning plate of three tartares: salmon, toro (tuna belly) and yellowtail. The kitchen copes impressively with classic specialities like nasu miso (deep-fried aubergine on a bamboo leaf topped with mirin-sweetened yellow miso) and jumps several borders for roast leg of wild rabbit with girolle sauce. As a pyrotechnic finale, order wild berry doriyaki with almond and plum wine sauce, which arrives at the table in flames. Service is 'young and groovy'. Equally groovy cocktails are alternatives to the wide-ranging wine list, where prices start at £15.

CHEF: Bubker Belkhit   PROPRIETOR: Janina Wolkow   OPEN: Mon to Fri L 12 to 2.45, all week D 6 to 11.30 (10.30 Sun)   CLOSED: bank hols   MEALS: alc (main courses £11.50 to £55). Set L £19.50 to £45, Set D 6 to 7 £27.50, Set D £65   SERVICE: 12.5% (optional)   CARDS: Amex, Delta, Diners, MasterCard, Switch, Visa DETAILS: 140 seats. Private parties: 160 main room, 30 private room. Vegetarian meals. No-smoking area. Wheelchair access (also WC). Music. Air-conditioned   ⊖ Green Park

Sushi-Hiro £
NEW ENTRY   map 12

1 Station Parade, Uxbridge Road, W5 3LD
TEL: 020 8896 3175   FAX: 020 8896 3209

COOKING 3
JAPANESE
£21–£31

'Well worth the drive to Ealing' is one reporter's considered view of this scrupulously clean little sushi joint opposite Ealing Common station (and no, he doesn't live in Acton).' Ever so friendly, smiling chefs' produce a wide variety of nigiri: the seven-piece deluxe set comprises tuna, organic salmon, surf clam, turbot and more besides. Pickled plums, gourds, radishes and fermented beans add diversity to the choice of maki rolls, and there are chirashi sets comprising bowls of sushi rice topped with seaweed, egg and fresh seafood. Assorted sashimi and bowls of miso soup complete the repertoire. Ingredients are 'sparklingly fresh' and rice is 'a cut above most other competitors in London', according to one with well-travelled taste buds. Prices across the board are remarkably low, but note that payment is by cash only. Drink beer, sake or something soft.

CHEF/PROPRIETOR: H Shimakage   OPEN: Tue to Sun 11 to 1.30, 4.30 to 9   MEALS: alc (main courses £5 to £14)   SERVICE: not inc   CARDS: none   DETAILS: 21 seats. Music. Air-conditioned   ⊖ Ealing Common

Sushi-Say ✱ £

map 12

33B Walm Lane, NW2 5SH
TEL: (020) 8459 2971 and 7512   FAX: (020) 8907 3229

COOKING 3
JAPANESE
£27–£76

The location may be downtown Willesden Green, but this spruce family-run restaurant succeeds in delivering Japanese food without compromise. The place hums every evening, and there's something very personal about its mood: chef Katsuharu Shimizu looks the part, while his wife presides over events in a kimono. Lunch plates and user-friendly set dinners are good value, while the regular menu encompasses sushi, sashimi, a host of appetisers and other staples from the traditional repertoire. Also check out the daily specials, which could include rarely encountered items such as deep-fried hairtail fish and hijiki seaweed with chopped vegetables. Wasabi ice cream sounds like an adventurous dessert, and you could cleanse your palate with the house digestif (vodka and pressed apple juice). Prices on the promising little wine list start at £9.95.

CHEF: Katsuharu Shimizu   PROPRIETORS: Katsuharu and Yuko Shimizu   OPEN: Sat and Sun L 1 to 3.15, Tue to Fri D 6.30 to 10.30, Sat and Sun D 6 to 11   MEALS: alc (main courses £6.50 to £19). Set L £8.20 to £12.80 (all 1 or 2 courses), Set D £18.30 to £28.80   SERVICE: not inc   CARDS: Amex, Delta, MasterCard, Switch, Visa   DETAILS: 36 seats. Private parties: 20 main room. Vegetarian meals. No smoking. Wheelchair access (also WC). No music. Air-conditioned   ⊖ Willesden Green

▲ Swissôtel The Howard, Jaan

map 13

Temple Place, WC2R 2PR
TEL: (020) 7836 3555   FAX: (020) 7240 7186

NEW CHEF
FRENCH/SOUTH-EAST ASIAN
£49–£108

The Howard's exterior belies a foyer that seems to have 'overdosed on opulent marble' and a light and spacious rectangular-shaped dining room with polished oak flooring, silk-upholstered chairs and floor-to-ceiling windows overlooking a central garden. Australian-born Paul Peters took over the kitchen as the Guide went to press, and he seems set to maintain the style of modern French dishes strongly influenced by South-east Asia. This translates into such starters as oriental mushroom consommé with Chinese chives, truffle and shiitake ravioli, and lobster salad with pickled daikon, cucumber, mango, paw-paw and yuzu dressing. Rack of lamb makes a reassuring main course, here served with aubergine caviar, pak choi, water chestnuts, miso and a natural jus, while puddings such as chocolate crème brûlée with raspberry sorbet steer a more European route. With only one bottle below £20 on the wine list – the bulk are well above £30 – older clarets and Super-Tuscans jostle with top New World wines.

CHEF: Paul Peters   PROPRIETOR: Swissôtel   OPEN: Mon to Fri L 12 to 2.30, all week D 5.45 to 10.30   MEALS: Set L £28 to £31, Set D £39 to £45   SERVICE: 12.5%   CARDS: Amex, Diners, MasterCard, Switch,

Visa DETAILS: 56 seats. 24 seats outside. Private parties: 90 main room, 10 to 130 private rooms. Car park. Children's helpings. No children under 4. Wheelchair access (also WC). Music. Air-conditioned ACCOMMODATION: 189 rooms, all with bath/shower. TV. Phone. Room only £295 to £650. Rooms for disabled. Baby facilities ⊖ Temple

Tamarind ※

map 15

20 Queen Street, W1J 5PR
TEL: (020) 7629 3561   FAX: (020) 7499 5034
WEBSITE: www.tamarindrestaurant.com

COOKING 3
MODERN INDIAN
£31–£99

On a quiet Mayfair side street, this swish and opulently decorated Indian restaurant in a low-ceilinged basement is comfortably in tune with its upper-crust W1 postcode. The kitchen scours the Subcontinent for inspiration, and the tandoor gets plenty of use – handling everything from king prawns and lamb cutlets to broccoli with paneer cheese. Seafood receives contemporary treatment: spicy herb-crusted John Dory was the dazzling high point of one thoroughly enjoyable meal. Elsewhere, innovation shows in appetisers like chicken breast in a crisp batter of lentils and rice-flour flavoured with ginger and curry leaves and accompanied by an avocado dip, while interesting vegetable dishes take in paneer with cherries in creamed tomatoes and fenugreek leaves. Rice and breads are 'well above normal standard', and desserts are the real thing. Prices are 'not cheap', and the wine list zooms skywards from house selections at £16.50.

CHEF: Alfred Prasad   PROPRIETOR: Indian Cuisine Ltd   OPEN: Sun to Fri L 12 to 2.45, all week D 6 to 11 MEALS: alc (main courses £13 to £26). Set L £14.95 (2 courses) to £16.95, Set D £48 to £65 (some min 6) SERVICE: 12.5% (optional), card slips closed   CARDS: Amex, Delta, Diners, MasterCard, Switch, Visa DETAILS: 100 seats. Private parties: 100 main room. Vegetarian meals. No children under 6. No smoking in 1 dining room. Music. Air-conditioned ⊖ Green Park (£5)

Tandoor

NEW ENTRY   map 12

232–234 Kingsbury Road, NW9 0BH
TEL: (020) 8205 1450   FAX: (020) 8205 6613
EMAIL: tandoorlondon@aol.com

COOKING 2
INDIAN
£31–£56

A 'barely converted' pub is the unexpected setting for this recently opened venue, which serves authentic Mughlai and North Indian food. Influences are drawn from the Awadhi, Rajasthani, Punjabi and Kashmiri traditions, say the owners, and the menu shows a neat balance of meat, fish, and vegetarian dishes. Chicken biryani is the real thing (sealed in a pot with pastry), and successful vegetables have included aloo jeera (potatoes and spinach laced with cumin), and khumb kaju mattar (mushrooms and peas in a cashew-based gravy). Breads – such as ultra-thin, folded romali roti – are not to be missed, and excellent kulfi is made on the premises. Drink beer or something from the minimal wine list. House wine is £10.95.

CHEF: Raman Sharda   PROPRIETOR: Nitu Khurana   OPEN: all week 12 to 3, 6 to 11   CLOSED: 25 Dec, 1 Jan MEALS: alc (main courses £6 to £13). Set L Mon to Fri £6.99 (1 course)   SERVICE: not inc   CARDS: MasterCard, Switch, Visa   DETAILS: 72 seats. 24 seats outside. Private parties: 50 main room, 30 to 50 private rooms. Car park. Vegetarian meals. No-smoking area. Wheelchair access (also WC). Music ⊖ Kingsbury (£5)

Tas £

33 The Cut, SE1 8LF

TEL: (020) 7928 1444   FAX: (020) 7633 9686

WEBSITE: www.tasrestaurant.com

COOKING 2

TURKISH

£21–£44

map 13

The Old Vic and the Festival Hall are within easy reach of this buzzily atmospheric Turkish brasserie, which scores with its bubbly service, music and keen prices. 'Tas' means a traditional Anatolian casserole pot: hence the presence of these comforting stomach-fillers on the menu. Recommended starters have included triangular borek pastries and patlican-biber kizartma (fried aubergines with peppers), and the kitchen also provides a healthy balance of salads, pilaffs, high-protein grills and fish specials like fried squid with walnut sauce. Desserts are traditional recipes, including kayisi tatlisi (home-made cream with sun-dried apricots, almonds and pistachios). A few gluggable Turkish wines pop up on the list. Villa Doluca is £10.95. There's a branch at 72 Borough High Street, SE1, tel: (020) 7403 7200, with a café close by.

The group's latest venture, Tas Pide, gives pride of place to 'pides' (boat-shaped Turkish versions of pizza): outlets are at 37 Farringdon Road, EC1, tel: (020) 7430 9721, and 20–22 New Globe Walk, SE1, tel: (020) 7928 3300. Another restaurant complex, Tas Gurme, is due to open in September 2004 at The Arches, 97–99 Isabella Street, SE1.

CHEF: Onder Sahan   PROPRIETORS: Onder Sahan, Ali Selim, Ismail Duman and Dervis Aslan   OPEN: all week 12 to 11.30 (10.30 Sun)   MEALS: alc (main courses £5.50 to £14.50). Set L and D £7.95 (2 courses) to £18.50   SERVICE: 10%   CARDS: Amex, Delta, MasterCard, Switch, Visa   DETAILS: 140 seats. 8 seats outside. Private parties: 55 main room. Vegetarian meals. No smoking in 1 dining room. Wheelchair access (also WC). Music. Air-conditioned   ⊖ Southwark

---

Tate Britain Restaurant

Millbank, SW1P 4RG

TEL: (020) 7887 8825   FAX: (020) 7887 8902

WEBSITE: www.tate.org.uk

COOKING 3

MODERN BRITISH

£34–£63

map 13

If the murals are your cup of tea, this must be one of London's prettiest dining rooms: 'ravishing rural murals bathe in a romantic golden glow', as one reader put it. Perhaps they inspire cooking based on seasonal and carefully sourced British produce. A new chef arrived in May 2004, and inspection showed the kitchen delivering food worthy of the setting, although the 'pleasant' service needed better coordination. Silky potato and watercress soup came with fresh pea shoots and perfectly coddled egg, but marinated herrings succumbed to a crudely seasoned curried dressing. Chargrilled spring vegetables and goats' cheese curd have been nicely assembled on sourdough toast, or else there might be herbed calf's liver with Swiss chard, runner beans and buttered carrots. Finish with simple but toothsome rhubarb and custard. One of the joys of dining here is dipping into one of the best wine lists in London. Since this is a lunchtime-only venue, options by the glass and half-bottle are important, and they are good and plentiful. The Francocentric list makes successful forays into other countries, and is always good value. Well-chosen house is £15.

CHEF: Andy Barber   PROPRIETOR: Tate Catering   OPEN: all week L only 12 to 3 (4 Sun)   CLOSED: 24 to 26 Dec   MEALS: alc L (main courses £11 to £18.50). Set L £17.50 (2 courses) to £20.50   SERVICE: not inc, card slips closed   CARDS: Amex, Delta, Diners, MasterCard, Switch, Visa   DETAILS: 90 seats. 20 seats outside. Vegetarian meals. Children's helpings. No-smoking area. Wheelchair access (also WC). No music. Air-conditioned ⊖ Pimlico £5

Tentazioni

map 13

2 Mill Street, SE1 2BD
TEL/FAX: (020) 7237 1100
WEBSITE: www.tentazioni.co.uk

COOKING 3
MODERN ITALIAN
£40–£63

This smart venue by converted warehouses in fashionable riparian Bermondsey has modern, Mediterranean-influenced décor and massive circular tables. The imaginative bilingual menu has appealing and flavoursome combinations – like smoked ricotta cheese with sun-dried tomatoes and potato gnocchi, myrtle-marinated stone bass with a timbale of courgette and prawns, and navarin of rabbit and artichokes with courgettes and mint. The distinctly modern cooking makes use of 'trad' Italian flavours and ingredients (witness roast fillet of cod with mustard seeds, porcini salad and blueberries) – for purists there's also a no-choice set-price 'traditional menu' offering regional cooking (e.g. Calabrian). Desserts range from traditional tiramisù to own-made ice creams and sorbets. The all-Italian wine list is peppered with good producers, and bottle prices start at £15.

CHEF: Riccardo Giacomini   PROPRIETORS: Maurizio Rimerici and Riccardo Giacomini   OPEN: Tue to Fri L 12 to 2.30, Mon to Sat D 7 to 10.45   CLOSED: 23 Dec to 2 Jan   MEALS: alc (main courses £12 to £19). Set L and D £26 to £36   SERVICE: 12.5%, card slips closed   CARDS: Amex, Delta, MasterCard, Switch, Visa   DETAILS: 50 seats. Private parties: 35 main room, 15 to 23 private rooms. Vegetarian meals. Children's helpings. Wheelchair access (not WC). Music   ⊖ London Bridge

Timo

map 13

343 Kensington High Street, W8 6NW
TEL: (020) 7603 3888   FAX: (020) 7603 8111

COOKING 3
ITALIAN
£41–£64

This long, narrow converted shop on two levels has grey-green painted walls, wooden floors, closely packed tables and low, brown suede banquettes. A popular neighbourhood restaurant, Timo serves well presented food made from good ingredients, although prices can seem high. Start, perhaps, with cod 'carpaccio' topped with pesto and mizuma leaves, before roast rack of lamb with a timbale of aubergine, red and yellow peppers and spinach. Pasta fans have choices ranging from linguine vongole to saffron gnocchi with prawns and broad beans. Desserts might include caramelised chestnuts, decorated with spun sugar, plus yoghurt mousse ice cream. Service is good, if a bit rapid. Wines are all-Italian, with the largest selection from Tuscany (including 'Super Tuscans' like Sassicaia and Solaia). Bottle prices move up swiftly from £16.50.

CHEF: Samuele Pacini   PROPRIETOR: Clubdown Ltd   OPEN: all week 12 to 2.30, 7 to 11 (10.30 Sun) CLOSED: 24 to 26 and 31 Dec, 1 Jan   MEALS: Set L £18.50 (2 courses) to £24.50, Set D £24.50 (2 courses) to £32.50   SERVICE: 12.5% (optional), card slips closed   CARDS: Amex, Delta, Diners, MasterCard, Switch, Visa   DETAILS: 55 seats. Private parties: 60 main room. Vegetarian meals. Children's helpings. No cigars. No-smoking area. Music. Air-conditioned   ⊖ High Street Kensington

To find a restaurant in a particular area use the maps at the centre of the book.

Tom Aikens ▼ ※

map 14

43 Elystan Street, SW3 3NT   COOKING **8**
TEL: 020 7584 2003   FAX: 020 7584 2001   MODERN FRENCH
WEBSITE: www.tomaikens.co.uk   £38–£107

The 'oh-so discreet frontage' of this former pub reveals a dining room showing a reassuring amount of self-confidence. It doesn't shout its concept from the rafters. Well-designed chairs at well-spaced and impeccably set tables; predominant colours of brown, black and cream; mirrors and fresh flowers: all serve to create the right mood. This is Chelsea, and don't you know it.

Tom and Laura Aikens appointed a new manager in the summer of 2004, and introduced a non-smoking policy to the dining room, otherwise, it is business as usual – the business of reaching the very top of the tree. Bread has impressed this year – green olive or onion and bacon, perhaps – and excellent butter gets its own marble slab. Fine technique is evident right from the off: amuse-gueule of quail's egg in Madeira jelly, or a chicken terrine. And then comes a pre-starter, of course, maybe a potato and truffle soup: a frothy velouté containing small cubes of spud, a thin crisp on top, and just the right amount of black truffle to inject some luxury. One reporter was reminded of a surgeon's dispensing bowl when confronted with the serving dish containing his starter, but lurking within might be two perfectly seared scallops with 'silky' braised Jerusalem artichokes, two tender pieces of 'baby' squid in the lightest of batters, and the 'blissful' contrasting texture of a confit duck wing. Scallops might also come as a salad with braised leeks, jabugo ham, leek and chervil jelly and hazelnut dressing. Presentation of dishes includes a liberal use of herbs and uncommon salad leaves, often in abundance ('a veritable garden'), and the 'herb du jour' was definitely chervil for one reporter, as it made an appearance in several places. Intelligent texture and flavour contrasts are to the fore, with braised shin of veal partnered with the roasted sweetbread, and pommes pureé, braised onions and caper and rosemary sauce. Sea bass fillet has been 'cooked to perfection', and might come with red mullet darne, black olive gnocchi, borlotti beans and pesto, or with a sesame and lime dressing and partnered with its own tartare with cucumber, an avocado pureé, coriander sauce and prawn beignet. Beignets figure large, in fact; perhaps a snail version with braised snails, red wine cassonade, potato soup and garlic as a starter. Desserts continue the theme of exploring particular ingredients and extracting contrasting textures while maximising flavours: grapefruit parfait, say, with grapefruit crisps, jelly and passion-fruit sauce, or another of caramelised pear with pear sorbet, chocolate mousse and Italian meringue. There are pre-desserts, petits fours (including excellent Madeleines), and decent coffee. Service is pretty much as you would expect at this level, and friendly with it. The sumptuous wine list looks beyond the obvious big names and wraps the core of Bordeaux and Burgundy in strong selections from elsewhere in France and beyond. A handful of well-chosen basics under £20 kicks things off.

CHEF: Tom Aikens   PROPRIETORS: Laura and Tom Aitkens   OPEN: Mon to Fri 12 to 2.30, 7 to 11   CLOSED: Christmas and New Year, bank hols, last 2 weeks Aug   MEALS: Set L £24.50 to £70, Set D £55 to £70 SERVICE: 12.5% (optional), card slips closed   CARDS: Amex, Delta, MasterCard, Switch, Visa   DETAILS: 55 seats. No smoking in dining room, permitted though discouraged in the bar. Wheelchair access (also WC). No music. No mobile phones. Air-conditioned   ⊖ South Kensington

---

※ *indicates there are some restrictions on smoking, though it is not banned altogether.*

Les Trois Garçons

map 13

1 Club Row, E1 6JX	COOKING 4
TEL: (020) 7613 1924 FAX: (020) 7012 1236	FRENCH
WEBSITE: www.lestroisgarcons.com	£41–£85

'This remains a marvellous place to take someone out for a festive occasion, to cheer them up or to impress them': a glowing endorsement from one reporter, who calls this flamboyantly burlesque dining room an asset to the area. Inside the converted pub 'you find a magical wonderland'; in the Caraveggesque chiaroscuro, coroneted stuffed animal heads protrude from walls, crystal chandeliers cascade from the ceiling and each table has its candle. The kitchen cooks in a French mode, perhaps prawns on braised chicory with tomato, garlic and coconut, or girolle soufflé, and even a classic nineteenth-century dish of Dover sole stuffed with herbs and truffles. Venison and duck breast might be garnished with foie gras and served with swede mash, salsify, mange-tout and port sauce. Note vegetables are extra. A chocolate pudding with cream and angel sauce was 'one to remember'. Service can seem 'snooty'. Classic French names top the wine list: think Burgundy, Alsace and Loire, plus gallons of claret. The short international selection that follows these seems like an afterthought, but a reasonably good one. Prices rise quite steeply from just under £20.

CHEF: Ade Adigun   PROPRIETORS: Michel Lasserre, Stefan Karlson and Hassan Abdullah   OPEN: Mon to Sat D only 7 to 10   MEALS: alc D (main courses £13.50 to £26). Set D £20 (2 courses) to £45   SERVICE: 12.5%   CARDS: Amex, Delta, Diners, MasterCard, Switch, Visa   DETAILS: 80 seats. Private parties: 80 main room, 16 private room. Vegetarian meals. No children under 12. No pipes. Wheelchair access (not WC). Music. Air-conditioned   ⊖ Liverpool Street

---

La Trompette ▮

map 12

5–7 Devonshire Road, Chiswick, W4 2EU	COOKING 6
TEL: (020) 8747 1836 FAX: (020) 8995 8097	FRENCH
	£36–£64

Down a Chiswick side street, a low awning and a potted hedge announce La Trompette. Inside, muted autumnal hues create an intimate, welcoming atmosphere, with angled lighting making each table an island of illumination. Here Ollie Couillaud's cooking combines comfort and variety, confidently deploying classic French ingredients and techniques. Breads draw praise, with walnut and raisin slices and black olive rolls standing out. One might begin with a hefty slice of ham hock and foie gras terrine with toasted brioche, or rolled, lightly seared tuna alongside 'fresh and tender' prawns. Main-course meats are carefully timed, whether black-leg chicken on the bone, with wild mushrooms and garlic potatoes, or slightly pink côte de boeuf served in a large dish with a multitude of shallots. Fish is as robustly treated as meat: perhaps crisp sea bream with butternut squash risotto and trompettes, or a starter dish of grilled halibut with Charlotte potatoes, chorizo and aïoli. A chocolate plate might generously involve no fewer than five items, including a take on Black Forest gâteau, or there might be a lemon tart (the filling of which, one diner felt, lacked a little acid bite). 'Fairly efficient, friendly' service adds class. The extensive wine list scours the world for good bottles from all regions; it caters for fashion victims and classicists with equal assurance, and even has imaginative options for diners on a tight budget. The 14 wines by the glass (£3.70 to £11.50) make a worthy introduction.

CHEF: Ollie Couillaud   PROPRIETORS: Nigel Platts-Martin and Bruce Poole   OPEN: all week 12 to 2.30 (12.30 to 3 Sun), 6.30 to 10.30 (7 to 10 Sun)   CLOSED: 24 to 26 Dec   MEALS: Set L £15 (1 course) to £21.50. Set L Sun £25. Set D £19 (1 course) to £32.50   SERVICE: 12.5% (optional), card slips closed   CARDS: Amex, Delta, MasterCard, Switch, Visa   DETAILS: 75 seats. 16 seats outside. Private parties: 60 main room. Vegetarian meals. Children's helpings. No cigars/pipes. Wheelchair access (also WC). No music. Air-conditioned   ⊖ Turnham Green

Tsunami ⚡✳   map 12

5–7 Voltaire Road, SW4 6DQ   COOKING 2
TEL: (020) 7978 1610   FAX: (020) 7978 1591   JAPANESE
                                                                   £33–£69

Tsunami 'is making a tidal wave in Clapham', observed a punning reporter about this easy-going Japanese restaurant incongruously located among the neighbourhood's railway sidings. A wave motif and large draped windows mark the spot, and the minimalist interior is broken up by impressive floral displays. The menu is upmarket, with sushi traditionally listed at the end and a sprinkling of crossover ideas such as flash-grilled scallops topped with chilli mayonnaise, or black cod in miso. Fish dishes make the most of top-quality raw materials, as in a trio of oysters and a 'classic presentation' of tuna sashimi. Tempura specialities are delivered with panache and – in earthier vein – there are 'juban' clay pots. Staff are eager and knowledgeable. Bizarrely named cocktails, saké and beer are alternatives to the workmanlike wine list, which has house recommendations from £12.

CHEF/PROPRIETOR: Ken Sam   OPEN: Mon to Fri 6 to 11, Sat 12 to 11   MEALS: alc (main courses £7 to £16.50)   SERVICE: 12.5% (optional), card slips closed   CARDS: Amex, Delta, MasterCard, Switch, Visa
DETAILS: 90 seats. 20 seats outside. Private parties: 90 main room. Vegetarian meals. Children's helpings. No smoking in 1 dining room. Occasional music. Air-conditioned   ⊖ Clapham North

Two Brothers £   【 NEW ENTRY 】   map 12

297/303 Regents Park Road, N3 1DP   COOKING 1
TEL: (020) 8346 0469   FAX: (020) 8343 1978   FISH 'N' CHIPS
                                                                   £22–£52

The Manzis' upmarket fish-and-chip restaurant/takeaway, a North London fixture since 1987, shows no sign of flagging. Ultra-fresh fish is the draw, fried to order in 'impressively unoily' batter or matzo meal; this comes with lashings of chunky chips and home-made tartare sauce, and you can add side orders of mushy peas or coleslaw. Other species are steamed or grilled, and blackboard specials like sardines with chicory and balsamic add variety. There is fish soup and marinated herrings to start, and old-fashioned delights like knickerbocker glory or bread-and-butter pud to finish. The fifties-style dining room is decorated in aquatic shades, with bare wooden tables and maritime pictures, service is 'absolutely first-rate', and house Cotes de Duras (from the owners' own vines) is £10.35.

CHEF/PROPRIETOR: Leon and Tony Manzi   OPEN: Tue to Sat 12 to 2.30, 5.30 to 10.15   CLOSED: bank hol Mons and succeeding Tues, 2 weeks Aug   MEALS: alc (main courses £8.50 to £18.50)   SERVICE: not inc, card slips closed   CARDS: Amex, Delta, MasterCard, Switch, Visa   DETAILS: 90 seats. Children's helpings. Occasional music. Air-conditioned   ⊖ Finchley Central

Ubon by Nobu

map 12

34 Westferry Circus, Canary Wharf, E14 8RR
TEL: (020) 7719 7800   FAX: (020) 7719 7801
WEBSITE: www.noburestaurants.com

COOKING 5
JAPANESE
£36–£145

Negotiating massive wrought-iron gates, then taking the lift from an unmanned foyer, gave one visitor 'the sense of being in London in the year 2050'. When reached, the fourth-floor dining room has a high 'wow factor': a vast, high-ceilinged space with full-height windows giving views of the Thames on three sides.

This sibling of Nobu in Mayfair offers an almost identical repertoire of modern and traditional Japanese dishes with occasional Peruvian influences – salmon tartare with caviar, lobster ceviche, yellowtail sashimi with jalapeño, squid pasta with garlic sauce, Dover sole with black bean sauce, and a comprehensive range of sushi, sashimi and tempura. And, as at its sibling, prices are high. Dishes are presented with beautiful simplicity, on green glass bowls full of crushed ice, in lacquered bento boxes or on opalescent plates, adorned with bamboo parchment scrolls, stalks of pickled ginger and tempura fruits. Fortunately, the food eats as well as it looks, featuring top-quality ingredients and expertly made delicate sauces. Staff add to the pleasure of dining here, with their enthusiastic and knowledgeable service – though be aware that 15% 'optional' service charge is added to the bills. To drink, there's a wide choice of saké and cocktails, plus wines from £26.

CHEF: Mark Edwards   PROPRIETOR: Nobuyuki Matsuhisa   OPEN: Mon to Fri L 12 to 2.15, Mon to Sat D 6 to 10.15   CLOSED: bank hols   MEALS: alc (main courses £5 to £29.50). Set L (min 12) £45 to £50, Set D (min 12) £70 to £90   SERVICE: 15% (optional)   CARDS: Amex, Delta, Diners, MasterCard, Switch, Visa   DETAILS: 120 seats. Private parties: 150 main room. Vegetarian meals. No cigars/pipes. No-smoking area. Wheelchair access (also WC). Music. Air-conditioned   ⊖ Westferry DLR (£5)

Uli

NEW ENTRY   map 13

16 All Saints Road, W11 1HH
TEL: (020) 7727 7511

COOKING 2
PAN-ASIAN
£30–£62

This Spartan white box of a dining room in the Notting Hill hinterland has a few mirrors on plain cream walls, bare wooden floorboards and tables laid with plain white cloths. Low-backed, cushioned wicker chairs are 'tolerably comfortable', '60s pop music plays quietly in the background, and service is overseen by a good-humoured Singaporean, assisted by several efficient and smartly dressed waitresses. The menu draws influences from across South-east Asia and the Orient, so there is Malay lamb curry alongside Singapore laksa and steamed Shanghai dumplings. A starter of Vietnamese-style steamed spring rolls contained shredded vegetables, prawns and chicken with a hint of green chilli, and a main-course special of Singapore chicken came with a vibrantly flavoured garlic and ginger sauce. A straightforward list of mostly New World wines starts at £10.

CHEF: Lillian Wong   PROPRIETOR: Frances Taylor   OPEN: Mon to Sat D only 6.45 to 11   MEALS: alc (main courses £7 to £15)   SERVICE: 12.5% (optional), card slips closed   CARDS: MasterCard, Switch, Visa   DETAILS: 40 seats. 20 seats outside. Private parties: 40 main room. Vegetarian meals. No cigars. Music (£5)

The Vale ✸ £

map 13

99 Chippenham Road, W9 2AB
TEL: (020) 7266 0990   FAX: (020) 7286 7224

COOKING **2**
MODERN BRITISH
£24–£46

Impressive flower displays and 'sensible' touches like proper napkins on unclothed tables help to create a good feeling in this smartly done-out brick building. Punters are attracted by its brasserie-style approach, with salads and pasta dishes (like oxtail and bone-marrow ravioli) in two sizes, agreeably priced set meals and a daily-changing all-sorts menu. Expect, say, celeriac soup with truffle oil, or tuna sushi, to start, followed by mains that run from paupiette of plaice with pink fir apple potatoes, lemon and saffron butter sauce to roast haunch of venison with bubble and squeak, braised red cabbage and horseradish cream. Finish with 'well-textured' ice creams or something like chocolate gâteau and Grand Marnier bavarois. The wine list is a good selection, with several half-bottles and twelve by the glass; house vin de pays is £10.50.

CHEF: Robin Tarver   PROPRIETORS: Robin Tarver and Francesca Melman   OPEN: Tue to Fri L 12.30 to 2.30, Sun brunch 11 to 3, Tue to Sat D 7 to 11   CLOSED: Christmas, Easter   MEALS: alc (main courses £8 to £15). Set L £12 (2 courses) to £15, Set D £15 (2 courses) to £18.50   SERVICE: 12.5% (optional), card slips closed   CARDS: Delta, Diners, MasterCard, Switch, Visa   DETAILS: 70 seats. Private parties: 34 main room, 14 to 34 private rooms. Vegetarian meals. Children's helpings. No smoking in 1 dining room. Wheelchair access (not WC). Occasional music. Air-conditioned   ⊖ Maida Vale (£5)

▲ Victoria

| NEW ENTRY | map 12

10 West Temple Sheen, SW14 7RT
TEL: (020) 8876 4238   FAX: (020) 8878 3464
WEBSITE: www.thevictoria.net

COOKING **2**
MODERN EUROPEAN
£28–£62

Beyond the bar, a pleasant, airy small room leads into a large, split-level conservatory with walled garden for summer dining beyond. Simplicity reigns: pale grey floorboards, plain white crockery, sensibly short menus. There's the odd Spanish influence, witness sauté of Jersey Royals mixed with piquillo peppers, sherry vinaigrette and wilted sorrel leaves, topped with a fried duck egg, and on Sundays there's always a roast from the rotisserie. Flavours may be intense (as in moist, tender braised pig's cheek with a rich potato cake and a sticky jus, or, for dessert, a concentrated pear and elderflower sorbet), and portions are large. Genuinely enthusiastic staff create a sense of relaxed friendliness. The 40-strong, reasonably priced wine list starts at £12.95, and Austrian Kremstal Grüner Veltliner is a 'delightful choice'.

CHEF: Darren Archer   PROPRIETORS: Mark Chester, Rex Chester and Darren Archer   OPEN: all week 12 to 2.30 (3 Sat, 4 Sun), 7 to 10 (9 Sun)   CLOSED: 4 days at Christmas   MEALS: alc (main courses £8 to £18) SERVICE: 12.5% (optional), card slips closed   CARDS: Amex, Delta, MasterCard, Switch, Visa   DETAILS: 75 seats. 50 seats outside. Private parties: 45 main room. Car park. Vegetarian meals. Children's helpings. Wheelchair access (not WC). No music   ACCOMMODATION: 7 rooms, all with bath/shower. TV. Phone. B&B £98.50. Baby facilities (£5)

The Guide's longest-serving restaurants are listed near the front of the book.

Villandry ▼ ✕

map 15

170 Great Portland Street, W1W 5QB
TEL: (020) 7631 3131   FAX: (020) 7631 3030
WEBSITE: www.villandry.com

COOKING 2
MODERN EUROPEAN
£31–£69

There are options aplenty at this Fitzrovia food emporium – peruse the shelves for some Italian or French delicacies, take breakfast from 8am, prop up the charcuterie counter and sample some of the excellent range of cured meats or cheeses, or eat and drink in the bustling bar. And then there is the main restaurant. Floor-to-ceiling windows and white walls ensure that the room is bright even on the dullest days, and the kitchen, at least in part, showcases the ingredients on the shelves next door. The regularly changing carte, Franco-Italian in style, may begin with pumpkin and rosemary soup, or a chicory, trevisse and hazelnut salad with anchovy dressing. Main courses might include grilled monkfish with shaved fennel, red onion and parsley salad, a wild mushroom and Jerusalem artichoke pie, and a rump of lamb with Puy lentils and Swiss chard. Alongside classic comfort puds like apple pie with clotted cream, or rice pudding with plum compote, there are cakes from the on-site pâtisserie. The bar menu might feature the likes of Brazilian street food, or lamb koftas with chilli dipping sauce, plus most of the same puddings.

Plenty of wines, from simple to serious, come by the glass (from £3.25) or the 500ml pichet. Beginning at £13.50, the main list herds well-chosen bottles into categories ('fresh', 'aromatic and piquant', etc.).

CHEF: Steve Evenett-Watts   PROPRIETORS: Martha Greene and Jeremy Sinclair   OPEN: all week L 12 to 3.30, Mon to Sat D 6 to 10.30   CLOSED: Christmas to New Year, bank hols   MEALS: alc (main courses £10.50 to £20)   SERVICE: 12.5% (optional), card slips closed   CARDS: Amex, Delta, Diners, MasterCard, Switch, Visa   DETAILS: 100 seats. Private parties: 125 main room. Vegetarian meals. Children's helpings. No smoking. Wheelchair access (not WC). No music. Air-conditioned   ⊖ Great Portland Street

Wapping Food

map 12

Wapping Hydraulic Power Station, Wapping Wall,
E1W 3ST
TEL: (020) 7680 2080
WEBSITE: www.thewappingproject.com

COOKING 3
MODERN EUROPEAN/MEDITERRANEAN
£36–£62

A restaurant in a disused hydraulic power station might seem the height of post-modernism, especially if the scheme also embraces an art gallery, video shows and huge machinery relics as *objets d'art*. Wapping Food's short daily menu reads like a fashionable shopping list: there may be fresh fig and Manchego salad with preserved lemons and roast almonds to start, then mains ranging from osso buco with risotto milanese to marinated marlin loin with pak choi, shredded vegetables, lime and chilli dressing. To finish, consider honeycomb ice cream, or dark chocolate torte with white chocolate sorbet. Brunch is served at weekends, and you can also graze on trendy nibbles in the bar. Three dozen or so table wines are Australian; bottles start at £14, and nine by the glass at £3.50.

CHEF: James Robson   PROPRIETOR: Wapping Restaurants Ltd   OPEN: all week L 12 (10 Sat/Sun) to 3 (3.30 Sat, 4 Sun), Mon to Sat D 6.30 to 11   CLOSED: 25 Dec to 2 Jan   MEALS: alc (main courses £12 to £17.50). Bar and Sat/Sun brunch menus available   SERVICE: not inc, 12.5% (optional), card slips closed   CARDS: Amex, Delta, Diners, MasterCard, Switch, Visa   DETAILS: 100 seats. 20 seats outside. Private parties: 120 main room. Car park. Wheelchair access (also WC). Occasional music   ⊖ Wapping

Wells ♥ ✳

30 Well Walk, NW3 1BX   COOKING 3
TEL: (020) 7794 3785   FAX: (020) 7794 6817   FRENCH
WEBSITE: www.thewellshampstead.co.uk   £31–£55

Near Hampstead Heath, the Wells is a pub 'gone gastro': chic downstairs bar and three small, modern dining rooms above. A starter croquette of oxtail topped with lightly fried quail's egg on red wine shallots ('pure bliss') exemplified a kitchen showing real confidence. Watercress and spinach soup comes with a poached egg and salted almonds, and 'fat, nicely browned' scallops with duxelles and some finely puréed parsnips. Main courses are well-conceived and accurately executed: witness a plate of lamb and liver with tender, truffled artichokes and crisp-browned gnocchi, or fried halibut with mussels, new potatoes and leek purée. Desserts might include apple Tatin with crème fraîche, and a dense gâteau Basque with the 'enlightened accompaniment' of spiced plums.

A fairly serious wine list plays to well-heeled locals, but there's plenty under and around £20. The main selection – arranged by style, with representatives of each sold by the glass – contains much that is modern and fashionable; the pricier 'reserve cellar' sticks to classic producers from Burgundy, Bordeaux and the Rhône.

CHEF: Andrew Gale   PROPRIETOR: Beth Coventry   OPEN: all week 12 to 2.45, 7 to 10.30   CLOSED: 24 and 25 Dec, 1 Jan   MEALS: Set L £14.50 (2 courses) to £19.50, Set D £24.50 (2 courses) to £29.50. Bar menu available   SERVICE: 12.5% (optional), card slips closed   CARDS: Amex, Delta, Diners, MasterCard, Switch, Visa   DETAILS: 50 seats. 25 seats outside. Private parties: 25 main room, 10 to 15 private rooms. Vegetarian meals. No smoking in 1 dining room. Wheelchair access (also WC). Music. Air-conditioned
⊖ Hampstead

William IV £

map 12

786 Harrow Road, NW10 5JX   NEW CHEF
TEL: (020) 8969 5944   FAX: (020) 8964 9218   MODERN EUROPEAN
                                       £26–£52

Once a boozer picking up passing trade from Harrow Road, the William IV has reinvented itself as a fully fledged gastro-pub. A major attraction at weekday lunchtimes is the enticing fixed-price deal: choose one course plus a glass of wine or a pint of beer for £8. The style of food seems less Italian than previously, and the new menu (as we go to press) advertises smoked haddock fish cakes with curry sauce and feta and Puy lentil salad among starters, followed by main courses such as grilled ribeye with chips, salad and béarnaise, or pappardelle with tomato sauce and pesto. Desserts are as straightforward as chocolate mousse or peach cheesecake. The wine list is broadly arranged by style ('big, bold and spicy' reds, for example), with prices from £11.50.

CHEF: Markus Georgiou   PROPRIETOR: Megamade Ltd   OPEN: all week 12 to 3 (4.30 Sat and Sun), 6 to 10.30 (11 Fri and Sat)   MEALS: alc exc Sun L (main courses £7.50 to £16). Set L Mon to Fri £8 (1 course, inc wine), Set L Sun £14 (2 courses) to £17, Set D Mon to Fri 6 to 7.30 £12 (2 courses)   SERVICE: not inc, card slips closed, 10% for parties of 5 or more   CARDS: Amex, Delta, MasterCard, Switch, Visa   DETAILS: 100 seats. 70 seats outside. Private parties: 100 main room, 20 to 100 private rooms. Vegetarian meals. Occasional music. No mobile phones   ⊖ Kensal Green

---

All entries, including Round-ups, are fully indexed at the back of the Guide.

Wiltons

map 15

55 Jermyn Street, SW1Y 6LX
TEL: (020) 7629 9955   FAX: (020) 7495 6233
WEBSITE: www.wiltons.co.uk

COOKING 5
TRADITIONAL ENGLISH
£48–£118

A measure of the indelible, inalienable old-style Britishness of Wiltons is that its head chef, nearly all the waiting staff and most of the wines (although not the menu language) are French. Its spruced-up but timeless aura of effortless professionalism is enhanced by the seating arrangements, which offer a choice of perching up high at the seafood bar, sitting in state in one of the hermetic-seeming booths upholstered in House of Commons green, or braving it at one of the tables in the middle of the back room. What one comes here for, primarily, are the quality-conscious renditions of Edwardian dining: game in season, crustacean cocktails, traditional varieties of fish (Dover sole, turbot), grills, sherry trifle, and savouries like anchovies on toast or angels on horseback. Some eyebrows might twitch at the sight of wild duck with peach sauce, or seared fillet of sea bass with fennel, and it is possible to have a rocket and Parmesan side-order these days, but what there is of noble tradition at Wiltons is done with consummate aplomb, though vegetables are extra. If you've a mind, you might finish with bitter chocolate and almond cake, but the likes of apple and plum crumble with cinnamon are probably the real shifters. Wines are a good selection at pneumatic mark-ups, with bottle prices from £24, glasses from £5.50.

CHEF: Jerome Ponchelle   PROPRIETORS: the Hambro family   OPEN: all week L 12 to 2.30, Mon to Sat D 6 to 10.30   CLOSED: 23 Dec to 3 Jan, bank hols   MEALS: alc (main courses £14 to £38)   SERVICE: not inc, card slips closed   CARDS: Amex, Delta, Diners, MasterCard, Switch, Visa   DETAILS: 80 seats. Private parties: 4 to 18 private rooms. Jacket and tie. Wheelchair access (also WC). No music. No mobile phones. Air-conditioned   ⊖ Green Park

Wolseley ▼ ⅚✳

NEW ENTRY   map 15

160 Piccadilly, W1J 9EB
TEL: (020) 7499 6996   FAX: (020) 7499 6888
WEBSITE: www.thewolseley.com

COOKING 3
INTERNATIONAL
£37–£72

Messrs Corbin and King know a thing or two about putting together a top-notch restaurant, with a shared past that includes Le Caprice and the Ivy (see entries). It will come as no surprise that they are back on the restaurant scene, or that they have hit the nail on the head once again. The former Wolseley garage (for those under 40: it was a car company) is a high-impact building - 'pause at the entrance to take in the whole place' is the advice. The high stone ceiling, curvaceous arches, marble floors and tall, black opal-effect columns are impressive, and it bustles with a serene elegance, and with more than a touch of Parisienne brasserie about the place. The menu reinforces this impression, even if a Vienniese café is frequently mentioned in dispatches – although that's probably down to the presence of both Wieners schnitzel and Holstein on the menu. The day is a long one: starting at 7am for breakfast, the café menu kicking in at 11.30, plus bar snacks and cocktails (until midnight), afternoon tea, and the à la carte menu available lunchtime and from 5.30. Start with something like a daily special of roast quail with a cep tart, little gem, and star anise sauce, or steak tartare with Poilâne toasts. A main-course hamburger comes on half a bun showing off the 'impressive slab of meat'. Fegato a la Veneziana has met with approval, and a red mullet escabèche (another daily special) came with carrot and shallot salad, and topped with tapenade with capers. The cover charge of £2 is an anachronism we could do without. Service has been mixed, but, as one reporter put it: 'considering some days they can serve 700 people, they are doing a good job.' A well-balanced Europhile wine list (from £14.50) makes all 28 bottles available by the glass. Reserve selections wheel out some famous and expensive names.

CHEFS: Chris Galvin and Ed Wilson   PROPRIETORS: Chris Corbin and Jeremy King   OPEN: all week 12 to 2.30, 5.30 to 11.30   MEALS: alc (main courses £9.25 to £18.50). Cover £2. Café menu and breakfast menus available   SERVICE: not inc   CARDS: Amex, Delta, Diners, MasterCard, Switch, Visa   DETAILS: 175 seats. Children's helpings. No smoking in 1 dining room Wheelchair access (also WC). No music. No mobile phones. Air-conditioned   ⊖ Green Park

Yatra ⁵⁄✳   map 15

34 Dover Street, W1S 4NF	COOKING 4
TEL: (020) 7493 0200 FAX: (020) 7493 4228	INDIAN
WEBSITE: www.yatra.co.uk	£26–£71

As Indian restaurants go, this refined Mayfair big-timer is an unusual place. Perhaps it's the burly doorman who polices the entrance, or the clubbers congregating in the bar before descending to the action in the basement Bollywood disco. By contrast, the main restaurant can seem quiet and underpopulated even on a Saturday night. The kitchen's heart is in the traditional world of exemplary tandooris and familiar curries, although there are nods to the new wave. Starters are given up-to-the-minute presentation: 'piquant' tawa masala Malabar red snapper has been particularly impressive. Main dishes revert to a simpler style where flavours are allowed to speak ('quite eloquently') for themselves. Rogan josh features lamb on the bone and a dose of ratanjot (the bark of a Kashmiri tree). Bengali fish curry brings together monkfish, aubergines and potatoes, and the kitchen put its fusion foot forwards for tandoori salmon with coriander risotto and Parmesan. Slow-cooked dhal makhani has excelled in the vegetable department, and shrikand is an intriguing dessert. House wines start at £14.75.

CHEF: Khishnapal Negi   PROPRIETOR: Mr Lalvani   OPEN: Mon to Fri L 12 to 3, Mon to Sat D 6 to 11 (11.30 Thur to Sat)   MEALS: alc (main courses £13.50 to £18.50). Set L £9.95 (2 courses) to £12.95 (inc wine). Bar menu available   SERVICE: 15% (optional)   CARDS: Amex, Delta, MasterCard, Switch, Visa   DETAILS: 80 seats. Private parties: 150 main room, 45 to 155 private rooms. Vegetarian meals. No smoking in 1 dining room. Wheelchair access (also WC). Music. Air-conditioned   ⊖ Green Park   £5

Yauatcha ♥ ⁵⁄✳   NEW ENTRY   map 15

15–17 Broadwick Street, W1F 0DL	COOKING 4
TEL: (020) 7494 8888 FAX: (020) 7494 8889	CHINESE
EMAIL: reservations@yauatcha.com	£41–£77

With the opening of Yauatcha in the vicinity of Berwick Street market, Midas man Alan Yau has once again shown his nerveless instinct for putting central London's less obvious culinary corners on the map. The design here, as at Hakkasan (see entry), is drop-dead cool, with opaque blue windows concealing a ground-floor space devoted to tea and snacks (feast your eyes on the pâtisserie counter). Downstairs is a dining room complete with fish tank in blue, low-slung chairs at wooden tables, and candles flickering in mirrored recesses.

The strict time limit on tables should just give you opportunity to explore the byways of a menu that deals in well-crafted, vibrantly seasoned dim sum. Scallop shumai, prawn and enoki dumpling, sea bass mooli roll, and – the star of the show – a spinach cube with prawn and water chestnut all dazzled at inspection, the seasonings judged to a nicety and the shellfish items perfectly timed. More substantial dishes may be more mainstream but are still capably rendered: XO seafood udon noodles are fresh and gutsy, stir-fried gai lan in ginger sauce has forthright flavour, and there are proper congee and cheung fun. Western desserts impress less, although iced melon soup with yoghurt sorbet should prove a welcome palate cooler. Staff slink about in uniforms, bringing a pleasing balance of warmth and savvy to the job. The sassy drinks list segues from cocktails to a succinct round-up of some of the world's trendiest wines arranged by style, and dares to include six rosés. Rocky Horror Cabernet Franc is no joke, but a sublimely good red. Prices start at £16.

CHEF: Soon Wah Cheong PROPRIETOR: Alan Yau OPEN: all week 12 to 10.45 (10.15 Sun) CLOSED: 25 Dec SERVICE: 12.5% (optional) CARDS: Amex, Delta, MasterCard, Switch, Visa DETAILS: 173 seats. Private parties: 120 main room. Vegetarian meals. No smoking. Wheelchair access (also WC). Music. Air-conditioned ⊖ Tottenham Court Road

Zafferano   map 14

15 Lowndes Street, SW1X 9EY   COOKING 6
TEL: (020) 7235 5800   FAX: (020) 7235 1971   ITALIAN
                                                            £42–£87

From the outside, Zafferano looks smart and serious. It's clearly a restaurant that aims for luxury but avoids high-minded posturing: visitors find the mood relaxed, and the layout of the two interconnecting rooms fashioned from an oddly shaped space adds to the domestic feel of the place. The kitchen's success depends on its raw materials, which are impeccably sourced and true to the season: first-course salads are a high point (artichokes with a well-balanced dressing, ultra-fresh crab with asparagus, French beans with squid and Taggiasche olives, for example).

The menu follows the traditional Italian four-course format, with pasta and risottos placed second. Nothing falters in this department, from veal shank ravioli with saffron ('a classic dish executed with some brio'), and tagliatelle with new season's white truffles shaved at the table, to a 'rich and silky' langoustine and courgette flower risotto. Fish main courses aim for direct simplicity – lobster is sautéed and served in its shell with vivid-green broad beans, while roast halibut comes with potatoes, peppers and basil. When it comes to meat, lamb cutlets might be chargrilled, while calves' sweetbreads are paired with spinach and asparagus. Tantalising desserts could embrace a refreshing assemblage of mango with mango sorbet and passion fruit, as well as fig tart. If there's a note of disapproval, it has to do with the overall cost, although staff continue to engender superlatives: 'as slick as ever under the guidance of maître d' Enzo' is a typical plaudit from one regular. The all-Italian wine list is notable for outstanding vintages of fine Piedmont and Tuscan wines – at a price (Tenuta dell' Ornellaia 1988 at £285, for instance). The rest of the list is kinder on the pocket, with some pedigree producers showing up. Prices start at £14.50 but soon jump over £20.

CHEF: Andy Needham PROPRIETOR: A To Z Restaurants OPEN: all week 12 to 2.30, 7 to 11 CLOSED: bank hols MEALS: Set L £23.50 (2 courses) to £32.50, Set D £29.50 (2 courses) to £41.50 SERVICE: not inc CARDS: Amex, Delta, Diners, MasterCard, Switch, Visa DETAILS: 50 seats. Vegetarian meals. No cigars/pipes. Wheelchair access (not WC). Music. Air-conditioned ⊖ Knightsbridge

Zaika 🍴 🎩

map 13

1 Kensington High Street, W8 5NP
TEL: (020) 7795 6533 FAX: (020) 7937 8854
WEBSITE: www.zaika-restaurant.co.uk

COOKING 3
MODERN INDIAN
£33–£94

Crowds pack the bar of this high-profile restaurant for serious cocktails, while others make their way to the vibrantly designed dining room. The man who put Zaika on the map, chef Vineet Bhatia, has moved on to open his own restaurant (see entry for Rasoi Vineet Bhatia). An inspection meal under the new chef revealed presentation to be as pretty as ever, and set-piece dishes are still classily executed from fine ingredients. A prawn platter, for example, involves a tandoori tiger prawn with coconut, a tiny mould of red onion and shrimp risotto, and a single prawn tempura. The trademark Westernisation of Asian classics also shows in the tomato ice cream served with tandoori butter chicken and in the wild mushrooms and truffle oil implanted into naan. Prices are sky-high and service is often 'overstretched', but impressive details such as 'genuinely good' chutneys, creamy raita, and pre-desserts like mango granita help to tip the balance. The vast wine list goes to town in France and Italy and shorter selection elsewhere are equally assured. Even some Indian wines have made the grade this year. Prices start at £16 and 16 by the glass give a decent glimpse of what is on offer.

CHEF: Sanjay Dwivedi PROPRIETORS: Cuisine Collection OPEN: Sun to Fri L 12 to 2, all week D 6 to 10.45
CLOSED: 25 and 26 Dec MEALS: alc (main courses £12.50 to £31.50). Set L £14.95 (2 courses) to £17.95,
Set D £38 to £85 (inc wine) SERVICE: 12.5% (optional), card slips closed CARDS: Amex, Delta, Diners,
MasterCard, Switch, Visa DETAILS: 80 seats. Private parties: 100 main room. Vegetarian meals.
Children's helpings. No cigars/pipes. Wheelchair access (not WC). Music. No mobile phones. Air-
conditioned ⊖ Kensington High Street

Zuma 🍷 ✳

map 14

5 Raphael Street, SW7 1DL
TEL: (020) 7584 1010 FAX: (020) 7584 5005
WEBSITE: www.zumarestaurant.com

COOKING 5
MODERN JAPANESE
£32–£98

Occupying a sizeable plot behind a Knightsbridge shopping complex, surrounded by unlovely office blocks, the location seems an odd one in which to find a contemporary Japanese restaurant designed like a Zen garden. Then again, perhaps it doesn't, as the mood of restrained opulence suits the clientele well, right down to the screened-off private dining areas with their sunken seating.

The menu is arranged into small appetiser dishes, salads, sushi, robata-grilled items, and tempura. Sashimi in their ice-cold glass bowl are uniformly fabulous. Soft-shell crab is another winner, sea-fresh in its crisp batter, with accompanying scorch from wasabi mayonnaise. Ribeye beef with daikon and ponzu sauce offers high-quality beef with a tiny bit of fat emphasising its flavour, while baby chicken marinated in barley miso and roasted over cedar wood is a revelation. Vegetable dishes, such as aubergine with dashi, grated radish and ginger, are both 'light and refreshing'. Desserts may not quite live up to what precedes them, but incidentals such as fluffy steamed rice and 'benchmark' green tea are as sound as a bell. Service is courteous and helpful and remains serene even in the thick of the evening trade. For those not exploring the extensive range of saké, there's a very good but not cheap wine list (from £19) arranged by grape variety and packed with droppable names. Ten or so come by the glass from £5.50. Rainer Becker opened a second restaurant in July 2004 - Roka, 37 Charlotte Street, W1; tel: (020) 7580 6464.

CHEF/PROPRIETOR: Rainer Becker   OPEN: all week 12 to 2.15 (2.45 Sun), 6 to 11 (10.30 Sun)   CLOSED: L 24 Dec, 25 and 26 Dec   MEALS: alc (main courses £4 to £30). Set L £8.50 to £21 (2 courses)   SERVICE: 12.5% (optional), card slips closed   CARDS: Amex, Delta, Diners, MasterCard, Switch, Visa   DETAILS: 130 seats. Private parties: 12 to 14 private rooms. Vegetarian meals. No smoking. Wheelchair access (also WC). Music. Air-conditioned   ⊖ Knightsbridge

London round-ups

With so many venues vying for attention, finding a place to eat out in London that offers the right blend of food, location, style and price to suit the occasion can often be very much down to potluck. This section aims to make choosing easier by providing details of a broad range of restaurants, bistros, cafés, hotel dining rooms, and so on, that are deserving of attention, though they do not merit a full entry. There are also one or two rising stars, well worth keeping an eye on, and in some cases establishments have been included here rather than in the main entries because of significant late changes or a lack of positive feedback. Reports on these places are particularly welcome. Brief details of opening times and prices are given in each entry where available.

Arancia   SE16
52 Southwark Park Road   map 13
(020) 7394 1751

Locally favoured Italian that scores with its cheery atmosphere, pleasant staff and low prices. Vibrant colours set the tone for an enticing regional menu that focuses on dishes from the south. Start with orecchiete, broccoli and chillies (£4.50), move on to baked sea bream with caponata (£9.25) and finish in style with ultra-rich chocolate semifreddo (£3.15). All-Italian wine list with plenty of 'gluggable' stuff from £9. Closed Mon and Sun.

Atlantic 66   SW9
66 Atlantic Road   map 12
(020) 7326 4920

Bright modern place opposite Brixton's market stalls, bringing foie gras and blue-fin tuna to a local crowd who might not fancy a trip 'up west'. Clever, concise menu with lots of contemporary twists and turns: seared scallops with pea purée, chilli and mint vinaigrette and chorizo (£7), roast rump of lamb with red pepper dauphinoise (£13.50) and milk chocolate brûlée with hazelnut biscotti (£4.50). A dozen wines by the glass and some good names on the list. Useful daytime offers. Open Fri and Sun L, Tue to Sat D.

L'Auberge   SW15
22 Upper Richmond Road   map 12
(020) 8874 3593

France comes to East Putney in Pascal Ardilly's staunchly Gallic restaurant. The menu spells out its wares in French (with English subtitles): start with ham and herb terrine with red onion marmalade (£5.50), proceed to navarin of lamb (£14.25) or grilled zander with Riesling sauce and conclude with individually crafted desserts like peach and apricot bavarois with blackcurrant coulis (£5). Three-course menu 'fixe' £16; assorted French wines from £11.50. Open Tue to Sat D only.

Avenue   SW1
7–9 St James's Street   map 15
(020) 7321 2111

Vast, high-ceilinged 'cavern of a place', its elegant bar dwarfed by the scale of the dining room beyond. The long menu of familiar items commands 'big league prices' and has served up scallops, potato cakes, sour cream and chives as a starter, followed by Parmesan chicken and vine tomatoes and, perhaps, chocolate semifreddo and honeycomb with pear gelato. All are delivered at a brisk pace by courteous young staff. House wine (£14.50) is the most affordable bet. Open all week.

Azou   W6
375 King Street   map 12
(020) 8563 7266

Morocco, Algeria and Tunisia are all represented on the menu at this small, bright restaurant. Starters might be good old hummus, or foul medames (£4), while for mains there are tagines and the usual couscous dishes with chicken, lamb, or merguez offered – the 'royal' version (£15.50) includes a bit of everything. French house wine is £10. Open Mon to Fri L and all week D.

Balham Bar & Kitchen   SW12
15–19 Bedford Hill   map 12
(020) 8675 6900

'Dead cool' is one enthusiastic verdict on this glass-fronted, stripped-wood venue, where 'retro bar chic' is the name of the game. Chef Martin Caws arrived from Le Pont de la Tour (see Main entry), too late for an inspection, but serious things are expected. The current menu breezes its way through 'small plates' (£4.50) and starters like asparagus with quails' eggs and hollandaise, before turning to duck cottage pie (£12) or grilled lobster and chips (£25); puddings (£5) might include raspberry fool. House wine £9.75 a carafe. Open all week (from breakfast at 8).

Barnsbury   N1
209–211 Liverpool Road   map 13
(020) 7607 5519

It may look like your average local from the outside, but 'chandeliers' constructed from inverted wine glasses indicate that this is no ordinary boozer. Organic wines feature on a global wine list, and the menu focuses on the Mediterranean, although devilled whitebait, Dorset Drum Cheddar, and summer pudding cheer for England. Otherwise expect chorizo and butter-bean salad, veal escalope with olive and sun-blush tomato couscous, then praline semifreddo. House wine is £12. Open all week.

Bertorelli's   WC2
44A Floral Street   map 15
(020) 7836 3969

As Italian as Puccini and handy for pre-show warm-ups and post-performance wind-downs after the opera. The culinary magnum opus embraces antipasti (from £4.75), pastas (linguine with clams and chilli, £7.50/£11.50), and high-protein 'secondi' such as involtini of rabbit with black olive paste and braised Savoy cabbage (£14.50). Pizzas also feature on the lighter caffé menu. All-Italian wine list. Branches at 19 Charlotte Street, W1, tel: (020) 7636 4174, and 11 Frith Street, W1, tel: (020) 7494 3491.

Brady's   SW18
513 Old York Road   map 12
(020) 8877 9599

For 15 years Luke and Amelia Brady have been serving fish and chips with class. The fish, as fresh as can be, is either done in batter or grilled and served with chips. Tuna, swordfish and sardines line up with cod, haddock and whole plaice (from £6.60 to £8.95). The blackboard menu lists starters such as cod's roe pâté, and anchovies with sweet herrings, both £3.25, and there's apple crumble or treacle tart (£2.20) to finish. House wine is £9.95. Open Fri L, Mon to Sat D.

The Burlington   W4
1 Station Parade   map 12
(020) 8995 3344

A second venture from Redmond Hayward (see Main entry for Redmond's, London), offering a pleasant, informal atmosphere. Straightforward bistro cooking shows up in duck liver parfait with red onion marmalade, and lamb shank with Puy lentils and mash, with a few forays in other directions represented by a platter of Spanish tapas, for example, or well-reported marinated pigeon breasts topped with foie gras and served with wet polenta and a rich game jus. The 50-bin wine list opens at £12. Closed Mon D.

Carluccio's Caffé   W1
8 Market Place   map 15
(020) 7636 2228

Antonio Carluccio's empire continues to grow (17 at the last count, including some outside London), and this original, just off Oxford Street, serving breezy modern Italian dishes in a buzzing canteen atmosphere, is a blueprint for the group. There are no surprises, but typical are 'good' breads, vegetable antipasti (£3.95), salads like tonno e fagioli (£5.50), 'excellent' pasta, and main courses ranging from lasagne to a rich lamb stew with cannellini beans (£9.25), with tiramisù and pannacotta to finish. House wine is £10.50. Open all week. (See www.carluccios.com for the other addresses).

Carpaccio   SW3
4 Sydney Street   map 14
(0207) 352 3433

'Excellent' carpacci (£9) front the menu in this Chelsea Italian, housed in a tight narrow dining room. Otherwise there are cold starters and pasta (tagliolini with sea bass and basil) before recommended main courses like tagliata di manzo (thinly sliced fillet steak piled with rocket, £14) and involtini di vitello (rolls of chargrilled veal with radicchio and smoked ham). Traditional Italianate desserts (£5) in the mould of pannacotta, tiramisù and cannelloni pancakes with orange cream. Italian regional wines from £12. Closed Sun.

Chapel   NW1
48 Chapel Street   map 13
(020) 7402 9220

Cheery, workmanlike boozer that 'gets better and better', according to one local supporter. Expect a packed house for drinks and imaginative food with 'intriguing Asian overtones'. Reporters have also singled out Western-style dishes such as thick butternut squash soup (£3.50), chicken breast stuffed with spinach and Parma ham (£11), and 'huge', accurately cooked ribeye steak with generous vegetables. A few simple desserts like raspberry bavarois (around £4). Global wine list with nine by the glass. Open all week.

Le Chardon   SE22
65 Lordship Lane   map 12
(020) 8299 1921

One-time grocer's shop (complete with original tiles), now trading as a local brasserie. The kitchen delivers speedy meals for the Dulwich crowd and looks to the French classics for moules marinière (£5.25), snails in herb and garlic butter, breast of guinea fowl with Roquefort sauce (£11.50) and praline mousse (£4.25). Occasional forays bring in Thai fishcakes, and a true-Brit roast is served on Sundays (to 5pm). Short, predominantly French wine list from £10.50. Open all week. Related to The Green (see Main entry, London).

Chez Liline   N4
101 Stroud Green Road   map 12
(020) 7263 6550

Recently renovated neighbourhood restaurant bringing Mauritian seafood cookery to the outer regions of Wood Green. Supplies are from the next-door fish shop, and the 'minute' kitchen delivers exotically

inclined 'cosmopolitan and inventive' food. Bouillon de crabe mourouck (light crab soup with sweet potatoes, £5.25) could start things off, before vivaneau à la Créole (red snapper with herbs, tomatoes and chilli, £11.75) or roast sea bass with fennel sauce. Ice cream with hazelnuts and honey is a noteworthy dessert. Revamped wine list from £10.75. Open Sat and Sun L, all week D.

Chor Bizarre   W1
16 Albemarle Street   map 15
(020) 7629 9802/8542

A glorious hotchpotch of Indian artefacts and furniture collected from bazaars around the Subcontinent, is backed up by cooking with a strong and roving regional accent. Try orange rasam (£3.50) a light soup from the south before moving north to a selection of Tandooris which include quail, salmon and lamb (£10–£20). Typical street fare, perhaps aloo tikki chaat (patties of potato, spiced lentils, and green peas) or Punjabi samosa are lighter options. Thalis start at £22. Wines are chosen to match the food with 20 by the glass (from £4). Closed Sun L.

Christopher's   WC2
18 Wellington Street   map 15
(020) 7240 4222

'Great' first-floor dining room with an American attitude and large windows opening onto the sights and sounds of Covent Garden. The menu pits transatlantic go-getters like Maryland crab cakes with red pepper mayo (£9) and blackened ribeye steak with buttermilk-fried onions, roast garlic and 'whipped' potatoes (£17) against ballottine of salmon and slow-roast belly pork with ginger soy broth. Desserts continue to steal the show, e.g. banana tart Tatin with rum and raisin ice cream. 'Choices of the month' are highlights on the extensive globetrotting wine list. Open Mon to Fri L and D, Sat and Sun L.

Chuen Cheng Ku   W1
17 Wardour Street   map 15
(020) 7734 3281 and 3509

This venerable Chinese warhorse is looking its age nowadays but continues to operate on several levels. Dim sum are still wheeled around on heated trolleys at lunchtime – 'now quite a rarity' – delivering true classics like rice gruel with pork and 100-year-old egg, although the sheer scale of the place can take its toll in the kitchen. Otherwise expect a lengthy Cantonese menu and a series of set menus ranging from £13 to £25 per person. Open all week.

Cru   N1
2–4 Rufus Street   map 13
(020) 7729 5252
In a converted warehouse south of that epicentre of Brit art, Hoxton Square, Cru sports a subdued, clubby look of dark wooden tables around a well-racked wine 'cellar'. Tapas are scrawled on a board, with more snacky things like eggs Benedict on the brunch menu, but the carte deals in things Mediterranean: creamed mussel and saffron soup, wood-oven-roast chicken breast on sun-dried tomato couscous (£12), and fig tart (£5). Good-value set lunch. Wines start at £13.50. Closed Mon.

Cumberland Arms   W14
29 North End Road   map 13
(020) 7371 6806
A relaxed atmosphere prevails as does a standard gastro-pub décor of wood floors, assorted furniture and big flowers all matched by a daily changing Mediterranean-style menu that reveals a 'sophistication above the norm' for such a venue. Casual dining is the thing, pasta and risotto are offered in two sizes, supported by roast chicken with orange and lime, couscous and apricots and parsley (£11), or grilled marinated lamb chops with sweet paprika, potato and beetroot gratin with sage and cream (£12.50). Lively wine list with house Italian at £10.50. Open all week.

Del Buongustaio   SW15
283–285 Putney Bridge Road   map 12
(020) 8780 9361
Animated Italian osteria where contemporary realisations of regional dishes are the kitchen's stock in trade. The set-price menu (two courses £17, three £21) promises specialities such as a platter of marinated vegetables with cheese, fish and bruschetta, then linguine with clams, tiger prawns and cherry tomatoes,

followed by roast rack of lamb with mint sauce. House wine is £13.50. Closed Sun.

Diwana Bhel Poori   NW1
121 Drummond Street   map 13
(020) 7387 5556
The pick of the crop in Drummond Street's 'Little India', close to Euston Station. Bhel-pooris are star turns, but fans also rave about bhajias, plump samosas and masala dosas. Vegetable curries and breads provide the back-up and there's always a daily special (channa battura on Monday, for example). Rock-bottom prices: no single dish more than £5, thalis £4.50–£6.25, lunchtime buffets £6.50 a head. Unlicensed, but tap water on the tables and supremely good lassi. Open all week, noon to midnight.

Earl Spencer   SW18
260–262 Merton Road   map 12
(020) 8870 9244
Semi-suburban gastro-pub that has been given a mainline injection of airy, bright décor without losing its traditional boozy charms. One highly rated meal included 'brilliant' roast monkfish cooked on the bone with parsley garlic butter and vegetables (£12) and Singapore-style braised rabbit leg with pak choi and steamed rice. The daily menu could start with deep-fried smoked haddock fritter (£5.50) or potted beef, while desserts may range from prune parfait to pear, plum and amaretti trifle (£4). Serviceable wines from £9.50. Open all week.

Ebury Wine Bar   SW1
139 Ebury Street   map 13
(020) 7730 5447
A doyen among London wine bars, established in 1959 and still maintaining its reputation. The wine list is a thoroughbred selection, with prices from £12 and no fewer than 30 offered by the glass. On the food front, the kitchen turns out up-to-the-minute dishes including Moroccan lamb kebabs with Arabic salad (£6) and seared tuna with beetroot relish and mustard beurre blanc (£15.75) alongside grills. To finish, there might be American griddle cakes with fresh banana and honeycomb butter (£5.25). Closed Sun L.

ECapital
W1
8 Gerrard Street map 15
(020) 7434 3838

Shanghai cuisine is the speciality in this smart, cheerful Chinatown eating house. Steamed 'little juicy buns', 'thousand-layer' pressed pig's ears and braised yellow eel are some of the intriguing items on offer. Elsewhere, the kitchen turns its hand to dishes from Canton, Peking, Hunan and even South-east Asia (Malaysian fried ho-fun noodles, for example): pig's liver and chicken hotpot, and beancurd stuffed with cuttlefish paste have impressed. 'Smiley', attentive staff. 'Excellent' unfermented Dragon Well tea; exclusively Burgunidan wine list (from £12). Open all week.

Efes Kebab House
W1
80 Great Titchfield Street map 15
(020) 7636 1953

In its thirtieth year, this consistent, reasonably priced restaurant is still one of the most cherished places for Turkish food in town. There's something for everyone, especially on the line-up of around 20 or so hot and cold meze (£3.80 to £4.20) ranging from carrots with yoghurt to deep-fried lamb's liver. Main dishes are built around impressive quantities of protein in the shape of kebabs: say, minced lamb every which way (£6.95), leg of chicken with peppers and mushrooms (£7.50), or various steaks (£12), all served with rice and salad. Closed Sun.

Electric Brasserie
W11
191 Portobello Road map 13
(020) 7908 9696

'A perfectly realised metropolitan experience' in surroundings that evoke an Art Deco Paris brasserie. The emphasis is firmly on décor, buzz and slick service, although the kitchen also aims to please. Fish, comfort food (coq au vin) and a few more complex ideas rub shoulders on the menu: roast sea bream with slow-roast fennel and sunblush tomatoes (£12.50) and red-wine poached pear with a cinnamon cone (£6) have been favourably received, although other dishes have faltered. Wines are tilted towards France; vin de pays is £13.50. Open all week.

Emile's
SW15
96 Felsham Road map 12
(020) 8789 3323

Laudable neighbourhood restaurant that has been feeding the Putney crowd since 1990. Monthly menus (£17.50 and £19.95) take their cue from the world larder: individual beef Wellington is a fixture, but main courses might extend to roast skate wing with sag aloo, oven-dried tomato and poppadom mille-feuille with garam masala butter sauce. Start with salmon and sorrel soufflé and finish with blackberry and ricotta cheesecake. Around 40 value-for-money wines from £10.50. Open Mon to Sat D only.

First Floor
W11
186 Portobello Road map 13
(020) 7243 0072

Huge blue baubles and a candelabra overflowing with wax are part of the theatrical décor in this well-worn dining room above a pub. Contemporary cooking with notably good starters and desserts, from globe and Jerusalem artichokes with preserved lemon and mustard leaves (£7.25) to chocolate tart with lime ice cream. In between, expect mains like monkfish with basil mash and Parma ham (£14.50). Short, realistically priced wine list. Closed Mon.

fish!
SE1
Cathedral Street map 13
(020) 7407 3803

Fish, steamed or grilled, is the business at this glass Victorian pavilion beside Southwark Cathedral, and right in the heart of the fabulous Borough Market (a must for all foodies). Ticks on the menu, which doubles as a place mat, indicate the selection available – perhaps monkfish, skate, lemon or Dover sole, Icelandic cod and organic salmon (£9.55 to £19.95) – served with your choice of spicy salsa, hollandaise, herb butter, red wine gravy or salsa verde. Starters take the form of devilled whitebait or dressed crab (£8.95). House French is £13.95. Open all week.

La Galette
W1
56 Paddington Street map 15
(020) 7935 1554

The premier spot in the capital to get a taste of Brittany. The eponymous buckwheat crêpes are served in simple and unfussy surroundings. Start with the soup du jour, or salmon rillettes, and move on to the galettes: forestière (£7.95) comes with a mix of mushrooms, crème fraîche and parsley, or a version with baked ham and cheese (£5.95). Desserts are crêpes, too, perhaps with chestnut cream or the legendary suzette (or there are ice creams). The excellent choice of Normandy and Breton ciders are ideal partners to the food; house wine is £11. Open all week.

Gilbey's   W5
77 The Grove   map 12
(020) 8840 7568

One of a trio of bistro/restaurants, with siblings in Amersham and Eton (see Round-ups, England). The conservatory and secluded garden are prime attractions and menus read well: starters like twice-baked smoked haddock soufflé (£7) could be followed by honey-roast duck breast with boulangère potatoes and glazed pear (£15), then chocolate and lavender tart with passion-fruit sorbet (£4.75). Two-course set lunches £8.95. Gilbey's imports French wine, and the list has plenty of attractive bottles at keen prices (from £10.45). Closed Sun D and all Mon.

Great Nepalese *   NW1
48 Eversholt Street   map 13
(020) 7388 6737

This most amenable of restaurants continues to serve Euston commuters, students and Camden Town locals with gutsy food. The menu has its share of standard Indian curries and tandoori dishes, but the Nepalese specialities are better. Typical are starters such as masco bara (deep-fried lentil pancakes), haku choyala (barbecued diced mutton), while mains run to pork flavoured with ginger, garlic, spices and fresh herbs (£5.95), and breast of duck cooked with mint, coconut and cream sauce (£11.50). House wine is £8.50. Open all week.

Havelock Tavern   W14
57 Masbro Road   map 12
(020) 7603 5374

Bustling neighbourhood pub serving the locals of Brook Green and conveniently located behind Olympia. Order and pay at the bar for pan-European dishes like steamed mussels and clams with cider, onion and crème fraîche (£6), roast chump of lamb with white-bean, tomato and red pepper stew (£12.50), and desserts such as grilled banana bread with vanilla ice cream and butterscotch sauce (£4). Real ales and a handy list of modern wines from £10. No credit cards. Open all week.

The Hempel   W2
31–35 Craven Hill Gardens   map 13
(020) 7298 9000

Some clue about pricing at this homage to minimalism may be gleaned from the fact that this is where rich and glossy folk hang out. And as the best way to remain exclusive is to charge the earth, expect to pay £9 for an odd assortment of Japanese and Mediterranean plates like a crudités platter, salad niçoise or two skewers of chicken or beef yakitori; better value are bento boxes (£15). Lunch is usefully served from noon to 6pm. House wine is £22. Closed Sun D.

Ikkyu   W1
67 Tottenham Court Road   map 15
(020) 7436 6169 and 636 9280

'Irresistible' Japanese café, in a cellar a few doors from Goodge Street station. Grab a table or sit at the counter and watch the action in the 'domestic-sized' kitchen. Weekday lunches are a snip (£6 to £8.50) for familiar sashimi, bowls of ramen noodles, a limited selection of sushi and other items like ten ju (a lacquered box with rice, a sweet dressing and mixed tempura, plus miso soup). A broader menu is available on the evening menu. 'Fantastically friendly' staff. Tea is free; house wine £11. Closed Sat and Sun L.

InterContinental, Le Soufflé   W1
1 Hamilton Place   map 14
(020) 7409 3131

Le Soufflé always manages to rise to the occasion in this ultra-chic hotel on Hyde Park Corner. New chef Geoff Haviland was due to take over the kitchen in September 2004; his cooking will – doubtless – continue in the modern French vein, with luxury ingredients and ambitious ideas much in evidence (no menus were available as the Guide went to press). Expect suitably professional service and a pedigree wine list peppered with vintage French classics. Open Tue to Fri L and D, and Sat D.

Istanbul Iskembecisi N16

9 Stoke Newington Road map 12
(020) 7254 7291

Simple, good-value Turkish eaterie whose signature dish, iskembe, is a traditional tripe soup to which you add salt, vinegar, lemon juice, pepper and dried chilli (£2.50). It is served until the early hours alongside meze of muska borek (light crisp pastries filled with feta and spinach), and garlicky ispanak salatesi (spinach in yogurt and olive oil), and mains of kebabs and grills, slow-cooked stews and casseroles. Turkish wines (£8.50) appear on a good value global list. Open all week.

Kasturi EC3

57 Aldgate High Street map 13
(020) 7480 7402

Modern Indian tucked away in the depths of Aldgate's cityscapes. The décor is upbeat and the kitchen aims high: expect a strong showing of tandooris and dishes from the North-west frontier, from ginger lamb chops (£5) to paneer tikka. Four kinds of biryani (from £8) share the stage with house specials such as murgh jaipuri (chicken breast rolls stuffed with minced meat) and ubiquitous dhansaks and Madras. Thalis from £14.95. Two dozen wines from £12.95. Open 11 to 11 Mon to Sat.

Lemonia NW1

89 Regent's Park Road map 13
(020) 7586 7454

Long-running Primrose Hill rendezvous serving great-value Greek-Cypriot food to an appreciative crowd. The kitchen knows its way around meze (from £3.25), kleftiko (£9.50) and chargrilled pork souvlaki, and springs a few surprises with specials like barbanouki (deep-fried baby red mullet) and hare stifado. Finish with baklava or rizogalo (rice pudding). Bestselling, bargain-price weekday lunches (two courses £7.25). Quaffable Greek-Cypriot wines, plus house French at £13.50 a litre. Closed Sat L and Sun D.

Little Bay EC1

171 Farringdon Road map 13
(020) 7278 1234

Peter Ilic's lively group of informal restaurants – don't expect much in the way of décor – are run to the same formula: prices are fixed so that main courses, for instance, are all £5.45 from noon to 7pm, and thereafter £7.95. Reporters hail this branch 'the cheapest place in the area'. Expect modern European cooking along the lines of steamed mussels, lemongrass, garlic and shallots, then 'well-timed' ribeye with vegetable purée and 'punchy' red wine and cep reduction. The varied wine list struggles to get above £20. Open all week. Also at 228 Belsize Rd, NW6, (020) 7373 4699.

Little Georgia E8

2 Broadway Market map 12
(020) 7249 9070

Outpost of genuine Georgian cooking in a converted pub close to the Regent's Park Canal. To start, try hachapuri (baked cheesebread stuffed with ricotta and mozzarella, £4.50) or catmis (a salad of chicken, spring onion, rice and cucumber). Mains hold fast to the rustic traditions of tabaka (fried poussin served with Georgian plum or 'ajica' spicy pepper paste) and kharcho (pork in walnut, garlic and herb sauce, £12). Old Tblisi wine (£12) is the preferred tipple. Open Tue to Sun D.

Livebait SE1

43-45 The Cut map 13
(020) 7928 7211

The original of a group that now has outlets in towns and cities across the land (see Round-up, Manchester). Like its relatives, this jam-packed venue close to the Old Vic goes for fish in a big way. Crowd-pleasing dishes include everything from squid tempura (£7) and chargrilled tuna with peppers, guacamole, sour cream and lime salsa (£14.50) to classic seafood platters and fish pie. Grills for carnivores. Good-value set menus (£14.50 to £18.50) between 2.30 and 7pm. Whites are the main players on the wine list, which kicks off at £11.50. Open all week.

Lobster Pot SE11

3 Kennington Lane map 13
(020) 7582 5556

Very French, very nautical and very idiosyncratic with its maritime sound effects and décor resembling a trawler cabin. Lobsters and extravagant plateaux de fruits de mer (£11.50/£22.50) top the bill, closely followed by gratinéed oysters with champagne sauce (£9.50) and grilled sea bass fillets with lemongrass and coconut sauce (£14.50); there are also meaty offerings such as roast rack of lamb with 'French' mint sauce. Check out the eight-course 'menu surprise'. Short Gallic wine list from £11.50. Closed Mon and Sun.

Loco   SE3
1 Lawn Terrace   map 12
(020) 8852 0700

This former fish! sports a new look and bright, breezy Italian menu. The formula here and at the Surbiton branch (see Round-up entry) is the same: things like prosciutto with buffalo mozzarella, bruschetta with tomatoes and basil (£4.25), or antipasti misti to start, and mains such as osso bucco milanese (£13.50), venison ravioli with mushrooms, and fillet of sea bass with braised fennel. Finish with pannacotta and raspberry sauce, or chocolate, hazelnut and Amaretto torta (£4.75). House Italian (£13.95) heads a short, varied list. Open Sat and Sun L and Tue to Sat D.

Lomo   SW10
222 Fulham Road   map 14
(020) 7349 8848

Almost a mini-cultural centre promising nightly live music, Spanish football at weekends and films on Sunday – not to mention classic grazing food in abundance. Tapas (£3–£6) run from tortilla to grilled squid salad; more substantial raciones (£7–£9) could include chicken livers in sherry, steamed octopus, and chorizo-stuffed courgettes. Crema Catalana (£3) is an appropriate finish. Bottled beers, cocktails and sherries by the glass, plus plenty of gutsy Iberian wines; prices from £10.95. Open all week from 5pm.

Lucky Seven   W2
127 Westbourne Park Road   map 13
(020) 7727 6771

Tom Conran's take on an American diner is a runaway success. There are no bookings, so expect to share a booth, and even to queue, for organic beefburgers every which way, and, to drink, malts and thick shakes. A cup of clam chowder (£3.95), chicken Caesar salad (£6.75)

and Foghorn Leghorn chicken burger with avocado, rocket, mustard mayo and cheese extend choice. Breakfast is 'two eggs any style' with hash browns and perhaps crispy bacon or home-made sausage, and there are buttermilk pancakes (£4.75) and heuvos rancheros. House wine £13.50. Open all week.

Mango Tree   SW1
46 Grosvenor Place   map 14
(020) 7823 1888

The location, not far from Victoria Station, means that this spacious, stylishly appointed Thai restaurant is handy for residents from the suburbs as well as the well heeled of Belgravia. The kitchen delivers competent renditions of somtum (green papaya salad), satays, shrimp cakes with plum sauce, curries such as green curry with sirloin (£13.95), and classic pad thai noodles. Prices are high. House wine is £19. Open all week.

Manna   NW3
4 Erskine Road   map 13
(020) 7722 8028

Definitely branching out from nut rissoles and vegetable lasagne, this Primrose Hill institution gets full marks for using far flung ideas for meatless dishes. Well-reported meals from the short, seasonal carte have included potato bondas (stuffed with pink chilli coconut chutney and served with coriander and ginger relish), whisky barbecue marinated grilled tofu on roasted garlic mash with onion rings and wilted greens (£12.50), and ricotta and chocolate flute (£5.95) for dessert. House wine £10.50. Open Sun L and Mon to Sun D.

Manzi's   WC2
1-2 Leicester Street   map 15
(020) 7734 0224

In business since 1928 (and not about to change its ways), the Manzi family's old-stager is now something of a West End institution. The menu promises fish cookery from days gone by in the shape of devilled whitebait (£4.50), poached skate with beurre noisette and capers (£15) and lobster thermidor, while desserts seldom stray from the classic mould of crème brûlée and sticky toffee pudding. Handy for theatreland and the West End nightlife;

accommodation available. House wine £12.50. Closed Sun.

Masala Zone
W1
9 Marshall Street
map 15
(020) 7287 9966
Earthy colours, Indian art, refectory tables and rapid turnaround of customers set the scene for this brisk-paced canteen close to Carnaby Street. Dishes from the open-to-view kitchen arrive in no particular order: say, aloo tikki chaat (potato cake with yoghurt and chutney), green chicken korma (£6.25), or a lamb thali (£9.70) served with vegetables, lentils and raita. Lunchtime salads and sandwiches include masala lamb burger (£6.25) and chicken tikka on ciabatta. Wines are from £10.25, or drink lassi. Open all week. A second branch is at 80 Upper Street, N1, tel: (020) 7359 3399.

Mehek
EC2
45 London Wall
map 13
(020) 7588 5043
'Jorokas' (antique wooden panels) hang on the yellow walls of this good-looking City Indian. Although the menu is straight out of the 'tikka masala' stable, Mehek is worth a visit for the good tandooris (including top-drawer king prawns, £12.50), a contingent of 'high street' curries from garlic chilli chicken to lamb pasanda (£7.50), plus a few specials like haash hyderabadi (marinated duck with sesame seeds, coconut and peanut sauce). Decent rice and breads (from £1). Pleasant service; respectable wines from £12.50. Open all day Mon to Fri; Sat D.

Mela
W1
152–156 Shaftesbury Avenue
map 15
(020) 7836 8635
'An intriguing, well-crafted Indian menu that raises expectations,' commented one visitor to this colourful restaurant. The results have been 'patchy', but gilafi seekh kebab (£4.50) is a decent version and naans are 'excellent'. Elsewhere, the kitchen aims for 'country-style cuisine' in the shape of gosht utthapams (fluffy rice pancakes with chargrilled lamb), and jhinga kalimirch (stir-fried prawns with moong lentils and grated coconut). Bargain snack lunches. Open all week. A sister restaurant, Chowki, is at 2–3 Denman Street, W1, tel; (020) 7439 1330.

Memsaheb
E14
65/67 Amsterdam Road
map 12
(020) 7538 3008/1177
Light and airy modern Indian restaurant that offers an up-to-date menu strong on regional accents. The menu draws inspiration from Goa for lamb xacuto (£6.95), Kerala for kingfish cooked in coconut milk (£9.95), southern India for konju papas (prawns with tamarind, mustard seeds and coconut), or there's Rajasthani khargosh (rabbit cooked in a mild sauce). Dhansaks, jalfrezis and bhunas are listed under 'all time favourites'. House wine is £8.40. Open Mon to Fri L and D, Sat and Sun D only.

Mezzanine
SE1
National Theatre
map 13
(020) 7452 3600
Timing is crucial if you have to be fed and watered before curtain up, but this place succeeds admirably. The format is flexible, menus are well thought out, and service is 'brisk and efficient'. The set-price menu (two courses £19.50, three £21.50) delivers smoked haddock and potato rösti, skewered lamb with chorizo, pappardelle, vegetables and puttanesca salsa, and summer pudding. Tables give Thames views or overlook the ground-floor musicians and spectators. Open Sat and matinée day L, Mon to Sat D.

Mirch Masala
SW16
1416 London Road
map 12
(020) 8679 1828
'Food Extraordinaire Halal' is the oddly westernised slogan for this cut-price suburban Indian. 'Warmers' (starters, £1.50–£7) embrace vegetarian samosas, chicken bhajias and masala fish, while 'coolers' (rice, breads and desserts from £1.50) complete the picture. In between are main-event 'steamers' including Deigi specialities, 'mix dishes' like jeera chicken and a host of karahis, from butter beans and methi (£3.50) to king prawns with mushrooms (£10). Sample lassi or BYO drink. Open all week noon to midnight. Also branches in Tooting and Soho.

Miyama   W1
38 Clarges Street   map 15
(020) 7499 2443

Fumio Miyama has run his Japanese restaurant of the old school for more than 20 years and, despite the prime Mayfair site, continues to maintain reasonable prices. The menu is as classic as they come, taking in zensai appetisers of such dishes as sunomono (octopus, mackerel and seaweed marinated in rice vinegar) and edamame (salted green beans), and grills, top-quality sashimi and sushi. Alternatively, order one of the set menus based on tempura, sushi, or teriyaki (£28 to £30). House wines start at £13. Closed Sat and Sun L.

Momo   W1
25 Heddon Street   map 15
(020) 7434 4040

Self-styled 'restaurant familial' that brings Morocco to Mayfair. The atmosphere is tailor-made for a 'super night out' and the food does its job. Couscous and tagines (from £14.50) form the backbone of the menu, with support from dishes like baked cod with melted shallots and tomato tian, wilted baby leaves and saffron-scented broth. Start with pastilla of pigeon (£10) and finish with sweet Maghrebi pastries. Some Moroccan wines appear on the wide-ranging list; prices from £18. 'Komia bar, tearoom and bazzar' next door. Closed Sun L.

Mon Plaisir   WC2
19–21 Monmouth Street   map 15
(020) 7836 7243

For more than 30 years, Alain Lhermitte's bistro has been a Covent Garden fixture and it's still just as Gallic as can be. The menu is a familiar run through coq au vin, carré d'agneau, and steak frites, with rabbit and sage terrine with apricot coulis (£7.50), and roast monkfish with pancetta and a saffron and red wine infusion (£16.95) giving a more contemporary feel. Pre- and post-theatre menus are £12.40 for two courses, and the sound French wine list opens at £11.50. Closed Sat L and Sun.

Moshi Moshi Sushi   EC2
Unit 24, Liverpool Street Station,   map 13
Broadgate
(020) 7247 3227

Moshi Moshi, the first kaiten restaurant in the UK, enjoys a great position overlooking the platforms of Liverpool Street Station. The conveyor belt snakes its way around the room delivering coloured plates (prices from £1.20 to £3.50): choose from a range of nigiri sushi, maki, and sashimi. Bento or donburi boxes, plus Japanese 'tapas' (gyoza, or 'excellent' tempura, perhaps) are ordered from friendly staff. Drink saké, or house wine from £11.50. There is another branch in Brighton (see Round-up entry), and the following addresses in London: 7-8 Limeburner Lane, EC4, tel: (020) 7248 1808; Waitrose, Canada Place, E14, tel: (020) 7512 9201; Kiosk 2B, Central Square, Broadgate, EC2, tel: (020) 7920 0077.

National Gallery, Crivelli's   WC2
Garden   map 15
Trafalgar Square
(020) 7747 2869

A room-with-a-view overlooking Trafalgar Square is the setting for this gallery-tourists' pit-stop on the first floor of the Sainsbury Wing. Choose anything from a sandwich in the bar/café to more elaborate restaurant dishes like rustic bean soup (£4.90), artichoke puffs, roast monkfish (£14.50) and 'admirable' pannacotta (£5). Set priced menus are available. Serious crowds can result in 'erratic service' and variable cooking. Italian wines from £11.25. Open all week L, also Wed D (5.30 to 7.15).

New Tayyabs   EC1
83–89 Fieldgate Street   map 12
(020) 7247 9543/6400

A lively café-style place with plain wooden tables, bright lighting and pulsing bhangra music. It's basic – 'you keep your plate throughout the meal' – and dishes arrive pretty much in whatever order the kitchen fancies. The cooking is Pakistani Punjabi, and the bulk of the menu comprises an extensive selection of karahi dishes ranging from chicken (£8.20) and prawns to dhal karela (bitter pumpkin). Start with chicken tikka (£2.40), and finish with rasmalai (£2).

Unlicensed, but you can BYO. Open all week,
D only.

New World W1

1 Gerrard Place map 15
(020) 7434 2508

'Cheerful, great fun and a landmark venue' for
'trolley' dim sum in Chinatown. Recent star
turns (from £2.20 each) have included
'unmistakably pungent' steamed tripe with
black beans and chilli, chicken wrapped in
bean curd rolls, pork balls each topped with a
Chinese mushroom, and made-to-order bowls
of soup noodles. The full menu is a Cantonese
heavyweight with abundant seafood and
main-dish prices from £6.50 to £16.50. Service
has been increasingly friendly of late. House
wine is £10.50. Open all week.

Old Delhi W2

48 Kendal Street map 13
(020) 7723 3335

There's more to this upmarket restaurant than
the name alone might suggest. The menu is
fairly evenly split between Iranian and Indian
dishes, so that hummus (£5.50), savoury
meatballs, gormeh sabsi (lamb stewed with
herbs and vegetables) and gaimeh (lamb with
split peas and dried limes) vie with a fairly
innovative monkfish tikka (£9.45) and the
more conventional dhal soup, rogan josh
(£10.25), and the usual accompaniments of
raita and poppadoms. Open all week.

Olé SW6

Broadway Chambers map 12
(020) 7610 2010

This tapas joint on the Fulham Broadway
packs them in nightly. Extensive menu with
an ambitious list of cold 'frias' and ensaladas
such as boquerones and goats' cheese salad
with quince and beetroot mousse. Hot
'calientes' leap from albondigas and patatas
bravas to rollitos de muslo de pato
escabechados y jamóon serrano (shredded
confit of duck and Serrano ham rolls, served
with couscous and port sauce). Prices from
£1.75 to £6.50. Finish with chocolate cream
tart (£4). Spanish wines from £11.10. Closed
Sun L.

The Perseverance WC1

63 Lamb's Conduit Street map 13
(020) 7405 8278

A combination of bustling, traditional pub
downstairs and more contemporary dining
room upstairs, where the short menu takes an
equally modern, flexible brasserie view of
things. Tomato and watermelon gazpacho
(£5.25) or crab tian with avocado, tomato and
herb salsa are typical starters, while main
courses run to pan-fried sea bass with salad
niçoise and herb jus (£13.95), with chilled
orange rice pudding and vanilla ice cream
(£5.50) to finish. House wine is £10.90. Closed
Sun D.

La Porte des Indes W1

32 Bryanston Street map 13
(020) 7224 0055

A 'pseudo-Indian fairytale', according to one
couple, who reported a 'fantastic experience of
unexpected dimensions'. Palm trees, orchid-
decorated tables, a pond and cascading
waterfall set the scene. The menu veers
between 'Les Indes Françaises' (côtes
d'agneau with a confit of red onions and malt
vinegar, £18) and authentic-sounding dishes
like Bombay chaat snacks (£6.50), tandoori
king prawns and Kashmiri braised lamb
shanks. Buffet-style lunches. Cocktails in the
themed Jungle Bar; 100-plus international
wines from £15.50. Closed Sat L.

Quaglino's SW1

16 Bury Street map 15
(020) 7930 6767

The impressive dining room is reached via a
sweeping grand entrance staircase and
dominated by a shellfish counter filled with
molluscs and crustacea that service the platters
of fruits de mer (£34), or plates of crab, lobster
or langoustines simply served with
mayonnaise. Good brasserie dishes like veal
chop with anchovy butter (£19.50) appear
alongside the likes of rôtisserie free-range
English chicken and Suffolk pork, but the
kitchen doesn't always live up to the grand
scale, and small portions niggle in reports.
House French is £14.50. Open all week.

Ragam W1
57 Cleveland Street map 15
(020) 7636 9098

The speciality at this affordable, cramped family-run restaurant is the vegetarian food of Kerala. Typical of dishes are masala dosai – a rice and flour pancake stuffed with potato – served with vegetable curry and coconut chutney (£3.80), uthappam (a potent pizza-style pancake), and dahi vada (gram flour doughnut in yoghurt). The rest of the menu is that of a non-vegetarian curry house, with the likes of butter chicken, lamb dhansak (£4.50), and keema aloo. Open all week.

Randall & Aubin W1
14–16 Brewer Street map 15
(020) 7287 4447

Once Soho's most distinguished butcher-cum-delicatessen, this white-tiled and marble-tabled emporium now deals in brasserie staples such as calf's liver, pancetta and mash (£15.50). The rôtisserie delivers spit-roast herb chicken (£10.50), whole dressed crab (£11.50) comes from the counter display of crustacea, or you could simply have a sausage, tomato and mustard baguette with frites (£6.70). Alternatively, splash out on fruits de mer for two, or 50g of caviar with blinis and fromage blanc. Another branch is at 329–331 Fulham Road, SW10, tel: (020) 7823 3515. Closed Sun L.

Rani N3
7 Long Lane map 12
(020) 8349 4386

Perhaps more modish West End brasserie than North London vegetarian restaurant, but the Pattnis' continue to deliver top-flight Gujarati cooking. Vivid, distinctive flavours are the kitchen's strengths, and attention to the smallest detail results in 'exemplary' potato bhajis and 'fulsome' breads. Apart from set meals, thalis, and a children's menu, it offers an enterprising list of curries, say banana methi, or akhaa ringal (with aubergine). Main courses £4.50 to £5.90. Open all week D and Sun L.

Rasa Travancore N16
56 Stoke Newington Church Street map 12
(020) 7249 1346

Opposite the original Rasa (see Main entry, London), this branch of the mini group has the trademark pink frontage, 'canteen-style' décor, and a menu that vigorously champions Keralan cuisine. Broadly based Syrian Christian cooking is the inspiration, with meat and seafood alongside vegetarian stalwarts. Recent successes have included roast duck tharavu (£7) and kappayyum meenum vevichathu (kingfish with tamarind and steamed tapioca root). Starters from £2.75, desserts such as pistachio kulfi (£2.50). Wines from £9.50; otherwise sample Rasa's own-label beer. Open Sun L, all week D.

Rasa W1 W1
6 Dering Street map 15
(020) 7629 1346

West End branch of a mini-group of Indian restaurants (see Main entry, London, and Round-up above), tucked behind New Bond Street. Like its relatives, this outlet is devoted to regional Keralan cooking, with a big contingent of trademark vegetarian specialities plus an increasing number of meat and fish dishes. Results have been variable, but splendid home-made pickles and breads (£2.50) seldom disappoint. Otherwise, the repertoire ranges from banana boli (deep-fried plantain, £4.25) to vadakkan koyi biryani with chicken and cashews (£10). House wine is £10.95. Closed Sun L.

Rebato's SW8
169 South Lambeth Road map 12
(020) 7735 6388

The grand señrita of London tapas bars and a Hispanic institution. The wooden and tiled front bar is dedicated to grazing, with temptations like hot chorizo rosario, patatas bravas, stuffed piquillo peppers with Galician cheese and more (prices from £3 per item). At the back is a formal dining room offering a Continental carte along the lines of prawns in filo (£4), paella valenciana (£14) and calf's liver and bacon. Red-blooded Spanish wine list with house Torres £9.95. Closed Sat L and Sun.

Red Pepper W9
8 Formosa Street map 13
(020) 7266 2708

Pizzas cooked in a wood-fired oven form the centrepiece of the menu at this 'cramped' Italian restaurant in a back street of Maida

Vale. Crusts are thin, and toppings, ranging from margherita to primavera, are generous. Alternatively, go for pasta such as linguine with tiger prawns and asparagus in sour thyme sauce (£9.50) or risotto primavera with Gorgonzola cream (£8). The all-Italian wine list starts at £12. Closed Mon to Fri L.

Rules   WC2
35 Maiden Lane   map 15
(020) 7836 5314

London's oldest restaurant offers within its amiably clubby confines a repertoire that ploughs pretty much the same furrow as when it opened 200 years ago. Seasonal game, thick-crusted pies and substantial puddings form the backbone, although there are occasional forays into the modern world, as in a salad of caramelised artichoke, roast rabbit, black pudding and Amontillado sherry (£8.95) and whole grilled sea bass with roast courgettes (£17.95). French house wine comes by the glass, jug or bottle (£14.95). Open all week.

The Social   N1
33 Linton Street   map 13
(020) 7354 5809

'Pubbily unpretentious' gastro-pub with relaxed atmosphere, staff 'well on top of the job', and an upstairs bar for sofa-sitting, drinking and pool. The food pulls crowds with a short menu dealing in grilled goats' cheese with tomatoes and red onion salad (£5) and grilled tuna with spinach, roast new potatoes and pomegranate salad (£11). Alternatively there's beef or lamb burgers, or chargrilled steak sandwich with chips (£8.50). Most wines on the short list are under £20. Open all week for D, L on Sat and Sun only.

Sofra   WC2
36 Tavistock Street   map 15
(020) 7240 3773

Incredible value for money and all-day opening are part of the attraction at this branch of a mini chain of Turkish eateries. The menus are flexible and meze stand out: salads, hummus, tabbouleh, imam bayaldi (savoury aubergines), and grilled halloumi can be ordered individually or as part of a mixed meze for £6.50, or there could be red lentil soup (£2.95), grilled fillets of lamb with oregano

(£8.95), and a dessert of fruit salad. Other branches with the same menu are at 18 Shepherd Market, tel: (020) 7493 3320, and 1 St Christopher Place, tel: (020) 7224 4080, both in W1. Open all week.

Spiga   W1
84–86 Wardour Street   map 15
(020) 7734 3444

Boisterous Soho joint with a high turnover, clean lines and populist Italian food. A wood-fired oven delivers pizzas (from £7.50) and there's a bunch of pasta dishes such as pappardelle with chicken livers and sage; alternatively choose a main course like sirloin steak with rocket salad and Parmesan (£14). Start with marinated salmon and balsamic dressing (£7.50) and finish with pannacotta. Italian wines from £3.30 a glass, £13 a bottle. Closed Sun L.

La Spighetta   W1
43 Blandford Street   map 15
(020) 7486 7340

On-the-ball basement Italian where classic pizzas from a wood-fired oven take centre stage. But the menu springs some pleasant surprises, with starters of octopus carpaccio with fennel salad and chives, and pan-fried goats' cheese with chicory, endive and blueberry sauce (£6.90). Vegetarian lasagne is made with wild mushrooms, aubergine and tomato sauce, or there's stuffed roast squid with warm French bean salad (£12.90). Chef's specials beef out the choice with seasonal treats like deep-fried courgette flowers stuffed with ricotta. House wine is £12.50. Closed Sun L.

Sutton Arms   EC1
6 Carthusian Street   map 13
(020) 7253 0723

On the ground floor is a die-hard backstreet boozer, upstairs is the plainly decked-out dining room. A new chef/proprietor was still finding his feet as the Guide was being compiled, but his seasonally inspired menus have plenty to offer. Smoked haddock and chive fishcake (£6) is a typical starter, before pan-fried duck breast with parsnip purée, caramelised onion and thyme sauce (£16.25) and desserts such as apple, raisin and cinnamon crème brûlée (£4.95). Minimal selection of international wines from £11. Open Mon to Fri.

Swag & Tails
SW7

10–11 Fairholt Street
map 14
(020) 7584 6926

Convivial pub/restaurant that suits its well-heeled location in a Knightsbridge mews. The ever-changing menu is an eclectic slate that pitches Caesar salad (£7/£10) and pork en croûte with black pudding and cider butter sauce (£12.95) against prawn, chilli and sesame fritters and crispy duck leg with ginger noodles, Asian greens and plum and soy dressing. Finish with Irish cheeses or a dessert like blood orange-curd tart with raspberry sorbet (£5.50). The well-chosen wine list has nine by the glass (from £3.10). Open Mon to Fri L and D.

Tate Modern, Café 7
SE1

Bankside
map 13
(020) 7401 5020

Café on the seventh floor of the gallery with great views over the Thames to St Paul's. Service gets its skates on for speedy pit-stops and the kitchen delivers breakfast, afternoon tea and lunches ranging from smoked haddock and crab rarebit (£8) to bigger dishes including herb-crusted veal with Mediterranean vegetables (£17). Finish with Neals Yard cheeses or something sweet like saffron-poached pear on ginger cake with pear sorbet (£4.50). Concise, palate-teasing wine list from £13. Open all week L, Fri and Sat D.

Thai Bistro
W4

99 Chiswick High Road
map 12
(020) 8995 5774

'Tom yum gong soup was excellent, as ever,' noted a regular at this popular Chiswick restaurant. Prices are fair, and dishes such as spicy prawns with a coconut red curry paste (£6.95), and papaya salad with its striking and balanced combination of strong chilli sensation and citrus richness are 'very fine indeed'. Pad Thai noodles (£6.95) get the thumbs up too. The short wine list suits the food and opens at £11.50. Closed Tue L and Thur L.

Thai Garden
E2

249 Globe Road
map 12
(020) 8981 5748

Utilitarian East End café/restaurant serving authentic Thai seafood and vegetarian dishes in equal measure. Noodle-based specialities such as pad thai (£4.50) and lard nata lay are skilfully prepared, likewise tom kar (cauliflower and coconut soup with galangal, £3.50), salad kak with peanut sauce, and light-textured seafood tempura (£5). Totally charming service, rock-bottom prices. Open Mon to Fri L, all week D.

Tokyo Diner
WC2

2 Newport Place
map 15
(020) 7287 8777

Richard Hills's bright Tokyo-inspired low-price eating house delivers basic Japanese-style curries, bento boxes comprising rice, sunomono, salmon sashimi, pickles and a main item such as chicken teriyaki (£11.50), and 'donburi' rice with seasoned egg plus chicken or salmon topping. Lunch specials – say, vegetable curry set (£5.70) – are served until 6.30pm, and there's a short, easy-on-the-pocket midnight menu served from 11.30pm. No booking, no tipping, and house wine is £6.90. Open all week.

La Trouvaille
W1

12A Newburgh Street
map 15
(020) 7287 8488

Explore the little-known byways of French regional cooking in this staunchly Gallic bistro off Carnaby Street. White radish with liquorice-flavoured sardines and smoked oyster jus, and braised pork belly with caramelised plums, shallots and white cabbage have featured, along with wacky desserts such as marinated pears with black truffle honey and tobacco ice cream. Wines are mostly from Southern France; vins de pays £14. Closed Sun D. Reports please.

Truc Vert
W1

42 North Audley Street
map 15
(020) 7491 9988

The dining area is part and parcel of a first-rate deli, and the sight and aroma of cheeses, hams, fruit and vegetables are enough to whet most people's appetites. You can come for breakfast, but lunch and dinner is what the set-up is all about. Plates of charcuterie and cheese are fixtures, as are main-course salads for lunch. Soup might be pumpkin and ginger, then chargrilled lamb cutlets with leek and parsley mash (£15.50), and lemon tart (£4.95) to finish. House wine is £12. Closed Sun D.

Vama   SW10
438 King's Road   map 13
(020) 7565 8500

Slick King's Road 'Indian Room' with pavement tables and a light, contemporary interior complete with an Indian 'fossil-stone' floor and handcrafted teak chairs. 'Untamed North-west frontier cuisine' promises the menu, which lists all manner of tandooris from praiseworthy marinated tiger prawns (£13.50) to cauliflower with broccoli (£7). Main dishes include some unusual items like crab and gourd kofta (£13.95) and kala chicken (roasted with cumin and black salt). Brunch at weekends. Twenty wines from £13. Open all week.

Vasco & Piero's Pavilion   W1
15 Poland Street   map 15
(020) 7437 8774

Vasco and Paul Matteucci's Italian warhorse has clocked up more than 30 years as a consistently reliable West End restaurant. Expect full-bodied cooking with Umbrian roots, 'hand-made' pasta including wild mushroom tortelloni with girolles, and other authentically unpretentious dishes such as herb-crusted cod with baby spinach and cannellini beans or pork milanese with baby artichokes and rocket. Finish with pannacotta or baked ricotta with plum compote. Lunch is à la carte (main courses from around £13); dinner is fixed price (£21/£25). Italian wines from £12.50. Closed Sat L and Sun.

Veeraswamy   W1
99–101 Regent Street   map 15
(020) 7734 1401

The Regent Street location means high prices are not unexpected. But main courses of Malabar lobster curry (£21.50) and sea bass pollichaddu (£15.50) are positive pointers to the kitchen's treatment of fine ingredients. While starters consist of idlis, pani puri and various kebabs, as well as an elaborate cod stuffed tandoori baby squid. Open all week.

Vivat Bacchus   EC4
47 Farringdon Street   map 13
(020) 7353 2648

Quirky basement near Smithfield Market that tries to sell South Africa to the denizens of EC4. The mood is easy-going and the kitchen comes up with creditable dishes like a terrine of foie gras, roast duck and chicken confit (£15.50), seared sirloin steak with green peppercorn and shallot butter (£17) and prosciutto-wrapped monkfish with braised fennel and piquillo peppers. Select cheese from the storage room and wander round the wine cellars if you want a decent drop to drink. Open Mon to Fri.

Wagamama   WC1
4A Streatham Street   map 15
(020) 7323 9223

You must know the format by now: tables are shared, no bookings are taken, and the menu is based on traditional Japanese ramen shops. Mainstays of the menu are three sorts of noodles – soba, udon and ramen – that might be teppan-fried or added to soups with accompaniments ranging from honey roast pork loin (£7.40) to chargrilled salmon fillet (£8.25). There are a few rice dishes, 'katsu' curries from £6.35, and side dishes such as yakitori. House wine is £11. This is the flagship of the ever-growing chain. Open all week.

Waterloo Bar and Kitchen   SE1
131 Waterloo Road   map 13
(020) 7928 5086

A magnet for theatregoers and commuters, next to the Old Vic and close to Waterloo station. Functional décor, great camaraderie and an upbeat pub-style menu. Expect soup, sandwiches and salads (seared tuna with coriander pesto, £5) followed by generous pastas and mains like marinated lamb steak with herb couscous (£13). Desserts might run to mango cheesecake (£4). Short wine list with house French £10.25. Open Mon to Fri L, Mon to Sat D. Reports please.

Yoshino

W1

3 Piccadilly Place   map 15
(020) 7434 3616

Discreet Japanese bolthole situated between Piccadilly and Regent Street. Sushi and sashimi are the main players, with a piscine inventory including otoro tuna, octopus, brill and sea bream; bento boxes extend the range, and there are a few side orders (D only) including edamame beans (£2) and fried tofu. Mini set menus are ideal for a speedy lunch (prices from £6 to £10), and you can finish with refreshing green tea sorbet (£4). Saké and spirits galore, plus a handful of wines from £12.80. Closed Sun.

Zetter

EC1

86-88 Clerkenwell Road   map 13
(020) 7324 4455

A newly converted Victorian warehouse (once the HQ of Zetter Football Pools), now a self-styled 'urban inn' with 59 bedrooms to boot. High quality ingredients are used for monthly menus with a rustic Italian heartbeat. Start with asparagus and marjoram risotto (£6.50), and move on to guinea fowl 'al mattone' with braised chard, grapes, roasted potatoes and aïoli (£14.50). Meals finish strongly with desserts like chocolate and Valpolicella pot (£5). Breakfast from 7; also weekend brunch. Open all week. Reports please.

England

Stephan Langton Inn 🍴

Friday Street, Abinger Common RH5 6JR
TEL: (01306) 730775
from A25 W of Wotton, turn S following signs for Leith Hill
and Friday Street; then turn sharp L signed Friday Street   COOKING 3
and follow very narrow road; turn right just before lake;   MODERN BRITISH
pub is after cottages   £30–£41

Named after the Archbishop who drew up the Magna Carta, the inn is reached via winding lanes along a wooded valley – but it's worth the effort. Posh frocks are not required, though: it's a relaxed, unstuffy pub-cum-restaurant with few decorative frills, although physical improvements are ongoing with the arrival of new tables and chairs, and the bar is the target next year. The menu has strong Mediterranean touches, with good balance and clear flavours throughout. Think colourful gazpacho, a sea bass ceviche with piquillo peppers, or Charentais melon with Serrano ham among the starters, then mains like roast cod with white beans and chorizo, or slow-roast pork with bubble and squeak, morcilla and piccalilli. If you've room, try white chocolate cheesecake with shortbread and strawberries, or maybe Taleggio and quince jam. A compact, global wine list offers a decent selection under £20, with nine by the glass from £2.95.

CHEF: Jonathan Coomb   PROPRIETORS: Jonathan Coomb and Cynthia Rajabally   OPEN: Sun L 12.30 to 3, Tue to Sat D 7 to 10   CLOSED: 2 wks winter, 24 Dec D, 31 Dec D, 1 Jan D   MEALS: alc (main courses £11 to £13). Bar L menu available Tue to Sun   SERVICE: not inc, card slips closed   CARDS: Delta, MasterCard, Switch, Visa   DETAILS: 50 seats. 50 seats outside. Private parties: 50 main room. Car park. Children's helpings. No smoking. Wheelchair access (not WC). Occasional music   £5

Drakes on the Pond 🍴

Dorking Road, Abinger Hammer RH5 6SA   COOKING 5
TEL/FAX: (01306) 731174   MODERN EUROPEAN
WEBSITE: www.drakesonthepond.com   £37–£82

The red-brick, two-storey building on the A25 puts on a modest outer appearance, but inside it's a different story: yellow walls hung with wildlife paintings and large mirrors, a dark red carpet with a fleur-de-lis pattern, and well-spaced white-clothed tables with tall vases containing single flowers provide an appropriately refined setting for some seriously ambitious cooking. Elaborate presentation and lots of intricate touches are the order of the day – as befits a chef who previously worked with Heston Blumenthal at the Riverside

Brasserie in Bray (see entry). Impressive technique and forceful flavours are found in a starter comprising a small heap of salmon confit, another of potato, chive and crab salad topped with salmon mousse, and a third of pressed baby leeks with a tender langoustine, a dollop of crème fraîche and a sprinkling of caviar. Among main courses, a signature dish of pork has stood out, comprising succulent slices of roast tenderloin on a strongly flavoured black pudding sauce with fondant potato and a square slab of melt-in-the-mouth braised belly topped with diced apple. In the evening a pre-dessert comes next – rhubarb compote for one diner – followed, perhaps, by attractively presented Granny Smith bavarois with an apple and basil sorbet, a mini doughnut on top, and surrounded by a drizzle of caramel sauce. Nine house wines, all under £20, open a varied, well-chosen list.

CHEF: Simon Attridge   PROPRIETORS: Tracey Honeysett and John Morris   OPEN: Tue to Fri L 12 to 1.30, Tue to Sat D 7 to 9.30   MEALS: Set L £17.50 (2 courses) to £21.50, Set D £30 (2 courses) to £49.50   SERVICE: not inc   CARDS: Delta, Switch, Visa   DETAILS: 32 seats. Car park. Vegetarian meals. No children under 10. No smoking. Wheelchair access (not WC). No music. No mobile phones. Air-conditioned

ADDINGHAM West Yorkshire
map 8

Fleece ¾ £

154 Main Street, Addingham LS29 0LY   COOKING 3
TEL: (01943) 830491   MODERN BRITISH
£25–£50

An informal gastro-pub offering table service, the Fleece has a lively list of traditional pub staples and sandwiches for casual diners, but the main interest is on the specials blackboard. Its enticing starter options embrace Bayonne ham, Pyrenean salami and wild boar teamed with Roquefort, or tuna carpaccio doused with porcini oil. Main courses include locally raised or rare-breed meats and clearly attributed seafood, but the treatments are international. Wrigglesworth mallard has been roasted with ginger and mandarin, while Islay king scallops may arrive with a tomato risotto and chilli salsa. Vegetables are extra (a good range, including sautéed fennel). Eleven house wines start at £2.50 a glass/£11.50 a bottle, and the list spreads across five continents, with France and Australia dominating the high end.

CHEFS: Matthew Brown and Andrew Wilkinson   PROPRIETOR: Chris Monkman   OPEN: Mon to Sat 12 to 2.15, 6 to 9.15, Sun 12 to 8   MEALS: alc (main courses £7 to £15). Bar menu available   SERVICE: not inc, card slips closed   CARDS: Delta, MasterCard, Switch, Visa   DETAILS: 60 seats. 60 seats outside. Private parties: 24 main room. Car park. Children's helpings. No smoking in 1 dining room. Wheelchair access (not WC). No music £5

ALDEBURGH Suffolk
map 6

Lighthouse ¾ £

77 High Street, Aldeburgh IP15 5AU   COOKING 3
TEL: (01728) 453377   FAX: (01728) 454510   MODERN BRITISH-PLUS
WEBSITE: www.lighthouserestaurant.co.uk   £24–£52

The Lighthouse seems something of an institution in this seaside town. Fish, first and foremost, is where it's at, although there's no shortage of meaty options, and the food is honest and simply cooked – which is good to see. Begin with dressed Cromer crab, ricotta cheesecake with coriander pesto, or fish soup, and move on to plump, succulent chicken breast wrapped in pancetta on spring onion mash, or roast cod fillet on brown shrimp risotto, and finish with 'excellent' bread-and-butter pudding. The international wine list offers ample choice, with some interesting selections. Prices open at £11.50.

CHEFS: Sara Fox, Guy Welsh and Leon Manthorpe PROPRIETORS: Sara Fox and Peter Hill OPEN: all week 12 to 2 (2.30 Sat and Sun), 6.30 to 10 CLOSED: 2 weeks Jan, 1 week Oct MEALS: alc (main courses £7 to £20.50). Set L and D £13.25 (2 courses) to £16.50 SERVICE: not inc, card slips closed CARDS: Amex, Delta, MasterCard, Switch, Visa DETAILS: 95 seats. 25 seats outside. Private parties: 45 main room, 14 to 25 private rooms. Vegetarian meals. No smoking. Wheelchair access (also WC). No music. No mobile phones. Air-conditioned (£5)

152 Aldeburgh ⅝✳

152 High Street, Aldeburgh IP15 5AX   COOKING 3
TEL: (01728) 454594 FAX: (01502) 731099   MODERN EUROPEAN
WEBSITE: www.152aldeburgh.co.uk   £30–£54

The team at 152 seem to have settled in very well since they took over in June 2003. The minimalist but stylish white and beige interior with light-coloured wooden tables and ladderback chairs eschews linen but glows noticeably in evening candlelight. Snack on a range of free nibbles, including good olives, while choosing between, say, fried scallops with sesame stir-fried vegetables, or a terrine of local game with home-made chutney, followed by a well-turned-out shoulder of lamb, with mixed beans and smoked bacon or seared gravad lax with fennel and baby beetroot. Desserts may run from the comfort of sticky toffee pudding with vanilla ice cream to the refinement of a trio of beautifully presented home-made sorbets – blackcurrant, pear and coconut – with fresh fruit more than just a garnish. A mostly European list of wines from Adnams in Southwold starts with £11 Spaniards from Telmo Rodríguez and stays mostly under £20.

CHEF: Garry Cook PROPRIETORS: Andrew Lister and Garry Cook OPEN: all week 12 to 3, 6 to 10 MEALS: alc (main courses £10.50 to £18) SERVICE: not inc CARDS: Amex, Delta, Diners, MasterCard, Switch, Visa DETAILS: 56 seats. 20 seats outside. Private parties: 60 main room. Vegetarian meals. No smoking. Wheelchair access (also WC). Music. No mobile phones (£5)

Regatta ⅝✳

171 High Street, Aldeburgh IP15 5AN   COOKING 2
TEL: (01728) 452011 FAX: (01728) 453324   SEAFOOD/EUROPEAN
WEBSITE: www.regattaaldeburgh.com   £24–£44

Carnivores and vegetarians are not forgotten at this cheerful, welcoming place, but fish, much of it straight from the beach, is the centrepiece. Freshness and simplicity dominate, from the wooden floors and cream-painted walls to the blackboards that list more of what's on offer than does the printed menu. Expect to find whole fish grilled straightforwardly, or plates of home-smoked prawns or salmon. In addition, first-class soup filled with a variety of fish in a rich stock; first-class chips; and a properly crisped, creamy brûlée show that skills go beyond basics. The good-value food is supplemented by decent wines starting at £10.50 and, champagne excepted, does not stray over £20.

CHEF: Robert Mabey PROPRIETORS: Robert and Johanna Mabey OPEN: all week 12 to 2, 6 to 10 (closed for D Sun to Tue in winter) CLOSED: 24 to 26 Dec, 31 Dec, 1 Jan MEALS: alc (main courses £8.50 to £12) SERVICE: not inc, card slips closed CARDS: Delta, MasterCard, Switch, Visa DETAILS: 90 seats. Private parties: 90 main room. Vegetarian meals. Children's helpings. No smoking in 1 dining room. No pipes. No music. No mobile phones. Air-conditioned

Juniper 🏅✳

21 The Downs, Altrincham WA14 2QD	COOKING **7**
TEL: (0161) 929 4008 FAX: (0161) 929 4009	MODERN FRENCH
WEBSITE: www.juniper-restaurant.co.uk	£35–£96

Altrincham may not be the most obvious place for a culinary upheaval to have started, but the earth has undoubtedly moved here in recent years. Paul Kitching has been in the first rank of that band of chefs, of whom Heston Blumenthal at the Fat Duck (see entry, Bray) is the evident torchbearer, who have redefined completely what it is possible to do within the haute cuisine format.

Juniper consists of a smart basement bar with comfortable armchairs and low tables and, on the floor above, a seductively lit, well-appointed restaurant. Bread is a straightforward choice of thickly sliced brown or white, with exemplary unsalted butter, but it is the last straightforward item you will be offered. Appetisers appear to be evolving to nothing, according to recent reports, the ingredients reduced to barely more than a squiggle of sauce or a plate of crumbs: four red dots of smoked salmon, puréed macaroni cheese, 'pizza without the base'. A strip of dried smoked salmon on scrambled egg arrives in a polystyrene cup.

By the time the ordered courses turn up, the palate has been softened up to expect anything, and its receptivity is usually rewarded. The versatility of fish is fully exploited, from the relative simplicity of a small piece of cod on tomato vinaigrette to a serving of turbot with a warm scallop, tomato and sultana risotto, and a quenelle of egg mayonnaise. The touch of genius was the application, to both turbot and scallop, of a light melon glaze: 'a dazzling partnership'. Nor do meat dishes lack for innovation: slow-baked duck breast comes with Christmas pudding, pear and balsamic vinegar, while 'very tender saddle of venison' is tricked out with Toulouse sausage, coloured rice and curried hollandaise. Desserts return us to the nursery, with miniature selections in fours and sixes, childhood flavours concentrated in the form of soufflés (perhaps of marzipan) and sorbets (sultana-studded hot cross bun). Petits fours include wedges of 'sublime' custard tart. There is a minority view – 'I did wonder when everyone was going to realise that the Emperor was wearing no clothes' – but there is no doubting the stunning technical virtuosity with which the cooking is accomplished. The enthusiasm of the staff is infectious.

For all the restless innovation of the food, the wine list is surprisingly classical in orientation, with Bordeaux and Burgundy to the fore. Mark-ups may frighten the horses, but the bidding starts at £16, and wines by the glass, from Bordeaux and Sicily, are £4.

CHEF/PROPRIETOR: Paul Kitching   OPEN: Tue to Fri L 12 to 2, Tue to Sat D 7 to 10   CLOSED: 1 week Feb, 2 weeks late summer   MEALS: alc (main courses £17 to £24). Set L £17.50 (2 courses) to £45, Set D £65   SERVICE: not inc, card slips closed   CARDS: Amex, Delta, MasterCard, Switch, Visa   DETAILS: 34 seats. Private parties: 30 main room. No smoking in 1 dining room. Music. Air-conditioned

---

'The waiter implied that "fregola" in crab fregola was an indicator of the postal code where the crab had lived. Upon further consultation with the kitchen, he said the term described the manner in which it was sautéed. We looked it up when we got home and it was neither in the Concise Oxford Dictionary or French dictionary nor the Larousse. According to an Italian dictionary, it essentially meant bonking crabs.' (On eating in London)

AMBLESIDE Cumbria   map 8

▲ Rothay Manor ♟ ⅚✳

Rothay Bridge, Ambleside LA22 0EH
TEL: (015394) 33605   FAX: (015394) 33607
WEBSITE: www.rothaymanor.co.uk
off A593 to Coniston, ¼m W of Ambleside

COOKING 3
MODERN BRITISH
£25–£53

The elegant white building is fronted by a landscaped garden and has an interior that is traditional in terms of furnishings and ornaments. Most visitors come here for old-fashioned hospitality and sound cooking rather than novelty. Lunch offers simple, good-value choices along the lines of soup, followed by fillet of salmon topped with crème fraîche and spring onions, or lambs' kidneys in Madeira sauce, with dinner being the main focus of attention. The format is generous to a fault, with a set-price menu delivering a range of Anglo-French dishes along the lines of foie gras and chicken liver parfait with Madeira jelly and toasted brioche, or home-made Cartmel Valley smoked mackerel pâté, followed by roast local pheasant with bread sauce and traditional gravy. The kitchen is obviously as happy with Cumbrian lamb and fillet of beef as with scallops and fillets of lemon sole. Nostalgic desserts might include strawberry mousse or champagne jelly with citrus and passion-fruit compote. Wines are a well-judged global selection at very fair prices. France is most exciting outside the major regions, while Australia and New Zealand turn up the best New World treats. Five house wines at £13 also come by the glass; in addition you can order half the contents of any bottle on the list.

CHEFS: Jane Binns and Colette Nixon   PROPRIETORS: Nigel and Stephen Nixon   OPEN: Mon to Sat 12.30 to 2, 7.30 to 9, Sun 12.45 to 1.30, 7.30 to 9   CLOSED: 3 to 29 Jan   MEALS: alc L (main courses £9.50). Set L Mon to Sat £16, Set L Sun £18.50, Set D £30 to £34. Light L menu available Mon to Sat   SERVICE: not inc   CARDS: Amex, Delta, Diners, MasterCard, Switch, Visa   DETAILS: 65 seats. Private parties: 34 main room. Car park. Vegetarian meals. Children's helpings. No children under 7 at D. No smoking. Wheelchair access (also WC). No music. Air-conditioned   ACCOMMODATION: 19 rooms, all with bath/shower. TV. Phone. B&B £70 to £155. Rooms for disabled. Baby facilities. Fishing

AMERSHAM Buckinghamshire   map 3

Artichoke ⅚✳   NEW ENTRY

9 Market Square, Amersham HP7 0DF
TEL/FAX: (01494) 726611
WEBSITE: www.theartichokerestaurant.co.uk

COOKING 4
MODERN FRENCH
£32–£101

Flanked by posh frock shops in what might nostalgically be called Old Amersham, the Artichoke is a tiny, beamed place with a wonky ceiling and white-painted brick walls, softly lit of an evening and easy on the eye. Laurie Gear's imaginative, often innovative cooking has brought new depth to the local dining scene. The eponymous vegetable goes, discreetly enough, into a terrine with venison and foie gras, accompanied by cognac fig chutney, while fat, sweet scallops are cleverly teamed with a rustic ragoût of flavourful, nutty salsify. Timing is good, as demonstrated by a piece of super-fresh turbot fillet with silky celeriac purée, poached leeks and bacon, sauced with red wine. Depth of flavour might be added by some unexpected ingredient, such as liquorice in the sauce to accompany Aberdeen Angus fillet, matched by a purée of beetroot and horseradish. A patient wait is rewarded by desserts such as a creamy, trifle-like combination of prunes, Granny Smith compote and yoghurt cream. Polite, efficient service is appreciated, and the background music thoughtfully chosen. A short, modern wine list focuses on France and the southern hemisphere, with bottle prices opening at £13.50 and wines by the glass from £3.75.

CHEF: Laurie Gear   PROPRIETORS: Laurie Gear and Jacqueline Dare   OPEN: Tue to Thur 12 to 2, 7 to 9.15, Fri and Sat 12 to 2, 6.45 to 9.30   CLOSED: 2 weeks Christmas, 1 week from Aug bank hol   MEALS: Set L £16.50 (2 courses) to £75, Set D £23.50 (2 courses) to £75   SERVICE: 12.5% (optional), card slips closed CARDS: Delta, MasterCard, Switch, Visa   DETAILS: 22 seats. 4 seats outside. Private parties: 26 main room. Vegetarian meals. Children's helpings. No smoking. Music

APPLETHWAITE Cumbria   map 10

▲ Underscar Manor 👻

Applethwaite CA12 4PH	COOKING 6
TEL: (01768) 775000 FAX: (01768) 774904	ANGLO-FRENCH
off A66, ½m N of Keswick	£40–£77

It's a surprise to find a grey Italianate villa, complete with campanile, at the foot of Skiddaw, just outside Keswick. Inside, though, all is as English as can be, with floral chintz, strikingly patterned carpets, and swagged drapes at the windows. The Harrisons, who also own Moss Nook (see entry, Manchester), run the place with great panache.

Equal panache goes into the menus on which every dish seems to consist of multiplicities of ingredients that nonetheless harmonise on the plate. A rösti-style spiced crab cake is fried and served with tomato salsa, orange segments and salad, for instance, or smoked salmon and Swiss cheese are combined in a hot soufflé on a sauce of sweet peppers, as first courses. The listing of mains is generally supplemented by one or two daily specials, described for you at the table. Angus fillet steaks, plain-grilled, peppered or topped with pâté de foie gras, are highly regarded by one reporter, and duck too elicits praise – perhaps for chargrilled breast served on cassoulet, with mashed potato and red wine sauce. Saucing and garnishing hold to classical principles, with corn-fed chicken appearing with wild mushrooms, baby leeks and wholegrain mustard, while the desserts use plenty of fruit, from a trio of apple items to a tuile basket of assorted sorbets. A few pedigree growers are thoroughly represented on the wine list, which includes reasonable representation of the non-European regions as well as catering for Francophiles. There is a fair amount of choice below £20.

CHEF: Robert Thornton   PROPRIETORS: Pauline and Derek Harrison and Gordon Evans   OPEN: all week 12 to 1, 7 to 8.30   CLOSED: 2 or 3 days after New Year   MEALS: alc (main courses L £14, D £21 to £25). Set L £28. Set D £38   SERVICE: not inc, card slips closed   CARDS: Amex, MasterCard, Switch, Visa   DETAILS: 50 seats. Private parties: 40 main room. Car park. Vegetarian meals. Jacket. No smoking. Occasional music. No mobile phones   ACCOMMODATION: 11 rooms, all with bath/shower. TV. Phone. D,B&B £110 to £250. No children under 12. Swimming pool

ARDINGTON Oxfordshire   map 2

▲ Boar's Head 👻

Church Street, Ardington OX12 8QA	COOKING 4
TEL/FAX: (01235) 833254	MODERN EUROPEAN
WEBSITE: www.boarsheadardington.co.uk	£36–£57

'It really does show when chef and proprietor are one and the same,' writes one diner of this old timber-framed pub in a 'quintessentially English village'. Inside, the three interlinking rooms are light and airy, but it is the output from the kitchen that really catches the eye. Bruce Buchan's menus focus on fresh, seasonal ingredients, locally produced wherever possible; fish comes daily from Newlyn, while meat, game and vegetables all come from within five miles. A spring selection from the three-course carte might begin with asparagus 'from the farm down the road' served on buttered brioche with grilled Parmesan; then a feuilleté of Cornish lobster with scallops, samphire and a 'mouth-wateringly good' bouillabaisse sauce. Buchan is big on fish but carnivores are well catered for: Angus beef fillet with kidneys in pastry and Dijon sauce is one option. To finish, there might be hot pistachio soufflé with iced chocolate cream, or a bitter chocolate fondant with chocolate sauce and vanilla ice cream, which scored highly at inspection. Wines start around £11 (check the blackboards for house wines), and peak with Château Pétrus '83, the price of which is discreetly left to the imagination; in between there's plenty from France and a brief international selection, plus some antique sherries.

CHEFS: Bruce Buchan and Simon Mildren PROPRIETORS: Bruce Buchan, Terry Chipperfield and Richard Douglas OPEN: all week 12 to 2, 7 to 9.30 (10 Fri and Sat) CLOSED: 27 to 30 Dec MEALS: alc (not Sun L; main courses £13.50 to £18.50). Set L Sun £18.50. Bar menu available except Sun L SERVICE: not inc CARDS: Amex, Delta, MasterCard, Switch, Visa DETAILS: 40 seats. Private parties: 26 main room, 10 to 15 private rooms. Car park. Children's helpings. No smoking in 1 dining room. Occasional music. No mobile phones ACCOMMODATION: 3 rooms, all with bath/shower. TV. Phone. B&B £65 to £120. Baby facilities (£5)

ARLINGHAM Gloucestershire

map 2

▲ Old Passage Inn 🍴✶

Passage Road, Arlingham GL2 7JR	COOKING 3
TEL: (01452) 740547 FAX: (01452) 741871	SEAFOOD
WEBSITE: www.fishattheoldpassageinn.co.uk	£29–£85

Don't stop when you reach Arlingham – the Old Passage is some way beyond the village, so continue across lush meadows all the way to the bank of the Severn, to its lowest crossing point, where this strikingly green-painted inn looks over the water. The dining room is a prime spot for watching the Severn Bore – a tidal surge that occurs once a day – but gives fine views at all times to complement the elegant brasserie-style décor, with mint-green walls, well-polished bare tables and plentiful palms in pots. The menu is almost exclusively fish and seafood, treated in simple but forthright fashion, with everything from battered Cornish haddock and chips to poached brill on buttered spinach with tomato concassé, caviar and saffron cream sauce. Contrasting flavours and textures are combined to good effect in starters such as smoked tuna with mayonnaise-dressed rocket and Parmesan shavings, while among main courses pan-fried mullet on pesto mash with tomato salsa has been a hit. Service is willing and friendly, and the short wine list features plenty of interesting choices from around the world while keeping prices sensible, starting with house Chilean red and white at £10.50 and £10.70 respectively.

CHEFS: Patrick Le Mesurier and Raoul Moore PROPRIETORS: the Moore family OPEN: Tue to Sun L 12 to 2, Tue to Sat D 7 to 9 (6.45 to 9.30 Fri and Sat) CLOSED: 24 to 30 Dec MEALS: alc (main courses £10.50 to £38.50) SERVICE: not inc, card slips closed CARDS: Amex, Delta, MasterCard, Switch, Visa DETAILS: 70 seats. 20 seats outside. Private parties: 12 main room, 5 to 12 private rooms. Car park. Vegetarian meals. Children's helpings. No smoking. Wheelchair access (also WC). Occasional music. No mobile phones. Air-conditioned ACCOMMODATION: 3 rooms, all with bath/shower. TV. Phone. B&B £55 to £95

▲ Amerdale House 🍴✸

Arncliffe, Littondale BD23 5QE	COOKING 4
TEL: (01756) 770250 FAX: (01756) 770266	MODERN EUROPEAN
WEBSITE: www.amerdalehouse.co.uk	£45–£54

Charming Amerdale House, in a remote and peaceful corner of the Yorkshire Dales, offers a quintessential English country-house experience. Both house and gardens are equally well cared for, and staff are 'always there when you need them' but never intrusive. Nigel Crapper's cooking uses first-class local produce, notably lamb from fell-grazing sheep and Gloucester Old Spot pork from a nearby farm, in a 'simple but effective' style. A leg of the aforementioned lamb might be roasted with rosemary and garlic and set on a bed of spinach, while confit duck is served on red cabbage with apple and cider, and lemon sole fillet is partnered with seared scallops and a creamy, mildly curried sauce. Dinner runs to four courses, with starters of warm black pudding and bacon salad, or grilled halloumi with tomatoes and capers, followed by an intermediary course of wild mushroom consommé, say, or smoked salmon and asparagus tart. Among desserts, apple strudel with custard has been 'better than any I have had in Austria'. Wines are a conservative selection but offer good variety and fair prices across the range, starting at £12.95.

CHEF: Nigel Crapper   PROPRIETORS: Paula and Nigel Crapper   OPEN: all week D only 7.30 for 8   CLOSED: mid-Nov to mid-Mar   MEALS: Set D £34.50   SERVICE: not inc, card slips closed   CARDS: MasterCard, Switch, Visa   DETAILS: 24 seats. Car park. No smoking. No music   ACCOMMODATION: 11 rooms, all with bath/shower. TV. Phone. D,B&B £162 to £170 (double room). Baby facilities

▲ Crab & Lobster 🍴✸

Dishforth Road, Asenby YO7 3QL	COOKING 3
TEL: (01845) 577286 FAX: (01845) 577109	FISH/MODERN EUROPEAN
WEBSITE: www.crabandlobster.co.uk	£38–£85

Now for something completely different: ephemera hanging from the old pub sign, lobster pots from walls, and a rocking horse on the roof mark this place out. From low-ceilinged bar to dining room and conservatory, the interior features an endearing riot of maritime-themed bric-à-brac, including a complete deep-sea diver's suit hanging from the roof. The dauntingly long, modern menu, a hardship for the hesitant, offers a preponderance of seafood (though there's plenty for carnivores too). Start with stir-fried mussels with chilli, lemongrass, ginger and coconut cream, then roast monkfish tail with leek and bacon mash and red wine prawn sauce, or crisp leg of duck confit, sausage and pancetta with Italian bean cassoulet. Puds run from plum pudding and rum sauce to baby brandy-snaps with ice cream. Service proves friendly and efficient, while the lively wine list kicks off with house wine from £15.

CHEF: Steve Dean   PROPRIETOR: Vimac Leisure   OPEN: all week 12 to 2.15, 7 to 9.30   MEALS: alc (main courses £13 to £30)   SERVICE: not inc   CARDS: Amex, MasterCard, Switch, Visa   DETAILS: 80 seats. Car park. Vegetarian meals. No smoking. Wheelchair access (also WC). Music   ACCOMMODATION: 12 rooms, all with bath/shower. TV. Phone. B&B £150 to £200. Rooms for disabled

▲ Callow Hall ♥ ※

Mappleton, Ashbourne DE6 2AA
TEL: (01335) 300900   FAX: (01335) 300512
WEBSITE: www.callowhall.co.uk

from Ashbourne market place take A515, at top of hill	COOKING **3**
turn W at crossroads with Bowling Green pub on left.	MODERN BRITISH-PLUS
Mappleton road is first on right after bridge	£31–£60

Callow Hall is a Victorian pile fashioned of Derbyshire stone in 42 acres of grounds amid rolling wooded hills overlooking the Dove Valley. It is a family-run enterprise of considerable warmth, with knowledgeable, efficient service a particular asset. Local fish, meat and game show up on a menu that works comfortably within the kitchen's capacity, ensuring consistency. The fixed-price format of four courses offers a fair range of choice, with starters including a crab and avocado tower dressed in lemon and dill, or celeriac soup with a swirl of tomato purée and garlic croûtons. After a choice of a fish dish or sorbet, main courses might take in 'tender and well-flavoured' duck confit on sweet potato rösti, or grilled fillet of sea bass with cucumber and mint chutney. Most desserts incorporate one of the home-made ices, such as cold chocolate soufflé with raspberries and chocolate chip ice cream. What at first seems a solid, traditional wine list, with good choice throughout France, takes a modern and pacy turn in the New World. Prices are modest, starting with £12 house wines, and with a good selection by the glass (including sherries) and plenty of half-bottles, this list is an all-round treat.

CHEFS: Anthony and David Spencer   PROPRIETORS: David, Dorothy, Anthony and Emma Spencer   OPEN: Sun L 12.30 to 1.45, Mon to Sat D 7.30 to 9.15   CLOSED: 25 and 26 Dec   MEALS: alc (main courses £16.50 to £19.50). Set L £22.50, Set D £39.50   SERVICE: not inc   CARDS: Amex, Diners, MasterCard, Switch, Visa   DETAILS: 80 seats. Private parties: 40 main room, 20 to 40 private rooms. Car park. Vegetarian meals. Children's helpings. No smoking. Wheelchair access (not WC). No music. No mobile phones   ACCOMMODATION: 16 rooms, all with bath/shower. TV. Phone. B&B £90 to £195. Rooms for disabled. Baby facilities. Fishing (£5)

Dining Room ※ | **NEW ENTRY** |

33 St John Street, Ashbourne DE6 1GP	COOKING **4**
TEL: (01335) 300666	MODERN BRITISH-PLUS
WEBSITE: www.thediningroomashbourne.co.uk	£34–£65

This 'unexpected little gem' (only six tables, so booking is recommended) is tucked away in a tiny sixteenth-century building off Ashbourne's busy one-way system. Enter via the back door, through the pretty courtyard and past the kitchen. Simple, contemporary furnishings in shades of green sit comfortably with old oak beams, a massive cast-iron range, and an original salt safe in the wall. Young proprietors Peter and Laura Dale impress with their dedication and fervour. Their menus take local and in-season shopping very seriously: an early summer dinner featured Lichfield Farm asparagus, Ashbourne quail, and vanilla-roasted Elmhurst strawberries. Artfully composed dishes are designed to explore a particular flavour from every angle – a starter of three fat slices of lightly curried scallop, the coral made into a pannacotta and the whole enhanced by 'a feathery foam' of cucumber and swirls of smoked curry oil. Intense flavours are concentrated in tiny slabs of jelly or sorbet: a dark amber disc of clove jelly and a scoop of pear sorbet provide counterpoints to 'tender and pink' quail breasts served with a perfectly timed soft-boiled quail's egg. An inspector's baked cod 'fell into gleaming curds, moist and full flavoured', and was nicely offset by carrot purée, spring vegetables and gently scented lemon gnocchi. Desserts are equally inventive, with imaginative home-made ice creams a highlight, while the all-British cheeseboard wins an honourable mention in dispatches, too. The compact, user-friendly wine list has house French at £12.95 and plenty of interest below £25.

CHEF: Peter Dale   PROPRIETORS: Peter and Laura Dale   OPEN: Tue to Sat 12 to 1.30, 7 to 8.30   CLOSED: 2 weeks from 26 Dec, 1 week Mar, 1 week Sept   MEALS: alc (main courses L £11 to £13, D £19.50 to £20.50). Set L £22. Set D (tasting menu; needs pre-booking) £40   SERVICE: not inc, card slips closed CARDS: Delta, MasterCard, Switch, Visa   DETAILS: 16 seats. Private parties: 16 main room. No children under 12. No smoking. Wheelchair access (also WC). No music. No mobile phones

ASHBURTON Devon   map 1

Agaric ✥

30 North Street, Ashburton TQ13 7QD   COOKING 4
TEL: (01364) 654478   MODERN BRITISH-PLUS
WEBSITE: www.agaricrestaurant.co.uk   £32–£56

Although Agaric is a touch unassuming from the outside, once you are through the door it makes a good impression with its small bar and more expansive, pleasant dining room, where light brown walls, bare wooden tables and rug-strewn floor strike a modern note. Nick Coiley is a keen advocate of local produce, but he looks to Europe and beyond for ideas: making taramasalata with home-cured turbot roe, turning crab into soup or packing it into a fishcake, and flavouring best end of Devon lamb with a North African marinade, yoghurt and duckah. Other appealing options might include crisp duck confit with five-spice, spiced plum sauce and mustard leaves, or perhaps pan-fried venison steak with celeriac purée, bacon, spiced red cabbage and red wine sauce. High-quality ingredients are handled with due respect, timing is good, and dishes are simply presented without frills. Desserts could include chocolate tart with blood orange and candied peel, and iced ginger meringue parfait with a brandy-snap and coffee sauce. A short list of wines balances value and quality. House Argentinian red and white are £12 a bottle, £2.75 a glass.

CHEF: Nick Coiley   PROPRIETORS: Nick and Sophie Coiley   OPEN: Wed to Fri L 12 to 2, Wed to Sat D 7 to 9.15   CLOSED: 22 Dec to 5 Jan, first week Feb, last 2 weeks Aug   MEALS: alc (main courses £11 to £17). Set L £11.50 (2 courses)   SERVICE: not inc, card slips closed   CARDS: Delta, MasterCard, Switch, Visa DETAILS: 32 seats. 20 seats outside. Private parties: 32 main room. Vegetarian meals. Children's helpings. No smoking. Wheelchair access (also WC). No music. No mobile phones

ASHFORD Derbyshire   map 9

▲ Riverside House ✥

Ashford in the Water DE45 1QF   COOKING 4
TEL: (01629) 814275   FAX: (01629) 812873   FRENCH-PLUS
WEBSITE: www.riversidehousehotel.co.uk   £39–£71

The hotel sits beside the A6 Bakewell to Buxton road by a delightful stretch of the River Wye, where those with a taste for pugilism may be found throwing bread for the ducks and trout to fight over. Clad in creepers without and decorated with welcome understatement within, the Riverside showcases the vibrant and impressive talents of chef John Whelan. Expect departures from the country-house norm, such as potato and ham chowder containing deep-fried spiced herring, or salmon fillet in a Thai marinade with vegetable couscous and a gazpacho dressing. A vanilla broth might be the medium for poached fillet of brill, while wild rabbit is presented two ways, the leg braised, the loin smoked, and accompanied by a risotto of smoked bacon and tomato. Good international cheeses are the alternative to desserts such as saffron-poached pear with vanilla pannacotta and a sun-dried cranberry compote. Service may not be entirely with it, but does its best. The wine list offers plenty of interest, even if the prices feel a bit stiff. Eleven house selections start at £16.95, £3.40 a glass.

CHEF: John Whelan   PROPRIETOR: Penelope Thornton   OPEN: all week 12 to 2, 6 to 9.30   MEALS: Set L Mon to Sat £18.95 (2 courses) to £26.95, Set L Sun £28.95, Set D £44.95. Conservatory menu available exc Sat D   SERVICE: not inc   CARDS: Amex, Delta, Diners, MasterCard, Switch, Visa   DETAILS: 40 seats. Private parties: 32 main room, 10 to 16 private rooms. Car park. Vegetarian meals. Children's helpings. No children under 12. No smoking. Wheelchair access (not WC). No music. No mobile phones ACCOMMODATION: 15 rooms, all with bath/shower. TV. Phone. B&B £80 to £250. No children under 12 (£5)

ASHWATER Devon
map 1

▲ Blagdon Manor 🍴

Ashwater EX21 5DF
TEL: (01409) 211224   FAX: (01409) 211634
WEBSITE: www.blagdon.com

COOKING 2
ENGLISH/MEDITERRANEAN
£27–£50

The homely farmhouse-like manor was mentioned in the Domesday Book, although the current building dates from the seventeenth century. An eclectic mix of personal family effects, original features such as a stone carved with the year 1683, and a cheerful colour scheme give the place the typically domestic atmosphere of a small family-run country hotel, which is precisely what it is. Steve Morey's cooking blends fashionable ingredients in elaborate combinations, and, despite arty 'nouvelle cuisine' presentation, portions are 'comfortingly adequate'. Butternut squash risotto with pan-fried guinea fowl, foie gras, crisp pancetta and roast garlic froth may sound like a culinary juggling act, but its reporter was impressed by the balance and intensity of flavours. Service is friendly and prompt, and wines are a varied, good-value bunch, with house wines £10.

CHEF: Steve Morey   PROPRIETORS: Liz and Steve Morey   OPEN: Wed to Sun L 12 to 2, Tue to Sat D 7 to 9 (Sun and Mon D residents only)   CLOSED: 2 weeks Jan to Feb, 2 weeks Oct to Nov   MEALS: Set L Wed to Sat £14 (2 courses) to £17, Set L Sun £19.50, Set D £26 (2 courses) to £30   SERVICE: not inc   CARDS: Delta, MasterCard, Switch, Visa   DETAILS: 30 seats. Private parties: 16 main room, 10 to 16 private rooms. Car park. Vegetarian meals. No children under 12. No smoking. Wheelchair access (not WC). No music   ACCOMMODATION: 7 rooms, all with bath/shower. TV. Phone. B&B £72 to £100. No children under 12

AYCLIFFE Co Durham
map 10

County 🍴

13 The Green, Aycliffe Village, Aycliffe DL5 6LX
TEL: (01325) 312273   FAX: (01325) 308780
WEBSITE: www.the-county.co.uk

COOKING 3
MODERN EUROPEAN
£32–£54

Chef/proprietor Andrew Brown runs this end-of-terrace Georgian/Victorian establishment as a bistro-style restaurant with pubby touches. Handpumps dispense real ales from a hatch in the bar, but most of the place is given over to food. The kitchen is equally at home with classic and new-fangled dishes. Free-range chicken casserole, or eggs Benedict with smoked haddock, provide old-school comfort, while warm salad of black pudding with spicy sausage, pine kernels and balsamic dressing, or chargrilled tuna with vanilla and basil risotto, should satisfy those with a taste for modern big-city food; vegetables are extra. Desserts return to familiar territory for crème brûlée and chocolate torte with Grand Marnier crème anglaise, and the short list of Old and New World wines includes house French at £11.45.

CHEF/PROPRIETOR: Andrew Brown   OPEN: all week L 12 to 2 (3 Sun), Mon to Sat D 6 (6.45 Sat) to 9.15
CLOSED: 25 and 26 Dec, 1 Jan   MEALS: alc (main courses £11 to £17). Bar menu available L and Mon–Fri
early D   SERVICE: not inc, card slips closed   CARDS: Amex, Delta, Diners, MasterCard, Switch, Visa
DETAILS: 90 seats. Private parties: 10 main room, 11 to 26 private rooms. Car park. Vegetarian meals.
Children's helpings. No-smoking area. No music. Air-conditioned

AYLESBURY Buckinghamshire

map 3

▲ Hartwell House 🛠

Oxford Road, Aylesbury HP17 8NL
TEL: (01296) 747444   FAX: (01296) 747450
WEBSITE: www.hartwell-house.com
on A418, 2m from Aylesbury towards Oxford

COOKING 5
BRITISH
£30–£90

The tone is set at Hartwell from the moment the porter in his lodge raises the barrier for you. This will be dining in the grand style, beneath a ceiling of three contiguous domes (making for some dramatic acoustics) and crystal chandeliers. While the cooking is very much in the country-house style, it attains a high level of sophistication and clarity. Freshness and scrupulous sourcing are also features (one supplier being the hotel's own garden). A salad of fine fresh prosciutto, or rillettes of smoked fish garnished with prawns, make for a light start, and may be followed by breast of Deben duck with a sauce of lemon and ginger chutney. A reader bemoaning today's tendency to stack components of a dish (because it 'often conceals ingredients to their disadvantage') nonetheless enjoyed an assemblage of slow-braised and eloquently flavoured venison shoulder, together with red cabbage, apple sauce and mashed potato. Matching soufflés and sorbets are favoured (an excellent pineapple variant has been mentioned), or there may be pear and cranberry bavarois encased in marzipan. Service has received mostly favourable notices. An immense wine list strong on French classics begins with house bottles from £16.50, and 12 wines by the glass from £4.50.

CHEF: Daniel Richardson   PROPRIETOR: Historic House Hotels Ltd   OPEN: all week 12.30 to 1.45, 7.30 to
9.45   MEALS: Set L £22 to £29, Set L Sun £32, Set D £25 (2 courses) to £46. Buttery L menu available
SERVICE: net prices, card slips closed   CARDS: Amex, MasterCard, Switch, Visa   DETAILS: 60 seats. 25
seats outside. Private parties: 60 main room, 12 to 60 private rooms. Car park. Vegetarian meals. No
children under 8. Jacket at D. No smoking. Wheelchair access (also WC). Occasional music. No mobile
phones   ACCOMMODATION: 46 rooms, all with bath/shower. TV. Phone. B&B £155 to £260. Rooms for
disabled. No children under 8. Swimming pool. Fishing

'The style of food is rather nouvelle cuisine with a package tour to Phuket and Tokyo carelessly thrown into the mix. The overall effect of both food and ambience is most definitely Lost in Translation.' (On eating in London)

BAGSHOT Surrey

map 3

▲ Pennyhill Park, Latymer Restaurant 🍽️ ✹

London Road, Bagshot GU19 5EU
TEL: (01276) 471774   FAX: (01276) 473217
WEBSITE: www.exclusivehotels.co.uk

COOKING **3**
MODERN EUROPEAN
£33–£98

Handy for Ascot, the Pennyhill Park hotel/spa/country-club complex has three restaurants. Through an imposing entrance hall, guarded by huge decorative lions, and along expensively decorated corridors is the flagship Latymer, where dramatic presentations, luxury ingredients plus jellied and foamed peripherals reflect the opulent surroundings.

Duncan Ray arrived in January 2004, so perhaps was still settling in when our inspector called. There was interesting workmanship (but overseasoning and some weak elements too) in starters like hay-baked sweetbreads with asparagus, morels and roast chicken jus, and confit chicken cannelloni with air-dried duck and amontillado jelly. To follow, a tasting plate of pork, the treatments of loin, belly and cheek redolent of Chinese cooking, or perfectly timed turbot presented with a shot glass of fennel foam on a mound of 'dentally dangerous' hazelnut and olive crumble. Puddings range from eccentric – 'peanut butter sandwich, raspberry jam, roast banana and chocolate, milk to drink' – to comparatively pedestrian. The wine list offers Pétrus, but nothing under £20.

CHEF: Duncan Ray   PROPRIETOR: Exclusive Hotels   OPEN: Tue to Fri and (Oct to May) Sun L 12 to 2.30, Tue to Sat D 7 to 11   MEALS: Set L £20 (2 courses) to £25, Set D Tue to Sat £50   SERVICE: not inc   CARDS: Amex, MasterCard, Switch, Visa   DETAILS: 36 seats. 30 seats outside. Private parties: 36 main room. Car park. Vegetarian meals. Children's helpings. No children under 12. No smoking. Wheelchair access (also WC). No music. No mobile phones. Air-conditioned   ACCOMMODATION: 123 rooms, all with bath/shower. TV. Phone. Room only £180 to £650. Rooms for disabled. Baby facilities. Swimming pool. Fishing

BAKEWELL Derbyshire

map 8

Renaissance ✹

Bath Street, Bakewell DE45 1BX
TEL: (01629) 812687
WEBSITE: www.renaissance-restaurant.com

COOKING **4**
FRENCH
£25–£53

Eric Piedaniel and his wife have transformed this attractive stone-built barn into a prime local destination for classic French cooking. They offer a short carte that displays plenty of technique, effort and enterprise. Asparagus cream soup might be glazed with a paprika hollandaise mousseline, and warm scallop terrine comes with a seafood and saffron sauce. Main courses continue the industrious theme: a trio of fish is served with Chablis, keta caviar and herbs on red pesto risotto, while braised pork fillet roulade gets a stuffing of red cabbage and Emmental. To finish, iced nougatine mousse wrapped in a honey biscuit vies for attention with warm banana and toffee tart crumble. One correspondent thought that the £14.95 set menu 'must be the best value in Britain'. The wine list puts emphatically Gallic selections alongside representatives from the rest of the world. House wine is £10.99.

CHEFS: Eric Piedaniel and J. Gibbard   PROPRIETORS: Mr and Mrs Eric Piedaniel, and Mrs D. Béraud   OPEN: Tue to Sun L 12 to 1.30, Tue to Sat D 7 to 9.30 (10 Sat)   CLOSED: 25 Dec, first 2 weeks Jan, first 2 weeks Aug   MEALS: Set L £14.95 to £25.95, Set D £14.95 (exc Fri and Sat) to £25.95   SERVICE: not inc   CARDS:

Amex, MasterCard, Switch, Visa DETAILS: 45 seats. Private parties: 60 main room, 1 to 25 private rooms. Vegetarian meals. Children's helpings. No smoking. Wheelchair access (not WC). Music

BARNSLEY Gloucestershire   map 2

▲ Village Pub ⬥ ⁵⚹

Barnsley, Cirencester GL7 5EF	NEW CHEF
TEL: (01285) 740421 FAX: (01285) 740929	MODERN BRITISH
WEBSITE: www.thevillagepub.co.uk	£30–£48

The name evokes bucolic antiquity, but this ancient Cotswold stone inn serves cosmopolitan pub food for the twenty-first century. Two former sous-chefs took over the running of the kitchen in summer 2004, so reports please. The menu is a short selection of tersely described dishes with a few eclectic flourishes: for example, roast quail with grilled courgettes and aubergine, a chicken and chorizo stew, or bream fillet with sweet-and-sour vegetables, basil and pine nuts; by contrast, beer-battered cod and chips are a salute to the old brigade. Desserts hop from banana and golden syrup bread-and-butter pudding to Greek yoghurt parfait with caramelised pineapple. Service could be better organized and more accommodating, but the helpfully annotated modern wine list, organised by style, causes no complaints; prices start at £12, and a dozen come by the glass. The owners' latest venture, Barnsley House Hotel – opposite the pub – has received mixed reports.

CHEFS: Gordon Jones and Vicki Lovegrove PROPRIETORS: Tim Haigh and Rupert Pendered OPEN: all week 12 to 3, 7 to 10 MEALS: alc (main courses £10.50 to £15.50) SERVICE: not inc CARDS: MasterCard, Switch, Visa DETAILS: 100 seats. 50 seats outside. Private parties: 30 main room, 10 to 30 private rooms. Car park. Vegetarian meals. Children's helpings. No smoking in 1 dining room. No music ACCOMMODATION: 6 rooms, all with bath/shower. TV. Phone. B&B £65 to £125

BARTON ON SEA Hampshire   map 2

▲ Pebble Beach ⁵⚹   NEW ENTRY

Marine Drive, Barton on Sea BH25 7DZ	COOKING 3
TEL: (01425) 627777 FAX: (01425) 610689	MODERN EUROPEAN/SEAFOOD
WEBSITE: www.pebblebeach-uk.com	£28–£57

The 'exceptional' views over sea, undulating headland and across to the Needles and the western tip of the Isle of Wight are a serious natural advantage, and Pebble Beach makes the best of them in the modern dining room and terrace. The kitchen – open to view – delivers simple modern treatments alongside classic French provincial fare, thanks to the talents of Pierre Chevillard, who has worked at Troisgros, the Crillon and Chewton Glen (see entry, New Milton). There's lots of seafood – Breton fish soup or Gigas rock oysters – then perhaps a brace of tasty mackerel roasted with lemon, caper berries and tomatoes, balsamic dressing and ample parsley garnish. Convinced carnivores get a good choice too, perhaps home-smoked duck and celeriac rémoulade, plus steak, or liver and bacon. Desserts seem rather an afterthought, but it pays to linger for the views. Wines focus on France, ranging from £3 a glass to a classy Clos de Vougeot at £95.

CHEF: Pierre Chevillard PROPRIETOR: Mike Caddy OPEN: all week 12 to 2 (2.30 Sat and Sun), 6.30 to 9.30 (10 Fri and Sat) CLOSED: 25 Dec D, 1 Jan D MEALS: alc (main courses £10 to £17.50). Light menu available (not Sat D) SERVICE: not inc CARDS: Amex, Delta, MasterCard, Switch, Visa DETAILS: 70 seats. 40 seats outside. Car park. Vegetarian meals. Children's helpings. No smoking. Wheelchair access (also WC). Music. No mobile phones. Air-conditioned   ACCOMMODATION: 3 rooms, all with bath/shower. TV. B&B £49.95 to £69.95 (£5)

BARWICK Somerset   map 2

▲ Little Barwick House ♥ ⅙✳

Barwick BA22 9TD
TEL: (01935) 423902   FAX: (01935) 420908
WEBSITE: www.littlebarwickhouse.co.uk
take first exit off A37 roundabout 1m S of Yeovil; Little
Barwick House ¼m on left

COOKING 6
MODERN ENGLISH
£31–£71

The house is a tall, white, flat-fronted, Georgian edifice of three storeys, sitting in well-maintained gardens and decorated in soothing, light pastel tones inside. Exposed floorboards in the dining room throw any sense of country-house chintz into relief, and there is a small, pleasant conservatory extension towards the back. Staff sashay about the place in tasteful designer costumes, emphasising the air of self-assurance that pervades both the service and the cooking.

Tim Ford goes for vibrancy and colour in dishes that mobilise Mediterranean technique and fine West Country materials. Cornwall supplies red mullet (grilled, with herb couscous and gazpacho sauce) and scallops (sautéed, with ratatouille and sauce vierge). Fish is a strong suit all round, perhaps comprising a main course of sea bass with sun-dried tomato risotto, but meat eaters are well looked after too. Roast breast of corn-fed guinea fowl comes with fine pasta and girolles, and braised red cabbage and beetroot beignets are the accompaniments for saddle of venison. The food delivers convincingly on the palate, as may be demonstrated in a dessert of dark chocolate and marinated prune gâteau served with prune and Armagnac ice cream, and there are also herb and spice ice creams (black pepper with pear tart, basil with raspberry sablé) for the adventurous. Starting with house bottles at £13.95, the sleek wine list is arranged by style, and deals properly with budget and middle-range options from all corners of the world before focusing on the cream of the crop. The extensive half-bottle list is very strong.

CHEFS: Tim Ford, Maxine Perrier and Trudy Gladman   PROPRIETORS: Tim and Emma Ford   OPEN: Wed to Sun L 12 to 2, Tue to Sat D 7 to 9.30   CLOSED: Christmas. New Year, 2 weeks Jan   MEALS: alc L (main courses £20 to £25). Set L £15.95 (2 courses) to £17.95, Set D £28.95 (2 courses) to £32.95   SERVICE: not inc, card slips closed   CARDS: MasterCard, Switch, Visa   DETAILS: 40 seats. 15 seats outside. Private parties: 56 main room, 2 to 16 private rooms. Car park. Vegetarian meals. Children's helpings. No smoking. No music. No mobile phones. Air-conditioned   ACCOMMODATION: 6 rooms, all with bath/shower. TV. Phone. B&B £65 to £120

BASLOW Derbyshire   map 9

▲ Cavendish Hotel, Gallery Restaurant ⅙✳

Baslow DE45 1SP
TEL: (01246) 582311   FAX: (01246) 582312
WEBSITE: www.cavendish-hotel.net

COOKING 3
MODERN EUROPEAN
£41–£71

Its position close to Chatsworth, with direct access to the surrounding parkland, ensures that the Cavendish is a peaceful hotel. Drinks arrive at comfortable chairs in the lounge, and there are two dining rooms: the Garden Room offering an all-day menu, and the slightly more formal Gallery Restaurant. 'Wonderful bucolic views' and Eric Marsh's collection of paintings momentarily distracted one visitor from Chris Allison's modern menu – but not for long. It takes inspiration from a wide variety of sources, turning out, for example, roast rump of Castlegate lamb with an apricot and lovage polenta cake and a rose petal glaze. Materials are particularly impressive, judging by an inspector's lightly cooked scallops and monkfish, and 'sweet and fibrous' English lamb shank. Technique is sound, as evidenced by a suprême of Cornish cod topped with goats' cheese rarebit on pea and mint risotto that had 'positive, refreshing flavours'. For dessert, lemon–curd bread-and-butter pudding is served with lemon meringue ice cream. Service is 'gently paced', and wines, arranged by style, are fairly priced. House wines from France and Chile start at £13.50.

CHEF: Chris Allison   PROPRIETOR: Eric Marsh   OPEN: all week 12.30 to 2, 7 to 10   MEALS: alc (main courses £16.50 to £20). Garden Room menu available   SERVICE: not inc, card slips closed   CARDS: Amex, Delta, Diners, MasterCard, Switch, Visa   DETAILS: 50 seats. Private parties: 50 main room, 4 to 16 private rooms. Car park. Vegetarian meals. Children's helpings. Jacket and tie. No smoking. Music. No mobile phones   ACCOMMODATION: 24 rooms, all with bath/shower. TV. Phone. Room only £103 to £168

▲ Fischer's Baslow Hall ♥ ⅚✶

Calver Road, Baslow DE45 1RR   COOKING 7
TEL: (01246) 583259   FAX: (01246) 583818   MODERN EUROPEAN
WEBSITE: www.fischers-baslowhall.co.uk   £36–£101

It may resemble an Elizabethan manor house, but in fact this tranquil dwelling was built in 1907 for a lucky clergyman. For the past 16 years it has been home to Max and Susan Fischer's well-appointed small hotel. The Peak District location (on the edge of the Chatsworth Estate), comfortable bedrooms, and gardens that just get 'better and better' make it 'an ideal place in which to unwind'. Pre-dinner drinks can be taken in the panelled hall amid sumptuous settees and a roaring fire, along with a generous assortment of hard-to-beat canapés.

Inspired teamwork from Max Fischer and Rupert Rowley in the kitchen produces consistently fine results. Ingredients (often local and organic) are first class, with the quality of meat coming in for particular praise: perfect crackling on honey-roast suckling pig for one reporter, well-sourced (and well-sauced) shoulder of lamb and 'impeccable' calf's liver for another, and 'pink, tender and very well-flavoured' roast grouse for a third. Dishes are frequently complex but never fussy, and flavours are finely tuned so that they balance rather than compete with each other: in a salad of sweetbreads, pig's trotter and a poached egg with truffle vinaigrette, for example, or a 'memorable' dish of roast scallops on a bed of celeriac and butternut squash.

Desserts such as apricot and pistachio strudel or Yorkshire forced rhubarb bavarois are 'well constructed and beautifully presented', while Rupert Rowley's enthusiasm for rare chocolate has produced some interesting offerings along the lines of organic wild Tanzanie chocolate soufflé with cherry ice cream. Service was 'relaxed and welcoming' for one reporter, 'rather on the starchy side' for another, but is generally pleasant and professional. Bordeaux and Burgundy set the standard for the wine list and the shorter selections from elsewhere keep the quality high. There's plenty on offer under £20 and five house wines from £15 also come by the glass.

CHEFS: Max Fischer and Rupert Rowley   PROPRIETORS: Max and Susan Fischer   OPEN: Tue to Sun L 12 to 1.30, Mon to Sat D 7 to 9.30 (Sun D residents only)   CLOSED: 25 and 26 Dec   MEALS: Set L Tue to Sat £17.50 (2 courses) to £22.50, Set L Sun £30, Set D Sun to Fri £30 (2 courses) to £35, Set D all week £59 to £69   SERVICE: not inc   CARDS: Amex, Delta, Diners, MasterCard, Switch, Visa   DETAILS: 68 seats. Private parties: 40 main room, 4 to 16 private rooms. Car park. Vegetarian meals. Children's helpings. No children

under 12 after 7pm. No smoking. No music. No mobile phones   ACCOMMODATION: 11 rooms, all with bath/
shower. TV. Phone. B&B £100 to £180. Baby facilities

▲ Bath Priory ⅚✳

Weston Road, Bath BA1 2XT	COOKING 4
TEL: (01225) 331922 FAX: (01225) 448276	MODERN FRENCH
WEBSITE: www.thebathpriory.co.uk	£40–£87

Set in spectacular gardens, the Priory is a grand-looking Gothic-style mansion on a not-so-grand scale, built in 1835 of the local honey-coloured stone. Originally a private residence, it is now run as a luxurious hotel, with an ornate décor featuring 'seriously patterned' wallpaper and a vast collection of animal-themed oil paintings. It makes a formal impression, although service, by a smartly dressed team of Frenchmen, is attentive and, for the most part, good-humoured. Executive chef Robert Clayton takes a fittingly serious-minded approach to cooking, creating attractively presented dishes of technical proficiency. Starters take in wild rabbit ravioli with Savoy cabbage, speck and a wild mushroom sauce, or a warm salad of three large pan-fried scallops, each topped with a ball of crisp caramelised apple and scattered with roast hazelnuts. Main courses range from sautéed turbot fillet with chive creamed potatoes, asparagus and girolle velouté to honey-roast Gressingham duck breast with fondant potato, confit shallots and Cassis sauce. To finish, choose between crisp plum tart with hazelnut ice cream and caramel sauce or a selection of first-class British and Irish cheeses. An inspection meal disappointed, with some dishes failing to make an impact (the duck above, for example). Wines are aimed squarely at high rollers, although there are a few bottles under £20.

CHEF: Robert Clayton   PROPRIETOR: Andrew Brownsword   OPEN: all week 12 to 1.45, 7 to 10   CLOSED: 18 to 23 Jan   MEALS: Set L £20 (2 courses) to £25, Set D £49.50   SERVICE: not inc   CARDS: Amex, Delta, Diners, MasterCard, Switch, Visa   DETAILS: 80 seats. Private parties: 64 main room. Car park. Vegetarian meals. Children's helpings. No smoking. Wheelchair access (also WC). Occasional music. No mobile phones   ACCOMMODATION: 27 rooms, all with bath/shower. TV. Phone. B&B £145 to £425. Rooms for disabled. Swimming pool

FishWorks ⅚✳

6 Green Street, Bath BA1 2JY	COOKING 3
TEL: (01225) 448707 FAX: (01225) 447562	SEAFOOD
WEBSITE: www.fishworks.co.uk	£28–£86

The FishWorks group (see entries, Bristol, Christchurch and London) seems to have struck on a formula that works, incorporating both a fishmonger and a restaurant. If customers take a shine to a particular fish, they can buy it whole from the counter and have it cooked for them on the premises. The philosophy, according to the owners, is to keep things simple. The Bath branch is in the centre of town, with the wet-fish counter at the front and the small blue and white contemporary restaurant behind. The menu features 'classic dishes' (salted Cantabrian sea anchovies, Dartmouth crab with salad and mayonnaise) as well as fish stew, cooked and raw shellfish, a selection of French oysters, and plenty more. Silky, luscious taramasalata ('the genuine article') has been singled out for particular praise, while other reporters note that the 'fish is always excellent'. Vegetables are not included in the price but are well reported. The wine list – mostly white – is carefully chosen to complement fish, with bottle prices starting at £15.25.

CHEF: Garry Rosser   PROPRIETOR: FishWorks plc   OPEN: Tue to Sat 12 to 2.30, 6 to 10.30, Sun 11 to 5
CLOSED: Christmas, bank hols   MEALS: alc (main courses £8.50 to £35)   SERVICE: not inc   CARDS: Amex,
Delta, MasterCard, Switch, Visa   DETAILS: 52 seats. 16 seats outside. Vegetarian meals. Children's
helpings. No smoking. Wheelchair access (not WC). Music. Air-conditioned

Hole in the Wall ✳

NEW ENTRY

16 George Street, Bath BA1 2EN   COOKING 2
TEL/FAX: (01225) 425242   MODERN BRITISH
WEBSITE: www.theholeinthewall.co.uk   £24–£46

Tucked away in the centre of Bath, the legendary Hole in the Wall has been under new
ownership since February 2004. The décor has changed little; the two basement rooms are
still dominated by a huge stone fireplace, although the colour scheme has been lightened
up with shades of cream and green. The cooking is seemingly more careful than it used to
be, and there is a distinct respect for the food served. The owners have gone for a simple
set-price menu on which dishes are briefly and sensibly described. There's a smattering of
local ingredients (Cornish cod, Gloucester Old Spot pork, West Country cheeses) and
modern takes on traditional combinations, such as pork with apple and Stilton Tatin. The
earthy flavour of Jerusalem artichokes shines through a soup enhanced with truffle oil and
chanterelles, while main courses might feature accurately roast cod fillet with crushed
potatoes and sauce vierge. Desserts such as passion-fruit tart with a matching coulis are put
together with a light touch. Service is eager to please, and the wine list offers a reasonably
priced (from £10.95), contemporary selection, with plenty by the glass.

CHEFS: Gerry Dowd and Marco Appel   PROPRIETOR: Guy Adams   OPEN: Mon to Sat 12 to 2.30, 5 to 10.30,
Sun 6 to 10   MEALS: Set L and D 5 to 6.30 £9.95 (2 courses) to £14.95, Set D £18.50 (2 courses) to £23.50
SERVICE: not inc   CARDS: MasterCard, Switch, Visa   DETAILS: 80 seats. Private parties: 80 main room, 6 to
15 private rooms. Vegetarian meals. Children's helpings. No smoking in 1 dining room. Music

Moody Goose ♀ ✳

7A Kingsmead Square, Bath BA1 2AB   COOKING 4
TEL/FAX: (01225) 466688   ENGLISH
WEBSITE: www.moody.goose.com   £29–£64

In a quiet square not far from the Theatre Royal, is this small, simple basement room with a
couple of under-pavement vaults, like little Nissen huts, off it. White linen and expensive
tableware bespeak serious intent, and Stephen Shore's menus read well, with interesting
but not wayward-sounding combinations and an enticing mixture of the earthy and the
refined: scallops come with parsnip purée and black pudding, and foie gras with boiled
ham. French technique is much in evidence, with a fair amount of saucing and some
complex accompaniments. At inspection a main course of pink-roasted partridge came
with roast pear, syrupy red cabbage and a rich, pungent gratin of Jerusalem artichokes.
Desserts shone too, in the forms of comforting apple and custard soufflé on toffee sauce, or
jasmine rice pudding topped with 'fantastically refreshing' clementine sorbet. Sometimes
the desire for strong visual presentation can have an impact on mouth-pleasing textures
(turrets of over-stiff parsnip purée each supporting a scallop, for example). A page of house
wines under £20, all also served by the glass, leads a global list of good names that quickly
reaches fairly high prices. A healthy range of dessert bottles rounds things off nicely.

CHEF: Stephen Shore   PROPRIETORS: Stephen and Victoria Shore   OPEN: Mon to Sat 12 to 1.30, 6 to 9.30
(10 Sat)   CLOSED: 25 Dec, bank hol Mons, 2 weeks Jan   MEALS: alc D (main courses £18.50 to £20). Set L

and D 6 to 7 £13 (2 courses) to £17.50, Set D £25   SERVICE: not inc   CARDS: Amex, Delta, Diners, MasterCard, Switch, Visa   DETAILS: 30 seats. Private parties: 16 main room, 6 to 8 private rooms. Vegetarian meals. Children's helpings. No children under 8. No smoking. Music

---

▲ Queensberry Hotel, Olive Tree Restaurant ▾ ✳

Russel Street, Bath BA1 2QF
TEL: (01225) 447928   FAX: (01225) 446065
WEBSITE: www.thequeensberry.co.uk

COOKING 5
MODERN BRITISH
£29–£61

Beneath a hotel consisting of three 'perfect Georgian Bath' terraced townhouses, this basement restaurant has swept away the old and brought in the uncompromisingly modern, with a glossy and ambitious makeover; neutral-coloured walls, wood floor and modern paintings are a world away from the chintz and conservatism of many of its local competitors. The owners (since 2003) have maintained continuity in the kitchen, with Jason Horne's team seemingly raising their game over the last year. Begin with steak and kidney pudding, pea purée and thyme jus, 'a triumphant illustration of the value of reviving an old English classic, giving it new refinement without losing its character'. Follow perhaps with roast wood pigeon, creamed cabbage, lentils and morel jus. Puddings, like pink elderflower jelly with rhubarb, poached pear and Poire William sorbet, are 'an absolute joy – seemingly artless combinations put together with a wonderfully light touch'. The vibrant wine list is arranged into styles with names such as 'raspberries and strawberries' or 'green, tangy and dry'. The monthly 'supplier's list' looks very good value, and a dozen interesting house wines from £13.50 are also offered by the glass.

CHEF: Jason Horne   PROPRIETORS: Laurence and Helen Beere   OPEN: Tue to Sun L 12 to 2, all week D 7 to 10.30   MEALS: alc (main courses £13 to £20). Set L £13 (2 courses) to £16.50, Set D £24 (2 courses) to £28   SERVICE: not inc   CARDS: Amex, Delta, MasterCard, Switch, Visa   DETAILS: 70 seats. Private parties: 24 main room, 10 to 24 private rooms. Vegetarian meals. Children's helpings. No smoking. Music. No mobile phones. Air-conditioned   ACCOMMODATION: 29 rooms, all with bath/shower. TV. Phone. Room only £100 to £285. Rooms for disabled. Baby facilities (£5)

▲ Royal Crescent, Pimpernel's ▾ ✳

16 Royal Crescent, Bath BA1 2LS
TEL: (01225) 823333   FAX: (01225) 339401
WEBSITE: www.royalcrescent.co.uk

COOKING 4
MODERN BRITISH
£41–£106

The Royal Crescent is probably Britain's finest Georgian terrace, and Pimpernel's occupies a Victorian building at the back of the eponymous hotel across a manicured garden. The formal dining room presents classic French cuisine with modern British touches, and flavour combinations are mostly light and harmonious. Set dinner starters could range from confit duck in maple and lime dressing with Cabernet vinegar reduction, to steamed langoustine with grape risotto and shellfish butter. Then perhaps beef tournedos with braised oxtail and Madeira jus – or poached brill fillet with squid pudding and tempura tentacles. Vegetarian choices, if limited, are substantially cheaper. To finish, expect complex creations like apricot crumble soufflé with almond ice cream and vanilla beignet, or maybe Eve's pudding with Calvados crème fraîche and apple ripple ice cream.

The wine list, as befits this address, is grand but elegantly proportioned, opening with a delightful range of food-friendly wines by the glass (£4 to £8). Except in the mainly French Classic section, the bottles are presented by style, with an engaging international line-up in each category. There is plenty of mileage in a £25 budget, with options under £20 and interesting halves.

CHEF: Steven Blake   PROPRIETOR: Von Essen Hotels   OPEN: all week 12.30 to 2, 7 to 10   MEALS: Set L £14 (2 courses) to £25, Set D £49   SERVICE: not inc   CARDS: Amex, Delta, Diners, MasterCard, Switch, Visa DETAILS: 60 seats. 45 seats outside. Private parties: 60 main room, 40 private rooms. Car park. Vegetarian meals. Children's helpings. No smoking. Wheelchair access (not WC). Occasional music. Air-conditioned ACCOMMODATION: 45 rooms, all with bath/shower. TV. Phone. B&B £210 to £840. Rooms for disabled. Baby facilities. Swimming pool

BEESTON Nottinghamshire   map 5

La Toque ✸✕

61 Wollaton Road, Beeston NG9 2NG   COOKING 3
TEL: (0115) 922 2268   FAX: (0115) 922 7979   FRENCH
WEBSITE: www.latoqueonline.co.uk   £29–£61

Set among Indian takeaways in a Nottingham suburb, the cuisine here lives up to the Gallic name, while drawing for its raw materials on British speciality producers discerningly chosen from near and far. Intricate menu descriptions means choosing dishes can take a fair while: a mere starter might be a piece of roast venison loin with Puy lentils, smoked bacon and shiitakes, garnished with toasted almonds and a Gorgonzola sauce. Proceed to baked sea bass with baby globe artichoke ragoût on balsamic spinach, or honey-glazed Gressingham duck breast with goats' cheese, a red onion tart and creamed cabbage and apple. Despite such elaboration, most of these assemblages are brought off with distinct panache. Desserts are a little simpler – perhaps chocolate-gratinated blood oranges served with passion-fruit sorbet. With strong runs of claret and Burgundy, the wine list will delight well-heeled aficionados, but there is choice under £20 too; four French house wines are £13.50 (£4.75 a glass).

CHEF: Mattias Karlsson   PROPRIETOR: Norman Oley   OPEN: Tue to Fri L 11.30 to 2.30, Tue to Sat D 6.30 to 10   CLOSED: second and third weeks Aug, 26 to 29 Dec, 1 to 6 Jan   MEALS: alc (main courses £16 to £19). Set L £11.95 (2 courses) to £16.95, Set D £18.95 (2 courses) to £24.95   SERVICE: 10% (optional)   CARDS: Amex, Delta, Diners, MasterCard, Switch, Visa   DETAILS: 40 seats. Private parties: 30 main room. Vegetarian meals. No children under 7. No smoking. Wheelchair access (also WC). Music. No mobile phones. Air-conditioned £5

BIDDENDEN Kent   map 3

West House

28 High Street, Biddenden TN27 8AH   COOKING 5
TEL: (01580) 291341   FAX: (01580) 292501   MODERN BRITISH
                                                                £33–£48

This partly tile-hung ancient building in a pretty and prosperous village provides very simple but exceptionally well-executed cooking. The compact daily-changing menu is concise and businesslike, rather than flowery ('breast of pigeon, chicken livers, onion and beetroot marmalade'; 'grilled skirt steak, oxtail ravioli and parsnip cream'). A first-time visitor was impressed by a starter of two caramelised scallops with cauliflower pannacotta and pancetta: 'tiny but exquisite in terms of texture, presentation and taste'. Perhaps because of the inherent simplicity, flavours are clear and contrasts strong, as in a casserole of wild boar with prune. Prune may reappear with Armagnac in a bread pudding, or you might finish with chocolate soufflé tart with caramel blood orange and Earl Grey ice cream. Graham Garrett emphasises seasonal ingredients, and his use of good raw materials, many of them local, is a strength. Some reporters have found the pace of service rather slow and the Muzak a little obtrusive. The Francophile wine list is several cuts above the average and follows interesting byways in the Midi; prices are reasonable and start with £11.95 vin de pays.

CHEF: Graham Garrett   PROPRIETORS: Graham Garrett and Jackie Hewitt   OPEN: Tue to Fri and Sun L 12 to 2, Tue to Sat D 7 to 9.30   CLOSED: 25 Dec, 1 Jan, 2 weeks summer   MEALS: alc L (main courses £12 to £16). Set D £28   SERVICE: 10% (optional), card slips closed   CARDS: Delta, MasterCard, Switch, Visa   DETAILS: 30 seats. Private parties: 30 main room. Car park. Children's helpings. No pipes/cigars. Wheelchair access (not WC). Music

BIRCH VALE Derbyshire   map 8

▲ Waltzing Weasel ⅖✳

New Mills Road, Birch Vale SK22 1BT   COOKING 1
TEL/FAX: (01663) 743402   ANGLO-MEDITERRANEAN
WEBSITE: www.w-weasel.co.uk   £28–£48

In the Peak District but hard by Greater Manchester, this is both country pub and restaurant. Italian leanings (sardine tapenade, or roast fennel, among starters) are balanced by bradan rost, or belly pork glazed with mustard, honey, Worcester and soy sauces. The Weasel is also evangelical about peasant stews, so daily specials range from pollo al chilindron to Persian mutton and orange koresh. More Anglophile desserts include treacle tart and bread-and-butter pudding. The set dinner brings local lamb, beef and game alongside tarte provençale and an Italian antipasti platter. House wines at £14.85 introduce a shortish, fully priced international list.

CHEF: Tracy Young   PROPRIETORS: Michael and Linda Atkinson   OPEN: all week 12 to 2, 7 to 9   MEALS: alc L (main courses £7 to £14). Set D £23.75 (2 courses) to £27.75. Bar menu available   SERVICE: not inc, card slips closed   CARDS: Delta, MasterCard, Switch, Visa   DETAILS: 36 seats. 20 seats outside. Private parties: 36 main room, 12 private room. Car park. Vegetarian meals. Children's helpings. No children under 8. No smoking. Wheelchair access (not WC). Occasional music. No mobile phones. Air-conditioned   ACCOMMODATION: 8 rooms, all with bath/shower. TV. B&B £48 to £108

BIRMINGHAM West Midlands   map 5

Bank ▼

4 Brindleyplace, Birmingham B1 2JB   COOKING 2
TEL: (0121) 633 4466   FAX: (0121) 633 4465   MODERN EUROPEAN
WEBSITE: www.bankrestaurants.com   £22–£86

The Midlands outlet of this little group (see entry, London) is every inch the urban brasserie, set fair and square in Birmingham's cool, fashionable playground known as Brindleyplace. It's a capacious, all-comers' venue with a trendy bar for cocktails and an open-plan dining area at the back dealing in breakfast, brunch and theatre deals (Symphony Hall and the New Rep are just a walk away), as well as offering customers a wide-ranging East/West carte peppered with modish culinary references. This is the world of chicken and shrimp 'nam' rolls, seared scallops with black pudding and potato mousseline, and roast rack of lamb with chorizo risotto, although there's also room for fish 'n' chips and sausage and mash. To finish, it's a toss-up between tiramisù, pannacotta and traditional puds. For those who make it past the cocktail list, a stimulating range of wines is presented by styles, now with an expanded line-up of 16 or so by the glass. Prices start at £12.25 but are not all bargains.

CHEF: Steve Woods   PROPRIETOR: Bank Restaurant Group   OPEN: Mon to Fri L 12 to 2.45, Mon to Thurs D 5.30 to 10.30, Sat and Sun brunch 11.30 to 2.30 (3 Sun), Fri to Sun D 5.30 to 11 (10 Sun). Breakfast from 7am   MEALS: alc (main courses £10 to £32). Set L and D £11.50 (2 courses) to £14. Breakfast and brunch menus   SERVICE: 12.5% (optional), card slips closed   CARDS: Amex, Delta, Diners, MasterCard, Switch, Visa   DETAILS: 150 seats. 60 seats outside. Private parties: 150 main room, 16 to 100 private rooms. Vegetarian meals. Children's helpings. No-smoking area. Wheelchair access (also WC). Music. Air-conditioned (£5)

Chung Ying Garden

17 Thorp Street, Birmingham B5 4AT

TEL: (0121) 666 6622   FAX: (0121) 622 5860

WEBSITE: www.chungying.co.uk

COOKING 1
CHINESE
£22–£58

Two golden statues deter evil spirits from the door here in Birmingham's Chinatown, close to city-centre clubland, New Street station and the Hippodrome. The menu encompasses 400 dishes (including 60 dim sum), and standards may fluctuate, although the kitchen can deliver some robustly flavoured food; specials, including paper-wrapped beef fillet, and a benchmark version of steamed eel with black bean sauce, particularly impressed an inspector. Otherwise, it's a long haul through the Cantonese repertoire for casseroles, hotpots, sizzlers, legions of one-plate rice and noodle dishes and seafood aplenty (from deep-fried oysters to halibut with shredded pork and mushrooms). House wines are £9.50 a bottle (£11.50 a litre).

CHEF/PROPRIETOR: Siu Chung Wong   OPEN: all week noon to 11.30 (10.30 Sun)   CLOSED: 25 Dec   MEALS: alc L and (exc Dec) D (main courses £7 to £36). Set L and D £14 (min 2) to £23 (min 4). Menu for Chinese diners available   SERVICE: not inc, card slips closed   CARDS: Amex, Delta, Diners, MasterCard, Switch, Visa   DETAILS: 380 seats. Private parties: 200 main room, 2 to 200 private rooms. Vegetarian meals. Wheelchair access (also WC). Music. Air-conditioned (£5)

▲ Hotel du Vin & Bistro ▮

25 Church Street, Birmingham B3 2NR

TEL: (0121) 200 0600   FAX: (0121) 236 0889

WEBSITE: www.hotelduvin.com

COOKING 3
MODERN EUROPEAN
£32–£56

In the imposing former Eye Hospital in the heart of the city, the Birmingham branch bears all the hallmarks of this swish but informal small chain of hotels (see entries in Brighton, Bristol, Harrogate, Tunbridge Wells and Winchester; a seventh is coming to Henley-on-Thames). The lavishly decorated Bubble Lounge is designed to resemble Venice's Florian's café, while the dining room, with its bare floorboards, wooden tables, and posters, has a simpler, genial feel. Classic bistro fare takes inspiration from France and Italy, with a few old favourites such as game pie and kedgeree thrown in. Ham hock terrine with piccalilli has pleased, as has calf's liver with shallot mash. Lest this sounds too meaty, vegetarians are well catered for, with a separate section of the menu. Round off with the impressive cheeseboard, or a tart such as pineapple and frangipane, or chocolate. The huge wine list raids every region for quality bottles and turns up affordable options from £11.50 seemingly at random along the way. Steer clear of famous names for the best value and also to taste interesting bottles you won't see anywhere else. Fans of dessert wines will be more than satisfied with the range on offer.

CHEF: Nick Turner   PROPRIETOR: Hotel du Vin Ltd   OPEN: all week 12 to 2, 6.30 to 10   MEALS: alc (main courses £14.50 to £17.50). Set L Sun £23.50   SERVICE: not inc   CARDS: Amex, Delta, Diners, MasterCard, Switch, Visa   DETAILS: 85 seats. 30 seats outside. Private parties: 60 main room, 10 to 25 private rooms. Vegetarian meals. Children's helpings. No smoking. Wheelchair access (also WC). No music ACCOMMODATION: 66 rooms, all with bath/shower. TV. Phone. Room only £120 to £395. Rooms for disabled. Baby facilities

Jessica's

NEW ENTRY

1 Montague Road, Edgbaston, Birmingham B16 9HN
TEL: (0121) 455 0999   FAX: (0121) 455 8222

COOKING 5
ANGLO-FRENCH
£35–£70

This latest addition to the burgeoning Birmingham culinary scene occupies the rear half of a solid red-brick Victorian house in leafy Edgbaston. It consists of two small dining rooms, one of which looks out on to a garden with a walled courtyard, lending the place the improbable feel of a country cottage. Pale wooden floors and French windows make it all feel fresh and new, and the cooking is by Glynn Parnell, formerly a sous-chef at Hibiscus (see entry, Ludlow).

An inspection meal began impressively with a finely textured gratin of ceps with a yolk of poached egg, a purée of shallots and a sharp mushroom-flavoured vinaigrette, a clever way of making straightforward ingredients stimulating and original. Another reporter enjoyed ballottine of foie gras with vanilla-dipped potatoes, apple purée, hazelnuts and rocket. Main courses deliver richness and subtlety together, as in pieces of milk-fed rabbit with pearl barley and a pistachio cream sauce, sharpened up cleverly with chicory, or Indian-spiced monkfish with red lentils and coconut cream. Desserts are similarly unafraid to mobilise challenging juxtapositions, adding peanut butter to a mille-feuille of pear with its own sorbet, while a warm chocolate pudding is tricked out with mango, pineapple and ginger ice cream. Engaging French service keeps people happy, but the wine list, sadly, won't inspire. Prices start at £13.95 for Muscadet and Côtes du Rhône.

CHEF: Glynn Parnell   PROPRIETORS: K. and D. Stevenson   OPEN: Tue to Fri L 12.30 to 2, Mon to Sat D 7 to 10   CLOSED: 1 week at Christmas, Easter week, last 2 weeks July   MEALS: Set L £15 (2 courses) to £21.50, Set D £29.95 to £42.50   SERVICE: not inc   CARDS: MasterCard, Switch, Visa   DETAILS: 36 seats. Private parties: 36 main room. Vegetarian meals. Children's helpings. No smoking. Music. No mobile phones. Air-conditioned

Metro Bar & Grill

73 Cornwall Street, Birmingham B3 2DF
TEL: (0121) 200 1911   FAX: (0121) 200 1611
WEBSITE: www.metrobarandgrill.co.uk

COOKING 2
MODERN EUROPEAN
£29–£53

Deep in the city's commercial centre, this live-wire place can get packed: although the bar can be a noisy scrum, there's some respite in the split-level dining room beyond. Starters might include crispy duck salad, while roast salmon with saffron potatoes and watercress could represent the seafood constituency. Other items might range from cherry tomato risotto with pesto and tapenade to braised shoulder of lamb with butter-bean and chorizo cassoulet. The classic brasserie-style menu also puts the rôtisserie and grill to work on, say, corn-fed chicken spit-roast with lemon, thyme and garlic, and chargrilled tuna with chilli, coconut and coriander noodles. Daily fish specials add variety, and, to finish, there might be something simple like fruit crumble. Ten champagnes fizz up the youthful wine list. House wines are £11.95.

CHEF: Matthew Knight   PROPRIETORS: Chris Kelly and David Cappendell   OPEN: Mon to Fri L 12 to 2.30, Mon to Sat D 6 to 9.30   CLOSED: bank hols   MEALS: alc (main courses £9 to £17). Bar menu available   SERVICE: not inc   CARDS: Amex, Delta, MasterCard, Switch, Visa   DETAILS: 120 seats. Private parties: 120 main room. Vegetarian meals. Wheelchair access (also WC). Music. Air-conditioned

Paris ⁵✕   NEW ENTRY

109–111 Wharfside, The Mailbox, Birmingham B1 1RF   COOKING 5
TEL: (0121) 632 1488   FAX: (0121) 632 1489   MODERN FRENCH
WEBSITE: www.restaurant-paris.co.uk   £38–£82

As its regeneration gathers pace, Birmingham is acquiring some smart new eateries to match. This one opened in 2003 in the Mailbox shopping complex (a funky new development), in high-ceilinged, extravagantly spacious premises with a predominantly brown colour scheme more Seine-side chic than canalside brummagem. Service is formal (surprisingly sedate and somewhat disjointed at inspection), but chef/patron Patrick McDonald scores well for culinary judgment.

Fish is top-notch. Seared scallops with truffle and potato are timed to a nicety, their juicy sweetness nicely pointed by the truffle, while a main course seafood fricassée with risotto nero and sauce bouillabaisse was 'devastatingly fresh and generous', the timing and technique effortlessly passing muster. Robustness characterises other main dishes: squab pigeon brésolles with roast shallots, fondant potato and Madeira jus, or pig's trotter stuffed with sage, onion and morels. Fine British and French cheeses are an optional precursor to desserts like hot passion-fruit soufflé with its own heavily sweetened sorbet, or crème brûlée with rhubarb done three ways – poached, puréed and as a sorbet. An ambitiously extensive wine list has many French treasures, and imaginative – if expensive – choices from elsewhere; bottle prices start at £17, and the six wines by the glass start at £4.50.

CHEF/PROPRIETOR: Patrick McDonald   OPEN: Tue to Sat 12 to 2.30, 7 to 10   CLOSED: 1 week Christmas, 1 week Easter, 2 weeks Aug   MEALS: alc (main courses £16.50 to £26). Set L £16.50 (2 courses) to £21.50   SERVICE: 12.5% (optional), card slips closed   CARDS: Amex, Delta, Diners, MasterCard, Switch, Visa   DETAILS: 42 seats. Private parties: 42 main room, 8 to 12 private rooms. Car park. Vegetarian meals. No Smoking. Wheelchair access (also WC). No music. No mobile phones. Air-conditioned

La Toque d'Or

27 Warstone Lane, Hockley, Birmingham B18 6JQ   COOKING 4
TEL/FAX: (0121) 233 3655   FRENCH
WEBSITE: www.latoquedor.co.uk   £32–£57

Located in what was once a metal rolling mill in Birmingham's jewellery quarter, La Toque d'Or aims to combine Didier Philipot's French technique with ingredients from an impressive roster of quality suppliers. The welcoming and hospitable atmosphere makes everybody feel at home amid slightly old-school décor that makes no concessions to contemporary minimalism. From the prix fixe menu start with mussel and saffron soup, in which float crostini topped with crab and aïoli, or alternatively with home-smoked salmon acerbically partnered with celeriac rémoulade, horseradish and capers. Seasonal dishes are chalked on a board and priced as supplements to the printed offerings, which may run to slow-braised rabbit with crushed potatoes, rillettes of the meat and a creamy Pommery mustard sauce, or Devon skate with wilted spinach, ruby grapefruit and dill butter. The duly patient will find the 20-minute wait for 'soufflé of the day' rewarded with a properly textured triumph. If you're pushed for time, try Amaretto pannacotta with pear confit. French house wines at £12.90 open a list that cherry-picks its way niftily around the world.

CHEF: Didier Philipot   PROPRIETOR: SSPG Consulting Ltd   OPEN: Tue to Fri L 12.30 to 1.30, Tue to Sat D 7 to 9.30   CLOSED: Christmas, New Year, Easter, 2 weeks Aug   MEALS: Set L £16.50 (2 courses) to £19.50, Set D £24.50   SERVICE: not inc   CARDS: Amex, Delta, Diners, MasterCard, Switch, Visa   DETAILS: 32 seats. Private parties: 40 main room. Vegetarian meals. Children's helpings. Wheelchair access (also WC). Music. No mobile phones. Air-conditioned

---

BIRTLE Greater Manchester   map 8

Waggon ✹ £   NEW ENTRY

131 Bury and Rochdale Old Road, Birtle BL9 6UE   COOKING 3
TEL: (01706) 622955   FAX: (01706) 620094   MODERN BRITISH
                                                              £21–£45

A converted pub on the main Bury to Rochdale road below the old hamlet of Birtle is where you'll find this Waggon. The ground floor has been opened up, with the bar and adjoining dining areas decked out with sturdy, stripped-wood tables. It's light and pleasant and has a modern edge without any pretensions of being designer led. The kitchen takes a modern and straightforward approach too, using locally sourced produce, and prices are reasonable, especially on the fixed-price menu. The simple repertoire takes in main courses of smoked cod risotto with parsley oil, and fillet of beef with sautéed potatoes, wild mushrooms and Madeira sauce, plus a couple of daily-changing fish specials: perhaps a tranche of 'fresh-tasting and perfectly cooked' turbot with a creamy mustard and tarragon sauce. Ginger sponge with custard, or lemon cake with lemon cheese bring things to a homely finish. Service copes well under pressure, and the atmosphere is buzzy. The compact, globetrotting wine list comes with useful notes; five house selections start proceedings at £10.95 a bottle, £2.75 a glass.

CHEF: David Watson   PROPRIETORS: Lorraine and David Watson   OPEN: Wed to Fri L 12 to 2, Wed to Sat D 6 (5 Sat) to 9.30, Sun 12.30 to 8.30 (food served all day)   CLOSED: 25 to 28 Dec, 1 and 11 Jan, last week July, first week Aug   MEALS: alc (main courses £8 to £15). Set L and D Wed to Fri £11.95 (2 courses) to £13.95   SERVICE: not inc, card slips closed   CARDS: Amex, Delta, MasterCard, Switch, Visa   DETAILS: 60 seats. Private parties: 50 main room, 8 to 24 private rooms. Car park. Vegetarian meals. Children's helpings. No smoking in 1 dining room. Wheelchair access (also WC). Music £5

BISHOP'S TACHBROOK Warwickshire   map 5

▲ Mallory Court ✹   NEW ENTRY

Harbury Lane, Bishop's Tachbrook CV33 9QB   COOKING 3
TEL: (01926) 330214   FAX: (01926) 451714   MODERN BRITISH
WEBSITE: www.mallory.co.uk   £42–£98

Comfort is the watchword at this well-maintained 1920s Lutyens-style country house. Handsome panelling, red floral carpets, tapestry curtains, linen and classy tableware give the dining room a formal air, although views over the gardens soften the effect, and courteous service is not at all stuffy. The menus display a leaning towards a classic style of cooking, with a degree of luxury to match the surroundings, starters taking in a dish of foie gras two ways – in a ballottine and pan-fried with pear. Among main-course highlights have been braised blade of beef with wild mushrooms and red wine sauce, and an elaborately crafted combination of well-timed red mullet, brandade croquette, and a nutty-flavoured scallop on smooth potato purée. Desserts end the meal in style – banana tarte Tatin with banana and lime sorbet, for example – although the well-kept, mainly French cheeses are a tempting alternative. Mark-ups are stiff on the extensive wine list, with few bottles under £20.

CHEF: Simon Haigh   PROPRIETOR: Sir Peter Rigby   OPEN: all week 12 to 2, 7 to 9.30   MEALS: alc D (main courses £18 to £28). Set L £19.50 (2 courses) to £25, Set D £39.50. Light L menu available   SERVICE: not inc   CARDS: Amex, Delta, Diners, MasterCard, Switch, Visa   DETAILS: 54 seats. 26 seats outside. Private parties: 104 main room, 2 to 104 private rooms. Car park. Vegetarian meals. No smoking. Wheelchair access (also WC). Occasional music   ACCOMMODATION: 29 rooms, 27 with bath/shower. TV. Phone. B&B £125 to £320. Rooms for disabled. Swimming pool

BLACKPOOL Lancashire   map 8

Kwizeen £

47–49 King Street, Blackpool FY1 3EJ	COOKING 2
TEL: (01253) 290045	MODERN EUROPEAN
WEBSITE: www.kwizeen.co.uk	£18–£53

Sited snugly on the inland side of the town centre, the orthographically challenged Kwizeen offers stylish modern food in spare surroundings. The concise menu, supplemented by a specials board, presses most of the right buttons. Salmon fishcakes are spiked with lime and coriander and served with sesame prawn toast, and robust appetites assuaged with starters like Cajun pork fillet with roast pineapple and a sauce of curried mango. Ginger butter sauce is a favoured accompaniment to fish, from sea bass to turbot, while the Aberdeen Angus steak comes with bubble and squeak and a £5 supplement. Puddings might include the likes of Baileys mascarpone cheesecake. A short, serviceable wine list opens with house French at £9.50.

CHEF: Marco Calle-Calatayud   PROPRIETORS: Marco Calle-Calatayud and Tony Beswick   OPEN: Mon to Fri L 12 to 1.15, Tue to Sat D 6 to 9   MEALS: alc (main courses £11 to £20). Set L £5.95 (2 courses)   SERVICE: not inc, card slips closed   CARDS: Delta, MasterCard, Switch, Visa   DETAILS: 40 seats. Private parties: 40 private room. Music. No mobile phones

BLAKENEY Norfolk   map 6

▲ White Horse Hotel ✸

4 High Street, Blakeney NR25 7AL	COOKING 1
TEL: (01263) 740574 FAX: (01263) 741339	MODERN BRITISH-PLUS
WEBSITE: www.blakeneywhitehorse.co.uk	£31–£55

Up the steepish High Street from the quay and the mudflats, this pub/restaurant is a focal point of the Blakeney scene. Separate kitchens feed the casual bar and the yellow-painted dining room, but raw materials are taken seriously throughout: game is from nearby estates, soft fruit and vegetables are grown locally and there's seafood in abundance. In the restaurant you might be offered Morston mussels in garlic sauce, venison with onion marmalade and pancetta, or griddled scallops with tagliatelle in a tomato and fennel broth. Timing is generally spot-on, witness daringly rare seared tuna loin with a Mediterranean salad, while desserts could feature vanilla crème brûlée and walnut tart. The British cheese menu reads well; so, too, does the affordable Adnams wine list, prices on which start at £12.95.

CHEF: Christopher Hyde   PROPRIETOR: Daniel Goff   OPEN: Tue to Sun D 7 to 9   CLOSED: 2nd and 3rd weeks Jan   MEALS: alc (main courses £10 to £20)   SERVICE: not inc   CARDS: Amex, Delta, MasterCard, Switch, Visa   DETAILS: 36 seats. Private parties: 36 main room. Car park. Vegetarian meals. Children's helpings. No smoking. Occasional music   ACCOMMODATION: 10 rooms, all with bath/shower. TV. Phone. B&B £20 to £100. Baby facilities £5

BODIAM East Sussex   map 3

Curlew ⅝✳   NEW ENTRY

Junction Road, Bodiam TN32 5UY	COOKING 2
TEL: (01580) 861394 FAX: (01580) 861396	MODERN EUROPEAN
WEBSITE: www.thecurlewatbodiam.co.uk	£27–£63

The Curlew is a white-painted clapboard pub, at a quiet crossroads, which operates pretty much as a restaurant these days, and reveals itself to be much bigger on the inside than you might expect. The kitchen has obvious Mediterranean leanings, with a modern menu of dishes based on long-established combinations of ingredients, along the lines of Mediterranean fish soup with rouille, smoked haddock risotto with saffron and curry oil, and 'marvellously melting' shank of lamb with spinach, herb mash and Madeira sauce. The cooking reveals good technical skills, while the service has let the side down. Wines are somewhat confusingly arranged, with bottles at £11.95 next to ones at £95. A separate page deals in wines by the glass from £3.25.

CHEFS: Andy Blyth, Robert Leeper and Tom Clarke   PROPRIETOR: Andy Blyth   OPEN: Tue to Sun L 12 to 2, Tue to Sat D 7 to 9.30   CLOSED: D 25 Dec, 26 Dec, 1 Jan, bank hols   MEALS: alc exc Sun L (main courses £13 to £20). Set L Sun £13.95 (2 courses) to £16.50. Light L menu available Tue to Sat   SERVICE: not inc, 10% for parties of 6 or more   CARDS: MasterCard, Switch, Visa   DETAILS: 68 seats. 20 seats outside. Private parties: 34 main room. Car park. Vegetarian meals. No smoking. Wheelchair access (not WC). Music. Air-conditioned

BOLTON ABBEY North Yorkshire   map 9

▲ Devonshire Arms, Burlington Restaurant ▮ ⅝✳

Bolton Abbey BD23 6AJ	
TEL: (01756) 710441 FAX: (01756) 710564	COOKING 5
WEBSITE: www.devonshirehotels.co.uk	MODERN BRITISH
at junction of A59 and B6160, 5m NW of Ilkley	£38–£108

A genteel separation of people is at work at this carefully renovated, lustrous country pile: the ramblers and tourists file leftwards into the brasserie, beer garden and general hustle and bustle, while the splashers-out veer right through the tree-lined car park and a main entrance full of fishing paraphernalia to the immaculate Burlington Restaurant, set with antique tables in various shapes and sizes.

As expected in this setting, Michael Wignall cooks grand, elegant, country-house dishes. A first course of rolled rabbit loin with pencil-sized cannelloni of osso buco, pea purée and button onions made an impact at inspection, as did a main course of cannon of sweetly tender lamb with tiny slices of liver, two sweetbreads, and many other small but powerfully flavoured items, including a battered anchovy. In between the two courses comes a soup – perhaps a delicate cream of butternut squash – and desserts are preceded by a sweet appetiser such as honey and lavender custard. The dessert itself might be something like a savarin of orange with orange parfait and blood orange sorbet. Service is mainly French and well drilled, with every last item in a dish being notified to you at table before you set about it. The wine list deftly manages to balance its imposing size with a welcoming approach. The trick is in the opening selection of 60 flavour-packed wines priced from £14 to just over £40, 23 of which come by the glass. For the committed and the curious the following pages light on some of the world's most celebrated wines, often in a range of vintages, but it may be more realistic to sniff out the many interesting options at less lofty prices.

CHEF: Michael Wignall   PROPRIETOR: the Duke of Devonshire   OPEN: Sun L 12 to 2, all week D 7 to 9.30 MEALS: Set L £27.50, Set D £58 to £75. Brasserie menu available all week L and D, bar menu available Mon to Sat L   SERVICE: not inc, card slips closed   CARDS: Amex, Delta, Diners, MasterCard, Switch, Visa DETAILS: 70 seats. 24 seats outside. Private parties: 6 to 90 private rooms. Car park. Children's helpings. No smoking. Wheelchair access (also WC). No music   ACCOMMODATION: 41 rooms, all with bath/shower. TV. Phone. B&B £160 to £380. Rooms for disabled. Baby facilities. Swimming pool. Fishing

BONCHURCH Isle of Wight · map 2

Pond Café ┃ NEW ENTRY ┃

Bonchurch Village Road, Bonchurch PO38 1RG
TEL/FAX: (01983) 855666
WEBSITE: www.pondcafe.com

COOKING 4
MODERN ANGLO-FRENCH
£26–£66

At the end of a steep, winding road carved into the cliffs, Bonchurch is a pretty little village with a picturesque church, and, directly opposite the village pond, this restaurant which has made quite a splash on the Isle. There's a small, neat terrace with a few tables outside, while inside, white walls with glass wall lights, dark leather chairs and white-damask-covered tables create a sophisticated, minimalist feel. Menus are led by local, seasonal produce, though the main source of inspiration in the cooking is the Mediterranean. Careful technique and well-balanced, restrained flavours mark out starters such as a ragoût of sweet, succulent mussels in a creamy sauce with lemon and garlic, and a warm salad of roast scallops with crispy bacon and a swirl of light avocado emulsion. Among main courses, 'plump, firm and meltingly tender' whole roast sea bass arrives with chunky, golden chips and hollandaise, while crisp roasted New Forest chicken, served on smooth, herby mash with a colourful mix of summer vegetables and a sharp sherry sauce, shows that meat is handled as competently as fish. Service is 'very personable', showing a good blend of social and professional skills. The wine list spans the world in under 30 attractively priced bottles and makes room for some sophisticated names. House French is £12.50.

CHEF/PROPRIETOR: David Thomson   OPEN: all week 12 to 3, 6 to 10   CLOSED: Mon and Sun D Nov to end Mar   MEALS: alc (main courses £10 to £22.50). Set L £19.50   SERVICE: not inc   CARDS: Amex, Delta, MasterCard, Switch, Visa   DETAILS: 30 seats. 16 seats outside. Private parties: 30 main room, 6 to 12 private rooms. Vegetarian meals. Children's helpings. Wheelchair access (not WC). Music. No mobile phones

'The waitresses seemed incapable of smiling, and even the question "Was everything OK?" was asked with body language and facial expression that seemed to mean, "If you don't like the food, nobody cares…".' (On eating in London)

BOROUGHBRIDGE North Yorkshire   map 9

Dining Room ▼ ⅝✳

20 St James's Square, Boroughbridge YO51 9AR   COOKING 4
TEL/FAX: (01423) 326426   MODERN BRITISH
                                                            £30–£45

In a terrace on Boroughbridge's Georgian main square, this is the kind of comfortable, relaxing place that attracts faithful regulars through its high standards, professionalism and warmth. Up a steep, narrow staircase is the bar-lounge: surprisingly large, with fireplace, deep-red walls, dark floorboards and an eclectic collection of sofas and armchairs. The ground-floor dining room has a more restrained and modern feeling, where white walls, blond-wood chairs and well-spaced white-clothed tables are set against a navy carpet. Lisa Astley ably handles front-of-house, while husband Chris cooks a sensibly compact, enticing menu, suitably contemporary and using sound quality produce carefully presented. After carrot, honey and ginger soup, or seared king prawns in a Thai-style sauce, there may be honey-roast confit of duck with an apple compote laced with Calvados, or pan-fried fillet of sea bass plus roast artichokes and a warm Mediterranean-style olive oil dressing. Finish with Yorkshire rhubarb and liquorice ice cream. The sound international wine list fits in with the grown-up modernity, starting at £12.50 and including a well-chosen handful of French classics. There are ten by the glass (from £3.20) and an impressive showing of half-bottles.

CHEF: Christopher Astley   PROPRIETORS: Christopher and Lisa Astley   OPEN: Sun L 12 to 2, Tue to Sat D 7 to 9.30   MEALS: alc L (main courses £10 to £14.50). Set D £20.95 (2 courses) to £24.95   SERVICE: not inc, card slips closed   CARDS: Delta, MasterCard, Switch, Visa   DETAILS: 32 seats. Private parties: 36 main room. Vegetarian meals. Children's helpings. No smoking. Wheelchair access (not WC). Music. No mobile phones   (£5)

BOUGHTON LEES Kent   map 3

▲ Eastwell Manor ⅝✳

Eastwell Park, Boughton Lees TN25 4HR
TEL: (01233) 213000   FAX: (01233) 213017   COOKING 3
WEBSITE: www.eastwellmanor.co.uk   ANGLO-FRENCH
on A251, 3m N of Ashford   £28–£99

Eastwell Manor is one of those grand old country houses that nowadays does much service as a venue for weddings and conferences. And with acres of immaculate formal gardens on the outside and swaths of Tudor oak panelling, tapestries and fireplaces within, it really looks the part. There are two dining options: the Brasserie, with its terrace for al fresco eating and live jazz band, and the Manor Restaurant, which offers the full-blown fine dining experience. Classic techniques inform the restaurant kitchen's straightforward modern British style, so starters range from a terrine of roast sardines to a warm salad of quail, roast sweetbreads and foie gras, while main courses take in pan-fried wild salmon fillet in mussel and basil broth alongside pot-roast squab pigeon with fricassee of peas and pancetta, and to finish there might be vanilla crème brûlée. The wine list is peppered with big names and three-figure price tags, but there is also room for a few more modest bottles, including a dozen house selections from £15.

CHEFS: Neil Wiggins, John Thorpe, Lloyd Cremer and Oliver Joyce   PROPRIETORS: Mr and Mrs J. Parrett
OPEN: Mon to Sat 12 to 2, 7 to 9.30 (10 Fri and Sat), Sun 12.30 to 2.30, 7 to 9.30   MEALS: alc (main courses
£25.50 to £38). Set L Mon to Sat £10 (2 courses) to £15, Set L Sun £24.50, Set D £37.50. Bar menu
available   SERVICE: not inc   CARDS: Amex, Delta, Diners, MasterCard, Switch, Visa   DETAILS: 70 seats.
Private parties: 82 main room, 6 to 120 private rooms. Car park. Vegetarian meals. Children's helpings.
Jacket and tie at D. No smoking. Wheelchair access (not WC). Music. No mobile phones
ACCOMMODATION: 62 rooms, all with bath/shower. TV. Phone. B&B £160 to £365. Rooms for disabled.
Baby facilities. Swimming pool (£5)

BOWNESS-ON-WINDERMERE Cumbria   map 8

▲ Linthwaite House ♥ ⅝✳

Crook Road, Bowness-on-Windermere LA23 3JA
TEL: (015394) 88600   FAX: (015394) 88601 | NEW CHEF |
WEBSITE: www.linthwaite.com   MODERN BRITISH
off B5284, ¾m S of Bowness, near Windermere golf club   £25–£66

The conservatory is probably the place to begin, with its fine views over Lake Windermere
towards the Fairfield and Coniston mountain ranges, but the rooms at Linthwaite are all
warm and welcoming. The two dining rooms have spacious tables with elegant lamps,
mirror-lined walls, and high-backed, comfortable chairs. Mike Bevans runs a tight ship out
front, chatting to guests with amiable ease, and, just as we go to press, he has appointed a
new chef. The format of a daily-changing, set-price dinner menu of modern British food,
with no supplements other than for cheese as an extra course, is likely to continue.
Previous menus have seen starters such as seared scallops with cauliflower purée and crisp
pancetta, or home-cured salmon dressed with lemon, shallots and chives, followed by an
intervening soup, then a main course such as venison from the Holker Hall estate with
beetroot cubes, a mashed potato and vegetable cake, and whole roast shallots. To finish,
there have been old favourites such as bread-and-butter pudding made with plenty of
custard and dried apricots. The wine list, starting at £16, is solid and fair value, with lots of
modern names and a particular penchant for New Zealand Sauvignon Blanc. A slate of
mature clarets rounds things off with a flourish.

CHEF: Simon Bolsover   PROPRIETOR: Mike Bevans   OPEN: all week 12.30 to 1.30, 7 to 9   MEALS: alc L
(main courses £6.50 to £15). Set L Mon to Sat £13.50, Set L Sun £17.95, Set D £42. Light L menu available
Mon to Sat   SERVICE: not inc, card slips closed   CARDS: Amex, Delta, Diners, MasterCard, Switch, Visa
DETAILS: 60 seats. 20 seats outside. Private parties: 40 main room, 16 to 40 private rooms. Car park.
Vegetarian meals. Children's helpings. No children under 7 after 7pm. No smoking. Wheelchair access
(also WC). Music. No mobile phones   ACCOMMODATION: 26 rooms, all with bath/shower. TV. Phone. B&B
£99 to £315. Rooms for disabled. Baby facilities. Fishing (£5)

BRADFORD West Yorkshire   map 8

Akbar's ⅝✳

1276 Leeds Road, Thornbury, Bradford BD3 8LF   COOKING 2
TEL: (01274) 773311   FAX: (01274) 785760   INDIAN
WEBSITE: www.akbars.co.uk   £18–£36

'An institution, almost a phenomenon', says one devotee who regularly makes a 90-mile
round trip to this cracking Bradford Indian. And it's 'an absolute hive of activity' in the bar
and packed dining halls, so be sure to book. Don't expect new-wave posturing; this
kitchen delivers gold-standard North Indian and Pakistani classics at knockdown prices,

with a few specials on top (lamb lumbet is cooked with chunks of homemade cheese). Meat is meltingly tender, and there's a telling use of spices throughout. Baltis loom large, starters continue to intrigue (chicken liver tikka, and squid in batter, for example), and prawn Madras is a definitive example of how to make a hot curry without rough edges or harshness. House wine is £6.95, otherwise drink bottled beer. There's also a younger sibling in Leeds (see entry).

CHEF: Talib Hussain   PROPRIETORS: Shabir Hussain and Nazir Ahmed   OPEN: all week D only 5 to 11.55   MEALS: alc (main courses £4.50 to £8.50). Set meals available (min 8)   SERVICE: not inc, card slips closed   CARDS: MasterCard, Switch, Visa   DETAILS: 250 seats. Private parties: 50 main room. Car park. Vegetarian meals. No smoking in 1 dining room. Wheelchair access (not WC). Music. Air-conditioned £5

Mumtaz 🎄 £ | **NEW ENTRY**

386–400 Great Horton Road, Bradford BD7 3HS | COOKING 1
TEL: (01274) 571861   FAX: (01274) 501201 | KASHMIRI
WEBSITE: www.mumtaz.co.uk | £19–£49

Finding Mumtaz, on Bradford's outer ring road, can be tricky, but bright neon signs help pinpoint the converted stone terrace. Beyond a take-away sales area with own-brand produce on display (pickles, sweets and ready meals), numerous dining areas on different levels have décor posher than the norm: marble floors and attractive modern furniture. The menu is essentially Kashmiri – with many karahi-cooked dishes, like cod in a pleasantly sharp pomegranate and garlic sauce – but draws on other regions for subtly spiced shami kebabs; crisp, non-greasy chicken pakoras; and rich, creamy vegetable korma. Alcohol is not allowed on the premises, but the salt lassi is recommended.

CHEFS: Tasawar Ali and Habib Yasin   PROPRIETOR: Mumtaz Khan Partnership   OPEN: all week 11am to midnight (1 Fri and Sat)   MEALS: alc (main courses £6.50 to £11.50). Set L £15.50, Set D £22.50   SERVICE: not inc   CARDS: Amex, Delta, Diners, MasterCard, Switch, Visa   DETAILS: 500 seats. Private parties: 350 main room, 1 to 350 private rooms. Vegetarian meals. Car park. No smoking. Wheelchair access (also WC). Music. Air-conditioned

BRAMPTON Cambridgeshire | map 6

▲ Grange Hotel 🍷 🎄

115 High Street, Brampton PE28 4RA | COOKING 2
TEL: (01480) 459516   FAX: (01480) 459391 | MODERN EUROPEAN
WEBSITE: www.grangehotelbrampton.com | £27–£51

Built as a private house in 1773, later a girls' school and now a hotel, restaurant and bar, this red-brick building is kept in good order and run by helpful, efficient staff. The menus offered in the modern dining room suggest a lively imagination at work in the kitchen: slow-cooked belly pork is paired with chargrilled king prawns and a blood orange and five-spice dressing, while pan-fried John Dory and sea bass come with a clam and artichoke casserole and wild garlic leaves. Completing the picture are desserts like plum tart with sherry syllabub, plus cheeses from Jeroboam's. Those wanting lunch in the comfortably sedate bar might be treated to satisfying dishes in similar vein, such as chargrilled cod with creamed parsnip and bacon rösti. To drink, there are East Anglian beers and a stimulating spread of wines by the glass at the head of a strong and good-value list arranged by grape variety.

CHEFS: Nick Steiger and Mark Caffrey PROPRIETORS: Nick and Susanna Steiger OPEN: Tue to Sun L 12 to 2 (2.30 Sun), Tue to Sat D 6.30 to 9.30 CLOSED: 26 Dec to 3 Jan MEALS: alc (main courses £7.50 to £17.50). Set L and D Tue to Thur £15 (2 courses) to £19.50. Bar L menu available all week SERVICE: not inc CARDS: Amex, Delta, MasterCard, Switch, Visa DETAILS: 40 seats. 12 seats outside. Private parties: 40 main room, 8 to 16 private rooms. Car park. Vegetarian meals. Children's helpings. No smoking. Wheelchair access (also WC). No music. No mobile phones ACCOMMODATION: 7 rooms, all with bath/shower. TV. Phone. B&B £65 to £90. Baby facilities (£5)

BRAMPTON Cumbria

map 10

▲ Farlam Hall ✱

Brampton CA8 2NG
TEL: (016977) 46234   FAX: (016977)46683
WEBSITE: www.farlamhall.co.uk
on A689, 2½m SE of Brampton (*not* at Farlam village)

COOKING 3
MODERN ENGLISH COUNTRY HOUSE
£47–£57

A partially creeper-covered country house with a tree-shaded stream running through the grounds, Farlam mixes elegant interiors with the kind of home-like feel in which a family-run hotel can specialise. The daily-changing, four-course dinner menus deal in the likes of confit duck leg on raspberry vinegar salad, or warm figs with Parma ham and goats' cheese, to start, followed by baked halibut on buttered spinach, sauced with white wine, cream and saffron, or best end of local lamb with rosemary, served with mashed potato and roast shallots. An English cheeseboard precedes a six-strong dessert menu, which ranges from dark chocolate tart to orange crème fraîche mousse with raspberry coulis. Five house wines at £17.95 (£4.75 a glass) introduce a list that spins briskly about the globe, and is mostly fairly priced.

CHEF: Barry Quinion PROPRIETORS: the Quinion and Stevenson families OPEN: all week D only 8 to 8.30 CLOSED: 25 to 30 Dec MEALS: Set D £34 SERVICE: not inc, card slips closed CARDS: MasterCard, Switch, Visa DETAILS: 40 seats. Private parties: 40 main room, 16 to 24 private rooms. Car park. No children under 5. No smoking. Wheelchair access (not WC). No music. No mobile phones ACCOMMODATION: 12 rooms, all with bath/shower. TV. Phone. D,B&B £137.50 to £285. Rooms for disabled. No children under 5

BRAY Berkshire

map 3

Fat Duck ▮ ✱

1 High Street, Bray SL6 2AQ
TEL: (01628) 580333   FAX: (01628 776188)
WEBSITE: www.fatduck.co.uk

COOKING 9
MODERN EUROPEAN
£52–£134

If a small village accommodates not one heavyweight restaurant, but two, they might as well be chalk and cheese. So, the Waterside Inn (see entry below) offers ultra-refined French classicism, the Fat Duck frontier-busting experimentalism. In a centuries-old house on a bend, in the lee of a large pub, the latter's solid wooden door opens into a low-ceilinged dining room filled with happy babble; here, ceremony is little stood upon, and it is the food that makes the splash.

Media brouhaha notwithstanding, Heston Blumenthal is not aiming to let anarchy loose upon the culinary world; rather, by the application of rigorous scientific procedure, to question traditional cooking techniques and to create tastes and textures that reawaken repressed gustatory memories, and the simple, unprejudiced receptivity of the child's palate. Fondly recollecting things like Pink Panthers (1960s strawberry-flavoured white chocolate chews) and butterscotch Angel Delight, he determinedly tries to induce regression to an earlier stage of taste (though he does not recreate those particular delicacies).

Two appetiser jellies arrive, orange and beetroot, with the instruction to eat the orange-coloured one first – but its sweet, vegetal pungency is that of beetroot, while the deep, purple-red one is made with blood orange. Pre-palatal expectations are neatly destabilised in preparation for what is to come, while registering the flavours the 'wrong' way round makes us think about them. Next, maybe an intriguing stiff mixture of chopped oyster, goats' cheese and truffle, wrapped in scales of paper-thin radish, sits alongside a rissole of fromage de tête and a quenelle of gribiche dressing. In another starter, lasagne encases a bright green pea purée containing fat langoustines, crisped julienne of pig trotter and black truffle, and sits in a caramelly brown stock reduction. The urge to amuse is never far away, and might surface in a main course of admirably tender veal kidneys cooked in Macvin, a fortified vin de liqueur of eastern France, but evoking another Mac, via its pile of croquette-like chips and spatter of intense brown 'ketchup'.

Incidentals evoke gasps and giggles, from the oyster in its shell set in passion-fruit jelly to the squidge of ice cream that turns out to be red-hot with mustard, and the presentations – especially on the Tasting Menu – are all part of the fun. (The green tea and lime mousse, which is sprayed onto a tablespoon and then sizzled in liquid nitrogen at the table, is surely one of the great restaurant performance dishes.) The sense of huge effort being expended, both in the kitchen and out front, is distinctly humbling, though, even if the lack of air-conditioning will prove a trial to some.

We wouldn't be performing our duty to our readers if we didn't mention that some find that sweetness (the preferred flavour category of pre-adolescence, after all) dominates many dishes, low serving temperatures can be poor friends of meat, and for a few it all seems like 'conceptualism run riot' – but perhaps these customers are simply discovering the limits of their individual gastronomic tolerance. Quite where wine fits into the picture is a mystery that may require some discussion with the wine waiter, who 'plainly loves her craft'. Several reporters have done well ordering from the 28 smart options by the glass (plus further ranges of sherries and dessert wines). Those who venture further will find an exquisite collection from famous and lesser-known regions of France, with stellar support from other countries. Prices are fairly high, with a baseline of £20.

CHEF/PROPRIETOR: Heston Blumenthal   OPEN: Tue to Sun L 12 to 2 (3 Sun), Tue to Sat D 7 to 9 (10 Fri and Sat)   CLOSED: 2 weeks at Christmas   MEALS: Set L £32.50, Set D £60 to £85 (whole table only)   SERVICE: 12.5% (optional), card slips closed   CARDS: Amex, Delta, Diners, MasterCard, Switch, Visa   DETAILS: 50 seats. Private parties: 40 main room. Children's helpings. No smoking. No music

Riverside Brasserie ▼ ⌂

Bray Marina, Monkey Island Lane, Bray SL6 2EB
TEL: (01628) 780553   FAX: (01628) 674312
WEBSITE: www.riversidebrasserie.co.uk

COOKING 3
MODERN EUROPEAN
£39–£60

Heston Blumenthal's other address in Bray is right on the Thames, part of the marina complex, and has outdoor tables on wooden decking making a summer lunch an immensely pleasant prospect. The ambience is of informal French village dining, with aluminium-topped tables outside and an industrious, open-plan kitchen the setting for the view of people drifting by on their boats.

Brasserie cooking is the order of the day, and the results are straightforward dishes with no illusions of grandeur. Potted pork with pickles, or baby leeks with hazelnuts and goats' cheese might be the curtain-raisers to poached salmon with lettuce and peas, or ribeye steak with bone marrow and first-class chips. Chicken liver and foie gras mousse has been 'exceedingly good, perfectly rich and balanced', while spaghettini with cockles is given extra kick by judicious use of chillies. Fine pastry work has produced dessert successes in the shapes of lemon and chocolate tarts, or there is pear poached in red wine. It is to be hoped that reports of sliding standards following a change of kitchen personnel in early 2004 marked only a momentary blip. The wine list is a compact line-up of quality bottles from £18. Not the cheapest, but there's no slack here.

CHEF: Garrey Dawson   PROPRIETORS: Heston Blumenthal, Lee Dixon and Alfie Hitchcock   OPEN: Tue to Sun L 12 to 3, Tue to Sat D 6.30 to 10   MEALS: alc exc Sun L (main courses £12 to £16). Set L Sun £23.50 (2 courses) to £28.50   SERVICE: 12.5% (optional)   CARDS: Amex, Delta, Diners, MasterCard, Switch, Visa   DETAILS: 40 seats. 80 seats outside. Private parties: 40 main room. Car park. Children's helpings. No cigars/pipes. Wheelchair access (not WC). Music

▲ Waterside Inn

Ferry Road, Bray SL6 2AT   COOKING 8
TEL: (01628) 620691   FAX: (01628) 784710   FRENCH
WEBSITE: www.waterside-inn.co.uk   £57–£187

From outside, the Waterside Inn is just a smart whitewashed cottage on the Thames, down a Berkshire lane. Inside, though, one is immediately reminded just how good service can be; meeting and greeting is a flawless balance of courtesy and warmth, and the chivalrous tone is worth relaxing into.

The cooking, jointly overseen by Michel Roux and son Alain, is profoundly classical. Many methods and presentations are straight Escoffier, lightly dusted with contemporary ingredients like galangal, pak choi and star anise. A serving-table is wheeled up, and a hunk of oxtail and one of beef cheek, glossy and black as rain-soaked logs, are lifted from copper pan to plate and the braising liquor (hours ago it was Beaujolais) spooned around, along with button onions, thick smoked lardons, tiny mushrooms, and a parsley-fringed lozenge of fried bread. The meats are luscious, sinewy but soft, crammed with exciting flavour. A November seasonal game pairing was similarly rewarding, both woodcock and venison judiciously high, and hence tender, served with glazed pumpkin and sauce poivrade.

First courses keep things light, with tomato and basil galette garnished with creamy scrambled egg, or a pretty-looking salad of expertly de-shelled lobster dressed in orange mayonnaise, dotted with Sevruga, and served with crunchy citrus couscous. Desserts, too, do their utmost to impress, with the mousse au chocolat unexpectedly secreting apricot coulis, while a tarte Tatin of juicy pear, gentled with cinnamon ice cream, is among the best to be had.

Dishes at these prices need to deliver consistent impact on the palate, and, for example, a spectacularly risen first-course soufflé of smoked haddock with a poached egg inside, and sparse pieces of fish rather lost amid billows of neutralising egg-white, failed to do so for one inspector, although the technical virtuosity was admired. Wines are all of a muchness, the list crowded with mature classics in three figures and four. Look to halves (from £11 for the proprietor's own Côtes de Provence) if resources can't compete. House wines are £32 to £48. This is a benchmark restaurant, inspiring both awe and warm loyalty in its inevitably well-heeled constituency.

CHEFS: Michel Roux and Alain Roux   PROPRIETOR: Michel Roux   OPEN: Wed to Sun 12 to 2 (2.30 Sun), 7 to 10   CLOSED: 26 Dec to 27 Jan   MEALS: alc (main courses £36 to £52). Set L £40 to £85, Set L Sun £56. Set

D £85   SERVICE: 12.5% (optional), card slips closed   CARDS: Amex, Delta, Diners, MasterCard, Switch, Visa   DETAILS: 75 seats. Private parties: 80 main room, 6 to 10 private rooms. Car park. Vegetarian meals. No children under 12. No cigars. Wheelchair access (not WC). No music. No mobile phones   ACCOMMODATION: 9 rooms, all with bath/shower. TV. Phone. B&B £160 to £205. No children under 12

BRIDGE Kent   map 3

White Horse Inn £✳

53 High Street, Bridge CT4 5LA	COOKING 4
TEL: (01227) 830249 FAX: (01227) 832351	MODERN BRITISH
WEBSITE: www.whitehorsebridge.co.uk	£24–£66

On the main road through this spread-out village, the White Horse is a substantial inn of some antiquity. Old beams are set off against dark red walls and dark polished floorboards in the bar, while the dining room has a bright and airy feel. Bar food keeps things simple but is a cut above average pub grub, while the restaurant menu shows more serious intentions. Local seasonal produce is to the fore – note the list of suppliers – although a broad range of contemporary influences are evident in Ben Walton's cooking. Pressed oxtail terrine with beetroot relish and mustard dressing is a typically forthright starter, and main courses continue in similar vein with a ragoût of fish and shellfish with tarragon, wild mushrooms and braised endive, or honeyed duck breast with braised Puy lentils and an apple and green peppercorn sauce. Meals are embellished with well-crafted canapés, appetisers, sorbets and petits fours, but save room for desserts such as prune and treacle tart with roast nut custard. The focus of the wine list is clearly on good-value easy-drinking modern wines to match the food. House selections are around £12.50.

CHEF: Ben Walton   PROPRIETOR: Alan Walton   OPEN: Tue to Sun L 12 to 2, Tue to Sat D 7 to 9   CLOSED: 29 and 30 Dec, 1 and 2 Jan   MEALS: alc exc Sun L (main courses £12.50 to £21). Set L Tue to Sat £12.50, Set L Sun £23.50, Set D Tue to Thur £19.50, Set D Fri and Sat £23.50. Bar menu available   SERVICE: not inc, card slips closed   CARDS: Delta, MasterCard, Switch, Visa   DETAILS: 35 seats. Private parties: 35 main room. Car park. Vegetarian meals. Children's helpings. No smoking. No music. No mobile phones   £5

BRIDPORT Dorset   map 2

Chez Cuddy £   NEW ENTRY

47 East Street, Bridport DT6 3JX	COOKING 2
TEL: (01308) 458770	MODERN EUROPEAN
	£23–£50

At the end of a row of shops, Chez Cuddy stands out for its stylish glass frontage next to the town's Chapel in the Garden. Inside is simple, uncluttered and minimalist, with well-spaced, white linen-dressed tables, a bar to one side, and plain walls hung with paintings (for sale) 'that for once are really worth looking at'. Young chef Adam Rendell utilises good raw materials alongside professional saucing and some bright, modern ideas. Crab and lime couscous, chilli jam and stir-fry vegetables could accompany crispy wild sea bass, while braised beans, Toulouse sausage and crispy cabbage might partner a confit lamb shank. Steamed fruit pudding with roast plums and vanilla sauce, and chocolate tart with candied kumquats follow the theme. Service is friendly and unpretentious (such as one would expect of a neighbourhood restaurant), while the short, simple global wine list comes in with bottles from £11.50 (£2.60 a glass).

CHEF: Adam Rendell   PROPRIETORS: Badir and Joanne Hadj-Aissa   OPEN: Mon to Sat L 12 to 2.30, Tue to Sat D 7 to 9.30   CLOSED: Tue to Thur D from Jan to Easter and during Nov   MEALS: alc (main courses L £6.50 to £9.50, D £9.50 to £15). Set L £12.50 (2 courses) to £15.50, Set D £25   SERVICE: not inc   CARDS: Amex, Delta, MasterCard, Switch, Visa   DETAILS: 36 seats. 4 seats outside. Private parties: 36 main room. Vegetarian meals. Children's helpings at L. No children under 10 in evening. No smoking area. Music

BRIGHTON & HOVE   East Sussex   map 3

▲ La Fourchette

105 Western Road, Brighton BN1 2AA   COOKING 2
TEL: (01273) 722556   FAX: (01273) 386710   FRENCH
WEBSITE: www.lafourchette-brighton.co.uk   £23–£43

A few doors down from its old location (now the North African focused Mascara, and under the same ownership), La Fourchette occupies a corner site with dark wood floors and tables and full-length glass windows allowing views of passing south-coast eccentrics. The menu is set out in two sections, meat and fish, and presentation shouts aspiration. Salads to accompany, say, duck pâté are 'crisp little salads, presented in dashing nouvelle style', and a single large crabmeat raviolo with buttered spinach, langoustine fumet and tarragon is artfully arranged on a large white plate. Moreover, ingredients are very fresh and well rendered: witness crisp-skinned 'roti' red mullet with tapenade, anchovies and garlic mashed potatoes, or excellent braised oxtail and accompanying courgettes. Desserts can be as French as chocolate charlotte with Chantilly cream, and service from a professional brigade keeps up a bustling pace. Bottles, from a decent wines list, start at £11.50.

CHEF/PROPRIETOR: Pascal Madjoudj   OPEN: all week L 12 to 2.30, Mon to Sat D 7 to 10.30   CLOSED: 26 Dec, 1 Jan   MEALS: alc (main courses £15). Set L £10 (2 courses) to £13   SERVICE: 10%   CARDS: Amex, Delta, Diners, MasterCard, Switch, Visa   DETAILS: 75 seats. Private parties: 40 main room. Vegetarian meals. No-smoking area. Wheelchair access (also WC). Music. Air-conditioned   ACCOMMODATION: 8 rooms, all with bath/shower. TV. Phone. Room only £60 to £150 (£5)

Gingerman

21A Norfolk Square, Brighton BN1 2PD   COOKING 2
TEL/FAX: (01273) 326688   MODERN EUROPEAN
                                                           £25–£54

Changes are afoot for the Gingerman team. While co-owner and executive chef Ben McKellar is involved in setting up a new restaurant within one of Brighton's seafront hotels (to open as we go to press), cooking at the original, small, pleasantly bustly venue is now led by McKellar's former sous-chef. Our inspector found perfectly competent renditions of foreign classics such as beef meatballs with spaghetti, or Thai red curry with monkfish, but not quite the sparkle for which the place was once justly celebrated. On a more ambitious night there may be warm rabbit salad with Puy lentils in hazelnut oil dressing, followed by smoked eel with spring onion mash, bacon and chive butter. It remains to be seen which way the menu will evolve. Desserts might include hot rhubarb soufflé with custard, or strawberry and white chocolate trifle. The wine list has fair choice below £20, with house wines – a Chilean Sauvignon Blanc and an Italian Merlot – £10.95 a bottle, £2.80 a glass.

CHEFS: Ben McKellar and David Keates   PROPRIETORS: Ben and Pamela McKellar   OPEN: Tue to Sat 12 to 1.45, 7 to 10   CLOSED: 2 weeks winter, 2 weeks summer   MEALS: Set L £12.95 (2 courses) to £14.95, Set D £22 (2 courses) to £25   SERVICE: not inc, 10% for parties of 6 or more   CARDS: Amex, Delta, Diners,

MasterCard, Switch, Visa   DETAILS: 35 seats. Private parties: 40 main room. Vegetarian meals. Music. Air-conditioned

▲ Hotel du Vin & Bistro ❙ ✳

2–6 Ship Street, Brighton BN1 1AD   COOKING 3
TEL: (01273) 718588   FAX: (01273) 718599   MODERN EUROPEAN
WEBSITE: www.hotelduvin.com   £32–£62

Brighton seems to have taken to the Hotel du Vin formula like a duck to water. Both bar and dining room are busy and buzzy most nights, and the combination of modern brasserie cooking and a serious wine list has proved a winning one, as elsewhere in the chain (see entries in Birmingham, Bristol, Harrogate, Tunbridge Wells and Winchester, with Henley-on-Thames to come). The global larder is raided for meals that might begin with a brochette of devilled duck hearts on couscous with apricot and coriander, or cecina (Spanish cured beef) rolled with fennel, rocket and goats' cheese. While there are some ups and downs in what is produced, the ideas are sparky enough, with maybe sautéed scallops and chorizo with braised split peas in red wine, or braised stuffed pig's trotter with truffled mash for main course. A list of 'Simple Classics' takes in anything from a plate of locally smoked salmon to cassoulet, and proceedings are rounded off with the likes of rhubarb fool, or lemon tart with raspberry sorbet. The wine list gives a masterful account of the global state of play. Wannabe classics like South Africa's Columella go head to head with the finest of the French establishment while at the other end of the spectrum there is plenty under £20 for the tighter of budget.

CHEF: Graham Ball   PROPRIETOR: Hotel du Vin Ltd   OPEN: all week 12 to 1.45, 6.30 to 9.45   MEALS: alc (main courses £14.50 to £19.50). Set L Sun £23.50   SERVICE: not inc   CARDS: Amex, Delta, Diners, MasterCard, Switch, Visa   DETAILS: 85 seats. 25 seats outside. Private parties: 36 main room, 2 to 14 private rooms. Vegetarian meals. Children's helpings. No smoking. Wheelchair access (also WC). No music. Air-conditioned   ACCOMMODATION: 37 rooms, all with bath/shower. TV. Phone. Room only £119 to £350. Rooms for disabled. Baby facilities

La Marinade ✳

77 St George's Road, Kemp Town, Brighton BN2 1EF   COOKING 1
TEL/FAX: (01273) 600992   MODERN EUROPEAN
WEBSITE: www.lamarinade.co.uk   £26–£53

This pleasant neighbourhood restaurant has primrose-yellow walls and lively, ingredients-led cooking. Nick Lang's rifles the world's larder, using everything from Spanish cured meats to obscure fungi; he also likes jazzing things up – tweaking potted shrimps with lemon and tarragon, or Mexicanising pork fillet with refried beans, sautéed plantain and mole sauce. Fillet of pike comes with a grain-mustard potato cake, capers, olives, Ortiz anchovies and beurre noisette, and roast milk-fed Pyrenean lamb rests on rocket and pecorino salad with roast Mediterranean vegetables and a pistachio and basil pesto. The pace slows with desserts like banana and sesame flambé, or crème brûlée. House Chileans are £10.95, and the short, world-spanning wine list offers choice under £20.

CHEF: Nick Lang   PROPRIETORS: Nick Lang and Kuldip Kaur   OPEN: Thur to Sat L 12 to 2.30, Tue to Sat D 6 to 10   MEALS: alc (main courses £13.50 to £17.50). Set L £15, Set D Tue to Thurs 6 to 7.15 £15   SERVICE: not inc, 12.5% for parties of 6 or more   CARDS: MasterCard, Switch, Visa   DETAILS: 40 seats. 10 seats outside. Private parties: 30 main room. Vegetarian meals. Children's helpings. No pipes/cigars. No smoking in 1 dining room. Wheelchair access (not WC). Music. 1 dining room air-conditioned

One Paston Place

GFG
2005
BRIGHTON + HOVE
COMMENDED

1 Paston Place, Brighton BN2 1HA
TEL: (01273) 606933   FAX: (01273) 675686
WEBSITE: www.onepastonplace.co.uk

COOKING **6**
MODERN EUROPEAN
£33–£80

In January 2004 the previous proprietors, the Emmersons, sold Brighton's star restaurant, having successively run and then owned it since the days when it was a subsidiary of Langan's Brasserie, London (see entry). The new chef is Francesco Furriello, a Neapolitan, who has brought some of the classical French technique for which the place was always renowned to menus that draw on Italian regionalism for inspiration, and the results are impressive.

The décor remains, for the time being, as before, a long, light, pine-floored room with many mirrors and well-spaced, smartly attired tables, but the level of culinary aspiration now seems rocket-fuelled. A crisp, flaky strudel filled with truffled mushroom purée, anointed with reduced balsamic and piped twirls of Parmesan cream, is a starter to assuage the keenest appetite, and yet the quantity is well judged. Another first course to impress has been a complicated tower of poached lobster, broccoli, tomato jelly and tapenade, surrounded by an expressively flavoured trail of lobster mayonnaise. If there was one blip at inspection it was with the slight overcooking of a piece of sea bass wrapped around langoustine mousse, but a dish of braised guinea fowl breast stuffed with foie gras, cleverly complemented by white asparagus ravioli and pieces of beetroot, was another undisputed winner. What inspires most confidence is the intimation that dishes have been properly road-tested from kitchen to arrival on the plate, an impression reinforced by desserts such as green apple bavarois with orange blossom ice cream, or soft chestnut cream interspersed with sablé biscuits, accompanied by earthy, intense pine-nut and orange ice cream. Service is enthusiastic but efficient with it. The wine list continues to develop, and while mark-ups are not the gentlest there are some fine bottles to be had. A quartet of French house wines comes at £16.50 and £17, or £4.25 and £4.50 by the glass.

CHEF: Francesco Furriello   PROPRIETOR: Gusto Ltd   OPEN: Tue to Sat 12.30 to 2, 7.30 to 9.30   MEALS: alc (main courses £19 to £24). Set L £16.50 (2 courses) to £19   SERVICE: not inc   CARDS: Amex, Delta, MasterCard, Switch, Visa   DETAILS: 40 seats. Private parties: 50 main room. Vegetarian meals. No children under 7. Wheelchair access (not WC). Music. No mobile phones. Air-conditioned

Sevendials

1 Buckingham Place, Brighton BN1 3TD
TEL: (01273) 885555   FAX: (01273) 888911
WEBSITE: www.sevendialsrestaurant.co.uk

COOKING **3**
MODERN EUROPEAN
£31–£43

The red-brick former bank building tapers to a point on one corner of the eponymous junction, and offers a muted, even sombre, interior of dark wood floor and undressed tables, a little leavened by changing artwork. After three years here Sam Metcalfe has now achieved a reasonable canter, with many dishes showing well. Roast loin of rabbit wrapped in Parma ham and stuffed with black pudding is a deftly rendered modern classic, and inspection dishes of spatchcocked quail on chopped Brussels sprouts, and pot-roasted halibut with button onions, mushrooms and spinach, were carefully timed and delivered plenty of punch. Desserts may well be the high point: don't miss Bakewell tart with clotted cream ice cream, or the passion-fruit bavarois. Service could do with waking up a little at busy sessions. Wines start at £12, and there's a good selection under £20.

CHEF/PROPRIETOR: Sam Metcalfe   OPEN: Tue to Sun 12 to 2.30 (12.30 to 3 Sun), 7 to 10 (9.30 Sun)   CLOSED: Christmas and New Year   MEALS: Set L Tue to Sat £10 (2 courses) to £25, Set L Sun £16.95, Set D £20 (2 courses) to £25   SERVICE: 12% (optional), card slips closed   CARDS: Amex, Delta, Diners, MasterCard, Switch, Visa   DETAILS: 75 seats. 50 seats outside. Private parties: 55 main room, 10 to 20 private rooms. Vegetarian meals. Children's helpings. No children after 7pm. No-smoking area. Wheelchair access (also WC). Music

Terre à Terre

71 East Street, Brighton BN1 1HQ	COOKING 3
TEL: (01273) 729051 FAX: (01273) 327561	GLOBAL VEGETARIAN
WEBSITE: www.terreaterre.co.uk	£31–£47

East Street is a prime Brighton location, between the Pavilion and the sea, on which this vegetarian restaurant has been a fixture for over ten years. The pale blue paintwork and large windows may well catch the eye of passing tourists, but the locals know what they have in Terre à Terre: 'surely one of the best vegetarian restaurants in the country'. The deceptively large premises is vibrant and contemporary within, and the same sense of creativity is apparent on the menu. This is modern vegetarian food, with the world as its oyster, delivering a lexicon of familiar and unfamiliar terms and ingredients in 'interestingly' named dishes: start with something as resolutely European as roast pumpkin risotto de Puy, or as African inspired as rizola (rice patties) served with Moorish slaw, tarragon mint and flat leaf parsley soft grain chop, finished with macadamia mayonnaise, Argan oil and mulberry caper hash. It isn't always obvious what is going to appear on the plate, but the composition and balance of each dish is usually successful, the flavours hit home, spicing is 'just so', and the friendly staff are always willing to help. Among main courses are 'kibbi our soles' (aubergine 'soles'), or 'yabba jabba beefy tea' (stuffed noodles), and the appealing desserts have included 'cigarillo majoolie' (a fried pastry filled with dates, frangipane and pomegranate, and served with frozen mint tea). Vegan dishes are marked as such, and the creativity does not cease with the drinks list: from cocktails to plenty of fresh juices, some interesting beers, and a wine list that starts at £15.25 (£4.10 per glass).

CHEF: Peter Winn   PROPRIETORS: Philip Taylor and Amanda Powley   OPEN: Wed to Fri L 12 to 3.30, Tue to Fri D 6.30 to 10.30, Sat and Sun 12 to 10.30   CLOSED: 25 and 26 Dec, 1 Jan   MEALS: alc (main courses L £7 to £12.50, D £11.50 to £12.50)   SERVICE: not inc   CARDS: Amex, Delta, Diners, MasterCard, Switch, Visa   DETAILS: 110 seats. 14 seats outside. Private parties: 20 main room. Vegetarian meals. Children's helpings. No smoking in 1 dining room. Wheelchair access (also WC). Music. Air-conditioned

BRIMFIELD Herefordshire   map 5

▲ Roebuck Inn   £

Brimfield SY8 4NE	COOKING 3
TEL: (01584) 711230 FAX: (01584) 711654	MODERN BRITISH
WEBSITE: www.theroebuckinn.com	£27–£47

On the Shropshire–Herefordshire border, the Roebuck still has some of the trappings of a local village pub, although the focus is now on its vividly coloured conservatory-style restaurant. Chef Jonathan Waters can clearly deliver the goods; his timing is assured, and the kitchen scores heavily with the quality of its raw materials: immaculate seared scallops on carrot and cumin purée with an orange dressing is a spot-on modern starter, while flavourful roast rack of lamb (with good fat) comes with cubes of roast sweet potato and a fine, stock-based vegetable broth. Several old stagers continue to grace the menu (fish pie, steamed steak and mushroom suet pudding), while simply conceived desserts include home-made ice creams and sorbets, marmalade queen of puddings, and three-chocolate terrine. Service is, 'in a word, nice'. The 40-plus wine list is peppered with good-value, interesting bottles, with four house recommendations at £11.

CHEF: Jonathan Waters   PROPRIETOR: Peter Jenkins   OPEN: all week 11.30 to 2.30, 6.30 to 8.30   MEALS: alc exc Sun L (main courses £10 to £17.50). Set L Sun £16.95   SERVICE: not inc, card slips closed   CARDS: Delta, MasterCard, Switch, Visa   DETAILS: 45 seats. Private parties: 45 main room. Car park. Children's helpings. No smoking. Occasional music   ACCOMMODATION: 3 rooms, all with bath/shower. TV. Phone. B&B £45 to £70

BRISTOL Bristol   map 2

Bell's Diner ♥ ⅝✶

1–3 York Road, Montpelier, Bristol BS6 5QB   COOKING 4
TEL: (0117) 924 0357   FAX: (0117) 924 4280   MODERN EUROPEAN-PLUS
WEBSITE: www.bellsdiner.co.uk   £36–£70

Looking coolly urbane and modern, in an area that is 'coming but not quite up', the physical appearance of Bell's Diner is in keeping with the kitchen's sophisticated repertoire. Fine raw materials, many of them local, include vegetables from a market garden outside Bristol, and Alan Sparks remains the main supplier of wild ingredients such as garlic, St George's mushrooms and woodland nettles. A high degree of technical competence suffuses everything, and although there is a daring element to combinations – teaming chocolate sauce with roast wood pigeon, and tangerine sorbet with asparagus – they are not outlandish. Starters include tournedos of monkfish with haricot beans, dried tomatoes and foie gras, and oysters with Bloody Mary, while main courses might take in roast Gressingham duck with sweet potato, braised turnips, baby onions, carrots and liquorice jus, or côte de boeuf with truffled potato purée, wild mushrooms, horseradish ice cream and a red wine jus. Chocolate features prominently among desserts, as in a fondant with parsnip ice cream (a combination that 'worked very well'), but there's also crème brûlée with rhubarb and beetroot. Service has been described as 'indefatigable'. One30, a funky tapas bar, is Christopher Wicks's latest venture in the city (see entry). The food-friendly wine list offers consistently high quality from around the world. Domaine du Trévallon from southern France gets a special feature, while house bottles at £12 are the budget range from another southern star, Mas de Daumas Gassac.

CHEFS: Christopher Wicks and Toby Gritton   PROPRIETOR: Christopher Wicks   OPEN: Tue to Fri L 12 to 2.30, Mon to Sat D 7 to 10   CLOSED: 24 to 30 Dec   MEALS: alc (main courses £13.50 to £18). Set L Tue to Thur £45, Set D Mon to Thur £45   SERVICE: 10% (optional), card slips closed   CARDS: Amex, Delta, MasterCard, Switch, Visa   DETAILS: 60 seats. Private parties: 20 main room. Vegetarian meals. Children's helpings. No smoking. Music   (£5)

Culinaria   [**NEW ENTRY**]

1 Chandos Road, Bristol BS6 6PG   COOKING 3
TEL/FAX: (0117) 973 7999   BISTRO
WEBSITE: www.culinariabristol.co.uk   £34–£44

Stephen and Judy Markwick used to own the renowned Markwicks restaurant in Corn Street, and are now back on the scene with an entirely different kettle of fish. Culinaria is a neighbourhood bistro, which also operates as a deli, offering prepared dishes to take away.

The interior is spacious and functional, with pale wood tables and plain floors. The weekly-changing menu is brief – four choices of starter and main course, plus six simple puddings – and the seasonal produce, much of it local, is of good quality. The robust yet refined flavours of starters such as ham hock terrine and chicken liver pâté might precede '70s-style classics such as chicken Basquaise, a generous portion flavoured with roasted red and yellow peppers and given a burst of flavour from chunks of orange. Finish with puddings such as gooseberry fool, or walnut and treacle tart with vanilla ice cream, or a couple of British cheeses. The wine list is short but interesting, with prices starting at £11.50.

CHEF: Stephen Markwick   PROPRIETORS: Stephen and Judy Markwick   OPEN: Fri and Sat L 12 to 2, Wed to Sat D 6.30 to 9.30   MEALS: alc (main courses £11.50 to £13.50)   SERVICE: not inc   CARDS: MasterCard, Switch, Visa   DETAILS: 30 seats. Vegetarian meals. Children's helpings. Wheelchair access (also WC). No music

Deason's ✸✶

43 Whiteladies Road, Clifton, Bristol BS8 2LS	COOKING 2
TEL: (0117) 973 6230	MODERN BRITISH
WEBSITE: www.deasons.co.uk	£29–£61

This tall Victorian end-of-terrace building isn't difficult to pick out on Whiteladies Road, with its large distinctive logo and name displayed high on the fascia. Neutral colours dominate much of the interior, with blond wood, fresh flowers and contemporary artwork. The overall effect is one of calm, which is assisted by well-spaced tables. Starters range from lemon and parsley sardines with roast plum tomato and olive oil sauce to confit duck leg with fig chutney and apricot dressing, while mains run to fried salmon fillet with crab and chargrilled fennel, or orange and ginger sausages with sautéed pig's liver and mash, or maybe a goats' cheese and butternut squash Tatin. For pudding, try baked polenta cake with citrus salad and basil ice cream. A fairly priced, thoroughly modern wine list eschews the big names but offers interesting bottles from across the world, starting at £13.75.

CHEF: Jason Deason   PROPRIETORS: Jason and Jodie Deason   OPEN: Tue to Fri L 12 to 2.30, Tue to Sat D 6.30 to 10.30   MEALS: alc (main courses L £8.50 to £12.50, D £13 to £20.50). Set D £17.50 (2 courses) to £21.50   SERVICE: 10% (optional), card slips closed   CARDS: Amex, Delta, Diners, MasterCard, Switch   DETAILS: 72 seats. 35 seats outside. Private parties: 45 main room, 12 to 45 private rooms. Vegetarian meals. Children's helpings. No smoking. Music. No mobile phones. Air-conditioned £5

FishWorks ✸✶

128 Whiteladies Road, Clifton, Bristol BS8 2RS	COOKING 3
TEL: (0117) 974 4433 FAX: (0117) 974 4933	SEAFOOD
WEBSITE: www.fishworks.co.uk	£28–£86

'A recipe for success' is how one inspector described the Bristol branch of FishWorks. The 'recipe' is to combine a quality wet-fish shop with a fish restaurant, and it's a formula that has been taken to Bath, Christchurch and London (see entries). The range of fish is enormous, from 'classic dishes' such as steamed River Fowey mussels with white wine and parsley or roast skate with black butter and capers to plates of fruits de mer heaped on ice. A daily specials board supplements the lengthy menu, and there are 'salads and sides' as accompaniments. The philosophy is to focus on light, fresh flavours. If customers are smitten by a particularly comely specimen in the shop, they can have it cooked to order on the premises. Reporters are enthusiastic about the quality of the fish, but value has not always been as highly rated. The wine list, however, has been put together creatively, focusing on fish-friendly whites from Galicia, Portugal and beyond. Bottle prices start at £15.25.

CHEFS: Matthew Prowse and Romero Costa   PROPRIETOR: FishWorks plc   OPEN: Tue to Sat 12 to 2.30, 6 to 10.30   CLOSED: Christmas, bank hols   MEALS: alc (main courses £8.50 to £35)   SERVICE: not inc CARDS: Amex, Delta, MasterCard, Switch, Visa   DETAILS: 54 seats. Vegetarian meals. Children's helpings. No smoking. Wheelchair access (not WC). Music. Air-conditioned

▲ Hotel du Vin & Bistro ▮ ✳

The Sugar House, Narrow Lewins Mead, Bristol BS1 2NU   COOKING 3
TEL: (0117) 925 5577   FAX: (0117) 925 1199   MODERN EUROPEAN
WEBSITE: www.hotelduvin.com   £33–£58

The Hotel du Vin Group continues its studied and considered expansion, with Henley-on-Thames next in their sights (see entries for Winchester, Brighton, Harrogate, Tunbridge Wells, Birmingham). At the Bristol site a seductively appealing feel is generated, with large bar, huge leather sofas and fashionable clientele. The restaurant (smoke-free, unlike the bar) has lots of pictures and posters – no trendy minimalism here. Bistro-style cooking occasionally nods to Italian influences – osso buco with saffron and gremolata, for example: luscious, rich, pink meat, enlivened by citrous gremolata. Pipérade comes with toasted country bread, while a spicy crab tian, based on first-class crab, may be complemented by pimentos and herb oil. Desserts feature unashamedly Anglo-centric comfort puds, such as a very superior spotted dick with custard, packed full of dried fruit and lightly spiced. Vegetables are extra, and some unevenness can affect the cooking at busy times, but service, from 'a rather formidable army of French staff', is willing and efficient. The substantial wine list, geographically arranged, is prefaced by sections flaunting champagne and 'prestige' bottles. The French listing doesn't linger excessively in Bordeaux and Burgundy and offers many good bottles from other regions; Italy and Spain fare well, while New World selections are good but less ambitious. Prices start at £13, and there's plenty under £20, though it's easy to get carried away.

CHEF: Rob Carr   PROPRIETOR: Hotel Du Vin Ltd   OPEN: all week 12 to 1.45, 6 to 9.45   MEALS: alc (main courses £10.50 to £17.50). Set L Sun £23.50   SERVICE: not inc   CARDS: Amex, Delta, Diners, MasterCard, Switch, Visa   DETAILS: 85 seats. Private parties: 60 main room, 10 to 30 private rooms. Car park. Vegetarian meals. Children's helpings. No smoking in restaurant, permitted in bar. Wheelchair access (also WC). No music   ACCOMMODATION: 40 rooms, all with bath/shower. TV. Phone. Room only £125 to £325. Rooms for disabled. Baby facilities

Lords ▾ ✳

43 Corn Street, Bristol BS1 1HT   COOKING 4
TEL/FAX: (0117) 926 2658   ANGLO-FRENCH
WEBSITE: www.lordsrestaurant.com   £35–£64

Down in a former bank vault in the financial quarter of old Bristol, reached via a marble staircase, Lords feels like a retreat from urban bustle. The chandeliers in the form of bunches of grapes may not be to everyone's taste, but Simon Searle's cooking has won firm converts. Tomato soup of rare, spicy intensity, and admirably chunky duck and foie gras terrine started off a lunch in fine style for one couple, nor did main courses of pork fillets sauced with white wine, and duck leg confit on lentils occasion any complaint either. Traditional European fish preparations have included provençale bourride as well as brill baked in cider with tomatoes, mustard and thyme. The crowd-pleasing approach that brings on seared calf's liver with mashed potato and smoked pancetta is bolstered at a meal's end by whisky and orange pannacotta with Drambuie sauce, or chocolate fondant pudding with vanilla ice cream. Enthusiastic and keen service is another asset, as is the wine list, including some 'very superior, excellent-value' options by the glass. Good pricing follows through to the bottles, where keenly chosen New World players rub shoulders with a handful of fine mature clarets and some well-chosen Burgundy.

CHEF: Simon Searle   PROPRIETORS: Hardev and Gurdip Singh   OPEN: Mon to Fri L 12 to 2, Mon to Sat D 6 to 9.45   MEALS: alc (main courses £15.50 to £20.50). Set L and D 6 to 7 £16.50 (2 courses) to £21 SERVICE: not inc   CARDS: Amex, Delta, MasterCard, Switch, Visa   DETAILS: 50 seats. Private parties: 30 main room. Vegetarian meals. Children's helpings. No smoking in 1 dining room. No music

▲ Michael Caines at the Bristol Marriott Royal ✳

NEW ENTRY

College Green, Bristol BS1 5TA
TEL: (0117) 910 5309   FAX: (0117) 910 5330
WEBSITE: www.michaelcaines.com

COOKING 4
MODERN EUROPEAN
£37–£90

The hotel itself enjoys a 'commanding' position in the centre of the city, with a lobby that is 'wonderfully grandiose without being pompous', and a dining room which pleasingly resembles an Italian piazza, with statues, stone arches and balconies from which Juliet should be whispering to Romeo. Michael Caines is not cooking here (he of Gidleigh Park, see entry Chagford, and the Royal Clarence, see entry Exeter), leaving the execution of his concept to Shane Goodway.

To start choose from the 'virginal purity' of pan-fried red mullet with Thai purée, or the 'earthy charms' of roast veal sweetbread with onion rings, cauliflower and garlic purée. Brill has been cooked perfectly, and a pan-fried fillet of sturgeon was, although diminutive, easily the star dish at inspection, served with leek fondue, caviar and vodka sauce. Vegetables are extra (and, given the portion sizes, are needed). Confit vine tomato with exotic fruit brunoise among the desserts might raise a few eyebrows; otherwise try three different takes on pineapple: pannacotta, carpaccio in vodka syrup, and with chilli in a sorbet. Four house wines at £16.50 are all there is under £20 on a concise international list, organised by grape variety and featuring two dozen champagnes.

CHEF: Shane Goodway   PROPRIETOR: Whitbread/Marriott   OPEN: Tue to Fri L 12 to 2.30, Mon to Sat D 7 to 10   CLOSED: 26 Dec to 7 Jan   MEALS: alc (main courses £17.50 to £28). Set L £17.50 (2 courses) to £21.50, Set D (whole table only) £57.50   SERVICE: not inc, card slips closed   CARDS: Amex, Delta, Diners, MasterCard, Switch, Visa   DETAILS: 70 seats. Private parties: 70 main room. Vegetarian meals. Children's helpings. No smoking. Wheelchair access (also WC). Music. No mobile phones. Air-conditioned ACCOMMODATION: 242 rooms, all with bath/shower. TV. Phone. Room only £149 to £305. Rooms for disabled. Baby facilities. Swimming pool

One30 £

NEW ENTRY

130 Cheltenham Road, Bristol BS6 5RN
TEL: (0117) 944 2442   FAX: (0117) 942 8913
WEBSITE: www.one30.co.uk

COOKING 2
MODERN EUROPEAN/TAPAS
£25–£46

Located in a 'bohemian' part of the city, One30 is a cavernous space with a no-nonsense, trendy look of wood floor, brick walls and exposed steel piping, with narrow teak tables and chairs softened, if that is the right word, by huge leather sofas in the bar area. The kitchen (the open-plan variety) knows how to put an enticing yet straightforward selection of dishes together. This sibling of Bell's Diner (see entry) deals in 'healthy-sized' tapas and eclectic modern European dishes on a good-value carte. Grazing through the former could produce 'beautifully crispy' patatas bravas, spiced aubergine salad, and fried goats' cheese with preserved lemons. Robust mains such as a 'devastatingly fresh' roasted skate wing with capers, parsley, crushed potatoes and broad beans, and a generously portioned dessert of roast almond tart with rosewater and cardamom ice cream, show standards remain high to the end. Service at inspection was slow but cheerful and courteous. House wine from Spain is £11.

CHEFS: Jake Platt, Johnny Evans and Christopher Wicks   PROPRIETORS: Chrisopher Wicks and William Bowen   OPEN: all week L 12 to 2.30, Mon to Sat D 6.30 to 11. Also open for breakfast/brunch, and all day for tapas   MEALS: alc (main courses £8 to £14.50). Tapas, breakfast and brunch menus available   SERVICE: not inc   CARDS: MasterCard, Switch, Visa   DETAILS: 70 seats. 25 seats outside. Private parties: 100 main room. Vegetarian meals. Children's helpings. Wheelchair access (also WC). Music (£5)

Quartier Vert ▼ ✷

85 Whiteladies Road, Clifton, Bristol BS8 2NT
TEL: (0117) 973 4482   FAX: (0117) 974 3913
WEBSITE: www.quartiervert.co.uk

COOKING 4
MEDITERRANEAN
£28–£63

While a determinedly southern European focus informs the cooking here, the admirable network of suppliers for seasonal British produce ensures that, in the words of one reporter, the place 'doesn't contribute to the fiction that we live in an eternal Mediterranean summer'. Choose from a number of separate eating areas for such first courses as roast pigeon breast with black pudding and braised lentils, or roast scallops with crushed minted peas and beurre blanc, before progressing to linguine of Cornish crab spiked with chilli and lemon, or Devon pork loin with roast carrots, curly kale, new potato mash and rosemary butter. High praise was lavished by one reader on a serving of confit lamb with pommes Anna, the 'fantastic mingling of lamb juices and soft potato making a sort of upmarket hotpot'. Finish with honeycomb ice cream in chocolate sauce, or one of the imaginatively chosen cheeses. Service is intelligent and on the ball. The wine list opens with a good range by the glass and, appropriately enough, is strongest in Mediterranean Europe. House Spanish red is £12.95, Italian white £13.95.

CHEFS: Barny Haughton and Jin Ren Huang   PROPRIETORS: Barny Haughton and Connie Coombes   OPEN: all week 12 to 3, 6 to 10.30   CLOSED: 1 week at Christmas, Sun D Oct to Apr   MEALS: alc (main courses £10.50 to £18.50). Set L £14.50 (2 courses) to £17.50. Café menu available   SERVICE: not inc, 10% for parties of 5 or more   CARDS: Delta, MasterCard, Switch, Visa   DETAILS: 80 seats. 25 seats outside. Private parties: 50 main room, 15 to 20 private rooms. Vegetarian meals. No smoking in 1 dining room. Music

riverstation ▼

The Grove, Bristol BS1 4RB
TEL: (0117) 914 4434   FAX: (0117) 934 9990
WEBSITE: www.riverstation.co.uk

COOKING 3
MODERN BRITISH-PLUS
£23–£60

A former police station in the historical harbour area, this waterside deli-bar and restaurant makes a striking impression with vast expanses of glass and steel. For light lunches, the more informal atmosphere downstairs is ideal, while the large, spacious dining room, with its terrace for al fresco dining, is equally unstuffy but also perfect for a special occasion (note that at weekends a more casual brunch menu operates). The modern approach applies equally to the cooking, where bright, bold flavours are the key to a simple but cosmopolitan style, starters ranging from fish soup with rouille to griddled tea-smoked quail with pak choi and a sesame and lime dressing, main courses from chargrilled ribeye with chips and béarnaise to roast cod with frijol negro beans, piquillo peppers, kale and almond aïoli. The wine list is a vibrant, up-to-the-minute global mix arranged by style, including ten astute house selections available by the glass from £3, £12 a bottle.

CHEF: Peter Taylor   PROPRIETORS: John Payne and Peter Taylor   OPEN: Mon to Fri 12 to 2.30, 6 to 10.30 (11 Fri), Sat 10.30 to 2.30, 6 to 11, Sun 12 to 3, 6 to 9   CLOSED: 24 to 26 Dec, 1 Jan   MEALS: alc (main courses £11.50 to £18). Set L Mon to Fri £11.50 (2 courses) to £13.75, Set L Sun £14 (2 courses) to £16.50. Deli-bar menu available   SERVICE: not inc, 10% for parties of 8 or more   CARDS: Delta, Diners, MasterCard, Switch, Visa   DETAILS: 120 seats. 20 seats outside. Private parties: 120 main room. Vegetarian meals. Children's helpings. No-smoking area. Wheelchair access (also WC). No music

BRITWELL SALOME Oxfordshire   map 2

The Goose ✳

Britwell Salome OX9 5LG   COOKING 4
TEL: (01491) 612304   FAX: (01491) 613945   MODERN EUROPEAN
                                                                         £25–£55

This modest sixteenth-century pub-turned-restaurant makes an informal yet upmarket stage for chef-patron Michael North's impressive cooking. Refurbished interiors are light and modern; blond-wood floors, matting, Roman blinds, pastel colours and white-clothed tables with solid, lightwood chairs create a relaxed, unpretentious atmosphere. The compact menu, too, is appealing and modern, flavours are clear and well defined, and portioning and presentation are as spot-on as the youthful service. Raw ingredients are from leading local suppliers: game from Well Place Manor Estate, for instance, which may appear as roast pheasant breasts with bubble and squeak and port jus, or quality breads from the De Gustibus artisan bakery in Abingdon. Fillets of Cornish red mullet and sea bream with grilled diver-caught scallop, soused vegetables and coriander cream might head the starters, alongside rillettes of confit Gressingham duck, while mains could feature a fillet of Scottish halibut with a green herb risotto, fennel and Noilly Prat velouté. To finish, maybe hot passion-fruit soufflé with glazed passion-fruit cream and passion-fruit sorbet. The compact, but comprehensive cellar yields 14 wines by the glass, 15 in half-bottles and vins de pays from £11.95.

CHEF: Michael North   PROPRIETOR: The Goose Restaurant Ltd   OPEN: all week L 12 to 2.30 (3 Sun), Mon to Sat D 7 to 9   MEALS: alc (main courses £14 to £17). Set L Mon to Fri £12 (2 courses) to £15. Bar menu available   SERVICE: not inc   CARDS: Amex, Delta, MasterCard, Switch, Visa   DETAILS: 50 seats. 30 seats outside. Private parties: 30 main room, 20 to 30 private rooms. Car park. Vegetarian meals. Children's helpings. No smoking in 1 dining room. Music £5

'The lady chef called through the kitchen hatch to my husband, asking if we were on holiday – and, on hearing that we were, grinned cheekily: "Well, smile then!" He wasn't amused. However, she got round him by (what else?) coming out and giving him a cuddle. He'd been on the receiving end of the occasional chefly handshake before, but this was his very first chefly cuddle. He rather thought he liked it.' (On eating in Wales)

BROADHEMBURY Devon map 2

Drewe Arms 🎇

Broadhembury E14 3NF
TEL: (01404) 841267

COOKING 3
SEAFOOD
£29–£52

In the 'somnolent' village of Broadhembury, north-west of Honiton, this cracking thatched pub takes straight-and-true fish cooking as its *raison d'être*, and the kitchen delivers: timing is sharp, accompaniments are complementary, not frivolous or overpowering, and there is nothing slapdash about its seemingly effortless results. Kerstin Burge hails from Sweden, hence the home-cured gravad lax and marinated herrings on the blackboard menus; otherwise, a tersely tasty line-up may embrace 'scallops – seared – mango chutney sauce', 'sea bream – orange and chilli', 'whole Dover sole – griddled – garlic butter'. As a finale, Swedish apple cake vies for attention with bread-and-butter pudding. There are also open sandwiches for those wanting a snack. Whites are a majority on the thoughtfully selected wine list, which starts with house French at £12.75.

CHEFS: Nigel and Andrew Burge   PROPRIETORS: Kerstin and Nigel Burge   OPEN: all week L 12 to 2, Mon to Sat D 7 to 9.15   CLOSED: 25 and 31 Dec   MEALS: alc (main courses £17). Bar sandwich menu available   SERVICE: not inc   CARDS: Delta, MasterCard, Switch, Visa   DETAILS: 45 seats. 50 seats outside. Private parties: 24 main room. Car park. Children's helpings. No smoking in 1 dining room. Wheelchair access (also WC). No music

BROADWAY Worcestershire map 5

▲ Dormy House 🎇

Willersey Hill, Broadway WR12 7LF
TEL: (01386) 852711   FAX: (01386) 858636
WEBSITE: www.dormyhouse.co.uk
just off A44, 3m E of Broadway

COOKING 3
MODERN EUROPEAN-PLUS
£31–£66

A view over three counties stretches around you from the garden of honey-coloured Dormy House, a country hotel done up in all the interior finery one expects in such surroundings, complete with large tapestry hanging on the dining room wall. Alan Cutler's style is centred on traditional English technique, shot through with the Mediterranean and oriental modes that comprise modern British cooking. Baked fillet of red mullet, crisp-skinned and fresh, comes with baby fennel and a tomato sauce to make a bright, refreshing starter. Main courses use quality meats to best effect, richly pairing Scottish beef fillet with a ragoût of oxtail and shallots, or supporting braised lamb shank with saffron and rosemary risotto, aubergine purée and a sauce infused with garlic. Finish with deep-fried filo parcels of apple and dried fruits, or, more simply, with the intensely flavoured, home-made ice creams (blackberry is the hot tip). Service could brush up its English. The wine list is good in France, but other selections look a bit off the pace. House red is £16, and a fair number come by the glass.

CHEF: Alan Cutler   PROPRIETOR: Mrs I.P. Sørensen   OPEN: Sun L 12 to 2, all week D 7 to 9.30   CLOSED: 25 and 26 Dec   MEALS: alc exc Sun L (main courses £20 to £22.50). Set L Sun £20.50. Bar menu available   SERVICE: not inc, card slips included   CARDS: Amex, Delta, Diners, MasterCard, Switch, Visa   DETAILS: 80 seats. 30 seats outside. Private parties: 160 main room, 10 to 160 private rooms. Car park. Vegetarian meals. Children's helpings. No smoking. No music. Air-conditioned   ACCOMMODATION: 47 rooms, all with bath/shower. TV. Phone. B&B £160 to £200. Baby facilities

▲ Lygon Arms ⅝✳

NEW ENTRY

Broadway WR12 7DU   COOKING **4**
TEL: (01386) 852255 FAX: (01386) 858611   FRENCH/EAST EUROPEAN
WEBSITE: www.the-lygon-arms.com   £52–£91

At the centre of a quiet Cotswold village, among a plethora of antique shops, is this old stone-built hotel. It is a veritable antique itself, particularly the great hall, now the main dining room, with its custard-coloured, barrel-vaulted ceiling and minstrels' gallery. Since early 2004 the kitchen has been under the leadership of Martin Blunos, who has in the past scored highly in the guide at his own restaurants in Bath and Bristol with a distinctive cooking style that blends high French with East European influences and a great deal of panache. His many commitments as lecturer, TV and radio personality mean he is not always present, and first impressions suggest that standards slip when he is not. However, his cooking still shows some of his old flair, with starters such as borsch terrine with sour cream, shredded beef and onion pirags (Latvian bread rolls), and confit salmon with lobster Russian salad and caviar dressing, and main courses of brill fillet with kipper mousse ravioli, Sauternes cream and curry oil, and roast best end and braised shoulder of lamb with tomato and thyme jus, featuring 'excellent, tasty meat'. To finish, there may be apricot froth with chocolate orange croquant biscuits and apricot sorbet. A dozen wines by the glass and two pages of 'sommelier's selections' open a wide-ranging and varied wine list that offers something to suit most budgets. House wines are £16.25.

CHEF: Martin Blunos PROPRIETOR: Furlong Hotel Group OPEN: Sun L 12.30 to 2, all week D 7.30 to 9.30 (6.30 to 10 Fri and Sat) MEALS: alc (main courses £17.50 to £26.50). Set L £26.50, Set D £39.50 SERVICE: not inc, card slips closed CARDS: Amex, Delta, Diners, MasterCard, Switch, Visa DETAILS: 60 seats. 24 seats outside. Private parties: 100 main room, 2 to 95 private rooms. Car park. Vegetarian meals. Children's helpings. No children under 6. No smoking in 1 dining room. Wheelchair access (also WC). No music. Air-conditioned ACCOMMODATION: 69 rooms, most with bath/shower. TV. Phone. B&B £119 to £495. Rooms for disabled. Baby facilities. Swimming pool

BROCKENHURST Hampshire

map 2

Simply Poussin ⅝✳

The Courtyard, Brookley Road, Brockenhurst SO42 7RB   COOKING **3**
TEL: (01590) 623063 FAX: (01590) 623144   MODERN BRITISH
                       £33–£50

Follow the sign on Brookley Road into the secluded courtyard to find the sibling restaurant of Le Poussin (see entry, Lyndhurst). The floor is of grey slate and the feel of the place is light and airy, the lack of formality enhanced by cartoons on the walls. A straightforward brasserie approach brings forth accomplished dishes such as a terrine of roast poussin (but of course) and foie gras with saladings and a mustardy dressing, and pot-roast loin and fillet of pork served with mashed potato, parsnips, carrots, and creamed cabbage. Fish eaters might opt for fillet of sea bass on a purée of Jerusalem artichokes, with sautéed girolles and a truffled beurre blanc. The rhubarb season has produced a fine cheesecake partnered by matching jelly and sorbet, or there may be cinnamon pannacotta with roast fruits. A concise, modern wine list opens with house Chileans at £13 (Sauvignon Blanc) and £15 (Merlot).

CHEF: Alex Aitken PROPRIETOR: Le Poussin Ltd OPEN: Tue to Sat 12 to 2, 7 to 10 MEALS: alc (main courses £10.50 to £14). Set L and D exc Sat D £10 (2 courses) SERVICE: 10% (optional), card slips closed

CARDS: Amex, Delta, MasterCard, Switch, Visa   DETAILS: 34 seats. 4 seats outside. Private parties: 30 main room. Car park. Vegetarian meals. Children's helpings. No children under 8 at D. No smoking. Wheelchair access (not WC). Music

BROMSGROVE Worcestershire   map 5

▲ Grafton Manor ⅚✗

Grafton Lane, Bromsgrove B61 7HA
TEL: (01527) 579007   FAX: (01527) 575221
WEBSITE: www.graftonmanorhotel.co.uk
off B4091, 1½m SW of Bromsgrove

COOKING 3
MODERN INDIAN/EUROPEAN
£28–£53

This ancient family pile is in an isolated spot at the end of a winding, narrow lane. Inside, it's all coats of arms, grand fireplaces, a sweeping staircase and high ceilings, although the dining room has a more domestic feel, with William Morris wallpaper and sentimental oil paintings. There's a strong Indian influence to the cooking, from nibbles of spicy prawn bhaji through to main courses of Bengal lamb curry and even desserts such as Hyderabadi apricots with mango and coriander sorbet. The rest of the menu has a more European character, as in a salad of chargrilled chicken breast with pancetta and blue cheese dressing, perhaps followed by pan-fried beef fillet on chargrilled leeks with minted broad beans. Execution is generally sound, but an inspection visit on what turned out to be the chef's night off proved uneven. Eight varied house selections under £15 open the France-centred wine list.

CHEF: Simon Morris   PROPRIETORS: the Morris family   OPEN: all week 12 to 1.30, 7 to 9.30   CLOSED: bank hols   MEALS: Set L Mon to Sat £20.50, Set L Sun £18.50, Set D £27.85 to £32.75   SERVICE: not inc, card slips closed   CARDS: Amex, Delta, Diners, MasterCard, Switch, Visa   DETAILS: 60 seats. Private parties: 60 main room. Car park. Vegetarian meals. Children's helpings. No smoking. Wheelchair access (also WC). No music. No mobile phones   ACCOMMODATION: 9 rooms, all with bath/shower. TV. Phone. B&B £85 to £150. Rooms for disabled. Baby facilities

BUCKLAND Oxfordshire   map 2

▲ Lamb at Buckland ⅚✗

Lamb Lane, Buckland SN7 8QN
TEL: (01367) 870484   FAX: (01367) 870675
WEBSITE: www.thelambatbuckland.co.uk

COOKING 2
MODERN BRITISH
£32–£57

True to its name, this pleasant Cotswold pub has lambs everywhere: as ornaments, as a carpet motif, and in various guises on the menu. Most of the action is on blackboards, and food orders are taken at the bar. Asparagus has been 'done absolutely to perfection', or there might be warm scallop, bacon and endive salad. Move on to a meaty roast pork with cep sauce, or tagliatelle con prataioli (with smoked bacon, field mushrooms, wood blewits, etc.), or seared sea bass on a prawn and asparagus risotto. Desserts are more typically English: steamed syrup sponge, perhaps, or a nostalgia-inducing junket. Service is informal and friendly, although a little brusque on occasion. A short, safe wine list runs from £15 to £28.

CHEF: Paul Barnard   PROPRIETORS: Paul and Peta Barnard   OPEN: Tue to Sun L 12 to 2 (2.45 Sun), Tue to Sat D 6.30 to 9.30   CLOSED: 24 Dec to 6 Jan   MEALS: alc (main courses £10.50 to £18.50). Set L Sun £19.95 (2 courses) to £22.95   SERVICE: not inc   CARDS: Delta, MasterCard, Switch, Visa   DETAILS: 65 seats. 32 seats outside. Private parties: 50 main room, 6 to 18 private rooms. Car park. Vegetarian meals.

Children's helpings. No smoking. Wheelchair access (not WC). Music   ACCOMMODATION: 1 room, with bath/shower. TV. Phone. D,B&B £70 to £145. Baby facilities

---

BUCKLERS HARD Hampshire   map 2

▲ Master Builder's House Hotel, Riverview Restaurant

Bucklers Hard SO42 7XB	COOKING 3
TEL: (01590) 616253 FAX: (01590) 616297	MODERN EUROPEAN
WEBSITE: www.themasterbuilders.co.uk	£34–£59

In an idyllic setting on the bank of the Beaulieu, the Riverview Restaurant thoroughly justifies its name, particularly in the summer, when full use is made of the large terrace for al fresco dining. The beamed lounge offers more of the same view, but from the comfort of bold-coloured sofas and armchairs and the warmth of a big inglenook in winter. The walls of the dining room, with its blond-wood floor and ceiling, are hung with alluring David Bailey photographs of 1960s stars. A light, straightforward but appealing menu charts a modern course and allows quality ingredients to shine, as in a fillet of sea bass with new potatoes and fennel, or roast duck breast with duck rillettes, glazed carrots and a sauce of green jasmine tea. Finish with classic tarte Tatin with cider sorbet. A French-led global mix of wines is arranged into price bands, starting with a dozen house options at £13.50 – perfectly shipshape if a little short on adventure.

CHEF: Dennis Rhoden   PROPRIETORS: Jeremy Willcock and John Illsley   OPEN: all week 12 to 3, 7 to 10   MEALS: alc (main courses £11 to £17)   SERVICE: not inc, card slips closed   CARDS: Delta, MasterCard, Switch, Visa   DETAILS: 70 seats. 80 seats outside. Private parties: 70 main room, 40 private room. Car park. Vegetarian meals. No music   ACCOMMODATION: 25 rooms, all with bath/shower. TV. Phone. B&B £130 to £235

BURFORD Oxfordshire   map 5

▲ Jonathan's at the Angel ⚡✳

14 Witney Street, Burford OX18 4SN	COOKING 5
TEL: (01993) 822714 FAX: (01993) 822069	MODERN EUROPEAN-BRASSERIE
WEBSITE: www.theangel-uk.com	£30–£61

One correspondent remembered this old Cotswold-stone building as an 'atmospheric little pub quietly tucked away off the High Street', but these days it pays its way as a self-styled brasserie-with-rooms. Current chef/proprietor Jonathan Lewis has retained the traditional inglenook, old beams and carved settle, although classical lamps now illuminate the dining room. Most attention focuses on the blackboard menu above the bar, which advertises a regularly changing list of specials. The kitchen seems equally at home with pan-fried fillet of plaice with asparagus as it does with breast of guinea fowl with lemongrass sauce and pilau rice. Starters such as chunky chicken and game terrine come with home-baked bread, which arrives on a board complete with a knife for DIY slicing. Main courses receive well-judged accompaniments – perhaps roast partridge with herb polenta or 'meltingly tender' medallions of pork with rosemary and sherry sauce. Vegetables are fine, and to finish, reporters have applauded praline mille-feuilles, as well as chocolate fondant with milk chocolate mousse and white chocolate ice cream – although the Angel delight dessert assortment is also hard to resist. Ten house wines by the glass open the well-annotated list, which gives equal prominence to France and the New World. Service here continues to let the side down, although the consensus is that this is a 'high-class' setup.

CHEFS: Jonathan Lewis and Dominic Ash   PROPRIETORS: Jonathan and Josephine Lewis   OPEN: Tue to Sun L 12 to 2, Tue to Sat D 7 to 9.30   MEALS: alc (main courses £11.50 to £19.50). Set L £14.50 (2 courses) to £18.50. Light L menu available   SERVICE: not inc, card slips closed   CARDS: Delta, MasterCard, Switch, Visa   DETAILS: 34 seats. 25 seats outside. Private parties: 40 main room. Vegetarian meals (notice required). Children's helpings. No smoking in dining room. Wheelchair access (not WC). Music. No mobile phones   ACCOMMODATION: 3 rooms, all with bath/shower. TV. Phone. B&B £70 to £98. No children under 9   (£5)

BURNHAM MARKET Norfolk   **map 6**

Fishes 🍸✳

Market Place, Burnham Market PE31 8HE   COOKING **4**
TEL: (01328) 738588   FAX: (01328) 730534   SEAFOOD
WEBSITE: www.fishesrestaurant.co.uk   £26–£76

There's a relaxed bistro feel to this light restaurant overlooking chestnut trees in the centre of Burnham Market. Matthew Owsley-Brown is a keen advocate of locally available ingredients, of which perhaps the most obvious is seafood: whole Dover sole, for example, with shrimps, capers, parsley and nut-brown butter, or a bourride of plaice, cod and skate. At inspection, grilled diver-caught scallops struggled to stand out against their accompanying finely chopped chorizo and preserved lemon, but the main course of roast wild sea bass ('very good, very fresh') wrapped in dried ham and served with an 'unctuous, al dente' saffron risotto, spinach and balsamic jus was a perfectly balanced dish. Care is taken with mixed vegetables (charged separately on both the fixed-price lunch and dinner menus), including a well-made hollandaise. Desserts are pretty straightforward, along the lines of sticky toffee pudding with caramel sauce and sticky pudding ice cream. On the wine list, fish-friendly whites outnumber reds, with prices from £11.95 and a few good choices by the glass.

CHEF: Matthew Owsley-Brown   PROPRIETORS: Matthew and Caroline Owsley-Brown   OPEN: Tue to Sun L 12 to 2, Tue to Sat D 6.45 to 9.30   CLOSED: 10 days before and during Christmas, 3 to 24 Jan, last week June   MEALS: Set L Tue to Sat £15.50, Set L Sun £13.50 (2 courses) to £17.50, Set D £30   SERVICE: not inc, card slips closed   CARDS: Delta, MasterCard, Switch, Visa   DETAILS: 42 seats. Private parties: 8 main room. No children under 6 after 8.30pm. No smoking. Wheelchair access (not WC). Music

---

▲ Hoste Arms 🍸 ✳

The Green, Burnham Market PE31 8HD   COOKING **2**
TEL: (01328) 738777   MODERN BRITISH
WEBSITE: www.hostearms.co.uk   £30–£57

The village of Burnham Market remains essentially unchanged since Georgian times, and so, externally, does this huge old coaching inn on the green. Inside, though, it's the very model of a modern country inn, having a popular traditional bar with real ales and real log fires, and a more formal dining room where a long, brasserie-style menu offers eclectic modern British cooking with Pacific Rim influences. There's steamed Brancaster mussels in white wine and cream, or venison, chocolate and pearl barley sausages with bubble and squeak, or maybe pot-roasted ham hock with apple and Dijon mustard mash, rubbing shoulders with rare seared tuna on pak choi, ginger and lemongrass, and chargrilled pork belly with honey and soy. Vegetables are extra. Puddings range from treacle tart to rice pudding brûlée with Asian spiced plum compote. A substantial and extensively annotated wine list starting at £10.95 balances affordable options with fine clarets and some special Australian bottles. Ten by the 175/250ml glass cover all bases for £2.70 to £6.80. Expansion of the kitchen team is planned as we go to press, with a head chef joining executive chef Andrew McPherson.

CHEF: Andrew McPherson   PROPRIETOR: Paul Whittome   OPEN: all week 12 to 2, 7 to 9   MEALS: alc (main courses £9 to £16.50)   SERVICE: not inc   CARDS: Delta, MasterCard, Switch, Visa   DETAILS: 140 seats. 70 seats outside. Private parties: 70 main room, 14 to 24 private rooms. Car park. Vegetarian meals. Children's helpings. No smoking in 1 dining room. No music. Air-conditioned   ACCOMMODATION: 36 rooms, all with bath/shower. TV. Phone. B&B £78 to £236. Rooms for disabled. Baby facilities

BURNSALL North Yorkshire   map 8

▲ Devonshire Fell

Burnsall BD23 6BT	COOKING 2
TEL: (01756) 729000 FAX: (01756) 729009	MODERN BRITISH
WEBSITE: www.devonshirehotels.co.uk	£29–£47

High on a hill overlooking the winding River Wharfe, this tall stone hotel makes much of its 'glorious location'. Originally a 'club for gentlemen mill owners', the place now looks swish and modern: there are creature comforts in the bar and a shade more formality in the conservatory dining room tacked on to the front of the building. You can choose to eat anywhere from a menu that offers wholesome brasserie mainstays like ham hock and potato terrine, Nidderdale lamb steak with carrot and swede purée, and Scottish salmon with red onion and fennel salad. Desserts include the likes of iced white chocolate parfait, or warm prune and hazelnut tart. The lengthy wine list is bracketed by price, with Spanish house selections at £11.95.

CHEFS: Neil Waterfield and Haydn Laidlaw   PROPRIETOR: the Duke of Devonshire   OPEN: all week 11.30 to 2.30, 6.30 to 10 (9.30 Sun)   MEALS: alc (main courses L £9.50 to £14, D £12 to £15.50). Bar menu available   SERVICE: not inc, card slips closed   CARDS: Amex, Delta, Diners, MasterCard, Switch, Visa   DETAILS: 50 seats. 18 seats outside. Private parties: 70 main room. Car park. Vegetarian meals. Children's helpings. No-smoking area. Wheelchair access (also WC). Occasional music   ACCOMMODATION: 12 rooms, all with bath/shower. TV. Phone. B&B £75 to £170. Baby facilities

BURTON ON THE WOLDS Leicestershire   map 5

Langs ⅚✳

Horse Leys Farm, 147 Melton Road, Burton on the	
Wolds LE12 5TQ	COOKING 3
TEL: (01509) 880980 FAX: (01509) 889018	MODERN EUROPEAN
WEBSITE: www.langsrestaurant.com	£23–£51

It may be a surprise to find this well-appointed restaurant out in the wolds that fringe the Soar, just east of Loughborough. It was originally a farmhouse, and there are echoes of the past in its original beamed dining room, although the adjoining Wold Suite (added in 2001) strikes a contemporary note, with its uplighters and metal-framed chairs. Gordon Lang ventures towards the Mediterranean for culinary ideas but doesn't seek to impress with outlandish fireworks. To start, expect anything from Moroccan-style red mullet to ham hock and feta salad, while main courses could range from spicy chicken skewers with chorizo and butter beans to salmon with Parma ham and seared scallops, via best end of lamb with grilled kidneys and rosemary potatoes. Desserts like crêpes suzette and raspberry crème brûlée make a fitting finale. Good-value Sunday lunches centre on traditional roasts, and the wine list is a well-balanced selection with house recommendations from £12.75.

CHEF: Gordon Lang   PROPRIETORS: Gordon and June Lang   OPEN: Tue to Fri and Sun L 12 to 2 (2.30 Sun), Tue to Sat D 7.15 to 9.45 (10 Sat)   MEALS: alc (not Sun L; main courses £11.50 to £17). Set L £13.50 (2 courses) to £14.95, Set D Tue to Thur £16.50   SERVICE: not inc, card slips closed   CARDS: Delta, MasterCard, Switch, Visa   DETAILS: 50 seats. 20 seats outside. Private parties: 50 main room. Car park. Vegetarian meals. Children's helpings. No smoking. Wheelchair access (also WC). No music. No mobile phones

BURY ST EDMUNDS Suffolk   map 6

Maison Bleue ✳   NEW ENTRY

30–31 Churchgate Street, Bury St Edmunds IP33 1RG   COOKING 2
TEL: (01284) 760623   FAX: (01284) 761611   SEAFOOD
WEBSITE: www.maisonbleue.co.uk   £28–£66

An attractive French seafood restaurant in the historical centre of Bury St Edmunds, Maison Bleue is indeed blue, outside and in, the marine tones reflecting the orientation of the menu. Smartly turned-out French staff deliver dishes of exemplary freshness: a cassolette of black tiger prawns with artichokes and asparagus in garlic butter, perhaps, or a colourful salad of crayfish with a dressing of celery and Granny Smith. Be sure to consider the *plat du jour*, which might be pan-fried gilthead bream with ratatouille, accompanied inventively by celeriac layered with foie gras, or go with a classic combination such as monkfish wrapped in Parma ham served on aubergine purée. There are one or two meat options too, as well as favourite desserts like crêpes suzette and tarte Tatin. The wine list makes an honest effort to bring in wines from the southern hemisphere alongside the French offerings. House wines start at £9.95 a bottle, £1.95 a glass.

CHEF: Pascal Canévet   PROPRIETOR: Régis Crépy   OPEN: Tue to Sat 12 to 2.30, 7 to 9.30 (10 Fri and Sat) CLOSED: Jan   MEALS: alc (main courses £9.50 to £18). Set L £7.95 (1 course) to £14.95, Set D £21.95 SERVICE: not inc   CARDS: Amex, Delta, MasterCard, Switch, Visa   DETAILS: 65 seats. Private parties: 36 main room, 14 to 22 private rooms. Vegetarian meals. No smoking. Wheelchair access (not WC). Music

BUSHEY Hertfordshire   map 3

St James ✳

30 High Street, Bushey WD23 3HL   COOKING 3
TEL: (020) 8950 2480   FAX: (020) 8950 4107   MODERN BRITISH
                                                                £31–£59

Red walls enhance the warm, rustic feeling of this now well-established and confident restaurant. Dishes avoid over-elaboration and are generously sized, accurately timed and reassuringly consistent. Some are robust combinations like a starter of calamari, mussels and chorizo; others are marked by subtlety and careful balance, as in a layering of vegetables between fillets of turbot accompanied by a tomato butter sauce, which provided 'elegant flavour combinations'. Carnivores can try pesto-crusted beef fillet, or roast duck breast with garlic cream spinach and rösti; vegetarians are well looked after, too. Puddings such as toffee and banana cake with vanilla ice cream and toffee sauce, or raspberry brûlée, make simple and satisfying endings. Wines start with house Italians at £12.95, but prices rise steeply, and the straightforward list is short of detail on provenances and vintages.

CHEF: Simon Trussell PROPRIETORS: Simon Trussell and Alfonso La Cava OPEN: Mon to Sat 12 to 2, 6.30 to 10 CLOSED: 25 Dec, bank hols MEALS: alc (main courses £15 to £20). Set L £13.95 (2 courses), Set D 6.30 to 7.30 £14.95 (2 courses) SERVICE: 12.5%, card slips closed CARDS: Delta, MasterCard, Switch, Visa DETAILS: 80 seats. Private parties: 65 main room, 35 to 44 private rooms. Vegetarian meals. No smoking in 1 dining room. Wheelchair access (also WC). Occasional music. No mobile phones. Air-conditioned

BUXTON Derbyshire   map 9

Columbine ✖

7 Hall Bank, Buxton SK17 6EW	COOKING 2
TEL: (01298) 78752 FAX: (01298) 71651	MODERN BRITISH
EMAIL: www.columbine@btinternet.com	£26–£41

This Georgian house – 'colourful to say the least' on the inside – offers seasonal menus and local sourcing, with quantity and quality in happy union. Readers commend the 'friendly, relaxed service and atmosphere'. There's a vegetarian carte with three choices per course; otherwise start with Cullen skink, or a juniper-tinged game terrine with melba toast and Cumberland dressing. Move on, perhaps, to a main-course sautéed brill fillet with a fricassée of shelled mussels, saffron and white wine, or there could be a boned and roast rack of lamb with 'mustard seed-glazed black pudding and button-onion gravy'. For pudding you might try honeyed brown bread ice cream with shortbread. The short, mainly New World wine list has Duboeuf house wines at £8.95 (£2.50/£3.10 per 175/250ml glass) and, barely venturing above £15, eschews arm-twisting mark-ups.

CHEF: Steve McNally PROPRIETORS: Steve and Kim McNally OPEN: Mon to Sat D only 7 to 9.30; other times by arrangement CLOSED: Tue Oct to May, 24 Dec to 2 Jan, Feb half-term, week before end-Aug bank hol MEALS: alc (main courses £11 to £14). Set D in July, Dec £17 (2 courses) to £19.50. Light L menu available Thur to Fri in July (Buxton Festival). Pre- and after-theatre menus available SERVICE: not inc, card slips closed CARDS: Delta, MasterCard, Switch, Visa DETAILS: 45 seats. Private parties: 18 main room, 10 to 18 private rooms. Vegetarian meals. No smoking in 1 dining room. Music

CAMBRIDGE Cambridgeshire   map 6

▲ Hotel Felix ✖

Whitehouse Lane, Huntingdon Road,	
Cambridge CB3 0LX	COOKING 2
TEL: (01223) 277977 FAX: (01223) 277973	MEDITERRANEAN
WEBSITE: www.hotelfelix.co.uk	£27–£71

The Felix is a stylish hotel not far from the city centre, a rather striking, bow-fronted grey edifice, although the Graffiti restaurant is in a single-storey extension beyond the car park. A Mediterranean bent informs the menus, which might begin with an appetiser selection of Italian breads with oil infusions and pesto. Recherché ingredients abound, so you might begin with baby octopus ceviche, served with cherry tomatoes and dandelion leaves, before going on to strawberry grouper with basil mash, fried baby squid, chorizo, sweet chilli and garlic. A certain robustness is evident, bringing on pot-roast haunch of wild boar with braised red cabbage, or blade of beef with celeriac purée, and the dessert options include warm spiced apple charlotte. Italian and French house wines at £11.50 and £12.50 lead off a carefully annotated and reasonably priced list.

CHEF: Stuart Conibear PROPRIETOR: Jeremy Cassel OPEN: all week 12 to 2, 6.30 to 10 (10.30 Fri and Sat, 9.30 Sun) MEALS: alc D (main courses £13 to £25). Set L £12.50 (2 courses) to £16.50. Café/bar L menu available SERVICE: not inc CARDS: Amex, Delta, Diners, MasterCard, Switch, Visa DETAILS: 50 seats. 70 seats outside. Private parties: 50 main room, 8 to 60 private rooms. Car park. Vegetarian meals. Children's helpings. No smoking. Wheelchair access (also WC). Music ACCOMMODATION: 52 rooms, all with bath/shower. TV. Phone. B&B £128 to £265. Rooms for disabled (£5)

Midsummer House 🍴✻

Midsummer Common, Cambridge CB4 1HA	COOKING **6**
TEL: (01223) 369299 FAX: (01223) 302672	MODERN FRENCH
WEBSITE: www.midsummerhouse.co.uk	£44–£119

In the conservatory dining room of this small Victorian house, vivid colours – vibrant yellow walls, red and blue upholstered chairs, bright, modern paintings – soften the formality of setting and service, perhaps echoing Daniel Clifford's penchant for subverting his classical French training with avant-garde ideas. Initially, diners get shot glasses of palate-cleansing potions: a green tea and lime foam, say, or cucumber and smoked salmon jelly topped with cauliflower froth. Then maybe a starter of snail tortellini with parsley jelly, garlic beignets and yeast cappuccino, or tiger prawns with squid cannelloni, caramelised cauliflower and crab, shellfish foam and maple syrup; after that, pigeon with a pastilla of cherries, sweet potato purée, chocolate jelly and sauce Valrhona. Desserts can astonish, too, whether caramel chocolate fondant with lime jelly and coriander purée, or iced Baileys cheesecake with coffee chocolate mousse and orange sorbet bubbles.

The audacity pays off, thanks to excellent raw materials, impeccable saucing and timing, and clean, pure flavours. Several reporters jib at the expense, though, and some are not convinced by each and every flavour combination, while most are impressed, praising 'serious attention to cooking and a lot of very nice extras'. With all the exciting flavours premium Bordeaux may not be ideal, although there's plenty listed. Alsace, Austria, Burgundy, Champagne and the Loire all provide more appropriate gems, and only South America is under-represented. There are budget bottles, but prices are mostly too high for comfort. A dozen-plus serious contenders come by the glass from £7.

CHEF: Daniel Clifford PROPRIETOR: Crown Group OPEN: Tue to Sat 12.15 to 1.45, 7 to 9.45 CLOSED: 23 Dec to 11 Jan, 1 week Easter, 15 Aug to 6 Sept MEALS: Set L £20 (2 courses) to £26, Set D £45 to (whole table only) £60 SERVICE: not inc, 12.5% for parties of 7 or more CARDS: Amex, Delta, MasterCard, Switch, Visa DETAILS: 50 seats. Private parties: 50 main room, 10 to 20 private rooms. Vegetarian meals. Children's helpings. No smoking. Wheelchair access (also WC). No music. Air-conditioned (£5)

Restaurant 22 🍴✻

22 Chesterton Road, Cambridge CB4 3AX	COOKING **2**
TEL: (01223) 351880 FAX: (01223) 323814	MODERN EUROPEAN
WEBSITE: www.restaurant22.co.uk	£36–£59

David Carter's popular restaurant (in the Guide last year as 'Twenty Two Chesterton Road') in a green-shuttered town house has all the intimacy of a candlelit Victorian living room. Modern European food is the order of the evening, and the concise fixed-price menu can run to five courses if you include the supplementary fish course (grilled tuna with pineapple and chilli salsa, for example) and the mixed-leaf salad that follows. You could open proceedings with smoked pigeon breast with onion ravioli in balsamic dressing, then plump for something robust – say, roast pork fillet with cabbage and smoked bacon in thyme sauce – before closing the show with perhaps pear and almond parfait with a miniature pear Tatin. A dozen limited-edition 'specials' gild the wine list, which puts France first but also offers fairly priced selections from elsewhere. Four house wines are £12.50 and £13.75.

CHEF: Martin Cullum   PROPRIETOR: David Carter   OPEN: Tue to Sat D only 7 to 9.45. Also open L during Dec   CLOSED: 1 week Christmas   MEALS: Set D £24.50   SERVICE: not inc   CARDS: Amex, Delta, Diners, MasterCard, Switch, Visa   DETAILS: 38 seats. Private parties: 26 main room, 7 to 12 private rooms. Vegetarian meals. No children under 10. No smoking. Occasional music. No mobile phones. Air-conditioned

The Volunteer 🅸🌟

60 Trumpington Road, Cambridge CB2 2EX	COOKING 4
TEL: (01223) 841675 FAX: (01223) 846741	MODERN EUROPEAN
WEBSITE: www.volunteerrestaurant.co.uk	£34–£54

NEW ENTRY

Under new ownership since mid-2003, the Volunteer has made the transition to full-on restaurant but retains the external features of a pub, and boasts a car park, a rare luxury in Cambridge. Inside, décor is stripped-down and understatedly neutral, with white linen on the tables and upholstered chairs adding a touch of smartness. Start perhaps with grilled asparagus and quail's egg salad, enhanced by small pools of pungent tomato sauce, or maybe a simple but convincing slab of chicken and foie gras parfait. Move on to 'excellently cooked' organic salmon on tender young spinach leaves and saffron velouté, or 'perfect' noisettes of beef melting on a potato rösti fired up with grated horseradish. Cheeses are well kept, or finish with something like hot chocolate fondant with pistachio ice cream. 'A veritable riot of textures and flavours, cleverly contrasting richness with simplicity' was one reporter's summation after a spring dinner. Straightforward, professional service pays attention to detail, and house wine seems excellent value, with crisp, fruity Sauvignon Blanc for less than £12. Three dozen bottles, half European, half Anglophone New World, include decent, cheap, all-round claret.

CHEF: David Rideout   PROPRIETORS: Nick and Vanessa Cross   OPEN: all week L 12 to 2.30, Mon to Sat D 7 to 9.30   CLOSED: 26 Dec to 2 Jan, bank hol Mons   MEALS: alc (main courses £13 to £18.50). Light L menu available   SERVICE: not inc, 10% (optional) for parties of 6 or more, card slips closed   CARDS: Delta, MasterCard, Switch, Visa   DETAILS: 52 seats. 16 seats outside. Private parties: 60 main room. Car park. Vegetarian meals. Children's helpings. No smoking. Wheelchair access (not WC). Occasional music (£5)

CANTERBURY Kent

map 3

Goods Shed

Station Road West, Canterbury CT2 8AN	COOKING 3
TEL: (01227) 459153	MODERN BRITISH
	£27–£50

The cavernous Goods Shed – hard by Canterbury West Station – was the first farmers' market in the country to open every day, and it now sports an admirable restaurant as well. The result is a ground-breaking, symbiotic partnership between produce and cooking. 'Slow-proved' bread is baked in-house, a wondrous array of fresh vegetables is supplemented by 'free food' (including alexanders and fungi), and everything is handled without posturing or flimflam. Recent successes from the blackboard menu have included seared pigeon breast set atop a large field mushroom, and asparagus with a poached local duck's egg, before fillet of sea bass with anchovy dressing, and top-drawer ribeye steaks. Visitors have also applauded puddings such as a flourless chocolate cake with milk chocolate ice cream. Service is as chatty and friendly as can be – although one reporter thought some extra staff training might not go amiss. To drink, there are pilsners from Canterbury's Hopdaemon Brewery, locally made ginger beer and cream soda (which have replaced Coke on the menu), and a clutch of wines from £12.

CHEFS: Rafael Lopez, Nick Packer and Robert Cooper PROPRIETOR: Susanna Atkins OPEN: Tue to Sun L 12 to 2.30 (3 Sat and Sun), Tue to Sat D 6 to 9.30 CLOSED: 25 Dec, 1 Jan MEALS: alc (main courses £8 to £17.50). Set L and D £27 SERVICE: not inc, card slips closed CARDS: Delta, Diners, MasterCard, Switch, Visa DETAILS: 75 seats. Car park. Vegetarian meals. Children's helpings. No-smoking area. Wheelchair access (also WC). No music

CARLISLE Cumbria
map 10

Number 10

10 Eden Mount, Stanwix, Carlisle CA3 9LY
TEL: (01228) 524183

COOKING 2
MODERN BRITISH
£29–£47

Number 10 remains, in the view of one reporter, pretty much what it has always been: an unpretentious, honest restaurant with a cosy warmth to the décor, serving a solid, tried and trusted repertoire of modern British food at reasonable prices. Local and regional materials play an increasing role – 'we try to use and support local people whenever possible,' writes Isabel Ferguson – from Allerdale goats' cheese to local lamb. The style of cooking embraces the likes of 'full-flavoured' curried mushroom pâté, twice-baked Gruyère soufflé, swordfish with salsa verde, ribeye steak baked in a rich Guinness and mushroom sauce, and vegetarian options such as an individual provençale tart filled with roast pepper, aubergine, tomato and courgette. Desserts might include lemon posset, or raspberry and amaretti trifle topped with Amaretto cream and toasted almonds. Service is friendly, and wines are priced from £11.

CHEF: Geoffrey Ferguson PROPRIETORS: Geoffrey and Isabel Ferguson OPEN: Tue to Sat D only 7 to 9.30 CLOSED: Feb, last week Oct MEALS: alc (main courses £11 to £17) SERVICE: not inc, card slips closed CARDS: Amex, Delta, MasterCard, Switch, Visa DETAILS: 24 seats. Private parties: 24 main room. Vegetarian meals. No smoking while others eat. Wheelchair access (not WC). Music

CARTMEL Cumbria
map 8

▲ L'Enclume ▼ ⁵⚹

Cavendish Street, Cartmel LA11 6PZ
TEL: (015395) 36362 FAX: (015395) 38907
WEBSITE: www.lenclume.co.uk

COOKING 7
MODERN EUROPEAN
£42–£143

Unusual, this place: 'perhaps one of the most exciting, innovative restaurants we have ever dined at'. L'Enclume is in an old smithy given a clean, modern redesign that preserves rusticity in white plastered walls and flagged floor, and offers seven smart and contemporary bedrooms. Tasting menus of seven to some twenty small courses are a speciality, but there is also a three-course carte for those who like choosing for themselves, and a set lunch.

Simon Rogan's innovative concepts are supported by sound techniques, impeccable sourcing of local supplies, and unusual spices and flavourings that bring vigour and surprise. One diner's pre-starter set the tone: a trio of shot glasses containing, respectively, purée of butternut squash topped by cumin froth, couscous with tomato under a square of black olive jelly, and pea velouté with a cigarette-shaped poppadom tuile. Poached, grilled and deconstructed quail, pink, tender and flavourful, came on a bed of spinach with caramelised tamarind, dabs of blackcurrant 'jam' and Darjeeling tea froth giving an 'exotic freshness'. Dishes are complex yet cohesive, and presentation exemplary: monkfish 'cinq saveurs' with sea-flavoured tortellini, parsnip and hazelnut oil foam and bitter caramel, for example, or Mr Little's beef fillet with good King Henry (wild spinach), parsnip and star anise purée and apple coulis. 'Cubes from land and sea' (lobster and scallops with chanterelles and a eucalyptus flavoured hollandaise) made quite an impression on one reader – a dish he 'possibly will never forget' – and humour is demonstrated by the serving of a 'Chinese style' white truffle custard in a take-away container marked 'No. 38' with a magic marker. One 'spectacular and dramatic' dessert has been upside-down coconut soufflé served with roast spiced pineapple, and mango chutney ice cream from a 'test tube'. If you fancy wine amid such culinary fireworks, a long international list is strong in both classical and modern styles; interesting bottles in the £20–£30 range include selections from Languedoc, Loire and Jura; 18 come by the glass from £3.50.

CHEF: Simon Rogan   PROPRIETORS: Simon Rogan and Penny Tapsell   OPEN: Tue to Sun L 12 to 1.30, Tue to Sat D 7 to 9.30   MEALS: alc (main courses £20 to £26). Set L £25, Set D £50 to £95 (all whole table only)   SERVICE: not inc   CARDS: Amex, Delta, Diners, MasterCard, Switch, Visa   DETAILS: 35 seats. 12 seats outside. Private parties: 30 main room. Vegetarian meals. No children under 12 at D. No smoking. Wheelchair access (not WC). No music. No mobile phones   ACCOMMODATION: 11 rooms, all with bath/shower. TV. Phone. B&B £110 to £200. Rooms for disabled

▲ Uplands ⚡

Haggs Lane, Cartmel LA11 6HD
TEL: (015395) 36248   FAX: (015395) 36848
WEBSITE: www.uplands.uk.com
2½m SW of A590, 1m up road opposite Pig and Whistle

COOKING 4
BRITISH
£26–£51

Described as 'our old reliable' by a pair of long-time admirers, Uplands is a stalwart of the Lakeland dining scene and Tom and Diana Peter celebrate 20 years here in 2005. As ever, guests arrive at 7.30 for aperitifs in the comfortable lounge before dinner at 8, and, although the repertoire may have been enhanced and updated in small ways over the years, the cooking is firmly set in its ways: rich, elaborate and comforting, as in a starter of poached scallops with lime and ginger served on a bacon, shallot and cognac sauce. The second course is always a generous tureen of soup to share: perhaps lightly curried parsnip and apple, served with a fresh-from-the-oven loaf of sweet, malty bread – 'not to be missed'. Main-course options typically take in baked fillet of halibut with cucumber, lemon and dill sauce, or pan-fried venison medallions with blackcurrant and juniper, all served with the same selection of five vegetables. Desserts are traditionally sweet and sticky, such as strawberry, raspberry and passion-fruit pavlova, and wines are a well-chosen, good-value bunch priced from £13.90.

CHEF: Tom Peter   PROPRIETORS: Tom and Diana Peter   OPEN: Fri to Sun L 12.30 for 1 (1 sitting), Tue to Sun D 7.30 for 8 (1 sitting)   MEALS: Set L £17, Set D £31.50   SERVICE: not inc, card slips closed   CARDS: Amex, Delta, MasterCard, Switch, Visa   DETAILS: 28 seats. Private parties: 28 main room. Car park. No children under 8. No smoking. No music   ACCOMMODATION: 7 rooms, all with bath/shower. TV. Phone. D,B&B £85 to £168. No children under 8 (£5)

CASTLE COMBE Wiltshire   map 2

▲ Manor House, Bybrook Restaurant 🍴✷

Castle Combe SN14 7HR	COOKING 3
TEL: (01249) 782206 FAX: (01249) 782159	ENGLISH
WEBSITE: www.exclusivehotels.co.uk	£37–£99

Castle Combe is the epitome of an old English village, and although the local manor house, a huge Georgian affair in acres of well-maintained gardens, looks much as it always has done it is no longer the home of the local lord, instead functioning as a classy country-house hotel, conference venue and golf club. Unsurprisingly, traditional country-house cooking is what to expect in the Bybrook Restaurant. Starters tend to be fairly simple but feature some interesting combinations, as in white onion and Sauternes soup, or seared scallops with crab mash and lemon oil, as well as a few French classics such as Bayonne ham with rémoulade and sauce gribiche. Main courses also show signs of boldness in flavour matching, beef fillet partnered with beetroot chutney and horseradish cream, grilled red mullet accompanied by Parmesan mash and aged balsamic vinegar, and elaborate desserts typically include chocolate and caramel mousse with chilled vanilla milkshake. Wine prices start around £20, and it would be easy to spend a lot more than that.

CHEF: Mark Taylor   PROPRIETOR: Exclusive Hotels   OPEN: all week 12 to 2, 7 to 10   MEALS: Set L Mon to Sat £16.95 (2 courses) to £18.95, Set L Sun £24.50, Set D Sun to Thur £35 to £65, Set D Fri and Sat £45 to £65. Bar menu available   SERVICE: not inc   CARDS: Amex, Delta, Diners, MasterCard, Switch, Visa DETAILS: 120 seats. 120 seats outside. Private parties: 80 main room, 2 to 80 private rooms. Car park. Vegetarian meals. Children's helpings. No smoking. Wheelchair access (not WC). No music. No mobile phones   ACCOMMODATION: 48 rooms, all with bath/shower. TV. Phone. B&B £185 to £750. Swimming pool. Fishing (£5)

CAUNTON Nottinghamshire   map 5

Caunton Beck 🍴✷ £

Main Street, Caunton NG23 6AB	COOKING 2
TEL: (01636) 636793 FAX: (01636) 636828	MODERN EUROPEAN
	£24–£48

Behind the modern-seeming exterior of this pub-restaurant lies a carefully restored Tudor cottage. There's no formality or pretension; order at the bar, then head for the dining area (or terrace, if the weather's kind). Begin with a local game terrine, plus fig and grape chutney, or perhaps pea and mint risotto laced with truffle oil. Among main courses 'simply grilled' ribeye steak with béarnaise sauce, and seared sea bass fillet on herb linguine have both been praised, though problems with the timing of vegetables and portion sizes were noted by one reporter. Puddings – which have included blackberry Eton Mess, a raspberry and elderflower jelly, and a dark chocolate and orange crème brûlée – are well received. Wines, listed in descending price order, offer plenty of choice under £20 and bottom out with the £11.50 house selection; there's a notable selection of pudding wines too.

CHEFS: Andrew Pickstock and Katie Crewe   PROPRIETOR: Wig & Mitre   OPEN: all week 8 to 11   MEALS: alc (main courses £9.50 to £17). Set L Mon to Sat £11 (2 courses) to £13.95, Set D Mon to Fri £11 (2 courses) to £13.95   SERVICE: not inc   CARDS: Amex, Delta, Diners, MasterCard, Switch, Visa   DETAILS: 90 seats. 40 seats outside. Private parties: 55 main room. Car park. Vegetarian meals. Children's helpings. No smoking. Wheelchair access (also WC). No music (£5)

CAVENDISH Suffolk   map 6

▲ George ⅝✳

The Green, Cavendish CO10 8BA	COOKING **3**
TEL: (01787) 280248 FAX: (01787) 281703	MODERN EUROPEAN
WEBSITE: www.georgecavendisn.co.uk	£28–£54

From the outside, this centuries-old country pub/restaurant looks a picture of calm rusticity, and its tastefully renovated interior creates just the right impression. That said, the frantic atmosphere, slow service and blaring pop music in the smoky bar are not to everyone's taste. Meals begin with 'stupendously good' home-baked bread, and the kitchen makes the most of good raw materials: witness sauté king scallops and chorizo with crisp celeriac and sherry dressing. Portions are on the large side, and a few mishaps have been noted, but Jonathan Nicholson is certainly a talented chef, and a dab hand at wild mushroom risotto and cassoulet. Hare, pistachio and prune terrine has also been applauded, while home-made sorbets are a pleasurable way to finish. The short wine list is a mixed bag from around the world; house wine is £9.95.

CHEF: Jonathan Nicholson   PROPRIETORS: Jonathan and Charlotte Nicholson   OPEN: Tue to Sun L 12 to 3, Tue to Sat D 6 to 10   MEALS: alc (main courses £10 to £19.50). Light L menu available Tue to Sat   SERVICE: not inc, 10% for parties of 8 or more   CARDS: Delta, MasterCard, Switch, Visa   DETAILS: 56 seats. 40 seats outside. Private parties: 30 main room, 8 to 16 private rooms. Vegetarian meals. Children's helpings. No smoking in dining room, permitted in the bar. Music   ACCOMMODATION: 5 rooms, all with bath/shower. TV. Phone. B&B £45 to £95. Baby facilities **£5**

CHADDESLEY CORBETT Worcestershire   map 5

▲ Brockencote Hall ⅝✳

Chaddesley Corbett DY10 4PY	COOKING **4**
TEL: (01562) 777876 FAX: (01562) 777872	MODERN FRENCH
WEBSITE: www.brockencotehall.com	£27–£84

'The most pleasant evening I've had at a posh country-house hotel for a long time, thanks to the super staff,' was one seasoned inspector's verdict on this French-owned hotel in 70 acres of parkland 'dotted with giant trees and flocks of sheep'. On the food front, Jérôme Barbançon shows confidence and has lots of good, modern ideas as well as a grasp of the right priorities – top-class local sourcing and sensitive timing and flavouring – to produce generous menus that range from frogs' legs with smoked kipper, potato, spring cabbage purée and almond butter, to Devon sea bass with lobster mousse ravioli, couscous, baby leeks and tarragon bisque. Perfectly timed scallops with lemon oil and a ragoût of shellfish with coriander and lime was an usual and really fresh idea for one reporter, who was further impressed by Barbary duck magret in cumin and lemon with apple compote and 'an exceptionally well-made' red wine reduction. Puddings include pineapple soufflé with passion-fruit sorbet, perhaps, or chocolate cannelloni with pistachio ice cream. The wine list plies most of its trade in France and accommodates differing pockets. House wines are priced from £14 to £17.

CHEF: Jérôme Barbançon   PROPRIETORS: Alison and Joseph Petitjean   OPEN: Sun to Fri L 12 to 1.30, all week D 7 to 9.30 (8.30 Sun)   CLOSED: first 2 weeks Jan   MEALS: alc (main courses £14.50 to £22.50). Set L Mon to Fri £13 (2 courses) to £20.20, Set L Sun £24.50, Set D £29.50 to £70   SERVICE: net prices, card slips closed   CARDS: Amex, Diners, MasterCard, Switch, Visa   DETAILS: 75 seats. Private parties: 50 main room, 10 to 30 private rooms. Car park. Vegetarian meals. Children's helpings. No smoking.

Wheelchair access (also WC). Occasional music. No mobile phones   ACCOMMODATION: 17 rooms, all with bath/shower. TV. Phone. B&B £96 to £180. Rooms for disabled. Fishing (£5)

▲ Gidleigh Park ▌ ✠

Chagford TQ13 8HH
TEL: (01647) 432367   FAX: (01647) 432574
WEBSITE: www.gidleigh.com   COOKING 8
from Chagford Square turn right at Lloyds Bank into Mill   MODERN EUROPEAN
Street, take right fork after 150 yards, follow lane for 1½m   £56–£116

The drive along the single-track road from the village of Chagford adds to the sense of anticipation created by a visit to Gidleigh, although, if you are a first-time visitor, it does not prepare you for the beauty of the spot. The black and white house is handsome enough by itself, with the view surely the reason it was built here in the first place. The gardens are majestic, the greeting is friendly, and the lounge the place to peruse the menus and take in the surroundings. The interior is rather grand, although not imposing, and warmth permeates the house – not the heat from the fires burning in the handsome stone fireplaces but a sense that this is a country home rather than country hotel. Start with an aperitif and amuse-bouche: sole goujons with tartare sauce, perhaps, and various little tartlets. The two traditional and rather plush panelled dining rooms are the setting for Michael Caines's cooking.

Lunch is a two- or three-course affair, offering two choices at each course and, not surprisingly, more straightforward in approach than dinner. Wild mushroom risotto with Parmesan, for example, has been as well made and comforting as you might expect, and was joined at starter stage by a light tian of crab and scallop mousse enlivened with a ginger and lemongrass sauce. A main course of pan-fried veal liver comes pink and perfect, served with asparagus, wild mushrooms and a thin balsamic vinegar sauce. Dinner sees the arrival of luxury ingredients and the raising of the stakes. Foie gras might appear in a soup with lentils, and black truffle in a tartlet of quail and quails' eggs also containing onion confit and smoked bacon, served with wild mushrooms and a light quail jus. Game when in season is a strong suit: for example, roast partridge partnered with braised chicory, quince and roast walnuts and a Gewürztraminer sauce.

There are reports of some mistimed fish cookery this year, with brill not living up to its crushed olive potatoes and ginger and vanilla jus for a couple of visitors. Desserts are a strength, with a palette of ice creams and sorbets somewhat of a speciality, and a lemon tart with lemon confit and candied zest with good pastry and a 'perfect degree of sharpness'. Service is formal but friendly and considered. Paul Henderson is rightly proud of his cellar full of 'the mature good stuff' – not just French classics but an encyclopaedic collection of California's finest. He also makes impassioned pleas on behalf of the fine but oft-ignored sherries and German wines on the list. Prices, including service, are fair, although there are no cheap options here (go for £20 South Africans if the budget's tight). Eight serious options come by the glass.

CHEF: Michael Caines   PROPRIETORS: Paul and Kay Henderson   OPEN: all week 12.30 to 2, 7 to 9   MEALS: Set L Mon to Thur £27 (2 courses) to £35, Set L Fri to Sun and bank hols £33 (2 courses) to £41, Set D £72.50 to £77.50. Light L menu available   SERVICE: not inc, card slips closed   CARDS: Amex, Delta, Diners, MasterCard, Switch, Visa   DETAILS: 35 seats. Private parties: 22 main room. Car park. No children under 7. No smoking. No music   ACCOMMODATION: 14 rooms, all with bath/shower. TV. Phone. D,B&B £270 to £975

▲ 22 Mill Street ✷

22 Mill Street, Chagford TQ13 8AW
TEL: (01647) 432244   FAX: (01647) 433101
WEBSITE: www.22millstreetrestaurant.co.uk

COOKING **6**
MODERN EUROPEAN
£33–£53

'All in all, the perfect small country restaurant,' is how one visitor summed up this engagingly unassuming and unpretentious ground-floor restaurant in a quiet corner of the village. Sedate the surroundings may be, but the cooking is anything but. At dinner, six courses from the no-choice set menu (£38, including service) might offer such appealing dishes as a salad of paprika-marinated duck, then sautéed globe artichoke, girolles and asparagus with Madeira and truffle oil velouté, before a main course of poached fillet of turbot with smoked haddock ravioli. The carte (£34 for three courses) might include fillet of mackerel with lemon-marinated fennel with parsley and pine nuts, or braised stuffed pig's trotter with roast belly pork and braised pig's cheek with apple and cabbage. Dishes are well judged, the timing spot-on, and diners are likely to leave feeling wonderfully spoilt, thanks to the atmosphere, friendly, helpful service, and the full array of amuse-bouche and petits fours, as well as the polite, restrained, yet hands-on presence of Duncan Walker. Prices are not low, but regular visitors feel they get value for money. The nicely judged wine list (not too long, not too short) holds plenty of interest, with the majority of bottles under £25. Prices start at £12.50.

CHEFS: Duncan Walker and Stephen Langstone   PROPRIETOR: Duncan Walker   OPEN: Wed to Sat L 12.30 to 1.45, Mon to Sat D 7.30 to 9   CLOSED: 2 weeks Jan, 1 week May   MEALS: Set L £21 (2 courses) to £24, Set D £29.50 (2 courses) to £38   SERVICE: net prices, card slips closed   CARDS: Delta, MasterCard, Switch, Visa   DETAILS: 22 seats. No smoking in 1 dining room. Occasional music. No mobile phones ACCOMMODATION: 2 rooms, both with bath/shower. TV. B&B £40 to £60

CHANDLER'S CROSS Hertfordshire   map 3

▲ The Grove, Colette's ✷   │ NEW ENTRY │

Chandler's Cross WD3 4TG
TEL: (01923) 807807
WEBSITE: www.thegrove.co.uk

COOKING **6**
MODERN EUROPEAN
£53–£104

The Grove is the biggest thing to hit Watford since . . . well, suffice to say it's a big deal round these parts. A few miles from the town at Chandler's Cross, The Grove was the seat of the Earls of Clarendon until 1920, but is now a hotel complex combining country-house hotel, golf club and fantasy office development. And strangely, the whole thing works.

At Colette's, the smartest of three restaurants on site, ambitious food makes liberal use of luxury ingredients, which is reflected in the price. Nonetheless, presentation does not eclipse taste, as seen with an airy disc of white crab meat topped by a generous layer of caviar with a zesty lemon cream, little cubes of cured tuna and dots of coriander dressing - the star starter at inspection. A salmon ballottine was less assured. Main-course lamb has also impressed: tender cutlet with braised shoulder in a rich olive jus and braised baby fennel, plus a small potato cake and some fresh spinach, or there might be Dover sole with cockles, clams, fresh linguini and herb juice. Desserts are highly elaborate but again full of flavour, with disparate elements – such as 'ethereally light' sticky toffee pudding, apple Tatin and caramel cinnamon ice cream – combining effectively on the plate. An outstandingly comprehensive wine list offers no change from 20 quid at the bottom end –

but if it's really good, they've probably got it. Keep tabs on the little things, like tea and water; these can add up to a considerable sum. Service from waiters in open-necked shirts is unusual: 'extraordinarily friendly, responsive but not the remotest bit deferential'.

CHEF: Christopher Harrod   PROPRIETOR: Ralph Trustees Ltd   OPEN: Sun L 12.30 to 3, Mon to Sat D 7 to 10.30   MEALS: alc (main courses £24 to £32). Set L Sun £35 to £50, Set D £65 (whole table only)   SERVICE: not inc   CARDS: Amex, Delta, Diners, MasterCard, Switch, Visa   DETAILS: 48 seats. Private parties: 30 main room, 12 to 20 private rooms. Car park. Vegetarian meals. Wheelchair access (also WC). Music. Air-conditioned   ACCOMMODATION: 227 rooms, all with bath/shower. TV. Phone. B&B £240 to £320 plus VAT. Rooms for disabled. Swimming pool

CHELTENHAM Gloucestershire   map 5

Le Champignon Sauvage ▼

24–26 Suffolk Road, Cheltenham GL50 2AQ   COOKING 8
TEL: (01242) 573449   FAX: (01242) 254365   FRENCH
WEBSITE: www.lechampignonsauvage.co.uk   £34–£76

There are no idyllic views of countryside, dramatic mountains or placid lakes to draw the crowds to Le Champignon Sauvage, situated as it is in the surroundings of suburban Cheltenham, but come they do for the excellent cooking. Inside, the serene colour scheme of primrose-yellow walls and cool blue upholstery, and tasteful collection of artworks on the walls, is a pleasantly bright and relaxed setting for what follows.

There's an unashamedly French attitude in evidence, but far from being a stuffy tribute to Escoffier the food here regularly has reporters reaching for words such as 'thrilling' and 'stupendous'. Hardly surprising: David Everitt-Matthias is a chef whose intense care and diligence are matched only by his supreme technical skill, creative flair and knack for inspired flavour combinations. These attributes are all evident in a starter of smooth-textured boudin noir studded with chunks of sweetbreads served in a warm salad with roast quail, the tender, pink breast meat thickly sliced, the neatly trimmed confit leg given a hint of sweetness from being dipped in Chinese spices.

If you think that sounds elaborate, main courses raise the stakes further, stuffing veal with snails and nettles, partnering roast pavé of lamb with sweetbreads, artichokes and powdered orange, and finishing a fillet of brill with white onion fondant and smoked eel cream. Roast pigeon breast combines well with 'sticky, gorgeous' ox cheeks in a dark, rich sauce with a hint of liquorice, and multitudinous accompaniments including chanterelles, crisp pak choi, baby turnips and potato purée. Desserts are equally elegantly presented but less elaborately constructed: a slab of roast pineapple, for example, with a scoop of herby, tangy pineapple and angelica sorbet. The midweek set-price dinner is considered 'unbelievably cheap' for this level of cooking, and service, headed by Helen Everitt-Matthias, is informed, friendly and confident. The mostly French wine list, opening with £11 house, is emphatically not priced to subsidise the food. There are good-value wines from reliable producers in all regions, with Burgundy and Bordeaux pushing on to greater heights. Australia, New Zealand and California cater for devotees of modern fruity styles.

CHEF: David Everitt-Matthias   PROPRIETORS: David and Helen Everitt-Matthias   OPEN: Tue to Sat 12.30 to 1.30, 7.30 to 9   CLOSED: 10 days at Christmas, 3 weeks June   MEALS: Set L and D £18 (2 courses; not Sat D) to £44   SERVICE: not inc   CARDS: Amex, Delta, Diners, Switch, Visa   DETAILS: 28 seats. Private parties: 22 main room. No smoking before 10pm at D. Wheelchair access (not WC). No music. No mobile phones   (£5)

Daffodil ✗

18–20 Suffolk Parade, Montpellier,
Cheltenham GL50 2AE
TEL: (01242) 700055   FAX: (01242) 700088
EMAIL: daffodilrest@c.s.com

COOKING **2**
MODERN EUROPEAN
£25–£59

A stylishly converted Art Deco cinema, 'striking and impressive', houses this 'fun' restaurant. Big-screen touches – a sweeping staircase to the Circle Bar, open-to-view kitchen (where the screen once was), and large dining auditorium in the stalls – create an upbeat mood. But if the setting celebrates the roaring '20s, the fashionable Mediterranean-style brasserie fare plays to a thoroughly modern audience. After perhaps a ricotta and mushroom soufflé, expect chargrilled chicken breast with polenta, sun-blushed tomato, sweetcorn and olives, say, or fillet of cod with basil and Parmesan crust, herb risotto and tempura prawns. Leave space for desserts like vanilla and coconut Condé with pan-seared pineapple. A short wine list starts at £12.90 a bottle and has eight by the glass.

CHEF: Andrew Palmer   PROPRIETORS: Marcel and Corinna Frichot   OPEN: Mon to Sat 12 to 2.30, 6.30 to 10
MEALS: alc D (main courses £13 to £20). Set L £12 (2 courses) to £14.50   SERVICE: not inc, 10% for parties
of 6 or more, card slips closed   CARDS: Amex, MasterCard, Switch, Visa   DETAILS: 150 seats. Private
parties: 150 main room. Vegetarian meals. Children's helpings. No smoking in 1 dining room. Wheelchair
access (also WC). Music

Lumière ▼ ✗

Clarence Parade, Cheltenham GL50 3PA
TEL: (01242) 222200
WEBSITE: www.lumiere.cc

COOKING **5**
GLOBAL
£49–£71

This 'little gem of a restaurant' in an unassuming side street near the bus station has a long, narrow dining room of minimalist elegance, with abstract artworks on oyster-coloured walls and modern table settings. The husband-and-wife formula works with precision here; Geoff Chapman creates original dishes in the kitchen, and his wife Lin, front-of-house, serves them with informed enthusiasm.

The food has classical roots and global range, and flavours are vibrant yet subtle. Menus start with a 'soup creation' (maybe mushroom velouté with courgette 'caviar', covered with a melting tarragon mayonnaise) and finish with 'one perfect cheese'. In between might be halibut with stir-fried Thai-style tiger prawns and toasted cashew noodles, or chargrilled springbok fillet (flown from Kenya) with sauce béarnaise, foie gras niblets and mushroom potato pavé. Excellent raw materials, harmonious combinations and perfect timing generally ensure accomplished results – witness an inspector's exceptionally tender and full-flavoured veal tournedos, complemented rather than eclipsed by the strong flavours of truffled mushroom duxelles, a rich red wine sauce and cracked pepper potatoes. Enterprising desserts like pecan torte with Bourbon ice cream, and lemon-lime tartlet with ginger and blueberry hint at Geoff Chapman's Pacific Rim background. Wine is one of Lin Chapman's passions, and she will 'come to the rescue' if you are hesitating over her highly personal list. Italy and California are well represented, prices start around £19, and value is good for uniformly high quality.

CHEF: Geoff Chapman   PROPRIETORS: Lin and Geoff Chapman   OPEN: Tue to Sat D 7 to 8.30   CLOSED:
first 2 weeks Jan, 2 weeks late summer   MEALS: Set D Tue to Thurs £27.50 (2 courses), Set D Tue to Sat
£34   SERVICE: not inc   CARDS: MasterCard, Switch, Visa   DETAILS: 28 seats. Private parties: 34 main
room. No children under 9. No smoking in dining room. No music. Air-conditioned

▲ Chester Grosvenor, Arkle ▮ ✳

Eastgate, Chester CH1 1LT   COOKING 7
TEL: (01244) 324024   FAX: (01244) 313246   EUROPEAN
WEBSITE: www.chestergrosvenor.com   £46–£96

Chester's hotshot restaurant just goes on getting better. The atmosphere in both the Library Bar and the main dining room is elegant and clubby, with brown tones predominating. Chairs in the style of Charles Rennie Mackintosh, and a screened skylight add to the feel of grand dining. A formidable standard of professionalism is set by staff, who are forthcoming with explanations of the dishes where needed and are clearly genuinely knowledgeable.

Simon Radley's cooking is in the modern French idiom, mobilising unexpected techniques and unafraid, for example, to offer a first-course pairing of veal sweetbreads and Scottish lobster, bolstered by chickpeas, almonds and spices, or – the outstanding starter at inspection – a piece of cod fillet pickled in verjuice, just cooked through and teamed with a foie gras fritter, raisins and a parsley cream sauce. Menu descriptions are precise enough to indicate the gender of the crab and to get the imagination ticking over: 'pig's foot studded with cheeks'? There is wit too: Ellel Grange chicken breast is steamed to preserve moistness, and served with buttered lettuce and a scrambled organic egg, put back in the shell, with crisp artichoke 'soldiers' for dipping. Aberdeen Angus beef fillet is lightly poached, sparingly sauced with horseradish sabayon and accompanied by a paper-thin ravioli containing tender braised ox cheek. Chocolate is a favoured dessert theme, labour-intensively worked to produce three cups in white, milk and dark and filled with different coffee mousses, or pasta might crop up again here, as tortellini encasing a sweet fruit filling, garnished with coconut sorbet and sauced with pomegranate butter, a roaring success at inspection. Strong espresso comes with impeccable petits fours.

The sommelier commendably asks for your price ceiling before guiding you through the wine list. If the sky is your limit it could take quite a while to filter through the pages of fine old Burgundy and Bordeaux and premium bottles from California, or order something from the superb champagne list to get you going. Ordinary mortals should home in on regional France, South America or South Africa. House wine is £15.50, and a dozen come by the glass.

CHEF: Simon Radley   PROPRIETOR: the Duke of Westminster   OPEN: Tue to Sun L 12 to 2.30, Tue to Sat D 7 to 9.30   CLOSED: 24 to 27 Dec   MEALS: Set L £25 (2 courses) to £30, Set D £45 (2 courses) to £60   SERVICE: 12.5% (optional)   CARDS: Amex, Delta, Diners, MasterCard, Switch, Visa   DETAILS: 50 seats. Private parties: 50 main room. Jacket and tie. No smoking. Wheelchair access (also WC). Music. No mobile phones. Air-conditioned   ACCOMMODATION: 80 rooms, all with bath/shower. TV. Phone. Room only £185 to £725. Rooms for disabled. Baby facilities

▲ Castleman Hotel ▮ ✳ £

Chettle DT11 8DB   COOKING 2
TEL: (01258) 830096   FAX: (01258) 830051   MODERN BRITISH
WEBSITE: www.castlemanhotel.co.uk   £25–£44

The Castleman is an attractive hotel with serene views, and a rather grand interior filled with 'beautiful plaster mouldings and walls lined with paintings', but with a distinctly unstuffy atmosphere. Locals and guests alike contribute to the general sense of relaxed cheer, presided over by Edward Bourke (his partner, Barbara Garnsworthy, is chef). In dishes such as chicken breast wrapped in Denhay ham with spiced honey mustard with cider and sage sauce, raw materials are of good quality. And timings, as in a starter of warm chicken liver and bacon salad with sherry vinegar dressing, are spot-on. Flavour combinations, too, are well judged: witness a dessert of banana and caramel ice cream with butterscotch sauce. 'Young staff are well trained, polite, cheerful and friendly,' wrote one visitor, and the wine list is 'an absolute joy' that combines a good international range with exceptionally reasonable prices. House wines are £10.

CHEFS: Barbara Garnsworthy and Richard Morris PROPRIETORS: Edward Bourke and Barbara Garnsworthy OPEN: Sun L 12 to 2, all week D 7 to 10 CLOSED: 25 and 26 Dec, Feb MEALS: alc D (main courses £8.50 to £15.50). Set L Sun £18 SERVICE: not inc, card slips closed CARDS: Delta, MasterCard, Switch, Visa DETAILS: 40 seats. Private parties: 50 main room. Car park. Vegetarian meals. Children's helpings. No smoking. Wheelchair access (also WC). No music ACCOMMODATION: 8 rooms, all with bath/shower. TV. Phone. B&B £50 to £85. Baby facilities

CHIEVELEY Berkshire
map 2

▲ Crab at Chieveley ✦
NEW ENTRY

Wantage Road, Chieveley RG20 8UE
TEL: (01635) 247550 FAX: (01635) 247440
WEBSITE: www.crabatchieveley.com

COOKING 2
SEAFOOD
£29–£93

This new venture from David and Jacqueline Barnard, previous owners of the Crab & Lobster in Asenby (see entry), opened in August 2003 after extensive refurbishment. This is no ordinary restaurant – it comes with a series of classy bedrooms in an attached tropical-style mews, the rooms designed to echo exotic locations and hotel rooms from around the world. Outside the white-painted building (it was once a pub) are a myriad of lobster pots, while, inside, the interconnecting rooms are decked out with pale floorboards, the beamed ceilings covered in fishing nets and cork floats, and throughout is all manner of bric-à-brac and *objets d'art*. The menu is a paean to seafood (which comes from Brixham market), taking in langoustines, oysters, mussels, lobster and crab, as well as meaty dishes such as oriental-spiced duckling. Galway smoked salmon, of excellent quality, makes a simple starter, followed perhaps by well-timed halibut with zingy seafood mash, or a generous portion of monkfish wrapped in Parma ham with tomato mash, while desserts might include an accomplished raspberry soufflé. Fourteen well-chosen basics at £15, or £3.75 a glass, set the tone for a canny wine list. Prices are not the cheapest, however.

CHEFS: David Moss and Neil Thornley PROPRIETORS: David and Jacqueline Barnard OPEN: all week 12 to 2.30, 6 to 10 MEALS: alc (main courses £11.50 to £35). Set L £13.50 (2 courses) to £16.50 SERVICE: not inc CARDS: Amex, Delta, MasterCard, Switch, Visa DETAILS: 100 seats. 160 seats outside. Private parties: 20 main room, 12 to 20 private rooms. Car park. Vegetarian meals. Children's helpings. No smoking. Occasional music. Air-conditioned ACCOMMODATION: 10 rooms, all with bath/shower. TV. Phone. B&B £100 to £150. Rooms for disabled

---

'[The proprietor] bustled back and forth, chattering incessantly to us, sometimes close at hand, sometimes from the opposite wall of the lounge, hovering and remarking, volubly agreeing or courteously demurring, but as persistent as an eager shih-tzu being collected from the kennels by its owners. Nice chap but a pest.' (On eating in Wales)

CHIGWELL Essex
map 3

Bluebell

117 High Road, Chigwell IG7 6QQ
TEL: (020) 8500 6282   FAX: (020) 8500 6942

COOKING 2
MODERN EUROPEAN
£30–£59

A bluebell on the High Road may sound unlikely, but this vibrant variety of neighbourhood restaurant brings a splash of culinary colour to Chigwell all year round. The dining room – in a whitewashed cottage – is modern and simple, with white-painted beams and walls and clothed tables set against a blue carpet. The set-price lunch menu (with bags of choice) and evening carte are supported by a wine list that coves the globe and has good choice under £20. Expect the likes of slow-baked English lamb shank with baby spinach, braised root vegetables, thyme croquettes and a rich rosemary and red wine jus, and familiar desserts perhaps headed up by tarte Tatin with cinnamon ice cream.

CHEF: Paul Korten   PROPRIETOR: Greg Molen   OPEN: Tue to Sun L 12 to 2 (4 Sun), Tue to Sat D 6.45 to 10 MEALS: alc D (main courses £15 to £20). Set L Tue to Sat £11.95 (2 courses), Set L Sun £18.95   SERVICE: not inc, card slips closed   CARDS: Amex, Delta, Diners, MasterCard, Switch, Visa   DETAILS: 95 seats. Vegetarian meals. Children's helpings. No cigars/ pipes. Occasional music. Air-conditioned

CHILGROVE West Sussex
map 3

▲ White Horse ▮ ⁵⨉
NEW ENTRY

Chilgrove PO18 9HX
TEL: (01243) 535219   FAX: (01243) 535301
WEBSITE: www.whitehorsechilgrove.co.uk

COOKING 3
MODERN BRITISH
£38–£64

A traditional, wisteria-clad old coaching inn this might appear on the outside, but its inner self is a light, bright, contemporary space with bare boards, pale-painted walls, and white-clothed tables in adjoining dining rooms smartly set with fresh flowers. The menus, too, follow modern lines, with hand-dived scallops combining with pancetta and a seafood risotto, and 'smooth, buttery, rich' paprika parfait of foie de volaille coming with a roast cherry compote as the 'perfect adjunct'. Main courses layer flavours in impressive fashion, partnering venison steak with a mandarin orange sauce and pumpkin pie, and breast of organic chicken with a novel combination of creamy Cheddar, chorizo and Turkish figs on a Marsala cream sauce. Bread rolls disappointed at inspection, and a lemon tart was redeemed by its brûlée topping. The wine list drips quality but doesn't groan under ludicrous mark-ups. Classic clarets lead the field, while shorter New World selections are spot on. Wines always come in mature vintages, but a few newer ones wouldn't go amiss. There's little under £20, although house wines are £13.50, and there's an impressive range of half-bottles.

CHEF: Juana Otero   PROPRIETOR: Charles Burton   OPEN: Tue to Sun L 12 to 2, Tue to Sat D 7 to 9   MEALS: alc (main courses £12.50 to £18)   SERVICE: 10%, card slips closed   CARDS: Delta, MasterCard, Switch, Visa   DETAILS: 60 seats. 30 seats outside. Private parties: 4 to 16 private rooms. Car park. Vegetarian meals. No smoking. Music. No mobile phones. Air-conditioned   ACCOMMODATION: 8 rooms, all with bath/ shower. TV. Phone. B&B £65 to £120. Rooms for disabled (£5)

'The chef [has been] allowed a pony tail because he's arty.' (On eating in Dorset)

Sir Charles Napier ▮ ⁵✳

Sprigg's Alley, Chinnor OX39 4BX
TEL: (01494) 483011   FAX: (01494) 485311
WEBSITE: www.sircharlesnapier.co.uk
take B4009 to Chinnor from M40 junction 6, turn right at
mini-roundabout and continue up hill for 2m to Sprigg's
Alley

NEW CHEF

ANGLO-FRENCH-PLUS
£35–£77

Take a look at the longest-serving list at the front of the book and you'll see that Julie Griffith's large, very old but prosperous-looking flint-and-brick restaurant has been in the Guide for 24 consecutive years. After completing the long climb up a narrow lane, reporters universally praise the tranquillity of the setting and the 'unbeatable ambience' of the restaurant, where sculptures catch the eye. In summer 2004 Richard Burkert joined as head chef, having worked at Kensington Place (see entry, London), among others. The kitchen makes almost everything from scratch (that is not about to change), and the quality of ingredients continues to impress. The new chef's menus show seared foie gras paired with a sweetcorn pancake to start, and then fillet of bream with borlotti beans, chilli, shrimps and tomato. Service is 'correct, very professional yet very individual', and they don't like to rush things. Eight well-chosen house wines are charged for the amount consumed pro rata to the bottle prices (from £18) – a welcoming start to a list that really wants diners to enjoy their wine. There are cracking little selections in each region running from the affordable to the iconic.

CHEF: Richard Burkert   PROPRIETOR: Julie Griffiths   OPEN: Tue to Sun L 12 to 2.30 (3.30 Sun), Tue to Sat D 6.30 to 10   CLOSED: 3 days at Christmas   MEALS: alc (main courses £11.50 to £27.50). Set L Tue to Sat £14.50 (2 courses), Set D Tue to Fri £16.50 (2 courses). Light L menu available Tue to Fri   SERVICE: 12.5% (optional), card slips closed   CARDS: Amex, Delta, Diners, MasterCard, Switch, Visa   DETAILS: 70 seats. 70 seats outside. Private parties: 45 main room, 10 to 45 private rooms. Car park. Vegetarian meals. Children's helpings. No children under 7 at D. No smoking in 1 dining room. Wheelchair access (not WC). Music. Air-conditioned

▲ Cotswold House, Juliana's Restaurant ♀ ⁵✳

The Square, Chipping Campden GL55 6AN
TEL: (01386) 840330   FAX: (01386) 840310
WEBSITE: www.cotswoldhouse.com

COOKING 6
MODERN BRITISH
£59–£71

This building on one corner of the town square, a hotel since the 1930s, was built in 1802 as a merchant's house. A majestic circular stairwell is the jewel of its interior, and the restaurant looks chic and inviting, with upholstered chairs and vases of flowers on well-spaced, white-decked tables.

Courteous, unrushed service enhances the enjoyment of Simon Hulstone's hugely accomplished cooking, which is full of fireworks. Deftly judged combinations have included seared duck foie gras with a Sauternes-poached pear and liquorice cream, or eloquently flavoured Orkney scallops with puréed cabbage, and a frothy sauce slicked with truffle oil and scattered with matchsticks of candied lemon. The enticements multiply at main-course stage, when sea bass may be twice-cooked (poached, then briefly roasted) and accompanied by fennel, Swiss chard and ham, or, for vegetarians, fettuccine comes with sweet potato, ceps and red onion, as well as 'shavings' of chestnut. More traditionally, Scottish beef fillet has been generous and well-timed, enriched with oxtail jus, and set off by baby leeks and wild mushrooms. Desserts are properly indulgent, with warm chocolate and banana tart, or tiramisù with amaretti ice-cream. Alternatively, try the award-winning artisanal British cheeses, which might include Ragstone, Sharpham and Cornish Blue. Truffles and tuiles come with good, strong coffee. This is a kitchen to watch. Simon Hulstone's team also cook at the hotel's Hicks' Brasserie, which has a more straightforward approach to the food and complements the main restaurant. The wine list turns up consistently good quality in its trot around the globe. For budget options stick to the Brasserie list from £12.50.

CHEF: Simon Hulstone PROPRIETORS: Christa Taylor and Ian Taylor OPEN: Sun L 12 to 2.30, all week D 7 to 9.45 MEALS: Set L Sun £15.50 (2 courses), Set D £45. Brasserie menu available all week L and D SERVICE: 10% (optional) CARDS: Amex, Delta, MasterCard, Switch, Visa DETAILS: 52 seats. 35 seats outside. Private parties: 70 main room, 15 to 40 private rooms. Car park. Vegetarian meals. Children's helpings. No smoking. Occasional music. No mobile phones. Air-conditioned ACCOMMODATION: 21 rooms, all with bath/shower. TV. Phone. B&B £115 to £595 (£5)

CHRISTCHURCH Dorset map 2

FishWorks

10 Church Street, Christchurch BH23 1BW COOKING **3**
TEL: (01202) 487000 FAX: (01202) 487001 SEAFOOD
WEBSITE: www.fishworks.co.uk £28–£86

This fishmonger-cum-restaurant is an upstairs, downstairs affair. On the ground floor, the catch of the day glistens in display cabinets, while upstairs is the disarmingly simple dining room. It is a combination that has proved successful in other branches in Bath, Bristol and London (see entries). 'Classic dishes' might include baked sea bass with roast garlic, rosemary, chilli and olive oil, while crustacea take in cockles, 'wild-caught' white prawns, clams, winkles and French oysters; among daily specials might be 'thoroughly satisfying' roast swordfish with rosemary and anchovy butter. Salads and vegetables such as tomatoes with mozzarella, basil and olive oil, and potatoes with butter and mint are charged extra and can push up the prices. A cheese plate of Yarg, Capricorn and Blue Vinney is a good alternative to desserts such as 'soufflé-like' baked chocolate pudding with cream. Wines are an imaginative lot, sourced from fish-friendly European regions such as Galicia and the Loire Valley. Prices start at £15.25.

CHEF: Nick Davies PROPRIETOR: FishWorks plc OPEN: Tue to Sat 12 to 2.30, 6 to 10.30 CLOSED: Christmas, bank hols MEALS: alc (main courses £8.50 to £35) SERVICE: not inc CARDS: Amex, Delta, MasterCard, Switch, Visa DETAILS: 44 seats. Vegetarian meals. Children's helpings. No smoking. Wheelchair access (not WC). Music. Air-conditioned

CLAYGATE Surrey map 3

Le Petit Pierrot

4 The Parade, Claygate KT10 0NU COOKING **3**
TEL: (01372) 465105 FAX: (01372) 467642 MODERN FRENCH
£20–£54

In a parade of shops, you can spot Le Petit Pierrot by the red blind shading the glass doors. Little changes here (a comfort and reassurance to some, but not to all), and the menu is as unmistakably French-inspired as ever. There may be an aumonière of wild mushrooms (baked in filo) with avocado sauce to start, or an adventurous half-pawpaw containing Thai-spiced prawn salad, then sautéed calf's liver with raspberries and raspberry vinegar, or a classic tournedos Rossini. Chocoholics may find it hard to resist the chocolate fondant with praline sauce (for two); otherwise French cheeses strike a savoury note. The all-Gallic wine list holds no surprises, although pricing is fair and there are plenty of half-bottles. House vin de pays starts at £11.75.

CHEFS: Jean-Pierre Brichot and Eric Plantureux   PROPRIETORS: Jean-Pierre and Annie Brichot   OPEN: Mon to Fri L 12.15 to 2.15, Mon to Sat D 7.15 to 9.15   CLOSED: 1 week Christmas, bank hols   MEALS: Set L £12.25 (2 courses) to £21.50, Set D £25.50   SERVICE: not inc   CARDS: Amex, Delta, MasterCard, Visa   DETAILS: 32 seats. Private parties: 34 main room. No children under 9. Wheelchair access (not WC). Occasional music. No mobile phones

CLIFFORD'S MESNE Gloucestershire
map 5

▲ Yew Tree Inn ▾ ⁵⁄✳

Clifford's Mesne GL18 1JS
TEL: (01531) 820719
WEBSITE: www.theyewtreeinn.co.uk

COOKING 3
MODERN EUROPEAN
£31–£55

'If you stand on top of May Hill on a clear day and slowly turn full circle, you'll find yourself taking in pretty much all of our grocery basket.' So writes Paul Hackett, chef/proprietor of this unstuffy country inn/restaurant in an updated sixteenth-century cider press overlooking the Leadon Valley. His claim is no idle boast, judging by dishes such as pot-roast breast of local pheasant with lentil and shallot sauce 'infused with rich forest fruits', or roast loin of Gloucester Old Spot pork with prune stuffing and mustard gravy. Fish is, of course, from further afield, but it's wisely chosen: for example, Brixham inshore cod and Cornish sea bass (which might be sautéed with vermouth and dill sauce). Desserts have included sticky toffee pudding with caramel sauce and mascarpone cream, and the 'grocery basket' is topped up with cheeses from the region's elite producers. The wine list is not short of premier-league players either, topped and tailed as it is by a long list of fizz, including the best from Champagne, and a cellar of mature clarets. In between you'll find around 20 by the glass, plenty of options under £20, and a fine list of smarter bottles that eventually homes in on Burgundy.

CHEF: Paul Hackett   PROPRIETORS: Paul and Anna Hackett   OPEN: Tue to Sun L 12 to 2, Tue to Sat D 7 to 9 CLOSED: 2 to 22 Jan, bank hols   MEALS: Set L and D exc Sun L £21.95 (2 courses) to £32, Set L Sun £14.75 (2 courses) to £18.75   SERVICE: not inc, card slips closed   CARDS: Delta, MasterCard, Switch, Visa DETAILS: 70 seats. 36 seats outside. Car park. Children's helpings. No smoking. Wheelchair access (also WC). Music   ACCOMMODATION: 2 rooms. TV. B&B £45 to £70

CLIPSHAM Rutland
map 6

Olive Branch ▾ ⁵⁄✳ £

Main Street, Clipsham LE15 7SH
TEL: (01780) 410355   FAX: (01780) 410000
WEBSITE: www.theolivebranchpub.com

COOKING 3
MODERN BRITISH
£21–£45

Inside this sensitively converted stone pub, in a pair of interconnecting rooms garlanded with hops and warmed on cool days by a fire crackling in the inglenook, Sean Hope's cooking intermingles rural Rutland and modern Europe. Alongside Lincolnshire sausages, mash and onion gravy might be mozzarella balls coated in polenta and crisply deep-fried, with cherry tomatoes and balsamic; and as well as a vibrantly flavoured composition of quick-fried brill fillet on potato rösti and creamed endive (plus a couple of lightly cooked scallops for good measure) there is roast beef, Yorkshire pudding and horseradish hollandaise. At a summer lunch a fine piece of salmon was served warm with niçoise accompaniments and a tomato sauce, while a bowl of cauliflower and Parmesan soup in January was properly, creamily nourishing. Meals end happily with well-made vanilla pannacotta and spiced poached plums, or maybe a chocolatey version of Eton Mess. Young staff keep up the pace, squeezing proficiently between tables. Look to blackboards around the bar for exciting wines from all over; the printed list is more workaday, although ten come by the glass. Prices are fair and start at £9.95.

CHEF: Sean Hope   PROPRIETOR: Rutland Inn Company Ltd   OPEN: all week L 12 to 2 (3 Sun), Mon to Sat D 7 to 9.30   CLOSED: 26 Dec, 1 Jan   MEALS: alc (main courses £9 to £15). Set L Mon to Sat £12.50. Set L Sun £15   SERVICE: not inc, card slips closed   CARDS: Delta, MasterCard, Switch, Visa   DETAILS: 45 seats. 30 seats outside. Private parties: 14 to 20 private rooms. Car park. Vegetarian meals. Children's helpings. No smoking in 1 dining room. Occasional music

COCKERMOUTH Cumbria
map 10

Quince & Medlar ✗

11/13 Castlegate, Cockermouth CA13 9EU   COOKING 2
TEL: (01900) 823579   VEGETARIAN
£38–£50

Confident in their role as guardians of one of Britain's long-standing vegetarian restaurants, Colin and Louisa Le Voi (here for 16 years) offer a warm welcome at this Georgian terrace. Many customers are omnivores drawn back again and again by imaginative cooking that avoids the usual vegetarian clichés; one regular roundly declared this 'certainly the best vegetarian restaurant I have been to ever'. There's an international dimension to Colin Le Voi's repertoire, with contemporary notes running through it: starters like Lebanese coconut pancakes with roast butternut squash and chilli pepper, for example, and a Moroccan-inspired main course of root vegetables and apricots, cooked with turmeric and paprika and served in a poppadom cone with saffron basmati and wild rice. Desserts are more familiar, say spiced apple cheesecake, or chocolate orange pie. The all-organic global wine list has fair prices.

CHEFS/PROPRIETORS: Colin and Louisa Le Voi   OPEN: Tue to Sat D only 7 to 9.30   CLOSED: 24 to 26 Dec, 1 Jan, 1 week mid-Feb, 1 week end-Oct   MEALS: alc (main courses £12.75)   SERVICE: not inc, card slips closed   CARDS: MasterCard, Switch   DETAILS: 26 seats. Private parties: 14 main room. No children under 5. No smoking. Music

CODFORD Wiltshire
map 2

▲ George Hotel £   NEW ENTRY

High Street, Codford BA12 0NG   COOKING 4
TEL: (01985) 850270   MODERN BRITISH
£25–£55

This old roadside inn in the Wylye Valley has taken on a new lease of life under the accomplished duo Boyd Mackintosh and Joanne Fryer, formerly of Howard's House (see entry, Teffont Evias). The unpretentiously refurbished dining room now has a

Mediterranean vibe; it's open-plan, and there's a drinkers' bar with the inevitable cigarette smoke. But the attraction here is what comes out of the kitchen: a modern British repertoire with plenty of class. Dishes are predominantly light and colourful with striking presentation, clear flavours and balanced combinations; raw materials are good, too. Start with a nicely presented warm tartlet combining well-timed pink wood pigeon, creamy wild mushrooms and coriander, or perhaps a hot salad of chicken livers, black pudding, buffalo mozzarella and pine nuts. It's nice to see gurnard among the mains, served perhaps as a competent modern take on fish 'n' chips, competing with pink and tender loin of lamb with Savoy cabbage and bacon. To finish, try a crème brûlée flavoured with Tahitian vanilla, or maybe a hot passion-fruit soufflé with strawberry cream. Service is bright, cheery and professional. A compact global wine list includes six half-bottles and house selections at £11.60 (£3 a glass).

CHEFS: Boyd McIntosh and Robert Fryer   PROPRIETORS: Boyd McIntosh, Joanne and Robert Fryer   OPEN: Wed to Mon 12 to 2, 7 to 9.30   MEALS: alc (main courses £7 to £19)   SERVICE: not inc, card slips closed   CARDS: Delta, MasterCard, Switch, Visa   DETAILS: 46 seats. 16 seats outside. Car park. Vegetarian meals. No-smoking area. Music. No mobile phones   ACCOMMODATION: 3 rooms, 2 with bath/shower. TV. B&B £45 to £70 £5

COLCHESTER Essex   map 6

Lemon Tree ✱ £

48 St Johns Street, Colchester CO2 7AD   COOKING 1
TEL/FAX: (01206) 767337   MODERN BRITISH
WEBSITE: www.the-lemon-tree.com   £18–£49

A chunk of Colchester's Roman city wall forms the back of Joanna and Patrik Minder's cheerful town-centre bistro, which also sports an al fresco eating area at the front. The kitchen takes a contemporary view of things, serving confit of duck, fig and foie gras terrine with red onion chutney, arranging grilled loin of monkfish on a three-bean and curly kale stir-fry, and offering vegetarians wild mushroom and ricotta ravioli in a tomato and artichoke sauce. Desserts, such as sticky toffee and date pudding, have drawn enthusiastic comments, and service continues in its own pleasant way. The wine list has been put together with an eye for interesting names and good value. House French is £10.95.

CHEF: Patrik Minder   PROPRIETORS: Joanna and Patrik Minder   OPEN: Mon to Sat 12 to 9.30 (10 Fri and Sat)   MEALS: alc (main courses £7 to £16.50). Set L £5.95 (1 course) to £9.95, Set D Mon to Thur £6.95 (1 course) to £12.95   SERVICE: not inc   CARDS: Amex, Delta, Diners, MasterCard, Switch, Visa   DETAILS: 80 seats. 50 seats outside. Private parties: 90 main room, 20 to 30 private rooms. Vegetarian meals. Children's helpings. No smoking in 1 dining room. Wheelchair access (also women's WC). Occasional music £5

COLERNE Wiltshire   map 2

▲ Lucknam Park ✱   NEW ENTRY

Colerne SN14 8AZ
TEL: (01225) 742777   FAX: (01225) 743536   COOKING 6
WEBSITE: www.lucknampark.co.uk   MODERN EUROPEAN
off A420 at Ford, 6m W of Chippenham   £44–£90

Lucknam Park dates from the late seventeenth century, although the façade that appears as you approach along the gloriously long tree-lined drive is principally Georgian. The interior décor aims to match the grandeur of the outward appearance – 'rather impressive in its over-voluptuousness', as one visitor put it – and the high-ceilinged dining room feels as cavernous as a ballroom. Service is somewhat stiff and formal, with lots of ceremonious napkin etiquette.

Hywel Jones, who last appeared in the guide at the ill-fated Pharmacy in London, was appointed head chef in January 2004. An early inspection meal found him still settling in, but, after a pre-starter of parsnip cappuccino, things started impressively with a boudin of sweetbreads – its crisp exterior contrasting with a melting middle – set on grated celeriac in a thick velouté flavoured assertively with truffle. Luxury ingredients are used in carefree fashion, as in a main course of pot-roast Anjou pigeon with a cabbage parcel of sweetbreads and pigeon livers, topped with a sliver of seared foie gras and girolles, and finished with a 'deliciously deep and powerful' jus of ceps and parsnips with a hint of truffle oil. Fish dishes have also been well reported – an impeccably fresh and sweet-tasting piece of turbot in a delicate, creamy shellfish broth with tender confit fennel, for example – and, to finish, elaborate desserts might include 'lemon three ways': a wedge of tart, a sorbet and a jelly. The wine list is focused on France with plenty of big-ticket Burgundies and clarets. Prices start at £17.50.

CHEF: Hywel Jones   PROPRIETOR: Lucknam Park Hotel Ltd   OPEN: Sun L 12.30 to 3, all week D 7 to 10.30 MEALS: Set L £20 (2 courses) to £27, Set D £45 (2 courses) to £55. Lounge L menu available   SERVICE: not inc, card slips closed   CARDS: Amex, Delta, Diners, MasterCard, Switch, Visa   DETAILS: 80 seats. 30 seats outside. Private parties: 64 main room, 2 to 30 private rooms. Car park. Vegetarian meals. Children's helpings. No children under 8. Jacket and tie. No smoking. Wheelchair access (also WC). Occasional music. No mobile phones   ACCOMMODATION: 41 rooms, all with bath/shower. TV. Phone. Room only £225 to £770. Rooms for disabled. Baby facilities. Swimming pool (£5)

COOKHAM Berkshire   map 3

Manzano's

19–21 Station Hill Parade, Cookham SL6 9BR   COOKING 4
TEL: (01628) 525775   SPANISH/MEDITERRANEAN
                                                                  £41–£50

Spanish paintings and mirrors on off-white walls set the mood in Richard and Deena Manzano's welcoming, homely restaurant in an unprepossessing row of shops. Lunchtime tapas (Monday to Thursday) reinforce the theme, and the full menu is suffused with Iberian influences: empanada gallega (a puff pastry 'flat pie' with tuna, peppers, tomatoes and onions), loin of pork with Rioja sauce infused with black pudding, onions and apple, and seared salmon 'escabèche' with crackling skin and a pickled dressing of pressed roast peppers and sherry vinegar – not to mention zarzuela and three versions of paella. Occasionally, the kitchen leaves Spain for flaked Cornish crabmeat with brandy and cream, or long-braised beef with beer, but returns to base for desserts like tarta de Santiago (almond tart with prunes soaked in Carlos I brandy). A quartet of house wines (at £11.95 and £12.95) heads the list, which features a creditable Spanish contingent and good-value alternatives from elsewhere.

CHEF: Richard Manzano   PROPRIETORS: Richard and Deena Manzano   OPEN: Mon to Fri L 12 to 2, Mon to Sat D 7 to 10   CLOSED: 2 weeks Aug, bank hols   MEALS: Set L £10 (2 courses), Set D £10 (2 courses) to £28. Tapas menu available Mon to Thurs L   SERVICE: 12.5%, card slips closed   CARDS: Amex, Delta, Diners, MasterCard, Switch, Visa   DETAILS: 35 seats. 12 seats outside. Private parties: 36 main room. Car park. Vegetarian meals. No-smoking area. Occasional music. Air-conditioned (£5)

▲ Inn on the Green ⁵⋇

The Old Cricket Common, Cookham Dean SL6 9NZ	COOKING **4**
TEL: (01628) 482638 FAX: (01628) 487474	MODERN BRITISH
WEBSITE: www.theinnonthegreen.com	£34–£74

This rambling, mock-Tudor inn is actually hidden from the eponymous village green behind a row of trees. A mixture of authentically ancient original features, reproduction fittings and austere contemporary furniture give the bar and dining room a mixed identity, as if it can't quite make its mind up whether it wants to be a traditional pub or a modern restaurant. There is no such confusion about the cooking. Executive chef and co-owner Gary Hollihead has his name emblazoned on the cover of the menu, although day-to-day running of the kitchen is in the hands of a team of able deputies who accurately reproduce their mentor's repertoire of upmarket, modern interpretations of classic dishes with some panache. Duck liver and foie gras parfait with chilli and red onion jam, or venison carpaccio with honey and soy dressing are typical of starters, while main courses take in seared tuna fillet on basil couscous with sauce vierge, and sautéed calf's liver and pancetta with creamed cauliflower. Soufflé – perhaps apricot – is a perennial highlight of desserts. The wine list shows a discerning eye for quality and features some interesting bottles, although hardly anything is under £20.

CHEF: Garry Hollihead   PROPRIETORS: Mark Fuller, Garry Hollihead and Andy Taylor   OPEN: Sat and Sun L 12 to 2.30, Tue to Sun D 7 to 9.30 (10 Sat, 9 Sun)   MEALS: alc exc Sun L (main courses £14.50 to £20). Set L Sat and D Tue to Thur and Sun £16.95 (2 courses) to £19.95, Set L Sun £23.50   SERVICE: 12.5% (optional) CARDS: Amex, Delta, MasterCard, Switch, Visa   DETAILS: 60 seats. 80 seats outside. Private parties: 80 main room, 6 to 40 private rooms. Car park. Vegetarian meals. No smoking in 1 dining room. Wheelchair access (also WC). Music. No mobile phones. Air-conditioned   ACCOMMODATION: 9 rooms, all with bath/ shower. TV. B&B £100 to £195 £5

▲ Corse Lawn House ▮ ⁵⋇

Corse Lawn GL19 4LZ	COOKING **2**
TEL: (01452) 780771 FAX: (01452) 780840	ANGLO-FRENCH
WEBSITE: www.corselawn.com	£31–£75

If your coach and horses are a little bespattered from the journey here, the large pond in front of this red-brick country house, owned by the Hine family of cognac fame, was designed originally as a washing facility. There are two dining areas within, the main restaurant and a less formal bistro, but the same style of food (think bruschetta of Mediterranean vegetables and mozzarella, chargrilled squid with rocket and chilli oil, and grilled ribeye with horseradish mash and béarnaise) is offered in both. Roast rump of lamb with crushed chickpeas, chorizo and red wine sauce suggests that, even when more involved, the cooking keeps its feet firmly on the ground. Finish with honey and walnut tart with toffee cream and vanilla ice cream. The excellent wine list, by contrast, sets off flights of fancy, with 30-odd pages of treats both young and mature, classically French and modishly global, but keen pricing and no-nonsense notes bring it happily back down to earth.

CHEFS: Baba Hine and Andrew Poole   PROPRIETORS: the Hine family   OPEN: all week 12 to 2, 7 (7.30 Sun) to 9.30   CLOSED: 24 to 26 Dec   MEALS: alc (main courses £13 to £28.50). Set L £17.50 (2 courses) to £19.50, Set D £29.50. Bistro menu available   SERVICE: not inc, card slips closed   CARDS: Amex, Delta, Diners, MasterCard, Switch, Visa   DETAILS: 60 seats. 30 seats outside. Private parties: 70 main room, 6 to 40 private rooms. Car park. Vegetarian meals. No babies in restaurant at D. Children's helpings. No smoking. Wheelchair access (also WC). Occasional music. No mobile phones   ACCOMMODATION: 19 rooms, all with bath/shower. TV. Phone. B&B £85 to £165. Rooms for disabled. Baby facilities. Swimming pool

CRAYKE North Yorkshire   map 9

▲ Durham Ox ⅝✦

Westway, Crayke, nr Easingwold YO61 4TE	COOKING 2
TEL: (01347) 821506 FAX: (01347) 823326	MODERN EUROPEAN
WEBSITE: www.thedurhamox.com	£26–£61

A genuinely welcoming atmosphere is one of the virtues of this old village pub on the edge of the Vale of York. Eat and drink casually in the beamed bar or choose the dressed-up formality of the blue-walled dining room. The kitchen supports local producers (and there's a shop on the premises where customers can buy their produce), and Jason Plevey can conjure up full-blooded flavours with it: witness a succulent terrine of free-range chicken and foie gras with celeriac salad and grain mustard mayonnaise, or braised osso buco with roast garlic, cherry tomatoes and herby polenta. Grills are an alternative to dishes such as baked cod with chorizo and Provençal vegetables, while desserts are old favourites like Ampleforth Abbey apple crumble and clotted cream. House wines are £10.95, and there's plenty of decent drinking for under £20.

CHEF: Jason Plevey   PROPRIETOR: Michael Ibbotson   OPEN: all week 12 to 2.30, 6 to 9.30 (10 Sat, 8.30 Sun)   CLOSED: 25 Dec   MEALS: alc (main courses £11 to £19). Set D Mon to Fri £7.95 (1 course) to £14.95   SERVICE: not inc, card slips closed   CARDS: Amex, Delta, MasterCard, Switch, Visa   DETAILS: 65 seats. 100 seats outside. Private parties: 35 main room, 10 to 16 private rooms. Car park. Vegetarian meals. Children's helpings. No smoking. Wheelchair access (not WC). Occasional music   ACCOMMODATION: 8 rooms, all with bath/shower. TV. B&B £60 to £160. Baby facilities

CRAY'S POND Berkshire   map 2

White Lion ⅝✦ £

Goring Road, Goring Heath, Cray's Pond RG8 7SH	COOKING 2
TEL: (01491) 680471 FAX: (01491) 681654	GLOBAL
WEBSITE: www.innastew.com	£25–£51

In a spread-out village north of Reading, this may look like a typical country pub, but these days it is known as a thriving pub/restaurant with a penchant for globally inspired food. Daily-changing menus please the diehards with devilled kidneys on toast, or grilled Torbay sole with caper butter and chips, but the main emphasis is on modern-sounding dishes from here, there and everywhere. On the menu grilled prawns with tabbouleh and feta salad, or cassoulet of duck with beans, chorizo and roast garlic, jostle tamarind-glazed salmon with curried noodle salad, and lamb chump chop with dhal and tsatsiki, while desserts veer from baked stuffed apple to coconut brûlée with banana samosa. The creditable wine list is organised by style and starts with house offerings at £11.95.

CHEFS: Robert Warham and Symon Reed   PROPRIETORS: Stuart and Caroline Pierrepont   OPEN: Tue to Sun L 12 to 2, Tue to Sat D 6 to 9.30   CLOSED: 25 and 26 Dec, 1 Jan   MEALS: alc (main courses £9 to £18).

Set L Sun £9.95 (1 course) to £15.95   SERVICE: not inc   CARDS: MasterCard, Switch, Visa   DETAILS: 64 seats. 40 seats outside. Private parties: 30 main room, 10 to 14 private rooms. Car park. Vegetarian meals. Children's helpings. No smoking. Music

CROSTHWAITE Cumbria · map 8

▲ Punch Bowl Inn ⅝✴ £

Crosthwaite LA8 8HR · COOKING 4
TEL: (01539) 568237   FAX: (01539) 568875 · MODERN BRITISH
WEBSITE: www.punchbowl.fsnet.co.uk · £23–£44

This rural Lakeland pub comes complete with real fires; low, beamed ceilings; well-kept real ales and an informal, relaxed atmosphere. But it is no ordinary country inn, as a glance at the upmarket modern British menu reveals. Starters of beetroot tart with goats' cheese and a basil and orange dressing, or crab and prawn gâteau with tomato, avocado, coconut relish and sweet chilli lime dressing, give way to roast lamb chump on horseradish mash with mint-dressed mixed beans and a thyme jus, or perhaps stuffed saddle of rabbit on goats' cheese mash with tomato tarragon jus, bacon and braised celery. Underlying the cooking are fine local produce and the skills of chef/proprietor Steven Doherty, honed at Le Gavroche (see entry, London). Steamed white chocolate pudding with vanilla anglaise and poached damsons is a typically sophisticated dessert idea. A daily specials board adds further choice to the already generous menu, and sandwiches are also served at lunchtime. The short wine list suits the pubby setting with plenty of options under £15, all served by the glass or pitcher, plus one or two smarter bottles.

CHEF: Steven Doherty   PROPRIETORS: Steven and Marjorie Doherty   OPEN: Tue to Sun L 12 to 2, Tue to Sat D 6 to 9   CLOSED: Four weeks Nov/Dec and 25 Dec   MEALS: alc (main courses £9 to £14). Set L Tue to Sat £10.95 (2 courses) to £13.95. Set L Sun £13.95 (2 courses) to £15.95. Set D Tue to Fri 6 to 7 £20 (2 courses)   SERVICE: not inc   CARDS: MasterCard, Switch, Visa   DETAILS: 70 seats. 20 seats outside. Private parties: 30 main room. Car park. Vegetarian meals. Children's helpings. No smoking. Wheelchair access (not WC). No music. No mobile phones   ACCOMMODATION: 3 rooms, all with bath/shower. TV. B&B £37.50 to £70

CRUDWELL Wiltshire · map 2

▲ Old Rectory ⅝✴

Crudwell SN16 9EP · COOKING 3
TEL: (01666) 577194   FAX: (01666) 577853 · MODERN BRITISH
WEBSITE: www.oldrectorycrudwell.co.uk · £32–£64

In a quiet Cotswolds village opposite the church, the Old Rectory is a typical Georgian building with a large walled garden. There are two comfortable sitting rooms with fires and a resident cat, while the large dining room has a restrained style, with limed-oak panelling, small pictures in gilt frames, and well-spaced tables with heavy white cloths, candles and flowers. The classic look is reflected in the formal presentation and creamy sauces that characterise the cooking, typified by roast chump of lamb with dauphinois potatoes, wild mushrooms and rosemary jus, or firm, juicy seared fillets of sea bass with basil mash, tomato fondue and mussels. Finish with British cheeses, or perhaps cappuccino crème brûlée with chocolate chip cookies. Set price meals apply at lunch, an à la carte for dinner. Wines are mainly French and represent a conservative selection, although prices are fair, starting at £12.95 for red and white Burgundy.

CHEF: Peter Fairclough   PROPRIETORS: Derek and Karen Woods   OPEN: all week 12 to 2, 7 to 9 (9.30 Fri and Sat)   MEALS: alc D (main courses £11.50 to £18.50). Set L £15.95 (2 courses) to £18.95. Light L menu available Mon to Sat   SERVICE: not inc   CARDS: Delta, MasterCard, Switch, Visa   DETAILS: 60 seats. Private parties: 40 main room, 2 to 26 private rooms. Car park. Vegetarian meals. Children's helpings. No children under 12 after 7pm. No smoking. Wheelchair access (not WC). Music. No mobile phones   ACCOMMODATION: 12 rooms, all with bath/shower. TV. Phone. B&B £75 to £169

CUCKFIELD West Sussex
map 3

Mansfields ⅝✳

1 Broad Street, Cuckfield RH17 5LJ	COOKING 2
TEL: (01444) 410222 FAX: (01444) 410333	MODERN EUROPEAN
	£29–£51

Mansfields, an unassuming house on the main street of this impeccably house-proud village, is made up of three small, dark-beamed dining rooms running into each other. The scale may be domestic, but what lifts this beyond the ordinary is the kitchen's attention to detail, a confident mastery of combinations and an awareness of seasonality. 'Excellent' fish soup, with a complexity of flavour, gets things off to a fine start, as does Somerset smoked eel accompanied simply by celeriac spiked with horseradish. Correctly timed monkfish with a herb-sharpened creamy mushroom sauce, and four pink lamb cutlets with ratatouille and a skilfully made jus flavoured with rosemary and thyme have been notable main courses. Vegetables get high praise, and among puddings might be intense chocolate crème brûlée, and praline ice cream with a 'voluptuous' hot toffee sauce. Service is attentive and intelligent, and prices on the routine wine list start at £10.75 and are far from rapacious.

CHEF: Günther Schlender   PROPRIETORS: Günther and Patricia Schlender   OPEN: Tue to Sat D only 7 to 9.30 (L for pre-booked parties only)   CLOSED: 26 Dec to first Sat Jan   MEALS: alc (main courses £10 to £16)   SERVICE: not inc, card slips closed   CARDS: Amex, Delta, MasterCard, Switch, Visa   DETAILS: 32 seats. Private parties: 12 main room, 12 to 32 private rooms. Vegetarian meals. Children's helpings. No smoking in 1 dining room. Music   £5

▲ Ockenden Manor ⅝✳

Ockenden Lane, Cuckfield RH17 5LD	COOKING 5
TEL: (01444) 416111 FAX: (01444) 415549	MODERN FRENCH
WEBSITE: www.hshotels.co.uk	£35–£104

The manor is at the bottom of a narrow lane in this exceedingly smart village. At the front is a small car park and a patch of lawn, although to the rear are nine acres of grounds. The tone is classic country house, the lounge accoutred with antique oils and the kinds of sofas into which you disappear, and one of the twin dining rooms boasts venerable dark oak panelling.

A number of fixed-price menus allows for flexible budget planning, and nobody will bat an eyelid if you hop from one to the other, such is the accommodating nature of the front-of-house team. Thickly cut salmon adorned with blobs of Avruga formed the centrepiece of a starter salad of exemplary freshness, supported by baby plum tomatoes, quail's eggs and diced potato in mayonnaise. A raviolo of wild mushrooms with melted Parmesan and ceps might be another way to begin. Combinations are carefully thought through, so that cubes of crisp-skinned duck breast gain hugely from their teaming with caramelised apples, Savoy cabbage, creamed celeriac and peppercorned roasting juices, or there may be a fillet of cod sent out as though it were roast lamb, with Puy lentils, confit garlic, button onions, French beans and a red wine sauce. A delicate touch distinguishes desserts such as lemon tart with blackcurrant sauce, or a lightly textured savarin filled with raspberries coated in coulis, dressed with clear, pale green mint syrup. Serious wines at serious prices mean you'll need to be ready to splash out – unless you stick to the dozen house selections, all at £17.50 or £3.95 a glass.

CHEF: Steve Crane   PROPRIETOR: Sandy Goodman   OPEN: all week 12.30 to 2, 7 to 9.30 (7.15 to 9 Sun) MEALS: Set L Mon to Fri £13.95 (2 courses) to £48, Set L Sat £16.50 (2 courses) to £48, Set L Sun £25.95, Set D £39 to £70. Bar menu available   SERVICE: not inc   CARDS: Amex, Delta, Diners, MasterCard, Switch, Visa   DETAILS: 45 seats. 20 seats outside. Private parties: 75 main room, 8 to 16 private rooms. Car park. Vegetarian meals. Children's helpings. No smoking. Occasional music. No mobile phones ACCOMMODATION: 22 rooms, all with bath/shower. TV. Phone. B&B £99 to £325 (£5)

DARGATE Kent

map 3

Dove

Plum Pudding Lane, Dargate ME13 9HB
TEL/FAX: (01227) 751360

COOKING 3
FRENCH
£32–£51

In a quiet and picturesque corner of Kent, not far from Canterbury, the Dove pulls in the punters with its good, unpretentious cooking and informal but efficient service. Scrubbed pine tables and wooden floors are just the ticket in these pub surroundings. Spot-on fish cookery has been reported, with wild sea bass accompanied by a powerful, yet simple, confit of fennel and red pepper – 'a marriage made in heaven'. Roast crown of pheasant has come on braised red cabbage, while a delicate, buttery pastry tart with wild mushroom and Bayonne ham filling was a definite success for one reader. An unctuous, oozing chocolate pudding has made a good finish. Vegetables and bread were the only weak elements reported this year. Beers from Shepherd Neame and wines starting at £12.50, with six by the glass and a decent selection under £20, contribute to the value.

CHEF: Nigel Morris   PROPRIETORS: Nigel and Bridget Morris   OPEN: Tue to Sun L 12 to 2, Wed to Sun D 7 to 9   MEALS: alc (not Sat L; main courses £13 to £18). Snack L menu available Sat   SERVICE: not inc, card slips closed   CARDS: Delta, MasterCard, Switch, Visa   DETAILS: 20 seats. 15 seats outside. Car park. No music

DARTMOUTH Devon

map 1

New Angel

NEW ENTRY

2 South Embankment, Dartmouth TQ6 9BH
TEL: (01803) 839425   FAX: (01803) 839567
WEBSITE: www.thenewangel.co.uk

COOKING 6
MODERN ANGLO-FRENCH
£50–£76

Formerly the Carved Angel, this venerable landmark was given a new lease of life in the spring of 2004 when it was taken over by John Burton-Race, most recently seen not in any restaurant kitchen but on TV in his own family kitchen in France. The place still has a lively, jolly atmosphere to go with views over the estuary from the upstairs dining room, where much wood is in evidence, from the pale painted floorboards to the dark, unclothed tables. Flexibility is the order of the day, with breakfast, brunch, and no pressure to eat a full three courses at lunch or dinner.

The sojourn in France has given John Burton-Race's cooking a simpler, homelier aspect, and though he is not a day-to-day presence in the kitchen, everything is handled with aplomb by Nigel Marriage and Robin Zavou. Excellent crisp bread rolls make a fine first impression, which is not dispelled by starters of rich, creamy terrine of duck and chicken liver with a complementary pear chutney and toasted brioche, or crab salad, featuring plenty of white and brown crab meat bound with a light creamy dressing and salad leaves in a vinaigrette containing tiny dice of avocado, tomato and grapefruit. Main courses show a similar blend of simplicity, sophistication and excellent technique, as in pink and tender rack of lamb with a herb crust, served with well-flavoured pea purée and a plum jus, or a simply grilled half-lobster with garlic and herb butter, the perfect freshness of the lobster apparent in its delicate flavour and tender meat. Among desserts, a dish of sugar-glazed raspberries encased in a thin wall of white chocolate and set on a creamy white chocolate mousse is 'an inspired mixture of textures and tastes'. France leads the way on a good wine list, including a dozen-plus by the glass and seasonal recommendations, but interesting choices elsewhere look better value.

CHEFS: John Burton-Race, Nigel Marriage and Robin Zavou PROPRIETOR: John Burton-Race OPEN: Tue to Sun L 12 to 2.30, Tue to Sat D 6.30 to 10.30 CLOSED: Jan MEALS: alc (main courses £16 to £26). Breakfast/brunch available Tue to Sun 8.30 to 11.30 SERVICE: not inc, 10% for parties of 8 or more CARDS: Delta, Diners, MasterCard, Switch, Visa DETAILS: 80 seats. Private parties: 30 main room, 30 to 40 private rooms. Vegetarian meals. Music. Air conditioned

DEDHAM Essex

map 6

▲ milsoms

Stratford Road, Dedham C07 6HW
TEL: (01206) 322795 FAX: (01206) 323689
WEBSITE: www.milsomhotels.com

COOKING 1
GLOBAL
£27–£57

Close to its more sophisticated sibling, Le Talbooth, milsoms is a different kind of place altogether. This rather grand Georgian building is home to a bustling bistro. Inside, it is a smart, modern split-level space, which fills up rapidly on weekend evenings; take a drink in the bar (where the food is ordered). Crab and crayfish crostini salad is alongside hummus and taramasalata among starters, while main courses are as cosmopolitan as salt-and-pepper squid with cucumber sambal; lamb shank with grain mustard mash; and linguine with baby artichokes and gorgonzola. The pudding menu runs from baked tamarillo with pannacotta to apple crumble and custard. House wines at £12 head a globe-trotting list that offers reasonable scope for under £20.

CHEF: Stas Anastasiades PROPRIETORS: Gerald and Paul Milsom OPEN: all week 12 to 2.15, 6 to 9.30 (10 Fri and Sat) MEALS: alc (main courses £8.50 to £16.50) SERVICE: not inc CARDS: Amex, Delta, Diners, MasterCard, Switch, Visa DETAILS: 80 seats. 80 seats outside. Private parties: 8 to 16 private rooms. Car park. Vegetarian meals. Children's helpings. No-smoking area. Wheelchair access (also WC). Music. Air-conditioned ACCOMMODATION: 14 rooms, all with bath/shower. TV. Phone. Room only £75 to £135. Rooms for disabled. Baby facilities

'[The waiter], a very Hugh Grant sort of chap who wasn't wearing a cravat but looked as though he'd be at home in one, came around to each table with a broad grin. [We] thought it was somebody we knew who'd just spotted us from across the room and was coming by to say hello.'
(On eating in London)

▲ Sun Inn ✹ £

NEW ENTRY

High Street, Dedham CO7 6DF

TEL: (01206) 323351   FAX: (01206) 323964

WEBSITE: www.thesuninndedham.com

COOKING 2
MEDITERRANEAN
£25–£41

In the heart of Constable country, this revamped fifteenth-century coaching inn wears a fashionable outfit. Old blackened timbers are reminders of the past, but the interior is now primrose-yellow, with ceiling spotlights, artwork and a menu that looks to Italy, Spain and Morocco for most of its inspiration. Tapas feature among the starters, along with contemporary combinations like roast butternut squash and red onion salad with rocket, hazelnut and feta. Main courses show a similar mixture of influences, with lamb tagine and Portuguese fish stew standing alongside 'terrific comfort food' such as slow-cooked rib of beef with red wine, rosemary and horseradish accompanied by celeriac and potato purée. Finish with Earls Colne ice creams or French cheeses. The lively modern wine list promises over a dozen by the glass. Prices start at £10.50 a bottle.

CHEF/PROPRIETOR: Piers Baker   OPEN: all week L 12 to 2.30 (3 Sat and Sun), Mon to Sat D 7 to 9.30 (10 Fri and Sat)   CLOSED: 25 to 27 Dec   MEALS: alc (main courses £7.50 to £12.50)   SERVICE: not inc, card slips closed   CARDS: MasterCard, Switch, Visa   DETAILS: 130 seats. 60 seats outside. Private parties: 25 main room, 10 to 30 private rooms. Car park. Vegetarian meals. Children's helpings. No smoking in 1 dining room. Music   ACCOMMODATION: 4 rooms, all with bath/shower. TV. B&B £55 to £150 ⓔ5⃝

DERBY Derbyshire

map 5

Darleys ✹

Darley Abbey Mills, Haslams Lane, Darley Abbey,
Derby DE22 1DZ

TEL/FAX: (01332) 364987

WEBSITE: www.darleys.com

off A6 2m N of city centre

COOKING 4
MODERN BRITISH
£27–£57

Jonathan and Kathryn Hobson took over Darleys at the end of 2003, and all is very well indeed. The terrific location by the River Derwent is a crowd-puller, while the kitchen – headed by Jonathan and long-serving chef Kevin Stone – is producing some fine modern British food. Quality appears consistent, and £15.50 buys a three-course lunch at which creative (and successful) ideas run from gently pickled slivers of mackerel on warm potato salad with spring onion-scented quenelles of crème fraîche, to a glazed tartlet of mozzarella, young leaf spinach and pine nuts with red onion salsa. A succulent, herb-crusted cod fillet impressed at inspection, the accompanying ratatouille delicate and beautifully executed. Vegetarians might choose tomato polenta on spring cabbage with a generous medley of crisp baby vegetables. At dinner things get more elaborate – perhaps a ballottine of chicken and lobster, squid ink linguine, sautéed baby leeks and chervil emulsion, or roast red mullet that comes with confit tomato risotto and tempura frogs' legs. Desserts might include an interesting sponge charlotte of rhubarb and stem ginger well complemented by a green apple sorbet, or a rich chocolate and Baileys pannacotta with warm fudge sauce. The international wine list offers plenty of choice under £20, with house selections from £14.

CHEFS: Jonathan Hobson and Kevin Stone   PROPRIETORS: Jonathan and Kathryn Hobson   OPEN: all week L 12 to 2.30, Mon to Sat D 7.30 to 10.30   MEALS: alc D (main courses £17 to £18.50). Set L £13.50 (2 courses) to £15.50   SERVICE: not inc   CARDS: Delta, MasterCard, Switch, Visa   DETAILS: 70 seats. 16

seats outside. Private parties: 70 main room. Car park. Vegetarian meals. Children's helpings. No smoking in 1 dining room. Wheelchair access (not WC). Music. No mobile phones. Air-conditioned £5

DINTON Buckinghamshire

map 3

La Chouette ♥ ⅝✳

Westlington Green, Dinton HP17 8UW
TEL: (01296) 747422

COOKING 4
BELGIAN
£25–£65

This charming restaurant in a converted pub is in picturesque Westlington Green, the western end of Dinton. Chef/patron Frederic Desmette, 'a genuine character', has been known to keep guests entertained with loquacious forays from the kitchen (he's also a wildlife photographer, with a keen interest in owls – hence the restaurant's name and a theme of its décor). His Belgian origins are apparent in pheasant Brabançonne, or a salad of Belgian grey shrimps enlivened with shredded apple and dressed with vinaigrette. The best dishes here can have diners in raptures – duck with morels being a case in point among main courses, and the chocolate sauce accompanying a vanilla ice cream was 'quite the best I have ever tasted' for one reporter. The serious wine list (all-French, bar one super-Tuscan) offers many excellent bins from famous and also lesser-known regions in multiple vintages. House bottles are just £13.50, but there's little else under £20.

CHEF/PROPRIETOR: Frederic Desmette   OPEN: Mon to Fri L 12 to 2, Mon to Sat D 7 to 9   MEALS: alc (main courses £13 to £16.50). Set L £13.50 to £36.50, Set D £26.50 to £36.50   SERVICE: 12.5% (optional), card slips closed   CARDS: Delta, MasterCard, Switch, Visa   DETAILS: 40 seats. Private parties: 40 main room. Car park. Children's helpings. No smoking in dining room. No music. No mobile phones

DORRIDGE West Midlands

map 5

▲ Forest ⅝✳

25 Station Approach, Dorridge B93 8JA
TEL: (01564) 772120   FAX: (01564) 732680
WEBSITE: www.forest-hotel.com

COOKING 4
MODERN FRENCH
£25–£53

Old and new blend seamlessly at this Victorian railway hotel, the ornate red-brick façade giving way to a stylish modern brasserie of spotlights, floorboards, plain tables and neutral tones. Amid an atmosphere of relaxed calm (in contrast to the popular bar area), James Pye delivers straightforward brasserie cooking along the lines of starters of ham hock terrine with leeks and sauce gribiche, wild mushroom risotto, and a warm salad of bacon, new potatoes and Brie, and main courses of John Dory poached in Shiraz with creamed celeriac and Savoy cabbage, and duck leg cassoulet with Toulouse and merguez sausages. One visitor was taken by a good-value Sunday lunch, praising roast rump of Scottish beef ('very good indeed') and a successful brioche bread-and-butter pudding. Wines, arranged by style, are a sound selection, with prices mostly pegged below £20 and a good choice by the glass.

CHEF: James Pye   PROPRIETORS: Gary and Tracy Perkins   OPEN: all week L 12 to 2.30, Mon to Sat D 6.30 to 10   CLOSED: 25 Dec   MEALS: alc exc Sun L (main courses £8.50 to £18). Set L Mon to Sat £10 (2 courses) to £15, Set L Sun £14.50 (2 courses) to £17.50, Set D Mon and Tue £12.50 (2 courses) to £17.50 (inc wine). Bar menu available   SERVICE: not inc   CARDS: Amex, Delta, MasterCard, Switch, Visa   DETAILS: 70 seats. 70 seats outside. Private parties: 24 main room, 10 to 150 private rooms. Car park. Vegetarian meals. Children's helpings. No smoking. Wheelchair access (also WC). Music. Air-

conditioned   ACCOMMODATION: 12 rooms, all with bath/shower. TV. Phone. B&B £62.50 to £97.50. Baby
facilities (£5)

DORRINGTON Shropshire   map 5

▲ Country Friends ⅍✳

Dorrington SY5 7JD	COOKING **6**
TEL: (01743) 718707	MODERN BRITISH
	£42–£56

In this half-timbered building beside the A49 south of Shrewsbury, the lounge and bar
have a relaxed and informal feel, while the smarter dining room has small but well spaced
tables and overlooks a garden to the rear. Charles Whittaker's cooking follows the purist's
credo of keeping things simple to accentuate the raw materials.

Start perhaps with a twice-baked soufflé of crab and Parmesan, or maybe a wild
mushroom risotto with confit duck and fig purée. Moving on, calf's liver has been paired
with a bean and sausage cassoulet, and venison presented on parsnip purée with beetroot
sauce; fillet steak has been topped with Welsh rarebit. Conclude with queen of puddings
and gin-and-lime-flavoured ice cream, or pistachio parfait with caramelised banana.
Lighter options are available à la carte at lunchtime. The style-organised wine list is short
and sweet, but provides interesting choices from across the world (including France). It
kicks off at £12.75, and there are five by the glass.

CHEF: Charles Whittaker   PROPRIETORS: Charles and Pauline Whittaker   OPEN: Wed to Sat 12 to 2, 7 to 9
(9.30 Sat)   CLOSED: Oct half term, 2 weeks end-July   MEALS: Set L and D £29.30 (2 courses) to £35.70.
Light L menu available   SERVICE: not inc   CARDS: Delta, MasterCard, Switch, Visa   DETAILS: 40 seats.
Private parties: 40 main room. Car park. No smoking. Wheelchair access (not WC). No music. No mobile
phones   ACCOMMODATION: 1 room, with bath/shower. D,B&B £95 to £135. No children

DURHAM Co Durham   map 10

Bistro 21 ⅍✳ £

Aykley Heads House, Aykley Heads, Durham DH1 5TS	NEW CHEF
TEL: (0191) 384 4354 FAX: (0191) 384 1149	MEDITERRANEAN
	£26–£51

A delightfully converted farmhouse on the northern edge of the city seems an unlikely
venue for a popular bistro, but '21' draws the crowds with its relaxed rustic-chic décor and
reliable cooking. Pink and grey walls, stripped floorboards and simple wood tables laid
with cloths convey something of a Mediterranean feel, helped on by a menu that includes
buffalo mozzarella with slow-roast vine tomatoes, rocket and pesto, or a sauté niçoise of
king prawns and calamari as starters. A new head chef joined the team too late for an
inspection, but the classic modern bistro cooking continues. Expect good-quality
ingredients in dishes like pan-fried calf's liver with red onion marmalade, Parma ham and
sage, or roasted cod fillet with pea purée, tomato salsa and straw potatoes. Desserts have a
traditional slant, with spotted dick and bay leaf custard, or treacle tart with mascarpone
sorbet. Specials supplement the main menu, while a sensibly priced wine list of 40-odd bins
starts with French house at £12. (See Newcastle and Ponteland for other restaurants in
Terry Laybourne's '21' stable).

CHEF: Paul O'Hara   PROPRIETOR: Terence Laybourne   OPEN: Mon to Sat 12 to 2, 7 (6 Sat) to 10.30
CLOSED: 25 Dec, bank hols   MEALS: alc (main courses £11 to £16.50). Set L £13 (2 courses) to £15.50

SERVICE: not inc   CARDS: Amex, Delta, Diners, MasterCard, Switch, Visa   DETAILS: 55 seats. 20 seats outside. Private parties: 55 main room, 10 to 30 private rooms. Car park. Vegetarian meals. No smoking. Music

EASTBOURNE East Sussex   map 3

Bonnicks 🍴   NEW ENTRY

55 Grove Road, Eastbourne BN21 4TX	COOKING 3
TEL: (01323) 416419 FAX: (01323) 416941	MODERN ENGLISH
WEBSITE: www.bonnicks.com	£28–£53

Bonnicks' fascia makes an elegant impact on this particular central street, and the interior reveals a long room with bold, contemporary art on plain walls; 'calm, cool, but with a touch of warmth'. Freebies abound, including, for one reporter, a clean-tasting leek soup with goats' cheese kicking things off very favourably. A starter of crisp-skinned salmon fillet sitting atop a smoked haddock confit was a good idea well executed, while fillets of brill with red wine sauce showed willingness to tackle bold flavourings. Meat dishes could include roast squab with Glenlivet and honey jus, or slow-braised beef with black pudding and parsnip purée. Among desserts, champagne jelly with raspberries, and a crème brûlée trio (strawberry and black pepper, vanilla, prune and Armagnac) have pleased, and an enthusiastic wine list, beginning at £13, has 16 by the glass and choice under £25.

CHEFS: Lawrence Bonnick and Nic Oarton   PROPRIETORS: Mark Fisher and Lawrence Bonnick   OPEN: Tue to Sat 12.30 to 2.30, 7 to 9.30   CLOSED: 26 Dec, 1 Jan, 2 weeks from 15 Feb   MEALS: Set L £11 (1 course) to £19, Set D £32   SERVICE: not inc, 10% for parties of 6 or more   CARDS: Amex, Delta, Diners, MasterCard, Switch, Visa   DETAILS: 34 seats. Private parties: 34 main room. Vegetarian meals. No smoking. Wheelchair access (not WC). Music. No mobile phones. Air-conditioned (£5)

▲ Grand Hotel, Mirabelle 🍷 🍴

King Edwards Parade, Eastbourne BN21 4EQ	COOKING 6
TEL: (01323) 412345 FAX: (01323) 412233	MODERN EUROPEAN
WEBSITE: www.grandeastbourne.com	£28–£76

Situated right on the seafront, the Grand Hotel lives up to its name. The tall, white, neo-classical building, all pillars and balustrades, covers an entire block and is set back from the road behind a semi-circular driveway and tall shrubs. The Mirabelle restaurant has its own separate entrance off a side street, and the vast dining room is on the first floor, a long narrow room with one end facing the sea. Predominantly pale pink décor is in keeping with the outer appearances, with heavily ruched net curtains, miles of flowery fabric, and ornate chandeliers – it is all reminiscent of a traditional ballroom, an effect enhanced by taped piano music.

The kitchen aims to live up to the setting with a grand cooking style laden with flourishes and luxury ingredients, and dishes are wheeled around on trolleys under silver domes – even the appetisers. Among starters, pike soufflé with smoked eel sauce is typical, the soufflé having a wobbly, mousse-like texture and a fresh, light taste that contrasts well with the stronger flavour of the sauce. To follow, cod comes on rösti potatoes and ratatouille, and well-flavoured duck breast with a sweet honeyed crust is served on a herby potato cake with baby beets and a sticky port sauce. Puddings are 'complex works of art': a pear tarte Tatin, for example, barely recognisable as such, comprises a scoop of intense cinnamon ice cream set on a pear purée encircled by cubes of jelly flavoured with pear liqueur and topped with crisp shortbread biscuit. The wine list has some very special bottles, even the almost unattainable Haelan Estate from California, but has less to satisfy more modest tastes (the French vins de pays range, including £17 house bottles, is the best bolthole). Value is variable, and some New World ranges could be better.

CHEF: Gerald Röser   PROPRIETOR: Elite Hotels   OPEN: Tue to Sat; 12.30 to 2, 7 to 10   CLOSED: First 2 weeks Jan   MEALS: Set L £12.50 to £19, Set D £35 to £55   SERVICE: net prices, card slips closed   CARDS: Amex, Diners, MasterCard, Switch, Visa   DETAILS: 50 seats. Private parties: 50 main room. Car park. Vegetarian meals. No children. Jacket and tie. No smoking in dining room. Wheelchair access (also WC). Music. No mobile phones. Air-conditioned   ACCOMMODATION: 152 rooms, all with bath/shower. TV. Phone. B&B £135 to £430. Rooms for disabled. Baby listening/sitting. Baby facilities. Swimming pool

EAST CHILTINGTON East Sussex

map 3

Jolly Sportsman ♥ ⅚✳

Chapel Lane, East Chiltington BN7 3BA
TEL/FAX: (01273) 890400
WEBSITE: www.jollysportsman.com

COOKING 3
MODERN EUROPEAN
£25–£55

Tucked away in the Sussex countryside, but within striking distance of both Lewes and Brighton, the Jolly Sportsman is a pub where 'ambition is considerable'. The décor and atmosphere are perhaps more modern bistro/brasserie than pub, but the decibels can certainly rise when the place is in full swing. Menus tend to be sensibly short with concise descriptions, and carefully sourced ingredients include the likes of Cornish gurnard and free-range chicken. The kitchen has delivered 'brilliant' slow-cooked lamb and fillet of halibut, and 'exquisite' puddings like spongy apricot and almond tart, and own-made ice creams generate 'amazed enthusiasm', according to one diner. The fixed-price lunch menu is good value, and the wine list works well at all levels, from a good house selection (£12 upwards) by bottle or glass through to ranges of considerable depth in Italy, Bordeaux and Burgundy plus a strong showing from the New World. Half-bottles abound.

CHEFS: Richard Willis and Bruce Wass   PROPRIETORS: Bruce and Gwyneth Wass   OPEN: Tue to Sun L 12.30 to 2 (3 Sun), Bank hol Mon L 12.30 to 3, Tue to Sat D 7 to 9 (10 Fri and Sat)   CLOSED: 4 days Christmas   MEALS: alc (main courses £9 to £17). Set L £11 (2 courses) to £14.75   SERVICE: 10%, card slips closed   CARDS: Delta, MasterCard, Switch, Visa   DETAILS: 80 seats. 40 seats outside. Private parties: 60 main room, 12 to 30 private rooms. Car park. Vegetarian meals. Children's helpings. No smoking. Wheelchair access (also WC). No music

EAST END Hampshire

map 2

East End Arms

Main Road, East End SO41 5SY
TEL: (01590) 626223
WEBSITE: www.eastendarms.co.uk
off B3054, 2m E of Lymington

COOKING 3
MODERN BRITISH/SEAFOOD
£32–£46

In a fine part of the New Forest, this unpretentious, popular local is so unassuming it could easily be missed. Pricing is simple, with starters at dinner such as devilled kidneys, or hake and salmon cake all at the same price. Main courses such as salmon pie with chunks of fresh-tasting fish topped with good mash, or an authentic version of chicken dansak clearly show the kitchen's culinary skills. At dessert stage, favourites like bread-and-butter pudding sit alongside interesting takes on traditional ideas, as in an upside-down apple crumble. Lunch is an even more straightforward affair of snackier items like salt-cod fishcakes and crab salad. A range of well-kept beers is supplemented by around 20 decent wines starting at £13.

CHEFS: Stuart Kitcher and Paul Sykes   PROPRIETOR: John Illsley   OPEN: Tue to Sun L 12 to 2, Tue to Sat D 7 to 9. No food 25 Dec, first 2 weeks Mar, first 2 weeks Oct   CLOSED: Tue after bank hols   MEALS: alc (main courses L £5.50 to £12, D £12)   SERVICE: not inc, card slips closed   CARDS: Delta, MasterCard, Switch, Visa   DETAILS: 34 seats. 60 seats outside. Car park. Children's helpings. Music

EAST GRINSTEAD West Sussex   map 3

▲ Gravetye Manor ▮ ✲

Vowels Lane, East Grinstead RH19 4LJ
TEL: (01342) 810567   FAX: (01342) 810080
WEBSITE: www.gravetyemanor.co.uk
Off B2110, 3 miles SW of East Grinstead

COOKING 6
MODERN BRITISH/FRENCH
£39–£88

This lovely Elizabethan manor house and garden ('a pleasure to visit at any time of the year') always felt like a grand establishment, humanised by the gentle presence of owner Peter Herbert. Now he has sold it, after 47 years. But devotees can relax, for he remains as consultant to the new owners, who just happen to be his former general manager Andrew Russell and head chef Mark Raffan. Early reports indicate little change; the décor still revolves around fine antiques and oak panelling, and the cooking continues to win praise.

Mark Raffan uses plenty of upmarket materials – panaché of seafood, for example, with cappuccino of lobster and summer truffles, or feuilleté of local wild duck with ceps – but such ingredients can be teamed with relatively humble ones: witness delicate Jerusalem artichoke mousse with lentil salad and winter vegetable crisps, or braised ox cheek with winter vegetables, creamed potatoes and braising juices enriched with red wine. Dishes that impressed at inspection included terrine of ham hock with sunblush tomatoes and sauce vierge, and tortellini of langoustines with spinach and lobster sauce. A star among desserts was a pleasantly restrained Brillat Savarin cheesecake with rhubarb. Extras may not be quite in the same league, but good bread comes in five different varieties. The wine list is a classical heavyweight – Bordeaux vintages going back over 40 years and swathes of Burgundy – but look out too for lively selections from Australia, New Zealand, South Africa and California. Wine prices – like the food prices – include service, and on that basis don't look too bad; house red is £16.

CHEF: Mark Raffan   PROPRIETORS: Andrew Russell and Mark Raffan   OPEN: all week 12.30 to 1.45, 7 to 9.30   CLOSED: 25 Dec D residents only   MEALS: Set L £27 to £52, Set D £37 to £52. Bar/garden menu available   SERVICE: net prices, card slips closed   CARDS: MasterCard, Switch, Visa   DETAILS: 45 seats. 12 seats outside. Private parties: 20 main room. Car park. Vegetarian meals. No children under 7. No smoking. No music. No mobile phones   ACCOMMODATION: 18 rooms, all with bath/shower. TV. Phone. Room only £100 to £325. No children under 7. Baby facilities. Fishing

EASTON GREY Wiltshire   map 2

▲ Whatley Manor ▼ ✲

Easton Grey SN16 0RB
TEL: (01666) 822888   FAX: (01666) 822888
WEBSITE: www.whatleymanor.com
S of B4040 2m W of Malmesbury

COOKING 7
MODERN EUROPEAN
£80–£116

The long, tree-lined drive through landscaped gardens sets the tone for what waits at the end: a spectacular country house of Cotswold stone (much of it of recent construction, contrary to appearances). The hotel has a full complement of modern facilities, including spa, boardroom and a luxurious cinema, plus two restaurants.

The more formal Dining Room, redecorated since last year, now has pale yellow shot silk on the walls, giving a lighter feel, and the chandeliers and green wall lamps have gone. Martin Burge worked under John Burton-Race at the Landmark, and his cooking is similar: top-quality ingredients in dishes that show a high level of complexity and 'superb' presentation. Among starters, for example, a whole quail is roasted, except the legs, which are confit and rolled with foie gras, then garnished with grapes and salad leaves in a walnut dressing, while hake ravioli is accompanied by langoustine tails in a sage-scented poultry jus. To follow, there might be pan-fried Scottish beef glazed in its juices and served with snails in parsley butter and a potato galette; or roast turbot wrapped in bacon, set on pak choi and moistened with a pork Sauternes jus. Desserts might take in a caramelised apple croustade filled with vanilla cassonade and butterscotch sauce, or lemon and orange curd-filled ravioli lying on a bed of pink grapefruit and mango under a coconut-foam quilt. Wines are truly international, spreading the net as far as England and India. There are some serious Bordeaux and lighter picks from around France, while other ranges, such as the Italian whites, can be spot-on. Prices start at £18.

Also under Burge's aegis, there's the more informal Le Mazot brasserie, with a more 'country-kitchen chintz' feel, pitch pine fittings and upholstered banquette seating. If the cooking is simpler and less aspirational, it is well presented and has been reported as 'memorable' (in the best sense).

CHEF: Martin Burge   PROPRIETOR: Christian Landolt   OPEN: Wed to Sun D only 7 to 10   MEALS: Set D £60 to £75 (min 2)   SERVICE: 10%   CARDS: Amex, Diners, MasterCard, Switch, Visa   DETAILS: 40 seats. Private parties: 30 main room. Car park. Vegetarian meals. No children under 12. No smoking. Wheelchair access (also WC). Occasional music. No mobile phones   ACCOMMODATION: 23 rooms, all with bath/shower. TV. Phone. B&B £275 to £1,700. Rooms for disabled. No children under 12. Swimming pool

EAST WITTON North Yorkshire   map 8

▲ Blue Lion

East Witton DL8 4SN   COOKING 3
TEL: (01969) 624273   FAX: (01969) 624189   MODERN BRITISH
WEBSITE: www.thebluelion.co.uk   £28–£51

A charming Wensleydale village of substantial stone-built houses, East Witton looks superficially as if the rest of the world has passed it by for the last 200 years. At its heart is this thriving pub, a big old coaching inn with a warm, cosy bar and separate dining room. In the bar, the flagstone floor, large open fire and simple wooden furniture keep up traditional appearances, while the long blackboard menu blends old and new ideas. Among starters might be bubble and squeak with black pudding and red wine sauce, or roast scallops with lemon risotto and Gruyère, and to follow poached smoked haddock on new potatoes, topped with poached egg and leek and mushroom sauce, or slow-roast belly pork with honey and apple sauce. The same menu in printed form is offered in the slightly more formal setting of the candlelit dining room. A list of around 90 wines opens with two pages of varied and good-value house selections, all available by the bottle (from £11.50), half-litre (£7.90) or glass (from £3).

CHEF: John Dalby   PROPRIETOR: Paul Klein   OPEN: Sun L 12 to 2.15, all week D 7 to 9.30   CLOSED: 25 Dec MEALS: alc D (main courses £8.50 to £17.50). Set L Sun £18.95   SERVICE: not inc   CARDS: Delta, MasterCard, Switch, Visa   DETAILS: 40 seats. 20 seats outside. Private parties: 40 main room, 10 to 25

private rooms. Car park. Vegetarian meals. Children's helpings. Wheelchair access (also WC). No music
ACCOMMODATION: 12 rooms, all with bath/shower. TV. Phone. B&B £53.50 to £89. Rooms for disabled. Baby facilities

ELLAND West Yorkshire   map 8

La Cachette ♥ £

31 Huddersfield Road, Elland HX5 9AW	COOKING 3
TEL: (01422) 378833 FAX: (01422) 327567	MODERN EUROPEAN
	£25–£52

'Value for money and a happy ambience' are the self-imposed watchwords at this lively, popular restaurant. It's the kind of place where loyal customers won't see favoured dishes disappear from the extensive menu without speaking up, which lends a kind of community feeling. Bistro-style dishes take in chicken and black pudding terrine with honey and mustard dressing; smoked haddock risotto with coriander and lime; and textbook beef stroganoff made with cream and brandy and served on rice. Grilled steaks come with black pepper or béarnaise sauces, and the puddings pull out all the stops for lemon-curd tart with raspberry compote, or milk chocolate and whisky mousse with chocolate shortbread. Happy staff help everyone feel at home, and the good-value wine list should keep all-comers smiling. Eight house wines from £10.95 are sold more by style than name – anyone for a glass of 'fun modern Aussie' red? – but it's by no means all novelty fare, with serious propositions from all regions.

CHEF: Jonathan Nichols   PROPRIETOR: CGL Partnership   OPEN: Mon to Sat 12 to 2.30, 6 to 9.30 (10 Fri and Sat)   CLOSED: 26 Dec to 6 Jan, last 2 weeks Aug   MEALS: alc (main courses £9 to £16). Set L £8.95 (2 courses), Set D Mon to Thur and 6 to 7 Fri and Sat £15.95 (inc wine). Light L menu available   SERVICE: not inc   CARDS: Delta, MasterCard, Switch, Visa   DETAILS: 80 seats. Vegetarian meals. Wheelchair access (not WC). Music. Air-conditioned

ELY Cambridgeshire   map 6

Old Fire Engine House ♥ ⅹ

25 St Mary's Street, Ely CB7 4ER	COOKING 1
TEL: (01353) 662582 FAX: (01353) 668364	TRADITIONAL ENGLISH FARMHOUSE
	£32–£49

In a homely setting within sight of the cathedral, this old stager still does things to a tried-and-tested formula of cheerful informality, typified by the fact that you need to wander through the kitchen to get to your table. Start with smoked salmon pâté, or dill-pickled herrings, before going on to one of the traditional roasts, such as herb-stuffed pork, or an adroitly handled fish dish like sea bass in watercress cream sauce. 'The potatoes alone are worth the distance we travel here,' write a pair of out-of-towners. Most puddings, which range from rhubarb and almond crumble to meringues or apple pie, are served with cream. The wine list debates the merits of every choice from the mainly French selection. It's a wonderful, individualistic effort and tremendously good value.

CHEF: Terri Baker   PROPRIETORS: Ann Ford and Michael Jarman   OPEN: all week L 12.15 to 2, Mon to Sat D 7.15 to 9   CLOSED: 24 Dec to 7 Jan, bank hols   MEALS: alc (main courses £14 to £17)   SERVICE: not inc   CARDS: MasterCard, Switch, Visa   DETAILS: 55 seats. 25 seats outside. Private parties: 35 main room, 10 to 24 private rooms. Car park. Vegetarian meals. Children's helpings. No smoking. No music

map 3

Fat Olives

30 South Street, Emsworth PO10 7EH   COOKING **3**
TEL: (01243) 377914   MODERN BRITISH
WEBSITE: www.fatolives.co.uk   £26–£48

One of a row of old stone fishermen's cottages a little way up from the harbour, the Murphys' small, uncluttered restaurant attracts solid local support for its friendly approach and unpretentiously interesting menus. The eponymous (and appreciated) green olives precede commended dishes like rabbit, prune and Armagnac terrine, then oxtail with swede and shallots in a rich, winey gravy, or maybe a bream, tiger prawn and monkfish bourride. Enterprising desserts take in Turkish Delight with white chocolate parfait, and a hearty sponge pudding of dates, pecans and ginger, served with cinnamon cream. The short wine list opens with Chilean house wines at £11.95 (£2.95 a glass), and manages a brisk jog-trot around the major countries.

CHEF: Lawrence Murphy   PROPRIETORS: Lawrence and Julia Murphy   OPEN: Tue to Sat 12 to 2, 7 to 10
CLOSED: 2 weeks Christmas, 1 week Oct   MEALS: alc (main courses £11 to £15.50). Set L £14 (2 courses)
to £18   SERVICE: not inc, card slips closed   CARDS: MasterCard, Switch, Visa   DETAILS: 28 seats. 10
seats outside. Private parties: 24 main room. Vegetarian meals. No children under 8. No smoking.
Wheelchair access (also WC). Music

▲ 36 on the Quay

47 South Street, Emsworth PO10 7EG   COOKING **6**
TEL: (01243) 375592   MODERN EUROPEAN
WEBSITE: www.36onthequay.co.uk   £36–£82

The Farthings' white-fronted quayside restaurant-with-rooms now also has a guest cottage just across the road. Views of peaceful comings and goings on the water set a relaxed tone, which is enhanced by the flowers, easy pastels and confident running of the dining room. Prize draw, though, must be Ramon Farthing's dazzling culinary talent, in evidence from canapés to petits fours. First courses read like mains, built as they are around central items such as John Dory, roast cod, or veal sweetbreads, but portions and combinations are carefully judged, so that they lead naturally on to the principal dish. Red mullet, presented on a courgette, tomato and thyme tart with crabmeat and a dressing spiked with lime, might precede Anjou pigeon, the breast and confit leg, accompanied by sticky pears, roasted foie gras, nutmegged spinach and fondant potato in a vanilla-scented gamey reduction, or – on a lighter note – seared scallops with bubble and squeak, crisp pancetta and a sauce combining vermouth and rosemary. A pre-dessert, which can be as labour-intensive as a micro-trifle of rhubarb, heralds the arrival of a tasting plate on a theme (passion fruit, perhaps), or banana ice cream with hazelnut biscuits, fig and orange pastries and a cardamom caramel sauce. If you can't choose, the ten-course taster menu awaits. Traditional France is the natural home of the wine list, but California and the southern hemisphere have also been efficiently cherry-picked for premium bottles, and there are some more affordable options from southern France and Chile. Mark-ups are high, but a spread of house bottles under £20 offers an escape route.

CHEF: Ramon Farthing   PROPRIETORS: Ramon and Karen Farthing   OPEN: Tue to Fri L 12 to 1.45, Mon to
Sat D 6.45 to 10   CLOSED: bank hols   MEALS: Set L £17.95 (2 courses) to £39.95, Set D £39.95 to £55
SERVICE: not inc   CARDS: Amex, Delta, Diners, MasterCard, Switch, Visa   DETAILS: 45 seats. 10 seats

outside. Private parties: 45 main room, 8 to 12 private rooms. Car park. Children's helpings. No smoking. Wheelchair access (not WC). Occasional music   ACCOMMODATION: 4 rooms, all with bath/shower. TV. B&B £60 to £110. Baby facilities

ERMINGTON Devon   map 1

▲ Plantation House, Matisse ⁵⅓✗

Totnes Road, Ermington PL21 9NS | NEW CHEF |
TEL: (01548) 831100   MODERN EUROPEAN
WEBSITE: www.plantationhousehotel.com   £38–£68

There is something timeless about this cream-painted Georgian former rectory on the main road just outside the village, with the care and luxury of the setting and décor echoed in the food. Chef Ashley Hutton has departed since the last edition of the Guide, and proprietor Alan Coby has taken a more active role in the kitchen, working alongside Daniel Gillard, a former sous-chef, giving some continuity; reports, please. The sourcing of ingredients – from local crab, beef and free-range ducks, to game and fish in season – is rightly a high priority here, and might turn up in breast of wood pigeon with its own consommé and shallot marmalade, then perhaps roast monkfish with bouillabaisse sauce, or local beef fillet with wild mushrooms, truffled potatoes and green beans. Among the sweets might be crème brûlée partnered by four variations on the theme of rhubarb. The broadly based wine list is packed with good names in all regions, but prices are on the high side. House wine is £14.95 (£3.95 a glass).

CHEFS: Alan Coby and Daniel Gillard   PROPRIETORS: Helen and Alan Coby   OPEN: Tue to Sat 12 to 2.15, 7 to 8.45   MEALS: alc (main courses L £13 to £16, D £18 to £20). Set D £36   SERVICE: not inc, card slips closed   CARDS: Amex, Delta, MasterCard, Switch, Visa   DETAILS: 32 seats. 24 seats outside. Private parties: 32 main room, 12 private room. Car park. Vegetarian meals. Children's helpings. No smoking. Music   ACCOMMODATION: 10 rooms, all with bath/shower. TV. Phone. B&B £50 to £119 (£5)

EXETER Devon   map 1

Brazz

10–12 Palace Gate, Exeter EX1 1JA   COOKING 3
TEL: (01392) 252525   FAX: (01392) 253045   MODERN BRASSERIE
WEBSITE: www.brazz.co.uk   £25–£48

This vast, airy cavern has a double-height circular aquarium reflected in a huge mirror at the top of the entrance stairs, beneath a blue domed ceiling twinkling with astral lights. The Brazz mini-chain (see Taunton, with the Wales Millennium Centre in Cardiff beckoning) deals in brasserie dishes. Chicken liver and foie gras parfait with red onion marmalade has 'rich, melting texture', or start with grilled Capricorn goats' cheese with baked figs; main courses run from generously salmon-laden fishcakes with creamed leeks to a large lamb shank coated in mint sauce with polenta. Cathedral pudding is a three-tiered chocolate extravaganza (ten per cent of its price goes to the Exeter Cathedral Music Foundation); lighter appetites might go for pannacotta with poached pear. Service is brisk and friendly, like the short, modern wine list that starts at £11.50 (£2.95 a glass).

CHEF: Simon Garbutt   PROPRIETOR: Brazz plc   OPEN: all week 12 to 3, 6 to 10.30 (11 Fri and Sat)   MEALS: alc (main courses £7.50 to £16)   SERVICE: 10% (optional), card slips closed   CARDS: Amex, Delta, Diners, MasterCard, Switch, Visa   DETAILS: 150 seats. Private parties: 150 main room. Vegetarian meals. Children's helpings. Wheelchair access (also WC). Occasional music. Air-conditioned

▲ Royal Clarence Hotel, Michael Caines Restaurant 🍷 ✸

Cathedral Yard, Exeter EX1 1HD	COOKING 5
TEL: (01392) 310031 FAX: (01392) 310032	FRENCH
WEBSITE: www.michaelcaines.com	£38–£84

This chic, uncluttered restaurant in an eighteenth-century hotel has panelled walls painted soft buttermilk and canvases inspired by the cathedral (visible through the front windows). There's an unpretentious atmosphere and knowledgeable, pleasantly pitched service too. Former sous-chef Simon Dow now heads the kitchen, translating Michael Caines's relatively simple but well-thought-out recipes with unfussy imagination, admirable timing and sound judgement. Menus teem with West Country produce: Red Ruby beef, local duckling, chicken from Ark Farm, near Crediton, Cornish lobster, local cheeses. Attention to detail shows in, for example, the crisp/soft textures in a first-course of quail with quails' eggs, celeriac, crisp belly pork and walnuts. Contrasts also figure in a ballottine of foie gras with wafer-thin slices of 'soused' beetroot and marinaded shiitake mushrooms, and in a main course of precisely cooked pan-fried sea bass paired with crushed olive potatoes, artichoke purée and a few saffron buttered baby onions. Finish with 'perfectly executed' roast peach and rhubarb soufflé, or a palette of home-made ice creams and sorbets. The 'exceptional-value' set lunch is also praised. A tempting line-up of house wines at £16 opens a decent list arranged by grape variety, with a handful of classics at the back.

CHEF: Simon Dow   PROPRIETORS: Andrew Brownsword and Michael Caines   OPEN: Mon to Sat 12 to 2.30, 7 to 10   MEALS: alc (main courses £16.50 to £30). Set L £19.50 (2 courses) to £23.50, Set D £31.50 (2 courses) to £36.50. Bar menu available   SERVICE: not inc, 12.5% for parties of 12 or more   CARDS: Amex, Delta, Diners, MasterCard, Switch, Visa   DETAILS: 70 seats. Private parties: 60 main room, 10 to 30 private rooms. Vegetarian meals. Children's helpings. No smoking. Wheelchair access (also WC). Occasional music. No mobile phones. Air-conditioned   ACCOMMODATION: 51 rooms, all with bath/shower. TV. Phone. B&B £105 to £185. Rooms for disabled. Baby facilities

---

Thai Orchid £   NEW ENTRY

Three Gables, 5 Cathedral Yard, Exeter EX1 1HJ	COOKING 2
TEL: (01392) 214215	THAI
WEBSITE: www.thaiorchidrestaurant.co.uk	£28–£54

A sixteenth-century building at the end of a row of rather grand terraced houses facing away from the cathedral is the peaceful setting for this smart, 'distinctly upmarket' Thai restaurant. It enjoys a loyal following, the mood is confident, and the cooking authentic. High-speed lunches hit the spot, and the full 140-dish menu covers a lot of familiar territory. Classic satays, fishcakes and spicy north-east Thai sausages are up to the mark, and the menu works its way through hot-and-sour salads, stir-fries, curries and noodles, picking up a few curiosities along the way: khai toon are steamed eggs, while kruang nai gai yang comprises chicken livers marinated in Thai spices. The thoughtfully assembled wine list includes a clever selection of aromatic whites. House wine is £13.

CHEFS: Subsuk and Chang   PROPRIETORS: Ron Shaw and Ubon Sarakhun   OPEN: Mon to Fri L 12 to 2, Mon to Sat D 6.30 to 10.30   CLOSED: 24 Dec to 8 Jan   MEALS: alc (main courses £7.50 to £9.50). Set L £7.50 (1 course) to £14.50 (2 courses), Set D £18.50 to £27 (all min 2)   SERVICE: 12.5% (optional), card slips closed   CARDS: Amex, Delta, MasterCard, Switch, Visa   DETAILS: 50 seats. Private parties: 24 main room, 8 to 10 private rooms. Music

FAIRFORD Gloucestershire   map 2

Allium 🍷 ✼

NEW ENTRY

1 London Street, Fairford GL7 4AH
TEL/FAX: (01285) 712200
WEBSITE: www.allium.uk.net

COOKING 6
MODERN EUROPEAN
£31–£69

The Grahams have moved some 60 miles from their former posts at Hampshire's Wickham Vineyard restaurant to set up this, their first independent venture. The two old stone buildings, situated at the bottom of the market square of this small Cotswold town, have received an impressive makeover, and the results are a serene and spacious dining room enlivened by modern art, which is for sale.

Out front, Erica Graham, displaying exceptional poise, knowledge and enthusiasm, makes a perfect ambassador for the kitchen, where husband James has sharpened his already admirable technical skills. His cooking has confidence, his ideas maturity, and 'you get the impression that he spends every spare moment of his life trying out new ideas'. One might begin with poached pigeon breast and endive Tatin – 'a nocturne in caramelisation and chicory' – then proceed to confit shoulder of lamb with sweetbread and tongue, or fillet of halibut, separated from a warm potato and bacon salad by a 'luscious and beautifully intense' purée of ceps. At inspection, all three courses were multi-faceted definitions of one of the main components, the meal ending convincingly with a sophisticated raspberry soufflé, raspberry sauce and raspberry sorbet. 'Value for money is terrific,' commented one reporter, the £17.50 lunch menu particularly so, and there's an eight-course gourmand dinner except on Sundays. The wine list opens with a wide range available by the glass or 50cl carafe. Bottles from £14 are an international mix arranged by style, with many options under £20 and plenty to tempt bigger spenders. Save some pennies for the exceptional selection of dessert wines.

CHEFS: James Graham and Nick Bartimote PROPRIETORS: James and Erica Graham and Nick Bartimote OPEN: Wed to Sun 12 to 2, 7 to 9 MEALS: Set L Wed to Sat £15 (2 courses) to £17.50, Set L Sun £17.50 (2 courses) to £19.50, Set D £25 (2 courses) to £42 (whole table only; not Sun) SERVICE: not inc, card slips closed CARDS: Delta, MasterCard, Switch, Visa DETAILS: 40 seats. Private parties: 40 main room, 8 to 12 private rooms. Vegetarian meals. Children's helpings. No smoking. Occasional music. No mobile phones (£5)

FARNBOROUGH Kent   map 3

Chapter One

Farnborough Common, Locksbottom,
Farnborough BR6 8NF
TEL: (01689) 854848   FAX: (01689) 858439
WEBSITE: www.chaptersrestaurants.co.uk

COOKING 5
MODERN EUROPEAN
£32–£75

A former hostelry in the mock-Tudor vein, Chapter One is now a long, beige restaurant lit by discreet ceiling spots, with chairs upholstered in midnight blue – a restful place given over to seriously stylish cooking in the modern French mode. Andrew McLeish, who trained at the Ritz (see entry, London), has imported a lustrous sense of polish to what he does here. Deep-fried veal sweetbreads with a basil minestrone sauce is a much-admired first course, as is a dish involving a tower of ham hock mixed with foie gras and tarragon, around which is poured an intense, frothy pea soup. Main courses tack to traditional methods, producing some stunning results. Glenarm salmon is roasted and accompanied by white asparagus, baby broad beans and a watercress sauce, while pork belly is appealingly slowly cooked and unctuously attended by creamed Savoy cabbage, foie gras and a purée of caramelised apple. Desserts can be as intricate as almond craqueline with white chocolate mousse and honeyed, spiced oranges or as straightforward as hot chocolate fondant with vanilla ice cream. France still dominates the wine list, but it now boasts a fair few quality growers. Prices start at £13.50, or £3.75 a glass. There's a sibling in Blackheath called Chapter Two (see entry, London).

CHEF: Andrew McLeish PROPRIETOR: Selective Restaurants Group OPEN: Mon to Sat 12 to 2.30, 6.30 to 10 (10.30 Fri and Sat), Sun 12 to 3, 6.30 to 9 CLOSED: 1 to 9 Jan MEALS: Set L £16 (2 courses) to £19.50, Set D £26.95. Brasserie L menu available Mon to Sat SERVICE: 12.5% (optional), card slips closed CARDS: Amex, Delta, Diners, MasterCard, Switch, Visa DETAILS: 120 seats. 20 seats outside. Private parties: 20 to 55 private rooms. Car park. Vegetarian meals. Children's helpings. No cigars/pipes. Music. Air-conditioned

FARNBOROUGH Warwickshire — map 5

Inn at Farnborough 🍴 — NEW ENTRY

Farnborough OX17 1DZ
TEL: (01295) 690615 FAX: (01295) 690032
WEBSITE: www.innatfarnborough.co.uk

COOKING 1
GLOBAL
£22–£57

Despite their reputation for food, the Robinsons strive to maintain the pubbiness of their Cotswold-stone inn on the main road through the village. Drinkers and diners mingle in the spacious interior, where pale neutral colours, flowers, evening candles and lots of wood – beams, floorboards and well-spaced tables – create a light, welcoming look. Trouble is taken over sourcing of raw materials, and the kitchen distinguishes itself with enthusiasm and honest effort, which stretches to first-class in-house-produced ice creams and excellent bread. The menus centre on appetising combinations: asparagus served with buttered spinach risotto and garlic- and lemongrass-scented wild mushrooms, while courgette ribbons, chive fondue and seared foie gras accompany fillets of turbot. Among desserts, vanilla pannacotta with liquorice ice cream and berries steeped in cognac has impressed. Value-led wines from across the world include around 10 by the glass from £2.75. House French is £10.95

CHEF: Trevor Burton PROPRIETORS: Anthony and Jo Robinson OPEN: all week 12 to 3, 6 to 10 MEALS: alc (main courses £11 to £19.50). Set L Mon to Sat and D Mon to Fri 6 to 7 £10.95 (2 courses) to £12.95 SERVICE: not inc CARDS: Amex, Delta, Diners, MasterCard, Switch, Visa DETAILS: 75 seats. 50 seats outside. Private parties: 100 main room, 2 to 18 private rooms. Car park. Vegetarian meals. Children's helpings. No smoking in 1 dining room. Wheelchair access (not WC). Music £5

FARNHAM Dorset — map 2

▲ Museum Inn 🍴 £

Farnham DT11 8DE
TEL: (01725) 516261 FAX: (01725) 516988
WEBSITE: www.museuminn.co.uk
off A354, 9m NE of Blandford Forum

COOKING 5
MODERN EUROPEAN
£29–£63

This historic red-brick building in Cranborne Chase is part nineteenth-century and part thatched and seventeenth-century. Nowadays it exudes a 'populist and relaxed' feel, with pale colours and natural materials setting the tone in the busy bar. The menu is based around judiciously sourced ingredients – Longhorn rump steak with organic watercress salad, milk-fed squab pigeon, Gloucester Old Spot pork – and dishes look pretty on the plate. Fish is often teamed with meat for vibrant modern combinations like roast cod with seared scallops, Parma ham, creamy potatoes and bouillabaisse juices, or fillet of John Dory with merguez sausage, beetroot and sauté potatoes. Tradition takes over when it comes to desserts such as crème caramel with strawberry and passion-fruit sorbet or rhubarb and ginger crumble. The same menu is also available (three sessions a week, bookable) in the barn-like, wooden Shed Restaurant, which one reporter thought 'a super combination of "country" and "contemporary" '. A bevy of good-humoured serving girls keep the mood buoyant. Eleven house wines (from £11) top the realistically priced list.

CHEF: Mark Treasure   PROPRIETORS: Vicky Elliot and Mark Stephenson   OPEN: Sun L 12 to 2, Fri and Sat D 7 to 9.30   CLOSED: 25 Dec, 26 Dec D, 31 Dec D   MEALS: alc (main courses £8.50 to £18.50)   SERVICE: not inc, card slips closed   CARDS: Delta, MasterCard, Switch, Visa   DETAILS: 90 seats. 40 seats outside. Private parties: 36 main room. Car park. Vegetarian meals. No children under 8. No smoking. Wheelchair access (also WC). No music. No mobile phones   ACCOMMODATION: 8 rooms, all with bath/shower. TV. Phone. B&B £65 to £120. Rooms for disabled. No children under 8

FAVERSHAM Kent   **map 3**

▲ Read's ▮

Macknade Manor, Canterbury Road,
Faversham ME13 8XE
TEL: (01795) 535344   FAX: (01795) 591200   COOKING **6**
WEBSITE: www.reads.com   MODERN BRITISH
on A2 Canterbury Road, ½m E of Faversham   £34–£95

Read's is a Georgian manor house with guest rooms, set in its own mature grounds, the kind of place in which you mustn't be surprised to spot pheasants having their own lunch at the edge of the lawn. With 25 years and more in the business, David and Rona Pitchford have perfected the personable, unceremonious approach that has delighted a generation of visitors, discernible here in everything from the good housekeeping to the welcoming and chatty staff.

The use of quality produce, much of it from the manor's own garden, shines through the menus, which are a mix of the old and nearly new. Langhirano Parma ham with a selection of vegetable crostini, Parmesan and rocket makes a punchy, modern, fresh-tasting dish, or there is the comfort quotient of a trio of smoked fish mousses – salmon, trout and mackerel – with horseradish cream and melba toast. Conscientious attention in the cooking reminds you why certain dishes have become classics: confit duck leg with roast winter vegetables and creamy mash is no menu makeweight, but has been properly looked after at every step of the way. Equally, slow-roast belly of organically reared pork on Savoy cabbage, with black pudding and caramelised apples, is a triumph of contrasting flavours and textures. Contrast also marks out a fine, unctuously rich chocolate fondant that comes with sharp-tasting yoghurt ice cream.

The wine list is a good example of the unpretentious approach here, opening with several pages of good-value international 'best buys' from £16 to £26. For those who wish to venture further, the full list will happily oblige with a strong range at the next level and onwards to classic Bordeaux in vintages back to 1970.

CHEF: David Pitchford   PROPRIETORS: Rona and David Pitchford   OPEN: Tue to Sat 12 to 2, 7 to 9.30 CLOSED: bank hols   MEALS: Set L £19.50, Set D £45 to £69 (inc wine)   SERVICE: not inc, card slips closed CARDS: Amex, Delta, Diners, MasterCard, Switch, Visa   DETAILS: 40 seats. 12 seats outside. Private parties: 60 main room, 20 to 36 private rooms. Car park. Children's helpings. No cigars/pipes. Wheelchair access (also WC). No music. No mobile phones ACCOMMODATION: 6 rooms, all with bath/shower. TV. Phone. B&B £120 to £150. Baby facilities (£5)

FAWSLEY Northamptonshire

▲ Fawsley Hall, Knightley Restaurant ♥ ⅝✳

Fawsley NN11 3BA
TEL: (01327) 892000   FAX: (01327) 892001
WEBSITE: www.fawsleyhall.com
1½m E of A361, 5½m S of Daventry

COOKING 5
MODERN EUROPEAN
£35–£81

This spectacularly beautiful Tudor house with Georgian and Victorian extensions is now a modern hotel, complete with conference, health and beauty facilities. This polished operation has a top-notch restaurant with an ambitious menu. Fortunately, chef Philip Dixon's flair matches his ambition, and the first-class materials at his disposal help in no small way, so everything from pasta, bread and ice creams to mousses, soufflés and sauces are technically sound and – more importantly – enjoyable to eat. Dinner menus offer half a dozen choices per course, typically kicking off with tian of pork belly with black pudding and beetroot chutney, or pear and goats' cheese tart with chestnut honey, then seared John Dory on a crab cake with roast root vegetables, or venison loin with mulled pear and chocolate sauce. To round off the meal, try a selection of Midlands cheeses, from Single Gloucester to Lincolnshire Poacher, or the black cherry and chocolate soufflé with dark chocolate ice cream. Ten house wines from £13.95 (£3.30 a glass) are billed as 'wines of the moment', and a selection of fine wines is discounted from a notional RRP and labelled 'affordable excess' (their prices are reasonable enough); the remainder of the list, arranged by style, is packed with goodies from all over.

CHEF: Philip Dixon   PROPRIETOR: Simon Lowe   OPEN: all week 12 to 2, 7 to 9.30   MEALS: alc (not Sun L; main courses L £12 to £14, D £14 to £28). Set L Sun £22.50, Set D £35. Bar menu available   SERVICE: 12.5% (optional), card slips closed   CARDS: Amex, Delta, Diners, MasterCard, Switch, Visa   DETAILS: 85 seats. 20 seats outside. Private parties: 80 main room, 80 to 140 private rooms. Car park. Vegetarian meals. Children's helpings. No smoking. Wheelchair access (also WC). Music. No mobile phones   ACCOMMODATION: 43 rooms, all with bath/shower. TV. Phone. B&B £140 to £390. Rooms for disabled

FERNHURST Surrey   map 3

King's Arms ⅝✳ £

Midhurst Road, Fernhurst GU27 3HA
TEL: (01428) 652005
WEBSITE: www.kingsarmsfernhurst.com
on A286, 1m S of Fernhurst on sharp bend

COOKING 2
MODERN BRITISH
£26–£47

Set amid rolling farmland, this Grade II listed seventeenth-century pub is endowed with all the obligatory rustic requisites, from hanging baskets to an inglenook. Top-notch real ales and lunchtime sandwiches reinforce the pubby image, although the place is now famed for its fully blown monthly-changing menus. On the one hand there are staunchly comforting dishes like toad-in-the-hole and devilled kidneys; on the other you might find grilled Mediterranean vegetable gâteau or roast monkfish with French beans and a mushroom and Jerusalem artichoke sauce. It's also worth checking out the daily specials, which could include Cajun chicken wings with chard and coriander salad or seared organic salmon fillet with buttered spinach and crab velouté. Finish with spotted dick, vanilla bavarois or well-selected English cheeses. House Chardonnay and Merlot are £11.

CHEFS: Michael Hirst and Sean Pay   PROPRIETORS: Michael and Annabel Hirst   OPEN: all week L 12 to 2.30, Mon to Sat D 7 to 9.30. No food 25 Dec   MEALS: alc (main courses £7.50 to £15)   SERVICE: not inc   CARDS: MasterCard, Switch, Visa   DETAILS: 44 seats. 60 seats outside. Private parties: 24 main room, 10 to 50 private rooms. Car park. Vegetarian meals. Children's helpings. No children under 14 after 7pm. No smoking in 1 dining room. Wheelchair access (not WC). No music

FERRENSBY North Yorkshire   map 9

▲ General Tarleton 🍴✳

Boroughbridge Road, Ferrensby HG5 0PZ	COOKING 4
TEL: (01423) 340284 FAX: (01423) 340288	MODERN BRITISH
WEBSITE: www.generaltarleton.co.uk	£26–£48

The death of Denis Watkins (see also the Angel, Hetton) in July 2004 is a loss to the British hospitality industry. This, his second pub/restaurant, had already passed into the stewardship of long-time chef and business partner John Topham, who runs the pub along the same lines, and to the same high standards. Situated only a few minutes' drive from the A1, the calm atmosphere is the perfect respite in a journey, or indeed well worth a trip for its own sake. Service has been described as 'gentle', and the main event is dinner, when a fixed-price menu offers starters like carpaccio and rocket salad before chargrilled rack of venison with creamed celeriac and a thyme and red wine jus, or seared fillet of sea bass with braised fennel, salsify and vanilla broth, rounding off with – say – chocolate truffle ravioli, or iced rhubarb crumble parfait. Sunday roasts have been appreciated, and there are plenty of good things to be had in the bar (pressed terrine of Yorkshire ham and foie gras, for example). The lengthy wine list includes a welcome and varied choice by the glass, some desirable Burgundies and house wines from £12.95.

CHEF: John Topham   PROPRIETORS: John and Claire Topham   OPEN: Sun L 12 to 1.45, Mon to Sat D 6 to 9.15 (6.45 to 9.30 Sat)   MEALS: Set L £17.50, Set D £29.50. Bar/brasserie menu available all week L and D   SERVICE: not inc   CARDS: Amex, Delta, MasterCard, Switch, Visa   DETAILS: 64 seats. 30 seats outside. Private parties: 30 main room, 2 to 36 private rooms. Car park. Vegetarian meals. Children's helpings. No smoking. Wheelchair access (not WC). No music   ACCOMMODATION: 14 rooms, all with bath/shower. TV. Phone. B&B £74.95 to £94.90

FLETCHING East Sussex   map 3

▲ Griffin Inn ♥ 🍴✳

Fletching TN22 3SS	COOKING 2
TEL: (01825) 722890 FAX: (01825) 722810	MODERN EUROPEAN
WEBSITE: www.thegriffininn.co.uk	£27–£54

This sixteenth-century country village pub has lots of local support, open fires, panelled main bar and wonderful views from the garden. High standards are obvious, from the range of local ales, via the excellent atmosphere, to the good service. It has a separate restaurant too, with menus notable for high-quality ingredients, often from local suppliers. Many dishes are roast or chargrilled, and there are frequent Italian and Mediterranean touches. For example, fennel and dolcelatte risotto, or a salad of Parma ham, rocket, and truffled mozzarella, may precede chargrilled fillet of beef with taleggio mash and pesto, or fried salmon with a salad of artichokes, olives, capers and saffron. Cheeses are English, and desserts aim to soothe – witness chocolate fondant with frozen white chocolate mousse, and vanilla pannacotta with griottine cherries. The wine list celebrates its release from the faux-leather binding of yore with an upbeat international selection underpinned by a dozen house bottles priced from £10.50 to £14.50 and also sold by the glass.

CHEF: Andrew Billings   PROPRIETORS: Nigel, Bridget and James Pullan   OPEN: all week 12 to 2.30, 7 to 9.30   CLOSED: 25 Dec   MEALS: alc (main courses £9.50 to £18.50). Set L Mon to Fri £12.50 (2 courses), Set L Sun £22.50. Bar menu available   SERVICE: not inc   CARDS: Amex, Diners, MasterCard, Switch, Visa   DETAILS: 60 seats. 30 seats outside. Private parties: 30 main room. Car park. Vegetarian meals. Children's helpings. No smoking. Wheelchair access (not WC). Occasional music. No mobile phones   ACCOMMODATION: 8 rooms, all with bath/shower. TV. B&B £50 to £120. Rooms for disabled. Baby facilities (£5)

FORTON Lancashire   map 8

Bay Horse Inn ⁵⋇

Bay Horse, Forton LA2 0HR
TEL: (01524) 791204
WEBSITE: www.bayhorseinn.com   COOKING 3
From M6 junction 33, take A6 for Preston; take second   MODERN BRITISH
left; pub is on right   £30–£53

This black-and-white gastro-pub in the hamlet of Bay Horse makes considerable use of Lancashire and Lakeland suppliers for dishes like suckling-pig sausages with orange, potato purée and HP sauce, or grilled langoustines with a mayonnaise flavoured with wild garlic from the banks of the River Cocker. These might figure among the specials chalked up on a blackboard. Meanwhile the carte proper might run to Morecambe Bay potted shrimps with brandy and chives, and then slow-cooked Goosnargh duckling with mash, roast fig and an elderberry wine and honey reduction, or seared salmon fillet with pak choi and sweet chilli dip. Portions are large, so not all will be able to round off their meal with, say pear and almond tart, or chocolate and passion-fruit délice with cappuccino ice cream. Wines take second place to the cooking, but the list offers decent value; house French are £11.95, and there are well-kept real ales too.

CHEFS: Craig Wilkinson, Matthew Illingworth and Adam Wood   PROPRIETORS: Brian, Mae and Craig Wilkinson   OPEN: Tue to Sun L 12 to 1.45 (1 Sat, 3 Sun), Tue to Sun D 7 to 9.15   CLOSED: 1 week Aug, 1 week Jan   MEALS: alc (main courses £12 to £18)   SERVICE: not inc, 10% for parties over 10   CARDS: Amex, Delta, MasterCard, Switch, Visa   DETAILS: 52 seats. 20 seats outside. Private parties: 26 main room, 14 to 26 private rooms. Car park. Vegetarian meals. Children's helpings. No smoking in 1 dining room. Wheelchair access (also WC). Music. No mobile phones

---

FOTHERINGHAY Northamptonshire   map 6

Falcon ▼ ⁵⋇

Fotheringhay PE8 5HZ   COOKING 3
TEL: (01832) 226254   FAX: (01832) 226046   MODERN EUROPEAN
WEBSITE: www.huntsbridge.com   £26–£56

This mellow-stone village inn by the meandering Nene is a genuine local and a food-pub combined – and it's only five miles west of the A1. The dining room and conservatory extension are decked out in green, floors are ochre, and smartly laid tables lend an air of modern comfort. Ray Smikle's food, fresh and flavourful, is unpretentious, generous and often colourful, and his modern repertoire travels the globe for inspiration. After sweet potato, plantain and roast pepper pot soup, you might find pork escalope with couscous salad and harissa alongside slow-braised lamb shank with mustard mash and cabbage, and homely sticky toffee, or queen of puddings, to finish. The Huntsbridge group (see Keyston, Madingley and Huntingdon for the others) goes in for imaginative, high-quality wine lists; here fourteen by the glass introduce an adventurous selection arranged by style and split into under £20 and 'top-class' bottles.

CHEF: Ray Smikle   PROPRIETORS: John Hoskins and Ray Smikle   OPEN: all week 12 to 2.15, 6.30 to 9.30
MEALS: alc (main courses £10 to £19). Set L Mon to Sat £11.50 (2 courses). Bar menu available   SERVICE:
not inc   CARDS: Amex, Delta, Diners, MasterCard, Switch, Visa   DETAILS: 75 seats. 35 seats outside.
Private parties: 60 main room, 20 to 30 private rooms. Car park. Vegetarian meals. Children's helpings.
No smoking. Wheelchair access (also WC). No music. No mobile phones

FOWEY Cornwall   map 1

▲ Marina Hotel,
Nick Fisher at the Waterside ⁂

17 Esplanade, Fowey PL23 1HY   COOKING 4
TEL: (01726) 833315   FAX: (01726) 832779   SEAFOOD
WEBSITE: www.themarinahotel.co.uk   £31–£79

Formerly the residence of the bishops of Truro, this smart pale-yellow-painted waterfront venue, in a 'stunning' setting on the esplanade, is now a splendidly refined hotel with an ambitious restaurant. The dining room is done out in navy blue and white, giving it a strongly nautical feel, enhanced by views over the estuary. The mood is formal, with service to match – though perhaps not sufficiently well trained to be convincing. The food makes a favourable impression, using good-quality fish and seafood in everything from simple, classic dishes such as fillet of Dover sole with mussels and mushrooms to exotic, elaborate modern options such as grilled tuna and melon salad with a hot-and-sour lime dressing, or John Dory with spring onions, tiger prawns, and a ginger and coriander broth. Non-fish options include beef fillet with red pepper pesto and asparagus, and desserts feature warm apple crumble with custard and rhubarb sorbet. Nine house wines from £16.25, all available by the large or small glass, open a good-quality but somewhat pricey list of around 70 bottles.

CHEF: Nick Fisher   PROPRIETOR: Steve Westwell   OPEN: all week 12 to 2, 6.45 to 9.15   CLOSED: Mon to Sat
L Oct to Apr   MEALS: alc (main courses L £10 to £16, D £12 to £28). Set D £34.50   SERVICE: not inc
CARDS: Amex, Delta, MasterCard, Switch, Visa   DETAILS: 40 seats. 25 seats outside. Private parties: 40
main room. Vegetarian meals. Children's helpings. No smoking. Music   ACCOMMODATION: 18 rooms, all
with bath/shower. TV. Phone. B&B £50 to £200. Fishing

FRAMPTON MANSELL Gloucestershire   map 2

White Horse £

Cirencester Road, Frampton Mansell GL6 8HZ
TEL: (01285) 760960   COOKING 2
on A419 7m W of Cirencester, beside turning to   MODERN ENGLISH
Frampton Mansell   £27–£45

More of a restaurant than a pub – though some reporters still comment that a certain smokiness goes with the territory – the White Horse seems to attract a young, casual crowd drawn by an easy-going style. The seasonally inspired round-the-world carte has taken on a degree more complexity, and ranges from tuna carpaccio rolled in fennel seeds and paprika with cucumber yogurt and lemon dressing, via pan-fried foie gras with a sweet potato pancake, crisp pancetta and a muscat butter, to slow-braised belly of pork with egg noodles, caramelised baby apples and soy and balsamic; ribeye steak comes more traditionally, with sautéed flat mushrooms and cracked black pepper sauce. Seafood comes from Looe in Cornwall, and shellfish are stored live in a large external tank to maximise freshness. There is usually a vegetarian option, and wines balance interest with good value, opening with house red and white at £11.50.

CHEF: Howard Matthews   PROPRIETORS: Emma and Shaun Davis   OPEN: all week L 12 to 2.30 (3 Sun), Mon to Sat D 7 to 9.45   CLOSED: 24 to 26 Dec, 1 Jan   MEALS: alc (main courses £9 to £14). Bar L menu available   SERVICE: not inc   CARDS: MasterCard, Switch, Visa   DETAILS: 53 seats. 50 seats outside. Car park. Vegetarian meals. Children's helpings. No pipes/cigars. No music

FRESSINGFIELD Suffolk

map 6

Fox and Goose ✦✱

NEW ENTRY

Fressingfield IP21 5PB
TEL: (01379) 586247   FAX: (01379) 586106
WEBSITE: www.foxandgoose.net

COOKING 3
MODERN BRITISH
£24–£62

Built around 1509 as a guild hall, this long, cream-plastered building beside the church became a pub in the eighteenth century, but is now wholeheartedly a restaurant. The 'atmospheric' dining room reflects the antiquity of the building, while contemporary touches are provided by some colourful artwork by local artists. Chef/proprietor Paul Yaxley's menu deals with some complex combinations – loin of lamb with artichoke purée, spinach, sauté potatoes, roast salsify, tarragon jus and tomato rouille, for example – all attractively presented, and with satisfying results. The soft textures and flavours of a fillet of sea bream on al dente artichoke risotto balanced by balsamic vinegar and small chunks of tomato made an excellent first course, and might be followed by fillet of beef on crushed peas with fondant potato, asparagus and a foie gras mousse. Finish with something as straightforward as a classic crème brûlée, or perhaps a strawberry and lemongrass mousse with an almond mirror biscuit and strawberry jelly. The cheerful and professional service has won plaudits. Fifty or so wines, selected with enthusiasm and knowledge, start at £12.50, with many below £20.

CHEFS: Paul Yaxley and Matthew Wyatt   PROPRIETOR: Paul Yaxley   OPEN: Tue to Sun 12 to 2, 7 to 9 (6.30 to 8.15 Sun)   MEALS: alc (not Sun L; main courses L £8 to £10, D £11 to £17.50). Set L £11.50 (2 courses) to £13.95, Set D £35 (whole table only). Light L menu available   SERVICE: not inc, card slips closed   CARDS: Delta, Diners, MasterCard, Switch, Visa   DETAILS: 50 seats. 12 seats outside. Private parties: 30 main room, 12 to 18 private rooms. Car park. Vegetarian meals. Children's helpings. No children under over 8 at D. No smoking. Wheelchair access (not WC). Music

---

'[We ordered a dish described as] "French corn-fed chicken breast with raw mangoes". We all spent the first ten minutes playing pin the tail on the mango. Even with our eyes open, we could not find the tiniest sliver, never mind the plural "mangoes" that the gastronomically litigious might demand from the menu description.' (On eating in London)

FRITHSDEN Hertfordshire map 3

Alford Arms £

Frithsden HP1 3DD	COOKING 2
TEL: (01442) 864480 FAX: (01442) 876893	MODERN BRITISH
WEBSITE: www.alfordarms.co.uk	£26–£46

This pretty Victorian inn enjoys a charmingly rustic setting overlooking the village green, with Ashridge Forest practically on the doorstep. Inside, a corner of the bar by a roaring log fire is reserved for drinkers, while the rest of the place is a cosy, intimate dining room with a countrified feel. Bold flavours in straightforward combinations are what the menus promise and what the kitchen delivers. Seared scallops with black pudding on saffron mash, Toulouse sausages with mash and roast onion gravy, and confit duck leg with Italian bean ragoût are the sort of thing to expect, with warm treacle and hazelnut tart to finish. Service is welcoming, enthusiastic and capable, and a short but effective wine list offers good variety, excellent value and plenty of choice by the glass.

CHEF: Damien Ng   PROPRIETORS: David and Becky Salisbury   OPEN: all week 12 to 2.30 (3 Sun), 7 to 10   CLOSED: 25 and 26 Dec, D 31 Dec, D 1 Jan   MEALS: alc (main courses £9.50 to £13.50)   SERVICE: not inc   CARDS: Amex, Delta, MasterCard, Switch, Visa   DETAILS: 70 seats. 82 seats outside. Car park. Vegetarian meals. Children's helpings. Music

FUNTINGTON West Sussex map 3

Hallidays ⁵⁄ₓ

Watery Lane, Funtington PO18 9LF	COOKING 2
TEL: (01243) 575331	MODERN BRITISH
	£28–£51

Three fifteenth-century thatched and flint-walled cottages are home to the Stephenson family's restaurant, where local and seasonal produce is deployed across the board. The kitchen's uncomplicated cooking style wins for honest food with no pretensions or flummery, 'and very pleased we are to have it', declares a regular. Typical choices are crostini of asparagus, Parma ham and mozzarella balls, or toasted scallops with salsa rossa to start, and main courses of a vivid saffron-sauced salmon fishcake with cucumber spaghetti, and sautéed calf's liver with a 'luscious' pool of Puy lentils in a good tarragon and red wine sauce. Vegetables might include a dish of broccoli with a light hollandaise and 'superb' cubed potatoes, while desserts run from tonka bean and Amaretto crème brûlée to fine apple tart with brandied raisins. The reasonably priced wine list opens with seven house selections from £10.50 to £14.

CHEF: Andy Stephenson   PROPRIETORS: Andy Stephenson and Peter Creech   OPEN: Wed to Fri and Sun L 12 to 1.30, Wed to Sat D 7 to 9   CLOSED: 2 weeks early Mar, 1 week late Aug   MEALS: alc L (main courses £15 to £16.50). Set L £14.50 (2 courses) to £17, Set D £24 (2 courses) to £28.50   SERVICE: not inc   CARDS: Delta, MasterCard, Switch, Visa   DETAILS: 28 seats. Private parties: 20 main room, 10 to 20 private rooms. Car park. No smoking in 1 dining room. Wheelchair access (also women's WC). No music

GALPHAY North Yorkshire
map 9

Galphay Inn £

Galphay HG4 3NJ
TEL: (01765) 650133
EMAIL: thegalphayinn@btopenworld.com

COOKING 3
MODERN BRITISH
£26–£45

Robert and Sam MacArthur have taken great pride in renovating this out-of-the-way stone pub a few miles from Ripon, and their caring approach extends to the food. The kitchen enthusiastically takes on board gutsy true-Brit favourites like potted Morecambe Bay shrimps and devilled kidneys, not forgetting a 'crock' of local lamb chops, which are seasoned with sea salt and herbs then served as 'crispy finger food'. The monthly inventory is fleshed out with globetrotting ideas such as skewers of Indonesian tempura prawns with hot-and-sour dipping sauce, and pan-fried chicken piccata with lemon and caper sauce and noodles. Familiar-sounding desserts might include sticky toffee pudding; otherwise finish with Yorkshire cheeses and home-made chutney. Lunchtime and early-evening menus stay firmly in pub territory with sandwiches, burgers, and ham and eggs. Around 30 good-value wines include half a dozen house choices from £3.20 a glass, £9.95 a bottle.

CHEF: Francisco Sandoval PROPRIETORS: Robert and Sam MacArthur OPEN: Wed to Mon 12 to 2, 6.30 to 9.30 MEALS: alc (main courses £9.50 to £16) SERVICE: not inc, card slips closed CARDS: Amex, Delta, Diners, MasterCard, Switch, Visa DETAILS: 44 seats. Private parties: 40 main room. Car park. Vegetarian meals. Children's helpings. No smoking in 1 dining room. Occasional music

GATESHEAD Tyne & Wear
map 10

▲ Eslington Villa

8 Station Road, Low Fell, Gateshead NE9 6DR
TEL: (0191) 487 6017 FAX: (0191) 420 0667
EMAIL: eslingtonvilla@freeuk.com
leave A1(M) at Team Valley Trading Estate, approach
Gateshead along Team Valley; at top of Eastern Avenue,
turn left into Station Road

COOKING 3
MODERN EUROPEAN
£24–£53

The villa in question is a substantial, brick-built mansion standing in a steep, mature garden that, at least in summer, obscures the fact that the view across the Team Valley is now of a trading estate. The Mediterranean-inspired fare of, say, slow-roast tomato tart with black olives, feta and olive oil may be the foundation, but the kitchen is perfectly at home with a dash of Eastern flavouring in home-cured duck breast with melon, soy sauce and pickled ginger. Materials are of top quality: note a simple dish of slow-roast pork leg that has impressed for its flavour, the meat perfectly paired with garlic and rosemary boulangère potatoes and an apple sauce spiced with cumin seeds. Honey-roast duck breast arrives pink and juicy on a large parcel of al dente Savoy cabbage containing spinach and a scattering of diced potato and carrot. Among puddings might be plum and almond tart, or pear and caramel bavarois with pistachio ice cream. Service is smooth and pleasant, and the 30-bottle wine list stays mostly under £20, starting at £11.50.

CHEF: Andrew Moore PROPRIETORS: Nick and Melanie Tulip OPEN: Sun to Fri L 12 to 2, Mon to Sat D 7 to 9.30 CLOSED: 4 days Christmas, 3 days New Year, bank hols MEALS: alc exc Sun L (main courses £10 to £17). Set L Mon to Fri £12.50 (2 courses) to £14.50, Set L Sun £16, Set D Mon to Fri £18.50 SERVICE: not inc CARDS: Amex, Delta, Diners, MasterCard, Switch, Visa DETAILS: 85 seats. 20 seats outside. Private parties: 60 main room, 4 to 30 private rooms. Car park. Vegetarian meals. Children's helpings. No smoking. Music ACCOMMODATION: 18 rooms, all with bath/shower. TV. Phone. B&B £59.50 to £74.50. Baby facilities £5

McCoys at the Baltic, Rooftop Restaurant ▮

Centre for Contemporary Arts, South Shore Road,
Gateshead NE8 3BA
TEL: (0191) 440 4949   FAX: (0191) 440 4950
EMAIL: mccoys@balticmill.com

COOKING 2
MODERN BRITISH
£31–£60

Pass between two massive iron slabs to enter the rooftop restaurant at Tyneside's premier art space, and remember to bring your head for heights with you. In the long, elegant, barrel-vaulted space, the modern British cooking hits occasional heights of its own. Wild mushroom tortellini in creamed Puy lentil soup is a straightforward way of starting, as might be game terrine with parsnip purée and fig crisps. Vanilla mash and peppered jus make a gentle backdrop for roast saddle of rabbit, while pancetta-wrapped monkfish comes with kedgeree, and there are a couple of vegetarian options as well. Chocolate tart of 'dense and serious' filling is accompanied by sharpening crème fraîche laced with Calvados, and there are English farmhouse cheeses with home-made chutney and walnuts. The wine list is modern and well chosen, and the large glasses help the wines show their best. House bottles from £14.50 find plenty of company under £20.

CHEF: Simon Wood   PROPRIETORS: Eugene McCoy, Marcus Bennett and Tom McCoy   OPEN: all week L 12 to 2.30, Mon to Sat D 7 to 10   MEALS: alc L (main courses £10.50 to £14.50). Set L £16.95 (2 courses) to £19.95, Set D £27 (2 courses) to £32   SERVICE: 10%   CARDS: Amex, Delta, MasterCard, Switch, Visa   DETAILS: 90 seats. Private parties: 80 main room, 10 to 30 private rooms. Vegetarian meals. Children's helpings. Wheelchair access (also WC). Music. Air-conditioned

---

GILLINGHAM Dorset   **map 2**

▲ Stock Hill 🍴

Stock Hill, Gillingham SP8 5NR
TEL: (01747) 823626   FAX: (01747) 825628
WEBSITE: www.stockhillhouse.co.uk
on B3081, 1m W of Gillingham

COOKING 5
MODERN EUROPEAN
£37–£57

The beech-lined drive leads to this lovingly restored late Victorian country-house hotel in an idyllic setting. Interiors reflect both the period and the Hausers' individual taste: time might have stood still in the nineteenth century. Dining room and sitting room both overlook the gardens and are filled with antiques, ornate mirrors, oil paintings, fine rugs and *objets d'art*. The sitting room has plump country sofas and armchairs, while the dining room is resplendent with powder pink walls, white table linen and comfortable upholstered seating. Nita runs front-of-house with practised professionalism, and Peter's passion is expressed through the kitchen's daily-changing set-price menus. Gloriously rich, full flavours make subtle use of high-quality ingredients that include vegetables and herbs from the hotel's kitchen garden. Peter is Austrian-born and -trained, and this shows in the highly accomplished, cultured dishes he produces: slow-cooked monkfish on a cheese tartine and an aged sherry vinegar sauce, perhaps, or grilled loin of rabbit wrapped in smoked bacon with a Napoleon potato beetroot flan. Preceding these might be poached lobster gâteau with root vegetable sabayon, or a roast boned quail on caramelised Bramleys. Beautifully crafted desserts are another attraction – bitter chocolate, Grand Marnier and crystallised ginger mousse, say, or house meringue Suchard. The wine list travels the globe and, though majoring on classical France, includes four from Austria, a decent selection of halves, and house bottles starting at £16.90.

CHEFS: Peter Hauser and Lorna Connor PROPRIETORS: Peter and Nita Hauser OPEN: Tue to Thur and Sun L 12.30 to 1.30, all week D 7.15 to 8.30 MEALS: Set L £25, Set D £35 SERVICE: not inc, card slips closed CARDS: MasterCard, Switch, Visa DETAILS: 24 seats. Private parties: 24 main room, 6 to 12 private rooms. Car park. Vegetarian meals. No children under 7. Children's helpings. No smoking. No music. No mobile phones ACCOMMODATION: 8 rooms, all with bath/shower. TV. Phone. D,B&B £110 to £300. No children under 7

GITTISHAM Devon   map 2

▲ Combe House ♥ ⅝✳

Gittisham EX14 3AD
TEL: (01404) 540400   FAX: (01404) 46004   COOKING 4
WEBSITE: www.thishotel.com   MODERN BRITISH
1½m off A30, 2m W of Honiton   £37–£84

Philip Leach runs the kitchen at this many-gabled Elizabethan manor house, where architectural grandeur does not translate into a stuffy ambience. The dedication to sourcing fine seasonal and often local ingredients is clearly a driving obsession, and the sylvan setting includes a large kitchen garden producing an array of herbs, vegetables and fruit. Begin with a woodsy pairing of ceps and leeks in an open ravioli sauced with cep velouté, or tempura oysters with celeriac and oyster soup, before moving on to pot-roast poussin simply paired with colcannon and wild mushrooms, or poached fillet of halibut with tagliatelle and pesto dressing. A six-course tasting menu is on hand if choices prove difficult. Puddings range from chocolate brownie with vanilla ice cream to pistachio bavarois with sesame tuiles and milk sorbet. France, in particular Bordeaux and – unusually – Chablis, is the first love of the wine list, with some well-chosen New World back-up. Half-bottles are in plentiful supply and six come by the glass. House wine is a rather steep £17.50.

CHEF: Philip Leach PROPRIETORS: Ken and Ruth Hunt OPEN: all week 12 to 2, 7 to 9.30 MEALS: Set L £18 (2 courses) to £22.50, Set D £36 to £51 SERVICE: not inc CARDS: Delta, MasterCard, Switch, Visa DETAILS: 60 seats. Private parties: 50 main room. Car park. Vegetarian meals. Children's helpings. No smoking. Wheelchair access (also WC). Music. No mobile phones ACCOMMODATION: 15 rooms, all with bath/shower. TV. Phone. B&B £99 to £295. Baby facilities. Fishing

GODALMING Surrey   map 3

La Luna ⅝✳

10–14 Wharf Street, Godalming GU7 1NN   COOKING 2
TEL: (01483) 414155   FAX: (01483) 418286   ITALIAN
WEBSITE: www.lalunarestaurant.co.uk   £25–£61

In the centre of town (Wharf Street can take some finding), La Luna's monochrome, minimalist interior sets black leather chairs and white table linen against wooden floors and white walls (plus one black one). It's cool and understated, with green leafy plants and floor-to-ceiling windows adding contrast. The traditional Italian cooking also has a modern edge, and menus (Italian with English subtitles) follow the seasons. There may be polenta with boneless leg of duck and porcini mushrooms to start, while home-made ravioli filled with braised pheasant in a shallot and game sauce could find a place among the pasta dishes, with oven-roasted monkfish tail, wrapped in sliced aubergine with a tomato tartare, wild leaves, capers and olives for a main dish. Italian apple tart with red fruits and vanilla ice cream makes a typical finish. The all-Italian wines include a couple of dozen under £25, among them house wines at £11.95, plus a long list of higher-priced heavyweights. We heard of the departure of co-chef Erik Michel as we went to press, so reports please.

CHEFS: Giovanni Puglisi and Laura Pasquini   PROPRIETORS: Daniele Drago and Orazio Primavera   OPEN: Tue to Sat 12 to 2, 7 to 10   CLOSED: 1st week Jan, 2 weeks Aug   MEALS: alc D (main courses £10.50 to £22). Set L £11.50 (2 courses) to £14.50   SERVICE: not inc   CARDS: Delta, MasterCard, Switch, Visa   DETAILS: 60 seats. Private parties: 28 main room. Vegetarian meals. Children's helpings. No smoking in 1 dining room. Wheelchair access (not WC). Music. No mobile phones. Air-conditioned   £5

GOLCAR West Yorkshire   **map 8**

▲ Weavers Shed ♥ ⚡✳

88 Knowl Road, Golcar HD7 4AN
TEL: (01484) 654284   FAX: (01484) 650980
WEBSITE: www.weaversshed.co.uk
on B6111, 2m W of Huddersfield via A62

COOKING 5
MODERN BRITISH
£25–£73

In the hills above Huddersfield, the group of buildings joined together to form Weavers Shed were once part of the West Riding textile industry, but now its business is that of restaurant-with-rooms. The bar/lounge is elegant and light, with comfortable seats and a huge range of cookery books to whet the appetite. The look of the dining room is more rustic, with low, beamed ceilings and stone floors. The atmosphere is relaxed, but one is left in no doubt that this is a serious operation. The menu changes monthly, and great play is made of home-grown produce and local sourcing (the restaurant has a kitchen garden and orchard and raises its own poultry).

Diners might be treated to an appetiser of 'gorgeous, creamy' potato and onion soup before moving on to a crisp potato and dill pancake with a 'moist and plentiful' filling of smoked trout, topped with a dollop of sour cream and a teaspoon of caviar. The appealing list of ingredients extends to main courses, which might include roast sea bass with creamed Puy lentils, crisp waffle potatoes, buttered Savoy cabbage and 'fluffy fish cream'. The restaurant's northern roots are perhaps most strongly felt on the dessert list, with the likes of parkin, served warm with clotted cream ice cream and a caramel and apple compote (a lovely, sticky, chewy concoction), and Yorkshire rhubarb served in various ways: a soufflé, jelly, sorbet and poached. 'Service throughout is friendly and enthusiastic.' The wine list proclaims a particular affection for the south of France and offers plenty of scope for exploring its fascinating wines. Good selections from the more traditional French regions and a global round-up add to the appeal.

CHEFS: Stephen Jackson, Ian McGunnigle and Cath Sill   PROPRIETORS: Stephen and Tracy Jackson   OPEN: Tue to Fri L 12 to 1.45, Tue to Sat D 7 to 9 (10 Sat)   CLOSED: 25, 26 and 31 Dec, 1 Jan   MEALS: alc (main courses £14 to £25). Set L £11.50 (2 courses) to £14.95   SERVICE: not inc   CARDS: Amex, MasterCard, Switch, Visa   DETAILS: 46 seats. Private parties: 40 main room, 24 private room. Car park. Vegetarian meals. No smoking. Music. No mobile phones   ACCOMMODATION: 5 rooms, all with bath/shower. TV. Phone. B&B £75 to £85. Baby facilities   £5

Leatherne Bottel

The Bridleway, Goring RG8 0HS
TEL: (01491) 872667   FAX: (01491) 875308   COOKING 3
WEBSITE: www.leathernebottel.co.uk   MODERN EUROPEAN
off B4009 heading N out of Goring   £34–£62

Sitting under parasols on the riverside terrace and looking over heat-hazed Oxfordshire in August reminded one couple why they keep coming here. Julia Storey's extensive menus are another reason, of course. We have good reports of spanking-fresh crayfish in lime and coriander broth; seared scallops with cherry tomatoes and pak choi dressed in balsamic; and asparagus just coming into its spring season, served with a poached egg and Parmesan. Meatier options might take in a cutlet of honey-glazed wild boar with roast squash and gingery apple purée, while desserts run the gamut from 'wonderfully rich' sticky toffee pudding to a selection of feather-light, exquisitely presented sorbets. Five house wines from £14.75 head a Francocentric list with gently ascending prices.

CHEF: Julia Storey   PROPRIETOR: Croftchase Ltd   OPEN: all week L 12.30 to 2 (2.30 Sat, 3.30 Sun), Mon to Sat D 7 to 9 (9.30 Fri and Sat)   MEALS: alc (main courses £17.50 to £20). Set D Mon to Fri £23.50. Light L menu available Mon to Fri   SERVICE: 10%, card slips closed   CARDS: Amex, MasterCard, Switch, Visa DETAILS: 48 seats. 80 seats outside. Private parties: 32 main room. Car park. Vegetarian meals. No children under 10. No pipes. Wheelchair access (not WC). No music. No mobile phones

▲ Borrowdale Gates Hotel 🎄

Grange CA12 5UQ
TEL: (017687) 77204   FAX: (017687) 77254   COOKING 3
WEBSITE: www.borrowdale-gates.com   MODERN BRITISH
off B5289, about 3m S of Keswick, 1/4m N of Grange   £28–£68

This country-house hotel at the southern end of Derwent Water has spectacular views of the surrounding valley and hills. The sights can be enjoyed from the large windows in the dining room and from the elegant garden; it's 'a slice of English perfection', as one visitor put it. A preponderance of pinks and greens characterises the décor, a colour scheme that's practically *de rigueur* in the Lakes. The many smaller connecting lounge areas are decorated with Lakeland scenes on the walls – 'not overtly huntin', shootin' and fishin',' according to one visitor, but decidedly unstuffy. Lunch is considered good value 'for this quality, setting and service'. Dinner is a more ambitious affair, for which the stops are pulled out to render dishes such as pressed rabbit confit with garlic and potato gratin, followed perhaps by local squab pigeon roasted with spices and served with caramelised fig Tatin and choux farcie, then banana bavarois with mango and pineapple salsa, passion-fruit sorbet and a rum and raisin caramel sauce. The wine list has plenty around the £20 mark in a well-balanced global selection.

CHEF: Justin Howe   PROPRIETORS: Colin and Carol Slaney   OPEN: all week 12.15 to 1.30, 7 to 8.45 CLOSED: Jan   MEALS: alc L Mon to Sat (main courses £7.50 to £12). Set L Sun £16.25, Set D £34.50 SERVICE: not inc   CARDS: Delta, MasterCard, Switch, Visa   DETAILS: 60 seats. 15 seats outside. Private parties: 24 main room. Car park. Vegetarian meals. No children under 7 at D. Children's helpings at L. No smoking. Wheelchair access (also WC). No music. No mobile phones   ACCOMMODATION: 29 rooms, all with bath/shower. TV. Phone. D,B&B £65 to £175. Rooms for disabled. No children under 7 (£5)

GRANGE MOOR West Yorkshire · map 8

Kaye Arms 🍴 £

NEW ENTRY

29 Wakefield Road, Grange Moor WF4 4BG
TEL: (01924) 848385   FAX: (01924) 848977
off A642 and B6118, 4m S of Dewsbury

COOKING 3
MODERN BRITISH
£27–£53

This popular black and white dining pub stands alone on the Huddersfield to Wakefield road close to Caphouse Colliery's Mining Museum. The traditionally decorated open-plan interior has a patterned carpet, a log fire, shelves lined with whisky bottles, and dark wooden tables covered with white cloths. Although there is a bar, this is very much a food-focused place. Chef Adrian Quarmby's approach is modern British: a simple lunch menu bolstered by a straightforward carte offering plenty of choice, including daily blackboard specials. Expect the likes of an 'excellent' Cheddar soufflé to start, followed by grilled fillet of sea bass with a spinach and thyme risotto cake and fennel, then lightly textured warm chocolate pudding with chocolate sauce and vanilla ice cream. Breads are home-made, while the wine list offers an interesting range of wines of the month and bin-ends from around £13. Service has been described as 'willing and helpful'.

CHEF: Adrian Quarmby   PROPRIETORS: Adrian and Niccola Quarmby, and Sarah Allott   OPEN: Tue to Sun 12 to 2, 7 to 9.30 (10 Sat)   CLOSED: 25 Dec to 3 Jan   MEALS: alc (main courses £9.50 to £18). Light L menu available Tue to Sat   SERVICE: not inc   CARDS: MasterCard, Switch, Visa   DETAILS: 90 seats. Car park. Vegetarian meals. No children under 14 at D. No smoking in 1 dining room. Music

GRASMERE Cumbria · map 8

Jumble Room 🍴 £

NEW ENTRY

Langdale Road, Grasmere LA22 9SU
TEL: (015394) 35188   FAX: (015394) 36088
WEBSITE: www.thejumbleroom.co.uk

COOKING 2
GLOBAL
£23–£60

From the outside it looks like a tea shop, but in fact, the Jumble Room is a cheerful, quality-driven place that 'simply makes one feel good'. Inside, it lives up to its name with bright orange/terracotta walls, jumble shop furniture, and wipeable table covers. Lunch has been given the thumbs up, with a Thai chicken wrap bursting with spicy lime and coriander flavours, and a fresh-tasting Moroccan-spiced king prawn salad vying with ginger pudding with custard, and hot chocolate brownie, to be the highlight of the meal. Dinner showcases some great local produce: Herdwick lamb kofta, for example, mixed with chilli, ginger, cumin, mint and preserved lemons, and local fillet steak rolled in black pepper served with roast red onion, warm Stilton salad and chips. Value for money extends to the short, varied wine list, which opens with house organic Rioja at £10.

CHEFS: Chrissy Hill, and David and Trudy Clay   PROPRIETORS: Andy and Chrissy Hill   OPEN: Wed to Sun 12 to 4, 6 to 9.30   CLOSED: 23 to 26 Dec, first 2 weeks Jan   MEALS: alc (main courses L £7 to £11, D £10 to £22)   SERVICE: not inc, card slips closed   CARDS: Delta, MasterCard, Switch, Visa   DETAILS: 40 seats. 8 seats outside. Private parties: 24 main room, 18 private room. Vegetarian meals. Children's helpings. No smoking. Wheelchair access (not WC). Music £5

▲ White Moss House ▮ ✱

Rydal Water, Grasmere LA22 9SE
TEL: (015394) 35295   FAX: (015394) 35516
WEBSITE: www.whitemoss.com
on A591, at W end of Rydal Water

COOKING 5
BRITISH
£45–£54

William Wordsworth, who once owned this classic Lakeland house at the head of Rydal Water, would doubtless recognise many of the carefully sourced ingredients on the current proprietors' menus: trout from Esthwaite Water, damsons from the Lyth Valley, shrimps from Morecambe Bay, and beef bred on the fells. Peter Dixon's restrained cuisine has a suitably timeless feel, and the repertoire changes little. The Dixons stick to what they know best, and do so in exemplary fashion.

Everyone sits down at eight to eat from a five-course menu with no choice before pudding. Soup – perhaps broccoli and basil, or courgette and chervil – is followed by a fish course that might be as simple as potted shrimps with asparagus, or a more complex soufflé of haddock and halibut. 'Top-notch' meat is beautifully timed, whether it's Lakeland mallard with a damson, port and Pinot Noir sauce, or rack of organic Herdwick lamb with a parsley, sage, rosemary and thyme crust (and its own certificate of origin). Light steamed puddings such as huntsman's pudding with Malmsey sauce, and Mrs Beeton's chocolate pudding, are 'justly celebrated', while raspberry meringue or blackcurrant ice cream provide cooler alternatives.

The Dixons have to be commended for squirrelling fine bottles away in the cellar for a few years before putting them on the wine list. Diners reap the twin benefits of a list of properly matured classics and eminently reasonable prices. Wines are grouped according to French regions, with international lookalikes following in the wake of the real thing. Seven house selections start at £10.95.

CHEFS: Peter Dixon and Ian Armstrong   PROPRIETORS: Susan and Peter Dixon   OPEN: Mon to Sat D only 8 (1 sitting)   CLOSED: Dec and Jan   MEALS: Set D £35.50   SERVICE: not inc, card slips closed   CARDS: MasterCard, Switch, Visa   DETAILS: 18 seats. Private parties: 18 main room. Car park. Vegetarian meals (with prior notice). Children's helpings. No smoking. Wheelchair access (not WC). No music. No mobile phones   ACCOMMODATION: 6 rooms, all with bath/shower. TV. Phone. D,B&B £75 to £198. Baby facilities. Fishing ⒺⒺ

GREAT GONERBY Lincolnshire   map 6

Harry's Place ✱

17 High Street, Great Gonerby NG31 8JS
TEL: (01476) 561780

COOKING 7
MODERN FRENCH
£61–£90

Apart from its sky-blue façade, the building is an ordinary residential house whose front parlour is devoted to serving guests – just ten of them, at three tables. The Hallam double-act is endowed with a special talent: service, from the 'balletic' Caroline Hallam, is polished, efficient, friendly and highly personal, and Harry himself appears at the end of dinner and does the rounds. And then there is the food.

Raw materials are seemingly never anything but perfect, and Harry's technical skills are impressive. The timing of fish is outstanding, while main-course compositions are assured, with masterful integration of peripheral elements: witness a supple and perfectly sealed fillet of wild Scottish salmon served with a sauce of Sauternes, Noilly-Prat and chives, not forgetting vegetables that are 'anything but routine'. Meat main courses are equally well timed: filleted loin of Cornish spring lamb with white wine, Madeira and tarragon sauce, for instance, comes 'very much on the pink side of pink'. A soup is normally an option among starters – 'complex and interesting' local asparagus, for example – and to finish there might be apricot soufflé or cherry brandy jelly with yoghurt and black pepper. Wine mark-ups on the short but decent handwritten list are high, with prices starting at £20 for Italian white, £26 for Australian red. Despite this, the feeling is that eating here is an experience that seems 'excellent value for money'.

CHEF: Harry Hallam   PROPRIETORS: Harry and Caroline Hallam   OPEN: Tue to Sat 12.30 to 2, 7 to 9
CLOSED: bank hols   MEALS: alc (main courses £27.50 to £32)   SERVICE: not inc   CARDS: Delta,
MasterCard, Switch, Visa   DETAILS: 10 seats. Private parties: 10 main room. Car park. Children's
helpings. No children under 5. No smoking. Wheelchair access (not WC). No music £5

GREAT MILTON Oxfordshire	map 2

▲ Le Manoir aux Quat' Saisons ✿✖

Church Road, Great Milton OX44 7PD   COOKING 9
TEL: (01844) 278881   FAX: (01844) 278847   MODERN FRENCH
WEBSITE: www.manoir.com   £68–£151

Twenty years ago Raymond Blanc embarked on his life's mission from this handsome stone manor house. We now see the results of all his work, energy and passion, and it is a sight to behold. Before crossing the threshold one can tell this is a place of serious intent and high standards, for the grounds are beautifully kept – but they also contribute some of the kitchen's finest vegetables, fruits and herbs. It's a short journey from garden to kitchen, so freshness is a given, and, as one visitor put it, 'the ingredients are the defining element here'.

There is a lack of stuffiness throughout, from the warm welcome at the door to service at table, which, though formal and correct, is friendly. Bread is offered at regular intervals: a generous choice including soda, beer, or pecan and raisin, each with distinct flavours and contrasting textures. After an amuse-bouche comes the *de rigueur* pre-starter – perhaps a vibrant watercress soup, which proved perfect for a spring evening. Starters can be as straightforward as a provençale tart topped with halved cherry tomatoes ('bursting with flavour'), confit of onions scented with thyme, and slivers of black olives, or as luxurious as a cannelloni of langoustines, packed with firm and sweet shellfish, accompanied by a perfectly seared scallop, a herb purée full of vigour, and a lemon sabayon light enough to enhance the main ingredient. While waiters dissecting both poached turbot and a corn-fed squab baked in a salt crust at table might make untidy surgeons, the latter dish proved to be a 'perfectly pink and lightly gamey bird', accompanied by creamy foie gras, thin slices of potato 'Maxim', cabbage with bacon, a scattering of morels, and some light meat juices spooned over by the waiter. Maximum flavour is drawn from sweet Romano peppers served with roasted Cornish sea bass, or from Trelough duck with a little foie gras and some gratin dauphinois.

There are many who feel desserts are a particular high point here; one found on the edible (biscuit) painter's palette of ice creams and sorbets 'the perfect vanilla ice cream and similarly sublime passion-fruit sorbet', while for another the caramel soufflé was the very best he had eaten. On a visit to Le Manoir expectations are high, on account of its deserved reputation and the high prices of meals (and accommodation), so any disappointments are proportionately intensified. Some readers report these back to us, but the preponderance of glowing reports demonstrates that the balance of cost versus value for money works out to be well and truly positive.

The wine list measures up to the calibre of the kitchen, but at a price: even house suggestions are around £25. Burgundy is documented not just village by village, but cru by cru, domaine by domaine, and top Bordeaux châteaux come in as many as nine different vintages. Beyond France the quality doesn't stint, with Australia, Italy and California all putting in star performances. Glass prices start at £6.

CHEFS: Raymond Blanc and Gary Jones   PROPRIETOR: Raymond Blanc   OPEN: all week 12.15 to 2.45, 7.15 to 9.45   MEALS: alc (main courses £37 to £40). Set L (not bank hols) £45 to £95, Set D (not bank hols) £95   SERVICE: not inc   CARDS: Amex, Delta, Diners, MasterCard, Switch, Visa   DETAILS: 100 seats. Private parties: 8 main room, 10 to 50 private rooms. Car park. Vegetarian meals. Children's helpings. No smoking. Wheelchair access (also WC). No music. No mobile phones. Air-conditioned   ACCOMMODATION: 32 rooms, all with bath/shower. TV. Phone. B&B £265 to £1,200. Rooms for disabled. Baby facilities

GREAT MISSENDEN Buckinghamshire   map 3

La Petite Auberge

107 High Street, Great Missenden HP16 0BB   COOKING 4
TEL: (01494) 865370   FRENCH
                                                                           £39–£54

This long-standing traditional French restaurant is in an unremarkable terrace at the south end of the High Street of this small Chilterns town. Two reports sum up its appeal, both from diners glad to have returned after too long an absence: one praised the consistent standards in classic dishes such as 'rich, smooth' foie gras terrine, and tender coquilles St Jacques in a light, buttery sauce on a bed of leeks; another found Mme Martel's welcome as warm as ever, and the service friendly, relaxed and unhurried. Menus rarely change, sticking to a tried-and-tested repertoire of simple, mostly traditional dishes. Starters range from soupe de poisson to marinated tuna in lemon juice, mains from sea bass with mustard sauce to venison noisettes with morello cherries and cranberry sauce, with tarte au citron or crème brûlée to finish. The short, exclusively French wine list is well chosen and offers a good selection under £20.

CHEF: Hubert Martel   PROPRIETORS: Mr and Mrs H. Martel   OPEN: Mon to Sat D only 7.30 to 10   CLOSED: 2 weeks Christmas, 2 weeks Easter   MEALS: alc (main courses £16 to £17)   SERVICE: not inc   CARDS: Delta, Diners, MasterCard, Switch, Visa   DETAILS: 30 seats. Private parties: 30 main room. Wheelchair access (also WC). No music

GREAT YELDHAM Essex   map 3

White Hart ♈ ⚹✳

Poole Street, Great Yeldham CO9 4HJ   COOKING 2
TEL: (01787) 237250   FAX: (01787) 238044   ANGLO-FRENCH-PLUS
WEBSITE: www.whitehartyeldham.co.uk   £24–£57

This large, handsome pub has been around for 500 years and has been welcoming diners for at least 150. Huge inglenooks, copious expanses of wooden beams, and bare wooden tables characterise the interior. At dinner a starter of fish soup has exhibited good depth of flavour, with a spicy bite. Main courses tend towards hearty dishes such as venison suet pudding, packed with tender, plentiful meat and served in a hard-to-finish portion, or beef medallion with mushrooms and a creamy pepper sauce. Desserts that have earned high praise include a fig tart with rum and raisin ice cream, based on delicate frangipane pastry, and an intense chocolate truffle cake with red fruit coulis. House wine is a pub-price £11.50, one of a dozen options also served by the glass. The full list, clearly arranged by style, motors on gently to finer things from France, Italy and the southern hemisphere. As well as Dicken's Brasserie in Wethersfield (see entry), John Dicken also owns Dick's Café (Townsford Mill, Halstead), in a converted mill that also houses an antiques centre.

CHEF/PROPRIETOR: John Dicken   OPEN: all week 12 to 2, 6.30 to 9.30   MEALS: alc (main courses £10 to £18). Set L Mon to Sat £10.50 (2 courses) to £14.50. Light menu available   SERVICE: not inc   CARDS: Amex, Delta, Diners, MasterCard, Switch, Visa   DETAILS: 150 seats. 50 seats outside. Private parties: 80 main room, 20 to 200 private rooms. Car park. Vegetarian meals. No smoking. Occasional music. No mobile phones

GRIMSBY N.E. Lincolnshire   map 9

Granary £   NEW ENTRY

Haven Mill, Garth Lane, Grimsby DN31 1RP   COOKING 1
TEL/FAX: (01472) 346338   SEAFOOD/MODERN EUROPEAN
WEBSITE: www.granarygrimsby.co.uk   £24–£51

Don't be fooled by the name of this establishment on the first floor of a converted 200-year-old waterside grain mill: the reason most people come to Ron and Mary Houghton's restaurant is to eat fish (although vegetarian or carnivore hangers-on are catered for as well). There's no printed menu: Mary lugs a big blackboard from table to table, provides explanations and takes orders. Dishes come and go at a rate of knots, but everything is cooked with disarming simplicity: salt cod brandade, and spicy fish soup (good for 'spoon-trawling') have been well received, while accurately timed mains range from halibut meunière to mackerel with sweet chilli sauce. Meat-fanciers might go for wild rabbit casserole with ceps and Muscat wine, and there's a trolley-load of everyday desserts for those with hollow legs. House wine is £10.

CHEF: Jon Warner   PROPRIETORS: Ron and Mary Houghton   OPEN: Mon to Fri L 12 to 2.15, Wed to Sat D 7 to 9   CLOSED: 3 to 18 July, 24 Dec to 2 Jan, bank hol Mons   MEALS: alc (main courses £8.50 to £22) SERVICE: not inc, card slips closed   CARDS: Amex, Delta, MasterCard, Switch, Visa   DETAILS: 90 seats. Private parties: 90 main room, 20 to 45 private rooms. Vegetarian meals. Children's helpings. No pipes/cigars. Music

GRIMSTON Norfolk   map 6

▲ Congham Hall ▼ ⅝✳

Lynn Road, Grimston PE32 1AH   COOKING 4
TEL: (01485) 600250   FAX: (01485) 601191   MODERN BRITISH/FRENCH
WEBSITE: www.conghamhallhotel.co.uk   £32–£75

A cream-painted Georgian manor house in 30 acres of parkland that include a notable herb garden, Congham Hall offers a traditional English country-house hotel experience. Its Orangery Restaurant has a muslin-tented skylight and large French windows that open onto a terrace with views over the flatlands between Peddars Way and the Wash. Pale coral walls are hung with prints of exotic fruits, and well-spaced tables come dressed in floor-length white linen. Fraser Miller runs the kitchen on modern British lines, exhibited in set-price lunches and dinners, including gourmand and vegetarian menus. Expect main-course dishes like pan-roasted sea bass served with ginger and spring onion risotto, crayfish and coriander tortellini, and a scallop infused velouté, or perhaps a saddle of venison with braised red cabbage, Jerusalem artichoke, pommes purée and a game jus. Raspberry soufflé with raspberry ripple ice cream could head the desserts list. A dinner inspection with the head chef off duty found flavours somewhat lacking, but 'friendly and intelligent, unstuffy' service by the restaurant manager helped redeem things somewhat. Wines are arranged into broad styles with astute choices for a range of pocket in each category. House wines at £18 are indicative of slightly steep prices.

CHEF: Fraser Miller   PROPRIETOR: Von Essen Hotels   OPEN: all week 12 to 1.45, 7 to 9.15   MEALS: Set L £13.50 (2 courses) to £31.95 (whole table only), Set D £31.50 (2 courses) to £48 (whole table only). Bar/terrace menu available   SERVICE: not inc, card slips closed   CARDS: Amex, Delta, Diners, MasterCard, Switch, Visa   DETAILS: 60 seats. 20 seats outside. Private parties: 60 main room, 4 to 20 private rooms. Car park. Vegetarian meals. Children's helpings. No children under 7 at D. No smoking. Wheelchair access (not WC). No music. No mobile phones   ACCOMMODATION: 14 rooms, all with bath/shower. TV. Phone. B&B £110 to £300. Baby facilities (£5)

HALIFAX West Yorkshire   map 9

Design House ✤ £   NEW ENTRY

Dean Clough, North Bridge, Halifax HX3 5AX
TEL: (01422) 383242 FAX: (01422) 322732
WEBSITE: www.designhouserestaurant.co.uk

COOKING 2
MODERN EUROPEAN
£23–£51

In the Dean Clough Mill complex, the Design House – contemporary as its name implies – sports flagstone floors, spotlights, silver panels on plain walls and trendy seating. Since 2003 Lee Marshall (former head chef at La Cachette, Elland; see entry), with Mark Mattock at the stove, has revitalised the venture via fixed-priced menus and a carte offering decent choice at reasonable prices. The modern brasserie-style fare runs from pan-fried turbot fillet with leeks, roast garlic and a red wine glaze, to classic steaks (fillet, sirloin or ribeye) with slow-roast tomato, home-made chips and various sauces – plus pasta, risotto and vegetarian options. Starters and puds include a tartlet of fried chicken livers, and deep-fried rice pudding with banana and butterscotch won tons. A compact global wine list starts with house from £11.50.

CHEF: Mark Mattock   PROPRIETOR: Lee Stevens Marshall   OPEN: Mon to Fri L 12 to 2.30, Mon to Sat D 6 to 9.30   MEALS: alc (main courses £6 to £20). Set L £8.95 (2 courses), Set D Mon to Fri 6 to 9.30, Sat 6 to 7 £12.95. Bar L menu available   SERVICE: not inc, 10% for parties of 15 or more   CARDS: MasterCard, Switch, Visa   DETAILS: 75 seats. 18 seats outside. Private parties: 125 main room. Vegetarian meals. No smoking. Wheelchair access (not WC). Music. No mobile phones. Air-conditioned

▲ Holdsworth House ✤   NEW ENTRY

Holdsworth, Halifax HX2 9TG
TEL: (01422) 240024 FAX: (01422) 245174
WEBSITE: www.holdsworthhouse.co.uk

COOKING 3
MODERN BRITISH
£27–£57

In this beautiful Jacobean manor house on the ridge between the Calder and the Aire the dining areas feature wood panelling, exposed beams, stone-mullioned windows and oil paintings on the walls. Begin with tasty, moist Loch Fyne smoked salmon with red onion and capers, or nicely soft linguine in cream sauce with chanterelle, shiitake and trompette mushrooms and hints of truffle oil. Follow up with roast lamb loin and aubergine caviar with red wine jus, or sea bass fillet on creamed pasta with leeks and tarragon. A 'grand selection of desserts' for sharing (deep-fried ice cream, baked egg custard, berry-topped almond tart, iced pistachio and lime bavarois and a powerfully minty chocolate fondant) makes for a good finish. Smart and correct service has been described as 'as from another time'. Starting with low-end Duboeuf at £12.75, a reasonably extensive list is strong on claret and Australia; there are ten by the glass.

CHEF: Gary Saunders   PROPRIETORS: Kim Pearson and Gail Moss   OPEN: Mon to Fri L 12 to 2, all week D 7 to 9.30   MEALS: alc (main courses £11 to £18). Set L £12.95 (2 courses) to £15.95, Set D Fri to Sun £27.50   SERVICE: not inc   CARDS: Amex, Delta, Diners, MasterCard, Switch, Visa   DETAILS: 50 seats. 10 seats outside. Private parties: 20 main room, 2 to 120 private rooms. Car park. Vegetarian meals. Children's helpings. No Smoking. Wheelchair access (also WC). Music. No mobile phones   ACCOMMODATION: 40 rooms, all with bath/shower. TV. Phone. B&B £95 to £160. Rooms for disabled. Baby facilities (£5)

▲ Shibden Mill Inn

Shibden Mill Fold, Shibden, Halifax HX3 7UL | NEW CHEF
TEL: (01422) 365840   FAX: (01422) 362971 | MODERN BRITISH
WEBSITE: www.shibdenmillinn.com | £29–£44

The restaurant at this welcoming pub is upstairs, reached via a staircase at the back of the bar. Beneath the vaulted ceiling, the ambience is cosy, and the food is what the management calls 'British at its best in the most British of settings'. A new head chef arrived in the kitchen too late in the day for an assessment, though you can expect something like saffron and leek risotto, followed by confit of duck leg with roasted beetroot and horseradish, and warm rice pudding with jam sauce to finish. An enterprising wine list keeps prices on the leash, opening with Hungarian Chardonnay and French Merlot at £9.90.

CHEF: Steve Evans   PROPRIETOR: S.D. Heaton   OPEN: Sun 12 to 7.30, all week D 6 to 9.30   CLOSED: 25 and 26 Dec pm, 1 Jan pm   MEALS: alc (main courses £10.50 to £15.50). Bar snack menu available   SERVICE: not inc, card slips closed   CARDS: Amex, Delta, MasterCard, Switch, Visa   DETAILS: 40 seats. 40 seats outside. Private parties: 70 main room, 2 to 10 private rooms. Car park. Vegetarian meals. Children's helpings. Music   ACCOMMODATION: 12 rooms, all with bath/shower. TV. Phone. B&B £65 to £115 (£5)

Monsieur Max ▼

133 High Street, Hampton Hill TW12 1NJ | COOKING 6
TEL: (020) 8979 5546   FAX: (020) 8979 3747 | FRENCH
WEBSITE: www.monsieurmax.co.uk | £40–£64

The unprepossessing frontage may not stop you in your tracks, but persevere. Despite some contemporary crossover dishes (such as octopus and ginger salad with fried ink risotto and citrus dressing), the kitchen's heart is in France, in a fillet of Aberdeen Angus beef en croûte with field mushroom mousseline, gratin dauphinois, and red wine and peppercorn sauce. For many, a meal here is a 'real treat', although some might quarrel with the complexity of the cooking. Baked fillet of line-caught South Coast sea bass has been served with several components: a seaweed crust, parsnips crushed with saffron, sardines, foie gras and squid, and sauce aigre-doux. There may be plenty of original ideas and novel presentations, but the focus is on sound culinary principles and traditional cooking methods. Desserts have included old-fashioned rice pudding with Madagascan vanilla and cognac caramel, and a strawberry soufflé that was 'worth the wait'. Service is cheerily described as 'very French' and 'leisurely', but some long waits are reported. The wine list focuses on France – where the south is the place for value – while other countries are relegated to supporting roles. Six house wines from £14.50 to £38.50 are marked up further by the glass.

CHEF: Alex Bentley   PROPRIETOR: Sunbow Ltd   OPEN: Sun to Fri L 12 to 2.30, all week D 7 to 9.30 CLOSED: 25 Dec   MEALS: Set L £20 (2 courses) to £35, Set D £37.50   SERVICE: 12.5% (optional), card slips closed   CARDS: Amex, Diners, MasterCard, Switch, Visa   DETAILS: 80 seats. Private parties: 90 main room. Children's helpings. No children under 8. Wheelchair access (not WC). No music. Air-conditioned

HAROME North Yorkshire   map 9

▲ Star Inn ♚ ✹ £

High Street, Harome YO62 5JE   COOKING 5
TEL: (01439) 770397   FAX: (01439) 771833   MODERN BRITISH
WEBSITE: www.thestaratharome.co.uk   £27–£60

The aptly named Star is seemingly straight out of Rural England Central Casting: a long, low, whitewashed, fourteenth-century building with a steep-sloping thatched roof. Inside, the flagged floors and warren of small, cluttered rooms are also what one expects, but Andrew Pern's busily inventive menus transcend the sleepy setting. Starters such as parsnip soup, enriched with sour cream and mildly flavoured with cumin, or crab and plum tomato salad with green herb mayonnaise and a Bloody Mary dressing, set the tone and combine exemplary freshness with sound technique. Flavour is built up robustly in main courses, partnering tender, gamey, pot-roasted partridge with Waberthwaite ham, pan-haggerty and a sticky stock reduction, or fashioning a Yorkshire blue risotto to accompany braised lamb shank and baked butternut squash. There are more homely dishes too, such as sausages and mash served in 'Yorkshire quantities', or a pressed terrine of local game, and such regional delicacies as crumbly, warm ginger parkin contrasted with a hot, spicy syrup and rhubarb ripple ice cream. Another way to finish might be with a decadently rich chocolate mousse on an orange biscuit base with orange sorbet. Vegetarians have their own menu, and everything is served up with obvious warmth and sincerity.

Reports rightly praise the wine list, which opens with over a dozen stylish options by the glass from £3 to £6, trips through France with flair, and picks some pearls out of other regions to boot. The Star at Scampston is a new venture run by Andrew and Jacquie at Scampston Hall, Malton. It's open from 10 to 5 and offers home-made cakes, snacks and light lunches, with much of the produce coming from the Hall's impressive gardens.

CHEF: Andrew Pern   PROPRIETORS: Andrew and Jacquie Pern   OPEN: Tue to Sun L 11.30 to 2 (12 to 6 Sun), Tue to Sat D 6.30 to 9.30   CLOSED: 2½ weeks in Jan   MEALS: alc (main courses £9.50 to £20)   SERVICE: not inc, card slips closed   CARDS: MasterCard, Switch, Visa   DETAILS: 36 seats. 20 seats outside. Private parties: 36 main room, 6 to 12 private rooms. Car park. Vegetarian meals. Children's helpings. No smoking. Music   ACCOMMODATION: 11 rooms, all with bath/shower. TV. B&B £90 to £195. Rooms for disabled

HARROGATE North Yorkshire   map 8

Attic ✹

62A Union Street, Harrogate HG1 1BS   COOKING 4
TEL: (01423) 524400   FAX: (01423) 523191   MODERN EUROPEAN
WEBSITE: www.attic-harrogate.co.uk   £21–£48

Hidden away down a narrow side street in the heart of the town, this aptly named restaurant – a former warehouse – is a welcoming, modern affair. Downstairs there's a smart, contemporary bar with sofas, tables and a flagstone floor, then it's upstairs to the 'light, airy' dining room. The long, atrium-like, minimalist space comes decked out with bare blond wooden tables and a matching wooden floor. The cooking continues the modern theme, approached via a 'bargain' set-price lunch and early-bird menu, plus a carte that changes every three weeks. Asparagus topped with ravioli surrounding a soft egg yoke and drizzled with truffle oil provides a twist on a classic combination to start, while crisp sea bass might be matched with tapenade and confit fennel, and roast leg of rabbit with seared foie gras and carrot purée at main-course stage. Muscavado sponge with an orange mousse – described by a reporter as 'posh nursery food' – might be among desserts. Service comes in for universal praise as 'excellent', while the sharp, modern wine list has helpful notes and eight house wines at £11.85.

CHEF: Joseph Horvath   PROPRIETOR: Chris Patchett   OPEN: Mon to Sat 12 to 2, 6.30 to 10   CLOSED: 25 and 26 Dec, 1 Jan   MEALS: alc (main courses £11 to £14.50). Set L and D 6.30 to 7.30 £9.50 (2 courses) to £11.50   SERVICE: not inc   CARDS: Amex, Delta, MasterCard, Switch, Visa   DETAILS: 56 seats. Private parties: 45 main room. Vegetarian meals. No smoking. Music. Air-conditioned (£5)

Drum and Monkey £

5 Montpellier Gardens, Harrogate HG1 2TF   COOKING 2
TEL: (01423) 502650   SEAFOOD
    £22–£59

In December 2003 this bastion of the Harrogate scene was taken over by Jan Fletcher, owner of Bryan's, an indefatigable chippy/restaurant in Leeds (see entry, Round-ups). At the Drum and Monkey the kitchen brigade has been retained and little seems to have changed: inside is a cosy, atmospheric bar (bedecked with fish-related art), which provides a preamble to meals in the 'regal-looking' upstairs dining room. Old-school seafood cookery is the order of the day, with a menu that puts its faith in classic ideas and rich flavours: poached sea trout with asparagus hollandaise, grilled sea bass with herb butter sauce, and smoked haddock florentine, for example. Salmon and watercress mousse remains a 'staple' starter, while vanilla ice cream with Madeira-soaked raisins is a still a favourite way to finish. House wines are £10.50.

CHEFS: Keith Penny and Selina Leamy   PROPRIETOR: Jan Fletcher   OPEN: Mon to Sat 12 to 2.30, 6.30 to 10.15   CLOSED: 24 Dec to 2 Jan   MEALS: alc (main courses £6.50 to £20)   SERVICE: not inc   CARDS: Delta, MasterCard, Switch, Visa   DETAILS: 58 seats. Wheelchair access (not WC). No music

▲ Hotel du Vin & Bistro ▮   NEW ENTRY

Prospect Place, Harrogate HG1 1LB   COOKING 3
TEL: (01423) 856800   FAX: (01423) 856801   MODERN EUROPEAN
WEBSITE: www.hotelduvin.com   £40–£59

The oenophile's hotel chain continues to lengthen, this link being forged in Harrogate. Beautifully uplit at night, this one is part of a trim terrace of Yorkshire-stone buildings overlooking the Stray, Harrogate's green heart. A hunting theme prevails inside, manifested in animal print cushions, table lights adorned with game bird feathers, and beastly heads fashioned from papier-mâché. The menus follow the formula established at the group's other branches (see entries in Birmingham, Brighton, Bristol, Tunbridge Wells and Winchester), with a modern brasserie vibe predominating. Kick things off with soft herring roes on toasted brioche with a properly piquant mustard beurre blanc or pigeon breast with lentils. After that, pink-roast venison loin has gone down well, served with crisp rösti and a cranberry jus to add both kinds of bite, while halibut may be intriguingly teamed with salsify and sauced with a gentle beurre rouge. Crème brûlée is right out of the textbook, a creamy, crunchy satisfaction, although the cheeses have been a bit fridgey. As at some of the other branches, the place has a real pulse to it, quickened by willing service. The wine list, too, is the equal of other branches. It covers the world in detail, even venturing into Corsica, and depth – over a dozen options in Australian Shiraz, say, or clarets back to 1982. Prices open at £12.50, and around 20 come by the glass, but value for money is variable.

CHEF: Gareth Longhurst   PROPRIETOR: Hotel du Vin Ltd   OPEN: all week 12 to 1.45, 6.30 to 9.45   MEALS: alc (main courses £14.50 to £16.50)   SERVICE: not inc, card slips closed   CARDS: Amex, Delta, Diners, MasterCard, Switch, Visa   DETAILS: 86 seats. 20 seats outside. Private parties: 10 to 60 private rooms. Car park. Vegetarian meals. Children's helpings. Wheelchair access (also WC). No music. Air-conditioned   ACCOMMODATION: 43 rooms, all with bath/shower. TV. Phone. Room only £95 to £225. Rooms for disabled. Baby facilities

HARROW Greater London   map 3

Golden Palace

146–150 Station Road, Harrow HA1 2RH   COOKING 4
TEL: (020) 8863 2333   FAX: (020) 8863 3388   CHINESE
                                                        £26–£72

Harrow has a thriving, though little-publicised, Chinese sub-culture, and this colourful restaurant in a parade of shops has become one of its focal points, with cooking that – on its day – can match the best in the capital. The kitchen has been known to falter, but there are no misgivings about the remarkable selection of immaculately executed dim sum. On Sunday Chinese families and out-of-towners descend on the Palace, queues stretch into the afternoon, and the set-up really shows its mettle. Stay with familiar steamed prawn dumplings and cheung fun, or plunge into the realms of goose feet with dried dough and satay sauce, or five-spiced beef belly (actually tripe served with Chinese turnip). Congee and 'beautifully textured' steamed rice in hotpot have passed with flying colours and – if you fancy something sweet – try fried bean curd pudding. The main menu offers a big selection of Chinese classics (from fried scallops with seasonal greens to roasted crispy chicken), backed up by challenging specials. A 'jolly crew' generally ensures service is on the ball, and house wines start at £10.50.

CHEF/PROPRIETOR: Gordon Ho   OPEN: Mon to Sat 12 to 11.30, Sun 11 to 10.30, bank hols 11 to 11.30   CLOSED: 25 Dec   MEALS: alc (main courses £5.50 to £30). Set L and D £16.50 to £24 (all min 2 or more)   SERVICE: 10%   CARDS: Amex, Delta, Diners, MasterCard, Switch, Visa   DETAILS: 150 seats. Private parties: 10 to 70 private rooms. Vegetarian meals. Wheelchair access (also WC). Music. Air-conditioned   ⊖ Harrow on the Hill

---

'The puddings were no longer served from a trolley, but that may have had to do with the fact the main dining room was taken by an enormous party of Rotarians. They still weren't individually shaped or portioned. I mean the puddings, not the Rotarians.' (On eating in Dorset)

HARWICH Essex
map 6

▲ Pier Hotel, Harbourside Restaurant ▼ ⅙✳

The Quay, Harwich CO12 3HH	COOKING 2
TEL: (01255) 241212 FAX: (01255) 551922	SEAFOOD/ENGLISH
WEBSITE: www.milsomhotels.com	£31–£61

From the first-floor Harbourside restaurant at the Pier (above the Ha'penny Pier Bistro) there's plenty to look at, including the ferries that ply across both the Stour estuary and the North Sea. Longstanding chef Chris Oakley's menus exploit fresh seafood landed at the harbour, perhaps in a hotpot of mussels with wild mushrooms and leeks to start, or in a main course of fried skate with capers and prawns in brown butter. Lobsters from a salt-water tank are a speciality, served in a seafood salad, or grilled with béarnaise sauce; meat-eaters may pick something like slow-braised shank of lamb in red wine sauce, and among the puds are Black Forest cheesecake, or chocolate and hazelnut parfait. France and the southern hemisphere predominate in the seafood-friendly wine list starting at £13.25, and additional 'guest' wines are a lively, modern bunch.

CHEF: Chris Oakley   PROPRIETORS: Paul and Gerald Milsom   OPEN: all week 12 to 2, 6 to 9.30   MEALS: alc (main courses £10.50 to £20.50). Set L £16 (2 courses) to £19   SERVICE: 10%, card slips closed   CARDS: Amex, Delta, Diners, MasterCard, Switch, Visa   DETAILS: 80 seats. 30 seats outside. Private parties: 80 main room, 40 to 80 private rooms. Car park. Vegetarian meals. Children's helpings. No smoking. Music. No mobile phones. Air conditioned   ACCOMMODATION: 14 rooms, all with bath/shower. TV. Phone. B&B £70 to £170. Baby facilities

HATHERSAGE Derbyshire
map 9

▲ George Hotel ⅙✳

Main Road, Hathersage S32 1BB	COOKING 4
TEL: (01433) 650436 FAX: (01433) 650099	MODERN BRITISH-PLUS
WEBSITE: www.george-hotel.net	£30–£66

The George Hotel's traditional exterior conceals 'cool, contemporary décor based on deliberate starkness' in its restaurant, George's. In this comfortable, attractive setting Ben Handley's cooking 'seems to go from strength to strength' as well as from continent to continent. The kitchen focuses largely on fresh Derbyshire raw materials, but has garnered praise for accurate timing of, for example, a starter of pan-roasted monkfish presented on a noodle salad and dressed with ginger and chilli, as well as mains of roast best end of lamb with garlic and thyme mash, or chargrilled sirloin. New England clam chowder has been described as 'the perfect comfort food'; tea-smoked duck breast has come on aromatic couscous; and seared diver-caught scallops have been perfectly seared on the outside and sweet and moist within. An inventive range of salads comes in two sizes, while vegetarians aren't short-changed with farfalle with chargrilled courgette, lime, mint and ricotta. Among desserts a banana tarte Tatin with caramel and brandy sauce has found favour, as has a red-wine-poached pear with a champagne sorbet. A couple of dozen wines from across the world start with Chilean varietals at £14.95 (£3.95 a glass), and rise to £27, though half of them stay under £20.

CHEF: Ben Handley   PROPRIETOR: Eric Marsh   OPEN: all week; 12 to 2.30, 7 to 10   MEALS: alc (main courses £10.50 to £19.95). Set L Sun £19.95   SERVICE: not inc, card slips closed   CARDS: Amex, Delta, Diners, MasterCard, Switch, Visa   DETAILS: 50 seats. Private parties: 80 main room, 8 to 80 private rooms. Car park. Vegetarian meals. Children's helpings. No smoking. Wheelchair access (not WC).

Music. No mobile phones   ACCOMMODATION: 19 rooms, all with bath/shower. TV. Phone. B&B £69 to £162 (£5)

HAWORTH West Yorkshire

map 8

▲ Weavers ⅝✳

13–17 West Lane, Haworth BD22 8DU
TEL: (01535) 643822   FAX: (01535) 644832
WEBSITE: www.weaversmallhotel.co.uk

COOKING 3
MODERN BRITISH
£26–£50

Mum, dad and son are in the kitchen and two daughters front-of-house in this knocked-through row of three nineteenth-century shops, busy with abundant knick-knacks and candlelit for a dark, moody feel. The cooking, a well-travelled, open-minded take on modern British, emphasises local produce. Thus menus and blackboards offer starters from terrine of black pudding, sausage, bacon and eggs with tomato and red onion marmalade, to a 'burger' of tuna, chickpeas and dill, while main courses range from Gressingham duck breast on bubble and squeak with orange and sherry sauce, to seared sea bass, scallops and tiger prawns on parsley risotto with shellfish and star anise broth. End on spiced apple crème brûlée, or fine Yorkshire cheeses for a savoury alternative. Fifty-odd international wines start at £11.50 and include eight by the glass (from £3).

CHEFS: Colin, Jane and Tim Rushworth   PROPRIETORS: the Rushworth family   OPEN: Wed to Fri and Sun L 12 to 2, Tue to Sat D 6.30 to 9   CLOSED: 10 days from Christmas   MEALS: alc (main courses £11 to £18). Set L £12.95 (2 courses) to £15.95, Set D Tue to Fri 6.30 to 7.30 £12.95 (2 courses) to £15.95   SERVICE: not inc   CARDS: Amex, Delta, Diners, MasterCard, Switch, Visa   DETAILS: 65 seats. Private parties: 12 to 45 private rooms. Vegetarian meals. Children's helpings. No smoking. Music. No mobile phones. Air-conditioned   ACCOMMODATION: 3 rooms, all with bath/shower. TV. Phone. B&B £55 to £90. Baby facilities (£5)

HAYDON BRIDGE Northumberland

map 10

General Havelock Inn ⅝✳

9 Ratcliffe Road, Haydon Bridge NE47 6ER
TEL: (01434) 684376   FAX: (01434) 684283
WEBSITE: www.generalhavelock.co.uk
on A69, 6m W of Hexham and 100yds W of junction with B6319

COOKING 2
MODERN EUROPEAN
£24–£48

The riverside location is one attraction of this old coaching inn; others include a friendly welcome, attentive service and a menu based on quality local ingredients. Since 1999 the Thompsons have built up a loyal following of customers who appreciate the value for money, and that much of the food is made on the premises – including bread, ice cream and petits fours. A three-course set lunch can be had for £14.25. At dinner (four courses for £25) chilled Galia melon with ginger and lime sorbet might precede honey-glazed duck breast on root vegetables with a mead-scented jus. 'Genuine minestrone, full of vegetables' is one dish that has earned high praise, as has chicken and leek terrine. Desserts might include warm walnut tart with crème fraîche, or chocolate, rum and raisin crème brûlée. The short wine list has a few interesting bottles; house French is £10.50.

CHEF: Gary Thompson   PROPRIETORS: Gary and Joanna Thompson   OPEN: Tue to Sun L 12 to 2, Tue to Sat D 7 to 9   MEALS: alc (main courses L £7 to £8.50, D £12 to £15.50). Set L £10.50 (2 courses) to £14.25, Set D £20.75 (2 courses) to £25. Bar L menu available   SERVICE: not inc, card slips closed   CARDS: Amex,

Delta, MasterCard, Switch, Visa DETAILS: 50 seats. 30 seats outside. Private parties: 40 main room. Children's helpings. No smoking in dining room. Wheelchair access (also WC). Occasional music £5

HAYWARDS HEATH West Sussex · map 3

Jeremy's

Borde Hill, Balcombe Road, Haywards Heath RH16 1XP
TEL: (01444) 441102 FAX: (01444) 443936
WEBSITE: www.homeofgoodfood.co.uk

COOKING 5
MODERN EUROPEAN
£32–£60

Jeremy Ashpool's restaurant, within pollinating distance of the gardens at Borde Hill House, is a model of relaxed restraint, an elegant and comfortable dining room serving stylish, modern, pan-European food that manages to avoid fashion clichés. There are fixed-price or à la carte menus offered – plus, on Tuesday nights, a menu dégustation that could transport you in six easy steps from tomato consommé with Kaffir lime leaves to a dessert assiette pairing Seville orange curd mille-feuille with chocolate and chilli mousse, with suggested wines to accompany each stage if you've a mind. A new chef joined in summer 2004, but this is Jeremy's Restaurant after all. Strong flavours are understood and allowed full rein, gratinating a truffled mushroom salad with blue cheese, adding spice to a vegetable ragoût, and teaming pheasant breast with roast chorizo, Jerusalem artichoke, red cabbage, a mousse of carrot and a juniper sauce. Some descriptions can sound complex (though not smoked haddock with spinach, new potatoes and grain mustard sauce), but what turns up on the plate convinces, through to the acerbic intensity of a dessert that combines pink grapefruit, orange and poached pear with sloe gin jelly. Monthly-changing recommendations lead off a wine list that nips assuredly around both hemispheres. Prices start at £12, or £2.90 a glass.

CHEF: Lee Cobb PROPRIETORS: Jeremy and Vera Ashpool OPEN: Tue to Sun L 12.30 to 2.30, Tue to Sat D 7.30 to 10 CLOSED: 1st week Jan MEALS: alc (not Sun L or Tue D; main courses £13 to £22). Set L £16.50 (2 courses) to £20.50, Set D Tue to Thurs £16.50 (2 courses) to £25 SERVICE: not inc CARDS: Amex, MasterCard, Switch, Visa DETAILS: 55 seats. 120 seats outside. Private parties: 55 main room, 60 to 120 private rooms. Car park. Vegetarian meals. Children's helpings. No smoking. Wheelchair access (not WC). Occasional music. No mobile phones £5

HELMSLEY North Yorkshire · map 9

▲ Feversham Arms Hotel | NEW ENTRY

Helmsley YO62 5AG
TEL: (01439) 770766 FAX: (01439) 770346
WEBSITE: www.fevershamarmshotel.com

COOKING 5
MODERN BRITISH
£30–£65

In a pretty part of North Yorkshire, within driving distance of York and heritage hot spots like Rievaulx Abbey, the Feversham Arms now lives very much in the present day. New owner Simon Rhatigan has a committed hands-on approach, and has transformed the place. Inside, it feels 'warm and rich', with pretty modern décor and a conservatory dining room done out in burgundy, with a tiled floor and quiet piano music.

The kitchen is headed by Charlie Lakin, formerly sous-chef at the Star Inn, Harome (see entry), and his professional touch is totally in keeping with the 'simple, uncomplicated class' of the set-up. Whitby fish and moorland game emphasise the Yorkshire connection, flavours are forthright and sauces are out of the top drawer: witness a deep bourguignon reduction used to accompany first-class ribeye steak on a bed of celeriac gratin. The sheer quality of the raw materials has also shown in slow-roast shoulder of lamb (so tender that it 'almost disintegrated on the roof of your mouth'). Starters might include smoked salmon, served hot on soft potato pancakes with crème fraîche, and among puddings might appear Yorkshire rhubarb and Bramley apple charlotte. The wine list is an extensive slate of some 100 bins, with fair prices from around £14.

CHEF: Charlie Lakin   PROPRIETOR: Simon Rhatigan   OPEN: Mon to Sat 12 to 2, 7 to 9.30, Sun 1 to 4, 7 to 9.30   MEALS: alc exc Sun L (main courses L £9 to £13, D £16 to £21). Set L Sun £15.25 (2 courses) to £17.95, Set D £30   SERVICE: not inc   CARDS: Amex, MasterCard, Switch, Visa   DETAILS: 55 seats. 30 seats outside. Private parties: 80 main room, 1 to 30 private rooms. Car park. Children's helpings. No children in restaurant after 8pm. No smoking. Wheelchair access (also WC). Music. No mobile phones   ACCOMMODATION: 17 rooms, all with bath/shower. TV. Phone. B&B £110 to £190. Rooms for disabled. Baby facilities. Swimming pool

HELSTON Cornwall   map 1

Morley's ⁵⚹

The Mews, 4 Wendron Street, Helston TR13 8PS	COOKING 2
TEL: 01326 564433	MODERN EUROPEAN
WEBSITE: www.morleyrestaurant.co.uk	£39–£47

The Morley-Smiths seek out local ingredients for their small mews restaurant but their culinary horizons are broad, with flavours drawn from all over the world. Menus demonstrate a knack for original combinations. Thus starters might include celery soup with a blue cheese beignet, while main courses run to roast chicken and pancetta on a chocolate and chilli sauce, and grilled gilt bream with seafood cakes and sweet-and-sour sauce. Desserts such as cashew and orange flower ice cream, or chilled almond soufflé, make a refreshing finish. Attractive presentation is singled out for praise, as is friendly, efficient service. The wine list covers some interesting ground and kicks off with Australian and German bottles at £11.50.

CHEF: Simon Morley-Smith   PROPRIETORS: Simon and Joanne Morley-Smith   OPEN: Tue to Sat D only 7 to 9   CLOSED: 26 Dec, all Jan   MEALS: Set D £22.95 (2 courses) to £27.95   SERVICE: not inc, card slips closed   CARDS: Delta, MasterCard, Switch, Visa   DETAILS: 26 seats. Private parties: 30 main room. Vegetarian meals. No smoking. Music (£5)

HEMINGFORD GREY Cambridgeshire   map 6

Cock ⁵⚹ £

47 High Street, Hemingford Grey PE28 9BJ	COOKING 2
TEL: (01480) 463609 FAX: (01480) 461747	MODERN BRITISH
WEBSITE: www.cambscuisine.com	£20–£45

In a charming village on the Great Ouse, this pub-with-restaurant makes a good stop-off for families. Sound local ingredients and a kitchen with the enthusiasm to cure its own ham point to higher-than-average culinary ambition. Sunday roasts such as exceptionally well-flavoured topside make for a refreshing simplicity, and fish might show up as a thick and fresh-tasting fillet of roast cod with wild mushroom sauce. A sure hand is behind puddings like 'delicious' pear crumble topped with butterscotch sauce with a scoop of vanilla ice cream. Service is pleasant, relaxed and informal, and the good-value wine list starts at £9.95 with a generous selection by the glass. A sister restaurant, the Crown & Punchbowl, is in Horningsea (see entry)

CHEF: Chris Brading   PROPRIETORS: Oliver Thain and Richard Bradley   OPEN: all week L 12 to 2.30, Mon to Sat D 6.45 to 9.30   CLOSED: 25 and 26 Dec, 1 Jan   MEALS: alc (main courses £9 to £16). Set L Mon to Sat £8.95 (2 courses) to £11.95, Set L Sun £14.95 (2 courses) to £17.95   SERVICE: not inc   CARDS: MasterCard, Switch, Visa   DETAILS: 60 seats. 30 seats outside. Private parties: 40 main room. Car park. Vegetarian meals. Children's helpings. No children under 8 at D. No smoking. Wheelchair access (not WC). No music (£5)

HENLEY-IN-ARDEN Warwickshire   map 5

Edmunds ✵

64 High Street, Henley-in-Arden B95 5BX	COOKING 5
TEL/FAX: (01564) 795666	MODERN BRITISH
	£26–£49

On an unusually broad and leafy part of the long main street through the village, this bay-windowed, steep-roofed, timbered and white-pebbledash sixteenth-century cottage restaurant proves quite a draw. Small, interlinked rooms in strong, warm colours create the backdrop for lots of dark wood – bare tables, heavy beams and stripped doors. Chef/proprietor Andy Waters' accomplished modern cooking uses 'quite exceptional' raw ingredients, while value for money is considered 'thoroughly applaudable'. Expect a salad of 'immaculate' seared scallops with asparagus, aubergine 'caviar' and red pesto dressing, or classic eggs Benedict to kick off a spring menu, while a rosette of Scottish beef with a forestière of ceps, pommes Anna and truffle jus could head up main courses. A warm tart of Valrhona chocolate with pistachio ice cream, or délices of Williams pear with walnut crisps holds up the style through to the finish. Service, overseen by Beverley Waters, is friendly and quite formal, and the wine list offers five by glass from £3.25 and house wines from £11.50 a bottle.

CHEF: Andy Waters   PROPRIETORS: Andy and Beverley Waters   OPEN: Tue to Fri L 12 to 1.45, Tue to Sat D 7 to 9.45   CLOSED: 5 weeks throughout the year; phone to check   MEALS: Set L £7.50 (1 course) to £15, Set D £24.50 (2 courses) to £26.95   SERVICE: not inc, card slips closed, 10% for parties of 6 or more   CARDS: Delta, MasterCard, Switch, Visa   DETAILS: 40 seats. Vegetarian meals. Children's helpings. No smoking. Wheelchair access (not WC)

HENLEY-ON-THAMES Oxfordshire   map 3

Three Tuns Foodhouse ✵ | NEW ENTRY |

5 Market Place, Henley-on-Thames RG9 2AA	COOKING 4
TEL: (01491) 573260	MODERN BRITISH
	£35–£59

Combining the virtues of a bar, restaurant and shop, this centuries-old hostelry in the centre of town also manages to function as a relaxed local pub with Brakspear ales on draught. Inside are three tiny beamed snugs with a motley assortment of retro 1950s furniture and paintings, and there's a tapas bar in the courtyard garden. Chef/proprietor Kieron Daniels is very much his own man and respects well-chosen ingredients and cooks with integrity. Presentation is bold and thoughtful, as in a long rectangular slice of white onion, Taleggio and Parmesan tart, or Herdwick lamb kofta with feta couscous and a mint and chermoula dressing. Fish is given vivid treatment (roast swordfish with grilled baby cuttlefish, squid and borlotti bean salad, for example), while show-stopping finales might include vanilla pannacotta with 'ephemeral' rose and strawberry jelly (a 'dream of a dessert,' according to one visitor). At lunchtime, a fiver will pay for one dish and a drink. The wine list includes plenty of interesting, quaffable stuff at realistic prices from £13.

CHEFS: Kieron Daniels and Michael Jones   PROPRIETOR: Kieron Daniels   OPEN: all week 12 to 2.30, 7 to 10 CLOSED: 25 Dec   MEALS: alc (main courses £10 to £17)   SERVICE: not inc   CARDS: MasterCard, Switch, Visa   DETAILS: 35 seats. 15 seats outside. Private parties: 35 main room, 15 to 40 private rooms. Vegetarian meals. Children's helpings. No smoking in 1 dining room. Wheelchair access (not WC). Occasional music (£5)

HEREFORD Herefordshire   map 5

▲ Castle House, La Rive ♥ ✱

Castle Street, Hereford HR1 2NW	COOKING 7
TEL: (01432) 356321 FAX: (01432) 365909	ANGLO-FRENCH
WEBSITE: www.castlehse.co.uk	£36–£81

In a quiet back street close to the cathedral, Castle House is a Grade II listed Georgian building with a pillared central porch jutting out from its elegant, symmetrical, custard-coloured façade. The yellow theme continues inside, with primrose shades dominating in the lounge, where a baby grand piano is squeezed in alongside plush sofas, and in the dining room, which has peaceful, leafy views through French windows over a stream. Tables are well spaced and generously dressed, and service is overseen by an efficient, courteous and considerate young manager and backed up by a well-drilled team.

This is a surprisingly modest setting for some rather grandiose cooking, in which dishes are typically built up in several layers of flavour and texture, and described in florid language on the menu. Among main courses, for example, a herb-crusted loin of lamb is presented as three slices of pink meat in a stack with 'epigram of the breast' (a thin slab of breadcrumbed meat), a seared half-kidney, a layer of spinach and another of foie gras, all on a base of sarladaise potatoes, surrounded with mounds of provençale vegetables and an olive and tarragon 'café au lait' (a 'luscious, immaculately flavoured' sauce). First-class raw materials and superb technical skills are evident in a starter of seared scallops featuring accurately timed shellfish on a risotto of peanut and lime providing harmonious textural and flavour contrasts, with soy-based 'Mikado' sauce and decorated with delicate satay and coriander 'straws'. Meals are embellished with a steady stream of appetisers, nibbles and between-course treats, which some have found a bit much after a while, but the pace is maintained through to desserts such as a delicately flavoured marmalade and whisky soufflé with rolled-oat crumble, marmalade and whisky ice cream and butterscotch caramel. A fine collection of Bordeaux is at the heart of the wine list. Otherwise it's a pick and mix of good and prestigious bottles with brief contributions from all over. Prices climb steeply from the £14.95 starting point.

CHEFS: Stuart McLeod and Gary Wheeler   PROPRIETORS: Dr and Mrs A. Heijn   OPEN: all week 12.30 to 2, 7 to 10   MEALS: alc D (main courses £18.50 to £24). Set L £21.95, Set D £49.95   SERVICE: not inc, card slips closed   CARDS: Amex, Delta, MasterCard, Switch, Visa   DETAILS: 26 seats. Private parties: 36 main room. Car park. Vegetarian meals. Children's helpings. No smoking. Wheelchair access (also WC). Music. Air-conditioned   ACCOMMODATION: 15 rooms, all with bath/shower. TV. Phone. B&B £100 to £225. Rooms for disabled. Baby facilities (£5)

'Whilst I like harp music and whilst she was good, I would have preferred to have had her more than three feet from my right elbow all night. Preferably in another room or another city.'
(On eating in the West Country)

▲ Angel Inn ♥ ⅍

Hetton BD23 6LT	COOKING **5**
TEL: (01756) 730263 FAX: (01756) 730363	MODERN BRITISH
WEBSITE: www.angelhetton.co.uk	£28–£55

As we were about to go to press the sad news of the death of Denis Watkins reached us. The Angel Inn is something of an institution – it has been a continual presence in the Guide since the 1985 edition – and the loss of Denis is a blow not just to the Yorkshire pub and restaurant scene, but nationally as well. Denis and Juliet Watkins ran it together for 21 years, and that wealth of experience has told over those years in the well-honed professionalism and good cheer for which the place has become known.

Bruce Elsworth is running it as we go to press. An L-shaped bar and a separate dining room hung with paintings are the options, but the cooking maintains the same no-nonsense approach in both. The sourcing of local ingredients remains a priority, with Lishman's prize-winning pork sausages on the bar menu, and much in the way of locally shot game in season. A long stayer has been the moneybag of seafood – prawns, scallops, cod and salmon wrapped in filo on a delicate lobster sauce – and fish specials are chalked on a board: roast halibut with mussels and tomatoes in a creamy broth, perhaps. Meat comes in for plaudits too, as was attested by reporters who enjoyed chargrilled beef fillet, which might come with creamed celeriac, lentil purée and a reduction of Shiraz. Puddings include the inevitable sticky toffee as well as pears poached in spiced red wine with cinnamon ice cream.

The Angel takes wine seriously, sourcing direct from quality producers in France and Italy, and keeps mark-ups under control. A compact global selection (with a special focus on Australia) fleshes out the list, and there are options aplenty by the glass and half-bottle. A supplementary venture across the road, the Wine Cave, acts as cellar and shop, and there is more parking space behind there too.

CHEF: Bruce Elsworth   PROPRIETOR: Juliet Watkins   OPEN: Sun L 12 to 2, Mon to Sat D 6 to 9   CLOSED: 25 Dec, 1 Jan, 1 week Jan   MEALS: alc exc Sat D and Sun L (main courses £11.50 to £17). Set L £20.90, Set D Mon to Fri 6 to 6.45 £13.20 (2 courses) to £16.50, Set D Sat £32.50. Bar menu available   SERVICE: not inc, card slips closed   CARDS: Amex, MasterCard, Switch, Visa   DETAILS: 56 seats. 40 seats outside. Private parties: 40 main room. Car park. Vegetarian meals. Children's helpings. No smoking in 1 dining room. Wheelchair access (not WC). No music. No mobile phones. Air-conditioned   ACCOMMODATION: 5 rooms, all with bath/shower. TV. Phone. B&B £120 to £170. Rooms for disabled

▲ Angel Inn ⅍

Angel Lane, Hindon SP3 6DJ	COOKING **3**
TEL/FAX: (01747) 820696	MODERN EUROPEAN
WEBSITE: www.theangelathindon.co.uk	£24–£50

This grey stone pub sits in a rural village only a mile from the A303. At the front are the open-plan bar and a lounge with comfy sofas, while diners should head through to the well-lit, cream-painted dining room, with its brick fireplace, high-backed chairs and square tables with slim, elegant cutlery. New owners have introduced minor changes in the format, but Matthew Laughton remains at the stoves and continues to impress. His upmarket country cooking ranges from homespun favourites like pan-fried calf's liver with crispy bacon and garlic mash ('the best liver I've tasted in years') to classic Italian peasant fare, such as rabbit leg poached in olive oil and served on tagliatelle with a creamy wild mushroom, bacon and watercress sauce. Start perhaps with herring roe fried with capers, bacon and lemon, or a red wine and radicchio risotto with lambs' kidneys, and finish with pineapple tarte Tatin with mango sorbet or the well-chosen selection of English cheeses. Wines are arranged by style with interesting selections from around the world, especially France; its fair prices start with four house wines from £10.50.

CHEF: Matthew Laughton   PROPRIETOR: Goldace Trading Ltd   OPEN: all week L 12 to 2.30, Mon to Sat D 6.30 to 9.30   MEALS: alc (main courses L £5.50 to £11, D £11 to £16.50)   SERVICE: not inc, card slips closed   CARDS: Amex, Delta, Diners, MasterCard, Switch, Visa   DETAILS: 64 seats. 20 seats outside. Private parties: 20 main room. Car park. Vegetarian meals. Children's helpings. No smoking in 1 dining room. Wheelchair access (also WC). Occasional music. No mobile phones   ACCOMMODATION: 8 rooms, all with either bath or shower. TV. Phone. B&B £30 to £75. Baby facilities

HINTON CHARTERHOUSE   Bath & N E Somerset   map 2

▲ Homewood Park 🔔✳

Hinton Charterhouse BA2 7TB
TEL: (01225) 723731   FAX: (01225) 723820   COOKING 5
WEBSITE: www.homewoodpark.com   MODERN BRITISH
off A36, 6m SE of Bath   £35–£76

An elegant Victorian pile resting in its 10 acres looking over the Limpley Stoke valley just south of Bath, Homewood is what most people would expect a country-house hotel to be. There are not one but three (interconnecting) dining rooms (named after sheep breeds to emphasise the pastoral note), into which local lamb, game, organic vegetables and cheeses, not to mention fish from the Cornish coast, pour from Jean de la Rouzière's industrious kitchen. Dishes are complex and ally French technique to modern British sensibility – teaming seared red mullet with battered squid, spicy Puy lentils and capers, or wrapping a main-course ballottine of quail in Parma ham and serving it with bittersweet caramelised chicory and puréed chestnuts. The seven-course tasting menu (with optional wine matchings) may well include roast loin of roe deer accompanied by turnip and sweet potato gratin and braised lettuce, the dish richly sauced with red wine. Desserts maintain the creative pace, offering the tempting contrast of a warm chocolate tart with raisin and Calvados ice cream and Amaretto crème anglaise. Service runs with friendly efficiency. The wine list's greatest depth is in France, and it has many classic bottles at country-house mark-ups; four house wines are £17.

CHEF: Jean de la Rouzière   PROPRIETOR: Alan Moxon   OPEN: all week 12 to 2, 7 to 9.30   MEALS: Set L £19.50 to £22.50, Set D £39.50 to £48   SERVICE: not inc   CARDS: Amex, Delta, Diners, MasterCard, Switch, Visa   DETAILS: 80 seats. 10 seats outside. Private parties: 85 main room, 10 to 85 private rooms. Car park. Children's helpings. No smoking. Wheelchair access (also WC). No music   ACCOMMODATION: 19 rooms, all with bath/shower. TV. Phone. B&B £120 to £270. Rooms for disabled. Baby facilities. Swimming pool

'Unfortunately, the style appeared to be an all too common version of East meets West fusion cuisine. It is the variety in which a chef spends a week's holiday passed out on a Thai beach and comes back instantly discovering religion.' (On eating in London)

HOLKHAM Norfolk map 6

▲ Victoria ✽

Park Road, Holkham NR23 1RU
TEL: (01328) 713230   FAX: (01328) 711009   COOKING 3
WEBSITE: www.victoriaatholkham.co.uk   MODERN EUROPEAN
on A149 3m W of Wells-next-the-Sea   £30–£53

In 1837 Thomas Coke rebuilt the Albemarle Arms on his Holkham estate and renamed it after the newly crowned monarch who had made him Earl of Leicester. The large flint-and-brick cube is architecturally undistinguished outside, but the décor inside has exotic colonial touches, particularly Indian and African, and the menu is similarly cosmopolitan. Among starters, deep-fried whitebait with garlic, lemon and parsley mayonnaise rub shoulders with chargrilled tuna, white radish and wasabi sorbet, while equally eclectic main courses include Holkham venison burger with cranberry chutney; grilled trout with broad beans, tomato and mint vinaigrette; and roast chicken with chorizo mash and black olive jus. To finish, hot chocolate fondant with griottine cherries and pistachio ice cream is one sweet-but-sophisticated option. Wines, arranged by style, are well-chosen, unpretentious and priced for all pockets, house selections starting at £12.50.

CHEF: Neil Dowson   PROPRIETORS: Tom and Polly Coke   OPEN: all week 12 to 2.30, 7 to 9.30   MEALS: alc (main courses £7.50 to £16)   SERVICE: not inc, 10% (optional) for parties of 6 or more   CARDS: Delta, MasterCard, Switch, Visa   DETAILS: 60 seats. 300 seats outside. Private parties: 40 main room. Car park. Vegetarian meals. Children's helpings. No smoking in 1 dining room. Wheelchair access (also women's WC). Music. No mobile phones   ACCOMMODATION: 11 rooms, all with bath/shower. TV. Phone. B&B £90 to £170. Rooms for disabled. Baby facilities £5

HOLT Norfolk map 6

Yetman's ♟ ✽

37 Norwich Road, Holt NR25 6SA   COOKING 4
TEL: (01263) 713320   MODERN BRITISH
WEBSITE: www.yetmans.net   £49–£65

In a terraced house on a busy main road, Yetman's aims for a striking visual impression, achieved by a combination of primrose-yellow walls, hung with many pretty prints, beneath a low ceiling. Peter Yetman is a great host, leading front-of-house with wit and a neat line in curtsying, so that everybody gets to feel like a regular. Alison, meanwhile, concentrates on the serious stuff, bringing a dash of Stateside style to East Anglia. For starters, Louisiana crab cakes come with red pepper mayonnaise, or there may be a green, green soup of asparagus, peas, herbs, lettuce and mint. Interesting meat treatments have involved marinating duck breast in Californian Black Muscat and partnering it with spiced figs, although apricot-stuffed lamb has been less memorable, while fillet of cod has been grilled and teamed with butter beans and aïoli. Neal's Yard cheeses might precede a pudding such as quince and apple pancakes, or a bombe of rhubarb and ginger. The wine list is short, sweet, modern and well-priced: just what the doctor ordered. Cheap house wines are spurned in favour of quality, so the baseline is a good Chilean Carmenère at £16.75. A changing line-up by the glass is listed on the menu.

CHEF: Alison Yetman PROPRIETORS: Peter and Alison Yetman OPEN: Sun L 12.30 to 2, Wed to Sat D 7 to 9.30 MEALS: Set L and D £28 (2 courses) to £38 SERVICE: not inc CARDS: Amex, MasterCard, Switch, Visa DETAILS: 32 seats. Private parties: 20 main room. Vegetarian meals. Children's helpings. No smoking. Wheelchair access (not WC). No music. No mobile phones

HONLEY West Yorkshire
map 8

Mustard and Punch

6 Westgate, Honley HD9 6AA
TEL: (01484) 662066   FAX: (01484) 660742
WEBSITE: www.mustardandpunch.co.uk

COOKING 3
MODERN EUROPEAN
£24–£54

In a converted shop front on a steep hill, Richard Dunn's smart, modern restaurant has a lively atmosphere, and an inventive menu. Things might kick off with a starter of tender, flavoursome roast quail, dressed with truffle oil and sitting on some pork belly, Jerusalem artichokes and pearl barley, followed by a towering presentation of roast turbot, braised lamb neck, buttered spinach and jus Parisienne. Steaks come with a choice of sauces – béarnaise, mustard seed velouté, or green peppercorn with brandy – and vegetables are extra; the home-made chips have been recommended. A pudding of rhubarb crumble might arrive in a pastry shell, topped with thyme-scented ice cream and custard, or there's that admirable Yorkshire institution, cheese and fruitcake. Good-value wines from around the world start at £10.95, with six by the glass. There is an excellent range of Belgian beers on offer, too.

CHEFS: Richard Dunn and Wayne Roddis PROPRIETOR: Richard Dunn OPEN: Tue to Fri L 12 to 2, Tue to Sat D 6 to 9.30 (10 Fri and Sat) CLOSED: 26 Dec to 8 Jan MEALS: alc (main courses £10 to £16). Set L £10.50 (2 courses), Set D Tue to Fri and 6 to 7 on Sat £16.95 SERVICE: not inc, card slips closed CARDS: Amex, MasterCard, Switch, Visa DETAILS: 55 seats. Private parties: 30 main room. Vegetarian meals. Music. Air-conditioned (£5)

HORNBY Lancashire
map 8

▲ Castle Hotel 🍴✱

49 Main Street, Hornby LA2 8JT
TEL: (015242) 21204   FAX: (015242) 22258
WEBSITE: www.thecastlehotel.uk.com

NEW CHEF
MODERN BRITISH
£56–£67

The 'castle' is in fact a Victorian folly that stands next to the church, opposite this sixteenth-century country house, formerly a coaching inn, on the main road through the village. The front part is a traditional bar, but the restaurant has its own entrance. Chef Paul Reed has departed so the dining room no longer bears his name. However, the cooking looks set to continue in a modern British vein, with local produce featuring strongly in starters such as locally caught trout with salmon and Morecambe Bay shrimps and creamy Lancashire cheese croûtons, while main courses typically range from chargrilled tuna steak on spring onion mash with lemon gravy to coriander- and pepper-crusted pork fillet on Stilton and walnut risotto with apple compote and cider jus. France accounts for around half the wines on the list, with the New World filling most of the rest. Prices start at £22.

CHEF: John Lyons PROPRIETOR: Sean Collidge OPEN: Thur to Sat D only 7 to 9.30 MEALS: Set D £39.95. Bistro menu available L and D SERVICE: 10% (optional) CARDS: Delta, MasterCard, Switch, Visa DETAILS: 150 seats. 20 seats outside. Private parties: 100 main room, 10 to 40 private rooms. Car park. Vegetarian meals. Children's helpings. No smoking. Wheelchair access (also WC). Music

ACCOMMODATION: 12 rooms, 9 with bath/shower. TV. Phone. B&B £50 to £90. Rooms for disabled. Baby facilities

HORNCASTLE Lincolnshire   map 9

Magpies

71–75 East Street, Horncastle LN9 6AA
TEL: (01507) 527004   FAX: (01507) 525068
WEBSITE: www.eatatthemagpies.co.uk

COOKING 5
MODERN BRITISH
£27–£43

The year 2004 has wrought big changes to Magpies; the name is the same, but not much else. Andrew Gilbert and Caroline Ingall took over at the beginning of the year and kicked off by spending four months on a thorough refurbishment, the results providing this custard-coloured row of terraced cottages with smart, uncluttered dining areas done out in rusty red and honey colours, and an attractive terrace for al fresco dining at the back. Experience gained at the Old Vicarage, Ridgeway (see entry) is apparent from the kitchen's output.

The evening set menu ('one of the nicest I have seen for some time ... very interesting without being outlandish') may offer seared monkfish with lemongrass curry soup, and pot-roasted guinea fowl flavoured with orange and honey to follow. Grilled salmon, gravad lax and spinach frittata, served with silky chive beurre blanc, made an excellent start to one dinner. Use of top-quality local produce is evident in Lincoln Red beef turning up as a main-course fillet roasted with candied garlic on a horseradish galette with baby carrots and red wine jus, which provided satisfying flavour combinations. A 'technically perfect' blueberry and white chocolate muffin with blueberry vanilla jelly and white chocolate ice cream is a good way to finish, and there are British cheeses served in 'prime condition'. The front-of-house team get the service just right. The magpie responsible for the wine list has a very discerning eye. It is packed with interesting bottles picked up from all over and offered at very good prices, starting with a house dozen from £9 to £19.

CHEF: Andrew Gilbert   PROPRIETOR: Caroline Ingall   OPEN: Sun L 12 to 2.30, Wed to Sat D 7 to 9.30 CLOSED: New Year, bank hols   MEALS: Set L Sun £18.50, Set D £26   SERVICE: not inc, card slips closed CARDS: MasterCard, Switch, Visa   DETAILS: 35 seats. 15 seats outside. Private parties: 40 main room. Vegetarian meals. Children's helpings by previous arrangement. No smoking. Wheelchair access (also WC). Music. No mobile phones. Air-conditioned

HORNDON ON THE HILL Essex   map 3

▲ Bell Inn

High Road, Horndon on the Hill SS17 8LD
TEL: (01375) 642463   FAX: (01375) 361611
WEBSITE: www.bell-inn.co.uk

COOKING 2
MODERN EUROPEAN
£32–£49

Nowadays the Bell, used by travellers crossing the Thames for 500 years, is 'handy for restoring the nerves' after the stresses of the M25 or a visit to Thurrock's Lakeside mega-mall. Book for the non-smoking restaurant, or eat the same menu in the bar (no booking, but arrive early). Cooking is inventive, with some combinations working better than others. Clam risotto with rocket froth and beetroot jelly, and Parma ham with pumpkin tarte Tatin and grilled figs have both won praise this year. Mains extend to fried red mullet with oxtail, watercress and spring onion, or maybe roast pheasant with tobacco jus – the less adventurous can find solace in beer-battered cod and other pub favourites. Successful puddings have included orange crème brûlée with rosemary and apricot sorbet. A cheerful, good-value little wine list includes a good spread of half-bottles.

CHEF: Finlay Logan   PROPRIETORS: John and Christine Vereker   OPEN: all week 12 to 1.45 (2.15 Sun), 6.45 to 9.45   CLOSED: 25 and 26 Dec, bank hols   MEALS: alc (main courses £12 to £14). Sandwich L and bar menus available.   SERVICE: not inc, card slips closed   CARDS: Amex, Delta, MasterCard, Switch, Visa DETAILS: 80 seats. 36 seats outside. Private parties: 12 main room, 14 to 36 private rooms. Car park. Vegetarian meals. Children's helpings. No smoking in restaurant; smoking permitted in bar. Wheelchair access (also WC). No music   ACCOMMODATION: 15 rooms, all with bath/shower. TV. Phone. Room only £50 to £100. Rooms for disabled. Baby facilities

HORNINGSEA Cambridgeshire   map 6

▲ Crown & Punchbowl ⁵⁄✱ £ | NEW ENTRY |

High Street, Horningsea CB5 9JG   COOKING 2
TEL: (01223) 860643   FAX: (01223) 441814   MODERN BRITISH
WEBSITE: www.cambscuisine.com   £25–£53

A thorough refurbishment with 'copious use of cream paint' has transformed this pub into a restaurant in the modern rustic style. It's under the same management as the Cock in Hemingford Grey (see entry), and is run to the same blueprint. The evening menu might offer potted pigeon on mixed leaves, or a rib-sticking salad of black pudding, bacon, croûtons and egg for starters. Meaty main courses – perhaps confit duck leg on a bed of braised red cabbage with orange sauce – are boosted by fish and sausage blackboard specials, and vegetarians might tuck into roast pumpkin curry in a filo basket with aubergine 'caviar'. A separate order of 'perfectly cooked' vegetables makes a good accompaniment, and seductive-sounding desserts such as a set liquorice cream with coconut, mango and mint might be upstaged by more traditional items like a top-notch sticky toffee pudding. The short wine list begins under £10 and offers ten by the glass.

CHEFS: Ben Renshaw and Richard Bradley   PROPRIETORS: Richard Bradley, Richard Day and Oliver Thain OPEN: all week L 12 to 2.30, Mon to Sat D 6.30 to 9 (9.30 Fri and Sat)   MEALS: alc D (main courses £10 to £18). Set L £9.95 (1 course) to £15.95   SERVICE: not inc   CARDS: Delta, MasterCard, Switch, Visa DETAILS: 75 seats. Private parties: 40 main room, 12 private room. Car park. Vegetarian meals. No smoking. Wheelchair access (also WC). No music   ACCOMMODATION: 5 rooms, all with bath/shower. TV. B&B £49.95 to £69.95. No children under 10. Baby facilities

HUDDERSFIELD West Yorkshire   map 9

Bradley's ⁵⁄✱

84 Fitzwilliam Street, Huddersfield HD1 5BB   COOKING 2
TEL: (01484) 516773   FAX: (01484) 538386   MEDITERRANEAN/MODERN BRITISH
                                                                £16–£51

Andrew Bradley's energy is 'awesome to behold', marvelled one visitor. 'He could be seen greeting customers, serving pre-meal drinks, taking orders, washing glasses ... and offering to find me a newspaper if I was unable to cope with the lone-diner syndrome.' His fertile mind also applies itself to theme evenings, a newsletter and more. Meanwhile, in the kitchen of this no-frills bistro, Eric Paxman focuses on a slate of global dishes that go from braised pig's cheek with cassoulet to pan-fried fillet of salmon with pak choi and a chilli, coriander and lime dressing – although Europe rules when it comes to desserts like white chocolate and orange parfait. Set-price lunch is reckoned to be 'the best deal in town', and the affordable wine list should make many friends. House French is £10.95.

CHEF: Eric Paxman PROPRIETOR: Andrew Bradley OPEN: Mon to Fri L 12 to 2, Mon to Sat D 6 (5.30 Fri and Sat) to 10 CLOSED: bank hols MEALS: alc (main courses £9.50 to £16.50). Set L £5.95 (2 courses) to £7.95, Set D £15.95 (inc wine) SERVICE: not inc CARDS: MasterCard, Switch, Visa DETAILS: 120 seats. Private parties: 120 main room, 40 to 60 private rooms. Car park (D only). Vegetarian meals. No smoking in 1 dining room. Wheelchair access (also WC). Music. Air-conditioned

Dining Rooms @ Strawberry Fair 🍴 ✸ £

14–18 Westgate, Huddersfield HD1 1NN   COOKING **2**
TEL: (01484) 513103   FAX: (01484) 428616   MODERN EUROPEAN
          £22–£46

Located on the first floor of the long-established crockery/kitchen shop Strawberry Fair, the Dining Rooms play to the gallery with a repertoire of modern brasserie-style lunches, as well as offering breakfast, sandwiches and afternoon tea. Pale cream walls, floorboards, modern lighting and high-backed brown leather chairs cut a contemporary edge to match the food. Glenn Varley took over the reins in the kitchen in October 2003, and his menus deliver a trendy nod to the Mediterranean in dishes like honey-roast Gressingham duck breast with chorizo and bean cassoulet, as well as the more traditional note supplied by Cumberland sausage with creamy mash and redcurrant and thyme gravy. Desserts follow suit, with crème brûlée vying for selection against spotted dick with custard. All the wines on the dozen-bottle list (priced from £10.55 to £14.45) come by the glass, while staff, clad in white aprons, are polite and professional.

CHEF: Glenn Varley PROPRIETOR: Phillip Harrison OPEN: Mon to Sat L only 11.30 to 4 MEALS: alc (main courses £6.50 to £12.50) SERVICE: not inc, card slips closed CARDS: Amex, Delta, MasterCard, Switch, Visa DETAILS: 48 seats. Private parties: 40 main room. Vegetarian meals. Children's helpings. No smoking. Wheelchair access (also WC). Music. No mobile phones. Air-conditioned

▲ Lodge Hotel ✸

48 Birkby Lodge Road, Birkby, Huddersfield HD2 2BG   COOKING **3**
TEL: (01484) 431001   FAX: (01484) 421590   MODERN EUROPEAN
WEBSITE: www.birkbylodgehotel.com   £32–£60

The Lodge Hotel – an ivy-clad nineteenth-century house with fascinating architecture – is one reporter's vision of an ideal home, with beautiful panelling and lots of creature comforts. The cooking has its heart in the modern European tradition, but there's an inkling of globalisation about some dishes. Starters might include a timbale of lobster bound with rice infused with coconut, green chilli and spring onion, as well as classic steak tartare, while main courses could leap from wild rabbit chasseur to John Dory with a Thai crab cake and pak choi. Desserts call into play the likes of warm banana flapjacks, and marbled chocolate tart with vanilla ice cream and home-made orange marmalade. Cheeses are many and varied. The wine list gives a fair account of the global picture, with plenty of good-value bottles starting at £12.95. Service is relaxed and friendly, though it proved a little intrusive for one reporter.

CHEF: Richard Hanson PROPRIETOR: Ian Barton OPEN: Sun to Fri L 12 to 2, all week D 6 to 9 CLOSED: bank hols exc 25 and 31 Dec, Easter MEALS: alc (main courses £12.50 to £17.50). Set L and D 6 to 7 £19.95 SERVICE: not inc, card slips closed CARDS: Amex, Delta, MasterCard, Switch, Visa DETAILS: 110 seats. 20 seats outside. Private parties: 70 main room, 10 to 20 private rooms. Car park. Vegetarian

meals. Children's helpings. No smoking. Wheelchair access (also WC). Music. Air-conditioned
ACCOMMODATION: 13 rooms, all with bath/shower. TV. Phone. Room only £50 to £120. Rooms for disabled.
Baby facilities

HULL Kingston upon Hull   map 9

Venn   NEW ENTRY

21 Scale Lane, Hull HU1 1LH	COOKING 2
TEL: (01482) 224004 FAX: (01482) 580507	MODERN BRITISH
WEBSITE: www.venn.biz	£49–£58

Venn sits shoulder to shoulder with some of Hull's liveliest bars in the middle of town, and
its brasserie at street level vies for attention with the offer of open sandwiches, salads, and
more substantial dishes such as risottos, steak and chips, and roast cod with chorizo and
parsley champ. The smart upstairs, split-level dining room has brown leather armchairs at
low (and close-together) tables of polished wood, and offers a striking modern menu,
available as we went to press only in the evenings. Start with seared scallops wrapped in
pancetta with sweet-pepper salsa, basil oil and a balsamic reduction, or a ravioli of smoked
ham and morels with asparagus and a truffle emulsion. Among main courses the prune and
Armagnac sauce with roast pork has been described as a 'syrupy perfection, the perfect
blend of light meat and rich dark sauce', or there might be firm-textured marinated brill
with pancetta, baby leeks and beurre rouge sauce. Puddings such as apple and cranberry
crumble are as smartly turned out as the friendly and knowledgeable staff. House wines are
£12, but there is choice of quality and price under £20.

CHEF: Paul Robinson   PROPRIETOR: Yummy Corporation Ltd   OPEN: Tue to Sat D only 7 to 10; open L 12 to
6 for brasserie menu, also restaurant menu by special arrangement   CLOSED: 26 Dec, 1 Jan   MEALS: Set
D £32 (2 courses) to £38. Brasserie menu available L and D   SERVICE: not inc   CARDS: Amex, Diners,
MasterCard, Switch, Visa   DETAILS: 80 seats. Private parties: 54 main room, 26 private room. Vegetarian
meals. Music. No mobile phones. Air-conditioned (£5)

HUNTINGDON Cambridgeshire   map 6

▲ Old Bridge Hotel ▮ ⅍

1 High Street, Huntingdon PE29 3TQ	COOKING 4
TEL: (01480) 424300 FAX: (01480) 411017	MODERN BRITISH
WEBSITE: www.huntsbridge.co.uk	£30–£59

A three-storey converted bank close to the bridge over the River Ouse is the setting for
this warmly commended 'Hotel, Restaurant, Bar and Business Centre'. It's the home base
of the Huntsbridge group (see also the Falcon, Fotheringhay; the Pheasant, Keyston, and
the Three Horseshoes, Madingley) and has the same flexible philosophy. You can choose
to eat in the Terrace amid summery pastel colours and *trompe l'oeil* paintings, or plump for
the intimate world of the refurbished, club-like dining room. The kitchen relies on an
ever-increasing network of local and regional suppliers, but the repertoire is worldwide in
scope. Sushi and sashimi rub shoulders with carpaccio and Portland crab with gnocchi,
while main courses could embrace hake fillet with a saffron-infused casserole of tomatoes,
mussels, potatoes and olives, braised beef bourguignonne, or roast pheasant with parsnip
purée, roast shallots and cavolo nero. Desserts sustain the momentum with, say, roast
pineapple with brioche, honey ice cream and a ginger and passion-fruit sauce.

The wine list is the biggest and best of all the Huntsbridge establishments. The same formula applies – adventurous options by the glass, then whites and reds divided into 'under £20' and 'top-class' categories – but the difference is in the sheer number of excellent bottles. Prices are fair, and the page of bin-ends is always worth a look.

CHEF: Martin Lee   PROPRIETOR: John Hoskins   OPEN: all week 12 to 2.30, 6 to 9.30   MEALS: alc (main courses £9.50 to £20). Set L Mon to Sat £12.50 (2 courses), Set L and D 6.30 to 7.30 £12 (2 courses) to £15.75, Set D £36   SERVICE: not inc   CARDS: Amex, Delta, Diners, MasterCard, Switch, Visa   DETAILS: 100 seats. 25 seats outside. Private parties: 80 main room, 20 to 50 private rooms. Car park. Vegetarian meals. Children's helpings. No smoking. Wheelchair access (not WC). No music. No mobile phones. Air-conditioned   ACCOMMODATION: 24 rooms, all with bath/shower. TV. Phone. B&B £85 to £195. Fishing

HUTTON MAGNA Co Durham   map 10

Oak Tree Inn ✳ £ | NEW ENTRY |

Hutton Magna DL11 7HH   COOKING 2
TEL: (01833) 627371   MODERN EUROPEAN
                                                        £27–£44

Claire and Alastair Ross make a great team in this enthusiastically run pub/restaurant: she works the bar and dispenses pints of real ale while he cooks. The menus are listed on a blackboard, and dishes are dictated by the market. You might open with a terrine of ham shank and duck confit with fig and orange chutney or opt for one of the warm salads (perhaps a parody of a greasy-spoon breakfast with sausage, bacon and egg). The modern European theme continues with main courses ranging from grilled halibut with 'hand-rolled' pesto spaghetti, artichokes and roast scallops or ribeye steak with mushrooms, white beans, bacon and cabbage, while desserts could include hot chocolate fondant with chocolate sauce. The wine list is a short, reasonably priced slate, with house Chilean at £9.90.

CHEF: Alastair Ross   PROPRIETORS: Claire and Alastair Ross   OPEN: Tue to Sun D only 6.30 to 8.30 (L bookings only)   CLOSED: 26 Dec, 1 week Jan   MEALS: alc (main courses £10.50 to £15.50)   SERVICE: not inc, card slips closed   CARDS: Delta, MasterCard, Switch, Visa   DETAILS: 20 seats. Private parties: 20 main room. Car park. Vegetarian meals. No smoking. Music. No mobile phones

ILKLEY West Yorkshire   map 8

Farsyde £

1–3 New Brook Street, Ilkley LS29 8DQ   COOKING 4
TEL: (01943) 602030   MODERN BRITISH
WEBSITE: www.thefarsyde.co.uk   £19–£43

Any apprehension felt by Farsyde's loyal band of followers about the move from underneath Betty's tea rooms to new premises opposite the parish church has been dispelled. Reporters note that the views are better, booth seats 'like the old Farsyde' have been constructed, and, more important, the cooking remains 'as consistent as ever'. Gavin Beedham's wide-ranging ideas are incorporated into a straightforward modern brasserie style that shows respect for good materials and sensitivity to achieving the right balance of flavours and textures. Examples include a rustic mushroom soup with a hint of whole-grain mustard, and a perfectly timed fillet of salmon on a pile of roast vegetables with a tomato and basil dressing. That same meal produced chorizo and bacon salad with chilli jam dressing, and chicken breast filled with Brie and accompanied by caramelised onions, sun-dried tomatoes and red pepper dressing. To finish there might be cherry cheesecake with brandy-snaps, or warm chocolate brownie with raspberry coulis. A global wine list opens with house French at £8.95.

CHEF/PROPRIETOR: Gavin Beedham OPEN: Tue to Sat 11.30 to 2, 6 to 10 CLOSED: 25 and 26 Dec, 1 and 2 Jan MEALS: alc (main courses L £4.50 to £9, D £11.50 to £15.50). Set L £12.95, Set D Tue to Thur 6 to 7.15 £12.95 (2 courses) SERVICE: not inc CARDS: Delta, MasterCard, Switch, Visa DETAILS: 82 seats. Vegetarian meals. No-smoking area. Wheelchair access (also WC). Music

INSTOW Devon **map 1**

Decks

Hatton Croft House, Marine Parade, Instow EX39 4JJ COOKING **2**
TEL: (01271) 860671 FAX: (01271) 860820 MODERN EUROPEAN
WEBSITE: www.decksrestaurant.co.uk £28–£62

A towering mast from an old schooner is the centrepiece of this nautically themed restaurant/bar, which makes the most of its superb beachfront setting and glorious views over the estuary to Appledore. Fish and meat get equal billing on the brief menu, which runs from grilled langoustines with garlic butter, and roast fillet of sea bass on spring onion mash, to pan-fried calf's liver with creamed noodles, and West Country beef fillet with a creamy pepper and red wine sauce. Vegetarians might be offered spinach and rocket risotto, while light lunches are tailor-made for holidaying families. Desserts are based around home-made ice creams, sorbets and chocaholic favourites. The wine list is a wordy tome of around 50 bins, with New World young bloods putting on a good show and plenty of house selections from £2.50 a glass, £9.75 a bottle.

CHEF/PROPRIETOR: Lee Timmins OPEN: Tue to Sat 12 to 2.30, 7 to 9.30 CLOSED: first week Nov, 24 to 26 Dec, 1 Jan MEALS: alc (main courses £12.50 to £20). Set L £18.50, Set D £21.50. Light L menu available SERVICE: not inc, card slips closed CARDS: Amex, Delta, MasterCard, Switch, Visa DETAILS: 48 seats. 30 seats outside. Private parties: 60 main room. Vegetarian meals. Children's helpings. No smoking in 1 dining room. Wheelchair access (also WC). Music. Air-conditioned

IPSWICH Suffolk **map 6**

Bistro on the Quay £

3 Wherry Quay, Ipswich IP4 1AS COOKING **2**
TEL/FAX: (01473) 286677 BISTRO
£24–£41

This quayside restaurant, accessed via Fore Street/Key Street, is a popular place and correspondingly lively. Fittingly, given its location, the menu leans heavily towards fish, but there is a decent choice of meat dishes, too. Chef/patron Anthony Brook's cooking is unpretentious and is served in a relaxed and informal atmosphere. There may be bang-bang chicken with peanut sauce, and then beef and herb sausages with spring onion mash, or else a starter of smoked prawns with garlic dip preceding tuna steak niçoise with béarnaise sauce, French beans, tomatoes and olives. From the fixed-price menu simple roast chicken breast has come with mushroom and tarragon sauce, and herb-crusted cod fillet with crushed peas, followed by date and walnut pudding with toffee ice cream. The brief wine list holds few surprises; house vin de pays starts at £10.95 a bottle.

CHEF: Anthony Brooks   PROPRIETORS: Anthony and Kathy Brooks   OPEN: all week L 12 to 2 (2.30 Sun), Mon to Sat D 6.30 to 9.30   CLOSED: 24 Dec to 3 Jan   MEALS: alc (main courses £7.50 to £14). Set L and D £9.95 (2 courses) to £12.50. 1-course £4.95 light L available   SERVICE: not inc   CARDS: Amex, Delta, MasterCard, Switch, Visa   DETAILS: 90 seats. Private parties: 20 to 30 private rooms. Vegetarian meals. Children's helpings. No pipes. Wheelchair access (also WC). No music £5

JEVINGTON East Sussex   map 3

Hungry Monk ❧✴

Jevington BN26 5QF
TEL/FAX: (01323) 482178   COOKING 2
WEBSITE: www.hungrymonk.co.uk   ENGLISH/PROVINCIAL FRENCH
on B2105, off A22 between Polegate and Friston   £42–£59

For 36 years The Hungry Monk has resisted 'going trendy'. Many regulars find it 'comforting that it doesn't change', although some lay charges of laurel-resting. Log fires and snug sitting rooms seem designed to smooth furrowed brows, as does the comforting food. 'Retro' bread rolls, hot from the oven, may precede starters like crab cakes, combining crisp exterior and softly textured interior and served with shallot, orange and saffron sauce. For main courses, medallions of aromatic pork ('good taste of pig') may come with traditional accompaniments of black pudding and apple. The Hungry Monk is a 'proper pudding place' (it's credited with 'inventing' the banoffi pie), so ice creams are own-made, and puds like custard tart with apricot compote continue to please. Service is notably friendly, helpful and relaxed, and an idiosyncratic wine list runs from England to Australia (and halves to magnums), with some mature clarets as its centrepiece.

CHEFS: Gary Fisher and Samantha Dimmick   PROPRIETORS: Nigel and Sue Mackenzie   OPEN: Sun L 12 to 2.30, all week D 6.45 to 10   CLOSED: 24 to 26 Dec, bank hols   MEALS: Set L £27.95, Set D £28.95   SERVICE: not inc, 12.5% for parties of 7 or more, card slips closed   CARDS: Amex, MasterCard, Switch, Visa   DETAILS: 40 seats. 8 seats outside. Private parties: 40 main room, 6 to 16 private rooms. Car park. Vegetarian meals. Children's helpings. No children under 5 in main dining room. No smoking in dining room. Music. Air-conditioned £5

KELSALE Suffolk   map 6

Harrisons ❧✴

Main Road, Kelsale IP17 2RF
TEL/FAX: (01728) 604444
on A12 outside village; going N look for sign for Carlton   COOKING 4
Industrial Estate and then turn left at lay-by after sharp   MODERN BRITISH
bend   £23–£49

This ancient thatched cottage shows its age in many ways – one visitor, a frequent returner over many years, was happy to find it still going strong, and brightened somewhat by a new coat of paint. Inside, expect a friendly atmosphere with helpful, pleasant service and a charming host who takes a flexible approach, happy to cater to the assorted whims of his customers, as reporters have testified. A bold, modern cooking style provides starters of steamed mussels in cumin and coriander, or deep-fried lambs' sweetbreads with basil mayonnaise and pickles, followed by slow-roast Aylesbury duck with rösti and red wine sauce, or roast sea bass with leeks and butter sauce. Sunday roast pork with crackling is a highlight, and among puddings might be vanilla cheesecake, or apple and quince tart. The wine list is a short but varied collection. Prices start at £10.95 for Sicilian white and Apulian red and rarely stray over £20.

CHEF: Peter Harrison   PROPRIETORS: Peter and Melanie Harrison   OPEN: Tue to Sat 12 to 2.30, 7 to 10   MEALS: alc (main courses £11.50 to £16). Set L £11.95 (2 courses) to £13.95   SERVICE: not inc, card slips closed   CARDS: Delta, MasterCard, Switch, Visa   DETAILS: 60 seats. 12 seats outside. Private parties: 26 main room, 10 to 24 private rooms. Car park. Vegetarian meals. Children's helpings. No smoking. Wheelchair access (not WC). No music. No mobile phones

KENDAL Cumbria

map 8

Bridge House ⁵⚹

1 Bridge Street, Kendal LA9 7DD
TEL/FAX: (01539) 738855
WEBSITE: www.bridgehousekendal.co.uk

COOKING 4
MODERN ENGLISH
£29–£55

One has to ring the doorbell at this elegant Georgian stone house run by the Pergl-Wilsons on a street corner just outside the town centre. The period charm continues inside, in the small ground-floor bar and in the two dining rooms upstairs (the front room overlooking the River Kent). Well-spaced tables with crisp white linen, contrasting with the backdrop of dark green wallpaper, are attended by a friendly young team under the discreet supervision of Alena. In the meantime Roger's modern, sensible-length menus focus on local and organic materials and keep things uncluttered and centred on main ingredients – perhaps in the form of Cumbrian air-dried ham with a red pepper mousse and Waldorf salad to start. Mains might include honey-roast breast of Lunesdale duck, its gravy enriched with soya, star anise and ginger, or grilled halibut fillet with asparagus, langoustines and a tarragon cream sauce. Finish with something like homely bread-and-butter pudding, or dark chocolate and ginger marquise with brandied cherries. The fairly substantial global list offers fair value, with six house wines at £11.50 (£3.50 a glass) and a welcome ten half-bottles.

CHEF: Roger Pergl-Wilson   PROPRIETORS: Roger and Alena Pergl-Wilson   OPEN: Tue to Sat 12.30 to 1.30, 6.30 to 9.30; bookings only   CLOSED: 24 to 26 Dec, 1 Jan   MEALS: alc D (main courses £10 to £17). Set L £13.50 (2 courses) to £17, Set D Tue to Fri £18.90   SERVICE: not inc, card slips closed   CARDS: MasterCard, Switch, Visa   DETAILS: 40 seats. Private parties: 24 main room, 12 to 24 private rooms. Vegetarian meals. Children's helpings. No smoking. Wheelchair access (not WC). Music

Déjà-vu ⁵⚹ £

124 Stricklandgate, Kendal LA9 4QG
TEL: (01539) 724843

COOKING 2
FRENCH BISTRO
£24–£53

Frances Wood's relaxed, great-value restaurant brings a hint of summery warmth and Mediterranean colour to a town best known for bracing outdoor exertions. She has abandoned Spanish theme nights so that the kitchen can concentrate wholeheartedly on delivering its own version of French bistro-style food with a few pan-European twists. The carte might open with lobster and crab ballottine on a saffron brioche, or a tartlet of Camembert, caramelised red onion and mango, before fennel- and basil-scented chicken breast with hazelnut sauce, or cannon of lamb with roast garlic and rosemary sauce. Desserts are mostly French classics like profiteroles and vanilla crème brûlée; otherwise opt for locally produced ice creams and sorbets. France heads the short international wine list, which kicks off with house selections from £11.75.

CHEF: Fabien Bellouère   PROPRIETOR: Frances Wood   OPEN: all week D only 5.30 to 9.30 (10 Sat)
CLOSED: 24 to 26 Dec, bank hols   MEALS: alc (main courses £8 to £17). Set D Mon to Thur 5.30 to 7.30
£10.95 (2 courses)   SERVICE: not inc, card slips closed, 10% for parties of 6 or more   CARDS: Amex, Delta,
MasterCard, Switch, Visa   DETAILS: 36 seats. Private parties: 40 main room. Vegetarian meals. Children's
helpings. No smoking. Wheelchair access (not WC). Music (£5)

KENILWORTH Warwickshire   map 5

Restaurant Bosquet ⅚✻

97A Warwick Road, Kenilworth CV8 1HP   COOKING 4
TEL/FAX: (01926) 852463   FRENCH
                                                                        £42–£58

It is easy to miss this small, terraced restaurant on the main road through Kenilworth, and parking can be a problem. But once found, the modern dining room, with its dark wooden floor, black faux-leather chairs, 'caffè latte wallpaper, cappuccino curtains and espresso blinds' makes a good impression, and Bernard Lignier's resolutely French cooking takes a benevolent approach. Things start as they mean to go on with excellent home-made bread and first-class green olives among the nibbles. The fine produce is allowed to shine in starters like crayfish tails and scallops in pastry with shellfish sauce, or fillet of Scottish beef with a confit of shallots and red wine sauce. Upmarket ingredients crop up from time to time, for example in a starter of lambs' sweetbreads, garnished with a sliver of black truffle and served with asparagus and some celeriac purée also containing truffle. Desserts seem to be a particular strength: witness ripe, tasty strawberries and raspberries with a boozy sabayon, or blueberry and almond tart. Service led by Jane Lignier is 'bright and friendly'. The wine list is exclusively French, with some classy, if pricey, bottles from the Rhône and Loire as well as fine Bordeaux and Burgundies. Four house selections are £14 and £14.50.

CHEF: Bernard Lignier   PROPRIETORS: Bernard and Jane Lignier   OPEN: Tue to Fri L (bookings only) 12 to 1,
Tue to Sat D 7 to 9.15   MEALS: alc (main courses £18 to £19). Set L and D Tue to Fri £28.50   SERVICE: not
inc   CARDS: Amex, MasterCard, Switch, Visa   DETAILS: 26 seats. Private parties: 30 main room.
Children's helpings. No smoking. Wheelchair access (not WC). No music. No mobile phones

Simpson's ♟

101–103 Warwick Road, Kenilworth CV8 1HL   COOKING 6
TEL: (01926) 864567   FAX: (01926) 864510   MODERN FRENCH
WEBSITE: www.simpsonsrestaurant.co.uk   £32–£70

The large windows on to the street offer passers-by a glimpse of the 'stylish' interior, where neutral colours set a contemporary note, and smartly attired staff 'operate very smoothly'. The big news is a move to Edgbaston is planned, and the good news for the residents of Kenilworth is that this site will remain as a Simpson's, albeit destined to become a bistro. This review, and mark for cooking, are pre-move. The kitchen likes to keep things simple, using pinpoint accuracy of timing, careful balance and pretty much faultless composition to make an impact. And make an impact it does. At inspection, the quality of raw materials – crab, smoked salmon, beef and asparagus – was 'outstanding'.

The menu descriptions are refreshingly to the point. Start with scallop ravioli with asparagus, broad beans, peas and Noilly-Prat sauce, or cep and potato risotto with aged

Parmesan, veal jus and truffle oil. To follow, there might be beef fillet on the bone, or baked sea bass with Puy lentils, fondant and grilled endive, and sauce épice. Finish perhaps with a plain-looking but technically perfect raspberry soufflé with raspberry ripple ice cream. The wine list picks fine names from France and beyond. A page of 'discovery wines' introduces some producers who may be less familiar, while the 17 house wines from £15 to £42 (and also by the glass) give a good overview of the quality here.

CHEFS: Andreas Antona and Luke Tipping   PROPRIETORS: Andreas and Alison Antona   OPEN: Tue to Sat 12.30 to 2, 7 to 10   CLOSED: Christmas and New Year, last 2 weeks Aug   MEALS: Set L £15 (2 courses) to £20, Set D £24.95 (2 courses) to £42.95   SERVICE: not inc, 10% for parties of 6 or more   CARDS: Amex, Delta, Diners, MasterCard, Switch, Visa   DETAILS: 65 seats. Private parties: 60 main room, 15 to 40 private rooms. Car park. Vegetarian meals. No-smoking area. Occasional music. No mobile phones. Air-conditioned

KEW Greater London   map 3

Glasshouse ▮ ✳

14 Station Parade, Kew TW9 3PZ
TEL: (020) 8940 6777   FAX: (020) 8940 3833

COOKING 5
MODERN BRITISH
£31–£80

Just far enough out to make you feel you've left London, yet still accessible by tube, the Glasshouse is in a parade of shops leading off from Kew Gardens station. Its long, many-windowed frontage makes it the kind of place that scores highly on summer evenings, and the light touch of Anthony Boyd's cooking, which extends to a children's lunch menu at weekends, draws firm plaudits. A starter course of black pudding served with caramelised endive, sauce soubise and a soft-poached egg was a triumph of gentle strength at an October lunch, as was a warm salad of wood pigeon on autumn vegetables dressed in truffle oil. Main courses keep an eye on the seasons, producing hearty fare such as navarin of venison with roast roots, chestnuts and cranberries in darkest January, and fish may be handled quite robustly, too, as when a fillet of cod is given a purée of carrot and swede, creamed Savoy cabbage and parsnip crisps. Attentive effort pays off in fine desserts, too, such as a textbook tarte Tatin, with its crisp pastry and finely judged caramelising, that comes with a contrasting dollop of crème fraîche. Service is as professional as it gets. Five sherries and a good spread of wines by the glass open proceedings on the long and stylish wine list. France, including good affordable options from the south, and Italy top the bill, but boutique wines from South Africa and a roll call of Australian and Californian greats show a sure grasp of life outside Europe.

CHEF: Anthony Boyd   PROPRIETOR: Larkbrace Ltd   OPEN: Mon to Sat 12 to 2.30, 7 (6.30 Fri and Sat) to 10.30, Sun 12.30 to 3, 7.30 to 10   CLOSED: 3 days at Christmas   MEALS: Set L Mon to Sat £12.50 (2 courses) to £17.50, Set L all week £25, Set D Mon to Thur £32.50 to £45, Set D Fri to Sun £32.50   SERVICE: 12.5% (optional), card slips closed   CARDS: Amex, Delta, MasterCard, Switch, Visa   DETAILS: 60 seats. Private parties: 65 main room. Vegetarian meals. Children's helpings Sat and Sun L. No smoking. No music. Air-conditioned ⊖ Kew Gardens

---

The text of entries is based on unsolicited reports sent in by readers, backed up by inspections conducted anonymously. The factual details under the text are from questionnaires the Guide sends to all restaurants that feature in the book.

KEYSTON Cambridgeshire

map 6

Pheasant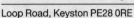

Loop Road, Keyston PE28 0RE
TEL: (01832) 710241
WEBSITE: www.huntsbridge.com

COOKING 2
MODERN EUROPEAN
£30–£61

'The Pheasant is a joy to behold,' wrote one reporter after visiting this long, white-painted thatched cottage. From the outside it is immediately welcoming, and the interior is smart and tasteful. New chef James Hepton-Claydon is developing less fancy dishes with simpler presentation than his predecessor. Expect a bedrock of modern British ideas with additions from France, Italy and beyond: thick slices of roast Goosnargh duck breast are matched with leg confit, cabbage, white-bean mash and truffle oil, while braised pork belly comes with noodles, cavolo nero and Thai broth. Plus-points are flexibility (have just a bowl of soup, a pudding, and a pint of Adnams beer for lunch) and the fact that there's always something interesting on offer, whether it be roast pumpkin risotto with oregano to start, or mango tart with lime sorbet to finish. Service is well groomed and unobtrusive. The Pheasant is one of the Huntsbridge Group's quartet of East Anglian pub/restaurants (see entries in Fotheringhay, Huntingdon and Madingley) and thus boasts one of the group's trademark characterful wine lists: brave options by the glass (including sherries), a page each of reds and whites under £20, and longer 'top-class' selections.

CHEF: James Hepton-Claydon   PROPRIETOR: Huntsbridge Ltd   OPEN: all week 12 to 2, 6.30 to 9.30   MEALS: alc (main courses £10 to £19). Set L Mon to Sat £9.95 (2 courses). Snack menu available   SERVICE: not inc   CARDS: Amex, Delta, Diners, MasterCard, Switch, Visa   DETAILS: 90 seats. 20 seats outside. Private parties: 35 main room, 30 private room. Car park. Vegetarian meals. Children's helpings. No smoking. No music. No mobile phones

KIBWORTH BEAUCHAMP Leicestershire

map 5

Firenze

9 Station Street, Kibworth Beauchamp LE8 0LN
TEL: (0116) 279 6260   FAX: (0116) 279 3646
WEBSITE: www.firenze.co.uk

COOKING 3
MODERN ITALIAN
£28–£80

The white pebbledash restaurant, standing on the village's only roundabout, is home to a small but not insignificant piece of Italy. The gold-washed and wine-red walls are crammed with Italianate drawings, paintings, and framed prints of architectural details. Then there's the menu. Ingredients are sparklingly fresh, and timing is spot-on, as in a simple-sounding starter of deep-fried squid and courgettes (pronounced 'stupendous' by the recipient) that made the most of a light batter, excellent timing, and contrasting flavours and textures. Main courses might include roast rack of lamb with sweetbreads, peas, pancetta, and a well-flavoured but not too reduced sauce. Finish with pannacotta (so good they named it thrice), or semifreddo al caffè. A set-price Menu Mercato operates on Tuesday to Thursday evenings, and a deli operates from here. Service is friendly, relaxed and well informed. Wines are strictly Italian and an effective showcase for the country's most talented producers. Prices, from £12.50, are fair, and 15 come by the glass.

CHEF: Lino Poli   PROPRIETORS: Lino and Sarah Poli   OPEN: Tue to Fri L 12 to 2, Tue to Sat D 7 to 10   CLOSED: 1 week at Christmas, 9 to 21 Apr, 8 to 24 Aug   MEALS: alc (main courses £7 to £30). Set L £10 (1 course), Set D Tue to Thur £15 (2 courses) to £25   SERVICE: not inc   CARDS: Delta, MasterCard, Switch,

Visa DETAILS: 70 seats. Private parties: 70 main room. Vegetarian meals. Children's helpings. No smoking in 1 dining room. Wheelchair access (not WC). Music

KINGHAM Oxfordshire   map 5

▲ Mill House

Kingham OX7 6UH
TEL: (01608) 658188   COOKING 5
WEBSITE: www.millhousehotel.co.uk   MODERN BRITISH-PLUS
just S of Kingham, off B4450 5m from Stow-on-the-Wold   £28–£48

A family-owned country hotel in the Evenlode valley near Chipping Norton, the Mill House Hotel has been substantially built up around the original stone miller's cottage and sits in seven acres of landscaped gardens. Chef Paul Haywood launched new set-price lunch and dinner menus at the beginning of 2004, which seems to have eliminated the plethora of supplements we mentioned last year. Start, perhaps, with seared scallops and roast pavé of cold smoked salmon on cucumber, crab and mint risotto, or pan-fried ox tongue on mushy peas with foie gras and red onion marmalade. Main courses are equally modern in approach, with halibut on sautéed gem lettuce with minestrone, or braised shoulder blade of Angus beef with creamed cabbage and oxtail. Desserts are as appealing as fine Braeburn apple tart with Calvados-soaked sultana ice cream and caramel sauce, but the serious cheeseboard, which presents British rarities such as Single Gloucester and Cerney Ash alongside the likes of Brie de Nangis and Crottin de Chavignol, should not be ignored. A fairly long international wine list offers plenty of scope, with a fair number of big names – Hochar, Muga, Mondavi and so on – alongside house selections from £12.75 and a reasonable choice of half-bottles.

CHEF: Paul Haywood PROPRIETOR: John Parslow OPEN: all week 12 to 2, 7 to 9.30 MEALS: Set L £12.50 (2 courses) to £28, Set D £28. Bar/terrace alc menu available SERVICE: not inc, card slips closed CARDS: Amex, Delta, Diners, MasterCard, Switch, Visa DETAILS: 80 seats. 24 seats outside. Private parties: 80 main room. Car park. Vegetarian meals. Children's helpings. Wheelchair access (also WC). Occasional music. No mobile phones ACCOMMODATION: 23 rooms, all with bath/shower. TV. Phone. B&B £85 to £140. Rooms for disabled. Baby facilities (£5)

KING'S LYNN Norfolk   map 6

Rococo   ⸢ NEW ENTRY ⸣

11 Saturday Market Place, King's Lynn PE30 5DQ   COOKING 3
TEL/FAX: (01553) 771483   MODERN BRITISH
                                                          £27–£60

After a spell cooking at a different address along the coast in Wells-next-the-Sea, Nick Anderson and his wife have moved back to their former premises amid a row of assorted old houses opposite the church on the main market square. The dining room has a pale wooden floor and mustard-coloured walls hung with abstract paintings, with an ancient brick fireplace and heavy black ceiling beams the visible signs of the building's antiquity. The cooking focuses on seasonal local produce given treatments ranging from traditional to exotic modern. A starter of crisp apple boudin salad with poached quail's eggs, Parma ham and red pepper sauce might be followed by Thai-glazed monkfish and tiger prawns with stir-fried pak choi, jasmine rice and coriander beurre blanc, or pink and tasty roast rack of lamb with crisp, fresh ratatouille vegetables, fragrant rosemary polenta and basil jus.

Finish with Cox apple pannacotta, or warm lemon tart with citrus caramel, although the latter was a disappointment at inspection. House selections on the wine list start at £15.75.

CHEFS: Nick Anderson and Tim Sandford   PROPRIETORS: Susannah and Nick Anderson   OPEN: Tue to Sat 12 to 2, 7 (6.30 Sat) to 10   MEALS: alc (main courses L £7 to £15, D £13 to £18.50)   SERVICE: not inc, card slips closed   CARDS: Delta, MasterCard, Switch, Visa   DETAILS: 40 seats. Private parties: 40 main room. Vegetarian meals. No smoking while others eat. Wheelchair access (also WC). Occasional music £5

KINGTON Herefordshire   map 5

▲ Penrhos Court 🍴✳

Kington HR5 3LH
TEL: (01544) 230720   COOKING 3
WEBSITE: www.penrhos.co.uk   MEDITERRANEAN
on A44, ½m E of Kington   £44–£55

Martin Griffiths and Daphne Lambert have run this isolated, ancient manor farm for over 30 years. The medieval cruck hall is rich in wood, from impressive half-timbering and ceiling beams to long polished tables, lighting is mainly from candles, and the great hearth has a winter log fire. The place has always had an unstuffy approach – Martin is an amiable host – and the Soil Association-certified kitchen reveals an ability to source unusually fine raw materials, many of them local or grown in the garden. The kitchen is not too ambitious but reveals a high degree of technical competence, and it rings interesting changes on its simple set menu, opening perhaps with carrot soup with ginger, then celeriac mousse, followed by fillet of sea bass with rösti and a ginger and chive cream sauce, with homely desserts like sherry and almond ice cream, or chocolate brownie. On the wine front, organic and biodynamic wines from Old and New World producers open at £16.40, but a £20 budget will leave you with a limited selection, especially among reds. It is perhaps part of the style that opening times to non-resident diners can be idiosyncratic, and, as it is a popular wedding venue in the summer, booking in June and July, in particular, may prove difficult.

CHEF: Daphne Lambert   PROPRIETORS: Daphne Lambert and Martin Griffiths   OPEN: all week D only 7.30 to 9.30   CLOSED: Jan   MEALS: Set D £31.50 to £33.50   SERVICE: not inc, card slips closed   CARDS: Amex, MasterCard, Switch, Visa   DETAILS: 70 seats. 200 seats outside. Private parties: 75 main room. Car park. Vegetarian meals. Children's helpings. No smoking. No music   ACCOMMODATION: 17 rooms, all with bath/shower. TV. Phone. B&B £65 to £135. Rooms for disabled. Baby facilities

KIRK DEIGHTON North Yorkshire   map 9

Bay Horse 🍴✳ £   NEW ENTRY

Main Street, Kirk Deighton LS22 4DZ   COOKING 3
TEL: (01937) 580058   FAX: (01937) 582443   MODERN EUROPEAN
                                                                     £24–£43

Karl Mainey (formerly of the Spice Box, Boston Spa, and Kings in Harrogate) and Stephen Ardern resurface at the refurbished Bay Horse, a 'classy, although still rustic, dining pub' just off the A1 north of Wetherby. Through the flagstoned bar, the main dining area sports a beige carpet, deep coral-pink walls, solid wooden furniture and a brick fireplace. Service is 'willing and pleasant', and informal handwritten menus are enticing and big on seafood. Classic bouillabaisse, or fried sea bass with lemongrass, star anise and rocket topped with lemon zest crème fraîche, co-star with more traditional chargrilled calf's liver, bacon and onions with creamy mash and port jus. Homely desserts (bread-and-butter pudding baked with marmalade, or chocolate truffle cake) provide the familiar finish. Breads are home-made, and a compact wine list (all under £20) has 20 by glass and French house at £10.95.

CHEF: Stephen Ardern   PROPRIETOR: Karl Mainey   OPEN: Tue to Sun L 12 to 2, Mon to Sat D 6 to 9.30 MEALS: alc (main courses L £7 to £11, D £12 to £13.50). Set D 6 to 7.30 £13.50 (2 courses)   SERVICE: not inc CARDS: Delta, MasterCard, Switch, Visa   DETAILS: 50 seats. 20 seats outside. Private parties: 50 main room. Car park. Vegetarian meals. Children's helpings. No smoking in 1 dining room. Wheelchair access (not WC). Occasional music

KIRKHAM Lancashire   map 8

Cromwellian

16 Poulton Street, Kirkham PR4 2AB   COOKING 3
TEL/FAX: (01772) 685680   MODERN BRITISH
                                                                    £33–£49

The Cromwellian is set back in a row of terraced cottages and, with its bubble-glass door and voile curtains, looks almost like a teashop. Small, homely and old-fashioned, it has a charm like that of going to old friends for dinner (though it's best to book). For eighteen years the Fawcetts – Josie behind the stove and Peter front-of-house – have offered wholesome, excellent-quality food and warm service at reasonable prices, accurately sensing customers' expectations and moving with the times, but not too fast. Escalope of salmon with spiced sweet potato mash and sweet chilli sauce sits alongside more familiar Aberdeen Angus fillet with a port and Stilton sauce, plus homely upside-down apple sponge pudding, or chocolate truffle torte. Wines, also fairly priced, start with house French or Spanish at £12 (£2.95 a glass).

CHEF: Josie Fawcett   PROPRIETORS: Peter and Josie Fawcett   OPEN: Wed to Sat D only 7 to 9   CLOSED: first 2 weeks Jan, 2 weeks Sept   MEALS: Set D £18 (2 courses) to £21.50   SERVICE: not inc, card slips closed   CARDS: Amex, Delta, MasterCard, Switch, Visa   DETAILS: 30 seats. Private parties: 10 main room, 10 to 12 private rooms. Vegetarian meals. No music

KNOSSINGTON Leicestershire   map 5

Fox & Hounds ✷ £   NEW ENTRY

6 Somerby Road, Knossington LE15 8LY   COOKING 2
TEL: (01664) 454676   FAX: (01664) 454031   MODERN BRITISH
WEBSITE: www.foxandhounds.biz   £22–£45

In farming and hunting country a few miles from Oakham, this three-storey yellow-stone pub pulls in a lively crowd of drinkers, diners and even hiking parties looking for sustenance. Bar food and fixed-price lunches are a bargain, but most interest focuses on the full carte. Mediterranean influences loom large, and the kitchen is very much at home with fish: witness a light-textured terrine of red mullet, scallops, roast tomatoes and rocket, or accurately timed fillet of sea bass served on a slice of grilled aubergine with red pepper salsa. Elsewhere, the choice extends to chicken liver parfait with balsamic onions, and roast rump of lamb with pea purée and mint dressing. Home-baked breads are highly rated, and desserts have included a good pannacotta with poached rhubarb. House French is £10.25.

CHEF/PROPRIETOR: Brian Baker   OPEN: Wed to Sun L 12 to 2.30 (12.30 to 3.30 Sun), Tue to Sat D 7 to 9.30 CLOSED: Feb (not confirmed; phone to check)   MEALS: alc exc Sun L (main courses £9 to £14). Set L Wed to Sat £9.95 (2 courses), Set L Sun £13.95. Bar L menu available   SERVICE: not inc   CARDS: MasterCard,

Switch, Visa   DETAILS: 35 seats. 30 seats outside. Private parties: 30 main room, 10 to 14 private rooms. Car park. Vegetarian meals. Children's helpings. No smoking in 1 dining room. No music. No mobile phones

LAMORNA Cornwall   map 1

▲ Lamorna Cove Hotel ⅚✳ ⬡

Lamorna Cove, Lamorna TR19 6XH	COOKING 3
TEL: (01736) 731411 FAX: (01736) 732316	ANGLO-FRENCH
WEBSITE: www.lamornacove.com	£30–£64

Between Penzance and Land's End, the Lamorna Cove Hotel enjoys beautiful views down a steep-sided valley to the sea. The hotel had an elegant and 'contemporary' makeover a few years ago and makes a fine setting for dinner. Japanese chef Hideki Koike is now running the kitchen, and, although some dishes bear the hallmarks of his heritage, he trained in the UK and the menus look more West than East. Start with clearly defined flavours in a plate of warm goats' cheese with tomato tortellini and a jus reduction of both tomato and basil, or carrot soup laced with coriander oil. A main course of well-timed cod has come with seafood chowder, and pork loin expertly glazed with ginger and soy is served with Japanese mushroom rice. Chocolate pot with pineapple sorbet makes a well-matched pudding, while caramelised banana with banana parfait is equally up to standard. The wine list lines up ten whites and ten reds under £20.

CHEF: Hideki Koike   PROPRIETORS: Peter and Tania Hopkinson   OPEN: all week 12.30 to 2, 7 to 9.30   CLOSED: first 3 weeks Jan   MEALS: alc (main courses L £10 to £16, D £12.50 to £21.50). Set L £15.95 (2 courses) to £21.50, Set D £21.20 (2 courses) to £27.50. Bar menu available   SERVICE: not inc, card slips closed   CARDS: Delta, MasterCard, Switch, Visa   DETAILS: 45 seats. 30 seats outside. Private parties: 45 main room. Car park. Vegetarian meals. No children under 14. No smoking. Wheelchair access (also WC). Occasional music   ACCOMMODATION: 12 rooms, all with bath/shower. TV. Phone. B&B £65 to £175. Rooms for disabled. No children under 14 (£5)

LANGAR Nottinghamshire   map 5

▲ Langar Hall ▼ ⅚✳

Langar NG13 9HG	COOKING 4
TEL: (01949) 860559 FAX: (01949) 861045	ENGLISH
WEBSITE: www.langarhall.com	£28–£75

The peaceful idyll of Langar Hall, a hotel that 'still feels like a family home', offers a 'strictly seasonal' menu and a chance to get away from it all. The kitchen does not overcomplicate dishes, but a lot of effort goes into sourcing decent materials, from local pike (served in a mousse with crayfish sauce) to Cropwell Bishop Stilton, lamb and game from the hotel grounds, and langoustines from Scotland. The lightness and 'cheesy punch' of a starter soufflé has impressed, as has accurately timed steamed fillet of brill with chervil sauce. Meat is equally well handled, as in slices of tender, tasty and pink chargrilled lamb with rosemary and garlic. Vegetables get the thumbs up, and among puddings have been an exemplary glazed lemon tart with crisp, fresh pastry, and an intense hot chocolate fondant with honeycomb ice cream. The wine list presents some interesting specials and bin-ends, a cellar of Bordeaux and a fair representation of grape-growing nations, mostly priced between £15 and £30.

CHEFS: Toby Garratt and Garry Booth   PROPRIETOR: Imogen Skirving   OPEN: all week 12 to 2, 7 to 10 (10.30 Fri and Sat, 8.15 Sun)   MEALS: alc D (main courses £13.50 to £20). Set L Mon to Sat £13.50 (2 courses) to £16.50, Set L Sun £24.50, Set D £25 to £30   SERVICE: 10% (optional), card slips closed   CARDS: MasterCard, Switch, Visa   DETAILS: 60 seats. 20 seats outside. Private parties: 50 main room, 6 to 20 private rooms. Car park. Vegetarian meals. Children's helpings. No smoking. Wheelchair access (not WC). Occasional music. No mobile phones   ACCOMMODATION: 12 rooms, all with bath/shower. TV. Phone. B&B £60 to £187.50. Baby facilities. Fishing (£5)

LANGFORD BUDVILLE Somerset   map 2

▲ Bindon Country House, Wellesley Restaurant 🦪 ⅚✷

Langford Budville TA21 0RU   COOKING 3
TEL: (01823) 400070   FAX: (01823) 400071   ANGLO-FRENCH COUNTRY-HOUSE
WEBSITE: www.bindon.com   £30–£66

Walks and open countryside in this part of Somerset help to make it a 'country retreat', and Bindon House plays the role of country hotel with traditional charm. There's a new chef at the stoves, although the thrust of the cooking remains largely unchanged. The kitchen delivers ambitious modern dishes, such as velouté of Jerusalem artichoke with a soft-poached quail's egg, and roast rack of local lamb with lavender jus, or pan-seared native sea bass with crushed potatoes and citrus jus. As a finish, both chocolate and chilli fondant with parsnip ice cream, and raspberry ripple soufflé with Sambuca ice cream show that this is a kitchen looking forward not backwards. The wine list is wide-ranging enough to include an English bottle (£17) among its house selection. The rest of the short list is arranged by style, with wines under £20 few and far between.

CHEF: Scott Dickson   PROPRIETORS: Lynn and Mark Jaffa   OPEN: all week 12 to 1.30, 7 to 9.30   MEALS: Set L £12.95 (2 courses) to £16.95, Set D £35 to £42   SERVICE: not inc, card slips closed   CARDS: Amex, Delta, Diners, MasterCard, Switch, Visa   DETAILS: 50 seats. 20 seats outside. Private parties: 50 main room, 6 to 25 private rooms. Car park. Vegetarian meals. Children's helpings. No smoking. Wheelchair access (not WC). Occasional music. No mobile phones   ACCOMMODATION: 12 rooms, all with bath/shower. TV. Phone. B&B £95 to £215. Rooms for disabled. Baby facilities. Swimming pool (£5)

LANGHO Lancashire   map 8

▲ Northcote Manor ♟ ⅚✷

Northcote Road, Langho BB6 8BE
TEL: (01254) 240555   FAX: (01254) 246568   COOKING 6
WEBSITE: www.northcotemanor.com   MODERN BRITISH
on A59, 9m E of M6 junction 31   £29–£87

Although only a few hundred yards from a busy roundabout on the A59, Northcote radiates as tranquil an air as one hopes for in a country house. It is comfortably appointed throughout, with the focal point the generously proportioned dining room done in gentle colours, with views of the appealing, slightly wild countryside that surrounds the Manor.

In June 2004 Matthew Harris became head chef, as predecessor Warwick Dodds departed for pastures new. The culinary philosophy of old has been sustained, however, making optimal use of local supply lines, with much in the way of organic produce and cooking it in ways guaranteed to turn Lancashire heads. Gourmet and tasting menus for the whole table allow a sweeping view of the style: Dublin Bay prawns with cucumber spaghetti, golden tomato relish, smoked paprika cream and caviar; turbot on mashed potato with a base of Jerusalem artichoke and a cube of pancetta; summer hotpot of Bowland lamb with a plethora of vegetables and carrot jus. These are intricately worked, impressive dishes. Vegetarians have their own richly inventive menus, while those eating from the regular carte might choose something as straightforward as plain-grilled Dover sole with new potatoes, or as elaborate as fillet, belly and bacon of Gloucester Old Spot pork with caramelised endive and celery purée. A fabulous dessert has been a soufflé of summer pudding fruits, partnered cleverly with liquorice ripple ice cream. The international wine list is switched on in all regions, including an unusually good line-up of Spanish reds, but with some fairly breathtaking prices. Nonetheless, six house wines from £16.75 and further options under £20 serve diners on a budget well enough.

CHEFS: Nigel Haworth and Matthew Harris PROPRIETORS: Craig Bancroft and Nigel Haworth OPEN: all week 12 to 1.30 (2 Sun), 7 to 9.30 (10 Sat) CLOSED: Dec 25, Jan 1 MEALS: alc (main courses £21.50 to £29.50). Set L Mon to Sat £17.50 to £20, Set L Sun £20, Set D £50. Breakfast (booking essential) also available, and afternoon tea Fri to Sun SERVICE: not inc CARDS: Amex, Delta, MasterCard, Switch, Visa DETAILS: 85 seats. Private parties: 85 main room, 2 to 40 private rooms. Car park. Vegetarian meals. Children's helpings. Jacket and tie. No smoking. Wheelchair access (not WC). Music. No mobile phones ACCOMMODATION: 14 rooms, all with bath/shower. TV. Phone. B&B £100 to £150. Rooms for disabled. Baby facilities

LAVENHAM Suffolk   map 6

▲ Great House ⁵⁄ₓ

Market Place, Lavenham CO10 9QZ	COOKING 2
TEL: (01787) 247431 FAX: (01787) 248007	FRENCH
WEBSITE: www.greathouse.co.uk	£26–£58

On the market square of this medieval village, one of Suffolk's showpieces, the whitewashed Great House looks diagonally across at the historic Guildhall. This is a well-supported French operation, run with commendable aplomb. Stuffed mussels in garlic butter, then guinea fowl with glazed apples and Calvados sauce, with fine lemon tart to finish, combined in a much-appreciated November dinner. Occasional more experimental dishes might unnerve some (red mullet with chocolate sauce, for example), but the performance is usually sound. The wide choice of French cheeses is commended, and Pernod in the crème brûlée sustains the Gallic tone. Wines – largely, but not exclusively, French – open at £10.20 (£2.10 a glass).

CHEF: Regis Crépy PROPRIETORS: Regis and Martine Crépy OPEN: Tue to Sun L 12 to 2.30, Tue to Sat D 7 to 9.30 (10 Sat) MEALS: alc (main courses £15 to £18). Set L Tue to Sat £14.95 (2 courses) to £16.95, Set L Sun £21.95, Set D Tue to Fri £21.95. Bar snack L available SERVICE: not inc CARDS: Amex, Delta, MasterCard, Switch, Visa DETAILS: 45 seats. 30 seats outside. Private parties: 60 main room. Children's helpings. No smoking in restaurant, permitted in bar. Music ACCOMMODATION: 5 rooms, all with bath/shower. TV. Phone. B&B £65 to £150. Baby facilities

£ means that it is possible to have a three-course meal, including coffee, half a bottle of house wine and service for £30 or less per person, at any time the restaurant is open, i.e. at dinner as well as lunch. It may be possible to spend considerably more than this, but by choosing carefully you should find £30 or less achievable.

LEAMINGTON SPA Warwickshire

map 5

Love's ⁵⅂✳

15 Dormer Place, Leamington Spa CV32 5AA
TEL/FAX: (01926) 315522
WEBSITE: www.lovesrestaurant.co.uk

COOKING **6**
MODERN EUROPEAN
£24–£58

In the centre of the town, with a car park conveniently located directly opposite, Love's stylish dining room is done out in a warm 'honey yellow', with suede high-backed chairs and some modern fixtures and fittings. Over the last couple of years Steve Love has refined and defined his cooking style, the dishes becoming more assured and less fussy while remaining highly labour-intensive. The kitchen's ambition (and its Francophile leaning) comes across clearly in combinations like seared scallops with a quenelle of pike mousse, frogs' legs and sauce verte – and technical skills are beyond reproach. Main courses are often duos, lamb arriving perhaps as 'luscious' braised shoulder and delicate fillet, 'even the fat quite gorgeous', with saffron couscous, a crisp deep-fried anchovy and 'excellent' sauce. One reader was impressed by the pairing of crisp-fried pickled onions accompanying a goats' cheese starter – a 'very upmarket ploughman's', he thought. To finish there might be a simple, intensely flavoured, feather-light raspberry soufflé ('a model of restraint') with chocolate sorbet. Service is observant and customer-focused. The cost is considered 'excellent value for money', and the wine list has plenty of choice under £25, with half a dozen house wines from £12.50 to £14.95.

CHEF: Steve Love   PROPRIETORS: Steve and Claire Love   OPEN: Tue to Sat 12 to 1.45, 7 to 9.30   CLOSED: first week Jan, 1 week Apr, last 2 weeks Aug   MEALS: Set L £13.95, Set D £25 (inc wine) to £37.50   SERVICE: 10% (optional), card slips closed   CARDS: Amex, MasterCard, Switch, Visa   DETAILS: 32 seats. Private parties: 35 main room. Vegetarian meals. No smoking. Music. No mobile phones

LEEDS West Yorkshire

map 8

Akbar's ⁵⅂✳ £

NEW ENTRY

15 Eastgate, Leeds LS2 7LY
TEL: (0113) 245 6566   FAX: (01274) 785760
WEBSITE: www.akbars.co.uk

COOKING **2**
INDIAN
£19–£35

No doubt buoyed by the continued success of Akbar's in Bradford (see entry), Shabir Hussain and Nazir Ahmed have added this branch in Leeds. Their new venture looks smart – but oddly Egyptian, with its Tutankhamun masks, hieroglyphics and cat statues alongside the usual greenery and twinkling lights. Fans of the Bradford original will be familiar with the menu, but there's always something to rave about. Benchmark chicken tikka and masala fish topped with cheese could start the ball rolling, before rishan lal ('totally tender' lamb in a thick rich sauce of onions, tomatoes and peppers), baltis, and chamgidar (chicken, lamb and minced beef in a chilli-spiked sauce). Orders are taken by beguilingly polite waiters, but chefs bring out the dishes. Drink bottled beer or house wine (£6.95).

CHEF: Talib Hussain   PROPRIETORS: Shabir Hussain and Nazir Ahmed   OPEN: all week D only 5 to 11.55   MEALS: alc (main courses £5 to £8.50). Party menus available   SERVICE: not inc, card slips closed   CARDS: MasterCard, Switch, Visa   DETAILS: 100 seats. Vegetarian meals. No smoking in 1 dining room. Music. Air-conditioned

Anthony's 🍷 ⅙✗

NEW ENTRY

19 Boar Lane, Leeds LS1 6EA
TEL: (0113) 245 5922
WEBSITE: www.anthonysrestaurant.co.uk

COOKING 7
MODERN EUROPEAN
£37–£60

A small earthquake has hit Leeds in the shape of Anthony's, a father-and-son venture that opened in early 2004. Anthony Flinn junior worked for a couple of years at the internationally lauded El Bulli near Barcelona, and aims to bring a bold splash of culinary enterprise to a city now handsomely supplied with fine dining options. The setting is a former nightclub opposite the Marriott Hotel. A ground-floor bar with floorboards stained in a striped pattern is a comfortable place in which to take aperitifs. The dining room is downstairs: another light, wood-floored space, with the tables situated in the back half of the room beyond the kitchen, and creative lighting contributing to the cool urban vibe.

'A new venture still developing' was the Flinns' modest summation of their efforts in summer 2004, in which case one can only hold one's breath at what may be to come. The menu is written in today's gnomic restaurant-speak – 'risotto of white onion, espresso, Parmesan air' or 'roast duck breast, olive oil, chocolate bonbons' – so while you wonder what may actually arrive on the plate, perhaps nibble on a poached baby cuttlefish in tomato vinaigrette. An Anjou squab first course comprised butter-soft rare meat on braised beetroot tops, alongside a raviolo of pickled garlic slivers; another paired both shades of crabmeat with white asparagus rémoulade, supported by 'unusual bursts of flavour' from pea shoots. Those chocolate bonbons sat atop upright cylinders of potato, with sliced nectarine an unexpected version of the expected fruity accompaniment to duck. Enoki mushrooms are dried and sprinkled on roast monkfish, which is given biting piquancy with pickled radishes, as well as artichoke and asparagus.

Ingenuity continues unabated into desserts such as the 'reconstructed apple Tatin', consisting of puddles of baked apple with vanilla parfait in a web of gossamer-thin pastry. A more conventionally rendered warm chocolate fondant is challengingly teamed with creamy peanut ice cream and a tuile fashioned of caramelised dried artichoke. Powerful espresso, thrilling nibbles and a choice of salted and unsalted butters with soft white bread give notice that the eye is not taken off the ball at any stage, making this all in all the most exciting arrival in the north of England for some years. The wine list is perhaps surprisingly down to earth – good names, reasonable value, arranged by style: can't say fairer than that. Moreover, it rounds off not with pages of exclusive clarets but with a slate of interesting imported beers.

CHEF: Anthony James Flinn   PROPRIETORS: Anthony Flinn and Anthony James Flinn   OPEN: Tue to Sat 12 to 2.30, 7 to 9.30 (10 Fri and Sat)   CLOSED: bank hol Tue   MEALS: alc (main courses £16 to £18). Set L £18.95 (2 courses) to £22.95   SERVICE: not inc   CARDS: MasterCard, Switch, Visa   DETAILS: 30 seats. Private parties: 30 main room. Vegetarian options upon request. No children under 5. No smoking in dining room, permitted in bar. Wheelchair access (also WC). Music. No mobile phones. Air-conditioned

Bibis Criterion

NEW ENTRY

Criterion Place, Leeds LS1 4AG
TEL: (0113) 243 0905   FAX: (0113) 243 7270
WEBSITE: www.bibisrestaurant.com

COOKING 3
ITALIAN
£29–£61

'Leeds wouldn't be Leeds without it,' maintains one devotee. Recent relocation to just off Sovereign Street, with a 24-hour car park above, doubled capacity, and the atmosphere is lively but not loud, informal (smart suits meet scruffy jeans), and food Italianate. Honest ingredients, cooked without pretension, are presented with interesting accompaniments. Starters extend to prawns in mango mayonnaise; bresaola with rocket, Parmesan and truffle oil; and Tuscan bean and pasta soup. Then expect combinations like roast guinea fowl, Muscat grapes and vin santo sauce; calf's liver and asparagus in basil butter; and Roman-style sucking pig alongside pizzas and pasta (scampi ravioli with tiger prawns and lobster sauce), plus blackboard fish specials. Then the usual sweet suspects and ice cream creations to finish. Half the short wine list is Italian (no Barolo though); Duboeuf house bottles are £14.

CHEF: Piero Vinci   PROPRIETOR: Oliver Teodorani   OPEN: all week 12 to 2 (3.30 Sun), 6 to 11.30 (5.30 to 10.30 Sun)   CLOSED: 25 Dec   MEALS: alc (main courses £7.50 to £18.50)   SERVICE: 10% (optional)   CARDS: Amex, Delta, MasterCard, Switch, Visa   DETAILS: 250 seats. 30 seats outside. Vegetarian meals. Children's helpings. Wheelchair access (also WC). Occasional music. Air-conditioned

---

Brasserie Forty Four

44 The Calls, Leeds LS2 7EW	COOKING 4
TEL: (0113) 234 3232 FAX: (0113) 234 3332	MODERN EUROPEAN
WEBSITE: www.brasserie44.com	£23–£60

This reliable brasserie, a doyen of the Leeds restaurant scene, keeps pace with fashion without ever becoming over-trendy. The simple dining room is predominantly white but enlivened by large, bright paintings, music is just the right side of loud, and the atmosphere is always bustling. That it appeals to a wide-ranging clientele is due to a crowd-pleasing menu. Steamed mussels on saffron risotto, or Whitby crab layered with sesame biscuits, Indian spices and pimento might get the ball rolling, while among main courses to impress have been a large, juicy, milky and tender veal escalope with a gremolata crust and Marsala sauce, and 'gorgeous' calf's liver, crisp on the outside, melting in the middle, served on creamed Savoy cabbage with smoky-flavoured lardons. Quirkier touches include a dish named 'East Meets West' (a combination of Bury black pudding, horseradish and Yorkshire pudding), while desserts include 'light-as-a-feather' chocolate and ginger sponge with white chocolate and lime parfait. What the wine list lacks in inspiration it makes up for in value, with the majority of bottles under £20.

CHEF: Jeff Baker   PROPRIETOR: Michael Gill   OPEN: Mon to Fri L 12 to 2, Mon to Sat D 6 to 10.30 (11 Fri and Sat)   CLOSED: bank hols   MEALS: alc (main courses £10.50 to £16). Set L and D 6 to 7.15 £11.50 (2 courses) to £14   SERVICE: 10% (optional), card slips closed   CARDS: Delta, MasterCard, Switch, Visa   DETAILS: 110 seats. Private parties: 110 main room, 12 to 50 private rooms. Vegetarian meals. No cigars/pipes. Music. Air-conditioned

---

Fourth Floor Café and Bar ▮ £

Harvey Nichols, 107–111 Briggate, Leeds LS17 6AZ	COOKING 4
TEL: (0113) 204 8000 FAX: (0113) 204 8080	MODERN BRITISH
WEBSITE: www.harveynichols.com	£26–£52

Like its London and Edinburgh siblings (see entries, Fifth Floor and Forth Floor), Leeds's Harvey Nichols wears a restaurant on its top floor. Reached via the deli, it has had a 'modest revamp' since last year, but the sleek, modern look remains. The restaurant prides itself on sourcing 70 to 90 per cent of its produce from Yorkshire, but these local ingredients are interpreted in cosmopolitan ways that draw on influences from across Europe and beyond. Starters such as gravad lax with pickled cucumber and sun-dried tomato salsa defy strict categorisation, while a main course such as chargrilled calf's liver with soft polenta, mozzarella, sage butter and caramelised shallot tart wears its heart on its sleeve. Desserts, such as trio of Yorkshire rhubarb (rhubarb and ginger sponge, vanilla and rhubarb pannacotta, rhubarb sorbet) show off the kitchen's seasonal slant. Vegetables are extra, but the prix fixe menus offer good value. The wine list bristles with quality and is bang up to the minute. Much is affordable only by platinum-pocketed corporate entertainers (especially some of the long list of champagnes), but £20 gives access to a worthwhile collection.

CHEF: Richard Allen   PROPRIETOR: Harvey Nichols   OPEN: all week L 12 to 3 (4 Sat and Sun), Thur to Sat D 5.30 (7 Sat) to 10   CLOSED: 25 and 26 Dec, 1 Jan, Easter   MEALS: alc (main courses £10 to £16). Set L Mon to Sat £15 (2 courses) to £18, Set brunch Sun (2 courses) £15, Set D £10.95 (2 courses) to £14.95. Bar menu available Mon to Sat   SERVICE: 10% (optional)   CARDS: Amex, Delta, Diners, MasterCard, Switch, Visa   DETAILS: 80 seats. 15 seats outside. Private parties: 200 (standing) main room. Children's helpings. No-smoking area. Wheelchair access (also WC). Music. Air-conditioned

Leodis ▼

Victoria Mill, Sovereign Street, Leeds LS1 4BJ	COOKING 3
TEL: (0113) 242 1010 FAX: (0113) 243 0432	BRASSERIE/MODERN BRITISH
WEBSITE: www.leodis.co.uk	£28–£61

This lively brasserie in a converted warehouse has played a full part in the renaissance of central Leeds's riverside for over a decade. Exposed iron beams and stone floor combine with glass partitions and strategic greenery to make an inviting place that combines a sense of fun with due professionalism. The daily-changing menus deal in well-wrought dishes that deliver plenty of punch. Scallops are lightly cooked and served in the shells, delicately glazed with Gruyère, monkfish is beer-battered and served with garlic and herb mayonnaise, and foie gras terrine comes with toasted brioche and sweet wine jelly. Finely judged timing distinguishes a mixture of seafood baked en papillote, while calf's liver with bacon and crunchy shallots is as tender as can be. Vegetables are separately charged for, and meals end triumphantly with blueberry mousse with lemon sorbet, or chocolate marquise. A reinvigorated wine list delivers a mix of affordable, intriguing and sought-after bottles from around the world, but is most astute in France and Italy. Eight by the glass, plenty of halves and magnums, good sparkling and dessert wines, and some fine old clarets ensure strength in depth.

CHEFS: Steve Kendell and John Wilks   PROPRIETORS: Martin Spalding, Steve Kendell and Phil Richardson   OPEN: Mon to Fri L 12 to 2, Mon to Sat D 6 to 10   CLOSED: 24 and 26 Dec, 1 Jan, bank hol Mons L   MEALS: alc (main courses £8 to £16). Set L £16.95, Set D Mon to Fri (and Sat 6 to 7.15) £16.95. Light L and Tapas L menus available   SERVICE: 10% (optional), card slips closed   CARDS: Amex, Delta, Diners, MasterCard, Switch, Visa   DETAILS: 180 seats. 60 seats outside. Private parties: 180 main room. Car park. Vegetarian meals. No cigars/pipes. Wheelchair access (also WC). Music

No. 3 York Place

3 York Place, Leeds LS1 2DR	COOKING 6
TEL: (0113) 245 9922 FAX: (0113) 245 9965	MODERN EUROPEAN
WEBSITE: www.no3yorkplace.co.uk	£31–£80

In a comparatively quiet street near the city centre, just around the corner from the landmark Metropole and Queen's hotels, No. 3 is a smartly furnished modern restaurant, sharing its location with a few other bars and clubs. Upfront it has a bar, while the long, narrow dining room is divided into two by a central spine, and there are brown banquettes, more intimate booths, and white walls decorated with mirrors and swirling stainless-steel designs. It's not a quiet temple either, but 'exudes an animated atmosphere' as it fills up, while service is personable, efficient and responsive. Martel Smith's modern approach is underpinned by a classical French theme and shows style on his menus. Fine materials are well handled, and dishes impress with clear flavours, workmanship and balance, and also with a skilful simplicity that avoids being too 'obviously attention-seeking'. Expect to start with the likes of caramelised galette of sea scallops with an endive tarte Tatin and red pepper vinaigrette, followed by main courses of roast fillet of beef with seared foie gras, ceps, celeriac purée and a red wine sauce, or fillet of brill poached in red wine, pommes purée, buttery spinach and salsify. To finish, hot apricot soufflé with almond ice cream and apricot and Cointreau jellies. The wine list, arranged by grape variety, focuses on thoroughbred bottles. Prices are not outlandish, but there are only occasional dips under £20. House red is £14, and six come by the glass.

CHEF: Martel Smith   PROPRIETOR: Mardenis Ltd   OPEN: Mon to Fri L 12 to 2, Mon to Sat D 6.30 to 10 MEALS: alc (main courses £13 to £20). Set L and D Mon to Fri 6.30 to 7.30 £14.50 (2 courses) to £18.50, Set D £45   SERVICE: 10%, card slips closed   CARDS: Amex, Delta, MasterCard, Switch, Visa   DETAILS: 50 seats. Private parties: 56 main room. Wheelchair access (also WC). Music. Air-conditioned

Pool Court at 42 £⭐

44 The Calls, Leeds LS2 7EW	COOKING 7
TEL: (0113) 244 4242 FAX: (0113) 234 3332	CLASSIC FRENCH/MODERN BRITISH
WEBSITE: www.poolcourt.com	£42–£88

Beside the Centenary footbridge that spans the river Aire, Pool Court is part of yet another phase of the city's redevelopment. The dining room is small and intimate rather than big-city brash, with a soothing riparian theme echoed in etched wavy lines at the windows and in a picture of water. Jeff Baker runs a highly industrious kitchen. Even at lunchtime there is much in the way of incidentals, with nibbles preceding an appetiser and petits fours with coffee. Bread is treated with exemplary solicitude: three loaves turn up on a trolley like cheeses; your choice is sliced on a small butcher's block before your eyes, and translated carefully to the side plate, with unsalted Echiré butter in attendance. The menu dishes aren't bad either: a November meal kicked off with a bowl of truffled seasonal game consommé adorned with a cabbage parcel of partridge, itself encasing an unusually expressive chicken mousse. Unfashionable cuts such as a chargrilled veal chop with Jerusalem artichokes and pickled girolles often feature, and calves' kidneys with trompette mushrooms and mashed potato suggest a willingness to explore the potentialities of offal. Fish specials, mentioned verbally, have included sea bass with Basque-style peppers, as well as Dover sole roasted whole and served with spinach and crisped ham. Variations on a banana theme worked well for one normally sceptical of such assemblages, its star components being a mille-feuille of mousse and a crisp-topped banana and rum crème brûlée. Service is exceptionally friendly, smiling through the occasional lapse, rather than putting on the kinds of airs that Yorkshire folk wouldn't tolerate. A fine wine list starts at £15.50 for a Chilean Chardonnay and a Californian Cabernet Franc, before ascending at a stately pace to the classé clarets and single-vineyard Burgundies. Quality is assured, even if prices press.

CHEF: Jeff Baker   PROPRIETOR: Michael Gill   OPEN: Mon to Fri L 12 to 2, Mon to Sat D 7 to 10 (8.30 Sat) CLOSED: bank hols   MEALS: Set L and D £25 (2 courses) to £59   SERVICE: 10%, card slips closed   CARDS: Delta, MasterCard, Switch, Visa   DETAILS: 38 seats. 18 seats outside. Private parties: 38 main room.

Vegetarian meals. No children under 3. No smoking. Wheelchair access (also WC). Music. No mobile phones. Air-conditioned

Simply Heathcotes ✖

Canal Wharf, Water Lane, Leeds LS11 5PS	COOKING 2
TEL: (0113) 244 6611 FAX: (0113) 244 0736	MODERN BRITISH
WEBSITE: www.heathcotes.co.uk	£26–£60

An old warehouse overlooking the Leeds–Liverpool canal is the charming setting for the Yorkshire branch of the Lancashire mini chain. Inside, it's a blend of old and new, with big wooden beams set off against swaths of glass and brushed steel, and window tables give views over the water. Various menu formulas encourage flexibility and informality, and the food aims for a broad appeal – modern and inventive but at the same time comfortingly familiar, choices ranging from roast chump of lamb with goats' cheese gnocchi and mint oil to grilled hake: a fine piece of fish carefully cooked, with aïoli, asparagus and roast tomatoes sprinkled with crunchy pine kernels. Among desserts, a light yet rich and buttery pear and almond tart has found favour. Prices on the compact, international wine list start at £13.50, and there are around ten wines by the glass.

CHEF: Simon Peacock   PROPRIETOR: Paul Heathcote   OPEN: all week 12 to 2.30, 6 to 10 (11 Sat, 9 Sun) CLOSED: bank hols   MEALS: alc (main courses £9 to £21.50). Set L and D 6 to 7 £9.50 (1 course) to £15.50 SERVICE: 10% (optional), card slips closed   CARDS: Amex, Delta, MasterCard, Switch, Visa   DETAILS: 130 seats. Private parties: 130 main room. Car park. Vegetarian meals. Children's helpings. No smoking. Wheelchair access (also WC). Music. Air-conditioned

Sous le Nez en Ville ▮ £

The Basement, Quebec House, Quebec Street,	COOKING 3
Leeds LS1 2HA	MODERN EUROPEAN
TEL: (0113) 244 0108 FAX: (0113) 245 0240	£28–£57

This basement restaurant has kept locals happy for years with its unpretentious bistro style, good-value set menu and interesting fish specials. Various nooks and crannies add character to what is otherwise a plainly decorated space, while prompt and efficient French staff ensure that everything runs smoothly. The robust cooking relies on fresh tastes rather than elaborate presentation for its impact and has a sprinkling of fusion flavours among the bistro classics. Thus, the menus might feature deep-fried Brie with warm pepper and mango chutney to start, then pork cutlet with sweet potato chips and beetroot jus, or roast salmon with a wasabi-dressed salad of king prawns, pak choi, watercress and lentils. Sticky desserts include banana and toffee parfait with caramelised bananas, and white chocolate and apricot bread-and-butter pudding. Of course, you could just come here for the wine – an encyclopedia of good and great bottles from France and around the world at refreshingly ungreedy prices. A dozen house wines from around £12 also come by the glass.

CHEFS: Andrew Carter and Andrew Lavender   PROPRIETOR: Sous le Nez Ltd   OPEN: Mon to Sat 12 to 2.30, 6 to 10 (11 Sat)   CLOSED: 24 Dec to 2 Jan   MEALS: alc (main courses £10 to £18.50). Set D 6 to 7.30 (7 Sat) £19.95 (inc wine). Bar menu available   SERVICE: not inc   CARDS: Delta, Diners, MasterCard, Switch, Visa   DETAILS: 95 seats. Private parties: 4 to 20 private rooms. Vegetarian meals. No cigars/pipes. Music. Air-conditioned

LEEK Staffordshire   map 5

▲ Number 64 ⅋✳

64 St Edward Street, Leek ST13 5DL	COOKING 2
TEL: (01538) 381900 FAX: (01538) 370918	MODERN BRITISH
WEBSITE: www.number64.com	£29–£63

This airy first-floor dining room with antique stained glass made one reporter feel as though 'invited over for lunch at Jane Austen's'. It fits into an elegant Georgian red-brick building along with a patisserie/food shop and cellar wine bar, all owned by local speciality food producer Cottage Delight. Mark Walker uses their jams and relishes in several dishes alongside Aberdeenshire beef, Yorkshire grouse, Shetland diver-caught scallops and Staffordshire cheeses. Imagination and skill show in a hearty cassoulet of pheasant with cabbage, bacon and Agen prunes, and in a rich starter of guinea-fowl terrine balanced by its orange and endive salad. And mandarin and golden syrup steamed pudding with praline ice cream makes a successful pairing. Ten house bottles at £9.95 open a well-spread list.

CHEF: Mark Walker   PROPRIETOR: Nigel Cope   OPEN: Tue to Sun L 12 to 2, Tue to Sat D 7 to 9   MEALS: alc (main courses £14.50 to £30). Set Sun L £15 (2 courses) to £20, Set D £39.95   SERVICE: not inc   CARDS: Amex, Delta, Diners, MasterCard, Switch, Visa   DETAILS: 50 seats. 20 seats outside. Private parties: 40 main room, 8 to 14 private rooms. Vegetarian meals. Children's helpings. No smoking. Music ACCOMMODATION: 3 rooms, all with bath/shower. TV. Phone. B&B £65 to £95. Baby facilities

LEICESTER Leicestershire   map 5

Opera House ▼ ⅋✳   NEW ENTRY

10 Guildhall Lane, Leicester LE1 5FQ	COOKING 2
TEL: (0116) 223 6666 FAX: (0116) 233 4704	MODERN EUROPEAN
WEBSITE: www.theoperahouserestaurant.com	£30–£71

Converted from two seventeenth-century cottages next to the cathedral, this black and white building served as an inn, jail and antique shop before becoming an ambitious modern restaurant. The dining room comprises a series of conjoined, brick-floored nooks, with a spiral staircase leading to a labyrinthine vaulted cellar. Ingredients are carefully sourced, whether potted Norfolk brown shrimps with Mrs O'Callaghan's soda bread, or locally reared fillet of beef with purple potatoes, glazed button onions, and spinach and watercress purée. Reporters have enjoyed sautéed mixed mushrooms in a puff pastry parcel with chive butter sauce, and an ample free-range chicken breast with Tuscan tomato and olive sauce. Desserts could be as uncomplicated as a brittle basket of mixed berries with praline ice cream. Ambition in wine choice is evident from a global mix of good names topped by a very smart 'private cellar'. At the other end of the spectrum six house wines from £13.50 also come by the glass.

CHEF: Alex Howard   PROPRIETORS: Noel and Val Weafer   OPEN: Mon to Sat 12 to 2, 7 to 10   CLOSED: 23 Dec to 3 Jan   MEALS: alc L (main courses £9 to £11). Set L and D £29.50 (2 courses) to £39.50   SERVICE: 10% (optional)   CARDS: Delta, Diners, MasterCard, Switch, Visa   DETAILS: 62 seats. Private parties: 20 main room, 8 to 14 private rooms. Vegetarian meals. Children's helpings. No smoking. Music. No mobile phones. Air-conditioned £5

'"Good evening," said the waitress as I arrived for lunch. Their computer was obviously on the same wavelength, since it billed me for a three-course dinner.' (On eating in Yorkshire)

The Boatyard

8/13 High Street, Leigh-on-Sea SS9 2EN | COOKING **2**
TEL/FAX: (01702) 475588 | MODERN EUROPEAN
WEBSITE: www.theboatyardrestaurant.co.uk | £27–£68

The boat-shaped bar and position overlooking the estuary recall the previous incarnation of this stylish, airy restaurant. Friendly, smart service creates the feeling one is in good hands, and the modern brasserie-style menu roams across Europe and beyond. Leek and goats' cheese tart sits happily alongside spicy squid in yellow curry among starters. The evening à la carte menu divides main courses into fish, meat and vegetarian, the four or five in each category typically including roast mullet stuffed with pine nuts and oyster mushrooms, grilled duck breast with crushed minted peas and sweet red wine jus, and field mushrooms stuffed with smoked mozzarella. The set-price lunch menu is shorter but covers a similar range. Five house wines at £12.95 open a varied and good-value list.

CHEF: Jonathan Luck   PROPRIETOR: John Cross   OPEN: Wed to Sun L 12 to 3 (4 Sun), Tue to Sat D 7 (6.30 Sat) to 10.30   CLOSED: 25 Dec, some bank hols   MEALS: alc D (main courses £15 to £20). Set L £10.95 (2 courses) to £14.95. Set L Sun £12.95 (2 courses) to £14.95. Cover £1.50   SERVICE: not inc, card slips closed   CARDS: Delta, MasterCard, Switch, Visa   DETAILS: 180 seats. Private parties: 40 main room. Car park. Vegetarian meals. No children after 9pm. Children's helpings. Wheelchair access (also WC). Music. Air-conditioned

▲ Lewtrenchard Manor 🍷 ✳

Lewdown EX20 4PN
TEL: (01566) 783222   FAX: (01566) 783332
WEBSITE: www.lewtrenchard.co.uk | COOKING **6**
off A30 Okehampton to Launceston road; turn left at | MODERN BRITISH
Lewdown | £29–£58

A splendid Jacobean building on Dartmoor's doorstep, formerly the home of the aristocratic Gould family, Lewtrenchard Manor makes the most of its countryside surroundings and offers plenty of scope for walks on the estate. Dining takes place in a period setting of dark wooden panelling and ancient portraits of serious-looking folk. First-class nibbles are served in the bar, then a set-price three-course dinner follows – in summer, perhaps in the colonnaded courtyard.

A seasonal menu from the skilled chef is heavy on local game in winter, featuring teal, woodcock, snipe and mallard, but lighter options predominate during the summer. All herbs and most vegetables come from the hotel's own walled garden. Consider starting with sautéed scallops with cep and artichoke purée and a chicken and rosemary reduction, or a tian of provençale vegetables with feta beignets. Main courses might include an interesting combination of seared tuna and deep-fried sole fillet served with saffron risotto and an orange and beetroot sauce. Puddings are no less convincing, among them coffee and Amaretto torte with coffee pannacotta and mascarpone ice cream. If the wine list seems unassuming on first inspection, look closer to discover a beautifully balanced French range and an astute international selection that concludes triumphantly in South Africa. Prices are customer-friendly, and six decent house options are £13 and £14 a bottle.

CHEF: Jason Hornbuckle   PROPRIETOR: Von Essen Hotels   OPEN: Tue to Sun L 12 to 1.30, all week D 7 to 9   MEALS: Set L £12 (2 courses) to £20, Set D £37.50. Light L and bar menus available   SERVICE: not inc   CARDS: Amex, Delta, Diners, MasterCard, Switch, Visa   DETAILS: 60 seats. 20 seats outside. Private parties: 30 main room, 8 to 25 private rooms. Car park. Children's helpings. No children under 8. No smoking. Wheelchair access (not WC). Music. No mobile phones   ACCOMMODATION: 9 rooms, all with bath/shower. TV. Phone. B&B £95 to £200. Rooms for disabled. No children under 8 (£5)

LEWES East Sussex   map 3

Circa

145 High Street, Lewes BN7 1XT   COOKING 3
TEL: (01273) 471777   FAX: (01273) 488416   FUSION
WEBSITE: www.circacirca.com   £29–£47

This dimly lit, many-windowed, quasi-Californian venue overlooks Lewes High Street. Witticisms abound: appetisers come on a slate dish with a fake $10,000 bill, while menus are on little clipboards. One reporter's crayfish tails with Stonegate cheese ravioli in a coconut bath with Marmited nuts offered something for everyone, the Thai-centred flavours just about hanging together, while five-spiced pork belly with blue crab samosas was another fascinating, and successful, starter. An inspector's seared venison was rather too well cooked, and its accompanying beet Anna perhaps over-inventive. Finish with desserts like double chocolate brownie and goats'-milk ice cream, or aniseed berries with runny honey ice. Winningly friendly service helps keep feet on the ground. Wines are more humdrum than the food, but offer geographical and numerical choice under £20, including house French Sauvignon and Merlot at £11.95. A sister fish restaurant - Circa Fish, no less - has opened round the corner at 9 Westgate, tel: (01273) 471333.

CHEF: Marc Bolger   PROPRIETOR: Ann Renton Biles   OPEN: Tue to Sat L 12 to 2.30 (2 Fri and Sat), D 6 (7 Fri and Sat) to 10   MEALS: alc L (main courses £12.50). Set L £12.95 (2 courses), Set D £24.50 (2 courses) to £27.50   SERVICE: 10% (optional), card slips closed   CARDS: Amex, Delta, Diners, MasterCard, Switch, Visa   DETAILS: 90 seats. Private parties: 90 main room. Vegetarian meals. Children's helpings. No smoking area. Wheelchair access (also WC). Music. Air-conditioned

LEYBURN North Yorkshire   map 8

▲ Sandpiper Inn ⅚✴ £   NEW ENTRY

Market Place, Leyburn DL8 5AT   COOKING 3
TEL: (01969) 622206   FAX: (01969) 625367   MODERN EUROPEAN
                                                            £25–£47

The Harrisons have made quite a name for themselves since taking over this stone-built pub/restaurant in 1999, and they have succeeded in preserving the homely feel of the place. Meals can be eaten in the bar or the adjacent restaurant, which is decked out with attractive olive-green walls and oak floorboards. The kitchen works to a menu of enticing modern dishes bolstered by a few specials. In the evening you might find warm goats' cheese on rocket and beetroot salad before loin of venison with crispy pancetta and green beans, or grilled sea bass on garlic and celeriac purée with forest mushrooms. Desserts range from bread-and-butter pudding to blackcurrant vacherin. Sandwiches and simpler dishes are served at lunchtime. Three dozen global wines offer plenty of affordable drinking from £11.

CHEF: Jonathan Harris   PROPRIETORS: the Harrison family   OPEN: Tue to Sat 12 to 2.30, 6.30 to 9 (9.30 Fri and Sat), Sun 12 to 2, 7 to 9   MEALS: alc (main courses L £7 to £12, D £9.50 to £15.50)   SERVICE: not inc, card slips closed   CARDS: Delta, MasterCard, Switch, Visa   DETAILS: 58 seats. 20 seats outside. Private parties: 40 main room. Car park. Vegetarian meals. Children's helpings. No children in restaurant after 8pm. Music. No mobile phones   ACCOMMODATION: 2 rooms, both with bath/shower. TV. B&B £55 to £85. Baby facilities

---

LIFTON Devon   map 1

▲ Arundell Arms ? ⅓✳

Lifton PL16 0AA   COOKING 5
WEBSITE: www.arundellarms.com   MODERN BRITISH
                                                                           £34–£63

This hotel has long catered to sportsmen of all sorts (today's rod and tackle room was a cockpit in the eighteenth century). For over 40 years Anne Voss-Bark has kept the place a firm favourite with those who come to Devon for shooting, riding and above all fishing (on the hotel's 20 miles of water, or on its angling courses).

Head chef Philip Burgess gives local suppliers pride of place on the daily-changing menu, and turns their sound materials into accomplished but simply presented modern British fare. The two- to four-course fixed-price menus may begin with lobster and baby vegetable salad, or a foie gras and chicken liver terrine, succeeded by a well-turned-out platter of lamb – contrasting saddle and chop – with dauphinois potatoes and accurately cooked vegetables (an alternative might be escalope of organic salmon with scallops, creamed girolles and celery flowers). An inspector's chocolate parfait was 'good, almost *parfait*', or try marinated prune fritters with cocoa sugar and vanilla sauce. The wine list provides a tidy balance of traditional and modern at very fair prices. Nine house wines from £13 also come by the glass, and half-bottles are well represented.

CHEFS: Philip Burgess and Nick Shopland   PROPRIETOR: Anne Voss-Bark   OPEN: all week 12.30 to 2, 7.30 to 9.30   CLOSED: 24 to 26 Dec D   MEALS: Set L £20 (2 courses) to £24, Set D £34 to £41. Bar alc menu available   SERVICE: not inc   CARDS: Amex, Delta, Diners, MasterCard, Switch, Visa   DETAILS: 70 seats. 25 seats outside. Private parties: 70 main room, 30 private room. Car park. Vegetarian meals. Children's helpings. No smoking. Wheelchair access (also WC). Music   ACCOMMODATION: 27 rooms, all with bath/shower. TV. Phone. B&B £52 to £136. Baby facilities. Fishing £5

LINCOLN Lincolnshire   map 9

Wig & Mitre ⅓✳

30–32 Steep Hill, Lincoln LN2 1TL   COOKING 1
TEL: (01522) 535190   FAX: (01522) 532402   MODERN BRITISH
WEBSITE: www.wigandmitre.com   £23–£54

In the old part of town among cobbled streets and within sight of the castle, the Wig & Mitre is a paragon of flexible dining, open all day, every day, with assorted dining and bar areas spread over two higgledy-piggledy floors. The main menu, available at all times, covers a variety of culinary styles (sometimes within a single dish), typically taking in sautéed scallops on coriander, peanut and garlic risotto, braised blade of beef with foie gras, onion mash and gravy, or a filo pastry tart of couscous and Mediterranean vegetables with cherry tomato confit and pistachio sauce. Breakfast, sandwiches and daily specials ensure that all bases are covered, and a short but wide-ranging wine list focuses on good-value drinking, bottle prices starting at £11.50.

CHEF: Valérie Hope PROPRIETORS: Michael and Valérie Hope, and Toby Hope OPEN: all week 8 to 11 MEALS: alc (main courses £9.50 to £18). Set L £11 (2 courses) to £13.95 SERVICE: not inc CARDS: Amex, Delta, Diners, MasterCard, Switch, Visa DETAILS: 135 seats. Private parties: 65 main room, 20 to 30 private rooms. Vegetarian meals. Children's helpings. No smoking. No music (£5)

LINTON West Yorkshire **map 8**

▲ Wood Hall

Trip Lane, Linton, Wetherby LS22 4JA
TEL: (01937) 587271 FAX: (01937) 584353
WEBSITE: www.handpicked.co.uk
go from Wetherby to Linton, then turn R opposite Windmill pub, continue 2m along single-track road

COOKING **3**
MODERN EUROPEAN
£29–£54

This imposing eighteenth-century hotel is set in 100 acres of rolling parkland at the end of a narrow road. Bold-patterned wallpaper, heavy curtains, a chandelier and a marble fireplace set a formal, traditional tone in the Georgian-style dining room, where well-spaced tables have fine views down to the Wharfe. Sensible-length set menus show a rather rich classically influenced style coexisting with modern ideas. Expect boneless saddle of grain-fed rabbit accompanied by fresh linguini, mustard cream and red wine jus, or braised fillet of turbot with scallop mousseline, girolle mushrooms and chive butter. Warm chocolate fondant served with a milk sorbet, or white chocolate crème brûlée with raspberries, could be hard to resist. The international wine list, ordered by style, has French house at £16.50 (but little else under £20) and decent selection by the glass and half-bottle.

CHEF: Lee Parsons PROPRIETOR: Hand Picked Hotels OPEN: Sun to Fri L 12.30 to 2 (Sun 10 to 3), all week D 7 (6.30 Sat) to 9.30 (9 Sun) MEALS: Set L £15 (2 courses) to £18.50, Set L Sun £18.50, Set D £32.50. Bar menu available SERVICE: not inc, card slips closed CARDS: Amex, Delta, Diners, MasterCard, Switch, Visa DETAILS: 60 seats. Private parties: 32 main room, 6 to 100 private rooms. Car park. Vegetarian meals. Children's helpings. No smoking. Wheelchair access (also WC). No music. No mobile phones ACCOMMODATION: 44 rooms, all with bath/shower. TV. Phone. B&B £135 to £280. Rooms for disabled. Baby facilities. Swimming pool. Fishing

LITTLE SHELFORD Cambridgeshire **map 6**

Sycamore House

1 Church Street, Little Shelford CB2 5HG
TEL: (01223) 843396

COOKING **3**
MODERN BRITISH
£35–£42

Domestically small-scale, the two linked, low-ceilinged dining rooms are 'bare bones without being minimalist': a plain, unpretentious look matching the homely and well-intentioned cooking of a country restaurant that opens only four sessions a week. Short, monthly-changing fixed-price menus carry simple descriptions of largely straightforward dishes. No froths or flourishes, just steamed asparagus on creamy-sauced noodles with 'excellent' salsa verde (for a May visitor), followed by a between-course salad ('something I rather wish I encountered more often'), then perhaps roast rack of lamb with creamed onions and translucent, very clear-flavoured red wine sauce, accompanied by a side dish of good, fresh vegetables, or goujons of plaice with parsley sauce. Desserts take in poppy-seed parfait with plum sauce, or steamed chocolate pudding with chocolate sauce. The short global wine list is cannily chosen and extremely good value. House red is reliable Côtes du Rhône from Guigal at £12.

CHEF: Michael Sharpe   PROPRIETORS: Michael and Susan Sharpe   OPEN: Wed to Sat D only 7.30 to 9
CLOSED: Christmas   MEALS: Set D £25   SERVICE: not inc, card slips closed   CARDS: Delta, MasterCard,
Switch, Visa   DETAILS: 24 seats. Private parties (not Fri/Sat): 24 main room. Car park. Vegetarian meals.
No children under 12. No smoking. No music (£5)

LIVERPOOL Merseyside   map 8

Chung Ku

Columbus Quay, Riverside Drive, Liverpool L3 4DB | NEW CHEF
TEL: (0151) 726 8191   FAX: (0151) 726 8190 | CHINESE
WEBSITE: www.chungku-restaurant.co.uk | £18–£72

Part of the in-vogue Columbus Quay development, this designer restaurant on two floors
should appeal equally to fans of modern architecture and those in search of Chinese food. A
new chef arrived too late for feedback or an inspection, but the repertoire seems much as
before. Its heart is in the Cantonese tradition, although the regular English-language menu
gives esoteric ingredients and challenging dishes a wide berth. Dim sum provide daytime
sustenance, and seafood is much in evidence. Appetisers range from soft-shell crab with salt
and pepper to crispy won ton, while main courses encompass everything from fried oysters
in black-bean and chilli sauce to sliced duck with ginger and spring onions. The short wine
list opens with house recommendations from £10.90. There is a branch on East Lancashire
Road, Carr Mill, St Helens, tel: (01744) 609868.

PROPRIETORS: Mr and Mrs Shum   OPEN: all week 12 to 11.30 (12 Fri and Sat, 10 Sun and bank hols)
MEALS: alc (main courses £9 to £26). Set L £9.50, Set D £19 to £35 (all min 2)   SERVICE: not inc   CARDS:
Amex, Delta, MasterCard, Switch, Visa   DETAILS: 400 seats. Private parties: 200 main room, 20 to 40
private rooms. Car park. Vegetarian meals. Wheelchair access (also WC). Music. Air-conditioned

▲ Hope Street Hotel,
London Carriage Works ▼

	NEW ENTRY
40 Hope Street, Liverpool L1 9DA	COOKING 5
TEL: (0151) 705 2222 FAX: (0151) 709 2454	MODERN BRITISH
WEBSITE: www.hopestreethotel.co.uk	£34–£62

The Hope Street Hotel is a grand building in the Venetian palazzo style, dating from 1860,
and the London Carriage Works is the name of its fine-dining restaurant and separate
brasserie, both on the ground floor. The carefully restored exterior, all arched windows
and cast-iron pillars, belies the modern, open-plan dining room within.

The daily-changing lunch and dinner menus contain much that is free-range or organic,
and efforts are made to source from local suppliers. Dishes tend to be well rounded in terms
of flavour combinations, and the cooking accomplished and complex. A main course of
Welsh beef, 'a beautifully cut fillet with a perfectly roasted crust encasing tender pink flesh',
came with wild mushrooms, an assiette of vegetables and a 'suitably rich' Madeira jus – 'a
real triumph'. Pressed terrine of game with a spicy fruit relish, herb salad and garlic toasts
makes an appealing starting point, and there could be chestnut and mushroom soup
scented with rosemary with Cashel Blue toasts. Desserts also display a degree of originality:
passion-fruit crème brûlée with a biscuit 'cannelloni' delicately flavoured with orange and
Muscat cream. Novelty features of the substantial wine list include a wholesale ban on
capital letters and a 'cult wine of the month' among the dozen-plus by the glass. But the
main selection is serious in intent with plenty in a classical vein. Prices start at £12.50. The

brasserie menu runs from sandwiches and salads, through to flash-fried chilli squid with pak choi, spring onion and nori rolls, and loin of free-range pork with Welsh rarebit, creamed Savoy cabbage and pease pudding.

CHEFS: Paul Askew and Matt Locke PROPRIETORS: David Brewitt, Paul Askew and Andrew Bentley OPEN: Sun to Fri L 12 to 3, Mon to Sat D 5 to 9.30 MEALS: Set L £16.95 (2 courses) to £21.95, Set D £23.95 (2 courses) to £29.95. Brasserie menu available SERVICE: not inc, card slips closed CARDS: Amex, Delta, Diners, MasterCard, Switch, Visa DETAILS: 70 seats. Private parties: 6 to 50 private rooms. Vegetarian meals. Children's helpings. No-smoking area. Wheelchair access (also WC). Music. Air-conditioned ACCOMMODATION: 48 rooms, all with bath/shower. TV. Phone. Room only £115 to £285. Rooms for disabled. Baby facilities (£5)

Other Place Bistro

29A Hope Street, Liverpool L1 9BQ
TEL/FAX: (0151) 707 7888

COOKING 3
MODERN EUROPEAN
£20–£45

Situated between the city's two cathedrals and just around the corner from the Philharmonic Hall, this unassuming bistro attracts its quota of culture vultures looking for affordable pre-theatre deals. It's also a godsend at lunchtime, when specials and light dishes are unlikely to stretch the wallet. Expect bistro food along the lines of coriander crab cakes with pineapple and chilli salsa before roast loin of Welsh lamb with celeriac and potato dauphinois, purple-sprouting broccoli and rosemary jus, or grilled cod fillet with lime-sautéed potatoes, fine beans and vanilla beurre blanc. Desserts such as rhubarb and custard tart or pannacotta with balsamic strawberries bring the curtain down, and the short wine list is a lively assortment of carefully chosen bottles, with house Chilean at £11.25. The Other Place Restaurant is at 141–143 Allerton Road, tel: (0151) 724 1234, and the Other Place Deli is nearby at 121 Allerton Road, tel: (0151) 724 7718.

CHEF: Rhian Cradock PROPRIETORS: David Thorneycroft, Sheila Benson, Sean Millar, Mark Benson and Philippa Feeney OPEN: Tue to Fri L 11.30 to 2.30, Tue to Sat D 6 to 10 CLOSED: bank hols MEALS: alc exc Fri and Sat D (main courses L £5 to £9, D £10 to £14). Set D Tue to Fri 6 to 7 £11.95 (2 courses) to £13.95, Set D Fri and Sat £20.95 (2 courses) to £24.95 SERVICE: not inc, card slips closed CARDS: Delta, MasterCard, Switch, Visa DETAILS: 54 seats. Private parties: 34 main room, 12 to 20 private rooms. Vegetarian meals. Children's helpings. No cigars/pipes. Music

Simply Heathcotes ⅝✳ £

Beetham Plaza, 25 The Strand, Liverpool L2 0XL
TEL: (0151) 2363536 FAX: (0151) 2363534
WEBSITE: www.heathcotes.co.uk

COOKING 3
MODERN BRITISH
£26–£50

Paul Heathcote's formula – modern British food with fine Lancashire produce running through it like the lettering in Blackpool rock – has this contemporary, glass-walled venue for its Liverpool showcase. Here you will find successful dishes like chargrilled artichokes on toast with hollandaise, shin of Bowland beef with beans and mashed potato, and seared red bream with pea and tomato concassé. The roast pork has excellent crackling, and the signature dessert – old-time Knickerbocker Glory in a tall glass – is irresistible to one regular. Pear and almond tart with raspberry ripple ice cream is another option. The helpfully descriptive wine list offers plenty of choice, though some will find the pricing's centre of gravity a touch high. House wines are £12.50 (French) or £13.50 (Chilean).

CHEF: Gavin Williams   PROPRIETOR: Paul Heathcote   OPEN: all week 12 to 2.30, 6 to 10 (11 Sat, 9.30 Sun)
CLOSED: 25 and 26 Dec, 1 Jan, bank hols   MEALS: alc (main courses £9 to £15). Set L £13.50 (2 courses) to
£15.50, Set D 6 to 7 £13.50 (2 courses) to £15.50. Snack menu available   SERVICE: 10% (optional), card
slips closed   CARDS: Amex, Delta, MasterCard, Switch, Visa   DETAILS: 100 seats. Private parties: 80
main room, 8 to 24 private rooms. Vegetarian meals. Children's helpings. No smoking. Wheelchair access
(also WC). Music. Air-conditioned

60 Hope Street ♥ ⌂

60 Hope Street, Liverpool L1 9BZ	COOKING 4
TEL: (0151) 707 6060 FAX: (0151) 707 6016	MODERN EUROPEAN
WEBSITE: www.60hopestreet.com	£27–£74

Snugly tucked at one end of a Georgian terrace within sight of the Anglican cathedral, not
far from Chinatown and the city centre, 60 Hope Street benefits from a sense of
unflustered cool. With its varnished floorboards, undressed tables and absence of curtains,
there isn't much to absorb sounds, but the modern city vibe – spread across the ground-
floor restaurant and basement café/bar – feels just right. Paul McEvoy cooks with
confidence, tossing chicken livers and button onions in a pomegranate dressing, and
pairing scallops and parsnips together with Old Spot bacon. There are foams, jus, creams
and reductions rather than sauces, but the combinations work and dishes are well
considered. Monkfish has gained from its teaming with pea risotto, white asparagus and a
Sauternes sauce, or there might be Goosnargh chicken breast with smoked garlic mash,
carrots, trompettes and sage cream. Top-notch desserts have included raspberry ripple
parfait with summer berry compote, and fine chocolate and pistachio fondant with an
almond tuile. Service manages things capably and cheerily. The wine list is not huge but
the 'understated class' of this international mix is well suited to the style of the place. House
red is £12.95, and there's something for all pockets, including some special bottles in the
'director's bin'.

CHEF: Paul McEvoy   PROPRIETORS: Colin and Gary Manning   OPEN: Mon to Fri L 12 to 2.30, Mon to Sat D 7
to 10.30   CLOSED: bank hols   MEALS: alc (main courses £14 to £25). Set L £12.95 (2 courses) to £15.95.
Café/bar menu available Mon to Sat noon to 10.30   SERVICE: not inc, 10% for parties of 8 or more
CARDS: Delta, MasterCard, Switch, Visa   DETAILS: 90 seats. Private parties: 90 main room, 10 to 30 private
rooms. Vegetarian meals. Children's helpings. No-smoking area. No music. Air-conditioned

▲ Ziba at the Racquet Club ♥ ✳

5 Chapel Street, Liverpool L3 9AG	NEW CHEF
TEL: (0151) 236 6676 FAX: (0151) 236 6870	MODERN BRITISH
WEBSITE: www.racquetclub.org.uk	£28–£53

Alongside gym, squash court and spa, the Racquet Club houses the transplanted Ziba. In
this vast, tall-windowed, wooden-floored space an infectious buzz is created, partly
through the use of a sound system. A new head chef, Neil Dempsey, joined in summer
2004, too late for an inspection. The style of cooking is set to continue, with the new lunch
menu featuring dishes as straightforward as Formby asparagus with Parma ham and rocket
to start, or perhaps red mullet with pickled red onion and pea salad, followed by confit
duck leg with roast sweet potato and mulled pears. The new dinner menu was not in place
as we went to press. Well-trained service maintains a smart pace. The good-value wine list
is arranged by styles and well attuned to modern palates, though good, mature fine wines
also have their place. House is £12.50, and ten come by the glass.

CHEF: Neil Dempsey   PROPRIETORS: Martin and Helen Ainscough   OPEN: Mon to Fri L 12 to 2.30, Mon to Sat D 6.30 to 10 (10.30 Sat)   MEALS: alc (main courses £9 to £18). Bar menu available   SERVICE: not inc   CARDS: Amex, Delta, MasterCard, Switch, Visa   DETAILS: 100 seats. Private parties: 80 main room, 6 to 30 private rooms. Children's helpings. No smoking in 1 dining room. Music. Air-conditioned   ACCOMMODATION: 8 rooms, all with bath/shower. TV. Phone. Room only £105 to £160. Swimming pool

LLANFAIR WATERDINE Shropshire   map 5

▲ Waterdine ⁵✻

Llanfair Waterdine LD7 1TU   COOKING 4
TEL: (01547) 528214   FAX: (01547) 529992   MODERN BRITISH
                                                          £28–£52

The village of Llanfair Waterdine may well sound at home in Wales, but this is Shropshire, with the principality just the other side of the River Teme. At this sixteenth-century inn near the church, the warren of tiny linked rooms – 'simple but comfortable, cosy and soothing', decorated with china cats, teapots, homely posies of flowers and watercolours for sale on the walls – is the setting for food that stretches well beyond the usual pub standard. The place can still be used as an inn (note the draught ales), but the dining room deals in modern cooking with its feet on the ground: say, artichoke risotto with paprika-roast tomatoes, or seared diver-caught scallops on tomato sauce with dressed leaves, then free-range chicken with spring vegetables and tarragon, or fillet of John Dory with tomato and basil sauce. Cheese consists of a wide choice of English and Welsh varieties, all in 'tasty condition'. Alternatively, go for rhubarb and ginger brûlée. Ken Adams is 'as well intentioned as ever', making his own bread and nibbles and buying meat from butchers accredited by the Rare Breeds Survival Trust. The wine list is a model of playing it straight, delivering a sound international selection at sensible prices, although with little to wow aficionados.

CHEFS: Ken Adams and James Kinghorn   PROPRIETOR: Ken Adams   OPEN: Tue to Sun L 12.15 to 1.45, Tue to Sat D 7.15 to 9   CLOSED: 1 week spring, 2 weeks autumn   MEALS: alc exc Sat D, Sun L (main courses £8.50 to £16.50). Set L Sun £18, Set D Sat £28   SERVICE: not inc, card slips closed   CARDS: MasterCard, Switch, Visa   DETAILS: 26 seats. Private parties: 16 main room. Car park. Vegetarian meals. No children under 8 at D. No smoking. No music   ACCOMMODATION: 3 rooms, all with bath/shower. TV. B&B £55 to £90. No children under 12

LONG CRENDON Buckinghamshire   map 2

▲ Angel Restaurant ♥ ⁵✻

47 Bicester Road, Long Crendon HP18 9EE   COOKING 1
TEL: (01844) 208268   FAX: (01844) 202497   MODERN BRITISH
                                                          £33–£60

Originally a village pub, this centuries-old listed building now functions as 'restaurant' rather than 'inn', with much of the space taken up by several distinctive dining areas and a conservatory. A specials board over the bar puts fish high on the agenda: gravlax is home cured, roast codling fillet is paired with sunblush tomato and olive fettucine, while Canadian perch comes on chargrilled vegetables in a Thai green curry sauce. The printed carte promises more in the way of meat and vegetarian options, such as fillet of Highland beef with cracked black pepper, confit of root vegetables and oxtail gravy, or vegetable sesame tempura with spring onion and ginger noodles, while desserts have included golden syrup and ginger pudding. The rather smart wine list deals mainly in French classics and good bottles from the New World, and it's not cheap. Just a handful of house wines come by the glass at £3.55 (£14.25 a bottle), but there is a decent range of half-bottles.

CHEFS: Trevor Bosch and Donny Joyce   PROPRIETORS: Trevor and Annie Bosch   OPEN: all week L 12 to 2.30, Mon to Sat D 7 to 9.30   MEALS: alc (main courses £14 to £22.50). Set L £16.95 (2 courses) to £19.95   SERVICE: not inc   CARDS: Amex, Delta, MasterCard, Switch, Visa   DETAILS: 75 seats. 20 seats outside. Private parties: 20 main room. Car park. Vegetarian meals. Children's helpings. No smoking in 1 dining room. Music. Air-conditioned   ACCOMMODATION: 3 rooms, all with bath/shower. TV. Phone. B&B £65 to £75. Baby facilities (£5)

LONG MELFORD Suffolk   map 6

Scutchers ⅚✳

Westgate Street, Long Melford CO10 9DP   COOKING 2
TEL: (01787) 310200   FAX: (01787) 375700   MODERN BRITISH
WEBSITE: www.scutchers.com   £32–£61

You can't miss this bright, lively restaurant's bold yellow exterior and red sign on the street outside. Inside, the open-plan, multi-level space has panelling, old beams, simple pine furniture and lots of prints of flowers on yellow walls. Nicholas Barrett's cooking follows suit, playing to the gallery with a lengthy modern bistro repertoire that includes some standards, like a rich thermidor sauce to partner a crayfish omelette starter, or bread-and-butter pudding served with apricot coulis and vanilla cream, and profiteroles with hot chocolate sauce. In between might be roast loin fillet of new season's English lamb with mint sauce and roast potatoes, or lobster casseroled with tomatoes, shallots and basil in white wine. Main courses come with green vegetables of the day, described as 'good to excellent' and 'very fresh'. Service is 'on the ball yet easy-going', while the wine list, grouped by grape variety, offers a good range by the glass (from £2.50) and half-bottle. The house selection starts at £12.50.

CHEFS: Nicholas Barrett and Guy Alabaster   PROPRIETORS: Nicholas and Diane Barrett   OPEN: Tue to Sat 12 to 2, 7 to 9.30   CLOSED: 24 to 26 Dec, 2 weeks Mar, 2 weeks Aug, bank hols   MEALS: alc (main courses £11 to £20)   SERVICE: not inc   CARDS: Amex, Delta, MasterCard, Switch, Visa   DETAILS: 70 seats. Private parties: 70 main room. Car park. Vegetarian meals. Children's helpings. No smoking. Wheelchair access (also WC). No music. Air-conditioned (£5)

LONGRIDGE Lancashire   map 8

Longridge Restaurant ⅚✳

104–106 Higher Road, Longridge PR3 3SY   COOKING 6
TEL: (01772) 784969   FAX: (01772) 785713   MODERN BRITISH
WEBSITE: www.heathcotes.co.uk   £28–£64

Paul Heathcote's cottage restaurant feels more at ease with itself in its lighter, brighter post-makeover version. The light colour scheme, high-backed chairs, and linen-covered tables create a smart and comfortable environment, but the service is 'breezily informal' and friendly. The food, rooted in Lancashire tradition, is technically accomplished, attractive and consistent, and often achieves excellence. Moreover, the price range for menu items is wide, so customers can tailor meals to their wallets.

A June starter could be asparagus propped against a drop scone bearing a quenelle of fried wild mushrooms and half an oeuf mollet, and goats' cheese may come as a croquette with deep-fried walnuts and endive salad. Main courses range from the comfortingly luxurious – roast loin of venison with caramelised beetroot tart and buttered potato – to the intriguing fried sole, sage and onion mashed potato, with creamed cauliflower and turkey juice. An impeccably fresh baked and breaded turbot surrounded by vegetables in a rich but clear-flavoured tomato butter sauce made 'a lovely dish: the very essence of spring flavours'. A sense of fun surfaces in a tongue-in-cheek trio of green-tea pannacotta, Eccles cake mille-feuille and digestive biscuit ice cream. (If that sounds too offbeat, there's likely to be an excellent, wobbly bread-and-butter pudding.) The wine list contains 'a really good choice of interesting wines from all over the world below £30' along with pricier options, and the Pinot Noir varietal section is particularly strong. House wines start at £13 (the set dinner includes half a bottle).

CHEFS: Paul Heathcote and Leigh Myers   PROPRIETOR: Paul Heathcote   OPEN: Tue to Fri L 12 to 2.30, Tue to Sat D 6 (5 Sat) to 10, Sun 12 to 9   CLOSED: 1 Jan   MEALS: alc (main courses £12 to £23.50). Set L £14 (2 courses) to £17, Set D Tue to Fri (Sat 5 to 6.30) £25   SERVICE: 10% (optional), card slips closed   CARDS: Amex, Delta, Diners, MasterCard, Switch, Visa   DETAILS: 70 seats. Private parties: 70 main room, 10 to 18 private rooms. Car park. Vegetarian meals. Children's helpings. No smoking in 1 dining room. Wheelchair access (not WC). Music (£5)

Thyme

1–3 Inglewhite Road, Longridge PR3 3JR   COOKING 3
TEL/FAX: (01772) 786888   MODERN EUROPEAN
                                                            £17–£45

Thyme is contemporary in attitude and operation, although it is perfectly possible to eat prawn cocktail and steak and chips, albeit in the form of a tian of prawns and crabmeat with crisp leaves and melba toast, and pan-fried ribeye with thick-cut chips and creamed peppercorn sauce. Alex Coward roams widely in his regularly changing menus, teaming Italian suckling pig with black pudding mash and red wine jus, and offering slow-braised kleftiko shoulder of lamb with oregano, rosemary, garlic and chickpeas. Occasionally, high-class comfort food makes an appearance, as in a starter of eggs Benedict with Parma ham and lightly minted hollandaise. Puddings are generally variations on a traditional theme: apricot bread-and-butter pudding with custard and vanilla ice, and Bramley apple and raspberry tart with almond crumble and sauce anglaise. A short wine list with a fair worldwide range opens with house white at £10.75 and red at £10.50. There is a second Thyme at the Sirloin Inn, Station Road, Hoghton; tel: (01254) 852293.

CHEF: Alex Coward   PROPRIETORS: Alex Coward and Wayne Keough   OPEN: Tue to Sat 12 to 2.30, 6 to 9.30, Sun 1 to 8   CLOSED: 26 Dec, 2 to 9 Jan   MEALS: alc (main courses £12 to £16). Set L £6.95 (2 courses) to £8.95, Set D 6 to 7.30 £7.95 (2 courses) to £9.95   SERVICE: not inc   CARDS: Amex, MasterCard, Switch, Visa   DETAILS: 45 seats. Private parties: 50 main room. Vegetarian meals. Children's helpings. Wheelchair access (also WC). Music. No mobile phones

LOOE Cornwall   **map 1**

▲ Talland Bay Hotel ⅝✕   **NEW ENTRY**

Porthallow, Looe PL13 2JB   COOKING 5
TEL: (01503) 272667   FAX: (01503) 272940   MODERN EUROPEAN
WEBSITE: www.tallandbayhotel.co.uk   £47–£56

The house is a 1930s gentleman's residence comfortably furnished in traditional country house style – 'chintz and fresh flowers everywhere' – and with wide picture windows

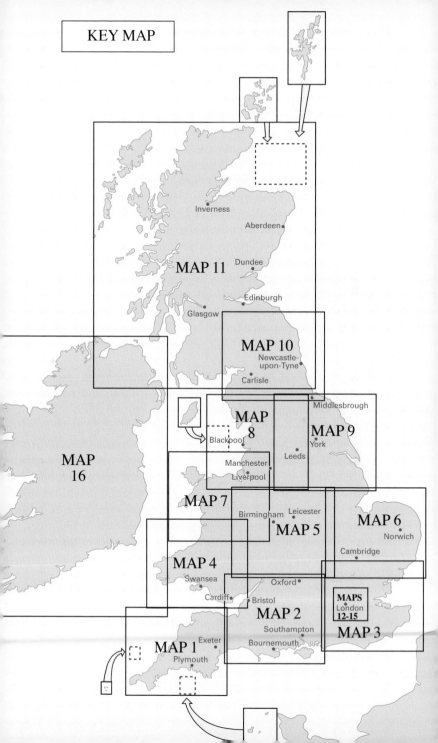

KEY MAP

MAP 11

MAP 10

MAP 16

MAP 8

MAP 9

MAP 7

MAP 5

MAP 6

MAP 4

MAP 2

MAPS 12-15

MAP 3

MAP 1

Inverness

Aberdeen

Dundee

Edinburgh

Glasgow

Newcastle-upon-Tyne

Carlisle

Middlesbrough

Blackpool

York

Manchester

Leeds

Liverpool

Birmingham

Leicester

Norwich

Cambridge

Swansea

Oxford

Cardiff

Bristol

London

Southampton

Bournemouth

Exeter

Plymouth

MAP 1

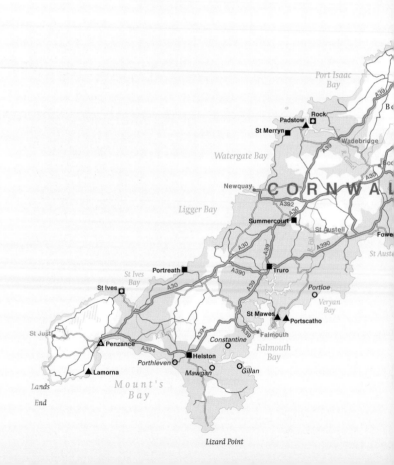

Lundy Isla

Isles of Scilly
28 miles WSW of Land's End

New
Grimsby
St Martin's ▲
○ *Tresco*
Hugh Town

B u
B

Port Isaac
Bay

Padstow ▲   Rock □
St Merryn ■
Wadebridge
B

Watergate Bay

Newquay   C O R N W A L

Ligger Bay

A392

Summercourt ■   St Austell   Fowe

St Auste

Portreath ■   Truro ■

St Ives
Bay
St Ives □

Portloe ○
Veryan
Bay

St Mawes ▲ ▲ Portscatho

St Just

Penzance △   Constantine ○   Falmouth

A394   Helston ■   Falmouth
Bay

Lamorna ▲   Porthleven ○   Mawgan ○   Gillan ○

Lands   M o u n t ' s
End   B a y

Lizard Point

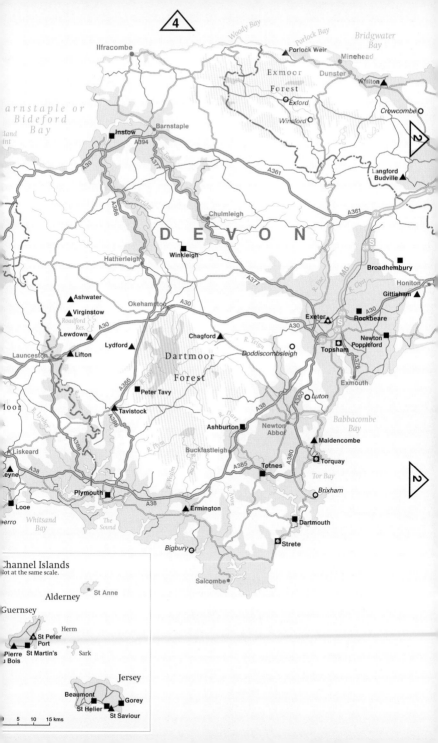

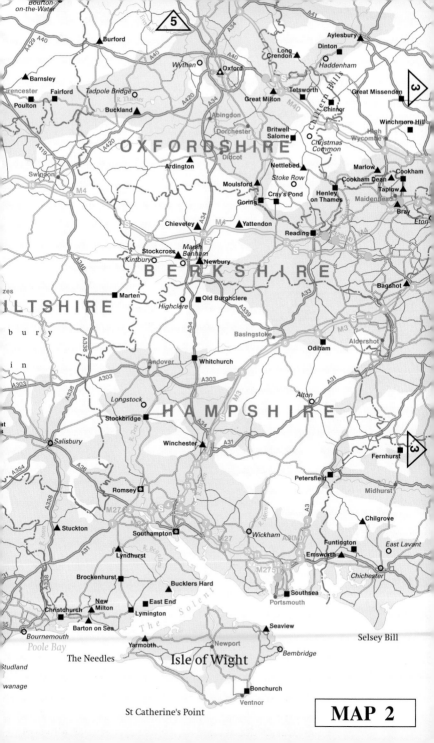

MAP 2

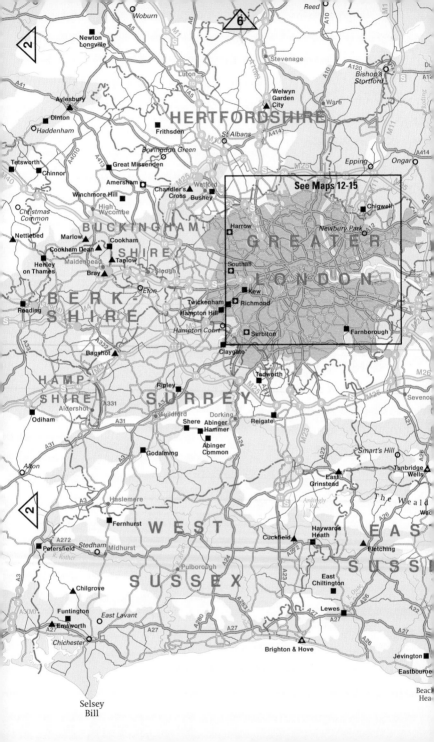

MAP 3

- ■ Restaurant
- ▲ Restaurant with accommodation
- ○ Round-up entry
- □ Combined main and
- △ round-up entries

| 0 | 5 | 10 miles |
| 0 | | 15 kms |

© Copyright

MAP 4

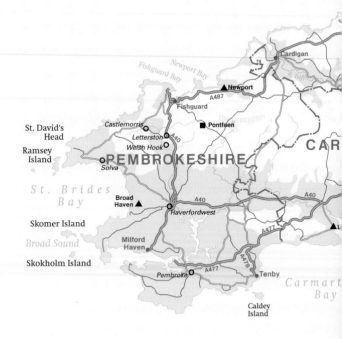

- ■ Restaurant
- ▲ Restaurant with accommodation
- ○ *Round-up entry*
- □ Combined main and
- △ round-up entries

| 0 | 5 | 10 miles |
| 0 | | 15 kms |

© Copyright

CARDIGAN

BAY

Cardigan

Newport Bay

Fishguard Bay

▲ Newport

A487

Fishguard

■ Pontfaen

St. David's
Head

Castlemorris ○

Letterston ○
A40
Welsh Hook ○

Ramsey
Island

○ **PEMBROKESHIRE**

Solva ○

CAR

*St. Brides
Bay*

**Broad
Haven** ▲

A40

Skomer Island

Haverfordwest ○

A40

A477

Broad Sound

Milford
Haven ●

A40

▲ L

Skokholm Island

A478

Pembroke ○

A477

Tenby ■

*Carmart
Bay*

Caldey
Island

BRIST

MAP 5

Legend:
- ■ Restaurant
- ▲ Restaurant with accommodation
- ○ *Round-up entry*
- □ Combined main and round-up entries
- △

0 — 5 — 10 miles
0 — 15 kms
© Copyright

Regions/Counties:
WREXHAM
STAFFORD-SHIRE
SHROPSHIRE
POWYS
WORCESTER-SHIRE
HEREFORD-SHIRE
GLOUCESTER-SHIRE
MONMOUTHSHIRE
WEST MIDLANDS

Places:
Lee
Worleston
Broxton
Crewe
Nantwich
Newcastle Under Lyme
Wrexham
Whitchurch
Stone
Stafford
Llanarmon Dyffryn Ceiriog
Oswestry
Llanfyllin
Telford
Wolverhampton
Dorrington
Norton
Church Stretton
Newtown
Holy Cross
Llanfair Waterdine
Bromfield
Ludlow
Kidderminster
Chaddesley Corbett
Bromsgrove
Presteigne
Brimfield
Dunhampton
Stoke Prior
Titley
Leominster
Ombersley
Kington
Knightwick
Worcester
Hay-on-Wye
Ullingswick
Malvern Wells
Evesham
Colwall Stone
Felinfach
Hereford
Corse Lawn
Winchcombe
Sellack
Crickhowell
Skenrith
Glewstone
Ross-on-Wye
Clifford's Mesne
Cheltenham
Gloucester
Shurdington
Llandewi Skirrid
Abergavenny
Monmouth
Arlingham
Painswick
Nantyderry
Clytha
Whitebrook

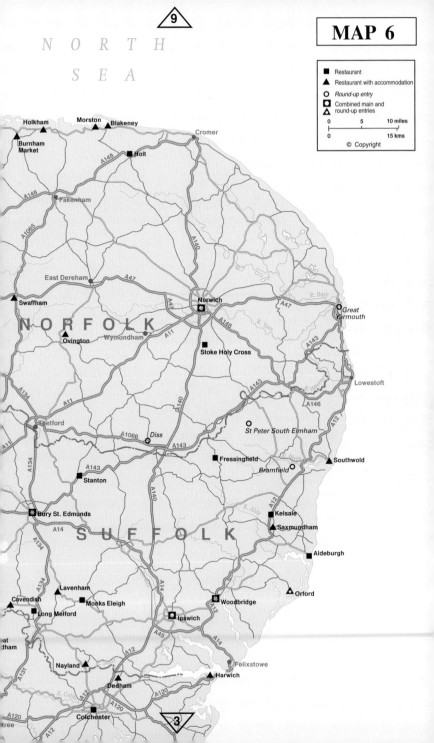

MAP 6

- ■ Restaurant
- ▲ Restaurant with accommodation
- ○ Round-up entry
- ◻ Combined main and
- △ round-up entries

| 0 | 5 | 10 miles |
| 0 | 15 kms | |

© Copyright

9

NORTH SEA

Holkham
Morston
Blakeney
Cromer
Burnham Market
Holt
A148
Fakenham
A148
A1065
East Dereham
A47
Swaffham
NORFOLK
Ovington
Wymondham
Norwich
Great Yarmouth
R. Bure
A140
A146
Stoke Holy Cross
A143
R. Yare
A134
A11
A47
Lowestoft
A143
A146
Thetford
A1066
Diss
St Peter South Elmham
A12
A143
Fressingfield
Southwold
A134
Stanton
Bramfield
A140
A11
Bury St. Edmunds
A14
SUFFOLK
Kelsale
Saxmundham
R. Alde
A12
A134
Lavenham
Aldeburgh
Cavendish
Monks Eleigh
A14
Orford
Long Melford
Woodbridge
A12
Ipswich
A131
A12
A45
A14
Nayland
Felixstowe
Dedham
Harwich
A120
Colchester
A120
A120
tree
R. Colne
3

MAP 7

- ■ Restaurant
- ▲ Restaurant with accommodation
- ○ *Round-up entry*
- □ Combined main and
- △ round-up entries

| 0 | 5 | 10 miles |
| 0 | | 15 kms |

© Copyright

IRISH

SEA

Holyhead Bay

Holyhead

Llyn Alaw

Red Wharf Bay

ISLE OF ANGLESEY

Holy Island

A55

▲ **Beaumaris**

Bangor

Anglesey

Foel Fras 942

Main Strait

A487

Caernarfon

Llanberis ■

Glyder Faw 999

Caer

Carne Moel-so

1085 Snowdon

Caernarfon

Bay

GWYNEDD

A487

Lleyn Peninsula

Portmeirion ▲ ▲ **Talsarnau**

Pwllheli ▲

Tremadog Bay

▲ **Harlech**

▲ **Abersoch**

Bardsey Sound

Penmaenpo

Bardsey Island

Barmouth ●

Cader Id

CARDIGAN

BAY

Mach

Aberdovey ▲

Aberystwyth

CEREDI

A487

▽ 4

MAP 8

- ■ Restaurant
- ▲ Restaurant with accommodation
- ○ Round-up entry
- □ Combined main and
- △ round-up entries

0	5	10 miles
0	15 kms	

© Copyright

△ 10

CUMBRI

Scafell Pike
977

▲ Grasmere

Wast Water

△ Ambleside

▲ Winderm

Windermere

Hawkshead

R. Esk

Bowness
Windere

▲ Near Sawrey

Crosthwaite ▲

R. Duddon

A5092

A595

A590

A595

A591

A592

Ulverston ▲

Cartmel ▲

Barrow-in-
Furness
Isle
of
Walney

Morecambe

Heysham

*Morecambe
Bay*

Forton ■

Fleetwood

Point of Ayre

Poulton-
le-Fylde ▲

R. Wyre

Ramsey Bay

Ramsey

Kirk Michael

Blackpool ■

Kirkham

Isle of

M55

Laxey Bay

Lytham St Anne's ▲

A583

Man

● Douglas

Glenmaye

A565

Port Erin

Southport □

Port St Mary

Calf of Man

A570

A59

Ormskirk

Skelmersdale

M58

MERSEYSIDE

Wallasey

Liverpool △

Oxton □ ● Birkenhead

7

*Conwy
Bay*

*Colwyn
Bay*

Llandudno ▲
○ *Glanwydden*
■ Colwyn Bay
Prestatyn

Rhyl

R. Merse

Beaumaris ●

A55

▲ Llansanffraid
Glan Conwy

A55

CONWY

Denbigh

7 FLINTSHIRE

Hawarden ●

Chester

A470

Foel Fras

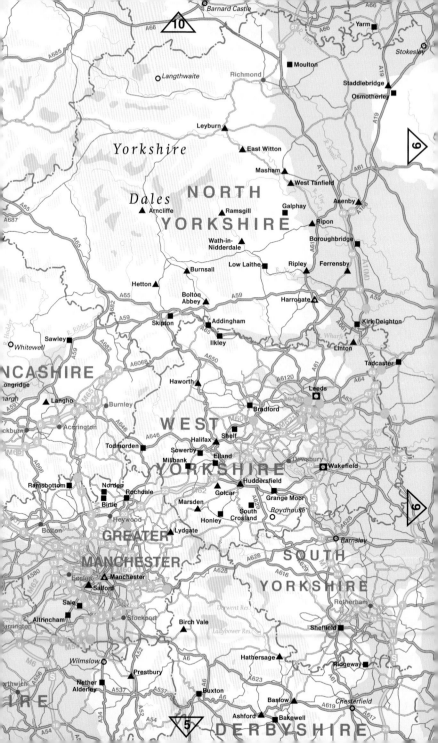

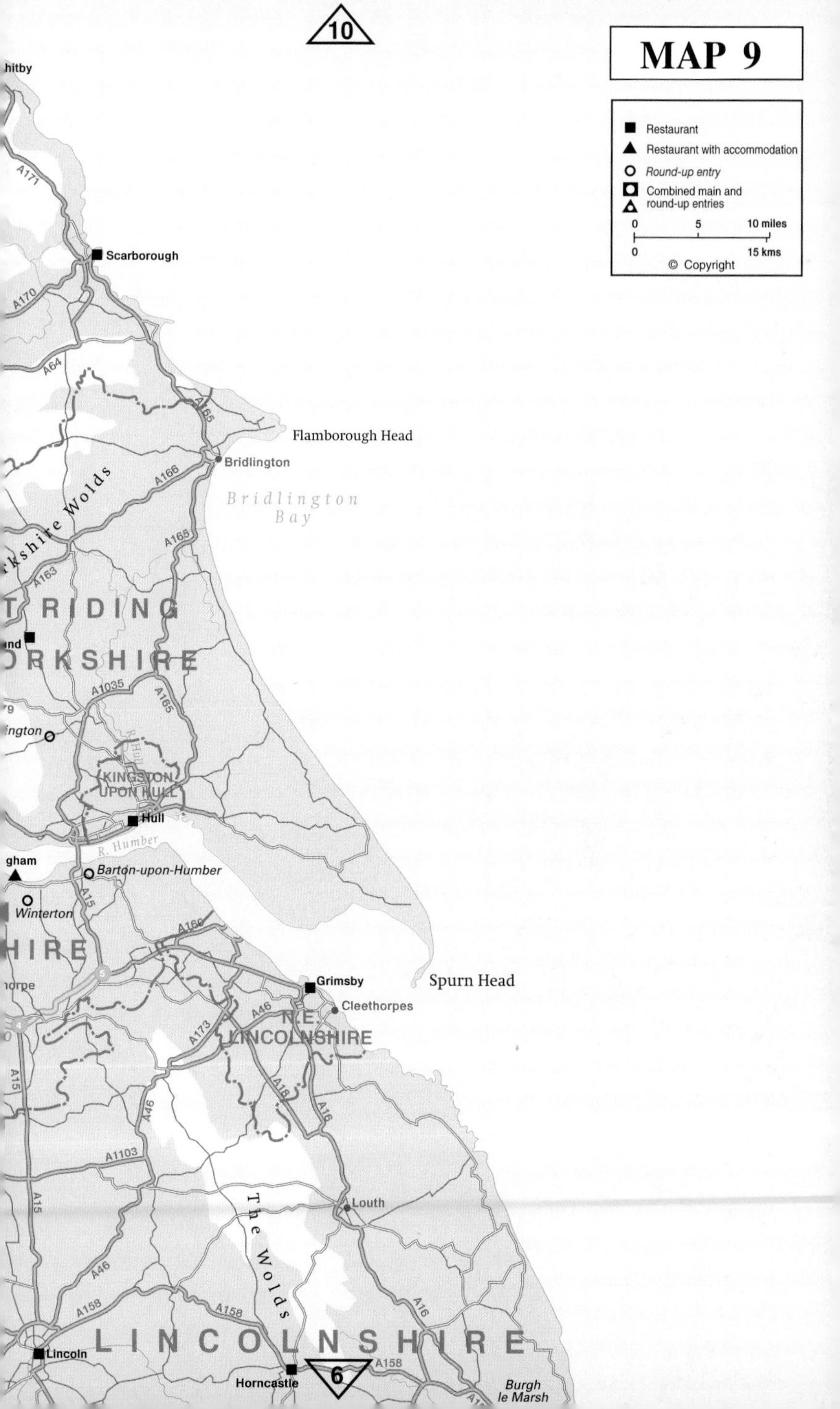

MAP 9

■ Restaurant
▲ Restaurant with accommodation
○ Round-up entry
□ Combined main and
△ round-up entries

| 0 | 5 | 10 miles |
| 0 | | 15 kms |

© Copyright

hitby

■ Scarborough

A171

A170

A64

Flamborough Head

○ Bridlington

Bridlington Bay

orkshire Wolds

A166

A163

A165

T RIDING

and ■

ORKSHIRE

A1035

A165

rg

ington ○

KINGSTON
UPON HULL

■ Hull

R. Humber

gham ▲

○ Barton-upon-Humber

A15

○ Winterton

A160

HIRE

■orpe

Grimsby ■

Spurn Head

Cleethorpes ○

A173   A46   N.E.
LINCOLNSHIRE

A18

A16

A15

A1103

A46

The Wolds

Louth ◆

A158

A46

A16

LINCOLNSHIRE

■ Lincoln

A158

A158

Horncastle

Burgh le Marsh

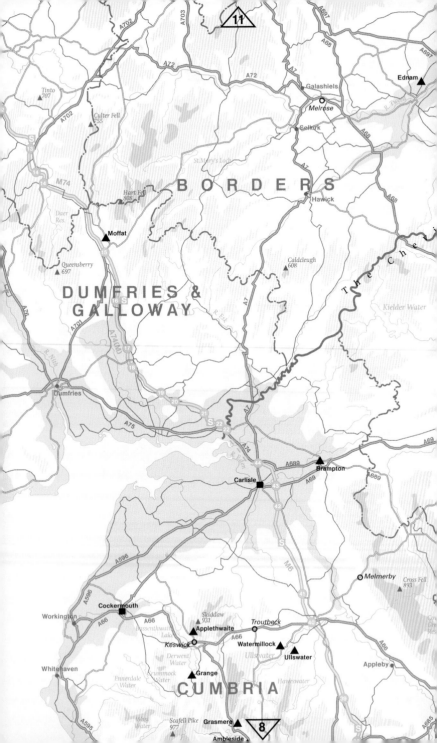

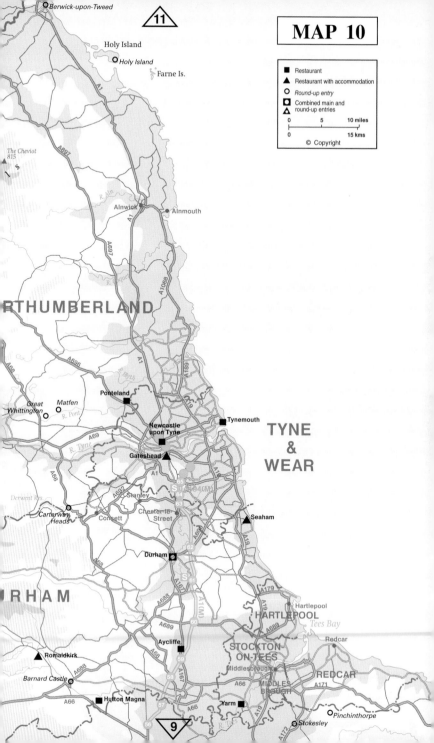

MAP 10

■ Restaurant
▲ Restaurant with accommodation
○ Round-up entry
▣ Combined main and round-up entries
△

| 0 | 5 | 10 miles |
| 0 | | 15 kms |

© Copyright

11

Berwick-upon-Tweed

Holy Island

Holy Island

Farne Is.

The Cheviot
815

A697

A1

Alnwick

Alnmouth

A697

A1068

R. Coquet

A1

RTHUMBERLAND

A696

R. Aln

Blyth

A189

A1

Great Whittington

Matfen

Ponteland

R. Pont

Newcastle upon Tyne

Tynemouth

A69

R. Tyne

Gateshead

A1

TYNE
&
WEAR

A68

Derwent Res.

A692

A1(M)

Stanley

Carterway Heads

Consett

Chester-le-Street

Seaham

A68

Durham

A19

A167

A179

URHAM

A688

A1(M)

Hartlepool

HARTLEPOOL

Tees Bay

A19

A689

A66

Aycliffe

STOCKTON-ON-TEES

Redcar

A68

A167

Middlesbrough

REDCAR

Romaldkirk

A688

MIDDLES
BROUGH

A171

Barnard Castle

A66

Hutton Magna

A167

Yarm

A19

A66

A172

Pinchinthorpe

Stokesley

9

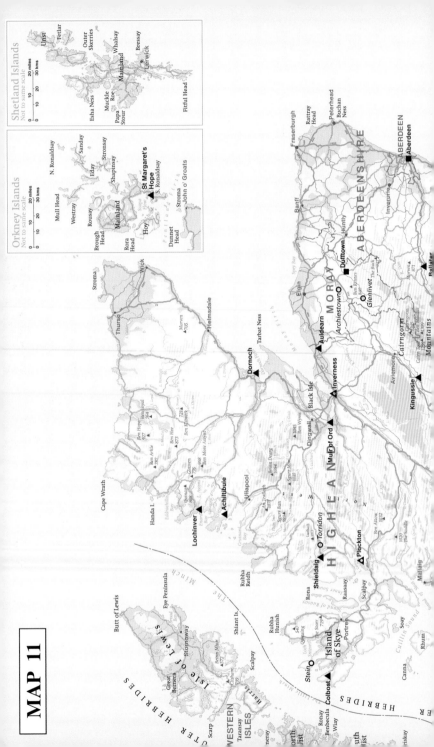

MAP 11

Shetland Islands
Not to same scale

0   10   20   20 miles
0   10   20   30 kms

Unst
Fetlar
Outer
Skerries
Whalsay
Bressay
Lerwick
Mainland
Esha Ness
Muckle
Roe
Papa
Stour
Fitful Head

Orkney Islands
Not to same scale

0   10   20   20 miles
0   10   20   30 kms

N. Ronaldsay
Westray
Sanday
Eday
Stronsay
Shapinsay
Brough
Head
Rousay
Mull Head
Mainland
Rora
Head
Hoy
St Margaret's
Hope
S. Ronaldsay
Pentland Firth
Stroma
John o' Groats
Dunnet Head

WESTERN
ISLES
OUTER HEBRIDES

Butt of Lewis
Eye Peninsula
Stornoway
Great
Bernera
ISLE OF LEWIS
Scalpay
Taransay
HARRIS
Scarp
Shiant Is.

The Minch

Stroma
Wick

Cape Wrath
Handa I.
Ben Hope
927
Ben Loyal
764
Ben Klibreck
873
Ben More
723
Eddrachillis
Bay
Lochinver
Quinag
808
Achiltibuie
Suilven
731
Glasven
776
Ben More Assynt
998
Ullapool

Thurso
Morven
705
Helmsdale
Dornoch
Tarbat Ness

HIGHLAND

Black Isle
Inverness
Dingwall
Ben Wyvis
1046
Muir of Ord

Elgin
MORAY
Auldearn
Archiestown
Dufftown
Ben Rinnes
840
Glenlivet
The Buck
Spey

Fraserburgh
Rattray
Head
Peterhead
Buchan
Ness

Banff
Huntly
ABERDEENSHIRE
Inverurie
ABERDEEN
Aberdeen

Aviemore
Cairngorm
Cairngorm
Mountains
Cairn Toul
1291
Ben Macdui
1309
Kingussie
Braeriach
1296

Morven
871
Ballater

Torridon
Shieldaig
Plockton
Ben Alligin
985
Beinn Eighe
1010
Sgurr Mòr
1110
An Teallach
1062
Sgurr Alasdair
1032

Rona
Raasay
Rubha
Hunish
The Storr
719
Portree
Island
of Skye
Scalpay
Soay
Cuillin Hills

Stein
Colbost
Loch Dunvegan
547

Rubha
Reidh
Gruinard
Bay
Loch Maree
Loch Broom

Mallaig
Kyle of Lochalsh
Loch Alsh
1020
The Saddle
Ben Aslow
1022

Canna
Rhum

North
Uist
Benbecula
South
Uist
Ronay
Wiay
Eriskay

The Minch
Sound of Raasay
Inner Sound

HEBRIDES

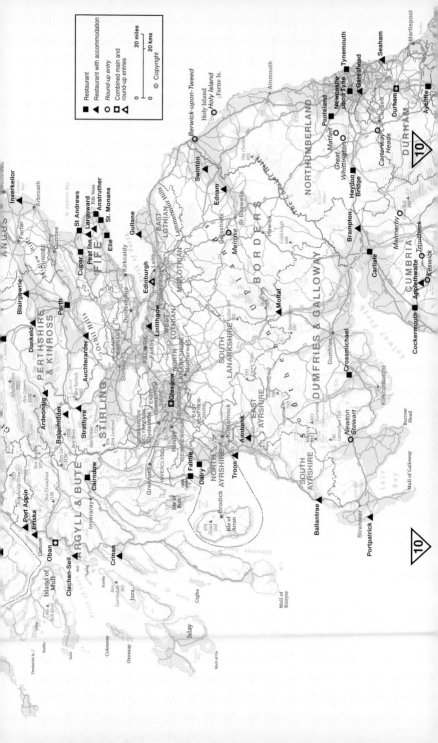

CHIGWELL

EDMONTON

Woodford

A112

A1010

A112

Hainault

A123

A1112

REDBRIDGE

A12

Mosaica

A503

Walthamstow

WALTHAM
FOREST

A104

A10

ILFORD

A124

Rasa Travancore

Istanbul Iskembecisi

A11

A118

A406

BARKING &
DAGENHAM

A123

Barking

A13

HACKNEY

Little
Georgia

Armadillo

NEWHAM

A102(M)

Thai Garden

A114

East Ham

HACKNEY

A11

New
Tayyabs

TOWER
HAMLETS

A13

A13

Poplar

Wapping Food

Royal China

Plateau

Ubon

Memsaheb

SOUTHWARK

A2

R. Thames

Thamesmead

Woolwich

A206

A205

A209

A202

A102(M)

Greenwich

Inside

A2

Chapter Two

GREENWICH

Loco

Lewisham

A20

A2

A210

LAMBETH

Franklins

The Green

Le Chardon

Babur Brasserie

A205

Eltham

Dulwich

Catford

A20

A205

A222

LEWISHAM

A2212

A211

Sidcup

Crystal Palace

A208

A205

BROMLEY

MAP 12

Beckenham

■ Restaurant

▲ Restaurant with accommodation

○ Round-up entry

0   5km

0   4 miles

A21

A208

A224

BROMLEY

© Copyright

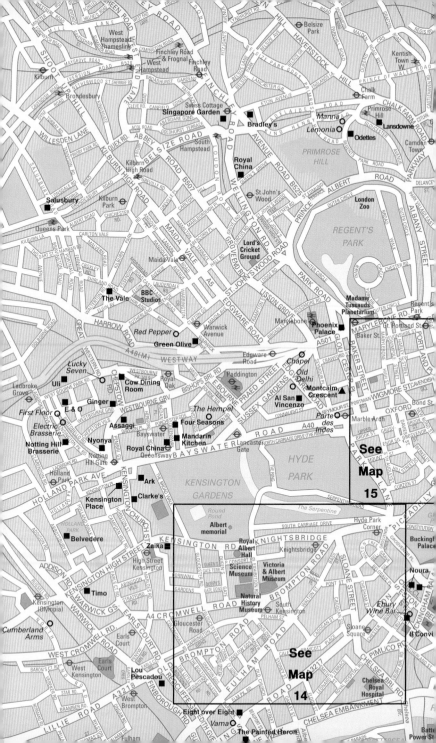

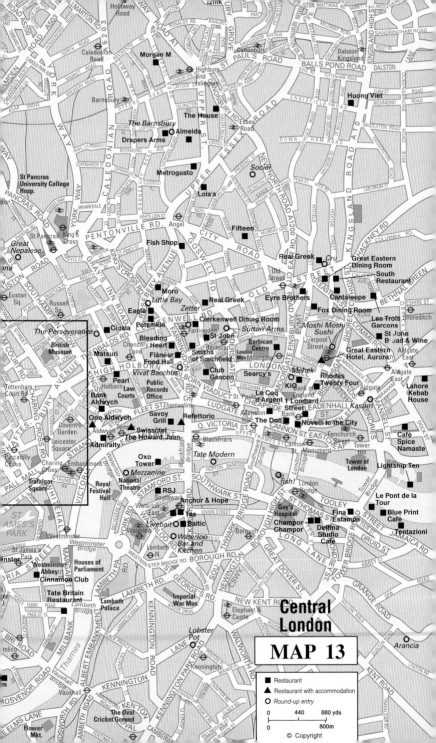

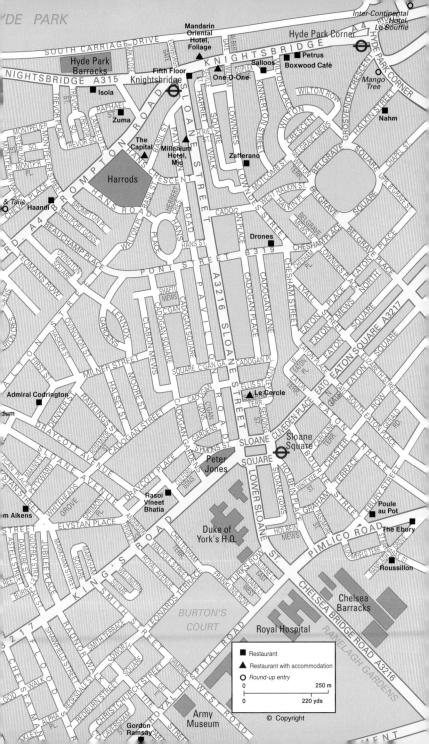

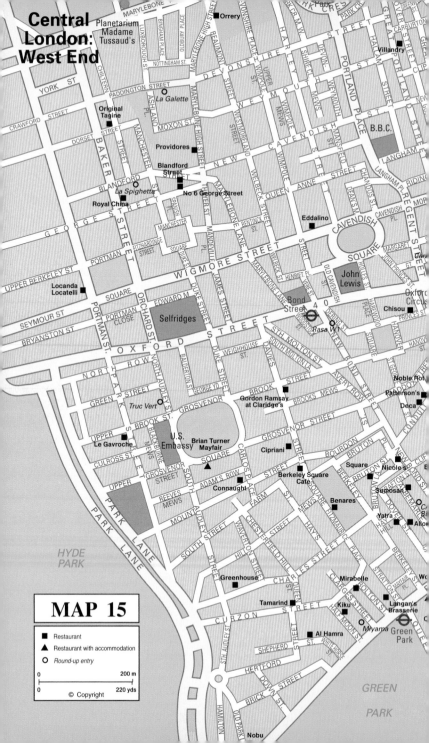

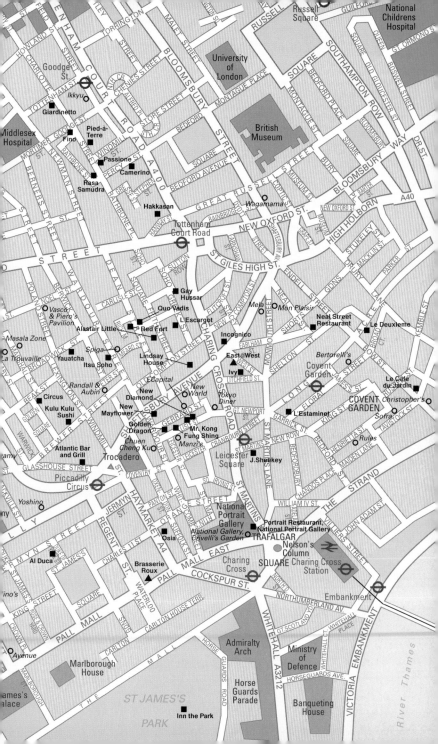

MAP 16

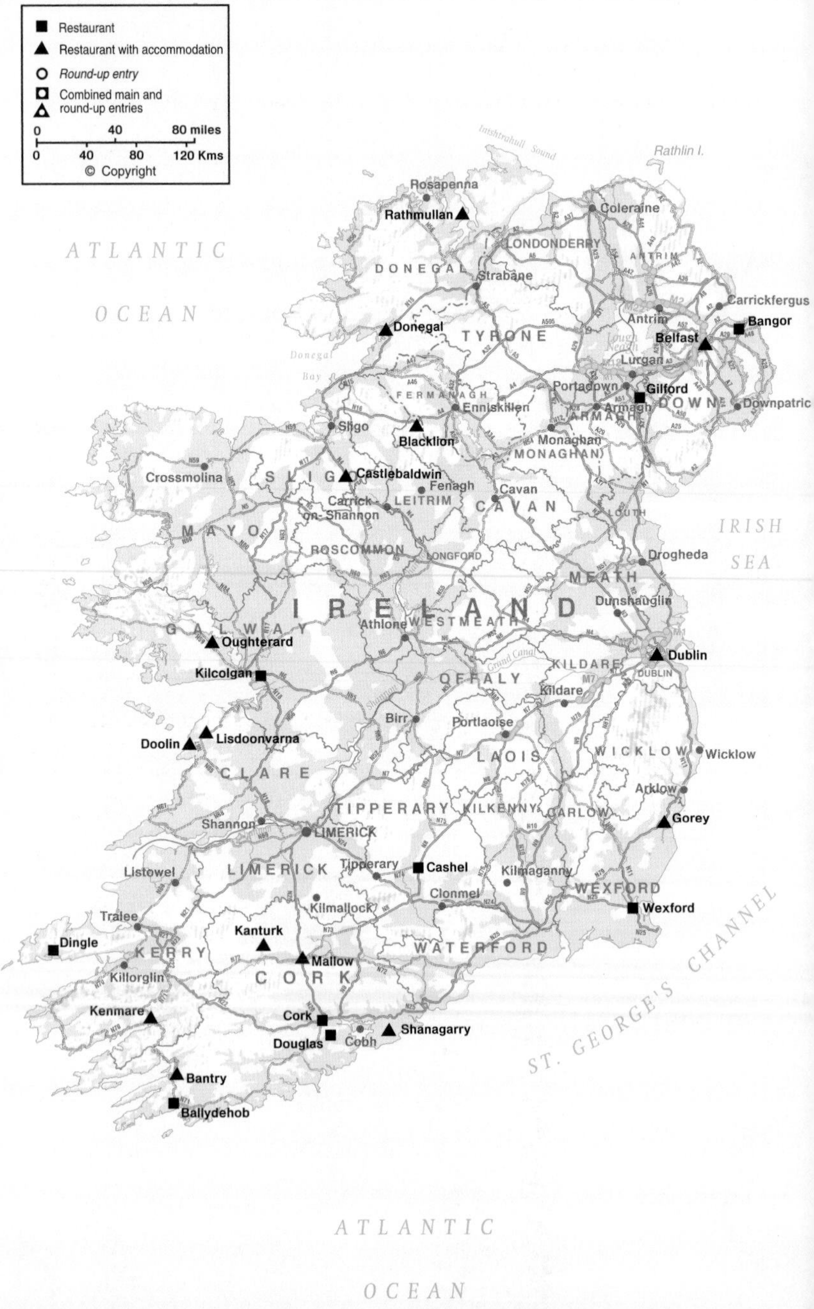

Legend:
- ■ Restaurant
- ▲ Restaurant with accommodation
- ○ Round-up entry
- ▣ Combined main and
- △ round-up entries

0   40   80 miles
0   40   80   120 Kms
© Copyright

ATLANTIC
OCEAN

Rathlin I.

Rosapenna
Rathmullan ▲
DONEGAL
Strabane
LONDONDERRY
Coleraine
ANTRIM
Carrickfergus
Antrim
Bangor ▲
Belfast ▲
Donegal ▲
TYRONE
Lurgan
Portadown ●
Gilford ▲
Donegal Bay
FERMANAGH
Enniskillen
Armagh
DOWN
Downpatric
Crossmolina
Sligo ●
Blacklion ▲
Monaghan
MONAGHAN
Castlebaldwin ▲
Fenagh
Cavan
SLIGO
Carrick-on-Shannon
LEITRIM
CAVAN
MAYO
ROSCOMMON
LONGFORD
Drogheda
IRISH SEA
IRELAND
Athlone
WESTMEATH
MEATH
Dunshaughlin
GALWAY
Oughterard ▲
Kilcolgan ■
OFFALY
KILDARE
Dublin ▲
DUBLIN
Kildare
Doolin ▲
Lisdoonvarna ▲
Birr
Portlaoise
LAOIS
WICKLOW
Wicklow ●
CLARE
Shannon ●
LIMERICK
TIPPERARY
KILKENNY
CARLOW
Arklow ●
Gorey ▲
Listowel
Tipperary
Cashel ■
Clonmel
Kilmaganny
WEXFORD
Tralee
Kilmallock
Wexford ■
Dingle ■
Kanturk ▲
WATERFORD
Killorglin
Mallow ▲
KERRY
CORK
Kenmare ▲
Cork ▣
Shanagarry ▲
Douglas
Cobh ●
Bantry ▲
Ballydehob ■

ST. GEORGE'S CHANNEL

ATLANTIC
OCEAN

taking in the 'breathtaking views' of Talland Bay. It is well looked after and feels welcoming; there's a conservatory for aperitifs and nibbles, and crisp white linen in the dining room. A new chef arrived in late 2003, and this is a kitchen to watch. Shay Cooper has learned much from his time with John Campbell at the Vineyard at Stockcross (see entry), and he is delivering well-balanced and technically accomplished food.

This is cooking as modern as it comes: a subtle white onion velouté, for example, with pearl barley and a confit of chicken tortellini is declared a 'triumph', and there is 'meltingly tender' roast quail accompanied by poached green grapes tasting delicately but pungently of balsamic vinegar. Fine materials are intelligently handled, notably in a dish of Caradon lamb fillet, cooked pink, accompanied by grilled figs, just wilted chicory, baby artichokes and a perfectly judged chocolate jus. To finish, mascarpone sorbet, poached cherries and Muscat granita was 'every bit as delicious as it sounds', or there could be smooth, creamy, black-flecked vanilla pannacotta accompanied by red wine jelly and spiced poached pear. There are tip-top British cheeses too. Service is discreet and well trained. Wines are arranged by style, with representatives of most available by the glass, and include some affordable clarets. Prices start at £14.50.

CHEF: Shay Cooper   PROPRIETORS: George and Mary Granville   OPEN: all week 12.30 to 2, 7 to 9   MEALS: Set D £32.50; light L menu   SERVICE: not inc, card slips closed   CARDS: Delta, MasterCard, Switch, Visa   DETAILS: 45 seats. 25 seats outside. Private parties: 40 main room. Car park. No children under 8. No smoking. Occasional music. No mobile phones   ACCOMMODATION: 23 rooms, all with bath/shower. TV. Phone. B&B £70 to £180. Baby facilities. Swimming pool

---

Trawlers on the Quay 🌟

Bullers Quay, East Looe PL13 1AH	COOKING 3
TEL: (01503) 263593	SEAFOOD
WEBSITE: www.trawlersrestaurant.co.uk	£36–£53

NEW ENTRY

Right on the quay, with views of buzzing harbourside activity, the pale-blue fronted Trawlers is right in the heart of the action, and wears its Cornishness with pride (even the bottled water is from Bodmin). With the fish market steps away, a menu that emphasises seafood is probably no surprise, although there are a couple of meat dishes and some vegetarian specials as well. Expect steamed Fowey mussels, a classic gratin of scallops with a light-textured sauce, and perfectly sautéed John Dory and brill, plus deftly handled Cajun spicing complementing bass, cod and succulent monkfish. Velvety leek and potato soup with puffy ham beignets, clean flavours in lemon posset and utterly correct crème brûlée show that skills don't stop at fish, as do 'truly delicious' breads and rich coffee with chocolate truffles. A modest but interesting wine list starts at £13.50, with most bottles below £20, and there are local beers and cider.

CHEF: Todd Varnadoe   PROPRIETORS: Nick Love and Mark Napper   OPEN: Tue to Sat D only 6.15 to 9.30   CLOSED: 25 and 26 Dec   MEALS: alc (main courses £13.50 to £18.50)   SERVICE: not inc   CARDS: MasterCard, Switch, Visa   DETAILS: 32 seats. 12 seats outside. Private parties: 50 main room. Vegetarian meals. No children under 6. No smoking. Wheelchair access (not WC). Music £5

Water Rail 🌟

Lower Market Street, Looe PL13 1AX	COOKING 2
TEL: (01503) 262314 FAX: (01503) 264814	SEAFOOD
	£34–£69

Seafood gets top priority in this rough-hewn cottagey restaurant a short stroll from the river and the beach. Richard Maior-Barron buys virtually all his fish direct from Looe market, and he handles the haul with due care and attention. His lobster tank is worth consideration; otherwise the standard menu trawls its way through whitebait, prawn cocktail, and grilled fillets of lemon sole. Daily specials add variety in the shape of flash-fried butterfly king prawns with lemongrass, garlic and coriander, followed by grilled fillet of wild sea bass with anchovy butter, and the kitchen returns to dry land for French onion soup, rack of Cornish lamb, and tenderloin of pork with apricot sauce. Nursery puddings like spotted dick are the order of the day when it comes to desserts. The wine list kicks off with a couple of Romanians: Chardonnay and Pinot Noir at £12.50.

CHEF: Richard Maior-Barron   PROPRIETORS: Richard and Denise Maior-Barron   OPEN: Wed to Mon D only 7 to 10 (9 winter)   CLOSED: 25 Dec, Jan   MEALS: alc (main courses £15.50 to £32.50)   SERVICE: not inc, card slips closed   CARDS: Amex, Delta, MasterCard, Switch, Visa   DETAILS: 24 seats. Vegetarian meals. No children under 10. No smoking. Music. No mobile phones ⓔ⑤

LOWER HARDRES Kent
map 3

Granville £
NEW ENTRY

Street End, Lower Hardres CT4 7AL
TEL: (01227) 700402   FAX: (01227) 700925

COOKING 3
MODERN EUROPEAN
£28–£52

Under the same ownership as the Sportsman in Whitstable (see entry), this old pub on a main road a few miles south of Canterbury follows a similar formula. The simple, uncluttered décor features neutral-coloured natural floor coverings, plain dark wooden furniture, and pale walls lined with attractive monochrome animal-themed linocuts. Most of the space is given over to dining, but there is a small lounge area and a pleasant garden to the rear where barbecues are held in summer. Simple, traditional cooking with modern twists is what to expect on the food front, carefully and skilfully prepared using high-quality materials. A large, succulent confit duck leg, for example, is served with a heady smoked chilli salsa and sour cream along with a heap of crisp shredded cabbage, while a large shoulder of lamb comes with exquisitely smooth, creamy mash and an intensely flavoured jus. Portions are large, but it's worth saving room for desserts: try the elegantly presented selection platter of nine small portions, including a delectably smooth chocolate mousse, a zesty rhubarb sorbet, and a rich, creamy coffee parfait. The concise selection of wines is listed on a blackboard. Prices start at £9.95, and seven are served by the glass.

CHEFS: Jim Shave, Ezra Gaynor and Denise Holness   PROPRIETORS: Gabrielle, Stephen, Philip and Damian Harris   OPEN: Tue to Sun L 12 to 2, Tue to Sat D 7 to 9   CLOSED: bank hols exc Good Fri   MEALS: alc (main courses £10 to £20). Bar L menu available Tue to Fri   SERVICE: not inc, 10% for parties of 6 or more   CARDS: MasterCard, Switch, Visa   DETAILS: 60 seats. Private parties: 30 main room. Car park. No-smoking area. Wheelchair access (also WC). Music. Air-conditioned

LOWICK Northamptonshire
map 6

Snooty Fox ⁵⁄₄✳
NEW ENTRY

16 Main Street, Lowick NN14 3BH
TEL: (01832) 733434   FAX: (01832) 733931

COOKING 3
MODERN BRITISH
£26–£59

A large, many-chimneyed honey-stone building in a tranquil village is the setting for this unpretentious, deservedly popular pub/restaurant. Clive Dixon moved here from the

Pheasant, Keyston (see entry), and has put the Snooty Fox well and truly on the map in an area of peaceful villages and lots of lakes and nature reserves. A rôtisserie and grill hold centre stage, and customers choose what they want from the display counter: steaks from well-hung Aberdeen Angus beef are cut and sold by weight and served with fat chips; otherwise go for corn-fed baby chicken, leg of new season's lamb, or Dover sole. Starters are fresh offerings like grilled sardines on roast tomato and fennel salad, daily specials run to uncompromisingly rustic braised lambs' hearts with gnocchi and chorizo, while desserts could be as simple as home-made vanilla ice cream with a 'DIY' glass of Pedro Ximénez sherry. The wine list comprises around 40 bins organised by style, with house selections from £12.50.

CHEF: Robert Clive Dixon   PROPRIETORS: Robert Clive Dixon and David Hennigan   OPEN: Wed to Sun L 12 to 2, Tue to Sat D 6.30 to 9.30   CLOSED: D 25 Dec, D 26 Dec, D 1 Jan   MEALS: alc (main courses L £7 to £16.50, D £9.50 to £20). Bar menu available   SERVICE: not inc, 10% for parties of 10 or more   CARDS: Delta, Diners, MasterCard, Switch, Visa   DETAILS: 90 seats. 50 seats outside. Private parties: 50 main room, 10 to 50 private rooms. Car park. Vegetarian meals. Children's helpings. No smoking in 1 dining room. Music

LOW LAITHE North Yorkshire   map 8

Dusty Miller

Low Laithe, Summerbridge HG3 4BU   COOKING 5
TEL: (01423) 780837   FAX: (01423) 780065   ANGLO-FRENCH
on B6165, 2m SE of Pateley Bridge   £34–£61

For one pair of reporters, the green, sunlit views seen while driving up Nidderdale are part of the joy of a trip to the Dusty Miller on a summer's evening. This is a pleasure in itself, but there's more to come at the cosily proportioned, smartly attired roadside restaurant. Here Elizabeth Dennison runs front-of-house with practised ease, while Brian cooks in highly polished, unpretentious Anglo-French mode. A Whitby crab salad may feature as a starter, a pair of contrasting terrines might sit side by side, or there could be a plate of ringingly fresh Loch Fyne oysters. Meat main courses are especially well reported, with crisply roasted duckling served Normandy-fashion with apples and Calvados a particular star. A salad dressed with Roquefort makes an indelibly Gallic partner for a piece of beef fillet, while English samphire accompanies wild trout from the Esk. Seasonal fruits pour forth in the form of pies, tarts and summer pudding at dessert stage, alongside alternatives such as bread-and-butter pudding and chocolate mousse. Every bottle on the handwritten wine list has earned its place for both quality and value, starting with the Côtes de Thongue house wines, Sauvignon and Syrah, at £12.90.

CHEF: Brian Dennison   PROPRIETORS: Brian and Elizabeth Dennison   OPEN: Tue to Sat D 7 to 11   CLOSED: 24 to 26 Dec, 31 Dec, 1 Jan, 1 week May   MEALS: alc (main courses £20 to £20). Set D £24   SERVICE: not inc   CARDS: Amex, Delta, MasterCard, Switch, Visa   DETAILS: 28 seats. Private parties: 28 main room, 6 to 18 private rooms. Car park. Children's helpings. No children under 9. Wheelchair access (not WC). Music

Prices quoted in the Guide are based on information supplied by restaurateurs. The prices quoted at the top of each entry represent a range, from the lowest price of a three-course meal with service and wine to the highest; the latter is inflated by 20 per cent to take account of likely price rises during the year of the Guide.

▲ Dinham Hall ⁵⁶✳

Dinham, By The Castle, Ludlow SY8 1EJ   COOKING **4**
TEL: (01584) 876464   FAX: (01584) 876019   MODERN EUROPEAN
WEBSITE: www.dinhamhall.co.uk   £39–£70

Barely a stone's throw from the castle and market square, this small, handsome grey-stone hotel dates from 1792, and has a country-house atmosphere. Lounges are small and traditionally furnished, while the dining room has the original oak-boarded floor, formal floral print curtains, pale yellow walls, tables with stiff white cloths and lovely views. Sensibly compact, modern menus show plenty of ambition, using fresh, top-quality produce. Expect Mediterranean influences in starters like roast quail on truffle and asparagus risotto, or perhaps red onion Tatin with goats' cheese and rocket salad. Among main courses, roast loin of rabbit might be wrapped in pancetta, stuffed with veal sweetbreads, and served with a port jus, while wild sea bass has come with saffron and vermouth sauce. A classic caramelised lemon tart with blackcurrant sorbet might head the desserts. The lengthy French-led wine list offers eight house bottles from £15.50 (£4.50 a glass), a selection of halves and a page of mature clarets.

CHEF: Peter James McGregor   PROPRIETORS: J.P. and J.E Mifsud   OPEN: Tue to Sun L 12.30 to 1.45, all week D 7 to 8.45   MEALS: alc L (main courses £14). Set D £35 to £42.50   SERVICE: not inc, card slips closed   CARDS: Amex, Delta, Diners, MasterCard, Switch, Visa   DETAILS: 24 seats. Private parties: 24 main room, 2 to 26 private rooms. Car park. Vegetarian meals. Children's helpings. No children under 8. No smoking. Wheelchair access (not WC). No music. No mobile phones   ACCOMMODATION: 13 rooms, all with bath/shower. TV. Phone. B&B £95 to £180. Baby facilities

Hibiscus ▼

17 Corve Street, Ludlow SY8 1DA   COOKING **8**
TEL: (01584) 872325   FAX: (01584) 874024   FRENCH
                                                              £39–£64

The restaurant doesn't exactly shout its presence to the world, despite its high-street location. Look for the hanging sign and unassuming yellow-beige frontage. Go through a door to the left of the hallway, marked Oak Room, and be greeted by Claire Bosi, who fronts the operation with calm assurance. The dining goes on in two small rooms, one oak-panelled, the other stone-walled, with tables decently spaced in both. The place has a highly civilised and pleasantly informal ambience.

Everything about Claude Bosi's food, from the signature appetiser of a neatly crowned egg containing a silky soup such as cabbage velouté, with some of the lightly coddled egg left in, to the vari-flavoured madeleines (honey and black pepper, hazelnut, pistachio) that come with coffee, impresses for its intelligence and flawless execution. Four fat langoustine tails arranged down a long plate are accompanied, boldly, by diced Nicola potato and a sauce containing sage and passion fruit. Black-leg chicken might appear in two services: first the crisp-skinned breast with peanut satay and baked banana, then the leg with a wedge of onion confit and some cumin-scented oil. The flavours and seasonings in these dishes turn out to counterpoint each other beautifully. Lighter lunch dishes have taken in Cornish cod poached in vin jaune with white beans and complementary purées of celeriac and quince. Once dessert stage is reached, vegetables are given full rein, with Jerusalem artichoke turning a crème brûlée into an earthy challenge, helped along by toasted oats and caramel ice cream, while apple tart is partnered with an ice cream of Puy lentils. In case your curiosity is not slaked at the same pace as your appetite, Monsieur Bosi is not shy about making appearances at the end of service, happy to discuss techniques and ideas with anyone who has time to linger.

To accompany all this, a manageable selection of quality wines both young and mature draws mostly on France and the New World. Much is under £30, and the handful of carefully chosen premium bottles would do any special occasion proud. House white starts at £14.50, red at £14.75, half-bottles are plentiful, and six come by the glass.

CHEF: Claude Bosi   PROPRIETORS: Claude and Claire Bosi   OPEN: Wed to Sat L 12.15 to 1.30, Tue to Sat D 7.15 to 9.30   CLOSED: 22 Dec to 15 Jan, 18 to 28 July   MEALS: Set L £19.50 (2 courses) to £25, Set D £42.50   SERVICE: not inc, card slips closed   CARDS: Delta, MasterCard, Switch, Visa   DETAILS: 28 seats. Private parties: 30 main room. Car park. Children's helpings. Wheelchair access (not WC). No music. No mobile phones

Merchant House 🍴

Lower Corve Street, Ludlow SY8 1DU
TEL: (01584) 875438
WEBSITE: www.merchanthouse.co.uk

COOKING 8
MODERN BRITISH
£40–£62

There's much praise for the Merchant House's down-to-earth style: no posh table settings, wine left to pour yourself, and a somewhat plain décor, albeit with plenty of eye-catching artefacts. It's all about the food and enjoying the company of one's dining companions without pomp or ceremony; all of which goes down well with the majority of Guide readers, judging by our postbag. Chef/proprietor Shaun Hill is an admirably level-headed fellow, a dedicated hands-on chef who cooks dinner five nights a week plus Friday and Saturday lunch, ably assisted front-of-house by wife Anja.

The simple and uncluttered presentation of dishes highlights the care and precision of his cooking. 'Fresh-as-a-daisy' diver-caught scallops, for example, are sautéed – the outside nicely toasted, the middle like mother-of-pearl – and served on lentils with a light but spicy and aromatic coriander sauce given a refreshing lift with a hint of lemon, while corn-fed squab pigeon is roasted and its distinctive but delicate flavour set off by the 'divine decadence' of a lightly cooked nugget of foie gras, and tender haricot beans in a light sauce of white wine, celery, streaky bacon, shallots, ribbons of cabbage and asparagus.

Risottos are a perennial highlight, perhaps with chunks of tender Jerusalem artichoke, parsley and a generous helping of girolles, fried quickly in olive oil then added to the rice at the last moment along with the pan juices. Offal is also used in imaginative ways, as in creamy calves' sweetbreads accompanied by tiny potato and olive cakes in a crisp breadcrumb coating, and a light mayonnaise-like dressing hinting of mustard. To finish, there might be Muscat crème caramel with prunes in Armagnac, a 'delicious reworking of prunes and custard', the crème perfectly wobbly, the fruit stewed in Earl Grey with a splash of Armagnac. Wines are a smart international bunch arranged by style and rounded off by a fine range of fruit eaux-de-vie. Prices are fair but house bottles are the only options under £20 –white is £15.50, while it's £17.50 for the red.

CHEF: Shaun Hill   PROPRIETORS: Shaun and Anja Hill   OPEN: Fri and Sat L 12.30 to 1.45, Tue to Sat D 7 to 8.45   MEALS: Set L £29, Set D £35   SERVICE: net prices, card slips closed   CARDS: Delta, MasterCard, Switch, Visa   DETAILS: 24 seats. No smoking. Wheelchair access (not WC). No music

▲ Mr Underhill's ♀ ⅚✳

Dinham Weir, Ludlow SY8 1EH	COOKING 7
TEL: (01584) 874431	MODERN EUROPEAN
WEBSITE: www.mr-underhills.co.uk	£47–£61

The past year has seen further accommodation added to this restaurant-with-rooms on the bank of the River Teme, including a new building on the site of an old mill with 'stupendous' views across the weir. The long, narrow dining room, with its décor of Bordeaux red, cream and white and the Bradleys' personal art collection, has a convivial atmosphere, and Judy Bradley runs the show with 'charm and humour'.

Dinner is a set price for five courses plus coffee and petits fours, with no hidden costs and no choice before dessert; Chris Bradley is careful to consult guests about likes, dislikes and special requirements. The cooking, which is entirely without affectation, shows an apparent simplicity that belies the considerable workmanship and faultless technique behind it. It also shows great creativity, not fixing on any single culinary style but following its own route.

Impressive incidentals – canapés of 'dainty, doll's-house-sized' cheese tarts and an appetiser of creamy broad bean soup topped with seared foie gras, for example – are overtures to the main event, which might commence with smoked haddock risotto, cooked gently and slowly for the rice to absorb the flavours of the fish and decorated with a zigzag of vivid green creamy spinach and chilli purée, a perfect blend of contrasting tastes, textures and colours. Pinpoint accuracy of timing and a delicate touch are called on again for a main course of 'moist, firm, snowy-white' halibut with 'sweet, melting' slow-roast pork in a subtle ginger and star anise sauce; and for a fillet of Marches beef, cooked to a deep rose-pink and served in a clear, light tarragon-infused jus with ceps redolent of musky woodland aromas, satin-smooth mash and creamy diced celeriac.

Just when you thought dinner couldn't get any better, along come the 'stellar-quality' desserts: perhaps pear poached with lemongrass and vanilla, its light, fresh flavour set off against a sweet, creamy pistachio parfait. The discerning wine list turns up treats at all price levels, and appropriate ageing and fair prices augment its considerable charm. One reporter applauded Judy Bradley's 'passion for fine Bordeaux', but this is a quality list throughout France and on into Italy, Australia, New Zealand and California. Six house wines from £13 to £15 also come by the glass, and half-bottles are many and interesting.

CHEF: Chris Bradley   PROPRIETORS: Chris and Judy Bradley   OPEN: Wed to Mon D only 7.15 to 8.15   CLOSED: some Mons, 1 week Jan, 1 week July   MEALS: Set D £36   SERVICE: not inc   CARDS: Delta, MasterCard, Switch, Visa   DETAILS: 26 seats. 26 seats outside. Car park. Children's helpings. No smoking. No music. No mobile phones   ACCOMMODATION: 9 rooms, all with bath/shower. TV. Phone. B&B £85 to £210. Fishing

LUND East Riding of Yorkshire   map 9

Wellington Inn ♀

19 The Green, Lund YO25 9TE	COOKING 3
TEL: (01377) 217294 FAX: (01377) 217192	MODERN BRITISH
	£31–£54

In the middle of a tiny village north of Beverley, this dyed-in-the-wool hostelry has all the warmth and good humour you might expect from a decent North Country pub. It also has a few surprises as regards food. Robust flavours are tempered with a light touch: witness starters such as Loch Fyne scallops with smoked bacon risotto and pesto, or warm Roquefort cheesecake with a poached pear and honey and balsamic syrup. Hearty main courses might include calf's liver with Toulouse sausage, crispy pancetta and sage and onion mash, or fillet of halibut with smoked mussel and smoked salmon kedgeree and lightly curried hollandaise. Bar food is served in a tastefully converted back room, while the main bar is a drinking-only zone in the evening. Real ales are on tap, and wines are an excellent-value modern selection, including interesting bottles from South Africa. House wines are £10.95 and six come by the glass.

CHEF: Sarah Jeffery   PROPRIETORS: Russell and Sarah Jeffery   OPEN: Tue to Sat D only 7 to 9.30   MEALS: alc (main courses £13 to £19). Bar menu available Tue to Sun L, Tue to Sat D   SERVICE: not inc, card slips closed   CARDS: Delta, MasterCard, Switch, Visa   DETAILS: 42 seats. Private parties: 42 main room, 8 to 12 private rooms. Car park. Vegetarian meals. No children under 16. Music. No mobile phones

LYDFORD Devon   map 1

▲ Dartmoor Inn

Lydford EX20 4AY
TEL: (01822) 820221   FAX: (01822) 820494
EMAIL: karen@dartmoorinn.co.uk

GFG 2005 DEVON COMMENDED

COOKING 4
MODERN BRITISH-PLUS
£25–£55

In 2004 Karen and Philip Burgess founded the Dartmoor Festival in their good-humoured, 'hidden treasure' of a pub. Their aim is to celebrate the region's history, customs and food, with the emphasis on all things local most evident in the kitchen, where much of the produce is from a network of trusted suppliers. What impresses is the refreshing simplicity of the food. There's also considerable deftness and skill at work, from faultless deep-frying (red mullet fritters clothed in 'positively floatingly light batter') to grilling ('ultra-fresh' mixed fish served with 'excellent' Maris Piper chips). On the meat front, you might find roast free-range duck with honey, raisins and Muscat sauce, or filet mignon on an 'inviting mattress' of potato and celeriac purée topped with whole baby carrots. Fritters resurface among desserts, along with, say, rhubarb and saffron crème brûlée. The well-spread wine list is a promising slate, with house recommendations from £11.75.

CHEFS: Andrew Honey and Philip Burgess   PROPRIETORS: Karen and Philip Burgess   OPEN: Tue to Sun L 12 to 2.15, Tue to Sat D 6.30 to 9.30   CLOSED: bank hols   MEALS: alc (main courses £9.50 to £19.50). Set L and D exc D Fri and Sat £12.50 (2 courses) to £15.95. Bar L menu available   SERVICE: not inc, card slips closed   CARDS: Delta, MasterCard, Switch, Visa   DETAILS: 75 seats. 20 seats outside. Private parties: 12 main room. Car park. Vegetarian meals. Children's helpings. No children under 5 at D Fri and Sat. No smoking. Occasional music. No mobile phones   ACCOMMODATION: 3 rooms, all with bath/shower. Prices on application. Phone £5

LYDGATE Greater Manchester   map 8

▲ White Hart Inn

51 Stockport Road, Lydgate OL4 4JJ
TEL: (01457) 872566   FAX: (01457) 875190
WEBSITE: www.thewhitehart.co.uk
on A6050, 3m E of Oldham

COOKING 4
MODERN ANGLO-FRENCH
£26–£54

In a picturesque setting opposite an ancient church and overlooking the Pennines, this handsome, sympathetically restored old inn has twenty-first-century credentials. Inside, smart brass signs guide you to the bar/brasserie or the restaurant, the latter decked out with dark walnut floorboards and a décor of pale aubergine and white. The modern cooking has a traditional anchor. In-house Saddleworth Sausage Company bangers (perhaps chicken and black pudding) come with a choice of mash and onion gravy, while the British farm cheeses (possibly featuring Burland Green and Shorrocks Tasty Lancashire) prove to be house specialities. More adventurous dishes could take in grilled fillet of sea bass with seared monkfish cheeks, caramelised fennel and wilted greens, or pan-fried fillet of beef with oxtail ravioli. Desserts embrace the familiar (sticky toffee pudding with butterscotch sauce) while extending as far as carrot and marzipan sponge with Amaretto ice cream. Youthful service is 'pleasant and eager'. A wide-ranging list of good-value wines is topped off by some smart Bordeaux; house wines are £14.75.

CHEF: John Rudden   PROPRIETORS: Charles Brierley and John Rudden   OPEN: Mon to Sat 12 to 2.30, 6 to 9.30, Sun 1 to 7.30   CLOSED: 25 and 26 Dec, D 1 Jan, 3 Jan   MEALS: alc (main courses £12 to £17). Set L Mon to Sat £10.50 (1 course) to £14.50, Set L Sun £14.50 (2 courses) to £18.25, Set D Mon to Thur 6 to 6.45 £10.50 (1 course) to £14.50   SERVICE: not inc, card slips closed   CARDS: Amex, Delta, MasterCard, Switch, Visa   DETAILS: 125 seats. 30 seats outside. Private parties: 150 main room, 12 to 38 private rooms. Car park. Vegetarian meals. Children's helpings. No smoking. Wheelchair access (also WC). Occasional music. No mobile phones. Air-conditioned   ACCOMMODATION: 12 rooms, all with bath/shower. TV. Phone. B&B £68.50 to £105. Baby facilities (£5)

LYMINGTON Hampshire   map 2

Egan's ⅚✳

24 Gosport Street, Lymington SO41 9BE   COOKING 2
TEL: (01590) 676165   MODERN BRITISH
                                                                    £22–£51

A tranquil environment of sage green, crisp linen and a relaxed atmosphere mark out Egan's, and the place remains popular with reporters. Generous portions of 'honestly made' food, alongside some complex combinations, are hallmarks of the modern bistro food. Poached fillets of brill, sea bass and turbot might grace the same plate, served as a main course with prawn risotto and lobster sauce, and everyone gets a side dish of correctly cooked vegetables. 'Supple and moist' slices of Cajun-spiced chicken might come in a starter salad with bacon, avocado, rocket, chard and strips of deep-fried vegetables, while a 'skilfully made' bordelaise sauce has partnered roast monkfish wrapped in pancetta with champ. Home-made bread is 'superb', and those who make it to dessert might go for pistachio crème brûlée. The short wine list offers a mix of Old World and New from £12.25, culminating in a well-annotated and well-chosen 'best of both worlds' selection of smarter bottles.

CHEF: John Egan   PROPRIETORS: John and Deborah Egan   OPEN: Tue to Sat 12 to 2, 6.30 to 10   CLOSED: 26 Dec to 2 Jan   MEALS: alc D (main courses £12 to £17). Set L £8.95 (2 courses) to £11.95   SERVICE: not inc   CARDS: MasterCard, Switch, Visa   DETAILS: 50 seats. 20 seats outside. Private parties: 50 main room. Vegetarian meals. Children's helpings. No smoking in dining rooms, permitted in bar. Music

---

'The place was virtually empty that evening, but this did not excuse the unutterably dismal Muzak playing: it was as if your old aunt has assembled all her favourite tracks on one interminable ''Hits from Hell'' album and let rip.' (On eating in London)

▲ Le Poussin at Parkhill 🍷 ✻

LYNDHURST Hampshire — map 2

Beaulieu Road, Lyndhurst SO43 7FZ
TEL: (023) 8028 2944   FAX: (023) 8028 3268
WEBSITE: www.lepoussin.co.uk

COOKING **6**
MODERN BRITISH
£50–£87

The white-painted Georgian country-house hotel is undergoing refurbishment. Any ongoing work should not affect the restaurant, where the conservatory-style room makes the best of the glorious views over the garden and parkland. The food's focus remains as before, with wild mushrooms and game finding their place alongside luxury items and top-notch meat and fish.

Alex Aitken's cooking runs mostly along classical lines – fillet of sea bass comes with leeks, a light butter sauce and creamy mashed potato, for example, though some imaginative pairings crop up in a starter of quail roasted pink and served off the bone with morel and thyme tea, or a main course of turbot roasted on the bone with girolles, a lavender sauce and saffron potatoes. First-class materials, spot-on timing and skilful saucing characterised an inspection meal, which opened with seared diver-caught scallops on cauliflower purée topped with caviar, served with scallop roe cappuccino, with the centrepiece a fillet of red mullet on confit potato with aubergine caviar. Desserts maintain interest: for example, in an intriguing 'best end' of pineapple in a pistachio praline crust with mango sorbet, coconut pannacotta and green tea syrup, or a Valrhona chocolate fondant with poached figs, pistachio ice cream and Banyuls syrup. Service is professional and knowledgeable. Wines are a profound classical collection that also showcases some of the leading properties in south-west France and some smart New World estates. A dozen good-value and interesting house wines open proceedings, priced from £14.50 and also sold by the glass.

CHEF: Alex Aitken   PROPRIETORS: Alex and Caroline Aitken   OPEN: all week 12 to 2.30, 6.45 to 10   MEALS: alc exc Sun L (main courses £22.50 to £26.50). Set L Mon to Sat £15 (2 courses), Set L Sun £25, Set D £35 to £55   SERVICE: 10% (optional), card slips closed   CARDS: Amex, Delta, MasterCard, Switch, Visa   DETAILS: 60 seats. Car park. Vegetarian meals. Children's helpings. No children under 8. No smoking. Wheelchair access (also WC). No music. No mobile phones. Air-conditioned   ACCOMMODATION: 19 rooms, all with bath/shower. TV. Phone. B&B £75 to £250. Rooms for disabled. Baby facilities. Fishing

Chicory

LYTHAM ST ANNE'S Lancashire — map 8

NEW ENTRY

5–7 Henry Street, Lytham St Anne's FY8 5LE
TEL: (01253) 737111   FAX: (01253) 739115

COOKING **4**
GLOBAL
£25–£52

Expansion is the name of the game at this vibrant modern restaurant bang in the centre of Lytham: the owners are planning a food hall around the corner and have opened a cocktail lounge above the dining room. Chicory's bright ochre façade is unmissable, and the interior is thoroughly contemporary. The kitchen works to a menu of complex dishes that can read 'more like your shopping list', but Gary Cartwright and co are sure of their ground. A recent inspection pinpointed high-quality raw materials and carefully balanced components: witness a starter of plump scallops with roast pumpkin risotto, crisp pancetta, and sage and sun-dried tomato pesto; the same applied to venison with incomparable turnip dauphinois, a spicy poached plum, a square of 'earthy' Brussels sprout rarebit, Cassis jus and straw potatoes. Desserts can be more run-of-the-mill, but home-baked breads and English cheeses receive high praise. Lunch is an affordable roll call of classic brasserie dishes. The roving, 50-strong wine list seeks out quality and value. Chilean house wines are £11.95.

CHEFS: Gary Cartwright, Richard Martin, Felix Santoni and Steven Shepard PROPRIETORS: Bevan Middleton, Gary Cartwright, Richard Martin and Felix Santoni OPEN: all week 12 to 2 (2.30 Sun), 6 to 9.30 (10 Fri and Sat) MEALS: alc exc Sun L (main courses L £7 to £12, D £14 to £18). Set L Sun £16.95, Set D Sun to Thur £16.95 SERVICE: not inc CARDS: Amex, Delta, MasterCard, Switch, Visa DETAILS: 65 seats. Private parties: 90 main room. Vegetarian meals. Children's helpings. No-smoking area. Wheelchair access (also WC). Music. Air-conditioned

▲ Dalmeny Hotel, Atrium £✷

19–33 South Promenade, Lytham St Anne's FY8 1LX COOKING 4
TEL: (01253) 712236 FAX: (01253) 724447 MODERN EUROPEAN
WEBSITE: www.dalmenyhotel.com £21–£51

Lytham lies cheek by jowl with the heady maelstrom of Blackpool, as is evident even at the Atrium, where Friday-night entertainment might bring you, 'fresh from his sell-out season at Blackpool Tower, our very own King of Swing, Tony Benedict'. Amid metropolitan-style restaurant design, the cooking fairly swings too, offering a starter of scallops paired with black pudding accompanied by deep-fried courgette strips and apple butter sauce, with perhaps pan-fried red mullet with citrus-spiked boulangère potatoes, braised baby chicory and mussel stew to follow. Local supplies include Lytham shrimps and Goosnargh duck, the latter perhaps honey-glazed and served with Savoy cabbage, a potato galette and thyme jus. Regional accents surface again in the apple and sultana crumble that comes with fritters of Lancashire cheese and vanilla ice cream, or you might opt for bitter chocolate tart with white chocolate and vodka sorbet. A concise list of modern classical wines opens at £10.95 and keeps prices reasonable throughout.

CHEF: Darren Pilling PROPRIETORS: the Webb family OPEN: all week D only 6 to 9.30 (9 Sun) CLOSED: 24 to 26 Dec MEALS: alc exc Fri (main courses £15 to £19). Set D 6 to 7.30 £9.95 (2 courses) to £12.50, Set D Sun to Thur £16.50, Set D Fri £25, Set D Sat £18.50 SERVICE: not inc CARDS: Amex, Delta, Diners, MasterCard, Switch, Visa DETAILS: 80 seats. Private parties: 100 main room. Car park. Vegetarian meals. No smoking. Wheelchair access (also WC). Music. Air-conditioned ACCOMMODATION: 128 rooms, all with bath/shower. TV. Phone. B&B £88 to £150. Rooms for disabled. Baby facilities. Swimming pool

MADINGLEY Cambridgeshire map 6

Three Horseshoes ♥ £✷

High Street, Madingley CB3 8AB
TEL: (01954) 210221 FAX: (01954) 212043 COOKING 4
WEBSITE: www.3horseshoes.windmillweb.net MEDITERRANEAN
of A1303, 2m W of Cambridge, close to M11 junction 13 £36–£59

A whitewashed, thatched country pub in an undisturbed village within cantering distance of Cambridge, the Three Horseshoes has a variety of dining areas, which become more alluring as you progress through to the shady, trestle-tabled garden at the back. Food is modern southern Mediterranean, with the occasional nod elsewhere. Starters embrace crab risotto with chilli, parsley, Chardonnay and crème fraîche, or bean and pea salad with shaved pecorino, dandelion, mint and Selvapiana olive oil, and main courses may feature monkfish with chargrilled asparagus and crushed new potatoes, or roast saddle of venison with grilled aubergine, braised spinach, ricotta and salsa rossa. It all makes for lustrous, highly polished dining, and the lively imagination that underpins it all also imbues desserts like quince and fig crumble with burnt caramel ice cream. Wines are a speciality, but the broad range by the glass seems to have gone a bit more mainstream than of old, though there's still plenty of magic in the 'under £20' and 'top-class' bottle selections. Other pub-restaurants in the Huntsbridge group are at Fotheringhay, Huntingdon and Keyston (see entries).

CHEF: Richard Stokes PROPRIETOR: Huntsbridge Ltd OPEN: all week L 12 to 2, Mon to Sat D (all week in summer) 6 to 9.30 CLOSED: 31 Dec and 1 Jan MEALS: alc (main courses £14.50 to £19.50). Bar snack menu available SERVICE: not inc CARDS: Amex, Delta, Diners, MasterCard, Switch, Visa DETAILS: 70 seats. 25 seats outside. Private parties: 55 main room. Car park. Vegetarian meals. Children's helpings. No smoking. Wheelchair access (not WC). No music

MAIDENCOMBE Devon

map 1

▲ Orestone Manor ♥ ✹

Rockhouse Lane, Maidencombe TQ1 4SX
TEL: (01803) 328098 FAX: (01803) 328336
WEBSITE: www.orestone.co.uk

COOKING 4
MODERN ENGLISH
£30–£71

This place, sitting in its own mature gardens between Torquay and Teignmouth, has a superb sea view and colonial/oriental notes in the décor that mark it out as somewhere special with an appealing quirkiness. Immaculate, knowledgeable service complements a confident kitchen that creates complex, imaginative and robust dishes. Babbacombe Bay, or others nearby, stocks much of the menu: unforgettable lobster with squid-ink tagliatelle, crab consommé with a purity of flavour, and John Dory with crushed potatoes were happy memories from one meal. Roast sweetbreads with smoked bacon, braised endive and black truffle sauce, or locally sourced beef fillet with wild mushroom, Stilton glaze and port jus epitomise the focus on rich, strong flavours. Honey nut roasted figs with lemon curd and prune ripple ice cream, or iced banana soufflé with warm butterscotch sauce, make a good finish. An international wine list, arranged by style, provides sound support to the kitchen's flourishes at a wide range of price levels. House is £14.95.

CHEFS: Anthony Hetherington and Darren Jory PROPRIETORS: Rose and Mark Ashton, Peter Morgan and Friedericke Etessami OPEN: all week 12 to 2, 7 to 9 MEALS: alc (main courses £18 to £24.50). Set L £14.95 (2 courses) to £17.50. Set L Sun £19.50. Terrace menu available SERVICE: not inc, 10% for parties of 8 or more CARDS: Amex, Delta, MasterCard, Switch, Visa DETAILS: 55 seats. 25 seats outside. Private parties: 65 main room, 6 to 19 private rooms. Car park. Vegetarian meals. Children's helpings. No smoking. Wheelchair access (also WC). Music. No mobile phones ACCOMMODATION: 12 rooms, all with bath/shower. TV. Phone. B&B £79 to £199. Rooms for disabled. Swimming pool (£5)

MAIDSTONE Kent

map 3

Souffle

31 The Green, Bearsted, Maidstone ME14 4DN
TEL/FAX: (01622) 737065

COOKING 3
MODERN BRITISH
£28–£58

The old village green area is 'a breath of fresh air' in Bearsted, nowadays a suburb of Maidstone. Housed in a tile-hung three-storey building with a well-planted summer dining area outside, this the sort of classy neighbourhood restaurant we would all like to have within staggering distance. Rye Bay scallops and black pudding set on a strip of soft, creamy mash with broad, elegant stripes of soft, bubbly yellow hollandaise and deep green parsley sauce on either side made an impression on one reporter – 'stunning to look at, perfectly balanced'. Nick Evenden's kitchen has shown a gentle way with the oriental spices in a spiced breast of duck, and good balance of textures and flavours in Parma ham-wrapped monkfish tail, crisp-crusted risotto cake and wilted spinach. Among sweets, a brownie with malt and Malteser ice cream has a high comfort factor. Karen Evenden's all-female waiting crew is 'organised, smooth, attentive and professional'. The wine list, which starts at £12.50 and peaks at £35, focuses mainly on France.

CHEF: Nick Evenden   PROPRIETORS: Nick Evenden and Karen Evenden   OPEN: Tue to Fri and Sun L 12 to 2, Tue to Sat D 7 to 9.30   MEALS: alc (main courses £16.50 to £18.50). Set L £13.50 (2 courses) to £16.50, Set D £22.50   SERVICE: 10% (optional), card slips closed   CARDS: Amex, Delta, MasterCard, Switch, Visa   DETAILS: 40 seats. 30 seats outside. Private parties: 50 main room, 10 to 25 private rooms. Car park. Vegetarian meals. Children's helpings. No pipes/cigars. Wheelchair access (also men's WC). Music. No mobile phones

MANCHESTER Greater Manchester   map 8

Establishment 🍴✳ | NEW ENTRY |

43–45 Spring Gardens, Manchester M2 2BG   COOKING 5
TEL: (0161) 839 6300   FAX: (0161) 839 6353   MODERN BRITISH
WEBSITE: www.establishmentrestaurant.com   £28–£63

Spring Gardens is filled with opulent Victorian buildings replete with marble columns and much ornate plasterwork. Establishment occupies one such building, offering a discreet, contemporary look that's a 'successful mix of antique and modern'. Ian Morgan, whose skill at Watersreach (see entry) was to interpret modern brasserie food and lift it to a higher level, now ratchets up his aspirations still further. This has proved a successful shift to a more formal environment and a rigorous strategy towards sourcing superior raw materials. Many of the main courses follow the contemporary fashion of pairing a prime cut of meat with a slow-cooked version of more humble but tastier parts of the animal or bird (double Cornish lamb cutlet, for example, with a cassoulet of beans, braised shoulder, spinach and sweetbreads), and fish is sometimes paired with meat (sautéed monkfish with Cumbrian ham, braised oxtail and salsify). Starters might take in frothy green pea and mint soup with smoked ham tortellini ('a classic combination'), and desserts score highly on presentation and flavour, from mille-feuille of raspberries with an 'intense' raspberry sorbet to an apple crumble soufflé with custard ice cream. The wine list is a lengthy one, with the best value among the Spanish and New World sections. Four house wines are £13.50.

CHEF: Ian Morgan   PROPRIETORS: Carl Lewis and Keith Raxter   OPEN: Mon to Fri (and Sat July and Aug) L 12 to 2.30, Mon to Sat D 7 to 10.30   CLOSED: Mon July and Aug   MEALS: alc (main courses £16 to £20). Set L £14 (2 courses) to £16.95   SERVICE: not inc   CARDS: Amex, Delta, MasterCard, Switch, Visa   DETAILS: 100 seats. Private parties: 100 main room. Vegetarian meals. Children's helpings. No smoking. Wheelchair access (also WC). Music

---

'*There was a wedding party in suits and smart spangly frocks and stoles, no less. Men in tuxedos, men in kilts and women in dresses to make even Liz Hurley blush – it was a heavy gaffer tape night.*'
(On eating in the West Country)

Glamorous Chinese £

Wing Yip Business Centre, Oldham Road, Ancoats,
Manchester M4 5HU
TEL: (0161) 839 3312   FAX: (0161) 839 8233

COOKING 2
CHINESE
£24–£59

Following the formula of a Chinese restaurant attached to a large supermarket with ample parking, this sprawling newcomer has rapidly been discovered by aficionados – thanks to a menu that suits traditionalists and those with specialist tastes. Lunchtime dim sum are a sound bet, although the best are on a Chinese menu (which may cause communication problems): many items have been endorsed, including steamed scallop dumplings and salt-and-pepper ribs. Elsewhere, roast meats have been variable, but the kitchen shows its mettle with 'authentically fatty' brisket and turnip casserole, braised fish with sliced pork, and roast suckling pig with jellyfish ('superb, though at £17 a portion it ought to be', mused the recipient). Singapore noodles and mixed seafood ho-fun are also recommended. The wine list includes plenty of bottles in the £15 bracket. House wine is £9.90.

PROPRIETOR: Tommy Hung   OPEN: Mon to Thur 11.30 to 11.30, Fri and Sat 11.30 to 12, Sun 11 to 11   MEALS: alc (main courses £7.50 to £17). Set L £5.95 (2 courses) to £9.95, Set D £15.50 to £32 (all min 2)   SERVICE: not inc, 10% for parties of 8 or more   CARDS: Amex, Delta, MasterCard, Switch, Visa   DETAILS: 600 seats. Private parties: 400 main room; private rooms also available. Car park. Vegetarian meals. Wheelchair access (also WC). Music. Air-conditioned

Greens

43 Lapwing Lane, West Didsbury, Manchester M20 2NT
TEL: (0161) 434 4259   FAX: (0161) 448 2098

COOKING 2
VEGETARIAN
£16–£33

The green awning and paint scheme are external evocations of the eclectic vegetarian menu within. The buzzy, intimate interior has a bistro feel (dark walls and wooden tables and chairs), which sits comfortably with the food. Starters like red hummus with a mixed salad and chargrilled flat bread show lively colour contrasts and clear flavours, while a tart of caramelised onion and grain mustard has come with Cornish Yarg melting over the top. Ambitious ideas and skilful execution have been noted in light-textured gnocchi with a well-judged creamy red pesto, both combining well with accurately cooked asparagus and peas. Sweets could include silky, vanilla-flecked crème brûlée, or chocolate and mint pie. Care is taken over details – generous slices of granary bread with dark olive oil, and decent espresso – and although Greens has no licence, bringing your own incurs no corkage.

CHEFS/PROPRIETORS: Simon Connolly and Simon Rimmer   OPEN: Tue to Fri and Sun L 12 to 2 (12.30 to 3.30 Sun), all week D 5.30 to 10.30   CLOSED: bank hols, 25, 26 and 31 Dec, 1 Jan   MEALS: alc (main courses £10 to £11). Set L £5.95 (1 course) to £10, Set D Sun, Mon and 5.30 to 7 Tue to Sat £12.50   SERVICE: not inc, 10% for parties of 6 or more, card slips closed   CARDS: Delta, MasterCard, Switch, Visa   DETAILS: 34 seats. Private parties: 34 main room. Vegetarian meals. Children's helpings. No cigars/pipes. Music

Koreana

40A King Street West, Manchester M3 2WY
TEL: (0161) 832 4330   FAX: (0161) 832 2293
WEBSITE: www.koreana.co.uk

COOKING 1
KOREAN
£30–£55

One of the few authentic Korean restaurants in the North, this family-run venue has been plying its trade since 1985. Sincere, charming service is one of its plus points, and the helpfully explained menu takes in all major aspects of the cuisine. Bulgogi and galbi (grilled at the table on a traditional hotplate) share the billing with soups, flash-fried bokum, casseroles (including a fearsome combination of meat, vegetables and transparent noodles laced with kim-chee pickle and chilli) and dolsot bibim bab (rice specialities served in a heated stoneware pot). Sushi puts in a token appearance, although you won't find it on the useful banquet menus. Drink Korean lager, saké or something from the wine list. House French is £8.95.

CHEFS: Mrs H. Kim and S. Nam   PROPRIETOR: Koreana Ltd   OPEN: Mon to Fri 12 to 2.30, 6.30 to 10.30 (11 Fri), Sat 5.30 to 11   CLOSED: 25 and 26 Dec, 1 Jan, bank hol L, 1 week Aug   MEALS: alc (main courses £6 to £14). Set L £5.50 to £8 (2 courses), Set D £9.90 (2 courses) to £18.90   SERVICE: not inc, card slips closed, 10% for parties of 8 or more   CARDS: Amex, Delta, Diners, MasterCard, Switch, Visa   DETAILS: 60 seats. Private parties: 60 main room. Vegetarian meals. Children's helpings. Occasional music (£5)

Lime Tree ▾ ⅙✳

8 Lapwing Lane, West Didsbury, Manchester M20 8WS	COOKING 3
TEL: (0161) 445 1217 FAX: (0161) 434 0574	GLOBAL
WEBSITE: www.thelimetreerestaurant.com	£22–£46

Regulars attest that this bustling neighbourhood restaurant 'does what it sets out to do and does it well'. The two rooms are warmly decorated in shades of blue, and well-spaced tables are serviced by a knowledgeable and friendly team. The shorter, simpler lunchtime carte prefigures an evening menu in a modern British style, where gravad lax partners smoked salmon mousse –'outstandingly clear and distinct' – and crab salad is dressed with orange and avocado. Attention is paid to seasons, and local supplies figure large in dishes such as mallard (praised for its flavour and texture) with black pudding, root vegetable mash, honey roast parsnips and a port jus, while scallops were 'as simple as possible', allowing the quality produce to shine. Warm chocolate torte, or amaretti sablés, might be among desserts. Fourteen wines of the month, a global mix, front a weighty list, much of it from Bordeaux, Burgundy and Italy; eight house options start at £10.95 (£2.75 a glass), and prices are fair. Service is friendly, knowledgeable and unfussy.

CHEFS: Jason Parker and Jason Dickenson   PROPRIETOR: Patrick Hannity   OPEN: Tue to Fri and Sun L 12 to 2.45, all week D 5.45 to 10.15   CLOSED: 25 and 26 Dec, 1 Jan   MEALS: alc (not Sun L; main courses £6.50 to £14.50). Set L £14.95, Set D 5.45 to 6.45 £14.95   SERVICE: not inc, 10% (optional) for parties of 6 or more   CARDS: Amex, Delta, MasterCard, Switch, Visa   DETAILS: 85 seats. 20 seats outside. Vegetarian meals. Children's helpings. No smoking in 1 dining room. Wheelchair access (not WC). Music

Little Yang Sing £ | NEW ENTRY |

17 George Street, Manchester M1 4HE	COOKING 1
TEL: (0161) 228 7722 FAX: (0161) 237 9257	CANTONESE
WEBSITE: littleyangsing.co.uk	£19–£57

Not so little any more, this busy L-shaped basement is 'probably the most attractive dining room in Chinatown', concludes a well-seasoned Mancunian. It's a favourite with Western customers, who appreciate its courteous staff, accessible menu, and extensive range of vegetarian dishes (spicy stir-fried yam with garlic, for example). The cooking is mainly Cantonese with a useful choice of dim sum (including not only salt-and-pepper ribs and deep-fried prawn balls but also curried minced beef samosas). Elsewhere, fillet steak and duck loom large, along with barbecued pork ('served hot'), roast crispy chicken, and dishes like pan-fried scallops with ginger and spring onions. The wine list is a 'sensible, practical document', with house vins de pays at £10.

CHEF: Kui Keung Yeung   PROPRIETOR: LYS Restaurants Ltd   OPEN: all week 12 to 12 (12.30 Fri, 1am Sat, 11 Sun)   CLOSED: 25 Dec   MEALS: alc (main courses £7.50 to £13). Set L £8.50 (2 courses) to £10.50, Set D £17 (min 2)   SERVICE: 10%   CARDS: Amex, Delta, MasterCard, Switch, Visa   DETAILS: 220 seats. Private parties: 100 main room, 60 to 75 private rooms. Vegetarian meals. Children's helpings. No-smoking area. Wheelchair access (also WC). Music. Air-conditioned

Le Mont ⚓

Urbis Centre, Cathedral Gardens, Manchester M4 3BG
TEL: (0161) 605 8282   FAX: (0161) 605 8283

COOKING 5
MODERN FRENCH
£35–£76

The spectacular steel-and-glass Urbis Centre, wedge-shaped in both plan and section, sits close to Victoria Station. Its attractions include a museum of Manchester life and this sleek, discreetly lit, trend-setting restaurant, which occupies the fifth (non-smoking) and sixth (smoking) floors. The latter's windows of frosted and clear glass afford breathtaking views, and since the opening in 2002 the menu-writer's Franglais has blossomed into French, with all accents present and correct (plus an English crib).

Robert Kisby oversees a menu that delivers modern brasserie cooking, yet avoids corporate anonymity by dint of sourcing fine materials. Bowland Forest heather-fed lamb (perhaps roasted in a herb crust and set on tomatoed flageolet beans and a rosemary jus) and Galloway beef (the rump steak in Hungarian-style paprika sauce, with pancetta, shallots and button mushrooms) score highly for quality, timing and generous quantity. A lighter note is apparent in fish dishes, such as a crumbed Dover sole fillet with girolles and a tarragon sauce, and there are unusual pasta options like linguini with mussels, smoked haddock and spiced cauliflower cream. With starters such as game terrine with berry vinaigrette, and perhaps chocolate tart with white chocolate sorbet to finish, the performance is strong throughout. Staff are 'impressive but not intrusive'. An extensive wine list starts at £17.50, though prices are more London than Manchester, but it includes many fine growers and takes its champagne quite seriously. Six wines by the glass are £4.25 to £5.25.

CHEF: Robert Kisby   PROPRIETOR: Manchester City Council   OPEN: Mon to Fri L 12 to 2.30, Mon to Sat D 7 to 10.30   MEALS: alc (main courses £13 to £28). Set L £14.95 (2 courses) to £29.50, Set D Mon to Fri £23.50 to £29.50   SERVICE: 10% (optional), card slips closed   CARDS: Amex, Delta, MasterCard, Switch, Visa   DETAILS: 74 seats. Private parties: 40 main room. Vegetarian meals. No smoking in 1 dining room. Wheelchair access (also WC). No music. Air-conditioned

Moss Nook

Ringway Road, Manchester M22 5WD
TEL: (0161) 437 4778   FAX: (0161) 498 8089
on B5166, 1m from Manchester Airport

COOKING 5
MODERN BRITISH
£29–£72

The Harrisons have been running Moss Nook with care and aplomb for over three decades now, and that wealth of experience shows in the unruffled style of service, which remains one of the great assets of the place. In an environment of warm red walls, Tiffany-style lights and lacy tablecloths, some modestly enterprising and careful cooking is offered. Starters mix and match traditional and experimental modes, so that seared scallops with deep-fried sesame cabbage and red pepper sauce appear among more familiar dishes like sautéed foie gras on rösti with truffle and Madeira sauce. Main courses bring on purées, stuffings and cream sauces to augment their fine central ingredients, which might include breast of Lunesdale duckling with orange, or best end of local lamb with pommes Anna, buttered spinach and sauce diable. Indulge yourself as the finishing line approaches with Tia Maria-laced tiramisù, or raspberries and whipped cream sandwiched between featherlight cinnamon wafers. As alternatives to the carte there are tasting menus at lunch (five courses) and dinner (seven). The wine list isn't all Bordeaux rouge and Bourgogne blanc, but gives a fair shake of the stick to the New World regions too; house Chardonnay and Syrah at £14 are Australian.

CHEF: Kevin Lofthouse   PROPRIETORS: Pauline and Derek Harrison   OPEN: Tue to Fri L 12 to 1.30, Tue to Sat D 7 to 9.30   MEALS: alc (main courses £19.50 to £22.50). Set L £19.50, Set D £36.50   SERVICE: not inc, card slips closed   CARDS: Amex, Delta, MasterCard, Switch, Visa   DETAILS: 65 seats. 20 seats outside. Private parties: 55 main room. Car park. Vegetarian meals. No children under 12. No pipes. No music. No mobile phones (£5)

Ocean Treasure £

Greenside Way, Middleton, Manchester M24 1SW   COOKING 2
TEL: (0161) 653 6688   FAX: (0161) 653 3388   CHINESE
WEBSITE: www.chiyip.co.uk   £22–£54

Take a city map to locate this solidly dependable and 'deservedly popular' Hong Kong-style eating house on the outskirts of Oldham, and keep your eyes peeled for its green glazed roof tiles. Daytime dim sum and business lunches are popular, while the full menu takes a regional trip from Canton to Szechuan. Seafood is the main player and reporters have enjoyed crisp fried soft-shell crab and steamed sea bass with ginger and spring onion, but the choice extends to sizzlers, bird's-nests, 'roasties' and stir-fries. A 'new' menu homes in on esoteric specialities – 'Mrs Spotty' beancurd, claypots, handmade noodles and dishes like crispy fried pork chop with lemongrass. Be warned: on Friday night there's a free live cabaret and disco. The wine list has been assembled with care; house wines start at £10.90.

CHEF: Chi Keung Wong   PROPRIETOR: Stewart Yip   OPEN: all week 12 to 11   MEALS: alc (main courses £7 to £11). Set L £4.50 (1 course) to £11.90, Set D £18 to £32 (most min 2)   SERVICE: not inc, card slips closed   CARDS: Amex, Delta, MasterCard, Switch, Visa   DETAILS: 380 seats. Private parties: 400 main room, 10 to 50 private rooms. Car park. Vegetarian meals. Wheelchair access (also WC). Music. Air-conditioned (£5)

Pacific ✳

58–60 George Street, Manchester M1 4HF   COOKING 2
TEL: (0161) 228 6668   FAX: (0161) 236 0191   CHINESE/THAI
WEBSITE: www.pacific-restaurant-manchester.co.uk   £28–£59

Two restaurants under one roof is the deal in this colourfully decorated building deep in Manchester's Chinatown: one specialises in Thai cooking, the other in Chinese, although our review and rating apply only to the latter. The menu is built around a mix-and-match policy for most dishes: decide on your chosen cooking method and pick an appropriate sauce or flavouring. Alternatively, you can graze your way through the extensive list of dim sum, which ranges from steamed minced lobster with bamboo shoot dumplings to breadcrumbed prawns and water chestnuts on a sugar cane stick. There are also intriguing house specials such as 'primrose conpay' (stir-fried dried scallops with egg, crabmeat and silver bean sprouts) and braised pork chops with lemongrass. House wines start at £10.50.

CHEF: Tim Wong PROPRIETOR: Special Charms Ltd OPEN: all week 12 to 10.45 MEALS: alc (main courses £8 to £15.50). Set L and D £19 to £35.50 (some min 2) SERVICE: 10% CARDS: Amex, Delta, Diners, MasterCard, Switch, Visa DETAILS: 250 seats. Private parties: 200 main room, 12 to 35 private rooms. Vegetarian meals. No smoking in 1 dining room. Wheelchair access (also WC). Music. Air-conditioned

Restaurant Bar & Grill £

14 John Dalton Street, Manchester M2 6JR
TEL: (0161) 839 1999 FAX: (0161) 835 1886
WEBSITE: www.individualrestaurants.co.uk

COOKING 2
GLOBAL
£23–£56

Popular, bold and buzzy, this two-floor venue sports a long bar and, upstairs, a restaurant with black leather seating, dark wooden flooring, white walls, and slick, helpful and friendly service. A Thai-style prawn fishcake starter, flavoured with authentic spices, might be joined by other modern stalwarts such as chicken Caesar salad, and 'gooey, oozy' prawn risotto. Moving on, main courses run to chargrilled chicken breast marinated in Malayan spices served with sweet potato, coconut and lime ('a lovely mix of flavours'), crispy duck with Chinese greens and a sesame and honey dressing, and, for those in search of something plainer, simply grilled fillet steak. A strongly flavoured and boozy dark chocolate and orange mousse impressed an inspector. The one-page wine list begins at £11.50 and presents a good choice of easy-drinking, youthful bottles.

CHEFS: Alan Earle and Dave Bright PROPRIETORS: Steve Walker, Vernon Lord and Iain Donald OPEN: Mon to Fri 12 to 2.45, 6 to 10.45, Sat and Sun 12 to 10.45 CLOSED: 25 and 26 Dec MEALS: alc (main courses £6 to £16.50). Bar menu available 12 to 7 (6 Sat and Sun) SERVICE: not inc, 10% for parties of 6 or more CARDS: Amex, Delta, Diners, MasterCard, Switch, Visa DETAILS: 150 seats. Vegetarian meals. Wheelchair access (also WC). Music. Air-conditioned

Second Floor ▮ [NEW ENTRY]

Harvey Nichols, 21 New Cathedral Street,
Manchester M1 1AD
TEL: (0161) 828 8898 FAX: (0161) 828 8815
WEBSITE: www.harveynichols.com

COOKING 4
MODERN BRITISH
£33–£67

Opened in August 2003 in the city centre, part of the Millennium Triangle development, the latest branch of Harvey Nics requires a shorter ascent than the five floors of London and four floors of Leeds and Edinburgh (see entries) to reach its restaurant, brasserie and bar. Tall windows and a gleaming black marble floor add an air of distinction to the main dining area, and the cityscape after dark (even from only two floors up) looks more opulent and variegated than it can ever have done in Manchester's history.

To these promising surroundings, Robert Craggs has weighed in with a multi-influenced menu that displays sound technique and some bright ideas. Slow-roast belly pork is served with a mound of tiny apple tarts as well as cumin mayonnaise, and seared foie gras may be presented with Agen prunes, parsnips and vanilla. Mackerel is not much seen as a main course, but comes here with pipérade, a polenta croquette and aged balsamic, while navarin of lamb is given extraneous white-bean purée and upstandingly flavoured saffron potatoes. A dab hand at pastry work brings on chocolate Rolo tart with candied pecans and crème fraîche, or there might be moreish warm banana cake with banoffi ice cream and caramel sauce. Service from a team of youngsters is 'enthusiastic and informative'.

The wine list is headed by own-label bottles from £13.50 and a stirring list of indulgent sparklers. The main sections are divided into New and Old World and arranged by style. And what a stylish list it is, reading like a directory of head-turners of the current world of wine. Prices aren't too scary either.

CHEF: Robert Craggs   PROPRIETOR: Harvey Nichols   OPEN: all week L 12 to 3, Tue to Sat D 6 to 10.30   MEALS: alc (main courses £10 to £18.50). Bar and brasserie menus available   SERVICE: 10% (optional), card slips closed   CARDS: Amex, Delta, Diners, MasterCard, Switch, Visa   DETAILS: 90 seats. Private parties: 160 main room. Vegetarian meals. No-smoking area. Wheelchair access (also WC). Music. Air-conditioned

Simply Heathcotes 🍷 ✈ £

Jacksons Row, Manchester M2 5WD	COOKING **2**
TEL: (0161) 835 3536 FAX: (0161) 835 3534	MODERN BRITISH
WEBSITE: www.heathcotes.co.uk	£26–£52

In a cavernous converted registry office in an alleyway in Manchester's theatreland, this Heathcote outpost (see also Leeds, Liverpool and Preston) delivers carefully cooked food in a bright, lively ambience. Local produce is emphasised, and veggies get a good deal. Start with a signature dish of black pudding, scallop, apple purée and mustard butter, or perhaps a nicely delivered butternut risotto with hazelnut dressing. Fine ingredients like Bowland lamb chump or pepper-seared salmon are allowed to shine without overcomplication. Desserts like raspberry trifle crème brûlée with raspberry sorbet show lightness of touch. A quite extensive wine list incorporates highish mark-ups: house wines are £13.50, but there's not much under £20; a dozen wines come by the glass.

CHEF: Oliver Casson   PROPRIETOR: Paul Heathcote   OPEN: all week 12 to 2.30, 5.30 to 10 (5.30 to 11 Sat, 6 to 9.30pm Sun)   CLOSED: 25 and 26 Dec, 1 Jan, bank hols except Good Fri   MEALS: alc (main courses £9.50 to £19.50). Set L £13.50 (2 courses) to £15.50, Set D 5.30 to 7 £13.50 (2 courses) to £15.50. Express menu available at L and 5.30 to 7   SERVICE: 10% (optional), card slips closed   CARDS: Amex, Delta, Diners, MasterCard, Switch, Visa   DETAILS: 150 seats. Private parties: 140 main room, 10 to 55 private rooms. Vegetarian meals. Children's helpings. No smoking in restaurant, permitted in lounge. Wheelchair access (also WC). Music. Air-conditioned

▲ Watersreach at the Golden Tulip 🍷 ✈

Waters Reach, Trafford Park, Manchester M17 1WS	COOKING **4**
TEL: (0161) 868 1900 FAX: (0161) 872 6556	GLOBAL
WEBSITE: www.goldentulipmanchester.co.uk	£26–£59

On open ground between Manchester United football stadium and Salford Quays, the unpretentious Golden Tulip Hotel has earned a reputation thanks to its restaurant. Watersreach reminds some people of a noisy 'canteen-like' brasserie, and the food neatly matches the setting. Michael Wilson has been promoted to top dog in the kitchen, and reports suggest that he is doing well. His wide-ranging menu seeks to please all-comers, whether they are looking for corned-beef hash with home-made tomato ketchup, fish 'n' chips, or something more contemporary. Best sellers are – according to the chef himself – warm duck confit with rocket and Manchego salad and pickled red onions, roast cod with herb risotto and a poached egg, and blade of beef with Vichy carrots and garlic mash. To finish, follow one correspondent's advice and try dark chocolate and rosewater cheesecake with a raspberry milkshake. The wine list takes up the international theme, with eight by the glass and house selections costing £12.95.

CHEF: **Michael Wilson**   PROPRIETOR: **Golden Tulip UK**   OPEN: **Mon to Fri L 12 to 2.30, all week D 6 to 10 (9.30 Sun)**   CLOSED: L bank hols   MEALS: alc (main courses £8.50 to £17). Set L and D 6 to 7.15 £12.95 (2 courses) to £14.95   SERVICE: 10%, card slips closed   CARDS: Amex, Delta, Diners, MasterCard, Switch, Visa   DETAILS: 84 seats. Private parties: 6 to 18 private rooms. Car park. Vegetarian meals. Children's helpings. No smoking. Wheelchair access (also WC). Music. No mobile phones. Air-conditioned   ACCOMMODATION: 160 rooms, all with bath/shower. TV. Phone. Room only £98 to £112. Rooms for disabled. Baby facilities (£5)

Yang Sing ▼

34 Princess Street, Manchester M1 4JY
TEL: (0161) 236 2200   FAX: (0161) 236 5934
WEBSITE: www.yang-sing.com

GREATER MANCHESTER
OF THE YEAR
RESTAURANT

COOKING **5**
CANTONESE
£34–£57

'Still probably the best overall dining experience in a UK Chinese restaurant,' concluded one devotee who knows his way around the scene. Yang Sing's success may be explained by the fact that ingredients are judiciously sourced and by Harry Yeung's policy of 'cooking everything he can at the last minute'. At the stove, he is an innovative trailblazer who works without compromise: scallops are steamed with green bean vermicelli and garlic; foil-wrapped boneless pork chop is baked in five spices with shallots; and he contrives a heart-warming winter lamb casserole with dried bean curd, water chestnuts and red dates. The kitchen also excels when it comes to staples from the standard 200-dish menu: 'superbly authentic' roast duck, steamed sole, and ho fun (rice sticks) with beef and black beans have all been endorsed. Dim sum (especially incomparable fried items) continue to receive plaudits, and the ever-changing repertoire of fascinating morsels helps to keep regulars on their toes: prawn dumplings in spicy Thai soup has been a winner, and look, too, for seafood with Chinese chives, and steak roll. Banquets and tailor-made special menus can be negotiated with knowledgeable staff. House wines (at £12.95) and 14 'special recommendations' make up a sounder wine list than you will see in most Chinese restaurants, but the range pushes on into fine Bordeaux and Burgundy and a few other goodies besides.

CHEF: **Harry Yeung**   PROPRIETOR: **Yang Sing Ltd**   OPEN: **all week 12 to 11.15 (11.45 Fri and Sat, 10.15 Sun)**   CLOSED: 25 Dec   MEALS: alc (main courses £8 to £12.50). Set D from £17.50 (min 2)   SERVICE: not inc   CARDS: Amex, Delta, MasterCard, Switch, Visa   DETAILS: 250 seats. Private parties: 250 main room, 20 to 250 private rooms. Vegetarian meals. Wheelchair access (also WC). Music. Air-conditioned

MARLOW Buckinghamshire   map 3

▲ Danesfield House, Oak Room ⬤ ✳

Henley Road, Marlow SL7 2EY
TEL: (01628) 891010   FAX: (01628) 890408
WEBSITE: www.danesfieldhouse.co.uk

COOKING **3**
ANGLO-FRENCH
£38–£103

Shock may be too strong a term for the feeling engendered by the first sight of Danesfield House, but its exuberantly ornate Victorian splendour certainly takes you by surprise. The interiors are just as grand, with vast stone fireplaces and an intricately carved minstrels' gallery. The Orangery brasserie in a conservatory overlooking the gardens has a cheaper, simpler menu than the Oak Room, where the mood is rather more formal. The 'posh hotel' cooking tends towards complexity, often pairing different treatments of the same main ingredient, such as confit rabbit in Gewurztraminer jelly with a salad of roast rabbit fillet for starters, and Gressingham duck with its own confit and a red wine jus to follow.

To finish, lemon tart is an inventive take on the standard, with a soft toffee-like filling under a crisp caramel lid, accompanied by a tequila and lime sorbet. Reporters generally feel that staff could be better trained, and wines are not the cheapest around, although house vins de pays are a relative bargain at £20.

CHEF: Steven Morris OPEN: all week 12 to 1.45, 7 to 10 MEALS: alc (main courses £18 to £27). Set L £18.50 (2 courses) to £24.50, Set D £39.50 to £65. Brasserie menu available SERVICE: not inc, card slips closed CARDS: Amex, Delta, Diners, MasterCard, Switch, Visa DETAILS: 39 seats. 20 seats outside. Private parties: 8 main room, 4 to 110 private rooms. Car park. Vegetarian meals. Children's helpings. No smoking. Wheelchair access (also WC). No music. No mobile phones ACCOMMODATION: 87 rooms, all with bath/shower. TV. Phone. B&B £190 to £300. Rooms for disabled. Baby facilities. Swimming pool (£5)

Vanilla Pod ⅍✕

31 West Street, Marlow SL7 2LS	COOKING 5
TEL: 01628 898 101 FAX: 01628 898 108	MODERN BRITISH
WEBSITE: www.thevanillapod.co.uk	£34–£75

Never judge a book by its cover. Behind the door of this tiny, quaint-looking brick-and-flint building is a vibrant space, with hot colours, vivid modern paintings, gauzily veiled windows, and top-quality china and glasses on crisp linen-clothed tables.

Michael Macdonald's cooking is innovative in its concepts, and the menus (there's a seven-course menu gourmand, a vegetarian menu and an à la carte) showcase food as vibrant as the setting. Seafood is a strength: among main courses, scallops might partner vanilla-braised fennel escabèche as a starter, while pan-roasted brill comes with lentils and braised oxtail in port. Meat cookery is also well rendered, as in a starter of roast squab, shiitake dauphinoise and port sauce that delivered rosy meat with a sweet musky flavour, or a salad of hare salad with beetroot, walnuts and a truffle, currant and port jus. The vegetarian menu sets the gold standard with pithiviers of Reblochon cheese and dauphinois potatoes with pickled fennel and parsley oil, followed by apple mash potatoes with etuvée of vegetables and woodland mushrooms. Desserts, too, are well considered: plum crème brûlée is accompanied by almond financier biscuits, while a dark chocolate 'soup' might be served with spiced bread and white chocolate sorbet. Service is polite and professional, and the wine list concentrates on France, with some carefully chosen New World examples; prices start at £16.50 and move swiftly up.

CHEF: Michael Macdonald PROPRIETORS: Michael and Stephanie Macdonald OPEN: Tue to Sat 12 to 2, 7 to 10 CLOSED: 24 Dec to 5 Jan, last week Aug and 1st week Sept MEALS: Set L £17.50 (2 courses) to £19.50, Set D £38 (2 courses) to £45 SERVICE: not inc CARDS: Amex, Delta, MasterCard, Switch, Visa DETAILS: 42 seats. Private parties: 34 main room, 8 private room. Vegetarian meals. Children's helpings. No smoking. Wheelchair access (not WC). No music

MARSDEN West Yorkshire   map 8

▲ Olive Branch ⅍✕

Manchester Road, Marsden HD7 6LU	
TEL: (01484) 844487	COOKING 3
WEBSITE: www.olivebranch.uk.com	MODERN ENGLISH
on A62, between Slaithwaite and Marsden	£24–£53

This friendly and efficient place in the south-western approaches to Huddersfield still exudes a certain pub atmosphere, largely because of the menu chalked on blackboards and specials pinned up on cards, but nowadays it operates as a restaurant. The 20-odd starters and 40-some main courses manage a neat balancing act that satisfies a range of tastes. Ambition and skill show up in robust innovations like a sweet chilli sauce with accurately cooked sea bass, and a glossy sauce with a whiff of chocolate accompanying rare-cooked medallions of venison. These sit alongside things more familiar hereabouts, such as 'The Steak Pie' complete with suet crust. A starter gâteau of Whitby crab and mango reflects the effort put into sourcing decent ingredients, and Belgian chocolate tart panders to the chocoholic tendency. On a wine list more interesting than many, Duboeuf house bottles are £11.95, and most of the others stay below £20.

CHEF: Paul Kewley   PROPRIETORS: John Lister and Paul Kewley   OPEN: Wed to Fri L 12 to 2, Tue to Sat D 6.30 to 9.30, Sun L and D 1 to 8.30   CLOSED: first 2 weeks Jan   MEALS: alc (main courses £11 to £17.50). Set L £10.95 (2 courses) to £13.95, Set D Tue to Thur and Sun (and Fri and Sat 6.30 to 7.30) £13.95 (2 courses) to £16.95   SERVICE: not inc, card slips closed   CARDS: Delta, MasterCard, Switch, Visa   DETAILS: 65 seats. 12 seats outside. Private parties: 40 main room, 12 private room. Car park. Vegetarian meals. No smoking in 1 dining room. Music   ACCOMMODATION: 3 rooms, all with bath/shower. TV. Phone. Room only £45 to £60. Baby facilities (£5)

MARTEN Wiltshire   map 2

Windmill

Salisbury Road, Marten SN8 3SH
TEL: (01264) 731372   FAX: (01264) 731284
On A338, 6½m SW of Hungerford

NEW CHEF
MODERN EUROPEAN
£29–£67

This yellow-fronted restaurant – named after the Wilton windmill half a mile away – sits lonely beside the A338. Inside, the woodwork is grey, the walls buttermilk or dusky pink, and the plethora of prints and paintings on them (some for sale) evokes undertones of art galleries and antique shops. Gary Fisher has been promoted from sous-chef to the top job, and the style of food is due to continue in the same vein. That has seen lambs' sweetbreads presented on home-made brioche, accompanied by asparagus, seedless green grapes and a veal stock reduction. Otherwise, start with something like smoked salmon, rocket and lemon risotto, and go on to breast of guinea fowl with creamed Savoy cabbage and foie gras sauce, or maybe a sea bass fillet with spinach and fennel, sauced with citrus. There's hot rice pudding in plum soup to finish. The international wine list is arranged by style and caters imaginatively for all pockets, starting at £12.90 and topped off by a long and strong fine wine selection for the gold card wielders. An impressive line-up by the glass compensates for the small number of half-bottles.

CHEF: Gary Fisher   PROPRIETOR: Chris Ellis   OPEN: Tue to Sun L 12 to 2, Tue to Sat D 7 to 9.15   CLOSED: 25 Dec, 1 Jan   MEALS: alc (main courses L £7.50 to £13, D £16 to £22.50). Set D Tue to Thurs £19.50 (2 courses). Light L menu available Tue to Sun   SERVICE: not inc   CARDS: Delta, MasterCard, Switch, Visa   DETAILS: 48 seats. 36 seats outside. Private parties: 48 main room, 10 to 14 private rooms. Car park. Vegetarian meals. Children's helpings. No smoking. Wheelchair access (not WC). Occasional music (£5)   •

Prices quoted in the Guide are based on information supplied by restaurateurs. The prices quoted at the top of each entry represent a range, from the lowest price of a three-course meal with service and wine to the highest; the latter is inflated by 20 per cent to take account of likely price rises during the year of the Guide.

MARTON North Yorkshire

map 9

Appletree ✕

Marton, nr Pickering YO62 6RD	COOKING **2**
TEL: (01751) 431457 FAX: (01751) 430190	MODERN BRITISH
WEBSITE: www.appletreeinn.co.uk	£25–£53

'A dedicated and professional place' was how one visitor summed up this amiable old village inn west of Pickering. And there's plenty of domestic industry here: the owners now have a shop counter within the pub selling all kinds of provisions produced by the kitchen. Lunch is reckoned very reasonable value, on account of well-considered dishes like spears of thin English asparagus on rösti with poached egg and chervil ('great for a summer lunch'), and gurnard fillets with buttered mash, black bean sauce and grilled tomatoes; marbled chocolate pyramid with Baileys chocolate mousse makes an eye-catching finale. Slightly pricier evening menus move up a gear for, say, a starter of caviar and prawn fishcake with papaya and sweet chilli sauce, and mains like lavender-scented rack of lamb with Mediterranean vegetables, tapenade and roast garlic gravy. The wine list is a workmanlike all-rounder with plenty by the glass; the cheapest bottles are £9.95.

CHEF: T.J. Drew   PROPRIETORS: Melanie and T.J. Drew   OPEN: Wed to Sun L 12 to 2 (2.30 Sun), Wed to Mon D 6.30 to 9.30 (7 to 9 Sun)   CLOSED: 25 Dec, 2 weeks Jan   MEALS: alc (main courses £9 to £18). Light L available Wed to Sat   SERVICE: not inc, card slips closed   CARDS: Delta, MasterCard, Switch, Visa DETAILS: 50 seats. 16 seats outside. Private parties: 26 main room, 6 to 10 private rooms. Car park. Vegetarian meals. Children's helpings. No smoking in 1 dining room. Music

MASHAM North Yorkshire

map 9

Floodlite

7 Silver Street, Masham HG4 4DX	COOKING **4**
TEL: (01765) 689000	ANGLO-FRENCH
	£22–£49

The Floods' idiosyncratic restaurant – a former shop on the street running north from the market square – has been a feature of Wensleydale since 1986. Change is slow here (something that regular returners relish), and the quirky, eccentric, endearing décor survives, from pink wallpaper and crystal chandelier to pot plants in the window and a display cabinet brimful of crockery. The restaurant's name plays on the owners' surname ('The family is so sweet,' says one reporter); wife Christine is found front-of-house, while Charles mans the stoves, cooking a lengthy carte that, like the décor, undergoes evolution rather than transformation. There are plenty of traditional favourites – like lobster bisque, prawn cocktail, mussels marinière à la crème, and a brandy-snap basket of fresh fruit sorbets – but newer ideas too: perhaps grilled duck breast with apple, ginger, honey and soy sauce, or seared fillet of sea bass with Mediterranean vegetable stew. Saucing is a strength, as are the use of quality ingredients and the good-value fixed-price menus. There's charming service, and the French-led, global wine list offers fair pricing, with six house bottles at £10.95 (£2.50 by glass) and a good selection of halves.

CHEF: Charles Flood   PROPRIETORS: Charles and Christine Flood   OPEN: Fri to Sun L 12 to 2, Tue to Sat D 7 to 9   MEALS: alc (main courses £11 to £19). Set L £12.95 (2 courses) to £14.95, Set D £16.25 (2 courses) to £18.75   SERVICE: not inc, card slips closed   CARDS: Amex, MasterCard, Visa   DETAILS: 36 seats. Private parties: 28 main room, 10 private room. Vegetarian meals. Children's helpings. No-smoking area. No music

▲ Swinton Park, Samuel's 🍴 ✳

Masham HG4 4JH

TEL: (01765) 680900   FAX: (01765) 680901

WEBSITE: www.swintonpark.com

1m SW of Masham

| NEW CHEF |
| MODERN BRITISH |
| £28–£54 |

The 200-acre grounds of this imposing pile bought by Samuel Cunliffe-Lister in the 1880s include a walled garden growing a wealth of fresh produce and, less than ten feet from the restaurant window, a deer park, which also plays its part in supplying the kitchen. A new head chef arrived in spring 2004. His modern menu has seen a starter of crab ravioli partnered with sautéed spinach and a spiced shellfish foam, then a main course of saltimbocca of rabbit with confit of pork belly, red onion Tatin and lavender jus, finishing with 'a theme of Yorkshire rhubarb' (or choose from the excellent selection of British, Irish and French cheeses). The good-value wine list is arranged by grape variety, with clued-up choices from all regions adding up to a profound collection of traditional and modern styles, starting at £14. By the glass, six reds and six whites are complemented by a host of sweet and fortified wines.

CHEF: Andrew Burton   PROPRIETORS: Mark and Felicity Cunliffe-Lister   OPEN: all week 12.30 to 2, 7 to 9.30   MEALS: Set L £14 (2 courses) to £18, Set D £32   SERVICE: not inc   CARDS: Amex, Delta, Diners, MasterCard, Switch, Visa   DETAILS: 60 seats. 16 seats outside. Private parties: 90 main room, 8 to 80 private rooms. Car park. Vegetarian meals. Children's helpings. No children under 12 at D. No smoking. Wheelchair access (also WC). Music. No mobile phones   ACCOMMODATION: 30 rooms, all with bath/shower. TV. Phone. B&B £100 to £350. Rooms for disabled. Baby facilities. Fishing (£5)

MEDBOURNE Leicestershire   map 5

▲ Horse and Trumpet

| NEW ENTRY |
| COOKING 6 |
| MODERN BRITISH |
| £27–£63 |

Old Green, Medbourne LE16 8DX

TEL: (01858) 565000   FAX: (01858) 565551

WEBSITE: www.horseandtrumpet.com

As the restaurant's name indicates, this three-storey thatched building of yellow sandstone was once a village pub. Dating from 1710, it opened in its present, sensitively converted form in 2003. In the lounge an old hipbath beside the inglenook fire serves as a log-basket, while the dining rooms on either side have light-coloured walls, low beamed ceilings and comfortably upholstered chairs.

David Lennox was a sous-chef at Inverlochy Castle (see entry, Fort William), so his cooking shows ambition – witness a roast chump of tender lamb with braised red cabbage and raisins, fondant potato and a cordon of mustard sauce, plus a thyme-infused jus. Portions, especially at lunch, are on the modest side, but dishes deliver concentrated flavour, as in a single raviolo of chopped Skye scallop, sitting on wilted greens and diced pineapple, with a frothy, truffled sauce. Interesting garnishes have included sweet-and-sour fennel wafers and avocado cream with a crab salad, while homely English rhubarb and custard might be teamed with an advocaat and ginger ice cream (other puddings come with ice cream containing mustard seeds). Service can look short-handed at busy times. The compact wine list offers a good range of flavours from £11.45, and half a dozen come by the small (125ml) glass.

CHEF: David Lennox   PROPRIETORS: David Lennox, Gary Magnani and Jim Bowes   OPEN: Tue to Sun L 12 to 1.30 (2.30 Sun), Tue to Sat D 7 to 9.30   MEALS: alc D (main courses £13 to £20). Set L £12 (2 courses) to

£15. Set L Sun £17 (2 courses) to £23   SERVICE: not inc   CARDS: Delta, Diners, MasterCard, Switch, Visa
DETAILS: 50 seats. 20 seats outside. Private parties: 25 main room. Vegetarian meals. Wheelchair access
(also WC). Music   ACCOMMODATION: 4 rooms, all with bath/shower. TV. Phone. B&B £55 to £65

MELBOURN Cambridgeshire   map 6

Pink Geranium ▯ ⅚✳

25 Station Road, Melbourn SG8 6DX	COOKING 5
TEL: (01763) 260215 FAX: (01763) 262110	MODERN BRITISH
WEBSITE: www.pinkgeranium.co.uk	£35–£74

With its thatched roof, pink colour scheme (inside and out), cottage garden and yards of
floral fabrics, the Pink Geranium is country restaurant personified. The food is a lot more
contemporary than the décor. Gordon Campbell takes a thoughtful and refined approach
to modern British cooking, serving appealing combinations of red mullet escabèche with
potato salad and saffron dressing, or a salad of air-dried Cumbrian ham with tête de moine
cheese and caper berry dressing to begin. The repertoire moves along gently with plenty of
original ideas and novel presentations, but the focus is on sound culinary principles and
traditional cooking methods, backed up by well-sourced raw materials. You might come
across main courses of Hungarian beef and venison goulash with fondant potato, roast
beetroot and sour cream, or pan-fried wild sea trout with chive potato purée, confit
tomatoes, braised leeks and pesto, with dark Valrhona marquise with white chocolate
sorbet for dessert. The combination of carte and fixed-price menu for both lunch and
dinner is worthy of note and certainly gives the kitchen a lot to do. The wine list is all
tickety-boo, with plenty of worthy names throughout France, Italy and the wider world.
Ten house recommendations start at a reasonable £12.95 and all come by the glass.

CHEF: Gordon Campbell   PROPRIETOR: Lawrence Champion   OPEN: Tue to Sun L 12 to 2, Tue to Sat D 7 to
9.30   CLOSED: 25 and 26 Dec, 1 Jan   MEALS: alc exc Sun L (main courses £17.50 to £26.50). Set L Tue to
Sat £16.50 (2 courses) to £21.50, Set L Sun £24.50, Set D Tue to Fri £21.50 (2 courses) to £27.50
SERVICE: 10% (optional), card slips closed   CARDS: Amex, Delta, MasterCard, Switch, Visa   DETAILS: 60
seats. Private parties: 50 main room, 4 to 14 private rooms. Car park. Vegetarian meals. Children's
helpings. No smoking. No music £5

▲ Sheene Mill ⅚✳

Station Road, Melbourn SG8 6DX	COOKING 3
TEL: (01763) 261393 FAX: (01763) 261376	GLOBAL
WEBSITE: www.sheenemill.co.uk	£35–£72

At this converted mill on the River Mel you overlook the old mill pond while pondering
Stephen Saunders' menus. These are based on organic ingredients sourced locally, and Far
Eastern and Mediterranean touches are evident – hence, tian of Cromer crab with
cucumber noodles and shiso leaves, or Greek salad with halloumi, olives and dried
tomatoes, as possible starters. Main courses take pedigree raw materials (Gloucester Old
Spot pork, Gressingham duckling, well-hung Aberdeen Angus beef, Welsh spring lamb,
Irish salmon) and respect their integrity: the salmon, for example, baked en croûte and
served with spinach and a Noilly Prat velouté; the duck teamed with chickpeas, shiitake
mushrooms and harissa spices. Finish with chocolate crème brûlée with lavender ice
cream, or iced raspberry soufflé. House wines are £13.50 to £16.50, with glass prices from
£4 to £6.

CHEFS: Steven Saunders and Adrian Doughty   PROPRIETORS: Steven and Sally Saunders   OPEN: all week
L 12 to 2 (2.30 Sun), Mon to Sat D 7 to 10   CLOSED: 25 Dec D, 26 Dec, 31 Dec L, 1 Jan   MEALS: alc (not Sun
L; main courses £10 to £26). Set L Sun £25. Snack menu available Mon to Fri   SERVICE: 10% (optional),
card slips closed   CARDS: Amex, Delta, MasterCard, Switch, Visa   DETAILS: 100 seats. 40 seats outside.
Private parties: 110 main room, 40 to 65 private rooms. Car park. Vegetarian meals. Children's helpings.
No smoking. Music at D. No mobile phones. Air-conditioned   ACCOMMODATION: 9 rooms, all with bath/
shower. TV. Phone. B&B £85 to £130. Baby facilities

MILLBANK West Yorkshire

map 9

Millbank ₤✳

Mill Bank Road, Millbank, Nr Sowerby Bridge HX6 3DY
TEL: (01422) 825588   FAX: (01422) 822080
WEBSITE: www.themillbank.com

COOKING 5

1m S of Sowerby Bridge, turn W off A58 at Triangle;
Millbank is ½m on L

MODERN EUROPEAN
£24–£51

'What a cool, slightly offbeat, funky place,' declared one reporter of this country pub and
restaurant in a beautiful rural setting. A change in ownership in late 2003 saw a team
including chef Glen Futter taking control, and the transition has been seamless. The low-
ceilinged dining room has wooden floors and close-packed square pine tables – 'not a horse
brass in sight!'

The lively menu has delivered a starter of smoked chicken and black pudding croquette,
crisp and ungreasy with 'the chicken smoked gently, so it didn't bully the other
ingredients'. Other starters might include a trio of roast king scallops, sweet and perfectly
cooked, set on a crisp cake of herb risotto with a rich pool of cauliflower purée underneath,
or linguini with white truffle sauce, poached egg and Parmesan. Sound sourcing is also
evident in main-course halibut, praised as 'squeaky-fresh', served perched on sheets of
green lasagne filled with shiitake mushrooms and artichoke hearts in a fennel cream sauce;
meat-eaters might go for pappardelle with venison and wild mushroom ragù. To finish, try
orange bread pudding with ginger and carrot ice cream, plus a sugar syrup containing
julienne of orange zest. If that's too sweet, there are Yorkshire cheeses and home-made
biscuits. Service is appropriately friendly and informal. The style-organised wine list scours
the world for interesting bottles and offers plenty under £20 (starting with £10.95 French
house wines), and includes a dozen by the glass. And the espresso is strong.

CHEF: Glen Futter   PROPRIETOR: Millbank (Halifax) Ltd   OPEN: Tue to Sun L 12 to 2.30 (12.30 to 4.30 Sun),
Tue to Sat D 6 to 9.30 (10 Fri and Sat)   CLOSED: first 2 weeks in Oct, first week in Jan   MEALS: alc (not Sun
L; main courses £9 to £15). Set L Tue to Sat £10.95 (2 courses), Set L Sun £13.25 (2 courses) to £16.95,
Set D Tue to Fri 6 to 7 £10.95.   SERVICE: not inc   CARDS: Delta, MasterCard, Switch, Visa   DETAILS: 50
seats. 12 seats outside. Private parties: 35 main room, 30 private room. Vegetarian meals. No-smoking
area. Wheelchair access (not WC). Music £5

MILTON ERNEST Bedfordshire

map 6

Strawberry Tree ₤✳

3 Radwell Road, Milton Ernest MK44 1RY

COOKING 6

TEL/FAX: (01234) 823633
EMAIL: strawberrytree_restaurant@yahoo.co.uk

MODERN EUROPEAN
£42–£65

Three specimens of *Arbutus unedo* (the evergreen strawberry tree) grow in the garden of
this seventeenth-century thatched building that once comprised a sweet shop and laundry

with a little cottage at the back. The Bona family opened it as a tea shop but have moved on apace, and their restaurant is now regarded as a gastronomic beacon. Sons Jason and Andrew hold sway in the kitchen and are always on the lookout for seasonal supplies: some organic vegetables are grown in the garden, game is local, the village fishmonger delivers seafood, and they have a liking for rare breeds (from Saddleback pork to White-Faced Woodland lamb).

This harvest festival of ingredients is used to telling effect for a short, classically inclined menu of meticulous dishes that are presented with an eye for geometry and visuals. Everything – including the service – is just so. As an opener you might choose warm fillet of mackerel with a colourful assemblage of beetroot, parsley, capers, pine nuts and horseradish cream, or pumpkin tortellini with sage, Parmesan, chestnuts and amaretti. Fine raw materials also take centre stage when it comes to main courses: roast free-range chicken is accompanied by lemon butter, wild mushroom risotto and truffle cream, while Dexter beef is simmered for five hours, then served with herb dumplings, parsnip purée and winter roots. As for desserts, expect the likes of warm bitter chocolate fondant with double cream sorbet, or almond crème brûlée with Yorkshire rhubarb. Around 30 wines make up the knowledgeably assembled list, which opens with house selections at £15.

CHEFS: Jason and Andrew Bona   PROPRIETORS: the Bona family   OPEN: Wed to Fri L 12 to 1.45, Wed to Sat D 7.30 to 9   CLOSED: 2 weeks Jan, 2 weeks summer   MEALS: alc L (main courses £14 to £18). Set D £38   SERVICE: not inc, card slips closed, 12.5% for parties of 8 or more   CARDS: Delta, MasterCard, Switch, Visa   DETAILS: 22 seats. Private parties: 18 main room, 8 private room. Car park. Vegetarian meals. Children's helpings. No smoking. Occasional music

---

MONKS ELEIGH Suffolk   map 6

Swan Inn 🍴✹ £

The Street, Monks Eleigh IP7 7AU   COOKING 3
TEL: (01449) 741391   MODERN EUROPEAN
                                                        £26–£52

This thatched, timber-framed building, with a history going back to medieval times, is still a village pub as well as a restaurant, and the main bar has been refurbished with a wood floor and warm colours. Otherwise it's business as usual for Carol and Nigel Ramsbottom: she works out front, he looks after the stoves. Seasonal East Anglian produce is put to good use: perhaps in Brancaster mussels steamed with coconut milk, chillies and coriander, or warm breast of woodcock with wild mushroom and crispy bacon salad and a Puy lentil dressing. The blackboard menu offers a roving repertoire covering everything from seared scallops on minted tabbouleh to a patriotically English apple and ginger pudding. Regional real ales are on draught, and the concise wine list from Lay & Wheeler begins with house at £10.50.

CHEF: Nigel Ramsbottom   PROPRIETORS: Carol and Nigel Ramsbottom   OPEN: Wed to Sun 12 to 2, 7 to 9 CLOSED: 25 and 26 Dec   MEALS: alc (main courses £9 to £20)   SERVICE: not inc, card slips closed   CARDS: Delta, MasterCard, Switch, Visa   DETAILS: 40 seats. Private parties: 25 main room, 12 to 25 private rooms. Car park. Vegetarian meals. Children's helpings. No smoking. No music   (£5)

New main entries are listed near the front of the book. Some may have appeared in earlier years (though not in the previous edition) or as a Round-up entry last year.

▲ Morston Hall ☻

Morston NR25 7AA	COOKING 6
TEL: (01263) 741041 FAX: (01263) 740419	MODERN BRITISH
WEBSITE: www.morstonhall.com	£37–£63

Morston Hall, built of flint and brick, is in a single-street village on the edge of salt marshes not far from the sea. It's the kind of country house that's run as much as possible as though it were a private dwelling, with its own kitchen garden supplying salad leaves and herbs, and the recently made-over dining room and conservatory done in calm colours and replete with interesting artefacts.

A no-choice dinner menu of four courses plus coffee (with Sunday lunch as the only midday option) is designed to show off the best of local produce, as well as the formidable skills of Galton Blackiston and his team; 'just about everything at this meal was classically perfect', summed up one reporter. A meaty starter is often the way, so that a spring menu opened with seared quail breast with ballottine of foie gras and poached rhubarb, before moving on to John Dory on pepper fondue, and then roast local beef fillet with stewed cabbage and béarnaise. Meals end with a choice of dessert or cheeses, the former perhaps a variation on a fruit theme, which might easily be blood orange (a tart, sorbet and jelly) as soon as strawberry. Some have questioned the balance in a meal that might kick off with braised lamb shoulder and proceed through a cheese soufflé to a piece of halibut, but the quality of what is presented and the technique that is brought to bear on it are not in doubt. Service is attentive, even if the pace may be a little more sedate than seems necessary. The thoroughly accessible wine list is arranged by grape variety and country, with interesting contrasts of Old and New World styles. Options by the glass are plentiful, and dessert wines are well worth a look.

CHEFS: Galton Blackiston, Samantha Wegg and Toby Runyland   PROPRIETORS: Tracy and Galton Blackiston   OPEN: Sun L 12.30 for 1 (1 sitting), all week D 7.30 for 8 (1 sitting)   CLOSED: 25 and 26 Dec, 1 to 26 Jan   MEALS: Set L £26, Set D £40   SERVICE: not inc, card slips closed   CARDS: Amex, Delta, Diners, MasterCard, Switch, Visa   DETAILS: 35 seats. Private parties: 40 main room, 10 to 14 private rooms. Car park. Children's helpings. No smoking before coffee. Wheelchair access (also WC). No music. No mobile phones   ACCOMMODATION: 7 rooms, all with bath/shower. TV. Phone. D,B&B £135 to £240. Baby facilities

▲ Beetle & Wedge ☻ ✗

Ferry Lane, Moulsford on Thames, Moulsford OX10 9JF	COOKING 4
TEL: (01491) 651381 FAX: (01491) 651376	ANGLO-FRENCH
WEBSITE: www.beetleandwedge.co.uk	£41–£69

The Thames-side setting of this charming hotel is a magnet whatever the season (as Jerome K. Jerome found when he lived here – he chronicled the escapades of his friends' visits in *Three Men in a Boat*). The formal conservatory Dining Room – in the main house – makes the best of the river views, and in summer opens onto the small garden (also used for al fresco dining). The popular, relaxed brasserie-style Boathouse alongside (focusing on chargrilled dishes like sirloin steak béarnaise) now has a brand new kitchen and riverside conservatory.

Richard Smith sources quality raw ingredients for his sensible-length, Anglo-French Dining Room carte. Expect the likes of a warm onion tart with sautéed foie gras and truffle sauce to start, while main courses might run to steamed escalope of halibut with lobster and fresh asparagus, or a fillet of Scottish beef with shallots and red wine sauce. Choose between classic crème brûlée or indulgent warm treacle sponge with real custard and vanilla ice cream to finish. Service is 'polite, attentive and polished', while the wine list reveals a keen interest in everything from 15 interesting house bottles under £20 to fine old clarets sourced at auction. In between are goodies from France (Alsace, Loire and Rhône giving strong support to the fuller selections from Bordeaux and Burgundy) and a smattering from elsewhere.

CHEFS/PROPRIETORS: Richard and Kate Smith OPEN: all week 12 to 1.45, 7 to 9.45 MEALS: alc (main courses £12.50 to £19.50). Cover £1. Booking essential SERVICE: not inc CARDS: Amex, Delta, Diners, MasterCard, Switch, Visa DETAILS: 65 seats. 30 seats outside. Private parties: 50 main room. Car park. Vegetarian meals. Children's helpings. No smoking in 1 dining room. Wheelchair access (also WC). No music. No mobile phones ACCOMMODATION: 10 rooms, all with bath/shower. TV. Phone. B&B £135 to £175. Baby facilities. Fishing

MOULTON North Yorkshire map 9

Black Bull Inn ♥

Moulton DL10 6QJ
TEL: (01325) 377289 FAX: (01325) 377422
EMAIL: sarah@blackbullinn.demon.co.uk

COOKING 4
SEAFOOD/MODERN BRITISH
£28–£67

Located just a mile from Scotch Corner, this is a food pub with the emphasis more on the food than pub. The traditional wood-panelled bar has a genteel atmosphere and a simple lunchtime menu. The popular restaurant, which has been established long enough to have acquired legendary status, occupies a converted Pullman railway carriage to the rear of the main building. Fish and seafood are the main focus of the long menus, which offer more than two dozen starters, divided into hot and cold, followed by a similar number of main courses. Choices feature plenty of classics such as moules marinière, shellfish bisque, lobster Newburg or thermidor, and poached salmon with asparagus and hollandaise. But the repertoire extends to more fashionable ideas, including griddled scallops with black pudding on sweet potato purée and oyster sauce, and king prawn and squid laksa. Non-fish dishes range from chateaubriand with béarnaise to duck, avocado, orange and pine-nut salad. The good-value wine list is appropriately biased towards whites and is strongest in France. Meat-eaters demanding red will find a satisfying selection from Bordeaux and the Rhône, and red Burgundies bridge both camps.

CHEF: Paul Grundy PROPRIETORS: A.M.C. and S.C. Pagendam OPEN: Mon to Fri L 12 to 2, Mon to Sat D 6.30 to 10.15 CLOSED: 24 to 26 Dec MEALS: alc (main courses £15.50 to £22.50). Set L £17.50. Bar L menu available SERVICE: not inc CARDS: Amex, Delta, Diners, MasterCard, Switch, Visa DETAILS: 100 seats. 20 seats outside. Private parties: 10 main room, 10 to 30 private rooms. Car park. Vegetarian meals. No children under 7. No music

NAYLAND Suffolk map 6

▲ White Hart ♥

11 High Street, Nayland CO6 4JF
TEL: (01206) 263382 FAX: (01206) 263638
WEBSITE: www.whitehart-nayland.co.uk

COOKING 3
MODERN EUROPEAN
£22–£54

In a village of picturesque, pastel-coloured and timber-framed houses by the Stour, this former coaching inn is owned by Michel Roux (see Waterside Inn, Bray). There's a bar, with more low-key eating out back, while the main dining room has a 'calm, gently formal atmosphere', tasteful pale yellow walls, cream-clothed tables and elegant, modern seating. Carl Shillingford's repertoire is European with French flair, and local and seasonal produce feature prominently. So expect 'attractively presented, well-balanced' dishes like roast monkfish, pancetta-wrapped and stuffed with lobster mousse, with sauce Nantua, or fried fillet of pork on tagliatelle with a truffle sauce. Finish perhaps with Seville orange bavarois and home-made mandarin sorbet. Occasional over-salting has been reported. Service is professional and fairly formal, and 14 house wines at £11 lay the foundations for a well-balanced international list.

CHEF: Carl Shillingford PROPRIETOR: Michel Roux OPEN: all week 12 to 2.30, 6.30 to 9.30 (10 Sat, 9 Sun) CLOSED: 26 Dec to 9 Jan MEALS: alc (main courses £10 to £16.50). Set L Tue to Sat £9.95 (2 courses) to £12.95, Set L Sun £14.60 (2 courses) to £18.90, Set D Sun to Fri £17.50 (2 courses) to £21.50. Bar L menu available SERVICE: not inc, 10% (optional) for parties of 6 or more CARDS: Amex, Delta, Diners, MasterCard, Switch, Visa DETAILS: 50 seats. 25 seats outside. Private parties: 76 main room, 10 to 33 private rooms. Car park. Vegetarian meals. Children's helpings. Wheelchair access (also WC). Music ACCOMMODATION: 6 rooms, all with bath/shower. TV. Phone. B&B £69 to £95. Baby facilities (£5)

NEAR SAWREY Cumbria   map 8

▲ Ees Wyke ✱

Near Sawrey LA22 0JZ
TEL/FAX: (015394) 36393   COOKING 2
WEBSITE: www.eeswyke.co.uk   BRITISH
on B5285 2m S of Hawkshead   £36–£44

A hop across Windermere on the ferry, then a short drive along steep lanes brings you to this elegant yet comfortable and friendly small hotel. A reporter found breakfast 'exceptional' and generous, but dinner is the main event, and the five-course menu has a strong local feel, with meat, game and smoked fish from nearby producers. Starters like wild mushrooms in creamy chervil sauce, or prawns in butter with garlic, lemon and parsley, precede a no-choice second course (perhaps smoked haddock and mushroom pancake) before mains of, say, game casserole with red wine and juniper, or pan-fried monkfish fillet with provençale sauce. Dessert options could include treacle tart with cream, or prune and Armagnac fool, and the finale is a selection from the well-kept cheeseboard. The kindly priced wine list starts at £12 for French and Australian house bottles.

CHEF: Richard Lee PROPRIETORS: Richard and Margaret Lee OPEN: all week D only 7 to 7.30 (1 sitting) MEALS: Set D £27 SERVICE: not inc, card slips closed CARDS: Amex, Delta, MasterCard, Switch, Visa DETAILS: 20 seats. 20 seats outside. Private parties: 20 main room. Car park. Vegetarian meals. No children under 12. No smoking. No music ACCOMMODATION: 8 rooms, 6 with bath/shower. TV. B&B £56 per person. No children under 12 (£5)

The cuisine styles noted at the tops of entries are only an approximation, often suggested to us by the restaurants themselves. Please read the entry itself to find out more about the cooking style.

NETHER ALDERLEY Cheshire · map 8

Wizard ⁵✱

Macclesfield Road, Nether Alderley SK10 4UB
TEL: (01625) 584000 FAX: (01625) 585105

COOKING 3
MODERN BRITISH
£31–£57

This secluded old-beamed hostelry in leafy surroundings, is more restaurant than pub, delivering modern British food in a traditional setting. Three dining areas vary in style and furnishings; two have flagstone floors and old wooden furniture, the other is more formal. The atmosphere – smart yet unpretentious and relaxed – is bolstered by attentive and friendly service. A repertoire of sensible length has some Mediterranean undertones, perhaps linguine with wilted rocket, pine nuts, cherry tomatoes and pesto, or seared sea bass fillet, avocado and spinach-leaf salad with a balsamic dressing, but also pork and leek sausages with mash and onion gravy. Desserts embrace cappuccino crème brûlée, or hot chocolate brownie with vanilla ice cream and raspberries, while the globetrotting wine list, laid out by style, has eight house bottles at £14.50.

CHEF: Paul Beattie PROPRIETOR: Bispham Green Brewery OPEN: Tue to Sun L 12 to 2, Tue to Sat D 7 to 9.30 MEALS: alc (not Sun L; main courses £9.50 to £19). Set L Sun £12.95 (1 course) to £18.95 SERVICE: not inc, card slips closed CARDS: Amex, Delta, MasterCard, Switch, Visa DETAILS: 90 seats. 12 seats outside. Private parties: 40 main room, 8 to 40 private rooms. Car park. Vegetarian meals. Children's helpings. No smoking in 1 dining room. Wheelchair access (also men's WC). Music

NETTLEBED Oxfordshire · map 2

▲ White Hart ⊗ ⁵✱

28–30 High Strett, Nettlebed RG9 5DD
TEL: (01491) 641245 FAX: (01491) 649018
WEBSITE: www.whitehartnettlebed.com

COOKING 3
MODERN BRITISH
£50–£86

This old brick and flint village inn is not as much of a pub as the name suggests. The ancient exterior contrasts with the minimalist modern décor inside, and most of the space is given over to the bistro, although the focal point of culinary operations (and the part to which the cooking score applies) is the restaurant, a small room with aubergine-coloured walls hung with a couple of abstract paintings. Seared scallops with a beetroot tart and onion purée has proved a colourful and clever combination, with accurately timed scallops next to a crisp puff pastry disc topped with thin slices of beetroot, while roast rack of lamb with ratatouille tian and pepper nage has provided good-quality meat, carefully cooked, in a smooth, creamy sauce with an intense pepper flavour. Finish perhaps with a well-made, delicately flavoured banana soufflé with toffee ice cream. Around 75 wines include everything from straightforward vins de pays at £14 to top-class Burgundies and Bordeaux with three-figure price tags, and there are ten wines by the glass.

CHEF: Nick Seckington PROPRIETOR: Robyn Jones OPEN: Thur to Sat D only 7 to 9 MEALS: Set D £35 to (tasting menu) £55. Bistro menu available L and D SERVICE: 12.5% (optional) CARDS: Diners, MasterCard, Switch, Visa DETAILS: 34 seats. 20 seats outside. Private parties: 34 main room, 18 to 46 private rooms. Car park. Vegetarian meals. No children. No smoking in 1 dining room. Wheelchair access (also WC). Music ACCOMMODATION: 12 rooms, all with bath/shower. TV. Phone. B&B £90 to £145. Rooms for disabled. Baby facilities

▲ Donnington Valley Hotel, Wine Press Restaurant 🍷

Old Oxford Road, Donnington, Newbury RG14 3AG
TEL: (01635) 551199   FAX: (01635) 551123
WEBSITE: www.donningtonvalley.co.uk

COOKING 2
MODERN BRITISH-PLUS
£28–£57

This friendly, modern hotel, sister to the Vineyard at Stockcross (see entry), is owned by Sir Peter Michael, who has wineries in the Napa and Sonoma Valleys. A striking interior design gives the restaurant a vaulted ceiling and an additional mezzanine level for its well-spaced, appropriately dressed tables. The modern carte has set pricing at dinner (with a few supplements) and could feature risotto of confit duck with spring onion and rocket to start, and pan-fried turbot with a white bean and vegetable cassoulet to follow. Finish with the likes of caramelised lemon tart with mascarpone and vanilla cream. The crisply presented wine list is thoroughly approachable, opening with an impressive range by the glass from £2.50 and moving on to bottles in various price bands below £20 before unveiling a fine global cellar that is strongest in California (naturally), Bordeaux and Italy.

CHEF: Kelvin Johnstone   PROPRIETOR: Sir Peter Michael   OPEN: all week 12 to 2, 7 to 10   MEALS: alc L (main courses £7.50 to £12.50). Set L £16 (2 courses) to £19, Set D £19 (2 courses) to £29.50. Bar menu available   SERVICE: not inc   CARDS: Amex, Delta, Diners, MasterCard, Switch, Visa   DETAILS: 120 seats. 12 seats outside. Private parties: 120 main room, 40 to 120 private rooms. Car park. Vegetarian meals. Children's helpings. No-smoking area. Wheelchair access (also WC). Music. No mobile phones. Air-conditioned   ACCOMMODATION: 58 rooms, all with bath/shower. TV. Phone. Room only £155 to £225. Rooms for disabled

Blackfriars Café Bar 🍴 £

Friars Street, Newcastle upon Tyne NE4 4XN
TEL: (0191) 261 5945   FAX: (0191) 261 9432
WEBSITE: www.blackfriarscafebar.co.uk

COOKING 2
GLOBAL
£20–£49

Sibling of Sidney's in Tynemouth (see entry), Blackfriars sits in a complex of medieval buildings that indeed once housed Dominicans. In today's refectory, with its well-spaced wooden tables, tiled floors, beamed ceilings and stone walls, there are no scriptural readings but thoroughly modern dishes with influences from the Mediterranean and far beyond. A starter of cherry tomato and goats' cheese tart Tatin with black olive tapenade, and mains of grilled salmon and champ, or Malaysian massaman lamb rump curry, show the range. Desserts stick closer to home, maybe a double chocolate soufflé with vanilla anglaise. The wine suggestions accompanying each dish on the menu come from a compact French/New World list that starts at £11 and stays largely under £20.

CHEF: Andy Drape   PROPRIETORS: Andy and Sam Hook   OPEN: Tue to Sun L 12 to 2.30 (3 Sun), Tue to Sat D 6 to 10   CLOSED: bank hols   MEALS: alc (not Sun; main courses £10 to £17). Set L Tue to Sat £8.50 (2 courses) to £10.95, Set L Sun and Set D Tue to Fri 6 to 7 £9.95 (2 courses) to £12.95   SERVICE: not inc, 10% (optional) for parties of 6 or more   CARDS: Delta, MasterCard, Switch, Visa   DETAILS: 65 seats. Private parties: 65 main room, 10 to 20 private rooms. Vegetarian meals. Children's helpings. No smoking. Wheelchair access (not WC). Music. Air-conditioned   (£5)

Café 21 🏮✶

19–21 Queen Street, Princes Wharf, Quayside,	COOKING 5
Newcastle upon Tyne NE1 3UG	BISTRO
TEL: (0191) 222 0755 FAX: (0191) 221 0761	£26–£62

An expansive, double-fronted glass façade at this brasserie means that you don't have to wonder what's going on behind the green door, as it's all pretty much on show. Wooden floors and a cool green ambience lend the place contemporary appeal, and the food follows on with innovation and confidence. Roast scallops on nori with black-bean vinaigrette is typical of the style, showing a nerveless way with non-Western ingredients. Impressive, too, at inspection was a main course of turbot fillet in a creamy stew of prawns, crayfish, broad beans, peas and asparagus, and, with an eye to the 'café' ethos, so was a piece of grilled halibut with tartare sauce and a bowl of chips. On the meat side, there might be slow-cooked lamb shoulder with courgettes provençale and marjoram, and substantial desserts have taken in spiced plums with toasted brioche, a chocolate doughnut with brandied cherries, and a perfectly softened roast pear with maple walnut ice cream. Service is friendly and on the cool side of efficient, perhaps necessarily so when there is so much eager custom to be handled. The wine list dashes about hither and yon, with the southern hemisphere getting a good look-in and Duboeuf house wines opening proceedings at £12.

CHEF: Christopher Dobson   PROPRIETORS: Terence and Susan Laybourne   OPEN: Mon to Sat 12 to 2.30, 6 to 10.30   CLOSED: bank hols   MEALS: alc (main courses £11.50 to £19.50). Set L £13 (2 courses) to £15.50   SERVICE: not inc   CARDS: Amex, Delta, Diners, MasterCard, Switch, Visa   DETAILS: 60 seats. Vegetarian meals. Children's helpings. No smoking in 1 dining room. Wheelchair access (not WC). Music. Air-conditioned

Fisherman's Lodge 🏮✶

Deep Dene House, Jesmond Dene, Jesmond,	
Newcastle upon Tyne NE7 7BQ	COOKING 6
TEL: (0191) 281 3281 FAX: (0191) 281 6410	SEAFOOD/MODERN BRITISH
WEBSITE: www.fishermanslodge.co.uk	£38–£103

This may be Newcastle, but the Lodge – a late Victorian villa up a long, woodland drive – feels a world away from urban bustle. Within, deep browns lend gravitas to the décor in the lounge and the two linked dining rooms. Bread studded with black pudding indicates that not everything is out of the classical repertoire, but dishes are thoughtfully composed, and skill shines through in bold, confident flavours. Ballottine of salmon comes with herbed fromage blanc, caviar and a shellfish cream. A potentially dainty starter of roast quail breast gains weight from a caramelised shallot tart, pancetta and a Barolo sauce. Opulent ingredients appear alongside the more everyday, so foie gras and choucroute support roast duck breast and celeriac, while more foie gras arrives with spiced pork belly, truffled mash and a white bean cassoulet.

The fashionable kindergarten tendency for puddings is alive and kicking in dishes such as banana soufflé with milkshake and 'iced banana crumble stack', or there may be Valrhona chocolate truffle cake with Baileys parfait and white chocolate mousse. The pace of service is agreeably brisk, without making anybody feel rushed. A 'top 20' page gives a tempting preview of a strong wine list that has good bottles from most regions, with France going the extra mile. House is £15.95, and, while there is no shortage of options under £20, prices overall are pretty steep.

CHEF: Paul Amer   PROPRIETORS: Tom and Jocelyn Maxfield   OPEN: Mon to Sat 12 to 2, 7 to 10.30
CLOSED: 25 and 26 Dec, 31 Dec L, 1 Jan, bank hols   MEALS: alc (main courses £21 to £36.50). Set L £22.50
SERVICE: not inc   CARDS: Amex, Delta, MasterCard, Switch, Visa   DETAILS: 65 seats. 16 seats outside.
Private parties: 40 main room, 4 to 14 private rooms. Car park. Vegetarian meals. Children's helpings. No
smoking. Wheelchair access (also WC). Music. No mobile phones

Treacle Moon

5–7 The Side, Quayside, Newcastle upon Tyne NE1 3JE
TEL: (0191) 232 5537   FAX: (0191) 221 1745
WEBSITE: www.treaclemoonrestaurant.com

COOKING 4
MODERN BRITISH
£41–£68

The arrestingly named Treacle Moon is on a street leading down to the quayside in this
rejuvenated district of Newcastle. It's a small venue with seating on two levels and fairly
muted décor, doing its business in the evening only, as the lunar reference might suggest. A
couple of specials on a blackboard supplement the printed menu, which is essentially
modern French with forays further East bringing on sautéed king prawns with sweet chilli
and coriander butter, or a main course of Malaysian vegetable curry with jasmine rice.
Otherwise, opt for the familiar likes of chicken liver and foie gras terrine accompanied by
pear poached in saffron and honey, followed perhaps by grilled sea bass with olive-crushed
potatoes and chorizo, or chargrilled beef fillet with dauphinois potatoes and caramelised
pancetta. Indulge yourself with desserts such as a chocolate and Cointreau tart with clotted
cream, or fig and ginger pudding with butterscotch sauce. Pacey service keeps things
moving, and a short, functional wine list is headed by a run of wines by the glass at £2.95 to
£3.50.

CHEFS: Neil Hawdon and Cyan Brace   PROPRIETOR: Tom Maxfield   OPEN: Mon to Sat D only 5.30 to 10
MEALS: alc (main courses £15 to £20)   SERVICE: not inc   CARDS: Amex, Delta, MasterCard, Switch, Visa
DETAILS: 27 seats. Private parties: 27 main room. Vegetarian meals. No smoking. Music. No mobile
phones. Air-conditioned

NEW MILTON Hampshire   map 2

▲ Chewton Glen

Christchurch Road, New Milton BH25 6QS
TEL: (01425) 275341   FAX: (01425) 272310
WEBSITE: www.chewtonglen.com
from A35 follow signs to Walkford and Highcliffe; take
second turning on left after Walkford down Chewton
Farm road

COOKING 5
MODERN EUROPEAN
£32–£120

The eighteenth-century mansion, remodelled along Palladian lines in the late Victorian
era, has it all – croquet lawn, hundreds of variegated fabrics in the interior design, spa
treatments, a range of complementary therapies to address every contemporary ill and so
forth. There's also an orchidaceous dining room with a tented ceiling in which a pianist
gives of his best, new chef Luke Matthews plies his trade, and whole regiments of staff
ensure it all proceeds smoothly, courteously and memorably.

The menu is accurately written and full of enticements: local lobster with Russian salad,
truffled tournedos with a Madeira jus, pan-fried sea bass with scallops, fennel and red wine.
Roast scallops as a first course are done proud with truffled mash, crisp bacon and lines of
earthy pea velouté, while a main dish of loin of veal is combined with tenderly roasted veal
sweetbreads and morels. Cheese is plentiful, well kept and knowledgeably served. The

sweeter of tooth will find the 20-minute wait well worth it for hot Valrhona chocolate fondant with its tuile basket of caramel ice cream, while the less patient might plunge straight into orange trifle. The wine list is a show stopper, but while a handful of bottles is under £20 many of the prices are heart stoppers. Its main focus is on top estates in Bordeaux, Burgundy and California, with strong support from Australia, Italy and Spain.

CHEF: Luke Matthews   PROPRIETORS: Martin and Brigitte Skan   OPEN: all week 12.30 to 1.45, 7.30 to 9.30 MEALS: alc L (main courses £20 to £35). Set L Mon to Sat £20, Set L Sun £36, Set D £57.50 to £100 (inc wine). Lounge and Pool Bar menus available   SERVICE: net prices, card slips closed   CARDS: Amex, Delta, Diners, MasterCard, Switch, Visa   DETAILS: 120 seats. 50 seats outside. Private parties: 80 main room, 4 to 120 private rooms. Car park. Vegetarian meals. Children's helpings. No children under 5. No smoking. Wheelchair access (also WC). Music. No mobile phones. Air-conditioned   ACCOMMODATION: 58 rooms, all with bath/shower. TV. Phone. Room only £199 to £780. Rooms for disabled. No children under 5. Swimming pool

---

NEWTON LONGVILLE Buckinghamshire   map 3

Crooked Billet ▮ ✳

2 Westbrook End, Newton Longville MK17 0DF   COOKING 3
TEL: (01908) 373936   FAX: (01908) 631979   MODERN BRITISH
WEBSITE: www.thebillet.co.uk   £32–£116

A fanatically researched and impressive wine list is the consuming passion of this pub in a village near Milton Keynes. It still has the air of a true village local, albeit with bar lunches running from posh sandwiches – lobster club, say, or steak with mustard mayonnaise and onions – to salads, pasta and a full three-course affair. Dinner in the restaurant could start with onion soup with a Stilton croûte and crispy shallots, or bubble and squeak tart with a poached egg, bacon and hollandaise, and go on to something like pan-fried fillet of sea bass with mash, deep-fried leeks and caviar cream, or rack of lamb in a mustard and parsley crust with swede mash and baby turnips. Finish with ice creams or sorbets or push the boat out and go for chocolate bread-and-butter pudding made with Armagnac-soaked raisins served with vanilla ice cream and custard. The wines are quite pricey, but the coup here is that all of them are available by the glass – sherries, fizz, everyday quaffers, fashionable names, global superstars, the lot. Listing is done by region, then again by minutely defined styles. Prices start at £14.50.

CHEF: Emma Gilchrist   PROPRIETORS: John and Emma Gilchrist   OPEN: Sun L 12.30 to 3, Tue to Sat D 7 to 10   CLOSED: 25 and 26 Dec, first 2 weeks Jan   MEALS: alc D (main courses £10 to £25). Set L Sun £18.95, Set D £50 to £85 (inc wine). Bar L menu available Tue to Sat   SERVICE: not inc, card slips closed   CARDS: Amex, Delta, MasterCard, Switch, Visa   DETAILS: 60 seats. 50 seats outside. Private parties: 8 main room. Car park. Vegetarian meals. Children's helpings. No smoking. Occasional music. No mobile phones

---

NEWTON POPPLEFORD Devon   map 1

Dawsons ✳   [NEW ENTRY]

6 Greenbank, High Street, Newton Poppleford EX10 0EB   COOKING 3
TEL: (01395) 568100   FAX: (01395) 568092   MODERN EUROPEAN/SEAFOOD
WEBSITE: www.dawsons-restaurant.co.uk   £27–£52

There's a prominent sign outside this small, cottage-style restaurant on a raised slip road beside the High Street. Chris Dawson, after working in some admired country-house kitchens, cooks here single-handedly, while wife Karen is the 'chatty, friendly' host in a 'light, pleasant room', with elegant table settings. Sensible-length, regularly changing fixed-price menus major on fish but offer meat choices too: perhaps rump of West Country lamb with an assiette of beans and fried sweetbreads. The whole operation is 'pleasantly understated', and dishes focus on flavour, balance and honest ingredients rather than presentational fireworks. Lunch is a light, 'fantastic-value' affair; dinner is slightly swisher, providing, say, roast sea bass with artichoke, French beans, sauté potatoes, basil oil and a chive crème fraîche. Desserts, perhaps a hot chocolate fondant, are paired with matching wines, while the main wine list (ordered by style) contains a good sprinkling of half-bottles, and house from £14.30.

CHEF: Chris Dawson   PROPRIETORS: Chris and Karen Dawson   OPEN: Tue to Sun L 12 to 1.30, Tue to Sat D 7 to 9   CLOSED: 25 Dec, most of Jan   MEALS: Set L £12.50 to £15 (2 courses), Set D £24.50 (2 courses) to £29.50   SERVICE: not inc, card slips closed   CARDS: Amex, Delta, MasterCard, Switch, Visa   DETAILS: 26 seats. Private parties: 18 main room, 2 to 12 private rooms. Vegetarian meals. Children's helpings. No smoking. Music. No mobile phones (£5)

NORDEN Greater Manchester

map 8

Nutters 👗✴

Edenfield Road, Norden OL12 7TW	COOKING 5
TEL/FAX: (01706) 650167	MODERN BRITISH
on A680 between Edenfield and Rochdale	£26–£53

Having wooed the crowds in his converted pub since 1993, gastronomic wonder boy Andrew Nutter upped sticks and moved his operation to new premises as this year's Guide was being compiled. Nutters now occupies a grand Victorian mansion in six and a half acres of parkland a mile down Edenfield Road. When the place is fully up to speed, it will open throughout the year for everything from afternoon teas on the terrace to full meals. Fans will also be relieved to know that Andrew has no plans to do away with his monthly masterclasses.

Judiciously sourced local ingredients are at the heart of the enterprise, and many dishes will ring reassuring bells with those who supported the original venue. Bury black pudding won tons with vegetable 'confetti' is a signature starter, or there might be something classical like flash-seared scallops with rémoulade and truffled sauce vierge. Main courses play a similar tune, from Goosnargh duck breast with carrot and potato dauphinois and beetroot crumble to a jokey modern take on an old Lancashire favourite in the shape of roast cod spiked with slivers of smoked garlic served with 'grandma's' potato scallops, snow pea purée and salt-and-vinegar sauce. Desserts could be as simple as assorted ice creams, and the cheese selection now runs to 80 specimens (many of which can be purchased from the new deli). The wine list is a big, beefy slate with a serious French presence, contributions from the New World and plenty of half-bottles. House wines are £11.95.

CHEF: Andrew Nutter   PROPRIETORS: Rodney, Jean and Andrew Nutter   OPEN: Tue to Sat and bank hol Mon 12 to 2, 6.45 to 9.30 (9.45 Sat), Sun 12 to 4, 6.30 to 9   MEALS: alc (main courses £13 to £17). Set L Mon to Sat £12.95 (2 courses) to £32, Set L Sun £19.95, Set D £32   SERVICE: not inc   CARDS: Amex, Delta, MasterCard, Switch, Visa   DETAILS: 158 seats. 60 seats outside. Private parties: 160 main room, 90 private room. Car park. Vegetarian meals. Children's helpings. No smoking. Wheelchair access (also WC). Music

The Guide always appreciates hearing about changes of chef or owner.

NORTON Wiltshire · map 2

Vine Tree 🅇

Foxley Road, Norton SN16 0JP
TEL: (01666) 837654   FAX: (01666) 838003
WEBSITE: www.thevinetree.co.uk

COOKING **3**
MODERN BRITISH
£30–£55

A tall white building with bright green shutters, the Vine Tree is in the Cotswolds a few miles from Malmesbury. The pair of ghosts that are said to roam the place, perhaps one for each of the two dining rooms, seem not to do anything to disturb people's enjoyment of Steve Smith's enterprising cooking. A real sense of brio invests dishes such as tea-smoked quail with foie gras on bacon salad, or artichokes filled with shrimps and herbs to start, while main courses bring European style to bear on fine English fare. Gressingham duck breast comes with ravioli of the leg meat, carrot fondant and truffled consommé, while sea bass is served with a risotto of scallops and leeks and a vanilla-scented sauce. 'Wardens in comfort' is a dessert that comprises a Williams pear poached in mulled claret served with home-made shortbread and a rosemary-infused chocolate sauce. The compact wine list keeps prices on a tight leash, opening at £10.75 a bottle, £2.95 a glass.

CHEF: Steve Smith   PROPRIETORS: Charles Walker and Tiggi Wood   OPEN: Mon to Sat 12 to 2 (2.30 Sat), 6 to 9.30 (10 Fri and Sat), Sun 12 to 3, 7 to 9.30 (12 to 10.30 summer)   CLOSED: 25 Dec   MEALS: alc (main courses £11 to £22)   SERVICE: not inc, card slips closed   CARDS: Amex, Delta, Diners, MasterCard, Switch, Visa   DETAILS: 75 seats. 70 seats outside. Car park. Vegetarian meals. Children's helpings. No smoking in 1 dining room. Wheelchair access (also WC). Music

NORWICH Norfolk · map 6

Adlard's

79 Upper St Giles, Norwich NR2 1AB
TEL: (01603) 633522
WEBSITE: www.adlards.co.uk

COOKING **5**
MODERN BRITISH
£34–£81

Off the inner ring road, just west of the city centre, with an understated white frontage and small, comfortable dining room, invigorated with bright modern paintings, Adlard's has some 20 years under its belt. Delightful service has always been, and remains, one of the assets of the place, while the cooking style has stayed broadly consistent, and dishes are both ample and fairly complex in conception.

A starter of smooth terrine of foie gras with compote of prunes was lauded by one reporter, or there might be roast red mullet with sweet fennel, calamari and sauce vierge. Scallops might feature in a currently fashionable pairing with cauliflower purée, as well as anchovy fritters, keta caviar and sorrel, to be followed by baked sea bass with a ragoût of mussels, white beans and saffron, in beurre blanc. Among meat main courses loin of pork has been wrapped in bacon, served with lentils and cabbage, and rump of lamb featured in a busy partnership with its sweetbreads, broad beans, mousserons, creamed endive and mint. Desserts run to vanilla cheesecake served with a compote and sorbet of apple, or chocolate moelleux with white chocolate ice cream. An expansive wine list explores the vinous world in thoroughgoing detail, with a pair of French whites and a Chilean red leading the bidding at £14.50, or £3.75 a glass.

CHEF: Tom Kerridge   PROPRIETOR: David Adlard   OPEN: Tue to Sat 12.30 to 1.45, 7.30 (7 Sat) to 10.30   CLOSED: Christmas, bank hols   MEALS: alc (main courses £16 to £23). Set L £19 (2 courses) to £21

SERVICE: not inc   CARDS: Amex, Delta, Diners, MasterCard, Switch, Visa   DETAILS: 42 seats. Private parties: 42 main room. Vegetarian meals. No pipes/cigars. Wheelchair access (not WC). No music. Air-conditioned

Merchant House 🍴

| NEW ENTRY |

8–10 St Andrews Hill, Norwich NR2 1AD
TEL: (01603) 767321

COOKING **3**
MODERN BRITISH/FRENCH
£27–£79

The Merchant House is a small property near St Andrew's Church in the city centre. The smart, expensive-looking décor and slightly formal atmosphere are relieved by friendly service. The menus are short but well balanced to provide a broad choice within a classic French style. Accurately seared scallops on crisp sautéed potatoes in a creamy mayonnaise dressing with a hint of truffle has been a highly enjoyable starter, while among main courses beef fillet is topped attractively with a wild mushroom raviolo and served on rösti with braised shallots and oxtail in a sweetly flavoured Madeira jus, and pan-fried halibut is a colourful dish, the moist, fresh-tasting fish set in a richly flavoured lobster bisque with angel hair pasta, and deep-fried battered scampi for textural contrast. A well-balanced lemon jelly is served as a pre-dessert before vanilla crème brûlée with crisp apple tuiles and an apple jus. The wine list is a good selection from around the world, with house wines £15.

CHEF: Andrew Rudd   PROPRIETOR: Kevin Gardner   OPEN: Tue to Sat 12 to 2, 7 to 9.30   MEALS: alc (main courses £16 to £20). Set meals (prices may vary): L £10.50 (2 courses) to £14.50, D £26 to £29   SERVICE: not inc   CARDS: Amex, Delta, MasterCard, Switch, Visa   DETAILS: 30 seats. Vegetarian meals. Children's helpings. No smoking in 1 dining room. Wheelchair access (also WC). Occasional music. Air-conditioned (£5)

Tatlers 🍴

21 Tombland, Norwich NR3 1RF
TEL: (01603) 766670   FAX: (01603) 766625
WEBSITE: www.tatlers.com

| NEW CHEF |
MODERN BRITISH
£30–£57

This Georgian town house near the cathedral has a relaxed, no-frills atmosphere, with four small dining rooms, bare wooden tables, and a selection of photographs and paintings by local artists on the walls. Chris Johnson joined as head chef too late for the Guide to inspect, but it seems likely that he will continue with the theme of simple, classic dishes based on excellent local produce. Expect to find the likes of Blakeney samphire with smoked salmon and lemon beurre blanc, roast chump of lamb in a provençale crust with sautéed sweetbreads and gratin dauphinois, and perhaps a straightforward pudding of English strawberries with cream and shortbread. The compact wine list focuses mainly on France and the New World, with 11 choices by the glass and Australian house wine at £12.75 a bottle.

CHEF: Chris Johnson   PROPRIETOR: Tatlers 2002 Ltd   OPEN: Mon to Sat 12 to 2, 6.30 to 10   CLOSED: 1 week at Christmas   MEALS: alc D (main courses £11 to £16.50). Set L £14 (2 courses) to £18   SERVICE: not inc, card slips closed   CARDS: Amex, Delta, Diners, MasterCard, Switch, Visa   DETAILS: 70 seats. Private parties: 30 main room, 6 to 30 private rooms. Vegetarian meals. Children's helpings. No smoking in 1 dining room. Music

NOTTINGHAM Nottinghamshire   map 5

▲ Hart's ⁵✳

1 Standard Court, Park Row, Nottingham NG1 6GN   COOKING 5
TEL: (0115) 911 0666   FAX: (0115) 911 0611   MODERN BRITISH
WEBSITE: www.hartsnottingham.co.uk   £25–£65

In the same ownership as Hambleton Hall (see entry, Upper Hambleton), Hart's is a contemporary styled restaurant and hotel in a Victorian building just off the main street of this historic city. Interiors are a kaleidoscope of bold colours – Mondrianesque paintings on brightly painted walls, plus large floral displays enhancing the informal, convivial mood. A modern vein also runs through menus, with flavour combinations as forthright as the décor; a starter of well-timed pan-fried squid is given a powerful kick with chorizo and set on basil-infused mash, while chicken liver parfait is complemented perfectly by a toasted pine-nut salad. Confident and accomplished handling of ingredients is evident also in such main courses as calf's liver with crisp bacon and shallot and sage sauce, or wild sea bass with roast artichokes and chanterelles, or confit duck with braised red cabbage. Hazelnut parfait with blood orange sorbet is a typical way to end a meal. Mark Gough is undoubtedly a talented chef, and, if standards can sometimes slip in his absence, by far the majority of reporters come away well satisfied. Wines, from £12, are an intriguingly varied bunch, mostly under £20.

CHEF: Mark Gough   PROPRIETOR: Tim Hart   OPEN: all week 12 to 2, 7 to 10.30 (9 Sun)   CLOSED: 26 Dec, 1 Jan   MEALS: alc (main courses £11.50 to £22.50). Set L £11.95 (2 courses) to £14.95, Set L Sun £18, Set D Sun £11.95 (2 courses) to £14.95   SERVICE: 12% (optional), card slips closed   CARDS: Amex, Delta, MasterCard, Switch, Visa   DETAILS: 80 seats. 20 seats outside. Private parties: 80 main room, 6 to 110 private rooms. Small car park (evenings only). Vegetarian meals. Children's helpings. No smoking. Wheelchair access (also WC). No music   ACCOMMODATION: 32 rooms, all with bath/shower. TV. Phone. Room only £112 to £225. Rooms for disabled. Baby facilities

▲ Hotel des Clos, Restaurant Sat Bains ♟ ⁵✳

Old Lenton Lane, Nottingham NG7 2SA   COOKING 7
TEL: (0115) 986 6566   MODERN EUROPEAN
WEBSITE: www.hoteldesclos.com   £39–£113

The hotel, at the end of a small lane next to a vast flyover, is comprised of a number of sensitively renovated low-slung Victorian houses, not far from the River Trent. In the restaurant, which bears the name of its talented chef, high-backed brown leather chairs and a mahogany wine cabinet create a masculine feel, with a stone floor and low ceiling adding a gentle touch of rusticity. No-choice dégustation menus at lunch and dinner supplement the main prix fixe, which itself keeps options limited to three per course, with the last a pair of dessert alternatives or cheese with oatcakes and fruit bread. Ingredients are tersely enumerated in the modern way, so that the tasting menus especially might be mistaken for shopping lists. Eye-catching combinations work: a single scallop is rubbed intensively with Indian spices and teamed with a medley of cauliflower (a beignet, purée, even an 'invigorating' carpaccio of the stuff with coriander salt), rabbit comes in a jelly with the texture of rillettes, with a light, greaseless black pudding fritter and a purée of carrot, while a main course of poached and roast wild duck is served with fine beans and hazelnuts and a sauce of Banyuls.

All these dishes evince genuine care in both conception and execution, suggesting that the striving for novelty is backed up by sound principle. Another reporter praises an assembly of Dover sole with Hereford snails, salsify and shiitakes for its revelatory juxtaposition of flavours. Top local Stiltons get a deservedly prominent outing, and meals are rounded off with the likes of a 'raviolo' fashioned from shaved pineapple filled with red fruits, or half a poached pear with liquorice ice cream. 'Exemplary, correctly attentive' service is what it's all about. The wine list is arranged by grape variety and packed with adept choices and informative annotations. Prices are on the high side, but there's plenty under £20 along with the £16 house wines. The 'glad to help' offer on the front of the list is backed up by 'helpful and knowledgeable' wine service.

CHEF: Sat Bains   PROPRIETORS: the Ralley family   OPEN: Tue to Fri L 12 to 1.45, Tue to Sat D 7 to 9.15   MEALS: Set L £20 (2 courses) to £35, Set D £45 to £75   SERVICE: 10% (optional), card slips closed   CARDS: Amex, Delta, Diners, MasterCard, Switch, Visa   DETAILS: 35 seats. Private parties: 20 main room, 8 to 15 private rooms. Car park. No children under 8. No smoking. Occasional music. No mobile phones. Air-conditioned   ACCOMMODATION: 9 rooms, all with bath/shower. TV. Phone. B&B £109 to £159. Rooms for disabled

Sonny's 🍷 🍞

3 Carlton Street, Hockley, Nottingham NG1 1NL   COOKING 3
TEL/FAX: (0115) 947 3041   GLOBAL
EMAIL: nottingham@sonnys.co.uk   £25–£61

The surroundings at this bright, airy and informal Hockley eatery are 'fresh and lively', a feeling that extends to the eclectic yet well-considered menu. Flavour combinations tend towards the classic, yet techniques often add a new twist, as in a starter of smoked salmon paupiette with fromage blanc mousse served with a dill sabayon. In a more classic vein, seared melt-in-the-mouth foie gras may come with pancetta, Puy lentils and toasted brioche, while moist, tender carpaccio is accompanied by rocket and Parmesan enlivened with high-quality balsamic dressing. Meats, too, are of good quality, as in a main-course rib of beef (for two), skilfully cooked and served with 'fabulous' chunky chips piled high to resemble a tower. Desserts might include orange tart with cardamom ice cream and bitter orange and vanilla sauce. Service is friendly and accommodating, and the wine list is imaginatively put together, with respected producers from the Old and New Worlds, at ungrasping prices, kicking in at £10.95 for southern French Terret and Merlot.

CHEF: Matt Vincent   PROPRIETOR: Rebecca Mascarenhas   OPEN: all week 12 to 2.30, 7 to 10.30   CLOSED: Christmas, bank hols   MEALS: alc exc Sun L (main courses £12.50 to £17.50). Set L Mon to Sat £12.95 (2 courses) to £15, Set L Sun £15.95 (2 courses) to £19.95, Set D Sun to Wed £15 (2 courses) to £19.50   SERVICE: 10% (optional), card slips closed   CARDS: Amex, Delta, Diners, MasterCard, Switch, Visa   DETAILS: 90 seats. Private parties: 80 main room. Vegetarian meals. Children's helpings. No-smoking area. Music. No mobile phones. Air-conditioned

World Service 🍴

Newdigate House, Castle Gate, Nottingham NG1 6AF   COOKING 3
TEL: (0115) 8475587   FAX: (0115) 8475584   MODERN BRITISH
WEBSITE: www.worldservicerestaurant.com   £24–£63

This city-centre venue is an oasis of calm, thanks to its high walls. The sheltered oriental-style patio garden is pleasant on a summer's evening, and the dining room has candlelit polished coconut tables, batik roof hangings and Indonesian face masks and vases. The cooking aims to match the surroundings – warm crab and smoked bacon tartlet with cauliflower and lime salad, or sweet potato and split pea soup with a feta and rosemary croûton showing the scope of starters. Main courses feature simple ideas, like pan-fried calf's liver with hash browns and home-made brown sauce, alongside more upmarket braised turbot with scallop and oyster velouté; to finish there might be classic crème brûlée, or treacle tart with clotted cream. Wines cover all regions, but better-quality bottles have stiff mark-ups. Basic house wines are £12.

CHEF: Preston Walker   PROPRIETORS: Ashley Walter, Philip Morgan, Chris Elson and Dan Lindsay   OPEN: all week 12 to 2.15 (3 Sun), 7 to 10 (9 Sun)   CLOSED: 26 Dec, 1 Jan   MEALS: alc (main courses £11.50 to £19.50). Set L £10.50 (2 courses) to £14, Set L Sun £12.50 (2 courses) to £17   SERVICE: 10% (optional), card slips closed   CARDS: Amex, Delta, Diners, MasterCard, Switch, Visa   DETAILS: 75 seats. 40 seats outside. Private parties: 32 main room, 12 to 30 private rooms. Car park (evenings only). Vegetarian meals. Children's helpings. No smoking in 1 dining room. Music

OAKHAM Rutland

map 5

▲ Nick's Restaurant, Lord Nelson's House ▼ ✕

11 Market Place, Oakham LE15 6DT
TEL/FAX: (01572) 723199
WEBSITE: www.nelsons-house.com

COOKING 4
MODERN BRITISH
£25–£55

This fourteenth-century timber-framed building has been converted with an eye to cosiness rather than ostentation, its interlinked dining rooms furnished with comfortably upholstered chairs and decent pictures. Nick Healey offers a menu that is strong on tradition but shows appreciable panache in the execution. Wood pigeon breast appears as a starter with roast celeriac, wild mushrooms and a port-spiked game jus, while seared scallops are teamed with gravad lax and saladings for another. Fish is a declared speciality, and might turn up in main courses such as olive-crusted salmon with king prawns and spinach in a lemon butter sauce, or monkfish in a Parma ham wrap accompanied by king scallops and shellfish sauce. One alternative might be cider-roast pork fillet served with cabbage and bacon, plus Calvados cream. Desserts may include lemon tart with raspberry coulis and mango sorbet, a white and dark chocolate torte, or sticky toffee pudding with clotted cream. Amanda Healy oversees good-humoured and well-paced service, and no-nonsense tasting notes give reliable guidance through a canny and reasonably priced wine list, starting at £10.95, that features plenty of options by the glass.

CHEF: Nick Healey   PROPRIETORS: Nick and Amanda Healey   OPEN: Tue to Sat 12 to 2.30, 7 to 9.30 CLOSED: 24 Dec to 8 Jan, 4 to 15 Apr   MEALS: alc (main courses £8 to £20).   SERVICE: not inc   CARDS: Delta, MasterCard, Switch, Visa   DETAILS: 46 seats. Private parties: 46 main room. Car park. Vegetarian meals. Children's helpings. No smoking. Wheelchair access (not WC). Music. No mobile phones ACCOMMODATION: 4 rooms, all with bath/shower. TV. Phone. B&B £65 to £90 (£5)

ODIHAM Hampshire

map 2

Grapevine

121 High Street, Odiham RG29 1LA
TEL: (01256) 701122
WEBSITE: www.grapevine-gourmet.co.uk

COOKING 3
ENGLISH/ITALIAN
£24–£49

Matthew Fleet's locally favoured neighbourhood bistro occupies a bow-windowed property on the High Street. Inside is a two-tiered dining room with subdued lighting and informal touches like paper napkins, prints and flowers. Italian-style brodetto, and poached fillet of beef (perhaps with tapenade, brandied raisins, beans and olive oil mash) head the popularity stakes, but the monthly-changing menus might also include non-Mediterranean alternatives such as confit of duck with roast apples and pears, or cod fillet in seaweed with pine nuts and sweet-and-sour vegetables, as well as something built around organic ingredients. Round off proceedings with banana mousse with caramelised banana, crème brûlée, or a selection of cheeses from the owner's delicatessen. Six house recommendations (from £12) top the lively wine list, which also features a couple of organic options.

CHEFS: David Bennett and Matthew Carroll   PROPRIETOR: Matthew Fleet   OPEN: Mon to Fri L 12 to 2, Mon to Sat D 6 to 10   CLOSED: 1 week at Christmas, bank hol Mons   MEALS: alc (main courses £11 to £17). Set L £9.95 (2 courses) to £13.95, Set D 6 to 7 £14.95 (inc wine)   SERVICE: not inc, 10% for parties of 8 or more   CARDS: Amex, Diners, MasterCard, Switch, Visa   DETAILS: 40 seats. Private parties: 50 main room. Vegetarian meals. Children's helpings. No cigars/pipes. Wheelchair access (not WC). Music. Air-conditioned

OLD BURGHCLERE Hampshire   map 2

Dew Pond ▾ ✖

Old Burghclere RG20 9LH	COOKING 4
TEL: (01635) 278408 FAX: (01635) 278580	ANGLO-FRENCH
WEBSITE: www.dewpond.co.uk	£41–£57

This homely country restaurant just off the A34 south of Newbury enjoys lovely views over rural Hampshire, and there's also a raised terrace for aperitifs on warm summer evenings. Overseeing each of two dining rooms from a central table is a bronze figure attended by a multitude of liqueur bottles. Uncomplicated cooking of mostly local materials is Keith Marshall's forte, and this might produce a caramelised onion tart with crisp Parma ham and basil to start, then perhaps fish of the day (steamed and sauced with Noilly Prat, cream and fresh herbs), or saddle of roe deer with fondant potato, wild mushrooms, spinach and red wine sauce. It's a well-balanced repertoire that focuses on perfecting the tried-and-true, rather than chasing novelty – which is why you may finish happily with apple and blackcurrant crumble with vanilla ice cream, or crème brûlée with a seasonal fruit salad. Staff are keen to help. A good-value, food-friendly international collection of wines is arranged by style, with 'notably fine' bottles adding extra polish. House is £13.50. Don't miss the regularly changing dozen wines by the glass at the back of the list.

CHEF: Keith Marshall   PROPRIETORS: Keith and Julie Marshall   OPEN: Tue to Sat D 7 to 9.30   CLOSED: 2 weeks Christmas, 2 weeks Aug   MEALS: Set D £28   SERVICE: not inc   CARDS: Delta, MasterCard, Switch, Visa   DETAILS: 50 seats. Private parties: 50 main room, 20 to 30 private rooms. Car park. Vegetarian meals. Children's helpings. No smoking. Wheelchair access (not WC). No music £5

OMBERSLEY Worcestershire   map 5

Venture In ✖

High Street, Ombersley WR9 0EW	COOKING 3
TEL/FAX: (01905) 620552	MODERN BRITISH/FRENCH
	£29–£53

Set among a clutch of half-timbered buildings in an ancient village bypassed by the main A449, the Venture In portrays its age with light beams, low ceilings and an inglenook.

'Gourmet' fish menus every other Wednesday show the kitchen's partiality for all things piscine (salmon and other items are smoked on the premises), and deliveries arrive six days a week. Meat is also given full consideration, thanks to a family butcher who provides the raw materials for dishes like fillet of beef with a mushroom and tarragon sauce, and best end of lamb with roast butternut squash and garlic sauce. Decent starters have included Stilton soufflé, and chicken liver terrine, while desserts could usher in chocolate marquise with raspberry coulis. The wine list ventures far and wide in search of interesting tipples. Five house recommendations are £12.

CHEF/PROPRIETOR: Toby W. Fletcher   OPEN: Tue to Sun L 12 to 2, Tue to Sat D 7 to 9.30   CLOSED: 2 weeks Feb, 2 weeks July   MEALS: Set L £16.95 (2 courses) to £19.95, Set D £30.50. Gourmet fish menus every other Wed £32   SERVICE: not inc, card slips closed   CARDS: Delta, MasterCard, Switch, Visa   DETAILS: 28 seats. Private parties: 35 main room. Car park. Vegetarian meals. No children under 10. No smoking. No music. No mobile phones. Air-conditioned

ORFORD Suffolk   map 6

▲ Crown and Castle, Trinity

Orford IP12 2LJ   COOKING 4
TEL: (01394) 450205   MODERN BRITISH-PLUS
WEBSITE: www.crownandcastle.co.uk   £30–£49

On the corner of the old market square, just yards from Orford Castle's magnificent Norman keep, is the Crown and Castle, an attractive, red-brick Victorian inn. Its restaurant, the Trinity, has two dining areas with wooden floors and tables, comfortable banquettes and a sophisticated, modern edge, all adding up to a distinctive yet relaxed atmosphere. Food writer Ruth Watson's modern menu, showcasing local produce, is divided into 'raw', 'cold' and 'hot' dishes that offer plenty of interest as well as a degree of flexibility. Starters tend toward the simple, predominantly cold or raw offerings, perhaps lime marinated, thinly sliced fresh tuna and a sweet and sour salad, while mains feature the likes of seared Orford-caught cod with 'zippy' Puy lentils and gingery pak choi, or rump of Suffolk lamb with saffron-roasted chunky root vegetables and salsa verde. A warm pecan nut and bourbon tart with 'proper' custard might make an alternative to well-kept British and Irish cheeses. The lengthy wine list is wide-ranging, highly individual and colour-coded; it includes 18–20 wines by glass, a good selection of half-bottles and Aussie house at £12.

CHEFS: Ruth Watson and Max Dougal   PROPRIETORS: David and Ruth Watson   OPEN: all week 12 to 2, 7 to 9 (9.30 Sat)   CLOSED: 4 to 6 Jan, Sun D from 7 Nov to 12 Dec and 9 Jan to 6 Feb   MEALS: alc D (main courses £10 to £16). Set L £15.50 (2 courses) to £23.50, Set L Sun £15.50 (2 courses) to £22.50 Set D Sat £27.50, light L available Mon to Sat   SERVICE: not inc   CARDS: Delta, MasterCard, Switch, Visa   DETAILS: 50 seats. 60 seats outside. Private parties: 8 to 14 private rooms. Car park. Vegetarian meals. Children's helpings. No children under 9. Wheelchair access (not WC). No music. No mobile phones   ACCOMMODATION: 18 rooms, all with bath/shower. TV. Phone. B&B £60 to £135. Rooms for disabled. Baby facilities

---

'[Lights] are gradually dimmed during the evening until towards the end you need a miner's lamp to read the dessert menu.' (On eating in London)

OSMOTHERLEY North Yorkshire   map 9

Golden Lion 🍴✴ £

6 West End, Osmotherley DL6 3AA   COOKING **3**
TEL: (01609) 883526   FAX: (01609) 884000   ENGLISH/FRENCH/ITALIAN
                £24–£48

This pub, bar and restaurant does many people very nicely, whether hikers tackling the Lyke Wake Walk, locals in for a pint of Timothy Taylor Landlord, or dressed-up Teessiders looking for a meal. Ambition is realistic, and the resulting clear focus much appreciated. The food covers pub fare bases, going in for modifications of tried and trusted favourites and producing main courses of steak and kidney pie with a suet crust, mashed potatoes and peas, and home-made chicken Kiev with chips and green salad. But the menu has wider appeal, running from white crabmeat with brown crab mayonnaise, and spaghetti vongole, to grilled sea bass, coq au vin, and roast rack of lamb with mint jelly gravy. Desserts tend to favour cakes and tarts, from a Middle Eastern orange cake with marmalade cream to fresh strawberry tart with crème pâtissière. A short, savvy wine list combines good quality and fair pricing and is backed up by four house wines at £12.

CHEF: Peter McCoy   PROPRIETORS: Peter McCoy, Christie Connelly and Belal Radwan   OPEN: all week 12 to 3, 6 to 9.30   CLOSED: 25 Dec   MEALS: alc (main courses £6.50 to £14)   SERVICE: not inc, card slips closed   CARDS: Diners, MasterCard, Switch, Visa   DETAILS: 90 seats. 20 seats outside. Private parties: 50 main room. Vegetarian meals. Children's helpings. No smoking in 1 dining room. Music

OSWESTRY Shropshire   map 7

▲ Sebastians 🍴✴

45 Willow Street, Oswestry SY11 1AQ   COOKING **3**
TEL: (01691) 655444   FAX: (01691) 653452   FRENCH
WEBSITE: www.sebastians-hotel.co.uk   £43–£56

This cheerily decorated establishment looks like a cross between a French bistro and an English tea room, but there's no ambiguity about its cooking. The monthly-changing menu sticks firmly to the provincial cuisine of France: champignons au Roquefort, pavé de boeuf au poivre, and filet d'agneau au galette de Provence, complete with a mid-meal sorbet and classic French cheeses to follow. If this strikes some as a little out of touch with the times, Sebastian Fisher wins plaudits for his sound technique and dedication to detail. Everything is made from scratch, including 'deeply impressive' puff pastry, which was the highlight of a painstakingly prepared apple tart with cinnamon ice cream and caramel sauce. The wine list draws equally from Europe and the New World, with house wines £12.95.

CHEF: Mark Sebastian Fisher   PROPRIETORS: Mark Sebastian and Michelle Fisher   OPEN: Tue to Sat D only 6.30 to 9.30   MEALS: Set D £30   SERVICE: not inc, card slips closed   CARDS: Amex, Delta, MasterCard, Switch, Visa   DETAILS: 35 seats. 20 seats outside. Private parties: 40 main room. Car park. Vegetarian meals. Children's helpings. No smoking. Wheelchair access (not WC). Music. No mobile phones ACCOMMODATION: 8 rooms, all with bath/shower. TV. Phone. Room only £65 to £75. Rooms for disabled. Baby facilities

OVINGTON Norfolk

map 5

▲ Brovey Lair ✸

NEW ENTRY

Carbrooke Road, Ovington IP25 6SD
TEL: (01953) 882706   FAX: (01953) 885365
WEBSITE: www.broveylair.com

COOKING 5
FUSIAN
£49–£59

'Definitely different' noted an inspector after visiting this chic café-with-rooms in the countryside near Watton. It is Mike and Tina Pemberton's home, and they run it in their own way: they open only when people book in advance; the menu is fixed; and the whole experience is like a convivial dinner party. The open-plan kitchen is stylish and contemporary, and the predominantly blond wood dining room overlooks the swimming pool. The food is in Asian-fusion style with a preference for fish and Japanese ideas, although Tina rings the changes. Ingredients are first-class, cooking is accurate, and 'healthy' flavours shine through. Dinner might begin with tuna carpaccio accompanied by pickled ginger, roast asparagus and rocket, followed by Portobello mushroom and miso soup displaying 'very fine flavours'. The centrepiece at one meal was teppan-grilled Cajun-spiced swordfish on 'attention-grabbing' orzo ('pasta rice') with myriad accompaniments. Finish with almond crusted ricotta and lemon cheesecake with strawberries and crème fraîche. The 'tempting and well-thought-out' wine list is priced from £14.50.

CHEF: Tina Pemberton   PROPRIETORS: Mike and Tina Pemberton   OPEN: all week D only 7.45 (1 sitting). Bookings only   CLOSED: 25 Dec   MEALS: Set D £37.50   SERVICE: 10%, card slips closed   CARDS: Amex, MasterCard, Switch, Visa   DETAILS: 20 seats. 10 seats outside. Private parties: 24 main room. Car park. Vegetarian meals. No children under 16. No smoking. Wheelchair access (also WC). Music. Air-conditioned   ACCOMMODATION: 2 rooms, both with bath/shower. TV. B&B £75 to £125. No children under 16. Swimming pool (£5)

OXFORD Oxfordshire

map 2

▲ Al-Shami ✸ £

25 Walton Crescent, Oxford OX1 2JG
TEL: (01865) 310066   FAX: (01865) 311241
WEBSITE: www.al-shami.co.uk

COOKING 1
LEBANESE
£23–£40

A plethora of hot and cold meze is the big draw for the town and gown who frequent this colourful, long-serving Lebanese restaurant. On the menu you will find tabbouleh and falafel cheek by jowl with more esoteric specialities like bastorma (cured fillet of beef) and zahra maqlia (fried cauliflower topped with sesame oil, parsley, garlic and lemon juice). Main courses rely on high-protein grills bolstered by a few fish and vegetarian options such as mujadara (rice and lentils with fried onions), while Arabic ice cream and Lebanese desserts complete the picture. The £1 cover charge pays for a harvest festival of salad vegetables. Arak and Almaza beer are alternatives to the short wine list, which is sure to please fans of Ch. Musar. House Lebanese is £11.99.

CHEF: Mimo Mahfouz   PROPRIETOR: Al-Shami Cuisine   OPEN: all week 12 to 11.45   MEALS: alc (main courses £7 to £12). Cover £1   SERVICE: not inc, 10% for parties of 6 or more   CARDS: MasterCard, Switch, Visa   DETAILS: 100 seats. Private parties: 50 main room, 50 private room. Vegetarian meals. No smoking in 1 dining room. Wheelchair access (also WC). Music   ACCOMMODATION: 12 rooms, all with bath/shower. TV. B&B £35 to £45 (£5)

Branca £

111 Walton Street, Oxford OX2 6AJ
TEL: (01865) 556111   FAX: (01865) 556501
WEBSITE: www.branca-restaurants.com

COOKING 1
MODERN ITALIAN
£27–£52

All-day opening, early-evening deals, and children's menus are part of the package at this 'pretty classless', live-wire brasserie. It's a favourite with the under-30s, although everyone is welcome and the mood benefits from tireless, friendly staff. Stone-baked pizzas and pasta are strong runners, along with risottos (butternut squash with Gorgonzola and caramelised onions has been enjoyed); the remainder is a contemporary mixed bag, including deep-fried squid with lemon and pine-nut dressing, grilled sea bass fillet with salsa verde and 'enough new potatoes to feed a football team', and free-range chicken with spiced potatoes and aïoli. Meals end well with desserts like hazelnut and praline semifreddo. Ten wines come by the glass, bottle (from £11.45) or 500ml pot.

CHEF: Michael MacQuire   PROPRIETORS: Paul Petrillo and Julian Rosser   OPEN: all week 12 to 11.30 (10.30 Sun)   CLOSED: 24 to 26 Dec   MEALS: alc (main courses £8.50 to £17). Set L Mon to Fri 12 to 5 £5.95 (1 course, inc wine), Set D Mon to Fri 5 to 7 £10 (2 courses, inc wine)   SERVICE: not inc, card slips closed, 10% for parties of 5 or more   CARDS: Amex, Delta, Diners, MasterCard, Switch, Visa   DETAILS: 110 seats. Private parties: 30 main room. Vegetarian meals. Children's helpings. No-smoking area. Wheelchair access (also WC). Music. No mobile phones. Air-conditioned

Cherwell Boathouse ▮ ✻

50 Bardwell Road, Oxford OX2 6ST
TEL: (01865) 552746

COOKING 2
MODERN ENGLISH/FRENCH
£23–£46

Locations seldom come as blissful as this. The Thames is a stone's throw from the glassed-in dining room, and punts (for hire) are drawn up just outside. The short menu – with just five choices per course – may start with good, fresh pan-fried scallops served with wild rocket, baby chard and crisp green beans, followed by roast breast of Barbary duck with dauphinois potatoes and a wild mushroom and shallot jus. Desserts are rather more workaday affairs: ice cream, sorbet, or cherry and almond tart, for example. Recent visits have left reporters less impressed with the cooking than in the past, with timings less accurate than they should be. The wine list continues to impress, though, with interesting options by the glass and a collection of established classics and modern upstarts, all at terrifically good prices. House wines open proceedings at £10.50.

CHEFS: Wayne Cullen and Mark Horton   PROPRIETORS: Anthony and John Verdin   OPEN: all week 12 to 2 (2.30 Sat and Sun), 6.30 to 10   CLOSED: 25 to 30 Dec   MEALS: Set L Mon to Fri £12.50 (2 courses) to £19.50, Set L Sat and Sun £21.50, Set D £23.50   SERVICE: not inc, 10% for parties of 6 or more   CARDS: Amex, Delta, Diners, MasterCard, Switch, Visa   DETAILS: 70 seats. 45 seats outside. Private parties: 120 main room, 10 to 50 private rooms. Car park. Vegetarian meals. Children's helpings. No smoking. Wheelchair access (also WC). No music (£5)

Chiang Mai Kitchen ✻

130A High Street, Oxford OX1 4DH
TEL: (01865) 202233   FAX: (01865) 250055
WEBSITE: www.chiangmaikitchen.co.uk

COOKING 2
THAI
£33–£50

A venerable timber-framed building dating from 1634 is the unlikely setting for this Thai restaurant down a tiny alleyway off the High Street. Appropriately, the interior is a cohesive East–West amalgam of ancient wood floors, panelling and native carvings. Ingredients are bona fide, the cooking is authentic, and the menu spans most aspects of the cuisine from salads and stir-fries to curries and noodles. Appetisers could include khanom jeep (steamed rice pastry dumplings) or mieng gai (spiced chicken and ground peanuts intended for wrapping in Thai spinach leaves), while mains cover everything from roast duck curry and seafood stir-fries to plentiful vegetarian options like tom yam het (clear mushroom soup) and Thai omelette. House wine is £10.50; otherwise drink Singha beer.

CHEF: Kamolwan Wright   PROPRIETOR: Helen O'Malley   OPEN: all week 12 to 2.30, 6 to 10.30   CLOSED: 25 Dec, bank hols   MEALS: alc (main courses £7 to £10.50)   SERVICE: not inc   CARDS: Amex, Diners, MasterCard, Switch, Visa   DETAILS: 80 seats. Vegetarian meals. No smoking in 1 dining room. Wheelchair access (not WC). No music   (£5)

Gee's ✦✱

61 Banbury Road, Oxford OX2 6PE — COOKING 2
TEL: (01865) 553540   FAX: (01865) 310308 — MODERN BRITISH
WEBSITE: www.gees-restaurant.co.uk — £27–£63

This light, appealing conservatory restaurant, with its fronds of greenery and white-draped tables, 'lifts the spirits'. Reporters confirm the consistency of the kitchen's output, although opinions on service can vary. Gee's delivers simply presented food, and due attention is paid to the seasons. One luncher was impressed by 'perfectly judged linguini with parsley and Parmesan'. The 'star dish' (weekly special) might be a wintry ham hock with mashed potato and parsley sauce, and sweets take in rice pudding and strawberry jam, or chocolate pot with orange shortbread. At weekends, a two-course set brunch could feature kedgeree, or grilled field mushrooms and poached eggs, and the set menus seem good value. The wine list, short but modish, has interesting selections; prices start at £12.75.

CHEF: Michael Wright   PROPRIETOR: Jeremy Mogford   OPEN: all week 12 (11 Sat and Sun) to 2.30 (3.30 Sun), 6 to 11   CLOSED: 25 and 26 Dec   MEALS: alc (main courses £8 to £20). Set L Mon to Fri £12.50 (2 courses) to £16.50, Set brunch Sat/Sun £19.50 (2 courses), Set D £20.95 (2 courses) to £24.95   SERVICE: not inc, 10% (optional) for parties of 5 or more   CARDS: Amex, Delta, MasterCard, Switch, Visa   DETAILS: 85 seats. 25 seats outside. Private parties: 85 main room. Vegetarian meals. Children's helpings. No smoking. Wheelchair access (also WC). Music. Air-conditioned

Lemon Tree — NEW ENTRY

268 Woodstock Road, Oxford OX2 7NW — COOKING 3
TEL: (01865) 311936   FAX: (01865) 514450 — MEDITERRANEAN
— £24–£61

After a spell as La Gousse d'Ail, this restaurant has been bought out and reopened with its original name by former owner Clinton Pugh. One visitor thought the split-level, mustard-yellow dining room had a 'rather southern-Italian feel' and there are plenty of Mediterranean influences on the menu. A healthy bias toward organic chicken, fish and salads is shown. Vine tomato tart with Mascarpone and basil is a typically professional starter, or there might be mackerel escabèche with sweet-pickled vegetables. Seafood is also represented by king prawn risotto with coriander and chilli oil, while beef from locally reared Charolais beasts turns up as burgers and fillet steak (with truffle and mushroom butter, red onion Tatin and chips). Puddings are decent versions of vacherin with summer fruits, and poached pear with cinnamon ice cream. House Australian is £12.95 on a list that also offers 11 by the glass from £3.25.

CHEF: John Pugsley   PROPRIETOR: Clinton Pugh   OPEN: Fri to Sun noon to 11, Mon to Thurs 6 to 11   MEALS: alc (main courses £9 to £19.50). Set L Fri and Sat £10.95 (2 courses) to £12.95. Tapas available in bar   SERVICE: not inc (though may change to an optional charge)   CARDS: Delta, MasterCard, Switch, Visa   DETAILS: 90 seats. Private parties: 100 main room. Car park. Vegetarian meals. Children's helpings. Wheelchair access (also WC). Music

OXTON Merseyside
map 8

Fraiche ✦

NEW ENTRY

11 Rose Mount, Oxton CH43 5SG
TEL: (0151) 652 2914
EMAIL: fraicherestaurant@yahoo.com

COOKING 6
MODERN FRENCH
£35–£66

Marc Wilkinson has cooked at this location before – around 14 years ago when it was Rondelle – and returns to the site after a spell working his way around various top kitchens across Britain. This new venture consists of a small dining room with a relaxed atmosphere and is decorated in subdued modern colours, with a deep-pile beige carpet, cream walls and coffee-coloured upholstery on the tall-backed chairs. Well-spaced tables are a good size and are laid with high-quality linen, glassware and cutlery. Marc's cooking is founded on classic French principles, but he is a chef with a strong sense of adventure, as is apparent in an unusual but enjoyable appetiser of egg with cream, maple syrup and chives served in an eggshell. To follow, plum tomato sorbet with watermelon salad and Cabernet dressing has proved a 'quite extraordinary' dish of harmoniously blended flavours, while top-quality scallops on a delicate butternut squash purée contrast well with a salad of diced fennel. Successes among main courses have included a vegetarian dish of roast walnut gnocchi with lemon confit, wild mushrooms, spinach and carrots, and an innovative take on loin of lamb: two thick slices of 'perfectly pink, melt-in-the-mouth' meat served with a cube of Earl Grey jelly, braised fennel, a ball of deep-fried battered sweetbreads and garnished with a delicate slice of garlic bread. More invention appears in the form of a pre-dessert coconut yoghurt foam with pineapple salsa, while dessert might be four large roast strawberries with pine kernels, mango sorbet and a rice pudding brûlée tart. Wines are priced according to a fixed mark-up policy, which means some real bargains are to be had at the top end. At the other end are house selections at £15.50.

CHEF/PROPRIETOR: Marc Wilkinson   OPEN: Sun L 12 to 1.45, Tue to Sat D 6.45 to 9 (9.30 Sat)   CLOSED: first week Jan   MEALS: Set L £21.50, Set D £24.50 (2 courses) to £39   SERVICE: not inc, card slips closed   CARDS: Delta, MasterCard, Switch, Visa   DETAILS: 20 seats. 10 seats outside. Private parties: 18 main room. Vegetarian meals. No smoking. Wheelchair access (not WC). No music. No mobile phones

PADSTOW Cornwall
map 1

The Ebb ✦

1A The Strand, Padstow PL28 8BS
TEL/FAX: (01841) 532565

COOKING 4
SEAFOOD-PLUS
£42–£51

Go through a whitewashed courtyard and up a flight of steps to reach this well-lit restaurant with its modern paintings and opaque glass-topped tables. Peter Scott oversees front-of-house while Karen cooks. Her fixed-price menus revolve around regular supplies of fish from the Cornish day boats, although local raw materials are often given an exotic makeover, as in starters of crab with a mango, peanut and bean sprout salad, or fish bhajia with tomato and tamarind jam. The Mediterranean has its say with main courses of whole sea bass baked in sea salt and rosemary served with slow-roast plum tomatoes and pesto. Away from the sea, you might find warm asparagus with white truffle oil and shaved Parmesan, followed by Chinese-style slow-roast belly pork with wok-fried sesame greens. Desserts stay close to home with plum crumble but may go walkabout for mint and cardamom meringues with ginger and basil cream. The wine list comes courtesy of West Country merchants, mark-ups are realistic, and there are six house selections from £14.

CHEF: Karen Scott   PROPRIETORS: Peter and Karen Scott   OPEN: Wed to Mon D only 7 to 9.30 (5 to 10 summer)   CLOSED: 10 Nov to 2 weeks before Easter   MEALS: Set D £25 (2 courses) to £29.50   SERVICE: not inc, card slips closed   CARDS: Delta, Switch, Visa   DETAILS: 60 seats. Private parties: 40 main room, 36 to 40 private rooms. Vegetarian meals. No children under 12. No smoking. Music. No mobile phones

Margot's 5⅙✳

11 Duke Street, Padstow PL28 8AB	COOKING 3
TEL: (01841) 533441	MODERN BRITISH
WEBSITE: www.margots.co.uk	£32–£44

'The Olivers have been busy!' noted a reporter. Not only have they freshened up Margot's pretty blue and white interior, but also they have opened a second branch, in the Tregea Hotel. The busy original is still going strong, and cheery staff add to the enjoyment of it all. Ultra-fresh seafood is a strong suit: 'vast' scallops come with smoked bacon and a pistachio dressing, while baked monkfish is paired with crisp Parma ham and a velvety fish sauce. The kitchen has also excelled with mushroom and chorizo risotto, and corn-fed chicken breast with spring onion mash and mustard sauce. As for desserts, it might be a toss-up between Eton Mess and saffron-poached pear with a sorbet and shortbread. The affordable wine list kicks off with house selections by the glass, carafe or bottle (£10.50 and £10.95).

CHEF: Adrian Oliver   PROPRIETORS: Adrian and Julie Oliver   OPEN: Wed to Sat L 12.30 to 2, Tue to Sat D 7 to 9   CLOSED: Nov, 25 to 27 Dec, Jan   MEALS: Set L £18.50 (2 courses) to £21.95, Set D £21.95 (2 courses) to £25.95   SERVICE: not inc   CARDS: Amex, Delta, MasterCard, Switch, Visa   DETAILS: 22 seats. Private parties: 22 main room. Children's helpings. No smoking. Wheelchair access (not WC). Music (£5)

▲ Rick Stein's Cafe 5⅙✳

10 Middle Street, Padstow PL28 8AP	COOKING 3
TEL: (01841) 532700 FAX: (01841) 532942	SEAFOOD
WEBSITE: www.rickstein.com	£34–£49

This 'most basic' of Rick Stein's food outlets is nonetheless a sound bet for reliably good fish and seafood. Set in an old fisherman's cottage, the knocked-through downstairs rooms decked out with bright paintings and light wood furniture, it's an attractively modern-looking dining room with a warm and welcoming atmosphere. Tables are packed in and the place is inevitably full at all times of day – and year – so expect a fair bit of hustle and bustle. There is also a small garden dining area. Short menus, simple and traditional, offer starters of smoked salmon with scrambled eggs, capers and onion, or mussels with chilli, tomato and parsley, followed by deep-fried plaice goujons with tartare sauce, or wild sea bass with roast tomatoes and fennel. There are meat and vegetarian options too, and the short, half-French wine list starts at £13.50.

CHEFS: Paul Harwood and Roy Brett PROPRIETORS: Rick and Jill Stein OPEN: all week 12 to 3, 7 to 10
CLOSED: 1 week at Christmas, May day MEALS: alc (main courses £8.50 to £15). Set D £19.50 SERVICE:
not inc CARDS: Delta, MasterCard, Switch, Visa DETAILS: 40 seats. 10 seats outside. Vegetarian meals.
Children's helpings. No smoking. Occasional music ACCOMMODATION: 3 rooms, all with bath/shower. TV.
Phone. B&B £85 to £105. Baby facilities

▲ St Petroc's Bistro 🍴✳

4 New Street, Padstow PL28 8EA	COOKING 3
TEL: (01841) 532700 FAX: (01841) 532942	BISTRO
WEBSITE: www.rickstein.com	£40–£55

'The hotel is the fifth-oldest building in Padstow,' Rick Stein, restaurateur, TV chef and
(seemingly) local historian, assures us. It was built by a chum of Sir Walter Raleigh, and
may or may not be haunted. With dining inside and out, the emphasis is on the celebrated
fish, although there is chicken with black pudding cooked in Muscat, as well as chargrilled
rump steak, on the menu. Grilled sea bass with beurre blanc, and starters such as mackerel
fishcakes with fennel, or salt-and-pepper squid with spring onion and chilli, are where the
heart is. Vegetables are extra. Finish with baked chocolate mousse, or a piece of
Montgomery Cheddar with pear and salad leaves. Wine prices start at £13.25, there's
choice under £20, and the list includes a couple of branded Stein blends from Australia.

CHEFS: Alistair Clive and Roy Brett PROPRIETORS: Rick and Jill Stein OPEN: all week 12 to 2, 7 to 10
CLOSED: 1 week at Christmas, May day MEALS: alc (main courses £11.50 to £16.50) SERVICE: not inc
CARDS: Delta, MasterCard, Switch, Visa DETAILS: 54 seats. 20 seats outside. Private parties: 54 main
room. Car park (for residents only). Vegetarian meals. Children's helpings. No smoking. Wheelchair
access (not WC). Music. Air-conditioned ACCOMMODATION: 10 rooms, all with bath/shower. TV. Phone.
B&B £90 to £180. Baby facilities

▲ Seafood Restaurant ▮

Riverside, Padstow PL28 8BY	COOKING 6
TEL: (01841) 532700 FAX: (01841) 532942	SEAFOOD
WEBSITE: www.rickstein.com	£50–£109

There are three Stein-owned establishments in Padstow listed in the Guide, and his name
also adorns a deli, pâtisserie, gift shop, cookery school and now a fish 'n' chip shop, but this
is the original venture, and remains the flagship. A spacious, white-walled place with a
conservatory out front, the atmosphere is enlivened by bright modern pictures and the
cheery, infectious attitude of the staff.

A wealth of piscatorial choice is offered, of unimpeachable freshness, as befits the
location, and there is an appealing mix of traditional simplicity and the influence of foreign
climes. Thus, langoustines on ice, or potted shrimps might preface a main course such as
chargrilled fillet of sea bass with tomato butter and vanilla vinaigrette, or fillets of Dover
sole with stir-fried red peppers, asparagus and wild garlic with a soy and sesame oil dressing.
That last, at inspection, delivered 'lovely, lean white flesh, bursting with the taste of the
sea', and followed a majestic first course of Irish black sea urchins served in the shell with
scrambled eggs on a bed of washed kelp. Platters of fruits de mer, served naturally with
mayonnaise and shallot vinegar, offer a crash course in marine biology, and the five-course
tasting menu (including coffee) is fulsomely praised, producing perhaps oysters with spicy
sausage, grilled langoustines, poached skate, sea bass, and a passion-fruit pavlova. That
some thought goes into desserts is evidenced by the take on bread-and-butter pudding,

made from saffron cake and served with stewed rhubarb on the side. The 18-strong house selection (from £16.50 to £23.75) could be all the wine list you need, but if you're in the mood for more the pin-sharp global list has plenty to entice.

CHEFS: Roy Brett and Stèphane Delourme   PROPRIETORS: Rick and Jill Stein   OPEN: all week 12 to 2, 7 to 10   CLOSED: 1 week at Christmas, May Day   MEALS: alc (main courses £17.50 to £44). Set L and D £50   SERVICE: not inc   CARDS: Delta, MasterCard, Switch, Visa   DETAILS: 110 seats. Children's helpings. No children under 3. Wheelchair access (not WC). No music. Air-conditioned   ACCOMMODATION: 14 rooms, all with bath/shower. TV. Phone. B&B £160 to £245 (double room). Baby facilities

PAINSWICK Gloucestershire

map 2

▲ Painswick Hotel ♥ ⁵⭒

Kemps Lane, Painswick GL6 6YB
TEL: (01452) 812160   FAX: (01452) 814059
WEBSITE: www.painswickhotel.com

COOKING 5
BRITISH
£30–£73

'Painswick village is as enchanting as the hotel brochure would have you believe,' and its Palladian former rectory is tucked away from the main through road on a narrow, winding lane. Lounge and bar are on the first floor, and the ground-level dining room has pale wood panelling, carpets and heavy printed curtains in traditional English style, and first-class white table linen. Live piano music may feature occasionally – which one reviewer found intrusive. There has been another change in ownership, but Kevin Baron continues at the stove.

The seasonal carte sees a main-course fillet of 'soft-textured and flavourful' Buccleuch beef with field mushroom beignets, oxtail dumplings and Pinot Noir sauce become akin to an assiette with the inclusion of an unannounced slice of tongue and celeriac purée. A 'good-sized chunk' of beautifully timed monkfish accompanied by crab rösti and a 'rough, almost nutty' pea purée has been enjoyed as a starter, and at dessert stage 'eye-catching presentation' and 'interesting flavour combinations' distinguished an English toffee jelly with honey pannacotta and Earl Grey granita. The daily Market Menu is more straightforward. Service from an English and French team has been 'bright, keen, and friendly'. A good international range of wines is strongest in France, with good bottles in mature vintages. House wines are £15, and six come by the glass.

CHEF: Kevin Barron   PROPRIETORS: Max and Jane Sabotini and Bob and Pauline Young   OPEN: all week 12.30 to 2, 7 to 9.30   MEALS: alc D (main courses £16.50 to £24). Set L £14 (2 courses) to £17, Set D £28 (2 courses) to £31. Light L menu available   SERVICE: not inc   CARDS: Amex, Delta, Diners, MasterCard, Switch, Visa   DETAILS: 40 seats. Private parties: 60 main room, 8 to 16 private rooms. Car park. Vegetarian meals. No smoking. Occasional music. No mobile phones   ACCOMMODATION: 19 rooms, all with bath/shower. TV. Phone. B&B £85 to £210 (£5)

PAULERSPURY Northamptonshire

map 5

▲ Vine House ⁵⭒

100 High Street, Paulerspury NN12 7NA
TEL: (01327) 811267   FAX: (01327) 811309
WEBSITE: www.vinehousehotel.com

COOKING 3
MODERN BRITISH
£43–£51

Vine House is a modest, rambling old stone restaurant-with-rooms. Inside, on varying levels, are a library-like drawing room, a small bar-lounge, and a creamy-walled dining room with beamed ceilings. It's a comfortable setting, in which the emphasis is firmly on the food. The menu is kept short, with three choices of starter, main course and dessert, all served on large white plates. A starter of fishcake with shallot, tomato and parsley velouté might be followed by medallions of local venison with turnips, smoked bacon and red wine sauce. End the meal with vanilla yoghurt sorbet with local honey-poached rhubarb, or the selection of farmhouse cheeses. Classical France accounts for much of a wine list that starts with French and Aussie house wines at £12.95.

CHEF: Marcus Springett PROPRIETORS: Marcus and Julie Springett OPEN: Thur and Fri L 12.15 to 1.45, Mon to Sat D 7 to 9.30 CLOSED: 1 week from 24 Dec MEALS: Set L and D £29.95 SERVICE: not inc CARDS: MasterCard, Visa DETAILS: 30 seats. Private parties: 30 main room. Car park. No smoking. Wheelchair access (not WC). No music ACCOMMODATION: 6 rooms, all with bath/shower. TV. Phone. B&B £59 to £85 (£5)

PAXFORD Gloucestershire   map 5

▲ Churchill Arms £

Paxford GL55 6XH	COOKING 4
TEL: (01386) 594000 FAX: (01386) 594005	MODERN EUROPEAN
WEBSITE: www.thechurchillarms.com	£25–£45

In an archetypal Cotswolds village full of honey-coloured stone buildings, this pub certainly puts on a rustic face and keeps up appearances with bare floorboards in the bar and decoration of the 'granny's attic' variety. Staff could exude a touch more personal warmth and hospitality, although there are no quibbles about the food itself. The kitchen's repertoire is forever changing, but the menu of full-blooded modern dishes might open with game terrine and home-made green tomato chutney, or vanilla risotto with Gruyère, smoked haddock and pancetta before, say, grilled flounder with sherry, rosemary and tomato; a comforting assemblage of pork belly with potato, chorizo and butternut broth, and soy and balsamic sauce; or – in more far-flung territory – monkfish with sweet-and-sour sauce and deep-fried okra. To finish, polenta tart with coffee parfait has been endorsed; otherwise there might be maple and mascarpone cheesecake. Some 20 eminently affordable wines are listed on a blackboard. Prices start at £10.50.

CHEFS: Sonya Brooke-Little and David Toon PROPRIETORS: Sonya and Leo Brooke-Little OPEN: all week 12 to 2, 7 to 9 MEALS: alc (main courses £7.50 to £14) SERVICE: not inc CARDS: Delta, MasterCard, Switch, Visa DETAILS: 60 seats. 60 seats outside. Vegetarian meals. Children's helpings. No music ACCOMMODATION: 4 rooms, all with bath/shower. TV. Phone. B&B £40 to £70

PENZANCE Cornwall   map 1

▲ Abbey Restaurant £✶

Abbey Street, Penzance TR18 4AR	COOKING 5
TEL: (01736) 330680 FAX: (01736) 351163	MODERN EUROPEAN
WEBSITE: www.theabbeyonline.com	£28–£61

Penzance has lost its end-of-the-line feel and is riding the wave of a Cornish renaissance. Ben and Kinga Tunnicliffe's smart restaurant and hotel – they also run the adjacent Abbey Hotel – are helping put the town on the foodie map, rivalling the county's big hitters, Padstow and St Ives. On a road leading down to the harbour, the hotel is an eye-catching shade of blue, while the low-key frontage of the restaurant gives no clues as to what lies within. On the ground floor is a windowless bar done out in vivid colours, while the upstairs dining room is all brightness and natural light: a contemporary space with black-and-white photos on the walls.

The menu, too, has an urbane, up-to-date feel. At lunch the carte may include twice-baked Cornish Yarg soufflé with apple chutney, then fried calf's liver with Jerusalem artichokes and caramelised shallots, followed by fig and banana crumble tart with clotted cream. At dinner a warm salad of smoked haddock comes with aïoli, Parmesan and soft-poached egg, and then an open raviolo of harlequin squash, spinach and pine nuts with tomato sauce and sage butter. Lemon meringue cheesecake with a blood orange water ice makes an impressive finish. The wine list has careful tasting notes and some very nice (and affordable) bottles, with Australian house from £11.

CHEF: Ben Tunnicliffe   PROPRIETORS: Ben and Kinga Tunnicliffe   OPEN: Fri and Sat L 12 to 1.45, Tue to Sat D 7.15 to 9.45   CLOSED: Jan   MEALS: alc (main courses £13.50 to £21.50). Set L and D, Nov, Feb and Mar £15 (2 courses) to £20   SERVICE: not inc   CARDS: Delta, MasterCard, Switch, Visa   DETAILS: 30 seats. Private parties: 22 main room. Vegetarian meals. No children under 10. No smoking. No music. No mobile phones. Air-conditioned   ACCOMMODATION: 8 rooms, 7 with bath/shower. TV. B&B £95 to £185

Harris's 🌶✕

46 New Street, Penzance TR18 2LZ	COOKING 2
TEL: (01736) 364408	ANGLO-FRENCH
WEBSITE: www.harrissrestaurant.co.uk	£41–£68

The Harrises have been at this site, just off the main street through the town, for more than 30 years. They aim to keep the cooking simple, although that doesn't mean that the locally sourced organic vegetables, seafood from Newlyn, local lobsters and seasonal game come to the plate unadorned. Combinations of flavours can be imaginative, as in medallions of venison with fresh beetroot, caraway seed and 'good-tasting, firm' wild mushrooms. In season, wild mushrooms may also appear in a risotto to accompany roast monkfish and white wine sauce, and daily fish specials may include grilled sea bass with red pepper sauce. To finish, try West Country cheeses or desserts ranging from Apfelstrudel to cold cream soufflé with a dark-chocolate basket and raspberry coulis. The wine list spans the globe, with some well-considered French bottles and dessert wines marking the high points; house wines start at £12.50.

CHEF: Roger Harris   PROPRIETORS: Anne and Roger Harris   OPEN: Tue to Sat 12 to 1.15 (light L to 2), 7 to 9.30; also Mon D in summer   CLOSED: 25 and 26 Dec, 1 Jan, 3 weeks winter   MEALS: alc (main courses £16 to £26.50). Light L menu available   SERVICE: 10%, card slips closed   CARDS: Amex, Delta, MasterCard, Switch, Visa   DETAILS: 40 seats. Private parties: 20 main room, 20 private room. 'Vegetarian dishes to order.' No children under 5. No smoking in 1 dining room. Occasional music. No mobile phones

▲ Summer House 🌶✕

Cornwall Terrace, Penzance TR18 4HL	COOKING 2
TEL: (01736) 363744 FAX: (01736) 360959	MEDITERRANEAN
WEBSITE: www.summerhouse-cornwall.com	£36–£46

You have to ring the doorbell to gain admittance to this little hotel in a side street not far from the seafront. Within is an elegant lounge furnished with antiques, and a small dining room leading into a walled garden. The daily-changing, essentially French menu makes good use of what's best at the market. Seafood figures prominently among starters, from seared scallops with rocket purée to pan-fried Isle of Skye salmon with mint-marinated courgettes. It makes an appearance at main-course stage, too, in the shape of roast monkfish with a light langoustine sauce, alongside perhaps rack of lamb, served pink, in a herby mustard crust. End on a Continental note with Normandy-style apple tart with Calvados cream Chantilly, or tiramisù. A 40-bottle all-Italian wine list starts at £14.

CHEF: Ciro Zaino   PROPRIETORS: Linda and Ciro Zaino   OPEN: Wed to Sun D only 7.30 to 9.30   CLOSED: Nov to early Mar   MEALS: Set D £24.50   SERVICE: 10%, card slips closed   CARDS: Delta, MasterCard, Switch, Visa   DETAILS: 22 seats. 20 seats outside. Private parties: 25 main room. No smoking. Music ACCOMMODATION: 5 rooms, all with bath/shower. TV. B&B £70 to £95. No children under 13

PETERSFIELD Hampshire
map 2

JSW 🍷 ✴

1 Heath Road, Petersfield GU31 4JE
TEL: (01730) 262030

HAMPSHIRE OF THE YEAR RESTAURANT

COOKING 6
MODERN BRITISH
£35–£55

A narrow, uncluttered room, Jake Watkins's restaurant makes the most of limited space. Wicker chairs seemingly lifted from a conservatory and walls in restful caffè latte and mushroom hues hung with excellent nude drawings make the interior view preferable to the one outside – hence the square geometrical patterns and giant JSW in the frosted glass of the frontage.

The cooking – impressive already when JSW opened in 2001 – is on the rise. The set menus are understated and deliver dishes of often astonishing quality (and dishes are the same at lunch and dinner, but lunch is £10 cheaper). Three plump scallops – gently cooked rather than seared, bedded on fresh-tasting pea purée and topped with pea shoots – sitting in a creamy, frothy pea and bacon velouté, was a top-drawer opener. Foie gras is roasted and partnered with a Tatin of shallots and Sauternes. Seasons are conscientiously observed, so a spring menu brought crushed Jersey Royals to accompany sea bass. Mashes and purées soften the edges of dishes, with truffled mash providing 'remarkably fragrant' support for crustily seared beef fillet with ceps and shallots, all in a copybook red wine sauce. Telling simplicity garnishes a subtly salted caramel mousse with crisp shards of walnut praline, adds apple to crème brûlée, or accompanies chocolate fondant with prune ice cream and an Armagnac-soaked prune. The wine list shows plenty of swagger in Bordeaux, Burgundy, Italy and Australia, and pushes beyond the common-or-garden in Spain, Alsace and Germany. Prices are less down-to-earth than they were, but diners on a budget still have choice enough under £20.

CHEF/PROPRIETOR: Jake Watkins   OPEN: Tue to Sat 12 to 1.30 (1 Sat), 7 to 9.30   CLOSED: 3 weeks at Christmas, 2 weeks July and Aug   MEALS: Set L £17.50 (2 courses) to £22.50, Set D £27.50 (2 courses) to £32.50   SERVICE: not inc   CARDS: Delta, MasterCard, Switch, Visa   DETAILS: 22 seats. Private parties: 23 main room. Vegetarian meals. No children under 6. No music. No mobile phones

PETER TAVY Devon
map 1

Peter Tavy Inn ✴ £

Peter Tavy PL19 9NN
TEL: (01822) 810348   FAX: (01822) 810835
off A386 Tavistock to Okehampton road, 2m NE of
Tavistock

COOKING 1
MODERN EUROPEAN
£21–£41

Originally a home for masons building the nearby church, this greatly extended fifteenth-century inn stands well off the beaten track down a tiny lane. Honest country pub cooking without fancy embellishments is the style at lunchtime, when the choice ranges from baguettes to game casserole with Stilton dumplings. In the evening, there's a touch more flair and invention in the shape of red mullet with olive and tomato salsa, or roast rack of lamb with minted gooseberry sauce followed by, say, apple and apricot crumble or Turkish delight with white chocolate mousse. West Country beers are an alternative to the affordable wine list, which starts from £8.75.

CHEFS: Stephen Byrne and Chrissie Kilfedder   PROPRIETORS: Graeme and Karen Sim   OPEN: all week 12 to 2, 6.30 to 9   CLOSED: 24 Dec D, 25 Dec, 26 Dec D, 1 Jan D   MEALS: alc (main courses L £6 to £10, D £8 to £16)   SERVICE: not inc, card slips closed   CARDS: Delta, MasterCard, Switch, Visa   DETAILS: 70 seats. 100 seats outside. Private parties: 44 main room. Car park. Vegetarian meals. Children's helpings. Children in separate dining area only. No smoking in 1 dining room. Music £5

PLUMTREE Nottinghamshire   map 5

Perkins ⅜ £   NEW ENTRY

Old Railway Station, Plumtree NG12 5NA   COOKING 2
TEL: (0115) 937 3695   FAX: (0115) 937 6405   MODERN BRITISH/FRENCH
WEBSITE: www.perkinsrestaurant.co.uk   £23–£45

A younger generation of Perkinses has taken charge at this converted Victorian railway station. One longstanding regular, 'never disappointed' with its bistro-style cooking, reports established tradition continues to be followed 'excellently and with much enthusiasm'; another commends the 'friendly and personal atmosphere'. Asparagus, served with a smooth, flavoursome hollandaise, has had perfect colour and faultless texture, while a main course mushroom mille-feuille was 'a winner'. Fish cookery has been praised, with chargrilled halibut 'spot-on' for timing, though vegetables are extra. Finish perhaps with simple raspberries and cream, or banana fritters with caramel sauce. Two-course weekday lunches cost under a tenner. The well-balanced wine list is very fairly priced; fruity Touraine Sauvignon is good value at £11.75.

CHEF: Marco Smeeth   PROPRIETORS: Tony, Wendy, Jonathan and David Perkins   OPEN: Tue to Sun L 12 to 2 (2.30 Sun), Tue to Sat D 6.45 to 9.45   MEALS: alc (not Sun L; main courses £9.50 to £14.50). Set L Tue to Sat £9.75 (2 courses). Set L Sun £13.50 (2 courses) to £16.95, Set D Tue to Thur £17.50. Bar menu available   SERVICE: not inc   CARDS: Delta   DETAILS: 73 seats. 24 seats outside. Private parties: 12 main room, 32 private room. Car park. Vegetarian meals. No smoking. Wheelchair access (not WC). Occasional music. Air-conditioned

---

PLYMOUTH Devon   map 1

Tanners ⅜   NEW ENTRY

Prysten House, Finewell Street, Plymouth PL1 2AE   COOKING 4
TEL: (01752) 252001   FAX: (01752) 252105   MODERN BRITISH
WEBSITE: www.tannersrestaurant.com   £26–£55

What is reputedly the oldest surviving domestic building in Plymouth manages to be both striking and approachable. Medieval England is the decorative theme – 'when the place is full it is easy to imagine a gathering of worthy burghers' – and solid refectory-style tables, tapestries, and quotes of 'varying impenetrability' scripted onto walls match the beamed ceilings, rough stone walls and floors, an illuminated well, and mullioned windows. Yet the food is far from retro, and brothers James and Christopher Tanner's short menus have elements of fashionable brasserie eating, with a bias towards fish. Cooking techniques and timing were spot-on at an inspection meal that started with red mullet teamed with sweet red and yellow peppers and a topping of tapenade, and a salad of 'fat, perfectly cooked' seared scallops with pancetta and chargrilled asparagus. 'Stunning' tournedos Rossini, and a Thai-style sea bass cooked in foil ('a triumph') have also found favour, and desserts might include a classic orange crème brûlée. Excellent home-made bread comes in for special mention, and the up-to-date globetrotting wine list opens with four house wines at £12.95.

CHEFS/PROPRIETORS: Christopher and James Tanner   OPEN: Mon to Sat 12 to 2.30 (2 Sat), 7 to 9.30
CLOSED: 25, 26 and 31 Dec, 1 Jan   MEALS: Set L £12.50 (2 courses) to £15, Set D £23 (2 courses) to £33.
Light L menu available   SERVICE: not inc   CARDS: Amex, Delta, Diners, MasterCard, Switch, Visa
DETAILS: 45 seats. 45 seats outside. Private parties: 30 main room, 10 to 25 private rooms. Vegetarian
meals. Children's helpings. No smoking. Wheelchair access (also WC). Music

PONTELAND Northumberland — map 10

Café 21 £

35 The Broadway, Darras Hall, Ponteland NE20 9PW
TEL/FAX: (01661) 820357

COOKING 4
MODERN EUROPEAN
£24–£57

Set in leafy Tyneside commuterland, this outpost of the Laybourne empire is a double-fronted bistro with smart, dark green awning, and a mirrored interior with tiled floors and crisp napery. Ian Lowrey's modern British carte also includes a listing of early-evening and Saturday lunch set meals. A simple bistro salad of Roquefort, pear and walnuts, straight from the classical repertoire, is joined by such starters as spicy beef salad with soy and chilli, or seared scallops with a salsa of mango and red onion. The same broad vision informs main courses, which run from sea bream with provençale vegetables and tapenade cream to a portion of plainly grilled halibut, and on to meat dishes that include sirloin steaks of good local beef, or medallions of venison with brandied cherries, walnuts and pasta. Meals end with pear, chocolate and almond tart, perhaps, or pistachio meringue filled with banana and passion fruit, or local cheeses. Friendly service and a keenly priced wine list complete the picture; house wines from Duboeuf are £11.70.

CHEF: Ian Lowrey   PROPRIETOR: Terence Laybourne   OPEN: Sat L 12 to 2, Mon to Sat D 5.30 to 10
CLOSED: bank hols   MEALS: alc (main courses £8.50 to £19.50). Set L Sat £12 (2 courses) to £14, Set D 5.30
to 7 £12 (2 courses) to £14   SERVICE: not inc   CARDS: Amex, Delta, Diners, MasterCard, Switch, Visa
DETAILS: 68 seats. Private parties: 68 main room. Vegetarian meals. Children's helpings. Wheelchair
access (also WC). Music

POOLE Dorset — map 2

▲ Mansion House ▼ ⅚✳

Thames Street, Poole BH15 1JN
TEL: (01202) 685666   FAX: (01202) 665709
WEBSITE: www.themansionhouse.co.uk

COOKING 3
MODERN BRITISH-PLUS
£28–£48

Mansion House, an elegant, red-brick Georgian building, has a loyal following, with a 4,000-strong dining club. 'Modern British with Asian influences' is how the owners describe the cooking style, and it is clear to see that ingredients are taken seriously here, from local lamb to lobsters and sea bass from Poole, and West Country cheeses. Consequently, the food makes a fresh impression, be it starters such as smoked haddock

Welsh rarebit with tomato salad, or main courses such as confit of duck with stir-fried vegetables and spiced plum sauce. There's plenty of choice for vegetarians, for example a green curry of beans, fennel and courgettes with a carrot and coriander spring roll and rice. Value for money extends to a wine list that has plenty under £20, topped off by some star turns from France and the New World. Service is thoroughly relaxed yet professional.

CHEF: Gerry Godden   PROPRIETORS: Jackie and Gerry Godden   OPEN: Sun to Fri L 12 to 2, Mon to Sat and Sun bank hol D 7 to 9.30   MEALS: Set L £17 (2 courses) to £19.25, Set D £21.95 (2 courses) to £27.45. Bistro menu available   SERVICE: not inc   CARDS: Amex, Delta, Diners, MasterCard, Switch, Visa DETAILS: 85 seats. Private parties: 100 main room, 14 to 36 private rooms. Car park. Vegetarian meals. Under-5s must eat at 7pm at D. Children's helpings. No smoking. Occasional music. Air-conditioned ACCOMMODATION: 32 rooms, all with bath/shower. TV. Phone. B&B £75 to £140. Baby facilities (£5)

PORLOCK WEIR   Somerset   map 1

▲ Andrew's on the Weir ⚜✳

Porlock Weir TA24 8PB	COOKING 4
TEL: (01643) 863300 FAX: (01643) 863311	MODERN EUROPEAN
WEBSITE: www.andrewsontheweir.co.uk	£27–£68

Brightly done in yellow and gold tones, with bay windows giving a grandstand view across the Bristol Channel, this is a restaurant of high local repute. A couple directed here by word of mouth were glad they took the advice: their fish soup contained three types of white fish and a decently fat scallop served in a frothy lobster bisque, while the main course, pink-cooked pigeon on a bed of ceps, surmounted by seared foie gras and white truffle, was worthy of the smartest metropolitan venues. Others might enjoy Exmoor venison pâté with red onion jam, or slow-roast Somerset pork with caramelised veal sweetbreads and Madeira jus, or Porlock Bay sea bass with basil tortellini and white wine velouté. For those with no sweet tooth, the dessert list includes a twice-baked cheese soufflé with balsamic dressing, alongside the likes of passion-fruit délice with crème fraîche sorbet and exotic fruits. Fine British cheeses have their own menu. The classy wine list, divided stylistically, starts with house wines from £10.75 and tops out with four vintages of Penfolds Grange.

CHEF: Andrew Dixon   PROPRIETORS: Andrew Dixon and Rodney Sens   OPEN: Wed to Sun L 12 to 2.30, Tue to Sat D 7 to 9.30   CLOSED: Jan   MEALS: Set L £12.50 (2 courses) to £15.50, Set D £28 (2 courses) to £35 SERVICE: not inc   CARDS: Amex, Delta, MasterCard, Switch, Visa   DETAILS: 30 seats. Private parties: 25 main room, 10 private room. Car park. Vegetarian meals. No children under 12. No smoking. Wheelchair access (not WC). Music. No mobile phones   ACCOMMODATION: 5 rooms, all with bath/shower. TV. B&B £65 to £120. No children under 12 (£5)

PORTREATH   Cornwall   map 1

Tabb's ⚜✳

Tregea Terrace, Portreath TR16 4LD	COOKING 2
TEL: (01209) 842488	MODERN BRITISH-PLUS
	£25–£55

Two-foot-thick granite walls lend a sense of permanence and rusticity to this former smithy in a tranquil Cornish village. Nigel and Melanie Tabb have a crusading attitude to local produce, which ensures regular supplies of fish and organic vegetables, top-drawer smoked cheese and seasonal game (a favourite option for Sunday lunch). Cornish hog's pudding with mushrooms, basmati rice and a garlic and sesame cream is a signature starter, while main courses leap from medallions of monkfish with chorizo, chilli and cherry tomato dressing to roast duck breast with onion, soy and sesame confit and five-spice jus. Bread, pasta and ice creams are made in-house, although chocolate is the real star when it comes to the final act. Four house wines from £10.95 head the affordable, round-the-world list.

CHEF: Nigel Tabb PROPRIETORS: Nigel and Melanie Tabb OPEN: Sun L 12.15 to 1.45, Wed to Mon D 7 to 9 CLOSED: 1 week Oct, 1 week Jan MEALS: alc D (main courses £11.50 to £20). Set L Sun £15, Set D £19.50 SERVICE: not inc, card slips closed CARDS: Delta, MasterCard, Switch, Visa DETAILS: 35 seats. Private parties: 35 main room. Vegetarian meals. Children's helpings. No smoking in dining room, permitted in bar. Wheelchair access (not WC). Music £5

PORTSCATHO Cornwall   map 1

▲ Driftwood 🛏

Rosevine, nr Portscatho TR2 5EW	COOKING 5
TEL: (01872) 580644 FAX: (01872) 580801	MODERN EUROPEAN
WEBSITE: www.driftwoodhotel.co.uk	£47–£56

The stylishly designed hotel perches above the sea like a piece of the driftwood that provides its name and decorative theme. There are panoramic views in the bright, airy dining room, where both tables and discreetly attentive staff are elegantly dressed. In February 2004 new chef Rory Duncan arrived, but standards have not wavered one iota. Local suppliers provide seasonal produce that is turned into fresh, light, modern dishes of strong appeal. Pea and courgette velouté, a piece of lightly cooked salmon in the middle, opened a spring dinner well, only to be bettered by a rolled saddle of rabbit topped with a piece of duck foie gras, dressed with celery and walnuts. Main-course choices are typically one vegetarian, one meat and two fish – exemplified by two large John Dory fillets on an underlay of crab and red pepper couscous with spinach, complemented by separate sauces of fennel and tomato. The meat might be roast rump of tender local lamb with fondant potato, shallot purée and a rosemary-scented sauce. The assiette of chocolate (moist sponge, rich parfait and white chocolate mousse) will ensnare many, or there may be lemongrass pannacotta with passion-fruit sorbet. The compact list is strong in southern hemisphere wines, with Chilean Sauvignon and Merlot opening the bidding at £13.

CHEF: Rory Duncan PROPRIETORS: Paul and Fiona Robinson OPEN: all week D only 7 to 9.30, booking essential CLOSED: Christmas, Jan MEALS: Set D £34 SERVICE: not inc, card slips closed CARDS: Amex, MasterCard, Switch, Visa DETAILS: 34 seats. 8 seats outside. Private parties: 34 main room. Car park. Vegetarian meals. Music. No mobile phones ACCOMMODATION: 11 rooms, all with bath/shower. TV. Phone. B&B £112.50 to £190

POULTON Gloucestershire   map 2

Falcon Inn

London Road, Poulton GL7 5HN	COOKING 4
TEL/FAX: (01285) 850844	EUROPEAN
WEBSITE: www.thefalconpoulton.co.uk	£29–£52

Refurbishment hasn't masked the essential character of the Falcon – effectively a pub with culinary aspirations – but it has introduced 'a stylish and contemporary interior'. There are real ales at the bar, but the main interest is in the cooking, which shows plenty of brasserie mainstays: everything from leg of duck confit with watercress and orange salad to chargrilled ribeye steak with garlic butter and home-made chips, or Gloucester Old Spot sausages with mash and onion gravy. The formula is a successful one – the menu changes every six weeks or so, supplies are as local as possible, and a blackboard of daily specials enlarges the choice. The results are good, according to one couple who were impressed by a Sunday lunch of 'rare and wonderfully tasty' Longhorn beef with Yorkshire pudding, and a rich, gamey venison carbonade. Puddings may be 'fairly traditional in range but very good in reality': sticky toffee pudding, say, or chocolate and hazelnut brownie with home-made milk chocolate and malt ice cream. A list of some 50-odd wide-ranging, well-sourced wines offers plenty of interest under £20. House French is £11.50.

CHEFS: Jeremy Lockley, Will Abraham and Robin Couling   PROPRIETORS: Robin Couling and Jeremy Lockley   OPEN: all week 12 to 2.30, 7 to 9   MEALS: alc (main courses £9 to £16). Set L Sun £15 (2 courses) to £20   SERVICE: not inc   CARDS: Delta, MasterCard, Switch, Visa   DETAILS: 60 seats. Private parties: 34 main room, 12 private room. Car park. Vegetarian meals. Children's helpings. No smoking in 1 dining room. Wheelchair access (also WC). Music   £5

POULTON-LE-FYLDE Lancashire   map 8

▲ River House

Skippool Creek, Thornton-Le-Fylde, Poulton-Le-
Fylde FY5 5LF
TEL: (01253) 883497   FAX: (01253) 892083
WEBSITE: www.theriverhouse.org.uk   COOKING 4
from roundabout junction of A585 and B5412 follow   FRENCH-PLUS
signs to Skippool Creek   £34–£58

Bill Scott has been cooking here for more years than he cares to admit. He produces robust dishes from a repertoire that tends towards comforting, tried and tested pairings such as sautéed chicken livers with marjoram, onions and mushrooms, or scallops lightly poached in a creamy, herby sauce for starters, and perhaps a main course of medallions of pork with green pepper sauce. There are culinary surprises, too, with a brace of breast of pigeon roasted rare, and a starter of salmon goujons in saké and teriyaki, but long-standing classics such as soufflé suissesse, chateaubriand with béarnaise, and beef schnitzel are as comforting and welcoming as the house itself. Puddings might include a rich dark chocolate mousse laced with Grand Marnier, or a choice of sorbets that runs to elderflower, as well as lemon curd and butterscotch ice creams. The wine list rarely mentions producers and is heavily, although not exclusively, skewed towards France, with affordable Languedoc-Roussillon helping to balance the usual heavyweight regions.

CHEF/PROPRIETOR: Bill Scott   OPEN: Mon to Sat D only 7.30 to 9.30   CLOSED: 25 and 26 Dec, 1 Jan   MEALS: alc (main courses £16 to £20). Set D £25   SERVICE: not inc   CARDS: MasterCard, Switch, Visa   DETAILS: 40 seats. Private parties: 40 main room. Car park. Vegetarian meals. No children under 7. Music ACCOMMODATION: 4 rooms, all with bath/shower. TV. Phone. B&B £70 to £90   £5

PRESTBURY Cheshire   map 8

▲ White House

The Village, Prestbury SK10 4DG   COOKING 4
TEL: (01625) 829376   FAX: (01625) 828627   MODERN BRITISH
WEBSITE: www.thewhitehouse.uk.com   £26–£67

Though it is understated on the outside, the interior of this eighteenth-century building is light, smart and thoroughly contemporary – cheery wooden tables, natural colours, and ceramics and glass sculptures by local artists. For over 20 years the kitchen has built up confidence and a range of local suppliers, and its output is imaginative and skilfully executed. Bold contrasts of flavour and texture, such as a risotto of avocado and rocket accompanied by feta fritters, or a main course of lamb with roast peppers, aubergine mash and minted tomato jus, come off as a result of careful judgement and excellent materials. The tasting plate of five 'British' desserts – including a rice pudding retaining firm grains, and a refined sticky toffee pudding – demonstrates a range of culinary skills and intelligence. The three-course set lunch looks good value, too. Informal but very professional service and subtle lighting reinforce the comfort factor. The wine list, starting at £13.95, settles for security and simplicity.

CHEFS: Ryland Wakeham and Richard Clarke   PROPRIETORS: Ryland and Judith Wakeham   OPEN: Tue to Sun L 12 to 2, Mon to Sat D 7 to 10   CLOSED: 25 Dec   MEALS: alc (not Sun L; main courses £12.50 to £19.50). Set L Tue to Thurs £14.95, Set L Sun £15.95, Set D Mon to Fri £16.50 (2 courses) to £19.50. Bar L menu available Tue to Sat   SERVICE: not inc, card slips closed   CARDS: Amex, MasterCard, Switch, Visa DETAILS: 70 seats. 12 seats outside. Private parties: 40 main room, 10 to 40 private rooms. Car park. Vegetarian meals. Children's helpings. No smoking in restaurant before 2pm and 10pm. Wheelchair access (not WC). Music. No mobile phones   ACCOMMODATION: 11 rooms, all with bath/shower. TV. Phone. Room only £40 to £130

PRESTON Lancashire   map 8

Simply Heathcotes

23 Winckley Square, Preston PR1 3JJ   COOKING **2**
TEL: (01772) 252732   FAX: (01772) 203433   BRASSERIE
WEBSITE: www.heathcotes.co.uk   £26–£62

One of the first openings in Paul Heathcote's early expansion beyond Longridge (see entry), the Preston restaurant is in a smartly affluent conservation district. Standards have varied as the chain has grown, but this kitchen is capable of turning out some good dishes. Minted pea soup is satisfying enough, the modern classic pairing of black pudding and scallops is well handled, pointedly supported by green apple purée and mustard butter, and pan-fried fillet of sea bass with fennel salad and black olive potatoes is a correctly timed main course. For dessert, treacle-dense Pedro Ximénez sherry is poured over vanilla ice cream with hot espresso, or there may be lemon-curd sponge pudding with clotted cream and raspberry sauce. Service is pleasant and efficient, and wines are a helpfully annotated modern assortment, starting at £13.50 a bottle.

CHEF: Paul Gray   PROPRIETOR: Paul Heathcote   OPEN: all week 12 to 2.30, 7 (6 Fri, Sat and Sun) to 10 (11 Fri and Sat, 9.30 Sun)   CLOSED: 25 and 26 Dec, 1 Jan, bank hol Mons   MEALS: alc (main courses £9.50 to £19.50). Set L and D Mon to Thur 7 to 7.45, Fri to Sun 6 to 7 £13.50 (2 courses) to £15.50   SERVICE: 10% (optional), card slips closed   CARDS: Amex, Delta, MasterCard, Switch, Visa   DETAILS: 90 seats. Private parties: 100 main room. Vegetarian meals. Children's helpings. No smoking. Wheelchair access (not WC). Music. Air-conditioned

---

Prices quoted in the Guide are based on information supplied by restaurateurs. The prices quoted at the top of each entry represent a range, from the lowest price of a three-course meal with service and wine to the highest; the latter is inflated by 20 per cent to take account of likely price rises during the year of the Guide.

Ramsons ▮ ⅄✖

18 Market Place, Ramsbottom BL0 9HT	COOKING 4
TEL: (01706) 825070 FAX: (01706) 822005	ITALIAN
WEBSITE: www.ramsons.org.uk	£42–£73

'Graduation to senior citizen persuaded me to reduce my working week to five days,' writes the indomitable Chris Johnson, but that sure won't stop him being much appreciated round these parts – 'Mr Johnson blazes a gourmet trail through the local wilderness,' as one local put it. The basement is the setting for the 'Hideaway' menu on Friday and Saturday nights, which is cooked by a separate chef (from a different kitchen) than are the menus for the main ground-floor restaurant. Chris's affinity with Italian cooking and talent for sourcing prime raw materials, locally and in Italy, are translated by Abdulla Naseem and Amy Bicknell with heartfelt directness in the ground-floor restaurant. And the kitchen deals in often simple, straightforward ideas, yet with an intelligent streak – as in wild nettle, wild garlic and truffle soup, or seared Shetland scallops with fennel purée and light saffron sauce. Much of the food runs along familiar (and not exclusively Italian) lines, taking in flash-fried fillet of beef with creamy mashed potatoes and two sauces, its everyman appeal also striking a balance between the richness of grilled lobster and Amalfi lemon sauce and the comfort of lasagne with meat and cheese sauce. Desserts can be a homage to Italy – ricotta and hazelnut gâteau with chocolate shavings – but organic Lancashire cheese waves the red rose. There's an 'Everyday' menu available in the restaurant (see below for availability), where you can eat up to three courses for a maximum of £20 at dinner.

The wine list is a winner not for any great breadth but for the passion with which Chris Johnson has scoured Italy and established links with the producers he features. It's worth sampling the 18 that come by the glass (£2.50 to £6) to tour the range of flavours from north to south; bottles start at £12.50.

CHEFS: Abdulla Naseem and Amy Bicknell   PROPRIETORS: Ros Hunter and Chris Johnson   OPEN: Wed to Sun L 12 to 2.30 (Sun 1 to 3.30), Wed to Sat D 6.30 to 9.30   CLOSED: 1 Jan   MEALS: alc (main courses L £8.50 to £12, D £14.50 to £19.50). Set D £39.50. 'Everyday' menu available Wed to Sat L, Wed to Thur D; 'Hideaway' menu available Fri and Sat D   SERVICE: not inc, card slips closed   CARDS: Delta, MasterCard, Switch, Visa   DETAILS: 36 seats. Vegetarian meals. No smoking. Music. No mobile phones (£5)

▲ Yorke Arms ▮ ⅄✖

Ramsgill, Pateley Bridge HG3 5RL	COOKING 7
TEL: (01423) 755243 FAX: (01423) 755330	MODERN BRITISH
WEBSITE: www.yorke-arms.co.uk	£29–£71

Traditional, unpretentious country pub in appearance, this is a serious, upmarket restaurant by intent, even if it is hidden away up the top of Nidderdale. The creeper-covered old inn facing the village green looks very neat – an impression confirmed by the well-kept snug bar or the comfortable drawing room where pre-dinner drinks are served. The dining room has a 'rustic but classy' feel, with old country dressers, an oversized mirror, bare floorboards with rugs, unclothed wooden tables and Windsor chairs.

The setting and warm welcome may elicit reporters' praise, but the food is the star. Meals start well with freshly home-baked breads and well-crafted appetisers, such as a savoury lobster pannacotta. Presentation can seem elaborate, but to good effect – witness a starter of three perfectly timed king scallops (crisp on the outside and nutty-flavoured, topped with a small heap of caviar and placed on a puddle of puréed butternut squash) flanked by two shelled langoustines on a dollop of pungent aïoli, and accompanied by a shot glass of tomato essence jelly of concentrated flavour. The same effort goes into main courses like herb-crusted roast guinea fowl, the moist breast meat set on a base of creamed leeks, accompanied by a herb-flecked sausage of leg meat and served with a cylinder of grilled polenta, peeled broad beans, intensely flavoured asparagus and a light sauce containing girolles. A ballottine of juicy, well-flavoured chicken with boudin blanc and crisp veal sweetbreads in a powerful stock reduction has made a similarly positive impression, and classy desserts have featured a clafoutis-style tart of marinated cherries with chocolate pannacotta. France, primarily Burgundy and Bordeaux, is the mainstay of the quality-focused wine list, while Italy, Spain and the New World countries turn in brief but well-chosen collections. Eight house bottles start at £13.50.

CHEFS: Frances Atkins and Roger Olive PROPRIETORS: Gerald and Frances Atkins OPEN: all week L 12 to 2 (2.30 Sun), Mon to Sat D 7 to 9 (9.30 Sat) MEALS: alc (main courses £17.50 to £22). Set L Mon to Sat £17.50. Set L Sun £26 (2 courses) to £32 SERVICE: not inc CARDS: Amex, Delta, Diners, MasterCard, Switch, Visa DETAILS: 60 seats. 30 seats outside. Private parties: 15 main room, 15 to 20 private rooms. Car park. Vegetarian meals. No children under 12. No smoking. Wheelchair access (not WC). Music. No mobile phones ACCOMMODATION: 12 rooms, all with bath/shower. TV. Phone. D,B&B £105 to £170. No children under 12 (£5)

READING Berkshire   map 2

London Street Brasserie

2–4 London Street, Reading RG1 4SE   COOKING 2
TEL: (01189) 505036 FAX: (01189) 505028   MODERN EUROPEAN
WEBSITE: www.londonstbrasserie.co.uk   £30–£65

Fast food dominates the Oracle Centre, but this old Toll House, overlooking the river, brings a lively modernity and much needed quality. An ambitiously long menu compiles local ingredients into multi-layered dishes like pheasant with Savoy cabbage, button onions, chestnuts, lardons and bread sauce, or a reporter's smoked salmon and halibut fishcakes rolled in oatmeal and served with spinach and a creamy chive beurre blanc. Italian charcuterie and bouillabaisse are among the starters, while puds include passion-fruit and mango pavlova, and spotted dick. Cocktails feature alongside a decent collection of wines starting at £13.50 that includes much under £20, a sprinkling of French classics, and a dozen by the glass.

CHEFS: Paul Clerehugh and Paul Brotherton PROPRIETOR: Paul Clerehugh OPEN: all week 12 to 11 MEALS: alc L 12 to 3 and D 6.30 to 11 (main courses £12 to £20). Set L and D 12 to 7 £13.50 (2 courses) SERVICE: not inc, 10% (optional) for parties of 10 or more CARDS: Amex, Delta, Diners, MasterCard, Switch, Visa DETAILS: 80 seats. 24 seats outside. Private parties: 80 main room, 20 to 40 private rooms. Vegetarian meals. Children's helpings. No pipes. Wheelchair access (also WC). Music. No mobile phones

Some restaurants leave credit card slips open even though they also make a fixed (or 'optional') service charge. The Guide strongly disapproves of this practice as it may result in consumers unknowingly paying twice for service.

REIGATE Surrey   map 3

Dining Room ✤

59A High Street, Reigate RH2 9AE	COOKING **3**
TEL/FAX: (01737) 226650	MODERN BRITISH
WEBSITE: www.tonytobinrestaurants.co.uk	£34–£70

A smart, understated sign marks out this restaurant on the busy High Street, the dining room reached by a flight of stairs. There's a cosmopolitan feel to the décor of soft leaf-green walls hung with modern landscapes, a constellation of lights in the cream-painted ceiling, and small white-clothed tables laid with attractive display plates. Tony Tobin's modern British cooking is infused with Mediterranean and Asian influences, so starters might feature seared scallops on a Thai crab cake with sticky rice alongside griddled black pudding with a compote of red onions, raisins and apples, topped with a soft-boiled egg. To follow, choices run from seared chicken fillet on tarragon tortellini to roast halibut with braised oxtail and a lemon and parsley dressing, and for dessert there might be sticky toffee pudding, or banana fritters with coconut sauce. The short, international wine list is chosen well for easy drinking by the glass or bottle, with prices starting at £14.95 for house French.

CHEF/PROPRIETOR: Tony Tobin   OPEN: Sun to Fri L 12 to 2.30, Mon to Sat D 7 to 10   CLOSED: 24 Dec to 2 Jan, bank hols   MEALS: Set L Mon to Fri £19.50, Set L Sun £28.50, Set D Mon to Thur £24.95 (2 courses) to £31.90, Set D Fri and Sat £32 (2 courses) to £38.95   SERVICE: 12.5% (optional), card slips closed   CARDS: Amex, Delta, MasterCard, Switch, Visa   DETAILS: 75 seats. Private parties: 75 main room. Vegetarian meals. Children's helpings. No smoking. Music. No mobile phones. Air-conditioned

RICHMOND Surrey   map 3

Burnt Chair ▾ ✤

5 Duke Street, Richmond TW9 1HP	COOKING **3**
TEL: (020) 8940 9488	GLOBAL
WEBSITE: www.burntchair.com	£33–£60

Being handy for Richmond Theatre, the Burnt Chair does pre-performance two-course set dinners here as well as the carte, and 'Mr Oo is always most welcoming', says one reporter for whom the global food warms the cockles. Menu descriptions run from resolutely European (chicken liver terrine) to deliberately esoteric (oriental vegetable bon bons, wasabi mayo). Otherwise, there might be crab charlotte with papaya and pepper gazpacho; tarte Tatin of lamb, apples, parsnips and tabbouleh; or salmon ceviche with mango, clams and lavender. Cheese – grilled crottin de chavignol with walnut and apple salad, perhaps – gets a section on the menu all to itself, while puddings range from pineapple and Serrano jelly with crème Chantilly to white chocolate and Galliano pavé. The restaurant stocks an encyclopaedic choice of Californian wine and is serious about Burgundies and single malt whiskies too. House wines are £14.75, and ten come by the glass, with more offered at lunchtimes. Lunch is in the offing as we go to press.

CHEFS: John Barry, Ivo Manni and Livio Te   PROPRIETOR: Weenson Andrew Oo   OPEN: Tue to Sat D only 6 to 11   CLOSED: 2 weeks at Christmas   MEALS: alc D (main courses £12.50 to £19.50). Pre-theatre D 6 to 7 £15, Set D Tue to Thurs £18 (2 courses) to £20. Cover £1   SERVICE: not inc   CARDS: Delta, MasterCard, Switch, Visa   DETAILS: 36 seats. Private parties: 36 main room. Vegetarian meals. Children's helpings. No smoking. No music ⊖ Richmond (£5)

RIDGEWAY Derbyshire   map 9

Old Vicarage ♥ ✖

Ridgeway Moor, Ridgeway S12 3XW
TEL: (0114) 247 5814
WEBSITE: www.theoldvicarage.co.uk
from A616 ¾m NW of Mosborough, turn W on B6054/   COOKING 7
B6388; in Ridgeway, turn S; restaurant ½m on left, nearly   MODERN BRITISH-PLUS
opposite church   £41–£80

Well-tended gardens and a fountain make an imposing foreground for this early-Victorian stone-built mansion, which would now look a trifle ostentatious as an archbishop's residence, let alone that of a mere vicar. The dining room affords a dramatic view of the floodlit grounds in the evening, and there is also a pleasant conservatory at the back. Tessa Bramley takes on a lot, devising menus, supervising the kitchen, and appearing out front to serve and chat, and readers attest that things continue to go from strength to strength.

The cooking is built on admirable principles, both in sourcing materials from local specialists and from further afield (olive oil is imported direct from a small grower on Crete), and in the execution. Spiced monkfish tail as a first course borrows from the Indian kitchen, arriving with a flat-topped cake of rice, mini poppadoms and a mildly curried coconut sauce, while foie gras terrine is given a fruity treatment, served with a mango dressing, Muscat jelly and a glass of sweet Muscat to accompany. Main-course descriptions run to three lines on the menus but are accurately reflected in what turns up, and the 'complexity and engineered layers of flavour' hit home. Roast fillet of Whitby cod comes on braised beans and pancetta with sweet-roasted squash and a cumin- and coriander-scented balsamic reduction, while properly crackled roast pork loin is successfully attended by roast apples, sprouting broccoli, a parsnip and ginger cake, and rhubarb butter sauce. Dessert trios such as a set of apple variations are favoured, or there may well be traditional plum pudding with cognac cream. 'Seamlessly smooth service' and top-notch incidentals ('amazing' spring onion and Gruyère bread, for example) add to the impact. Wines, grouped by style, are a well-chosen, international mix with a European focus at the top end. Six house bottles, also available by the glass, start at £17.50, and prices overall are on the high side.

CHEFS: Tessa Bramley and Nathan Smith   PROPRIETOR: Tessa Bramley   OPEN: Tue to Fri L 12.30 to 2.30, Tue to Sat D 7 (6.30 Sat) to 9.45   CLOSED: 26 Dec, 31 Dec to 7 Jan, bank hols   MEALS: Set L £25 (inc wine) to £48, Set D £48   SERVICE: not inc, card slips closed   CARDS: Delta, MasterCard, Switch, Visa   DETAILS: 46 seats. 16 seats outside. Private parties: 50 main room, 10 to 20 private rooms. Car park. Vegetarian meals. No smoking. Wheelchair access (also WC). Occasional music. No mobile phones

RIPLEY North Yorkshire   map 9

▲ Boar's Head ♥ ✖ £

Ripley HG3 3AY   COOKING 3
TEL: (01423) 771888   FAX: (01423) 771509   MODERN BRITISH
WEBSITE: www.boarsheadripley.co.uk   £28–£56

This foursquare inn in Ripley's cobbled square offers a choice. The bistro's hearty à la carte features, say, beef and ale casserole in a Yorkshire pudding, or pork and leek sausages, flanked by starters like a warm venison sausage and wild mushroom salad, and sweets like milk chocolate mousse with mango coulis. The restaurant (crimson walls and oil paintings, starched tablecloths and upholstered chairs) serves restrained, modish 'set' meals; price is determined by the main-course choice. That might be seared sea bass fillet on a baby vegetable nage with star anise and Brie-filled won tons, or fillet of beef with gratinated mushrooms and truffle oil. Top and tail your selection with mussel soup, or warm quail salad, and maybe 'Boozy' Bakewell, or Irish coffee soufflé with vanilla ice cream and espresso sauce. France is the strongest suit in a global wine list picked with care and an eye for value; house Chileans are £12.25.

CHEF: Jason Main   PROPRIETORS: Sir Thomas and Lady Emma Ingilby   OPEN: all week 12 to 2, 7 to 9
MEALS: alc bistro (main courses £9 to £15). Set D restaurant £18.95 to £31.95   SERVICE: not inc   CARDS:
Amex, Delta, MasterCard, Switch, Visa   DETAILS: 40 seats. Private parties: 20 private room. Car park.
Vegetarian meals. Children's helpings. No smoking. Wheelchair access (also WC). Music. No mobile
phones   ACCOMMODATION: 25 rooms, all with bath/shower. TV. Phone. B&B £99 to £140. Rooms for
disabled. Baby facilities. Fishing

RIPLEY Surrey   map 3

Drake's Restaurant ✶

NEW ENTRY

The Clock House, High Street, Ripley GU23 6AQ   COOKING 7
TEL: (01483) 224777   FAX: (01483) 222940   MODERN FRENCH
WEBSITE: www.drakesrestaurant.co.uk   £32–£69

The Clock House, an imposing three-storey Georgian building, has gone through several changes of ownership and identity in recent years, but now it is well and truly on the map. Steve and Serina Drake, following on from their success at Drakes on the Pond in Abinger Hammer (see entry), have got off to a flying start here. The dining room has an understated elegance, plainly decorated in shades of green and dimly lit, with generously spaced tables laid with silver cutlery and decorative plates. But it's the cooking that draws the plaudits.

Steve Drake creates luxurious dishes where apparent simplicity belies the effort that goes into them. A starter assiette of seafood, for example, incorporates pan-fried hake, lightly grilled red snapper and 'eye-poppingly good' scallops, each component impeccably fresh and perfectly timed, accompanied by a beurre rouge and a decadently creamy cauliflower purée with a hint of truffle. Presentation is a strong point, as in a main course featuring five neat mounds of duck, each a work of art in itself, including the pink, juicy, crisp-skinned roast breast on an earthy celeriac purée, a confit drumstick coated in a stickily reduced jus, a braised thigh wrapped in a cabbage leaf, and a nugget of seared foie gras on darkly caramelised onions. Roast sea bass, cooked just beyond rare and tasting sweet and fresh, is served with saffron potatoes, slivers of poached fennel strewn artfully around the plate, and bouillabaisse, the last given glorious deep orange hues from generous use of saffron. Pear poached in wine with cinnamon parfait and roasted pistachios provides interesting contrasts of flavour and texture and makes a light, refreshing way to end a meal. The wine list offers a fair selection of reasonably priced bottles, starting at £14 for house French.

CHEF: Steve Drake   PROPRIETORS: Steve and Serina Drake   OPEN: Tue to Fri L 12 to 1.30, Tue to Sat D 7 to
9.30   CLOSED: Christmas, 2 weeks Aug   MEALS: Set L £16 (2 courses) to £19, Set D £30 (2 courses) to £36
SERVICE: not inc   CARDS: Delta, MasterCard, Switch, Visa   DETAILS: 34 seats. Private parties: 34 main
room, 6 to 10 private rooms. Vegetarian meals. No children under 12. No smoking. No music. No mobile
phones £5

The Guide always appreciates hearing about changes of chef or owner.

▲ Old Deanery ⅓✗

NEW ENTRY

Minster Road, Ripon HG4 1QS
TEL: (01765) 600003   FAX: (01765) 600027
WEBSITE: www.theolddeanery.co.uk

COOKING 2
MODERN BRITISH
£23–£62

Last in the Guide in 1996, this revamped seventeenth-century manor house adjacent to the cathedral shows its new modern credentials with polished floorboards, pale wooden tables, and high-backed brown leather dining chairs. The kitchen draws on regional produce, serving a range of seafood from crab omelette, via pan-fried scallops with pea purée, to fillet of sea bass with crushed new potatoes, roast tomato and horseradish butter sauce. It also enrols the likes of roast loin of Nidderdale lamb (served with linguine, asparagus and minted pea foam), while the lunch menu deals in modern classics, delivering such things as fish 'n' chips with mushy peas, grilled ribeye with chips, mushrooms and tomatoes and so on. Desserts tend to explore the toffee and chocolate end of the spectrum, but there may be an unusual lemongrass-scented rice pudding with white chocolate sorbet. 'Professional and down to earth' is what most people would ask of service. The wine list is arranged by style, with house selections at £13.50

CHEF: Barrie Higginbotham   PROPRIETOR: Express Terminals Ltd   OPEN: all week L 12 to 2, Mon to Sat D 7 to 9.30   CLOSED: 25 Dec   MEALS: alc (main courses L £5 to £10, D £12.50 to £20)   SERVICE: not inc, card slips closed   CARDS: Delta, MasterCard, Switch, Visa   DETAILS: 50 seats. 28 seats outside. Private parties: 50 main room, 12 to 20 private rooms. Car park. Vegetarian meals. No smoking. Wheelchair access (also WC). Music   ACCOMMODATION: 11 rooms, all with bath/shower. TV. Phone. B&B £85 to £125

▲ Roade House ⅓✗

16 High Street, Roade NN7 2NW
TEL: (01604) 863372   FAX: (01604) 862421
WEBSITE: www.roadehousehotel.co.uk

COOKING 4
MODERN BRITISH
£30–£57

Originally a roadside inn, pebbledashed and painted red, the Roade House has a somewhat old-fashioned feel both outside and in. Curtains depicting the Battle of Hastings and large gilt-framed paintings make striking focal points in the dining room, and the 'friendliness and sincerity' of the owners is a big plus. The menus tend towards a reassuringly familiar modern British style with a few flamboyant touches to pique the interest of the more gastronomically adventurous. A terrine of rabbit with hazelnuts is typical of starters, while main courses run to grilled fillet of sea bass with prawn and fennel risotto, and roast rump of lamb featuring 'pink and moist' meat sliced into a fan and served with a minted béarnaise and lyonnaise potatoes. Wines are a modest collection with not so modest prices, although five house selections start at an eminently reasonable £12.

CHEFS: Chris Kewley and Steve Barnes   PROPRIETORS: Chris and Sue Kewley   OPEN: Tue to Fri and Sun L 12 to 1.45 (2 Sun), Mon to Sat D 7 to 9.30   CLOSED: Christmas, bank hols   MEALS: alc D (main courses £15.50 to £21). Set L Tue to Fri £16 (2 courses) to £19, Set L Sun £21   SERVICE: not inc   CARDS: Amex, Delta, MasterCard, Switch, Visa   DETAILS: 45 seats. Private parties: 50 main room. Car park. Children's helpings. No smoking. Wheelchair access (also WC). Occasional music. Air-conditioned   ACCOMMODATION: 10 rooms, all with bath/shower. TV. Phone. B&B £58 to £80. Rooms for disabled. Baby facilities

ROCHDALE Greater Manchester · map 8

After Eight 🗲

2 Edenfield Road, Rochdale OL11 5AA
TEL/FAX: (01706) 646432
WEBSITE: www.aftereight.uk.com

COOKING 3
MODERN BRITISH
£30–£52

Traditional virtues and a 'mini country-house hotel feel' continue to define proceedings at Geoff and Anne Taylor's personably run stone house in a leafy part of Rochdale. Inside, everything is 'absolutely immaculate', and the food tries to keep pace with current trends without resorting to gimmickry. Baked sea bream with layers of beef tomato and feta and a colourful black olive and yellow pepper vinaigrette kicked off an inspection, before a benchmark slow-roast lamb shank accompanied by lambs' kidneys, sherry sauce and minted pea risotto. A beautiful-looking raspberry parfait on a chocolate sponge soaked in eau-de-vie with home-made chocolate ice cream shows plenty of skill in the dessert department. There's also a separate vegetarian menu and an admirable selection of carefully nurtured North Country cheeses. The well-spread global wine list includes particularly enjoyable house wines at £11.90.

CHEF: Geoff Taylor PROPRIETORS: Geoff and Anne Taylor OPEN: Tue to Sat D only 7 to 9.30 CLOSED: 25 and 26 Dec, 1 Jan MEALS: alc (main courses £12 to £17) SERVICE: not inc CARDS: Amex, Delta, Diners, MasterCard, Switch, Visa DETAILS: 45 seats. Private parties: 30 main room, 10 to 20 private rooms. Vegetarian meals. Children's helpings. No smoking. Music £5

ROCK Cornwall · map 1

Black Pig

NEW ENTRY

Rock Road, Rock PL27 6JS
TEL/FAX: (01208) 862622
WEBSITE: www.blackpigrestaurant.co.uk

COOKING 7
MODERN BRITISH
£36–£80

The Black Pig (it's named after a local trawler) doesn't *look* like a top-class restaurant from the outside. It's a neat, low brick building set back from the road, at the edge of a small shopping centre in this tiny village across the Camel estuary from Padstow. Inside is a long, narrow dining room, light and bright, with crisply dressed tables, and a display of modern paintings on loan from the gallery in Padstow.

Seasonal, local produce, natural flavours and avoidance of gimmickry are the watchwords of young Nathan Outlaw, formerly of the Vineyard at Stockcross (see entry), who set up here in 2003. Bread of superlative quality is home-made from a starter culture derived from fermented fruit, and sets the tone for meals that might begin with a piece of seared cured salmon, accompanied by fennel and wild mushroom risotto and horseradish dressing, or a superlative foie gras parfait served with walnut toast and an intense rhubarb chutney. Carte, set-lunch and tasting menus are written in ingredients-list fashion, with no information on how dishes are cooked or assembled, but with local suppliers credited. At inspection 'Cornish lamb' proved to be roast rack and braised neck end, both yielding in texture, bedded on Savoy cabbage and creamy garlic mash, the jus given punch with shallots and thyme; 'cod' was sea-fresh, perfectly timed, and served on crunchy kale, with a feather-light potato pancake. Not the least asset of the cooking is its holy-grail combination of lightness and resonance, an impression continuing into desserts such as a cube of electrifying orange jelly, served with sliced almond bread and banana ice cream, or a similarly intense mousse of tart green apple, with shimmering pink rhubarb sorbet. Fine shortbread and chocolate truffles come with satisfying coffee, and service is professionally coordinated by co-owners Colin Morris and Nicki Tigwell. The short, functional wine list is predominantly French and southern-hemisphere, opening with half a dozen house wines from £14 (£3.75 a glass).

CHEF: Nathan Outlaw PROPRIETORS: Nicki Tigwell, Colin Morris and Nathan Outlaw OPEN: Tue to Sat (and Mon, Apr to Sept) 12.30 to 2, 7 to 9.30 (9 Oct to Mar) CLOSED: 25 and 26 Dec, 2nd week Nov to 2nd week Dec MEALS: alc (main courses £20 to £21.50). Set L £17.50 (2 courses) to (whole table only) £50, Set D (whole table only) £50 SERVICE: not inc CARDS: Amex, MasterCard, Switch, Visa DETAILS: 36 seats. 16 seats outside. Private parties: 32 main room. Car park. Vegetarian meals. No children under 12. Music. No mobile phones (£5)

ROCKBEARE Devon
map 1

Jack in the Green ✳

London Road, Rockbeare EX5 2EE
TEL: (01404) 822240 FAX: (01404) 823445
WEBSITE: www.jackinthegreen.uk.com

COOKING 2
GLOBAL
£28–£45

Standing beside the old A30, a few miles outside Exeter, this white-pebbledash inn is a favourite destination for travellers in the area. The interior is a series of rooms with lots of pubby paraphernalia and a definite bias towards food. Restaurant customers are offered a concise fixed-price menu that might open with celeriac and chestnut soup or scallops with saffron vanilla cream and finish with a splendid orange assiette. Reporters have also approved of main courses like fillets of John Dory with Savoy cabbage and bacon butter sauce, and loin of venison with butternut squash and shallot purée. Simpler dishes are served in the bar, along with a serious line-up of West Country real ales, and the well-spread wine list opens with house selections from £9.75.

CHEFS: Matthew Mason and Craig Sampson PROPRIETOR: Paul Parnell OPEN: Mon to Sat 12 to 2, 6 to 9.30, Sun 12 to 9.30 CLOSED: 25 Dec to 5 Jan MEALS: Set L Mon to Sat £19.45 (2 courses) to £24.75, Set L Sun £15.50 (2 courses) to £19.30, Set D £19.45 (2 courses) to £24.75. Bar menu available SERVICE: not inc CARDS: Delta, MasterCard, Switch, Visa DETAILS: 140 seats. 20 seats outside. Private parties: 80 main room, 16 to 80 private rooms. Car park. Vegetarian meals. Children's helpings. No toddlers at D. No smoking. Wheelchair access (also WC). Music. Air-conditioned

ROMALDKIRK Co Durham
map 10

▲ Rose and Crown ✳

Romaldkirk DL12 9EB
TEL: (01833) 650213 FAX: (01833) 650828
WEBSITE: www.rose-and-crown.co.uk

COOKING 3
TRADITIONAL ENGLISH
£25–£48

The presence of walkers and their dogs in the bar testifies to the relaxed mood in this traditional stone-built pub next to the church. Eat something straightforward like wild boar sausages with Puy lentils in the 'brasserie' or head for the elegant restaurant, where more ambitious four-course deals are the order of the day. Starters such as black pudding risotto with grilled pancetta precede a soup (cream of haggis, for example); main courses could range from baked baby halibut with local Cotherstone cheese and cream and red onion marmalade to heartily traditional roast duckling with leek and bacon pudding, prune and apricot compote and gravy 'from the roasting tin'. To finish, choose between North

Country cheeses and desserts like vanilla cheesecake. The helpfully described wine list includes a handy assortment of halves and ten by the glass. Chilean house selections are £12.95.

CHEFS: Christopher Davy and Andrew Lee PROPRIETORS: Christopher and Alison Davy OPEN: Sun L 12 to 1.30, all week D 7.30 to 9 CLOSED: 24 to 26 Dec MEALS: Set L £15.95, Set D £26. Bar menu available SERVICE: not inc, card slips closed CARDS: MasterCard, Switch, Visa DETAILS: 24 seats. 24 seats outside. Private parties: 20 main room. Car park. Vegetarian meals. Children's helpings. No children under 6. No smoking. Wheelchair access (also WC). No music. No mobile phones ACCOMMODATION: 12 rooms, all with bath/shower. TV. Phone. B&B £75 to £124. Rooms for disabled. Baby facilities (£5)

ROMSEY Hampshire   map 2

Three Tuns 🍷 ✗

58 Middlebridge Street, Romsey SO51 8HL   COOKING 3
TEL: (01794) 512639   FAX: (01794) 514524   MODERN BRITISH
                                                           £32–£51

'Contemporary, cosmopolitan and upmarket' succinctly describes this remodelled old-world hostelry, now transformed into a tasteful modern gastro-pub. Flagstone floors, beams and timbers are reminders of its former life, although much of the décor is uncluttered and informally sophisticated. New chef Matt Appleton has done stints in several southern counties' kitchens including Chesil Rectory (see entry, Winchester) and continues where his predecessors left off. He offers classy cooking with brasserie inclinations, along the lines of pavé of halibut with saffron and mussel risotto and rocket pesto, or guinea fowl 'cooked two ways' with braised Savoy cabbage. To start there might be a terrine of ham hock and foie gras, while desserts could run to rice pudding parfait with cardamom syrup. Drink real ale or something from the concise wine list; house wine is £10.

CHEF: Matt Appleton PROPRIETOR: Belinda Baker OPEN: all week L 12 to 2.30, Mon to Sat D 7 to 9.30 MEALS: alc (main courses £13 to £17). Bar L menu available Mon to Sat SERVICE: not inc, card slips closed CARDS: Amex, Delta, MasterCard, Switch, Visa DETAILS: 50 seats. 60 seats outside. Private parties: 30 main room. Car park. Vegetarian meals. Children's helpings. No smoking. Wheelchair access (not WC). Music. Air-conditioned

ROSS-ON-WYE Herefordshire   map 5

Pheasant at Ross 🍷 ✗

52 Edde Cross Street, Ross-on-Wye HR9 7BZ   COOKING 2
TEL: (01989) 565751   COUNTRY COOKING
                                                           £37–£50

This creeper-covered terraced property in the town centre is a welcome highlight in an area not overly blessed with culinary hot spots. Eileen Brunnarius takes care of matters in the kitchen while Adrian Wells holds court in the compact dining room, which looks like a cross between a French bistro and 'granny's attic', with crocheted table covers, bowls of artificial fruit and heavily embossed wallpaper. A starter of Hereford Hop cheese soufflé with salad dressed with walnut oil – 'a gorgeous combination and superbly executed' – epitomises the admirable dedication to local produce combined with a broad gastronomic outlook that also turns up fillets of red gurnard on Savoy cabbage in red wine sauce, and duck cooked slowly in a pot and served simply in its own richly flavoured juices. Classic desserts might include 'deliciously light' bread-and-butter pudding.

The wine list has no truck with the notion of classics and relies instead on the admirable criteria of flavour and value, with Germany, Italy and Spain some of the most fruitful hunting grounds. House wine is another banned concept, but prices start at £13.50. Sherries and other aperitifs are a passion, and a number of wines come by the glass. Choose by style or by variety, or more likely with enthusiastic expert guidance from Adrian Wells.

CHEF/PROPRIETOR: Eileen Brunnarius   OPEN: Fri and Sat D only 7 to 9   MEALS: alc (main courses £15 to £17)   SERVICE: not inc   CARDS: Amex, MasterCard, Switch, Visa   DETAILS: 20 seats. Private parties: 24 main room. Vegetarian meals. Children's helpings. No smoking. Wheelchair access (not WC). Music ⓔ5

ROWDE Wiltshire   map 2

George & Dragon ✱ £

High Street, Rowde SN10 2PN   COOKING 3
TEL: (01380) 723053   FAX: (08700) 118301   SEAFOOD
EMAIL: gd-rowde@tiscali.co.uk   £21–£55

The George & Dragon appears simple, rustic and unassuming – an impression reinforced by its beams and bare tables. Tim Withers's passion is fish cookery, and his well-considered, unflashy dishes have pulled in the punters since 1989. Daily supplies from Cornwall are the starting point for plentiful specials that might include red gurnard in beer batter with coriander chutney, roast hake with peppers and aïoli, or perhaps simply grilled whole lemon sole. The standard menu also pleases carnivores and vegetarians alike, with venison sausages and mustard sauce, or cheese soufflé baked with Parmesan and cream. Wind up with rhubarb and honey saffron custard, or pear and chocolate tart with crème fraîche. Wines are a decent selection at fair mark-ups, with eight by the glass (from £2.50) and bottle prices starting at £10.

CHEFS: Tim Withers and Kate Patterson   PROPRIETORS: Tim and Helen Withers   OPEN: Tue to Sat 12 to 2, 7 to 9   CLOSED: 25 Dec, 1 Jan   MEALS: alc (main courses £7.50 to £20). Set L £10 (2 courses) to £12.50   SERVICE: not inc   CARDS: MasterCard, Switch, Visa   DETAILS: 40 seats. 20 seats outside. Private parties: 8 main room. Car park. Vegetarian meals. No children after 9pm. Children's helpings. No smoking. No music. No mobile phones

RYE East Sussex   map 3

Landgate Bistro ✱ £

5–6 Landgate, Rye TN31 7LH   COOKING 4
TEL: (01797) 222829   MODERN BRITISH
WEBSITE: www.landgatebistro.co.uk   £23–£38

Coming up for its quarter century, this unpretentious restaurant is still 'friendly, casual, honest and committed'. Inside two joined-together brick buildings just outside Rye's medieval walls is a deep, narrowish room with wooden tables and evocative photos of Romney Marsh on the walls. Precision fish cooking is a highspot, including subtle, satisfying salmon and salt cod fishcakes, followed by the utter simplicity of poached fillet of turbot, or a combination of superb scallops and 'zingy' brill in an orange and vermouth sauce. Seasonal sourcing, from a network of good local suppliers built up over many years, shows in plenty of game and good vegetables (extra) and in mains like wild rabbit with mustard and rosemary, griddled Old Spot cutlets, or lamb chump with butter beans, bacon and basil. Among creamy-rich puddings might be lemon and sherry syllabub, or Jamaican chocolate cream. With wines starting at £9.90, and eight offered by the (not over-large) glass at under £3, pricing for the tight, intelligent range from consistently decent growers is very fair.

CHEF: Toni Ferguson-Lees   PROPRIETORS: Nick Parkin and Toni Ferguson-Lees   OPEN: Tue to Sat D only 7 to 9.30 (10 Sat)   CLOSED: 2 weeks Christmas, 1 week summer   MEALS: alc (main courses £10 to £13.50). Set D Tue to Thur £17.90   SERVICE: net prices, card slips closed   CARDS: Delta, MasterCard, Switch, Visa DETAILS: 30 seats. Vegetarian meals. Children's helpings. No smoking. Music

---

ST IVES Cornwall   map 1

Alba Restaurant ✳️

Old Lifeboat House, Wharf Road, St Ives TR26 1LF   COOKING 3
TEL: (01736) 797222   FAX: (01736) 798937   MODERN EUROPEAN
WEBSITE: www.alba-restaurant.co.uk   £25–£53

After refurbishment, both storeys of the old lifeboat house are now given over to the restaurant, with the glass frontage affording majestic views over the harbour where much of the restaurant's fish is landed. Minimally dressed pale wood tables sit comfortably with the straightforward culinary approach, offering perhaps a mixture of fine shellfish in a hot, chilli-fired, marinière-type broth as a starter, or grey mullet with Puy lentils, flavoured with preserved lemon and coriander, as a main. Accompaniments can occasionally overpower the main ingredients, but the flavour combinations make sense. Beef bourguignon is made with local meat, and served with horseradish mash. A plate of strawberry desserts has included 'a wonderfully silly pink-swirled wobble' of a pannacotta, and a baby hazelnut meringue with strawberry compote that converted a meringue-hater. Informal service pleases, as will the breakfast menu, and the imaginatively chosen wine list has some appealing bottles, starting from £11.95 (£3 a glass).

CHEF: Grant Nethercott   PROPRIETOR: Harbour Kitchen Co Ltd   OPEN: all week 12 to 3 (2.30 winter), 6 (6.30 winter) to 10   CLOSED: 25 and 26 Dec, Sun and Mon D Nov to 24 Dec and 5 Jan to Mar   MEALS: alc (main courses £7 to £17)   SERVICE: not inc   CARDS: Amex, Delta, MasterCard, Switch, Visa   DETAILS: 60 seats. Private parties: 40 main room, 25 private room. Vegetarian meals. Children's helpings. No smoking. Wheelchair access (also WC). Music. Air-conditioned

---

Pickled Fish ✳️ £

3 Chapel Street, St Ives TR26 2LR   COOKING 3
TEL: (01736) 795100   MODERN BRITISH
                                                                       £24–£45

Paintings by local artists line the blue walls of this modest, glass-fronted restaurant – a reminder that this is artistically minded St Ives. Despite the name, seafood doesn't steal the limelight on the menu, although you will find plenty of modern piscine ideas like Cornish line-caught mackerel with pancetta and tapenade dressing, or grilled fillets of John Dory with pea and rosemary purée and a lobster reduction. Back on land, the choice extends to roast maize-fed chicken breast with orange-glazed fennel and a chorizo cream sauce, and balsamic-glazed winter vegetable tarte Tatin with beetroot compote and rocket pesto. There's also a separate menu for vegans. Bringing up the rear are appealing desserts like elderflower-scented baba with home-made stem ginger ice cream, or iced apple and poppy seed parfait. BYO wine (there's an off-licence nearby).

CHEF: Ben Reeve   PROPRIETORS: Ben and Jennifer Reeve   OPEN: Tue to Sat and Mon July and Aug D only 7 to 10   MEALS: alc (main courses £12 to £18)   SERVICE: not inc, card slips closed   CARDS: Delta, MasterCard, Switch, Visa   DETAILS: 30 seats. Private parties: 30 main room. Vegetarian meals. Children's helpings. No smoking. Music. No mobile phones. Air-conditioned (£5)

Porthminster Beach Café 🍴✳

Porthminster Beach, St Ives TR26 2EB	COOKING 4
TEL/FAX: (01736) 795352	GLOBAL/SEAFOOD
WEBSITE: www.porthminstercafe.co.uk	£28–£50

Views across the sandy beach and out over the bay are part of the appeal of this relaxed, jolly and very popular place. The covered, heated outside terrace comes into its own on hot summer days but is also used at other times when the dining room is full (book early if you want a table by the windows). The stylish modern cooking further enhances the beauty of the spot. An accomplished fusion of Mediterranean and Pacific Rim themes, predominantly seafood-oriented, runs through the menus. Tiger prawn risotto, pan-seared scallops with lemon miso and saffron-braised fennel, and veal sweetbreads on mushroom and pancetta marmalade with roasted yams and sage show the broad scope of starters, and main courses are similarly varied, taking in John Dory with black olive crushed potatoes and salsa verde, grilled turbot with fried cassava and chermoula paste, and crispy duck with steamed pak choi, sweet-and-sour broth and tamarillo chutney. Finish perhaps with crème brûlée scented with lime and candied ginger. Service is slick yet personal, and Italian house wines are £10.95.

CHEFS: Michael Smith, Fabian Christoph and Ben Day   PROPRIETORS: James Woolcock, David Fox, and Roger and Timothy Symons   OPEN: all week 12 to 3.30, 6 to 10.30   CLOSED: from 1 Nov to 2 weeks before Easter   MEALS: alc (main courses £8 to £18)   SERVICE: not inc   CARDS: Delta, MasterCard, Switch, Visa   DETAILS: 60 seats. 60 seats outside. Vegetarian meals. No smoking. Occasional music

ST KEYNE Cornwall   map 1

▲ Well House ▼ 🍴✳

St Keyne PL14 4RN
TEL: (01579) 342001   FAX: (01579) 343891
WEBSITE: www.wellhouse.co.uk
on B3254, 3m S of Liskeard; at end of village near church
follow sign to St Keyne Well

NEW CHEF
MODERN BRITISH
£35–£61

This rural Victorian house feels more cosmopolitan than rustic, with its stylish décor and furniture, and 'cool and contemporary' dining room; it 'could easily be a town house in Hampstead', thought one reporter. The modern feel is reflected in the food, which is built around fresh, mainly Cornish ingredients. However, our inspection meal took place while Matthew Corner (who cooked here since 1999) was still at the stoves; he has now left and sous-chef Glen Gatland has moved into the top job – too late for the Guide to receive any feedback on his performance. However, an early menu yielded dishes such as ham hock and pea risotto with a poached egg and thyme oil, a trio of Cornish seafood with tomato, saffron and fennel beurre blanc, and fresh cherry clafoutis with lemon-curd ice cream, giving every indication that the refined, modern approach to cooking, based on classic techniques, will continue. The wine list features substantial collections from Bordeaux and Burgundy as well as good-value offerings from elsewhere, especially Australia and New Zealand. Four house wines are £12.50.

CHEF: Glen Gatland   PROPRIETORS: Nick Wainford and Ione Nurdin   OPEN: all week 12 to 1.30, 7 to 8.30   MEALS: Set L £18.50 (2 courses) to £23.50, Set D £32.50   SERVICE: not inc, card slips closed   CARDS: Delta, MasterCard, Switch, Visa   DETAILS: 36 seats. 20 seats outside. Private parties: 40 main room. Car park. Vegetarian meals. Children's helpings. No children under 8 at D. No smoking. Wheelchair access (also WC). No music. No mobile phones   ACCOMMODATION: 9 rooms, all with bath/shower. TV. Phone. B&B £75 to £170. Rooms for disabled. Baby facilities. Swimming pool

---

ST MARGARET'S AT CLIFFE Kent   map 3

▲ Wallett's Court 🌢✳

Westcliffe, St Margaret's at Cliffe CT15 6EW	COOKING 3
TEL: (01304) 852424 FAX: (01304) 853430	ANGLO-FRENCH
WEBSITE: www.wallettscourt.com	£32–£73

Just a mile inland from Kent's chalk cliffs, surrounded by gentle hills and fields, Wallett's Court is a treasure-trove of unmolested seventeenth-century rusticity, complete with wonky floors and worm-holed timbers. Chef Stephen Harvey buys well and brings a dash of creative flair to his cooking. Plump Pacific tiger prawns are spiked with smoked garlic and lime and served with roasted pepper jam, while main-course meats are of outstanding quality: perhaps roast rack of Romney Marsh lamb glazed with cardamom, cumin, coriander and turmeric, or horseradish-crusted chargrilled Aberdeen Angus fillet. While good rhubarb crème brûlée with crystallised ginger ice has been let down by a rather too sour lime and green tea compote, hot chocolate fondant oozes in all the right places and is teamed with fine pistachio ice cream. A chaotically arranged but decent wine list opens with classy house French and Chilean at £14.95, or £4.25 a glass.

CHEF: Steven Harvey   PROPRIETORS: the Oakley family   OPEN: Tue to Fri and Sun L 12 to 2, all week D 7 to 9   MEALS: Set L £17 (2 courses) to £19.50, Set D £35. Bar menu available   SERVICE: not inc   CARDS: Amex, Delta, Diners, MasterCard, Switch, Visa   DETAILS: 70 seats. Private parties: 40 main room, 6 to 40 private rooms. Car park. Vegetarian meals. No children under 8 after 8pm. Children's helpings. No smoking. Wheelchair access (not WC). Occasional music. No mobile phones   ACCOMMODATION: 16 rooms, all with bath/shower. TV. Phone. B&B £79 to £159. Rooms for disabled. Baby facilities. Swimming pool (£5)

ST MARTIN'S Isles of Scilly   map 1

▲ St Martin's on the Isle 🌢✳

Lower Town, St Martin's TR25 0QW	COOKING 5
TEL: (01720) 422092 FAX: (01720) 422298	MODERN EUROPEAN
WEBSITE: www.stmartinshotel.co.uk	£57–£98

Whether you travel by helicopter and launch, plane or boat, the general consensus is that this elegant establishment is well worth the effort. The restaurant's floor-to-ceiling window makes the most of the breathtaking views, while a sunny yellow and sea-blue colour scheme creates a welcoming feel.

If the setting is exhilarating, the same can be said of Stewart Eddy's cooking, which gives a suitably light but subtle treatment to daily deliveries of seafood, fished from the clear waters around the island. Plump scallops are quickly seared and served with an artichoke, tomato and fine bean salad, with plenty of fresh herbs and a 'lovely, subtle dressing'. Cornish brill, 'perfectly timed to preserve its natural taste', comes with a potage of spring vegetables, mussels and tarragon, resulting in a light dish full of complementing flavours. The focus may be on seafood, but meat is also handled in exemplary fashion: witness an inspector's 'very accomplished' roast loin of veal with a properly moist and creamy wild mushroom risotto and a light rosemary jus. Desserts benefit from the same sureness of touch and often have a fruity theme: vanilla crème brûlée with a sablé of raspberries and raspberry yoghurt sorbet, perhaps, or chocolate tart with orange salad and orange blossom ice cream. Service runs smoothly, with a personal touch. The shortish wine list is a little on the pricey side but includes ten wines by the glass from £2.85.

CHEF: Stewart Eddy   PROPRIETORS: Peter and Penny Sykes   OPEN: all week D only 7 to 9   CLOSED: Nov to Feb   MEALS: Set D £43.50. Bar L menu available   SERVICE: not inc, card slips closed   CARDS: Amex, Delta, Diners, MasterCard, Switch, Visa   DETAILS: 80 seats. Private parties: 100 main room, 2 to 25 private rooms. Vegetarian meals. Children's helpings. No children under 9. No smoking. No music. No mobile phones   ACCOMMODATION: 30 rooms, all with bath/shower. TV. Phone. D,B&B £115 to £320. Rooms for disabled. Baby facilities. Swimming pool. Fishing

ST MAWES Cornwall
map 1

▲ Rising Sun ⅚✸

The Square, St Mawes TR2 5DJ	COOKING 4
TEL: (01326) 270233 FAX: (01326) 270198	MODERN EUROPEAN
WEBSITE: www.innsofcornwall.com	£39–£47

Comfy sofas in the bar and yacht-like wooden floors and striped awnings in the dining room give this restaurant-with-rooms a feeling of informality. Reports consistently and unreservedly praise Ann Long's careful, imaginative cooking. A velvety soup of parsnip, ginger and coconut achieved a brilliant un-analysable balance, while wrapping monkfish in bacon retained both the bacon's succulence and the moistness of the fish. And roast salt chicken, stuffed with sage and onion forcemeat and moistened with a wine sauce, has been welcomed as 'chicken as it used to taste'. Flashy complication is kept off the plate, but behind-the-scenes effort goes into excellent sourcing and the preparation of complex bases for sauces, such as crab and lobster accompanying Dover sole and sea bass. A hint of 1970s nostalgia, raspberry and oatmeal meringue, reminds one how good those early forays into indigenous cookery could be when executed with the panache found here. Quiet passion has gone into assembling the list of 50-odd wines from around the globe; prices start at £11, and a dozen are available by the glass.

CHEF: Ann Long   PROPRIETOR: R.J. Milan   OPEN: all week D only 7 to 9.30   MEALS: Set D £30. Bar menu available   SERVICE: not inc, card slips closed   CARDS: MasterCard, Switch, Visa   DETAILS: 40 seats. 50 seats outside. Private parties: 65 main room. Car park. Children's helpings. No smoking. No music. No mobile phones   ACCOMMODATION: 8 rooms, all with bath/shower. TV. Phone. B&B £50 to £130

▲ Hotel Tresanton

Lower Castle Road, St Mawes TR2 5DR	COOKING 4
TEL: (01326) 270055 FAX: (01326) 270053	MODERN EUROPEAN
WEBSITE: www.tresanton.com	£39–£59

Originating in the 1940s as a yacht club, this cluster of split-level buildings was given the designer makeover a few years ago, and is wearing pretty well. Head for the first floor, where the public rooms offer breathtaking views over the bay. Chef Paul Wadham trades in sophisticated brasserie dishes designed to appeal to a smart set, marshalling organic meats and vegetables and local seafood, and pulling off some notable successes. Dover sole is simply seared to achieve both crispness and tenderness and partnered with diced tomato, green beans and olives, as a first course, while a main-course fish might be exquisitely presented cod, served with mussels and peas in a wine bouillon. As to meat, there could be grilled pork fillet with caramelised apples, or resonantly flavoured chicken breast on shredded Savoy cabbage with carrots and baby turnips. Favoured desserts include chocolate brownie with Amaretto ice cream, and there are fine farmhouse cheeses. Service at inspection was somewhat haphazard and nonchalant, although cordial enough. France and Italy get about equal cracks of the whip on the imaginative wine list, which opens at £13.50.

CHEF: Paul Wadham   PROPRIETOR: Olga Polizzi   OPEN: all week 12.30 to 2.30, 7 to 9.30   MEALS: Set L £20 (2 courses) to £26, Set D £35. Light L menu available   SERVICE: not inc, card slips closed   CARDS: Amex, Delta, MasterCard, Switch, Visa   DETAILS: 50 seats. 60 seats outside. Private parties: 40 main room. Car park. Vegetarian meals. Children's helpings. Wheelchair access (not WC). No music   ACCOMMODATION: 29 rooms, all with bath/shower. TV. Phone. B&B £187 to £265. Baby facilities

ST MERRYN Cornwall   map 1

Ripley's ✾✖

St Merryn PL28 8NQ   COOKING 5
TEL: (01841) 520179   FAX: (01841) 521641   MODERN BRITISH
                                                              £31–£51

A small photogenic hamlet, a little inland from the north Cornish coast, is home to Paul Ripley's yellow-fronted restaurant. It's all on a Lilliputian scale, with a tiny, bisected dining room and a modest, enclosed back garden. What isn't at all modest is the reach of the culinary ambition, which is capable of taking the breath away at the nerveless panache with which it handles the best of local seasonal produce. Oriental modes, as in seared scallops with a salad of rice noodles, ginger and coriander, are mixed with Mediterranean, such as pumpkin risotto with crisp pancetta and shaved Parmesan, and the results seem uniformly engaging. Curry spices and saffron add aromatic allure to a main course of roast monkfish and mussels, while local pheasant in winter turns up as the breast accompanied by grapes, wild mushrooms and foie gras. Puddings are as rich as they come, with clotted cream anointing pear, chocolate and almond tart, and warm gingerbread served with dried fruit compote and honey ice cream. Service is sharp and straightforward, as is the wine list, which covers Europe and the southern hemisphere with brisk aplomb. Six house wines start at £10.95 a bottle, £3 a glass.

CHEF/PROPRIETOR: Paul Ripley   OPEN: Fri and Sat L 12 to 1.30, Tue to Sat D 7 to 9.30   CLOSED: 1 week at Christmas. Phone to check winter opening times   MEALS: Set L £15 (2 courses) to £20, Set D £25.50 (2 courses) to £30.50   SERVICE: not inc, card slips closed   CARDS: Delta, MasterCard, Switch, Visa   DETAILS: 30 seats. Private parties: 8 main room. No smoking. Music. No mobile phones

---

Some restaurants leave credit card slips open even though they also make a fixed (or 'optional') service charge. The Guide strongly disapproves of this practice as it may result in consumers unknowingly paying twice for service.

SALE Greater Manchester map 8

Hanni's £

4 Brooklands Road, Sale M33 3SQ COOKING **2**
TEL: (0161) 973 6606 FAX: (0161) 972 0469 EASTERN MEDITERRANEAN
£28–£48

Hanni himself is often found overseeing proceedings in this family-run neighbourhood restaurant adjacent to Brooklands Metrolink station. This is a genuinely welcoming place delivering sound food with a strong eastern Mediterranean slant, and it continues to offer excellent value for money. The kitchen stays with what it knows, so expect a recognisable run of meze to start, including sarma (stuffed vine leaves), tabbouleh, and foul medames. Rich, flavoursome kleftiko with okra has been cooked to a T; otherwise there are six versions of couscous and a brigade of high-protein grills and kebabs ranging from Tunisian meatballs to marinated poussin. Desserts like baklava and halva are enjoyable 'without setting any rivers on fire'. Good-value wines from Greece, Turkey, the Lebanon and Israel show up on the affordable list. House wine is £11.95.

CHEF: Mr Hoonanian PROPRIETORS: Mohamed Hanni and Jennifer Al-Taraboulsy OPEN: Mon to Sat D only 6 to 10.30 (11 Fri and Sat) CLOSED: 25 and 26 Dec, 1 Jan, Good Fri, Easter Mon MEALS: alc (main courses £11.50 to £15.50). Set D 6 to 7 £11.95 (2 courses) SERVICE: not inc, card slips closed, 10% for parties of 7 or more CARDS: Amex, Delta, MasterCard, Switch, Visa DETAILS: 50 seats. Private parties: 50 main room. Vegetarian meals. Children's helpings. Wheelchair access (not WC). Music. Air-conditioned

SALFORD Greater Manchester map 8

▲ Lowry Hotel, River Room – Marco Pierre White 🍷

50 Dearmans Place, Chapel Wharf, Salford M3 5LH COOKING **4**
TEL: (0161) 827 4041 FAX: (0161) 827 4001 FRENCH
WEBSITE: www.roccofortehotels.com £35–£64

The restaurant is on the second floor of the Lowry in its riverside setting not far from Manchester city centre. Chic contemporary design (David Collins and Olga Polizzi) makes a refined backdrop for the brasserie-style cooking overseen by David Woolf in the name of MPW himself. Good things come of it too: an effective Caesar salad had 'a good dressing and a few anchovies but no other extraneous fripperies', while black pudding on bubble and squeak with a soft-poached egg is almost pure Lancashire but for the chopped pancetta that finds its way into the b&s. Sea bass, perhaps served with boulangère potatoes and a sauce vierge, has been so 'strikingly fresh' as to be beyond reproach, although a serving of steamed turbot wasn't quite so superb. More challenging ideas include grilled calf's liver with caramelised cauliflower purée and lime jus, while Eton Mess comes with wild strawberries as well as plenty of whipped cream. Dairy-free and full vegan menus are also offered, and the large service brigade is friendly and on the ball. Wine prices reflect the stylish surroundings (house is £16), but the succinct global selection is consistently interesting with suitable bottle age on many.

CHEF: David Woolf PROPRIETOR: Rocco Forte OPEN: Wed to Sun L 12 (12.30 Sat and Sun) to 2.30 (3.30 Sun), all week D 6 to 10.30 MEALS: alc (main courses £9 to £30). Bar menu available SERVICE: 10% CARDS: Amex, Delta, Diners, MasterCard, Switch, Visa DETAILS: 126 seats. 40 seats outside. Private parties: 22 main room, 8 to 22 private rooms. Car park. Vegetarian meals. Children's helpings. No-smoking area. Wheelchair access (also WC). Music. No mobile phones. Air-conditioned

ACCOMMODATION: 165 rooms, all with bath/shower. TV. Phone. B&B £189 to £1,255. Rooms for disabled. Baby facilities

SAPPERTON Gloucestershire · map 2

Bell at Sapperton 🍴 ✖

Sapperton GL7 6LE
TEL: (01285) 760298 FAX: (01285) 760761
WEBSITE: www.foodatthebell.co.uk

COOKING 4
MODERN EUROPEAN
£30–£54

'This comes pretty close to one's archetypal dream pub,' enthused one happy visitor to this stylish, prosperous-looking Cotswold-stone inn. Even so, you won't find anything remotely 'trad pubby' on the menu, the descriptions on which are to the point and sometimes vaguely poetic (for example, blade of local beef 'braised in its own goodness'). Chef Ivan Reid, who previously worked at the Churchill Arms in Paxford (see entry), clearly has high ambitions and has some striking, unusual flavour combinations to prove it. The presentation of starters such as brandade with seared scallops in scapece (lemon, peppers, garlic and mustard seed) is very good, as is the execution in terms of texture and timing. For main courses, the blackboard menu might list pan-fried wild sea bass served with roasted globe artichoke and a vanilla and red wine sauce. Semolina budino (rhubarb cake) might feature among desserts alongside more familiar sticky toffee pudding. Service is observant and cheerful, as befits the relaxed and unpretentious atmosphere. The revamped wine list is organised by style, and there are some pretty decent bottles to be had, most for under £20.

CHEF: Ivan Reid PROPRIETORS: Paul Davidson and Pat Le Jeune OPEN: all week 12 to 2, 7 to 9.30 (9 Sun) CLOSED: 25 Dec, D 26 Dec, D 31 Dec MEALS: alc (main courses £10.50 to £18) SERVICE: not inc CARDS: MasterCard, Switch, Visa DETAILS: 70 seats. 70 seats outside. Private parties: 12 main room, 12 private room. Car park. Vegetarian meals. Children's helpings. No Children under 10 at D. No smoking in 1 dining room. Wheelchair access (also WC). No music. No mobile phones

SAWLEY Lancashire · map 8

Spread Eagle ✖ £

Sawley BB7 4NH
TEL: (01200) 441202 FAX: (01200) 441973
WEBSITE: www.the-spreadeagle.co.uk

COOKING 3
MODERN BRITISH
£20–£46

In a rural setting beside the Ribble upstream of Clitheroe, this black and white seventeenth-century stone inn may be 'halfway to everywhere', but some reporters wish it nearer still. Various menu options include an excellent-value set-price lunch, and all show off the kitchen's penchant for gutsy flavours in elaborate combinations, as in starters of caramel-glazed melon with coconut cream and rum syrup, or smoked salmon with spiced aubergine dressing and a poached egg. A dozen main-course choices might feature seared sea bass on buttered spinach with shrimps and a creamy chicken essence, and roast pork fillet with apple purée and smooth piccalilli velouté, while desserts are sophisticated creations such as white-wine-poached pear with almond pannacotta and lemon jelly. The revamped wine list is arranged by grape variety, with plenty of affordable choices and a few special bottles besides. Four house wines are £10 to £11.25 a bottle, and ten come by the glass.

CHEF: Greig Barnes   PROPRIETORS: Nigel and Ysanne Williams   OPEN: Tue to Sun L 12 to 2, Tue to Sat D 6 to 9   MEALS: alc exc Sun L (main courses £9.50 to £16.50). Set L Tue to Fri £9.25 (2 courses) to £12.20, Set L Sun £12.50 (2 courses) to £15.75, Set D 6 to 7pm Tue to Fri and Sun £10.25 (2 courses) to £13.20; Set D other times £11.50 (2 courses) to £14.45. Bar L available Tue to Sat   SERVICE: not inc, card slips closed   CARDS: Amex, MasterCard, Switch, Visa   DETAILS: 180 seats. Private parties: 100 main room, 10 to 50 private rooms. Car park. Vegetarian meals. Children's helpings. No smoking. Wheelchair access (also WC). Music (£5)

SAXMUNDHAM Suffolk   map 6

▲ Bell Hotel ⁵⨉

31 High Street, Saxmundham IP17 1AF	COOKING 4
TEL/FAX: (01728) 602331	ANGLO-FRENCH
EMAIL: thebell@saxhighstreet.fsnet.co.uk	£22–£45

At the Bell, right by the town hall, the Blackburns (Andrew at the stoves, Catherine front-of-house) have been ringing the changes since they arrived in 2002. The smart, modern, understated dining room, with its green and white décor, has already been refurbished, and the conservatory-style lounge filled with pink-cushioned Lloyd Loom-style cane furniture; work continues on the bedrooms.

Andrew's sensibly compact menus offer a mixture of classic and contemporary, English and French dishes, utilising fresh local produce in soundly balanced combinations: for example, a galantine of guinea fowl with foie gras and truffle vinaigrette to start, or polenta with casseroled wild mushrooms. Continuing the theme might be venison with a liquorice sauce, red cabbage and fondant potato, or perhaps fillet of halibut poached in red wine with creamed celeriac and Savoy cabbage. Finish with iced praline parfait with figs marinated in white wine and rum. Courteous service and value for money are hallmarks here, and the value extends also to wines: a French-led global list that has few bottles over £20 and house wines starting at £9.50.

CHEF/PROPRIETOR: Andrew Blackburn   OPEN: Tue to Sun L 12 to 2, Tue to Sat D 6.30 to 9   CLOSED: 25 Dec D, 26 Dec, 1 Jan, 1 week Feb, 1 week Oct   MEALS: alc (main courses £8.50 to £16). Set L £10.50 (2 courses) to £13.50, Set D £16. Bar L menu available   SERVICE: not inc, card slips closed   CARDS: Delta, MasterCard, Switch, Visa   DETAILS: 26 seats. 15 seats outside. Private parties: 26 main room, 8 to 40 private rooms. Vegetarian meals. No smoking. No children under 8 after 7.30. No music   ACCOMMODATION: 10 rooms, all with bath/shower. TV. B&B £40 to £80. Baby facilities

SCARBOROUGH North Yorkshire   map 9

Lanterna ⁵⨉

33 Queen Street, Scarborough YO11 1HQ	COOKING 3
TEL/FAX: (01723) 363616	ITALIAN
WEBSITE: www.lanterna-ristorante.co.uk	£33–£99

The white truffle of Piedmont holds a place of honour in Giorgio and Rachel Alessio's long-running, 'reassuringly familiar' restaurant. It occupies an entire section of their predominantly Piedmontese menu, which also features a clutch of risottos prepared using Carnaroli rice, hand-made pasta and other classics. Many provisions are imported direct from Italy, but when it comes to fish Giorgio simply makes early-morning trips to pick the best from Scarborough's market: expect anything from sea bream with lemon butter sauce or grilled sea bass with herbs to Scarborough woof. Reporters have also praised king prawns in white wine and garlic, and fillet steak Mussolini (with a sauce of Taleggio, cream and grappa), while, as a novel finale, sweet nettle pudding has been deemed 'a great success'. The wine list is an oenophile's tour around the Italian regions, with house wine opening the account at £10.50.

CHEF: Giorgio Alessio   PROPRIETORS: Giorgio and Rachel Alessio   OPEN: Mon to Sat D only 7 to 10   CLOSED: 2 weeks Oct, 25 and 26 Dec, 1 Jan   MEALS: alc (main courses £12.50 to £37)   SERVICE: not inc, card slips closed   CARDS: Delta, MasterCard, Switch, Visa   DETAILS: 30 seats. Private parties: 35 main room. Vegetarian meals. No children under 2. No smoking in 1 dining room. Wheelchair access (not WC). Music. Air-conditioned

SEAHAM Co Durham   map 10

▲ Seaham Hall ♥ ✱

Lord Byron's Walk, Seaham SR7 7AG   NEW CHEF
TEL: (0191) 516 1400   FAX: (0191) 516 1413   MODERN EUROPEAN
WEBSITE: www.seaham-hall.com   £31–£105

This clifftop Georgian mansion where Byron was married in 1815 has manicured gardens overlooking the North Sea; the interior, though, is seriously modern, with two large dining rooms done up in 'restful shades of beige' opening onto a terrace. Chef Matthew Weedon has departed and replaced, as we went to press, by his former sous-chef. The choice is either menu du jour or à la carte, and dinner might begin with roast Skye scallops and minestrone, or foie gras and leek terrine with truffle bouillon. Luxury ingredients are packed into the mains (as you'd hope at dish prices nearing 30 quid): for example, veal fillet with mushroom ravioli, red wine sauce and morels, or turbot fillets with wild mushroom risotto and cep velouté. Desserts might include something like apple Tatin, yoghurt sorbet and caramel. There have been niggles with service and with second-hand smoke in the bar. The wine list is lengthy and good, though mark-ups on established names can be alarming (£40 for Musar, £60 for Cloudy Bay Sauvignon). Of the many smart bottles the smartest of all are grouped into 'private cellar' sections.

CHEF: John Schwartz   PROPRIETORS: Tom and Jocelyn Maxfield   OPEN: all week 12 to 2.30, 7 to 10   MEALS: alc (main courses £26 to £29). Set L £17.50 (2 courses) to £20, Set L Sun £27, Set D £40 to £65. Light L menu available   SERVICE: not inc   CARDS: Amex, Delta, Diners, MasterCard, Switch, Visa   DETAILS: 60 seats. 20 seats outside. Private parties: 12 main room, 12 to 120 private rooms. Car park. Vegetarian meals. Children's helpings. No smoking. Wheelchair access (also WC). Music. No mobile phones. Air-conditioned   ACCOMMODATION: 19 rooms, all with bath/shower. TV. Phone. B&B £195 to £525. Rooms for disabled. Baby facilities. Swimming pool (£5)

SEAVIEW Isle of Wight   map 2

▲ Seaview Hotel ✱

High Street, Seaview PO34 5EX   COOKING 3
TEL: (01983) 612711   FAX: (01983) 613729   ANGLO-FRENCH
WEBSITE: www.seaviewhotel.co.uk   £24–£44

This hotel draws savvy locals, visitors, and the seafaring set with its civilised, 'cheerful' character and stress on island produce. A nautical theme pervades its bars and two contrastingly styled dining rooms (the smaller, navy-blue front room is non-smoking) which offer a mix of modern dishes with occasional classical influences. Expect, say, fillet of Isle of Wight beef with château potatoes, spinach and hollandaise; Godshill duck breast with a leg confit, golden raisin jus and rösti potatoes; or herb-crusted cod with sautéed

Savoy cabbage and Mornay sauce. You could start with beef broth, or soft roes on toasted brioche, and end on queen of puddings. Service proves friendly and chatty, and the wine list classically French biased, with Corney & Barrow house red £11.95 a bottle.

CHEF: Michael Green   PROPRIETOR: Techaid Facilities Ltd   OPEN: all week 12 to 1.30, 7.30 to 9.30 CLOSED: 4 days at Christmas   MEALS: alc (not Sun L; main courses £10.50 to £17.50). Set L £16.95. Bar menu available   SERVICE: net prices, card slips closed   CARDS: Amex, Delta, Diners, MasterCard, Switch, Visa   DETAILS: 70 seats. 50 seats outside. Private parties: 40 main room, 30 private room. Car park. Vegetarian meals. Children's helpings. No children under 5 after 7.30. No smoking in 1 dining room. Wheelchair access (not WC). No music. No mobile phones. Air-conditioned   ACCOMMODATION: 17 rooms, all with bath/shower. TV. Phone. B&B £55 to £170. Baby facilities

SELLACK Herefordshire   map 5

Lough Pool Inn 🍴

Sellack HR9 6LX	COOKING **4**
TEL: (01989) 730236 FAX: (01989) 730462	MODERN EUROPEAN
off A49, 3m NW of Ross-on-Wye	£31–£52

True to its pub roots, this black, white and brick building has picnic tables in the garden and real ales on draught in the flag-floored bar. Eat here or make your way to the yellow-ochre, non-smoking dining room, with its rough plaster walls and chunky wooden furniture. One menu serves the whole place and displays an admirable commitment to local produce along with a feel for combining diverse flavours: shank of saltmarsh lamb, for example, might be served with cranberries, baby figs and Moroccan tagine sauce. You might also find pan-fried haggis with swede and carrot mash, or seared tuna with pak choi, red pepper salsa and sesame potatoes. There's also a fondness for the zest and bite of home-made chutneys: a courgette version accompanies Welsh rarebit, while beetroot is a foil for black pudding fritters. Desserts focus on wholesome cakes, puddings and contrasting ideas like chestnut parfait with warm apricot compote. The thoughtfully chosen list of four dozen wines now sports succinct tasting notes; ten house wines start at £12.50 (£2.95 a glass).

CHEF: Chris Leeton   PROPRIETOR: Stephen Bull   OPEN: all week 12 to 2, 7 to 9   CLOSED: 25 Dec, 26 Dec D; Sun D and Mon from 3 Oct to 2 Apr   MEALS: alc (main courses £11 to £16)   SERVICE: not inc, card slips closed   CARDS: Delta, MasterCard, Switch, Visa   DETAILS: 80 seats. 35 seats outside. Private parties: 30 main room. Car park. Vegetarian meals. Children's helpings. No smoking in restaurant, permitted in bar. Wheelchair access (not WC). No music

SHAFTESBURY Dorset   map 2

▲ Wayfarers 🍴

Sherborne Causeway, Shaftesbury SP7 9PX	COOKING **4**
TEL/FAX: (01747) 852821	MODERN EUROPEAN
on A30 2m W of Shaftesbury	£29–£64

'Sherborne Causeway' (a stretch of A30 just outside Shaftesbury) makes a prosaic setting for this converted inn that is now a cosy restaurant, complete with a giant hearth, paintings and a striking metal sculpture of a 'very lively' cock in one corner of the dining room. Clare Newton is a courteous hostess and Mark cooks. He takes care and time over every detail, from amuse-gueules and excellent bread to arty arrangements on the plate. Immaculately fresh raw materials receive elaborate treatment, as in wild pigeon breast with garlic-roasted beetroot, celeriac dauphinoise and morels in a rich, truffle-scented demi-glace. Pairing fish with meat is a favourite device, for example roast spiced langoustines with pork confit, or hot scallop mousseline with seared scallops and dried ham 'croquant' on a pea and bacon purée. Desserts are also complex creations: hot raspberry and apple 'tarte fine' comes with caramelised marzipan, Amaretto syrup and crème fraîche sorbet. The weekday Bistrot menu is 'ridiculously good value', likewise the mainly French wine list, which includes seven house selections from £12.

CHEF: Mark Newton   PROPRIETORS: Clare and Mark Newton   OPEN: Tue to Fri and Sun L 12 to 1.30, Tue to Sat D 7 to 9.15   CLOSED: 2–3 weeks after Christmas, 2–3 weeks Jun/July   MEALS: alc (main courses £16.50 to £17.50). Set L and D Tue to Fri £17.95, Set L Sun £21.50   SERVICE: not inc, card slips closed   CARDS: Amex, Delta, MasterCard, Switch, Visa   DETAILS: 34 seats. 8 seats outside. Private parties: 34 main room. Car park. No children under 8 at D. No smoking before 10.15pm. Wheelchair access (also assisted women's WC). No music   ACCOMMODATION: 1 room, with bath/shower. B&B £55 to £70. No children under 12 (£5)

SHEFFIELD South Yorkshire   map 9

Blue Room Brasserie

798 Chesterfield Road, Woodseats, Sheffield S8 0SF   COOKING **2**
TEL: (0114) 255 2004   MODERN EUROPEAN-PLUS
                                                            £27–£55

Christian Kent has given the Blue Room a contemporary look with neutral walls, a bleached-wood floor and lots of 'student art' canvases dotted around. Some reporters feel standards have dropped here lately, but the place still manages to hold its own as a high-volume suburban brasserie. Crowd-pleasers like corned beef hash with fried egg, fish 'n' chips with pea purée, and a successful version of braised lamb shank share the stage with more cosmopolitan ideas like fried foie gras with Yorkshire pudding and truffle-scented mash as a starter, or angel hair pasta with tiger prawns, Parmesan and roast tiger prawn oil. There's also a full menu for vegetarians (Puy lentil and spinach curry, for example). Staff are well-meaning, and the wine list is a cheerful worldwide slate, with four house recommendations at £11.95 and lots of choice below £20.

CHEF/PROPRIETOR: Christian Kent   OPEN: Tue to Sat D only 6 to 10.30 (11 Sat)   CLOSED: bank hols   MEALS: alc (main courses £8 to £17). Set D £19.95 to £24.95   SERVICE: not inc   CARDS: Delta, Diners, MasterCard, Switch, Visa   DETAILS: 130 seats. Private parties: 120 main room, 12 to 40 private rooms. Car park. Vegetarian meals. Children's helpings. Wheelchair access (also WC). Music. Air-conditioned (£5)

Browns ⌒

289 Abbeydale Road South, Dore, Sheffield S17 3LB   COOKING **3**
TEL: (0114) 235 0101   MODERN BRITISH
WEBSITE: www.carriagesrestaurant.co.uk   £31–£50

Carriages has become Browns, but what's in a name? Things are carrying on as before in this former shop on the edge of town. The tastefully turned-out restaurant is the setting for John Mahoney's well-judged food, where starters might include smoked salmon with new potato salad, and pork and duck terrine with peach chutney. Portions tend to be large: a roast chicken potage with oven-dried wild mushrooms contained almost a whole crisp-skinned chicken breast. Well-sourced meats have included a meltingly tender, well-hung fillet steak, served with sweet potato chips and black pudding, or there might be roast saddle of rabbit with chorizo, or fried red mullet with a courgette tart and niçoise dressing.

Finally, diners can choose between English and French cheeses, or opt for a selection of fruit sorbets, or the innovative-sounding chocolate and mascarpone stack with vanilla ice cream. Wines are evenly divided between the Old and New Worlds, with house Vin de Pays d'Oc at £11.90.

CHEF: Jon Mahoney PROPRIETOR: Cary Brown OPEN: Sun L 12 to 2.30, Wed to Sat D 6.30 to 10 CLOSED: 2 weeks Jan, bank hols MEALS: alc D (main courses £10 to £16). Set L Sun £21.95 SERVICE: not inc, card slips closed CARDS: Delta, MasterCard, Switch, Visa DETAILS: 50 seats. Private parties: 60 main room. Car park. Children's helpings. Wheelchair access (also WC). Music

Curator's House 🗶

NEW ENTRY

Botanical Gardens, Clarkehouse Road, Sheffield S10 2LN
TEL/FAX: (0114) 268 7788
EMAIL: curatorshouse@fsmail.net

COOKING 1
MODERN BRITISH
£34–£48

A tearoom and café serving visitors to the surrounding Botanical Gardens during the day – with a lunchtime menu of sandwiches, salads, a soup, and perhaps prawn fritters with chilli jam and cucumber relish – the Curator's House shifts up a few gears in the evenings to become a popular, full-on restaurant. Successful starters have included perfectly seared scallops with salad and a lemongrass and coconut dipping sauce, and calf's liver on butter-bean purée with crispy bacon. Fish from Brixham might show up as fillet of cod in a mild curried sauce, and 'tasty and tender' fillet of beef might come with potato, artichoke and tarragon dauphinois. Finish with coffee crème brûlée, or banana tarte Tatin. Service is pleasant and efficient, and the wine list has a few interesting bottles, with most under £20, starting at £10.50.

CHEF: Paul Crossland PROPRIETORS: Malcolm and Lesley Donaldson OPEN: all week L 11.30 to 2.30, Tue to Sat D 7 to 10 CLOSED: 25 Dec MEALS: alc (main courses L £4.50 to £8.50, D £14 to £16) SERVICE: not inc, card slips closed CARDS: Delta, Diners, MasterCard, Switch, Visa DETAILS: 54 seats. 28 seats outside. Private parties: 54 main room. Vegetarian meals. Children's helpings. No smoking. Wheelchair access (also WC). Music. Air-conditioned

Greenhead House 🗶

84 Burncross Road, Chapeltown, Sheffield S35 1SF
TEL: (0114) 246 9004

COOKING 2
MODERN EUROPEAN
£29–£59

Part of the draw of this restaurant in a seventeenth-century house is attentive service from enthusiastic owners. The dining room has a rustic, country-house feel, and well-spaced tables are laid with fresh flowers in bowls. Dinner is four courses, priced according to the main-course choice. It's not the most ambitious cooking around but the food is carefully prepared using good local produce. Start with a salad of baby leeks with anchovies, capers, quail's eggs and Cabernet Sauvignon vinaigrette, before an intermediary small pot of cassoulet with Toulouse sausage, then perhaps grilled Mediterranean fish with pistou and tomato confit, or sautéed medallions of venison with a little venison pie, apple purée and beetroot sauce. Desserts range from warm chocolate pancakes with rum syrup to pear tart with vanilla cream. There's plenty under £20 on the compact but varied wine list, and some interesting fine wines for those with more to spend.

CHEF: Neil Allen PROPRIETORS: Neil and Anne Allen OPEN: Fri L 12 to 1, Wed to Sat D 7 to 9 CLOSED: Christmas to New Year, 2 weeks Easter, 2 weeks Aug MEALS: alc L (main courses £8.50 to £9). Set D £33.50 to £38 SERVICE: not inc, card slips closed CARDS: Amex, Delta, MasterCard, Switch, Visa

DETAILS: 32 seats. 6 seats outside. Private parties: 30 main room. Car park. Vegetarian meals. Children's helpings. No children under 7. No smoking. Wheelchair access (not WC). No music

Rafters

220 Oakbrook Road, Nether Green, Sheffield S11 7ED
TEL/FAX: (0114) 230 4819
WEBSITE: www.raftersrestaurant.co.uk

COOKING 4
MODERN BRITISH
£40–£52

This first-floor restaurant above a shop – accessed via a side entrance – does indeed have a high-pitched ceiling with wooden rafters, plus smartly set tables, high-backed chairs and exposed red-brick walls hung with foodie pictures and plates. The modern, fixed-price menu changes every six weeks and showcases locally sourced, quality ingredients, including organics, via high-calibre dishes where the visual presentation enhances anticipation. After a tian of honey-glazed ham hock, or a wild salmon and baby leek terrine, there might be chargrilled fillet of Angus beef with a samosa of oxtail braised in Kelham Island Pale Ale, oven-roasted shallots and burgundy jus, or baked fillet of Whitby cod with a mussel and clam chowder and artichoke mash. Finish with bread-and-butter pudding layered with dried winter fruits and accompanied by a butterscotch sauce and vanilla ice cream. A globetrotting wine list of three dozen bins, arranged by style, offers helpful tasting notes and prices predominantly under £20; French house bottles are £11.50.

CHEFS/PROPRIETORS: Marcus Lane and Michael Sabin OPEN: Wed to Sat and Mon D only 7 to 9.30 CLOSED: 25 and 26 Dec, 1 to 10 Jan MEALS: Set D £27.50 SERVICE: not inc, card slips closed CARDS: Amex, Delta, MasterCard, Switch, Visa DETAILS: 40 seats. Private parties: 40 main room. Vegetarian meals. No children under 5. No-smoking area. Music. No mobile phones. Air-conditioned

Richard Smith at Thyme ♥

32–34 Sandygate Road, Crosspool, Sheffield S10 5RY
TEL: (0114) 266 6096
WEBSITE: www.thymeforfood.com

COOKING 4
MODERN BRITISH/MEDITERRANEAN
£29–£77

Sheffield can't match its northern rivals Manchester and Leeds when it comes to numbers of good restaurants, but it's catching up. This lively and popular neighbourhood restaurant in a suburb to the west of the city centre goes some way to bridging the gap. A bar area at the front gives way to a 'cool, minimalist' dining room in pale shades of blue and grey with bare wooden tables and high-backed upholstered chairs. The kitchen is behind an opaque glass screen to the rear. The cooking makes good use of Yorkshire produce from well-respected suppliers in a contemporary bistro style. Fish dishes have been particularly well reported, including roast hand-dived scallops, 'fresh, lightly golden and drizzled with good olive oil', served with a fiery chorizo and chickpea relish, a dollop of aïoli and ciabatta; 'classic' fish 'n' chips, a decent rendition using Whitby haddock in crisp beer batter; and a blackboard special of roast cod with crushed potatoes, confit garlic and tomato essence. Service is pleasantly informal. The wine list sweeps from a range of easy-going gluggers under £15 to some smart bottles, taking in along the way astute choices from all over. There is a spin-off café at 490–492 Glossop Road, Broomhill.

CHEFS: Simon Wild and Tim Vincent PROPRIETORS: Richard and Victoria Smith OPEN: all week 12 to 2, 6 to 10 CLOSED: D some Suns MEALS: alc (main courses £8 to £24). Set L and D £18 (2 courses) to £23, Set D Mon to Fri 6 to 7 £15 SERVICE: not inc CARDS: Amex, MasterCard, Switch, Visa DETAILS: 80

seats. Private parties: 70 main room, 8 to 30 private rooms. Vegetarian meals. Children's helpings. Wheelchair access (also WC). Music

SHELF West Yorkshire   map 8

Bentley's ✦

12 Wade House Road, Shelf HX3 7PB   COOKING 4
TEL: (01274) 690992   FAX: (01274) 690011   MODERN BRITISH
                                                                           £19–£59

Once a two-up, two-down terraced cottage, and still featuring flagstone floors and fireplace, this eponymous restaurant continues to pull in the crowds. There's a small bar on the ground floor and, above it, the carte comes chalked on a blackboard, then it's downstairs to the two simply decorated basement dining rooms. Paul Bentley's compact menus veer towards the familiar, delivering the likes of rack of English lamb with minted béarnaise, mashed peas and jus, but they step out occasionally into the realms of roast cod with pequillo peppers and a herb salsa. Main-course lobster is a house speciality, and desserts continue the theme with ginger moggy parkin with treacle and custard on the one hand, and plum Tatin with clotted cream and chilled sauce anglaise on the other. Service is polite and friendly, while the short, reasonably priced wine list is ordered by style, kicking off with four house wines at £9.95 and £12.95.

CHEFS: Paul Bentley and Anthony Bickers   PROPRIETORS: Paul and Pamela Bentley   OPEN: Tue to Fri L 12 to 2, Tue to Sat D 6.30 to 9.30   CLOSED: 25 and 26 Dec, first week Jan   MEALS: alc (main courses £10.50 to £17). Set L £9.95 (2 courses) to £10.95, Set D £45 (min 2)   SERVICE: not inc, card slips closed   CARDS: Delta, MasterCard, Switch, Visa   DETAILS: 65 seats. Private parties: 25 main room. Vegetarian meals. Children's helpings. No smoking. Music. Air-conditioned

SHEPTON MALLET Somerset   map 2

▲ Charlton House Hotel, Mulberry Restaurant ♥ ✦

Charlton Road, Shepton Mallet BA4 4PR
TEL: (01749) 342008   FAX: (01749) 346362   COOKING 5
WEBSITE: www.charltonhouse.com   MODERN BRITISH
1m E of Shepton Mallet on A361 towards Frome   £35–£95

Barely outside the urban spread of Shepton Mallet, this is a grand house done throughout in burnished red and gold, with a trout lake and croquet lawn in the grounds and a fountain before the main entrance. The cooking, under the aegis of Adam Fellows, aims to rise to the splendid occasion, with big flavours, grand presentations, luxury ingredients and lots of little extras. Start perhaps with a crisp parcel of brandade with pipérade and pesto, or a finely executed tartlet of sea bass, Mediterranean vegetables and tapenade with a coulis of red peppers and cardamom. Mains can be even more complex, but the effort pays off, as in a serving of venison stew with butternut squash purée alongside venison loin with celeriac, button onions and a jus combining red wine and bitter chocolate. 'Jumbo quail' seems to be a new species, and is appositely partnered with black pudding and a nage of apples and Calvados. Pleasing desserts have included a composition of winter fruits, taking in pear and blackberry crumble, a fruit gratin, mandarin sorbet and an apple and fig samosa, served with mulled wine. Service is highly efficient and good-humoured to boot. The wine list measures up, too, with an imaginative selection arranged by style that runs all the way up to top-class Bordeaux in mature vintages and includes a good number of half-bottles. Eighteen wines by the glass are a stylish mix, but they carry heavy mark-ups on the bottle price.

CHEF: Adam Fellows   PROPRIETORS: Mr and Mrs R.J. Saul   OPEN: all week 12.30 to 2, 7.30 to 9.30   MEALS: Set L £16 (2 courses) to £49.50, Set D £49.50 to £60. Light L menu available   SERVICE: not inc, 10% for parties of 8 or more   CARDS: Amex, Delta, Diners, MasterCard, Switch, Visa   DETAILS: 60 seats. 20 seats outside. Private parties: 90 main room, 8 to 140 private rooms. Car park. Vegetarian meals. Children's helpings. No smoking. Wheelchair access (also WC). Music. No mobile phones. Air-conditioned ACCOMMODATION: 25 rooms, all with bath/shower. TV. Phone. B&B £112.50 to £400. Rooms for disabled. Swimming pool

SHERBORNE Dorset   map 2

The Green 🍴   NEW ENTRY

3 The Green, Sherborne DT9 3HY   COOKING 2
TEL: (01935) 813821   MODERN EUROPEAN
WEBSITE: www.thegreen.info   £26–£47

There's no village green here nowadays, just a small street off the A30 in the middle of town. But this friendly, informal neighbourhood restaurant would suit a village green, with its old, ochre-coloured stone, green paintwork and window boxes over bay windows. Inside are a couple of giant beams, simple but stylish décor and the 'biggest old flagstones ever'. Michael Rust's sensible-length, modern menus offer cooking that is both simple and attractive: freshly prepared and consistently presented ('small, neat, colourful') dishes using sound local ingredients. There might be asparagus and hollandaise to start, then beef fillet on 'silky and luscious' celeriac mash with red wine jus, artichokes, fine beans, golden beets and shallots, or wild bass on creamed fennel with new potatoes. Pistachio crème brûlée with strawberries and shortbread has featured among desserts, while the reasonably priced wine list offers plenty under £20, and house from £12.95. Wife Judith oversees 'friendly and willing' service.

CHEF: Michael Rust   PROPRIETORS: Michael and Judith Rust   OPEN: Tue to Sat 12 to 2, 7 to 9   CLOSED: 25 Dec, 2 weeks Jan/Feb, 1 week Jun, 1 week Sept, bank hols   MEALS: alc L (main courses £9 to £15). Set D £16.95 (1 course) to £27.50   SERVICE: not inc, card slips closed   CARDS: Delta, MasterCard, Switch, Visa DETAILS: 40 seats. 10 seats outside. Private parties: 10 to 21 private rooms. Vegetarian meals. Wheelchair access (not WC). Occasional music. No mobile phones

SHERE Surrey   map 3

Kinghams 🍴

Gomshall Lane, Shere GU5 9HE   COOKING 3
TEL: (01483) 202168   MODERN ENGLISH
WEBSITE: www.kinghams-restaurant.co.uk   £31–£59

In a picturesque village just off the A25 east of Dorking, this ancient, half-timbered, red-brick building with a tiled roof is something of a 'romantic little hideaway'. Its two small rooms with low, dark beams and tiny windows are separated by a large fireplace, and white-clothed tables are set against blue fabrics and magnolia walls. In such surroundings, chef-patron Paul Baker's menus – set lunch and dinner, daily-changing fish specials (perhaps roast cod fillet with chorizo, pancetta and baby prawns) and carte – surprise with their modernity. One might start with open ravioli of lambs' sweetbreads with pea and marjoram sauce, move on to fillet of lamb wrapped in aubergines, red peppers and fennel, bound with a rosemary mousse in a light lamb jus (vegetables extra), and finish with chocolate, pear and vanilla torte with kumquat and blueberry salad. Staff are 'exceptionally pleasant' and hard-working, and a pretty cottage garden offers fair-weather dining. The balanced wine list, with helpful notes, starts with French house at £11.95.

CHEF/PROPRIETOR: Paul Baker   OPEN: Tue to Sun L 12.15 to 2.30, Tue to Sat D 7 to 9.30   CLOSED: 25 Dec to 5 Jan   MEALS: alc (main courses £11 to £20). Set L £14.95 (2 courses), Set D £15.95 (2 courses)   SERVICE: not inc   CARDS: Amex, Delta, Diners, MasterCard, Switch, Visa   DETAILS: 48 seats. 20 seats outside. Private parties: 48 main room, 20 to 28 private rooms. Car park. Vegetarian meals. No smoking. Wheelchair access (not WC). No music (£5)

SHIPHAM Somerset   map 2

▲ Daneswood House �✳

Cuck Hill, Shipham BS25 1RD
TEL: (01934) 843145   FAX: (01934) 843824
WEBSITE: www.daneswoodhotel.co.uk   COOKING 2
off A38 2½m N of Axbridge; hotel is on left at S end of   MODERN BRITISH
village   £31–£64

This former Edwardian homeopathic hydro has fine views over the Mendips. Décor in the dining room reflects its origins, with heavily patterned wallpapers, sentimental china figurines and ornately framed pictures, while menus offer an ambitious version of modern British cooking. Elaborate starters such as tuna carpaccio with fennel and cucumber blinis, wasabi ice cream and ginger dressing appear alongside simpler things like wild rabbit terrine with carrot marmalade. Main courses continue in similar fashion with breast of pheasant and confit leg with wild mushroom roulade in a corn, lentil and cabbage broth, or poached medallion of beef with foie gras, creamed wild mushrooms and garlic mash, and to finish there might be macadamia nut tart with clotted cream ice cream, or rhubarb and ginger blancmange. The list of mostly French wines opens with 16 house selections priced from £10.95.

CHEF: Ross Duncan   PROPRIETORS: David and Elise Hodges   OPEN: all week 12 to 2, 7 to 9.30 (8 Sun) CLOSED: 24 Dec to 2 Jan   MEALS: alc (not Sun L; main courses £15 to £22). Set L Sun £17.95 (2 courses) to £19.95, Set D Fri £29.95 (whole table)   SERVICE: not inc, 10% for parties of 10 or more, card slips closed CARDS: Amex, Delta, Diners, MasterCard, Switch, Visa   DETAILS: 50 seats. Private parties: 35 main room, 10 to 14 private rooms. Car park. Vegetarian meals. Children's helpings. No smoking. Wheelchair access (also WC). Music   ACCOMMODATION: 17 rooms, all with bath/shower. TV. Phone. B&B £89.50 to £150. Baby facilities (£5)

SHURDINGTON Gloucestershire   map 5

▲ The Greenway ✿ ✳

Shurdington GL51 4UG   COOKING 5
TEL: (01242) 862352   FAX: (01242) 862780   MODERN FRENCH
WEBSITE: www.the-greenway.co.uk   £37–£131

The Greenway is a beautiful old Cotswold-stone manor house with 'stupendous' views over steeply rising hills from its conservatory dining room. By contrast, the décor is rather more sedate, albeit in a fairly posh way, and service is 'very smart, very French'. Meals open with a succession of fancy appetisers – perhaps a tartlet of scrambled egg and caviar – setting the tone for some ambitious and remarkably elaborate cooking. A starter of roast tuna belly, for example, gives the fish a curried breadcrumb crust and partners it with a salsa of diced mango, chilli and red onion, arranged on the plate around an exclamation mark of creamy mango purée and a separate tiny pile of wafer-thin slices of tuna carpaccio. Main courses show the kitchen's style off to full effect: Barbary duck breast with wild mushroom lasagne, confit duck leg and a chestnut faggot, roast peaches, seared foie gras and red wine sauce, the individual components carefully executed though perhaps too disparate for the dish to work as a whole. Portions are small, so you may need a pudding along the lines of vanilla pannacotta with Granny Smith sorbet, poached rhubarb, apple beignets and rhubarb syrup. The wine list is a weighty tome but finds little room for bottles under £20, although house New Zealand is £18.50.

CHEF: Kenny Atkinson   PROPRIETOR: Von Essen Hotels   OPEN: all week 12 to 2, 7 to 9.30   MEALS: Set L Mon to Sat £15.50 (2 courses) to £45, Set L Sun £25 to £45, Set D £45 to £90   SERVICE: not inc   CARDS: Amex, Delta, Diners, MasterCard, Switch, Visa   DETAILS: 45 seats. 24 seats outside. Private parties: 56 main room, 4 to 22 private rooms. Car park. Vegetarian meals. No smoking. Wheelchair access (also WC). Music. No mobile phones   ACCOMMODATION: 21 rooms, all with bath/shower. TV. Phone. B&B £99 to £280. Rooms for disabled (£5)

SKIPTON North Yorkshire   map 8

Le Caveau ⅋✳ £

86 High Street, Skipton BD23 1JJ   COOKING 2
TEL/FAX: (01756) 794274   ANGLO-FRENCH
                                                                                     £23–£50

As its name suggests, Le Caveau is a cellar restaurant (a 'super little place') tucked away beneath a shop in the centre of town. Steep stairs descend to the stone walls and barrel-vaulted ceiling of the diminutive dining room. Although the building may be centuries old, the seasonal carte – bolstered by blackboard specials – moves with the times, supported by traditional values. Richard Barker uses well-sourced local ingredients: venison (served with spiced red cabbage and a redcurrant and port jus) and beef (sirloin steak with a pink peppercorn sauce) from the Yorkshire Dales, and cheeses from Skipton's market. Blueberry frangipane tartlet, or dark chocolate truffle cake tempt at dessert. Service is good humoured and unstuffy, and prices on the compact wine list rarely stray over £20. House Duboeuf is £10.95.

CHEF: Richard Barker   PROPRIETORS: Brian Womersley and Richard Barker   OPEN: Tue to Fri 12 to 1.45, 7 to 9.30 (Sat 5.30 to 9.45)   CLOSED: 25 Dec, first week Jan, first week June, 2 weeks Sept   MEALS: alc (main courses L £7 to £15, D £10 to £18)   SERVICE: not inc   CARDS: Amex, Delta, MasterCard, Switch, Visa   DETAILS: 30 seats. Private parties: 30 main room, 10 to 16 private rooms. Vegetarian meals. No smoking. Music (£5)

SOUTHALL Greater London   map 3

Brilliant ⅋✳ £

72–76 Western Road, Southall UB2 5DZ   COOKING 3
TEL: (020) 8574 1928   FAX: (020) 8574 0276   NORTH INDIAN
WEBSITE: www.brilliantrestaurant.com   £24–£59

From small beginnings in 1975, the Anand brothers' Southall restaurant now incorporates outside catering and, in private parties, karaoke – not to mention a licence for weddings.

The menu shows a few influences from the family's native Kenya, but the lion's share is a spicy assortment of classics like palak lamb (with spinach), meat kofta, mattar paneer, and various biryanis. Regulars continue to endorse the kitchen's efforts, especially in the evening. Tandoori prawns with a zingy marinade make a fine starter, and methi chicken is a 'tried and trusted' favourite. Vegetables include karahi Mexican mix as well as highly rated aloo chollay (chickpeas and potatoes) and aloo gobi. Rice is a strong point, and chapatis and garlic naan fare well in the bread department. Indian beers and lassi suit the food; otherwise there's a minimal wine list from £9.

CHEF: D.K. Anand   PROPRIETORS: K.K. and D.K. Anand   OPEN: Tue to Fri L 12 to 3, Tue to Sun D 6 to 11.30   MEALS: alc (main courses £4.50 to £15). Set L and D £17.50 (min 10)   SERVICE: not inc, card slips closed   CARDS: Amex, Delta, Diners, MasterCard, Switch, Visa   DETAILS: 250 seats. Private parties: 120 main room, 80 to 130 private rooms. Car park. Vegetarian meals. No smoking in 1 dining room. Wheelchair access (also WC). Music. Air-conditioned (£5) ·

Madhu's £

39 South Road, Southall UB1 1SW COOKING 3
TEL: (020) 8574 1897   FAX: (020) 8813 8639 NORTH INDIAN
WEBSITE: www.madhusonline.com £24–£60

This family-run restaurant has been a Southall fixture for almost 25 years, and despite a fire at South Road in 2002, their culinary supremacy in the area shows no signs of waning. Madhu's glitzy décor may resemble W1 Indian, but the food is a staunchly traditional blend of Punjabi and Kenyan: look for the 'M' logo on the glossy menu, which highlights specialities like nyamah choma (a Masai warrior dish of marinated lamb ribs) and mogo jeera (fried cassava with cumin seeds). The standard repertoire is also fully represented by the likes of meat samosas, methi chicken, and king prawn masala, while home-made kulfi with almonds is reckoned to be in a class of its own. Plenty of thought has gone into the wine list, which begins with house Bordeaux at £8.

CHEFS: Harsandeep Bhanot and J.P. Singh   PROPRIETORS: Sanjay and Sanjeev Anand   OPEN: Mon and Wed to Fri L 12 to 3, Wed to Mon D 6 to 11.30   CLOSED: 25 Dec, L bank hols   MEALS: alc (main courses £6 to £12). Set L £17.50, Set D £20   SERVICE: not inc, card slips closed   CARDS: Amex, Delta, Diners, MasterCard, Switch, Visa   DETAILS: 102 seats. Private parties: 45 main room, 20 to 30 private rooms. Vegetarian meals. Wheelchair access (also WC). Music. Air-conditioned (£5)

SOUTHAMPTON Hampshire map 2

Oxfords £

35/36 Oxford Street, Southampton SO14 3DS NEW CHEF
TEL: (023) 8022 4444   FAX: (023) 8022 2284 MODERN EUROPEAN
WEBSITE: www.oxfordsrestaurant.com £28–£48

Not the same establishment as the Oxford Brasserie (next door at No. 33), Oxfords is nonetheless a contemporary brasserie and bar. It's popular, relaxed and buzzy, with fair-weather pavement seating under large awnings. The large, smart interior has polished-wood tables and light-wood floor, plain walls are hung with large mirrors and artwork, and there are leafy plants, ceiling fans, and Venetian blinds on the big front windows. There was a change in the kitchen team after our inspection, but the menu continues in the same vein. You can expect to start with something like smoked haddock and chive fishcakes with beurre blanc, followed by roast corn-fed chicken with baby vegetables, creamed mash and Madeira jus. Daily fresh fish proves ever-popular, and desserts run to caramelised lemon tart with crème fraîche. A 50-strong wine list starts at £11.95 and offers 16 by the glass.

CHEFS: Nick Smith and Kevin Anfield PROPRIETORS: Simon Foderingham and Jimmy Hajiantoni OPEN: all week L 12 to 2.15, Mon to Sat D 6 to 10 (10.30 Fri and Sat) CLOSED: 25 and 26 Dec MEALS: alc (main courses £8.50 to £16) SERVICE: not inc, 10% for parties of 7 or more CARDS: Amex, MasterCard, Switch, Visa DETAILS: 100 seats. 40 seats outside. Private parties: 120 main room. Vegetarian meals. No-smoking area. Wheelchair access (also WC). Music. Air-conditioned

SOUTH CROSLAND West Yorkshire   map 8

King's Arms 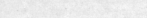   NEW ENTRY

23/25 Midway, South Crosland HD4 7DA   COOKING 4
TEL: (01484) 661669 FAX: (01484) 660427   MODERN EUROPEAN
                                                                       £23–£53

Besides the fantastic moorland views, service that strikes the right balance, and the comfort afforded by a wood-burning stove on a winter's day, the King's Arms delivers uniformly good cooking. Start perhaps with a properly traditional French fish soup and rouille, or maybe with seared king scallops, grilled halloumi and chorizo. Moving on, roast cod is given the provençale treatment, poached chicken comes with morel tagliatelle and asparagus, and an attractively fanned duck breast with spinach and a mound of cassoulet is made with good Toulouse sausage. Finish off with a triangular wedge of rhubarb cheesecake with strawberry coulis and custard, or just a simple trio of home-made ice creams (the whisky and ginger comes recommended). Reasonable mark-ups characterise the intelligently composed wine list, which starts at £10.95 for Chardonnay. The kitchen also serves up sandwiches and an enticingly written list of simpler dishes.

CHEFS: Edd Bowen and Richard Greenway PROPRIETOR: Tracy Lightowlers OPEN: Tue to Fri and Sun L 12 to 2 (4 Sun), Tue to Sat D 6 to 9 (9.30 Fri and Sat) MEALS: alc (not Sun; main courses £5 to £18). Set Sun L £12 (2 courses) to £15. Light menu available Tue to Thurs. SERVICE: not inc CARDS: MasterCard, Switch, Visa DETAILS: 42 seats. Private parties: 42 main room. Car park. Vegetarian meals. Children's helpings. No smoking. Wheelchair access (also men's WC). Music

SOUTHPORT Merseyside   map 8

Warehouse Brasserie £

30 West Street, Southport PR8 1QN   COOKING 3
TEL: (01704) 544662 FAX: (01704) 500074   GLOBAL
WEBSITE: www.warehousebrasserie.co.uk   £20–£51

This smart and individualistic warehouse conversion is reportedly a gathering place for the North-west's glitterati, so weekend diners need to book (and there's a two-hour time limit on tables). Marc Vérité's assured and eclectic contemporary cuisine offers good Lancashire produce on the monthly-changing menus (roast Goosnargh duckling with orange and green peppercorn sauce, and rump of Bowland lamb with roast garlic and tarragon cream), while Eastern and Western influences show in chicken satay salad, and Mexican chicken pasta (involving guacamole and coriander). Fish features too, perhaps as smoked haddock served in a mussel and spinach chowder. Top and tail a meal with Parma ham and asparagus with a soft-boiled egg, and banana doughnuts with chocolate sauce. An enterprising wine list runs from Pays d'Oc varietals at £10.95 to California's Opus One at £195, offering decent choice under £20.

CHEF: Marc Vérité PROPRIETOR: Paul Adams OPEN: Mon to Sat 12 to 1.45, 5.30 to 10 MEALS: alc (main courses £6.50 to £16.50). Set L £8.95 (2 courses) to £10.95, Set D Mon to Thur £10.95 (2 courses) to £13.95 SERVICE: not inc, 10% for parties of 8 or more CARDS: Amex, Delta, MasterCard, Switch, Visa DETAILS: 128 seats. Private parties: 80 main room, 10 to 18 private rooms. Vegetarian meals. Children's helpings. No cigars/pipes. Music. Air-conditioned

SOUTHSEA Hampshire   map 2

Bistro Montparnasse

103 Palmerston Road, Southsea PO5 3PS	COOKING 3
TEL: (023) 9281 6754	MODERN EUROPEAN
WEBSITE: www.bistromontparnasse.co.uk	£26–£46

'Exciting' is how one visitor described the menu at this determinedly bistro-style eatery not far from the sea. Indeed, chef Kevin Bingham is not afraid to try his hand at original combinations for some dishes while keeping to the traditional for others. A well-presented starter of Serrano ham-wrapped pigeon breast has been accompanied by potato salad and balsamic and champagne sauce ('enjoyably piquant'), and herb-crusted fillet of wild salmon of 'excellent flavour' enhanced by a punchy reduction of sun-dried tomatoes and cream. On the menu might also be seared scallops and clam chowder with noodles, followed by chargrilled Gressingham duck breast with spicy plum compote. Desserts tend towards the traditional, such as vanilla crème brûlée and sticky toffee pudding. Service is young, enthusiastic and prompt, and the colourful décor is decidedly pleasant. The wine list is short but not without interest. House wines start proceedings at £12 a bottle.

CHEF: Kevin Bingham PROPRIETORS: John Saunders and Kevin Bingham OPEN: Tue to Sat 12 to 1.45, 7 to 9.30 CLOSED: 25 and 26 Dec, 1 Jan, first 2 weeks Mar, first 2 weeks Oct MEALS: Set L £13 (2 courses) to £16, Set D £20 (2 courses) to £25. Light L menu available SERVICE: not inc CARDS: Amex, Delta, MasterCard, Switch, Visa DETAILS: 34 seats. Private parties: 34 main room, 12 to 30 private rooms. Vegetarian meals. Wheelchair access (not WC). Music

SOUTHWOLD Suffolk   map 6

▲ Crown Hotel ▮ ✳

90 High Street, Southwold IP18 6DP	NEW CHEF
TEL: (01502) 722275 FAX: (01502) 727263	MODERN BRITISH-PLUS
WEBSITE: www.adnams.co.uk	£30–£46

The flagship of Adnams, the brewer and wine merchant, tries to be all things to all people in sought-after Southwold. Restaurant customers head for the airy, duck-egg blue dining room, where fixed-price menus change daily and there are suggested wines for each course. New head chef Sue Miles took charge of the kitchen in June 2004. Open with a warm salad of beetroot, pancetta and pigeon, then perhaps steamed brill with white bean cassoulet and grain mustard, and finish with summer pudding with fruits. Similar, brasserie-style food (tarragon chicken with herb rice, for example) is served in the adjoining bar, which can become frantically busy at peak times. The global wine list really pushes the boat out in France, including special older bottles for the highest high days. Prices look good further down the list; house bottles run from £11.25, and 17 by the glass neatly span the flavour spectrum.

CHEF: Sue Miles PROPRIETOR: Adnams Brewery plc OPEN: all week 12.30 to 1.30, 7.30 to 9 MEALS: Set L £18.50 (2 courses) to £21.50, Set D £24 (2 courses) to £29. Bar menu available SERVICE: not inc CARDS: Delta, MasterCard, Switch, Visa DETAILS: 60 seats. 12 seats outside. Car park. Vegetarian meals. Children's helpings. No children under 7 at D. No smoking. Wheelchair access (also WC). No music. No mobile phones ACCOMMODATION: 14 rooms, 13 with bath/shower. TV. Phone. B&B £77 to £162. Baby facilities

SOWERBY West Yorkshire
map 8

Travellers Rest ⅝✗

Steep Lane, Sowerby HX6 1PE
TEL: (01422) 832124 FAX: (01422) 831365

COOKING 3
MODERN BRITISH-PLUS
£21–£49

High on a hill overlooking Halifax, this pub-restaurant has its stone walls, flagged floors and log fires set off with modern colours and fabrics, and supplements straightforward bar food with more ambitious, polyglot restaurant dishes served in a long, many-windowed room. Crottin goats' cheese is crusted with tapenade and served with beetroot and chilli oil, while boudin noir comes with chorizo hash and sauce gribiche. Look to the specials board for fish of the day, or pick from the printed menu meats such as roast rack of salt-marsh lamb on flageolet beans and peas with a 'pesto' of garlic and mint. Finish on a high with the likes of Dundee pudding with Drambuie custard, or stewed plum and sloe gin trifle. The compact, fairly priced wine list starts off with Chilean house wines in three colours at £9.25 and peaks with a £25 Californian pinot.

CHEFS: Darren Collinson and Lee Coulter PROPRIETOR: Caroline Lumley OPEN: Sat and Sun L 12.30 to 3, Wed to Sun D 6 to 9.30 (10 Sat, 8 Sun) MEALS: alc (main courses £8.50 to £17). Set L Sun £15.95 (2 courses) to £19.95, Set D Wed to Thur 6 to 8 £12.95. Bar menu available SERVICE: not inc CARDS: Delta, MasterCard, Switch, Visa DETAILS: 50 seats. 40 seats outside. Private parties: 100 main room. Car park. Vegetarian meals. No children under 6. No smoking. Wheelchair access (not WC). Music

STADDLEBRIDGE North Yorkshire
map 9

▲ McCoy's

The Cleveland Tontine, Staddlebridge DL6 3JB
TEL: (01609) 882671 FAX: (01609) 882660
WEBSITE: www.mccoysatthetontine.co.uk
6m NE of Northallerton, at junction of A19 and A172

COOKING 5
BISTRO
£27–£62

The Tontine is a fine, stone-built, early nineteenth-century inn on a major junction of the A19 – once a stopover for those travelling between Newcastle and York. The stone-floored, dimly lit basement bistro (with a lighter, modern conservatory) meets the needs of the McCoy brothers' many supporters, who appreciate the comfortable, unstuffy feel created by 'wobbly sofas, ancient cats'.

Marcus Bennett's accomplished bistro cooking covers both classic and contemporary modes. The former offers anything from a straightforward lunch of chicken liver pâté with plum chutney, and minute steak with poivre sauce, chips and salad, to dinner of seafood pancake, and Dover sole with Montpellier butter. But the combination of flexibility and professionalism is seen throughout, and there is no shortage of bright yet appealing ideas. If beef Wellington is too familiar, then there is ample choice elsewhere, from king scallops with sautéed wild rocket, tomato fondue, roast garlic, cream and basil oil, to roast corn-fed chicken with rösti, buttered spinach, roast asparagus, petits pois, pancetta, wild mushrooms and foie gras cream. Desserts are on a par: note pannacotta with mango ice cream and baby fruit salad, or a trio of milk and white chocolate with orange jelly and passion-fruit syrup, as well as spotted dick with golden syrup. Prices on the short but well-chosen wine list start at £14.95 but soon leap over the £20 barrier.

CHEF: Marcus Bennett PROPRIETORS: Tom and Eugene McCoy OPEN: all week 12 to 2 (2.30 Sun), 6.45 to 9.45 CLOSED: 25 and 26 Dec, 1 Jan MEALS: alc (main courses L £9 to £14, D £17.50 to £19). Set L Mon to Sat £12.95 (2 courses) to £14.95, Set L Sun £17.95 SERVICE: not inc CARDS: Amex, Delta, Diners, MasterCard, Switch, Visa DETAILS: 70 seats. Private parties: 70 main room, 10 to 50 private rooms. Car park. Vegetarian meals. Children's helpings. Music ACCOMMODATION: 6 rooms, all with bath/shower. TV. Phone. B&B £80 to £100

STAITHES North Yorkshire   map 9

▲ Endeavour ✸

1 High Street, Staithes TS13 5BH	COOKING 3
TEL: (01947) 840825	MODERN BRITISH/SEAFOOD
WEBSITE: www.endeavour-restaurant.co.uk	£31–£48

In the narrow main street of a particularly picturesque fishing village, Endeavour (named after local boy James Cook's ship) has blue walls and tablecloths echoing the colours of the sea, and a homely atmosphere of gentle amiability. The menus, firmly emphasising locally caught fish and shellfish (though meat eaters and vegetarians aren't forgotten), change daily depending on what's available from the Staithes boats or the quays in Whitby and Scarborough. The cooking favours simplicity, allowing the freshness of the ingredients to shine. So expect Staithes crab bisque, then roast Whitby turbot fillet with an apple and Calvados sauce, or perhaps a cassoulet of halibut, squid, scallops, smoked bacon and cannellini beans, while crème brûlée with raspberries could feature among the home-made desserts. Almost all the bottles on the compact global wine list are under £20; house Chilean or Oz are £10.95.

CHEFS/PROPRIETORS: Brian Kay and Charlotte Willoughby OPEN: Tue to Sat D only 7 to 9 CLOSED: 25 and 26 Dec, 1 Jan MEALS: alc D (main courses £11 to £16) SERVICE: not inc CARDS: Amex, Delta, MasterCard, Switch, Visa DETAILS: 36 seats. Private parties: 16 main room, 16 private room. Car park. Vegetarian meals. No smoking. Music. No mobile phones ACCOMMODATION: 3 rooms, all with bath/shower. TV. B&B £65 to £75. (£5)

STAMFORD Lincolnshire   map 6

Oakhouse Restaurant ✸   NEW ENTRY

11 All Saints Place, Stamford PE9 2AR	COOKING 2
TEL: (01780) 756565 FAX: (01780) 761371	MODERN BRITISH
WEBSITE: www.oakhouserestaurant.com	£24–£55

Having made a success of the World Service (see entry, Nottingham), Chris Elson and Ashley Walter recently teamed up with André Vazquez for their second venture. The Oakhouse is a shopfronted premises with opaque windows, a rough-hewn stone and timber interior on two levels, and a sun terrace for al fresco meals. Visitors can expect good value and capable cooking, as in one reporter's pleasing lunch of sunblush tomato and artichoke risotto, lightly roasted fillet of haddock with parsley and shellfish ragoût, and ungreasy apple beignets with vanilla mascarpone and spiced toffee sauce. In the evening, the kitchen also gets to work on, say, roast Gressingham duck breast with fondant potatoes

427

and sour cherry sauce and creates its own version of chicken Kiev. The comprehensive, global wine list is fairly priced from £11.75.

CHEFS: Dan Powell and Chris Elson   PROPRIETORS: André Vazquez, Chris Elson and Ashley Walter   OPEN: all week L 12 to 2.30 (3 Sun), Mon to Sat D 6.30 to 10   MEALS: alc exc Sat and Sun L (main courses £10 to £17.50). Set L Mon to Fri £9.95 (2 courses) to £13.50, Set L Sat and Sun £13.50 (2 courses) to £16.75, Set D Mon to Thur £14.50 (2 courses) to £17.50   SERVICE: not inc, 10% for parties of 8 or more   CARDS: Amex, Delta, MasterCard, Switch, Visa   DETAILS: 90 seats. 50 seats outside. Private parties: 90 main room, 12 to 20 private rooms. Vegetarian meals. Children's helpings. No smoking in 1 dining room. Wheelchair access (also WC). Music

STANTON Suffolk

map 6

Leaping Hare

Wyken Vineyards, Stanton IP31 2DW
TEL: (01359) 250287   FAX: (01359) 252372
From Ixworth bypass, turn E off A143 and follow brown signs for Wyken Vineyards

NEW CHEF
MODERN EUROPEAN
£31–£53

Vineyard, restaurant, café, shop – it's all way off the beaten track and beautifully tranquil (with llamas, sheep and ancient trees). The fabulously impressive barn housing the restaurant has lashings of bare wood and lots of glass and light. A new chef started in summer 2004, so too late for any feedback. The Hare's own excellent produce – sold here via the Saturday farmers' markets – remains the focus of the menu. After grilled sardines with Wyken mizuna and rocket and lemon mayonnaise, there's truffled local mushroom risotto, or roast Wyken rack of lamb with sauté niçoise and salsa verde. End with three English cheeses, or warm honey and walnut tart with crème fraîche, or both. A short, reasonably priced wine list (including four from Wyken Vineyards from £14.50) favours champagne and reds, and there's their own cider and ale, too. More basic menus are offered mornings and afternoons.

CHEF: Nick Claxton-Webb   PROPRIETORS: Kenneth and Carla Carlisle   OPEN: all week L 12 to 2.30, Fri and Sat D 7 to 9.30   CLOSED: 24 Dec to 5 Jan   MEALS: alc (main courses £9 to £16). Morning/afternoon menus available   SERVICE: not inc, 10% (optional) for parties of 8 or more, card slips closed   CARDS: Delta, MasterCard, Switch, Visa   DETAILS: 70 seats. 20 seats outside. Private parties: 70 main room. Car park. Vegetarian meals. Children's helpings. No smoking. Wheelchair access (also WC). No music. No mobile phones £5

STATHERN Leicestershire

map 5

Red Lion Inn £

2 Red Lion Street, Stathern LE14 4HS
TEL: (01949) 860868   FAX: (01949) 861579
WEBSITE: www.theredlioninn.co.uk

COOKING 2
MODERN BRITISH-PLUS
£20–£48

The dining room at this sister establishment of the Olive Branch at Clipsham (see entry) was the skittle alley. Now it's a homely showcase for inventive modern dishes making the most of fine local raw materials. 'Home and away' starters include terrine of local game with Cumberland sauce, and deep-fried battered tiger prawns with sweet-and-sour noodle salad. Among mains might be fried wild sea bass with saffron mash and griddled fennel, alongside calf's liver and bacon with buttered spinach and marjoram jus. British cheeses, sticky toffee pudding, or crème brûlée and nectarine compote round things off. An array of wines from £10 (£2.50 a glass) to £20 is supplemented by 'fine and rare' bottles for those naughty but nice occasions.

CHEF: Phil Lowe   PROPRIETORS: Ben Jones, Sean Hope and Marcus Welford   OPEN: all week L 12 to 2 (3 Sun), Mon to Sat D 7 to 9.30   CLOSED: 1 Jan   MEALS: alc (main courses £8.50 to £15.50). Set L £9.50 (2 courses) to £11.50, Set L Sun £14.50   SERVICE: not inc, card slips closed   CARDS: Delta, MasterCard, Switch, Visa   DETAILS: 60 seats. 30 seats outside. Private parties: 20 main room. Car park. Vegetarian meals. Children's helpings. Wheelchair access (not WC). Occasional music

STOCKBRIDGE Hampshire   map 2

Greyhound ♟ ⅝✳

31 High Street, Stockbridge SO20 6EY   COOKING 4
TEL: (01264) 810833   FAX: (01264) 811184   MODERN BRITISH
                                                                   £39–£67

This is a rustic yet sophisticated restaurant in pub's clothing – London-style cuisine with the River Test slipping through the back garden. The clubby lounge has leather sofas, and the dining space, with its clothless wood tables and brown high-back leather chairs, has low beams, inglenooks, polished-wood floors and a small bar.

Since last year ownership has changed, and former chef Darron Bunn is now chef-patron. His seasonal modern British carte, with classical roots, is sensibly compact and appealing, and has 'definitely moved up a gear'. (And service, a source of complaints in late 2003, seems to be unpretentiously efficient under the new management.) Expect accomplished, well-presented, light dishes with quality ingredients: perhaps haricot blanc soup with truffle oil to start, or risotto of Dorset crab with clams, followed by roast pheasant with choucroute and Madeira sauce, or maybe pan-fried turbot, queen scallops, confit bacon and a sauce lie de vin (vegetables are extra). Classic warm chocolate fondant with pistachio ice cream makes a rich finish. The wine list provides a good mix of easy drinking and heavyweights. Always strong on French classics, it seems to have embraced the New World with renewed vigour; southern France and Argentina provide the six house wines by the glass.

CHEF/PROPRIETOR: Darron Bunn   OPEN: all week L 12 to 2.30, Mon to Sat D 7 to 9.30. Light L, garden (summer) and Sun brunch menus available   CLOSED: 25 and 26 Dec, 1 Jan   MEALS: alc (main courses £12.50 to £21.50)   SERVICE: 10% (optional), card slips closed   CARDS: Delta, MasterCard, Switch, Visa   DETAILS: 45 seats. 20 seats outside. Private parties: 40 main room. Car park. Vegetarian meals. Children's helpings. No smoking. Wheelchair access (not WC). Music

STOCKCROSS Berkshire   map 2

▲ Vineyard at Stockcross ▮

Stockcross RG20 8JU
TEL: (01635) 528770   FAX: (01635) 528398   COOKING 8
WEBSITE: www.the-vineyard.co.uk   ANGLO-FRENCH
just off A4, 2m W of Newbury on B4000   £36–£94

The setting is splendidly dramatic: a modern Californian-style villa with ostentatious opulence in large measure. This starts with a fire and water sculpture in the garden area in front of the building and continues in the Art Deco-style split-level dining room, where widely spaced tables are dressed with tall, elegant floral displays and lighting subtly changes colour over the course of the evening.

The food lives up to the setting. Luxury ingredients are used in abundance, but the real impact of dishes comes from the way in which flavours and textures are brought together. John Campbell is one of the finest exponents of the scientific approach to gastronomy, ensuring that even the most surprising combinations are successful; in addition, dishes are beautifully presented with a minimum of fuss. Among starters, roast Anjou squab is partnered by black treacle and celeriac, while roast scallops are paired more conventionally with shellfish ravioli. Among main courses, sea bass comes with parsnip and vanilla purée, pea soubise and tomato jelly, while the saddle and confit shoulder of lamb are served with red cabbage, Venezuelan chocolate and bacon and hazelnut dressing. Meals finish with a choice from the fine selection of British and French cheeses or desserts such as chocolate délices with basil ice cream and hazelnut clafoutis, or coffee pannacotta with citrus salad and pink grapefruit sherbet. Service has come under fire from some reporters for its leisurely pace and the practice of hiding wine bottles out of reach. Sir Peter Michael is an established producer of premium wines in California, and half of the magnificent wine list is devoted to these and many other fine bottles from around the state, some of them rare. The second volume covers the rest of the world in lavish detail and is not neglectful of options under £20, which are usefully summarised on the back pages.

CHEF: John Campbell PROPRIETOR: Sir Peter Michael OPEN: all week 12 to 2, 7 to 9.45 MEALS: Set L £17 (2 courses) to £55, Set D £25 (2 courses) to £65 SERVICE: not inc CARDS: Amex, Delta, Diners, MasterCard, Switch, Visa DETAILS: 70 seats. 20 seats outside. Private parties: 140 main room, 40 to 140 private rooms. Car park. Vegetarian meals. Children's helpings. No-smoking area. Wheelchair access (also WC). Music. No mobile phones. Air-conditioned ACCOMMODATION: 49 rooms, all with bath/shower. TV. Phone. B&B £245 to £635. Swimming pool. Fishing

STOKE HOLY CROSS Norfolk

map 6

Wildebeest Arms ▼

NEW ENTRY

82–86 Norwich Road, Stoke Holy Cross NR14 8QJ
TEL: (01508) 492497 FAX: (01508) 494353
EMAIL: mail@animalinns.co.uk

COOKING 2
MODERN EUROPEAN
£25–£55

Outside this neat-looking roadside pub south of Norwich palms in terracotta pots give a clue to the exoticism inside. Masks, musical instruments and other 'Africana' adorn the long bar/dining room, and the kitchen is open to view. Set menus, specials and a 'tasting' menu provide flexibility and choice, and results on the plate can be impressive: 'beautifully timed' seared scallops with warm apple boudin and guacamole made a fine starter, while hot raspberry soufflé with strawberry sorbet has been a very acceptable dessert. In between, expect anything from grilled fillet of sea bass with sauté potatoes, roast artichokes, buttered samphire and sauce vierge, to ribeye steak with a Gruyère and herb crust, 'house chips' and aïoli. Smart, slick service matches the cosmopolitan feel. Wines run to several pages of very good options and are tremendously good value. A dozen or so house bottles at £11.95 open proceedings, while the final flourish of 'wines for indulgence and special occasions' definitely measures up to the billing.

CHEF: Daniel Smith PROPRIETOR: Henry Watt OPEN: all week 12.30 to 2.30, 7 to 10 CLOSED: 25 and 26 Dec MEALS: alc (main courses £11 to £18.50). Set L Mon to Sat £11.95 (2 courses) to £14.95, Set D Sun to Fri £15 (2 courses) to £18.50, Set D all week £29.50 (whole table) SERVICE: not inc, card slips closed CARDS: Amex, Delta, MasterCard, Switch, Visa DETAILS: 60 seats. 30 seats outside. Private parties: 60 main room. Car park. Vegetarian meals. Children's helpings. No-smoking area. Wheelchair access (not WC). Music. Air-conditioned

▲ Kings Arms £

The Square, Stow-on-the-Wold GL54 1AF	COOKING 2
TEL: (01451) 830364 FAX: (01451) 830602	MODERN EUROPEAN
WEBSITE: www.kingsarms-stowonthewold.co.uk	£27–£45

A tall building with mullioned windows on the market square, this old stone pub is an 'interesting mix of ancient and modern'. Downstairs is pubbier, with its bar counter, while upstairs has a 'wine wall' – bottles are displayed on shelves with price tags around their necks (house wines check in at £12 a bottle). High ceilings, dark floorboards and exposed stone abound, while, upstairs, some walls are painted deep claret, and dark wooden tables come with 'highly individual' seating. Peter Robinson's daily-changing blackboard menus make the best of local, seasonal produce. Flavours are 'robust and rich', the approach is straightforward: grilled sardines with gremolata and pine nuts, followed by roast brill with capers, chilli and lemon, or spaghetti with chorizo, tomatoes and olives; finish with pannacotta with raspberries.

CHEF: Peter Robinson   PROPRIETORS: Louise and Peter Robinson   OPEN: all week 12 to 2.30, 6 to 9.30 (10 Sat)   CLOSED: D 25 and 26 Dec, 1 week mid-May, 1 week mid-Oct   MEALS: alc (main courses £9 to £13.50)   SERVICE: not inc, card slips closed   CARDS: Delta, MasterCard, Switch, Visa   DETAILS: 70 seats. Private parties: 10 main room. Car park. Vegetarian meals. Children's helpings. Music   ACCOMMODATION: 10 rooms, all with bath/shower. TV. Phone. B&B £70 to £100

▲ Royalist Hotel, 947AD Restaurant

Digbeth Street, Stow-on-the-Wold GL54 1BN	COOKING 4
TEL: (01451) 830670 FAX: (01451) 870048	MODERN BRITISH
WEBSITE: www.theroyalisthotel.co.uk	£35–£73

The previous incumbents have returned to Australia, and the Royalist has a new owner and a new kitchen brigade under Darren Le Feuvre, former sous-chef at Lords of the Manor, Upper Slaughter (see entry). The interior of the restaurant, housed in an ancient building (dating back to AD 947), has been tastefully refurbished and feels unstuffy and relaxed.

Talent and ambition are at work here. Dishes are straightforward, presentation is uncluttered, and the quality of raw materials is consistently high. Appetisers, such as vichyssoise with smoked haddock, are top-drawer; tasty starters include seared scallops with petite ratatouille and tomato sorbet; and in a main-course rump of Cotswold lamb with flageolet purée and an anchovy beignet a generous portion of lamb also has a confit garlic clove on top and a bed of fresh spinach underneath. Finish, perhaps, with a skilfully made dessert of biscuit glacé with passion-fruit and banana sorbet. The capable young sommelier, also new, is in charge of an international wine list that includes a nice line in affordable Bordeaux and Burgundy; ten house selections start at £14.80.

The attached Eagle & Child pub offers a brasserie menu.

CHEF: Darren Le Feuvre   PROPRIETOR: Peter Rowan   OPEN: Tue to Sat 12 to 2, 7 to 9 (9.30 Fri and Sat)   MEALS: alc D (main courses £17 to £18). Set L £18 (2 courses) to £22. Brasserie menu available   SERVICE: 10%, card slips closed   CARDS: Delta, MasterCard, Switch, Visa   DETAILS: 30 seats. Private parties: 30 main room, 14 to 16 private rooms. Car park. Vegetarian meals. No children under 7 at D. No smoking. Music. No mobile phones   ACCOMMODATION: 8 rooms, all with bath/shower. TV. Phone. B&B £50 to £180. Baby facilities

Margaux ⁵⁄ₓ

6 Union Street, Stratford-upon-Avon CV37 6QT	COOKING 3
TEL/FAX: (01789) 269106	ENGLISH/MEDITERRANEAN
WEBSITE: www.restaurantmargaux.co.uk	£32–£52

Tucked away down a side-street in the centre of town, Margaux is as geared up for the pre-theatre trade as you would expect in Stratford. It is run with consummate panache by Maggie Brebner, for whom no personal endearment is too expansive to bestow on customers. Chef Shaun Brebner has departed since the last edition of the Guide, but reports suggest that standards are being maintained. Duck livers on onion mash, brill fillet in a Thai-type sauce of coconut milk, and noteworthy sea bass in saffron cream sauce with black olive couscous have all drawn plaudits, while meat dishes might include beef bourguignon served with mash and green beans. Finish with white peach parfait, or vanilla and white chocolate brûlée with espresso ice cream. A 20-bottle slate of wines opens at £12.50.

CHEF/PROPRIETOR: Maggie Brebner   OPEN: Tue to Sat 12 to 2, 6 to 10   CLOSED: 25 and 26 Dec, 1 Jan
MEALS: alc (main courses £11 to £18)   SERVICE: not inc, 10% for parties of 10 or more   CARDS: Amex,
Delta, MasterCard, Switch, Visa   DETAILS: 50 seats. Private parties: 30 main room, 12 to 18 private
rooms. Vegetarian meals. Children's helpings. No smoking in 1 dining room. Music

Kings Arms ⁵⁄ₓ   [NEW ENTRY]

Dartmouth Road, Strete TQ6 0RW	COOKING 4
TEL: (01803) 770377	SEAFOOD
	£24–£53

Painted white and with a splendid cast-iron balcony overlooking the road, the Kings Arms is hard to miss. It has become more of a 'restaurant with pub' than the other way around, and the focus is on local seafood – crabs and lobsters from Start Bay, for instance – and produce – organic herbs and lettuce, local meat and game – from Devon suppliers. A small cup of intense, delectable crab bisque might precede starters such as plump, fresh, juicy Brixham scallops with Puy lentils and scallion vinaigrette, or soused mackerel with a tart rhubarb jelly (the rhubarb is grown in the chef's garden). The menu shows influences from around the globe, as in a signature dish of Galician-style roast cod on a chorizo, pepper and potato stew, or spicy poached wild sea bass in a Thai broth with lemongrass, lime leaves, coriander and chilli, which impressed an inspector. For dessert, there are local cheeses or orange and passion-fruit tart with vanilla ice cream. Service is attentive and the atmosphere jolly. Ten wines are available by the glass from the short wine list. Bottle prices start at £12.50.

CHEF: R. Dawson   PROPRIETORS: R. Dawson and V. Heath   OPEN: Tue to Sun L 12 to 2, Tue to Sat D 7 to 9
CLOSED: 25 and 26 Dec, last 2 weeks Feb, last 2 weeks Oct   MEALS: alc D (main courses £16.50). Set L
£12.95. Bar menu available   SERVICE: not inc   CARDS: Amex, Delta, MasterCard, Switch, Visa   DETAILS:
30 seats. 50 seats outside. Private parties: 30 main room. Car park. Vegetarian meals. No smoking. No
music. No mobile phones (£5)

▲ Three Lions ▼ ✿

Stuckton, Fordingbridge SP6 2HF
TEL: (01425) 652489   FAX: (01425) 656144
WEBSITE: www.thethreelionsrestaurant.co.uk
1m SE of Fordingbridge, off A338 but not signposted   COOKING 6
from it; just S of Fordingbridge turn E and follow sign   ANGLO-FRENCH
down a narrow country lane.   £28–£60

The Womersleys' restaurant-with-rooms, a former pub on the edge of the New Forest, has plenty of enthusiastic supporters. Mike Womersley has built up a network of local suppliers for game, fruit and vegetables, and he aims for balance and intensity in his cooking, respecting the natural flavours of ingredients, and avoiding superfluous flounce both on the plate and in his menu descriptions. So ravioli of wild mushrooms is basically just that: three pillows of tender pasta encasing an earthy mousseline mixture, with sliced mushrooms bound in cream surrounding them. Quickly cooked chicken livers and kidneys go into a filo pastry basket to make another hugely eloquent first course, while fish alternatives might be sautéed scallops and shrimps, or smoked haddock galette. Main courses centre on the principal ingredient, whether it be well-trimmed roast pork with a couple of bits of impeccable crackling, loin of lamb with leeks, or cod baked with tomato and basil. These are accompanied straightforwardly by a choice of vegetables or salad (extra). You finish with the likes of treacle and hazelnut tart, which balances its delightfully squidgy filling with a crisp pastry shell, or the signature liquid-centred chocolate pudding, both accompanied by fine vanilla ice cream. Coffee could do with a little beefing up, but essentially this is a supremely professional operation. The wine list is short but well-chosen and offers fair value; 11 house bottles from £12.75 to £19.50 kick things off.

CHEF: Mike Womersley   PROPRIETORS: Mike and Jayne Womersley   OPEN: Tue to Sun L 12 to 2, Tue to Sat D 7 to 9.30 (10 Sat)   MEALS: alc (main courses £14.50 to £17). Set L Tue to Fri £15.75   SERVICE: not inc CARDS: Delta, MasterCard, Switch, Visa   DETAILS: 60 seats. 15 seats outside. Private parties: 60 main room, 10 to 25 private rooms. Car park. Vegetarian meals. Children's helpings. No smoking in dining room. Wheelchair access (not WC). No music. No mobile phones   ACCOMMODATION: 4 rooms, all with bath/shower. TV. B&B £59 to £95. Rooms for disabled. Baby facilities (£5)

▲ Plumber Manor ✿

Sturminster Newton DT10 2AF
TEL: (01258) 472507   FAX: (01258) 473370
WEBSITE: www.plumbermanor.com   COOKING 2
from Sturminster Newton, take road for Hazelbury Bryan;   ANGLO-FRENCH
hotel is on left after 2m   £31–£44

This seventeenth-century manor, the ancestral home of the Prideaux-Brunes, is 'English to the backbone'. Inside, it is evident this is a family home, with portraits lining the walls of the upstairs gallery. You'd be right to think that tradition has an important role here, so the menu doesn't exactly move with the times (be prepared for some rich sauces). At dinner, a smoked duck and chicken breast salad might precede a suitably traditional lemon sole Véronique. Desserts, such as Bakewell tart, or French pear tart, strike the English and French notes of the rest of the menu. France, though, is the main focus of the list of kindly priced wines starting from £12.50, including plenty of half-bottles. Service is a very personal affair, with 'courteous and witty attendance' impressing one visitor.

CHEF: Brian Prideaux-Brune PROPRIETOR: Richard Prideaux-Brune OPEN: Sun L 12.30 to 1.45, all week D 7 to 9 CLOSED: Feb MEALS: Set L £19.50, Set D £25 SERVICE: not inc CARDS: Amex, Diners, MasterCard, Switch, Visa DETAILS: 65 seats. Private parties: 45 main room, 12 to 45 private rooms. Car park. Vegetarian meals. Children's helpings. No smoking. Wheelchair access (also WC). No music ACCOMMODATION: 16 rooms, all with bath/shower. TV. Phone. B&B £90 to £160. Rooms for disabled. Baby facilities

SUMMERCOURT Cornwall · map 1

Viner's Bar and Restaurant ✻ £ · ☐ NEW ENTRY

Carvynick, Summercourt TR8 5AF
TEL: (01872) 510544 FAX: (01872) 510468

COOKING 4
MODERN EUROPEAN
£21–£52

Guide readers may recall Kevin Viner from his days at Pennypots in Maenporth, or before, and he is much lauded in the county, and beyond. His most recent venture has taken him to the former Foxes Revenge pub among the timeshare cottages of Carvynick, and this new Viner's has already become 'an adornment to the area', as one local reporter put it. The building now has a farmhouse feel, although subtle pale green shades lighten up the mood, and there's a trimmed-down approach to things culinary, with gimmick-free food and no pressure to follow the conventions of a three-course meal. Twice-baked West Country cheese soufflé is 'a fluffy masterpiece', pot-roast shoulder of Cornish lamb comes with a thyme and red wine sauce straight out of Provence, and pan-fried cod is paired with chorizo, sunblush tomatoes and pesto. Pennypots bread-and-butter pudding still graces the menu; otherwise try chocolate temptation ('a mousse with knobs on!'). The wine list is an apposite slate, with realistic mark-ups and 13 house wines, all £10.50, served by the glass.

CHEF: Kevin Viner PROPRIETORS: Jane and Kevin Viner OPEN: Sun L 12.30 to 3, Mon to Sat D 6.30 to 9.30 CLOSED: 4 weeks winter. Possible reduced opening hours winter; phone to enquire MEALS: alc D (main courses £11 to £20). Set L £10.95 (2 courses) to £12.95. Bar menu available SERVICE: not inc, card slips closed CARDS: Delta, MasterCard, Switch, Visa DETAILS: 55 seats. 40 seats outside. Private parties: 60 main room, 20 private room. Car park. Vegetarian meals. Children's helpings. No smoking. Wheelchair access (not WC). No music

SURBITON Surrey · map 3

French Table

85 Maple Road, Surbiton KT6 4AW
TEL: (020) 8399 2365 FAX: (020) 8390 5353
WEBSITE: www.thefrenchtable.co.uk

COOKING 4
FRENCH/MEDITERRANEAN
£26–£55

The brilliant-white and purple paintwork of the French Table marks the restaurant out from the parade of shops one road back from the Thames. A recent refurbishment in shades of cream, plum and purple, with crisply dressed tables, underscores the sense that this is a neighbourhood restaurant with high aspirations. The menu tends to the Mediterranean-inspired end of French cuisine, with ingredients to match: deep-fried salsify, for example, or ballottine of cod with brandade. A vein of unusual ingredients – cocoa bean purée, Tarbais beans, smoked vegetables (some sourced direct from France) – enlivens the menu.

A starter of roast haddock topped with Gruyère and a poached egg, and a main course of caramelised pork belly with pommes Anna and beetroot raviolo have earned praise. Desserts such as bavarois of cinnamon with pear ice cream, and lemon tart with blueberry sorbet are of equally high quality. Service is relaxed, confident and charming. Good value extends to the well-conceived wine list, where prices start at £11.75. A second branch, the Food Room, has opened at 123 Queenstown Road, London SW8; tel (020) 7622 0555.

CHEF: Eric Guignard   PROPRIETORS: Eric and Sarah Guignard   OPEN: Wed to Fri and Sun L 12 to 2.30, Tue to Sat D 7 to 10.30   CLOSED: 24 and 25 Dec, first week Jan, last 2 weeks Aug   MEALS: alc D (main courses £10.50 to £15). Set L Wed to Fri £12.50 (2 courses) to £15.50, Set L Sun £16.50   SERVICE: 12.5% (optional), card slips closed   CARDS: Delta, MasterCard, Switch, Visa   DETAILS: 48 seats. Vegetarian meals. Children's helpings. No-smoking area. Wheelchair access (not WC). Music. Air-conditioned

SUTTON GAULT Cambridgeshire   map 6

▲ Anchor Inn ⚙ | NEW ENTRY |

Sutton Gault, Ely CB6 2BD
TEL: (01353) 778537   FAX: (01353) 776180
WEBSITE: www.anchor-inn-restaurant.co.uk   COOKING 3
off B1381 Sutton to Earith road, just NW of Sutton, 7½m   MODERN BRITISH
W of Ely   £31–£52

It's Fenland: starkly desolate and flat save for the raised banks of dead-straight 'cuts'. Hence, the warren of little linked rooms constituting this dining pub looks onto a grassy slope up to the New Bedford River. Food looks the other way, as far as Italy and the Mediterranean, showing up-to-date credentials on menu and specials board: fennel and orange salad with salmon and smoked haddock terrine, pesto mash and balsamic dressing with baked salmon, etc. Mingled with the modern are old-fashioned favourites: grilled bacon-wrapped dates with mustard cream sauce, or ribeye with onion, mushrooms and sauté potatoes. Raw materials are spot-on: 'seriously flavoursome, well-hung and beautifully timed' roast lamb chump came with ratatouille, buttered spinach, fondant potato and tomato jus in a meal beginning with mackerel fillets with roast Mediterranean vegetables, and completed by lemon polenta cake with mascarpone. A decent international wine list has plenty of options under £20.

CHEF: Kerrif Mayes and Barbara Jordan   PROPRIETORS: Robin and Heather Moore   OPEN: all week 12 to 2, 7 to 9 (6.30 to 9.30 Sat)   CLOSED: 26 Dec   MEALS: alc (main courses L £7.50 to £16.50, D £11.50 to £16.50). Set L Sun £16.50 (2 courses) to £19.95. Light L menu available Mon to Fri   SERVICE: not inc   CARDS: Amex, Delta, MasterCard, Switch, Visa   DETAILS: 70 seats. 30 seats outside. Private parties: 30 main room. Car park. Vegetarian meals. Children's helpings. No smoking in 1 dining room. Wheelchair access (also WC). No music. No mobile phones   ACCOMMODATION: 2 rooms, both with bath/shower. TV. Phone. B&B £50 to £110

SWAFFHAM Norfolk   map 6

▲ Strattons ⚙

4 Ash Close, Swaffham PE37 7NH   COOKING 4
TEL: (01760) 723845   FAX: (01760) 720458   MODERN EUROPEAN
WEBSITE: www.strattonshotel.com   £48–£58

Sited in the glorious Breckland region of forests and ancient heaths that straddles Norfolk and Suffolk, Strattons does its level best to play a harmonious role in the local ecosystem.

The Scotts proudly source wild game and local pork and poultry and glean the provender of trout lakes and asparagus patches, with wild mushrooms from the forest floor. The dining room isn't a basement, being only half-submerged, but the atmosphere is one of calm elegance. In spring the seasonal menu offered Cromer crab cooked to a Brittany recipe with local brown nut mushrooms in port to start, followed by grilled halibut with brown shrimp risotto, 'frizzled' mâche and Parmesan, or roast pork tenderloin in wild garlic leaves and bacon served with bubble and squeak and a Bramley apple tartlet. The menus sensibly keep things short, with three choices each of starter and main, one of the latter always a vegetarian option, such as root vegetable roulade with chilli jam. Finish with mango and passion-fruit meringue, or prune pudding with vanilla ice cream. The wine list, illustrated by the owners themselves, is also extensively annotated and starts with house Vins de Pays d'Oc, a Sauvignon Blanc (£12.90) and a Merlot (£13.90).

CHEFS: Vanessa Scott and Maggie Cooper PROPRIETORS: Les and Vanessa Scott OPEN: Mon to Sat D only 7 to 9 CLOSED: 24 to 26 Dec MEALS: Set D £37.50 SERVICE: not inc, card slips closed CARDS: MasterCard, Switch, Visa DETAILS: 20 seats. 4 seats outside. Private parties: 20 main room. Car park. Vegetarian meals. Children's helpings. No smoking. Occasional music. No mobile phones ACCOMMODATION: 8 rooms, all with bath/shower. TV. Phone. B&B £80 to £200. Baby facilities

TADCASTER North Yorkshire   map 9

Singers £✷

16 Westgate, Tadcaster LS24 9AB | NEW CHEF |
TEL: (01937) 835121   MODERN EUROPEAN
WEBSITE: www.singersrestaurant.co.uk   £24–£37

Not sewing machines but music is the theme at Philip Taylor's friendly and professional 'little gem' of a place – hardly more than a white-painted stone cottage – that has been brightening Tadcaster for ten years now. Results of a refurbishment – light mushroom-coloured walls, new tables and 'more comfortable' chairs – have met with approval, but it is the departure of the chefs that is potentially the biggest upheaval. The good news is that early reports on the new team are encouraging. A passion for decent food still emanates from the kitchen, and good relationships with local suppliers ensure consistent quality. Start, perhaps, with a warm tartlet of smoked haddock with wilted spinach and Cheddar rarebit, then on to something like crisp roasted duck breast with fondant potato, blueberry and port sauce, and finish with rhubarb mascarpone cheesecake with strawberries and a coulis. Sound wines, from 'soprano whites' to 'bass reds', form a small international chorus that starts at £10.95 and is modestly priced all through the scale.

CHEFS: Adam Hewitt and John Appleyard PROPRIETOR: Philip Taylor OPEN: Tue to Sat D only 6 to 9.30 CLOSED: 1 week at Christmas MEALS: Set D Tue to Fri 6 to 7 £14.95, Set D Tue to Thur £12.95 (1 course) to £16.95 (2 courses), Set D Tue to Sat £20.95 SERVICE: not inc, card slips closed CARDS: Delta, MasterCard, Switch, Visa DETAILS: 38 seats. Private parties: 38 main room. Vegetarian meals. No smoking. Wheelchair access (not WC). Music. Air conditioning

---

'A bewildering selection of sorbets and ice creams was presented on the table. We asked what flavours were included. "Oh, it changes every day," said the waiter with finality. Strangely, we were more interested in that day's selection than what had been offered, for example, during the 1966 World Cup Final.' (On eating in London)

Gemini ✷

28 Station Approach, Tadworth KT20 5AH   COOKING 3
TEL/FAX: (01737) 812179   MODERN EUROPEAN
WEBSITE: www.gemini-restaurant.com   £33–£63

Behind the hanging sign and the spruce, big-windowed exterior is a long, thin dining room with pale yellowy walls and well-spaced white-clad tables surrounded by comfortable upholstered chairs. The kitchen shows good technical grasp, and first courses can be a high spot, with finely balanced flavourings in a creamy pea, asparagus and pancetta soup coming in for praise, along with a comforting 'Gemini breakfast salad' that included decent black pudding and a perfectly oozing poached egg. A baked cod fillet on mussel, smoked bacon and tomato risotto might be a fishy option among filling main dishes like quail stuffed with basil-flavoured goats' cheese with a cheesy mash and spicy tomato relish, and Tuscan lemon cake with basil sorbet could typify the puddings. Service can be haphazard. A fair selection of wines starts at £12.55, and five are available in two sizes of glass; the short bin-end list could be worth a glance.

CHEF/PROPRIETOR: Robert Foster OPEN: Tue to Fri and Sun L 12 to 2, Tue to Sat D 7 to 9.30 CLOSED: 2 weeks Christmas MEALS: Set L Tue to Fri £11.50 (1 course) to £17.90, Set L Sun £17.95 (1 course) to £20.95, Set D Tue to Fri £25.90 (2 courses) to £34.90, Set D Sat £38.50 SERVICE: not inc CARDS: Amex, Delta, Diners, MasterCard, Switch, Visa DETAILS: 50 seats. 12 seats outside. Private parties: 50 main room. Vegetarian meals. Children's helpings. No children under 12 at D. No smoking. Wheelchair access (not WC). Music (£5)

▲ Cliveden, Waldo's ✷

Taplow SL6 0JF
TEL: (01628) 668561   COOKING 7
WEBSITE: www.clivedenhouse.co.uk   MODERN EUROPEAN
off A4, 2m N of Taplow on Cliveden road   £90–£121

How much grandeur can you take? Cliveden is Berkshire's very own Xanadu, built for the philandering second Duke of Buckingham in the year London was burning down, and crammed with the pick of European fine art when the Astors bought it in the nineteenth century. The notability of past eras, in politics and the arts, have dallied within its portals, and as you sashay up the quarter-mile drive, to be ushered through the glorious public rooms by uniformed footmen, its inherited splendour is hard to resist.

The basement restaurant, Waldo's, is where the main action is. Niggles about the dress code and the occasional over-attentiveness of staff should soon subside with the arrival of Mark Dodson's supremely assured, inspiring food. Dishes that might appear delicate turn out to be full of impact, as was the case with an inspector's puff pastry-lidded copper pan, which concealed a ragoût of lightly cooked lobster in white wine cream spiked with lemongrass. Apple and vanilla are productively combined to dress a serving of smoked salmon, and the sensitive treatment of fish extends into main courses such as potato-scaled fillet of red mullet in a vegetable broth. Menu descriptions are pleasingly unflorid, so that 'loin of lamb with a crown of asparagus, tarragon jus' may barely hint at what is to come. Meanwhile, Aberdeen Angus fillet comes with thick-cut chips and not one but three sauces. A pre-dessert (perhaps strawberries set in champagne jelly) announces the arrival of such richnesses as a duo of cherry crumble and treacle tart served with mascarpone ice cream. Note that a 'donation' to the National Trust is automatically added to the bill. The wine list is a treasure, but only for the prodigiously resourced, with its lashings of Burgundy at sky-high prices, and even Californian Chardonnays ascending into three figures. Wines by the glass are £6.50 to £14.50.

CHEF: Mark Dodson   PROPRIETOR: Von Essen Hotels   OPEN: Tue to Sat D only 7 to 9.30   MEALS: Set D £65 to £75. Cover £4   SERVICE: not inc   CARDS: Amex, Delta, Diners, MasterCard, Switch, Visa   DETAILS: 24 seats. Car park. No children under 12. Jacket and tie. No smoking. Wheelchair access (not WC). Music. No mobile phones. Air-conditioned   ACCOMMODATION: 39 rooms, all with bath/shower. TV. Phone. B&B £225 to £895. Swimming pool

TAUNTON Somerset   map 2

Brazz ⅚ £

Castle Bow, Taunton TA1 1NF   COOKING 1
TEL: (01823) 252000   FAX: (01823) 336066   MODERN BRASSERIE
WEBSITE: www.brazz.co.uk   £25–£53

Brazz is a big, bold and noisy offshoot of the Castle Hotel (see entry below), occupying another part of the same building. Much of the cavernous L-shaped room is given over to the bar area, with its comfortable sofas and long counter. In the smart dining area a brasserie menu takes in everything from calf's liver with bacon, mash and onion gravy to roast skate wing with Mediterranean vegetables and chorizo, or half a kilogramme of moules marinière with chips and mayonnaise. There is also a choice of simple sandwiches and snacks, while desserts tend to be rich and chocolatey. The short wine list keeps prices mostly under £20 and offers a dozen wines by the half-litre, large or small glass. House French is £11.50. There's another Brazz in Exeter (see entry), and, while the Bristol branch has closed, a new one is due to open in the new Cardiff Opera House.

CHEFS: Richard Guest and Simon Beaumont   PROPRIETOR: Castle Hotel (Taunton) Ltd   OPEN: all week 12 to 3, 6 to 10.30 (11 Fri and Sat)   MEALS: alc (main courses £7.50 to £16)   SERVICE: 10% (optional)   CARDS: Amex, Delta, Diners, MasterCard, Switch, Visa   DETAILS: 100 seats. 4 seats outside. Private parties: 120 main room. Car park. Vegetarian meals. Children's helpings. No smoking. Wheelchair access (also WC). Occasional music. Air-conditioned

▲ Castle Hotel ♥ ⅚

Castle Green, Taunton TA1 1NF   COOKING 7
TEL: (01823) 272671   FAX: (01823) 336066   MODERN BRITISH
WEBSITE: www.the.castle.hotel.com   £33–£72

The venerable castellated building can trace its lineage back to Norman times, and when the Victorian wisteria covering its façade is in bloom it is a striking sight. The public rooms are marked by thoroughgoing opulence (just take a gander at the Rose Room cocktail bar), and the dining room is a vision in shimmering crimson, with ornately framed mirrors and works by the much-loved (and local) artist Beryl Cook on show.

A choice of fixed-price and à la carte menus is offered. Organic wheat for the rolls is stone-ground at a water mill near Wells, giving an early indication of the commitment to quality. Presentations can be novel: ballottine of foie gras has a soup of potato and wild garlic poured over it at the table. Risotto of Brixham crab and tomato is redolent of the sea, and is accompanied cleverly by cubes of tomato jelly, which melt into the dish, producing a sharp and refreshing effect. More of the West Country catch informs a main course of sea bass served with baked garlic, cauliflower purée and a chicken jus, the intensely fresh and well-timed fish sitting on an underlay of tender sprouting broccoli. Calf's liver has made a fine main dish, too, teamed with crisp bacon, steamed kale and a light but rich onion purée. Divertingly named desserts have included 'Foolish Rhubarb' and 'Orange! Orange! Orange!', the latter a spectacular assemblage of ice cream, buttery sablé biscuits, segments in Grand Marnier, and a glass of something resembling 'a superior buck's fizz'. The wine list gets under way with a good selection by the glass, including an outstanding range of sherries. The main selection focuses seriously on France, with flashes of brilliance in the short slates from elsewhere. Prices start at £13.50 for a Californian Cabernet Sauvignon.

CHEF: Richard Guest   PROPRIETORS: the Chapman family   OPEN: all week 12.30 to 2.15, 7 to 10   MEALS: alc (main courses £18 to £22.50). Set L and D £12.50 (1 course) to £22.50 (inc wine)   SERVICE: 12.5% (optional), card slips closed   CARDS: Amex, Delta, Diners, MasterCard, Switch, Visa   DETAILS: 70 seats. 30 seats outside. Private parties: 80 main room, 12 to 30 private rooms. Car park. Vegetarian meals. Children's helpings. No smoking. Wheelchair access (also WC). No music. No mobile phones   ACCOMMODATION: 44 rooms, all with bath/shower. TV. Phone. B&B £120 to £200. Rooms for disabled. Baby facilities

Willow Tree 👍✗

3 Tower Lane, Taunton TA1 4AR
TEL: (01823) 352835

COOKING 6
MODERN BRITISH
£33–£58

Though it opened only in September 2002, in a rather ancient white-plastered building just off Tower Street, the Willow Tree has quickly earned a dedicated following. Pastry skills and saucing are especially lauded, as are the 'really beautiful' raw materials. An immense amount of care and skill goes into the likes of pithiviers of confit oxtail and caramelised onion with celeriac purée and red wine jus, or such main courses as seared tuna with Nanjing rice and baked squash filled with sautéed spinach and served with beetroot coulis. Such ideas are innovative, but the underlying skills are rooted in classical technique (chef Darren Sherlock spent over a decade with the Roux brothers).

The two very small (non-smoking) rooms have beamed ceilings and tastefully simple décor. Front-of-house is run by Sherlock's thoroughly capable and knowledgeable partner Rita Rambellas. When she tells you about the pudding (an assiette of lemon, say, consisting of tarte au citron, steamed lemon sponge and organic lemon sorbet), she also tells you the price – and prices here (though up a bit on last year) are very reasonable, especially given the quality. The relatively short wine list, covering all the bases, reflects the restaurant's unpretentious approach; three good sherries are served by the glass, and bottle prices start at £11.95.

CHEF: Darren Sherlock   PROPRIETORS: Darren Sherlock and Rita Rambellas   OPEN: Tue to Sat D only 6.30 to 10   CLOSED: 4 weeks from 25 Dec   MEALS: alc D (main courses £13 to £19)   SERVICE: not inc   CARDS: Delta, MasterCard, Switch, Visa   DETAILS: 25 seats. 12 seats outside. Private parties: 25 main room, 2 to 18 private rooms. Vegetarian meals. No smoking. Wheelchair access (not WC). Music. No mobile phones

Occasional music *in the details at the end of an entry means live or recorded music is played in the dining room only rarely or for special events.* No music *means it is never played.*

TAVISTOCK Devon   map 1

▲ Horn of Plenty ⅙⅞

Gulworthy, Tavistock PL19 8JD
TEL/FAX: (01822) 832528   COOKING **6**
WEBSITE: www.thehornofplenty.co.uk   GLOBAL
3m W of Tavistock on A390, turn right at Gulworthy Cross   £28–£64

This small, creeper-covered, country-house restaurant-with-rooms has all the right
ingredients in the abundance its name suggests. Set in five acres of gardens and orchards
overlooking the Tamar valley, it has bags of 'homely charm', fine bedrooms and a
distinguished kitchen at its very heart. Comfortable, welcoming lounges have fires and
'smart-casual' décor, while the L-shaped dining room sports a conservatory extension to
take full advantage of the wonderful views. There are fresh flowers everywhere, and staff
are appropriately 'professional and friendly, efficient and unfussy'. There's true
'professionalism about the kitchen' also, with Peter Gorton's modern, set-price menus
'full of freshness and flavours', backed by accurate timings, balance and fine attention to
detail from canapés through to petits fours. Roast wild wood pigeon breast with a sweet
potato hash and balsamic dressing could start a lunch, followed by roast tenderloin of pork
with potato rösti and red wine sauce, or 'tender' roast loin of Devonshire lamb with basil-
flavoured mash, wild mushroom salsa and a red wine and garlic froth. Finish, perhaps, with
a light chocolate and hazelnut parfait with crème anglaise. The French-led and influenced
wine list is complemented by a decent New World selection, with a 10-strong house line-
up from £13.50 a bottle.

CHEF: Peter Gorton   PROPRIETORS: Paul Roston and Peter Gorton   OPEN: Tue to Sun L 12 to 2, all week D 7
to 9   CLOSED: 24 to 26 Dec   MEALS: Set L £18.50 to £23.50, Set D £39.50   SERVICE: not inc, 10% for
parties of 10 or more   CARDS: Amex, Delta, MasterCard, Switch, Visa   DETAILS: 60 seats. 15 seats
outside. Private parties: 70 main room, 2 to 15 private rooms. Car park. Vegetarian meals. Children's
helpings. No smoking. Wheelchair access (also WC). Occasional music. No mobile phones
ACCOMMODATION: 10 rooms, all with bath/shower. TV. Phone. B&B £105 to £200. Rooms for disabled.
Baby facilities (£5)

TEDDINGTON Surrey   map 12

Wharf

22 Manor Road, Teddington TW11 8BG   COOKING **2**
TEL: (020) 8977 6333   FAX: (020) 8977 9444   MODERN BRITISH
WEBSITE: www.walk-on-the-water.co.uk   £27–£57

This Thames-side restaurant now has an upstairs private dining room called 'first floor'
and, downstairs in the main dining area, a larger canopied area for al fresco dining. The
relaxed atmosphere and stylish setting carry over into the fish-slanted menu, which cherry-
picks global flavours and ingredients with an emphasis on Asian cooking. So Thai seafood
salad with lime leaves, coriander and pink ginger, might precede chilli-seared salmon with
tom yam noodles and Asian vegetables. Elsewhere, there might be Continental-style
brandade with poached egg and wilted spinach, or, for vegetarians, risotto al funghi with
truffle oil. Carnivores may get a look-in with an assiette of charcuterie, then cumin-crusted
lamb with couscous, and bread-and-butter pudding or chocolate tart with Grand Marnier
crème fraîche might be among the sweets. The wine list, starting at £12.25, has well-
chosen bottles from Old and New Worlds, with 14 by the glass.

CHEF: Nick Marfe   PROPRIETOR: Ray Neve   OPEN: all week 12 to 3.45, 6.30 to 9.45 (9.15 Sun)   MEALS: alc (main courses £9.50 to £18). Set L £13 (2 courses) to £16, Set D £16 (2 courses) to £19   SERVICE: 12.5% (optional), card slips closed   CARDS: Amex, Delta, MasterCard, Switch, Visa   DETAILS: 120 seats. Private parties: 120 main room, 20 to 80 private rooms. Car park. Vegetarian meals. Children's helpings. No-smoking area. Wheelchair access (also WC). Music. Air-conditioned

TEFFONT EVIAS Wiltshire   map 2

▲ Howard's House ⅚✗

Teffont Evias SP3 5RJ
TEL: (01722) 716392   FAX: (01722) 716820
WEBSITE: www.howardshousehotel.co.uk   COOKING 3
off B3089, W of Dinton and 9½m W of Salisbury,   MODERN BRITISH-PLUS
signposted Chicksgrove   £35–£66

If you have socks, prepare them to be charmed off now. Teffont Evias is unreconstructed English countryside, down to the tiny stream and undulating topiary that form the boundary of this seventeenth-century dower house. In a primrose dining room with an eye-catching, gilt-framed mirror, Nick Wentworth's cooking exudes and inspires quiet confidence. Roast wood pigeon on crushed peas with garlic foam was a 'fresh and interesting' starter at inspection, its flavour combinations persuasive. Foaming sauces are a must-do, it seems, as another – composed this time of apples and Calvados – appears in support of braised belly and roast fillet of local pork, the impressive meat almost outshouted by rather solid, mustard-hot mash. Roast halibut with buttered leeks and lemon marmalade is an offbeat fish option, and meals conclude with the likes of rum pannacotta sprinkled with sea-green sugar crystals, served with tiny roast pears and lavender sorbet. Staff are relaxed, friendly and positively happy, and the wines deal exhaustively with France before heading anywhere else. House wines are £13.25 and £16.50.

CHEF: Nick Wentworth   PROPRIETOR: Noele Thompson   OPEN: Tue to Thur and Sat and Sun L 12.30 to 2, all week D 7.30 to 9   CLOSED: 5 days at Christmas   MEALS: alc D (main courses £20 to £23). Set L £18.50 (2 courses) to £22.50, Set D £23.95   SERVICE: not inc   CARDS: Amex, Delta, MasterCard, Switch, Visa   DETAILS: 30 seats. 12 seats outside. Private parties: 40 main room. Car park. Children's helpings. No smoking. Wheelchair access (not WC). No music. No mobile phones   ACCOMMODATION: 9 rooms, all with bath/shower. TV. Phone. B&B £95 to £165. Baby facilities

TETBURY Gloucestershire   map 2

▲ Close Hotel ⅚✗   NEW ENTRY

Long Street, Tetbury GL8 8AQ   COOKING 4
TEL: (01666) 502272   FAX: (01666) 504401   MODERN BRITISH
WEBSITE: www.theclose-hotel.com   £32–£72

This relaxed, laid-back family-run hotel makes pleasing first impressions. Tables in the smart dining room are set with quality china, green candles in silver holders, and flowers, and service is knowledgeable, pleasant and enthusiastic. The cooking doesn't let the side down. The carte offers five well-balanced choices per course, the style leaning towards classic French but with a few fashionably exotic touches. To start, ravioli of blue cheese with braised celery and walnut vinaigrette shows skill in the preparation and provides plenty of flavour in the eating, while herb-crusted cod features impeccably fresh fish carefully cooked and served on a bed of sunblush tomatoes with chervil. To follow, fillet of beef has been well received, the pink, tender meat topped with a slice of flash-fried foie gras and accompanied by a pair of flavoursome faggots of the blade and a creamy mushroom and tarragon fricassee. Desserts extend to rhubarb crumble soufflé with rhubarb and custard ice and strawberry and rhubarb compote. House wines start at £16.50, with half a dozen served by the glass.

CHEF: Ellery Powell PROPRIETOR: Greene King OPEN: all week 12 to 2, 7 to 9.30 MEALS: alc D (main courses £24.50). Set L £17.50, Set D £28.50 SERVICE: not inc, card slips closed CARDS: Amex, Delta, Diners, MasterCard, Switch, Visa DETAILS: 40 seats. 20 seats outside. Private parties: 20 main room, 10 to 20 private rooms. Car park. Vegetarian meals. No smoking. Occasional music. No mobile phones ACCOMMODATION: 15 rooms, all with bath/shower. TV. Phone. B&B £100 to £160

Trouble House 🍴✹

Cirencester Road, Tetbury GL8 8SG
TEL: (01666) 502206   FAX: (01666) 504508
WEBSITE: www.troublehouse.co.uk
on A433 1½m NE of Tetbury

COOKING 5
MODERN EUROPEAN
£31–£56

A historical run of bad luck gave this rural seventeenth-century inn its name, but that was long ago, and now it is a peaceful spot. Sympathetic refurbishment makes the most of the traditional features of the three public rooms, including log fires and low-beamed ceilings, yet adds touches of sophistication, with sofas in the bar area and newspapers and magazines provided. The feel is relaxed and unpretentious, though; diners happily share the space with drinkers, and, this being a proper pub at heart, food is ordered at the bar. Menus are a sensible length and keep things simple without thereby sacrificing interest, focusing on showing off the good raw materials. Start with crab linguini with olive oil and Parmesan, hot-smoked sea trout with sun-dried tomatoes, or a salad of duck breast and beetroot, before moving on to pork tenderloin with prunes and plums, jugged hare with swede mash, or perhaps pan-fried red mullet with linguini and baked peppers. To finish, the fine cheeseboard is a tempting alternative to pink grapefruit terrine, or rich dark chocolate muffins. Wines are an attractive mixture of bottles from France and the New World, with prices starting at £12.25.

CHEF: Michael Bedford PROPRIETORS: Michael and Sarah Bedford OPEN: Tue to Sun L 12 to 2, Tue to Sat D 7 to 9.30 (also 1 May to 31 Sept Sun D 7 to 9) CLOSED: 25 Dec to 4 Jan MEALS: alc (main courses £12 to £16) SERVICE: not inc, 10% for parties of 10 or more CARDS: Amex, Delta, MasterCard, Switch, Visa DETAILS: 50 seats. 24 seats outside. Car park. Vegetarian meals. Children's helpings. No children under 14 in bar. No smoking in 1 dining room. Wheelchair access (not WC). Music

TETSWORTH Oxfordshire   map 2

Swan at Tetsworth

High Street, Tetsworth OX9 7AB
TEL: (01844) 281182   FAX: (01844) 281770
WEBSITE: www.theswan.co.uk/restaurant.htm

COOKING 4
MODERN EUROPEAN
£32–£53

Forty showrooms of antiques under one roof attract visitors to this listed Elizabethan coaching inn, which is one of those ancient buildings that looks remarkably modern for its age. Browsing antiques, combined with reading the papers and enjoying a good lunch, is 'a great prospect', according to one couple who spent a lazy Sunday meandering through the place and dining amid period paintings and antique furniture in the atmospheric wood-floored restaurant. Sunday lunch may be traditional, but at other times the kitchen draws on modern European and home-grown ideas, from open ravioli of king prawns and mussels, or pan-fried salmon with baby leeks and tapenade, to mushroom and tarragon soup and ribeye steak with parsnip and horseradish purée. Waiters announce the list of puddings, which might include chocolate truffle cake; otherwise there's a selection of English cheeses. A blackboard over the bar advertises four house wines at £12.75, and the full list runs to around 50 keenly priced bins organised by style.

CHEF: Naseem Salam PROPRIETOR: Swan Holdings Ltd OPEN: all week L 12 to 2.15 (3.30 Sun), Tue to Sat D 7 to 9.15 (9.45 Sat) CLOSED: 25 and 26 Dec MEALS: alc (main courses £10.50 to £17) SERVICE: not inc; 10% for parties over 10 CARDS: Delta, MasterCard, Switch, Visa DETAILS: 55 seats. 20 seats outside. Private parties: 55 main room, 8 to 14 private rooms. Car park. Children's helpings. No-smoking area. Wheelchair access (not WC). Music (£5)

THORNBURY South Gloucestershire — **map 2**

▲ Thornbury Castle

Castle Street, Thornbury BS35 1HH
TEL: (01454) 281182 FAX: (01454) 416188
WEBSITE: www.thornburycastle.co.uk
off B4061, at N end of town

NEW CHEF
MODERN EUROPEAN
£39–£73

Thornbury Castle was built in 1551 and embraces the baronial feel enthusiastically, with open fires, panelling, tapestries and suits of armour. It feels sophisticated and moneyed. Chef Nick Evans departed and was replaced by Steven Rimmer as the Guide was going to press, although the menu looks set to remain much the same. First-class ingredients, imaginative presentation and sound cooking skills are to be expected, whether in a starter of sautéed Isle of Skye scallops accompanied by cauliflower purée, black pudding and chicken juices, main courses such as roast cannon of local lamb with veal sweetbreads, ratatouille and aubergine caviar, and a dessert of elderflower jelly with raspberry compote and raspberry sorbet. House wines start at £18 and include Thornbury Castle Müller-Thurgau.

CHEF: Steven Rimmer PROPRIETOR: Von Essen Hotels OPEN: all week 12 to 2, 7 to 9.30 (10 Fri and Sat) MEALS: Set L £22.50, Set D £42.50 SERVICE: not inc CARDS: Amex, Delta, Diners, MasterCard, Switch, Visa DETAILS: 46 seats. Private parties: 30 main room. Car park. Children's helpings. No smoking. Wheelchair access (also WC). Music. No mobile phones ACCOMMODATION: 25 rooms, all with bath/shower. TV. Phone. B&B £80 to £370

TITLEY Herefordshire — **map 5**

▲ Stagg Inn

Titley, Nr Kington HR5 3RL
TEL: (01544) 230221 FAX: (01544) 231390
WEBSITE: www.thestagg.co.uk

COOKING **5**
MODERN BRITISH
£23–£52

The Stagg, with its pale yellow brick frontage, sits cheerfully at the foot of a slope. Inside are more autumnal colours, log fires and a bread oven evoking a sense of bygone times, and front-of-house runs with warm enthusiasm under Nicola Reynolds. Fine local suppliers send such ingredients as free-range veal, wild hare, fruit and vegetables to the kitchen, where they receive due respect. A pair staying here in summer found much to write home about, including crab cake with avocado salad, powerfully impressive artichoke soup with white truffle, and a dessert – passion-fruit jelly with a sabayon – so exquisite that the recipe was sought (and happily given). Another diner's seared scallops were boldly dressed in black pepper oil and teamed with parsnip purée, and skill in sourcing local supplies has shown in 'excellent, full-flavoured' roast organic pork, served at Sunday lunch with a textbook chunky apple sauce. Ice creams like hazelnut or blackberry score high for flavour and texture, and cinnamon-spiked bread-and-butter pudding, crammed with dried fruit, was dubbed 'a schoolboy's delight'. The wine list offers stress-free choice: enjoyable drinking at fair prices from £11.90, nothing unaffordably grand, some useful food-matching hints and ten (plus five sweeties) by the glass.

CHEF: Steve Reynolds   PROPRIETORS: Steve and Nicola Reynolds   OPEN: Tue to Sun L 12 to 2, Tue to Sat D 6.30 to 10   CLOSED: first 2 weeks Nov, 25 and 26 Dec, 1 Jan, 1 week Feb, Tue after bank hols   MEALS: alc exc Sun L (main courses £12.50 to £17). Set L Sun £13.50. Bar snack menu available exc Fri/Sat D and Sun L   SERVICE: not inc, card slips closed   CARDS: Delta, MasterCard, Switch, Visa   DETAILS: 50 seats. 12 seats outside. Private parties: 28 main room. Car park. Children's helpings. No smoking. No music ACCOMMODATION: 4 rooms, all with bath/shower. TV. B&B £50 to £90

TODMORDEN West Yorkshire
map 8

Old Hall 🍴

Hall Street, Todmorden OL14 7AD
TEL: (01706) 815998   FAX: (01706) 810669

COOKING 2
MODERN BRITISH
£24–£55

Todmorden's historical Old Hall has just the right blend of comforting, manor-house antiquity and stylish contemporary features: no wonder it's popular with wedding parties. The kitchen's honest approach and lack of trickery are also greatly appreciated by reporters. Straightforward lunch dishes like leek and Gruyère tart have been cooked to a turn, and the evening menu follows suit. Local ingredients pop up everywhere, from a warm salad of Bury black pudding with chorizo and caramelised apple to poached Goosnargh chicken breast with crispy bacon and a cabbage and shiitake broth – not forgetting seasonal game and weekend fish specials. To finish, Yorkshire parkin with ginger sauce and rhubarb ice cream neatly fits the north-country bill. Service receives fulsome praise – likewise the knowledgeably assembled wine list, which holds some 'real crackers' at competitive prices. Six house recommendations start at £10.95.

CHEF: Chris Roberts   PROPRIETORS: Nick and Madeleine Hoyle   OPEN: Tue to Sun L 12 to 2 (2.30 Sun), Tue to Sat D 7 to 9 (9.30 Sat)   CLOSED: 25 and 26 Dec, first week Jan, day after bank hols   MEALS: alc (main courses £11 to £16.50). Set L Tue to Sat £8.50 (2 courses), Set L Sun £11.95 (2 courses) to £14.95 SERVICE: not inc, card slips closed   CARDS: Delta, Diners, MasterCard, Switch, Visa   DETAILS: 70 seats. 20 seats outside. Private parties: 60 main room, 8 to 24 private rooms. Vegetarian meals. Children's helpings. No smoking. Music. No mobile phones

TOPSHAM Devon
map 1

La Petite Maison 🍴
NEW ENTRY

35 Fore Street, Topsham EX3 0HR
TEL/FAX: (01392) 873660
WEBSITE: www.lapetitemaison.co.uk

COOKING 4
MODERN BRITISH
£32–£45

Aptly named, the two dining rooms in this elderly white-stuccoed building are indeed small, with a bow window and unusual curvature of the main room bringing character to the space. The greeting from Mrs Pestell instantly warmed one visitor arriving on a bitter night. Much importance is given to local produce, and West Country names pepper the menu: Lyme Bay crab in a tian with ginger and coriander, for example, or 'full of flavour' Exmoor lamb in a main course with parsnip and potato mash, ratatouille and a red wine and rosemary jus. A starter of juicy chicken livers came cooked rare, complemented by an agreeable balsamic dressing, while a 'sensational' crab galette was encased in perfect puff pastry and accompanied by a delicate thermidor sauce. A main course of breast of guinea fowl was partnered by 'delicious' leg confit and Parmesan, herb and saffron risotto. Bread and ice creams are made on the premises. Puddings such as tarte Tatin and pear poached in red wine and cinnamon maintain the momentum. Prices are far from greedy, and service is amiable and efficient. The good-value wine list features a few bottles from Devon vineyards. House wines, a Sauvignon Blanc and a Cabernet Sauvignon from France, are £11.95.

CHEFS: Douglas and Naomi Pestell PROPRIETORS: Douglas and Elizabeth Pestell OPEN: Tue to Sat D only 7 to 10. L bookings only Apr to Sept, Oct to Mar MEALS: Set L £16.95 (2 courses) to £20.95, Set D £22.95 (2 courses) to £27.95 SERVICE: not inc CARDS: Delta, MasterCard, Switch, Visa DETAILS: 30 seats. Private parties: 26 main room. Vegetarian meals. No smoking. Music £5

TORQUAY Devon

map 1

No 7 Fish Bistro £

7 Beacon Terrace, Torquay TQ1 2BH	COOKING 1
TEL: (01803) 295055	SEAFOOD
WEBSITE: www.no7-fish.com	£27–£50

Graham and Jill Stacey's set-up has 'no pretensions other than to be a first-class family-run fish bistro' – although it also exudes a touch of 'smart, simple seaside chic'. Supplies come mainly from Brixham, and the emphasis is on daily specials: you may even get to meet the fish you have chosen. One of the regular stars is an assortment of monkfish, cod *et al* coated in tempura batter; otherwise you might find queenie scallops, grilled Dover sole, and Star Point crab plus a few more showy ideas like whole sea bass roasted with olive oil, herbs and garlic. The 'excellent value' extends to the wine list, which includes a decent range of house wines from £10.

CHEFS: Oliver and Paul Stacey PROPRIETORS: Graham and Jill Stacey OPEN: Wed to Sat L 12.15 to 1.45, Tue to Sat D 7 to 9.45 (6 to 10.15 summer); also open Mon D June and Oct, Sun and Mon D July to Sept CLOSED: 1 week Nov, Christmas and New Year, 2 weeks Feb MEALS: alc (main courses £10 to £17.50) SERVICE: not inc CARDS: Amex, Delta, MasterCard, Switch, Visa DETAILS: 38 seats. Private parties: 20 main room. Vegetarian meals. Children's helpings. Wheelchair access (not WC). Music. No mobile phones. Air-conditioned £5

TOTNES Devon

map 1

Effings ⁵⚡

50 Fore Street, Totnes TQ9 5RP	COOKING 4
TEL: (01803) 863435 FAX: (01803) 863505	MODERN EUROPEAN
EMAIL: info@effings.co.uk	£30–£57

Just five pine tables at the back of a delicatessen – an 'Aladdin's cave of delights' – prove a top draw for Totnes's food lovers. It's a hybrid emporium run with 'panache and devotion to excellence', offering a whole range of home-made vacuum-packed meals to take away alongside pâtés, terrines, savoury and sweet tarts, and ice creams and sorbets. The tables are used throughout the day for light dishes and snacks, but at lunchtime they're upgraded with blue cloths, and the daily-changing menu gets chalked on a blackboard. Nigel Marriage has moved on to the New Angel (see entry, Dartmouth), and Karl Rasmussen has been joined in the kitchen by Karen Miller. They make the best use of the abundant local larder, with fresh, good-quality produce a hallmark of the compact menu (a choice of three starters and main courses and one dessert). Start with a soup – cream of local cauliflower, perhaps, with white truffle oil, morels and chives – followed by main courses of corn pancakes with pan-fried foie gras and roast pears in an apple and chive reduction, or roast loin of local pork glazed with thyme and Torquay honey served with baked plums. Quality extends to the tiny wine list, where two house wines are £13.75 (£3.75 a glass), while service is 'warm, friendly and efficient'.

CHEFS: Karl Rasmussen and Karen Miller   PROPRIETORS: Jacqueline Williams and Michael Kann   OPEN: Mon to Sat L only 12 to 2.15   CLOSED: bank hols   MEALS: alc (main courses £11 to £24). Light menu available 9.30 to 12, 2.30 to 5   SERVICE: net prices, card slips closed   CARDS: Delta, MasterCard, Switch, Visa   DETAILS: 14 seats. Private parties: 14 main room. Children's helpings. No smoking. Wheelchair access (also WC). No music. No mobile phones. Air-conditioned

Wills Restaurant ✶✗

3 The Plains, Totnes TQ9 5RY

NEW CHEF

TEL: (0800) 056 3006   FAX: (01803) 864682   MODERN EUROPEAN
WEBSITE: www.eiaddio.com   £39–£66

Egyptologist and explorer William Wills was born in this Regency town house, and its current incumbents have filled the place with an amazing collection of wacky and ethnic artefacts. A new chef arrived in July 2004, so reports please. Local ingredients, free-range meat and organic fruit and vegetables show up on their dinner menu, which might open with clams and mussels served with linguini in a garlic, olive oil and chilli sauce, followed by a confit of duck legs with savoy cabbage, pancetta and a caramelised bittersweet sauce, or pan-fried halibut with a mussel and samphire sauce. For dessert, there's perhaps dark chocolate fondant with white chocolate ice cream. Representatives from the Sharpham vineyard add a touch of local colour to the global wine list. House French is £12.50. Bistro-style food is available in the adjoining café.

CHEFS: Tom Cook and Craig Purkiss   PROPRIETORS: Philip Silvester and Jenny Priest   OPEN: Tue to Sat D only 7 to 9.30   MEALS: alc (main courses £15 to £22). Café L and D menu available   SERVICE: not inc CARDS: Amex, Delta, MasterCard, Switch, Visa   DETAILS: 28 seats. Private parties: 24 main room, 6 to 14 private rooms. Vegetarian meals. Children's helpings. No smoking. Wheelchair access (also WC). Music £5

TRURO Cornwall   map 1

Café Citron ✶✗ £

76 Lemon Street, Truro TR1 2PN   COOKING 3
TEL: (01872) 274144   FAX: (01872) 274145   MODERN EUROPEAN
WEBSITE: www.cafecitron.co.uk   £21–£44

Until recently this bright blue-fronted brasserie was the more informal half of a dual enterprise that included Sevens restaurant, listed in last year's Guide, next door. Sevens has now closed, although the premises are used as an overflow when the place gets busy (which is often). Gavin Young takes a flexible approach to feeding the crowds, serving tapas-style dishes all day (roast chorizo and potato, and fried squid with smoked paprika, for example), plus full lunch and dinner menus and daily specials, mostly fish, listed on a blackboard. The cooking aims for a broad appeal, with main courses at dinner ranging from slow-cooked lamb shank with basil-crushed potatoes and rosemary sauce to baked monkfish with marinated Mediterranean vegetables and warm fennel cream. Lunch is slightly simpler – perhaps fishcakes with tomato beurre blanc – and desserts include warm chocolate pudding with orange ice cream. Prices on the modest wine list start at £9.50. There are Citron Vite deli/patisseries in Truro, Falmouth and Penzance (take-away only).

CHEF: Gavin Young   PROPRIETORS: David and Jane White   OPEN: Mon to Sat 12 to 3, 6 to 9.30 (10 Fri and Sat)   CLOSED: 25 Dec, 1 Jan   MEALS: alc (main courses L £6 to £7, D £11 to £16.50)   SERVICE: not inc, card slips closed   CARDS: Delta, MasterCard, Switch, Visa   DETAILS: 120 seats. Private parties: 90 main room, 15 to 40 private rooms. Vegetarian meals. Children's helpings. No smoking in restaurant, permitted in bar. Wheelchair access (also WC). Music

---

TUNBRIDGE WELLS Kent   map 3

▲ Hotel du Vin & Bistro ▮ ✳

Crescent Road, Tunbridge Wells TN1 2LY | NEW CHEF |
TEL: (01892) 526455   FAX: (01892) 512044   MODERN EUROPEAN
WEBSITE: www.hotelduvin.com   £33–£63

This branch of the Hotel du Vin & Bistro mini chain (see entries in Birmingham, Brighton, Bristol, Harrogate and Winchester) seems to have settled into an easy familiarity within its surroundings – and when a place works this well, that's no bad thing. There is a new chef, but things continue unabated; menus are of a manageable size, with straightforward descriptions. There are few surprises in terms of combinations: a plate of Serrano ham for a starter, for example, is served with rémoulade, while a meaty main course of braised shin of beef might be teamed with saffron risotto and salsa verde. Meat-free dishes such as pithiviers of potato, cream and garlic or pipérade go beyond paying mere lip service to vegetarians. A 'simple classics' section lists the likes of cassoulet de Toulouse and kedgeree. Service has been described as 'a smooth machine, but with character and individual attention to detail'. Wine, inevitably (given the name), is another important cog in the well-oiled machine, with pages of French classics, a good range from Austria, all the trendiest names in Spain, and much more. Prices start at £12.50 and around ten come by the glass, but value for money is variable.

CHEF: Matt Green-Armytage   PROPRIETOR: Hotel du Vin Ltd   OPEN: all week 12 to 1.45, 7 to 9.45   CLOSED: L 31 Dec   MEALS: alc (main courses £10.50 to £18). Set L Sun £23.50   SERVICE: not inc   CARDS: Amex, Delta, Diners, MasterCard, Switch, Visa   DETAILS: 80 seats. 44 seats outside. Private parties: 84 main room. Car park. Vegetarian meals. Children's helpings. No smoking. Wheelchair access (also WC). No music   ACCOMMODATION: 35 rooms, all with bath/shower. TV. Phone. Room only £89 to £250. Baby facilities

---

Thackeray's ✳

85 London Road, Tunbridge Wells TN1 1EA   COOKING 6
TEL: (01892) 511921   FAX: (01892) 527561   MODERN FRENCH
WEBSITE: www.thackeraysrestaurant.co.uk   £26–£83

This white-painted Georgian-style house on Tunbridge Wells Common (floodlit at night), once the home of the novelist, is a 'professional, slick restaurant'. 'Coolly elegant',

ENGLAND

its contemporary tones of beige, grey and cream are paired with original oak floorboards, modern paintings, brown suede banquettes and white linen cloths. Richard Phillips has a Marco Pierre White pedigree and brings a cosmopolitan edge to proceedings. His is a serious kitchen, menus are imaginative and a 'delight to read', dishes are attractively presented, and ingredients are impeccably sourced. Service is 'well rehearsed' and knowledgeable, with a touch of theatre delivered by staff pouring sauces at table, as seen with a Sauternes sauce added to a starter of hay-smoked veal sweetbreads wrapped in Parma ham with braised leeks, or raspberry coulis poured in to the centre of a perfect raspberry soufflé with a matching sorbet. In between might come 'fresh, firm, creamy' wedges of roast John Dory with truffle and mushroom risotto and Jerusalem artichoke velouté, or marinated pork cooked three ways (braised, roasted and confit) with 'wonderful' black pudding and a grain mustard and apple sauce. The well-chosen wine list fits the bill, with around half a dozen offered by the glass and a 13-bottle 'Thackeray's Selection' from £12.95 to £24.75.

CHEF: Richard Phillips   PROPRIETORS: Richard Phillips and Paul Smith   OPEN: Tue to Sun L 12 to 2.30, Tue to Sat D 6.30 to 10.30   MEALS: alc exc Sun L (main courses £16 to £23.50). Set L Tue to Sat £12.95 (2 courses) to £13.95, Set L Sun £24.50, Set D £55   SERVICE: 12.5% (optional)   CARDS: Amex, Delta, Diners, MasterCard, Switch, Visa   DETAILS: 54 seats. 30 seats outside. Private parties: 54 main room, 6 to 16 private rooms. Vegetarian meals. Children's helpings. No smoking in 1 dining room. Wheelchair access (not WC). Music. Air-conditioned

TWICKENHAM Greater London   map 3

A Cena

418 Richmond Road, Twickenham TW1 2EB   COOKING 2
TEL/FAX: (020) 8288 0108   ITALIAN
                                                                                                       £22–£54

Just over the bridge on the road out of Richmond, this handy neighbourhood restaurant hides behind a discreet frontage with only its name to mark the spot. The casual setting of bare boards, gilt mirrors and wooden church chairs suggests elegance on a budget, and the food is genuine Italian with a few imaginative touches. The well-balanced, daily menus keep one eye on the calendar, with specialities like asparagus with a fried egg and prosciutto, marinated lobster with chilli and lemon spaghetti, and marinated veal cutlet with slow-cooked fennel and cherry tomatoes, plus desserts such as pannacotta with raspberries. Affordable fixed-price lunches involve, say, milk-braised pork with sage and olive oil mash. Start with an invigorating aperitif like rhubarb schnapps and check out the grappas and digestifs to finish. In between, pick from a good spread of Italian wines starting at £12.50, with seven by the glass.

CHEF: Nicola Parsons   PROPRIETORS: Tim and Camilla Healy   OPEN: Tue to Sun L 12 to 2.30, Tue to Sat D 7 to 10.30   CLOSED: 25 and 26 Dec, last 2 weeks Aug   MEALS: alc exc Sun L (main courses £13 to £18). Set L Tue to Sat £10 (2 courses) to £12, Set L Sun £12 (2 courses) to £15   SERVICE: not inc   CARDS: Amex, Delta, MasterCard, Switch, Visa   DETAILS: 55 seats. Vegetarian meals. Children's helpings. No cigars/pipes. Wheelchair access (not WC). Music. Air-conditioned

---

The cuisine styles noted at the tops of entries are only an approximation, often suggested to us by the restaurants themselves. Please read the entry itself to find out more about the cooking style.

Brula

43 Crown Road, St Margaret's, Twickenham TW1 3EJ
TEL: (020) 8892 0602   FAX: (020) 8892 7727
WEBSITE: www.brulabistrot.com

COOKING 2
FRENCH
£21–£51

Rated highly for service and informality as well as for its food, this stylish, unpretentious neighbourhood restaurant knows its market and 'serves that market supremely well', offering 'value for money that is very hard to beat'. This is the place for some old-style French dishes, whether snails provençale, pork and veal terrine, or onglet steak and chips. Those who yearn for more modern food can choose the likes of a salad of Jersey Royals and spring onions with smoked haddock rillettes and crisp bacon, roast fillet of lemon sole with endive and citrus crème fraîche, and vanilla parfait with warm cherry compote. House vins de pays are £11.

CHEF: Bruce Duckett   PROPRIETORS: Lawrence Hartley and Bruce Duckett   OPEN: all week 12.30 to 2.30, 7 to 10.30   CLOSED: 24 to 26 Dec, 1 Jan   MEALS: alc (main courses £9.50 to £14). Set L £10 (2 courses) to £12   SERVICE: not inc   CARDS: Delta, MasterCard, Switch, Visa   DETAILS: 40 seats. 6 seats outside. Private parties: 40 main room, 10 private room. Vegetarian meals. No cigars/pipes. Wheelchair access (not WC). No music

McClements 🍷 🕮 ✂

2 Whitton Road, Twickenham TW1 1BJ
TEL: (020) 8744 9610   FAX: (020) 8744 9598

COOKING 6
FRENCH
£32–£87

A curved parade of shops on the road between station and rugby ground houses John McClements' two restaurants (see also Ma Cuisine, below). At this one, the flagship, the interior has been spruced up, though retaining a cream-and-beige suburban feel, and Daniel Woodhouse arrived in January 2004 from the kitchens at Tom Aikens (see entry, London). A strategic rethink has eliminated multifarious intermediate extras, lowered prices (except for the tasting menu) and returned emphasis to the quality of the main menu dishes. These can be stunning: a brilliantly light raviolo of lobster, boldly accompanied by black pudding and a smear of apple sauce, or a partnership of plump, crisp langoustines with pieces of pork belly, chicken wing and tiny, tasty leaves of watercress. Accompaniments don't always live up to main ingredients – rather bland butter beans came with superb roast loin of veal – but there is plenty that pleases in fillet of turbot with confit turnips and salsify, or braised pig's head with pickled vegetables and a salt and vinegar crisp. Crisps crop up later too: chocolate ones with cakey-textured dark chocolate mousse, or an apple version with a roast apple. Formal, professional service impresses. Many bottles on the wine list are pitched at big spenders, but close scrutiny reveals numerous interesting options under and around £20 from less mainstream regions. A good range by the glass starts at £5.

CHEF: Daniel Woodhouse   PROPRIETOR: John McClements   OPEN: Tue to Sat 12 to 2.30, 7 to 10 (10.30 Fri and Sat)   MEALS: Set L Tue to Fri £18, Set L Sat £29.50, Set D £29.50 to £55   SERVICE: 10% (optional), card slips closed   CARDS: Amex, Delta, Diners, MasterCard, Switch, Visa   DETAILS: 45 seats. Vegetarian meals. Children's helpings. No smoking. Wheelchair access (not WC). Music. Air-conditioned

Ma Cuisine £

6 Whitton Road, Twickenham TW1 1BJ
TEL: (020) 8607 9849

COOKING 3
FRENCH REGIONAL
£22–£40

As the name might indicate, this is an 'uncompromisingly authentic' French bistro, with a black and white marble floor and gingham-patterned coverings on the tightly packed tables, serving appealing cuisine bourgeoise. The fact that it is in Twickenham and the owner is John McClements (see preceding entry) is by the by. Home-made boudin noir is finely textured and gently spiced ('a sausage of sophistication and distinction'), while skate rillettes comes as a cuboid assemblage of shredded fish and olive oil. If the dishes are of bourgeois origins, they have nonetheless been through finishing school, as witness the discreet bed of choucroute underlying sticky-sweet, slow-cooked belly pork. Classic veal schnitzel has been 'crisp and succulent', and main courses are fully garnished (dauphinois potato has lashings of garlic). Tarte Tatin is a sound version, and there is also chocolate pot with coffee cream, or strawberries in peppered vodka cream. Good service, along with a short, largely French wine list with house wines at £11.50 (white) and £12.50 (red), completes the picture.

CHEF/PROPRIETOR: John McClements   OPEN: all week L 12 to 2.30, Mon to Sat D 7 to 10.30   MEALS: alc (main courses £9 to £13.50). Set L Mon to Fri £12   SERVICE: 10% (optional), card slips closed   CARDS: Delta, MasterCard, Switch, Visa   DETAILS: 60 seats. 12 seats outside. Private parties: 30 main room. Vegetarian meals. Children's helpings. Wheelchair access (also women's WC). Music. No mobile phones. Air-conditioned

TYNEMOUTH Tyne & Wear

map 10

Sidney's ⅝✳ £

3–5 Percy Park Road, Tynemouth NE30 4XN
TEL: (0191) 257 8500   FAX: (0191) 257 9800
WEBSITE: www.sidneys.co.uk

COOKING 3
MODERN BRITISH-PLUS
£20–£48

Sidney's lies downriver from the rush of Newcastle, home to its sister, the Blackfriars Café Bar (see entry). Bright décor, helpful and relaxed service and simple but well-judged cooking all create a fresh, modern feel. Sourcing is taken seriously: a properly hung steak accompanied by sausage and seared calf's liver, or cod served tandoori-style with saffron pilaf typify the marrying of local ingredients with carefully controlled flavourings. Basics like apple crumble or silky crème brûlée are on the lunch and early evening set menus, while specials and the main menu bring more complex and original combinations like poached saffron pear with cranberry and lime mousse. Around 25 wines range from £11 to £25, and food/wine pairings for main-menu dishes are helpfully suggested.

CHEF: Samantha Mowbray   PROPRIETORS: Andy and Sam Hook   OPEN: Mon to Sat 12 to 2.30, 6 to 10   CLOSED: bank hols exc Good Friday   MEALS: alc (main courses £10.50 to £17). Set L £7 (1 course, Mon to Fri) to £10.95, Set D 6 to 7 Mon to Fri £9.95 (2 courses) to £12.95   SERVICE: not inc, 10% for parties of 6 or more   CARDS: Amex, Delta, MasterCard, Switch, Visa   DETAILS: 50 seats. Private parties: 30 main room, 10 to 22 private rooms. Vegetarian meals. Children's helpings. No smoking. Music. Air-conditioned £5

Three Crowns

Bleak Acre, Ullingswick HR1 3JQ
TEL: (01432) 820279   FAX: (08700) 515338
WEBSITE: www.threecrownsinn.com
from A417 turn E (signposted Ullingswick), then straight
on through village for 1½m

COOKING **4**
MODERN BRITISH
£24–£45

Feel your way through tortuous Herefordshire lanes to Brent Castle's self-described 'rustic, wobbly, red-brick-and-beamed country pub'. The well-balanced menu has a user-friendly structure (starters are all one price, mains another, and desserts a third), and there's plenty to keep the palate alert. Openers generally feature a soufflé (Little Hereford cheese and spinach, for example) along with, say, warm asparagus and Jersey Royal salad with a fried duck egg, while main courses bring into play marinated rump of Cornish lamb (with a kidney kebab, braised lettuce, peas and soft garlic sauce) as well as baked cod with crab and Parmesan crust, confit tomatoes, ratatouille and saffron mash. To conclude, choose between English cheeses and Continental desserts like Muscat crème caramel with Armagnac and Agen prunes. Fixed-price lunches tread a plain-and-simple path, and a blackboard of pricier 'specials' tops up the Italian-accented list of around 30 creditable wines, which includes six house selections from £13.75.

CHEFS: Brent Castle, Jon Howe and Dan Cross   PROPRIETOR: Brent Castle   OPEN: Tue to Sun L 12 to 2.30, Tue to Sat D (all week April to Oct) 7 to 9.30   CLOSED: 2 weeks from 25 Dec   MEALS: alc (main courses £14.50). Set L £10.95 (2 courses) to £12.95   SERVICE: not inc, card slips closed   CARDS: MasterCard, Switch, Visa   DETAILS: 45 seats. 24 seats outside. Private parties: 45 main room. Car park. Vegetarian meals. Children's helpings. No cigars/pipes. Wheelchair access (also WC). No music (£5)

▲ Sharrow Bay 🍸 ⭐

Ullswater CA10 2LZ
TEL: (01768) 486301   FAX: (01768) 486349
WEBSITE: www.sharrow-bay.com
2m from Pooley Bridge on E side of lake, on road
signposted Howtown and Martindale.

COOKING **6**
ENGLISH
£51–£77

Everywhere at Sharrow Bay feels as comfortable and opulent as can be, not least the dining room, which has ormolu finishings, swagged curtains and a splendid view of the lake ('birds cavort, yachts tack, steamboats ply, and in the distance, Helvellyn broods'). In the five-course lunches and six-course dinners (which still include a mid-meal sorbet) the commitment to excellence is unwavering. Soufflé suissesse is a crusty-domed magnificence concealing spinach and onion, the forthright flavour of Stilton aided and abetted by Parmesan. Crab and scallops form an eggy galette topped with asparagus and sauced with creamy Martini and lemon, and meats are of formidable quality. Pork has come as the tenderloin and slow-roasted belly, along with braised red cabbage and black pudding, while slow cooking also made a triumph out of lamb shoulder, served with a soft raviolo of the sweetbreads in a rosemary- and thyme-infused reduction. Steamed syrup sponge is 'as wartime plain as can be' (though the custard bristled with vanilla seeds), or there might be chocolate and pecan tart. Cumulatively, it is all very rich, but most people reckon it's worth girding the loins for.

The wine list comes up trumps whether you are seeking good value or untrammelled extravagance, which is a fair tribute to the scale of the cellar and the integrity of pricing. All the classics are there, including good ranges from the Loire and Alsace, alongside fashionable bottles such as L'Ecole No. 41 Semillon from Washington (£24). Prices start at £16.95, and 16 come by the glass.

CHEFS: Colin Akrigg and Johnnie Martin   PROPRIETOR: Von Essen Hotels   OPEN: all week 1 to 1.30, 8 to 8.30   MEALS: Set L £38.25, Set D £49.25   SERVICE: not inc, card slips closed   CARDS: Amex, Delta, MasterCard, Switch, Visa   DETAILS: 60 seats. Private parties: 35 main room. Car park. Vegetarian meals. No children under 13. Jacket and tie. No smoking. Wheelchair access (also WC). No music. No mobile phones. Air-conditioned   ACCOMMODATION: 25 rooms, 21 with bath/shower. TV. Phone. D,B&B £150 to £235. Rooms for disabled. No children under 13

ULVERSTON Cumbria
map 8

▲ Bay Horse ✸

Canal Foot, Ulverston LA12 9EL
TEL: (01229) 583972   FAX: (01229) 580502
WEBSITE: www.thebayhorsehotel.co.uk
from A590 turn SE at N edge of Ulverston and follow
signs to Canal Foot

COOKING 4
COUNTRY-HOUSE
£28–£62

Ignore the factory buildings as you follow the lane towards this inviting pub/restaurant and anticipate the expansive views of Morecambe Bay sands that can be admired from the veranda or the conservatory dining room. Lunchtimes bring carte or fixed-price meals in the latter, or the bar menu is a big hit, with its jazzy sandwiches on home-baked bread and heart-warming dishes like grilled Waberthwaite sausages with date chutney. A la carte dinner in the restaurant shows all the fingerprints of co-owner John Tovey: the curtain rises at 8, and customers are treated to a menu of country-house dishes that are loyal to the Lakeland food network. Typically, you might begin with potted shrimps or smoked chicken and avocado salad, before rack of Holker Estate saltmarsh lamb with garlic and rosemary, or pan-fried tuna with lemon and prawn butter; finally, you can close the show in true Tovey style with sticky toffee pudding, or chocolate Mascarpone cheesecake. South Africa is a major player on the serious, well-constructed wine list; prices start at £15.50.

CHEF: Robert Lyons   PROPRIETORS: John Tovey and Robert Lyons   OPEN: Tue to Sun 12 to 1.30, all week D 7.30 for 8 (1 sitting)   MEALS: alc (main courses £22.50 to £24). Set L £17.95, Set D £27.50. Bar L menu available   SERVICE: not inc, card slips closed   CARDS: Amex, Delta, MasterCard, Switch, Visa   DETAILS: 50 seats. 20 seats outside. Private parties: 30 main room. Car park. Vegetarian meals. No children under 12. No smoking. Wheelchair access (also WC). Music. No mobile phones   ACCOMMODATION: 9 rooms, all with bath/shower. TV. Phone. D,B&B £80 to £190. No children under 12

UPPER HAMBLETON Rutland
map 6

▲ Hambleton Hall ♀ ✸

Upper Hambleton LE15 8TH
TEL: (01572) 756991   FAX: (01572) 724721
WEBSITE: www.hambletonhall.com

COOKING 7
MODERN BRITISH
£34–£110

Hambleton is the kind of country-house hotel to which people return enthusiastically. Its drawing room is 'alone worth the visit', according to a regular, for its views over Rutland

Water and a terraced, topiary garden. Aaron Patterson's menus follow the seasons (with the odd anachronism, such as chocolate-sauced venison in April), and autumn seems a particularly smart bet for a visit, when the 'Festival of Game' comes into play. A kitchen garden is on hand to supply vegetables, salad leaves, herbs and some soft fruits, and it all comes together in a style of gently speculative cooking that emphasises freshness. Make that 'startling freshness' in the case of a reporter's tagliatelle of crayfish with saffron and chervil, a 'simple-looking yet beguiling' first course. Combinations can be novel, as with a partnership of borscht and poached langoustines, or soused aubergine and plums with sautéed foie gras. Main-course meats are properly hung to maximise flavour and juiciness and are royally treated on the plate, so that honey-roast breast of Goosnargh duck comes with a little pie of its leg meat in a sauce of orange and ginger. Winter might bring on hare Wellington, sauced with prunes and Armagnac, while fish favourers might opt for turbot served with a risotto of clams, tomato and (unseasonal) asparagus and grain mustard sauce.

Flawless simplicity distinguishes desserts such as thin apple tart on a base of luxurious, even 'sybaritic', crème pâtissière, or light, almost foamy-textured passion-fruit soufflé. The cost is high, and one inspector queried whether it constitutes value for money, especially given an experience of some disappointing pasta in a raviolo with foie gras, and over-dominant lemon in a starter of roasted scallop with a velouté of asparagus and Scottish chanterelles. Our postbag, though, suggests most visitors are eager to return. Service is attentive and friendly. Bordeaux, Burgundy and California are the chief interests of the wine list, with illustrious bottles aplenty. But there is a good showing from most regions, and the list caters to all sizes of wallet, starting from £15 on the opening page of the engaging 'Wines of the Moment'.

CHEF: Aaron Patterson PROPRIETORS: Tim and Stefa Hart OPEN: all week 12.30 to 1.30, 7 to 9.30 MEALS: alc (main courses £25 to £39.50). Set L Mon to Fri £18.50 (2 courses) to £27, Set L Sun £36, Set D £35 to £55. Snack menu available SERVICE: no service expected CARDS: Amex, Delta, Diners, MasterCard, Switch, Visa DETAILS: 64 seats. Private parties: 64 main room, 2 to 24 private rooms. Car park. Vegetarian meals. No smoking. Wheelchair access (not WC). No music ACCOMMODATION: 17 rooms, all with bath/shower. TV. Phone. B&B £160 to £600. Rooms for disabled. Baby facilities. Swimming pool

UPPER SLAUGHTER Gloucestershire   map 5

▲ Lords of the Manor

Upper Slaughter GL54 2JD	COOKING 6
TEL: (01451) 820243 FAX: (01451) 820696	MODERN FRENCH
WEBSITE: www.lordsofthemanor.com	£36–£93

Pint-sized Upper Slaughter, some four miles south-west of Stow-on-the-Wold, has at its heart this harmonious sprawl of honey-hued stone that started out as a rectory in the mid-seventeenth century, but has been much extended since. The surprisingly small dining room enjoys a view of the walled garden at the back, and is hung with an array of family portraits in oil.

Les Rennie took over the stoves here in May 2004, arriving from Ynyshir Hall in Eglwysfach, Powys (see entry). He brings to the very traditional confines of the Manor a dash of modernity, serving seared foie gras with tamarind ice cream, or Gressingham duck breast with celeriac confit and chocolate oil, and supplementing the short printed menu with daily dishes. One of these was our inspector's main course of slow-roasted beef fillet, comprised of three cylinders of meat topped with chanterelles, garnished with beetroot, celeriac and foamy pea purée in a richly intense stock reduction. A neat and classically inspired arrangement of unilaterally browned scallops with niçoise salad ingredients made a fresh and appetising starter, while desserts aim to keep the taste-buds awake, rather than lull them to sleep, by means of summer fruit jelly with passion-fruit consommé and lemon verbena sorbet, or chocolate-coated black cherry mousse with matching sorbet and coulis. Very smooth, professional service inspires confidence. Diners on a budget will struggle with a wine list that offers barely a drop below £20 and very little under £25 (house white is £22). Quality, however, is not an issue, with premium names throughout Europe, including top English bottles, and solid ranges elsewhere.

CHEF: Les Rennie   PROPRIETOR: Empire Ventures   OPEN: all week 12.30 to 1.45, 7 to 9.15   MEALS: alc D (main courses £27 to £39.50). Set L £16.95 (2 courses) to £19.95, Set L Sun £21. Bar/terrace menu available (not Sun L)   SERVICE: 12.5% (optional), card slips closed   CARDS: Amex, Delta, Diners, MasterCard, Switch, Visa   DETAILS: 50 seats. 25 seats outside. Private parties: 50 main room, 8 to 30 private rooms. Car park. Vegetarian meals. Children's helpings. No children under 7. No smoking. Wheelchair access (also women's WC). No music   ACCOMMODATION: 27 rooms, all with bath/shower. TV. Phone. B&B £100 to £310. Rooms for disabled. Baby facilities

UPTON SCUDAMORE Wiltshire   map 2

▲ Angel Inn 🍴   [NEW ENTRY]

Upton Scudamore BA12 0AG   COOKING 4
TEL: (01985) 213225   FAX: (01985) 211119   MODERN BRITISH
WEBSITE: www.theangelinn-wiltshire.co.uk   £27–£49

At the heart of a hamlet on the edge of Salisbury Plain, the Angel is a large, neat-looking country inn. Inside is a series of linked rooms on slightly different levels, including a long, narrow, high-ceilinged bar and a sizeable dining area with well-spaced tables bearing single flowers, bare old floorboards, honey-coloured walls and a civilised atmosphere. Chef Paul Suter offers a printed menu backed up by blackboards of desserts and daily specials (mostly fish). His cooking is simple and unpretentious, focused on bringing the best out of quality produce with careful, skilful preparation. Among starters, luscious, melting and impeccably fresh seared Brixham scallops are set off with a well-balanced sweet chilli jam – hot but not overpoweringly so, and not too jammy either – and crisp, peppery salad leaves in a slightly sweet mustard dressing, while main courses range from whole grilled Dover sole with lemon butter to seared saddle of venison, the well-hung flavoursome meat cooked precisely and served with bubble and squeak and a fruity blueberry jus. To finish, warm pear tart with chocolate sauce and vanilla ice cream is a highly individual – and successful – take on a classic dessert. House vins de pays are £12.95, £3 a glass.

CHEF: Paul Suter   PROPRIETORS: Carol and Tony Coates   OPEN: all week 12 to 2, 6.30 to 9.30   CLOSED: 25 and 26 Dec, 1 Jan   MEALS: alc (main courses L £8 to £13, D £11.50 to £18)   CARDS: MasterCard, Switch, Visa   DETAILS: 80 seats. 30 seats outside. Private parties: 30 main room. Car park. Vegetarian meals. Children's helpings. No smoking. Music   ACCOMMODATION: 10 rooms, all with bath/shower. TV. Phone. B&B £60 to £78

If 'vegetarian meals' is noted in the details at the end of an entry, this means that a restaurant routinely lists at least one vegetarian starter and main course on menus. Other restaurants, however, may offer good vegetarian choices if you let them know in advance, so it is worthwhile phoning to enquire.

VIRGINSTOW Devon

map 1

▲ Percy's ❦

Coombeshead Estate, Virginstow EX21 5EA
TEL: (01409) 211236   FAX: (01409) 211460
WEBSITE: www.percys.co.uk
follow signs to Percy's at Coombeshead from Gridley
corner on A388, or from B3218 at Metherell Cross
junction

COOKING 4
MODERN BRITISH
£39–£72

'It is not often when arriving early for lunch you are asked whether you would like to feed the lambs first,' commented one reporter approvingly. But then not many restaurants are at the heart of an accredited organic farm. The Bricknell-Webbs grow (and rear) much of their own produce on the tranquil Coombeshead Estate yet still find time to run a chefs' school and offer accommodation. The light, bright, contemporary architectural styling belies the building's 400 years. A modern extension includes a zinc bar opening on to a decked patio, while the dining room in the older part of the house has a low ceiling and a dark wood and cream décor. In the interests of freshness and seasonality, the menus are kept short, with just four choices per course. Fish, bought direct from the boats at Looe, is given simple treatments: steamed turbot with béarnaise sauce, and pan-fried monkfish accompanied by a julienne of vegetables and ginger. Lavender and rosemary are popular flavourings, the former appearing in a jus with roast home-reared lamb, the latter in an ice cream with lemon tart and raspberries. Unlike the menu, the brief wine list doesn't highlight organic choices. Prices start at around £14.

CHEF: Tina Bricknell-Webb   PROPRIETORS: Tony and Tina Bricknell-Webb   OPEN: all week 12 to 1.30, 7 to 9.30   MEALS: Set L £20 (2 courses) to £25.50, Set D £40   SERVICE: not inc   CARDS: Delta, MasterCard, Switch, Visa   DETAILS: 40 seats. Private parties: 24 main room, 12 to 14 private rooms. Car park. No children under 12. No smoking. Wheelchair access (also WC). Occasional music   ACCOMMODATION: 8 rooms, all with bath/shower. TV. Phone. D,B&B £115 to £290. No children under 12. Fishing

WADHURST East Sussex

map 3

▲ Best Beech Inn

Mayfield Lane, Best Beech Hill, Wadhurst TN5 6JH
TEL: (01892) 782046   FAX: (01892) 785092
WEBSITE: www.bestbeech.net
on B2100, midway between Mark Cross and Wadhurst

COOKING 3
MODERN EUROPEAN
£25–£51

This tile-hung country pub has undergone many transformations, including life as an early petrol station. Nowadays it fills stomachs, and to seriously good effect. Quality ingredients from local suppliers create a firm base for imaginative cooking that draws inspiration from Europe. Michael Weir's bold but not overfussy approach shows in a cauliflower risotto accompanying seared scallops, making an alternative to black pudding with apple crisps, foie gras and apple jus among the starters, and in mains of sea bass on a truffle mash with roast beetroot and spinach, or fried venison loin with roast apples, broad beans and a port-and-brandy jus. Puddings are more conventional, with prune and Armagnac brûlée, and vanilla pannacotta with berry compote. A fairly eclectic wine list stays largely under £25, starting with six house bottles from £10.95 (£2.95 a glass).

CHEF: Michael Weir   PROPRIETOR: Roger Felstead   OPEN: all week L 12 to 2, Mon to Sat D 7 to 9   MEALS: alc (not Mon D; main courses L £7 to £15, D £15 to £17). Set L Mon to Sat and Set D Mon to Thur £12.95 (2 courses) to £14.95, Set L Sun £12.95 (2 courses) to £16.95. Bistro L menu available   SERVICE: not inc, 10% for parties of 7 or more   CARDS: MasterCard, Switch, Visa   DETAILS: 65 seats. 32 seats outside. Private parties: 32 main room, 28 to 32 private rooms. Car park. Vegetarian meals. Children's helpings. No children under 10 in main restaurant. Wheelchair access (not WC). Occasional music   ACCOMMODATION: 7 rooms, 5 with bath/shower. TV. Phone. B&B £39.90 to £79.90 £5

WAKEFIELD West Yorkshire   map 9

Brasserie Ninety Nine ※   NEW ENTRY

Trinity Business Park, Turner Way, Wakefield WF2 8EF   COOKING 2
TEL: (01924) 377699   FAX: (01924) 375100   MODERN BRITISH
                                                                      £26–£74

The 'odd location' shouldn't deter you from seeking out this modern brasserie in a business park close to Wakefield city centre. Brushed-metal walls, etched glass, and tiled floors send out all the right modish signals, and the food is in tune with its surroundings. A few retro ideas (whitebait, pear Belle Hélène) and comfort dishes (black pudding with a poached egg) vie for attention with modern stuff based on spanking-fresh raw materials: chargrilled calf's liver with pancetta and a borlotti bean stew, for example, or roast cod with tapenade. A light touch is evident in items like fishcake with cucumber and rocket salad, and fig and almond tart. The reasonably priced wine list includes house French at £12.50.

CHEF: Jon Coxon   PROPRIETORS: Neal Parkin and Jon Coxon   OPEN: all week 9 to 10.30 (8.30 Sun)   MEALS: alc (main courses £9 to £35). Set L £8.99 to £10.99 (2 courses), Set D 5.30 to 7 £15.95   SERVICE: not inc, 10% for parties of 8 or more   CARDS: Amex, Delta, Diners, MasterCard, Switch, Visa   DETAILS: 120 seats. 20 seats outside. Private parties: 40 to 120 private rooms. Car park. Vegetarian meals. Children's helpings. No smoking. Wheelchair access (also WC). Music. Air-conditioned £5

WARWICK Warwickshire   map 5

Findons ※

7 Old Square, Warwick CV34 4RA   COOKING 2
TEL: (01926) 411755   FAX: (01926) 400453   MODERN EUROPEAN
WEBSITE: www.findons-restaurant.co.uk   £36–£60

Findons occupies the ground floor of a Georgian town house in a small square, facing St Mary's Church. Ornate gilt-framed mirrors, dripping cut-glass chandeliers and reproductions from art's 'greatest hits' decorate lemon-yellow walls. Rosemary Findon oversees the 'warm', if youthful service team in an 'unpretentious and friendly' manner, while husband Michael cooks. His crowd-pleasing menus have a definite Mediterranean tinge, so expect the likes of prosciutto, fresh fig and Parmesan with strawberry and mango vinaigrette to start, then perhaps a breast of Gressingham duck with baked aubergine, tapenade and baby plum tomatoes, and a raspberry crème brûlée finish. The sensibly priced, compact wine list starts with Spanish house at £12.95.

CHEF: Michael Findon   PROPRIETOR: Findon & Williams Ltd   OPEN: Mon to Sat D only 6.30 to 9.30   CLOSED: 26 to 31 Dec   MEALS: alc (main courses £13 to £19). Set D £15.95 (2 courses)   SERVICE: not inc, 10% (optional) for parties of 6 or more   CARDS: Delta, MasterCard, Switch, Visa   DETAILS: 40 seats. 20 seats outside. Private parties: 36 main room, 8 to 14 private rooms. Vegetarian meals. No children under 11. No smoking in 1 dining room. Wheelchair access (not WC). Music £5

▲ Rampsbeck Country House Hotel ▼ ⅍

Watermillock CA11 0LP   COOKING 4
TEL: (017684) 86442   FAX: (017684) 86688   ANGLO-FRENCH
WEBSITE: www.rampsbeck.fsnet.co.uk   £38–£69

The spectacular views across Ullswater from 18 acres of grounds seem reason enough to visit the attractive dining room of this eighteenth-century hotel. Comfortable armchairs and sofas await in the lounges for aperitifs and canapés, while the dining room is set out with pink tablecloths, comfortable chairs and fine tableware. It's relaxing and welcoming, backed by friendly, professional and unobtrusive service. The modern Anglo-French menus rise to the occasion with flair, embracing top-notch local ingredients and luxury items that provoke an agony of choice: perhaps a starter assiette of Périgord foie gras with balsamic dressing, or pan-fried John Dory fillets with squat lobster and saffron risotto to start. Deep-fried monkfish with spaghetti carbonara and a shellfish dressing, and poached organic Bresse chicken with a chicken, foie gras and macadamia nut boudin with cep-flavoured essence maintain the trend. Finish in style with a hot raspberry soufflé accompanied by arctic roll and a compote of raspberries. For all the grandeur of the setting, the wine list is engagingly unpretentious, sticking mostly to affordable bottles from around the world. Wines are sorted into detailed style categories – medium-bodied, soft, neutral, or crisp, fruity, for example – and all have a useful tasting note.

CHEF: Andrew McGeorge   PROPRIETORS: Tom and Marion Gibb   OPEN: all week 12 to 1, 7 to 8.30 CLOSED: early Jan to mid-Feb   MEALS: Set L £28, Set D £39 to £46. Bar L menu available   SERVICE: not inc, card slips closed   CARDS: Delta, MasterCard, Switch, Visa   DETAILS: 40 seats. Private parties: 65 main room, 8 to 15 private rooms. Car park. Children's helpings. No smoking. No music. No mobile phones ACCOMMODATION: 19 rooms, all with bath/shower. TV. Phone. B&B £65 to £240

▲ Sportsman's Arms ▼ ⅍

Wath-in-Nidderdale, Pateley Bridge HG3 5PP   COOKING 4
TEL: (01423) 711306   FAX: (01423) 712524   ANGLO-FRENCH
off B6265, 2m NW of Pateley Bridge   £36–£53

This cheery Yorkshire hostelry is reached via a narrow bridge off the main Dales road. The bar and lounge are a picture of informal conviviality, while a distinct air of Sunday best (antique furniture and a collection of outsized wall clocks) prevails in the dining room, although the service here is as relaxed. An inventive streak runs through the cooking, bringing on a salad of black pudding, haggis and pancetta to start, followed perhaps by breast of guinea fowl with seared scallops in curry-seasoned wild mushroom sauce. Simpler lunch dishes have included mousse de canard with sharp, home-made chutney, good tomato and fennel soup, and beef rib with Yorkshire pudding, onion gravy and a dollop of white-hot horseradish dressing. Fish specials from east coast boats are shown separately, and meals end with blackcurrant-packed summer pudding of great intensity, a slice of home-made fruit pie with fine, thick, short pastry, or chocolate and mocha surprise. The wine list offers a rewardingly broad range of good choices at very fair prices, starting from £13.20. The major passion is for France, including some treats among the cheaper Rhône reds.

CHEFS: Ray Carter and Seth Marsland   PROPRIETORS: Ray and Jane Carter   OPEN: all week L 12 to 2, Mon to Sat D 7 to 9   CLOSED: 25 Dec   MEALS: alc (main courses £14.50 to £17)   SERVICE: not inc, card slips closed   CARDS: MasterCard, Switch, Visa   DETAILS: 45 seats. 30 seats outside. Private parties: 50 main room, 12 private room. Car park. Vegetarian meals. Children's helpings. No smoking in restaurant, permitted in lounge and bar. Wheelchair access (also WC). No music   ACCOMMODATION: 11 rooms, all with bath/shower. TV. Phone. B&B £50 to £100

WELWYN GARDEN CITY Hertfordshire   map 3

▲ Novelli at Auberge du Lac

Brocket Hall, Lemsford, Welwyn Garden City AL8 7XG   COOKING 6
TEL: (01707) 368888   FAX: (01707) 368898   MODERN FRENCH
EMAIL: auberge@brocket-hall.co.uk   £42–£110

In the grounds of Brocket Hall – now hotel and golf course rather than country seat – this eighteenth-century former hunting lodge is the setting for Jean-Christophe Novelli's cooking. His style ranges wide, although the point of departure is classic French. His passion for pairing unusual flavours and textures shows in a starter of steamed scallops with open cardamom, truffled winter spinach, orange vanilla syrup and coffre feuilleté, while a main-course wood-smoked steamed tournedos of monkfish is teamed 'osso-bucco-style' with braised oxtail, caramelised onions and Barolo jus. This food is full of playful enthusiasm, as in roast stuffed saddle of rabbit, served with a braised caramelised leg, soufflé cutlet, liver and chestnut mousse and mustard cream sauce. Although Novelli commutes between here and London Capital Club (a sister property in the City; see entry under Novelli in the City, London), where he also runs the kitchen, he remains in command at Brocket Hall. At inspection a virtuoso performance included a ravioli of poached duck egg with wild mushrooms, nutmeg-infused spinach and French grain mustard velouté, and poached turbot with saffron jacket fondant and shellfish provençale fondue, with the extra vegetables cooked 'to absolute perfection'. A 'light and perfect' iced milk chocolate and Amaretto parfait with chocolate almond truffle is a star among desserts. The wine list's quality in depth covers top producers from all over France, old vintages from Bordeaux and voguish names from around the world. But, with prices zooming up from £20, value is more debatable; diners on a budget can stick with the very good range by the glass from £6 or go for set lunches, which include two glasses of wine.

CHEF: Jean-Christophe Novelli   PROPRIETOR: CCA International   OPEN: Tue to Sun L 12 to 2.30, Tue to Sat D 6.45 to 10   MEALS: alc (main courses £25 to £38). Set L Tue to Fri £28.50, Set L Sat/Sun £35, Set D £35 to £65   SERVICE: 10% (optional), card slips closed   CARDS: Amex, Delta, Diners, MasterCard, Switch, Visa   DETAILS: 70 seats. 70 seats outside. Private parties: 70 main room, 4 to 20 private rooms. Car park. Vegetarian meals. Children's helpings. No pipes/cigars. Music. No mobile phones. Air-conditioned   ACCOMMODATION: 16 rooms, all with bath/shower. TV. Phone. Room only £150 to £170

WEST BAY Dorset   map 2

Riverside Restaurant ♥ ⁵✳

West Bay DT6 4EZ   COOKING 3
TEL: (01308) 422011   FAX: (01308) 458808   SEAFOOD
                                                                 £25–£70

When it opened some 40 years ago, the Riverside was an old-style seaside café, but under the Watsons' stewardship it has evolved into an unaffected restaurant devoted to fresh fish. 'Simplicity is part of its charm,' observed one visitor, no doubt referring to the waterside location and the refreshingly plain décor as well as the food. Seafood platters vie for attention with fish and chips or roast salmon fillet with basil hollandaise, although the kitchen also goes walkabout for Moroccan prawns with tabbouleh salad and Greek-style baked brill. Meat and vegetarian dishes are there if you really need them – perhaps roast chicken suprême with mushroom risotto, or baked courgette mousse with roast Mediterranean vegetables – and a sizeable contingent of desserts covers everything from treacle tart to pineapple carpaccio with coconut sorbet. Staff are 'wonderfully informal and jovial' – and the fish-friendly and pocket-pleasing wine list certainly gives them something to smile about.

CHEFS: Chris Ansell, Nic Larcombe, R. Wolverson and Natalie Andrews   PROPRIETORS: Arthur and Janet Watson   OPEN: Tue to Sun L 12 to 2.15, Tue to Sat D 6.30 to 9 (check evening opening Feb, Mar and Nov). Open all bank hol weekends Easter to late Aug   CLOSED: late Nov to mid-Feb   MEALS: alc (main courses £9.50 to £25). Set L Mon to Fri £13.50 (2 courses) to £16.50 (not available July, Aug and bank hols) SERVICE: not inc, card slips closed   CARDS: Delta, MasterCard, Switch, Visa   DETAILS: 70 seats. 30 seats outside. Private parties: 80 main room, 10 to 22 private rooms. Vegetarian meals. Children's helpings. No smoking. Wheelchair access (also women's WC). Occasional music

WEST TANFIELD North Yorkshire   map 9

▲ Bruce Arms ⁵✳

Main Street, West Tanfield HG4 5JJ	COOKING 4
TEL: (01677) 470325	MODERN ENGLISH
WEBSITE: www.brucearms.com	£30–£52

It may feel like an upmarket pub, but the Bruce Arms plies its trade as a 'bistro-with-bedrooms' – complete with an astonishing assortment of eye-catching decorative paraphernalia, including tennis racquets, foreign banknotes and an old laundry rack. Jan Smith holds sway out front, while husband Geoff mans the stoves. The kitchen has access to decent supplies of local meat: fillet of Masham beef might be served with pesto and a mild garlic sauce, while roast loin of Well lamb is scented with fresh tarragon. Fish comes from a merchant in Hartlepool – hence the presence of fillets of Dover sole with east coast crab in filo with hollandaise. Starters range from parsley soup with shallots and croûtons to smoked haddock rarebit, and the line-up of desserts has included sticky toffee pudding and lemon posset. A 'premier' selection provides some vintage alternatives to the competitively priced wine list. Ten house recommendations start at £3.25 a glass, £11.95 a bottle.

CHEF: Geoff Smith   PROPRIETORS: Geoff and Jan Smith   OPEN: Sun L 12 to 2, all week D 6.30 to 9.30 MEALS: alc (main courses £12 to £17)   SERVICE: not inc, card slips closed   CARDS: MasterCard, Switch, Visa   DETAILS: 50 seats. 12 seats outside. Private parties: 30 main room. Car park. Vegetarian meals. Children's helpings. No smoking in 1 dining room. Music. No mobile phones   ACCOMMODATION: 3 rooms, all with bath/shower. TV. B&B £40 to £60

WETHERSFIELD Essex   map 6

Dicken's Brasserie ⁵✳

The Green, Wethersfield CM7 4BS	COOKING 2
TEL: (01371) 850723 FAX: (01371) 850727	MODERN BRITISH
WEBSITE: www.dickensbrasserie.co.uk	£33–£50

A spruce three-storey building with its ground-floor bow windows overlooking the village green makes a picture-postcard setting for this smart/casual venue that serves unfussy brasserie food to the accompaniment of jazzy background music. A number of dishes can be ordered as starters or main courses (roast pigeon salad with black pudding and smoked bacon, for example), and there are grills for the raging carnivore; the remainder is an assortment of old favourites and contemporary ideas, ranging from steak and kidney pie to baked cod fillet on warm new potato and spinach salad with braised fennel and ratatouille sauce. Likewise, desserts span everything from apple and mincemeat tart to tiramisù. A handful of champagnes open the brief list, which has house selections from £10.95.

CHEF/PROPRIETOR: John Dicken   OPEN: Tue to Sun L 12 to 2, Tue to Sat D 6.30 to 9.30   MEALS: alc (main courses £11 to £16)   SERVICE: not inc   CARDS: Delta, MasterCard, Switch, Visa   DETAILS: 50 seats. Private parties: 40 main room, 12 to 20 private rooms. Car park. Vegetarian meals. No smoking. Music. No mobile phones

WHITBY North Yorkshire   map 9

Magpie Café ⁵⚹ £

14 Pier Road, Whitby YO21 3PU   COOKING 2
TEL: (01947) 602058   FAX: (01947) 601801   SEAFOOD
WEBSITE: www.magpiecafe.co.uk   £18–£46

This unpretentious, busy seafood café – painted a distinctive magpie black and white – on the harbourside has achieved a continuous entry in the Guide for 25 years, a testament to its quality. In fact, its popularity means that queuing for a table is inevitable; should it rain, the owners even provide umbrellas. The menus concentrate on the fruits of the sea, with up to ten varieties of Whitby fish available daily, so there's no doubting the freshness. Daily specials bolster the repertoire, and you may be seduced by Mediterranean-style haddock on a bed of penne, lobster thermidor, or 'incomparably fresh' deep-fried cod or halibut, described by a reporter as having 'the best and crispiest batter I've ever tasted', with chips and tartare sauce. 'Staff are wonderful', and the good-value list of predominantly white wines opens with house French at £9.95.

CHEFS: Ian Robson and Paul Gildroy   PROPRIETORS: Ian Robson and Alison McKenzie-Robson   OPEN: all week 11.30 to 9 (6.30 Sun Nov to Mar)   CLOSED: 20 to 26 Dec, 9 Jan to 4 Feb   MEALS: alc (main courses £5 to £19)   SERVICE: not inc, card slips closed   CARDS: Delta, MasterCard, Switch, Visa   DETAILS: 100 seats. Private parties: 50 main room. Vegetarian meals. Children's helpings. No smoking. Occasional music. Air-conditioned (£5)

WHITCHURCH Hampshire   map 2

Red House ⁵⚹

21 London Street, Whitchurch RG28 7LH   COOKING 3
TEL: (01256) 895558   FAX: (01256) 895966   GLOBAL
                                                                                 £26–£48

Think white, not red, and you'll find this sixteenth-century inn at the centre of town, close to the river and Whitchurch's working silk mill. The pebble-dashed exterior does include two red doors, and diners want the one labelled lounge bar and restaurant (the other leads to the public bar). Low beams, floorboards and large mirrors on yellow walls create space and light, while unclothed polished-wood furniture maintains relaxed informality. Short, modern-focused menus deliver attractive, colourful dishes, incorporating quality ingredients and balanced flavours: perhaps seared scallops with pea and mint purée and crispy Serrano ham to start, then lamb fillet with spinach and roast pepper mousse and sweet potato fondant. Service is enthusiastic and well-informed, and the compact, global wine list offers reasonable prices, helpful notes and a nine house bottles from £10.75.

CHEFS: Shannon Wells and Pete Nash   PROPRIETORS: Shannon and Caroline Wells   OPEN: all week 12 to 2, 6.30 (7 Sun) to 9.30   MEALS: alc (main courses £7 to £16.50)   SERVICE: not inc, 10% for parties of 8 or more, card slips closed   CARDS: MasterCard, Switch, Visa   DETAILS: 30 seats. 40 seats outside. Private parties: 30 main room. Car park. Vegetarian meals. Children's helpings. No children under 12. No smoking. No music

WHITSTABLE Kent   map 3

Sportsman ⅝⋇

Faversham Road, Seasalter, Whitstable CT5 4BP   COOKING 4
TEL: (01227) 273370   FAX: (01227) 262314   MODERN EUROPEAN
                                                                     £30–£49

A fresh lick of paint has given this remote marshland pub an outer appearance to match the simple look of its large, open-plan bar. Bare floorboards, chunky pine furniture and a jolly landlord give the place an informal atmosphere. The kitchen delivers some classical flavour combinations, and as far as possible uses only ingredients sourced from within ten miles, including plenty of fish and seafood. A small and sweet-flavoured grilled lobster and 'beautiful' skate have come in for praise, but the repertoire runs to Brussels sprout soup with a native oyster, confit pork belly with apple sauce, and crispy duck with smoked chilli salsa and sour cream. Among desserts, lemon tart with thin, crisp pastry has been a highlight. A short but diverse and well-chosen wine list mostly sticks to bottles under £20, including three at £9.95. Five wines are available by the glass. There is a new sister operation, The Granville, just outside of Canterbury (see entry, Lower Hardres).

CHEFS: Stephen Harris and Dan Flavell   PROPRIETORS: Stephen, Philip and Damian Harris   OPEN: Tue to Sun L 12 to 2 (3 Sun), Tue to Sat D 7 to 9   CLOSED: 25 Dec   MEALS: alc (main courses £10 to £17)   SERVICE: not inc, card slips closed, 10% for parties of 6 or more   CARDS: Delta, MasterCard, Switch, Visa   DETAILS: 50 seats. Car park. Children's helpings. No smoking in 1 dining room. Wheelchair access (not WC). Occasional music

Wheelers Oyster Bar £

8 High Street, Whitstable CT5 1BQ   COOKING 2
TEL: (01227) 273311   SEAFOOD
                                                                     £22–£46

Behind the cheery blue and pink shopfront you'll find a happy atmosphere among the customers tucking into the fresh seafood at this tiny restaurant. The front part is a seafood bar where shellfish platters, salads and tapas-style small dishes are served. The main dining room is to the rear, a small parlour with knick-knacks filling up every surface. The seasonally changing menus focus on seafood straight from the boats done up in an ambitious, modern British style with some heartfelt European influences: roast scallops on Puy lentils with lemon and thyme rösti and pancetta, for example, or baked hake on brandade with charred baby leeks and peppers topped with a soft-boiled egg and mustard dressing. Bring your own wine: there's an off-licence across the road and corkscrews are provided.

CHEF: Mark Stubbs   PROPRIETOR: Delia Fitt   OPEN: Thur to Tue 1 to 7.30 (8 Sat, 7 Sun)   CLOSED: 25 Dec, 2 weeks Jan   MEALS: alc (main courses £13.50 to £16). Light menu available   SERVICE: not inc   CARDS: none   DETAILS: 20 seats. Private parties: 16 main room. Wheelchair access (not WC). No music

Williams & Brown Tapas ✹ £

48 Harbour Street, Whitstable CT5 1AQ	COOKING 2
TEL: (01227) 273373	TAPAS
	£25–£38

NEW ENTRY

A small dining room with full-height picture windows on two sides gives views of the daily hustle and bustle of this small seaside town. White walls and a large mirror at the back add to the light and spacious feel. Menus offer tapas, treated more as a style of cooking than a style of eating, but the fundamentals are as authentic as any tapas bar in Spain: pungently smoked boquerones (anchovies); pata negra ham from acorn-fed sows; juicy, tender chicken with lemon and garlic; cured beef with sweet, succulent roasted beetroot; and modern versions of tortilla made with chickpeas and greens. The regular menu is supplemented by a list of seafood specials (crab claws with aïoli, for example), and a clutch of wines, mostly Spanish, is listed on a blackboard, prices starting at £12.95.

CHEFS: Chris Williams, David Brown and Ricardo Cordovez   PROPRIETORS: Chris Williams and David Brown   OPEN: Wed to Sun L 11.45 to 2 (2.30 Sat, 2.45 Sun), Mon and Wed to Sat D 5.45 to 9.15 (10.30 Sat)   MEALS: tapas £3.95 to £7.95   SERVICE: 10% (optional)   CARDS: none   DETAILS: 45 seats. Private parties: 20 main room. Vegetarian meals. No smoking. Music. No mobile phones. Air-conditioned

WHITTLESFORD Cambridgeshire   map 6

Tickell ♥ ✹

1 North Road, Whittlesford CB2 4NZ	COOKING 5
TEL: (01223) 833128 FAX: (01223) 835907	MODERN FRENCH
	£30–£77

The Tickell's cobalt blue exterior hides touches of eccentricity: Gothic-style doors and windows, a boldly coloured dining room, a jungly-verdant conservatory, and a terrace beside a large pond with plashing fountain. It all presents plenty to ponder, as do Spencer Patrick's classical French fixed-price menus, which have brought a splash of big-city panache to this sleepy part of Cambridgeshire.

A signature starter has been roast foie gras, sometimes with poached Muscat grapes, sometimes with creamed lentils and a spicy red wine sauce – and that propensity for luxury ingredients extends to adding white truffle oil to the artichoke velouté, or offering Sevruga and blinis Moscow-style. Simpler things are done well too, though: readers have praised dishes such as wild mushroom risotto with Parmesan, and moules marinière (as well as the value of the lunch menu). Even more substantial main dishes include veal noisette with sweetbreads, pommes dauphinoise and sauce diable, and grilled gilt-head bream with palourdes and herb velouté. Finish with a tarte Tatin of pineapple seasoned with cracked black pepper, or maybe chocolate fondant with pistachio ice cream. Be sure to study the full wine list, sourced from pioneering and highly individual wine merchants Noel Young; virtually every bottle on it is a gem. Prices start at £13.95, and there are six by the glass.

CHEF: Spencer Patrick   PROPRIETOR: Tickell Management Co.   OPEN: Tue to Sun L 12 to 2, Tue to Sat D 7 to 9   CLOSED: 25 Dec and 1 Jan   MEALS: Set L £14.50 (2 courses) to £19.50, Set D £34.50   SERVICE:

12.5% (optional), card slips closed   CARDS: Amex, Delta, MasterCard, Switch, Visa   DETAILS: 40 seats. 20 seats outside. Private parties: 50 main room. Car park. Vegetarian meals. No children under 12 Tue to Sat. No smoking. Wheelchair access (not WC). Music. No mobile phones

---

WILLITON Somerset   map 2

▲ White House ▾ ⌘

11 Long Street, Williton TA4 4QW	COOKING 6
TEL: (01984) 632777	ENGLISH/MEDITERRANEAN
	£53–£82

A pristine white façade, white shutters, and palms and mimosas gracing the forecourt give this classic Georgian house a Mediterranean air. Inside are well-chosen modern and antique furniture and oil paintings enough for a small gallery, and the dining room overlooks a courtyard with more palms, fig trees and abundant clematis. Long-standing owners Dick and Kay Smith are 'really lovely' people, and modest with it, though they have much to be proud of. Kay Smith, cooking in a classic Mediterranean style, makes good use of meticulously sourced supplies. Among starters, garlicky smoked haddock brandade with smoked eel and beetroot is more than a collection of first-rate individual components; each tasting fresh and distinct, it is also a strikingly effective combination of flavours. A main course of pan-fried suprême of guinea fowl with caramelised apples and Calvados sauce sounds more conventional, but the skin is cooked separately until crisp and used to garnish the perfectly timed meat. Desserts keep up the standards, a crisp, chewy, nutty almond meringue filled with cream and a light apricot purée proving the point at inspection. The Med occasionally makes its presence felt on the good-value and thoroughly civilised wine list, adding a southern twist to fine collections from Bordeaux, Burgundy, the Loire and Germany; some good modern choices turn up elsewhere too. House white is £14.75.

CHEFS/PROPRIETORS: Dick and Kay Smith   OPEN: all week D only 7 to 8.30   CLOSED: Nov to mid-May   MEALS: Set D £40   SERVICE: not inc   CARDS: none   DETAILS: 22 seats. Private parties: 6 main room. Car park. Children's helpings. No smoking while others eat. No music   ACCOMMODATION: 10 rooms, 9 with bath/shower. TV. Phone. B&B £55 to £120. Baby facilities

---

WINCHCOMBE Gloucestershire   map 5

5 North Street

5 North Street, Winchcombe GL54 5LH	COOKING 6
TEL: (01242) 604566 FAX: (01242) 603788	MODERN EUROPEAN
	£32–£68

The Ashenfords' small restaurant, with its compact, beamed dining room, is located in the centre of this handsome village, all mellow Cotswold stone and home to Sudeley Castle to boot. With deep red walls and a tiled fireplace, 5 North Street has a comfortable, almost domestic feel, although the cooking will remind you that you are anywhere but at home. A tower made up of cauliflower purée, a roasted scallop and a piece of sautéed foie gras, surrounded by dots of beetroot syrup, is as rewardingly complex as modern restaurant food gets, and has become a signature starter. That's from the more expensive prix-fixe menu, as is a main course of Old Spot pork with crackling, fondant potato, stuffed cabbage and a cider jus, while the cheaper options might include as a starter an evening take on a cooked breakfast, combining scrambled eggs, baked beans and a superior 'brown sauce' with a sausage of pigeon and tarragon. Desserts have taken in coconut milk rice pudding with caramelised pineapple, and a 'presentation' of chocolate items that should keep a cocoa addict going. Service, led by Kate Ashenford, is assured and amicable. The short wine list is steadily improving, and starts in southern France at £11.95, or £2.75 a glass.

CHEF: Marcus Ashenford   PROPRIETORS: Marcus and Kate Ashenford   OPEN: Wed to Sun L 12 to 2, Tue to Sat D 7 to 9   CLOSED: 1st 2 weeks Jan   MEALS: alc (main courses L £9.50 to £12, D £12 to £17). Set D £21.50 to £45. Light L dishes available   SERVICE: not inc, card slips closed   CARDS: Delta, MasterCard, Switch, Visa   DETAILS: 26 seats. Private parties: 26 main room. Vegetarian meals. Children's helpings. No music

▲ Wesley House 🍳 ✱

High Street, Winchcombe GL54 5LJ	COOKING 3
TEL: (01242) 602366 FAX: (01242) 609046	MODERN BRITISH
WEBSITE: www.wesleyhouse.co.uk	£28–£68

Dating from 1435, Wesley House looks its age, with a half-timbered black and white façade and, inside, dark beams, rough white-painted plaster walls and a huge old brick fireplace. The cooking makes much use of local supplies, although culinary inspiration is from across Europe, particularly the Mediterranean. Among starters, a single seared scallop is set on a tomato and courgette fondue with a streak of well-made tapenade dressing and garnished with crisp-fried onion ribbons, while main courses range from pan-roast salmon with butter-bean casserole to good-quality, flavoursome duck breast with Swiss chard, toasted hazelnuts, roughly crushed potatoes and a light Madeira jus. Finish perhaps with almond and cherry pithiviers with vanilla ice cream. The compact, good-value wine list opens with ten house selections from £14 a bottle, also available by the large or small glass.

CHEF: Martin Dunn   PROPRIETOR: Matthew Brown   OPEN: all week L 12 to 2, Mon to Sat D 7 to 9   CLOSED: 25 and 26 Dec   MEALS: alc L (main courses £12.50 to £18). Set L Mon to Sat £12.50 (2 courses) to £16, Set L Sun £18.50 (2 courses) to £21.50, Set D £29.50 (2 courses) to £35. Bar and Sun brunch menus available SERVICE: not inc   CARDS: Amex, Delta, MasterCard, Switch, Visa   DETAILS: 55 seats. 12 seats outside. Private parties: 60 main room. Vegetarian meals. Children's helpings. No smoking. No music. No mobile phones   ACCOMMODATION: 6 rooms, all with bath/shower. TV. Phone. D,B&B £90 to £180. Baby facilities (£5)

WINCHESTER Hampshire   map 2

Chesil Rectory 🍳 ✱

1 Chesil Street, Winchester SO23 8HU	COOKING 6
TEL: (01962) 851555	MODERN BRITISH
	£50–£73

In a city of venerable buildings, the striking half-timbered Chesil Rectory is as venerable as they come, dating from the mid-fifteenth century. Inside, the décor is simple, with dark beams and timbers set off against plain white walls hung with a few low-key artworks. Tables are widely spaced and dressed with heavy linen, elegant glassware and single orchids, and seating is large, comfortable leather armchairs. In charge of proceedings is the knowledgeable, charming and enthusiastic co-proprietor, who maintains a relaxed atmosphere while the kitchen turns out some seriously luxurious food.

At inspection, a starter galette of seared scallops and foie gras demonstrated pinpoint accuracy in the cooking of first-rate materials, the shellfish sticky and sweetly flavoured with a crisp, browned crust and seductively melting in the middle, while, to follow, roast halibut with boulangère potatoes, caviar and clams showed similar textbook skills. While the cooking is technically impressive, the tendency to play it safe and rely on luxury ingredients for impact perhaps does not show off the kitchen's considerable skills to their best. That said, a Rossini-style Aberdeen Angus fillet on crisp caramelised parsnip rösti with port gravy left its reporter grasping for superlatives. Wines favour France but not to the exclusion of some classy bottles from elsewhere. Mark-ups are not excessively steep, and there are also good choices at the lower end of the price scale, with the house selection of eight bottles starting at £16.

CHEF: Robert Quéhan   PROPRIETORS: Carl and Anna Reeve, Julia and and Robert Quéhan   OPEN: Sat L 12 to 1.30, Tue to Sat D 7 to 9   MEALS: Set L £30 (2 courses) to £35, Set D £45   SERVICE: not inc, 12.5% for parties of 7 or more   CARDS: Amex, Delta, Diners, MasterCard, Switch, Visa   DETAILS: 45 seats. Vegetarian meals. No smoking in 1 dining room. Music £5

▲ Hotel du Vin & Bistro ♦

Southgate Street, Winchester SO23 9EF	COOKING 4
TEL: (01962) 841414 FAX: (01962) 842458	MODERN EUROPEAN
WEBSITE: www.hotelduvin.com	£35–£62

It may be the oldest in this boutique chain (see entries in Birmingham, Brighton, Bristol, Harrogate and Tunbridge Wells), with the formula repeated at every branch, but the setting still manages to remain fresh and the civilised restaurant exudes the right air of informality without any stuffiness. It's also a 'paradise for a vinophiles', with prints of just anything and everything associated with wine'. The food is contemporary without being too fashionable, its clearly focused Mediterranean perspective evident in an assiette of duck with lentils and chorizo, and braised lamb neck with ratatouille, basil mash and olive jus. Seafood is a strength: among highlights have been seared scallops with Jerusalem artichoke and crispy pancetta, seared tuna with baby spinach, haricots verts and balsamic dressing, and roast cod with Jerusalem artichoke and roast salsify. At its best the kitchen's simple approach and light touch have produced delicate flavours and spot-on execution. Sadly, Eddie Grey is scheduled to move on to the forthcoming Henley-on-Thames branch when it opens during the currency of the guide. Service is charming, professional and helpful. The wine list remains triumphant, giving a spirited account of all regions with a mix of bargains, classics and modish bottles jumbled up together. Mark-ups can be high, but there is value to be had, with prices starting at £12.

CHEF: Eddie Grey   PROPRIETOR: Hotel du Vin Ltd   OPEN: all week 12 to 1.45, 7 to 9.45   MEALS: alc (main courses £14.50 to £17.50). Set L Sun £24.50   SERVICE: not inc   CARDS: Amex, Delta, Diners, MasterCard, Switch, Visa   DETAILS: 65 seats. 20 seats outside. Private parties: 48 main room, 8 to 48 private rooms. Car park. Vegetarian meals. Children's helpings. No cigars/pipes. Wheelchair access (also WC). No music   ACCOMMODATION: 23 rooms, all with bath/shower. TV. Phone. Room only £105 to £225. Rooms for disabled. Baby facilities

▲ Wykeham Arms ⚡✳

75 Kingsgate Street, Winchester SO23 9PE	COOKING 2
TEL: (01962) 853834 FAX: (01962) 854411	INTERNATIONAL
	£28–£49

Playing on its proximity to the oldest public school in the land, the Wykeham Arms oozes ancient-rooted Englishness and mild eccentricity. No need to fear institutional food here, though; the kitchen may please with simple, unpretentious 'Wyk' cottage pie, chicken and leek soup and fruit crumbles, but it also masters the complexities of breast of chicken on a risotto of bacon, butternut squash and Savoy cabbage with a tomato and grain mustard chutney and rocket pesto. There is a base of local produce, like Hampshire Down lamb and game, but influences from all over are detectable, and you could move from gravad lax to tuna loin with tapenade and couscous to tiramisù terrine. And to drink, Gale's ales vie for attention with a world-spanning 100-bin wine list that starts at £11.95 (and has fair mark-ups thereafter) and includes a range of halves, and 20 by the glass.

CHEFS: Alex Jones, Jamie Binch and Justin Mundy   PROPRIETORS: Peter and Kate Miller   OPEN: all week L 12 to 2.30, Mon to Sat D 6.30 to 8.45   CLOSED: 25 and 26 Dec, 1 Jan D   MEALS: alc (main courses £5.50 to £17.50). Set L Sun £14.50 (2 courses) to £18.50. Light L menu available   SERVICE: not inc, card slips closed   CARDS: Amex, Delta, MasterCard, Switch, Visa   DETAILS: 80 seats. 80 seats outside. Car park. Vegetarian meals. No children under 14. No smoking. No music. No mobile phones   ACCOMMODATION: 14 rooms, all with bath/shower. TV. Phone. B&B £50 to £120. No children under 14

WINCHMORE HILL Buckinghamshire   map 3

Plough   NEW ENTRY

Winchmore Hill HP7 0PA   COOKING 3
TEL: (01494) 721001   FAX: (01494) 728105   MODERN BRITISH
                                                             £22–£64

Overlooking the village green, this long, white-painted building has scored a hit with locals since new owners took over in January 2003. A stylish oak front door and standard shrubs on either side hint at its upmarket appeal. Inside is unexpectedly contemporary, the metropolitan-concept bar featuring a stainless-steel-topped counter and trendy leather seats, while the large dining room has a granite floor, scrubbed beams and timbers, high-backed chairs and banquettes and modern polished-wood tables. The sensibly compact menu, underpinned by a classical theme, fits the bill perfectly. Choose pan-fried foie gras on braised Puy lentils and wilted greens to start, and fillet of Buchan beef with pommes Anna, sautéed girolles and a truffle jus to follow, while Valrhona chocolate marquise with cherry sorbet and griottines winds things up. Ingredients are sound, presentation is colourful, and service from an attentive and youthful team is relaxed and informal. The wine list has a yen for serious bottles at high prices, but keeps its balance with enough everyday fare from £12.95 and an impressive line-up by the glass.

CHEF: Saleem Ahmed   PROPRIETOR: Darren Newby   OPEN: all week 12 to 2.30, 6 to 10   MEALS: alc (main courses £12 to £20). Set L £9.50 (2 courses) to £11.50   SERVICE: 12.5% (optional), card slips closed   CARDS: Amex, Delta, MasterCard, Switch, Visa   DETAILS: 75 seats. 30 seats outside. Private parties: 60 main room. Car park. Children's helpings. Occasional music. No mobile phones. Air-conditioned £5

WINDERMERE Cumbria   map 8

▲ Gilpin Lodge ⁵✳

Crook Road, Windermere LA23 3NE
TEL: (015394) 88818   FAX: (015394) 88058   NEW CHEF
WEBSITE: www.gilpin-lodge.co.uk   MODERN BRITISH
on B5284, 2m SE of Windermere   £32–£70

This country-house hotel sits in 20 acres of tranquillity on the back road from Kendal to Windermere. Chintzy and comfortable, it has antiques and crisp, white napery – plus some luxuries on three-course lunch and five-course dinner menus. A new chef arrived in July

2004, and we're told the style of food is set to continue. This has seen substantial pre-prandial nibbles followed in the dining room by starters like terrine of globe artichoke mousseline with frisée leaves and Stilton and walnut dressing. After a second course – maybe homely parsnip soup in a Lilliputian tureen – comes a sorbet, then mains like seared sea bass with creamed salsify, asparagus and chive-scented sauce. Finish with plum and apple crumble with vanilla sauce anglaise. Wine mark-ups seem fair, with plenty in the £20–£30 range and lots of halves; house bottles start at £14.50, and nine come by the glass (£4–£5).

CHEF: Simon Crannage   PROPRIETORS: John and Christine Cunliffe   OPEN: all week 12 to 2.30, 6.45 to 9.15. Light L menu available   MEALS: Set L £14.75 (2 courses) to £19.50, Set L Sun £23, Set D £42.50   SERVICE: not inc   CARDS: Amex, Delta, Diners, MasterCard, Switch, Visa   DETAILS: 60 seats. 20 seats outside. Private parties: 30 main room, 10 to 30 private rooms. Car park. Vegetarian meals. No children under 7. No smoking. Wheelchair access (not WC). No music. No mobile phones   ACCOMMODATION: 14 rooms, all with bath/shower. TV. Phone. B&B £140 to £250. No children under 7

▲ Holbeck Ghyll ♦ ⅝✸

Holbeck Lane, Windermere LA23 1LU
TEL: (015394) 32375   FAX: (015394) 34743
WEBSITE: www.holbeckghyll.com   COOKING 7
from A591 3m N of Windermere, turn E (Holbeck Lane,   MODERN BRITISH/FRENCH
signposted Troutbeck); hotel is ½m on left   £43–£81

The last climb from the main road gives this nineteenth-century mansion sumptuous views across Lake Windermere towards the Old Man of Coniston and the Langdale Pikes (there's a telescope in one of the lounges for closer inspection). Understated interiors eschew chintziness for a restrained taste that includes oak panelling in the dining room cheerily offset by giraffes and elephants on the pelmets.

First-rate breads and dainty, well-made nibbles introduce David McLaughlin's self-assured cooking, and a new sense of dishes honed to an impressive pitch marked our inspection. A langoustine and lentil velouté appetiser ('knockout stuff') prefigured a salad of warm langoustines with lobster and celeriac rémoulade, its flavour deepened with a judicious hint of truffle oil, and an altogether superior tripartite terrine (rabbit, foie gras and chicken) with a neat quenelle of gribiche dressing cleverly hovered between rusticity and refinement. Prime cuts of prime quality comprise main-course listings: Périgord duck breast, say; best end of lamb; veal fillet with butternut squash, broad beans and baby leeks; or sea bass, skin scored and crisped, plus aubergine caviar of improbable intensity and a red pepper and tomato sauce stippled with basil oil. The fine materials and craftsmanship making the food so enjoyable, and the unsparing attention to detail, reappear in dessert assiettes (of up to five items) that offer yet more discoveries; a lemon plate offered a wedge of lemon tart, a parfait, a mousse, a sorbet, and a scoop of ice cream further sharpened by passion-fruit sauce.

Expertly drilled service 'runs at a well-judged pace, with no lurches or longueurs', and the wine list picks out some of the finer things in life, whether from France, Italy or further afield (though the fair spread of half-bottles is resolutely Gallic). There's little below £20 (house wines start at £18.50) but you can spoil yourself for well under £30.

CHEF: David McLaughlin   PROPRIETORS: David and Patricia Nicholson   OPEN: all week 12.30 to 2, 7 to 9.30   MEALS: Set L £29.50, Set D £47.50. Light L menu available   SERVICE: not inc, card slips closed   CARDS: Amex, Delta, Diners, MasterCard, Switch, Visa   DETAILS: 65 seats. 25 seats outside. Private parties: 30 main room, 18 private room. Car park. Vegetarian meals. Children's helpings. No children under 8 at D.

No smoking. Wheelchair access (not WC). No music. No mobile phones ACCOMMODATION: 21 rooms, all with bath/shower. TV. Phone. B&B £125 to £260. Rooms for disabled. Baby facilities (£5)

Jerichos ⁵⋇

Birch Street, Windermere LA23 1EG	COOKING 5
TEL/FAX: (015394) 42522	MODERN BRITISH
EMAIL: enquiries@jerichos.co.uk	£34–£52

It doesn't take too much to strike a blow for vivid modernity in the tranquil environs of Lake Windermere, but Jerichos does it with style, thanks to its arresting interior décor and its contemporary British cooking. Mediterranean influences are most notable, resulting in chorizo and black pudding salad with a poached egg, shaved Parmesan and a garlic cream vinaigrette, or risotto of chicken, shiitakes and thyme with a reduction of balsamic, perhaps followed by roast loin of Lunesdale lamb on garlic and rosemary mash, with caramelised onions and a red wine sauce. The lamb itself is 'top class, very tender and cooked rosy-pink, with a good amount of crisp fat'. A deep mental breath is required to take in the lengthy menu specifications, which might include 'seared fillet of cod with coarse-grain mustard and mushroom crust, on creamed new potatoes, with peppered French beans, caramelised fennel and reduced white wine cream sauce'. After that lot, relax with raspberry and lemon crème brûlée, or chocolate fudge cake with chocolate whisky sauce. The wine list is arranged along food-matching principles, which will disorientate some, but there are many fine bottles on it, with prices starting at £12.50 and decent choice at under £20.

CHEFS: Chris Blaydes and Tim Dalzell PROPRIETORS: Chris and Jo Blaydes OPEN: Tue to Sun D only 6.45 to 9.30 CLOSED: Last 2 weeks Nov, first week Dec, 24 to 26 Dec, 1 Jan MEALS: alc (main courses £14 to £17) SERVICE: not inc CARDS: Delta, MasterCard, Switch, Visa DETAILS: 36 seats. Private parties: 28 main room. Vegetarian meals. No children under 12. No smoking. Music

▲ Miller Howe ⁵⋇

Rayrigg Road, Windermere LA23 1EY	COOKING 4
TEL: (015394) 42536 FAX: (015394) 45664	ENGLISH COUNTRY-HOUSE
WEBSITE: www.millerhowe.com	£29–£64

The Lake District is synonymous with scenery, and here Miller Howe lacks nothing. The northern third of England's longest lake stretches out before pre-prandial drinkers in the conservatory; it is visible too from the glittering dining room (whither all repair at 8pm for four courses plus intermediate sorbet) until descending dusk turns the windows to reflecting the ormolu hangings and *trompe l'oeil* balustrade dado.

The cooking still has some of that glitter. Braised ox tongue with parsley purée and a red wine essence came in a nice, sticky stack one spring evening, while roast wild duck (meaty, pink breast and delightfully fatted confit leg) with celeriac mash, and a vegetarian dish of beetroot Tatin on expert flattened puff, well-matched with goats' cheese, made strong impressions at inspection. Elsewhere, a sense of flagging effort, and of some dishes not matching their menu specifications, undermines overall performance. Warm chocolate fondant with liquorice ice cream is an accomplished dessert, though, made with good chocolate and full of balanced, considered flavours. The wine list is strong in the New World, especially South Africa, though under £20 there's not much beyond three of the six house bottles. Service is routine and somewhat sleepy.

CHEF: Paul Webster PROPRIETOR: Charles Garside OPEN: all week; 12.30 to 1.30, 8 (1 sitting) MEALS: Set L Mon to Sat £17.50. Set L Sun £19.95, Set D £39.50 SERVICE: 10% (optional), card slips closed

CARDS: Amex, Delta, MasterCard, Switch, Visa   DETAILS: 64 seats. Private parties: 64 main room, 6 to 20 private rooms. Car park. Vegetarian meals. No children under 8. Jacket and tie. No smoking. Wheelchair access (also WC). Music. No mobile phones. Air-conditioned   ACCOMMODATION: 15 rooms, all with bath/shower. TV. Phone. D,B&B £80 to £175. (£5)

WINDERMERE Devon

▲ Samling ⁵✗

Ambleside Road, Windermere LA23 1LR
TEL: (015394) 31922   FAX: (015394) 30400
WEBSITE: www.thesamling.com
3m N of Windermere turn E off A591 opposite water
sports centre; hotel 300yds on R

COOKING 6
MODERN BRITISH
£59–£91

This grand old house, white-painted with prominent barge boards on its three gables, sits in 60-odd acres and looks over Lake Windermere to the fells beyond. The interior is discreetly modern, low-key and generally peaceful, the dining room comfortably understated with high-backed chairs and good linen. The kitchen takes 'all the care over ingredients and preparation' one might hope for from its set menus, but without any showiness or pretence. Our inspector found its output 'light in quantity yet deep in flavour': witness a pigeon breast paired with seared foie gras on a bed of choucroute, the plate awash with beetroot and juniper jus. Other starters could include veal sweetbreads with endive, and red mullet with sea urchin foam. A main-course best end of local Herdwick lamb has been presented in tiny, delicate morsels alongside 'hotpot vegetables' and fondant potato, and John Dory in a cosmopolitan-sounding partnership with crab cannelloni, bouillabaisse sauce, confit artichokes and baby fennel. Flavours are likely to be intense and cooking accurate. Desserts seem less complex, but pear Tatin ('oozing gooey richness') with liquorice ice cream should appeal, as might an assiette of chocolate and praline.

Service is calm and proficient, and serious effort has gone into the wine list: a hefty tome that presents good, safe bottles from well-known sources alongside plenty of less obvious choices and some charming oddities. It offers quality and quantity for sure, but few options under £20, or £5.50 by the glass.

CHEF: Chris Meredith   PROPRIETOR: Tom Maxfield   OPEN: all week 12 to 1.45, 7 to 9.30   MEALS: Set L £45, Set D £45 to £60   SERVICE: not inc, card slips closed   CARDS: Amex, MasterCard, Switch, Visa   DETAILS: 22 seats. Private parties: 22 main room. Car park. Children's helpings. No smoking in dining room. Music. No mobile phones   ACCOMMODATION: 11 rooms, all with bath/shower. TV. Phone. B&B £175 to £405

WINKLEIGH Devon   map 1

Pophams ⁵✗

Castle Street, Winkleigh EX19 8HQ
TEL: (01837) 83767

COOKING 5
MODERN BRITISH
£37–£50

If good things come in small packages, then this minuscule, ten-seater must-book restaurant in the centre of the village is exceptional. It's much like eating in your own kitchen, really – friendly and convivial, with just three green-and-white-check clothed tables, a bring-your-own wine policy (no corkage charge), openings of just two lunchtimes a week, and a cash and cheques only rule. Melvyn and Dennis have doubled as chef and host for almost two decades – Melvyn at the stove and Dennis serving – sticking to the same winning formula and each day chalking on the blackboard the menu, which Dennis explains in detail. It's a simple, sensible-length affair that keeps within the operating limitations, utilising top-quality local ingredients, cooked with faultless timing, in effective combinations. Expect the likes of fresh salmon and cod fishcakes with a red pepper sauce, or warm onion tart with crème fraîche to start, and perhaps roast fillet of local beef with shiitake mushrooms and Madeira sauce to follow. An 'out of this world' sticky toffee pudding with clotted cream could be among the desserts. 'It's a fun experience, and the service is attentive and efficient', with Dennis looking after your wine.

CHEF: Melvyn Popham   PROPRIETORS: Dennis Hawkes and Melvyn Popham   OPEN: Thurs and Fri L only 11.45 to 2.30   CLOSED: Feb   MEALS: alc (main courses £16.50 to £18)   SERVICE: not inc   CARDS: none DETAILS: 10 seats. No children under 16. No smoking. Occasional music. No mobile phones. Air-conditioned

WINTERINGHAM North Lincolnshire   map 9

▲ Winteringham Fields ⁵⁄ₓ

Winteringham DN15 9PF   COOKING 9
TEL: (01724) 733096   FAX: (01724) 733898   PROVINCIAL FRENCH/SWISS
WEBSITE: www.winteringhamfields.com   £50–£118

There's a buzz in the air at Winteringham Fields. Long-running kitchen extension work has been completed, and newly promoted head chef Robert Thompson has injected a sense of youthful enthusiasm into the operation to complement the maturity and experience of Germain Schwab, one of the most talented chefs in Britain. Front-of-house, changes are less visible, although a few new appointments have sharpened up an already pretty impeccable service team, anchored by long-serving and knowledgeable specialists – overseen by the matchless Annie Schwab – who all relate skilfully and pleasantly with customers.

The classically orientated cooking is underpinned by pinpoint timing, 'stunning confidence' and technical proficiency, impeccable raw materials, and the careful artistry of the presentation. It's adventurous enough and visually stimulating enough to generate excitement, yet balanced by finely honed discipline. A lightly steamed pavé of brill, for example, embedded with a pair of langoustines, topped with a brill and mushroom mousse and set on a mound of Puy lentils in a puddle of Nantua sauce was the highlight of one reporter's meal, although it saw off stiff competition from wild boar loin cutlets with crab apple and a restrained stock sauce, and roast Aberdeen Angus fillet on wild mushroom risotto redolent of Parmesan, finished with a marchand de vin sauce and pak choi moistened with slicks of hollandaise.

Desserts reveal the full extent of the kitchen's culinary dexterity, as in a trio of pyramids of decreasing size featuring a chocolate fondant, its contents oozing out satisfactorily when the outer surface is breached, Christmas pudding ice cream, and a small pyramid of tangerine jelly. Prices are at the top end of the national spectrum, but then so is the quality, and if there is any lingering doubt over value, bear in mind that you get a lot for your money – not just a guaranteed 'special occasion' but plenty of food too. Meals start with a succession of three pre-starter appetisers – perhaps including a blini 'tart' of mango salsa and langoustine, then a slice of 'rich, fishy, oily' red mullet liver terrine – and puddings are preceded by a beautifully crafted miniature dessert, such as a small passion-fruit soufflé spiked with a miniature ice cream cone and accompanied by a shot glass of coconut and pineapple granita. And to round off the meal, coffee is served with a panoply of impressive petits fours. Reporters are unanimous in their verdict that this is worth every penny.

Reports confirm that the wine selection can confidently be entrusted to the sommelier, but the list is not so vast as to be unmanageable. Bordeaux and Burgundy are fine but also kept in proportion, while other regions are generally short but assured. Prices start at £20, but mark-ups are high.

CHEFS: Germain Schwab and Robert Thompson   PROPRIETORS: Annie and Germain Schwab   OPEN: Tue to Sat 12 to 1.30, 7 to 9.30   CLOSED: 2 weeks at Christmas, last week Mar, first 10 days Aug   MEALS: alc (main courses £30 to £33). Set L £27 (2 courses) to £31, Set D £38 to £70   SERVICE: not inc, card slips closed   CARDS: Amex, Delta, MasterCard, Switch, Visa   DETAILS: 42 seats. Private parties: 10 main room, 6 to 10 private rooms. Car park. No smoking. Wheelchair access (not WC). No music. No mobile phones   ACCOMMODATION: 10 rooms, all with bath/shower. TV. Phone. B&B £90 to £195. Rooms for disabled. No children under 8 exc babes in arms

WITCHFORD Cambridgeshire   map 6

▲ Needhams ✸

186 Main Street, Witchford CB6 2HT	COOKING 2
TEL/FAX: (01353) 661405	MODERN EUROPEAN
WEBSITE: www.needhamsrestaurant.co.uk	£27–£50

Luke and Verity Pearson have been busy redecorating their unostentatious converted farmhouse and tracking down more local and organic suppliers. Their regularly changing menu embraces European and occasional Oriental influences, and some unusual and interesting pairings occur – grilled sea trout is served with pickled red cabbage, while liquorice finds its way into a blackcurrant crème brûlée. To begin, home-cured bresaola might rub shoulders with a tian of sweet Indian spiced vegetables with mung bean salad, while main courses could veer from roast breast of guinea fowl with caramelised onion and grape tart and sauté foie gras to stuffed aubergine with wild rice, pine nuts, crème fraîche and tomato confit. As a finale, consider cardamom and honeycomb parfait, or treacle tart with rum-soaked sultanas. House wines are £10.25.

CHEF: Luke Pearson   PROPRIETORS: Luke and Verity Pearson   OPEN: Tue to Sun L 12 to 2, Tue to Sat D 7 to 9 (6.30 to 9.30 Sat)   MEALS: alc (not Sun; main courses £12 to £16.50). Set L Sun £17.25   SERVICE: not inc CARDS: Amex, Delta, MasterCard, Switch, Visa   DETAILS: 60 seats. Private parties: 90 main room, 20 to 90 private rooms. Car park. Vegetarian meals. Children's helpings. No smoking. Wheelchair access (also WC). Music. No mobile phones   ACCOMMODATION: 2 rooms, available Fri and Sat only. TV. Room only £40 to £60 (£5)

WOODBRIDGE Suffolk   map 6

Captain's Table ✸ £

3 Quay Street, Woodbridge IP12 1BX	COOKING 3
TEL: (01394) 383145 FAX: (01394) 388508	MODERN EUROPEAN
WEBSITE: www.captainstable.co.uk	£23–£43

Among the attractions of this unpretentious café-style venue is its walled garden, a prize spot for al fresco dining in summer. If the weather isn't so good, the three linked dining areas are pleasant enough, with a casual atmosphere and simple décor featuring prints of French vineyard scenes on magnolia walls. The eclectic bistro cooking aims for good value and broad appeal, and the kitchen takes pride in making good use of some top-notch local produce, notably fish and seafood, and vegetables and herbs 'picked that very morning'. Deep-fried tiger prawns in pastry with a herb mayonnaise dip, twice-baked mussel soufflé with thermidor sauce, and slow-roast duck leg confit with pea purée and red wine sauce are typical, with simpler options such as shepherd's pie, or chargrilled ribeye with chips, and various sandwiches at lunchtime. The majority of wines on the short list are under £15, with house French £9.95.

CHEF: Pascal Pommier   PROPRIETORS: Jo and Pascal Pommier   OPEN: Tue to Sun and bank hol Mon L 12 to 2 (3 Sun high season and bank hols), Tue to Sat and bank hol Sun and Mon D 6.30 to 9.30 (10 Fri and Sat)   CLOSED: 2 weeks early Jan   MEALS: alc (main courses £7 to £15.50)   SERVICE: not inc, card slips closed   CARDS: Delta, MasterCard, Switch, Visa   DETAILS: 50 seats. 30 seats outside. Private parties: 34 main room, 19 to 34 private rooms. Car park. Vegetarian meals. Children's helpings. No smoking. Wheelchair access (not WC). No music

WORLESTON Cheshire   map 7

▲ Rookery Hall ❧✳

Worleston CW5 6DQ   COOKING 4
TEL: (01270) 610016   FAX: (01270) 626027   MODERN EUROPEAN
WEBSITE: www.handpicked.co.uk/rookeryhall   £34–£87

Built with Jamaican sugar money in 1816, the hall is a stolid edifice on two floors. One pair of lucky guests gets to sleep in a four-poster bed made in the 1830s, and all who eat here will enjoy the original dining room, with its ornate plaster mouldings, mahogany panelling, and leather-upholstered chairs. Quality British ingredients such as Aberdeen Angus beef from the Buccleuch estate, together with Continental luxuries like foie gras, inform the gently experimental approach of Craig Malone. A trio of roast scallops is presented on individual mounds of champ with a parsley and garlic velouté for a refined, precisely executed first course. Local goats' cheese forms the topping for a warm tartlet cleverly served with a dressing combining raisins and balsamic. Main-course meats are well looked after, offering lamb two ways, the loin roasted, the neck braised with split peas, while roast monkfish is enjoyably given the full treatment, with pancetta, mash, roast foie gras and a sauce of oyster and sweet Muscat. A creative streak runs through desserts such as milk chocolate risotto with toasted pine nuts and basil syrup, rhubarb and ginger soup, or pancakes filled with mashed banana and white chocolate served with banana ice cream. The youthful staff are well drilled and amiable. A lengthy wine list is grouped by style, with prefatory notes and quotes heading each section. Choices are mostly good and prices correspondingly hefty. Wines by the glass start at £4.50, and a list of knocked-down bin-ends is worth a look.

CHEF: Craig Malone   PROPRIETOR: Hand Picked Hotels   OPEN: Sun to Fri L 12.30 to 1.45, all week D 7 to 9.30 MEALS: alc D (main courses £16.50 to £25.50). Set L £15 (2 courses) to £20, Set D Mon to Thur £37.50. Bar menu available   SERVICE: not inc   CARDS: Amex, Delta, Diners, MasterCard, Switch, Visa   DETAILS: 60 seats. 30 seats outside. Private parties: 60 main room, 10 to 30 private rooms. Car park. Vegetarian meals. Children's helpings. No smoking. Wheelchair access (also WC). No music. No mobile phones   ACCOMMODATION: 46 rooms, all with bath/shower. TV. Phone. Room only £85 to £150. Rooms for disabled. Fishing

WRIGHTINGTON Lancashire   map 8

Mulberry Tree ❧✳

9 Wrightington Bar, Wrightington WN6 9SE   COOKING 4
TEL/FAX: (01257) 451400   MODERN BRITISH
                                                                           £29–£50

This spacious, open-plan pub conversion stays true to its Lancashire setting by avoiding unnecessary fripperies of décor and having local boy and co-owner Mark Prescott at the stoves. Simple pub dishes are served in the main bar, but ambitious, yet modestly priced, cooking is offered in a pair of more formal dining rooms. Black pudding and Lancashire cheese might be combined in a tart with hot ketchup, and followed by roast sirloin of beef with Yorkshire pudding, but there is also a global undertow that might take in deep-fried Thai-style squid with chilli dipping sauce, steamed asparagus served with chorizo and chilli-spiced egg, and slow-roast belly pork with white bean ribollita and a Parmesan crisp. A generosity of approach shows in hearty portions and multiple rich flavours. Desserts end things on a luxurious note: rum baba with red fruits, or double yoghurt mousse with exotic fruit salad and a sesame tuile. A thoughtfully chosen wine list offers plenty of variety, and a fair range of half-bottles. House wines are £13.50 (£3.15 a glass).

CHEF: Mark Prescott PROPRIETORS: James Moore and Mark Prescott OPEN: Mon to Sat 12 to 2, 6 to 9.30 (10 Fri/Sat), Sun 12 to 9.30 CLOSED: 26 Dec and 1 Jan MEALS: alc (main courses £9.50 to £17). Set L Sun £17.95. Bar menu available SERVICE: not inc CARDS: Delta, MasterCard, Switch, Visa DETAILS: 80 seats. Private parties: 80 main room. Car park. Vegetarian meals. Children's helpings. No smoking. Wheelchair access (not WC). Music. Air-conditioned

WYE Kent
map 3

▲ Wife of Bath ⭐

4 Upper Bridge Street, Wye TN25 5AF
TEL: (01233) 812540
WEBSITE: www.wifeofbath.com

COOKING 2
MODERN EUROPEAN
£32–£69

Wye is a charming old village between Ashford and Canterbury, its narrow, twisting streets lined with buildings of varying degrees of antiquity. At its centre is this fittingly old-fashioned restaurant-with-rooms, which is more of a small country-house hotel in style. It has a comfortably appointed dining room with large, well-spaced tables laid with well-starched, good-quality tablecloths, silver cutlery and white candles in gilt candlesticks. The eclectic modern European cooking style produces starters of rillettes of pigs' trotters with ravigote dressing, and seared scallops on cauliflower and rosemary purée, and main courses of roast pork fillet with sage and black pudding mash, and pan-fried fillets of sea bass with mussel and saffron velouté. Interesting British and Irish cheeses make an appealing alternative to desserts such as vanilla pannacotta with rhubarb compote. House selections at £14 open a rather conservative wine list.

CHEF: Robert Hymers PROPRIETORS: Andrew and Nicola Fraser OPEN: Tue to Sat 12 to 1.30, 7 to 9.30 MEALS: alc (main courses £16 to £22.50). Set L £13 (2 courses) to £19, Set D Tue to Thur £24.50 SERVICE: not inc CARDS: Amex, Delta, MasterCard, Switch, Visa DETAILS: 50 seats. Private parties: 50 main room. Car park. Children's helpings. No smoking. Wheelchair access (not WC). No music. No mobile phones ACCOMMODATION: 5 rooms, all with bath/shower. TV. Phone. B&B £45 to £95. Rooms for disabled

YARM Stockton-on-Tees
map 10

Chadwick's

104B High Street, Yarm TS15 9AU
TEL: (01642) 788558 FAX: (01642) 788344

COOKING 4
GLOBAL
£24–£50

This self-styled Continental café stands at one end of Yarm's broad main street and fits in well with the atmosphere of this attractive little town. Large windows look over the street, and the décor tends towards the fashion for angular lines, plain wooden furniture, and plentiful mirrors to give a pleasantly light feel. Separate lunch and dinner menus cater for different modes of dining, lunch being a much more informal affair with various sandwiches, simple pasta dishes and pizzas with interesting toppings such as wasabi vegetables and sashimi tuna, or lamb kofta, harissa, tomato and raita. In the evening, starters take in anything from twice-baked Swiss cheese soufflé to bruschetta of chicken livers and mushrooms, while main courses range from calf's liver with bacon and bubble and squeak to pork souvlaki with Greek salad and a feta spring roll. The short wine list features 30 wines under £30 and a further dozen 'fine wines' above £30. House Duboeuf is £11.50.

CHEFS: David Brownless and Steven Conyard   PROPRIETORS: David Brownless and D. Beattie   OPEN: Mon to Sat 11.30 to 2.30, 5.30 to 9.30. Also open 1 Sun L per month   CLOSED: 25 and 26 Dec, 1 Jan, bank hol Mons   MEALS: alc (main courses L £6.50 to £9.50, D £12 to £16.50). Tapas menu available 5.30 to 6.30   SERVICE: not inc, 10% for parties of 12 or more   CARDS: MasterCard, Switch, Visa   DETAILS: 70 seats. Private parties: 70 main room. Vegetarian meals. Children's helpings. No-smoking area. Music. Air-conditioned

YARMOUTH Isle of Wight   map 2

▲ George, Brasserie ▼

Quay Street, Yarmouth PO41 0PE   COOKING 3
TEL: (01983) 760331   FAX: (01983) 760425   MODERN BRITISH
WEBSITE: www.thegeorge.co.uk   £38–£61

The former governor's house dates from the seventeenth century and maintains a luxurious feel not typically associated with seaside hotels. It offers two options for dining, both under the guidance of Kevin Mangeolles: the spacious brasserie, with its excellent views over the gardens to the Solent, and the more formal restaurant. The atmosphere in the brasserie (to which the score relates) is relaxed, and the cosmopolitan approach to food might bring warm squid and ruby chard salad with chilli and lime dressing before braised belly pork with green peppercorn sauce, Savoy cabbage and butternut squash. Organic salmon, crab and orange spring rolls with a hazelnut dressing have been praised for their 'delicious and unusual' flavours, and apple soufflé with Calvados ice cream pronounced 'wonderful'. A page each of interesting red and white wines are topped and tailed by a baker's dozen of house wines at £13.50 (also by the glass) and a collection of older clarets. More reports, please, on the restaurant.

CHEF: Kevin Mangeolles   PROPRIETORS: John Illsley and Jeremy Willcock   OPEN: Brasserie all week 12 to 3, 7 to 10; Restaurant Tue to Sat D only 7 to 10   MEALS: Brasserie alc (main courses £15 to £17); Restaurant Set D £45   SERVICE: not inc, card slips closed   CARDS: Delta, MasterCard, Switch, Visa   DETAILS: Brasserie: 80 seats. 100 seats outside. Private parties: 40 main room, 10 to 40 private rooms. Vegetarian meals. Children's helpings. Wheelchair access (not WC). No music; Restaurant: 40 seats. Private parties: 20 main room, 20 private room. Vegetarian meals. No children under 10. Wheelchair access (not WC). No music. Air-conditioned   ACCOMMODATION: 17 rooms, all with bath/shower. TV. Phone. B&B £130 to £235

YATTENDON Berkshire   map 2

▲ Royal Oak ⁙✳

The Square, Yattendon RG18 0UG   NEW CHEF
TEL: (01635) 201325   FAX: (01635) 201926   MODERN BRITISH
EMAIL: oakyattendon@aol.com   £34–£59

The handsome old inn is on what passes for the main square of this affluent village a few miles west of Pangbourne. It consists of a bar/brasserie and separate restaurant, and you might like to note that it doesn't have a car park. Service has been polished and personable. As we go to press Jason Gladwin is due to be replaced in the kitchen by Jamie Mould, formerly at Cliveden (see entry, Taplow), joined by the newly promoted former sous-chef Richard Terry. The menu is bound to undergo some changes under the new team, and details are not available as we finalise this edition. Previously, the ambitious cooking has shown a decided cosmopolitan edge, with starters like a warm salad of goats' cheese with kohlrabi and Seville orange dressing, followed poached boneless Cornish sole with seared scallops glazed with a light mustard and tarragon velouté. Among the desserts has been milk chocolate marquise with espresso prunes and fromage blanc sorbet. Wines starts at £14 and there's plenty of choice, though options under £20 are limited. Reports please.

CHEFS: Jamie Mould and Richard Terry   PROPRIETOR: Rocco Ltd   OPEN: all week 12 to 2 (2.30 Fri to Sun), 7 to 9.30 (10 Fri to Sun)   CLOSED: 1 Jan   MEALS: alc (main courses £13 to £19). Set L £20 (2 courses) to £23.50   SERVICE: 10% (optional), card slips closed   CARDS: Amex, Delta, MasterCard, Switch, Visa   DETAILS: 60 seats. 40 seats outside. Private parties: 100 main room. Vegetarian meals. No children under 6. No smoking in 1 dining room. No music   ACCOMMODATION: 5 rooms, all with bath/shower. TV. Phone. Room only £95 to £140. Baby facilities

YORK North Yorkshire   map 9

▲ Blue Bicycle 🌂✳

34 Fossgate, York YO1 9TA	COOKING 3
TEL: (01904) 671696 FAX: (01904) 677688	MODERN EUROPEAN/SEAFOOD
WEBSITE: www.thebluebicycle.com	£29–£63

Although in the city centre, the Blue Bicycle feels insulated from all the hurly-burly. Its busy ambience appeals to many reporters, who also endorse the interesting and generally sound cooking offered on its main carte and supporting blackboards. Successful starters have included juicy king prawns carefully cooked in garlic and chilli with saffron noodles and lime salad, and haggis, neeps and tatties with a whisky cream. Main-course halibut on a seafood and black truffle couscous earned praise too. Fish dishes predominate – salmon, cod, swordfish, mussels, scallops and more – but beef fillet figures too, and fried duck breast with noodles and stir-fry vegetables. Finish with pineapple Tatin and liquorice ice cream. Nearly 80 interesting wines start at £13, and 18 come by the glass (£3.50 from £5.50).

CHEF: Kenny Noble   PROPRIETOR: Anthony Stephenson   OPEN: all week 12 to 2.30, 6 to 9.30 (9 Sun) CLOSED: 25 and 26 Dec, 1 Jan   MEALS: alc (main courses £8 to £22)   SERVICE: 10% (optional)   CARDS: MasterCard, Switch, Visa   DETAILS: 73 seats. Vegetarian meals. Children's helpings. No smoking. Wheelchair access (not WC). Music at Sat D   ACCOMMODATION: 1 room, with bath/shower. TV. B&B £150.

Melton's 🍷 🌂✳

7 Scarcroft Road, York YO23 1ND	COOKING 5
TEL: (01904) 634341 FAX: (01904) 635115	MODERN EUROPEAN
WEBSITE: www.meltonsrestaurant.co.uk	£26–£57

'If we lived in York, we would probably visit Melton's every week,' says a fan. 'Real thought goes into providing a top-class restaurant experience.' The aim of chefs Michael Hjort and Jon Coates is simple: 'to make every effort to source good local and seasonal ingredients and to cook and serve them with integrity.' Each dish has a number of components; the skill of the chefs and their team here lies in ensuring that all of those parts come together on the plate. Starters range from crab with rocket and crème fraîche on a blini to a salad of home-smoked chicken with herbs. Main-course rack of Towthorpe lamb is marinated like game and served with parsnip purée and boulangère potatoes with kale, and roast monkfish is served with anise-scented meat juices, fennel and crushed new potatoes. Among desserts, hot raspberry soufflé has hit the spot, as has Victoria plums on a filo base with caramel sauce. Young but professional staff show a genuine interest in guests' enjoyment without being intrusive. Honest and helpful annotations are a useful guide through a well-researched and good-value wine list.

CHEFS: Jon Coates and Michael Hjort   PROPRIETORS: Michael and Lucy Hjort   OPEN: Tue to Sat L 12 to 2, Mon to Sat D 5.30 to 10   CLOSED: 3 weeks at Christmas, 1 week Aug   MEALS: alc (main courses £11.50 to £19). Set L and D 5.30 to 6.15 £17   SERVICE: not inc   CARDS: Delta, MasterCard, Switch, Visa   DETAILS: 42 seats. Private parties: 36 main room, 2 to 18 private rooms. Vegetarian meals. Children's helpings. No smoking in 1 dining room. Wheelchair access (not WC). Music. No mobile phones. Air-conditioned (£5)

Melton's Too 🗑 ✻ £

25 Walmgate, York YO1 9TX	COOKING 2
TEL: (01904) 629222 FAX: (01904) 636677	MODERN EUROPEAN
WEBSITE: www.meltonstoo.co.uk	£22–£40

Melton's Too is the more casual sister establishment of Melton's (see above). The interior, described by some as 'spartan', can be cramped, but the buzzy atmosphere generally makes up for the lack of space. The food is not showy or complicated, being based on good, simple flavour combinations. The daily specials are the place to look for the best dishes, say some cauliflower soup with cheesy garlic bread, or 'brilliant' chicken roasted with garlic and herbs accompanied by new potatoes. Desserts might include an 'excellent' winter fruit crumble. Tapas-style dishes are served in the bar area. Service has been described in the past as both 'pleasant' and 'perfunctory' but seems to have stabilised as 'very good' of late. The 'excellent value' has been noted, helped by a moderately priced list of a dozen or so wines, with a pair of organic Italian bottles opening the bidding at £10.80.

CHEF: Steve Holding   PROPRIETORS: Michael and Lucy Hjort   OPEN: all week 10.30 to 10.30 (9.30 Sun) CLOSED: 2 days at Christmas, 1 Jan   MEALS: alc (main courses £5.50 to £12). Sandwich, brunch and tapas menus available   SERVICE: not inc   CARDS: Delta, MasterCard, Switch, Visa   DETAILS: 140 seats. Private parties: 40 main room, 25 to 40 private rooms. Vegetarian meals. Children's helpings. No smoking in 1 dining room. Wheelchair access (also WC). Music. Air-conditioned (£5)

▲ Middlethorpe Hall ✻

Bishopthorpe Road, York YO23 2GB	COOKING 3
TEL: (01904) 641241 FAX: (01904) 620176	MODERN ENGLISH
WEBSITE: www.middlethorpe.com	£28–£69

A hugely imposing William and Mary country house just outside York, Middlethorpe was once home to Lady Mary Wortley Montagu. It sits in 20 acres of parkland complete with small lake and ha-has and provides a highly formal setting for Martin Barker's painstaking cooking. Dishes look spare: a single scallop, of 'delicious flavour', comes just browned and borne along on salsify purée with strands of crisped artichoke, while the tiny leg and rolled breast of quail make another first course, served with a miniature 'cassoulet' of snails and wild mushrooms. Daube of beef is brought up to date with parsnips, pomme purée and parsley oil, and desserts marshal the likes of hot chocolate fondant with pistachio ice cream, or vanilla pannacotta with fig jam. Exciting sorbets, perhaps of passion fruit or lemongrass, get an enthusiastic nod. A lengthy list of fine classic wines has plenty of choice, with house selections from £14.50.

CHEF: Martin Barker   PROPRIETOR: Historic House Hotels Ltd   OPEN: all week 12.30 to 2.30, 7 to 9.45   MEALS: alc L exc Sun (main courses £8.50 to £15). Set L Sun £23.50, Set D £37.95 to £46.50   SERVICE: net prices, card slips closed   CARDS: Delta, MasterCard, Switch, Visa   DETAILS: 56 seats. 24 seats outside. Private parties: 56 main room, 56 to 100 private rooms. Car park. Vegetarian meals. No children under 8. Jacket. No smoking. Wheelchair access (also WC). No music. No mobile phones   ACCOMMODATION: 29 rooms, all with bath/shower. TV. Phone. Room only £109 to £370. Rooms for disabled. No children under 8. Swimming pool

---

Rish

7 Fossgate, York YO1 9TA
TEL: (01904) 622688   FAX: (01904) 671931
WEBSITE: www.rish-york.co.uk

COOKING 6
MODERN BRITISH
£31–£101

This glass-fronted restaurant, on a lovely old street in the centre of York, is flooded with light and bears the hallmarks of contemporary design, from cream leather upholstery to muted modern art. Gavin Aitkenhead, latterly at Winteringham Fields (see entry, Winteringham), was appointed head chef in December 2003, and the kitchen's output seems to have moved up several gears as a result. An amuse-bouche of confit lobster made an inspector's heart soar, and was followed by a trio of duck ('a real thing of beauty'): a ball of dense rillettes, a pink-roast slice of breast rolled in spices, and a sliver of pan-fried foie gras on a diminutive slice of brioche, with a few splodges of sloe gin sauce for contrast. Equally impressive has been another starter of seared scallops with warm scallop and ginger jelly, morel velouté and baby leeks. Main courses maintain the high standards. Roast lobster might arrive on pipérade next to a courgette flower beignet in a slick of fennel cream, the slightly sour flavours of the peripherals accurately balancing the sweetness of the shellfish, while slow-roast belly pork, with summer vegetables, pea and truffle purée and a 'deeply savoury and unctuous' sauce, has made as much of an impact. If these don't finish you off, go for the hot raspberry charlotte with rhubarb and Sauternes ice cream – which 'looked fairly ordinary but tasted gorgeous'. Wines run from £13 for house basics to world-famous bottles, with a range of 17 by the glass.

CHEF: Gavin Aitkenhead   PROPRIETORS: Maria and Sam Abu Rish   OPEN: all week 12 to 2.30, 7 (6.30 Fri and Sat) to 10   CLOSED: 25 to 27 Dec, 1 and 2 Jan   MEALS: alc D (main courses £12.50 to £22.50). Set L £15 (2 courses) to £18.50, Set D £70   SERVICE: not inc, 10% for parties of 8 or more   CARDS: Amex, Delta, MasterCard, Switch, Visa   DETAILS: 64 seats. Private parties: 20 main room. Vegetarian meals. Children's helpings. No smoking. Wheelchair access (not WC). Music

Scotland

map 11

Silver Darling ✸

Pocra Quay, North Pier, Aberdeen AB11 5DQ
TEL: (01224) 576229   FAX: (01224) 588119

COOKING 6
SEAFOOD
£34–£67

Set in an old quayside house by the harbour entrance, this aptly named seafood restaurant ('silver darling' is Aberdonian for herring) offers stunning views of sea, coastline and sky, not to mention the bustling marine traffic. A metal spiral staircase ascends to the bright, cheerful dining room, with its huge all-round windows (and sunny yellow blinds) that supply those super views. Didier Dejean's enticing lunch menu and evening carte, the latter in French with English translations, ebb and flow with the fruits of the sea as they become available (there are token land-based options too, for those who must). Freshness and quality of raw materials are givens here, timings are accurate, and a fine balance between complexity and clean flavours is maintained. Expect Mull of Kintyre roast turbot with braised celery, pan-fried ceps, and a cep and black truffle sauce, or pan-fried medallions of monkfish with squid, wilted spinach leaves and fish roe, served with a squid ink sauce. Starters might include wood mushroom and langoustine minestrone, or duck foie gras ravioli and trompettes; desserts get proper attention too, perhaps a cinnamon-flavoured pear sandwiched between filo layers and served with maple sauce and crumbled pecans. Service has proved polished and unobtrusive, while the compact wine list, predominantly French and naturally white-focused, offers house Bergerac at £16.50, plus eight wines by glass from £3.50.

CHEF: Didier Dejean   PROPRIETORS: Didier Dejean and Karen Murray   OPEN: Mon to Fri L 12 to 1.30, Mon to Sat D 7 to 9.30   CLOSED: 23 Dec to 7 Jan   MEALS: alc (main courses L £9.50 to £12.50, D £18.50 to £21.50)   SERVICE: not inc, card slips closed   CARDS: Amex, Delta, Diners, MasterCard, Switch, Visa   DETAILS: 55 seats. Private parties: 50 main room. Vegetarian meals. Children's helpings. No smoking. Music

map 11

▲ Summer Isles Hotel ▮ ✸

Achiltibuie IV26 2YG
TEL: (01854) 622282   FAX: (01854) 622251
WEBSITE: www.summerisleshotel.co.uk
take A835 to Drumrunie, 10m N of Ullapool, then single-track road for 15m; hotel 1m past Achiltibuie on left

COOKING 5
MODERN EUROPEAN
£28–£62

Readers who have made the journey along a meandering single-track road to this remote hotel on Scotland's west coast consider it worth the journey – and the fairly hefty prices. The low, whitewashed building, with splendid views over the Summer Isles, offers 'a marvellous amount of nothing to do', according to owners Mark and Gerry Irvine, but there are plenty of recommended walks to help work up an appetite for the no-choice, five-course dinner. Most ingredients are produced or caught locally, and in these surroundings, that means a great deal of fresh fish – particularly at lunchtime, when platters of locally smoked salmon, mixed seafood, and Tanera Bay langoustines and spiny lobsters are on offer. The dinner menus are simple but certainly not lacking in sophistication. Starters might be monkfish tails wrapped in filo, or fish soup, then there is more fish (scallops with vermouth, buttery champ, leeks and basil, or plainly grilled halibut with herbs), followed by a meat course: perhaps a successful dish of duck breast on spiced baked apple with a wine sauce, or roast venison with pancetta and juniper. Desserts are wheeled in on a trolley, and the exemplary selection of cheeses is 'in beautiful condition' (one reporter was pleased to be given the opportunity to choose whether to have cheese before or after pudding). Thirty red Bordeaux under £30 set the tone for a long wine list which focuses on classical France but always has an eye for value. New World selections are much shorter but with plenty of inspiring bottles. Prices start at £12, and terrific bargains like 1996 Bandol from Domaine Tempier at £18 crop up here and there. Wines available by the glass vary according to each night's menu.

CHEF: Chris Firth-Bernard   PROPRIETORS: Mark and Gerry Irvine   OPEN: all week L 12.30 to 2, D 8 (1 sitting) CLOSED: 18 Oct to 23 Mar   MEALS: alc L (main courses £11 to £30). Set D £46. Bar menu available SERVICE: net prices, card slips closed   CARDS: MasterCard, Switch, Visa   DETAILS: 30 seats. Private parties: 8 main room. Car park. Children's helpings. No children under 8. No smoking. No music. No mobile phones   ACCOMMODATION: 13 rooms, all with bath/shower. Phone. B&B £75 to £240. No children under 8. Fishing

ANNBANK South Ayrshire   map 11

▲ Enterkine Country House 🍴✹

Annbank KA6 5AL
TEL: (01292) 520580   FAX: (01292) 521582   COOKING 4
WEBSITE: www.enterkine.com   MODERN EUROPEAN
on B742 just N of Annbank   £31–£61

This impressive white 1930s building up a long, tree- and rhododendron-lined drive has the intimate, relaxed atmosphere of a private country residence: 'tasteful, comfortable and peaceful'. Interiors are well kept and elegant. The lounge (open fire, plump sofas and armchairs and large windows looking over unspoilt countryside) is in soothing shades of green and cream, while one of the dining rooms has yellow walls, a sage green carpet and elegantly set tables. Service is 'smart and professional but also welcoming and friendly'; note men must wear a jacket and tie. There are set-price menus with about five choices per course. Weekend dinners are 'real special-occasion' affairs with four listed courses, plus canapés, amuse bouche, pre-dessert and profiteroles with coffee all included; weekday dinners are three courses. Fresh local produce, simplicity and elegant presentation are hallmarks, with starters such as an appetising casserole of perfectly cooked mussels with a cream sauce and tomato concassé. Among main courses might be a flavoursome combination of tender roast herbed chicken with wild mushroom risotto, braised leeks, Parmesan and a red wine sauce, and for dessert there's white chocolate raspberry mousse with chocolate syrup. Wines are strongest in France, and six house bottles start at £18 (£4.95 a glass).

CHEF: Douglas Smith   PROPRIETOR: Oswald Browne   OPEN: all week 12 to 2, 7 to 9   MEALS: Set L £12.50 (2 courses) to £16.50, Set D £18.50 (2 courses) to £37.50   SERVICE: not inc, 10% for parties of 6 or more, card slips closed   CARDS: Amex, Delta, Diners, MasterCard, Switch, Visa   DETAILS: 70 seats. Private parties: 70 main room, 6 to 20 private rooms. Car park. Vegetarian meals. Children's helpings. Jacket and tie. No smoking. Wheelchair access (also WC). Music. No mobile phones   ACCOMMODATION: 6 rooms, all with bath/shower. TV. Phone. B&B £55 to £150. Rooms for disabled. Baby facilities. Fishing

ANSTRUTHER Fife

map 11

Cellar ▮ ⅚✳

24 East Green, Anstruther KY10 3AA
TEL: (01333) 310378   FAX: (01333) 312544

COOKING 6
MODERN SEAFOOD
£31–£63

Always a popular spot with visitors to St Andrews golf course, the Cellar has adorned the Fife dining scene for over 20 years; yet Peter Jukes – simultaneously chef/proprietor, father to four daughters and trainer of up-and-coming young chefs – remains as enthusiastic as ever. Despite the fairly sophisticated look to the décor, the atmosphere remains decidedly relaxed, and you may have to argue with the resident cat to get a chair in the lounge.

The cooking, too, shows an assured blend of sophistication and homeliness, epitomised by a starter of lobster and sea trout quiche with salad in a smoked lobster dressing. The menu doesn't change significantly or often, but the repertoire has been finely honed over the years, and the serious-minded approach is based on a strict attention to detail, particularly with regard to the seasons, and a responsible attitude to current issues in food such as dwindling fish supplies. Thus 'simple dishes are turned into something excellent'. Omelette of smoked haddock, or terrine of Gressingham duck, pistachios and green peppercorns with a spiced pear chutney might be followed by grilled halibut fillet with greens, pine nuts, chopped bacon and hollandaise sauce; or pan-fried beef fillet with wild mushrooms, lyonnaise potatoes and Dijon mustard sauce. Among tempting dessert options might be warm date and ginger sponge with cinnamon ice cream. The wine list has a very personal feel, with Bordeaux, Burgundy and Alsace the main areas of interest in France, and Australia leading the New World pack. Quality is high, and particular favourites turn up in a range of vintages. House wines are £15, and a good range of half-bottles complements the line-up of seven by the glass.

CHEF: Peter Jukes   PROPRIETORS: Peter and Susan Jukes   OPEN: Wed to Sat L 1 to 1.30, Tue to Sat D 7 to 9 (also Sun L and D June to Sept)   MEALS: Set L £15.50 (2 courses) to £18.50, Set D £28.50 (2 courses) to £38.50   SERVICE: not inc   CARDS: Amex, Delta, Diners, MasterCard, Switch, Visa   DETAILS: 42 seats. Private parties: 42 main room, 20 private room. Children's helpings. No smoking. Wheelchair access (not WC). Occasional music. No mobile phones

ARDEONAIG Stirling

map 11

▲ Ardeonaig Hotel ▮ ⅚✳

NEW ENTRY

Ardeonaig FK21 8SU
TEL: (01567) 820400   FAX: (01567) 820282
WEBSITE: www.ardeonaighotel.co.uk

COOKING 3
SOUTH AFRICAN/SCOTTISH
£27–£56

From the owners of Fish Hoek (see entry, London) comes this new venture, which could hardly provide a greater contrast: a hotel overlooking Loch Tay reached by a rutted and precipitous road. The tranquil dining room commands fine waterside views, and the interior was variously scented at inspection by both a peat-burning fire and a colossal show of lilies.

Pete Gottgens is South African, and he applies his home technique to the best that Scotland can offer. Bobotie spring rolls are light and crisp, encasing a spicy minced lamb and served with the imported Mrs Ball's chutney; Pinotage wine goes into a sauce for rich, gamey, locally shot wood pigeon; and white stumpnose, a Cape fish, is chargrilled and served with red peppers, rock salt and olive oil, its skin just crisped – 'I savoured every fresh, flaking morsel'. Monkfish, by contrast, might be curried with prawns and banana, while red-legged partridge in season is partnered by spicy Malay-style vegetables. Hot chocolate fondant is well served by its vanilla ice cream, or there may be crunchy-topped apple crumble presented in a small pan. Reliable names mingle with some limited-edition specials on a wine list that puts its faith 100 per cent in the cream of the South African crop, from a slate of delicious fizz right through to the good old-fashioned port styles and brandies.

CHEF: Pete Gottgens   PROPRIETORS: Pete and Sara Gottgens   OPEN: all week 12 to 2, 6 to 10   MEALS: alc (main courses £9.50 to £17.50). Set L and D £25.50 (2 courses) to £47.50. Bistro menu available   SERVICE: not inc   CARDS: MasterCard, Switch, Visa   DETAILS: 30 seats. 24 seats outside. Private parties: 40 main room. Car park. Vegetarian meals. No smoking. Music. No mobile phones   ACCOMMODATION: 20 rooms, all with bath/shower. Phone. B&B £45 to £220. No children under 12. Fishing

AUCHTERARDER Perthshire & Kinross   map 11

▲ Andrew Fairlie at Gleneagles

Auchterarder PH3 1NF   COOKING 7
TEL: (01764) 694267   FAX: (01764) 694163   MODERN FRENCH
WEBSITE: www.gleneagles.com   £79–£115

Andrew Fairlie's restaurant, which is an autonomous business within the Gleneagles Hotel, combines a traditional approach to service – understated courtesy the abiding tone – with modernism in the design. Full-drop, light brown curtains divide the expansive space into bar and dining room, and the menu is a stylishly produced booklet, with prices noted discreetly at the back.

The food is best described as modern French, but there is no tendency to the outlandish or to overt technical wizardry here, just an assured way with contemporary cooking built on the solid foundation of quality ingredients. Among starters, a slice of ballottine of foie gras is complemented by a spoonful of apricot and grapefruit chutney, truffled cream and pain Poilâne, and the house speciality is home-smoked Scottish lobster served in the shell and dressed in lime and herb butter. The kitchen is justly proud of its lamb from the Glenearn estate, which may be roasted and served with crisply grilled polenta and half a kidney flavoured with tarragon mustard and bedded on onion relish. Fish alternatives might include a classic pairing of sea bass with champagne sauce, or halibut with bourride and aïoli. Waits of 25 minutes are necessary for the cooked desserts: perhaps hazelnut pithiviers with ginger ice cream, or luxuriously textured caramel soufflé with a quenelle of shyly flavoured vanilla ice. Service from ladies in rakish pink cravats is impressively precise and full of enthusiasm for the food. Bread has been poorly reported, though, and the background jazz Muzak has been too loud for some, especially in the bar.

A wine list of indubitable pedigree contains many fine bottles. Those with three figures to spend are furnished with an embarrassment of choice. Those with less than £25 will just be embarrassed, unless they look to the wines by the glass, although these start at £7.50 and stop at £13.50 for a *grand cru* St-Emilion from a poor vintage. Accommodation is available in the hotel, of course.

CHEF/PROPRIETOR: Andrew Fairlie   OPEN: Mon to Sat D only 7 to 10   MEALS: Set D £55 to £75   SERVICE: not inc   CARDS: Amex, Delta, Diners, MasterCard, Switch, Visa   DETAILS: 40 seats. Car park. Vegetarian meals. No children under 12. No smoking. Wheelchair access (also WC). Music. No mobile phones

AULDEARN Highland

map 11

▲ Boath House 🕏

Auldearn IV12 5TE	COOKING 5
TEL: (01667) 454896 FAX: (01667) 455469	FRANCO-SCOTTISH
WEBSITE: www.boath-house.com	£41–£72

In 20 acres of grounds, this country-house hotel is marked from the road by a discreetly designed modern stone sign, the first clue to the 'elegance with a modern twist' that defines Boath House. A Georgian mansion, it is grand yet not over-imposing. The entrance hall mixes bright modish colours and paintings with the classical structure, while the lounge continues the theme, enhanced by plush chairs and sofas and modern decoration. The dining room itself is relatively small but elegantly proportioned, with a bay window overlooking lake and gardens. Service is 'exemplary', and Don and Wendy Matheson are friendly and chatty hosts.

Charles Lockley's daily-changing five-course dinner menu offers choice only at main-course and dessert stage on a modern but classically inspired repertoire. An opening potage – following canapés in the lounge – could be cauliflower velouté with Avruga caviar and might be followed by steamed rabbit loin with foie gras on crushed peas and trompettes. Roast saddle of blackface lamb with celeriac purée, parsnip crisps and a white wine sauce might show up at main-course stage. Cheese precedes dessert of, for example, double-chocolate brownies with mascarpone sorbet. The wine list is biased towards France, seasoned with bottles from here, there and everywhere. Six house wines from £14.50 are a fresh, modern bunch.

CHEF: Charles Lockley   PROPRIETORS: Don and Wendy Matheson   OPEN: Thurs to Sun L 12.30 to 1.30, all week D 7 to 8.15   MEALS: Set L £27.50 to £32.50, Set D £45   SERVICE: not inc   CARDS: Amex, Delta, MasterCard, Switch, Visa   DETAILS: 30 seats. Private parties: 30 main room, 6 to 8 private rooms. Car park. Children's helpings. No smoking. Wheelchair access (also WC). Occasional music. No mobile phones   ACCOMMODATION: 6 rooms, all with bath/shower. TV. Phone. B&B £110 to £220. Rooms for disabled. Baby facilities. Fishing

BALLANTRAE South Ayrshire

map 11

▲ Glenapp Castle

NEW ENTRY

Ballantrae KA26 0NY	
TEL: (01465) 831212 FAX: (01465) 831000	COOKING 3
WEBSITE: www.glenappcastle.com	FRENCH
off A77 2m S of Ballantrae	£15–£85

This baronial mansion has a glorious view across the Firth of Clyde to Ailsa Craig and Arran. Dinner is a taste of grand country living (lunch consists of soup and sandwiches), and pricing reflects the luxury ingredients and the exclusive atmosphere – impressive setting and diligent, smiling service are integral to the experience. Strengths of the simple cooking are fresh, good-quality raw materials, impeccable timing and elegant presentation, although the no-choice dinners may lack balance, with scant vegetation to cut their richness. Start with an appetiser of foie gras on crackers, then move through trout terrine, and 'wonderfully tender' blanquette of quail, pause over a lavender sorbet before the main event: perhaps a few bites of local lobster, perfectly cooked and simply presented. After local soft cheese, whisky-soaked and rolled in oatmeal, finish on chocolate fondant with rice ice cream. An international mix of 17 house wines are arranged by style and priced at £19.50. Otherwise France rules the roost, with the most convincing support coming from Australia.

CHEF: Tristan Welch PROPRIETORS: Graham and Fay Cowan OPEN: all week 1 to 2.30, 7 to 9 CLOSED: 1 Nov to 1 Apr MEALS: Set L £15, Set D £55 SERVICE: not inc, card slips closed CARDS: Amex, Delta, MasterCard, Switch, Visa DETAILS: 40 seats. Private parties: 20 main room. Car park. Children's helpings. Wheelchair access (also WC). No music. No mobile phones ACCOMMODATION: 17 rooms, all with bath/shower. TV. Phone. D,B&B £255 to £515. Rooms for disabled. Cots, baby listening, highchairs (£5)

BALLATER Aberdeenshire   map 11

▲ Balgonie Country House 𝄞✳

Braemar Place, Ballater AB35 5NQ	COOKING **4**
TEL/FAX: (013397) 55482	MODERN SCOTTISH
WEBSITE: www.balgonie-hotel.co.uk	£32–£58

The ambition of this Edwardian house, built on a family rather than a palatial scale, is signalled by four carefully tended acres of grounds, including a croquet lawn and a statue of an African shepherd boy. Enter the house to find light public rooms with a comfortable small country-house feel and interesting books lying around. In the kitchen, a clear sense of purpose is evident from the sourcing of good materials and a balanced menu with well-defined ideas. The output varies from smoked ham hough (hock) and brawn terrine, to pork fillet wrapped in Parma ham with creamed potatoes, red cabbage marmalade, turnip and apple purée, and red wine sauce. A degree of comfort is apparent in some dishes: smoked haddock and pea risotto with Parmesan oil, or a tower of fried cod with sautéed potatoes, wild mushrooms, leeks, chorizo, and a fish nage. Desserts have included a 'very appealing' chocolate marquise with pistachio parfait and raspberry sorbet. Service is attentive, discreet and personable. The wine list shows a preference for France, especially Burgundy and Bordeaux, with few bottles under £20. Beaujolais-Villages opens proceedings at £15.75.

CHEFS: John Finnie and William Steele PROPRIETORS: John and Priscilla Finnie OPEN: all week 12.30 to 2 (reservations only), 7 to 9 CLOSED: 6 Jan to 12 Feb MEALS: Set L £19.50, Set D £35 SERVICE: not inc, card slips closed CARDS: Amex, Delta, Diners, MasterCard, Switch, Visa DETAILS: 30 seats. Private parties: 30 main room. Car park. Children's helpings. No smoking. Wheelchair access (also WC). Occasional music ACCOMMODATION: 9 rooms, all with bath/shower. TV. Phone. B&B £50 to £135 (£5)

▲ Darroch Learg ▼ 𝄞✳

Braemar Road, Ballater AB35 5UX	COOKING **6**
TEL: (013397) 55443 FAX: (013397) 55252	MODERN SCOTTISH
EMAIL: info@darroch-learg.demon.co.uk	£31–£64

The substantial late-Victorian mansion offers comfortable, well-appointed and welcoming public rooms with leafy views out to Glen Muick from the conservatory extension dining room. There's a certain opulence and comfort to David Mutter's cooking, too, which is neither traditional nor cutting edge but gives a sense of well-sourced materials handled with confidence. Native supplies play an essential role in the kitchen's success, from Deeside hare to Ayrshire ducks, squabs and guinea fowl. Smoked salmon, mussels and scallops from Loch Fyne are given a fair crack, too, perhaps in the form of tortellini of Arbroath smokie with roast sea scallops, Sauternes sauce and curry oil. Precision timing is characteristically applied to roast calves' sweetbreads with Jerusalem artichoke purée, mushroom tuile and St George's mushrooms, and the prime quality of ingredients also impressed an inspector who was taken by the 'superb flavour' of medallion of Balmoral venison.

A real understanding of textures and flavours was apparent in a main course of guinea fowl with tagliatelle, broad beans and a creamy morel sauce, while desserts maintain interest: a smooth and 'roundly lemony' lemon tart, and a delicately crusted classic vanilla crème brûlée. Bread is home-made and 'straightforwardly unflavoured', and service is well informed. The wine list shows a sure touch in Bordeaux and Burgundy, and doesn't automatically plump for the grandest bottles. Italy looks nicely balanced and South Africa is particularly well chosen among the good New World ranges. The 'brief encounters' page of one-off oddities is definitely worth a look. Prices kick off around £18 but there are a lot of good-value bottles in the mid-20s.

CHEF: David Mutter   PROPRIETORS: the Franks family   OPEN: Sun L 12.30 to 2, all week D 7 to 9   CLOSED: Christmas, last 3 weeks Jan   MEALS: Set L £21, Set D £37.50 to £43.50   SERVICE: net prices, card slips closed   CARDS: Amex, Delta, Diners, MasterCard, Switch, Visa   DETAILS: 48 seats. 8 seats outside. Private parties: 62 main room. Car park. Children's helpings. No smoking. Wheelchair access (not WC). No music   ACCOMMODATION: 17 rooms, all with bath/shower. TV. Phone. B&B £65 to £165. Rooms for disabled. Baby facilities

BALQUHIDDER Stirling   map 11

▲ Monachyle Mhor ⁵⧓

Balquhidder FK19 8PQ	COOKING 5
TEL: (01877) 384622 FAX: (01877) 384305	MODERN SCOTTISH
WEBSITE: www.monachylemhor.com	£29–£58

It's worth allowing plenty of time to get here. The narrow road winds through six miles of 'hauntingly lovely' glen, skirting the water's edge and passing sheep and Highland cattle, before you arrive at this pink-painted country house. In such a remote setting, it's hardly surprising that local produce dominates the menu, and the level of industry behind the operation is impressive – the owners gather wild mushrooms, cure meat, and make their own sausages. These are put to good use in an ambitious cooking style that shows some elaborate touches while allowing the superlative quality of the ingredients to shine through. Meals might start with a classic velvety, creamy cauliflower soup finished with a trickle of pungent white truffle oil, the result 'dreamy and decadent', or perhaps accurately timed kidneys, juicily pink, bursting with flavour and set on a balsamic onion and fine bean tart with chorizo and mustard dressing. Among main courses, 'superb' roast sirloin is a fixture, served with roseval potatoes, 'confit' carrots and buttered leeks, although equally tempting alternatives might include 'utterly fresh' baked cod fillet, golden brown and flaky-textured, served with smoked garlic mash and hollandaise. To finish, subtly flavoured iced Amaretto with chocolate mousse has made a good impression. A good little wine list is arranged by grape variety, with separate sections of 'oddballs'. House white is £13, red £14.50.

CHEFS: Tom Lewis and Selwyn October   PROPRIETORS: Tom and Angela Lewis   OPEN: all week 12 to 1.45, 7 to 8.45   CLOSED: 9 Jan to mid-Feb   MEALS: alc exc Sun L (main courses L £9.50 to £14.50, D £14.50 to

£18.50). Set L Sun £21.50, Set D £37. Light L menu available SERVICE: not inc CARDS: MasterCard, Switch, Visa DETAILS: 40 seats. 20 seats outside. Private parties: 24 main room, 6 to 12 private rooms. Car park. Vegetarian meals. Children's helpings. No children under 12. No smoking. Wheelchair access (also WC). No music. No mobile phones ACCOMMODATION: 11 rooms, all with bath/shower. TV. Phone. B&B £55 to £150. No children under 12. Baby facilities. Fishing

BLAIRGOWRIE Perthshire & Kinross   map 11

▲ Kinloch House � ✷

Blairgowrie PH10 6SG
TEL: (01250) 884237 FAX: (01250) 884333   COOKING 5
WEBSITE: www.kinlochhouse.com   SCOTTISH
on A923, 3m W of Blairgowrie   £28–£61

The Allens' country-house hotel in Perthshire (they previously owned Airds at Port Appin in Argyll, see entry) is run with characteristic care and attention to detail. A walled kitchen garden supplies fresh produce and herbs, while in the spacious and extremely comfortable dining room there is pretty china and pristine cutlery. In the kitchen Bill McNicol charges those plates with premium ingredients, prepared simply so as to emphasise their pedigree. Lobster ravioli are served with creamed leeks and a classic shellfish sauce, while scallops are lightly fried and served on a herby salad dressed in pesto. A soup, perhaps straightforward carrot and coriander, intervenes before the main course, which may be fillet of hare with Puy lentils, red cabbage, root vegetables and a port sauce, or one of the celebrated gigantic fillet steaks, accompanied by seared foie gras, potato rösti and caramelised onions, sauced with Madeira. Recline at the end into such luxuries as a Mirabelle plum soufflé with marzipan ice cream, or alternatively a plate of Scottish and English cheeses. Bordeaux and Burgundy are the wine list's main focus – even the half-dozen wines by the glass veer towards French classics – though there's something of note from all points of the compass. Half-bottles are taken seriously too.

CHEF: Bill McNicol PROPRIETORS: the Allen family OPEN: all week 12 to 2, 7 to 9 CLOSED: 17 to 29 Dec MEALS: Set L £18.50, Set L Sun £22, Set D £39. Snack/light L menu available SERVICE: not inc, card slips closed CARDS: Amex, Delta, MasterCard, Switch, Visa DETAILS: 40 seats. Private parties: 20 main room. Car park. Vegetarian meals with prior notice. Children's helpings. No smoking. Wheelchair access (also men's WC). No music. No mobile phones ACCOMMODATION: 15 rooms, all with bath/shower. TV. Phone. D,B&B £90 to £330. Rooms for disabled. Swimming pool

CAIRNDOW Argyll & Bute   map 11

Loch Fyne Oyster Bar ✷ £

Clachan, Cairndow PA26 8BL
TEL: (01499) 600236 FAX: (01499) 600234   COOKING 2
WEBSITE: www.loch-fyne.com   SEAFOOD
on A83, at head of Loch Fyne   £23–£64

'Environmental care' and 'sustainability' are watchwords for the Loch Fyne chain, and this, the original outlet, sets an admirable example as it seeks to conjure up 'the food, atmosphere and spirit of Argyll'. At the very head of the sea loch, this can be a magnet for the crowds, but service keeps its cool. Local seafood is the main theme, with plates of oysters, mussels and organic smoked salmon topping the bill of fare. When cooking is involved, it's rarely more complicated than milk-poached smoked haddock with egg, or skewered king scallops wrapped in bacon. Away from fish, a network of 'artisan' producers provides the raw materials for, say, venison fillet with Cassis and red wine sauce. Youthful whites dominate the reasonably priced wine list; house French is £10.95.

CHEFS: Tracy Wyatt and Ahamed Haja   PROPRIETOR: Loch Fyne Oysters Ltd   OPEN: all week 9 to 8.30 (7.30 Nov to Mar)   CLOSED: 25 and 26 Dec, 1 and 2 Jan   MEALS: alc (main courses £5.95 to £25)   SERVICE: not inc   CARDS: Amex, Delta, Diners, MasterCard, Switch, Visa   DETAILS: 120 seats. Private parties: 40 main room. Car park. Vegetarian meals. Children's helpings. No smoking. Wheelchair access (also WC). Occasional music. No mobile phones (£5)

CLACHAN-SEIL Argyll & Bute   map 11

▲ Willowburn Hotel ⁵✳

Clachan-Seil, by Oban PA34 4TJ
TEL: (01852) 300276   FAX: (01852) 300597
WEBSITE: www.willowburn.co.uk
from Oban take A816 S for 8m; then take B844, following   COOKING 3
signs for Seil Island and Luing, for 7m; after hump-   MODERN SCOTTISH/FRENCH
backed bridge Willowburn is approx ¼m on left   £42–£51

Cross the road bridge south of Oban to Seil Island and admire the images of the mainland hills mirrored on the surface of Clachan Sound through the windows of the dining room of this idyllically located restaurant-with-rooms, a long, low, whitewashed building. The daily-changing menu is based around raw materials sourced from the surrounding waters and hills, with vegetables and fruit from the garden or from local growers. A starter of lamb fillet in a herb brioche was praised by one reporter, and this might be followed by a soup – tomato consommé, for instance – and then a main course of, say, bacon-wrapped roast beef fillet in a rosemary crust with a girolle and Madeira sauce, or baked halibut with prawn butter and a creamy grapefruit sauce. Choose something fruity at dessert stage: rhubarb, pear and basil cobbler, or redcurrant and raspberry tartlet. Some good bottles show up on the carefully compiled wine list, on which annotations convey the owners' enthusiasm. Prices start at £12.50.

CHEF: Chris Wolfe   PROPRIETORS: Jan and Chris Wolfe   OPEN: all week D only 7 for 7.30   CLOSED: Dec, Jan and Feb   MEALS: Set D £32   SERVICE: not inc, card slips closed   CARDS: Delta, MasterCard, Switch, Visa   DETAILS: 20 seats. Car park. Vegetarian meals. No children under 8. Children's helpings. No smoking. Music. No mobile phones   ACCOMMODATION: 7 rooms, all with bath/shower. TV. D,B&B £72 to £150. No children under 8

COLBOST Highland   map 11

▲ Three Chimneys ▼ ⁵✳

Colbost, Dunvegan, Isle of Skye IV55 8ZT
TEL: (01470) 511258   FAX: (01470) 511358   COOKING 5
WEBSITE: www.threechimneys.co.uk   MODERN SCOTTISH
on B884, 4m W of Dunvegan   £39–£84

In romantically remote environs in the far north-west of Skye, the Spears' restaurant-with-rooms does justice to its setting. It offers the kind of package you would expect in a smart country restaurant in France, with an air of polish bright enough to suit a city address and yet belonging specifically right here. Chic modern furnishings offset the rough-cast shell of the converted crofters' cottages, and the haunting views over Loch Dunvegan exercise their own evocative appeal.

Shirley Spear delivers 'refined, poised' cooking, in the words of a reporter, a style well suited to lunch dishes such as 'creamy yet subtle' shellfish bisque; twice-baked, generously filled haddie and prawn soufflé with excellent saladings from nearby Glendale; and lemon and almond roulade with passion-fruit sorbet and hot chocolate sauce. In the evenings the choice expands to a potential four-course format, with soup or shellfish intervening between such options as lambs' kidney croustade with Ayrshire bacon sauced with mustard and cream sherry, and grilled fillet of turbot with lemon butter, accompanied by seared scallops, fine beans and a sauce of Seville orange. Hot marmalade pudding with Drambuie custard is a long-staying dessert, or there might be rhubarb and ruby orange compote with stem ginger ice cream. Service is 'formally correct' as well as friendly. The wine list has a certain metropolitan swagger and favours top-quality bottles. In France, serious collections of Bordeaux and Burgundy are spiced up by the smartest names from the south and a worthwhile showing from Alsace, and there's a good range of half-bottles; shorter selections elsewhere are fresh and modern. House wines start at a hefty £17.95.

CHEF: Shirley Spear   PROPRIETORS: Eddie and Shirley Spear   OPEN: Mon to Sat L 12.30 to 2, all week D 6.30 to 9.30   CLOSED: 13 to 19 Dec, 9 to 28 Jan, L Nov to end Mar   MEALS: Set L £18 (2 courses) to £25, Set D £48 to £55   SERVICE: not inc, 10% for parties of 10 or more   CARDS: Amex, Delta, MasterCard, Switch, Visa   DETAILS: 30 seats. 8 seats outside. Private parties: 15 main room. Car park. Vegetarian meals. Children's helpings. No children under 8 at D. No smoking. Wheelchair access (not WC). No music   ACCOMMODATION: 6 rooms, all with bath/shower. TV. Phone. B&B £145 to £215. Rooms for disabled. Baby facilities

CRINAN Argyll & Bute   **map 11**

▲ Crinan Hotel, Westward Restaurant ⑤✗

Crinan PA31 8SR   COOKING **5**
TEL: (01546) 830261   FAX: (01546) 830292   MODERN EUROPEAN
WEBSITE: www.crinanhotel.com   £56–£67

The restaurant's name should orientate you as you gaze over Crinan towards the mountains of Mull, with the Gulf of Corryvreckan (the second largest whirlpool in the western hemisphere) in the middle distance. If you're up early enough, you may see the fishing fleet heading out towards the Atlantic side of Jura. Some of their catch will land up at the hotel, where Ben Tish runs an impeccably quality-conscious kitchen. Humanely reared meats, organic salads and fruits, and bread baked on the premises from organic flour, all find their way onto the fixed-price menus of four courses plus coffee.

Start with a fricassee of lobster, cockles and mussels with herb spaghetti in a champagne velouté, or oxtail and pancetta ravioli, before going on to wild sea bass with crab pithiviers and Swiss chard. There are meats – perhaps rump of Argyll lamb with roasted sweetbreads and chèvre dauphinois – but the first love is clearly seafood, which is why the intermediate course will so often be something like a shellfish potage with fennel and chives. Desserts end things with a flourish, the hot apple tart accompanied by beignets, a granita and Sauternes cream. Service seems to vary a little, with one reporter in May getting a new team still requiring some bedding in. The wine list, which is annotated in an entertaining and helpful style, has many fine growers and négociants. Prices open at £16 (red) and £16.50 (white).

CHEF: Ben Tish   PROPRIETORS: Frances and Nick Ryan   OPEN: all week D only 7 to 8.30 (9 summer)   MEALS: Set D £42.50. Bar menu available L   SERVICE: not inc, card slips closed   CARDS: MasterCard, Switch, Visa   DETAILS: 40 seats. 20 seats outside. Private parties: 60 main room, 40 to 50 private rooms. Car park. Children's helpings. No smoking. Wheelchair access (also WC). Occasional music

ACCOMMODATION: 20 rooms, all with bath/shower. TV. Phone. D,B&B £75 to £300. Rooms for disabled. Baby facilities

CROSSMICHAEL Dumfries & Galloway   map 11

Plumed Horse ✹

Main Street, Crossmichael DG7 3AU	COOKING 6
TEL: (01556) 670333	MODERN EUROPEAN
WEBSITE: www.plumedhorse.co.uk	£32–£58

'I doubt there is a more improbably sited really good restaurant in Britain,' commented one visitor to this unassuming building on the main road through the village. Inside, however, its credentials are not in doubt as one encounters crisp linen, deep carpets, immaculate table settings and food to match. 'The value is remarkable,' says an inspector of the downstairs restaurant (there's also a brasserie upstairs, which broadens the appeal even further). Helpings are generous, components are first-rate, and serious skill goes into many dishes: witness an elaborate and intensely flavoured smoked salmon and oyster soup, served with caviar and a centrepiece of smoked salmon. Start perhaps with an interesting, leek-wrapped terrine combining smoked ham, black pudding and foie gras with Cumberland sauce. Moving on, one might find monkfish fillet paired with Jerusalem artichoke purée, scallops and shellfish butter: accurate treatment of fine ingredients giving 'delightful textures and vivid flavour'. Meat-eaters might favour braised breast of organic veal with foie gras, sautéed sweetbreads, carrots and morels. Puddings run to a prune and Armagnac parfait with apricot sorbet – subtle but clear tastes well balanced – or an 'aggressively chocolatey' tart accompanied by coffee, Cognac and raisin ice cream. Visitors can expect a hearty welcome from chef/proprietor Tony Borthwick, who on quiet evenings sometimes doubles as head waiter. Wines begin at £12.50; the mainly European list seems most at home in France, and has venerable clarets and white Burgundies at the top end.

CHEFS: Tony Borthwick and Russell Robertson PROPRIETOR: Tony Borthwick OPEN: Tue to Fri and Sun L 12.30 to 1, Tue to Sat D 7 to around 9 CLOSED: 25 and 26 Dec, 2 weeks Jan, 2 weeks Sept MEALS: alc Tue to Sat (main courses £19). Set L £20, Set L Sun £22; brasserie £19 (two courses) to £22.50 SERVICE: not inc, card slips closed CARDS: Delta, MasterCard, Switch, Visa DETAILS: 18 seats. Private parties: 18 main room, 24 private room. No smoking. Wheelchair access (also WC). Occasional music. No mobile phones. Air-conditioned

CUPAR Fife   map 11

Ostlers Close ♥ ✹

25 Bonnygate, Cupar KY15 4BU	COOKING 5
TEL: (01334) 655574	MODERN SCOTTISH
WEBSITE: www.ostlersclose.co.uk	£32–£57

After extensive refurbishment, Ostlers Close now has an attractive, modern interior, worthy of the contemporary Scottish cooking served within. Jimmy and Amanda Graham have given it a cleaner, less cluttered style without losing its intimacy. After 24 years, their philosophy in the kitchen remains unchanged: to buy the best possible local produce and treat it simply, so that the ingredients speak for themselves. Meat is of fine provenance (free-range Glamis duck, Tamworth pork and Jacob sheep), eggs are from a local farm, and there is plenty of game in season. Fish is treated with a light touch: 'perfectly cooked' roast cod served with a well-judged Arbroath smokie risotto, or nicely seasoned lemon sole fillets with sauce vierge and asparagus. Baskets of own-picked wild mushrooms are on display in autumn and may be stir-fried to serve with a herb potato scone and red onion marmalade or used to accompany 'really excellent' roast saddle of roe venison. Desserts range from the homely (upside-down apple and bramble crumble with bramble mascarpone ice cream) to the cosmopolitan (vanilla and orange pannacotta with toasted pineapple and passion-fruit sauce). The handwritten wine list offers a well-chosen international selection at very reasonable prices, with some smart bottles in the mix. Good Chilean house red is £14.50.

CHEFS/PROPRIETORS: James and Amanda Graham   OPEN: Sat L 12.15 to 1.30, Tue to Sat D 7 to 9.30
CLOSED: 25 and 26 Dec, 1 and 2 Jan, 2 weeks Oct   MEALS: alc (main courses L £11 to £12.50, D £18 to £19)
SERVICE: not inc   CARDS: Amex, Delta, MasterCard, Switch, Visa   DETAILS: 26 seats. Private parties: 26
main room. Children's helpings. No children under 6 at D. No smoking. Wheelchair access (also WC). No
music. No mobile phones

DALRY North Ayrshire   map 11

Braidwoods ▼ ⁵⁄✳

Drumastle Mill Cottage, Dalry KA24 4LN
TEL: (01294) 833544   FAX: (01294) 833553   COOKING 6
WEBSITE: www.braidwoods.co.uk   MODERN SCOTTISH
1m off A737 Dalry to Saltcoats road   £29–£63

Keith and Nicola Braidwood took advantage of their annual three-week closure in January 2004 to redecorate, as a way of celebrating ten years of operations. The style is now a little brighter and more modern than old hands will remember it, but is still in keeping with the rugged venerability of the converted mill cottages in which this highly accomplished restaurant is housed. The culinary style continues in its successful vein of Scottish produce cooked with sensitivity and care, in presentations that avoid unnecessary complexity. Rillettes of potted oak-smoked salmon come with cucumber salad and melba toast as one way of starting. Soups are well received, perhaps involving Arbroath smokies and leeks with saffron and chives, and are served as an intermediate course at dinner, with the alternative of something like a mini Caesar salad with smoked chicken. Among the regional riches are Highland red deer, served with Jerusalem artichoke purée and morels, and turbot caught off the west coast, robustly accompanied by Savoy cabbage and smoked bacon. A selection of British farmhouse cheeses from a justly celebrated cheesemonger is the savoury alternative to desserts such as cinnamon pannacotta with apple compote and caramel sauce, or pecan parfait with sharp raspberry coulis. The whole approach is one of quiet, attentive courtesy, and the absence of both canned music and cigarette smoke has prompted a positive response from reporters. Half a dozen 'seasonal selections' open a wine list with a quality-first approach and French classics to the fore, so it takes a moment to realise that there are also good options under £20 from around the world. Only four come by the glass, but half-bottles are plentiful.

CHEFS/PROPRIETORS: Keith and Nicola Braidwood   OPEN: Wed to Sun L 12 to 1.45, Tue to Sat D 7 to 9
CLOSED: 25 and 26 Dec, first 3 weeks Jan, first 2 weeks Sept   MEALS: Set L Wed to Sat £16 (2 courses) to
£19, Set L Sun £25, Set D £32 to £36   SERVICE: not inc, card slips closed   CARDS: Amex, Delta, Diners,
MasterCard, Switch, Visa   DETAILS: 24 seats. Private parties: 12 main room. Car park. No children under
12 at D. No smoking. No music. No mobile phones

DORNOCH Highland

map 11

▲ 2 Quail ✗

Castle Street, Dornoch IV25 3SN
TEL: (01862) 811811
WEBSITE: www.2quail.com

COOKING 4
MODERN EUROPEAN-PLUS
£49–£59

2 Quail is set discreetly in a Victorian terrace of substantial sandstone houses, and its elegant, book-lined interior exudes a house-proud domesticity that extends from sparkling top-quality glasses in the small dining room to cotton hand-towels in the loos. Similar dedication, along with consistency in execution, animates the kitchen: details like an appetiser of tangy tomato consommé receive the same attention as the main acts. A densely packed, moist venison terrine (its richness perfectly complemented by blueberry chutney), a faultlessly cooked fillet steak with a well-balanced sherry and truffle gravy, and a fresh, accurately timed sea bream fillet with braised fennel and a vermouth butter sauce exemplify well-sourced ingredients brought together with classic restraint. Among the sweets 'seriously classy ice creams – far too good for children' stand out for their understated sweetness and clear flavours. France accounts for two-thirds of a concise wine list, which starts with £13.95 for Vin de Pays d'Oc and finishes with mature clarets and carefully chosen white Burgundies.

CHEF: Michael Carr   PROPRIETORS: Michael and Kerensa Carr   OPEN: Tue to Sat (Nov to Mar, Thur to Sat) D 7.30 to 9.30. Booking advisable   CLOSED: 25 and 26 Dec, 2 weeks Feb/Mar, bank hols   MEALS: Set D £35.50   SERVICE: not inc   CARDS: Amex, Delta, MasterCard, Switch, Visa   DETAILS: 14 seats. Private parties: 10 main room. Children's helpings. No smoking. Occasional music. No mobile phones ACCOMMODATION: 3 rooms, all with bath/shower. TV. Phone. B&B £65 to £105. No children under 8 exc babies. Baby facilities

DUFFTOWN Moray

map 11

La Faisanderie

2 Balvenie Street, Dufftown AB55 4AD
TEL: (01340) 821273
WEBSITE: www.dufftown.co.uk/lafaisanderie.htm

COOKING 2
FRANCO-SCOTTISH
£22–£52

In this two-level restaurant close to the town's central clock tower, the menu reflects Eric Obry's background by offering a French-accented take on local produce, especially game, presented in robust, unfussy combinations. Starters of galantine of game, smoked salmon with lime and pink peppercorn dressing, or snails gratinée, may lead on to civet of wild boar with black olives, some salmon cutlets with lime butter sauce, or onglet steak with shallot confit. Cranachan crème brûlée, or iced whisky and chestnut soufflé, are tasty developments of the auld alliance theme. Complementing the food, Mandy Bestwick's thoughtful, unintrusive service, along with simple, restful décor, enhance customer contentment, and wines start at £9.90 with plenty under £20 on the all-French list.

CHEF: Eric Obry   PROPRIETORS: Mandy Bestwick and Eric Obry   OPEN: Thur to Mon (Nov to Mar Fri to Sun) L 12 to 1.30, Wed to Mon (Nov to Mar Thur to Mon) D 6.30 to 8.30 (7 to 9 Fri and Sat)   MEALS: alc (main courses £9 to £17). Set L £11.20 (2 courses) to £14.10, Set D £22   SERVICE: not inc, card slips closed CARDS: Delta, MasterCard, Switch, Visa   DETAILS: 26 seats. Private parties: 14 main room. Children's helpings. Wheelchair access (also WC). Music

DUNKELD Perthshire & Kinross map 11

▲ Kinnaird ⅚✳

Kinnaird Estate, by Dunkeld PH8 0LB
TEL: (01796) 482440   FAX: (01796) 482289
WEBSITE: www.kinnairdestate.com
from A9 2m N of Dunkeld, take B898, signposted
Kinnaird, for 4½m

COOKING **6**
MODERN EUROPEAN
£47–£83

There can't be many places with an estate as extensive as Kinnaird is able to call its own – all 9,000 acres of it. It's an early twentieth-century mansion of some magnificence, but run with a personalised approach that makes visitors feel at home, from the front-door welcome to the winter log fire to warm new arrivals in winter.

The cooking occupies the centre ground of country-house opulence, with nibbles, an appetiser and a pre-dessert all included in the fixed-price dinner menu. A round slice of duck and foie gras ballottine with Sauternes jelly and fine beans is appealing in its straightforward richness, and a main course of 'very fresh, perfectly cooked' halibut at inspection benefited from its partnering with a cylinder of potato containing a truffled quail's egg, rocket and dried tomatoes. While there is no stinting on luxuries, the simpler, earthier things are done well too: squab pigeon with purple-sprouting broccoli, oatmeal and walnuts makes a hearty main course. Accompaniments deepen the impact of dishes, as they should, so that best end of spring lamb comes with artichokes, lamb's tongue and Calvados and rhubarb couscous, and desserts display the same degree of creativity in black fig carpaccio with a port reduction and marzipan ice cream, or hot date soufflé ('brimming with flavour') served with coffee ice cream. Hundreds of delightful wines are listed from all countries, with France dominant, and there's also an excellent list of half-bottles. But prices are high whether you are after mature Bordeaux or an everyday quaffer: £20 is the baseline. Six come by the 250ml glass for £7.50.

CHEF: Trevor Brooks   PROPRIETOR: Constance Ward   OPEN: all week 12.30 to 1.45, 7.15 to 9.30   MEALS: Set L £30, Set D £50. Light L menu available   SERVICE: not inc, card slips closed   CARDS: Amex, MasterCard, Switch, Visa   DETAILS: 36 seats. Private parties: 36 main room, 15 to 36 private rooms. Car park. Vegetarian meals. No children under 12. Jacket and tie at D. No smoking. Wheelchair access (also WC). No music. No mobile phones   ACCOMMODATION: 9 rooms, all with bath/shower. TV. Phone. D,B&B £225 to £425. Rooms for disabled. No children under 12. Fishing

EDINBURGH Edinburgh map 11

Atrium ⅚✳

10 Cambridge Street, Edinburgh EH1 2ED
TEL: (0131) 228 8882   FAX: (0131) 228 8808
WEBSITE: www.atriumrestaurant.co.uk

COOKING **3**
MODERN EUROPEAN
£30–£66

This is a good place to 'impress any visitor to the city', according to one reporter who thought the smart and mellow dining room with its flickering oil lamps contrasted nicely with the lively sister operation, 'blue', upstairs (see Round-ups). Based on well-sourced ingredients, the cooking mixes traditional and global influences: seared scallops with chilli, lemongrass and ginger syrup, roast lamb with salsa verde, and rhubarb and banana crumble have all appeared on a single dinner menu. Simpler items such as hot-smoked salmon tart, followed by duck confit with garlic mash, and then tarte Tatin might crop up on the good-value fixed-price lunch menu, where the wine list is drawn on to good effect with a recommended glass for each dish. Striking monthly selections, a wide range of sherries and further interesting suggestions by the glass open the full version – an imaginative and well-focused global selection – while an impressive range of sweeties rounds things off. Quality is never in doubt, but it is just a bit hard on the pocket.

CHEFS: Neil Forbes and Andrew Jenkins   PROPRIETORS: Andrew and Lisa Radford   OPEN: Mon to Fri L 12 to 2, Mon to Sat D 6 to 10 (all week L and D during Festival)   CLOSED: 25 and 26 Dec, 1 Jan   MEALS: alc (main courses £16 to £22). Set L £9.50 (1 course) to £17.50, Set D £25   SERVICE: not inc, 10% for parties of 5 or more   CARDS: Amex, Delta, Diners, MasterCard, Switch, Visa   DETAILS: 80 seats. Private parties: 180 main room. Vegetarian meals. Children's helpings. No smoking. Wheelchair access (also WC). No music. Air-conditioned

▲ Balmoral, Number One

1 Princes Street, Edinburgh EH2 2EQ	COOKING 6
TEL: (0131) 557 6727 FAX: (0131) 557 3747	MODERN EUROPEAN
WEBSITE: www.roccofortehotels.com	£36–£117

The overall effect of this basement bar and dining room is one of space and comfort. This is a first-class operation matched by a kitchen working to demanding technical standards, servicing an evening carte (and tasting menu) that wraps its luxuries in appealing guises: ravioli of celeriac and truffle with spiced wild mushrooms, or langoustine in maccheroncini pasta with curried bisque. But the appeal of Jeff Bland's food is that it is essentially uncomplicated, although he invariably manages to produce the magic that transforms the materials into something exciting. While his style has a broadly European thrust, raw materials are sourced within Scotland, and there's an individuality that defies pigeonholing. Each dish has its own focus: tranche of halibut served with parsley mash and scallop and mussel bouillabaisse; roast loin of Perthshire venison with fondant potato and juniper jus; and noisette of veal Orloff with sautéed foie gras, cocotte potatoes and white wine glaze. Even at dessert stage flavour combinations are carefully considered, as in chilled cantaloupe melon soup with exotic fruit salad and mango sorbet, or white chocolate and raspberry soufflé with raspberry ripple ice cream. The wine list is weighted towards French classics but has most zip in Chile, Australia and New Zealand. Italy holds up well too. Very little comes in under £20, however, and mark-ups are generally on the high side. Six by the glass are £6 to £6.50.

CHEF: Jeff Bland   PROPRIETOR: Rocco Forte Hotels   OPEN: Mon to Fri L 12 to 2, all week D 7 to 10 (10.30 Fri and Sat)   CLOSED: first week Jan   MEALS: alc (main courses £22.50 to £25). Set L £16.50 (2 courses) to £19.50, Set D £55 to £85 (inc wine)   SERVICE: not inc, 12.5% for parties of 6 or more   CARDS: Amex, Delta, Diners, MasterCard, Switch, Visa   DETAILS: 60 seats. Private parties: 80 main room. Children's helpings. No-smoking area. Wheelchair access (also WC). Music. No mobile phones. Air-conditioned ACCOMMODATION: 188 rooms, all with bath/shower. TV. Phone. Room only £195 to £340. Rooms for disabled. Baby facilities. Swimming pool

▲ The Bonham 🍴✕

35 Drumsheugh Gardens, Edinburgh EH3 7RN	COOKING 3
TEL: (0131) 623 9319 FAX: (0131) 226 6080	MODERN EUROPEAN
WEBSITE: www.thebonham.com	£26–£62

The Victorian and contemporary meet with timeless appeal in the smart oak-panelled and wooden-floored dining room of this fashionable boutique town-house hotel, cutting a tranquil city oasis. Likewise, the chef's classical training provides a solid base but equally doesn't curb the adventure of the menu's modern European accent. The approach is via set-price lunch (noted as particularly reasonable at weekends, when it includes a bottle of house wine) and an evening carte. On the latter, expect seared hand-dived scallops with a cream of cauliflower, niçoise, olive and pine-nut dressing to start, and main courses along the lines of seared sea bass with sweet potato mash, vegetable stir-fry and an oregano and tomato butter sauce. Finish in classical style with hot caramel soufflé or cappuccino crème brûlée. The short annotated wine list struts the globe, starting in Australia at £14.50 a bottle (£4 a glass).

CHEF: Michel Bouyer   PROPRIETOR: Peter Taylor   OPEN: all week 12 to 2.30 (12.30 to 3 Sun), 6.30 to 10 MEALS: alc D (main courses £17 to £21.50). Set L Mon to Sat £12.50 (2 courses) to £15, Set L Sun £15 (min 2, inc wine). Snack menu available   SERVICE: not inc, card slips closed   CARDS: Amex, Delta, Diners, MasterCard, Switch, Visa   DETAILS: 52 seats. Private parties: 60 main room, 1 to 70 private rooms. Car park. Vegetarian meals. Children's helpings. No smoking. Wheelchair access (also WC). Music ACCOMMODATION: 48 rooms, all with bath/shower. TV. Phone. B&B £108 to £195. Rooms for disabled. Baby facilities

Café St Honoré ✒

34 NW Thistle Street Lane, Edinburgh EH2 1EA
TEL: (0131) 226 2211
WEBSITE: www.cafesthonore.com

COOKING 2
MODERN BISTRO
£25–£51

A little piece of *fin de siècle* France is not what you might expect to find on one of Edinburgh's narrow cobbled streets, but Café St Honoré offers just that. With its black and white tiled floor, huge mirrors and candles on paper-covered tables, it is everybody's idea of a traditional French bistro, with a bustling atmosphere and snappy service to match. Despite a few Gallic classics (duck leg confit, navarin of lamb, beef bourguignonne), however, the daily-changing menu takes its inspiration from a different quarter. Contemporary-sounding dishes might include smoked haddock risotto to start, followed by rabbit with bacon, olives, and chocolate sauce, or tuna with parsnip rösti, prawns and spring onions. Desserts such as bread-and-butter pudding with marmalade and brown bread ice cream are firmly in the British comfort-food category. The well-priced wine list starts with eight house wines at £10.50 a bottle.

CHEFS: Christopher Colverson and Garrett O'Hanlon   PROPRIETORS: Christopher and Gill Colverson OPEN: all week 12 to 2.15, 5.30 (6 Sat and Sun) to 10   CLOSED: 3 days at Christmas, 3 days at New Year MEALS: alc (main courses L £9 to £14.50, D £14.50 to £20). Set D Mon to Fri 5.30 to 6.45 £13.50 (2 courses) to £18   SERVICE: not inc, 10% for parties of 8 or more   CARDS: Amex, Delta, Diners, MasterCard, Switch, Visa   DETAILS: 48 seats. Private parties: 42 main room, 8 to 16 private rooms. Vegetarian meals. Children's helpings. No smoking in 1 dining room. Wheelchair access (also women's WC). Music

▲ Channings ✒

15 South Learmonth Gardens, Edinburgh EH4 1EZ
TEL: (0131) 315 2225   FAX: (0131) 332 9631
WEBSITE: www.channings.co.uk

COOKING 2
MODERN SCOTTISH
£29–£58

Behind the discreet façade is a smartly decorated interior, which manages to stay true to its Victorian roots. A gilded hand points the way down brass-capped stairs to Channings, the hotel's main restaurant. Chef Hubert Lamort's attractively presented food delivers appealing juxtapositions of good ingredients and satisfying textural combinations. One might start with roast pumpkin and honey soup with Szechuan pepper foam, followed by pink sea bream with creamed butter endive, purple potato purée and a reduction of sweet wine and orange, or roast pheasant served in its own juices with fig purée, a potato croquette and pancetta crisps. Among desserts, seasonal fruit might be presented as a crumble and sorbet combination. Wines are arranged by grape type with plenty of international flavours but only a handful of bottles under £20. The hotel also houses Ochre Vita, a 'Mediterranean' restaurant, its kitchen also run by chef Lamort.

CHEF: Hubert Lamort   PROPRIETOR: Peter Taylor   OPEN: Tue to Sat 12 to 2, 6.30 to 10   MEALS: alc D (main courses £12.50 to £22). Set L £16 (2 courses) to £19   SERVICE: not inc, card slips closed   CARDS: Amex, Delta, Diners, MasterCard, Switch, Visa   DETAILS: 36 seats. 24 seats outside. Private parties: 36 main room, 10 to 20 private rooms. Vegetarian meals. No smoking. Music. No mobile phones ACCOMMODATION: 46 rooms, all with bath/shower. TV. Phone. B&B £101 to £175. Baby facilities

David Bann ✳ £

56–58 St Mary's Street, Edinburgh EH1 1SX
TEL: (0131) 556 5888   FAX: (0131) 556 8074
WEBSITE: www.davidbann.com

NEW ENTRY

COOKING 2
VEGETARIAN
£23–£36

'This looks like a place for fun,' thought one reporter, noting the trendy lighting and colours at this stylish bar and restaurant. Nori timbale with wild mushroom teriyaki is one example of the successful creations emerging from a kitchen that adapts modern cooking techniques to vegetarian cuisine. For the main course, pistachio and lentil koftas are gently flavoured and stylishly presented; simpler souls might settle for a nicely creamy mixed vegetable risotto, featuring broad beans, rocket, chard and fennel. Conclude with hot chocolate pudding and white chocolate sauce, or Amaretto cheesecake. The wine list begins in Gascony for under £11 and rises to just over £20. Commendably, they've taken the effort to check the vegetarian credentials of all wines served, many of which are suitable for vegans.

CHEF/PROPRIETOR: David Bann   OPEN: all week 11 to 10 (10.30 Fri and Sat)   CLOSED: 25 and 26 Dec, 1 and 2 Jan   MEALS: alc (main courses £7 to £11)   SERVICE: not inc, 10% (optional) for parties of 8 or more CARDS: Amex, Delta, MasterCard, Switch, Visa   DETAILS: 86 seats. Private parties: 80 main room, 30 to 40 private rooms. Children's helpings. No smoking from 12 to 2 and from 6 to 10. Wheelchair access (not WC). Music. Air-conditioned   £5

First Coast ✳ £

99–101 Dalry Road, Edinburgh EH11 2AB
TEL: (0131) 313 4404   FAX: (0131) 346 7811
WEBSITE: www.first-coast.co.uk

COOKING 1
MODERN SCOTTISH
£21–£43

The area near Haymarket station seems to be on the up, and several decent restaurants in Dalry now cater for the younger people moving in. First Coast aims to turn out 'no-nonsense food', without over-elaborate presentation, priced to encourage customers to return. An 'excellent, flavoursome' starter of sliced roast aubergine wrapped round apricot chutney and topped with feta and pine nuts might be followed by lamb and mussel pie, or grilled sole with Gruyere and Dijon mustard sauce. Round things off with a homely jam roly-poly and custard. Staff are 'enthusiastic and eager to please', and Chilean house wines cost £9.95.

CHEF: Hector MacRae   PROPRIETORS: Hector and Alan MacRae   OPEN: Mon to Sat 12 to 2, 5 to 11 CLOSED: 25 and 26 Dec, 1 Jan   MEALS: alc D (main courses £7 to £17). Set L and D 5 to 6.30 £10 (2 courses) to £12.50. Light L menu available   SERVICE: not inc   CARDS: Delta, MasterCard, Switch, Visa   DETAILS: 55

seats. Private parties: 50 main room, 15 to 20 private rooms. Vegetarian meals. No smoking in 1 dining room. Wheelchair access (not WC). Music. Air-conditioned (£5)

Fishers in the City ▮ ⊁ £

58 Thistle Street, Edinburgh EH2 1EN	COOKING 2
TEL: (0131) 225 5109 FAX: (0131) 225 5434	SEAFOOD
WEBSITE: www.fishersbistros.co.uk	£24–£61

Fishers in the City has become something of an Edinburgh business institution. Sister restaurant to the Round-up entry in Leith, City has a pleasantly relaxed atmosphere and a modish daily-changing menu that centres largely on fish and seafood. Treatments range from the traditional (Arbroath smokies; fishcakes with lemon and chive mayonnaise; fish soup combining rich stock and chunky pieces of fish, mussels and prawns) to the more exotic (lasagne of seafood with Thai seasonings; king prawn, salmon and monkfish pakora with beetroot, horseradish, raita and peach sambal). Meat lovers might be drawn to a pan-fried fillet steak with brandy sauce, while vegetarians are treated to a daily menu. Plenty of options by the glass and a stack of tempting bottles under £20 mean that there's no need to blow the budget on wine, but, equally, the 'fine wine' list offers good value for top-quality bottles and could easily lead you astray.

CHEF: Brendan Sugars   PROPRIETORS: James Millar and Graeme Lumsden   OPEN: all week 12 to 10.30 CLOSED: 25 and 26 Dec, 1 Jan   MEALS: alc (main courses £8.50 to £25.50). Brunch menu available Sun 12 to 4   SERVICE: not inc   CARDS: Amex, Delta, Diners, MasterCard, Switch, Visa   DETAILS: 75 seats. Private parties: 40 main room. Vegetarian meals. No smoking in 1 dining room. Wheelchair access (also WC). Music. Air-conditioned

Forth Floor ▮

Harvey Nichols, 30–34 St Andrews Square, Edinburgh EH2 2AD	COOKING 4
TEL: (0131) 524 8350 FAX: (0131) 524 8351	MODERN BRITISH
WEBSITE: www.harveynichols.co.uk	£35–£70

Harvey Nichols' Scottish outpost boasts magnificent views from the 'ultra-modern' dining room taking in most of Edinburgh. You can't quite see the Forth, but they couldn't resist the pun. It's a slick operation: service is beyond reproach, and both wine and incidentals have impressed. While a few ideas may have been imported from the mother ship, the menu knows it's north of the border, with some local ingredients on display and a starter of Cullen skink a nod to classic Scottish cuisine. France and Italy appear side by side among starters, courtesy of wild mushroom risotto; gnocchi with sun-blush tomatoes and toasted pine nuts; and foie gras with Sauternes jelly and brioche. Main-course veal fillet wrapped in pancetta and sage has been 'cooked to perfection', and poached halibut might get the tarragon and Dijon treatment, served with crab ravioli and spring greens. Desserts range from rice pudding with raspberry jam through rhubarb charlotte to fig crumble tart with 'excellent' Amaretto ice cream. The long wine list shows impeccable pedigree throughout, whether in Old World or New, and pricing is realistic. Own-label house wines are £13.50, and ten come by the glass. If a bottle of bubbly seems *de rigueur*, don't just scream for Bolly – there are at least 40 other options.

CHEF: Stuart Muir   PROPRIETOR: Harvey Nichols   OPEN: Tue to Sun L 12 to 3 (3.30 Sat and Sun), Tue to Sat D 6 to 10.30   MEALS: alc (main courses £12.50 to £22.50). Brasserie menu available   SERVICE: 10%, card slips closed   CARDS: Amex, Delta, Diners, MasterCard, Switch, Visa   DETAILS: 85 seats. Private parties: 85 main room. Vegetarian meals. Wheelchair access (also WC). Music. Air-conditioned

Haldanes ▾ ✹✲

39A Albany Street, Edinburgh EH1 3QY
TEL: (0131) 556 8407   FAX: (0131) 556 2662
WEBSITE: www.haldanesrestaurant.com

COOKING 2
MODERN SCOTTISH
£35–£69

Despite its city-centre location, Haldanes has a quiet and calm atmosphere and an elegant décor that gives the basement dining room a country-house feel. Options such as baked salmon fillet with asparagus and lemon sabayon, or roast breast of guinea fowl with braised Savoy cabbage and Puy lentils, display the kitchen's classic French leanings, although certain dishes could hardly be more Scottish if they wore a kilt and played the bagpipes: a baked filo parcel of haggis with roast neeps and a whisky sauce, for example. At inspection the kitchen's ability fell somewhat short of ambition, the latter indicated by the prices charged. Whoever assembled the wine list clearly had plenty of fun picking out quotable witticisms but also put some serious thought into selecting a stylish New World range to set against the solid line-up from France. Ten or so house wines are £13 to £16 and also come by the glass.

CHEFS: George Kelso and Steven Faulkener   PROPRIETORS: George and Michelle Kelso   OPEN: Mon to Fri L 12 to 1.30, all week D 6 to 9.30   MEALS: alc D (main courses £17 to £24). Set L and D 6 to 7 £17.50 (2 courses) to £23.50   SERVICE: not inc   CARDS: Amex, Delta, Diners, MasterCard, Switch, Visa   DETAILS: 60 seats. Private parties: 26 main room, 10 to 26 private rooms. Vegetarian meals. Children's helpings. No smoking. Occasional music (£5)

Kalpna ✹✲ £

2–3 St Patrick Square, Edinburgh EH8 9EZ
TEL: (0131) 667 9890

COOKING 3
INDIAN VEGETARIAN
£16–£41

Since 1982 Ajay Bhartdwaj has ploughed a highly distinctive furrow in this utilitarian Indian vegetarian restaurant. His food is a lively cocktail of regional ideas, the main component being Gujarati ('with a touch of Rajastani'). It's a fascinating mix, with starters ranging from samosas and sev puri to aloo firdoshi (potato barrels stuffed with pistachios, raisins and coriander). Main courses are equally interesting: hader chuman is a hot-and-sour mélange of sun-dried tomatoes, home-made cheese and baby corn with green chillies and seasonal vegetables, while khumb masala is built around mushrooms, coconut milk and tomatoes. Matka kulfi (made and served in a traditional clay pot) heads the desserts, and thalis (including a vegan version) are for one person. Drink Indian beer or consider the short, realistically priced wine list starting at £9.95.

CHEF/PROPRIETOR: Ajay Bhartdwaj   OPEN: Mon to Sat L 12 to 2 (2.30 May to Sept), Mon to Sat D (all week May to Sept) 5.30 to 11   CLOSED: 24 and 25 Dec, 1 Jan   MEALS: alc (main courses £5 to £13). Set L £5.50 (2 courses), Set D £10.50 (no set meals during Festival)   SERVICE: 10%, card slips closed   CARDS: MasterCard, Visa   DETAILS: 65 seats. Private parties: 60 main room, 20 to 22 private rooms. Vegetarian meals. No smoking. Wheelchair access (not WC). Occasional music

'It is sad that ... this chef is so let down by his support team .... He's a talented chef: Get Him Out of There!!!!!!!!!' (On eating in the Home Counties)

Martins ▮ ✸✖

70 Rose Street North Lane, Edinburgh EH2 3DX
TEL: (0131) 225 3106
WEBSITE: www.edinburghrestaurants.co.uk

NEW CHEF
MODERN BRITISH
£32–£71

Martins, still going strong after twenty years, has remained undeterred by recent access problems caused by building work in the vicinity. Rising above it all, the founding proprietors are still much in evidence and make 'exemplary hosts'. Since the last Guide a new kitchen regime has arrived, too late for us to send an inspector, though menus from the new team promise starters along the lines of terrine of confit duck, pigeon and shiitake mushroom with a fig and apple chutney, and main courses such as fillet of halibut with creamed leeks, saffron risotto and a butter sauce. Desserts might take in vanilla pannacotta with biscuit tuile and exotic fruit coulis, or opt for unpasteurised cheeses. No smoking and no Muzak cheers reporters. Opening with a house range at £14, the individual wine list extends to a well-chosen pick and mix from all over, mostly at fair prices. France has most to offer with affordable Burgundy backed up by good bottles from the Loire and the south.

CHEFS: Daniel Schlegel and Anna Holden   PROPRIETORS: Martin and Gay Irons   OPEN: Tue to Fri L 12 to 2, Tue to Sat D 7 (6.30 Sat) to 10   CLOSED: 4 wks from 24 Dec, 1 week May/Jun, 1 week Sep/Oct   MEALS: alc (main courses L £10, D £17 to £26). Set L £15 (2 courses) to £20   SERVICE: not inc, 10% (optional) for groups of 6 or more   CARDS: Amex, Delta, Diners, MasterCard, Switch, Visa   DETAILS: 58 seats. Private parties: 30 main room, 8 to 20 private rooms. Vegetarian meals. No smoking. Wheelchair access (not WC). No music. No mobile phones

Off the Wall

105 High Street, Edinburgh EH1 1SG
TEL: (0131) 558 1497
WEBSITE: www.off-the-wall.co.uk

COOKING 4
MODERN SCOTTISH
£32–£72

Occupying a first-floor dining room with arched leaded windows overlooking the Royal Mile, this warmly coloured restaurant raises the spirits with its quiet attention to detail and air of calm. The food is deceptively simple, with no unnecessary fuss or trimmings, just high-quality materials lightly and confidently handled. David Anderson has built his thoughtful modern style on a classic base – seen in a starter terrine of pork cheek with shallots, orange and grapefruit salad, orange vinaigrette and glazed beetroot, and main courses of breast of duck with creamed red onions, wild mushrooms, pommes Anna, and grand veneur sauce. All in all he offers an appealing menu with a choice of fish options (seared fillet of sea bass with mussels, buttered leeks, roast asparagus and hot tartare sauce, for example), excursions into game, and an emphasis placed on rare breeds such as Middle White pork as well as the usual Scottish beef, lamb, veal and so forth. Typical of desserts are chocolate torte with mint ice cream, glazed oranges and mint chocolate sauce, and coconut parfait with mango, Amaretto anglaise and red berry sorbet. The globetrotting wine list is arranged in price order, but only a handful are under £20. House recommendations are £13.95.

CHEF: David Anderson   PROPRIETORS: David Anderson and Aileen Wilson   OPEN: Mon to Sat 12 to 2, 7 (6 June to Sept) to 10 (all week 12 to 2, 5.30 to 11 during Festival)   CLOSED: 25 and 26 Dec, 1 and 2 Jan   MEALS: alc D (main courses £20 to £22). Set L £16.50 (2 courses) to £19.95   SERVICE: not inc   CARDS: Amex, Delta, MasterCard, Switch, Visa   DETAILS: 44 seats. Private parties: 44 main room. Children's helpings. No-smoking area. No cigars/pipes. Occasional music   (£5)

Restaurant Martin Wishart

54 The Shore, Leith, Edinburgh EH6 6RA
TEL: (0131) 553 3557   FAX: (0131) 467 7091
WEBSITE: www.martin-wishart.co.uk

COOKING **7**
MODERN FRENCH
£37–£92

The restaurant occupies pride of place on the Shore development at Leith, overlooking the water and a mix of architecture. Tables are decked out in white linen and flowers, and if you've an appetite for it there is a constant soundtrack of classical background music. Reports attest that the cooking is achieving heights of dizzying refinement of late, apparent as soon as the appetisers arrive: deep-fried pork cheek, celeriac and truffle soup, truffled risotto, and a little cone of intensely flavoured salmon mousse have all been enjoyed this year. The standard thus set, the menu dishes manage to maintain this pace. Lobster tortellini with sautéed queenies and leeks packs sensational punch, the frothy lobster sauce emphasising the richness of the pasta filling. Beignets of skate and caviar are ungreasy and elegantly presented, dotted with a balsamic dressing and accompanied by a couple of scallops. Soft textures, bold seasoning and rich sauces define dishes such as a traditional daube of beef cooked in red wine, served with winter roots and potato purée. Chicken stock is the base for a reduction sauce that has brilliantly offset a dish of John Dory fillets with roast salsify. Quality of even the simplest preparations shines forth, so that pannacotta is expertly rendered, accompanied by mixed berries and good raspberry sorbet, as is the more complex coffee and chocolate brûlée, partnered with concentrated coffee ice cream and white chocolate 'cappuccino' that comes with a coloured plastic straw to drink it through. Service is highly professional, with the sommelier singled out for special praise. A French-orientated wine list at fairly plutocratic mark-ups doesn't give much quarter, with prices opening at £18 for a basic Côtes du Rhône red.

CHEF/PROPRIETOR: Martin Wishart   OPEN: Tue to Fri L 12 to 2, Tue to Sat D 7 to 10   MEALS: alc (main courses £22.50 to £24.50). Set L £18.50 to £55, Set D £48 to £55   SERVICE: not inc   CARDS: Amex, Delta, MasterCard, Switch, Visa   DETAILS: 45 seats. Private parties: 45 main room. Vegetarian meals. No smoking before 2.30pm and 10.30pm. Wheelchair access (also WC). Music. No mobile phones

Rogue £

67 Morrison Street, Edinburgh EH3 8BU
TEL: (0131) 228 2700   FAX: (0131) 228 3299
WEBSITE: www.rogues.uk.com

COOKING **3**
MODERN EUROPEAN
£24–£41

One reporter likened the interior of this loud, contemporary brasserie to a darkened spaceship ready to take off. It certainly wears an austere minimalist face with its white linen cloths, subdued lights glimmering from the dark ceiling and staff dressed in obligatory black. The menu offers a choice of 'light mains' (salade niçoise, *et al*) and more full-blooded ideas like pork belly with sweet potato and pineapple. Pasta includes some intriguing combinations, including penne with braised rabbit, chorizo and mushrooms, while the section headed 'a new direction' offers exotica: say, swordfish with baked papaya, rice and green curry sauce. You could begin with leek and Fontina cheese tartlet and finish with passion-fruit parfait. The wines are an interesting collection (from £12.75), although more choice by the glass would be welcome.

CHEF: Wyatt Shevloff   PROPRIETOR: David Ramsden   OPEN: Mon to Sat 12 to 2.30, 6 to 11   MEALS: alc (main courses £6 to £11)   SERVICE: not inc, card slips closed   CARDS: Amex, Delta, MasterCard, Switch, Visa   DETAILS: 96 seats. Private parties: 96 main room. Vegetarian meals. Wheelchair access (also WC). Music. Air-conditioned

Skippers Bistro

1A Dock Place, Leith, Edinburgh EH6 6LU
TEL: (0131) 554 1018   FAX: (0131) 553 5988
WEBSITE: www.skippers.co.uk

COOKING **1**
SEAFOOD
£19–£61

Part of the Edinburgh scene for two decades, this informal fish bistro wears its colours on its sleeve. Nautical memorabilia cover its red-painted walls, a homely atmosphere prevails, and the kitchen's philosophy is simple: take top-quality seafood from Scottish waters, handle with the minimum of culinary interference, and serve. Fishcakes come with home-made tartare sauce, while sea bass is roasted whole with lemon, garlic and rosemary. Occasionally there are forays abroad for, say, grilled fillet of red mullet with couscous salad, and meat eaters get a look in with confit of duck on garlic and rosemary mash. Bargain basement specials (one dish plus a drink) from £5 are a great lunchtime deal, and there's brunch on Sundays. The wine list slightly favours whites, and house Duboeufs are £10.50.

CHEFS: Mary Walker and Matt Flitney   PROPRIETORS: Gavin and Karen Ferguson   OPEN: all week 12.30 to 2 (2.30 Sun), 7 to 10   CLOSED: 1 week at Christmas   MEALS: alc (main courses L £7 to £18, D £13 to £23). Set L Mon to Sat £7.50 (2 courses) to £15.50, Set brunch Sun £12.50 (2 courses) to £15.50, Set D Mon to Thur £16.50 (2 courses) to £19.50   SERVICE: not inc   CARDS: Amex, Delta, MasterCard, Switch, Visa   DETAILS: 55 seats. Private parties: 40 main room, 15 to 30 private rooms. Vegetarian meals. Wheelchair access (also WC). Music. No mobile phones

Tower Restaurant

Museum of Scotland, Chambers Street,
Edinburgh EH1 1JF
TEL: (0131) 225 3003   FAX: (0131) 220 4392
WEBSITE: www.tower-restaurant.com

COOKING **2**
SEAFOOD/MODERN BRITISH
£31–£85

The setting could hardly be more dramatic. It's a rooftop restaurant with fine views towards the castle, which is obligingly floodlit at night. An up-tempo brasserie-style menu is offered: oysters are poached and dressed with hollandaise, penne comes with Portobello mushrooms and artichokes, and John Dory with saffron mash, sweet peppers and rosemary. Bad timing upset one or two dishes at inspection, but a Roquefort, onion and tomato tart had good flavour, and soft-textured cranachan parfait was garnished with good raspberries. The wine list is arranged in price bands with a host of good choices at each level (unless, that is, you were determined to spend over £100 on a bottle of white). Even if mark-ups are on the high side, there is plenty at the bottom end (starting with house at £13.75) and 11 tempting choices by the glass. Older vintages show serious intent at more rarefied altitudes.

CHEF: David Haetzman   PROPRIETOR: James Thomson   OPEN: all week 12 to 11   CLOSED: 25 and 26 Dec   MEALS: alc (main courses L £9.50 to £22, D £15 to £24.50). Set L and D 5 to 6.30 and 10 to 11 £9.95 (2 courses)   SERVICE: not inc, card slips closed   CARDS: Amex, Delta, Diners, MasterCard, Switch, Visa   DETAILS: 90 seats. 70 seats outside. Private parties: 90 main room, 12 to 50 private rooms. Vegetarian meals. No smoking. Wheelchair access (also WC). Music. Air-conditioned

---

'I asked the maitre d' for the bill as he was strolling past our table, and he wheeled round on his heels. "Now hang on a minute!" he spat. "I've been listening to you all evening and now it's time for you to listen to me!" (Pregnant pause ensued). "Now – can I get you anything else?" Very, very odd.'
(On eating in London)

Valvona & Crolla Caffè Bar ❙ ⁵⁄₊ £

19 Elm Row, Edinburgh EH7 4AA
TEL: (0131) 556 6066   FAX: (0131) 556 1668
WEBSITE: www.valvonacrolla.com

COOKING 3
ITALIAN
£22–£47

The Continis run what is in effect a great café – as well as a delicatessen, wine merchant, and cookery shop. Apart from Festival time (when it opens in the evening), the café serves from breakfast to tea, with lunch taking centre stage. Produce imported from Milan dictates a repertoire of dishes of straightforward Italian cooking, much of it in either rustic or domestic mould: home-made Italian pork, beef and pine-nut meatballs in a Vitale tomato sugo, for example, or grilled polenta with herb sausages, pan-fried Italian greens and mostarda di frutta – but incorporating the best Scottish produce, too, in dishes such as pasta with James Dickson's oak-smoked salmon with cream and dill, and new season's Scottish asparagus with bruschetta and Stracchino cheese. Pizzas can come with mozzarella di bufala, air-dried beef and rocket, the children's menu is a model of its type, and Italian classics among desserts include pannacotta, and crumbly lemon polenta cake, as well as Italian ice cream and cheeses. Valvona & Crolla is one of the UK's leading Italian wine specialists (with good ranges from other countries too), and the deal here is that you can buy anything at shop price then pay £4 corkage to enjoy it in the café. So for £20 you could indulge in, say, a top-class Chianti Classico by Felsina. Alternatively pick from a range of 18 or so by the glass starting at £2.75. A sister café is due to open in the city in September 2004: The Walk, 11 Multree's Walk.

CHEF: Mary Contini   PROPRIETORS: Philip and Mary Contini   OPEN: Mon to Sat 8 to 6, Sun 11 to 6.30 (L served 12 to 3). Open Thurs to Sat D during Festival and special events (bookings only)   CLOSED: 25 Dec, 1 Jan   MEALS: alc (main courses £8 to £15)   SERVICE: not inc, 10% for parties of 6 or more   CARDS: Amex, MasterCard, Switch, Visa   DETAILS: 80 seats. 10 seats outside. Private parties: 60 main room. Vegetarian meals. Children's helpings. No smoking. Wheelchair access (also WC). Music. Air-conditioned

Vintners Rooms ♟ ⁵⁄₊

NEW ENTRY

The Vaults, 87 Giles Street, Leith, Edinburgh EH6 6BZ
TEL: (0131) 554 6767   FAX: (0131) 555 5653
WEBSITE: www.thevintnersrooms.com

COOKING 4
FRENCH
£29–£56

What must qualify as a romantic setting *par excellence*, with its wooden panelling and fire, this eighteenth-century centre for the wine trade mixes informal but knowledgeable service with excellent French cooking. Technical accomplishment is matched by seriously good sourcing of fine ingredients to produce, for instance, starters of perfectly cooked veal sweetbreads with profiteroles and sauce cévenol, and sweet-tasting seared scallops wrapped in pancetta with cider beurre blanc. Main courses continue in similar vein: moist, flavoursome monkfish in Bayonne ham with clams and parsley sauce, or fillet of Aberdeen Angus with foie gras and sauce Diane. Tarte Tatin was 'the real thing' for one reporter, while 'excellent' cheeses provided an enticing alternative for another. If the venue's history suggests a stuffy old-fashioned wine list, fear not, for alongside the classics it plunders regional France, the New World and lesser-known corners of Europe with a gleeful sense of adventure. Mature vintages, fair prices and a good selection of half-bottles complete the picture.

CHEF: Patrice Ginestière   PROPRIETOR: Vintners Rooms Ltd   OPEN: Tue to Sun L 12 to 2 (2.30 Sun), Tue to Sat D 7 to 10   MEALS: alc D (main courses £15 to £19). Set L £13 (2 courses) to £16.50   SERVICE: not inc, 10% for parties of 5 or more   CARDS: Amex, Delta, MasterCard, Switch, Visa   DETAILS: 46 seats. Private parties: 34 main room. Vegetarian meals. Children's helpings. No smoking in 1 dining room. Wheelchair access (not WC). No music

▲ Witchery by the Castle

Castlehill, Royal Mile, Edinburgh EH1 2NF
TEL: (0131) 225 5613 FAX: (0131) 220 4392
WEBSITE: www.thewitchery.com

COOKING 4
MODERN SCOTTISH
£26–£85

The historic building by the gates of Edinburgh Castle is a magical place. Of the two extravagant dining rooms, the Witchery is the more dramatic – gothic in feel with its gilded leather screens, tapestries, antique church candlesticks, and oak panelling – while the Secret Garden's painted ceiling and doors and views onto a topiary- and urn-filled terrace capture something of the rococo. The kitchen, by contrast, is rooted in sharp modernity. Douglas Roberts's use of ingredients can be straightforward, sometimes very clever, but never overdone: witness main-course roast breast of Gressingham duck with a kale and prune tart and pomme cocotte, or pan-roasted wild sea bass teamed with fennel à la grecque, ham hough ravioli and citrus jus. Starters read like an inventory of high-impact flavours – garden pea velouté with goats' cheese grissini, or roast salt cod with parsley purée, ruby grapefruit and pine kernels – while puddings vary from a classic poached pear Belle Hélène to a modern-day passion-fruit and mascarpone trifle. The wine list comes in a heavy black binder, fat as a book of spells. The basic house dozen by bottle (from £13.75) or glass is unpretentious and fair value. The immense full list conjures up a stimulating global range from good everyday bottles to the very grandest (in numerous vintages), all annotated with commendable clarity.

CHEF: Douglas Roberts PROPRIETOR: James Thomson OPEN: all week 12 to 4, 5.30 to 11.30 CLOSED: 25 and 26 Dec MEALS: alc (main courses £14 to £35). Set L £9.95 (2 courses), Set D (2 courses) 5.30 to 6.30 and 10.30 to 11.30 £9.95 SERVICE: not inc, card slips closed CARDS: Amex, Delta, Diners, MasterCard, Switch, Visa DETAILS: 110 seats. 20 seats outside. Private parties: 60 main room, 40 to 50 private rooms. Vegetarian meals. Music. 1 dining room air conditioned ACCOMMODATION: 7 rooms, all with bath/shower. TV. Phone. B&B £250

EDNAM Borders map 11

▲ Edenwater House

Ednam TD5 7QL
TEL: (01573) 224070 FAX: (01573) 226615
WEBSITE: www.edenwaterhouse.co.uk

COOKING 4
MODERN BRITISH
£41–£49

Jacqui Kelly cooks, and husband Jeff is 'mine host' in this four-square converted manse next to the church. Appreciative visitors give thanks for 'the graciousness of the service, the attention to detail and the unpretentious elegance and comfort of the place'. The restaurant, 'lovingly put together' in shades of green, makes a pleasant setting for a four-course dinner at 8. Like many Lakeland hotels, the menu here is fixed-price with no choice and a sometimes variable running order, but the overall style can be gauged from the meal that one reporter much enjoyed. Baked monkfish wrapped in smoked salmon opened the show, before roast pheasant breast stuffed with Ardennes pâté and grapes with diced root vegetables in cream sauce. Next came a savoury – goats' cheese and Gorgonzola melted onto a toast wedge – and proceedings concluded with a fruity assemblage of strawberries, apricots and blueberries with crème anglaise gratinée. Jeff Kelly knows his wines and is keen to recommend bottles from his thoughtfully assembled list; 'table wine' is £12.50.

CHEF: Jacqui Kelly   PROPRIETORS: Jacqui and Jeff Kelly   OPEN: Thu to Sun D only 8 (1 sitting)   MEALS: Set D £32.50   SERVICE: net prices, card slips closed   CARDS: Delta, MasterCard, Switch, Visa   DETAILS: 16 seats. Private parties: 16 main room. Car park. No children under 10. No smoking. Occasional music. No mobile phones   ACCOMMODATION: 4 rooms, all with bath/shower. TV. B&B £40 to £95. No children under 10

ELIE Fife
map 11

Sangster's ♟ ✳
NEW ENTRY

51 High Street, Elie KY9 1BZ
TEL/FAX: (01333) 331001
EMAIL: brucesangster@aol.com

COOKING 4
MODERN BRITISH
£27–£54

In a smartly painted converted house on the High Street, Sangster's reminded one reporter of a typical French village restaurant. Once inside, though, the look is more like a smart Scottish lounge, with sofas, wooden tables, and some modern paintings on the walls (as well as Bruce Sangster's many awards and medals). The set-price menus are modern, interesting and 'daringly short', with, at dinner, three starters, two intermediate courses, four mains and three desserts; prices are very fair. A starter of Isle of Mull scallops with brown lentil, cardamom and coriander sauce gives a little Asian inspiration to some fine Scottish ingredients, and a main-course dish of a generous tranche of Parmesan tart with a compote of tomatoes and pesto looks to mainland Europe. Other main courses have included loin of Glen Isla venison served with a compote of red cabbage, gratin potatoes and red wine and juniper sauce, and roast fillet of monkfish has come with crab and lobster risotto. An intense, complex pudding of milk chocolate tart with vanilla-poached pear, hazelnut praline and an orange and caraway tuile was the highlight of dinner for one reporter. Service is affable but can struggle under pressure. Brisk upbeat selections from Old World and New line up on the good-value wine list. House bottles are £14.

CHEF: Bruce Sangster   PROPRIETORS: Bruce and Jacqueline Sangster   OPEN: Wed to Fri and Sun L 12.30 to 1.45, Tue to Sat D 7 to 9.30   CLOSED: 25 and 26 Dec, 1 and 2 Jan   MEALS: Set L Wed to Fri £15.50 (2 courses) to £17.50, Set L Sun £18.75, Set D £22 (2 courses) to £30   SERVICE: not inc, card slips closed   CARDS: Delta, MasterCard, Switch, Visa   DETAILS: 28 seats. Private parties: 16 main room. No children under 12. No smoking. No music. No mobile phones

ERISKA Argyll & Bute
map 11

▲ Isle of Eriska ✳

Ledaig, Eriska PA37 1SD
TEL: (01631) 720371   FAX: (01631) 720531
WEBSITE: www.eriska-hotel.co.uk
off A828, 12m N of Oban

COOKING 6
SCOTTISH
£48–£57

If the urban bustle of Glasgow or Edinburgh should happen to pall, the Isle of Eriska may fit the bill. This professionally run hotel is named after the western island on which it stands, since the family that owns it also own the island. That makes for plenty of the right sort of tranquillity, with the thwock of croquet balls and the nightly feeding of wild badgers on the terrace by the staff among the diversions.

Not only the badgers, but guests too are fed nightly, in the form of Robert MacPherson's fixed-price menu of five courses plus coffee. A pair of options each for starter and second course might embrace terrine of pig cheek, duck confit and shallots, served with a salad of duck breast and black olives, followed by John Dory with grilled asparagus and nettle sauce, or a soup such as tomato consommé with basil dumplings. Main courses offer a choice of three, ranging one February evening from leg of Scots lamb carved at the table, saddle of roe deer with an artichoke and skirlie gâteau and morel jus, or turbot on white bean purée, with seared squid and spinach. After a dessert such as pistachio and griottine parfait with macerated Agen prunes, a trolley of farmhouse cheeses is wheeled forth to round things off. Burgundies from Louis Latour, Rhônes from Jaboulet, Upper Loire wines from Ch. du Nozet and Alsace from Trimbach ensure the French section leads off the list in fine, if rather monothematic, style. There are plenty of half-bottles, and house wines come in at £9.60, or £3 for a small glass.

CHEF: Robert MacPherson   PROPRIETORS: the Buchanan-Smith family   OPEN: all week D only 8 to 9
MEALS: Set D £38.50   SERVICE: not inc, card slips closed   CARDS: Amex, Delta, MasterCard, Switch, Visa
DETAILS: Private parties: 20 main room, 10 to 20 private rooms. Car park. Vegetarian meals. Children's helpings (high tea for children 6pm). No smoking. Wheelchair access (also WC). No music. No mobile phones. Air-conditioned   ACCOMMODATION: 19 rooms, all with bath/shower. TV. Phone. B&B £135 to £305. Rooms for disabled. Baby facilities. Swimming pool. Fishing

FAIRLIE North Ayrshire   map 11

Fins 🍴✱

Fencefoot Farm, Fairlie KA29 0EG	COOKING 2
TEL: (01475) 568989 FAX: (01475) 568921	SEAFOOD
WEBSITE: www.fencebay.co.uk	£27–£65

Bernard and Jill Thain's passion for curing fish explains the smokehouse and shop attached to their cottagey little restaurant on the coast road. 'Cute touches' like pottery fish emphasise the seafood theme in their homely dining room, where the mood is relaxed and staff add a cheerful note to proceedings. The menus are based around fresh supplies from local waters, and the kitchen keeps things simple: shelled squat lobster tails are served with garlic butter, while fillets of sea bass come on a warm Mediterranean salad. Juicy fillet steak with bacon and mushrooms is a token concession to meat eaters. Portions are generous, whether it's a bowl of Cullen skink to start, or two slabs of ginger and Grand Marnier parfait to finish. White wines understandably outnumber reds on the wine list; house bottles are £11.30.

CHEFS: Jane Burns and Gary Brown   PROPRIETORS: Jill and Bernard Thain   OPEN: Tue to Sun L 12 to 2.30, Tue to Sat D 7 to 9.30   CLOSED: 25 Dec, 1 Jan   MEALS: alc (main courses L £9 to £28, D £13 to £28) SERVICE: not inc, card slips closed   CARDS: Delta, MasterCard, Switch, Visa   DETAILS: 50 seats. Private parties: 50 main room. Car park. No children under 7 at D. No smoking. Wheelchair access (also WC). Music. No mobile phones

FORT WILLIAM Highland   map 11

Crannog 🍴✱ £

Town Pier, Fort William PH33 6PD	COOKING 2
TEL: (01397) 705589 FAX: (01397) 700134	SEAFOOD
WEBSITE: www.crannog.net	£26–£56

Book well in advance to guarantee a window table at this charming loch-side restaurant. The chalet-like building with white walls and a steeply pitched red-tiled roof stands literally above the water, on a short pier, and views are as mouthwatering as the first-class fish and seafood that land daily at Crannog's doorstep. The in-house smokery produces impressive results – as in a salmon platter featuring the fish hot-smoked, cold-smoked and gravad lax style – and the rest of the menu mostly keeps things equally simple: piles of langoustines in garlic butter, or braised skate with sweet chilli sauce. A blackboard lists a handful of daily specials such as baked bream in Noilly Prat, and to finish there might be 'tipsy laird', a traditional Scottish trifle with Drambuie and raspberries. A few non-fish dishes, also locally sourced, ensure all-comers are catered for, and house wines at £13.95 open a short, mostly white list.

CHEF: Gary Dobbie   PROPRIETOR: Finlay Finlayson   OPEN: all week 12 to 2.30 (3 June to Aug), 6 to 9.30 (10 June to Aug)   CLOSED: 25 Dec, 1 Jan   MEALS: alc (main courses £8.50 to £20)   SERVICE: not inc   CARDS: MasterCard, Switch, Visa   DETAILS: 65 seats. Private parties: 40 main room. Car park. Vegetarian meals. Children's helpings. No smoking in 1 dining room. Wheelchair access (also WC). Occasional music

▲ Inverlochy Castle ⁵⧗

Torlundy, Fort William PH33 6SN
TEL: (01397) 702177   FAX: (01397) 702953
WEBSITE: www.inverlochycastlehotel.com
3m N of Fort William on A82

COOKING 6
MODERN EUROPEAN
£45–£86

Set in pine woodland amid gardens pink with rhododendrons, with Ben Nevis for a backdrop and its own loch teeming with rainbow trout in the foreground, this nineteenth-century 'big hoose' beguiled even Queen Victoria (staying here on a sketching and painting trip, she found it quite 'romantic', apparently). Inside are crystal chandeliers, ornately framed pictures and mirrors on rich wallpapers, and a trio of grand dining rooms where scrupulous formality reigns (a jacket and tie are required), and service is a model of expertly trained precision.

Matthew Gray rises to the stately occasion with daily-changing menus that combine classical French technique with today's more speculative culinary mode. A seared tranche of turbot might turn up with glazed belly pork and rocket these days, while sea bass comes decked in a Parmesan crust and sauced with basil-scented velouté. There is boldness in first courses as robust as slow-cooked beef shin with green bean relish and Cabernet Sauvignon vinegar, and as whimsical as Skye crab with pannacotta and a Granny Smith apple wafer. Between first and main courses comes a soup, such as lightly spiced butternut squash, and meals conclude with novelties like spiced pineapple tart with hot chocolate ice cream, or angel food poppyseed cake with blueberry compote. High prices and broad range characterise a wine list that not only gives France its due but also takes the rest of the wine world seriously. House wines are £25 to £35 (£4.50 to £5.50 a glass).

CHEF: Matthew Gray   PROPRIETOR: Inverlochy Castle Ltd   OPEN: all week 12.30 to 2, 7 to 9.15   CLOSED: 6 Jan to 12 Feb   MEALS: Set L £23.50 (2 courses) to £28.50, Set D £52.50. Light L menu available   SERVICE: not inc, card slips closed   CARDS: Amex, MasterCard, Switch, Visa   DETAILS: 50 seats. Private parties: 50 main room, 2 to 50 private rooms. Car park. Children's helpings. Jacket and tie. No smoking. Wheelchair access (not WC). Music. No mobile phones   ACCOMMODATION: 17 rooms, all with bath/shower. TV. Phone. B&B £205 to £395. Baby facilities. Fishing

'Our companion really enjoys pouring his own beer. A dutiful waiter thought his duty extended to filling every guest's glass at pain of death. Fortunately, the ensuing confrontation stopped just short of the nude wrestling match between Oliver Reed and Alan Bates in Women in Love.*'*
(On eating in London)

Brian Maule at Chardon d'Or ▼ ⅝✻

176 West Regent Street, Glasgow G2 4RL
TEL: (0141) 248 3801   FAX: (0141) 248 3901
WEBSITE: www.brianmaule.com

COOKING 4
FRENCH/MEDITERRANEAN
£29–£64

A little outside the city's central hub is this ambitious restaurant and Edinburgh high-flyer, stamped very firmly and copiously with the chef/proprietor's identity. The bar and dining room aim for a cool, modern feel, although elbowroom seems at a premium and the lighting, from overhead spots turned way down and from tealights, has veered towards 'Stygian gloom' in the opinion of one. Modern European dishes are the name of the game, with a starter of warm flakes of ham hock with Puy lentils in a fruity dressing showing the kitchen's paces at inspection. A main course of roast beef fillet has been impeccably timed, served in a classic red wine reduction with girolles and superbly textured roast potatoes, while gratin dauphinois is the accompaniment for braised shank of lamb. Other items have pleased less – smoked salmon tartlet, for instance – but an unmodified vanilla crème brûlée, made in the textbook fashion, has been beautifully executed. House red at £14.50 has come in for praise, while the main wine list stretches the budget but provides a cogent account of the global state of play, with smart clarets and Burgundy to top things off.

CHEF/PROPRIETOR: Brian Maule   OPEN: Mon to Fri L 12 to 2, Mon to Sat D 6 to 10 (10.30 Sat)   CLOSED: 2 to 18 Jan, bank hols   MEALS: alc (main courses £14.50 to £19.50). Set L and D 6 to 7 £14.50 (2 courses) to £17.50   SERVICE: not inc, 10% for parties of 8 or more   CARDS: Amex, Delta, MasterCard, Switch, Visa   DETAILS: 90 seats. Private parties: 90 main room, 6 to 26 private rooms. Vegetarian meals. No smoking. Music. No mobile phones

Buttery ⅝✻   [NEW ENTRY]

652 Argyle Street, Glasgow G3 8UF
TEL: (0141) 221 8188   FAX: (0141) 204 4639
EMAIL: ia.fleming@btopenworld.com

COOKING 5
MODERN SCOTTISH
£35–£72

Under new ownership since 2002, the Buttery, one of Glasgow's most intimate and atmospheric restaurants, is back on form. In terms of décor not much has changed; the main eating area still recalls an old library, and the dark mahogany bar remains, curlicues and all. Chef Willie Deans's cooking employs a complex interweaving of many precisely cooked items, as in a light starter of delicately poached pear and fanned Charentais melon with jewel-like pomegranate seeds, grape slices, shards of chicory, Parma ham, crumbled Dunsyre blue cheese and avocado dressing. Well-judged flavours show up in a main course that combines translucent roast turbot, 'dazzlingly white and buttery' chargrilled cod and sea bass with cumin fritters, set off by luscious roast tomatoes; and for carnivores there might be loin of sika venison accompanied by potato and leek cake, pear and elderberry compote and allspice berry sauce. Bread is own-made soda bread. For dessert, there might be banana and toffee pudding with candied fruit, served with violet-petal ice cream (with a piercing note of violet flavour), or Franco-Scottish cheeses with home-made walnut biscuits or oatcakes. Tea and coffee are excellent, and service is skilled and unobtrusive. The wine list, arranged by price and drawing on wine regions the world over, has a decent by-the-glass selection (£4 to £5.50); bottle prices start at £16.

CHEF: Willie Deans   PROPRIETOR: Ian Fleming   OPEN: Tue to Fri L 12 to 2, Tue to Sat D 6 to 10   CLOSED: 25 and 26 Dec, 1 and 2 Jan   MEALS: alc L (main courses £12 to £14). Set L £16 (2 courses), Set D £34 (2

courses) to £38   SERVICE: not inc   CARDS: Amex, Delta, MasterCard, Switch, Visa   DETAILS: 60 seats.
Private parties: 40 main room, 6 to 30 private rooms. Car park. Vegetarian meals. Children's helpings. No
smoking. Wheelchair access (not WC). Music. Air-conditioned (£5)

Café Ostra ✱ £

	NEW ENTRY

The Italian Centre, 15 John Street, Glasgow G1 1HP
TEL: (0141) 552 4433   FAX: (0141) 552 1500
WEBSITE: www.cafeostra.com

COOKING 1
SEAFOOD
£22–£58

Set in the Italian Centre near Glasgow's revitalised Merchant City, Café Ostra is a cool-
green, all-day venue with an upper dining area and seats outside. Like its elder sister Gamba
(see entry, Glasgow), this new addition to The Marshall/Tomkins' burgeoning bar/
restaurant empire takes seafood as its theme, although there's a simpler approach to things.
Breakfast savouries start the day, while the full menu takes in everything from warm oysters
with Parmesan cream to spaghetti with chilli, crab and coriander, alongside specials like
cod with olives, peas and mussels. Carnivorous alternatives come in the guise of, say, ribeye
steak with béarnaise; Bakewell tart is a typical dessert. The short, reasonably priced wine list
includes 11 by the glass from £3.30. Bottle prices start at £11.95.

CHEF: John Gillespie   PROPRIETORS: Derek Marshall and Alan Tomkins   OPEN: all week 11 (12 Sun) to 10
(10.30 Fri and Sat)   CLOSED: 25 and 26 Dec, 1 and 2 Jan   MEALS: alc (main courses £5 to £18). Set L 12 to
6 £12.95 (2 courses, inc wine)   SERVICE: not inc, 10% for parties of 6 or more   CARDS: Amex, Delta,
MasterCard, Switch, Visa   DETAILS: 100 seats. 100 seats outside. Private parties: 60 main room, 16 to 26
private rooms. Vegetarian meals. Children's helpings. No smoking in 1 dining room. Music. Air-
conditioned

Étain ♥

	NEW ENTRY

The Glasshouse, Springfield Court, Glasgow G1 3JX
TEL: (0141) 225 5630   FAX: (0141) 225 5640
WEBSITE: www.conran.com

COOKING 3
MODERN FRENCH
£33–£62

This 'elegant, subtly lit', modern city-centre dining room behind the pulsating Zinc Bar in
Princess Square – accessed by glass elevator – brings Conran fine dining and style to the
Glasgow restaurant scene. Hallmark designer interiors, stiff white napery, 'professional,
well-informed and courteous' service, plus a relaxed atmosphere create the inspired
backdrop for Geoffrey Smeddle's modern French cooking. The approach, using the best of
Scottish produce, is via 'value' set-price lunch and dinner cartes and a six-course Epicurean
Menu. Expect the likes of a classically inspired threesome consisting of 'delicate' ballottine
of foie gras with lemon confit and toasted pain Poilâne to start, and warm chocolate and
amaretti fondant with Baileys ice cream to finish. In between, a fillet of Scottish beef with
shallot purée, broad beans and an oxtail and red wine sauce, or maybe herb-crusted halibut
with braised baby gem lettuce and a mussel and bacon velouté. The wine list offers a good
mix of fruity modern standards, famous names and serious bottles right up to top-class
mature claret. Prices are mostly fairly high, but there's reasonable choice under £20 and
ten come by the glass.

CHEF: Geoffrey Smeddle   PROPRIETOR: Conran Restaurants Ltd   OPEN: Sun to Fri L 12 to 2.30 (3 Sun),
Mon to Sat D 7 (6.30 Fri and Sat) to 11   CLOSED: 25 Dec, 1 Jan   MEALS: Set L £16 (2 courses) to £18.50,
Set L Sun £23.50, Set D £24 (2 courses) to £35   SERVICE: 12.5% (optional), card slips closed   CARDS:
Amex, Delta, MasterCard, Switch, Visa   DETAILS: 60 seats. Private parties: 80 main room. No children
under 8. Wheelchair access (also WC). Music. No mobile phones. Air-conditioned

Gamba ⁵⧱

225A West George Street, Glasgow G2 2ND	COOKING **3**
TEL: (0141) 572 0899 FAX: (0141) 572 0896	SEAFOOD
WEBSITE: www.gamba.co.uk	£29–£69

Gamba is not easy to find, so it's worth watching out for the small metallic fish over the entrance to this lively basement seafood restaurant on a corner. The mood of relaxation and enjoyment is buttressed by a menu showing a catholic competence and a broad range of influences and ingredients; there's tuna and salmon sashimi with soy dip, wasabi and pickled ginger among the starters, while main courses range from grilled lemon sole with lemon butter to seared scallops with beetroot and pink peppercorns. For all its simplicity, the cooking makes a favourable impression with the quality and freshness of ingredients, as in a reporter's salad of 'freshest, plumpest mussels and ripest, sweetest melon' with a sweet balsamic dressing. A couple of non-fish options are included, and to finish there might be Bakewell tart with coconut ice cream. Wine prices starting at £15 (and with five house wines by the glass from £4.20) soon top £20. Café Ostra (see entry, Glasgow) is under the same ownership.

CHEF: Derek Marshall   PROPRIETORS: Derek Marshall and Alan Tomkins   OPEN: Mon to Sat 12 to 2.30, 5 to 10.30   CLOSED: 25 and 26 Dec, 1 and 2 Jan   MEALS: alc (main courses £12 to £22). Set L £13.95 (2 courses) to £16.95, Set D 5 to 6.30 £15 (2 courses)   SERVICE: not inc, 10% for parties of 6 or more   CARDS: Amex, Delta, MasterCard, Switch, Visa   DETAILS: 66 seats. Vegetarian meals. No children under 14. No smoking until after 2 (L) and 10 (D). Music. No mobile phones. Air-conditioned (£5)

Rogano ⁵⧱

11 Exchange Place, Glasgow G46 6LT	COOKING **3**
TEL: (0141) 248 4055 FAX: (0141) 248 2608	SEAFOOD
WEBSITE: www.rogano.co.uk	£27–£89

Notable for its splendid 1935 Art Deco interior, this city-centre restaurant (with attached café and oyster bar) offers a stable menu of simple dishes that give Scottish themes a French accent. There are starters like seared pigeon breast with Puy lentils, or baked goats' cheese in oatmeal with a fig compote, and mains like roast venison with butternut rösti cake, but fish is the speciality, and the thing to go for; buying is excellent and the kitchen lets the ingredients shine. There's Rockefeller oysters, or seared scallops with celeriac and horseradish rémoulade, then perhaps large perfectly timed langoustines with garlic butter, or pesto-crusted halibut complemented by roast tomatoes. Desserts take in crème brûlée and a pre-plated cheese selection. Service is formal, and, with Muscadet at £25 the cheapest wine on the conservatively chosen, white-leaning list, economical bottles are few.

CHEF: Andrew Cummings   PROPRIETOR: Spirit Group   OPEN: all week 12 to 2.30, 6.30 to 10.30   CLOSED: 25 and 31 Dec, 1 and 2 Jan   MEALS: alc (main courses £18.50 to £34). Set L £16.15. Bar and café menus available   SERVICE: 12.5% (optional), card slips closed   CARDS: Amex, Delta, Diners, MasterCard, Switch, Visa   DETAILS: 70 seats. Private parties: 70 main room, 8 to 25 private rooms. Vegetarian meals. No smoking before 2pm L, 10pm D. Wheelchair access (not WC). Music. No mobile phones. Air-conditioned (£5)

78 St Vincent 🍴 ✂

78 St Vincent Street, Glasgow G2 5UB
TEL: (0141) 248 7878   FAX: (0141) 221 1874
WEBSITE: www.78stvincent.com

COOKING 2
MODERN SCOTTISH
£27–£74

One of the most imposing settings for a comfortable evening meal in the city centre, with lofty ceilings and a white marble staircase leading up to the mezzanine (smokers' section), 78 is styled like a French brasserie with intimate dining booths, dark wood and professional service to boot. The kitchen's appetite for Pacific Rim fusion treatments seems to have waned under the new head chef, although subtle touches of fusion remain: a star anise jus to accompany haggis, neeps and tatties, for instance. One can expect good Scottish ingredients given the modern Scottish treatment with some Continental leanings, such as wild venison carpaccio with peppercorn and Parmesan tuile, rocket salad and raspberry vinaigrette. Finish with simple desserts, and pick from a wine list that takes in Old and New Worlds, with prices from £13.95 or £3.70 per glass.

CHEF: Simon Ridge   PROPRIETORS: Julie Williams and Frederick Williams   OPEN: all week 12 to 3, 5 to 10 (10.30 Fri and Sat)   CLOSED: 1 Jan   MEALS: alc (not Sat D; main courses L £7 to £11, D £12.50 to £22.50). Set L £12.50 (2 courses) to £15.50, Set D £26.95 (2 courses) to £31.95   SERVICE: not inc, 10% (optional) for parties of 6 or more   CARDS: Amex, Delta, Diners, MasterCard, Switch, Visa   DETAILS: 100 seats. Private parties: 100 main room, 12 to 16 private rooms. Vegetarian meals. Children's helpings. No smoking in 1 dining room. Wheelchair access (also WC). No music. No mobile phones (£5)

Stravaigin 🍷 ✂

28 Gibson Street, Glasgow G12 8NX
TEL: (0141) 334 2665   FAX: (0141) 334 4099
WEBSITE: www.stravaigin.com

COOKING 3
GLOBAL
£35–£65

If you are looking for good 'craic' along with fusion food cooked with some flair, at reasonable prices, this is one of the best choices in the city (or try Stravaigin 2; see below). The buzzy basement café/bar/restaurant just below Gilmorehill attracts a lively, youthful clientele. Exotic flavours sometimes blur, but imaginative efforts are made, and local ingredients are well sourced. Starters may pair peppery morcilla with light, creamy cauliflower pannacotta and seared west coast scallops. An inspector was impressed with a main course of coconut and peanut laksa with seared bream, Loch Etive mussels and prawn dumplings, in which the mussels contrasted piquantly with the luscious peanut and coconut flavours. A refreshing passion-fruit jelly with lime and ginger bavarois and Gewurztraminer sorbet might round off the array of flavours. The enthusiastically annotated wine list is packed with fresh, modern flavours and some interesting foodie options from older European regions.

CHEF: Alan Doig   PROPRIETOR: Colin Clydesdale   OPEN: Fri to Sun L 12 to 2.30 (café bar menu only), Tue to Sun D 5 to 11   CLOSED: 25 and 26 Dec, 1 Jan   MEALS: alc (main courses L £7 to £17, D £13.50 to £21.50). Set D 5 to 7.30 (7 Fri and Sat) £13.95   SERVICE: not inc   CARDS: Amex, Delta, Diners, MasterCard, Switch, Visa   DETAILS: 75 seats. Private parties: 75 main room. Vegetarian meals. Children's helpings. No smoking before 10pm. Music. Air-conditioned

'The décor...is extraordinary. It looked like what I could imagine to be the canteen of the East German secret police c. 1980.' (On eating in London)

Stravaigin 2 🍴 £

8 Ruthven Lane, Glasgow G12 9BG	COOKING 3
TEL: (0141) 334 7165 FAX: (0141) 357 4785	GLOBAL
WEBSITE: www.stravaigin.com	£24–£44

Stravaigin 2, the second of Colin Clydesdale's Glasgow restaurants (see above), has its feet firmly on Scottish soil, but the menu embraces the flavours of the world. It's an informal place, at once laid back and spot on. The menus take in all-day breakfasts at weekends, a dedicated list of burgers (ostrich, beef and chicken), a set-price menu, and the carte. Dishes are not shy, retiring types: witness the likes of hot Louisiana crab, okra and rice fritters with tomatillo drizzles, or Chennai (Madras) chicken curry with mango and lime leaf chutney, chilli peanut sprinkles and chapatis. Or how about a fish supper with 'big chips and real tartare sauce' for the ardent traditionalists? The kitchen shows enough deftness and skill to keep this global approach from falling into the trap of being jack of all trades, master of none. Australia kicks off the short wine list at £13.25 a bottle.

CHEF: Daniel Blencowe   PROPRIETOR: Colin Clydesdale   OPEN: all week 12 (11 Sat and Sun) to 11 CLOSED: 25 Dec, 1 Jan   MEALS: alc (main courses £8 to £14.50). Set L and D 5 to 7 £11.95 (2 courses) to £14.95   SERVICE: not inc   CARDS: Amex, MasterCard, Switch, Visa   DETAILS: 70 seats. Private parties: 35 main room, 20 to 35 private rooms. Vegetarian meals. Children's helpings. No smoking 12 to 2 and 5 to 10. Wheelchair access (also WC). Music. Air-conditioned £5

Ubiquitous Chip 🍷

12 Ashton Lane, Glasgow G12 8SJ	COOKING 4
TEL: (0141) 334 5007 FAX: (0141) 337 1302	SCOTTISH
WEBSITE: www.ubiquitouschip.co.uk	£37–£72

Plumb in the middle of Glasgow's West End, between the university and Botanic Gardens, the Chip is a long stayer with a fiercely loyal customer base. A conservatory patio makes an appealing location for summer dining and expands the space available in both the ground-floor bistro and the more informal first-floor venue. Ronald Clydesdale cooks an inventive menu, with a strong regional accent and some fine ingredients adding depth. Tender braised Perthshire pig's cheek comes with a delicately truffled potato omelette and wild mushroom sauce, a hearty enough start at a winter lunch, and a main course of breast and confit leg of duck with peppered potatoes and balsamic-pickled morello cherries has been described as 'a very fine mix of ingredients expertly handled'. Fish eaters might opt for the aromatic intrigue of salmon smoked with Darjeeling tea, served with cabbage washed in Riesling, and other ideas – for example, crusted chocolate brûlée accompanied by a poached pear seasoned with chilli – are generally as good. Finely tuned service helps things along, and almost all reporters praise the 'serious, impressive, unpretentious, ungreedy' wine list. Lots of smart Bordeaux and, much rarer, an extensive collection of German wines crown a long, quality-focused international list that includes a broad and affordable range by the glass.

CHEF/PROPRIETOR: Ronald Clydesdale   OPEN: Mon to Sat 12 to 2.30, 5.30 to 11, Sun 12.30 to 3, 6.30 to 11 MEALS: Set L Mon to Sat £21.80 (2 courses) to £26.80, Set L Sun £17.95 (inc wine), Set D £32.80 to £37.80. Upstairs and bar menus available   SERVICE: not inc   CARDS: Amex, Delta, Diners, MasterCard, Switch, Visa   DETAILS: 70 seats. 60 seats outside. Private parties: 60 main room, 20 to 60 private rooms. Vegetarian meals. Children's helpings. Wheelchair access (also WC). No music. No mobile phones. Air-conditioned

▲ Greywalls Hotel ▮ ⁵⁄₊✳

Muirfield, Gullane EH31 2EG	COOKING 4
TEL: (01620) 842144 FAX: (01620) 842241	MODERN BRITISH
WEBSITE: www.greywalls.co.uk	£59–£70

Greywalls, built for a keen golfer (one Alfred Lyttelton) in the early twentieth century, is the only remaining Sir Edwin Lutyens-designed house in Scotland. In the Second World War the house was requisitioned as a place of rest and relaxation for fighter pilots from nearby Drem airfield. During this time the sunken garden, originally designed by Gertrude Jekyll, was the scene of many a wild party. Nowadays the hotel is rather calmer, with the feel of a gracious country home. The atmosphere is not as stuffy as the jacket-and-tie-for-men policy suggests, and staff are friendly, helpful and professional.

Simon Burns chooses ingredients carefully from local suppliers and aims for dishes that are not over-sauced. Carpaccio of Highland venison may be served with pink peppercorn dressing, while lightly smoked Eyemouth lobster may be simply accompanied by Jersey Royal potatoes, and cannon of Scottish lamb by a 'confit' of tomato and wild garlic. To finish, an impressive choice of mature British and Irish cheeses with home-made oatcakes are alternatives to the likes of caramelised pear with hazelnut parfait. The bufferish appearance of the wine list – lashings of lovely old claret and Burgundy interspersed with saucy limericks – tells only half the story: there are rich pickings in the New World, too, and the house selections, from £16.50, are as modern as you could wish.

CHEF: Simon Burns   PROPRIETORS: Giles and Ros Weaver   OPEN: all week D only 7.30 to 9   CLOSED: Nov to Mar   MEALS: Set D £45   SERVICE: not inc, card slips closed   CARDS: Amex, Delta, Diners, MasterCard, Switch, Visa   DETAILS: 50 seats. 10 seats outside. Private parties: 50 main room, 2 to 20 private rooms. Car park. Vegetarian meals. Jacket and tie. No smoking. Wheelchair access (also men's WC). No music   ACCOMMODATION: 23 rooms, all with bath/shower. TV. Phone. B&B £135 to £265. Rooms for disabled. Baby facilities (£5)

La Potinière ⁵⁄₊✳

Main Street, Gullane EH31 2AA	COOKING 6
TEL/FAX: (01620) 843214	MODERN BRITISH
WEBSITE: www.la-potiniere.co.uk	£28–£56

In the United States this small restaurant four miles south-west of North Berwick would be called a Mom and Pop operation. It is a two-hander of singular charm and affability that sets out to make the most of Scotland's natural larder, and on busy evenings one of the chefs may bring your dish to the table personally.

There are fixed-price menus for both lunch and dinner, with the three courses of midday expanding to four in the evening when a no-choice intermediate dish – such as a warm Parmesan tart served with baby plum tomatoes, rocket and pesto – comes between starter and main. Begin perhaps with a fillet of lemon sole rolled around a mousse of scallops, or a slice of chicken, ham and leek terrine served with salad leaves dressed in truffle oil, before proceeding to main courses of seared monkfish on smoked salmon risotto with green vegetables and champagne sauce, or roast fillet of Scots beef with a dauphinoise of potato and celeriac, winter roots and a Madeira jus. Round things off with hot coconut rice pudding with caramelised banana and passion-fruit ice cream, or a plate of fabulous cheeses. The evolving wine list, an interesting selection, opens with four house bottles from £15.50 to £18 (£3 to £4 a glass).

CHEFS/PROPRIETORS: Mary Runciman and Keith Marley   OPEN: Wed to Fri and Sun L 12.30 to 2, Wed to Sat D 7 to 9 (booking essential)   CLOSED: 24 to 28 Dec, 3 to 21 Jan   MEALS: Set L £15.50 (2 courses) to £18, Set D £35   SERVICE: not inc, card slips closed   CARDS: MasterCard, Switch, Visa   DETAILS: 28 seats. Private parties: 28 main room. Car park. Children's helpings. No smoking. Wheelchair access (not WC). No music. No mobile phones

INVERKEILOR Angus   map 11

▲ Gordon's 🌟

32 Main Street, Inverkeilor DD11 5RN	COOKING 5
TEL/FAX: (01241) 830364	MODERN SCOTTISH
WEBSITE: www.gordonsrestaurant.co.uk	£29–£69

In Inverkeilor, a small village on the coast road from Montrose to Arbroath, is this warm and welcoming husband-and-wife-run restaurant; she organises front-of-house, he stays behind the scenes in the kitchen. The beamed ceiling, exposed stone walls, bare floorboards and open fire reflect the building's former incarnation as a pub, though tables are set in more formal restaurant style with crisp cloths and sparkling glassware. The menu offers a well-balanced and interesting selection of dishes in an ambitious modern style with a prevailing Scottish character. Among starters, a cauliflower soup had 'tremendous depth of flavour', enhanced by a light-handed touch of truffle oil, while a main-course pairing of sea bass and halibut was set on a pea and saffron risotto and finished with a well-judged red pepper sauce. A creative streak is evident in novel combinations such as venison loin with candied salsify, white bean and bitter chocolate jus. To finish, there are excellent ripe Scottish cheeses served with home-made oatcakes, while the sweet-toothed might opt for the splendid sticky toffee pudding. Nearly all the wines on the compact list are priced in the £13 to £25 bracket, and three of them come by the glass.

CHEFS: Gordon and Garry Watson   PROPRIETORS: Gordon and Maria Watson   OPEN: Wed to Fri and Sun L 12 to 1.45, Tue to Sat D 7 to 9   CLOSED: first 3 weeks Jan   MEALS: Set L £16 (2 courses) to £20, Set D £32 to £46   SERVICE: not inc   CARDS: Delta, MasterCard, Switch, Visa   DETAILS: 24 seats. Private parties: 20 main room. Car park. No smoking. Wheelchair access (not WC). No music. No mobile phones ACCOMMODATION: 3 rooms 2 with bath/shower. TV. B&B £47 to £90. No children under 12

INVERNESS Highland   map 11

▲ Culloden House Hotel, Adams Restaurant 🌟

Culloden, Inverness IV2 7BZ	
TEL: (01463) 790461 FAX: (01463) 792181	
WEBSITE: www.cullodenhouse.co.uk	COOKING 2
from Inverness take A96 to Nairn, turn right after 1m, then	INTERNATIONAL
left at Culloden House Avenue	£52–£63

This grand Palladian mansion postdates the older house where the Young Pretender slept before the battle fought a couple of miles away in 1745. Nonetheless, it still makes an opulent impression, with its glistening chandeliers, marble pillars and fireplaces and Adam plaster reliefs. Though straightforward and unpretentious, the cooking does not lack imagination. A salad of Orkney crab comes with asparagus, onion and lime zest and lemon jelly, preceding perhaps a cauliflower and smoked bacon soup, while cutlets of Highland lamb are topped with black pudding and peach and served with a rosemary jus, or Gressingham duck breast is stuffed with raisin mousse and set on beetroot purée with a Marsala jus. Desserts might take in strawberry parfait, or white chocolate crème brûlée with passion-fruit water ice. The wine list focuses on the major French regions and the classier end of the New World spectrum, but prices are pitched high, and there's very little below £25.

CHEF: Michael Simpson PROPRIETOR: North American Country Inns OPEN: all week 12.30 to 2, 7 to 9 CLOSED: 25 Dec MEALS: alc L (main courses £12 to £18). Set D £38. SERVICE: not inc CARDS: Amex, Delta, Diners, MasterCard, Switch, Visa DETAILS: 60 seats. 60 seats outside. Private parties: 60 main room, 2 to 26 private rooms. Car park. Vegetarian meals. Children's helpings. No children under 10. No smoking. No music. No mobile phones ACCOMMODATION: 28 rooms, all with bath/shower. TV. Phone. B&B £85 to £279. No children under 10 (£5)

Restaurant Chez Christophe ⁑

	NEW ENTRY
16 Ardross Street, Inverness IV3 5NS	COOKING 4
TEL/FAX: (01463) 717126	MODERN FRENCH
WEBSITE: www.chezchristophe.co.uk	£41–£66

Just five or so minutes' walk from Inverness's main tourist attractions, Restaurant Chez Christophe is conveniently situated for visitors to the town, although, as it has just 16 seats, it would be wise to book in advance. The décor has something of a formal edge, although the atmosphere is relaxed. Christophe Magie's menus offer an enticing repertoire of new and traditional French dishes using fine Scottish produce. There are umpteen intermediary courses, and the style and delivery are 'quite classic French'. Take an 'outstanding' starter of duck foie gras slices roasted in a green apple liqueur and served with sweet apple caramel and 'petite salade verte', or a main course of sautéed fillet of Aberdeen Angus beef, topped with confit shallots and accompanied by traditional gratin potatoes, Comte cheese and Bayonne ham. Finish with warm chocolate fondant gâteau with vanilla and mascarpone ice cream. The all-French wine list is a fairly pricey affair, starting at £16.

CHEF: Christophe Magie PROPRIETORS: Christophe and Carol Magie OPEN: Tue to Sat D only 7 to 9 CLOSED: Christmas, 15 Feb to 3 Mar, 10 to 26 July MEALS: Set D £23.95 (2 courses) to £39.50 SERVICE: not inc, card slips closed CARDS: Delta, MasterCard, Switch, Visa DETAILS: 16 seats. Private parties: 16 main room, 6 to 12 private rooms. No children under 12. No smoking. Wheelchair access (also WC). Music. No mobile phones

Rocpool £

1 Ness Walk, Inverness IV3 5NE	COOKING 3
TEL/FAX: (01463) 717274	MODERN EUROPEAN
WEBSITE: www.rocpool.com	£21–£51

This brasserie (and all-day tapas bar) on the west bank of the Ness, decorated in hot orange and indigo, is named after a famous Sydney restaurant. The cooking aims high; on the dinner carte, start perhaps with a warm salad of black pudding and artichoke with 'frizzled' chorizo and grain mustard, before proceeding to soy- and ginger-glazed duck breast with maple-roasted sweet potato wedges and baby pak choi. A special 'Fish on Friday' menu has now been introduced, featuring the likes of brill with a garlic and citrus crust, crushed new potatoes and passion fruit, or king scallops and clams dressed in white wine, lemon and capers. You might finish with something like lemon posset with raspberries. A sheet of classic cocktails supplements the briskly functional wine list, which opens with ten by the glass from £3.25 and South African varietals at £12.50 a bottle.

CHEF: Steven Devlin PROPRIETORS: Adrian and Susan Pieraccini and Stephen Devlin OPEN: Mon to Sat L 12 to 2.30, 6 to 10 MEALS: alc (main courses £7 to £17). Set L £7.95 (2 courses) SERVICE: not inc, card slips closed CARDS: Delta, MasterCard, Switch, Visa DETAILS: 55 seats. Private parties: 55 main room. Vegetarian meals. Children's helpings. No cigars. Music. Air-conditioned £5

KILLIECRANKIE Perthshire & Kinross map 11

▲ Killiecrankie House Hotel ♥ ✳

Killiecrankie PH16 5LG
TEL: (01796) 473220 FAX: (01796) 472451
WEBSITE: www.killiecrankiehotel.co.uk
off A9, 3m N of Pitlochry on B8079

COOKING 3
GLOBAL
£44–£53

Built as a dower house in 1840 and converted into a hotel a century later, Killiecrankie House benefits from a beautiful wooded setting by the River Garry. Tim and Maillie Waters have gradually made 'subtle changes' to the place since arriving in 2001, and their efforts have hit the right note with visitors. Eat casually in the popular conservatory bar or put on your glad rags for dinner in the restaurant, where menus are fixed-price and appropriate wines are suggested for each main course. Typically, you might begin with terrine of corn-fed chicken with spring onions and walnuts, before loin of Perthshire lamb with lyonnaise potatoes and grilled Stornoway black pudding, or goujons of sea bream and prawns in tempura batter with noodles. Desserts such as vanilla brûlée with caramelised banana are followed by cheeses and coffee with hand-made petits fours. Tim Waters's wine expertise, much appreciated by reporters, spills over into the informative and opinionated commentary that runs through his well-chosen and good-value list. New World countries are the main focus, though house red at £13.90 hails from southern France.

CHEFS: Mark Easton and Ryan Young PROPRIETORS: Tim and Maillie Waters OPEN: all week D only 7 to 8.30 CLOSED: 3 Jan to 13 Feb, Tue to Thur Nov to Mar MEALS: Set D £23 (2 courses) to £33. Bar L and D menu available SERVICE: not inc, card slips closed CARDS: Delta, MasterCard, Switch, Visa DETAILS: 34 seats. Private parties: 16 main room, 12 private room. Car park. Vegetarian meals. Children's helpings. No children under 9 at D. No smoking. Wheelchair access (not WC). No music. No mobile phones ACCOMMODATION: 10 rooms, all with bath/shower. TV. Phone. D,B&B £79 to £218. Rooms for disabled. Baby facilities £5

KINGUSSIE Highland map 11

▲ The Cross ♥ ✳

Tweed Mill Brae, Ardbroilach Road, Kingussie PH21 1LB
TEL: (01540) 661166 FAX: (01540) 661080
WEBSITE: www.thecross.co.uk

COOKING 5
MODERN BRITISH
£41–£55

Kingussie is the bucolic setting for the Youngs' restaurant-with-rooms, a former water mill of rustic charm and character, surrounded by beautiful grounds. It may be off the beaten track, but the pick of Scotland's produce manages to find its way to the door, including fish from Skye, game from Newtonmore, meat from Aberfoyle, and cheeses from Edinburgh specialist Mellis. The drill is a monthly-changing, fixed-price menu of five courses. A soup – perhaps lobster, or turnip and garlic – might kick things off before three choices each of second and main courses. Menu descriptions are pleasingly laconic, offering 'grouse, pea purée, brambles', or 'scallops, cauliflower purée, basil oil', before a choice usually of one fish and two meats for main course. These have taken in turbot with wild mushrooms, spinach and mash, as well as traditional rack of lamb with Savoy cabbage and dauphinois potatoes. After a selection of British cheeses, a choice of three desserts is furnished, possibly pannacotta, pear and almond tart, or chocolate parfait. Informal service comes with a smile. A page of sherries by the glass bodes well for the wine list. France fulfils the promise with a well-chosen selection that stretches beyond the standards to the south and Alsace. Other countries are similarly confident with the same balance of good-value wines under £20 and special bottles. The dessert wine list is unusually good.

CHEFS: Becca Henderson and David Young   PROPRIETORS: David and Katie Young   OPEN: Tue to Sat D only 7 to 8.30   CLOSED: Christmas, Jan   MEALS: Set D £28.50 (2 courses) to £38.50   SERVICE: net prices, card slips closed   CARDS: Amex, MasterCard, Switch, Visa   DETAILS: 24 seats. Private parties: 30 main room. Car park. Children's helpings. No smoking. Wheelchair access (also WC). No music. No mobile phones   ACCOMMODATION: 8 rooms, all with bath/shower. Phone. B&B £65 to £180

LARGOWARD Fife   map 11

▲ Inn at Lathones 🕏✗

By Largoward, St Andrews KY9 1JE	COOKING 2
TEL: (01334) 840494 FAX: (01334) 840694	MODERN EUROPEAN
WEBSITE: www.theinn.co.uk	£30–£64

Little expense has been spared to give this ancient coaching inn a colourful and comfortable interior. The cooking majors on locally sourced ingredients (though there's ostrich too, with honey and pink peppercorn sauce) and is admirably simple. It ranges from creamy roast parsnip soup, or confit duck leg, via unpretentious basics like grilled haddock and Mornay sauce, to cinnamon apple crumble with double cream, or iced nougat with passion-fruit sauce. Lunchtime specials, based on the dinner menu, are especially good value. The wine list offers a sound selection under £20 before bringing on the heavy guns in both the Old World and the New World sections; eight come by the glass.

CHEF: Marc Guibert   PROPRIETORS: Nick and Jocelyn White   OPEN: all week 12 to 2.30, 6 to 9.30   CLOSED: 25 and 26 Dec, 3 to 16 Jan   MEALS: alc (main courses £10.50 to £22). Set L £12.50 (2 courses) to £15.50. Set D £28 (pre-theatre) to £42   SERVICE: not inc, card slips closed   CARDS: Amex, Delta, Diners, MasterCard, Switch, Visa   DETAILS: 40 seats. Private parties: 5 to 50 private rooms. Car park. Vegetarian meals. Children's helpings. No smoking. Music. No mobile phones   ACCOMMODATION: 13 rooms, all with bath/shower. TV. Phone. B&B £100 to £200. Rooms for disabled. Baby facilities

LINLITHGOW West Lothian   map 11

▲ Champany Inn 🍷

Champany Corner, Linlithgow EH49 7LU	
TEL: (01506) 834532 FAX: (01506) 834302	COOKING 5
WEBSITE: www.champany.com	SCOTTISH
2m NE of Linlithgow at junction of A904 and A803	£37–£96

Steak is king here, at what is essentially a temple to the delights of the Aberdeen Angus (though other Scots staples – West Coast scallops, Shetland smoked salmon and Highland black pudding – also feature). The dining room (across the yard from the more economical Chop and Ale house) has stone walls hung with Victorian oil paintings and a high, vaulted wooden ceiling. Bare mahogany tables carry fine glassware and copper jugs.

Starters, largely fishy, include a modern but convincing take on prawn cocktail, grilled piri-piri prawns, and salmon grilled or (hot- or cold-) smoked. For full flavour the beef is hung for three weeks in controlled conditions, and the various different steaks are then expertly trimmed and cooked with the pinpoint accuracy to be expected at the prices charged (serious beef aficionados can have their meat cut to order from a display cabinet). Vegetables are extra. There are lamb, chicken and sausage main dishes, too, for eaters of lesser meats, and lobster, salmon and cod if required, but just a salad for veggies. Desserts might range from old-fashioned favourites like rice pudding with strawberry jam to perhaps a dark chocolate and gingerbread torte. Whether you are eating seafood or steak, the wine list has a vast array of indulgent choices. And, alongside a long list of French classics, there's a rare selection of South Africa's best on offer here. Diners on a tight budget will feel squeezed, but not completely excluded.

CHEFS: Clive Davidson, David Gibson and Kevin Hope   PROPRIETORS: Clive and Anne Davidson   OPEN: Mon to Fri L 12.30 to 2, Mon to Sat D 7 to 10   CLOSED: 25 and 26 Dec, 1 and 2 Jan   MEALS: alc (main courses £17.50 to £35.50). Set L £16.75 (2 courses) to £23.50. Chop and Ale House menu available   SERVICE: 10%, card slips closed   CARDS: Amex, Delta, Diners, MasterCard, Switch, Visa   DETAILS: 50 seats. 20 seats outside. Private parties: 50 main room, 6 to 30 private rooms. Car park. No children under 8. Wheelchair access (also WC). No music   ACCOMMODATION: 16 rooms, all with bath/shower. TV. Phone. B&B £105 to £125. Rooms for disabled

LOCHINVER Highland   map 11

▲ Albannach ▼ ✸✲

Baddidarach, Lochinver IV27 4LP   COOKING 6
TEL: (01571) 844407   MODERN SCOTTISH
WEBSITE: www.thealbannach.co.uk   £52–£63

The Albannach presents a romantic appearance: tall, tower-like and looking out over a mountainous vista. Inside, it has been decorated in the Scottish baronial style, with deep wine reds and bottle greens, tartan prints, and the occasional antlered stag's head. It makes sense anywhere, but here particularly, to use local produce, and Colin Craig and Lesley Crosfield are rightly proud of their materials: seafood 'supplied by friends locally', organic vegetables and eggs from nearby crofts, and wild or free-range meat and game. Dinner is a no-choice five-course menu, which typically takes in guinea fowl with confit of garlic, shallots, juniper, spinach and wild mushrooms, considered by a reporter to be 'divine, and great fun to have as a starter instead of a main dish'. Red pepper soufflé with red onion marmalade could follow, then baked fillet of halibut on croft-grown greens with duck egg hollandaise, asparagus, fennel, potatoes and sorrel. Cheese consists of a Scottish and French variety, while desserts have included a buttery apple tart with Calvados and apple gelato and butterscotch sauce. Success is helped by 'lovely' home-baked bread, top-notch appetisers and petits fours, and 'delightful, intelligent' service. France is the first love of the good-value wine list, with the traditional regions spiced up by a handful of bottles from St Chinian in the south. Short selections from other countries turn up plenty of good names. House white is £12.50, and there's an exceptional range of half-bottles.

CHEFS/PROPRIETORS: Colin Craig and Lesley Crosfield   OPEN: Tue to Sun D only 8 (1 sitting)   CLOSED: mid-Nov to mid-Mar   MEALS: Set D £42   SERVICE: not inc   CARDS: Delta, MasterCard, Switch, Visa   DETAILS: 16 seats. Private parties: 18 main room. Car park. No children under 12. No smoking. No music. No mobile phones   ACCOMMODATION: 5 rooms, all with bath/shower. TV. Phone. D,B&B £105 to £234. Rooms for disabled. No children under 12

Limetree ⅚✕

High Street, Moffat DG10 9HG	COOKING 2
TEL: (01683) 221654 FAX: (01683) 221721	MODERN BRITISH
WEBSITE: www.limetree-restaurant.co.uk	£25–£35

Located at the top end of the High Street, the Limetree has an immaculate interior – simple, cream-painted stone walls and metal-framed chairs – plus friendly and unobtrusive service (and sometimes intrusive music), and food that aims to forsake fuss and focus on flavour. Much therefore hangs on sourcing skills, and here the kitchen performs well, with carefully prepared smoked pigeon complementing black pudding in one starter at inspection. Excellent mustard-roasted potatoes came with accurately timed, if carelessly plated pork, and a well-executed orange crème caramel also demonstrated genuine skills. Decent sherries and dessert wines, topping and tailing a small but pleasingly marked wine list that starts from £10.95 and has choice under £20, underline the good value offered at this useful stop on the road north, or south.

CHEF: Matt Seddon PROPRIETORS: Matt and Artemis Seddon OPEN: Sun L 12.30 to 2.30, Tue to Sat D 6.30 to 9 CLOSED: 2 weeks Oct MEALS: Set L £12.50 (2 courses) to £15.75, Set D £15.75 (2 courses) to £19.50 SERVICE: not inc, card slips closed CARDS: Delta, MasterCard, Switch, Visa DETAILS: 25 seats. Private parties: 25 main room. Car park. Vegetarian meals on request. Children's helpings. No smoking. Wheelchair access (not WC). Music

▲ Well View ⅚✕

Ballplay Road, Moffat DG10 9JU	COOKING 4
TEL: (01683) 220184 FAX: (01683) 220088	FRANCO-SCOTTISH
WEBSITE: www.wellview.co.uk	£23–£44

Towards Moffat's eastern edge, this hotel stands in its peaceful half-acre with an air of tranquillity. It's a restored Victorian villa, impeccably run, the lounge done in sedate pastels, the dining room all floral murals. The formula is a familiar and successful one: a fixed menu with choice only at dessert stage, served in the evenings and at Sunday lunch. A typical menu might proceed from a salad of melon, Parma ham and avocado with a balsamic dressing, to roast rump of Annandale lamb on a mustard and mint mash with a Madeira and redcurrant jus. After a pause for the cheeses, the enticing pudding choice might be chocolate heather cream pot, lemon meringue pie, and crème brûlée. John Schuckardt mans front-of-house with gravitas and finesse. After concentrating on France, the wine list nips quickly around a few other areas (including Washington state); house French is £14 a bottle, £3 a glass.

CHEFS: Janet and Lina Schuckardt PROPRIETORS: Janet and John Schuckardt OPEN: Sun L 12.15 to 1.15, all week D 6.30 to 8 MEALS: Set L £16, Set D £30 SERVICE: none, card slips closed CARDS: Amex, Delta, MasterCard, Switch, Visa DETAILS: 20 seats. Private parties: 20 main room, 6 private room. Car park. No children under 6 at D. No smoking. No music. No mobile phones ACCOMMODATION: 6 rooms, all with bath/shower. TV. B&B £60 to £110. Baby facilities (£5)

'Two perfectly pleasant but slightly bored waitresses . . . disappeared for large amounts of time into the kitchens, reducing us to fits of giggles about being abandoned.' (On eating in Cornwall)

▲ Dower House ✳

Highfield, Muir of Ord IV6 7XN	COOKING 2
TEL/FAX: (01463) 870090	MODERN BRITISH
WEBSITE: www.thedowerhouse.co.uk	£48–£57

An endearingly ramshackle-looking house with a low-slung roof, the Dower House is home to the Aitchisons' set-price-dinner operation. Arrive at 7.30 for a drink, then sit down to a three-course dinner that might start with well-timed halibut with lemon, capers and parsley, before going on to beef fillet with caramelised onions, sautéed potatoes and steamed broccoli. Another night might produce Arbroath smokie with leeks, followed by loin of lamb with roast cherry tomatoes. It's all as homely as can be, and all the more appreciated for that. Finish with well-kept Scottish cheeses or the day's dessert, which could be an expertly risen raspberry soufflé. The wine list accords about equal billing to France and the southern hemisphere, with Languedoc house wines £17.

CHEF: Robyn Aitchison   PROPRIETORS: Robyn and Mena Aitchison   OPEN: all week D only 8 (L by arrangement)   CLOSED: Nov   MEALS: Set D £35   SERVICE: not inc, card slips closed   CARDS: MasterCard, Switch, Visa   DETAILS: 25 seats. Private parties: 25 main room. Car park. Children's helpings. No children under 6. No smoking. Wheelchair access (also WC). No music. No mobile phones   ACCOMMODATION: 5 rooms, all with bath/shower. TV. Phone. B&B £65 to £150. Rooms for disabled. Baby facilities

Ee-Usk £

North Pier, Oban PA34 5QD	COOKING 2
TEL: (01631) 565666 FAX: (01631) 570282	SEAFOOD
EMAIL: eeusk.fishcafe@virgin.net	£24–£50

Now in a brand new, red-roofed building on the North Pier, incorporating the harbourmaster's office, Ee-Usk makes the most of amazing views over Oban Bay and the Sound of Kerrera. The name is the Gaelic for fish, so it is no surprise that the menu focuses on 'super-fresh seafood', with everything bar sea bass and sea bream provided by trusted local fishermen. The catch can depend on 'the vagaries of the weather', but there were no disappointments for one visitor who raved about his Loch Etive mussels and 'oozingly tender' creel-caught langoustines with ginger and chilli dip. The kitchen also tackles cod and chips with pea and pancetta purée, and wild halibut with creamed leeks. Chargrilled Scotch fillet steak is the token non-fish option, and lemon cheesecake or clootie dumpling typify the desserts. The handy little wine list naturally favours whites; house selections are £10.50 (£2.75 a glass).

CHEF: Marianne Macdonald   PROPRIETORS: the Macleod family   OPEN: all week 12 to 3, 6 to 9   CLOSED: 25 and 26 Dec, 1 Jan   MEALS: alc (main courses £7.50 to £16.95)   SERVICE: not inc   CARDS: Delta, MasterCard, Switch, Visa   DETAILS: 100 seats. 40 seats outside. Private parties: 25 main room. Children's helpings. No children under 14 after 8pm. No-smoking area; no pipes/cigars. Wheelchair access (also WC). Music

'Muzak of a truly hideous standard haunts the dining room, giving the impression that you are stuck in the elevator from hell.' (On eating in London)

▲ Peat Inn 🍷 ⅙☀

Peat Inn KY15 5LH
TEL: (01334) 840206   FAX: (01334) 840530   COOKING 5
WEBSITE: www.thepeatinn.co.uk   SCOTTISH
at junction of B940 and B941, 6m SW of St Andrews   £33–£75

David and Patricia Wilson have been running their former coaching inn in the centre of
the village for over 30 years. You enter through a tiny lobby into a cosy reception room
complete with log fire, deep sofas and thick curtains, and proceed from there to the huge-
windowed dining room, with its views on to the garden. The Wilsons were
conscientiously sourcing fresh Scottish produce from small suppliers long before others
caught on, and are still doing so with vigour. Two king scallops are roasted, set on fanned
thin slices of potato, and accompanied by leeks, smoked bacon pieces and pea purée to
make a delightfully balanced starter; crab from Anstruther is dressed Asian-style in
coriander and lime; or there might be the elegant simplicity of lobster salad with avocado.
Three slices of 'truly outstanding' venison were the highlight of an April visit, supported by
shredded red cabbage topped with mashed blue potato. Desserts might take in caramelised
apple draped in its sauce offset by cinnamon ice cream, or lemon parfait with contrasting
orange sorbet. Coffee comes with chocolatey petits fours.

Praise be to the wine list, a Francophile selection but with global alternatives at every
stop. It's not huge, but it's packed with well-chosen, food-friendly wines, including
mature bottles at good prices. Useful background information and vintage assessments
make choice a doddle. House wines are £16, and while only two come by the glass, the
excellent selection of half-bottles proved just the job for one reporter.

CHEFS: David Wilson and Richard Turner   PROPRIETORS: David and Patricia Wilson   OPEN: Tue to Sat
12.30 for 1, 7 to 9.30   CLOSED: 25 Dec, 1 Jan   MEALS: alc D (main courses £16 to £21). Set L £22, Set D
£32 to £48   SERVICE: not inc, card slips closed   CARDS: Amex, Delta, MasterCard, Switch, Visa   DETAILS:
48 seats. Private parties: 24 main room, 12 to 14 private rooms. Car park. Vegetarian meals. Children's
helpings. No smoking. Wheelchair access (also WC). No music. No mobile phones   ACCOMMODATION: 8
rooms, all with bath/shower. TV. Phone. B&B £80 to £165. Rooms for disabled

Let's Eat ⅙☀ £

77 Kinnoull Street, Perth PH1 5EZ   COOKING 3
TEL: (01738) 643377   FAX: (01738) 621464   MODERN EUROPEAN
WEBSITE: www.letseatperth.co.uk   £26–£50

Tony Heath's bistro/restaurant remains 'something of a stalwart on the Perth eating scene',
although at a recent inspection meal the cooking seemed to have lost some of its spark.
Perennial favourites like smoked haddock chowder and chargrilled Inverurie ribeye please
traditionalists, but the kitchen also moves with the times, offering breast of local wood
pigeon with truffled tagliatelle, oyster mushrooms, pine nuts and spinach, or roast cod
studded with rosemary and pancetta served on pecorino mash – plus some intriguing
blackboard specials. As a finale, choose between, say, iced hazelnut praline parfait with
glazed banana or steamed ginger pudding with vanilla sauce and rhubarb ice cream. The
global wine list has plenty of drinkable stuff for under £20. House wines begin at £11.75.

CHEFS: Tony Heath, Graeme Pallister and Tomi Burns   PROPRIETORS: Tony Heath and Shona Drysdale
OPEN: Tue to Sat 12 to 2, 6.30 to 9.30   CLOSED: 25 and 26 Dec, last 2 weeks Jan, middle 2 weeks July
MEALS: alc (main courses L £9 to £12, D £10 to £18.50)   SERVICE: not inc, card slips closed   CARDS: Amex,
MasterCard, Switch, Visa   DETAILS: 65 seats. Private parties: 70 main room. Vegetarian meals. Children's
helpings. No smoking. Wheelchair access (also WC). Occasional music. No mobile phones (£5)

63 Tay Street 🍷 ✻

63 Tay Street, Perth PH2 8NN   COOKING 4
TEL: (01738) 441451   FAX: (01738) 441461   MODERN SCOTTISH
WEBSITE: www.63taystreet.co.uk   £29–£49

'On a beautiful sunny day, the view across the Tay to the autumn-coloured slopes opposite
this elegant modern restaurant made the visit particularly memorable,' wrote one happy
visitor. It is Jeremy Wares's cooking that is the main attraction, though, and his use of 'first-
class' ingredients and the 'deceptively simple but well-balanced and vibrant' menu
continue to draw praise.

At inspection, a starter of chicken terrine with onion marmalade, nicely seasoned and
studded with apricots, preceded chargrilled fillet of beef served with a well-judged black
pepper sauce. The menus are not overly long (sensibly so), but the sweet-toothed are still
likely to have difficulty deciding between the likes of date and fig pudding with
butterscotch sauce, or nougat glacé with a pistachio tuile. Service, from 'absolutely
charming' staff, tends toward the formal. The interior, with its crisp white walls and
wooden floor, is fresh and uncluttered. The wine list is perfectly attuned to the setting.
Eight house wines from £11.25 a bottle kick off a well-chosen modern international
selection arranged by styles.

CHEF: Jeremy Wares   PROPRIETORS: Shona and Jeremy Wares   OPEN: Tue to Sat 12 to 2, 6.30 to 9
CLOSED: last week Dec, first week Jan, last week June, first week July   MEALS: alc (main courses L £8.50,
D £15 to £18)   SERVICE: not inc, card slips closed   CARDS: Amex, MasterCard, Switch, Visa   DETAILS: 32
seats. Private parties: 32 main room. Vegetarian meals. No smoking. Wheelchair access (also WC). No
music (£5)

PITLOCHRY Perthshire & Kinross   map 11

Port-na-Craig

Port-na-Craig, Pitlochry PH16 5ND   COOKING 2
TEL: (01796) 472777   FAX: (01796) 481259   MODERN BRITISH
WEBSITE: www.portnacraig.com   £27–£45

This simply decorated inn is handy for those beating along the A9; it sits by the river just
below Pitlochry's theatre. The atmosphere is pleasant and festive, relaxed and informal,
and young chef Jamie Thewes has produced some 'delicious and individual' food. Local
and seasonal produce is emphasised, including herbs and some unusual fruit varieties from
the family's old walled kitchen garden. Start with a delicate venison salad and mustardy
celeriac rémoulade, or scallop salad with bacon and nut butter dressing; follow with a
substantial lamb shank with couscous, or salmon with hollandaise and spinach. As a finale,
one reporter's orange and cardamom pannacotta with orange salad was 'truly divine' and
perfectly textured, though Amaretto and almond tart with caramelised apples might run it
close. A couple of dozen wines start with house bottles from Gascony and the Gard at
£10.50 (£3 a glass).

CHEF: Jamie Thewes PROPRIETORS: the Thewes family OPEN: Tue to Sun L 12.30 to 2 (1 to 2.30 Sun), Tue to Sat D 6 to 9 MEALS: alc (main courses £7.50 to £15.50) SERVICE: not inc, 12.5% for parties of 6 or more CARDS: Delta, MasterCard, Switch, Visa DETAILS: 38 seats. 40 seats outside. Private parties: 20 main room, 12 to 20 private rooms. Car park. Vegetarian meals. Wheelchair access (also women's WC). No music

PLOCKTON Highland — map 11

▲ Plockton Hotel £ — NEW ENTRY

Harbour Street, Plockton IV52 8TN — COOKING **2**
TEL: (01599) 544274 FAX: (01599) 544475 — MODERN SCOTTISH
WEBSITE: www.plocktonhotel.co.uk — £20–£48

It's a pleasure to encounter skilful fish cookery in such a beautiful seaside location, and the Plockton Hotel's restaurant delivers some good stuff with minimal fuss. By electing to eat similar fare in the bar, one can enjoy a marvellous view across the bay. Four 'super' Plockton prawns (aka langoustines) with Marie-Rose sauce, or a ramekin of 'delicious and subtle' smoked mackerel with tomato gratin get a meal off to a promising start. Straightforward treatment of quality local produce delivers main courses of halibut steak with lemon butter ('wonderful'); monkfish and bacon brochette; and Highland venison casseroled in red wine with juniper berries, herbs and redcurrant jelly. Finish things off in appropriate style with whisky, honey and oatmeal ice cream, or local cheeses. Service is knowledgeable and friendly, and all the bottles on the compact wine list are under £15, with house Duboeuf £8.75.

CHEF: Alan Pearson PROPRIETORS: Mr and Mrs T. Pearson, and Alan Pearson OPEN: Mon to Sat 12 to 2.15, 6 to 9.15, Sun 12.30 to 2.15, 6 to 9 CLOSED: 25 Dec, 1 Jan MEALS: alc (main courses £6.50 to £18) SERVICE: not inc, card slips closed CARDS: Amex, Delta, MasterCard, Switch, Visa DETAILS: 60 seats. 30 seats outside. Private parties: 55 main room. Vegetarian meals. Children's helpings. No smoking. Wheelchair access (not WC). Occasional music. No mobile phones ACCOMMODATION: 11 rooms, all with bath/shower. TV. Phone. B&B £40 to £90. Rooms for disabled. Baby facilities

PORT APPIN Argyll & Bute — map 11

▲ Airds Hotel

Port Appin PA38 4DF
TEL: (01631) 730236 FAX: (01631) 730535 — COOKING **4**
WEBSITE: www.airds-hotel.com — MODERN BRITISH
2m off A828, on E shore of Loch Linnhe — £33–£74

There are stunning views across Loch Linnhe to Mull and Lismore from the windows of this white-painted eighteenth-century inn, and the dining room makes the very best of them; or you may prefer to soak up the scene from the water's edge. The hotel is traditionally and comfortably furnished - including the obligatory stag's head - and original artwork hangs in the restaurant. Dinner is four courses (vegetarians have their own menu), and the cooking is what you might expect given the country-house setting. Starters make the most of kitchen luxuries: for example, a guinea fowl, wild mushroom, foie gras and dill sausage with Puy lentils and truffles, or ravioli of lobster and langoustine with shellfish sauce. A soup such as cream of spinach and apple precedes the main course, which could be robustly traditional (roast loin of venison with red cabbage, celeriac purée and a thyme and juniper sauce), or a reworked classic (seared fillet of salmon with honeyed aubergine and hollandaise). Desserts maintain the balance with date pudding and butterscotch sauce, alongside vanilla mousse with poached berries and raspberry coulis. Burgundy is the main feature of the wine list, with short round-ups from the rest of France and a toe dipped in to other countries. Australia looks good, and the house selection is a tempting international mix from £16 to £23 with five by the glass.

CHEF: Paul Burns   PROPRIETORS: Shaun and Jenny McKivragan   OPEN: all week 12 to 2, 7.30 to 8.30
CLOSED: 5 to 26 Jan   MEALS: Set L £17.95 (2 courses) to £21.95, Set D £45. Light L available   SERVICE: not inc, card slips closed   CARDS: Delta, MasterCard, Switch, Visa   DETAILS: 36 seats. Private parties: 36 main room, 6 to 12 private rooms. Car park. Vegetarian meals. Children's helpings. No children under 8 at D. No smoking. No music. No mobile phones   ACCOMMODATION: 12 rooms, all with bath/shower. TV. Phone. D,B&B £160 to £360. Rooms for disabled. Baby facilities

▲ Pierhouse 🍴✸

Port Appin PA38 4DE	COOKING 3
TEL: (01631) 730302 FAX: (01631) 730400	SEAFOOD
WEBSITE: www.pierhousehotel.co.uk	£24–£68

The singular-looking building was once the residence of the pier master, who oversaw the then plentiful water traffic that went up and down Loch Linnhe. It now houses a comfortable small hotel and seafood restaurant, where the likes of oysters, deep-fried whitebait, or herring marinated in whisky are among the plain and simple but vibrantly fresh starters. Nor do main courses get needlessly elaborate but satisfy in the old-fashioned way by means of steamed haddock with sautéed potatoes, salmon on noodles with spinach cream, or crowded platters of shellfish and smoked salmon. There is also a full list of meat dishes, and ice creams, sorbets or local cheeses to finish. Seven house wines open a reasonably wide-ranging list with Vin de Pays d'Oc Chardonnay and Merlot at £11.50.

CHEF: Rita Thomson   PROPRIETORS: David and Liz Hamblin   OPEN: all week 12.30 to 2.30, 6.30 to 9.30
CLOSED: 25 and 26 Dec   MEALS: alc (main courses L £10 to £20, D £10.50 to £25)   SERVICE: not inc
CARDS: Delta, MasterCard, Switch, Visa   DETAILS: 70 seats. 24 seats outside. Car park. Vegetarian meals. Children's helpings. No smoking. Wheelchair access (also WC). Music   ACCOMMODATION: 12 rooms, all with bath/shower. TV. Phone. B&B £35 to £110. Baby facilities (£5)

PORTPATRICK Dumfries & Galloway   **map 11**

▲ Knockinaam Lodge 🍷 🍴✸ | NEW ENTRY |

Portpatrick DG9 9AD	
TEL: (01776) 810471 FAX: (01776) 810435	COOKING 5
WEBSITE: www.knockinaamlodge.com	MODERN EUROPEAN
off A77, 2½m S of Portpatrick	£32–£69

The grey-stone Victorian lodge is gloriously sited amid wooded hills and manicured lawns in the majestically tranquil Rhins of Galloway. Tony Pierce has cooked here since 1994, though the present owners took over only in 2003. His French-influenced cooking uses a four-course format, with no choice until the alternatives of dessert or cheese, to build up an array of bold, impressive flavours. A winter meal kicked off with piping hot wild mushroom and truffle velouté with smoked ham hock, preceding 'splendidly fresh' grilled salt cod in a light beurre blanc evanescently flavoured with rosemary. A main-course paupiette of corn-fed chicken shared the plate with a supporting cast including Puy lentils, asparagus and foie gras, while warm almond tart with a single roasted fig and a 'perfectly delicious dollop' of Amaretto sabayon made a fitting finale (the alternative being outstanding British and French cheeses, served with dried apricots). Service is mostly efficient, although can take a while to get in gear. Bordeaux and Burgundy lead the way in the wine list, and it's good to see affordable clarets between the big names (1995 Fourcas-Hosten at £26, for example). Other regions are patchier and can lean heavily on a small number of producers, but there are plenty of good bottles.

CHEF: Tony Pierce   PROPRIETORS: David and Sian Ibbotson   OPEN: all week 12 to 2, 7 to 9.30   MEALS: Set L £30, Set L Sun £22.50, Set D £45. Bar L menu available   SERVICE: not inc   CARDS: Amex, MasterCard, Switch, Visa   DETAILS: 40 seats. 18 seats outside. Private parties: 40 main room, 20 private room. Car park. Vegetarian meals upon request. Children's helpings. No children under 12 after 7. No smoking. Wheelchair access (not WC). No music.   ACCOMMODATION: 9 rooms, all with bath/shower. TV. Phone. D,B&B £125 to £350. Baby facilities (£5)

ST ANDREWS Fife   map 11

Seafood Restaurant ♥

NEW ENTRY

Bruce Embankment, St Andrews KY16 9AB   COOKING 4
TEL: (01334) 479475   FAX: (01334) 479476   SEAFOOD
WEBSITE: www.theseafoodrestaurant.com   £39–£77

New sibling to the Seafood Restaurant in St Monans (see entry), this striking, contemporary glass structure makes quite a statement, perched on the sea wall looking out on the water. Inside, glass walls offer stunning sea views, there's a central open-to-view kitchen, generous-sized tables are draped in white linen atop turquoise-green under-cloths, and smart, high-backed chairs provide comfort. Friendly and upbeat staff are clad in black, while the kitchen delivers a fashionably modern, lively seafood repertoire (with one option for carnivores): a starter of crab and langoustine risotto partnered by avocado 'ice cream' and shellfish sauce, say, and main courses of seared fillet of cod with chorizo, sun-blush tomatoes, beans, and garlic and herb butter; or steamed fillet of turbot topped with a foie gras and truffle mousse with Sauternes sauce. Finish with chocolate mousse with chocolate and chilli tuiles, honey ice cream, saffron and orange jelly, and caramel sauce: a dessert that 'tasted as good as it looked'. The wine selection is similar to that at St Monans, so expect a quality selection from £16 that's as up to date as the cooking. But look out, too, for interesting older bottles like the 1988 Hugel Riesling Jubilee at £40.

CHEFS: Craig Millar and Neil Clarke   PROPRIETORS: Craig Millar and Tim Butler   OPEN: all week 12 (12.30 Sun) to 2.30, 6.30 to 10   CLOSED: 25 and 26 Dec, 1 Jan   MEALS: Set L £20 (2 courses) to £30, Set D £30 (2 courses) to £50   SERVICE: not inc   CARDS: Amex, Delta, MasterCard, Switch, Visa   DETAILS: 60 seats. 36 seats outside. Private parties: 72 main room. Wheelchair access (also WC). No music. No mobile phones. Air-conditioned

---

ST MARGARET'S HOPE Orkney   map 11

▲ The Creel ⅙✳

Front Road, St Margaret's Hope KW17 2SL   COOKING 7
TEL: (01856) 831311   SEAFOOD/MODERN SCOTTISH
WEBSITE: www.thecreel.co.uk   £43–£54

Perched on the edge of a picturesque bay on South Ronaldsay, the Creel may not be the easiest place in the Guide to get to, but this doesn't stop people beating a regular path to its door. 'If only it wasn't a two-day drive and a boat ride away,' lamented one reader, who nevertheless plans to return.

The main draw is fish of unbeatable freshness, prepared with quiet skill by chef/proprietor Alan Craigie. His short, simple menus are an education for anyone who has never ventured beyond salmon and cod. There might be roast wolf fish and steamed megrim with Puy lentils, deep-fried sea witch with parsley sauce, and steamed tusk with seared scallops, leeks, ginger and cannellini beans. Tope, torsk and forkbeard have featured too. The fish is always precisely cooked – all the more commendable considering that sometimes there are three varieties with contrasting densities in a single dish – and beautifully but unfussily presented. Soups are the 'crowning achievement': full-bodied langoustine bisque with a generous garnish of five sweet langoustine tails has been considered 'world class', while a rich, reddish-brown partan bree is a 'superlative' example of this local speciality, 'so full of shreds of white meat that it was almost a crab stew'. Meat alternatives have included seaweed-fed North Ronaldsay mutton, served in a trio of grilled fillet, pot-roast shoulder and home-made sausage. Supporting roles are ably filled by freshly baked beremeal bannocks, well-dressed salads, and excellent local potatoes. For dessert, home-made ice creams (with Orkney strawberries in season) are a speciality, while a trio of rhubarb puddings, including a jelly 'of just the right consistency' and a refined version of a crumble, has pleased. The wine list is thoughtfully put together and refreshingly priced, with house Australian £14.50 and little in excess of £25.

CHEF: Alan Craigie   PROPRIETORS: Alan and Joyce Craigie   OPEN: all week D only 7 to 8.30   CLOSED: mid-Oct to mid-April; and Mon April, May and Sept   MEALS: alc (main courses £17 to £17.50)   SERVICE: not inc, card slips closed   CARDS: MasterCard, Switch, Visa   DETAILS: 36 seats. Private parties: 36 main room, 8 to 16 private rooms. Car park. Children's helpings. No smoking. Wheelchair access (also WC). No music   ACCOMMODATION: 3 rooms, all with bath/shower. TV. B&B £55 to £90. Baby facilities

ST MONANS Fife   map 11

Seafood Restaurant ♥ ✷

16 West End, St Monans KY10 2BX	COOKING 5
TEL: (01333) 730327 FAX: (01333) 730508	SEAFOOD
WEBSITE: www.theseafoodrestaurant.com	£34–£68

Blink and you might miss it, if you are coming at the place via its main entrance, which is on a narrow road leading to the harbour. The converted pub is most clearly visible from the seashore. Once inside, however, you will find a wholeheartedly welcoming ambience, with many of the old decorative features retained, and majestic views out over the Forth. Not much of the erstwhile pub catering style has been retained, though Scottish fish and shellfish remain the mainstays of the chic, modern menus. Linguine is mixed with mussels and caviar and sauced with white wine, while a timbale of kiln-roasted and smoked salmon, accompanied by crème fraîche with shallots and chives, is another simple but effective starter. Meaty treatments of main-course fish have included top-notch monkfish served with truffled cauliflower purée and curried aniseed oil, and grilled fillet of turbot with oxtail and foie gras ravioli and a wild mushroom ragoût in red wine. There is generally one main-course option for meat eaters. A streak of inspired creativity produces desserts such as a warm soup of berries and saffron with poached pear and 'electrifyingly flavourful' lemon sorbet, or the odd but successful balsamic ice cream partnering a bitter chocolate tart. Organic beer from the Black Isle Brewery is an eye-catcher, while the wine list pitches straight in with quality bottles, which means the bidding opens at £16; pricing nonetheless is mostly reasonable for the quality. The list is nicely weighted towards seafood-friendly whites; reds are an odd mix with rather too many prestige bottles. Under the same ownership is the Seafood Restaurant in St Andrews (see entry).

CHEFS: Craig Millar and George Scott   PROPRIETORS: Craig Millar and Tim Butler   OPEN: Tue to Sun L 12 to 2.30 (12.30 to 3 Sun), Tue to Sat D 6.30 to 9.30   CLOSED: 25 and 26 Dec, 1 and 2 Jan   MEALS: Set L £16 (2 courses) to £20, Set D £25 (2 courses) to £35   SERVICE: not inc, card slips closed   CARDS: Amex, Delta, MasterCard, Switch, Visa   DETAILS: 44 seats. 32 seats outside. Private parties: 50 main room. Car park. Children's helpings. No smoking. Wheelchair access (also WC). No music. No mobile phones

SHIELDAIG Highland   map 11

▲ Tigh an Eilean Hotel ⅓✳ | NEW ENTRY |

Shieldaig IV54 8XN   COOKING 3
TEL: (01520) 755251   FAX: (01520) 755321   MODERN SCOTTISH
EMAIL: tighaneileanhotel@shieldaig.fsnet.co.uk   £45–£58

'The house opposite the island' sounds prosaic, but the magical approach to this straightforward white-painted pub/hotel in a hamlet by the sea could figure in *The Lord of the Rings*. There's nothing mythical about the food, though. At inspection, beetroot soup, unobtrusively hinting of cumin, made a fine starter along with 'juicy and sweet' langoustines in a risotto. Fish and seafood are delivered to the kitchen each day: perhaps fillet of cod on crushed peas with tapenade, or scallops with Serrano ham and a hazelnut and coriander beurre blanc. Succulent pork tenderloin with mustard sauce, and pink, tender local rack of lamb in a herb crust show that meat cookery is just as deftly handled. Chocolate cake with lemon mousse makes a light but richly satisfying finale, with well-chosen Scottish and Continental cheeses an alternative. Incidentals like bread and appetisers are well reported, and a sensibly sized wine list centres on France but strays further afield into both Old and New Worlds. Three house wines are £11.95 and £14.95.

CHEFS: Christopher Field and N. Keevil   PROPRIETORS: Christopher and Cathryn Field   OPEN: all week D only 7 to 8.30   CLOSED: end Oct to end Mar   MEALS: Set D £35. Bar menu available   SERVICE: not inc CARDS: Delta, MasterCard, Switch, Visa   DETAILS: 26 seats. Vegetarian meals. Children's helpings. No smoking. No music. No mobile phones   ACCOMMODATION: 11 rooms, all with bath/shower. B&B £55 to £120. Baby facilities (£5)

STRATHYRE Stirling   map 11

▲ Creagan House ⅓✳

Strathyre FK18 8ND   COOKING 4
TEL: (01877) 384638   FAX: (01877) 384319   FRENCH/SCOTTISH
WEBSITE: www.creaganhouse.co.uk   £32–£44

The original seventeenth-century farmhouse has been lavishly upgraded, with nothing less than a baronial dining hall at its heart. Here, before the grand fireplace, some well-wrought Scottish cooking is served, with fish and seafood from Skye, Aberdeen Angus beef, Perthshire lamb and regional cheeses constituting the mainstays of the ambitious menus. Halibut has been served on a purée of Jerusalem artichokes with prawn beignets and lemongrass cream, to show that time has not stood still. Guinea fowl might be given a more obviously French treatment, perched on a croûte combining foie gras, bacon and grapes, in a sauce of wild mushrooms and Marsala. The handling of ingredients seems spot-on, whether for beef medallions, lamb cutlets, or a trio of fish – turbot, monkfish and salmon – in which each specimen is separately sauced. Challengingly rich desserts are the alternatives to those cheeses. Eight house selections, from an eminently reasonable base of £9.90, open a traditional but thoughtfully compiled wine list.

CHEF: Gordon Gunn   PROPRIETORS: Gordon and Cherry Gunn   OPEN: all week D only 7.30 (1 sitting)
CLOSED: 6 to 25 Nov, 23 Jan to 4 Mar; on Thurs from 1 April 2005   MEALS: Set D £22.50 to £26.50
SERVICE: not inc, card slips closed   CARDS: Amex, MasterCard, Switch, Visa   DETAILS: 14 seats. Private
parties: 35 main room. Car park. Children's helpings. No children under 10 at D. No smoking. Wheelchair
access (not WC). No music. No mobile phones   ACCOMMODATION: 5 rooms, all with bath/shower. B&B £60
to £100. Rooms for disabled. Baby facilities (£5)

STRONTIAN Highland   map 11

▲ Kilcamb Lodge ▮ ⅚✳

Strontian PH36 4HY   COOKING 4
TEL: (01967) 402257   FAX: (01967) 402041   SCOTTISH/FRENCH
WEBSITE: www.kilcamblodge.co.uk   £29–£54

Kilcamb Lodge is a tastefully restored country house on the edge of Loch Sunart, rather
dwarfed by the rising wooded hills behind. A rose-pink colour scheme makes the dining
room easy on the eye, as do the candles of an evening. Neil Mellis is all for regionalism in
his cooking, with seafood and game from the Highlands and Islands prominently featured.
'Sweet, fresh and tender' mussels from Loch Etive are steamed and sauced with cider,
saffron and shallots to make an 'out-and-out star' starter, while an early-summer menu
delivered gazpacho jelly with avocado mousse and basil oil. Next in the four-course format
comes a soup or sorbet, not always a convincing interlude, before the main-course trio of
meat, fish and vegetarian options. Roast breast of goose is a rarity, here caramelised and
served with braised red cabbage, roast shallots and intense thyme gravy. Fish might be
monkfish marinated in chilli, lime and coriander and accompanied by rösti, spinach and
beurre blanc. Lemon and raspberry posset with raspberry sorbet has proved an enjoyable
dessert. The wine list is arranged by grape variety with a briefing on styles to introduce each
section. Bottles are well chosen and mostly affordable, starting at £12.50. Eight come by
the glass.

CHEF: Neil Mellis   PROPRIETORS: Sally and David Fox   OPEN: Tue to Sun L 12 to 2.30, all week D 7.30 to
8.30   CLOSED: 5 Jan to 14 Feb   MEALS: alc L exc Sun (main courses £9 to £13.50). Set L Sun £14.50, Set D
£35   SERVICE: not inc, card slips closed   CARDS: Amex, Delta, MasterCard, Switch, Visa   DETAILS: 30
seats. Private parties: 30 main room. Car park. Vegetarian meals. No children under 12. No smoking.
Music. No mobile phones   ACCOMMODATION: 12 rooms, all with bath/shower. TV. Phone. B&B £55 to
£220. No children under 12

SWINTON Borders   map 11

▲ Wheatsheaf ⅚✳

Main Street, Swinton TD11 3JJ   COOKING 3
TEL: (01890) 860257   FAX: (01890) 860688   MODERN SCOTTISH
WEBSITE: www.wheatsheaf-swinton.co.uk   £25–£55

New owners (since 2003) Chris and Jan Winson are creating a good impression at their
welcoming inn overlooking the green in a pleasant village just north of Coldstream, and
they are benefiting from reliable back-up at the stoves. Long-serving chef John Keir is loyal
to Scotland's larder, and his cooking shows a sure touch. Black pudding fritters with
cranberry and orange sauce have been delicately handled; likewise grilled goats' cheese
salad with balsamic dressing. Main courses could include 'nicely balanced' corn-fed
chicken breast with pak choi and pancetta in soy sauce, or braised Border lamb shank on
squash and Gruyère mash, while desserts might feature iced Malteser parfait. Some of these

dishes also appear on the pub-style lunch menu, along with Eyemouth haddock and thick chips 'made from good local potatoes'. The reasonably priced, 100-strong wine list has eight house selections at £11.95.

CHEF: John Keir   PROPRIETORS: Chris and Jan Winson   OPEN: all week 12 to 2, 6 to 9 (8.30 Sun)   CLOSED: 24 to 26 Dec, Sun D in Dec and Jan   MEALS: alc (main courses L £7.50 to £13, D £11 to £18), light L menu available Mon to Sat   SERVICE: not inc   CARDS: Delta, MasterCard, Switch, Visa   DETAILS: 50 seats. Private parties: 30 main room, 16 to 30 private rooms. Car park. Vegetarian meals. Children's helpings. No smoking. No music   ACCOMMODATION: 7 rooms, all with bath/shower. TV. Phone. B&B £62 to £120. Baby facilities £5

TROON South Ayrshire   map 11

▲ Lochgreen House ⅚✻

Monktonhill Road, Southwood, Troon KA10 7EN   COOKING 5
TEL: (01292) 313343   FAX: (01292) 318861   FRANCO-SCOTTISH
WEBSITE: www.costleyhotels.co.uk   £35–£55

Thirty acres of trademark manicured gardens surround this white-painted early twentieth-century country house, which seems to be a product of the Scottish Arts and Crafts school of architecture. Like other establishments in the elite Costley group, it is immaculate. The hotel has been dramatically enlarged, but Andrew Costley still holds sway in the kitchen and the cooking impresses with its professionalism, elegance and impeccable presentation.

Dinner runs to four courses, with starters setting the tone: luxurious roulade of confit duck and foie gras with wild kumquat and orange dressing, and seared local scallops with their own mousseline, tomato, beurre blanc and champagne foam both won over our inspectors. Next, a 'dinky' timbale of haggis, neeps and tatties with whisky and chive sauce gives a new twist to the auld Scottish cliché, and the kitchen's assured way with fish resurfaces in a main-course ensemble of seared, lightly cured salmon topped with a pastry parcel of leeks and langoustine, together with asparagus spears and a buttery Shiraz sauce. Desserts like red mango parfait with tropical fruit in a lime and lemongrass syrup look as enticing as they sound, and well-trained, smartly groomed staff add to the all-round sense of occasion. An extensive, well-priced wine list impressed an inspector, though unfortunately the hotel opted not to send us the list for detailed assessment; nor did it return our questionnaire and thus some of the information below may not be accurate.

CHEF: Andrew Costley   PROPRIETOR: Costley and Costley Hoteliers Ltd   OPEN: Sun L 12 to 2, all week D 7 to 9   MEALS: alc L (main courses £7.50 to £12). Set L Sun £22.50, Set D £35   SERVICE: not inc, card slips closed   CARDS: Amex, Delta, MasterCard, Switch, Visa   DETAILS: 80 seats. 50 seats outside. Private parties: 120 main room, 12 to 80 private rooms. Car park. Vegetarian meals. No smoking. Wheelchair access (also WC). Music. No mobile phones. Air-conditioned   ACCOMMODATION: 44 rooms, all with bath/shower. TV. Phone. B&B £70 to £85. Rooms for disabled

---

MacCallums Oyster Bar

The Harbour, Troon KA10 6DH   COOKING 3
TEL: (01292) 319339   SEAFOOD
WEBSITE: www.maccallums.co.uk   £28–£56

The location – right by the harbour – is tailor-made for an oyster bar, and this relaxed high-ceilinged dining room makes the most of its views. The owners also run a wet fish shop in Glasgow, so expect impeccable freshness from daily deliveries. In addition to oysters, attentive 'smiley' staff in blue aprons deliver all manner of fish and shellfish cooked with simple confidence: no-frills smoked haddock rarebit, or grilled langoustines with garlic butter, alongside more complex sea bass with crayfish salsa and tomato sauce, or sole tempura with courgette and fennel ragout and dill cream sauce. Pot-roast poussin with honey-glazed root vegetables is a sop to meat lovers, while desserts are elaborately dressed-up things like chocolate torte with Cointreau syrup. The wine list has whites aplenty and reasonable prices from £11.60.

CHEFS: Scott Keenan and Stuart Wilson PROPRIETORS: John and James MacCallum OPEN: Tue to Sun L 12 to 2.30 (3.30 Sun), Tue to Sat D 7 to 9.30 MEALS: alc (main courses £9.50 to £20.50) SERVICE: not inc CARDS: Delta, MasterCard, Switch, Visa DETAILS: 43 seats. Private parties: 43 main room. Car park. Children's helpings. Wheelchair access (not WC). Music

Wales

map 4

▲ Harbourmaster Hotel 🍴 ✴

Pen Cei, Aberaeron SA46 0BA   COOKING 2
TEL: (01545) 570755   FAX: (01545) 570762   MODERN WELSH
WEBSITE: www.harbour-master.com   £26–£54

Reporters confirm that this refurbished Grade II listed building by the quay is 'justifiably gathering momentum' since Glyn and Menna Heulyn arrived on the scene. Their hands-on approach is appreciated, and the place benefits from attentive, Welsh-speaking staff. The bilingual policy extends to the menu, which proudly advertises the sources of most of its native ingredients – from Nevern goose to organic Nantclyd eggs. Fish is a strong suit, and reporters have recommended linguine with New Quay crab, prawns with lemon and thyme butter, and halibut on a bed of smoked haddock and asparagus risotto; meat eaters meanwhile might be treated to haunch of Coed-y-Brenin venison with chorizo mash. Cheeses are patriotic, and desserts could feature, say, blueberry and Brazil nut brûlée. The moderately priced wine list (from £11.50) includes some interesting names. Ten come by the glass.

CHEF: Sara Griffiths   PROPRIETORS: Glyn and Menna Heulyn   OPEN: Tue to Sun L 12 to 2, Mon to Sat D 6.30 to 8.45   CLOSED: 24 Dec to 10 Jan   MEALS: alc (main courses £9.50 to £16.50)   SERVICE: not inc, card slips closed   CARDS: Delta, MasterCard, Switch, Visa   DETAILS: 40 seats. Car park. Vegetarian meals. No smoking. Wheelchair access (also WC). Music   ACCOMMODATION: 7 rooms, all with bath/shower. TV. Phone. B&B £55 to £105. No children under 5

map 7

▲ Penhelig Arms Hotel 🍷 ✴

Terrace Road, Aberdovey LL35 0LT   COOKING 2
TEL: (01654) 767215   FAX: (01654) 767690   BRITISH
WEBSITE: www.penheligarms.com   £24–£55

Affectionately dubbed 'the Pen' by regulars, this three-storey inn overlooking the Dovey estuary owes much to the personal attention of its long-standing custodians, Robert and Sally Hughes. Local ingredients are a priority, and their kitchen is bolstered by organic meat, salad leaves from a neighbourhood smallholder, and supplies of fish from the boats. Pub standards like lamb's liver and bacon, and haddock 'n' chips remain firm favourites, but the kitchen has also pleased visitors with whole grilled mackerel, and Welsh lamb cutlets with chilli and tomato sauce. Mediterranean flavours add zing to dishes like chard salad with buffalo mozzarella, cherry tomatoes and olives, and grilled fillet of plaice with pancetta and tapenade, while desserts could usher in pannacotta, summer pudding, and apricot frangipane tart. Robert Hughes's enthusiasm for wine is a boon for customers. The 'give-away' prices put a huge range within the reach of ordinary mortals, and those wines are a very well-chosen international selection, regularly updated with new finds. Eighteen house bottles from £10.50 also come by the glass. 'Worthy of a London restaurant at half London's prices,' concluded a reporter.

CHEFS: Bronwen Shaw, Jason Griffiths and Sarah Gerrard   PROPRIETORS: Robert and Sally Hughes
OPEN: all week 12 to 2.15, 7 to 9.30   CLOSED: 25 and 26 Dec   MEALS: alc L (main courses £8 to £14). Set L
Sun £15, Set D £26   SERVICE: not inc   CARDS: Delta, MasterCard, Switch, Visa   DETAILS: 40 seats. 20
seats outside. Private parties: 24 main room. Car park. Vegetarian meals. Children's helpings. No
smoking. No music. Air-conditioned   ACCOMMODATION: 14 rooms, all with bath/shower. TV. Phone.
D,B&B £66 to £150. Baby facilities (£5)

ABERSOCH Gwynedd   map 7

▲ Porth Tocyn Hotel 🍴

Bwlch Tocyn, Abersoch LL53 7BU
TEL: (01758) 713303   FAX: (01758) 713538
WEBSITE: www.porth-tocyn-hotel.co.uk   COOKING 4
on minor road 2m S of Abersoch through hamlets of Sarn   MODERN EUROPEAN
Bach and Bwlch Tocyn   £29–£56

Besides the stupendous views across Cardigan Bay, what continues to please here are the relaxed informality, 'comfy sofas' and serious, innovative cooking. Evolutionary changes have brought both physical renovation (lavatories and car park) and further opening up to Pacific Rim culinary influences. Combinations at dinner have shown deft and original touches: wok-fried basil and chilli squid on vegetable spaghetti with aubergine raita; a fine Thai soup based on good chicken stock sharpened with lemon; an excellent pawpaw and balsamic ice cream; and interestingly flavoured bread (including Dijon and black pepper). Closer to home come duck liver pavé with plum and orange compote; a carefully cooked tournedos with a sweet-and-sour onion topping; and nursery favourites like orange and almond sponge pudding. 'Light bite' lunches are popular – Welsh rarebit, perhaps, or duck and spring onion filo rolls – and there's an all-you-can-hold set-price buffet lunch on Sundays. Around 70 wines from across the world start with six house selections from £13.50, and further up the scale are some slightly older clarets and white Burgundies.

CHEFS: Louise Fletcher-Brewer and Douglas Hull   PROPRIETORS: the Fletcher-Brewer family   OPEN: Sun L
12.15 to 1.45, all week D 7.30 to 9 (7.15 to 9.30 when busy)   CLOSED: mid-Nov to mid-Mar   MEALS: buffet
L Sun £20.50, Set D £29.50 (2 courses) to £36. Light L menu available Mon to Sat   SERVICE: not inc, card
slips closed   CARDS: MasterCard, Switch, Visa   DETAILS: 50 seats. 30 seats outside. Car park.
Vegetarian meals. Children's helpings; no very young children at D. No smoking. Wheelchair access (also
WC). No music. No mobile phones   ACCOMMODATION: 17 rooms, all with bath/shower. TV. Phone. B&B
(continental breakfast) £60 to £149. Rooms for disabled. Baby facilities. Swimming pool

---

BASSALEG Newport   map 4

Junction 28 🍴 £

Station Approach, Bassaleg NP10 1LD
TEL: (01633) 891891   FAX: (01633) 895978   COOKING 2
from M4 junction 28 take A468 towards Caerphilly, turn   MODERN EUROPEAN
right at Tredegar Arms and take first left   £21–£42

Almost as bustling as the nearby M4 intersection it's named after, this converted railway station proves a popular commute for local diners. The interior, far from traditional, is in old-colonial style, with palm trees, oriental statues, overhead fans and bamboo furniture. The cooking is hearty and honest and more contemporary, offering a lengthy carte of homely dishes with a modern tilt. After lamb's sweetbreads on a balsamic-dressed salad, or a Mediterranean vegetable and crab strudel, proceed to mains of seared halibut steak paired with spicy sweet-pepper marmalade and basil pesto, or veal sausages on a truffle mash with a creamy wild mushroom sauce. Sticky toffee pudding with toffee sauce and vanilla ice cream might figure among familiar desserts. Set meals are good value, too, and a short but well-spread wine list starts with house wines at £11.50 (£2.25 a glass).

CHEFS: Jon West and Jean Payz   PROPRIETORS: Richard Wallace and Jon West   OPEN: all week L 12 to 2 (4 Sun), Mon to Sat D 5.30 to 9.30   CLOSED: last week July, first week Aug   MEALS: alc Mon to Sat (main courses £8 to £16). Set L Mon to Sat £7.95 (1 course) to £11.45, Set L Sun £10.95 (2 courses) to £12.95, Set D 5.30 to 7 £12.95   SERVICE: not inc, card slips closed   CARDS: Amex, Delta, MasterCard, Switch, Visa   DETAILS: 160 seats. Private parties: 50 main room, 12 to 14 private rooms. Car park. Vegetarian meals. No smoking. Wheelchair access (also WC). Music. Air-conditioned

BEAUMARIS Isle of Anglesey   map 7

▲ Ye Olde Bulls Head ♥ ✻

Castle Street, Beaumaris LL58 8AP	COOKING 4
TEL: (01248) 810329 FAX: (01248) 811294	MODERN EUROPEAN
WEBSITE: www.bullsheadinn.co.uk	£46–£55

Just a stone's throw from the town's majestic medieval castle, the Bulls Head is a historical inn of many parts. Its restrained classical frontage belies the variety and richness inside: the darkly traditional bar and a light, modern brasserie (with its own chef) occupy the ground floor, while the contemporary-style restaurant is upstairs. The daily fixed-price menu puts great store by carefully sourced native ingredients, from Conwy mussels to smoked Anglesey beef. To start, a terrine of local smoked bacon with grape chutney might vie for attention with the 'seductive odours' of Thai-style scallops with coconut milk. Main courses usher in medallions of Snowdonia venison with Puy lentils, girolles and a tart cranberry sauce, or steamed fillet of Menai sea bass with seafood chowder, while professionally executed desserts feature the likes of baked fig and honey tart with hazelnut praline cream, and steamed Agen prune pudding. Service is well paced and unobtrusive. Whoever chooses the wine and sets the prices deserves a pat on the back, if not a full knighthood, for putting the customer first. There are neat selections from most parts of the world, with a fuller focus on France (also the main source for the good number of half-bottles). House wines are £14.75. The restaurant's chef departed as we were going to press, but co-proprietor Keith Rothwell is a steadying hand in both kitchen and dining room.

CHEF: Keith Rothwell   PROPRIETOR: Rothwell & Robertson Ltd   OPEN: Mon to Sat D only 7 to 9.30 CLOSED: 25 and 26 Dec, 1 Jan   MEALS: Set D £32. Brasserie menu available L and D   SERVICE: not inc CARDS: Amex, Delta, MasterCard, Switch, Visa   DETAILS: 45 seats. Private parties: 25 main room. Car park. Vegetarian meals. No children under 7. No smoking. No music. No mobile phones ACCOMMODATION: 13 rooms, all with bath/shower. TV. Phone. B&B £67 to £97. Baby facilities

---

'Service alternately makes you feel sorry for one member of staff while waiting to punch the next one.' (On eating in London)

---

map 4

▲ Druidstone ⚡✻ £

Druidston Haven, Broad Haven SA62 3NE
TEL: (01437) 781221   FAX: (01437) 781133
WEBSITE: www.druidstone.co.uk   COOKING 1
from B4341 at Broad Haven turn right at sea; after 1½m   GLOBAL
turn left to Druidston Haven; hotel ¾m on left   £25–£48

This rambling stone hotel, perched on the cliff-top overlooking a rugged seascape, is an idiosyncratic, one-off place with an 'utterly laid-back atmosphere, as if time had stood still'. The downstairs bar, a 'throwback to the '60s', attracts a broad mix of customers, while the dining room's wooden floorboards, open fire and upright piano maintain an air of informality. The lack of pretence extends to the cooking, where decent raw materials and unfussy presentation reign. There's an occasional nod to exoticism in, say, Cajun pan-fried salmon with king prawn and lime, but the more familiar predominates with the likes of fried pork fillet with caramelised apples, red onion and Pant Mawr cheese. Banoffi pie, or hot chocolate fudge cake, makes a typical homely finish, while a compact global wine list offers reasonable prices and house wines from £8.40.

CHEFS: Rod and Angus Bell, Donna Banner and Jon Woodhouse   PROPRIETORS: Rod, Jane and Angus Bell
OPEN: Sun L 12.30 to 2.30, Mon to Sat D 7.30 to 9.30   MEALS: alc (main courses £10 to £19). Bar menu
available   SERVICE: not inc, card slips closed   CARDS: Amex, Delta, MasterCard, Switch, Visa   DETAILS:
36 seats. 30 seats outside. Private parties: 36 main room, 8 to 12 private rooms. Car park. Vegetarian
meals. Children's helpings. No smoking. Wheelchair access (not WC). No music   ACCOMMODATION: 11
rooms, 4 with bath/shower. B&B £38 to £124. Rooms for disabled. Baby facilities

                                    map 7

▲ Tan-y-Foel ⚡✻

Capel Garmon, nr Betws-y-coed LL26 0RE
TEL: (01690) 710507   FAX: (01690) 710681
WEBSITE: www.tyfhotel.co.uk   COOKING 5
take turning marked Capel Garmon and Nebo from A470   MODERN BRITISH-PLUS
about halfway between Betws-y-coed and Llanrwst   £50–£60

A luxury country hideaway with majestic views over the Conwy Valley and Snowdonia, Tan-y-Foel is not as hidebound and traditional as outer appearances might suggest. The bold, contemporary décor is an essay in shades of brown, with linen and hessian wall coverings in the lounge, and rough cream plaster walls hung with wooden carvings set off against a beamed ceiling in the dining room. Square tables are comfortably spaced, adding to the elegant impression.

Choice is limited to two alternatives per course on the three-course dinner menu, although anyone staying more than a couple of days will be pleased to note that they change daily. Main-course options usually include something relatively down-to-earth and domestic, such as rack of salt-marsh lamb with wild garlic and bacon bubble and squeak, alongside a more exotic dish – perhaps roast turbot with nasi goreng made from local brown shrimp, finished with pak choi, a fried quail's egg and Mussaman sauce. Starters typically include smoked salmon-stuffed lemon sole mousse, and to finish there might be warm chocolate mousse with star anise ice cream. Service is serene and .

professional, and wines are a well-chosen and fairly priced international bunch, with house selections starting at £16.

CHEF: Janet Pitman   PROPRIETORS: Mr and Mrs P.K. and J.C. Pitman   OPEN: all week D only 7.30 to 8.15
CLOSED: Dec, limited opening Jan   MEALS: Set D £35   SERVICE: not inc   CARDS: MasterCard, Switch, Visa
DETAILS: 12 seats. Car park. No children under 7. No smoking. No music. No mobile phones
ACCOMMODATION: 6 rooms, all with bath/shower. TV. Phone. B&B £99 to £160. No children under 7

CARDIFF Cardiff   map 4

Armless Dragon ✿ £

97–99 Wyverne Road, Cathays, Cardiff CF24 4BG   COOKING 2
TEL: (029) 2038 2357   FAX: (029) 2038 2055   MODERN WELSH
WEBSITE: www.armlessdragon.co.uk   £19–£57

A recent facelift has lightened up the mood at Paul and Martine Lane's unostentatious neighbourhood bistro, but their crusading approach to local produce and contemporary Welsh cuisine is as strong as ever. Meals now begin with a choice of palate-teasing platters: assortments of little dishes built around the themes of 'land' (smoked Monmouthshire chicken), 'sea' (Pembrokeshire spider crab tart; sewin pancakes with dill yoghurt) and 'earth' (vegetarian based – e.g. crispy laver balls with ginger-pickled vegetables or Glamorgan sausage with piccalilli). Main courses take up the baton with a seafood version of cawl, or braised and roast kid with mustard mash and wild mushrooms. To finish, try white chocolate and hazelnut cheesecake, or tackle the giant bara brith bread-and-butter pudding. The well-spread wine list has plenty of quality drinking for under £20. 'Everyday' bottles start at £8.90.

CHEF: Paul Lane   PROPRIETORS: Paul and Martine Lane   OPEN: Tue to Fri L 12 to 2, Tue to Sat D 7 to 9 (9.30
Fri and Sat). Also open Mon D by arrangement, Sat L for home rugby internationals   CLOSED: 25 Dec, 1
Jan   MEALS: alc (main courses £12 to £20). Set L £10 (2 courses) to £12, Set D £27 (inc wine)   SERVICE:
not inc, card slips closed   CARDS: Delta, MasterCard, Switch, Visa   DETAILS: 50 seats. Private parties: 50
main room. Vegetarian meals. Children's helpings. No smoking. Wheelchair access (not WC).
Music £5

Da Castaldo ✿

5 Romilly Crescent, Canton, Cardiff CF11 9NP   COOKING 2
TEL: (029) 2022 1905   FAX: (029) 2022 1920   MODERN ITALIAN
WEBSITE: www.dacastaldo.com   £23–£55

Rubbing shoulders with a row of local shops in the suburb of Canton, Da Castaldo has bright, stylish décor, and in terms of what appears on the plate Antonio Castaldo aims to 'uphold authentic Italian traditions within a modern style'. Spaghetti al cartoccio (baked in parchment with shellfish, cherry tomatoes and white wine), and pork fillet in a chestnut and honey sauce with roast vegetables, certainly fit the bill. Bread, served with garlicky green and black olives, was commended by an inspector, and saucing, too, seems to be a strength. Desserts might include torta di mela, apple and cinnamon crumble, or perhaps a hot chocolate soufflé. Service is relaxed and friendly. The Italian half of the shortish wine list offers the best value; house wines start at £10.50.

CHEF: Antonio Castaldo   PROPRIETORS: Antonio and Cheryl Castaldo   OPEN: Tue to Sat 12 to 2, 7 to 10
(10.30 Sat)   MEALS: alc (main courses £11 to £16.50). Set L £10 (2 courses) to £13.50, Set D Tue to Thur
£20   SERVICE: not inc, card slips closed   CARDS: Delta, MasterCard, Switch, Visa   DETAILS: 45 seats.

Private parties: 50 main room. Vegetarian meals. Children's helpings. No smoking. Wheelchair access (not WC). Music. Air-conditioned £5

Da Venditto

7–8 Park Place, Cardiff CF10 3DP   COOKING 2
TEL: (029) 2023 0781   FAX: (029) 2039 9949   MODERN ITALIAN
WEBSITE: www.vendittogroup.co.uk   £30–£66

Housed on the ground floor of two imposing stone Victorian town houses, this modern Italian restaurant uses marble, stainless steel and cherry wood to make a stylish impression. Paper-thin slices of poached veal come with creamy tuna sauce and capers for a first-course deconstruction of vitello tonnato, while scallops and squid are appealingly dressed with rosemary-scented oil. Rump of salt-marsh lamb has been carefully timed and partnered with buttered spinach, and desserts have included lemon ricotta cake with mascarpone. Grumbles concentrate on the high cost (side orders are essential as main courses are only sparsely garnished), augmented by the unexpected charges for incidentals such as bread and olives. A list with maps helps you get your bearings on the contemporary Italian wine scene, opening with house wines from Campania at £14.50, or £4.50 a glass.

CHEFS: Mark Freeman and Ifan Dunn   PROPRIETOR: Toni Venditto   OPEN: Mon to Sat 12 to 2.30, 6 to 10.45   CLOSED: bank hols   MEALS: alc (main courses £16.50 to £18.50). Set L £14.50 (2 courses) to £18, Set D 6 to 7 and 10 to 10.45 £19.50 (2 courses), Set D £27.50 (2 courses) to £37.50   SERVICE: not inc, 10% for parties of 6 or more   CARDS: Amex, Delta, MasterCard, Switch, Visa   DETAILS: 55 seats. Private parties: 70 main room. Car park (D only). Vegetarian meals. Children's helpings. No pipes. Wheelchair access (also WC). Music. No mobile phones. Air-conditioned

Le Gallois

6–10 Romilly Crescent, Canton, Cardiff CF11 9NR   COOKING 5
TEL: (029) 2034 1264   FAX: (029) 2023 7911   MODERN FRENCH-PLUS
WEBSITE: www.legallois-ycymro.com   £29–£75

WALES GFG 2005 COMMENDED

A smooth operation front and back delivering confident, complex cooking in a modern Gallic style, Le Gallois continues to raise its game. Chef/patron Padrig Jones (the Welshman of the place's name) seeks out quality raw materials; he sources produce each week from the markets of Paris, and uses the best local stuff he can find. The smart dining room with large picture windows (a conversion of three suburban shops) is a worthy setting for a starter such as sautéed scallops with belly pork, boudin noir, quail's egg, confit tomato and honey jam: each element 'perfectly cooked and a perfect foil to the others'. At an inspection meal oxtail bourguignon with monkfish was a combination as successful as it was unexpected; and a mascarpone sorbet and rhubarb, orange and champagne jelly supplemented by a tuile incorporating large flakes of hot Szechuan pepper was inspired. A pre-dessert lemon posset preceded an intensely flavoured raspberry and goats' cheese soufflé with goats' milk ripple ice cream. Service by young Frenchmen is generally deft and unobtrusive, as well as knowledgeable and forthcoming when necessary. Unsurprisingly, only a quarter of the wine list's 80-odd bins, from £14 upwards, come from outside French borders.

CHEF: Padrig Jones   PROPRIETORS: the Jones and Dupuy families   OPEN: Tue to Sat 12 to 2.30, 6.30 to 10.30   CLOSED: 1 week at Christmas, 1 week Aug   MEALS: alc (main courses £10.50 to £22). Set L £17.95, Set D £30 (2 courses) to £35   SERVICE: not inc, 10% for parties of 6 or more, card slips closed   CARDS:

Amex, MasterCard, Switch, Visa   DETAILS: 60 seats. Private parties: 60 main room. Car park. Vegetarian meals. Children's helpings. No pipes/cigars. Wheelchair access (also WC). Occasional music. Air-conditioned

Izakaya Japanese Tavern 🌣

Mermaid Quay, Cardiff Bay, Cardiff CF10 5BW	COOKING 3
TEL: (029) 2049 2939 FAX: (029) 2049 2969	JAPANESE
WEBSITE: izakaya-japanese-tavern.com	£14–£53

An *izakaya* might be considered the Japanese equivalent of Spain's tapas bar, and this informal, friendly venue overlooking Cardiff Bay captures the spirit of such places perfectly, albeit with the focus mainly on eating. Bamboo screens, low tables, paper lanterns and illuminated beer signs certainly help it to look the part, and illustrated menus come with advice on ordering. Choice is wide, taking in skewered dishes (such as yakitori), sushi and sashimi in individual portions or as selection platters, and assorted tempura, noodles and vegetables – pick a few dishes at a time, then come back for more when you are ready. Reporters recommend choosing individual dishes rather than opting for the set menus, and tempura usually comes in for praise; extras such as miso soup, rice and pickles can be ordered separately. To drink, there's a range of hot and cold sakés, plum wine, shochu or Japanese beers, as well as house wines at £10.90 a bottle.

CHEFS: Yoshiko Evans and Peter Mansbridge   PROPRIETORS: Iestyn and Yoshiko Evans   OPEN: all week 12 to 2, 6 to 10.30 (Sun 1 to 9.30)   CLOSED: 24 and 25 Dec, 1 Jan   MEALS: Set L £5.90, Set D £17 to £26   SERVICE: not inc   CARDS: Amex, Delta, Diners, MasterCard, Switch, Visa   DETAILS: 90 seats. 8 seats outside. Private parties: 80 main room, 6 to 25 private rooms. Vegetarian meals. No smoking in 1 dining room. Wheelchair access (also WC). Music

Woods Brasserie

The Pilotage Building, Stuart Street, Cardiff CF10 5BW	COOKING 4
TEL: (029) 2049 2400 FAX: (029) 2048 1998	MODERN EUROPEAN
	£34–£58

Hard by Cardiff Bay, Woods is in the thick of a revitalised part of Cardiff, with contemporary architecture springing up all around. And its cool, bright interior, with wicker-chaired bar and wood-floored restaurant hung with bold modern paintings, fits this setting well. A take on Caesar salad is what you might expect, and heads a seasonally changing menu of dishes in the textbook brasserie idiom. Yellowfin tuna on coriandered fennel with caper vinaigrette should awaken the tastebuds, and this might be followed by roast poussin with potato gratin, or Aberdeen Angus two ways (the fillet chargrilled and the shin braised) in a jus containing smoked bacon. Traditionalists can opt for wild mushroom risotto with Parmesan, or even house fish 'n' chips, before ending on apple and red berry crumble with vanilla ice cream. Consistent quality, 'very adequate' portions and friendly staff make this a regular favourite with one pair of out-of-towners. The wide-ranging and intelligently chosen wine list offers ten by the glass, and bottle prices from £14.10. Sean Murphy is executive chef here and at Choice Produce's other restaurant, the Old Post Office in St Fagans (see entry).

CHEFS: Sean Murphy and Nathan Brown   PROPRIETOR: Choice Produce Ltd   OPEN: Mon to Sat 12 to 2 (3 Sun), 7 to 10   CLOSED: 25 and 26 Dec, 1 Jan, occasional Sun eves in winter, bank hol Mon D   MEALS: alc (main courses £9.50 to £18)   SERVICE: not inc, 10% (optional) for parties of 6 or more, card slips closed   CARDS: Amex, Delta, Diners, MasterCard, Switch, Visa   DETAILS: 70 seats. 30 seats outside. Private parties: 45 main room, 25 private room. Vegetarian meals. Children's helpings. No pipes/cigars. Wheelchair access (also WC). Music. No mobile phones. Air-conditioned

CLYTHA Monmouthshire

map 2

▲ Clytha Arms ▼ ⁵⁄ₓ

Clytha NP7 9BW
TEL: (01873) 840206   FAX: (01873) 840209
WEBSITE: www.clytha-arms.com
off old Abergavenny to Raglan road, S of A40, 6m E of
Abergavenny

COOKING 3
MODERN WELSH
£28–£54

Hidden away in the countryside not far from the River Usk, this former dower house fulfils the dual roles of informal pub and restaurant. The popular bar throngs with locals playing draughts and table skittles while enjoying the decent range of ales and bar snacks. By contrast, the calmer, carpeted lounge comes in farmhouse style, with a high settle, leather sofa and a fireplace. The restaurant continues the theme, with an assortment of white-clothed tables. The Cannings use quality local ingredients to produce carefully cooked, and generous, modern dishes with the occasional Mediterranean twist: wild boar in red wine with chorizo, or pork tenderloin paired with roast peppers and mozzarella, for example. The long pudding list may provoke an agony of decisions; a 'super' cinnamon and almond cake with honey ice cream did the trick for one visitor. The wine list shifts gear smoothly from ten pub-style house bottles at £11.95, or £2.20 a glass, to a range fit to grace the smartest tables, including a good spread of half-bottles, and all at reasonable prices.

CHEFS: Andrew and Sarah Canning   PROPRIETORS: Andrew and Beverley Canning   OPEN: Tue to Sun and bank hol Mon L 12.30 to 2.30, Tue to Sat D 7 to 9   CLOSED: 25 Dec   MEALS: alc (main courses £11 to £19). Set L and D £15.95 (2 courses) to £17.95. Bar L menu available Tue to Sat   SERVICE: not inc   CARDS: Amex, Delta, Diners, MasterCard, Switch, Visa   DETAILS: 100 seats. 50 seats outside. Private parties: 60 main room, 6 to 20 private rooms. Car park. Vegetarian meals. Children's helpings. No smoking. No music   ACCOMMODATION: 4 rooms, all with bath/shower. TV. Room only £50 to £90. Baby facilities (£5)

COLWYN BAY Conwy

map 7

Café Niçoise £

124 Abergele Road, Colwyn Bay LL29 7PS
TEL/FAX: (01492) 531555
WEBSITE: www.cafe-nicoise.co.uk

COOKING 3
MODERN EUROPEAN
£25–£47

An unprepossessing exterior in downtown Colwyn Bay conceals an intimate interior, a cheerful atmosphere and a kitchen producing intelligently unfussy combinations from good, locally sourced ingredients. Starters include cauliflower soup with Parmesan croûtons, or venison sausage with celeriac purée and red wine sauce. Mains encompass roast darne of salmon with Conwy mussels, or loin of Welsh lamb with creamed cabbage and smoked bacon; vegetarians will welcome ratatouille and Parmesan-filled samosas with roast tomato coulis. Ice creams (perhaps lemon with lemon tart and lemon anglaise, or honey and almond with a white-wine-poached pear) are noteworthy. European-focused wines start at £10.50 and go to £30-plus for a couple of French classics, but choice and value are sound and fair throughout.

CHEF: Chris Jackson PROPRIETORS: Colin and Eileen Kershaw OPEN: Wed to Sun L 12 to 1.45, Wed to Sat D 7 to 9.45 CLOSED: 25 and 26 Dec, 1 week Jan, June and Nov MEALS: alc (main courses £11 to £15.50). Set L Sun £12.75 (2 courses) to £15. Light L menu available SERVICE: not inc, card slips closed CARDS: Amex, MasterCard, Switch, Visa DETAILS: 26 seats. Private parties: 26 main room. Vegetarian meals. Children's helpings. Music (£5)

CRICKHOWELL Powys
map 4

▲ Bear Hotel 💱✳

High Street, Crickhowell NP8 1BW
TEL: (01873) 810408   FAX: (01873) 811696
WEBSITE: www.bearhotel.com

COOKING 2
MODERN WELSH
£32–£55

The food in the medieval dining room of this fifteenth-century coaching inn combines the up-to-date and the traditional. Roquefort and basil mille-feuille with walnut and shallot vinaigrette, or pressed game terrine might feature among starters, while main courses of sweet potato mash and kumquat sauce teamed with crispy belly pork, or rack of Welsh lamb in Dijon mustard and hazelnut crust, demonstrate the culinary range of the kitchen. Fish is not ignored: witness sea bass fillet with crab and ginger risotto and tomato salsa. Desserts can be as comforting as home-made apple and whinberry pie. Beginning with French and German house bottles at £10.50, the wine list is grouped by grape variety, irrespective of country; a sweetness/fullness code helps one take advantage of the choice under £20.

CHEFS: Brian Simmonds and Ross Williams PROPRIETORS: Stephen and Judy Hindmarsh OPEN: Sun L 12 to 2, Tue to Sat D 7 to 9.30 MEALS: alc (main courses £12.50 to £21). Bar and children's menus available SERVICE: not inc CARDS: Amex, Delta, MasterCard, Switch, Visa DETAILS: 80 seats. 40 seats outside. Private parties: 60 main room. Car park. Vegetarian meals. Children's helpings. No smoking in 1 dining room. Wheelchair access (also WC). Music. Air-conditioned ACCOMMODATION: 33 rooms, all with bath/shower. TV. Phone. B&B £55 to £105. Rooms for disabled

Beaufort 💱✳
NEW ENTRY

Beaufort Street, Crickhowell NP8 1AD
TEL: (01873) 810402

COOKING 1
MODERN EUROPEAN
£28–£51

Originally one of Crickhowell's many staging posts, this old town-centre inn has been sympathetically transformed into a smart modern restaurant. The ground-floor dining room feels fresh and inviting, with its wooden floors and vibrant contemporary canvases; there's also a walled garden for al fresco meals. Heather Matthews is a capable cook, her talents showing in, say, a terrine of smoked chicken on balsamic-dressed leaves with marinated mushrooms, and honey-glazed noisettes of lamb with blackcurrant and onion marmalade. Bresaola and other home-cured items are a feature, a daily fish special broadens the range, and desserts might include strawberry pavlova. Service is caring and unhurried. Low prices are a feature of the well-spread wine list, which opens with house French at £12.

CHEF: Heather Matthews PROPRIETORS: Ian Pateshall-Ward and Robert Owen OPEN: Wed to Sun L 12 to 2.30, Tue to Sat D 7 to 9.30 MEALS: alc (main courses £8.50 to £15) SERVICE: not inc, card slips closed CARDS: Amex, Delta, MasterCard, Switch, Visa DETAILS: 44 seats. 20 seats outside. Private parties: 16 main room. Vegetarian meals. No smoking in 1 dining room. Wheelchair access (not WC). Music

▲ Nantyffin Cider Mill Inn ♥ ✻

Brecon Road, Crickhowell NP8 1SG
TEL: (01873) 810775
WEBSITE: www.cidermill.co.uk
1½m W of Crickhowell at junction of A40 and A479

COOKING 2
MODERN WELSH-PLUS
£23–£57

Born as a drovers' inn some five centuries ago, this pink-washed hostelry is still in the business of dispensing sustenance and good hospitality. The strength of the enterprise is its enduring commitment to local and regional produce, including organic and free-range meat and poultry from the proprietors' farm in Llangynidr. Slow-roast lamb shank with mustard mash and rosemary and garlic sauce has impressed, as has an outstandingly flavoursome duck breast served with creamed parsnips, caramelised oranges and duck jus. The kitchen displays 'a sure touch in concept and execution', which extends to fish specials such as seared king scallops with minted pea purée, and grilled razor clams with parsley sauce. Desserts span everything from sticky toffee pudding to tiramisù. 'Uniformly smiley' staff add to the convivial mood of the place. The wine list, marshalled into style sections, is a model of efficiency – not too long, carefully annotated and with every bottle well chosen. It's decent value, too.

CHEF: Sean Gerrard   PROPRIETORS: Sean Gerrard, and Glyn and Jess Bridgeman   OPEN: all week 12 to 2.30, 6.30 to 9.30   CLOSED: Sun D and Mon (exc bank hols) Sept to July   MEALS: alc (main courses £7.50 to £17). Set L (exc Sat and Sun) £10 (2 courses) to £12.95, Set D (exc Fri and Sat) £10 (2 courses) to £12.95   SERVICE: not inc, card slips closed   CARDS: Amex, Delta, MasterCard, Switch, Visa   DETAILS: 100 seats. 60 seats outside. Private parties: 60 main room. Car park. Vegetarian meals. Children's helpings. No smoking. Wheelchair access (not WC). No music

DOLGELLAU Gwynedd   **map 7**

Dylanwad Da ♥ ✻ £

2 Ffôs-y-Felin, Dolgellau LL40 1BS
TEL: (01341) 422870
WEBSITE: www.dylanwad.co.uk

COOKING 2
BISTRO
£27–£44

A convivial atmosphere prevails at this unpretentious town-centre restaurant, its long dining room simply furnished with blond wooden tables and high-backed chairs. Dylan Rowlands's broadly based bistro-style cooking extends from Hungarian red pepper and tomato soup, via Moroccan lamb stew with couscous, to Castile-style chicken with tomato sauce, peppers and chorizo. Good-quality ingredients are the backbone, and treatments are generally straightforward: fillet of hake, for example, comes with a creamy pesto sauce, and sirloin steak from Welsh beef is classically garnished with onions, tomatoes and mushrooms. A vegetarian dish might be spinach and cream cheese pancake with a sun-dried tomato sauce, and for afters there's lemon-curd ice cream with marmalade sauce, or rhubarb meringue crush. Service is friendly and understated. Wines are good value, and the short selection has been picked with a sharp eye. Some smart 'cellar specials' add class.

CHEF/PROPRIETOR: Dylan Rowlands   OPEN: Thurs to Sat (and Tue and Wed summer and bank hols) D only 7 to 9   CLOSED: Feb   MEALS: alc (main courses £10 to £15)   SERVICE: not inc   CARDS: none   DETAILS: 28 seats. Private parties: 28 main room. Vegetarian meals. Children's helpings. No smoking. Wheelchair access (not WC). Music. No mobile phones (£5)

▲ Ynyshir Hall ♦ ✻ ⌂

Eglwysfach SY20 8TA
TEL: (01654) 781209   FAX: (01654) 781366   COOKING **7**
WEBSITE: www.ynyshir-hall.co.uk   MODERN BRITISH
off A487, 6m SW of Machynlleth   £43–£79

'The ultimate in rural cosseting' is how one reporter described this agreeable country hideaway. From the long, white Tudor house, bucolic views of lush shrubberies and smooth lawns contrast with the rugged background of surrounding hills. The Reens, who have run Ynyshir for 15 years, have created a sophisticated and convivial interior, with a clever mix of vibrant colours, matched fabrics, dramatic paintings and well-tended antiques. In the dining room, well-spaced tables are adorned with pale pink brocade, high-backed chairs are comfortably padded in rich green, and napkins tied with blue ribbon are 'so stiffly starched that they crack when unfolded'.

In new chef Adam Simmonds (formerly of Greenway, Shurdington - see entry), the Reens have appointed a worthy successor to Les Rennie. His acute visual sense and imaginative technical skills ensure that dishes have a drama equal to that of the surroundings. Terrine of moist, firm pigeon, silky-textured foie gras and celeriac, for example, is almost jewel-like in appearance, with a perfect combination of flavours and textures given a further lift with an explosion of flavour from a garnish of dried grapes and dabs of coffee oil. Slow cooking is a favoured technique that achieved impressive results in salt-marsh Welsh lamb that had 'a melt-in-the-mouth texture and intense flavour'. Steaming is also used to great effect: fillet of cod was 'pure white, fresh and springy' after being steamed over lemon thyme, lime leaves and lemongrass, its flavour distinct enough to hold its own against multiple garnishes (lemon and fennel risotto, 'a doll's house portion' of confit of clams, a miniscule vodka jelly and a froth of vodka sauce). Desserts achieve the same standard of consistency and flair. A 'tasting of strawberries' was a skilful selection of tiny offerings, including a jelly topped with a hat of dried strawberry, a 'silky-smooth' parfait, and a strawberry soufflé enlivened with a shake of black pepper, all 'zinging with refreshing clean flavours'. Don't expect any bargains on the wine list, but prepare to be seduced if fine Bordeaux or Burgundy in mature vintages is your thing. Top bottles crop up in all French regions, while Italy and Australia lead the way internationally. The dozen house wines from £18 to £35 are no makeweights and also come by the glass.

CHEF: Adam Simmonds   PROPRIETORS: Rob and Joan Reen   OPEN: all week 12.30 to 1.30, 7 to 8.45 CLOSED: Jan   MEALS: Set L £30, Set D £48. Bar menu available L   SERVICE: not inc, card slips closed CARDS: Amex, Delta, Diners, MasterCard, Switch, Visa   DETAILS: 26 seats. Private parties: 26 main room, 16 private room. Car park. Vegetarian meals. No children under 9. No smoking. Wheelchair access (not WC). Occasional music. No mobile phones   ACCOMMODATION: 9 rooms, all with bath/shower. TV. Phone. B&B £95 to £375. No children under 9

▲ Felin Fach Griffin ✻

Felinfach LD3 0UB   COOKING **3**
TEL: (01874) 620111   FAX: (01874) 620120   MODERN BRITISH
WEBSITE: www.eatdrinksleep.ltd.uk   £32–£53

Just off the A470 some four miles north-east of Brecon, this sturdy rough-stone pub could be mistaken for a farmhouse from outside – even though its interior now resembles a 'fairly trendy version of something out of *Country Living*'. The kitchen depends on a network of local supplies (from wild venison to organic salad leaves) for a repertoire that fizzes with bright ideas: pan-fried scallops served with asparagus and black pepper butter, for example. Main courses exploit robust earthy flavours, as in rump of lamb with Puy lentils, chorizo and colcannon, or ox liver with cannellini beans, grain mustard and dauphinoise potatoes. Puddings run to dark chocolate mousse or poached pears in red wine, and 'deeply professional' home-baked soda bread and admirable Welsh cheeses underpin the crusading, quality-conscious approach. The short, well-considered wine list opens with Sicilian house selections at £10.95.

CHEF: Ricardo van Ede PROPRIETOR: Charles Inkin OPEN: Tue to Sun L 12.30 to 2.30, all week D 7 to 9.30 (Sat 6.30 to 10pm, Sun 7 to 9) CLOSED: 25–26 Dec, last week Jan, first week Feb MEALS: alc (main courses £9.50 to £15.50) SERVICE: not inc, card slips closed CARDS: Delta, MasterCard, Switch, Visa DETAILS: 50 seats. 30 seats outside. Private parties: 30 main room, 10 to 20 private rooms. Car park. Vegetarian meals. Children's helpings. No smoking in 1 dining room. Wheelchair access (also WC). Music ACCOMMODATION: 7 rooms, all with bath/shower. Phone. B&B £57.50 to £115

HARLECH Gwynedd — map 7

▲ Castle Cottage ⁵✳

Y Llech, Harlech LL46 2YL
TEL: (01766) 780479 FAX: (01766) 781251
WEBSITE: www.castlecottageharlech.co.uk

COOKING 2
MODERN WELSH
£38–£56

Close to Harlech Castle, the Cottage is a homely restaurant-with-rooms offering food that is generous and unpretentious. Following canapés in the bar you could pursue the porcine theme of the décor and start your meal with air-dried Carmarthen ham, which comes with roasted butternut squash, pine nuts and Parmesan shavings; alternatively go for a creamy chowder of mussels, prawns and sweetcorn. Main courses take in pesto-crusted monkfish brochette on buttered spinach with tomato sauce, or grilled Welsh ribeye with a classic green peppercorn and cognac cream sauce. Keeping clear of culinary ruts, the kitchen might add tarragon to the crème brûlée, or serve treacle tart with berries and Drambuie cream. The compact, serviceable wine list has a good selection of halves, and opens at £13.

CHEFS: Glyn Roberts and Ryland Britland PROPRIETORS: Glyn and Jacqueline Roberts OPEN: all week D only 7 to 9.30 CLOSED: 3 weeks Jan MEALS: Set D £26 SERVICE: not inc, card slips closed CARDS: Delta, MasterCard, Switch, Visa DETAILS: 45 seats. Private parties: 45 main room. Vegetarian meals. Children's helpings. No smoking. Wheelchair access (not WC). Music. No mobile phones ACCOMMODATION: 8 rooms, all with bath/shower. TV. B&B £35 to £90. Baby facilities (£5)

HAWARDEN Flintshire — map 7

Hawarden Brasserie £

68 The Highway, Hawarden CH5 3DH
TEL: (01244) 536353 FAX: (01244) 520888
WEBSITE: www.brasserie1016.com/hawarden

COOKING 2
MODERN EUROPEAN
£21–£47

Refurbishment has softened the mood of this friendly village brasserie: the walls are cream, and chunky pine chairs are grouped around closely packed tables. The kitchen continues to offer assured cooking, and the menus are accurately pitched to the local market. 'Express' weekday lunches do the trick with sandwiches, salads and dishes like pork steaks on mustard mash, while the carte has featured some well-wrought dishes like sea bass fillets on mascarpone risotto with asparagus tempura and tomato hollandaise. Starters could include an interesting terrine of salmon, potato and Gruyère, although desserts such as strawberry shortbread cheesecake have produced a lukewarm response. The 26-bottle wine list does its job, with good value across the board and six house offerings from £9.95. Messrs Jones and Bates also own Brasserie 10/16 (see Round-ups, Chester).

CHEF: Mark Jones   PROPRIETORS: Neal Bates and Mark Jones   OPEN: Tue to Fri and Sun L 12 to 2, all week D 6 to 9.15 (9.30 Fri and Sat)   MEALS: alc (main courses L £6 to £17, D £10 to £17). Set D exc after 7pm Sat £9.90 (2 courses)   SERVICE: not inc   CARDS: Amex, MasterCard, Switch, Visa   DETAILS: 40 seats. 6 seats outside. Private parties: 25 main room. Car park. Vegetarian meals. Children's helpings. No cigars. Occasional music. No mobile phones. Air-conditioned

HAY-ON-WYE Powys
map 4

▲ Pear Tree ✸

6 Church Street, Hay-on-Wye HR3 5DQ
TEL: (01497) 820777
WEBSITE: www.peartreeathay.co.uk

COOKING 4
GLOBAL
£31–£49

'Warmth' sums up Rod and Penny Lewis's style, emanating from the two interlinked dining rooms as well as the informed, attentive service, and the whole approach, from the kitchen as well, seems confident and skilful. Rod Lewis sets an example in the art of serving unfussy food using good ingredients, and much is sourced locally: for example, neighbouring farms are the source of lamb and beef via a local butcher with his own slaughterhouse. The weekly-changing carte is a model of simplicity and clarity, with a line in seafood that includes salmon rillettes with apple and beetroot relish, and steamed fillet of hake with Parmesan mash and a saffron, seafood and dill cream sauce. Elsewhere, Rod Lewis's time in Australia and California might be evident in chargrilled Hereford rump steak with Cajun-spiced potatoes, thyme-scented tomatoes, and sour cream with chives, or roast pork fillet with stir-fried greens, oriental spices, and jasmine rice. Finish with pannacotta with rhubarb compote, or local cheeses with home-made chutney, chilli jam and digestives. Around 30 wines offer a broad choice and plenty of drinking under £20, with house French £12.

CHEF: Rod Lewis   PROPRIETORS: Rod and Penny Lewis   OPEN: Sat L 12 to 2, Tue to Sat D 7 to 9   MEALS: alc (main courses £11 to £16)   SERVICE: not inc, card slips closed   CARDS: MasterCard, Switch, Visa DETAILS: 32 seats. 24 seats outside. Private parties: 32 main room. Vegetarian meals. Children's helpings. No smoking. Music   ACCOMMODATION: 3 rooms, all with bath/shower. B&B £40 to £100. Baby facilities (£5)

HENDRERWYDD Denbighshire
map 7

White Horse Inn ✸
NEW ENTRY

Hendrerwydd, nr Denbigh LL16 4LL
TEL: (01824) 790218
WEBSITE: www.white-horse-inn.co.uk
signposted off B5429 between Llandyrnog and
Llanbedr, 5m SE of Denbigh

COOKING 2
MODERN EUROPEAN
£24–£53

Fires burn in the grates and 'native Welsh voices assert their individuality' in the bar of this buzzy rural pub. By contrast, the dining room has been likened to a West End art gallery, with its modern, minimalist tones, stone and marble sculptural objects, and panels of grey illustration. The kitchen seeks out Welsh produce and subjects it to global treatment: Conwy mussels are served with a Thai green sauce, beef fillet is transformed into carpaccio, and Llanbedr spring lamb steaks become kleftiko. A salad of grilled black pudding ('the best ever') and bacon makes a satisfying starter, while apple crumble, or lemon sponge pudding with that genuine home-made touch, could prove a good finale. Vintage 'cellar selections' broaden the enthusiastically collated wine list. House wines are £10.95.

CHEFS: Ruth Vintr, Chris Hurst and Graham Ryder   PROPRIETORS: Ruth and Vit Vintr   OPEN: Tue to Sun 12 to 2.30, 6 to 9.30   CLOSED: bank hols   MEALS: alc (main courses £7 to £19). Bar menu available   SERVICE: not inc, card slips closed   CARDS: Delta, Diners, MasterCard, Switch, Visa   DETAILS: 55 seats. 25 seats outside. Private parties: 35 main room. Car park. Vegetarian meals. Children's helpings. No smoking. Wheelchair access (not WC). No music. No mobile phones (£5)

LAUGHARNE Carmarthenshire   map 4

▲ The Cors 🌟

Laugharne SA33 4SH   COOKING 2
TEL: (01994) 427219   MODERN WELSH
                                                          £26–£49

Dylan Thomas pilgrims visiting Laugharne might consider booking their place at this atmospheric Victorian villa in three acres of enchanting gardens. The Cors is Nick Priestland's home, where he shows off his talents as host, gardener and chef. He cooks only three nights a week (plus Sunday lunch) and makes sound use of local ingredients for his uncomplicated Anglo-Welsh menu: tournedos of organic Carmarthenshire black beef is served with green peppercorn sauce, while roast rack of salt-marsh lamb could be accompanied by samphire and rosemary jus. Start with Caesar salad or chargrilled sardine fillets, and finish with something like lemon tart or crème brûlée. Two dozen wines provide interesting drinking at fair prices, starting at £10.95.

CHEF/PROPRIETOR: Nick Priestland   OPEN: Sun L 12 to 3, Thur to Sat D 7 to 10   CLOSED: first 2 weeks Oct   MEALS: alc (main courses L £9 to £15, D £14 to £19)   SERVICE: not inc   CARDS: none   DETAILS: 28 seats. 12 seats outside. Private parties: 22 main room, 8 to 12 private rooms. Car park. Vegetarian meals. No children under 8. No smoking in 1 dining room. Wheelchair access (not WC). Music. No mobile phones   ACCOMMODATION: 2 rooms, both with bath/shower. B&B £35 to £75

LLANBERIS Gwynedd   map 7

Y Bistro 🌟

43–45 High Street, Llanberis LL55 4EU   COOKING 2
TEL: (01286) 871278   FAX: (01286) 871634   MODERN WELSH
WEBSITE: www.ybistro.co.uk   £34–£55

At the foot of Mount Snowdon, behind a shop-front exterior, Y Bistro is an old-fashioned, homely, lace-curtain kind of place, with a hodgepodge collection of chairs and sofas in the parlour and the dining room walls hung with local scenes. Nerys Roberts has been behind the stoves for some 25 years, and her unfussy, daily-changing menu – headlined in Welsh with English translations – revels in a commitment to fresh, seasonal local produce: perhaps Welsh mountain lamb served with a herb crust, potato rösti and blackberry and red wine sauce, or roasted Anglesey pheasant breast with leek, white wine and Puy lentil sauce. Bara brith bread-and-butter pudding with cinnamon ice cream continues the homely theme, while the short, reasonably priced wine list includes some patriotic Welsh bottles; house wines from £10.50.

CHEF: Nerys Roberts   PROPRIETORS: Danny and Nerys Roberts   OPEN: Mon to Sat D only 7.30 to 9.45 CLOSED: Closed Mon and Tue in winter   MEALS: alc (main courses £13.50 to £18)   SERVICE: not inc, card slips closed   CARDS: Delta, MasterCard, Switch, Visa   DETAILS: 40 seats. Private parties: 42 main room. Vegetarian meals. Children's helpings. No smoking in 1 dining room. Wheelchair access (not WC). No music (£5)

LLANDEWI SKIRRID Monmouthshire   map 4

Walnut Tree Inn

Llandewi Skirrid NP7 8AW
TEL: (01873) 852797   FAX: (01873) 859764   COOKING 5
WEBSITE: www.thewalnuttreeinn.com   MEDITERRANEAN/ITALIAN
on B4521, 3m NE of Abergavenny   £31–£92

The pebbledash building looks much the same outside, with a few cast-iron tables for clement weather, but the inside has had a soothing makeover. Rag-rolled mushroom tones lend an appealing cottagey feel to the dining room, with groups of small, black-framed paintings offering a modern counterpoint. Tables are bare wood. Known as a beacon of Italian gastronomy under previous chefs, the formula remains in safe hands under new boy Spencer Ralph's tutelage. Leek and potato soup is garnished with pancetta, grilled focaccia accompanies smoked duck breast, and there is a range of tempting pasta options. Then again, skewered pigeon breasts with couscous and minted yoghurt suggest a willingness to light out into new territory, and a reporter's lunchtime main course of rarely encountered pollack with pearl barley risotto and a salad of blood oranges and fennel made a powerful case for itself, with fresh, meaty, big-flaking fish, creamy grains with a top note of artichoke, and a refreshing, if slightly extraneous, salad. Otherwise, osso buco milanese is still available, as is roast leg of Welsh lamb with rosemary potatoes and greens, and there is semifreddo al torroncino with dark chocolate sauce to finish, or poached pear with praline ice cream and a toasted slice of dense panettone. Service is capable and friendly. House wines are £13.50, and around ten are served by the glass.

CHEF: Spencer Ralph   PROPRIETOR: Francesco Mattioli   OPEN: Tue to Sun and bank hol Mon L 12 to 2.30, Tue to Sat and bank hol Mon D 7 to 9.30   MEALS: alc (main courses £11 to £35). Set L £16.50 (2 courses) to £19.50   SERVICE: not inc   CARDS: MasterCard, Switch, Visa   DETAILS: 70 seats. 15 seats outside. Private parties: 30 main room, 25 to 35 private rooms. Car park. Vegetarian meals. Children's helpings. No-smoking area. Wheelchair access (not WC). No music. Air-conditioned

---

LLANDRILLO Denbighshire   map 7

▲ Tyddyn Llan ▮ ⅝✳

Llandrillo LL21 0ST
TEL: (01490) 440264   FAX: (01490) 440414   COOKING 7
WEBSITE: www.tyddynllan.co.uk   MODERN BRITISH
on B4401, 4½m S of Corwen   £32–£65

The Webbs' restaurant-with-rooms is a grey building of slate and stone in the lee of the Berwyn mountains at the edge of the village of Llandrillo, on a road leading nowhere in particular. Clipped hedges and a fountain ornament the gardens, while the interior favours an understated approach, with the two dining rooms done in subtle blue-grey, and there are plenty of deep sofas for sinking into after dinner. Bryan Webb, who once cooked at Hilaire in London, has gone thoroughly native here, offering a tartlet of leek and laverbread among the copious nibbles, themselves leading up one night to an appetiser bowl (no mere coffee cup) of intense watercress soup. Webb's cooking has always been about making an impact with surprisingly economical means, which is to say that the quality of materials is allowed to speak for itself, in presentations that contain just as many elements as they need to. 'Succulent and flavoursome' roast Welsh black beef, perhaps with Yorkshire pudding, has been perfectly timed, as has osso buco served with saffron risotto. Oysters are gratinated under a 'beautifully blistered' smooth Stilton layer with laverbread, cream and egg, while the vegetable relish and rocket that accompany another starter of griddled scallops are just what the shellfish require. The conception of dishes may seem to be nothing out of the ordinary – rabbit stuffed with black pudding in mustard sauce, sea bass in lemon butter – but the execution and the almost teasing depth of flavour win converts.

Equally straightforward are desserts such as earthy-flavoured port and blackcurrant jelly with a scoop of 'very fresh, decadent cream', or an ungarnished trio of caramel ice cream and coconut and raspberry sorbets of searing intensity. Over a dozen wines by the glass open a strong and good-value list arranged by style that effortlessly spans the range from budget Italian basics to top bottles from Bordeaux and California. Even the list of half-bottles pulses with quality. Service, though willing, was disappointing at inspection with rather too many interruptions.

CHEF: Bryan Webb   PROPRIETORS: Bryan and Susan Webb   OPEN: Fri to Sun L 12.30 to 2 (2.30 Sun), all week D 7 to 9.30. Hours may vary between Nov and Mar; phone to check   CLOSED: 16 to 27 Jan   MEALS: Set L Fri and Sat £17.50 (2 courses) to £23.50, Set L Sun £19.50, Set D £29.50 (2 courses) to £40   SERVICE: not inc   CARDS: Delta, MasterCard, Switch, Visa   DETAILS: 35 seats. 10 seats outside. Private parties: 65 main room, 10 to 40 private rooms. Car park. Children's helpings. No smoking. Wheelchair access (also WC). Occasional music. No mobile phones   ACCOMMODATION: 13 rooms, all with bath/ shower. TV. Phone. B&B £65 to £90. Rooms for disabled. Baby facilities

LLANDUDNO Conwy   map 7

▲ Bodysgallen Hall ▼ ✵

Llandudno LL30 1RS
TEL: (01492) 584466   FAX: (01492) 582519
WEBSITE: www.bodysgallen.com
off A470, 2m SE of Llandudno; follow brown road sign

COOKING 4
MODERN BRITISH
£30–£70

This seventeenth-century pile stands in 200-acre grounds and offers country-house luxe, with crackling fires in chintzy lounges and occasional tables with country magazines to skim while nibbling olives. John Williams, who ran Sol in Shrewsbury in its heyday, arrived in late 2003, and his cooking has made an impact in the interlinked dining rooms, where a pianist tinkles out the standards. A chicken sausage, containing the odd bit of bright orange lobster flesh and tightly bound in Parma ham, is served in a buttery reduction to start, while twice-baked goats' cheese soufflé comes with spiced melon chutney. With main courses the kitchen teams a moist, fresh fillet of sea bass with roast scallops, home-made tagliatelle and a shellfish bisque sauce, or accompanies a breast of guinea fowl with a boudin of the leg meat. Fashionable spicy desserts surface in a most convincing peppered pineapple tart with star anise ice cream, or there's a more mainstream chocolate cherry pudding. Good petits fours, and an intensely flavoured mid-meal sorbet (cassis, say) as an optional extra round out the experience, and the service's unhurried pace is fitting in the context. A calmly confident wine list presents a well-balanced portfolio from around the world. House bottles start at £14.50 and six come by the glass.

CHEF: John Williams   PROPRIETOR: Historic House Hotels   OPEN: all week 12.30 to 1.45, 7.30 to 9.30 MEALS: Set L £17 (2 courses) to £20, Set L Sun £22, Set D £37.50   SERVICE: net prices, card slips closed CARDS: Delta, MasterCard, Switch, Visa   DETAILS: 60 seats. Private parties: 55 main room, 12 to 40 private rooms. Car park. Vegetarian meals. No children under 8. Jacket required. No smoking. Wheelchair access (also WC). No music. No mobile phones. Air-conditioned   ACCOMMODATION: 35 rooms, all with bath/shower. TV. Phone. B&B £125 to £300. Rooms for disabled. No children under 8. Swimming pool

---

▲ St Tudno Hotel, Terrace ▮ ✳

Promenade, Llandudno LL30 2LP
TEL: (01492) 874411   FAX: (01492) 860407
WEBSITE: www.st-tudno.co.uk

NEW CHEF
MODERN EUROPEAN
£27–£63

Martin and Janette Bland have been busy of late, radically revamping and redesigning the restaurant belonging to their hotel on Llandudno promenade. It now has a new name (the Terrace) and a distinctly Italian look, with columns, balustrades and murals of Lake Como lining the walls. Italian-made chandeliers hang from the centre of three recessed ceiling areas, and an octagonal lion's head fountain completes the scene. As we go to press Steven Duffy, a former sous-chef here, has returned to take charge of the kitchen. Previously it has been easy to spot a few Mediterranean influences on the menus (wild mushroom risotto with shaved Parmesan and truffle oil, pan-fried monkfish with Parma ham), with the net cast further afield for roast cod fillet with lemongrass velouté, couscous and asparagus; desserts have run to lemon and lime pannacotta with orange caramel sauce and an almond biscuit. Reports on the new chef would be welcome. The wine list has had no Italianate makeover, though; it sticks to its winning formula of French classics complemented by short selections from around the world. Special extended selections from the Blands' favourite producers add interest, and there are numerous options by the glass and half-bottle.

CHEF: Steven Duffy   PROPRIETORS: Martin and Janette Bland   OPEN: all week 12.30 to 1.45, 7 to 9.30 (9 Sun)   MEALS: alc D (main courses £16.50 to £21). Set L Mon to Sat £17.50, Set L Sun £17.95. Bar L menu available   SERVICE: not inc   CARDS: Amex, Delta, Diners, MasterCard, Switch, Visa   DETAILS: 60 seats. Private parties: 50 main room. Car park. Vegetarian meals. Children's helpings. No children under 5 at D. No smoking. Wheelchair access (not WC). No music. No mobile phones. Air-conditioned ACCOMMODATION: 18 rooms, all with bath/shower. TV. Phone. B&B £60 to £290. Baby facilities. Swimming pool £5

LLANGAMMARCH WELLS Powys   **map 4**

▲ Lake Country House ▮ ✳

Llangammarch Wells LD4 4BS
TEL: (01591) 620202   FAX: (01591) 620457
WEBSITE: www.lakecountryhouse.co.uk
at Garth, 6m W of Builth Wells, turn off B483 on to B4519,
then take first right

COOKING 4
MODERN BRITISH
£39–£64

The house is a towering Victorian hotchpotch, half-timbered in the upper storeys and verandahed below. Rhododendron-lined pathways and riverside walks are among the charms of its extensive grounds, as is the three-acre lake that gives the place its name. Inside, all is as grand as can be, with oceans of space between tables in the distinctly humbling dining room. Bold experimentation and vivid flavours characterise Sean Cullingford's cooking. After a no-choice soup, a warm tart of scallops and creamed leeks with tomato sorbet and sauce verte might be one way of proceeding, while a new spin is put on old luxuries in the form of smoked foie gras parfait with Sauternes jelly, shallot marmalade and an olive brioche. If there is a feeling that nothing is quite left alone – beef fillet is marinated in treacle and chilli, set on polenta mixed with sweetcorn and pancetta, served with onion fritters, and sauced with red pimento – that nonetheless indicates the pains the kitchen is prepared to take to impress its target constituency. Finish with something like a parcel of banana and white chocolate with sweet mango chutney and coconut sorbet. The wine list balances all sorts of good-value quality bottles from southern France and New World countries (although pricing is not consistent) against a very serious collection of clarets in mature vintages. Decent house is £17.50 a bottle.

CHEF: Sean Cullingford PROPRIETORS: J.P. and J.E. Mifsud OPEN: all week 12.30 to 2, 7.30 to 9.30 MEALS: Set L £24.50, Set D £37.50 SERVICE: not inc, card slips closed CARDS: Amex, Delta, Diners, MasterCard, Switch, Visa DETAILS: 40 seats. 12 seats outside. Private parties: 80 main room. Car park. Vegetarian meals. Children's helpings. No children under 8 at D. No smoking. Wheelchair access (also WC). No music. No mobile phones ACCOMMODATION: 19 rooms, all with bath/shower. TV. Phone. B&B £99 to £130. Rooms for disabled. Baby facilities. Fishing

LLANRHIDIAN Swansea

map 4

Welcome to Town 🍴

Llanrhidian, Gower SA3 1EH
TEL/FAX: (01792) 390015
WEBSITE: www.welcometotown.co.uk

COOKING 3
CLASSICAL/MODERN WELSH
£26–£56

This whitewashed stone building looks down from the Gower Peninsula on the creek-laced saltmarsh of the Loughor estuary, dotted with sheep and cocklers. The kitchen takes full advantage of local produce – from laverbread and fish to lamb and soft fruit – for a short carte (plus blackboard specials) including perhaps Roquefort soufflé with walnuts and pears, or a salad of seared hand-dived scallops with pancetta and balsamic, then main courses of fillet of Welsh Black beef on polenta with a ragoût of wild mushrooms and sauce Bercy. Desserts embrace tiramisù, and hot chocolate fondant with pistachio ice cream and white chocolate sauce. Fixed-price lunches show similar aspirations, as in fillet of sea bream on saffron risotto and sauce vierge. The wine list starts with house bottles at £11.50 and five by the glass from £2.50.

CHEF: Ian Bennett PROPRIETORS: Ian and Jay Bennett OPEN: Tue to Sun L 12 to 2, Tue to Sat D 7 to 9.30 CLOSED: 25 and 26 Dec, 1 Jan, last two weeks Feb MEALS: alc (main courses £11 to £20). Set L £12.25 (2 courses) to £15 SERVICE: not inc, card slips closed CARDS: MasterCard, Switch, Visa DETAILS: 40 seats. 20 seats outside. Private parties: 30 main room. Car park. Vegetarian meals. Children's helpings. No smoking in dining room. Wheelchair access (not WC). Music. No mobile phones (£5)

LLANSANFFRAID GLAN CONWY Conwy

map 7

▲ Old Rectory Country House 🍷 🍴

Llanrwst Road, Llansanffraid Glan Conwy LL28 5LF
TEL: (01492) 580611 FAX: (01492) 584555
WEBSITE: www.oldrectorycountryhouse.co.uk

COOKING 5
MODERN FRENCH/BRITISH
£55–£66

Looking across the river to Conwy Castle and Snowdonia, this Victorian house is beguilingly remote, and at the end of the road is a warm welcome from the effusively friendly Vaughans. There is a comfortable feel to the place, with cabinets of antique porcelain and silver, oil paintings on the walls and a baby grand piano piled high with books. Menus offer no choice, so necessarily take a fairly conservative approach, but are well balanced and carefully constructed; the style is decidedly French, with Mediterranean leanings (though native flavours make themselves felt). Things might begin with a wild mushroom tart with Madeira sauce, or a fine, well-flavoured and accurately cooked wild sea bass fillet on a ragoût of Mediterranean vegetables. To follow, a mint-crusted rack of Welsh mountain lamb might be served on minted boulangère potatoes, with ratatouille wrapped in a cabbage leaf and rich, sticky beetroot, or a roast guinea fowl breast could be stuffed with goats' cheese and spinach; the assiette of desserts might include meringue filled with blackberry compote and praline ice cream. There's a very good range in both traditional and modern styles on the wine list, with clear tasting notes for guidance. Some bottles are nicely aged, others a bit long in the tooth. Prices are fair and half-bottles plentiful.

CHEFS: Wendy Vaughan and Chris Jones   PROPRIETORS: Michael and Wendy Vaughan   OPEN: Tue to Sat and bank hol Sun, D only, 7.30 for 8 (1 sitting)   CLOSED: Dec 15 to Jan 15   MEALS: Set D £39.90   SERVICE: not inc, card slips closed   CARDS: Delta, MasterCard, Switch, Visa   DETAILS: 14 seats. Private parties: 12 main room. Car park. Children's helpings. No children under 5. No smoking. Wheelchair access (not WC). No music. No mobile phones   ACCOMMODATION: 6 rooms, all with bath/shower. TV. Phone. B&B £79 to £169. No children under 5 exc babes in arms.

LLANWRTYD WELLS Powys   map 4

▲ Carlton House 🔔✖

Dolycoed Road, Llanwrtyd Wells LD5 4RA	COOKING 6
TEL: (01591) 610248 FAX: (01591) 610242	MODERN BRITISH
WEBSITE: www.carltonrestaurant.co.uk	£33–£63

In a pint-sized spa town, Carlton House is a three-storey hotel, painted deep red, with just a handful of rooms. The interior is comfortably domestic, to the extent of having family photographs in the sofa-filled lounge, oriental ceramics on the dining room mantelpiece, and cut-glass decanters on the Welsh dresser. Mary Ann Gilchrist runs a one-woman kitchen for which husband Alan is the perfect advocate. An expert communicator, he may, as one reader thought, appear to be just pottering about out front, but the timing of service is impeccable and his knowledge of wines inspires confidence. Fine Welsh produce informs the menus, which offer a nice mix of the homely and the experimental: winter vegetable soup garnished with crisped bacon sounds familiar enough, but how about a poached egg deep-fried in a Parmesan crust, served on Carmarthen ham and creamed spinach? A crab cake gently spiced with coriander and chilli is anointed with butter and numerous tiny brown shrimps to make a simple starter that for one visitor left an indelible impression. Rack of lamb arrives with a heap of couscous, roast ratatouille vegetables and a warm slick of puréed tomatoes streaked with basil oil. This is sound cooking, built on coherent principles and first-class raw materials. Sticky toffee pudding with its own sauce is an unadorned object lesson, or there may be mango jelly with a sorbet of lemon, lime and vodka. House wines from Chile at £11.50, or £3.25 a glass, head up a pedigree list that includes over 20 halves.

CHEF: Mary Ann Gilchrist   PROPRIETORS: Alan and Mary Ann Gilchrist   OPEN: Mon to Sat D only 7 to 8.30   MEALS: alc (main courses £22 to £26). Set D Mon to Thur £19.95 (2 courses) to £24.50   SERVICE: not inc, card slips closed   CARDS: Delta, MasterCard, Switch, Visa   DETAILS: 14 seats. Private parties: 14 main room. No smoking. No music   ACCOMMODATION: 6 rooms, 5 with bath/shower. TV. B&B £45 to £80. Baby facilities

MACHYNLLETH Powys — map 4

▲ Wynnstay ⚡✕

Maengwyn Street, Machynlleth SY20 8AE	COOKING **3**
TEL: (01654) 702941 FAX: (01654) 703884	MODERN WELSH
WEBSITE: www.wynnstay-hotel.com	£23–£47

Praise for Gareth Johns's cooking at this rambling old coaching inn is not unanimous this year, but one reader found the problem with his seasonal menus 'was deciding what not to have'. Careful sourcing of local produce is evident in scallops wrapped in Carmarthen ham, and with a fillet of brill in Borth prawn bisque that 'conveyed the natural flavour of the fish'. Meat main dishes may include Dyfi Valley lamb with Puy lentil gravy, or Middle White pork tenderloin with spiced apple and black pudding. Start with local game and pork terrine, or Borth shrimps with chilli and tomato; and rhubarb tart with lemon custard ice cream, or chocolate truffle with ginger sauce make a good finish. The annotated wine list favours Italy and starts at £12.

CHEFS: Gareth Johns and James Hamilton   PROPRIETORS: Charles Dark and Sheila Simpson   OPEN: all week 12 to 2, 6 to 9   MEALS: alc (not Sun L; main courses £8 to £16). Set L Sun £8.95 (1 course) to £12.95   SERVICE: not inc, card slips closed   CARDS: Amex, Delta, Diners, MasterCard, Switch, Visa   DETAILS: 60 seats. Private parties: 70 main room, 15 to 20 private rooms. Car park. Vegetarian meals. Children's helpings. No smoking. Wheelchair access (also WC). Occasional music   ACCOMMODATION: 23 rooms, all with bath/shower. TV. Phone. B&B £50 to £100. Baby facilities (£5)

NANTGAREDIG Carmarthenshire — map 4

▲ Four Seasons ⚡✕

Nantgaredig SA32 7NY	
TEL: (01267) 290238 FAX: (01267) 290808	COOKING **3**
WEBSITE: www.fourseasonswales.co.uk	MODERN BRITISH
on B4310, ½m N of Nantgaredig	£37–£44

Set in a group of converted farm buildings, this pleasant and spacious restaurant is done out in an informal country-kitchen style – slate flagstones and old-fashioned iron stove. The set dinner is grounded in local supplies, offering dishes that are consistently imaginative and technically assured. Progress from the relative sophistication of smoked salmon and smooth laverbread tart set off by a fresh and appetising cream cheese sauce, via a hearty and tender shank of lamb with red peppers, tomatoes and a thick, well-flavoured red wine sauce, to crispy yet melting home-made meringue carefully balanced with sharp damsons and a honey ice cream served at a well-judged barely freezing temperature. Everything going on in the kitchen is open to view from the tables, through a large open hatch, and there is no demarcation of tasks either, with the chef/proprietor sisters combining culinary and serving skills with equal élan. The wine list's emphasis is mainly on France, with mark-ups very fair at every level; house French is £12.

CHEFS/PROPRIETORS: Charlotte Pasetti and Maryann Wright   OPEN: Tue to Sat D only 7.30 to 9.30   MEALS: Set D £27.50   SERVICE: not inc, card slips closed   CARDS: Delta, MasterCard, Switch, Visa   DETAILS: 45 seats. 10 seats outside. Private parties: 50 main room. Car park. Vegetarian meals. Children's helpings.

No smoking. Wheelchair access (not WC). Occasional music   ACCOMMODATION: 6 rooms, all with bath/ shower. TV. B&B £55 to £90. Rooms for disabled. Baby facilities. Swimming pool

NANT-Y-DERRY Monmouthshire   map 2

Foxhunter ⅝✳

Nant-y-derry NP7 9DN	COOKING 4
TEL: (01873) 881101 FAX: (01873) 881377	MODERN EUROPEAN
WEBSITE: www.thefoxhunter.com	£35–£64

This old stone, Grade II listed building with a 'fresh and modern' dining room is the surprisingly contemporary setting for Matt Tebbutt's daily-changing menu, where good local raw materials are subject to imaginative treatments. Seasons are followed, and attention to detail shows up in the 'superb' bread and the ice creams. Dinner might start with a hake brandade with poached egg and saffron hollandaise, and lunch with tagliolini with wild duck sauce and aged pecorino. Roast lamb has been accompanied by an intensely flavoured cold cucumber relish and hot aubergine salad, and on the set menu chargrilled monkfish has come with creamy mash and sautéed spinach. An inspector's December was brightened by a dessert of Christmas fruits, fat and juicy, soaked in Marsala with a Greek yoghurt ice cream. Tasty house varietals at £13.50 (£2.50 a glass) open a shrewdly chosen, wide-ranging wine list with good choice either side of £20.

CHEF: Matt Tebbutt   PROPRIETORS: Matt and Lisa Tebbutt   OPEN: Tue to Sat 12 to 2.30, 7 to 9.30   CLOSED: 25 and 26 Dec, 2 weeks Feb   MEALS: alc (main courses £11 to £18). Set L Tue to Fri £18 (2 courses) to £22. Sat brunch menu available   SERVICE: not inc; 10% for parties of 8 or more   CARDS: Delta, MasterCard, Switch, Visa   DETAILS: 60 seats. 15 seats outside. Private parties: 60 main room, 36 private room. Car park. Vegetarian meals. Children's helpings. No smoking. Wheelchair access (also WC). Music

NEWPORT Newport   map 2

Chandlery

77–78 Lower Dock Street, Newport NP20 1EH	COOKING 4
TEL: 01633 256622 FAX: 01633 256633	MODERN EUROPEAN
WEBSITE: www.chandleryrestaurant.co.uk	£22–£54

This listed Georgian townhouse, until recently a ships' chandlery, is now a relaxed, light and airy modern restaurant on two floors that 'seems to go from strength to strength'. The remodelling has retained the building's high ceilings, old fireplaces and staircase, while introducing an eclectic mix of wooden furniture that blends sympathetically with the period. There are sofa areas on both floors to relax in, and the décor's clean, minimalist edge is balanced by an intimate atmosphere and warm, well-informed service.

The regularly changing menus – modern but underpinned by classical traditions – promote well-sourced, quality Welsh produce: lobster and crabs from Pembroke, venison from Brecon and Welsh black beef. Attention to detail shows in soft, succulent rump of Welsh lamb with pithiviers of goats' cheese, ratatouille and basil mash, and grilled halibut with a cockle and laverbread beignet (good enough to make a course of its own) and tomato and chive velouté. From a highly praised wild mushroom risotto starter to hot chocolate fondant with white chocolate and rosemary ice cream, standards are high. The compact, annotated wine list comes in predominantly under £20, with French house from £10.95.

CHEF/PROPRIETOR: Simon Newcombe   OPEN: Tue to Fri L 12 to 2, Tue to Sat D 7 to 10   CLOSED: 24 Dec to 4 Jan   MEALS: alc (main courses £9.50 to £17). Set L £9.95 (2 courses) to £12.95. Light L menu available   SERVICE: not inc, 10% (optional) for parties of 8 or more, card slips closed   CARDS: Amex, Delta, MasterCard, Switch, Visa   DETAILS: 80 seats. Private parties: 40 main room, 10 to 40 private rooms. Car park. Vegetarian meals. Children's helpings. Wheelchair access (also WC). Music. Air-conditioned

NEWPORT Pembrokeshire   map 4

▲ Cnapan 🎇

East Street, Newport SA42 0SY	COOKING 2
TEL: (01239) 820575	MODERN BRITISH
WEBSITE: www.online-holidays.net/cnapan	£22–£45

Watch out for Wales's two Newports: the industrial city east of Cardiff, and this one, a small town of a thousand souls in the Pembrokeshire National Park in west Wales. If you look for Cnapan in the wrong one, you will miss out on Judith Cooper's accomplished, enticing cooking, which focuses on organic veg, local seafood (perhaps served in a chunky, spicy chowder) and meats like prime Welsh black beef, which might come as strips of fillet in a brandy-strengthened cream sauce. Outside influences make an appearance in Thai fishcakes with chilli and lime pickle, or in chicken breast with coconut, coriander and lime, and meals end with the likes of chocolate crunch with pistachios and sour cherries, or perhaps Welsh cheeses. A competitively priced wine list opens with house wines at £10.

CHEF: Judith Cooper   PROPRIETORS: Eluned and John Lloyd and Michael and Judith Cooper   OPEN: Wed to Sat and Mon L 12 to 2, Wed to Mon D 6.45 to 9   CLOSED: Christmas, Jan, Feb   MEALS: alc (main courses £7 to £16)   SERVICE: not inc, card slips closed   CARDS: Delta, MasterCard, Switch, Visa   DETAILS: 35 seats. 35 seats outside. Private parties: 35 main room. Car park. Vegetarian meals. Children's helpings. No smoking. Wheelchair access (also WC). Music. No mobile phones   ACCOMMODATION: 5 rooms, all with bath/shower. TV. B&B £42 to £70. Baby facilities

PENMAENPOOL Gwynedd   map 7

▲ Penmaenuchaf Hall ♥ 🎇

Penmaenpool LL40 1YB	COOKING 2
TEL: (01341) 422129 FAX: (01341) 422787	MODERN BRITISH
WEBSITE: www.penhall.co.uk	£27–£67

Twenty-one acres of landscaped gardens and woodland overlooking the breathtaking Mawddach estuary surround this imposing Victorian mansion. Attentive, friendly service and comfortable dining chairs enhance the leisurely pace of the dining room, while the cooking style aims for lightness and modernity. Reported hits have included a well-presented warm salad of ham and herb gnocchi, a lunch main course of smoked haddock and leek pie, and carefully made pear frangipane tart with almond ice cream. More daring turns, such as roast monkfish with a vanilla and orange sauce, may not be as reassuring to quite the degree that Welsh black beef fillet with shallots and red wine will be. An intermediate course – perhaps a silky bean velouté with morels – comes free. Cheeses are a Celtic farmhouse selection, served with tomato chutney, while coffee and petits fours are a class act. Wines are a well-balanced selection centred on France, including plenty of half-bottles, and reporters have praised the sensible pricing. An informative introduction to sherry and a line-up of affordable fizz increase the temptation to indulge.

CHEFS: Justin Pilkington, and Anthony and Tim Reeve PROPRIETORS: Lorraine Fielding and Mark Watson OPEN: all week 12 to 2, 7 to 9.30 (9 Sun) MEALS: alc D (main courses £20 to £24.50). Set L £14.95 (2 courses) to £15.95, Set D £32.50. Light L menu available Mon to Sat SERVICE: not inc, card slips closed CARDS: Delta, Diners, MasterCard, Switch, Visa DETAILS: 34 seats. 8 seats outside. Private parties: 50 main room, 8 to 16 private rooms. Car park. Vegetarian meals. Children's helpings. No children under 6. No smoking. Wheelchair access (also WC). Music ACCOMMODATION: 14 rooms, all with bath/shower. TV. Phone. B&B £75 to £180. No children under 6 exc babes in arms. Baby facilities. Fishing £5

PONTDOLGOCH Powys   map 7

▲ Talkhouse ⁵⁄✳

Pontdolgoch SY17 5JE
TEL: (01686) 688919   FAX: (01686) 689134   NEW CHEF
WEBSITE: www.talkhouse.co.uk   MODERN BRITISH
on A470, about 1½m NW of Caersws   £34–£48

While retaining its country-inn good looks – a pubby bar, old photographs, polished oak tables, a comfortable, homely sitting room – the emphasis is nonetheless on food. Owner Stephen Garratt has taken over in the kitchen, notification coming too late for us to inspect the results of his work. His daily-changing menus, however, reveal a brisk run through the modern European repertoire with more than a nod to timeless French techniques and Mediterranean influences. Starters might include pan-fried soft-shell crab with its own bisque, or Carmarthen ham with toasted Pantysgawn goats' cheese, while main courses might deliver rack of local spring lamb on dauphinois potatoes. Puddings, meanwhile, bring forth classics such as lemon tart and crème brûlée. Six wines of the month are offered by the glass from £2.10 and by the bottle from £12, and there is plenty of interest on the rest of the well-chosen list, with reasonable choice under £20.

CHEF: Stephen Garratt PROPRIETORS: Stephen and Jackie Garratt OPEN: Tue to Sun L 12 to 2, Tue to Sat D 6.30 to 9 CLOSED: 2 weeks early Jan MEALS: alc (main courses £13 to £16). Light L menu available SERVICE: not inc CARDS: MasterCard, Switch, Visa DETAILS: 30 seats. Private parties: 30 main room. Car park. No children under 12. No smoking. Music ACCOMMODATION: 3 rooms, all with bath/shower. TV. B&B £70 to £95. No children

PONTFAEN Pembrokeshire   map 4

Tregynon Farmhouse ⁵⁄✳

Gwaun Valley, nr Fishguard SA65 9TU
TEL: (01239) 820531   FAX: (01239) 820808
WEBSITE: www.tregynon-cottages.co.uk
at junction of Narberth-to-Fishguard B4313 and B4329,   COOKING 2
take B4313 towards Fishguard, then take first right, and   MODERN BRITISH
follow brown signs   £36–£47

Coming to this fourteenth-century farmhouse in deepest Pembrokeshire, with its wood fire in the inglenook, grandfather clock and cheerful atmosphere, 'is like taking a step backwards in time'. There's no written menu for the straightforward, wholesome cooking, which is based on local and home produce – the latter including bread, smoked meats and water from their own spring. The style is typified by loin of pork with apple in a light cream and mustard sauce, accompanied by lemon-infused mashed carrots, or fried haddock fillet with a crab and butter sauce. A starter might be sautéed chicken liver and bacon salad, with chestnut and maple tart, or home-made ice creams, to finish. The menu changes daily and anyone eating here every night for a week won't come across the same dish twice, or even a vegetable cooked the same way. The short wine list is well annotated and offers decent choices fairly priced, starting around £12 (£2.25 a glass). Three self-catering cottages are available.

CHEFS: Peter and Jane Heard and Gemma Cox   PROPRIETORS: Peter and Jane Heard   OPEN: Tue, Fri and Sat D 7.30 to 8.30, booking essential   CLOSED: 31 Dec   MEALS: Set D £26.95   SERVICE: not inc   CARDS: Delta, MasterCard, Switch, Visa   DETAILS: 20 seats. Private parties: 14 main room, 2 to 6 private rooms. Car park. Vegetarian meals. No children under 8. No smoking. Wheelchair access (also WC). Music

PORTMEIRION Gwynedd   map 7

▲ Hotel Portmeirion ♥ ✸

Portmeirion LL48 6ET
TEL: (01766) 772440   FAX: (01766) 771331   COOKING 4
WEBSITE: www.portmeirion-village.com   MODERN WELSH-PLUS
off A487, signposted from Minffordd   £25–£58

Clough Williams-Ellis's Italianate 1920s village, into which an admission charge is payable if you haven't a reservation, is a fantasy set in aspic. It doesn't make much sense in the dark, so go on a light evening or for lunch to get its measure. At its heart, straight on down the hill from the entrance gateway, is the hotel, where Billy Taylor oversees the culinary activities, offering some gently imaginative country-house cooking in the curving, white-walled, pine-floored dining room.

An inspection turned up evidence of sound meat cookery, with honey-roast Gressingham duck breast inspiringly accompanied by creamed Savoy cabbage, roast kohlrabi, crisp pancetta and a turbo-charged reduction of Calvados, while Pen Llyn lamb of exemplary tenderness came with caramelised garlic cloves, leeks and red wine. These might be preceded by chargrilled scallops with spinach and lemon risotto and a beurre blanc enriched with smoked salmon, the kind of rich-sounding dish that turns out agreeably light on the plate, while the full presentational stops are pulled out for desserts such as blackcurrant sorbet in a brandy-snap basket with champagne sauce, or two-tone chocolate bavarois with caramel sauce and a tall isosceles triangle of dark chocolate. Fine petits fours come with coffee, although appetisers and vegetable side dishes need overhauling. Service has tended towards the forgetful, but the attitude is willing enough. House wines have proved more than satisfactory, but those who venture further into the list will discover plenty of affordable Bordeaux and a sound international selection with oceans of choice under £20.

CHEFS: Billy Taylor, David Doughty and Steven Stevens   PROPRIETOR: Portmeirion Ltd   OPEN: all week 12 to 2, 6.30 to 9   CLOSED: 4 to 28 Jan   MEALS: Set L £14.50 to £16.50, Set D £32.50 (2 courses) to £37.50   SERVICE: not inc, card slips closed   CARDS: Amex, Delta, Diners, MasterCard, Switch, Visa   DETAILS: 100 seats. Private parties: 100 main room, 20 to 30 private rooms. Car park. Vegetarian meals. Children's helpings. No smoking. Wheelchair access (also WC). No music. No mobile phones   ACCOMMODATION: 51 rooms, all with bath/shower. TV. Phone. Room only £135 to £190 (double room). Rooms for disabled. Baby facilities. Swimming pool (£5)

'The bellydancer swept into the room with a flourish. Most female diners beamed and clapped to the music. Some lads, who had previously been behaving badly, only stared embarrassingly into their drinks, as if their mums had just come to do the hokey pokey.' (On eating in Sussex)

PWLLHELI Gwynedd   map 7

▲ Plas Bodegroes ▮ ✝

Nefyn Road, Pwllheli LL53 5TH
TEL: (01758) 612363   FAX: (01758) 701247   COOKING 6
WEBSITE: www.bodegroes.co.uk   MODERN WELSH
on A497, 1m W of Pwllheli   £30–£64

Plas Bodegroes is a beautiful late-eighteenth-century house in a woodland setting that gives it a pleasantly secluded feel. Inside, it is altogether more contemporary, with spotlights and modern paintings on deep duck-egg blue walls, yet the place still has an old feel and bags of character. In short, it is civilised, and, along with the slick, attentive service, everything adds up to 'an extremely comfortable and enjoyable place to stay'.

Chris Chown's cooking shows a similar blend of old and new, his style incorporating fresh ideas and fashionable flavours. There's a nod to North Africa in a starter of pigeon and bacon pastilla with seared pigeon breast, duck liver and pine nuts, plus a hint of the Far East in scallop and sea trout tartare with sea bass sashimi, herring caviar and cucumber pickle; more homespun ideas also appear, though, such as Cardigan Bay scallops baked with leek and laverbread. Among main courses, grilled fillet of Welsh beef with mushroom and horseradish crust has been a hit, and other options typically run to pork tenderloin with bacon and black pudding and an apple and Calvados sauce, or poached sea trout with lime hollandaise. Bara brith and butter pudding puts a local twist on the old dessert favourite, or there might be prune and Armagnac parfait on a brandy-snap disc sitting - 'occasionally skating' - on toasted hazelnuts. The wine list offers well-rounded selections from all regions. Bordeaux and Burgundy are given due respect; Alsace is a highlight and signals a focus on food-friendly wines. House wines are £14.50 and many bottles are under £20. Plentiful half-bottles compensate for a lack of options by the glass.

CHEF: Chris Chown   PROPRIETORS: Chris and Gunna Chown   OPEN: Sun L only 12 to 2.30, Tue to Sat D 7 to 9 (9.30 Sat in summer)   CLOSED: Dec to Feb   MEALS: Set L Sun £17.50, Set D £38   SERVICE: not inc CARDS: MasterCard, Switch, Visa   DETAILS: 40 seats. Private parties: 40 main room, 12 to 16 private rooms. Car park. No smoking. Wheelchair access (also WC). Occasional music   ACCOMMODATION: 11 rooms, all with bath/shower. TV. Phone. B&B £45 to £160. Baby facilities

REYNOLDSTON Swansea   map 4

▲ Fairyhill ▮ ✝

Reynoldston SA3 1BS
TEL: (01792) 390139   FAX: (01792) 391358   COOKING 4
WEBSITE: www.fairyhill.net   MODERN WELSH
off A4118, 1½m NW of Reynoldston   £32–£63

At the heart of the Gower peninsula, in 24 acres of gardens and woodland, the creeper-clad house is early Georgian, although the restaurant extension is of more recent vintage. Black-sweatered staff establish a classy, professional tone when visitors arrive, and this is maintained in the two formally attired dining rooms. An inventive way with pedigree Welsh ingredients distinguishes the menus, which have turned up true triumphs such as a trio of seared scallops with black fettucine in a pool of vivid yellow saffron sauce, and suprême of 'unbelievably tender' Gressingham duck with root vegetable gratin and a spiced plum salsa. Laverbread has proved a success when used as the base for a sauce to accompany a mille-feuille of sea trout and prawns, and the crackling on roast pork loin is both crisp and light. Treacle pudding is the star among desserts, partnered with orange ice cream and crème anglaise. Details are good, as in the now-famous appetiser of deep-fried Penclawdd cockles and the home-made breads. Bordeaux and Burgundy are explored in sumptuous depth in the 39-page wine list, but all parts of the world are given serious attention and, while prestige bottles abound, the range below £20 has been chosen with care.

CHEFS: Paul Davies and Bryony Jones   PROPRIETORS: Paul Davies and Andrew Hetherington   OPEN: all week 12.30 to 2, 7.30 to 9 (8.15 Sun)   CLOSED: 1 to 21 Jan   MEALS: alc L (main courses £12 to £18.50). Set L £14.95 (2 courses) to £18.95, Set D £29.50 (2 courses) to £37.50   SERVICE: not inc, card slips closed   CARDS: Delta, MasterCard, Switch, Visa   DETAILS: 60 seats. 20 seats outside. Private parties: 40 main room, 4 to 40 private rooms. Car park. Children's helpings. No children under 8. No smoking. Music   ACCOMMODATION: 8 rooms, all with bath/shower. TV. Phone. B&B £120 to £245. No children under 8

ST FAGANS Cardiff   map 4

▲ Old Post Office 🍴 ⁵✳

Greenwood Lane, St Fagans CF5 6EL   COOKING 3
TEL: (029) 2056 5400   FAX: (029) 2056 3400   MODERN EUROPEAN
WEBSITE: www.old-post-office.com   £30–£57

Although the old post office building fronts the road, the restaurant is an 'ultra-modern extension' accessed via gardens and a car park around the back. From blond wooden floors and brown leather chairs in the small bar, to the terracotta walls and white-clothed tables of the upmarket, conservatory-style dining room, there's a 'stylish and professional but relaxed feel' to proceedings. The cooking is as contemporary as the surroundings, featuring fixed-price menus that aim high. A terrine of rabbit and foie gras with grape chutney and toasted brioche won praise from one reviewer, while main courses of pan-fried turbot are accompanied by a saffron and mussel broth, and fillet of Welsh Black beef comes with fondant potato, spinach, asparagus and a rich red wine jus. Desserts are 'elaborate, piled creations': perhaps raspberry mille-feuille with pistachio ice cream and chocolate sauce. Service is 'friendly and professional', while the compact wine list kicks off at £14.95. Woods Brasserie, Cardiff (see entry), is under the same ownership and shares executive chef Sean Murphy.

CHEFS: Sean Murphy and Wesley Hammond   PROPRIETOR: Choice Produce Ltd   OPEN: Thur to Sun L 12 to 2, Wed to Sat D 7 to 9.30   MEALS: Set L £12.50 (2 courses) to £15.95, Set D £27.50 (2 courses) to £32.50   SERVICE: not inc   CARDS: Amex, Delta, Diners, MasterCard, Switch, Visa   DETAILS: 28 seats. 20 seats outside. Private parties: 30 main room. Car park. No smoking. Wheelchair access (also WC). Music. No mobile phones. Air-conditioned   ACCOMMODATION: 6 rooms, all with bath/shower. TV. Phone. B&B £55 to £75. Rooms for disabled (£5)

SALEM Carmarthenshire   map 4

Angel ⁵✳

Salem, nr Llandeilo SA19 7LY   COOKING 2
TEL: (01558) 823394   MODERN BRITISH
                                                                            £26–£50

Images of angels share the space with plants in this refurbished pub/restaurant next to the chapel that gives the village its name. Rod Peterson has settled in well and pleases his customers with no-nonsense bar lunches of potato and leek soup, and spiced lamb sausages with mash. In the evening he takes a more ambitious view of things, when pine-kernel soufflé, and seared fillets of wild Carmarthen Bay sea bass with a warm salad of new potatoes, mushrooms, spinach and mozzarella are typical of his output. Welsh ingredients also form the basis of dishes like medallions of beef in a tarragon rarebit crust with cannellini beans and chorizo, while Tregaron strawberries might appear as an accompaniment to pannacotta. The reasonably priced, international wine list has house recommendations from £9.45.

CHEF: Rod Peterson   PROPRIETORS: Rod Peterson and Liz Smith   OPEN: Sun L 12 to 2, Tue to Sat D 6.45 to 9   MEALS: alc (main courses L £8 to £12, D £13 to £18). Bar L menu available   SERVICE: not inc   CARDS: Delta, MasterCard, Switch, Visa   DETAILS: 60 seats. Private parties: 80 main room. Car park. Vegetarian meals. Children's helpings. No smoking. Music

---

SKENFRITH Monmouthshire   map 2

▲ Bell at Skenfrith ♥ ✸

Skenfrith NP7 8UH | NEW CHEF |
TEL: (01600) 750235   FAX: (01600) 750525   MODERN BRITISH
WEBSITE: www.skenfrith.com   £29–£53

A whitewashed and slate-roofed seventeenth-century coaching inn, the Bell stands in a picturesque setting on the bank of the River Monnow overlooking the ruins of twelfth-century Skenfrith Castle – a pleasant spot for a day trip out from Cardiff. Original features are prominent throughout – flagstone floors and an open fireplace – but pale yellow walls that are set off with mirrors, light oak and brushed-chrome fittings give both the bar and separate dining room a distinctly contemporary feel. A new chef started in summer 2004 too late for an assessment for this edition, but previously the traditional brasserie-style fare has produced seared scallops with a sharply flavoured dressing of capers and sun-dried tomatoes, sirloin with béarnaise, and a classic version of steak and kidney pie made with well-flavoured, best-quality steak in a rich gravy. Desserts have included apricot bread-and-butter pudding with clotted cream. Reports on the new man, please. Dozens of half-bottles are a special feature of the intelligently chosen, global wine list, along with a stunning range of old cognac and other brandies. The main bottle line-up pitches interesting options at all levels, from £10 house wine to fine-vintage Bordeaux; over a dozen come by the glass.

CHEF: Kurt Fleming   PROPRIETORS: Janet and William Hutchings   OPEN: all week 12 to 2.30, 7 to 9.30 (9 Sun)   CLOSED: Mon Nov to Mar   MEALS: alc (main courses £11 to £18)   SERVICE: not inc, card slips closed   CARDS: Amex, Delta, MasterCard, Switch, Visa   DETAILS: 80 seats. 20 seats outside. Private parties: 50 main room, 20 to 50 private rooms. Car park. Vegetarian meals. No children under 8 at D. Children's helpings. No smoking. Wheelchair access (also WC). Occasional music   ACCOMMODATION: 8 rooms, all with bath/shower. TV. Phone. B&B £85 to £150. Fishing

---

SOUTHERNDOWN Vale of Glamorgan   map 4

Frolics ✸ | NEW ENTRY |

Beach Road, Southerndown CF32 0RP   COOKING 1
TEL/FAX: (01656) 880127   MODERN EUROPEAN
EMAIL: dougwindsor@aol.com   £21–£60

A converted corner shop on the narrow lane leading down to Dunraven Bay, Frolics dishes up stylishly simple, nicely presented and mostly successful food with plenty of Welsh ingredients. There's a French bistro feel, and the Bristol Channel provides a maritime backdrop. Tables on the ground floor are preferable to those in the basement. Start with wok-fried king prawns, pak choi and battered herb garnish, or scallops à l'orange with rocket tempura. Mains might include Welsh beef fillet on mushroom polenta and port sauce, or a soufflé of local goats' cheese. Puddings, like summer pudding with elderflower ice cream, are accomplished, and there's a good range of modern wines, with six by the glass.

CHEF/PROPRIETOR: Doug Windsor OPEN: Tue to Sun L 12 to 2.30, Tue to Sat D 6.30 to 10 MEALS: alc (main courses £6 to £22). Set L £8.95 (2 courses) to £11.95 SERVICE: not inc, 10% (optional) for parties of 8 or more CARDS: Amex, Delta, Diners, MasterCard, Switch, Visa DETAILS: 50 seats. 15 seats outside. Private parties: 32 main room, 15 to 30 private rooms. Car park. Vegetarian meals. Children's helpings. No smoking before 2.30 L and 9 D. Occasional music. No mobile phones £5

SWANSEA Swansea   map 4

La Braseria £

28 Wind Street, Swansea SA1 1DZ   COOKING 1
TEL: (01792) 469683   FAX: (01792) 456334   SPANISH
WEBSITE: www.labraseria.com   £26–£58

Swansea's answer to a Spanish bodega must rank as one of the busiest venues in town; it's also one of the largest now that it has absorbed the premises next door. The procedure is simple: find a table, note its number, then order at one of the counters. Displays of meat and poultry are on the ground floor, seafood is upstairs, where the choice ranges from oysters to red snapper; finally, take your pick from the salad bar. Chargrilling is the favourite cooking technique, but the kitchen also goes in for deep-frying and baking. Steamed asparagus makes a good starter, and there is a selection of ready-made puddings to finish. Service is on the ball, and the vast choice of mainly Spanish and French wines (from £10.50) includes many bargains.

CHEF: Ian Wing PROPRIETOR: Manuel Tercero OPEN: Mon to Sat 12 to 2.30, 7 to 11.30 CLOSED: 25 and 26 Dec, 1 Jan MEALS: alc (main courses £9 to £24). Set L £8 (2 courses). Bar tapas menu available SERVICE: not inc, card slips closed CARDS: Amex, Delta, Diners, MasterCard, Switch, Visa DETAILS: 205 seats. Private parties: 120 main room. Vegetarian meals. Wheelchair access (also WC). Music. Air-conditioned

Didier & Stephanie's

56 St Helens Road, Swansea SA1 4BE   COOKING 3
TEL: (01792) 655603   FAX: (01792) 470563   FRENCH
                                                                       £22–£47

Subtle lighting and greenery set the welcoming tone at this homely French restaurant. The cooking – regional and seasonal – is what you might expect in many a French village or suburb: Agen prunes go into the rabbit terrine, there's creamy green Puy lentil soup, while roast shank of lamb comes with garlicky tomato coulis, and pheasant Parmentier is reinforced with port. Fish is well handled, with Dover sole treated to prawns and mushrooms, while the salmon is cooked on one side only and saffron-sauced. A couple of vegetarian main courses remind you you're not in France after all, and meals end with tarte Tatin or mango crème brûlée. The wine list is stoutly Burgundian (it includes Burgundian cider) and, bar champagnes and a couple of clarets, consigns the rest of the wine world to 'Other reds/whites'. Nonetheless, there's choice under £20, and house wines are £11.

CHEFS/PROPRIETORS: Stephanie Danvel and Didier Suve OPEN: Tue to Sat 12 to 2, 7 to 9 CLOSED: 2 weeks at Christmas/New Year, 2 weeks early Sept MEALS: alc D (main courses £12 to £14). Set L £7.70 (1 course) to £12.70 SERVICE: not inc, card slips closed CARDS: Delta, MasterCard, Switch, Visa DETAILS: 28 seats. Private parties: 28 main room. Children's helpings. Music

Hanson's

Pilot House Wharf, Trawler Road, Swansea SA1 1UN
TEL: (01792) 466200

COOKING 3
MODERN BRITISH/SEAFOOD
£24–£53

The first-floor restaurant is located on a wharf right next to where the trawlers come in, with much of the fish bought directly from the boats. Once in the kitchen, it is chalked up on the specials board, and treated with care and proper timing in the cooking. A spring speciality is garfish, a tasty green-boned oddity like a very streamlined swordfish. Main menu offerings take in king prawn brochette with sauce indienne and pilaff rice, or pasta accompanied by smoked haddock and seafood with chive cream sauce, plus a handful of meat dishes like Welsh beef fillet with leek and cheese glaze, sauced with port and Stilton. Vegetarians are not forgotten, and to finish, there is white chocolate and raspberry torte, or crème brûlée with fresh berries. The modestly proportioned wine list is usefully annotated, and opens with house vins de pays at £10.95.

CHEFS: Andrew Hanson and Gareth Bagley PROPRIETORS: Andrew Hanson and Helen Tennant OPEN: Tue to Sun L 12 to 2, Mon to Sat D 6.30 to 9.30 CLOSED: 24 Dec D, 25 and 26 Dec, bank hols MEALS: alc (main courses £10 to £20). Set L £10.95 (2 courses) to £13.95 SERVICE: not inc CARDS: Delta, MasterCard, Switch, Visa DETAILS: 50 seats. Private parties: 50 main room. Vegetarian meals. Children's helpings. Music (£5)

TALSARNAU Gwynedd

map 7

▲ Maes-y-Neuadd ❢ ⁵✳

Talsarnau LL47 6YA
TEL: (01766) 780200 FAX: (01766) 780211
WEBSITE: www.neuadd.com
off B4573, 1m S of Talsarnau

COOKING 4
MODERN WELSH
£24–£55

Anyone with a romantic streak warms to this slate-roofed granite pile (its name means 'Meadow Mansion'), which has sweeping views to Snowdonia and over Cardigan Bay. Inside, it is 'surprisingly cosy and intimate, with none of the stuffiness of a grand mansion'. The convivial bar offers a lunchtime carte, while the more formal dining room is the setting for the grander four-course set dinner. The kitchen's approach is grounded on produce from its own garden (some of it available for sale) and Welsh suppliers, and – from an initial canapé of creamy goats' cheese on rye bread right through to decent fudge with the coffee – one senses imagination allied to practicality. Robust flavours in a chicken and guinea-fowl terrine, and crispy-skinned but moist local bass served with an onion chutney, were highlights of an inspection dinner, as were home-grown vegetables and pink and tender Welsh lamb noisettes with a mushroom duxelles and rosemary mash. The grand finale, cheeses from Snowdonia and three separate puddings – perhaps well-made ice creams and sorbets, rhubarb and lemon tart, and a pineapple fritter with butterscotch sauce

– literally rounds out the diner. The revamped wine list has much to commend it. In tune with modern tastes, Australia has been pushed to the top of the list and the range by the glass (including Glyndwr from Wales) has been extended to eight. A page of options under £16 will satisfy value-hunters, while France caters for serious lovers of Bordeaux and Burgundy.

CHEF: Peter Jackson   PROPRIETORS: Peter and Lynn Jackson, and Peter and Doreen Payne   OPEN: all week 12 to 1.45, 7 to 8.45   MEALS: alc L Mon to Sat (main courses £7 to £11). Set L Sun and Thurs £12.95 (2 courses) to £15.25. Set D £31 to £35. Tapas and light meal menus available   SERVICE: not inc   CARDS: Amex, Delta, MasterCard, Switch, Visa   DETAILS: 60 seats. 20 seats outside. Private parties: 50 main room, 2 to 15 private rooms. Car park. Vegetarian meals. Children's helpings. No children under 8 after 7pm. No smoking. Wheelchair access (also WC). Occasional music. No mobile phones   ACCOMMODATION: 16 rooms, all with bath/shower. TV. Phone. B&B £65 to £201. Rooms for disabled. Baby facilities

WHITEBROOK   Monmouthshire   map 2

▲ Crown at Whitebrook ▸ ※

Whitebrook NP25 4TX
TEL: (01600) 860254   FAX: (01600) 860607
WEBSITE: www.crownatwhitebrook.co.uk   COOKING 6
leave A466 at Bigsweir bridge, 6m S of Monmouth; follow   MODERN EUROPEAN
signs to Whitebrook; hotel is 2m on left   £31–£51

New owners have been busy upgrading this restaurant-with-rooms set in the Wye Valley, but James Sommerin remains at the stoves, delivering his appealing mix of fine materials, enterprising ideas and skilful handling. Preliminaries take place in a comfortable, country-style lounge-bar with sofas and a big stone fireplace; meals in a large, rustic dining room with plenty of exposed beams in ceiling and walls. Service is 'cheerful and efficient'. Although the food owes much to classical ways, an innovative streak shows up in, for example, a starter of caramelised orange-infused lobster served with seared squid and tomato and wild mushroom consommé, and in a main courses of maple-glazed turbot with a crab beignet, fennel, and peanut sauce, and seared breast of black leg chicken, stuffed thigh with an asparagus and broad bean ragoût and truffle foam. A variety of perspectives can be explored on one plate – a delicate construction of duck tournedos, duck 'guissard' tortellini and vanilla-braised duck heart made for an exhilarating starter for one reader, and guinea fowl gets equal consideration with a terrine, set consommé and sausage. A good way to finish might be rich chocolate and almond fondant with iced Cointreau sabayon, or a 'study of rhubarb', comprising rhubarb three ways: a finely textured and tart rhubarb sorbet, a creamy pannacotta, and a 'sweet and luscious' warm soup. The Crown's 'recommended wines' start with house bottles at £12.50 and mostly stay the right side of £20. Overall, there is plenty of good value drinking before the heavy-hitters take to the field. Reds in particular run to some serious bottles, with further options in halves.

CHEF: James Sommerin   PROPRIETOR: Jonathon Davies   OPEN: Wed to Sun L 12 to 1.45, Wed to Sat D 7 to 9   MEALS: alc L (main courses £11 to £15). Set D £30   SERVICE: not inc, card slips closed   CARDS: MasterCard, Switch, Visa   DETAILS: 32 seats. Car park. Vegetarian meals. No children under 12. Jacket and tie required. No smoking. Wheelchair access (not WC). Occasional music. No mobile phones   ACCOMMODATION: 10 rooms, all with bath/shower. TV. Phone. D,B&B £80 to £140. No children under 12

Channel Islands

Bistro Soleil

La Route de la Haule, Beaumont, St Peter JE3 7BA   COOKING **4**
TEL: (01534) 720249   FAX: (01534) 625621   BISTRO/SEAFOOD
WEBSITE: www.aboutjersey.net/eat/bistro_soleil   £25–£49

This aptly named bistro is 'bright, sunny and airy', with yellow walls reflecting a 'sea-fresh' feel, and large windows looking across the beachside walkway, through the masts of sailing boats and on out to sea. The relaxed, casual atmosphere and bare-wood tables and floors (there's also a small courtyard patio outside) belie the kitchen's serious intentions. Equally sunny modern menus offer plenty of choice and put the freshest local ingredients to good use, handling these with intelligent simplicity. Unsurprisingly, the availability of the fruits of the sea rules – there may be local lobster, crab or diver-caught scallops (simply fried in a beurre blanc) or sea bass and brill (again fried but paired with colcannon potatoes and coriander oil). Bistro favourites appear too, such as fried calf's liver with black pudding, field mushrooms, crispy bacon and roast cherry tomatoes, while puddings might include a 'high-quality' dark chocolate and poached pear tart with thick Jersey cream and a duo of orange and Grand Marnier and chocolate sauces. The global wine list is laudable for its range of good-value bottles, with a mere handful over the £20 threshold and four house from £10.95.

CHEF: Ian Jones   PROPRIETOR: Chris Power   OPEN: Tue to Sat L 12.15 to 2, Sun L 12.30 to 2.30, Tue to Sat D 6.45 to 9.30 (9 Oct to Mar)   CLOSED: 25 and 26 Dec, 1 Jan   MEALS: alc (not Sun L; main courses £12 to £16.50). Set L £15.85 to £16.85, Set D £32. Terrace menu available in summer   SERVICE: not inc, 10% for groups of 10 or more   CARDS: Amex, Delta, MasterCard, Switch, Visa   DETAILS: 60 seats. 40 seats outside. Private parties: 60 main room. Car park. Vegetarian meals. Children's helpings. No pipes/cigars. Wheelchair access (not WC). Music. Air-conditioned

Jersey Pottery, Garden Restaurant 🔪✳

Gorey JE3 9EP   COOKING **2**
TEL: (01534) 850850   FAX: (01534) 856403   MODERN BRITISH/SEAFOOD
WEBSITE: www.jerseypottery.com   £28–£68

A major tourist attraction, the pottery caters for the crowds with several eating options. After a tour of the workshop, grab coffee and cake in the café or take an informal meal in Spinnakers Bar and Grill. For more of an occasion, there's the Garden Restaurant, surrounded by landscaped grounds. Trellises are covered in lush greenery, and the glass roof gives a feel of the outdoors (you can actually eat outside on a leafy patio in summer). Local fish and seafood are the mainstay of the extensive menu, either dressed up in modern, exotic combinations, such as tempura coconut king prawns with spicy noodle salad, or done in simple, classic style, such as plainly grilled Dover sole with herb butter, or lobster thermidor. There are plenty of meat and vegetarian options too, and a varied wine list with prices starting at £12.95.

CHEFS: Tony Dorris and Roger White   PROPRIETORS: the Jones family   OPEN: Wed to Sun and bank hol Mon L 12 to 2.30, Wed to Sat and bank hol Mon D 7 to 9.30   CLOSED: Jan   MEALS: alc exc Sun L (main courses £11 to £31.50). Set L £15.50 (2 courses) to £19.50, Set D £19.95 (2 courses) to £25   SERVICE: net prices, card slips closed   CARDS: Amex, Delta, Diners, MasterCard, Switch, Visa   DETAILS: 280 seats. 50 seats outside. Private parties: 280 main room, 10 to 100 private rooms. Car park. Vegetarian meals. Children's helpings. No smoking. Wheelchair access (also WC). Music

Suma's

Gorey Hill, St Martin, Gorey JE3 6ET
TEL: (01534) 853291   FAX: (01534) 851913

COOKING **5**
MODERN EUROPEAN
£21–£58

A table by the window (or on the terrace under a parasol in fine weather) with stunning views over the harbour and Mont Orgueil Castle is surely a top spot on the island. The popular, modern restaurant is a sibling of Longueville Manor in St Saviour (see entry); its interior is predictably stylish, with pale wood and white tones, elegant place settings and a bright, fresh minimalist feel that complements that superb harbourside location. The kitchen takes an equally modern approach, offering an appealing repertoire of well-executed, refined yet uncomplicated dishes that reflect the island's abundant local larder. So expect fried local scallops with saffron potato and black pudding to start, with perhaps roast fillet of brill served on a lasagne of crab, spring onions and greens, or oven-roasted rump of lamb niçoise with sautéed potatoes, to follow. The sweet-toothed may find it hard to ignore a summery apple and peach Tatin partnered by an orange sorbet, or classic hot chocolate fondant with Baileys ice cream. Breads are home-made, service is efficient and unobtrusive, while a lively wine list offers a choice from around the globe organised by price, with plenty of bottles under £20, house from £8.50 and a good selection by glass.

CHEF: Daniel Ward   PROPRIETORS: Malcolm Lewis and Sue Dufty   OPEN: all week 12 to 2.30, 6.15 to 9.30   CLOSED: 23 Dec to 20 Jan   MEALS: alc (main courses £12 to £21). Set L and D 6.15 to 7 £12.50 (2 courses) to £15   SERVICE: net prices, card slips closed   CARDS: Amex, Delta, Diners, MasterCard, Switch, Visa   DETAILS: 45 seats. 16 seats outside. Private parties: 40 main room. Vegetarian meals. Children's helpings. Music. No mobile phones. Air-conditioned

ST HELIER Jersey   map 1

Le Chambertin   NEW ENTRY

20 Beresford Street, St Helier JE2 4WN
TEL: (01534) 877912

COOKING **5**
MODERN FRENCH
£22–£54

Behind the food market in St Helier, Le Chambertin's long, thin dining room is strong on Provençal atmosphere, but fresh and modern too, with warm yellow walls, a creamy stone floor and heavy white chairs. The walls are adorned with wine memorabilia, with special attention paid to the 30-odd acres in Burgundy after which the restaurant is named.

The cooking is rural Gallic, with the lightest contemporary touch, and the quality of the materials is what shines. You might start with a bowl of snails, cooked with leeks, garlic and cream, or Périgord foie gras with caramelised apples in a port reduction, then tackle one of the Charolais beef or veal dishes – perhaps a huge piece of beef fillet with oxtail jus, sautéed fennel and Jersey Royals in season, highly rated for textural combinations and generosity. Our inspector applauded salted, thinly sliced, raw sea bass marinated in lime, garnished with smooth avocado purée and presented on a fish-shaped plate, while main-course turbot might come in a red wine reduction with spinach and spring onions. Homely desserts include soufflés and mousses, a cake of white chocolate, caramelised almonds and pear, as well as 'refreshing and lively' sorbets (passion-fruit, say, or raspberry). Service, slick and businesslike rather than warm, copes well. Although no wine list was supplied to the Guide before we went to press, an inspector described it as a 'serious list with serious prices too', with a focus on France and some bottles for the budget-minded too. The details below may not be fully accurate as our questionnaire was not returned.

CHEF/PROPRIETOR: Laurent Dauce   OPEN: Mon to Sat 12 to 2, 7 to 9   CLOSED: 1 week Christmas and New Year, bank hol Mon   MEALS: alc (main courses £12 to £16). Set L and D £12.50 to £30   SERVICE: not inc CARDS: MasterCard, Visa, Switch   DETAILS: 40 seats. Vegetarian meals. Children's helpings. Occasional music. Air-conditioned

ST MARTIN'S Guernsey   map 1

Auberge ⁵⅍

Jerbourg Road, St Martin's GY4 6BH	COOKING 5
TEL: (01481) 238485 FAX: (01481) 710936	MODERN BRITISH
WEBSITE: www.theauberge.gg	£27–£48

A few miles from St Peter Port, on the road to Jerbourg Point, this converted pub has been smartly redesigned in bold, bright, minimal style, with a full-length window overlooking the bay. Its blond wood tables, smart bar and live music may give the hallucinatory feeling that you are in some mainland city centre, until you turn once more to the sumptuous clifftop view.

Paul Olliver's simple and eclectic modern cooking stresses seafood, seasonality and freshness. Lunch might start with duck rillettes with a kumquat and red onion marmalade and move on to pan-fried local scallops and king prawns with crispy bacon, garlic butter and scallion mash. Dinner might bring on a foie gras terrine, sharply supported by goats' cheese and apple jelly, followed by more of those oriental notes in seared tuna with pak choi, water chestnuts and a prawn spring roll. Meat and seafood often turn up on the same plate, whether it be chorizo in the mash to accompany sea bass, or crab ravioli with roast pork loin. Head-turning desserts include coffee mousse served with mini-doughnuts, or warm fruit compote with mulled wine ice cream. A brief wine list covers most bases, opening with house Australian red at £10.95 and French Chardonnay at £11.95.

CHEF: Paul Olliver   PROPRIETOR: Ian Irving-Walker   OPEN: all week 12 to 2, 7 to 10   CLOSED: Sun D from 1 Nov to 31 Mar   MEALS: alc (main courses £10 to £14.50). Set L £11.95 (2 courses)   SERVICE: not inc CARDS: Amex, Delta, Diners, MasterCard, Switch, Visa   DETAILS: 70 seats. 30 seats outside. Private parties: 80 main room. Car park. Vegetarian meals. Children's helpings. No smoking in restaurant, permitted in bar. Wheelchair access (not WC). Occasional music. Air-conditioned

ST PETER PORT Guernsey   map 1

▲ La Frégate   `NEW ENTRY`

Les Cotils, St Peter Port GY1 1UT   COOKING **4**
TEL: (01481) 724624   FAX: (01481) 720443   MODERN EUROPEAN
WEBSITE: www.lafregatehotel.com   £26–£58

This frigate is berthed high in the narrow, winding streets of Guernsey's main town, looking down on the bay and the 800-year-old Castle Cornet. Within a period, oak-panelled hotel, the restaurant is a contrast: cool, airy and contemporary, with bare boards, abstract paintings in marine tones, and Zen-like floral arrangements. Apart from good-value set meals, Neil Maginnis offers a lengthy carte on which fish shares equal billing with meat. Seared local scallops come on a warm crab tian in lime and coriander butter, making a 'rich yet delicate, perfectly judged' starter. Pancetta adds crispness to accurately timed calf's liver with caramelised shallots in a red wine jus, while duck made a breathtaking high point for one diner, the breast peppered, cooked pink, and attended by honey-roast vegetables and a sauce enriched with foie gras. Vegetable extras are well handled, and there is the pleasingly retro touch of serving crêpes suzette, all oranged and lemoned and flamed up with Grand Marnier, as it would have been half a century ago. Good incidentals include full-throttle espresso. A deeply classical French-led wine list has some scary prices, but offers plenty of choice below £20 as well. Half a dozen house selections are £13.50.

CHEF: Neil Maginnis   PROPRIETOR: Guernsey Summer Holidays Ltd   OPEN: all week 12.30 to 2, 6.30 to 9   MEALS: alc (not Sun L; main courses £11 to £34). Set L £16.50, Set D £23.50   SERVICE: not inc   CARDS: Amex, Diners, MasterCard, Switch, Visa   DETAILS: 80 seats. 30 seats outside. Private parties: 75 main room, 2 to 32 private rooms. Car park. Vegetarian meals. No music. Air-conditioned   ACCOMMODATION: 13 rooms, all with bath/shower. TV. Phone. B&B £85 to £180. Rooms for disabled. Baby facilities

ST PIERRE DU BOIS Guernsey   map 1

▲ Café du Moulin ⁵⁺

Rue du Quanteraine, St Pierre du Bois GY7 9DP   COOKING **4**
TEL: (01481) 265944   FAX: (01481) 267343   MODERN EUROPEAN
WEBSITE: www.cafedumoulin.com   £39–£63

Café du Moulin is tucked away in a secluded valley among high-hedged lanes, so leave it to a local taxi driver to get you there. It's a simple place, occupying a converted granary alongside a beautifully restored watermill; there's a tiny bar and a beamed dining room, tastefully decorated in shades of beige with white-clothed tables and an old armoire in the corner. Christophe Vincent, originally from the French Alps, trained under Albert Roux, and his à la carte and six-course gourmand menus follow the seasons to showcase the best of local and continental ingredients. The modern focus has a classical underpinning and plenty of luxury items; crab ravioli, for instance, with a herb sauce and garlic oil, or ballottine of foie gras with orange jelly and toasted gingerbread to start. Calves' sweetbreads, paired with an orange and Grand Marnier sauce, or a pot-au-feu of rabbit with crab tortellini, continue the theme, while classics like crème brûlée deliver the finish. Though some inconsistencies have been noted, most reporters are delighted with both service and cuisine. The well-chosen wine list has an understandable Francophile leaning and starts at £12.

CHEF/PROPRIETOR: Christophe Vincent OPEN: Wed to Sun L 12 to 2, Tue to Sat D 7 to 9 CLOSED: 2 weeks Nov, 2 weeks Mar MEALS: alc (main courses £16 to £22). Set L £35, Set D £35 SERVICE: not inc CARDS: Delta, Diners, MasterCard, Switch, Visa DETAILS: 37 seats. 24 seats outside. Private parties: 40 main room. Car park. Vegetarian meals. Children's helpings. No smoking. Wheelchair access (not WC). Music ACCOMMODATION: 3 rooms, all with bath/shower. TV. Room only £200 to £650. Rooms for disabled. No children under 8

ST SAVIOUR Jersey map 1

▲ Longueville Manor

St Saviour JE2 7WF COOKING **5**
TEL: (01534) 725501 FAX: (01534) 731613 MODERN EUROPEAN
WEBSITE: www.longuevillemanor.com £27–£88

This small-scale country-house hotel has an elegant stone façade with an eighteenth-century French feel. Inside a 'hushed, comfy lusciousness' pervades lounges with deep sofas, open fires and antiques. In the oak-panelled non-smoking dining room, or the modern-feeling smoking one, four dinner menus give wide choice: menu du jour (summer only), à la carte, and (both for whole tables) 'Taste of Jersey' and a gourmet menu. Successes from the carte have been simple classics like fillet of Angus beef bordelaise with fondant potatoes, white asparagus and ceps, and well-balanced 'surf-and-turf' combinations like grilled Jersey king scallops with honey-glazed belly pork, boudin noir and cider butter sauce, or local sea bass with chicken confit, langoustines, baby summer vegetables and Jersey Royals. Not everything comes off – for example, an indeterminate foie gras ice cream in an assiette of foie gras and roast quail. Inventive and elegant presentation is exemplified by a pyramid chocolate coulant with condensed milk sorbet ('sculptural, elegant, creative and bloody tasty'), and professional, enthusiastic service balances county-house charm with the haute-cuisine formality.

Dominating the long wine list is a substantial collection of clarets spanning many vintages, plus top bottles elsewhere in France and short, sound ranges from other countries. An impressive range by the glass (£4 to £14.75) and modern house wines from £16 add further zing.

CHEF: Andrew Baird PROPRIETORS: Malcolm Lewis and Susan Dufty OPEN: all week 12.30 to 2, 7 to 9.30 MEALS: alc (main courses £28 to £30). Set L £12.50 (2 courses) to £15. Set D £55 to (whole table only) £65. Snack menu available SERVICE: net prices, card slips closed CARDS: Amex, Delta, Diners, MasterCard, Switch, Visa DETAILS: 70 seats. 40 seats outside. Private parties: 70 main room, 2 to 24 private rooms. Car park. Vegetarian meals. Children's helpings. No smoking in 1 dining room. Wheelchair access (not WC). No music. No mobile phones ACCOMMODATION: 30 rooms, all with bath/shower. TV. Phone. B&B £170 to £500. Rooms for disabled. Baby facilities. Swimming pool

Northern Ireland

map 16

Shanks ▯ ✳

The Blackwood, 150 Crawfordsburn Road,
Bangor BT19 1GB
TEL: (028) 9185 3313 FAX: (028) 9185 2493
WEBSITE: www.shanksrestaurant.com

COOKING 5
MODERN EUROPEAN
£35–£70

This particular part of the Clandeboye estate features a rolling golf course as well as the Millars' stylish restaurant. When you have admired the Hockney theatre pictures on the walls, you can watch players teeing off outside.

Robbie Millar uses plenty of local produce, much of it organic, including the Clandeboye estate's venison. That might take pride of place among main courses, served with potato fondant, spiced red cabbage, creamed morels and baby leeks. Also on the seasonal menus will be things like grilled tuna with roast peppers, saffron and pine-nut couscous and aubergine and chorizo chutney. Dishes are nothing if not complex, with even the seared foie gras teamed with carrot puree and poached grapes, as well as the expected Sauternes jus and toasted brioche. Separate vegetarian menus show similar pains being taken, and desserts are multi-layered too: orange and pink grapefruit gratin comes with Orange Muscat sabayon and Campari sorbet, while ginger, sherry and raisins all find their way into a 'traditional crème brûlée'. The service delivering all this is characterised by high formality. The wine list strikes a neat balance between modern pizzazz and classical poise and includes up-to-the-minute names like Girardin in Burgundy and Henschke in Australia; house wines start at £15.

CHEF: Robbie Millar PROPRIETORS: Robbie and Shirley Millar OPEN: Tue to Fri L 12.30 to 2.30, Tue to Sat D 7 to 10 CLOSED: 24 to 26 Dec, Easter Sun to Wed, 1st 2 weeks July MEALS: Set L £19 (2 courses) to £23, Set D Tue to Thur £19 (2 courses) to £42 SERVICE: not inc, 10% for groups of 6 or more CARDS: Amex, Delta, MasterCard, Switch, Visa DETAILS: 65 seats. Private parties: 65 main room, 10 to 36 private rooms. Car park. Vegetarian meals. Children's helpings. No smoking. Wheelchair access (also WC). Music. Air-conditioned

map 16

Aldens ▯ £

229 Upper Newtownards Road, Belfast BT4 3JF
TEL: (028) 9065 0079 FAX: (028) 9065 0032
WEBSITE: www.aldensrestaurant.com

COOKING 4
MODERN IRISH
£26–£60

Aldens is out in the suburbs of the city, a fair way from the centre. The smart exterior features lots of opaque plate glass, framed in dark blue and grey, and few traces remain of the building's former life as a supermarket. Inside, too, the décor tends to blue and charcoal tones, with bare wooden floors.

Cath Gradwell is Roux-trained and has worked with Paul Rankin among others. Her menus offer a varied choice of international tastes and flavours, from Thai-spiced steamed cockles, via Charentais melon with Parma ham, to seared foie gras with sweetcorn pancake. Main courses could run from duck breast fanned on potato rösti with cherries, to roast hake, and on to Cajun pork chop on Louisiana rice. For a sweet note to end on, try hot passion-fruit meringue or baked tamarillos with raspberry coulis and vanilla ice cream. The professional service is a strong point. A baker's dozen of good-value and interesting house wines from £13 is backed up by serious bottles from around the world that favour restrained, food-friendly styles.

CHEF: Cath Gradwell   PROPRIETOR: Jonathan Davis   OPEN: Mon to Fri L 12 to 2.30, Mon to Sat D 6 to 10 (11 Fri and Sat)   CLOSED: 2 weeks July, bank hols   MEALS: alc (main courses L £6 to £16, D £9 to £17). Set D Mon to Thur, and Fri 6 to 6.45 £16.95 (2 courses) to £21.95   SERVICE: not inc   CARDS: Amex, Delta, Diners, MasterCard, Switch, Visa   DETAILS: 70 seats. Private parties: 80 main room. Vegetarian meals. Wheelchair access (also WC). Music. Air-conditioned

Cayenne ▼

7 Ascot House, Shaftesbury Square, Belfast BT2 7DB   COOKING 4
TEL: (028) 9033 1532   FAX: (028) 9026 1575   FUSION
WEBSITE: www.cayennerestaurant.com   £24–£60

Paul and Jeanne Rankin's stylish city-centre restaurant aims to provide a 'dynamic mix of hot and funky food in a cool urban atmosphere', and pulls it off with aplomb. Light from flower-like orange lanterns adds to the mood in the buzzing dining room. Service is 'excellent in all respects – efficient and calm, attentive but not intrusive', and food makes an equally positive impression. Among starters, foie gras with charred figs on brioche, and smoked salmon with cucumber and curry sauce have made quite an impact, or try Strangford mussels in spicy tomato and coriander broth. Then main courses take in dishes as simple and traditional as sirloin steak with Roquefort butter, crispy garlic potatoes and green beans, as well as a more unusual Cambodian seafood hotpot with udon noodles; among desserts might be ginger parfait with warm rhubarb compote. Wines are listed by grape, with Riesling and Tempranillo sections fingering the pulse of wine fashion. The main list (from £12.75) offers fair value, though top bottles are heavily marked up; the short 'fine wine' selection is rather special.

CHEFS: Paul Rankin, Andy Rea and Danny Millar   PROPRIETORS: Paul and Jeanne Rankin   OPEN: Mon to Fri L 12 to 2.15, all week D 6 (5 Sun) to 10.15 (11.15 Fri and Sat, 9 Sun)   CLOSED: 25 and 26 Dec, 12 July, 1 Jan   MEALS: alc (main courses L £11 to £18, D £11 to £22.50). Set L and D 6 to 6.45 £12 (2 courses) to £15.50   SERVICE: not inc, 10% (optional) for parties of 6 or more, card slips closed   CARDS: Amex, Delta, Diners, MasterCard, Switch, Visa   DETAILS: 120 seats. Private parties: 70 main room, 18 private room. Vegetarian meals. Children's helpings. No-smoking area. Wheelchair access (also WC). Music. Air-conditioned

Metro Brasserie £

13 Lower Crescent, Belfast BT7 1NR   COOKING 2
TEL: (028) 9032 3349   FAX: (028) 9032 0646   MODERN EUROPEAN
WEBSITE: www.crescenttownhouse.com   £24–£50

One of two dining rooms in the 'smart, friendly' Crescent Hotel near the University,

Metro has light-coloured stripped-wood floors and burgundy walls exuding a feeling of warmth. Customers relax at amply proportioned marble-topped tables. A good-value early-bird menu offers brasserie standards like mussels steamed in white wine, chicken liver pâté, chargrilled ribeye steak or bangers and mash. Ordering à la carte you might get rare beef salad with confit celery and Cashel Blue fritters, with simple fried skate wing to follow, or prawn and mango spring roll with coriander, mint and soya, then confit duck on curried couscous. There's a separate vegetarian menu. Comforting desserts include sticky toffee pud or pannacotta, and the modest international wine list stays below £20.

CHEF: Stephen Taylor-Winter   PROPRIETOR: Wine Inns Ltd   OPEN: all week, D only 5.45 (5 Sun) to 9.30 (10 Fri and Sat, 8.30 Sun)   CLOSED: 24 to 26 Dec, 1 Jan, 11 to 13 July   MEALS: alc D Mon to Sat (main courses £10 to £17). Set D Sun and 5.45 to 7.15 Mon to Sat £11.95 (2 courses) to £13.95. Bar L menu available   SERVICE: not inc, card slips closed   CARDS: Amex, Delta, MasterCard, Switch, Visa   DETAILS: 75 seats. Private parties: 27 private room. Vegetarian meals. Children's helpings. Wheelchair access (also WC). Music. Air-conditioned   ACCOMMODATION: 17 rooms, all with bath/shower. TV. Phone. B&B £50 to £145. Rooms for disabled. Baby facilities

Nick's Warehouse

35 Hill Street, Belfast BT1 2LB	COOKING 5
TEL: (028) 9043 9690 FAX: (028) 9023 0514	MODERN IRISH
WEBSITE: www.nickswarehouse.co.uk	£25–£52

'Warehouse' is no lie. The place was built as a bonded whiskey store for the Bushmills distillery in 1832, and sits in an engaging district of old Belfast, all cobbled streets and red-brick period charm. Local supplies, such as crabs from Dundrum and the wares of the enigmatic 'wild boar and rare pig lady', inform the menus of both the Upstairs Restaurant (lunches only) and the less formal Anix below. Fish is a strong point, as was discovered by a reporter who ate a bowl of Thai-style clear fish soup with mussels and lemongrass, followed by sea bass with peppers and a 'very fresh, simple and delicious' parsley sauce. That rare pig might show up as pork loin with roast garlic and creamed lentils, or there may be Moroccan spiced beef with carrot and orange salad and a yoghurt and cumin dressing. Meals end with the likes of pannacotta, ice creams or cheeses. Service can seem a bit stretched at busy sessions. The businesslike listing of typical brasserie wines is supplemented by slates of fine wines and a Spanish collection. House wines are £11.95 (£3 a glass).

CHEFS: Nick Price, Gerard Sands and Sean Craig   PROPRIETORS: Nick and Kathy Price   OPEN: Mon to Fri L 12 to 3, Tue to Sat D 6 to 9.30 (10 Fri and Sat)   CLOSED: 25 to 28 Dec, 1 Jan, 12 and 13 Apr, 3 May, 12 July   MEALS: alc (main courses £6.50 to £17.50). Restaurant Upstairs L menu available Tue to Fri   SERVICE: not inc, 10% (optional) for parties of 5 or more   CARDS: Amex, Delta, Diners, MasterCard, Switch, Visa   DETAILS: 180 seats. Private parties: 90 main room, 10 to 50 private rooms. Vegetarian meals. Children's helpings. No children after 9.30. No cigars/pipes. Wheelchair access (also WC). Music. Air-conditioned

Rain City

33–35 Malone Road, Belfast BT9 6RU	COOKING 3
TEL: (028) 9068 2929 FAX: (028) 9068 2060	INTERNATIONAL
	£26–£49

Rain City is open all day (serving breakfast from 9 till noon), and the Rankins – who also own Cayenne in Belfast (see entry) – claim US West Coast influence 'in both menu and décor'. It does have the casual feel of a vaguely retro student hangout, though customers span a broad age range, perhaps because the place is child-friendly (there's a 'kiddies' menu', and children's drinks are topped up gratis). No surprise, then, that the carte offers Caesar salad, chargrilled steaks, nachos and seafood chowder alongside steamed Dundrum mussels, pasta dishes and Cumberland sausages and mash. Puds include blueberry and apple crumble, and lemon tart with raspberry sauce. Cooking is very simple, though patchy in places, and the short wine list seldom strays above £25, with bottle prices from £11.50.

CHEFS: Andrew Rea and Gareth Magill   PROPRIETOR: Paul Rankin   OPEN: all week 9am to 10.30   CLOSED: 25 Dec   MEALS: alc (main courses £7 to £14)   SERVICE: not inc, 10% (optional) for parties of 6 or more   CARDS: Amex, Delta, Diners, MasterCard, Switch, Visa   DETAILS: 90 seats. 25 seats outside. Private parties: 50 main room, 50 private room. Vegetarian meals. Children's helpings. No-smoking area. Wheelchair access (also WC). Music. Air-conditioned

Restaurant Michael Deane

36–40 Howard Street, Belfast BT1 6PF
TEL: (028) 9033 1134   FAX: (028) 9056 0001
WEBSITE: www.michaeldeane.co.uk

COOKING 6
MODERN EUROPEAN-PLUS
£58–£90

This cosmopolitan restaurant behind City Hall has a brasserie downstairs, which has a lively atmosphere, friendly, white-aproned waiters and a repertoire ranging from fish and chips with mushy peas to slow-cooked pork belly with white beans and harissa. The cooking mark above, however, applies to the upstairs dining room, where the mood is a little more sombre with rather more formal service.

If the tone is meant to suggest a serious approach to food, it is not misplaced. At the heart of Michael Deane's cooking is a solid grounding in classic techniques, but, rather than restricting his style, this acts as a springboard for his creative flair – apparent in starters such as spiced scallops with kedgeree of cucumber, sticky rice, aubergine caviar and curry oil. High standards are required to pull off such audacious cooking, and high standards are consistently achieved, praise coming in for turbot with white chocolate sauce and peas, and Clonakilty black pudding with foie gras and langoustines in balsamic, as well as a more conventional beef fillet with a 'sensational' thyme sauce. Desserts make less impact but the excellent selection of French cheeses is a tempting alternative. A dozen 'sommelier's choices' from £19 to £38 set the tone for a wine list about half of which is devoted to high-end French wines; for sub-£20 bottles turn to the New World pages towards the back.

CHEF/PROPRIETOR: Michael Deane   OPEN: Wed to Sat D only 7 to 9.30   CLOSED: 25 Dec, 1 Jan, 1 week July   MEALS: Set D £33 (2 courses) to (whole table only) £59   SERVICE: not inc, 10% (optional) for parties of 6 or more   CARDS: Amex, Delta, MasterCard, Switch, Visa   DETAILS: 35 seats. Private parties: 35 main room. Vegetarian meals. No pipes/cigars. Music. No mobile phones. Air-conditioned

Ta Tu

701 Lisburn Road, Belfast BT9 7GU
TEL: (028) 9038 0818   FAX: (028) 9038 0828
WEBSITE: www.ta-tu.com

COOKING 2
MODERN EUROPEAN
£26–£46

This chic, minimalist 'Bar and Grill' is on Belfast's south side beyond the university. Location and design are crowd-pullers, so expect high decibels in the atrium-style bar;

alternatively seek sanctuary in the more sedate restaurant area. Local supplies of 'extra-hung' beef, organic vegetables and daily fish deliveries underpin menus in tune with the times. Smoked pancetta and cod chowder, and crispy pork and shiitake dumplings with sesame and ginger dip give way to five-spiced Barbary duck breast with Szechuan pickled cucumber salad, and seafood hotpot with chorizo, chickpeas and new potatoes. Desserts are mostly European classics like apple pannacotta or pavlova. Fifteen wines come by the glass (£3.25 to £4.95) from a globetrotting list that starts at £11.50.

CHEF: David Harding   PROPRIETOR: Bill Wolsey   OPEN: all week 12 to 9.45 (8.45 Sun)   CLOSED: 25 and 26 Dec, 12 July   MEALS: alc (main courses L £7 to £11, D £13 to £15.50). Bistro D menu available   SERVICE: not inc, 10% (optional) for parties of 6 or more   CARDS: Amex, Delta, Diners, MasterCard, Switch, Visa   DETAILS: 115 seats. 30 seats outside. Private parties: 65 main room, 50 private room. Vegetarian meals. Children's helpings. Wheelchair access (also WC). Music. Air-conditioned (£5)

GILFORD Co Down
map 16

Oriel ⚡✕

NEW ENTRY

2 Bridge Street, Gilford BT63 6HF
TEL: (028) 3883 1543   FAX: (028) 3883 1180
WEBSITE: www.orielrestaurant.com

COOKING 4
MODERN IRISH
£35–£76

The focus is on food, not furnishings, in this small-town restaurant. 'The tasting menu is a real treat,' says one visitor, for whom Oriel has no equal in Ireland. The modern Irish cooking shows strong French influences, hence the weekly deliveries of luxury items from Rungis Market in Paris. Organic vegetables are sourced locally, as is meat, and local seafood is delivered daily. The results on the plate have included 'as good a Caesar salad as we have had anywhere', roast supreme of chicken with Clonakilty black pudding and spring onion mash (a main-course winner), and a 'beautifully browned' roast monkfish fillet with saffron potatoes, spring vegetables and delicate but underpowered lobster cream. Puddings really stand out, for presentation as well as flavour: warm vanilla bean rice pudding, with mango soup and mango sorbet, for example. Service is satisfactory despite a few niggles and a marked reluctance on one occasion to serve tap water. France gets top billing on the wine list, but there's reasonable scope beyond its borders, and house bottles hover around £15.

CHEFS: Damian Tumilty and Paul Heron   PROPRIETOR: Barry Smyth   OPEN: Sun L 12.30 to 2.30, Tue to Sat D 6.30 to 9.30   CLOSED: 25 and 26 Dec, 2 weeks Jan, 2 weeks July   MEALS: alc D (main courses £17 to £23). Set Sun L £21, Set D (min 6 or whole table) £50   SERVICE: not inc, card slips closed   CARDS: Amex, Diners, MasterCard, Switch, Visa   DETAILS: 45 seats. Private parties: 40 main room, 8 to 14 private rooms. Vegetarian meals. Children's helpings. No smoking. Music. No mobile phones. Air-conditioned

Republic of Ireland

We have not given marks for cooking for the Republic of Ireland entries (all found on map 16) because of a shortage of reports, and we have shortened the amount of factual information provided. Please do give us feedback should you visit. To telephone the Republic from mainland Britain, dial 00 353 followed by the number listed, but dropping the initial 0. Prices are quoted in euros.

BALLYDEHOB Co Cork

Annie's

Main Street, Ballydehob
TEL: (028) 37292

Dano and Anne Barry's friendly little restaurant stands opposite the village phone box and the local pub – with whom they have a 'unique arrangement': customers may order their meal while at the pub and be called over to table when the food's ready. The Barrys point out that 'everything is made on the premises' and that local produce forms the backbone of their menus. Ideas are totally free of pretence: seafood salad or sautéed lambs' kidneys in filo to start, then grilled whole black sole or roast rack of lamb with rosemary jus, followed by a dessert such as hot chocolate fudge cake. Around 50 respectable wines open with South African Paarl Heights at €17.

OPEN: Tue to Sat D only 6.30 to 10; closed Oct bank hol, Nov   DETAILS: alc (main courses €23 to €27). Set D €40 to €45

BANTRY Co Cork

▲ Larchwood House

Pearsons Bridge, Bantry
TEL: (027) 66181

The lady of the house is also the chef at the Vaughans' modest, creeper-clad guesthouse, which comes complete with a luxuriant, semitropical garden. Sheila's five-course dinners display lots of fruity flourishes; a warm salad with duck and ginger might open the show before carrot and peach soup; an intermediary pear and melon cocktail precedes centrepieces such as roast pheasant with cranberry and wine sauce or fillet of hake with avocado sauce, and proceedings conclude with desserts such as apple and raisin crumble. A handful of fine wines add gloss to the 40-strong international list. House French is €22.

OPEN: Mon to Sat D only 7 to 9; closed Christmas week   DETAILS: Set D €40. B&B €40 to €80

▲ *means accommodation is available.*

BLACKLION Co Cavan

▲ Macnean Bistro

Main Street, Blacklion
TEL: (071) 9853022   FAX: (071) 9853404

Neven Maguire's small hotel and bistro is a welcome oasis in the gorgeous wilderness of the northwest of Ireland. His cooking is firmly in the modern Irish vein, with special game menus a seasonal highlight. Goats' cheese is crisp-fried in a walnut coating, and served with roast peppers and chilli jam, as one way of starting, after which there may be wild salmon with carrot and cumin purée and prawn velouté, or Thornhill duckling (sautéed breast and confit leg) with creamed Savoy cabbage and ginger jus. Desserts look a treat: passion-fruit pannacotta comes with poached strawberries and raspberry ice cream. A short but broadly based wine selection opens with a choice of eight house wines from €15.95.

OPEN: Sun L 12.30 to 4, Thurs (Wed in high season) to Sun D 6.30 to 9.30   DETAILS: alc D (main courses €21 to €22). Set L €27, Set D €55. B&B €35 to €40

CASHEL Co Tipperary

Chez Hans

Moor Lane, Cashel
TEL/FAX: (062) 61177

Chez Hans continues to emphasise the strength of local produce, and although modern trends are acknowledged they are made to complement rather than dominate what is offered. Chargrilled boned quail with niçoise salad and honey and soy dressing is one such example, while poached Irish salmon is teamed with a risotto of Dublin Bay prawns, mussels, crabmeat and chilli. More straightforward are dishes such as roast breast of chicken stuffed with creamed leeks and Cashel Blue and served with chasseur sauce, and desserts like glazed lemon tart. House wine is €23.50. Under the same management is Café Hans, an all-day eatery serving salads, open sandwiches, and simple dishes like grilled lamb cutlets with mushroom sauce.

OPEN: Tue to Sat D only 6 to 10; closed 24 to 26 Dec, last 2 weeks Jan   DETAILS: alc (main courses €19 to €32). Set D €32 to €45

CASTLEBALDWIN Co Sligo

▲ Cromleach Lodge

Castlebaldwin, via Boyle
TEL: (071) 916 5155   FAX: (071) 916 5455   WEBSITE: www.cromleach.com
signposted from Castlebaldwin on N4

The waters of Lough Arrow and the peaks of Carrowkeel Cairns are visible from this family-run country-house hotel, but visitors are also lured by the prospect of Moira Tighe's cooking. She procures organic and local produce for dinner menus that mix and match classic and contemporary ideas. Roast quail is stuffed with morels as a starter, while a refreshing sorbet sharpens the palate for – say – free-range duck breast with onion purée and plum glaze or wild salmon on smoked haddock brandade with mustard sauce. Take your leave with iced nougat parfait. Residents also have the option of an eight-course tasting menu. House wines are €23.95, and six wines are served by the glass, starting at €6.50.

OPEN: all week D only 7 to 8.30 (6.30 to 8 Sun); closed 1 Nov to 7 Feb   DETAILS: Set D €60. B&B €139 to €376

CORK Co Cork

Crawford Gallery Café

Emmet Place, Cork
TEL: (021) 4274415

The busy, upmarket bistro in the city art gallery offers a mixture of traditional and trendy fare on weekly-changing lunch menus, with all the ingredients either sourced locally or grown by Isaac Allen himself. A crispy salmon cake served with herbed mayonnaise and salad might precede spicy sausage and lentil stew seasoned with rosemary and bay, or steamed mussels Thai-style with coconut milk, chilli and coriander. Finish with chocolate ice cream and marshmallows, or spiced pear tart. A short wine list has Duboeuf house wines at €17.50 but goes up only as far as €35 for Blanquette de Limoux.

OPEN: Mon to Sat L only 12.30 to 2.30 (3 Sat)   DETAILS: alc (main courses €12 to €14). Set L €20

DINGLE Co Kerry

Half Door

3 John Street, Dingle
TEL: (066) 9151600   FAX: (066) 9151883   EMAIL: halfdoor@iol.ie

Deep in the south-west, Dingle sits on a windswept peninsula, and it seems only right and proper that Teresa O'Connor's first love is freshest fish and seafood. The fixed-price and à la carte menus are supplemented by a plethora of daily specials, and treatments are simple: mussels are steamed and served with garlic sauce, lobsters chosen from the tank are boiled or served thermidor, while scallops are sautéed and given a saffron sauce as a main course. Finish with bread-and-butter pudding or fruit pavlova. A tempting, expansive wine list opens with a broad selection of house wines from €20.

OPEN: Mon to Sat 12.30 to 2.30, 6 to 10   DETAILS: alc (main courses €12.50 to €50). Set L €32, Set D €36.50

DONEGAL Co Donegal

▲ Harvey's Point

Lough Eske, Donegal
TEL: (074) 9722208   FAX: (074) 9722352   WEBSITE: www.harveyspoint.com

Former chef Franck Pasquier has returned to head the kitchen of this chalet-style country-house hotel overlooking Lough Eske, but the formula of four-course dinners with a strong European accent remains. Start with feuilleté of wood pigeon with celeriac purée, quail's eggs and game sauce, before choosing a soup or sorbet. Next up might be escalope of Atlantic salmon with leek fondue, truffle mash and a light champagne cream, which could be followed by chocolate marquise with mint ice cream and orange crème anglaise. Europe also has the edge over the New World on the dependable wine list. House selections start at €19.50.

OPEN: all week 12.30 to 2.30, 6.30 to 9.30; closed Sun D, Mon and Tue Nov to Mar exc Christmas and New Year   DETAILS: alc (main courses €17 to €30). Set L €25 to €30, Set D €47 to €50. B&B €114 to €250

DOOLIN Co Clare

▲ Ballinalacken Castle

Coast Road, Doolin
TEL/FAX: (065) 707 4025   WEBSITE: www.ballinalackencastle.com

Doolin is a sprawl of pubs, holiday homes and hotels, and this particular hotel has part of an ancient ruined castle next to it. Inside, the atmosphere is well-kept Victorian, with ladderback chairs and heavy drapes, and landscape pictures on the dining room walls. Frank Sheedy offers some enterprising starters, as in tian of crab with red pepper relish, crab claws and a balsamic and citrus dressing, or a smoked salmon crème brûlée with a Parmesan and sesame seed crust, as well as intelligently conceived main courses like roast monkfish with a soft herb crust, served with peperonata and lemon and thyme butter. Luxurious desserts might include dark and white chocolate mousse cake with mint and chocolate ice cream and a strawberry and cappuccino sauce. House Vins de Pays d'Oc are €18.50.

OPEN: Wed to Mon D only 6.45 to 8.45   DETAILS: alc (main courses €20 to €28). B&B €80 to €176

DOUGLAS Co Cork

Lovetts

Churchyard Lane, Well Road, Douglas
TEL: (021) 4294909

A mini directory of trusted local suppliers testifies to the provenance of the food served in this conscientiously run enterprise. Galway oysters and mussels, venison, free-range chickens and more find their way on to the brasserie menu and the restaurant carte. Ardsallagh goats' cheese, tomato and walnut muffin with yoghurt and pesto dressing is a newcomer, while Bresnan's rack of lamb with mint oil and roast seasonal vegetables remains a stalwart of the repertoire. Daily fish specials might include baked cod with crab and chive sauce, and vegetarians have their own menu. Desserts revolve around seasonal tarts, ice creams and 'something chocolate'. House wines are €18.75.

OPEN: Tue to Sat D only 6.30 to 9.30; closed 1 week at Christmas, first 2 weeks Aug   DETAILS: alc (main courses €19 to €36)

DUBLIN Co Dublin

Bleu

Joshua House, Dawson Street, Dublin 2
TEL: (01) 676 7015   FAX: (01) 676 7027   WEBSITE: www.onepico.com

Paul McDonald is the chef charged with bringing Eamonn O'Reilly's vision of modern bistro fare to this offshoot of One Pico (see entry). Crab forms the basis of a tian starter that includes tomato tartare, apple crème fraîche and pickled cucumber, while seared scallops are the main component of a dish taking in apple and cashew nut dressing, mesclun salad and glazed baby vegetables. Bright ideas among main courses include an unusual take on fish and chips, here teamed with pea and basil purée and sauce gribiche, and loin of lamb stuffed with boudin noir and served with fondant potato, mushroom and Madeira onion tart and red wine sauce. Warm chocolate and port tart with Banyuls and orange chocolate ice cream catches the eye for dessert. House wine is €22.

OPEN: Mon to Sat 12 to 3, 6 to 11   DETAILS: alc (main courses €14.50 to €25). Set L €20 to €25, Set D €25 to €30

▲ Browne's Brasserie

22 St Stephen's Green, Dublin 2
TEL: (01) 638 3939   FAX: (01) 638 3900   WEBSITE: www.brownesdublin.com

Occupying a prime site on St Stephen's Green, Browne's is an elegant hotel, the dining-room designed in fin-de-siècle Parisian style, complete with an updated version of Manet's image of the bar at the Folies Bergères. What is offered is modern brasserie cooking, not too ambitious, but with plenty of materials produced in-house. Roast salt cod arrives in a bowl of creamy clam chowder, while a fillet of home-smoked salmon is perfectly timed, teamed with spring onion mash, and sauced with red wine and mustard seeds. The hearty of appetite might opt for cabbage-wrapped loin of venison with foie gras, celeriac purée and red wine sauce. Finish with fig and pistachio tart or chocolate fondant. A serviceable wine list contains a few safe bets, as well as the odd eye-catching bin-end. The restaurant did not return our questionnaire, so not all the details below may be accurate.

OPEN: Sun to Fri L 12.30 to 3, all week D 6.30 to 11 (10 Sun and bank hols)   MEALS: alc (main courses €19.50 to €29.50). Set meals also available. B&B €170 to €350

Chapter One

18–19 Parnell Square, Dublin 1
TEL: (01) 873 2266   FAX: (01) 873 2330   WEBSITE: www.chapteronerestaurant.com

A flight of stone steps leads down to this spacious basement restaurant under the Writers' Museum. The menu deals in modern luxuries and reworkings of classics. Brandade with cauliflower purée is served with lemon and dill jelly and Avruga caviar, terrine of foie gras and squab pigeon is dressed with fig vinegar, while roast scallops are accompanied by creamed organic leeks, pumpkin purée, bordelaise of duck, and dauphine potatoes. A charcuterie trolley delivers west Cork ham with celeriac and mustard, and a selection of west Cork salami, while desserts range from orange jelly with basil and orange mousse and chocolate sorbet to warm blueberry financier served with sauce anglaise. The quality-conscious wine list kicks off with house French at €20 and ends with a couple of pages of fine wines, culminating in top clarets.

OPEN: Tue to Fri L 12.30 to 2.30, Tue to Sat D 6 to 10.45; closed 2 weeks at Christmas, Good Fri, first two weeks Aug   DETAILS: alc (main courses €26.50 to €32). Set L €25.50 to €28.50

▲ Clarence Hotel, Tea Room

6–8 Wellington Quay, Dublin 2
TEL: (01) 407 0800   FAX: (01) 407 0818   WEBSITE: www.theclarence.ie

The whimsically named Tea Room restaurant offers cooking by Antony Ely, whose style continues to promote the finest that Ireland can produce, teamed with French technique. Fricassee of pork might come with lyonnaise sausage, Jerusalem artichoke, morels, snails and Madeira, and fillet of Angus beef with horseradish mash and bourguignonne garnish. Risotto of Périgord truffles with Parmesan is from the more classical end of his repertoire, as is ballottine of chicken with glazed artichoke, roast button onions, langoustine and thyme. Desserts might include pistachio soufflé with hot cherry sauce, or an assiette of rhubarb. Notable vintages of the leading estates in Bordeaux are available for big spenders. Quality is high throughout the list, particularly Australia and the USA. Prices start at around €26, and 18 by the glass or pichet give a good selection across the range.

OPEN: Sun to Fri L 12.30 to 2.30, all week D 6.30 to 10.30; closed D 24 Dec, 25 and 26 Dec   DETAILS: Set L €26 to €30, Set D €41.50 to €70. Room only €325 to €2,100

L'Ecrivain

109A Lower Baggot Street, Dublin 2
TEL: (01) 661 1919   FAX: (01) 661 0617   WEBSITE: www.lecrivain.com

Not far from St Stephen's Green, this is a 'carefully manicured', contemporary dining room serving food that treads a path between 'novelty and tradition'. Dishes involve plenty of finely honed workmanship, but the results are genuinely unfussy: witness a 'tasting' of Connemara lamb with smoked loin, kidney croquette, herb sausage and swede purée or a baked medallion of hake wrapped in Parma ham with white-bean and basil cassoulet and tapenade. Desserts keep pace with, say, chocolate Manjori dome and Kirsch-marinated griottine cherries. The big, bulky wine list is peppered with pedigree vintages. Twenty house recommendations from €25 are the most affordable bets.

OPEN: Mon to Fri L 12.30 to 2, Mon to Sat D 7 to 10.30 (11 Fri and Sat); closed Christmas, Easter, bank hols
DETAILS: alc (main courses €38 to €40). Set L €30 to €35, Set D €60

Eden

Meeting House Square, Temple Bar, Dublin 2
TEL: (01) 670 5372   FAX: (01) 670 3330   WEBSITE: www.edenrestaurant.ie

The most memorable nights at Eden are in summer, when films are screened on the opposite wall of Meeting House Square, a table on the terrace here affording an enviable view. Contemporary cooking with firm Irish roots brings on Carlingford oysters with a dipping sauce of carrot juice, chives and ginger, and main courses such as Castletownbere scallops with squash, leeks and rocket in spaghetti, or braised lamb shank with tomato and basil jus, baked sliced aubergine and mash. There are hazelnuts in the bread-and-butter pudding, and cinnamon and apple in the crème brûlée. A single-page wine list does the job, with bottles from €22, glasses €5.75.

OPEN: all week 12.30 (12 Sat and Sun) to 3, 6 to 10.30; closed 25 Dec to 2 Jan, bank hols   DETAILS: alc (main courses €17.50 to €29). Set L €19 to €22, Set D €22 to €38

Les Frères Jacques

74 Dame Street, Dublin 2
TEL: (01) 679 4555   FAX: (01) 679 4725   WEBSITE: www.lesfreresjaques.com

The site of this long-standing city-centre restaurant is as prime as they come, next to the

Olympia Theatre and facing the castle. Traditional French cuisine is the stock in trade, with fish, seafood and seasonal game the strong suits. Turbot is sauced with red wine butter, monkfish is wrapped in Parma ham, or there may be roast Barbary duck with kumquat confit. Start perhaps with native oysters, or home-cured salmon with anchovy mayonnaise. Quality French and Irish cheeses might precede desserts such as orange and lemon tart with mascarpone cream. Wines start at €18.50.

OPEN: Mon to Fri L 12.30 to 2.30, Mon to Sat D 7 to 10.30 (11 Fri and Sat); closed 25 Dec to 2 Jan, bank hols
DETAILS: alc (main courses €15 to €36). Set L €17 to €22, Set D €35

▲ Halo at the Morrison

Ormond Quay, Dublin 1
TEL: (01) 887 2400   FAX: (01) 887 3185   WEBSITE: www.morrisonhotel.ie

Pass through the stark minimalism of the Morrison Hotel and into the vast double-height, split-level restaurant – this may lack windows but certainly sets out to impress with its dark wooden floors and sheets of darkly hued metal. The evening carte follows suit with a well-reported tian of crabmeat with vegetable salad, wasabi and a chive cream, carrot and lemongrass vinaigrette featuring in the starting line-up, while main courses might roll out fillet of beef with duxelles ('the request for rare beef singularly met') accompanied by smoked bacon and asparagus ragoût, mushroom mash and a foie gras and pepper sauce. House wine kicks in at €25, with six by the glass from €4.60.

OPEN: Sat and Sun L 12.30 to 3.30, all week D 7 to 10   DETAILS: alc (main courses €24.50 to €33). Set D €32 to €60. Room only €140 to €280

Jacob's Ladder

4 Nassau Street, Dublin 2
TEL: (01) 670 3865   FAX: (01) 670 3868   WEBSITE: www.jacobsladder.ie

Views over the hallowed lawns and playing fields of Trinity College may distract the eye at this restrained, first-floor dining room. Focus on the food and you will notice that lunches, fixed-priced dinners and the eight-course Menu Surprise all inhabit similar culinary worlds, with supplies from artisan Irish producers given free rein. Cep brûlée with cep purée is a typically creative starter, while main courses could include fillet of sole with scallion risotto, bay carrots and lovage foam. As a refreshing finale, try lemon cup with cinnamon-infused blood oranges and blood orange sorbet. Eight wines by the glass (€4.75) open the respectable list.

OPEN: Tue to Sat 12.30 to 2.30 (2 Sat), 6 to 10; closed 2 weeks at Christmas, 1 week Aug, bank hols
DETAILS: alc (main courses €13.50 to €32.50). Set D €37

Mermaid Café

69–70 Dame Street, Dublin 2
TEL: (01) 670 8236   FAX: (01) 670 8205   WEBSITE: www.mermaid.ie

A couple of doors up from Dublin's Olympia Theatre and opposite the castle, this casual, modern-looking café does a great service to playgoers, sightseers and locals alike. The menus change regularly, and the repertoire sounds a contemporary note: chargrilled spatchcock quail with balsamic Puy lentils and rocket might precede sea bass fillet with basil, crab peperonata and tapenade, and you could finish with the day's ice cream, ginger and cranberry crème brûlée, or a brace of Irish cheeses. Six house wines from €19.95 head the affordably priced list.

OPEN: all week 12.30 to 2.30 (3.30 Sun), 6 to 11 (9 Sun); closed 24, 25 and 31 Dec, 1 Jan, Good Fri
DETAILS: alc (main courses €16 to €30). Set L €20 to €24

One Pico

5–6 Molesworth Place, Dublin 2
TEL: (01) 676 0300   FAX: (01) 678 8576   WEBSITE: www.onepico.com

Not far from St Stephen's Green and the city centre, this chic, contemporary restaurant is a stylish showcase for Eamonn O'Reilly's sophisticated and thoroughly modern cooking. Seared tuna escabèche is served with sweet potato aïoli, olives, fennel and coriander, while roast loin of venison is paired with a scallop and shiitake brochette, beetroot purée, braised cabbage, blackberry and juniper. Typically involved desserts might include spiced pineapple Tatin with coconut ice cream, chilli syrup and Malibu froth. The substantial wine list has a good showing from both the Old and New Worlds, with prices from €26.

OPEN: Mon to Sat 12.30 to 2.30, 6 to 10.30; closed bank hols   DETAILS: alc (main courses €14.50 to €29.50). Set D €30 to €75

Restaurant Patrick Guilbaud

21 Upper Merrion Street, Dublin 2
TEL: (01) 676 4192   FAX: (01) 661 0052   WEBSITE: www.restaurantpatrickguilbaud.ie

Located within the Merrion Hotel, a solid Georgian building with a modern feel, this barrel-vaulted dining room is light and airy, predominantly cream, with pillars on two sides. The menus include a carte plus various set-price options, the most exciting being a nine-course 'Sea and Land' dinner that offers an innovative take on traditional Irish cooking: Galway Bay oysters in Guinness jelly with oyster cream, for example. The rest of the repertoire is 'full of interest in a more generally modern way', taking in roast partridge breast with spätzli and chanterelles in a foie gras sauce, or roast John Dory with pears, butternut squash and a hazelnut tuile. Inventive desserts have included 'ace' honey-roast figs with ras el hanout ice cream and dried fruit couscous. The 'going for broke' wine list features lots of swanky bottles at 'frightening' prices as well as a few more affordable options, although prices start at €36.

OPEN: Tue to Sat 12.30 to 2.15, 7.30 to 10.15; closed first week after Christmas, 17 Mar, Good Fri
DETAILS: alc (main courses €36 to €54). Set L €30 to €45, Set D €79 to €130

Roly's Bistro

7 Ballsbridge Terrace, Dublin 4
TEL: (01) 668 2611   FAX: (01) 660 8535   EMAIL: ireland@rolysbistro.ie

At the heart of Dublin's business quarter, Roly's is a versatile all-rounder, with a large-scale dining room and a diverse clientele. The bistro designation reflects the informal atmosphere as well as the straightforward cooking style that blends modern and traditional ideas, with starters ranging from potato and garlic soup to crispy Thai chicken spring rolls. Among main courses, traditional Kerry lamb and vegetable pie with thyme-roast parsnips vies for attention with pan-fried Dublin Bay prawns Newburg with fennel-scented wild rice, and pudding choices could include chocolate truffle tart with nougat parfait and orange tuiles. There are ten wines by the glass, and bottle prices start at €19.95.

OPEN: all week 12 to 3, 6 to 10   DETAILS: alc (main courses L €12 to €19, D €19 to €27). Set L €18.50

Shanahan's on the Green

119 St Stephen's Green, Dublin 2
TEL: (01) 407 0939   FAX: (01) 407 0940   WEBSITE: www.shanahans.ie

The accent is Irish-American, the mood is animated and there's an air of super-efficiency about this contemporary restaurant on two floors overlooking St Stephen's Green. Certified Angus steaks of every description and weight are the prime contenders on the menu, with hash browns and bowls of crispy onion 'strings' as must-have side orders. Alternatively, kick off with Galway oysters Rockefeller or Caesar salad before pork shank with melted cabbage and leeks or roast skate with a clam and smoked bacon emulsion. Typical desserts include an assiette of mini crème brûlées. The wine list, generally arranged by grape variety, is a serious tour of the wine-producing world, with quality and interest encountered at every turn. Prices run from €23 for a Coteaux du Languedoc rosé to €3,000 for a 1961 Ch. Haut-Brion. Eight by the glass give a good range.

OPEN: Fri L 12.30 to 2, all week D 6 to 10.30; closed 22 Dec to 12 Jan   DETAILS: alc (main courses €37 to €45). Set L €45

Thornton's

128 St Stephen's Green, Dublin 2
TEL: (01) 478 7008   FAX: (01) 478 7009   WEBSITE: www.thorntonsrestaurant.com

In the Fitzwilliam Hotel, up three flights of stairs, with splendid views over St Stephen's Green, Thornton's offers refined haute cuisine in a pleasingly unceremonious atmosphere. Local and organic ingredients form the backbone of the menus, with two shades of asparagus – the white whole, the green in a bavarois – dressed up in truffle hollandaise, or braised lobster in its own consommé with celeriac cream to start, followed perhaps by Wicklow lamb with a courgette clafoutis and spinach and garlic sauce. Fruit parfait is fashioned into a pyramid and adorned with glazed berries to make an eye-catching dessert, and the extensive list of fine wines contains many mature bottles. Wines by the glass start at €8.

OPEN: Tue to Sat 12.30 to 2, 7 to 10.30; closed 2 weeks at Christmas   DETAILS: alc (main courses €45). Set L €30 to €120, Set D €65 to €120

GOREY Co Wexford

▲ Marlfield House

Courtown Road, Gorey
TEL: (055) 21124   FAX: (055) 21572   WEBSITE: www.marlfieldhouse.com

Set amid expansive grounds a mile out of town, this lordly country mansion benefits from a working kitchen garden, which supplies chef Henry Stone with seasonal pickings. The four-course dinners might open with a tian of avocado and prawns with gazpacho and fried beetroot before a salad, sorbet – avocado, for instance – or soup (Tuscan bean, for example). Main courses range from roast rack of lamb and braised shank with balsamic-roast celeriac to salmon fillet with rösti, wilted wild garlic, asparagus and hollandaise, while desserts could feature poached pear with ginger ice cream and chocolate sauce. France looms large on the lengthy wine list, although other countries also have their say. House selections are €25.

OPEN: Sun L 12.30 to 1.45, all week D 7 to 9 (9.30 Sat, 8 Sun); closed mid-Dec to Feb   DETAILS: Set L €36, Set D €58. B&B €135 to €750

KANTURK Co Cork

▲ Assolas Country House

Kanturk
TEL: (029) 50015   FAX: (029) 50795   WEBSITE: www.assolas.com
signposted from N72, NE of Kanturk, 8m W of Mallow

The Bourke family have been custodians of this seventeenth-century manor since 1915, and its current incumbents are well versed in the traditions of hospitality. Local supplies and home-grown produce find their way into the kitchen, where Hazel Bourke keeps guests satisfied with five-course dinners. Begin with locally smoked salmon on a hot potato cake before roast free-range duck breast with spicy pear or baked John Dory with bacon and parsley sauce. Desserts and local cheese are followed by coffee in the drawing room. Bottles from French family vineyards take pride of place on the all-European wine list. House Côtes du Rhône from Guigal is €22.

OPEN: all week D only 7 to 8; closed 1 Nov to 1 Apr   DETAILS: Set D €49. B&B €104 to €280

KENMARE Co Kerry

▲ Park Hotel Kenmare

Kenmare
TEL: (064) 41200   FAX: (064) 41402   WEBSITE: www.parkkenmare.com

Pre-dinner drinks outside on the terrace, looking across the water towards the hills beyond, formed the prelude to what one diner summed up as a 'memorable and outstanding experience'. The imaginative and finely crafted modern Irish cooking lives up to the splendour of the setting: chicken and lobster terrine has been an outstanding starter, while main courses extend to veal medallion with tarragon and chanterelle mousse, forest mushroom risotto and onion jus, and baked hake wrapped in bacon on colcannon with mussel and clam chive cream sauce. Finish with a selection of Irish cheeses or perhaps a gratin of seasonal berries with champagne sabayon. As well as famed estates in Bordeaux and Burgundy, the wine list features top producers from other French regions as well as California and Australia. The more budget conscious can choose from the house selections, priced from €22 to €25.

OPEN: all week D only 7 to 9; closed 1 to 23 Dec, 2 Jan to 12 Feb   DETAILS: alc (main courses €18 to €32). B&B €230 to €265

The Guide is totally independent, accepts no free hospitality, and survives on the number of copies sold each year.

▲ Sheen Falls Lodge

La Cascade, Kenmare
TEL: (064) 41600   WEBSITE: www.sheenfallslodge.ie
follow signs for Glengariss from Kenmare; hotel signposted after about ½m

Bag a table by the window if you can to enjoy the dramatic spot-lit evening backdrop of river and falls, although the views from all sides are pretty lush. New chef Alan McGrath has maintained the formidable standards set by predecessors here, turning out finely timed monkfish with aubergine purée, provençale vegetables and bouillabaisse sauce, as well as fillet of beef with a pudding of ox cheek, truffled mash, broad beans and girolles. First-course salads (perhaps of prawns, wild asparagus, organic leaves and preserved lemon) are immaculately presented, and meals end with the likes of a 'vertical mille-feuille' of chocolate and hazelnuts, or Irish cheeses with Parmesan biscuits. A wine list of the highest pedigree opens with house selections from €8.50 a glass.

OPEN: all week D only 7 to 9.30   DETAILS: alc (main courses €33.50 to €38). Set D €65. Room only €275 to €1,800.

KILCOLGAN Co Galway

Moran's Oyster Cottage

The Weir, Kilcolgan
TEL: (091) 796113   FAX: (091) 796503   WEBSITE: www.moransoystercottage.com

Take your pick from 'locally grown' oysters, Dingle crab or smoked wild salmon in this amicable little all-day restaurant within reach of Galway Bay. Alternatively, call in for anything from a bowl of seafood chowder (made to a sixth-generation recipe), garlic mussels, or something more exotic like tempura prawns with sweet chilli dip. Open sandwiches go well with a cup of coffee, baked ham should satisfy carnivorous cravings, and you can finish with cheesecake or ice cream. The short wine list has prices from €15.30.

OPEN: all week 12 to 10; closed 25 to 27 Dec, Good Fri   DETAILS: alc (main courses €12 to €38)

LISDOONVARNA Co Clare

▲ Sheedy's

Lisdoonvarna
TEL: (065) 7074026   FAX: (065) 7074555   WEBSITE: www.sheedys.com

Organically grown herbs and vegetables are ever-present on the menu at John and Martina Sheedy's pleasant country-house hotel and restaurant, and nearly all of what is bought in comes from local suppliers. They are put to good use in a modern cooking style with broad appeal, starters taking in roast St Tola goats' cheese on a chickpea cake with beetroot salad, and main courses ranging from roast rump of lamb with wild mushrooms, pearl barley and thyme gravy to seared salmon with baby leeks and lemon butter sauce. Sticky toffee pudding with butterscotch sauce and vanilla ice cream is a typical dessert. House wine is €19.

OPEN: all week D only 6.45 to 8.45; closed mid-Oct to mid-Mar   DETAILS: alc (main courses €18.50 to €25). B&B €90 to €180

MALLOW Co Cork

▲ Presidents' Restaurant, Longueville House

Mallow
TEL: (022) 47156   FAX: (022) 47459   WEBSITE: www.longuevillehouse.ie
3m W of Mallow on N72 Killarney road turn right on to Ballyclough road

A 500-acre wooded estate surrounds the O'Callaghans' elegant Georgian mansion, and the hotel kitchen is guaranteed supplies from its own farm, walled garden and the Blackwater river. 'Sumptuous' four-course dinners might begin appetisingly with Atlantic oysters and sorrel granita, before a middle course like pumpkin soup. Mains usher in, say, roast mallard with Jerusalem artichoke mousse, sloe and cep sauce, and then comes a dessert such as apple tartlet 'minute' with nougat ice cream. The owners import wine direct from vineyards as far apart as France and South Africa. Prices start at €25.

OPEN: all week D only 6.30 to 8.45; closed 1 week at Christmas, mid-Feb to early Mar   DETAILS: alc (main courses €25 to €28). Set D €50 to €65. B&B €90 to €360

OUGHTERARD Co Galway

▲ Currarevagh House

Oughterard, Connemara
TEL: (091) 552312   FAX: (091) 552731   WEBSITE: www.currarevagh.com
4m NW of Oughterard on Hill of Doon lakeshore road

The Hodgsons' sympathetically run hotel in sumptuous Connemara has a deliciously Edwardian feel and works to an unchanging and successful formula. A dinner gong sounds at 8pm to announce the serving of a five-course, no-choice menu. One example comprised spinach and feta bake, seafood tart, breast of duck marinated in honey and ginger, served with pommes Anna and carrots, baked pineapple with butterscotch sauce, Irish cheeses, and then coffee. House wines from €17.50 head up a France-led list.

OPEN: all week D only 8 (1 sitting); closed mid-Oct to Easter   DETAILS: Set D €39. B&B €82.50 to €210

RATHMULLAN Co Donegal

▲ Rathmullan House

Rathmullan
TEL: (074) 91 58188   FAX: (074) 91 58200   WEBSITE: www.rathmullanhouse.com

This family-run country house on Lough Swilly offers imaginative and refined modern Irish cooking using the best Donegal produce, including organically grown vegetables, fruit and herbs from its own walled gardens. Typical dishes on the daily-changing set-price menu include roast fillet of pork with braised belly in soy and ginger served with baby pak choi and olive oil mash, and turbot fillet with clams and roast langoustines, parsley, lemon oil and a tomato and chicken stock glaze. The chocolate plate, featuring a mini chocolate tart, white chocolate mousse and rich dark chocolate brownies, ends meals on a decadent note. An extensive international wine list opens with four house selections from €20.

OPEN: all week D only 7 to 8.45   DETAILS: alc (main courses €20 to €30). Set D €45. B&B €70 to €250

▲ Ballymaloe House

Shanagarry
TEL: (021) 465 2531   FAX: (021) 465 2021   WEBSITE: www.ballymaloe.com
2m outside Cloyne on Ballycotton road

When it opened in 1964, the Allen family's enterprise was a standard-bearer for the Irish cookery renaissance. Domestic industry is the guiding principle in their kitchen, and abundant produce is harvested from the hotel's garden. You might kick off with chilled ruby beetroot soup before moving on to bruschetta of Fran Fraser's exotic mushrooms. Keenly sourced Irish produce also dictates main courses, whether it's grilled wild Atlantic salmon with chilli, parsley and garlic oil or free-range chicken braised in St-Véran and cream, served with freshly cut asparagus. Farmhouse cheeses and a trolley of puddings make a fitting finale. House wines start at €19.

OPEN: all week 1 to 1.30, 7.30 to 9; closed 23 to 27 Dec   DETAILS: Set L €35, Set D €58. B&B €115 to €290

La Riva

Crescent Quay, Wexford
TEL: (053) 24330   WEBSITE: www.larivarestaurant.com

'Excellent and imaginative cooking in a pleasantly informal atmosphere' sums up the appeal of Warren Gillen's waterside restaurant. Inspiration comes from home and abroad in a modern cooking style that offers pan-fried Clonakilty black pudding with bacon, onion and a mustard seed jus for a starter alongside a spring roll of chicken, basil, tomato and mozzarella. Main-course choices typically range from roast marinated chicken breast with mustard mash, oyster mushrooms and tarragon velouté to slow-roast Barbary duck leg with a raisin, cognac and marjoram reduction, and meals might end with iced Guinness bread parfait with drunken fruits. House Chilean wines are €19.70.

OPEN: Sun L 12.30 to 2.30, all week D 6 to 10.30; closed last week Feb   DETAILS: alc (main courses L €10 to €12, D €17 to €22.50). Set L €22.50 (2 courses), Set D €28.50 to €34.50

Round-ups

Looking for a suitable place to eat can be a lottery, especially if you are travelling around the country with no set plans in mind. The Round-up section is intended to provide some interesting gastronomic possibilities, whether you find yourself in an unfamiliar city centre or a rural outpost. Pubs are becoming increasingly valuable as sources of high-quality food, but the listings below also include modest family-run enterprises in country towns, bustling café/bars and ethnic restaurants in big cities, and a sprinkling of hotel dining rooms in all parts of the land. Dip into this section and you are almost bound to find somewhere that suits your needs and pocket. Entries are based mainly on readers' recommendations, supported where appropriate by inspectors' reports. Sometimes restaurants appear in the Round-ups instead of the main entry section because seasonal closures or weekly openings limit their usefulness, or because late changes in the kitchen or to ownership have occurred, or because feedback this year has been thin on the ground. Reports on these are especially welcome, as they help to broaden our coverage of good eating places in Britain. The entries below are arranged alphabetically by locality within England, Scotland, Wales and the Channel Islands.

England

● **ALTON** (Hampshire)
Alton Grange Hotel, Truffles Restaurant
London Road, (01420) 86565. Country hotel that continues to do sterling service as a charming local institution. Luxury, elaboration and florid descriptions abound on the menu, which might advertise pan-fried foie gras with white onion purée and an apple and ginger reduction (£9), and panaché of fish and shellfish cooked in a Chardonnay broth scented with star anise and orange (£8.50), with lemon verbena ice cream cannelloni with a warm compote of berries to finish (£7). The wine list embraces Old and New World wines and some high prices; house wine is £12.95. Accommodation. Open all week.

● **AMBLESIDE** (Cumbria)
Drunken Duck Inn Barngates, (015394) 36347. Lakeland hot-spot greatly favoured by walkers, real ale fans (the Barngates Brewery is on-site) and those looking for new-wave pub food. Typically complex dishes might include quail confit and garlic tartlet with sauté foie gras and cep oil dressing (£8), and grilled sea bass fillet on rhubarb and vanilla risotto with plum vinaigrette (£14) followed by roasted figs in port with goats' cheese ice cream (£6.25). Also note the cheese menu and the wide-ranging wine list, which includes 20

by the glass. Accommodation available. Open all week.

● **AMERSHAM** (Buckinghamshire)
Gilbey's 1 Market Square, (01494) 727242. Locally popular 'cottagey' wine bar/restaurant in a converted seventeenth-century grammar school with a pleasant courtyard garden. Modern bistro-style cooking, taking in crab and crayfish cake with watercress salad (£6), herb-roasted poussin with tarragon butter sauce (£14.50) and desserts like Malibu pannacotta (£5). Two-course lunches Mon-Sat, £11. Gilbey's are specialist importers of French wines and many bottles are well below market price (house Sauvignon Blanc £10.45). Open all week. (There are branches at 82-83 High Street, Eton, Berks, tel (01753) 854921/ 855182 and in Ealing (see entry, London Round-up).)

● **BARNARD CASTLE** (Co Durham)
Blagraves House 30 The Bank, (01833) 637668. Centuries-old listed residence that continues to do sterling service as a family-run restaurant. Regularly changing menus offer a slate of classic dishes with a few modern twists, as in tortellini of game with Stilton in a vegetable broth (£5.25), roast chicken breast with sage and fennel crust (£11.75), and grilled fillet of sea bass with cumin and saffron. Fixed-price menu also

available Tue to Fri (£19.95). House wine £10.95. Open Tue to Sat D.

● **BARNSLEY** (South Yorkshire)

Blah Blah Blah 1 Market Hill, (01226) 734195. 'A welcome addition to the Barnsley central scene', with a kitchen headed by émigrés from the Fourth Floor, Harvey Nichols in Leeds (see entry). Hot panini and 'chunky sarnies' (from £4) are handy for snacking, but the menu extends to salads and hot dishes ranging from penne with Parma ham and chilli jam to roast salmon fillet with chive mash and white wine sauce (£8.50). A few simple desserts like treacle tart. Duboeuf house wine is £8.95. Open Mon and Tue 11.30 to 2.30, Wed to Sat 11.30 to 6.30.

● **BARTON UPON HUMBER** (North Lincolnshire)

Elio's 11 Market Place, (01652) 635147. Choose between the covered courtyard and the intimate dining room in this long-serving Humberside favourite. Pizzas and other trattoria staples are regulars, but 'one can rarely fault' Elio's fresh fish specials: tagliolini with baby clams and chilli (£5.55), a trio of grilled tuna, halibut and salmon with olives and capers (£16), and ever-popular Dover sole have all been appreciated. Chocolate trifle (£4.75) is a popular dessert. All-Italian service and a decent regional wine list, with prices from £11.50. Accommodation. Open Mon to Sat D.

● **BATCOMBE** (Somerset)

Three Horseshoes Batcombe, (01749) 850359. Look for Batcombe church if you are aiming for this spacious, food-orientated Somerset stone pub. Fish specials like grilled tuna with wild mushrooms and spiced sauté potatoes add fizz to the menu, which offers the likes of smoked chicken, smoked duck and avocado salad (£5.75) and medallions of beef with Devon Blue cheese glaze and shallot jus (£17). Finish with apple and blueberry crumble or crème brûlée with cherries (£4.50). West Country real ales and some very decent wines from £11.40. Open all week.

● **BATH** (Bath & N. E. Somerset)

Firehouse Rotisserie 2 John Street, (01225) 482070. Vibrant cooking with a transatlantic accent is the deal in this buzzy city-centre venue. The eponymous rôtisserie and grill deliver everything from Texas-spiced chicken

with jalapeño coleslaw and hickory-smoked barbecue dip (£10.95) to Pacific crab and salmon cakes with avocado salsa. Pizzas emanate from a brick-fired oven, and there are 'small plates' of Caesar salad with tempura shrimps (£8.50) and stone-baked mozzarella in prosciutto. 'Slick informal service.' House wine is £12.95. There's a branch in Anchor Square, Bristol, tel: (0117) 915 7323. Closed Sun D.

Hop Pole 7 Albion Buildings, (01225) 446327. One of the few places in Bath where you can eat outside, this dining pub – with restaurant housed in a former skittle alley – is popular whatever the weather. Lunch brings pub stalwarts like home-cooked ham, egg and chips (£6.95) and sausages and mash (£7.95), but the short dinner menu reveals more ambition: begin with duck rillettes and pickles (£4.95), before chump of local lamb, Greek salad and salsa verde (£12.95) or well-reported roast belly pork. Finish with dark chocolate mousse (£4.95). House wine is £10.50. Closed Mon.

Woods 9–13 Alfred Street, (01225) 314812. The Woods have been custodians of this 'elegant' restaurant since 1979 and the place continues to please. The kitchen pulls in ideas from everywhere, say a starter of lemon and chilli polenta, marinated sardines and red pepper reduction (£5.75) from the carte, to a well-reported chicken ballottine with pork and apricot stuffing from the set lunch menu (two courses £9.50). There's also a good-value weekday dinner menu (£14.50 for two courses). House wine £13.75. Closed Sun D.

● **BATTLE** (East Sussex)

Pilgrims 1 High Street, (01424) 772314. Once a shelter for pilgrims visiting the abbey, this historic Wealden hall house is now a crusader for local produce, offering all kinds of options, including breakfast, afternoon teas and cocktails with canapés. Seared Rye Bay scallops with balsamic dressing and Appledore salad leaves (£8.50) makes a decent starter, while main courses take in saddle of Brightling venison with rhubarb compote and spinach (£18.50) or blackened whole sea bass with herbs. Seasonal local berries figure among desserts, along with white chocolate and praline trifle (£5.75). House French £10.95. Closed Sun D.

● **BEMBRIDGE** (Isle of Wight)
Net Sherbourne Street, 01983 875800. New owners have started well at this casual, modern-looking restaurant in the centre of – reputedly – 'the largest village in Britain'. Fish from the Bembridge boats is a good bet (grilled lobster with garlic butter and whole sea bass have been appreciated), otherwise the menu tries to please all-comers with burgers and wraps (from £5.50), pasta (from £7.25) and chargrills like lamb steaks marinated in rosemary, garlic and balsamic vinegar (£11). Good home-made sweets like tarte au citron. 'Bouncy ambience', friendly young staff and fairly priced wines. Open Tue to Sat L and D, Sun L.

● **BERWICK-UPON-TWEED**
(Northumberland)
No 1 Sallyport Off Bridge Steet, (01289) 308827. Not a restaurant, but a 'mini-boutique hotel' offering B&B and 'rustic French provincial suppers' by prior arrangement (three courses £27.50). Join other guests round a big oak table, help yourself from the tureen of soup before hearty main courses based on local produce (leg of Lammermuir lamb with bacon, mint, red wine and tomatoes); conclude with warm lemon tart or some Keen's cheddar. No wine list, but BYO (£1 corkage per person). Open all week D only.

● **BIGBURY-ON-SEA** (Devon)
The Oyster Shack Milburn Orchard Farm, Stakes Hill, (01548) 810876. A summertime favourite, where you can sit outside and enjoy impeccably fresh fish served by laid-back young staff. Avon oysters au naturel are fine (six for £5), but also look for specials like crab soup, 'lordly' Dover sole (£13), and brill with creamy crayfish sauce. Finish with St Emilion chocolate pot (£4) or local ice creams. Bring your own wine (£2 corkage). Open Tue to Sun; check directions.

● **BIRKENHEAD** (Merseyside)
The Station 24-28 Hamilton Street, (0151) 647 1047. Ideally sited adjacent to Hamilton Square station, this enterprising set-up comprises a food store, brasserie and hotel rolled into one. New chef Kevin Perry is staying on track with a straightforward menu

that runs from confit of duck salad (£4.50) through roast monkfish with salsa verde and provençale potatoes (£13) to chocolate and lime cheesecake (£3.50). Carefully selected, interesting wines from £12. Open Tue to Sat L, Wed to Sat D. Under the same ownership as Ziba at the Racquet Club (see Main entry, Liverpool).

● **BIRMINGHAM** (West Midlands)
Lasan 3–4 Dakota Buildings, (0121) 212 3664. Cream walls, bare tables and sculptural white chairs create a cool, very contemporary and smart look for this modern Indian restaurant. The short menu mixes familiar samosas, lamb rogan gosht, and chicken jalfrezi (£8.95), with more unusual dishes such as pan-fried red mullet on kachamber salad with lemon oil (£4.60), and pan-fried black bream with spinach, baby aubergine and mild malabari sauce (£8.25). House wine is £13.95. Open Mon to Sat D only.
Le Petit Blanc 9 Brindleyplace, (0121) 633 7333. 'A welcome addition to the good food cognoscenti of the district' is one verdict on this brasserie in upwardly fashionable Brindleyplace. Like other branches (see Round-ups under Cheltenham, Manchester, Oxford and Tunbridge Wells), it offers speedy lunches, fixed-price deals, children's menus and many dishes with the Raymond Blanc stamp. Expect deep-fried goats' cheese with French bean salad (£6.50), roast rack of Cornish lamb with grilled aubergine (£17), and desserts such as lemon parfait with cherry coulis (£5). Predominantly French wines from £12.95. Open all week.
San Carlo 4 Temple Street, (0121) 633 0251. A modern city-centre ristorante/pizzeria offering a menu that is a long run through pizzas, pasta and trattoria classics like saltimbocca alla romana. All tastes are indulged here, whether it's for prawn cocktail, spaghetti bolognese (£6) and fillet steak Rossini, or linguine with clams and prawns, calf's liver pan-fried with sage, white wine and butter (£13), or a vegetarian pizza (£9). Service, and kitchen, may wilt under pressure. House wines start at £15. Open all week.
Zinc Unit 6, Regency Wharf, (0121) 200 0620. Overlooking Birmingham's fashionably reborn Canal Basin, this branch of Zinc is instantly recognisable as part of the Conran

empire. The décor is emblazoned with trademark design features and the bar is a grazer's paradise for those who like tapas and 'light bites'. Steaks and crustacea feature on the restaurant menu, alongside crispy duck spring roll (£6.50), sea bass fillet with buttered leeks and new potatoes (£14.50) and passion-fruit tart (£4). Compact, keenly priced wine list (from £12.50) with almost everything by the glass. Open all week; Sun drinks only after 8pm.

● **BISHOP'S STORTFORD** (Hertfordshire)
Lemon Tree Water Lane, (01279) 757788. Relaxed restaurant tucked away in a Georgian terrace just off the town's main drag. Distinctively named '7lt' one-course lunches are a snip at £7.95 (including a drink), and fixed-price menus provide plenty of options. The kitchen turns its hand to wide-ranging bistro dishes such as Caesar-style salad with crisp Parma ham (£6.50), breast of duck with black pudding, Puy lentils and roast beetroot (£13), and iced strawberry semifreddo with macerated strawberries (£4.50). House wines from £11. Closed Sun D and Mon.

● **BISPHAM GREEN** (Lancashire)
Eagle & Child Malt Kiln Lane, (01257) 462297. Hop-garlanded beams set the tone in this rural country pub a few miles off the M6. From the 'pub grub' menu and more promising daily specials board, reporters have applauded sea bass fillet with chickpeas, shrimps and capers (£12) and a mighty helping of sautéed suckling pig with paprika, button onions and mushrooms. Start with smoked chicken and wild mushroom risotto (£5) and finish with raspberry tart (£4). Creditable real ales and a workmanlike wine list from £10. Open all week.

● **BODSHAM** (Kent)
Froggies at the Timber Batts School Lane, (01233) 750237. Deeply rural, fifteenth-century English village pub now in the hands of a well-respected French chef/proprietor. Blackboard menus (written in word-perfect untranslated Français) focus on country classics like moules farcies (stuffed mussels, £6.50), selle d'agneau rôti (roast saddle of lamb, £16), and sole de Douvres meunière, with desserts including tarte Tatin and profiteroles (£5) to follow. Bar meals, good real ales, local cider and regional Gallic wines

from £12 – not forgetting 'perfect views'. Closed Sun D and all Mon. Reports please.

● **BOURNEMOUTH** (Dorset)
Bistro on the Beach Southbourne Coast Road, (01202) 431473. Celebrating its tenth birthday this year, this beachside 'bistro with attitude' is a snack bar during the day, and morphs into a 'candlelit' restaurant on Wednesday to Saturday evenings (and Tue in summer). Set meals (£16.50 for two courses, £18.50 for three) offer plenty of options and concentrate on local ingredients, maybe beetroot and cumin soup with soured cream, followed by grilled black bream fillet, orange and bean sprout salad and honey dressing. House wine is £10.95.
Chef Hong Kong 150 Old Christchurch Road, (01202) 316996. Yellow walls and red lanterns add colour to the simple and unfussy dining room of this popular (including among members of the Chinese community, judging by our visit) Chinese restaurant. The food is the star here, along with the genuinely warm and friendly service. Dim sum is the real thing, but the main menu also delivers to a high standard: stuffed bean curd with minced prawn in oyster sauce (£5.95) has impressed, or there is sliced honey-roast pork Chinese style (£5.25), and roasted duck in plum sauce (£.6.25). House wine is £9.95.
Westbeach Pier Approach, 01202 587785. Superbly located right on the promenade and with large windows overlooking the beach, this modern restaurant is clearly on good form – judging by recent reports. Fish is a strength, with daily-changing specials ranging from petit fruit de mer (£10) to oven-baked John Dory stuffed with ginger, lime and coriander (£18), but lunch brings a prime burger with all the trimmings (£8.50), and the fixed-price evening menu (£21.95 for two courses, three £24.95) can include steak with béarnaise sauce. To finish, brownies are highly recommended. Open all week.

● **BOURTON-ON-THE-WATER** (Gloucestershire)
Dial House The Chestnuts, (01451) 822244. Personable family-run Costwold hotel with a pretty cottage garden and a seventeenth-century sundial in its porch. New chef Daniel Bunce spends time transforming good raw materials into dishes like warm terrine of

goats' cheese with dried figs and chive oil (£7), halibut fillet with fennel barigoule, caramelised garlic and langoustine beignet (£19), and iced honey and muesli parfait with praline ice cream (£8). House wine £12.95. Open all week.

● **BOVINGDON GREEN** (Buckinghamshire)
Royal Oak Bovingdon Green, (01628) 488611. Younger brother of the Alford Arms (see Main entry, Frithsden), with a cosy real ale bar and a flexible attitude to food. Pick from the regular menu or daily specials board, and eat anywhere. Fashionable 'small plates' are handy at lunchtime (warm monkfish tart with béarnaise sauce, £6.50), while those with bigger appetites could choose braised pork belly with chickpea, butterbean and chorizo stew (£11.25), or roast vegetable Wellington. Close proceedings with, say, Walnut Whip fool (£4.75). Well-spread, drinkable wines from £10.75. Open all week.

● **BRAMFIELD** (Suffolk)
Queen's Head The Street, (01986) 784214. The naming of suppliers adds a twist to the menus in this Suffolk-pink pub/restaurant overlooking Bramfield's unusual thatched village church. Local and organic ingredients play their part in dishes like Aldeburgh asparagus with melted butter (£4), Northend Farm Gloucester Old Spot pork steaks with blackcurrant sauce (£11), and mackerel with gooseberry sauce. Finish with Larksfield Cottage apple crumble or home-made ice cream. Real ales and wines come courtesy of Adnams of Southwold. Three-tiered, child-friendly garden. Open all week.

● **BRIGHTON & HOVE** (East Sussex)
Due South 139 Kings Road Arches, (01273) 821218. Underneath the arches and between the two piers, Due South is right in the heart of the seafront action, with terrific views out to sea from the outside terrace. The original arched ceiling lends character, and the kitchen is open to view from the small downstairs bar. Start with red mullet fillets with lemon pickle (£7.95), then tenderloin of pork with potato and garlic purée and Middle Farm cider cream sauce (£12.95), and finish with summer pudding with vanilla cream. Local ingredients are prominent on the menu; house wine is £12.95. Open all week.

Momma Cherri's Soul Food Shack 11 Little East Street, (01273) 774545. Tucked away on the fringes of the Laines, just back from the seafront, is Brighton's little bit of soul. Both food and music can be experienced in this small, lively restaurant with basic décor, warm service and character by the bucket-load. Brunch is recommended – the 'real soul food breakfast' (£7.50) capable of reviving those flagging from the excesses of the night before. Otherwise it runs the gamut from jambalaya (£13) to Lupita's fajita's (£10.50), and from B.J.'s Southern fried catfish to soulful veggie lasagne bake (£9). Drink US beers or wines starting at £11.50. Open Fri to Sun L, all week D.

Moshi Moshi Sushi Bartholomew Square, (01273) 719195. Sussex branch of the London-based sushi group (see London Round-up), following the same formula. Colour-coded plates (priced from £1.25 to £3.50) pass by on the conveyor belt (kaiten), with nigiri, maki and sashimi as the main contenders. Also 'double-decker' bento boxes (£14.50), and a selection of hot and cold Japanese tapas, from gyoza dumplings and yakitori to kakuni (marinated poached tuna with ginger and soy dressing). Drink, beer, saké or wine (from £11.50). Closed Mon.

● **BRIXHAM** (Devon)
Pilgrims Restaurant 64B Fore Street, (01803) 853983. Promising family-run venue in touristy, nautical Brixham, designed to look like the cabin of an ancient galleon (i.e. the Mayflower). Local fish in the shape of seafood chowder (£5.50), grilled scallops with Thai spices and roast skate wing in Moroccan tomato sauce (£12.75); also sauté Devon duck breast with cumin and ratatouille and desserts such as crème brûlée with rhubarb compote (£4.75). Extravagantly described wines from £10.50. Open Thurs to Sat L, Tue to Sat D.

● **BROMFIELD** (Shropshire)
Cookhouse Bromfield, (01584) 856565. This restaurant on the A49 north of Ludlow meets a wide range of culinary needs. The 'interesting, buzzing' brasserie-cum-café runs through the repertoire from croque-monsieur (£6.95) and fish and chips to smoked haddock rarebit and slow-roast shank of lamb (£8.95), while the more formal restaurant offers a set-price menu (three courses £25) of things like local organic

smoked salmon with honey, mustard and dill sauce, grilled lemon sole with asparagus, and vanilla crème brûlée. House wine is £10.75. Open all week.

● **BROXTON** (Cheshire)
Frogg Manor Nantwich Road, (01829) 782629. Hundreds of imitation frogs, nostalgic recorded music and a larger-than-life host create the mood in this lavishly furnished, bourgeois Georgian manor. Eccentric menus, but sound cooking based on decent local ingredients. Expect, say, black pudding Winston Churchill (with poached egg), chicken Cleopatra (cooked in goats' milk with mild curry sauce), whole turbot, and pear Malibu (with cream Florentine and drizzled chocolate). Table d'hôte £20/£25, dinner menu '30 guineas'. Accommodation available. Open Sun L and all week D by reservation.

● **BURGH ĪE MARSH** (Lincolnshire)
Windmill 46 High Street, (01754) 810281. Trips to Normandy provide ingredients and inspiration for the menus in the Fleischers' friendly restaurant a few miles from Skegness. You could start with black pudding and bacon on creamed leeks, proceed to braised oxtail in red wine sauce or poached salmon hollandaise, and close the show with home-made apple and Calvados ice cream. Home-baked bread uses flour from the listed windmill nearby. Three courses £20-£24, house wines from £10.95 and vintage ports aplenty. Open Sun L and Tue to Sat D.

● **BURY ST EDMUNDS** (Suffolk)
The Angel Hotel 3 Angel Hill, (01284) 714000. Creeper-clad fifteenth-century coaching inn that is a fixture of Bury's social scene. Views of the Norman gates are to be had in the formal Abbeygate Restaurant, where you will find modern European cooking. Fixed-price dinners (£26.50) could take in salmon boudin with pink ginger beurre blanc, breast of duck with roasted apricots and thyme, and vanilla cheesecake with rhubarb compote. Twenty-two wines by the glass from £3.20 (£12.95 a bottle). Alternatively, eat casual brasserie food in the subterranean Vaults. Open all week.

● **CAMBER** (East Sussex)
The Place New Lydd Road, (01797) 225057. 'A unique position in the SE', across the road from Camber Sands dunes and close to Pontins holiday camp. Equally geared up for young holidaying families and business conferences. Locally sourced ingredients, including fish 'from non-threatened species': expect anything from dressed crab with aïoli (£7.50) and roast sea bream with tamarind, lemongrass, ginger and garlic to grilled guinea fowl with salsa verde, braised peas and organic mash (£13). Finish with a brûlée or pavlova (£4.50). Two dozen keenly priced wines from £10.95. B&B accommodation in 18 rooms. Open all week L and D.

● **CANTERBURY** (Kent)
Lloyd's 89–90 St Dunstan's Street, (01227) 768222. Stylish-looking contemporary venue right by Westgate's impressive medieval stone arch. The monthly menu concentrates on French-inspired dishes in the shape of duck foie gras with summer fruit chutney (£8), followed by salmon in puff pastry with pommes dauphinois and tarragon sauce (£14.75) or roast rack of lamb. Desserts in similar vein might range from caramelised banana bavarois (£6.50) to a special 'chocolate plate'. Fixed-price lunch menus £10/£13.50. Two dozen wines from £13.75. Open all week.

● **CARTERWAY HEADS** (Northumberland)
Manor House Inn Carterway Heads, (01207) 255268. Derwent Water is just a walk away from this rough-hewn stone pub, which also boasts stunning views over the surrounding countryside. Blackboard specials augment the standard menu, which might run along the lines of warm salad of smoked bacon and mange-tout (£4.50), Cajun-blackened salmon with salsa (£12), and lamb cutlets with port and cranberry jus, plus desserts such as fig and almond cake (£3.50). Well-kept real ales and some very drinkable wines from £10.50. Accommodation available. Open all week.

● **CASTLE DONINGTON** (Leicestershire)
Nags Head Inn Hill Top, (01332) 850652. A reliable pit-stop if your destination is Castle Donington motor-racing circuit or East Midlands airport. The kitchen does a good line in upbeat pub food, with dishes like bacon and poached egg salad with garlic croûtons (£5.25), blackened swordfish with crème fraîche and lime (£15) or duck breast with pak choi and curry oil. Snacks and sandwiches are served lunchtimes and early evening; desserts could run to chocolate rum torte. Most wines

on the shortish list are under £20. Open Mon to Sat L and D.

● **CHELTENHAM** (Gloucestershire)
Mayflower 32–34 Clarence Street, (01242) 522426. Cheltenham's Chinese favourite, run by the Kong family since 1982. Mother and son work the kitchen, and their familiar menus carefully avoid esoteric ingredients. Sesame prawn toasts (£5.50) and sizzling mixed seafood (£12.50) have been well received; otherwise expect anything from roast duck with ginger and spring onions to braised bean curd and vegetable hotpot. Accessible set menus, and a global wine list offering plenty of choice, with house French £11.95. Open all week.

Le Petit Blanc Queen's Hotel, (01242) 266800. Lively brasserie in what was once the ballroom of Cheltenham's elegant Queen's Hotel. It follows the chain formula (see Round-ups under Birmingham, Manchester, Oxford and Tunbridge Wells) with flexible menus, a positive attitude to kids and good-value fixed-price deals offering dishes such as lamb croquants with potato salad, poached baby plaice with spring vegetables, and desserts like nougat and apricot parfait. Main-course prices from the carte are around £10.50 to £17.50. The wine list is Raymond Blanc's personal selection from the new breed of French vineyards; prices from £12.95. Open all week.

● **CHESTER** (Cheshire)
Brasserie 10/16 Brookdale Place, (01244) 322288. Cheerful informality is a bonus at this sibling of the Brasserie, Hawarden (see Main entry, Wales). The kitchen soaks up influences from near and far, but recent results have been patchy. Chicken, chorizo and sun-dried tomato salad (£4), roast cod with mash, red pepper jam and pesto (£10) and desserts such as profiteroles or raspberry ripple cheesecake show the style. All sorts of daytime offers, from 'classic sandwiches' to a 'two-course rapido'. House wines from £9.95. Open all week.

● **CHESTERFIELD** (Derbyshire)
Old Post Restaurant 43 Holywell Street, (01246) 279479. Located in the market town of Chesterfield the Old Post is set in a fifteenth-century building, and run by a 'dedicated and hardworking couple'. Home-made bread and a moderately priced wine list support a menu

that offers the likes of lasagne of red mullet, quail's eggs and champagne sabayon (£6.50) and ballotine of pheasant and foie gras (£17). Desserts have included an enjoyable treacle tart. Open Tue to Fri and Sun L, Tue to Sat D.

● **CHICHESTER** (West Sussex)
Comme Ca 67 Broyle Road, (01243) 788724. Treat yourself to a spell of French leave in Michel and Jane Navet's converted pub. Resolutely Gallic menu with English subtitles, along the lines of Gascogne duck foie gras terrine with apple and grape chutney (£8), roast local sea bass with rosemary velouté (£13.50), and chateaubriand with béarnaise and red wine sauce (£30 for two), followed by 'desserts du moment' (£6). Traditional 'French family lunches' on Sun; also handy for pre-and post-theatre dinners. Open Wed to Sun L, Tue to Sat D.

● **CHRISTMAS COMMON** (Oxfordshire)
Fox and Hounds Christmas Common, (01491) 612599. Nicknamed 'The Top Fox', this Chilterns hostelry has been transformed from country inn to high-profile gastro-pub without sacrificing its time-honoured virtues. Food is high on the agenda. Curried parsnip soup (£5.50) and steak and kidney pie please the die-hards, while more adventurous palates might be stimulated by goats' cheese crostini with basil oil, pan-fried tuna with Asian coleslaw (£13) and pork medallions with black pudding, baby spinach and nutmeg mash, followed by pannacotta. Brakspears ales and 30 affordable wines from £11. Open all week.

● **CHURCH STRETTON** (Shropshire)
The Studio 59 High Street, (01694) 722672. Former artist's studio, now a restaurant with hands-on owners offering a good line in straightforward food based on good ingredients. There's a refreshing simplicity about local asparagus with hollandaise sauce, roast monkfish with griddled Mediterranean vegetables and tomato and basil sauce, and strawberry and cream meringue stack. Main courses £12.95 to £15.95. Wines open at £10.95 and struggle to get above £20. Open Tue to Sat D and Sun L.

● **COLWALL STONE** (Herefordshire)
Colwall Park Walwyn Road, (01684) 540000. Sprawling mock-Tudor village inn, now a popular hotel in the grand-bourgeois Victorian fashion. Chef James Garth returned

to head the kitchen shortly before our deadline, but his menu promises the likes of seared scallops with cauliflower purée and sherry caramel (£7.25), and roast fillet of Hereford organic pork with cabbage and bacon, apple fondant and sage juices (£17), followed by hot apricot soufflé with coconut and rum ice cream (£8). Interesting wine list with house selections £12.99. Open Sun L and all week D.

● **CONSTANTINE** (Cornwall)
Trengilly Wartha Nancenoy, (01326) 340332. One couple discovered this 'jovial' country inn while 'walking on the coastal path from Penzance to Plymouth'; others might need a map or directions. The location – in a remote wooded valley – is a big plus, but most seek it out for the high standard of food and drink. Menus take account of local produce eg. roast beetroot and Vulscombe goats' cheese salad (£4.50), confit of Cornish lamb with haricot bean and gammon ragoût (£13), and chocolate terrine with brandied cherries and clotted cream. Beers, ciders and an enthusiastically assembled wine list from £10.50. Accommodation available. Open all week.

● **CORSCOMBE** (Dorset)
Fox Inn Corscombe, (01935) 891330. Old thatched pub in a web of winding lanes, with climbing roses out front and lots of country artefacts inside. Fish specials are the main attraction – say, Thai-style hot shellfish with crab, clams and prawns (£18.50) or whole grilled plaice with herb butter. Otherwise, the kitchen turns its hand to warm salad of black pudding and bacon (£6.50) and rump steak with wild mushroom sauce, followed by a handful of desserts (around £3.50). Worldwide wine list, with prices from £11. Open all week.

● **CROWCOMBE** (Somerset)
The Carew Arms Crowcombe, (01984) 618631. A comprehensive makeover is breathing new life and vigour into this 'time-warp gem' of a village pub. Chef Barrie Tucker's CV includes stints at Chez Nico and the Castle Hotel, Taunton (see Main entry) and it shows: expect a classy mix of modern and traditional dishes, e.g. crab remoulade with celeriac mayonnaise (£5.75) and chicken breast with creamed leeks and black pudding (£10.50), followed by desserts like home-made Turkish delight (£4.50). Fifty-strong wine list peppered with reputable vintages; prices from £11. Accommodation available. Open all week. Reports please.

● **DIDMARTON** (Gloucestershire)
Kings Arms Inn The Street, (01454) 238245. The kitchen at this seventeenth-century coaching inn cares about ingredients (local venison, and locally made sausages, for example), with the cooking revolving around seasonal menus. Dishes have a contemporary flavour as in salad of roasted artichoke, fresh asparagus and pesto (£5.95), pan-fried fillet of sea bass on seafood risotto with lemon and saffron dressing (£12.95), or roast breast of Gressingham duck with pak choi, banana shallots and quince (£15.50). House wines start at £10.95 with 14 by the glass. Accommodation. Open all week.

● **DISS** (Norfolk)
Weavers Wine Bar Market Hill, (01379) 642411. Set in a heavily timbered fifteenth-century building that was once a chapel, Weavers serves the denizens of Diss with flexible, good-value eating options. Steak, kidney and mushroom pie is familiar enough, but more novel is lightly poached breast of pigeon with fresh mango and sweet cherry tomatoes with Muscatel glaze and curry oil. Vegetarians have a choice of four or so main courses. Menu prix fixe is £16.95 for three courses, house wine £11.95. Open Tue to Fri L and Mon to Sat D.

● **DODDISCOMBSLEIGH** (Devon)
Nobody Inn Doddiscombsleigh, (01647) 252394. Quaint-looking fifteenth-century thatched inn famed for its breathtaking selection of more than 50 West Country cheeses, around 200 whiskies and a gargantuan 800-strong wine list (including over 20 by the glass). Restaurant dinner menus advertise a smoked fish platter with beetroot salad (£6), silverside of veal with ratatouille (£11.50) and stem ginger pudding with ginger sauce (£5). Similar dishes can be eaten more cheaply in the bar. Accommodation available. Restaurant open Tue to Sat D only; bar food available every day.

● **DONHEAD ST ANDREW** (Wiltshire)
Forester Lower Street, (01747) 828038. Smartly thatched, lovingly re-vamped

Wiltshire village inn offering fine real ales and modern pub food. New chef Tom Shaw worked at the Angel Inn, Hindon (see Main entry), and his talents show in dishes like pan-fried Brixham crab cake with piri-piri dressing (£6.75), roast saddle of venison with braised red cabbage and sloe gin, and – for vegetarians – tagliatelle with artichokes and oyster mushrooms (£9). Warm poached pear with caramelised figs is a typical dessert. Two dozen wines from £10.95. Open all week.

● **DORCHESTER** (Dorset)

Sienna 36 High West Street, (01305) 250022. Tiny, bright new restaurant run as a husband-and-wife double act. Modern paintings, orange fittings and frosted glass windows provide the backdrop for some enthusiastically endorsed cooking. Typical dishes are tartlet of roast baby beets, spinach and spring onion with mascarpone and Parmesan, fillet of turbot with tagliatelle, langoustines, saffron and peas, then orange terrine with kumquat marmalade. Lunch from £13, dinner from £24. France looms large on the well-spread wine list; bottles from £12. Closed Sun and Mon.

● **DUNHAMPTON** (Worcestershire)

Epic Bar/Brasserie Ombersley Road, (01905) 620000. One of Patrick McDonald's group of chic Midlands brasseries. Like its relatives, the menu races through starters (antipasti, £6.75), salads, pasta (salmon and basil tagliatelle, £6/£10) and pizzas. There are also more substantial items like Moroccan-style spiced lamb with couscous (£14) and a few puddings including hot chocolate fondant (£5.75). Organic children's menu. Forty wines from £11.25. Open all week (drinks only Sun D). Branches in Stoke Prior (see Round-up entry) and at Station Road, Whitacre Heath, Warwickshire, tel: (01675) 462181.

● **DURHAM** (Co Durham)

Almshouses Palace Green, (0191) 3861054. 'Lovely setting, ancient building, part old-fashioned tea shop, part restaurant', noted one correspondent. Dishes from the world larder such as tofu, olive and walnut pâté (£5), lamb curry, and roast fillet of smoked haddock with saffron risotto and roasted tomatoes (£6.50) could be followed by lemon and almond polenta cake (£2.50). Filled rolls and cakes; coffees and teas, too; house wine £11.50.

Handy for the cathedral. Open all week 9am to 5pm (8pm June-Aug).

Pump House Farm Road, Haughall (0191) 386 9189. Seafood and steak restaurant in a converted Victorian pump house on the fringes of Durham. Old-style 'faded red' décor, but a mix of classic and contemporary dishes from Caesar salad and 'surf and turf' to aromatic duck leg on oriental risotto (£6.50) and monkfish in Parma ham with ratatouille and pesto (£14.50), plus desserts like chocolate tart with orange custard (£5). Cocktails, champagnes and a short list of global wines from £12.50. Open all week.

● **EAST COKER** (Somerset)

Heylar Arms Moor Lane, (01935) 862332. In a 'wonderful village setting' surrounded by thatched cottages, this cheerful hostelry strikes a good balance between dining and its status as the village pub. The likes of roasted rack of North Petherton lamb flies the flag for local produce on the seasonal restaurant menu (three courses for £23.50), which runs to deep-fried Capricorn goats' cheese, roast breast of corn-fed chicken with runner beans, Parmentier potatoes and tarragon cream, and gooseberry and rhubarb fool. Lighter meals run to soup, ploughman's and fishcakes. House wine is £10.95. Accommodation. Open all week.

● **EAST LAVANT** (West Sussex)

Royal Oak Pooks Lane, (01243) 527434. Transformed from a one-room village local into a sophisticated pub/restaurant with a cosy atmosphere and a good line in modern food. Start with duck spring roll, glass noodles and cucumber salsa (£7), move on to salmon and cod fishcakes with spinach and parsley sauce (£12.50) and finish with, say, orange and passion-fruit tart with caramelised kiwi fruit (£5.50). Bar snacks also served at lunchtime. House wines from £11. Handy for Goodwood and the South Downs; accommodation available. Open all week.

● **EPPING** (Essex)

Clocktower 4 Station Road, (01992) 575707. 'A classy act in an area not known for its restaurants.' Breakfast and light meals are served till 5, with a full menu from noon until close. Recent successes have included mixed mushrooms in garlic butter (£4.50), herb-crusted tuna with new potatoes and olives

(£12), and warm chocolate brownie with ice cream and chocolate sauce (£3.50). Attentive staff in 'perpetual motion'. House wine £11.50. Open all week from 11am. The original is at Budworth Hall, Chipping Ongar.

● **ETON** (Berkshire)

Gilbey's 82-83 High Street, (01753) 855182. Auspiciously sandwiched between Eton College and Windsor Castle, close to the Thames, this is one of a trio of all-round bar/ bistros (see Round ups, Amersham and London). The formula is much the same, with two-course lunches (£10.95) and a menu that embraces smoked salmon and sole roulade (£6.50), pan-roasted duck breast with pak choi, sweet potato and mango and chilli salsa (£14.50) and roasted pear brûlée (£5). The wine list revolves around French bottles imported directly by the Gilbey Group (prices from £10.55). Open all week.

● **EVESHAM** (Worcestershire)

Evesham Hotel Cooper's Lane, (01386) 765566. John Jenkinson and family have resided in this idiosyncratic Cotswold hotel since 1975. Their kitchen goes walkabout for lively menus peppered with quirky names and global inventions, viz. Chinese-style fritters with pork and sweetcorn (£5.75), keema meatballs, 'king crusty' (salmon and crab cake with lime butter sauce, £14) and spiced Sangria jelly (£4.75). The drinks list is a wonder to behold: over 600 wines catalogued in three photograph albums, aperitifs, hangover cures and other specialist beverages. Open all week L and D.

● **EXETER** (Devon)

Carved Angel Café 21A Cathedral Yard, (01392) 210303. Lively, modern all day café that takes an international route on its menu. Start the day with smoked salmon and scrambled eggs (served between 9am to midday), or hold on until lunch when soup and sandwiches vie with omelettes, goats' cheese salad and oriental duck confit pizza. Dinner brings caramelised onion tart (£5.50), turbot with Thai-style curry (£13.95), and cappuccino crème brûlée. House wine is £11.75. Closed Sun D.

St Olaves Hotel Mary Arches Street, (01392) 217736. Grade II listed Georgian merchant's house, now an intimate hotel in the oldest part of the city within walking distance of the cathedral. Fixed-price dinners (£26/£29.50) could open with game terrine and beetroot chutney, before fillet of sea bass with orange-roast salsify or wild mushroom risotto. Desserts like baked lemon-curd Alaska, and Bramley apple crumble are followed by West Country cheeses. Pub-style bar menu also available. House wine is £14. Open all week.

● **EXFORD** (Somerset)

The Crown Exford, (01643) 831554. There's a comfortable, old fashioned look to this gabled building set in a tiny village in the heart of Exmoor National Park. Dinner in the restaurant (£32.50 for three courses) could include slow-roasted fillet steak served with fricassee of artichokes, wild mushrooms and Madeira jus, followed by a 'clean tasting' consommé of summer fruit, orange jelly and sorbet. Food in the Crown bar offers simpler ideas, say minute steak with onion tart and salad (£8.95). House wine £14.95 (£3.50 a glass.) Open all week D and Sun L.

● **FOWEY** (Cornwall)

Fowey Hall Hotel & Restaurant Hanson Drive, (01726) 833866. Grand hotel high above the estuary with some of the most desirable views in town. Fixed-price menus (lunch £17.50, dinner £32.50) feature Cornish fish, ranging from Fowey oysters to grilled mackerel with plum tomato and tarragon polenta and pesto dressing. Local meat is deployed for dishes like grilled lamb cutlets with rosemary potatoes and a tartlet of creamed leeks, while peach tart with Calvados crème fraîche could appear for dessert. Substantial wine list including plenty of classic names; house selections from £15.50. Open all week.

Old Quay House 28 Fore Street, (01726) 833302. A thorough refurbishment in 2002 has brought the Old Quay House back to life as a smart and contemporary hotel. Natural colours and modern touches are in keeping with the building. The kitchen turns out a modish menu where seared local scallops are partnered with chorizo, broad-bean salad and lime oil as a starter (£6.50), and loin of Cornish lamb is stuffed with coriander and pine nuts and served with rosemary potatoes, spinach and red wine jus (£19.50). House wine is £11.50. Open Fri to Sun L, Tue to Sun D.

● **GEDNEY DYKE** (Lincolnshire)
Chequers Main Street, (01406) 362666. A beacon in the remote Fenland outback, a few miles inland from the Wash. Fish shows up in the shape of, say, crab and Parmesan tartlet with cucumber and balsamic dressing (£6); there's also a fondness for rare breeds (e.g. roast leg of Gloucester Old Spot pork with black cherry sauce, £10.50), while vegetarians might be offered spinach pancakes filled with provençale vegetables served with asparagus sauce. East Anglian real ales and a sizeable wine list with prices from £9.95. Closed Mon.

● **GILLAN** (Cornwall)
Tregildry Hotel Gillan, (01326) 231378. Glorious views over Falmouth Bay are a prime attraction at this family-run hotel high on the cliffs. Dinner menus change daily (four courses £25), although chargrilled ribeye steak is always available. Start with Cornish fish soup, before wild venison steak with cranberry sauce, tagliatelle and smoked bacon; desserts such as local ice creams or chocolate and Grand Marnier mousse are followed by West Country cheeses. House wines are £12.50. Open all week D only Mar to Oct.

● **GLEWSTONE** (Herefordshire)
Glewstone Court Glewstone, (01989) 770367. 'Croquet and Pimms are a happy pastime', say the owners of this lovingly run country-house hotel among orchards overlooking the Wye Valley. The kitchen employs local and organic produce for an international repertoire that encompasses crab cakes with sweet chilli sauce (£6), plates of tapas and grilled canon of Welsh lamb with leek and mint timbale and claret gravy (£14). Puddings range from ice creams to grape crème brûlée (£4.75). Lighter meals in the Bistro. Well-chosen wines from £11. Open all week.

● **GOOSNARGH** (Lancashire)
Solo Goosnargh, (01772) 865206. Since 1986, this comfortable restaurant in an eighteenth-century cottage has been a boon to the area. The cooking is consistent, soups are 'always smooth' and steak is 'some of the best'; otherwise look for piri-piri prawns (£6.25), pork loin with apples, sultanas and brandy (£13.75) and sea bass fillet with spring onions,

ginger and white wine. House wine £11.90. Open Sun L and Tue to Sat D.

● **GREAT HINTON** (Wiltshire)
The Linnet Great Hinton, (01380) 870354. Seriously re-vamped local Wiltshire watering hole, now an open-plan set-up with restaurant aspirations. Chef/landlord Jonathan Furby produces ambitious bistro-style dishes including chicken liver and roast black pudding parfait (£4.75), poached salmon fillet on a langoustine risotto with dill sauce (£11.75) and a gâteau of roasted artichokes, leeks, smoked cheese and sun-dried tomatoes. Desserts could feature plum and orange crème brûlée (£4.50). Light lunches available. Around 50 wines from £10.95. Open Tue to Sun L and D.

● **GREAT WHITTINGTON** (Northumberland)
Queens Head Great Whittington, (01434) 672267. Extended stone-built inn, in a charming village, where the emphasis is placed firmly on dining. The kitchen does a good line in modern food, with tempura of cod fillet showing up alongside honey-roast gammon with caramelised onions, Dijon mash and mustard sauce (£12). Start with deep-fried black pudding with salad and apple and raisin chutney (£6) or game terrine with red onion compote (£5.50). Wines start at £12.50. Closed Sun D and Mon.

● **GREAT YARMOUTH** (Norfolk)
Seafood Restaurant 85 North Quay, (01493) 856009. Old-school fish cookery in a converted pub by Yarmouth Quay. The Kikis family has been in residence since 1979 and a few native Greek dishes spice up their well-tried menu: prawn cocktail (£6) and goujons of plaice (£10) rub shoulders with the likes of wild sea bass, chilli, garlic and soy. Meat-eaters could be offered beef stroganoff, and desserts (£5) are veterans like raspberry pavlova. Whites rule the waves on the international wine list; prices from £9.75. Closed Sat L and all day Sun.

● **GRIMSTHORPE** (Lincolnshire)
Black Horse Inn Grimsthorpe, (01778) 591247. Dating from 1717, this fine inn stands in the lee of historic Grimsthorpe Castle. New owners have given the place a more relaxed feel. The menus change quarterly, but typical offerings might include smoked chicken with tapénade and quail's eggs (£5) and grilled tuna

steak with Mediterranean vegetables (£14), followed by desserts like strawberry cheesecake. The wine list is a serious slate promising many vintage treasures; house wines £11.95. Accommodation available. Closed Sun D.

● **HADDENHAM** (Buckinghamshire)
Green Dragon 8 Church Way, (01844) 291403. It may look like just another village pub, but this 350-year old hostelry now serves up interesting renditions of dishes old and new. Steak and kidney suet pudding (£9.95) sticks with tradition, but confit of duck leg with honey and black pepper glaze and pineapple chutney (£6.95) and fillet of monkfish, crushed new potatoes with chorizo and fish bisque (£13) give a modern twist to the menu. Fixed price deals for dinner (£11.95) on Tue and Thur are popular. House wine is £11.50. Closed Sun D.

● **HAMPTON COURT** (Surrey)
Hamptons Mitre Hotel, Hampton Court Road, (020) 8979 4740. Promising newcomer in a plum location within the Mitre Hotel, opposite Hampton Court Palace. Views of the Thames from the stunningly adorned dining room provide an enviable, 'romantic backdrop' to proceedings. Chef Russell Pollard worked for Marco-Pierre White, and the menu has noticeable MPW fingerprints. Reporters have endorsed chargrilled English asparagus with Parmesan and olive oil (£7.50), followed by poached fillet of smoked haddock with new potatoes and poached egg (£16.50), and crème brûlée with summer berries (£6.50). Closed Sat L, Sun D. Reports please.

● **HARROGATE** (North Yorkshire)
Quantro 3 Royal Parade, (01423) 503034. Contemporary brasserie that adds some fizz to the Harrogate scene with its typically forthright menu of classic and modern European dishes. Roast red mullet on saffron and caper vinaigrette (£4), whole wood pigeon on creamed cabbage with Madeira sauce, plus desserts like orange frangipane tart (£4.50) show the style. One-course lunches around £6 and 50 modern wines from £11.90 – including plenty by the glass. Open Mon to Sat. There's a sister restaurant at 62 Street Lane, Leeds; tel: (0113) 2888063.

● **HARROW** (Greater London)
Ram's 203 Kenton Road, (020) 8907 2022. Great-value Indian vegetarian food in bright minimalist surroundings a short walk from Kenton tube station. The Gujarati city of Surat is the inspiration for the menu, which has myriad starters like bhel puris (£3.20), patras and stuffed banana bhajias before specialities such as spinach paneer (£4.50), mung bean curry and dhal dokri. Interesting breads and ultra-cheap thalis, plus additional Surti specialities at weekends. Drink lemon soda, lassi or beer; house wine is £9.20 a bottle. Open all week.

● **HATFIELD PEVEREL** (Essex)
Blue Strawberry The Street, (01245) 381333. Essex 'bistrot' (with a new chef) in an old timbered house three miles from Chelmsford. Expect modern international dishes like swordfish niçoise or Chinese-spiced mussels (£6.50), followed by organic salmon with mango, lime and coriander couscous or rosemary-roasted rack of lamb (£15.50), plus desserts such as toffee and banana crème brûlée. Fixed-price weekday lunches from £9.50 (one course); set dinners (Mon-Thur, £18.95). Closed Sat L and Sun D.

● **HEREFORD** (Herefordshire)
Cafe @ All Saints All Saints Church, High Street, (01432) 370415. Enterprising café run as a fund-raising sideline for the upkeep of All Saints medieval church. The menu changes daily, but there's always a soup (fennel, green pea and mint £2.25) plus quiche, ploughman's, salads and a couple of hot dishes such as field mushroom and Dorothy Goodbody's ale pie with smoked Cheddar mash and Savoy cabbage (£6). Home-baked tarts and cakes (cranberry and marzipan, for example) are just the ticket with Italian Illy coffee; alcoholic beverages also available. Open Mon to Sat 8.30am to 5.30pm.

● **HEYTESBURY** (Wiltshire)
Angel High Street, (01985) 840330. Ancient coaching inn that's currently cutting a well-groomed look thanks to new owners and major refurbishment. Upmarket, chic tones are matched by a menu built around the chargrill – popeseye, ribeye, sirloin and fillet, served with a choice of flavoured butters or sauces – the carte (only available in the evening) calls other main courses 'alternative

choices'. These run to pan-fried liver with dry cured bacon and mash (£13.50), or whole roasted bream with café de Paris butter (£14.95). Accommodation. Open all week.

● **HIGHCLERE** (Hampshire)
Yew Tree Hollington Cross, (01635) 253360. Seventeenth-century inn that has been remodelled in sympathetic contemporary style. The kitchen follows the modern 'dining-pub' route with an emphatically upmarket menu: pigeon breast appears as a starter with green pea purée, port and tarragon jus (£7.25), mains might include sesame seed-coated salmon steak on basil risotto (£14) or fillet of beef with home-made chips and blue cheese sauce; desserts could feature chocolate and hazelnut semifreddo (£5). Custom-made 'vodka shots' and a compact wine list (from £10.95). Accommodation available. Open all week.

● **HOLY CROSS** (Worcestershire)
Bell and Cross Holy Cross, (01562) 730319. Tall-fronted, listed pub at the foot of the Clent Hills, with a bustling traditional bar and several dark-hued dining rooms. The long menu is supplemented by a fistful of hearty modern specials: for example, ham hock pâté with brandy, plum and fig compote (£5.50), daube of Cornish lamb with spicy sausage, and roast Highland cod with smoked haddock brandade and balsamic tomato (£12). Desserts range from treacle tart to tiramisù (£5). House wines from £11. Open all week.

● **HOLY ISLAND** (Northumberland)
Crown and Anchor Hotel The Market Square, (01289) 389215. Promising pub reached from the mainland by a tidal causeway (check local papers for times) offering a good line in straightforward food based on sound ingredients. Menus and blackboards offer sweet-cured mackerel fillets (£4.60), or fresh Holy Island crab (£6.80), and mains of stuffed breast of maize-fed chicken with herb sauce (£11.40) with passion-fruit cheesecake to finish. Interesting wines struggle to get over £20, otherwise drink Deuchars IPA. Closed Mon and Sun D.

● **HOUGHTON CONQUEST** (Bedfordshire)
Knife & Cleaver The Grove, (01234) 740387. More of a restaurant-with-rooms than a country pub, this place is worth noting in an area with few decent eating places. The

kitchen does a good line in reasonably priced bar food, like pork and Stilton sausages with parsnip and honey mash (£6.50), while fish is a big player on the menu offered in the conservatory dining room: say, grilled sea bass fillets with potatoes roasted with thyme and anchovies (£18). Alternatives might include duck confit or beef fillet Rossini. Good selection of wines under £20. Accommodation. Closed Sun D and bank hol Mon D.

● **HYTHE** (Kent)
Hythe Bay Fish Restaurant Marine Parade, (01303) 267024. A prime beachside location at this 'cheerful' restaurant, with a terraced area for al fresco dining, pulls in the crowds. Naturally, fish is the main focus on a menu that delivers pan-fried garlic prawns, plaice fillets with sautéed potatoes and warm apple and apricot strudel on its weekday 'quick lunch' menu (2 courses £10.95). Alternatively go for the shellfish platter of whelks, oysters, crab, prawns and cockles (£16.50). A blackboard lists the catch of the day. Service has been reported as 'unflappable'. The fish-friendly wine list opens at £11.95. Open Tue to Sun L (Mon L summer only) and Wed to Sat D.

● **ILMINGTON** (Warwickshire)
Howard Arms Lower Green, (01608) 682226. Four centuries old, this upmarket village pub serves up contemporary food along the lines of stuffed polenta mushrooms with tarragon and yoghurt sauce (£5), chargrilled spicy marinated lamb with sweet potato mash (£13.50) and cappuccino mouse with hazelnut biscotti (£5). Old favourites like beef, ale and mustard pie and steaks also put in an appearance. Creditable real ales and a good list of wines from £10.90. Open all week.

● **IPSWICH** (Suffolk)
Galley 25 St Nicholas Street, (01473) 281131. Lively bistro-style restaurant in the centre of town. The menu takes a tour for confit of duck salad braised in saké and star anise with pomegranate dressing (£8), and chargrilled pork loin coated in North African spices with wholegrain mustard sauce (£16), while desserts tip their hat to owner Ugur Vata's native land with home-made Turkish delight, and yoghurt caramel with currants and roasted pine nuts (£6). House wine is £12.95.

Closed Sun and Mon. There's a branch at 21 Market Hill, Woodbridge; tel: (01394) 380055.

● **KESWICK** (Cumbria)
Swinside Lodge Grange Road, (01768) 772948. Majestically situated Lakeland hotel with new owners – although chef Clive Imber has been retained. Four-course dinners (£29.50) are 'served smoothly': you might begin with an Asian-style salad and crispy seafood dumplings before leek soup with white truffle oil. Roast Gressingham duck breast with kumquat relish, black pudding and ginger sauce is a typical main course, and desserts could feature iced dark chocolate parfait with Kirsch cherries. House wine £11.50. Open all week D only.

● **KING'S LYNN** (Norfolk)
Riverside 27 King Street, (01553) 773134. Converted 500-year-old timbered building, now an Arts Centre and restaurant overlooking the Ouse. Lunch is a crowd-pleasing deal, with dishes ranging from dressed Norfolk crab (£6.25) to wild boar and Puy lentil casserole (£9.25). Seasonal fixed-price dinners (£22.50/£27.50) expand the theme with mains like roast organic salmon fillet, English asparagus and tarragon sauce and desserts such as pecan pie. 'Prompt, kind service'. The 'Riverside Wine Club' meets regularly, and the restaurant list is broadly-based slate with house selections £11.50. Closed Sun.

● **KINTBURY** (Berkshire)
Dundas Arms 53 Station Road, (01488) 658263. Small hostelry run since 1967 by David Dalzell-Piper, famed for its setting wedged between the Kennet and Avon Canal and the River Kennet (eat outside in fair weather) and for its mighty 200-strong wine list (from around £13.50). Home-potted shrimps (£6.60) and grilled ribeye with chips and mushrooms (£13.50) are tried and trusted favourites, or try grilled tuna steak with mango, orange and chilli salsa (£13), with iced coffee and praline mousse (£5) for pudding. No food Sun L or Mon D; closed Sun D.

● **KNIGHTWICK** (Worcestershire)
The Talbot Knightwick, (01886) 821235. The Clifts are an industrious family, brewing beer, making jams and pickles, growing vegetables – what they can't make or grow they buy locally. Their fourteenth-century inn is quite

the hub of the community, with food a distinct version of home cooking. Dinner is fixed price (£24.95), along the lines of hot-smoked eel with horseradish sauce, then hare leg casserole or pot-roast grouse, with cider cake or spiced apple and date tart to wind things up. House wine is £9.75. Open all week.

● **LANCASTER** (Lancashire)
Simply French 27A St Georges Quay, (01524) 843199. Originally a quayside warehouse for imported mahogany, now a cavernous, rough-walled restaurant with a Gallic accent. Lunch menus promise asparagus with hazelnut and balsamic dressing (£4) followed by seared dorade with sweet chilli and orange butter (£6.50) or something from the grill; apple and vodka sorbet (£2) makes a suitably refreshing finale. Similar – but more expensive – dishes in the evening ('early bird' offers from 6–6.30pm). House wine is £11.95. Open Fri, Sat and Sun L and all week D.

● **LANGTHWAITE** (North Yorkshire)
Charles Bathurst Inn Arkengarthdale, (01748) 884567. Revamped eighteenth-century village pub famed for its location close to the Pennine Way. Short modern menus take inspiration from far and wide, offering duck noodle salad with cashew nuts and Thai vinaigrette (£5.50), Chinese-style strips of beef fillet with noodles and black-bean sauce (£10.50), and, closer to home, roast grouse with ham and horseradish sauce (£19). Desserts can be as traditional as spiced plum and apple crumble (£3.50), and cheeses are from Wensleydale. House wine £8.95. Accommodation. Open all week.

● **LEEDS** (West Yorkshire)
Bryan's 9 Weetwood Lane, (0113) 278 5679. Legendary chippie-cum-restaurant that has been dispensing the real McCoy since 1934. Haddock is king in these parts and you choose your own size, from 'baby' to 'jumbo' (prices from £7 to £13.25); otherwise plump for hake, halibut or – perhaps – grilled salmon steak. Finish with treacle sponge or peach Melba (£3.50), if you have room. 'Senior citizen' deals every day until 5.30 (£5.75). House wine from £11.60; otherwise drink tea or John Smith's beer. Open all week.
Cactus Lounge St Peter's Square, (0113) 243 6553. Upbeat Mexican joint on the ground floor of the Yorkshire Dance Centre;

convenient for theatre-goers to the nearby Playhouse, with a pre-theatre deal at £9.95 (2 courses and a drink). Expect classic nachos (from £4) and various dips with tortilla chips, followed by meat or vegetarian chimichangas (£9), fajitas, burritos and enchiladas. Drink beer or dip into the minimal wine list (prices from £9.95). Closed Sat L and Sun.

Dough 293 Spen Lane, West Park (0113) 278 7255. Neighbourhood bakery by day and rustic, brick-walled bistro by night. Surroundings are cramped, but dressed-down conviviality prevails. Main man Andrew Newsome dons his whites for dinners (including a sorbet) that might run to mussel soup with seafood ravioli, chicken breast stuffed with spring onions and lime, and hot chocolate fondue with pistachio ice cream. Prices start at £16.95 for two courses and £21.95 for three. Polite, prompt service; BYO drink (there's 'a great off-licence opposite'). Bistro open Tue to Sat.

Little Tokyo 24 Central Road, (0131) 2439090. Simon and Helen Wong's dedicated little enterprise now includes a Japanese garden with a bridge over a carp pond. 'The root and spice of healthy eating' says the menu, which focuses on all-in-one bento boxes (from £10.25), bolstered by a few starters (avocado tempura, £4), sushi and assorted noodles. There are also Japanese curries and nutritious 'munchies munchies' (the 'vegan's paradise' comprises tofu, mushrooms, lotus root, mountain yam and daikon). Weekday lunches £5.50. Drink tea, beer or saké; house wine is £9.50. Closed Sun.

Olive Tree Oaklands, 55 Rodley Lane, (0113) 256 9283. A Victorian house on the outer ring road has been home to George Psarias's Greek Cypriot taverna since 1986. Prices are modest for the traditional array of meze, including a full range of dips, dolmades and falafel. Reports have praised lamb moussaka (£10), or there could be chargrilled salmon, or souvlaki (£11). Baklava heads the range of traditional puddings. The two-course lunch menu is excellent value at £6.95. Greece and Cyprus dominate the wine list; house wine is £11.95. Open all week.

Raja's 186 Roundhay Road, (0113) 2480411. Street-corner Indian close to a local Bangladeshi Community Centre in Roundhay's ethnic enclave (a couple of miles from the city centre). Functional, suburban décor, an open-to-view kitchen and food that is die-hard 'traditional British Indian restaurant fare'. The menu trots its way through tandooris, chicken Punjabi (£5.75), lamb biryani et al: don't miss the deeply flavoured dhal (£3) and expertly made naan bread (£1). 'Smiley and accommodating' service. Open Mon to Fri L and all week D.

Room Bourse Courtyard, Boar Lane, (0113) 242 6161. Young 'fashion destination' with striking contemporary design, regular DJs and bags of informal style. Deliberately 'British retro' evening menu with starters (£5) such as Waldorf salad and 'posh' Spam terrine, followed by main courses (£14) including corn-fed chicken Kiev, duck 'pot noodle', and sea bass florentine. Desserts (£4.50) like Black Forest chocolate fondant are in keeping. Lighter all-day menu (to 6pm). Book for cocktails in the basement 'Bedroom' or eat al fresco in the courtyard. Shortish wine list with house Spanish from £12.50. Closed Sun.

● **LICHFIELD** (Staffordshire)

Chandlers Corn Exchange, Conduit Street, (01543) 416 688. This former corn exchange is given an ecclesiastical air by its stained glass windows and vaulted ceilings. Generous brasserie-inspired menus include a carte, a three course set lunch (£11.95), and 'supper prix fixe' offering, for example, sautéed calamari and prawns with sweet chilli spaghetti, poached salmon salad and herb de provence potatoes, and ice coup glace and brandy snap, all for £16. Fish specials – roasted skate wing, vodka, lemon and prawn butter (£9.50) – are listed separately. House French is £10.95. More reports please. Open all week.

● **LIDGATE** (Suffolk)

Star Inn The Street, (01638) 500275. At face value this is a traditional country pub, with a board floor and an inglenook, but the landlady hails from Catalonia and brings an unexpected flash of Mediterranean colour to the menu. Long, daily-changing blackboards turn up grilled squid (£6), scallops Santiago (£12.50), and paella (£11.50), as well as old favourites such as lasagne. Spain dominates the reasonably priced (from £12) wine list. Open all week (drinks only Sun D).

● **LITTLE BARROW** (Cheshire)
Foxcote Inn Station Lane, (01244) 301343.
Originally the Railway Inn, now more of a
restaurant than a traveller's watering hole.
Seafood steals the show on the blackboard
menu: bacon-wrapped hake stuffed with
salmon with a shellfish beurre blanc and crispy
leeks, for example. Fixed-prices lunches
(£7.95/£9.95) are particularly good value for
avocado, Stilton and pear salad, slow-braised
belly pork with Chinese-spiced sweet-and-
sour vegetables or breaded plaice goujons and
chips, before vanilla pannacotta with
caramelised banana. Wines start at £9.95.
Closed Sun D.

● **LITTLEPORT** (Cambridgeshire)
Fen House 2 Lynn Road, (01353) 860645.
Born in 1987 and 'still thriving', according to
visitors who returned after 16 years away.
Dinner in this smart Georgian residence is
fixed-price for three courses (£28.75), with
cheese as a complimentary extra. David
Warne looks to France for most of his ideas,
starting with grilled goats' cheese on
provençale vegetables, before rolled saddle of
lamb with onion sauce and Madeira gravy,
then desserts like spiced apple tartlet with
Calvados custard. Sixty wines from £13.75.
Open Fri and Sat D only (must book); other
times by arrangement.

● **LIVERPOOL** (Merseyside)
Puschka 16 Rodney Street, (0151) 708 8698.
Promising 'classy and intimate' restaurant
with the feel of a friendly neighbourhood
haunt, thanks to 'welcoming and obliging
staff'. Lunch is café-orientated, say hummus,
mussels and chips, or chicken and bacon
Caesar with fresh anchovies, but dinner shows
more ambition with recommendations
including terrine of smoked trout and smoked
salmon (£5.90), chargrilled breast of duck with
leek and potato cake and caramelised onion
marmalade (£14.50), and rich chocolate
mascarpone cake (£4.95) to finish. House
wine £10.90. Open Tue to Sun L and Tue to Sat
D.

● **LONGSTOCK** (Hampshire)
Peat Spade Inn Longstock, (01264) 810612.
Impeccable sourcing of raw materials, many of
them organic, defines this popular Hampshire
pub close to the River Test. Appearing on the
short, modern carte could be cabbage and

bacon soup (£4.50), organic lamb rogan josh
(£8.50), and local free-range bangers and
mash (£8) as well as good vegetarian choices.
Organic house wine at £11.25 and nine by the
glass. Open Wed to Sun L, Wed to Sat D.

● **LOWER ODDINGTON** (Gloucestershire)
Fox Inn Lower Oddington, (01451) 870555.
Civilised Cotswolds pub in idyllic setting, with
flagstone floors, an open fire and pleasant
garden. The kitchen puts its faith in well-tried
country cooking based on seasonal
ingredients, beginning with a soup (leek and
potato, for example) before, say, steak and
kidney pie (£9.50), or whole lemon sole with
capers and lemon butter (£12.75). To finish
there could be raspberry and white chocolate
tart (£4.50). Six wines come by the glass. Open
all week.

● **LUDLOW** (Shropshire)
Retro 11 Corve Street, (01584) 878777. A
recent addition to Ludlow's gastronomic
legions, run by David Wilson-Lloyd (ex-
Roebuck, Brimfield, see Main entry).
Welcome for its reasonably priced 'pub-style'
dishes, including scallops with minted pea
purée and tomato sauce (£6.50), braised beef
with Guinness (£10), and pecan and maple
streusel cheesecake (£5). Modest, well-
sourced wine list from £12. Situated on the
ground floor of a stately Georgian brick
residence with an expansive rear garden;
accommodation is planned. Open Wed to Sun
L, Tue to Sat D.

● **LUTON** (Devon)
The Elizabethan Inn Fore Street, 01626
775425. In a quiet Devon backwater, this
village pub has been given a new lease of life
by owners Nick Powell and Anne Gibbs.
There's a promising extensive chalkboard
menu which ranges from a traditional smooth
chicken liver parfait, or Dover sole with capers,
lemon and herb dressing, to more modish
duck in ginger, soy and hoisin sauce.
Elsewhere expect mixed seafood risotto with a
smooth tomato sauce, and homespun sweets
like sticky toffee pudding with caramel sauce.
Main courses £7.50 to £14.25 and affordable
wines start at £9.95. Open all week.

● **MAIDEN NEWTON** (Dorset)
Le Petit Canard Dorchester Road, (01300)
320536. Homely, 'consistent oasis' run by a
likeable husband-and-wife team: she

generates a friendly atmosphere out-front, while he cooks. Candlelit fixed-price dinners (£24.50/£28) yo-yo between Euro-classics (Portland crab Thermidor, local venison with red wine, thyme and port sauce) and more exotic ideas (Gressingham duck breast with chilli and five-spice sauce, rack of lamb with minted couscous). Finish with sticky toffee pudding or basil ice cream and mango sorbet with mango and kiwi salsa. Around three dozen affordable wines from £13.95. Open Tue to Sat D and first and third Sun for L.

● **MALVERN WELLS** (Worcestershire)

Planters 191–193 Wells Road, (01684) 575065. Two evenings a week, Sandra Pegg and chef Chandra de Alwis bring a taste of south-east Asian home cooking to this English country town. Order the five-course Rijstaffel ('rice table', £19.50 a head) if you are in a group; otherwise pick from the short menu, which could list vaday (Sri Lankan lentil rissoles, £4.50) and pork curry with roasted spices and coconut milk (£9.50) along with crispy murtaba bread (£2.75), stir-fried noodles and nasi goreng rice (£6.25). Reasonably priced wines from £12. Open Fri and Sat D only.

● **MANCHESTER** (Greater Manchester)

Bridge 58 Bridge Street, (0161) 834 0242. The 'gastro-pub' comes to Manchester in the shape of this reborn venue, which bridges the gap between city watering hole and informal restaurant. The kitchen treats local ingredients with style and generosity: witness Bury black pudding, potato cake and poached egg (£4.25), breast of chicken with wild garlic and wilted greens in smoked bacon broth (£7.95), and ribeye steak with homemade 'duck fat' chips. For afters, consider lemon tart or stem ginger pudding (£3.50). Fairly priced wines from £10. Open all week.

Bridgewater Hall, The Charles Hallé Room Lower Mosley Street, (0161) 950 0000. Linked to the concert hall and only open for evening meals before and after performances: chef Robert Kisby whizzes back and forth from his main base at Le Mont (see Main entry, Manchester). Menus are fixed price (£16.95/£21.50) and potage 'Yehudi Menuhin' is a fixture. Otherwise, start with seared calf's liver and red onion confit, move on to cold poached salmon with cucumber tagliatelle, asparagus

and egg mayonnaise, and finish with caramelised banana crêpe or something from the cheese menu. Wines from £12.45.

Kosmos 248 Wilmslow Road, (0161) 225 9106. Here for nigh on 24 years, TV cook and chef/patron Loulla Astin continues to produce authentically Greek dishes at this popular taverna. Dishes range from a selection of Metzethes – complete meals served in three stages – to meat moussaka (£9.50) and lamb kebabs (£9.80). More unusual offerings take in yemitsa (tomatoes and peppers stuffed with rice, pumpkin seeds and dried fruit) and fassolia yiahini (cannelloni beans casseroled with carrots, celery and tomatoes). Greece and Cyprus dominate the wine list, with house wine at £13. Open all week D only.

Livebait 22 Lloyd Street, (0161) 817 4110. Vaulted Victorian building with retro tiled décor, smiley staff and a menu that goes for fish in a big way. Start with a plate of 'excellent' oysters or a bowl of Scottish mussels (£5.50/£8.50), then choose from shellfish platters, grilled exotica and classics like smoked haddock on herb mash with poached egg (£12.75). Meat and vegetarian alternatives; fish 'n' chip lunches £5 (12–5pm, Mon–Sat). Short list of seafood-friendly wines from £11.50. Open all week.

Lounge 10 Tib Street, (0161) 834 1331. An extravagant mix of over-the-top décor and live music creates a restaurant buzz and certainly draws the crowds. The short menu follows suit, with plenty of up-to-the-minute offerings: asparagus soup with goats' cheese tortellini (£6.50), fricassee of turbot with mushrooms, spring onions and chive potatoes (£18), and spiced bitter chocolate truffle cake with an orange compote (£6). Prices are on the high side, but the wine list offers affordable drinking, opening with house wine at £11.95. Closed Sun and Mon.

Market Restaurant 104 High Street/Edge Street, (0161) 834 3743. Retro-style décor, jazz and original cooking are the selling points in this idiosyncratic long-runner just off Piccadilly. The menu changes every six weeks and the repertoire is a 'home-and-away' mixed bag, taking in pork terrine and anchovy butter (£6), fillet of salmon with green lentils and salsa verde (£15) and mushroom strudel with watercress sauce. Finish with chocolate pavlova (£5.25) or 'old-fashioned' bread pudding. 'Excellent' Belgian beers, plus cocktails and great-value wines from £7.95. Open Wed to Fri L, Wed to Sat D.

Midland Hotel Peter Street, (0161) 236 3333. Grand Edwardian city-centre hotel evoking a bygone era. The kitchen was in a state of flux as we went to press, but expect a lengthy carte with classic French roots and modern flourishes: chateaubriand sits alongside chicken cutlet with sweetcorn and spring onion risotto (£20), for example. Start with, say, seared scallops with vanilla dauphinoise and mint dressing (£15), and try banana and five-spice Tatin (£7.50) as a finale. France dominates the wine list, with prices from £16. Open Mon to Sat D only. Reports please.

New Emperor 52–56 George Street, (0161) 228 2883. Creditable alternative to some of the big players in the heart of Manchester's Chinatown, with a spacious open-plan dining room and a lengthy menu that meanders through the Cantonese repertoire. Expect familiar dim sum (around £2.50), casseroles, roast meats, one-plate rice and noodles, plus dishes ranging from duck with Chinese mushrooms and king prawns with cashews to steamed minced pork with dried squid (mains from £7). Banquet menus from £25 per person; house wine around £10. Open all week.

Palmiro 197 Upper Chorlton Road, (0161) 860 7330. Reporters continue to praise this striking modern Italian in a low-rent part of the city. The short menu displays a refreshing lack of reliance on pasta – there may be just linguine with sugo d'anitra (£5.25) – but the kitchen has produced swordfish carpaccio on mint and crushed peas to start, and chicken and spinach rotolo with carrot and courgette roast (£12.75) and Sicilian fish couscous as main courses, and Venetian rice pudding to finish. Italian wines from £9.75 make an interesting list. Open Sun L and all week D.

Le Petit Blanc 55 King Street, (0161) 832 1000. 'A fine example of a cosmopolitan brasserie' in the energetic heart of the city, notable for its informal setting, friendly service and fair prices. Like other branches, it aims for flexibility and has an enthusiastic attitude towards children. The menus are bolstered by daily specials like duck confit terrine with

mustard dressing (£6.50) and pan-fried salmon with cucumber beurre blanc (£15.50), while desserts could run to bourbon vanilla crème brûlée (£5.50). The wine list favours forward-looking French producers, with prices from £12.95. Open all week. See also Round-ups under Birmingham, Cheltenham, Oxford and Tunbridge Wells.

Stock 4 Norfolk Street, 0161 839 6644. Italian food rather than share-dealing is now the name of the game in this contemporary restaurant occupying Manchester's opulent Stock Exchange Hall (note the huge domed ceiling and marble pillars). Open with tiger prawns in garlic butter with lemon risotto (£8.25) or a dish of pasta (from £6.50), before tackling osso buco Milanese (£17.50), stuffed boneless quails on Mediterranean couscous or something from the list of fish specials. Comprehensive all-Italian wine list, with prices from £16. Closed Sun.

Tai Pan Brunswick House, 81–97 Upper Brook Street, (0161) 273 2798. Away from the city centre and Chinatown, towards the university, this Chinese emporium encompasses a supermarket and wholesaler with a substantial restaurant above. Celebrated for its dim sum – steamed scallop dumplings, char siu bau, prawns in rice paper, and so on – there's also a list of familiar roast meats (£7.50 to £9.50), and one-plate rice and noodle dishes. Several set-price dinner and banquet menus (£15 to £30.50) are aimed mainly at Western tastes. Open all week.

That Cafe 1031 Stockport Road, (0161) 432 4672. Converted terraced house where Alison Eason and co please the punters with their weekly menus of bright modern dishes. Expect the likes of bruschetta with griddled Cajun chicken and roast red peppers (£6.75) and seafood risotto topped with a fennel fritter (£15), followed by nectarine and meringue parfait. House wine £10.25. Early-evening menus (two courses £11, Tue–Fri); live jazz first Wed of each month. Open Sun L and Tue to Sat D.

Zinc The Triangle, Hanging Ditch, (0161) 827 4200. With a weekday 'Express' lunch menu delivering the likes of coq au vin and mash for £8, a weekday prix fixe (£10 for two courses) running from noon to 7pm, as well as a carte offering everything from Caesar salad and risottos to hamburger and steaks, this is a useful destination for informal eating. Linguine with sea bass and shellfish is a good version, and crème brûlée is a classic. Part of the Conran mini-chain, with bags of style and good service. House wine is £12.50. Open all week.

● **MARSH BENHAM** (Berkshire)
Red House Marsh Benham, (01635) 582017. Hefty timbers, a thatched roof and other remnants of the past add character to this old red brick building (formerly the Water Rat pub). The kitchen shows a creative streak with gratin of crab and grapefruit with hollandaise (£8.50) and almond-crusted sea bream fillet with stir-fried vegetables and orange-infused sauce (£16). Also expect meat dishes such as chargrilled veal loin with Mediterranean mash, tomato Tatin and sauce vierge, plus desserts like vanilla crème brûlée (£5). Fixed-price 'bistro' menu. House wines £13.50. Closed Sun D and all Mon.

● **MATFEN** (Northumberland)
Matfen Hall Matfen, (01661) 886500. A model of early nineteenth-century baronial splendour in a 200-acre estate close to Hadrian's Wall. Meals are served in the Library and Print Room, where the diverse carte takes in Cheddar and spinach soufflé (£6), before home-bred lamb Wellington with red wine and rosemary jus (£19), or baked duck breast with pesto mash, port and redcurrant sauce. Bringing up the rear are desserts like pear Tatin with stem ginger ice cream (£5.50). Well-chosen international wine list; house French £14.95. Open Sun L and all week D.

● **MAWGAN** (Cornwall)
New Yard Trelowarren, (01326) 221595. A mile-long drive leads deep into the Trelowarren Estate, where visitors will find this categorically French restaurant housed in a converted coach house. The kitchen takes a serious view of things. You might find pan-fried smoked cod fillet topped with peppered cream with a walnut dressing (£7), as well as sirloin steak and lobster, or Cornish lamb with a goats' cheese and basil parcel and celeriac salad (£17). Finish perhaps with lemon soufflé and cinnamon ice cream. House wines are £12.50. Open all week L and Tue to Sat D. Reports please.

● **MELMERBY** (Cumbria)
Village Bakery Melmerby, (01768) 881811. Breakfasts of oak-smoked Inverawe kippers and bacon sandwiches sit alongside quality lunchtime cold meat platters served with organic breads (£6.95), and mixed vegetable soup (£4.50); drawing visitors back time and time again. After almost 30 years the Village Bakery is still in the vanguard of organically minded ventures, and the hub of the restaurant remains the wood-fired oven used for everything, from breads to pies and good things such as rich fruit cake (£2.25) and gingerbread. House wine £9.75. Open all week L.

● **MINCHINHAMPTON** (Gloucestershire)
Sophie's Restaurant 20 High Street, (01453) 885188. Country cooking 'as it is in France' served in a laid-back, thoroughly English, Grade II listed building. Sophie Dominique Craddock's French family roots are the inspiration behind her market-led, daily changing menus: typical lunch dishes might include bacon, spinach and asparagus tart (£7) and lamb steak with Puy lentils (£11) followed by baked apricot, peach and Calvados meringue (£4.50). Alternatively choose from a selection of fish dishes, say, wild sea bass with roasted tomatoes (£13) or Basque fish stew with saffron risotto (£13). Directly imported Languedoc wines star on the 100 per cent Gallic list; prices from £9.95. Open Tue to Fri L and Sat D.

● **NAILSWORTH** (Gloucestershire)
Mad Hatters 3 Cossack Square, (01453) 832615. 'Local' and 'organic' are the rallying calls in the Findlay's likeable neighbourhood restaurant-with-rooms. Ever-changing, French-inspired menus feature a few fixtures like fish soup with rouille (£4.75) but ring the seasonal changes with venison and pork terrine, monkfish wrapped in prosciutto with peperonata (£17) and pork à l'indienne, followed by home-made desserts like pannacotta with poached pears (£5). Organic beers and a 100 per cent organic wine list from £11. Open Wed to Sun L, Wed to Sat D.

● **NEWARK** (Nottinghamshire)
Café Bleu 14 Castle Gate, (01636) 610141. 'Spectacularly designed' riverside bistro close to the castle ruins. Tables outside are at a premium, and the 'happy' atmosphere is

helped along by regular live music. Visitors have enjoyed pan-seared halibut with cockles and mussels in fish stock, and duck with rhubarb compote; otherwise opt for, say, blade of Aberdeenshire beef with buttered Savoy cabbage and foie gras sauce (£14). Start with wild rocket and globe artichoke risotto (£5) and end with the Café Bleu chocolate plate (£6.50). Around 40 youthful wines from £9.95. Closed Sun D.

● **NEWBURY PARK** (Essex)
Curry Special 2 Greengate Parade, (020) 8518 3005. Culture and cuisine share the limelight at this colourful Indian restaurant set over two floors. Bollywood movies play on a screen downstairs, while the smartly turned-out and mostly Asian clientele create a buzzy atmosphere. The menu majors in the familiar, although standards are high: 'excellent' onion bhajias and samosas, to start, while tandooris are a feature for mains alongside the likes of whole methi chicken (£34), karahi king prawns (£9.75) and masala lamb (£5.50). Basic wine list and Kenyan beers. Open Tue to Fri L and Tue to Sun D.

● **NORTON** (Shropshire)
Hundred House Hotel Bridgnorth Road, (01952) 730353. Red-brick Georgian hotel (with additions) amicably run by the Phillips family since 1986. Mother Sylvia tends the lovely gardens, father Henry is at the helm and son Stuart mans the stoves. Menus are dominated by generously proportioned specials like mussels with coriander and chilli (£7), Szechuan-peppered venison with soy, red wine and shiitake sauce (£19) and brown bread ice cream with autumn fruits (£5). Lighter meals in the brasserie. A dozen global house wines from £12.95. Open all week.

● **NORWICH** (Norfolk)
Delia's Restaurant and Bar Norwich City Football Club, River End, Carrow Road, (01603) 218705. The Canaries are in the Premiership, so there is going to be a bit of a buzz around the place this year. Delia Smith's influence on the football club extends to this restaurant and bar, open only on Saturday evenings. Dinner might start with deep-fried lobster tails with a chunky tartare sauce, or duck rillettes with a confit of cranberries and granary toast. Main courses like pot-roasted venison with Shrewsbury sauce precede desserts such as mincemeat and almond tart with vanilla bean ice cream (£27.50 for 3 courses). Open Sat D only.

● **NOTTINGHAM** (Nottinghamshire)
Bees Make Honey 12 Alfreton Road, (0115) 978 0109. Homespun café a few minutes walk from the Playhouse and Theatre Royal. Blackboard menus offer a motley assortment of dishes with French/Mediterranean influences, from shellfish soup with smoked paprika (£4.95) to fillet steak (£18.95). Vegetarians are well served by, say, sweet potato fritters with Thai sauce, or spinach and vegetable pie (each £12.95), while desserts range from treacle tart to white chocolate cheesecake (£4.50). Unlicensed, but BYO. No credit cards. Open Tue to Sat D only.

● **ONGAR** (Essex)
Smiths Fyfield Road, (01277) 365578. Opened in 1958 and still going strong, this swish modern venue is expanding to cope with its popularity. 'Famous for fish' proclaims the menu, which veers between skate and cod fillet cooked every which way (£12.50) to crab Mornay and specials like steamed turbot with spring onion, ginger and soy. Starters like sardines with salsa verde (£6), a few alternatives for meat eaters (fillet steak béarnaise, for example), and desserts such as strawberry tart (£5.75). Forty wines including house French at £12. Closed Mon.

● **ORFORD** (Suffolk)
Butley-Orford Oysterage Market Hill, (01394) 450277. 'Just the same as always,' noted a regular of this basic eatery, which serves up Butley Creek oysters, own-smoked salmon, mackerel and sprats, fresh fish and 'noteworthy' puddings. The selection of smoked fish and oysters (£9.50) is a must have, then perhaps some griddled sardines or squid, but leave room for the 'outstanding' rum cake (£3.90). Wine (£12.95) produced on the local Rendlesham estate 'goes with everything on the menu'. Expect queues during high season. Open all week exc Sun to Thur D in winter.

● **OXFORD** (Oxfordshire)
Aquavitae 1 Folly Bridge, (01865) 247775. Glossy basement Italian with mirrored walls in a 'gorgeous' position right by the riverbank (eat outside when the weather allows). Long orthodox menu kicking off with a modern take on Parma ham with rocket (£8.50) or fresh

orecchiette with tomato sauce before, say, monkfish with a lively salad, steak or tortelloni stuffed with pumpkin (£10.50); finish with zabaglione (£5). 'University portions' and quaffable Italian regional wines. Closed Mon L.

Fishers 36/37 St Clements, (01865) 243003. 'A supporter of the RNLI and sustainable fishing' declares the menu, suggesting that the restaurant lives up to its name. Baked, grilled, poached and smoked are treatments seen in dishes like Cornish scallops (£7.50), Welsh sea bream served whole with roasted garlic and herb oil (£14.50) and Irish salmon steak with lemon hollandaise (£12.50). Only roasted Barbary duck is the exception to the fishy rule. Shellfish platters and a special early evening menu (£20 two courses) are available. Fish-friendly wines start at £10.95. Closed Mon L.

Liaison 29 Castle Street, (01865) 242944. Popular oriental restaurant housed in a 'Tudor-looking' building in the city centre. The menu cuts a broad swath through the Chinese, Malaysian and Thai repertoires for an extensive assortment of capably prepared dishes: hoi nam chicken with sweet chilli sauce (£7), and bean curd hotpot (£6.50) have been well received by reporters. Otherwise expect fillet of beef, and plenty of seafood. House wine is £9.50. Open all week.

Le Petit Blanc 71–72 Walton Street, (01865) 510999. The godfather of Raymond Blanc's group of family-friendly provincial brasseries (now jointly owned by Loch Fyne). A fresh white and blue décor and a menu that shows many of M. Blanc's fingerprints: wild mushroom fricassee (£8), hot-smoked Duart salmon with beetroot carpaccio (£13), and a croustillant of ice creams and sorbets (£5.25) are typical. Fixed-price menus and children's deals too. Wines aim to 'reflect the current renaissance of the French vineyard', plus a few interlopers from elsewhere; prices from £12.95. Open all week. There are branches in Birmingham, Cheltenham, Manchester and Tunbridge Wells (see Round-ups).

Sojo Restaurant 6–9 Hythe Bridge Street, (01865) 202888 Sited in this growing little Chinatown, two shop fronts have merged into one open-plan restaurant simply decorated in black with soft wall lighting. This is where 'brains and good food go together', thought

one reporter, noting the place was packed with students. Reports focus on dim sum (£2.50 to £5.80) – a good, fresh sui mei (pork dumplings), congee, and pan-fried chicken – but there is also an extensive carte with things like Mongolian sizzling dish (£12), and steam boat (£34.50 for two people). Open all week. More reports please.

● **PENZANCE** (Cornwall)
Bay Restaurant, Mount Prospect Hotel
Britons Hill, (01736) 363117. Friendly, family-run hotel with 'stimulating' views of Penzance Harbour and Mount's Bay from the contemporary dining room. Seasonal menus focus on 'the sea' (tian of Newlyn crab, guacamole 'jumble salad' and new potatoes, £15.50), 'the land' (herb-crusted best end of spring lamb with rosemary, port and beetroot jus) and 'the garden' (local asparagus, potato and mint frittata). Start with steamed langoustines and basil aïoli (£8.50); finish with iced banana parfait and caramelised banana (£5.50). Lighter dishes served lunchtimes and early evening. Wines from £12.95. Closed Sun L in winter.

● **PINCHINTHORPE** (Redcar & Cleveland)
Brewhouse Bistro Pinchinthorpe Hall, nr Guisborough, (01287) 630200. Fascinating set-up built around a seventeenth-century country manor, complete with its own organic microbrewery, organic kitchen garden, restaurant and unpretentious pubby bistro. Home-grown and local produce surfaces in the shape of twice-baked courgette and goats' cheese soufflé (£4.95), saddle of venison with celeriac purée, butternut squash and wild mushroom sauce, or pan-fried sea bass with buttered vegetables and dill cream (£13.25). Finish with comforting rhubarb crumble and 'real custard'. Hotel accommodation in the original hall. Well-balanced wine list from £12.50. Open all week. Reports please.

● **POLPERRO** (Cornwall)
Kitchen The Coombes, (01503) 272780. Unassuming Cornish seaside refuge, dedicated to feeding the influx of seasonal holidaymakers. The Kitchen conjures up globally inspired dishes like oak-smoked duck with melon, home-pickled ginger, sesame and soy dressing (£6), and Goan-style lamb Xacutti (£12.50). Fish lovers might be tempted by brill with orange and basil butter sauce, and

vegetarians by spicy 'quorn' in coriander Masala. Desserts (£4.50) could include Cointreau chocolate pot. Around three dozen wines from £12.50. Note: no cheques. Open Tue to Sun, Apr to Sept D only (ring to check).

● **PORTHLEVEN** (Cornwall)

Critchards The Harbourside, (01326) 562407. Veteran seaside restaurant in a converted mill overlooking the harbour. Fish from the Cornish ports takes pride of place on the Critchards' well-tried menu and specials list; successes have included decent soups (from seafood chowder to woodland mushroom), Russian-style salmon ceviche (£6.50) and pan-fried fillets of red gurnard (perhaps with olive oil, garlic and parsley, £14). Chocolate, Grand Marnier and praline torte is a typical dessert (£5). Reasonably priced, fish-friendly wines from £13.95. Accommodation available. Open Mon to Sat D only (check winter closures).

● **PORTLOE** (Cornwall)

Lugger Hotel Portloe, (01872) 501322. Hospitable little hotel in a minuscule fishing village with enviable vistas and a cliffside terrace overlooking Veryan Bay. Fixed-price dinners (three courses £37.50) might kick off with asparagus and herb bavarois or tempura of Dublin Bay prawns before seared cod on spring onion mash with chorizo and curry oil or entrecôte steak with rösti and sauce Diane. Desserts have included crème brûlée. Sunday lunch has also passed muster. House wines from £16.50 to £18.50. Open all week.

● **RAMSGATE** (Kent)

Surin 30 Harbour Street, (01843) 592001. Understated, with the look of a simple café, this small Thai restaurant delivers a long, familiar repertoire of freshly prepared dishes. Popular items such as satays, tom yum soups, roast duck curry and glass noodle salads are augmented by a few less common specialities. Look for whole steamed sea bass with garlic, chilli and lime (£11.95), or deep-battered salmon in sweet and sour sauce (£6.75). Drink locally brewed own-label Thai-style beer. Service can be slow. Open Tue to Sat L and Mon To Sat D.

● **REED** (Hertfordshire)

Cabinet Reed, (01763) 848366. Tastefully refurbished, sixteenth-century country pub tucked away off the A10 south of Royston.

Real ales in the bar; challenging modern food in the restaurant, with its 'stripped back' décor and daily-changing menu. Reporters have applauded Caesar salad with garlic croûtons and poached egg (£6), grilled beef fillet with celeriac and apple mash and poached garlic sauce (£20) and an eye-catching dessert involving blackberry jelly with a mille-feuille of Baileys ice cream (£6). Well-chosen wines from £12.50. Open Tue to Sat L and D, Sun D.

● **RICHMOND** (Surrey)

Chez Lindsay 11 Hill Rise, (020) 8948 7473. Celebrate the glories of traditional Breton cooking in Lindsay Wotton's long-running neighbourhood restaurant. Galettes made from organic flour are a firm favourite (£3–£9), with fillings from egg and ham to queen scallops and leeks. Seafood also appears in the form of palourdes, winkles with aïoli, halibut and shellfish casserole, and king prawns with Muscadet (£13.75). Meat alternatives like braised lamb shank, plus sweet crêpes to finish (from £3). Fixed-price Breton cider menu (£15.75); mainly French wines from £11.50. Open all week.

Petersham Hotel Nightingale Lane, (020) 8939 1084. Everyone raves about the stupendous location, with its 'unbeatable' views over the Thames and Petersham Meadows; the food in this awesome Victorian folly also receives plaudits. Expect intricate modern dishes along the lines of pan-fried red mullet with peppercorn risotto and aubergine crisps (£8.50), brioche herb-crusted lamb with a faggot, roast garlic and watercress mousse (£18.50) and banana crème brûlée (£5.50). Sunday lunch is a well-reported, leisurely repast (£26). Heavyweight wine list, with prices from £17.50. Open all week.

● **ROCK** (Cornwall)

St Enodoc Hotel Rock, (01208) 863394. Bold Mediterranean design and stunning views are plus-points at this revamped hotel. Expect elaborate cooking and fish in abundance: start with seared scallops on celeriac purée with crisp prosciutto and truffle oil (£9.50) before, say, pan-fried sea bass with chive mash, wild mushrooms, green beans and rosemary butter (£20) or guinea fowl with lemon, fennel seeds and black olive game jus. Desserts are a high point: glazed lemon tart (£7) or a little chocolate and thyme pot with ginger tuiles, for example. 'Eminently quaffable' wines from £15. Open all week.

● **ROMSEY** (Hampshire)
Bertie's 80 The Hundred, (01794) 830708. Brightly coloured paintings set the tone in this former coaching inn. Danny Carter's jazzed-up bistro menus mix familiarity with invention, as in smoked chicken spring roll with chilli jam (£6), escalope of salmon with Parmesan mash and spiced tomato sauce (£12) and sweets like honeycomb parfait with toasted banana bread (£5.50). Light lunches and snacks also available. Ten house wines from £3.10 a glass, £11.95 a bottle. Accommodation available. Closed Sun.

● **ROYDHOUSE** (West Yorkshire)
Three Acres Inn Roydhouse, (01484) 602606. Emley Moor TV mast acts as a homing beacon to this big roadside hostelry known for panoramic views and a four-pronged operation: restaurant, seafood bar, deli and hotel. A culinary mix punctuates the lengthy menu: hot crispy Peking duck with egg noodles and Chinese greens, crispy Japanese chicken with chilli sauce and stir-fried greens (£6), lobster thermidor, and pot-roast wood pigeon with peas, pancetta and Puy lentils (£13). Wines are priced from £11.95. Accommodation. Open all week.

● **ST ALBANS** (Hertfordshire)
Sukiyaki 6 Spencer Street, (01727) 865009. Just off the marketplace, Mr and Mrs Wakai's little restaurant is the perfect place in which to discover domestic-style Japanese food. As they can't guarantee absolute freshness, raw fish is not served, but there's yakitori, kushikatsu, or miso soup (£2.20) before chicken with teriyaki sauce (£8.50) or prawn and vegetable tempura (£11.50). Prices are reasonable: a five-course sukiyaki dinner is £24.50, for example. House wine is £10.50. Open Tue to Sat.

● **ST IVES** (Cornwall)
Porthgwidden Beach Café (01736) 796791. Sister of the Porthminster Beach Café (see Main entry, St Ives), also with a fabulous location 'overlooking the elemental crashing waves'. 'English seaside' collides with Mediterranean fusion now that chef Mick Smith has re-joined the kitchen; the menu spans everything from Moroccan-inspired tapas plates (£5) and lamb tagine (£11.50) to local lemon sole grilled with paprika and

'Cornish know-how'. 'Sunny and delightful staff' match the setting. Breakfast, cream teas and a sizeable drinks list for young and old alike; house wine is £9.50. Open all week.

Tides Café 6 The Digey, (01736) 799600. Tucked down a side street, this trendy café of slate floors, metal and mosaic tables, and driftwood mirrors has an easy-going air. The open-to-view kitchen works to a lively menu of cosmopolitan dishes along the lines of a platter of mixed tapas or seared scallops with Serrano ham and salad (£11) for lunch, and duck and fig brochette with feta and summer leaves (£14) or whole baked trout with thyme, rosemary and bay butter sauce for dinner. House wine £12.95. Open Mon to Sat summer, closed end Oct to end Feb exc Christmas and New Year.

● **ST PETER SOUTH ELMHAM** (Suffolk)
St Peter's Hall and Brewery St Peter South Elmham, (01986) 782322. A visually stunning and historically fascinating venue in a converted medieval manor house (complete with a moat). The set-up comprises a ground-breaking brewery with organic allegiances, plus a pub/restaurant festooned with antique furnishings. Expect simple modern dishes such as seared duck liver salad with bacon and pine nuts (£5) and baked turbot fillet with mussels, garlic and chorizo (£14.50), plus desserts like lemon tart with mandarin sorbet (£5). Tip-top draught and bottled beers; 40 very decent wines from £9.95. Open Mon to Sun L and D.

● **SALISBURY** (Wiltshire)
LXIX 69 New Street, (01722) 340000 A quick Latin translation will leave you with the number of this light and airy bar/bistro, which is 'coming up', according to some reporters. Specials such as sea bass fillet on crunchy Japanese-style salad add more possibilities to the bistro-style menu, which roams about for starters and 'quick bites' like filo-wrapped Brie parcels and fruit compote (£5.75) and mains such as Mexican-style chicken wraps with salsa and fries (£8.25). Green Thai fish curry has been enjoyed, and crème brûlée has shown up well among the choice of desserts. Thirty wines from £10.25. Closed Sun.

● **SHAFTESBURY** (Dorset)
Fleur De Lys Bleke Street, (01747) 853717. A well-liked local rendezvous with a new home

in a former 'girls' boarding house'. The owners now offer accommodation, the atmosphere remains sociable, and French-inspired cooking is still the order of the day. Luxury-tinged menus promise the likes of lobster and asparagus salad with lemon and truffle dressing (£10.50) and chargrilled fillet of local beef with wilted spinach, broad beans and a morel sauce (£21.50) followed by butterscotch crème brûlée (£6). House wine is £14. Pleasant courtyard garden. Open Wed to Sun L, Mon to Sat D.

● **SHEPTON MALLET** (Somerset)
Blostins 29–33 Waterloo Road, (01749) 343648. February 2005 marks the twentieth anniversary of Nick and Lynne Reed's tried-and-tested country restaurant. Their fixed-price menus (£15.95 and £17.95) make reassuringly familiar reading: start with warm salad of chicken and smoked bacon, move on to fillet of hake with roasted fennel and butter sauce, and conclude with iced lemon meringue with summer fruits. Also note seasonal specials like escalope of veal with Portabella mushrooms and Marsala. House wines are £10.95. Open Tue to Sat D only.

● **SINNINGTON** (North Yorkshire)
Fox and Hounds Sinnington, (01751) 431577. Pleasantly civilised village pub with a quiet, domestic air and tone of cosy comfort. Traditions are upheld at lunch with steak and Guinness pie (£7.95) and battered haddock and chips, but the evening repertoire takes off rapidly into the realms of pan-seared halibut fillet with a warm salad of roasted fennel, salmon, monkfish and basil (£13.45), and slow roast belly pork with roast garlic and cracked chilli sauce. The short wine list opens with house selections at £11.50. Open all week.

● **SMART'S HILL** (Kent)
Spotted Dog Inn Smart's Hill, (01892) 870253. Picturesque fifteenth-century country inn that makes good use of local, and seasonal produce (Penshurst lamb, Hildenborough pork and bread from Rushbridge family bakery). Dishes have a contemporary flavour as in Brie-glazed roasted vine tomato and pesto crostini (£4.95) before, say, rump of lamb, celeriac dauphinois, asparagus and bramble jelly reduction (£16.75), with local strawberry mille-feuille with mint and vanilla Chantilly cream for

afters. There's a Sunday barbecue in fine weather. Wines are well spread and affordable, £10.50. Closed Sun D.

● **SOUTHALL** (Greater London)
Gifto's Lahore Karahi 162–164 The Broadway, (020) 8813 8669. A noisy, frantically busy canteen occupying a sprawling ground-floor premises on Southall's Broadway. The cooking is full-blooded Pakistani and the tandoor is fired up for everything from chicken wings (£4.50) to tilapia and pomfret. Bhel puri and other 'chat-pata' snacks are also available (£1.50-£2.50), alongside a healthy showing of familiar and esoteric curries like tinda gosht (baby pumpkin with lamb, around £7). Also note the tawa specials cooked on a hotplate. Unlicensed, but you can BYO. Open all week.

● **SOUTHAMPTON** (Hampshire)
White Star Tavern 28 Oxford Street, (023) 8082 1990. Housed in a former hotel for ocean-going passengers, this contemporary, pubby bistro is a hive of activity. Informality reigns at lunch, when you can choose anything from a light snack (a club sandwich with chips, for example) to beef and mushroom casserole with green beans and pommes purée (£11). Dinner brings crab and cucumber risotto, followed by beef sirloin with fondant potato, baby vegetables and foie gras jus (£15), then tiramisù with a cinnamon doughnut (£6.50). House wine £11.50. Open all week.

● **SOUTHPORT** (Merseyside)
Tyndall's 23 Hoghton Street, (01704) 500002. 'Unlike any other restaurant in Southport,' noted a reporter about this converted town house. Local ingredients like shrimps and black pudding take their place on the straightforward carte alongside sautéed lambs' kidneys in red wine sauce (£6.75), breast of chicken in wild mushroom sauce (£11.75), and whole baked sea bass on a bed of fennel. Set-price menu (£24.95) on Saturdays. Thirty international wines from £12.95. Open Tue to Sat D.

● **STEDHAM** (West Sussex)
Hamilton Arms School Lane, (01730) 812555. Authentically decked-out Thai restaurant/takeaway in a Sussex country pub. The Nava Thai offers a traditional 100-dish menu covering all the staples from soups to

stir-fries, curries and noodles. Typical offerings are keow grob (crispy pork won tons, £4.40), hot-and-sour rare beef salad, and gung pao (grilled king prawns with chillies and fish sauce, £7.60), plus Anglo-Thai desserts like bananas in syrup (£4). One-plate meals and a few pub-grub die-hards in the bar. Eclectic wines include bottles from Monsoon Valley, Thailand; house French £9.25. Closed Mon.

● **STOKE BRUERNE** (Northamptonshire)
Bruerne's Lock 5 The Canalside, (01604) 863654. Likeable restaurant overlooking the Grand Union Canal with menus offering a mixed bag of popular dishes along the lines of salmon roulade, beef tournedos Rossini (£18.85), and Baileys bread-and-butter pudding. The kitchen also gets to grips with chargrilled fillet of red snapper with Cajun spiced parmentier potatoes, and poached fillet of turbot with broccoli and scallion mousse and lemon and anchovy cream (£17.75). Good choice for vegetarians. Praiseworthy wines. Open Wed to Sun L and Tue to Sat D.

● **STOKE PRIOR** (Worcestershire)
Epic' Bar Brasserie 68 Hanbury Road, (01527) 871929. This is the prototype of erstwhile TV chef Patrick McDonald's small chain of brasseries, which bring a dash of urban chic to rural locations, Output from this cosmopolitan kitchen ranges from deep-fried dim sum (£5.75) to Moroccan spiced lamb, couscous and cucumber yoghurt (£13.95), taking in wild mushroom and chive risotto (£5.75) and fillet steak au poivre (£17.75) along the way. 'Fully organic' ice creams are an alternative to hot chocolate fondant and vanilla pannacotta. An equally wide-ranging wine list opens at £11.25. Closed Sun D. A second branch is in Dunhampton (see Round-up entry), and a third at Station Road, Whitacre Heath, Warwickshire; tel: (01675) 462181.

● **STOKE ROW** (Oxfordshire)
Crooked Billet Newlands Lane, (01491) 681048. Remote, rambling old country pub – 'you would never stumble upon this place accidentally' – that has the type of menu 'where it takes ages to decide because so much sounds so good': baby squid pan-fried with chilli, garlic, chorizo and spinach (£5), perhaps, then beef fillet with seared foie gras, rösti, wild mushrooms and red wine jus (£18),

or venison and venison kidney pudding with haggis mash, followed by sherry trifle (£6). Reliable, wide-ranging wines from £12.95. Open all week.

● **STOKESLEY** (North Yorkshire)
Chapters 27 High Street, (01642) 711888. The restaurant in Alan and Catherine Thompson's welcoming three-storey hotel has a strong contemporary feel and the cooking is 'polished': begin with ham hock terrine and home-made chutney (£5.50) before roast monkfish, mustard mash and chive butter; finish with a classic dessert like raspberry crème brûlée (£4.50) or lemon tart. Around 30 reasonably priced wines from £10.50. Closed Sun and Mon. A tapas bar was due to open in the hotel as we went to press.

● **STOW ON THE WOLD** (Gloucestershire)
Hamiltons Brasserie Park Street, (01451) 831700. A new chef started at this handsome brasserie in July 2004, so reports please. The menu has previously followed a broadly European path, from crab risotto with lemon butter (£5.50), and creamed spinach and Gruyère tartlet served with a warm tomato vinaigrette (£5.50) among starters. Main courses have included baked organic salmon with English asparagus, buttered Jersey royals and aïoli (£12), and for dessert chocolate and espresso tart with pecan nut and maple ice cream (£6). Closed Sun D.

● **STRATFORD-UPON-AVON** (Warwickshire)
Russons 8 Church Street, (01789) 268822. Small, town centre bistro with an easy-going, family friendly feel courtesy of caring owners. The long menu specialises in fish and seafood like starters of tiger prawns wrapped in filo with a Cantonese spicy kung po dipping sauce (£6.50), and mains of whole baked dorade with basil oil, Greek salad and new potatoes (£13), but there are plenty of non-fish options such as duck confit and bangers and mash. Soft toffee and mascarpone cheesecake will fill up any corners. House wines are £11.95. Open Tue to Sat L and D.

● **STRETE** (Devon)
Laughing Monk Totnes Road, (01803) 770639. Converted Victorian schoolhouse, now a personally run restaurant favoured by locals and holidaymakers alike. Devon produce shows up on the menu in the shape of, say, baked goats' cheese layered with puff

pastry and roast red onions (£5.50) and roast herb-crusted rack of lamb with aubergine and fig confit and a port and rosemary jus (£14.75). The dessert trolley has been enthusiastically recommended. Well-chosen, affordable wines from £10.95. Open Tue to Sat D plus L last Sun in month autumn and winter.

● **STUDLAND** (Dorset)
Shell Bay   Ferry Road, (01929) 450363. A simply amazing location – facing Poole harbour with views to Brownsea Island – goes hand-in-hand with an informal 'beachy' feel at this usefully placed restaurant (there's not a lot else in the vicinity). There's seating inside and out, and the short, fish-led menu has served up praiseworthy chilled gazpacho (£5) and whole plaice with chunky chips (£13). Chargrilled medallions of Scotch fillet on lyonnaise potatoes (£18) and a vegetarian dish offer further choice. House wine £11.50. Open all week.

● **SURBITON** (Surrey)
Loco   61–63 Brighton Road, (020) 8399 2441. An open kitchen is the focal point of this pleasant neighbourhood restaurant. All things Italian dictate the menu, which opens with Parma ham, rocket and Gorgonzola (£5.50) and concludes with strawberries with balsamic and mascarpone (£5). In between, expect pasta (linguine with pesto, £4.25/£7.75) and main courses like grilled swordfish with marinated aubergine, red pepper and olive sauce (£12). Italy also heads the short wine list, with prices from £12.95. Open Fri and Sat L and Tue to Sat D. Branches at Blackheath (see Round-up entry) and 222 Munster Road, Fulham, SW6; tel: (020) 7381 6137.

● **SUTTON ON THE FOREST** (North Yorkshire)
Rose & Crown Inn   Main Street, (01347) 811333. New owners are aiming for a 'rural-bistro' feel at this well-heeled village pub. Bare tables and paper napkins set the tone and the kitchen delivers creditable modern dishes like ballotine of chicken, foie gras and rabbit (£7), a mighty plateful of Barbary duck breast with Paris Brown mushrooms, salsify, green beans and potato galette (£13.50) followed by iced nougatine parfait with citrus consommé. Real ales and plenty of drinkable wines under £20. Open Tue to Sat and Sun L.

● **SWANAGE** (Dorset)
Cauldron Bistro   5 High Street, (01929) 422671. 'Since we opened, the atmosphere has often felt like a dining club!' notes Terry Flenley, chef/proprietor of this popular bistro. Daily deliveries of South Coast fish dictate the handwritten menu, which offers specials like fillet of wild halibut with roast tomatoes and thyme and garlic butter (£15.50). Start with a salad of seared king scallops (£7) and conclude with chocolate truffle cake (£4.50). Meaty alternatives could run to sirloin of naturally reared bison with horseradish mash. House wines from £10.95. Open Thur to Sun.

● **TADPOLE BRIDGE** (Oxfordshire)
Trout   Tadpole Bridge, (01367) 870382. The setting – on the banks of the river Thames – may be dyed-in-the-wool traditional but the food in this county pub/restaurant fizzes with fashionable flourishes. Polenta and carpaccio of tuna add a touch of modernism to short menus, which are bolstered by blackboard specials. Trout comes as tartare and gravadlax (£5.25), venison is teamed with fig tart and sautéed cabbage (£15.95), or there's tomato and black olive risotto with roasted vegetables and Parmesan. The 80-strong wine list includes 10 house wines from £9.95. Accommodation. Closed Sun D.

● **TETBURY** (Gloucestershire)
Calcot Manor, Gumstool Inn   Tetbury, (01666) 890391. All-day, brasserie-style 'inn' attached to a swanky Georgian country house hotel complete with formal gardens and its own spa. The flexible, fairly priced menu casts its net wide for 'ample' and 'generous' dishes to suit all appetites: avocado with prawn mousse, crème fraîche and dill (£6), Asian duck salad with pickled ginger (£7.50 or £10.50), Hungarian goulash and Thai lamb curry (£12) show the style. Substantial wine list with a dozen offerings by the glass (from £4). Open all week.

● **TOPSHAM** (Devon)
Galley   41 Fore Street, (01392) 876078. Fish cookery with a twist is Paul Da-Costa-Greaves's passion in this converted cottage overlooking the Exe estuary. Supplies from the Devon boats are the impetus for menus that plunder the globe for inspiration. Consider red mullet fillets 'towered on' mixed pasta (£8.50), John Dory with Bombay

potatoes, coriander and spiced mango (£20) and – perhaps – the 'Seductress' (aka baked lemon and vanilla cheesecake). Six champagnes by the glass (from £5.95) and organic tipples aplenty. Accommodation in self-styled 'cabins'. Closed Mon L.

● TORQUAY (Devon)

Mulberry House 1 Scarborough Road, (01803) 213639. Since 1985, Lesley Cooper has been performing minor miracles in this spick-and-span Victorian terraced house. Her distinctive brand of home cooking is based on top-drawer ingredients, and her menus change daily. Expect to pay around £25 for three courses such as smoked ham rissoles with apple sauce, slow-roast free-range Devon duck with cherry brandy sauce, and sherry trifle or crème brûlée. House wine £10. Booking essential. Accommodation. Open Fri to Sun L, Wed to Sat D (residents only Mon and Tue D).

● TRESCO (Isles of Scilly)

Island Hotel Tresco, (01720) 422883. Sophisticated hotel with awesome views and a wondrous setting on the 'island of flowers'. Fixed-price 'gourmet dinners' (£37.50 for three courses) offer classical hotel cooking along the lines of John Dory fillet in puff pastry with white Burgundy sauce, then honey-glazed Barbary duck with dauphinoise potatoes and Griottine cherries, followed by Island fruit salad with citrus sorbet. Buffet lunches on the terrace (weather permitting). Well-annotated, all-round wine list with prices from £16. Open all week.

● TROUTBECK (Cumbria)

Queens Head Hotel Townhead, (015394) 32174. A traditional coaching inn that's worth knowing about if you plan to take in the views over Troutbeck Valley. Light lunches include pan-fried pork schnitzel set on creamy garlic noodles (£5.95), or steamed mussels with garlic and herbs (£5.25), while dinner promises hearty dishes of shank of English lamb braised with red wine and rosemary (£10.50) or suprême of chicken with leek champ and mustard cream. Set dinner menu £15.50 for three courses. Fine real ales and creditable wines from £10.80. Accommodation. Open all week.

● TUNBRIDGE WELLS (Kent)

Le Petit Blanc Five Ways, Lime Hill Road, (01892) 559170. The latest branch of a mini chain founded by Raymond Blanc overlooks the town's Victoria Shopping Centre. Like its relatives, this outlet delivers accessible brasserie food along the lines of chicken liver and foie gras parfait (£7) and sea bream fillet with bouillabaisse sauce (£16.50), followed by desserts such as hot chocolate fondant with pistachio ice cream (£6.50). The wine list is M. Blanc's tribute to the rebirth of French vineyards; prices from £12.95. Open all week. Other branches in Birmingham, Cheltenham, Manchester and Oxford (see Round-ups).

● WAKEFIELD (West Yorkshire)

Wolski's Monarch House, George Street (01924) 381252. Spread over three floors, Wolski's combines an informal bar/brasserie, a smarter restaurant, and a banqueting/ conference facilities. The restaurant specialises in lobster offering crab and lobster soup (£6.95) as a warm up before roast lobster with parsley butter or lobster Thermidor (£13.95-£19.95). Alternatively plump for roast rack of lamb, served pink, with baby cottage pie and redcurrant sauce (£15.95) or cumin spiced ostrich. Light lunches and early evening meals are served in the bar. House wines start at £11.95. Closed Sun.

● WALKINGTON (East Riding of Yorkshire)

Manor House Northlands, (01482) 881645. Long-established timber-clad country house hotel where new owners are trying hard to make their mark. Two formal dining rooms (one overlooking the lawned garden). Fixed-price menus (£34.50 plus supplements) based around good-quality Yorkshire produce: fillet of beef with wild mushroom ravioli, for example. Start with lobster bisque and a tian of crabmeat; finish with, say, lemon and lime cheesecake. House wines from £12.50. Closed Sat L and all Sun.

● WARWICK (Warwickshire)

Rose and Crown 30 Market Place, (01926) 411117. Revitalised town-centre inn that's home to real ales, affordable wines and innovative food. A flexible menu opens with breakfast and continues all day, drawing crowds to the bustling, cosmopolitan space. Salmon fishcake, dill and white wine sauce (£8.50), and confit duck leg, creamed cabbage and cinnamon aniseed sauce (£11.50), are typical of the bistro style. Alternatively, there's the pick-and-mix deli board with cheeses, charcuterie and the like. House French £10.50. Open all week.

● **WESTFIELD** (East Sussex)

Wild Mushroom Woodgate House, Westfield Lane, (01424) 751137. A 'splendid variety' of home-baked breads have impressed visitors to Paul and Rebecca Webbe's restaurant in a Victorian house. The kitchen spreads its wings for menus that might work their way through tiger prawn, aubergine and courgette tempura with Thai dressing (£7) and poached loin of organic lamb with bean panaché, tomato and basil jus (£15.50), before returning home for summer pudding with sweetened cream (£5). House wines from £10.95. Open Tue to Fri and Sun L, Tue to Sat D.

● **WEYMOUTH** (Dorset)

Abbotsbury Seafood Bar Abbotsbury Oyster Farm, Ferrybridge (01305) 788867. Right on the edge of the sea near Portland Bill, this small restaurant is an outlet for the Abbotsbury Oyster Farm. Alongside mussels (steamed in white wine sauce) and oysters (au naturel, or grilled with garlic, herbs and lemon butter), there's a wide selection of very fresh fish from a 'day boat', but bad weather can mean no supplies. Baked cod with herb and citrus crust is typical (£14.95), or really push the boat out and have a Portland crab and shellfish feast (£42.90 for 2 to 4 people). Wine is chalked up on a blackboard with house bottles £9.95. Open Tue to Sun L and Thur to Sat D.

Perry's 4 Trinity Road, (01305) 785799. Fish is the first choice in this family-run restaurant overlooking the harbour. The kitchen casts off with shellfish soup (£4.50) and cruises on to baked halibut with saffron and mussel sauce or grilled lemon sole with chips (£15). Meat eaters are offered alternatives like beef fillet with mustard sauce, while desserts are favourite things such as raspberry and white chocolate mousse (£4.75). Vins de pays £10.50. Open Tue to Fri and Sun L and Mon to Sat D (plus Sun D Apr to Sept).

● **WHITEWELL** (Lancashire)

Inn at Whitewell Whitewell, Forest of Bowland, (01200) 448222. Lighting is 'predictably dim' at this upmarket, rambling inn to suit the 'olde worlde' feel of roaring fires, cosy rooms, tapestry seats, antique furniture and sporting prints. Eat Barnsley chops or excellent fish and chips in the bar, or dine in the restaurant on terrine of braised ham hock (£6), roast cannon of Bowland lamb with split pea and peppercorn purée (£16.50), and chocolate pot with spiced orange biscuit (£4.20). Fair mark ups on a creditable wine list. Accommodation. Open all week.

● **WHITSTABLE** (Kent)

Whitstable Oyster Fishery Co Royal Native Oyster Stores, (01227) 276856. Converted Victorian warehouse and oyster store, now a beachside restaurant devoted to fish. Whitstable natives and rock oysters top the bill, and the blackboard menu keeps things simple with jellied eels (£5), Norfolk potted shrimps (£7), and deep-fried local dabs with mayo, plus chargrilled mackerel with tomato salsa (£12.50), and whole Portland cock crab (£17.50). There's a bar for pre- and post-prandial drinks at weekends. Beers courtesy of the Whitstable Brewery, plus a cluster of wines from £11.95. Closed Mon.

● **WICKHAM** (Hampshire)

Old House The Square, (01329) 833049. Handsome, creeper-clad and well-appointed Georgian town house that now boasts three dining rooms. The kitchen concentrates mainly on European-inspired dishes including twice-baked Roquefort soufflé with pear and walnut cream (£6), roast turbot and dill tagliatelle (£15.25) and honeyed duck breast with lavender and lentil jus and Savoy cabbage. Suggested dessert wines are listed alongside sweets like plum frangipane with toasted almond ice cream. Nine house wines (from £12.95) head a 60-strong list. Accommodation available. Closed Sun D.

● **WILMSLOW** (Cheshire)

Heddy's 102 Water Lane, (01625) 526855. Neighbourhood prices, authentic cooking and friendly service ensure that Heddy's affable pan-Middle Eastern restaurant gets packed with regulars. Extensive menu with a 'lovely range of meze' (from £7.50), plus main events like 'immense' couscous Maroccain (£11.95) and marinated baked sea bass stuffed with parsley and garlic. Baklava and other desserts (£2.50/£3) are par for the course. Global wine list (from £11.95) with some intriguing

Lebanese selections. Reports please. Open Mon to Sat.

● **WINDERMERE** (Cumbria)

Kwela's 4 High Street, (01539) 444954. Named after shanty town jazz, this fascinating place brings modern African cooking to a touristy Lakeland honey-pot. Starters like Ivorian plantain loaf could precede Western Cape seafood potje (a light stew topped with bulgar wheat, £12.75) or Sengalese-style guinea fowl with beetroot 'jallof'. Pannacotta is given a twist with Red Bush tea (£4.25) or you could finish with coconut tart and apricot 'porcupines'. Breakfasts and light lunches during the holiday season. Short, eclectic wine list from £10. Open Sat and Sun L, Tue to Sun D.

● **WINSFORD** (Somerset)

Royal Oak Inn Winsford, (01643) 851455. With its thatched roof and attractive village setting, this ancient inn is a rather appealing spot. Light lunches, along the lines of soup, sandwiches, ploughman's and sausage and mash are served in the bar (£3.95–£12.50), while more ambitious evening meals (£24.50 for three courses) are offered in the restaurant: say, pigeon and venison terrine with spiced pear chutney followed by chargrilled suprême of chicken with wilted spinach, light herb oil and cherry tomatoes, all rounded off with West Country cheeses. House French is £11.45. Accommodation. Open all week.

● **WINTERTON** (North Lincolnshire)

The George, O'Connor's Restaurant Market Hill, (01724) 732270. Modest, but aspiring restaurant bedecked with curios and bric-a-brac above a stoically traditional Lincolnshire town pub. The kitchen buys locally and aims high, with exquisite pre-starter 'tasters' before, say, a salad of black pudding, fried quail's egg and Calvados sauce (£4.75). Mains could feature grilled sea bass with a medley of root vegetables and lemon butter sauce (£15.75), while desserts have included a 'really steamy' brioche bread-and-butter pudding with marmalade sauce (£4.25). Limited but well chosen wines from £11.95. Open Wed to Sat D and Sun L.

● **WOBURN** (Bedfordshire)

Paris House Woburn Park, (01525) 290692. Unique timbered house that stands imposingly in the grounds of Woburn Park. Peter Chandler's cooking is classical French all the way, although it comes at a price. The £55 carte buys dishes that work their way from confit of duck with orange salad, via lamb cutlets with tarragon sauce, to tarte Tatin with vanilla ice cream. Set lunches (£20-£30) ease the financial burden, although the platinum-card wine list takes no prisoners; house vin de pays is £16. Closed Sun D and all day Mon.

● **WOLVERHAMPTON** (West Midlands)

Bilash Tandoori 2 Cheapside, (01902) 427762. Enterprising Indian in the centre of town opposite the Civic Centre, specialising in custom-built dishes that are noticeably different from the provincial curry-house norm. The wide-ranging menu includes starters like Goan coconut pancake (£5) and chicken pancake, while everyday tandooris are eclipsed by creative ideas such as maach diya masala (grilled marinated sea bass with warm tomato 'salsa', mint and yoghurt) and beef and chilli stir-fry (£12.50). Promising, up-to-the-minute wine list. Closed Sun.

● **WOODBRIDGE** (Suffolk)

Riverside Quayside, (01394) 382587. The oldest cinema in the country, updated for sound and comfort, is just part of the package at this Suffolk success story. There's also a restaurant delivering accurate, unpretentious cooking that takes in lunchtime tapas as well as fixed-price menus (two courses £15, three £20) featuring spiced crab salad and guacamole, chargrilled Adnams pork chop with crispy black pudding, plus Suffolk strawberries and crème chantilly to finish. Creditable selection of wines by the glass (from £3); house wines £12. Closed Sun D.

● **WORCESTER** (Worcestershire)

Brown's 24 Quay Street, (01905) 26263. Converted eighteenth-century grain mill by the Severn that has been a fixture of the Worcester scene for many years. There has been a change in ownership, but the long-serving kitchen team continues. Anglo-French fixed-price lunch and dinner menus (£18.95 and £38.50).Grilled sea bass fillets with leeks, bacon and cider vinaigrette is a typical starter, before chargrilled quail and pearl barley risotto; desserts like white chocolate and raspberry parfait precede the cheeseboard. Global wine list with house recommendations £12.95. Open Tue to Fri and Sun L, Tue to Sat D.

● **WYTHAM** (Oxfordshire)

White Hart Wytham, (01865) 244372. A favourite out-of-town destination for those seeking a pub with bright, modern décor and a menu to match. Self-styled 'divine' salads might include chargrilled summer vegetables with rocket pesto and devilled walnuts (£9), while classic mains could range from lamb steak with red wine, thyme jus and mint salsa (£15) to fishcakes with wasabi crème fraîche and herb salad. Start with carpaccio of beef and finish with pear and almond tart with vanilla ice cream (£5). House wine £11. Open all week.

Scotland

● **ARCHIESTOWN** (Moray)

Archiestown Hotel Archiestown, (01340) 810218. This village on the banks of the River Spey has the eponymous hotel at its heart. A 'comfortable and country-house feel' pervades. The bistro looks rather less traditional. The à la carte menu might start with leek and potato soup (£4), or warm salad of chicken livers with local chanterelles and raspberries. Local produce also figures large in main courses: guinea fowl perhaps, or loin of venison with dauphinoise potatoes, raspberries and black pudding (£15.50). Finish with a dessert from the blackboard or a selection of Scottish cheeses. Closed Sun D.

● **EDINBURGH** (Edinburgh)

Blue Bar Café 10 Cambridge Street, (0131) 221 1222. 'Urban chic' sums up this cool, casual brasserie above the Traverse Theatre and close to Usher Hall. Culture vultures and others hunting for a prime deal appreciate its flexibility: have anything from a quick light dish (grilled sardines with plum tomato salad, £5.75) to three courses. Duck confit with black pudding mash (£9.50) and roast smoked haddock with sauté potatoes, rocket and truffle oil (£9.95) have passed muster, but sweets may disappoint. Well-chosen wines, 'pretty painless' prices. Open Mon to Sat (also Sun during Festival).

Centotre 103 George Street, (0131) 2251550 This spin off from Valvona and Crolla is centrally located (hence the name) in a former banking hall and has a 1950s retro feel despite the grandness of Doric columns. Open all day, the menu ranges from coffee and cake through sandwiches to full meals. Early reports indicate that the kitchen needs time to settle down, but ravioli filled with spinach and ricotta with sage butter (£6.95), half lobster with spaghettini (£19.95), and 'excellent' pannacotta got the thumbs up from one reporter. Creditable Italian wine list is fairly priced. Open all week.

Fishers 1 Shore, (0131) 554 5666. This former pub premises retains an informal approach and offers a generous choice of dishes which roll over from day to day, putting fish centre stage. Keep it simple with a bowl of fish soup or steamed west coast mussels in white wine, garlic and cream (£8.95), or opt for more exotic ideas along the lines of tempura soft-shelled crab, Asian vegetables and red Thai coconut sauce (£5.75), and whole Moses perch with warm courgette, rosemary and smoked garlic salad (£14.95). House wine £10.75. Open all week.

Shore 3–4 Shore, (0131) 553 5080. One-time seamen's pub, now a casual fish bar-cum-restaurant by Leith waterside. Fresh ingredients, accurate cooking and globally inspired dishes like grilled sardines with caper and lemon butter (£5), Finnan 'haddie' topped with chorizo and Mozzarella (£12), and seared scallops with coconut, chilli and Kaffir lime leaves (£15.25). Limited meat and vegetarian options. House wine £11.30. Open all week.

Suruchi 121 Constitution Street, 0131 554 3268. Indian regional dishes translated into broad Edinburgh patois is the novel idea behind this restaurant, which also makes a feature of food festivals and jazz. 'Sterters' ('tae get yer juices gaun') might include salmon tikka (£5) and vegetarian haggis fritters, while curries could run to achar gosht ('lamb cookit with ginger in a yoghurt and picle mixter-maxter', £8.75), or Goan prawns. Good range of rice and breads. House wine £10.50. Closed Sun L. The original branch is at 14a Nicolson Street; tel: (0131) 556 6583.

● **GLASGOW** (Glasgow)
Café Gandolfi 64 Albion Street, (0141) 552 6813. Bold furniture, stained glass, and a trendy buzz give a European air to this crowded and jolly all-day café. Quality and invention are the hallmarks of the menu, from breakfast to such dishes as Stornoway black pudding with mushrooms and pancakes (£5.50), Arbroath smokies baked with tomatoes and cream, smoked venison with gratin dauphinois (£11.50), and linguine with Italian sausage and tomato ragù (£7.75). Baguettes, sourdough sandwiches and scones also available. Open all week.

● **GLENLIVET** (Moray)
Minmore House Glenlivet, (01807) 590378. Substantial, but unshowy country-house hotel in four acres of landscaped gardens close to Blairfindy Castle and the Glenlivet Distllery. There's no printed menu, but chef/proprietor Victor Janssen explains what's available on the nightly four-course dinner (£35): expect dishes along the lines of butternut squash soup, a tranche of hot-smoked salmon with hollandaise, Gressingham duck breast with two kinds of potato and vegetables, then raspberry crème brûlée. South African wines figure prominently on the list. Open all week.

● **INVERNESS** (Highland)
Dunain Park (01463) 230512. Imposing grey-stone Georgian mansion, now an easy-going family-friendly hotel with charming owners. Dinner in the plush restaurant is a classical four-course affair beginning with a soup (wild mushroom for example) before, say, smoked haddock rarebit on sliced tomatoes (£7). Mains range from sea bass with squid tagliatelle, white wine and parsley jus (£17) to herb-crusted fillet of lamb with rosemary sauce. To finish, choose from the array of ready-made desserts (£7) laid out on the sideboard. Quality wine list at fair prices. Open all week D only.

● **MELROSE** (Borders)
Burt's Hotel Market Square, (01896) 822285. Family-run hotel built in 1722 and very much the hub of the town. Bar snacks are commendable, as are more formal meals in the restaurant. Here, set menus (three courses £29.75) pair traditional Scottish ingredients with modern ideas, as in a parfait of lobster, monkfish and salmon with cracked black pepper, coriander seed, lemon dressing and truffle-scented salad, and pan-fried sea bass on chive and spring onion mash with tomato coulis. House wine £12.25. Open all week.

● **NEWTON STEWART** (Dumfries & Galloway)
Kirroughtree Hotel (01671) 402141. Imposing eighteenth-century mansion, now a country-house hotel cosseted in well-tended grounds. Formal four-course dinners (£32.50) are based on Scottish produce: typically, start with ham mousse with sweet pepper sauce before carrot and butternut squash soup. Move on to sea bream fillet with turned potatoes, tomato confit, asparagus and sauce vierge and conclude with, say, Drambuie parfait and Glayva sauce or Scottish cheeses. Reasonably priced international wine list. Open all week.

● **OBAN** (Argyll & Bute)
Waterfront 1 Railway Pier, (01631) 563110. 'From the pier to the pan...as fast as we can!' runs the motto of this converted seaman's mission overlooking Oban Bay. Locally landed seafood is - of course - the main business and menus are dictated by the catch and the weather. Expect lobster and crab bisque (£5), seared scallops with bacon and leek risotto (£15.50 main course) or haddock and chips, plus fillet steak for meat-eaters. Finish with cheese, ice creams or crème brûlée (£4.25). Light, one-course meals lunchtime and early evening; house wine £11.99. Open all week.

● **PLOCKTON** (Highland)
Plockton Inn Innes Street, (01599) 544222. Refreshingly down-to-earth village inn a few doors from the seafront. No grandeur, no makeovers, but a 'marvellously restful' atmosphere and fine fish (including delights from the owners' smokehouse). Seafood platters (£6.50/£14) are a decent bet, soups such as smoked haddock chowder (£3) are honestly made, and the kitchen also handles everything from Thai mussels to haggis with clapshot (£7). To finish, home-made frozen cranachan has been 'a poem'. Scottish real ales and around 20 global wines. Accommodation. Open all week.

● **STEIN** (Highland)
Loch Bay 1-2 Macleod Terrace, (01470) 592235. The white-painted Loch Bay restaurant enjoys a 'magnificent setting' close

to the water's edge. Local seafood is the order of the day, unadorned, and allowed to shine. The lobster platter has been 'exemplary', the shellfish as fresh as one reporter has ever had. The blackboard displays the day's catch. Organic salmon comes poached or grilled (£11.50), and Loch Bay king prawns dressed and served cold (£19), or grilled with garlic butter (£20.50). Finish with clootie dumpling (£4.25) or Scottish cheeses (£5.25). Closed Sat L and all day Sun.

● **STONEHAVEN** (Aberdeenshire)
Tolbooth Old Pier, (01569) 762287. Relaxed restaurant above a small museum on the north side of Stonehaven harbour. Good views are to be had from the windows of the pleasant, wood-floored dining room. Fish dominates, as in salmon mousse topped with home-cured salmon (£5.25) or pan-fried medallions of monkfish with chorizo in smoked garlic and saffron sauce (£15.50). There are meat

alternatives like pot-roast haunch of venison with rich port and orange sauce; desserts run to banana and walnut pudding (£5). House wine £11.95. Open Tue to Sat L and D.

● **TORRIDON** (Highland)
Loch Torridon Hotel Loch Torridon, (01445) 791242. Wondrously remote baronial country hotel in untamed Highland countryside, where the mountain walks are 'second to none'. Seasonal fixed-price menus (£39) take account of Scottish produce including sea trout, Shetland mussels and Black Isle beef. Expect complex dishes like steamed wild sea bass stuffed with langoustine mousse served with sauerkraut, a panaché of vegetables, herb bouillon and caviar, followed by - perhaps - a slice of strawberry and Champagne jelly with black sesame tian. 'Bright, well informed staff' and an extensive wine list with prices from £16.75. Open all week D only.

Wales

● **BETWS-Y-COED** (Conwy)
Ty Gwyn Hotel Betws-y-coed, (01690) 710383. Ty Gwyn (the 'white house') is a venerable coaching inn set in a 'Victorian honeymoon village' at the heart of the Snowdonia National Park. The kitchen satisfies with asparagus served with warm hollandaise (£4.25), and grilled Conwy salmon with dry Vermouth and sweet basil butter sauce (£13), together with specials (Thai-marinated Welsh lamb chops). Vegetarian options might include savoury fried Brie with sage and hoisin sauce. House wine is £12. Open all week.

● **BRECON** (Powys)
Barn at Brynich Brynich, (01874) 623480. Part of a busy complex alongside the A470, serving visitors to the Brecon Beacons National Park (children's play area and camp site available). Local ingredients get a good outing, whether it's bresaola of Welsh Black beef (£5), confit of Llangynidr duck on rhubarb and vanilla compote (£12) or rainbow trout with smoked bacon and wild mushrooms. The flame-grill delivers a few keenly priced, retro classics like pork steak Diane, while desserts could include chocolate

marquise. Everyday wines from £7.95. Open all week (closed Mon in winter).
Tipple 'n' Tiffin Theatr Brychieniog, (01874) 611866. 'Shared eating' is encouraged in the Gudsell's casual café-style venue in the Brecon Theatre. They support local and organic produce in a big way and their kitchen is keen on hot-smoking and oak-roasting. Dishes are all priced from £6–£8, whether it's deep-fried Penclawydd cockles with salsa and crispy bacon, goats' cheese and spinach terrine or game sausages on root mash. Finish with local ice creams or a home-made dessert like chocolate espresso crème brûlée (£4). Short, sharp wine list with prices from £11. Closed Sun.

● **CARDIFF** (Cardiff)
Gilby's Old Port Road, (029) 2067 0800. Open-beamed barn of a place, on the rural edge of west Cardiff, which offers an 'enormous' range of menus dealing in orthodox choice and robust portions. Prawn cocktail and fish 'n' chips are likely options from the fixed-price lunch (two courses £12.50), 'Simply Fish' (two courses £20) delivers langoustine and saffron risotto and halibut Mornay, and the carte features lobster thermidor, chargrilled steaks, and grilled

organic Orkney salmon. Sticky toffee pudding makes a familiar finale. House wines from £12.95. Closed Sun D and Mon.

Le Monde 60 St Mary's Street, (029) 2038 7376. Tables cannot be booked in advance, so the deal is to wander about to see what's on offer from the displays of fish (sold by weight), meat and salads, then join the queue. The chargrill dominates the cooking – say, beef kebab (£10.75) or crawfish tail – while sea bass is cooked in rock salt (£13); all come with a choice of fries, jacket or new potatoes. Start perhaps with a pint of shrimps (£4.25) or home-made game pâté. House wine £11.95. Closed Sun.

● **CASTLEMORRIS** (Pembrokeshire)
Tides Restaurant Llangloffan Farm, (01348) 891383. Immaculate modern restaurant/ coffee shop in a barn attached to Llangloffan Farm and Cheese Centre. Café food at lunchtime, more ambitious 'dinner-party' stuff in the evening. Seafood fares well, as in seared Cardigan Bay scallops with honey and soy dressing (£7) and line-caught sea bass with lobster and vanilla sauce; otherwise go for organic fillet steak with red wine sauce. Finish with sticky toffee pudding (£4.75) – and don't forget the cheeses. House wine £9.95. Open Apr to Oct Mon to Sat L and Wed to Sat D; Nov to Mar Fri and Sat D.

● **GLANWYDDEN** (Conwy)
Queen's Head Glanwydden, (01492) 546570. The Queen's Head draws crowds from near and far, thanks to its civilised pubby atmosphere, good food and decent wines. The extensive menu sounds a patriotic note, whether it's grilled local fish (£16.50), Conwy pork and leek sausages, or rack of Welsh lamb (£12.75). Treatments, however, are global: for example, seared Anglesey king scallops with hummus, tortilla chips and sweet chilli dip, Jamaican chicken curry, and spring onion and sweetcorn risotto. House wine is £13.50 a litre. Open all week.

● **LETTERSTON** (Pembrokeshire)
Something's Cooking The Square, (01348) 840621. Take in the 'fish facts' while perusing the menu in this great-value fish 'n' chip joint. Cod, line-caught haddock (£6–£8) and plaice can be poached or deep-fried in 'rice cones'; otherwise, batter rules. Fishcakes (£5), dressed crab and whole sea bass are also on show,

along with a few non-seafood items like gammon steak. Banana 'boats', pineapple fritters and fruit crumble to finish (£3.25); everyday wines from £9.50. On the Fishguard-Haverfordwest road and a godsend for families on holiday. Closed Sun and Mon.

● **LLANARMON DYFFRYN CEIRIOG** (Wrexham)
West Arms Llanarmon Dyffryn Ceiriog, (01691) 600665. Originally licensed as a hotel in 1670, this is now a thoroughly up-to-the-minute stopover in a remote part of the Ceiriog valley. Welsh ingredients have their say on the bar menu and the local theme is followed through in the restaurant, where fixed-price dinners (£27.95/£32) take in guinea fowl terrine with basil chutney, herb-crusted fillet of organic lamb with wild mushrooms and red wine sauce, and caramel delice with raspberry compote. Open all week.

● **LLANFYLLIN** (Powys)
Seeds 5 Penybryn Cottages, (01691) 648604. Mark Seager cooks and Felicity oversees events in this tastefully decorated, beamed cottage restaurant. Good-value, fixed-price evening menus (£21/£23) move confidently from warm goats' cheese salad and filo parcels of crab with papaya salsa via fillet steak and steamed chicken breast with butter beans to crème brûlée and treacle tart. Service is 'fast without being rushed'. The wine list is a comprehensive slate running to 165 bins, with prices from £11. Open Thur to Sun L and Wed to Sat D.

● **LLANWRTYD WELLS** (Powys)
Lasswade Country House Station Road, (01591) 610515. Edwardian residence near Llanwrtyd Wells station, now a welcoming family-run country-house hotel. The concise dinner menu (three courses £22.55, plus VAT) stays close to home for locally smoked organic salmon with apple and horseradish cream, slow-roast shoulder of new season's mountain lamb on a bed of orange-scented butter beans, and sautéed hedgerow fruits doused in Welsh birch wine. A couple of organics show up on the creditable wine list; vin de pays is £9.95. Open all week D only.

● **PEMBROKE** (Pembrokeshire)
Old Kings Arms 13 Main Street, (01646) 683611. Reputedly Pembroke's oldest hostelry, run by the Wheeler family for over

50 years. The kitchen makes good use of indigenous supplies for a restaurant menu that could list hot cockles with laverbread and bacon (£6), pan-fried Welsh Black fillet steak with mushrooms (£17), seared lamb fillet on wilted greens with port and redcurrant sauce, and simple puddings like apple pie (£3.60). Sandwiches and light meals in the bar. Fifty wines from £8.75. Open all week.

● **ROCKFIELD** (Monmouthshire)
Stone Mill Rockfield, (01600) 716273. Unpretentious restaurant housed in a remote sixteenth-century cider mill. The kitchen applies a few generous modern twists to Italian classics, as in linguine with spring vegetables and pesto (£5), or fillet of Monmouthshire Black beef with risotto rösti, wild mushrooms, broad beans and chargrilled radicchio (£17). Desserts (£4.75) could include lemon and almond cake with mascarpone cream. Six house wines (£11) head the compact list. Accommodation in self-catering cottages. Open Sun L, Tue to Sat L and D.

● **SOLVA** (Pembrokeshire)
The Old Pharmacy 5 Main Street, (01437) 720005. Menus rather than medicines now catch the eye in Martin Lawton's relaxed, one-time chemist's shop. Fish is a strong suit (anything from Solva crab and lobster to marlin and red snapper); otherwise the kitchen dispenses global dishes like warm salad of pan-fried tofu with lemongrass and ginger (£6), Preseli lamb sausages with butterbean casserole (£15.50) and Tunisian citrus cake (£5). Warm, happy atmosphere, 'wonderful service'. Three dozen very decent wines from £11.90. Open all week D only.

● **SWANSEA** (Swansea)
Fredericks 654–656 Mumbles Road, (01792) 368900. Bright and modern good looks distinguish this restaurant, part of the Carlton Hotel. The cooking takes inspiration from local ingredients in an up-to-date style that's grafted on to a classic French base. Laverbread pikelet is topped with cockles, leeks and Carmarthen ham with white wine sauce (£4.50), while plump mussels may come as traditional marinière. Cod fillet on spinach with scallops and mussels and a white wine and chervil sauce (£15) is typical, and properly hung fillet steak is first rate. The set lunch (two

courses £11.95) is a bargain. Closed Sun and Mon.

Knights 614–616 Mumbles Road, (01792) 363184. Diners here have panoramic views of Swansea Bay to go with their plates of locally caught fish and seafood. Dishes range from reliable favourites like lobster, prawn and melon cocktail and Dover sole with herb butter (£19) to the more exotic chargrilled Cajun shark steak with chilli jam and garlic mayonnaise (£12.50). Meat lovers can tuck into chargrilled kangaroo kebabs, or roast guinea fowl with redcurrant and strawberry sauce (£13). The set lunch is good value (two courses £9.50). House wines from £11.75. Closed Sun D.

Mermaids 686 Mumbles Road, (01792) 367744. Busy coffee lounge-cum-restaurant on the famous 'Mumbles mile seafront'. Minimalist décor, canteen-style layout and quotes from Dylan Thomas inscribed on the walls. Welsh ingredients and eclectic ideas like cockle fritters with smoked salmon, garlic and laverbread in Cajun chilli batter (£7), and roast rack of salt marsh lamb with rosemary, apricot and celery sauce (£15). Dark and white chocolate torte with butterscotch sauce (£4.50) for afters. Reasonably priced wines; many New World bottles. Mon to Sun L, Tue to Sat D (summer all week D).

P.A.'s 95 Newton Road, (01792) 367723. Lively, long-serving wine bar in the commercial centre of Mumbles. The full menu changes fortnightly, but expect dishes like duck liver and brandy parfait (£5) followed by baked chicken with honey, lemon and thyme (£12.50) or rack of Welsh lamb on scallion mash with puttanesca sauce, plus desserts such as dark chocolate, orange and Grand Marnier truffle cake. Also look for daily fish specials like medallions of monkfish and king prawns with chilli, tomato and coriander. Cut-price lunches; house wine £9.95. Closed Sun D.

● **TREDUNNOCK** (Monmouthshire)
Newbridge Inn Tredunnock, (01633) 451000. Remote, quirkily decorated pebbledash inn by a bridge over the River Usk. High-quality raw materials (from crayfish to Carmarthenshire beef) figure on a menu that covers locally smoked duck and orange salad (£6.25), cannon of Welsh lamb with

ratatouille and rosemary jus (£18.50), and Cornish fish specials like sea bass on Mediterranean couscous with bouillabaisse sauce. Desserts could include glazed orange tart with strawberry and mint salad (£5). Wines from £12.50. Accommodation. Open all week.

● **WELSH HOOK** (Pembrokeshire)
Stone Hall Welsh Hook, (01348) 840212. Martine Watson has been in residence at her 600-year-old manor house for 20 years and has developed a successful formula of serving prime local materials in French classic style. Tartiflette combines Pembrokeshire potatoes and Welsh bacon with Reblochon cheese (£6.75), and best end of Welsh lamb comes with garlic and redcurrants (£17.25), and there are profiteroles to finish. A good-value four-course menu is £24; and the (almost) all-French wine list opens at £13.10. Accommodation. Open Tue to Sat D.

Channel Islands

● **ST PETER PORT** (Guernsey)
Da Nello 46 The Pollet, (01481) 721552. Rough stone, shipwreck beams, high-backed chairs and white-clothed tables all come together in a bustling formality – Italian-style. Pasta dishes abound, as do copious veal and beef dishes on a menu that's a veritable line-up of trattoria favourites. Well-reported wild mushroom risotto or cannelloni (£6.25) open proceedings, with calf's liver and bacon (£12), or grillade of fish and shellfish (£48 for two), among main courses. House Italian is £9.95. Open all week.

London restaurants by cuisine

Boundaries between national cuisines can be blurred, so the restaurants listed below are classified by the predominant influence, although there may be some crossover. The headings are in many cases more generalised than the brief cuisine descriptions given at the tops of the entries themselves, and restaurants without a single overriding influence are not included on the list at all. This list contains main entries only.

Australian
Osia, SW1

British
Brian Turner Mayfair, W1
Franklins, SE22
Rhodes Twenty Four, EC2
St John, EC1
Smiths of Smithfield: Top Floor, EC1
Tate Britain Restaurant, SW1
Wiltons, SW1

Chinese
Four Seasons, W2
Fung Shing, WC2
Golden Dragon, W1
Hakkasan, W1
Mandarin Kitchen, W2
Mr Kong, WC2
New Diamond, WC2
New Mayflower, W1
Nyonya, W11
Phoenix Palace, NW1
Royal China, W1
Yauatcha, W1

Danish
Lundum's, SW7

East European/ Eurasian
Baltic, SE1
Gay Hussar, W1
Potemkin, EC1

Seafood
Back to Basics, W1
Fish Hoek, W4
Fish Shop, EC1
FishWorks, W4
J. Sheekey, WC2
Lou Pescadou, SW5
One-O-One, SW1

French
Admiralty, WC2
Almeida, N1
Aubergine, SW10
Berkeley Square Café, W1
Bistro Aix, N8
Bleeding Heart, EC1
Brasserie Roux, SW1
Brasserie St Quentin, SW3
The Capital, SW3

Le Cercle, SW1
Chez Moi, W14
Club Gascon, EC1
Le Colombier, SW3
Le Coq d'Argent, EC2
Crowthers, SW14
Drones, SW1
L'Escargot, Ground Floor, W1
L'Escargot, Picasso Room, W1
L'Estaminet, WC2
L'Etranger, SW7
Le Gavroche, W1
Gordon Ramsay, SW3
Gordon Ramsay at Claridge's, W1
Incognico, WC2
Mirabelle, W1
Morgan M, N7
Orrery, W1
Patterson's, W1
Pearl, WC1
Le Petit Max, SW11
Pétrus, SW1
Pied-à-Terre, W1
Plateau, E14
La Poule au Pot, SW1
Putney Bridge Restaurant, SW15
Racine, SW3
Ritz Hotel, W1
Roussillon, SW1
RSJ, SE1
Savoy Grill, WC2
Sketch, W1
South, EC2
Square, W1
Swissôtel The Howard: Jaan, WC2
Tom Aikens, SW3
Les Trois Garçons, E1
La Trompette, W4
Wells, NW3

Fusion/pan-Asian
e&o, W11
East@West, WC2
Eight Over Eight, SW3
Great Eastern Dining Room, EC2
Providores, W1

Greek
Real Greek, N1

Real Greek Souvlaki and Bar, EC1

Indian/Pakistani/ Bangladeshi
Babur Brasserie, SE23
Benares, W1
Café Spice Namaste, E1
Calcutta Notebook, SW18
Chutney Mary, SW10
Cinnamon Club, SW1
Ginger, W2
Haandi, SW3
Lahore Kebab House, E1
Painted Heron, SW10
Parsee, N19
Radha Krishna Bhavan, SW17
Rasa Samudra, W1
Rasoi Vineet Bhatia, SW3
Red Fort, W1
Salloos, SW1
Sarkhel's, SW18
Tamarind, W1
Tandoor, NW9
Yatra, W1
Zaika, SW7

Indian vegetarian
Kastoori, SW17
Rasa, N16
Sabras, NW10

Indonesian/Straits/ Malaysian
Champor-Champor, SE1
Singapore Garden, NW6
Uli, W11

Italian
Al Duca, SW1
Alloro, W1
Al San Vincenzo, W2
Ark, W8
Assaggi, W2
Camerino, W1
Cecconi's, W1
Cipriani, W1
Il Convivio, SW1
Eddalino, W1
Enoteca Turi, SW15
Giardinetto, W1
Green Olive, W9
Isola, SW1

continued . . .

Locanda Locatelli, W1
Metrogusto Islington, N1
Neal Street Restaurant, WC2
Olivo, SW1
Passione, W1
Philpott's Mezzaluna, NW2
Phoenix, SW15
Quo Vadis, W1
Refettorio, EC4
River Café, W6
Salusbury, NW6
Sardo, W1
Tentazioni, SE1
Timo, W8
Zafferano, SW1

Japanese
Café Japan, NW11
Chisou, W1
Itsu, SW3 and W1
Kiku, W1
K10, EC2

Kulu Kulu Sushi, W1
Matsuri High Holborn, WC1
Nobu, W1
Sumosan, W1
Sushi-Hiro, W5
Sushi-Say, NW2
Tsunami, SW4
Ubon by Nobu, E14
Zuma, SW7

North African/ Middle Eastern
Adams Café, W12
Al Hamra, W1
Noura Brasserie, SW1
Numidie, SE19
Original Tagines, W1

South American
Armadillo, E8
Cantaloupe, EC2

Fina Estampa, SE1

Spanish
Cambio de Tercio, SW5
Cigala, WC1
Fino, W1
Moro, EC1

Thai
Blue Elephant, SW6
Nahm, SW1

Turkish
Iznik, N5
Tas, SE1

Vegetarian
Gate, W6

Vietnamese
Huong-Viet, N1

New entries

These restaurants are new main entries in the Guide this year, although some may
have appeared in previous years, or in the Round-ups last year.

London
Allium, SW1
Anchor & Hope, SE1
Bentley: 1880, SW7
Brackenbury, W6
Calcutta Notebook, SW18
Le Cercle, SW1
Champor-Champor, SE1
Chisou, W1
Cipriani, W1
The Ebury: Dining Room, SW1
Eight Over Eight, SW3
L'Etranger, SW7
Franklins, SE22
Giardinetto, W1
Inn the Park, SW1
Inside, SE10
Lahore Kebab House, E1
Morgan M, N7
Mosaica @ the lock, N17
New Mayflower, W1
Notting Hill Brasserie, W11
Novelli in the City, EC4
Numidie, SE19
Nyonya, W11
Painted Heron, SW10
Patterson's, W1
Le Petit Max, SW11
Pétrus, SW1
Plateau, E14
Rasoi Vineet Bhatia, SW3
Refettorio, EC4
Rhodes Twenty Four, EC2
St John Bread & Wine, E1
Sushi-Hiro, W5
Tandoor, NW9

Two Brothers, N3
Uli, W11
Victoria, SW14
Wells, NW3
Wolseley, W1
Yauatcha, W1

England
Amersham, Artichoke
Ashbourne, Dining Room
Barton on Sea, Pebble Beach
Bath, Hole in the Wall
Birmingham, Jessica's
Birmingham, Paris
Birtle, Waggon
Bishop's Tachbrook, Mallory
    Court
Bodiam, Curlew
Bonchurch, Pond Café
Bradford, Mumtaz
Bridport, Chez Cuddy
Bristol, Culinaria
Bristol, Michael Caines at the
    Bristol Marriott Royal
Bristol, One30
Broadway, Lygon Arms
Bury St Edmunds, Maison Bleue
Cambridge, The Volunteer
Chandler's Cross, The Grove:
    Colette's
Chieveley, Crab at Chieveley
Chilgrove, White Horse
Codford, George Hotel
Colerne, Lucknam Park
Dartmouth, New Angel
Dedham, Sun Inn

Eastbourne, Bonnicks
Exeter, Thai Orchid
Fairford, Allium
Farnborough, Inn at
    Farnborough
Fressingfield, Fox and Goose
Grange Moor, Kaye Arms
Grasmere, Jumble Room
Grimsby, Granary
Halifax, Design House
Halifax, Holdsworth House
Harrogate, Hotel du Vin & Bistro
Helmsley, Feversham Arms
    Hotel
Henley-on-Thames, Three Tuns
    Foodhouse
Horningsea, Crown &
    Punchbowl
Hull, Venn
Hutton Magna, Oak Tree Inn
King's Lynn, Rococo
Kirk Deighton, Bay Horse
Knossington, Fox & Hounds
Leeds, Akbar's
Leeds, Anthony's
Leeds, Bibis Criterion
Leicester, Opera House
Leyburn, Sandpiper Inn
Liverpool, Hope Street Hotel:
    London Carriage Works
Looe, Talland Bay Hotel
Looe, Trawlers on the Quay
Lower Hardres, Granville
Lowick, Snooty Fox
Lytham St Anne's, Chicory

Manchester, Establishment
Manchester, Glamorous
Chinese
Manchester, Little Yang Sing
Manchester, Second Floor
Medbourne, Horse and Trumpet
Newton Poppleford, Dawsons
Norwich, Merchant House
Ovington, Brovey Lair
Oxford, Lemon Tree
Oxton, Fraiche
Plumtree, Perkins
Plymouth, Tanners
Ripley, Drake's Restaurant
Ripon, Old Deanery
Rock, Black Pig
Sheffield, Curator's House
Sherborne, The Green
South Crosland, King's Arms
Stamford, Oakhouse
Restaurant

Stoke Holy Cross, Wildebeest
Arms
Strete, Kings Arms
Summercourt, Viner's Bar and
Restaurant
Sutton Gault, Anchor Inn
Tetbury, Close Hotel
Topsham, La Petite Maison
Upton Scudamore, Angel Inn
Wakefield, Brasserie Ninety
Nine
Whitstable, Williams & Brown
Tapas
Winchmore Hill, Plough

Scotland
Ardeonaig, Ardeonaig Hotel
Ballantrae, Glenapp Castle
Edinburgh, David Bann
Edinburgh, Vintners Rooms
Elie, Sangster's

Glasgow, Buttery
Glasgow, Café Ostra
Glasgow, Étain
Inverness, Restaurant Chez
Christophe
Plockton, Plockton Hotel
Portpatrick, Knockinaam Lodge
St Andrews, Seafood
Restaurant
Shieldaig, Tigh an Eilean Hotel

Wales
Crickhowell, Beaufort
Hendrerwydd, White Horse Inn
Southerndown, Frolics

Channel Islands
St Helier, Le Chambertin
St Peter Port, La Frégate

Northern Ireland
Gilford, Oriel

Budget eating

At the restaurants below it is possible to have a three-course meal, including coffee,
half a bottle of wine and service, for £30 or less per person, at any time the restaurant is
open, i.e. at dinner as well as lunch. It may be possible to spend considerably more
than this, but by choosing carefully you should find £30 or less achievable

London
Adams Café, W12
Anchor & Hope, SE1
Anglesea Arms, W6
Babur Brasserie, SE23
Brackenbury, W6
Café Japan, NW11
Calcutta Notebook, SW18
Chisou, W1
Eagle, EC1
Ealing Park Tavern, W5
Four Seasons, W2
Fox Dining Room, EC2
Gate, W6
Golden Dragon, W1
The Green, SE22
Huong-Viet, N1
Iznik, N5
Kastoori, SW17
K10, EC2
Kulu Kulu Sushi, W1
Lahore Kebab House, E1
Lansdowne, NW1
Lou Pescadou, SW5
Mandarin Kitchen, W2
Mr Kong, WC2
New Diamond, WC2
New Mayflower, W1
No. 6 George Street, W1
Numidie, SE19
Nyonya, W11
Phoenix Palace, NW1
Potemkin, EC1
Radha Krishna Bhavan, SW17

Rasa, N16
Real Greek, N1
Real Greek Souvlaki and Bar,
EC1
Sabras, NW10
Salusbury, NW6
Sarkhel's, SW18
Sushi-Say, NW2
Sushi-Hiro, W5
Tas, SE1
Two Brothers, N3
The Vale, W9
William IV, NW10

England
Addingham, Fleece
Aldeburgh, Lighthouse
Birtle, Waggon
Blackpool, Kwizeen
Bradford, Mumtaz
Bridport, Chez Cuddy
Brimfield, Roebuck Inn
Bristol, One30
Caunton, Caunton Beck
Chettle, Castleman Hotel
Clipsham, Olive Branch
Codford, George Hotel
Colchester, Lemon Tree
Cray's Pond, White Lion
Crosthwaite, Punch Bowl Inn
Dedham, Sun Inn
Durham, Bistro 21
Elland, La Cachette
Exeter, Thai Orchid

Farnham, Museum Inn
Fernhurst, King's Arms
Frampton Mansell, White Horse
Frithsden, Alford Arms
Galphay, Galphay Inn
Grange Moor, Kaye Arms
Grasmere, Jumble Room
Grimsby, Granary
Halifax, Design House
Harome, Star Inn
Harrogate, Drum and Monkey
Hemingford Grey, Cock
Horningsea, Crown &
Punchbowl
Huddersfield, Dining Rooms @
Strawberry Fair
Hutton Magna, Oak Tree Inn
Ilkley, Farsyde
Ipswich, Bistro on the Quay
Kendal, Déjà-vu
Kirk Deighton, Bay Horse
Knossington, Fox & Hounds
Leeds, Akbar's
Leeds, Fourth Floor Café and
Bar
Leeds, Sous le Nez en Ville
Leyburn, Sandpiper Inn
Liverpool, Simply Heathcotes
Lower Hardres, Granville
Manchester, Glamorous
Chinese
Manchester, Little Yang Sing
Manchester, Ocean Treasure

Manchester, Restaurant Bar & Grill
Manchester, Simply Heathcotes
Monks Eleigh, Swan Inn
Newcastle upon Tyne, Blackfriars Café Bar
Osmotherley, Golden Lion
Oxford, Al-Shami
Oxford, Branca
Paxford, Churchill Arms
Peter Tavy, Peter Tavy Inn
Plumtree, Perkins
Ponteland, Café 21
Ripley, Boar's Head
Rowde, George & Dragon
Rye, Landgate Bistro
St Ives, Pickled Fish
Sale, Hanni's
Sawley, Spread Eagle
Skipton, Le Caveau
Southall, Brilliant
Southhall, Madhu's
Southampton, Oxfords
Southport, Warehouse Brasserie

Stathern, Red Lion Inn
Stow-on-the-Wold, Kings Arms
Summercourt, Viner's Bar and Restaurant
Taunton, Brazz
Torquay, No 7 Fish Bistro
Truro, Café Citron
Twickenham, Ma Cuisine
Tynemouth, Sidney's
Whitby, Magpie Café
Whitstable, Wheelers Oyster Bar
Whitstable, Williams & Brown Tapas
Woodbridge, Captain's Table
York, Melton's Too

Scotland
Cairndow, Loch Fyne Oyster Bar
Edinburgh, David Bann
Edinburgh, First Coast
Edinburgh, Fishers in the City
Edinburgh, Kalpna
Edinburgh, Rogue

Edinburgh, Valvona & Crolla Caffé Bar
Fort William, Crannog
Glasgow, Café Ostra
Glasgow, Stravaigin 2
Inverness, Rocpool
Oban, Ee-Usk
Perth, Let's Eat
Plockton, Plockton Hotel

Wales
Bassaleg, Junction 28
Broad Haven, Druidstone
Cardiff, Armless Dragon
Colwyn Bay, Cafe Niçoise
Dolgellau, Dylanwad Da
Hawarden, Hawarden Brasserie
Swansea, La Braseria

Northern Ireland
Belfast, Aldens
Belfast, Metro Brasserie

The Good Food Club 2004

With many thanks to all those who contributed to the 2005 Guide.

Dr K.R. Aberdour
Dr A.H Abrahams
Mr David Adam
Mrs J.R.S. Adams
Mr Robert Adams
Robert and Margaret Adams
Max Ahern
Mr Martin Ainsworth
Mr and Mrs M. and S. Alexander
Rosemary Alexander
Mr J. Allan
Margaret Allen
Kerry Allison
Tim Ambrose
Kurt and Kiki Angelrath
Sir Michael Angus
Cynthia Archer
Colin Arnold
Jack and Mireille Attas
Martin Attewell
G.U. Austin
Graham Avery
Janet Awty
Michael Awty
Martin Baglee
Jacqueline Bagnall
David Baker
Mr R.W. Baker
Charlie Ballantayne
Peter Ballantyne
Mrs H. Barclay
Alan and Dorothy Barker
John Barker
K.J. Barker
E. Barratt
Jean Barrett
Mrs E.A. Barwood
Mr D.R. Bass
S. Batcup
Mr and Mrs A. Bates
David Battye
William Bavin
Jane Baxter
K. Baxter
Conrad Bayliss
Derek Bayntun
Mre C.G. Beauchamp
Prof. Frank Bechhofer
Mr F.R. Beckett
Mrs J. Bega
Mrs D. Bellerby
John Bence
Dr Peter Benczeller
Daphne Bennett
Tim Bent
Ivan Berardi

Petra Bercakova
Gabriele Berneck
Mr W.J. Best
Nick Bevan
Kathy Bichan
Betty and Chris Birch
Mr and Mrs A.R.H. Birchwood
Matt and Esther Bird
P.F. Bird
Mr R.G. Birt
J. Bishton
Ann Black
Mr C.T. Blackburn
Mrs V. Blackburn
Mr and Mrs J.L. Blakey
Mrs J.A. Blanks
Barbara Blatchley
Neville and Sonia Blech
Edward Blincoe
Mr and Mrs S. Bliss
J.A. Bluett
Mr and Mrs J.L. Blyth
Mr K.W. Blyth
Steven Bobasch
Mr K.W. Bogle
Christopher Bolton
Mr N.J. Bonham-Carter
Dr Ben Booth
S. Botfield
Mrs S.E. Bourne
Mr A.J. Bowen
John Boynton
Anthony Bradbury
Mr M. Brady
Roger Braithwaite
Claire Brayne
J. Bream
Mr B. Brears
Roisin Bresnihan
Mr and Mrs Edwin Brew
Robert Bridges
Mr and Mrs John Brierley
Mr C.M. Brinton
Roma Bromley
Cindy Brook
Nick Brookes
Douglas Brooks
Col. J.M. Browell
Mrs B. Brown
H.E. Brown
William Bruton
Isobel Bryan
R.W. Buckle
Daphne Bullock

Michael Bunce
B.K. Bunker
Mr and Mrs Bureeson-Wilde
Paul Burke
Mr M.H. Burr
Richard Bush
Paul Butler
Ronald Buyers
Amanda Cadwallader
Nicholas Caiger
Alan Caine
C.J.B. Campbell
Jane Campbell
Mrs M.E.F. Carmichael
Bruno Carpanini
Mr K. Carslaw
Mr J.A.H. Cartwright
Ann Marie Carver
Ms S.C. Cassells
Mr R.H. Cassen
Joanne Cassidy
Dr R.E. Catlow
Mr and Mrs M.F. Cave
Peter Cavey
Mr P.D. Cetti
Christopher Stephen Challener
Harry Chambers
Josephine Champsaur
Chris Chapman
Mr H.B. Chicken
Patricia Chopard
Lesley Clare
Daniel Clark
Mr M.M.A. Clark
Mr and Dr S. Clark
Tricia Clarke-Jervoise
Mr C.L. Clarkson
John Clegg
K. Cleveland
Mrs P.D. Cliff
Gillian Clinton
Miss E.A. Cochrane
Mrs H Cochrane
Roger Cockbill
Richard Coe
Prof. and Dr. Cohen
Dr Vivienne Cohen
Shirley Coker
K.J. Coleman
Michael Coleman
Mr N.P. Coley
Prof Joe Collier
D.W.F. Collins
Hannah Colton
Mr R.T. Combe
Mr M. Comninos
Lt. Col B.P. Concannon

C.S. and J. Cooke
Juliann and Linda Cooke
Peter Coombs
H.G. Cooper
Richard Cooper
Stephen Cooper
Ron and Sheila Corbett
Mr P.M.A. Corke
Mrs H.T Corry
Mr and Mrs Costa
Paul Costi
Mr S. Cowan
James Coward
Sally Cox
Mrs C. Crackwell
R. Cradick
G. Craig
Mr R.D. Cramond
Mrs J.M. Crewe
Niall and Gloria Crookdahe
G. Crossgrove
Gill Cruchley
R.J. Cuff
R.S. Curless
Ruth Curson
Mike Cushman
Dr Stan Da Prato
W.J.A. Dacombe
Mrs J. Dacre
Alexander Dainty
Mr M. Dallas
Mr and Mrs J.O. Dalzell
Mrs Richard Dannatt
Jane Davidson
Alun Davies
Duncan Davies
Lynda Davies
Mr S.T. Davies
Chrisopher Davis
Peter Davis
Dr and Mrs R.P.R. Dawber
Mr and Mrs Keith Dawson
Mr M.J. Day
Sarah Day
Sheila De Voil
Nigel Deacon
Ms N.C. Dee
James Delahooke
Joseph Dent
John Diley
Mr G.M. Dobbie
M.L. Dodd
M.H. Dods
Mr and Mrs W. Dolan

Helen Donkin
Liz and Phil Donnelly
Tony Dorran
Mr and Mrs R.C. Douglas
Jim Downer
Tony Downs
Dr Peter Drader
A.S.P. Drake
Mr and Mrs M. Draper
Mr D.R. Drucquer
David Duckham
Dr Andrew Dunn
Mr and Mrs P.L. Dunning
Claude Duval
Chris Dyson
Colin Eastaugh
John Eastwood
Mrs M.P. Eaves
Peter Ede
T.P. Edsall
Aileen Edwards
Alan Edwards
John Elder
Joanne Eley
Mr G. Elflett
Colin Elliot
Derrick and Margaret Elliot
Lynn Elliott
Robert Ellis
D. Emery
Mr and Mrs John Ette
Mr John Ette
Mrs John and Rosy Ette
Catherine Evans
D. Evans
J. Evans
J.S. Evans
Peter Evans
Mrs V. Evans
Andrew Everhale
Jenkinson Family
Ann Farrow
David Fearnley
Diane Fenton
Mildred Ferguson
William Ferguson
Jane Fernley
John Ferrewy
David and Barbara Le Fevre
Mr L.A. Fielding
Mr Neville Filar
A.V. Filby
T.C. Flanagan
Kim Fleming
David Foot
Colin Forbes
Rosie Ford
Christopher Forman
Mrs P.L. Forrest
Gordon and Brenda Foster

Alan Foward
Mr R.J.N. Fowler
Mrs M. Frame
Anthea France
Gordon Franklin
Harold Franks
Jackie Freke
Dr D.J. Frost
Peter Fry
Mr and Mrs B.D. Fuller
Mr and Mrs Tony Gamble
Mrs K. Garden
R.J. Garlick
Dr Ian Gavin
Tim Gay
Neil Gershon
Mr P. Gibbs
Trisha and Andrew Gilbrewwy
Peter Gittins
B. Glover
Roger Glover
Mr and Mrs S.C. Glover
Mr and Mrs N. Godley
Richard and Barbara Gold
Joy and Raymond Goldman
Marion and Richard Goldwater
Mr P.J Goodale
C. Goodall
Ken Goody
Alison Gooseacre
Mr D. Gordon
Mr M. Gordon-Russell
Terry Gorman
John Gorman-Charlton
Blake Gorst
Mrs R. Gostellon
Mr and Mrs A. Gough
Dr P.E. Gower
Ronnie Graham
David Grant
Mr M Grantham
John Gravey
Mr T.G. Green
Jim Greenwood
Mr W.N. Greenwood
Conal Gregory
Mrs C. Grey
Mr R.F. Grieve
David Griffith
Rev William Griffiths
Jenny Grimes
Mr N.M. Grimwood
Mrs S.P. Griscom
Lieut K.R. Groves
K.R. Groves
A.D. Grumley-Grennan
Ray Gudge
David Gunn

Pamela and Raymond Guy
Vivien Haigh
Mr and Mrs Hall
Dr Bryan Hall
C.J Hall
Tom Halsall
J. Hamilton
John Hammond
Gordon Hands
Mrs M. Hansford
Janie Harding-Edgar
Tim Harper
P. Harrington
Malcolm Harris
Raymond Harris
Mr C. Harrold
Peter Hartland
Mr J.D. Hartley
C.I. Harvey
E.S Harvey
Dr Peter Harvey
Peter Harvey
Pamela Hastings
Charles Hawes
Peter Hayman
S.B.L Hayman
Mrs S. Haywood
Mr and Mrs R. Hazlerigg
David and Anthea Head
Revd. Canon Neil Heavisides
T.P. Heavisides
Dr Ann Henderson
Joan Henry
Mr N.F. Henshaw
Dr's Geoffrey and Joselen Heron
Dr Andrew Herxheimer
Jennifer Hicks
Tony Hickson
Paula Higgins
Sarah and Chris Higgins
Robert Hill
Wendy Hillary
Michael Hindle
Eric Hinds
J.M. Hinds
Leslie Hoare
Mr and Mrs P.A. Hoare
Philip Hodgson
P.B. Homer
David Honeyball
Mrs I.P. Honeywood
Mr and Mrs Honour
Mrs J. Hope
Mr Hopper
Mr and Mrs John Hornsby
Mr and Mrs Ray Horrocks
Ian Howarth

Mr and Mrs A. and E. Howe
Mr D.P. Howell
Mr and Mrs E. Howson
Mr and Mrs A. Hubbard
Bob Hughes
Gerald Hughes
Jon Hughes
L.U.M. Hughes
M. Hughes
Sarah Hughes
Mrs Richard and Fran Hull
Kathryn Humphreys
Dr B.J. Hunt
Peter Hunt
Dr Tim Hunt
Mr P. Huntingdon
Mrs J. Huntley
Mr T.J. Hypher
Sarah Ilott
Dr G.B. Jackson
Monica Jackson
Ms C. Jansen
Prof. Barrie Jay
Brenda Jeeves
M.F. Jeeves
Alan Jefferson
Mr and Mrs Jenkins
Philip and Pamela Jenkins
Valerie Jenkins
John Jenkinson
Jean Jennings
Paul Jerome
David Jervois
Nigel Jestico
Mr B.M. Joce
Victoria Joel
Alan Johnson
Anna Johnson
Margaret Johnston Jones
Chris Jones
David Jones
Douglas Jones
Mrs H.M. Jones
Mel Jones
Peter Jones
Neil and Linda Jordan
Peter Jordan
Mr M.R Judd
G. Kahan
Leo Katzen
Dr Leon Kaufman
Mrs P. Kay
Richard Kay
Chris Keeling
Mr and Mrs J.O. Keir
Mr A. Kellett-Long
Dr Deirdre Kelly
Roger Kenber
Kenneth Kendall
Roger Kendall
Rosalind Kent
Clive Kerridge

Margaret Kershaw
Lynda Kettle
Elizabeth Key
Sheila Keynton
Mr and Mrs J.H. Kilby
Miss E. Kim
Anthony King
W.M. Kingston
Alison Kinnear
Maria Kitt
Robin Knapp
Sylvia Knapp
Mr and Mrs Knight
Mrs A Knight
C.H. Knight
Ra Knight
Jonathon Knights
R.G.A. Knott
Peter Knowles
Mr C. Kone
Mr P. Krause
Mr I. Laidlaw-Dickson
J.J. Laithwaite
Mr J.W. Lambeth
Lynden Lane
Mr P. Lane
I. Langford
Richard Lawrence
Nicholas Laws
Mr A. Lawson
B.S. Lawson
Michael Le Pour
    Trench
Alan Leaman
Peter Lecois
Geoffrey Lee
Dr Robbie Lendrum
Dr Andrew Leonard
W. and E. Leslie
James Lethem
Lionel Leventhal
B.K. Levy
Alan Lewis
D.E. Lewis
John Lewis
Mr and Mrs G.R. Ley
Mr B.N. Liddiard
D.J. Lindsay
David Lipsey
Chris Lloyd
Janet Lockett
James Long
Mr and Mrs P.A.
    Lowater
Julian Lowe
Jeremy Lucas
Tony Lucas
Dr Arthur Lui
Dr P.J. Lutman
Mr and Mrs Lyttelton
Peter Macaulay
M.W.B. MacEacharn
Mr J.B. MacGill
Martin Machan
Mr A.J. Macintosh
Tessa Mack

Mrs S.A. Mackenzie
Mrs M. Mackley
Helen Maclennan
Marcia Macleod
Mr C.B. Madderson
Patrick Mallon
Adrienne Malmesi
Julia Mann
Paul Manners
Mr M.B. Manser
David Mansfield
Susan Mansfield
Barbara Marasco
J. Marchal
Jacques Marchal
M. Marcian
David Mariano
I.M. Marks
Dr Charles Markus
E.S. Marriott
June Marsden
Mr S.P. Marshall
Rosamond Marshall-
    Smith
Pamela Marston
Mr and Mrs G.D. Martin
Hugh Martin
Roy Mathias
Scott Mathieson
Gavin Matthew
Ms K. Mattingly
Colin Mattocks
Mike Maughan
Ian May
John and Teresa Mc
    Sweeney
G.J. Mcallister
Mike Mccann
Karen Mcconville
Sean Mcdermott
Mr M.L. Mcdougall
Cynthia McDowall
Kate McDowall
George Mcdowell
Michael Mcevoy
Tim Mcewen
Charles McFeeters
Colin and Lilian
    McGhee
Gill Mckee
Mr and Mrs Maurice
    Mckee
Dr and Mrs J.G.
    McLaggan
Andrew McPherson
Philip Medcalf
Philip and Alison
    Midwinter
Carole Mills
Mrs S.B. Milne
Joan and David
    Mitchell
Margaret Mitchell
Pauline Mobey
Jan Moir
Mr N. Monk

Wendy Montague
S.R. Montgomery
Mrs P. Moore
R.B.R. Moore
R.E. Moors
Norma and Francis
    Moran
Martin Morgan
Michael Morgan
Veronica Morgan
Michael Morison
Mrs A. Morris
David Morrison
John Morrison
Anne Muers
Mr and Mrs William
    Mullins
Mrs A. Myers
David Mylroie
Mr and Mrs Natton
Chris and Vicki Naylor
Jitka Netopilova
Adrian and Maggie
    Newell
Mrs P.M. Newton
Rosina Nichols
Bryan Nicholson
A. Nightingale
Mr and Mrs David
    Nightingale
Paula Nimmo
Mick Noble
Craig Nolan
D.A. Norman
Dr J. Norman
Mr J.G. Norris
Sarah Norton
Paul Nossell
C.E. Nuttall
Rona Nuttall
Miss V.M. Nuttall
Laurence O'Donnell
Jane and Kevin
    O'Mahoney
M.D. Oakley
Anthony Ogden
Mr S. Oliver
Liz Orr
Mr and Mrs Orton
Mr and Mrs R.E.
    Osborne
T. Osborne
Meriel Packman
Andrew Palmer
Mr D. Palmer
M. and L. Pangels
Dennis Parker
Dr R.B. Parker
Richard and Andrea
    Parker
Mr J.H Parkin
J.D. Parsons
T.G. Parsons
Mrs C. Patrick
John Patrick
Chris Pearson

David Pearson
M.C. Pendered
Mr Owain Peredur
    Tomos
Robert Perry
B. Perryman
Chris Philips
Ian Phillips
V.M. Phillips
Mr R.L. Pickering
A.M. Pickup
Richard Pierce
Captain Michael Pigot
David Pilling
Mary Pimm
George Pincus
Michael Pitel
Christopher Pitt
Mrs J. Plante Cleall
Prof Peter Plesch
David Poole
Mr and Mrs R.J.M
    Pope
R.L. Poutney
Miss J. Powell
L.M. Pratier
Prof and Mrs G.M.
    Pratt
Noemi Press
L. Preston
J. Procter
Mrs C. Pudney
Robert Pullar
Martin Pursall
R.G. Pursey
Mrs G. Pusey
Dr Michael Quigley
William Rankin
Mr and Mrs Graham
    Ransome
Kervern and Val
    Rapkin
Sylvia Rawlins
Mrs A. Redfern
Prof W.D. Redfern
A. Reed
John and Jenny Reid
Alan Reynolds
Edgar Rich
Frank and Pam Rich
Dallas Richards
Lady J. Richards
Dr T.M. Richards
Mr C.J. Richardson
Gary Richardson
Heather Richardson
Malcolm and Dawn
    Richings
Professor Joel
    Richman
Carol Riddick
Mr and Mrs R. Ring
Gordon Ringrose
Mr G. Roberts
Derek Robinson
Harry Robinson

Josephine Robinson
N. Robinson
Sally Rosenegk
Michael Rowland
Peter and Jenny
  Rowland
Mr and Mrs D.
  Rowlands
Prof. David Rowley
Mr and Mrs Ian Royle
Mr J.S. Rutter
Ilse Ryder
K. Saalson
Keith Salway
Dr C. Saunders
A.A. Schiff
Susan Schonfield
Elliot Schwartz
Esme Scott
Paul Scott
A.G. Searle
David Sefton
Paul Sellers
Dr John Senior
Cliff and Ann-Marie
  Sharp
John and Kate Sharp
John Sharpe
Dr J.T.R. Sharrock
Mr and Mrs K. Shaw
W. Shelton
Ian Shepherdson
Charles Sheppard
Mr and Mrs G. Short
S. Singh
Andrew Skeet
Mr and Mrs R W
  Skinner
Fred Slegg
David Sleight
Alan Sloan
John and Kate
  Smallwood
Mr and Mrs J.E. Smart
Margaret Smart
Mrs J. Smith
Peter Smith
P. Snaith
Robert Southgate
Mrs M. Spearman
Alan Spedding
Justin Spence
Mrs L. Spencer
Robert Spooner
John and Lynne
  Stanbury
Christine Stanley

Mr J. Stanley-Smith
Jeremy Stanley-Smith
John Start
Bruce Statham
Charles Stead
M. Stearn
Mrs G.M. Stein
John Stein
Prof Chris Stephens
Alan Stevens
John Stevenson
Capt and Mrs J.S.
  Stewart
Dr and Mrs James
  Stewart
David Stocker
Mr M.H. Stone
Sybil Stone
Sue Storey
J.C. Stot
John Stott
Julian Struthers
  Danskin
Adele and Alan
  Summers and Black
Mr and Mrs. Supran
A.M. Sutton-Scott-
  Tucker
Sarah Swallow
Andrew Swindells
Brenda Symes
Keith Symons
Mrs E.M. Talbot
Mr and Mrs Tate
Mrs A.C. Taylor
George Taylor
J.D. Taylor
Mrs J.L. Taylor
Jean Taylor
T.W. Taylor
Dr Diana Terry
Diana Terry
Dr B. Thawayasingam
Alan Thomas
Dr B.H. Thomas
Francis Thomas
Mr and Mrs P. Thomas
E. Thompson
Mrs B.J. Thomson
Mr and Mrs Gavin
  Thomson
Mrs J.E. Thornton
Howard Thrift
Mr and Mrs Thurlow
Mr and Mrs P.E.
  Tingley
Mr Terence Titmus

Paul Todd
Barry Tomlinson
John Tomlinson
Roy Towler
Dr J. Towner
Barbara Trendall
A. Treweeke
Capt J.C.M. Troughton
Nigel Tubbs
P.E. Tucker
J. Tudor-Craig
Charles Turner
Mr R.L. Turner
Siobhan Turner
Stanley and Sue
  Turner
Paul Tuthill
Alan Tye
Mrs B. Tytko
Mrs G.U. Unwin
John Urry
Roger Utley
A.W. Vernon-Harcourt
Mr R. Vicar
Anthony Vigurs
Michael Waggett
Mr P.H. Wainman
Mrs A.M. Walden
Adam Walford
Tom and Angela
  Walford
M.G. Walker
Sarah Walker
Stephen John Walker
Ian Waller
Dr Robert Waller
Adrian Walsh
Mrs M.E.M. Walsh
Capt P.J. Walsh
Mrs A. Warburton
Sally Ward
Mr A.J. Wardrop
Mr R.A. Wartnaby
Mr and Mrs J.S.
  Waters
Steve Waters
Mr K.R. Waterworth
Mr and Mrs Watkins
Mr David Watters
Dr M Webb
Patricia Webb
W.J. Webber
Marcia Webster
Mr J.F.M. West
M.J. West
Sue Westmore
T. Weston

Mr T.J.M. Weston
Mrs M. Weston-Smith
Mr W.J. Wetenhall
Stacey Whatling
Joanne Whelan
Dr G.T. Whitaker
Maggie and John
  Whitaker
Martin White
Sue and John White
Mrs M. Whiteman
Elizabeth Whitethread
John Whittaker
Paul Whittard
David Whittle
Mr and Mrs S. Whittle
Jill Wight
Mr Wightman
Mr and Mrs Wilkes
Mr H. Wilkinson
Sue Wilkinson
Mr P. Willer
Mr and Mrs Williams
Mr J.R. Williams
Jeremy Williams
John Williams
Stephen Williamson
Mr and Mrs M.J.
  Williets
Drs. A. and C. Wilson
Craig Wilson
Mr and Mrs E. Wilson
M. Wilson
John Window
Mr J. Winecor
Brian and Fiona
  Wiseman
Dr N.P. Woffenden
E.E. Wolfe
Canon and Mrs Eric
  and Sandra Woods
Alan Worsdale
Margaret Worsley
Terry Worster
Brenda Wright
John Wright
Keith Wright
Margaret Wright
T.E. Wright
J. Wyllie
Miss C. Wyn-Jones
Mr B.D. Yates
Mr and Mrs A.H Young

Index of entries

Index of entries

Names in bold are main entries. Names in italics are Round-ups.

To the Editor *The Good Food Guide*
FREEPOST, 2 Marylebone Road, London NW1 4DF

Or send your report by electronic mail to: *goodfoodguide@which.net*

From my personal experience the following establishment should/should not be included in the Guide (please print in BLOCK CAPITALS):

_____

_____

Telephone_____

I had lunch/dinner/stayed there on (date) _____

I would rate this establishment _____ out of ten.

please continue overleaf

My meal for ___ people cost £_____ *attach bill where possible*

☐ Please tick if you would like more report forms

I am not connected in any way with management or proprietors, and have not been asked by them to write to the Guide.
Name and address (BLOCK CAPITALS, please)

_____

_____

Signed _____

As a result of your sending us this report form, we may send you information on *The Good Food Guide* and *The Which? Guide to Good Hotels* in the future. If you would prefer not to receive such information, please tick this box ☐.

Report Form

To the Editor *The Good Food Guide*
FREEPOST, 2 Marylebone Road, London NW1 4DF

Or send your report by electronic mail to: *goodfoodguide@which.net*

From my personal experience the following establishment should/should not be included in the Guide (please print in BLOCK CAPITALS):

_____

_____

Telephone_____.

I had lunch/dinner/stayed there on (date) _____

I would rate this establishment _____ out of ten.

please continue overleaf

My meal for ___ people cost £_____ *attach bill where possible*

☐ Please tick if you would like more report forms

I am not connected in any way with management or proprietors, and have not been asked by them to write to the Guide.

Name and address (BLOCK CAPITALS, please)

_____

_____

Signed _____

Report Form

To the Editor *The Good Food Guide*
FREEPOST, 2 Marylebone Road, London NW1 4DF

Or send your report by electronic mail to: *goodfoodguide@which.net*

From my personal experience the following establishment should/should not be included in the Guide (please print in BLOCK CAPITALS):

_____

_____

Telephone_____

I had lunch/dinner/stayed there on (date) _____

I would rate this establishment _____ out of ten.

please continue overleaf

My meal for ___ people cost £_____ *attach bill where possible*

☐ Please tick if you would like more report forms

I am not connected in any way with management or proprietors, and have not been asked by them to write to the Guide.
Name and address (BLOCK CAPITALS, please)

Signed _____

As a result of your sending us this report form, we may send you information on *The Good Food Guide* and *The Which? Guide to Good Hotels* in the future. If you would prefer not to receive such information, please tick this box☐.

Report Form   2005

To the Editor *The Good Food Guide*
FREEPOST, 2 Marylebone Road, London NW1 4DF

Or send your report by electronic mail to: *goodfoodguide@which.net*

From my personal experience the following establishment should/should not be included in the Guide (please print in BLOCK CAPITALS):

_____

_____

Telephone _____

I had lunch/dinner/stayed there on (date) _____

I would rate this establishment _____ out of ten.

please continue overleaf

My meal for ___ people cost £_____ *attach bill where possible*

☐ Please tick if you would like more report forms

I am not connected in any way with management or proprietors, and have not been asked by them to write to the Guide.
Name and address (BLOCK CAPITALS, please)

_____

_____

Signed _____

As a result of your sending us this report form, we may send you information on *The Good Food Guide* and *The Which? Guide to Good Hotels* in the future. If you would prefer not to receive such information, please tick this box ☐.

Report Form

To the Editor *The Good Food Guide*
FREEPOST, 2 Marylebone Road, London NW1 4DF

Or send your report by electronic mail to: *goodfoodguide@which.net*

From my personal experience the following establishment should/should not be included in the Guide (please print in BLOCK CAPITALS):

_____

_____

Telephone_____

I had lunch/dinner/stayed there on (date) _____

I would rate this establishment _____ out of ten.

please continue overleaf

My meal for ___ people cost £_____ *attach bill where possible*

☐ Please tick if you would like more report forms

I am not connected in any way with management or proprietors, and have not been asked by them to write to the Guide.

Name and address (BLOCK CAPITALS, please)

_____

_____

Signed _____

Report Form   2005

To the Editor *The Good Food Guide*
FREEPOST, 2 Marylebone Road, London NW1 4DF

Or send your report by electronic mail to: *goodfoodguide@which.net*

From my personal experience the following establishment
should/should not be included in the Guide (please print in
BLOCK CAPITALS):

_____

_____

                          Telephone_____

I had lunch/dinner/stayed there on (date) _____

I would rate this establishment _____ out of ten.

please continue overleaf

My meal for ___ people cost £_____ *attach bill where possible*

☐ Please tick if you would like more report forms

I am not connected in any way with management or proprietors, and have not been asked by them to write to the Guide.
Name and address (BLOCK CAPITALS, please)

_____

_____

Signed _____

As a result of your sending us this report form, we may send you information on *The Good Food Guide* and *The Which? Guide to Good Hotels* in the future. If you would prefer not to receive such information, please tick this box ☐.

Report Form

To the Editor *The Good Food Guide*
FREEPOST, 2 Marylebone Road, London NW1 4DF

Or send your report by electronic mail to: *goodfoodguide@which.net*

From my personal experience the following establishment should/should not be included in the Guide (please print in BLOCK CAPITALS):

_____

_____

Telephone_____

I had lunch/dinner/stayed there on (date) _____

I would rate this establishment _____ out of ten.

please continue overleaf

My meal for ___ people cost £_____ *attach bill where possible*

☐ Please tick if you would like more report forms

I am not connected in any way with management or proprietors, and have not been asked by them to write to the Guide.
Name and address (BLOCK CAPITALS, please)

_____

_____

Signed _____

As a result of your sending us this report form, we may send you information on *The Good Food Guide* and *The Which? Guide to Good Hotels* in the future. If you would prefer not to receive such information, please tick this box ☐.